P9-DFP-681

in a Crowd.

We'd like to express our sincere thanks to all of the marketing professors and students who have used our text over the years. Your feedback, ideas, and support are the most important ingredients that go into this book. We never lose sight of the fact that our work "stands out in a crowd" because of you.

Thanks!

Philip Kotler   *Gary Armstrong*

Catalina Ainsworth

253-380-8437

Reviewers Agree That Kotler and Armstrong's Text

STANDS OUT IN A CROWD

"This text is one of the best overall undergraduate marketing texts I have seen, because it incorporates more real-world applications of marketing concepts than any others I have used. This text does a good job of presenting marketing theory that is based on academic literature, without excessive jargon or 'lists' that students think they should memorize. The videos and cases go well with the material."

"I think Kotler and Armstrong really have a tiger by the tail in emphasizing relationships as their dominant theme."

"The authors do a superb job of covering customer value. It is certainly a conspicuous cornerstone of the book. The concept is well integrated in each chapter I reviewed."

"The underlying value-creation theme is excellent. The section on brand strategy is thorough, provides good examples, and students can relate to it. Great idea to place positioning in with the product—FINALLY a book that did this!"

"I have aggressively sought to utilize various assessment tools in my curriculum and have been very pleased with the Kotler/Armstrong support and value added materials. I find the students often list them as 'most helpful' in course evaluations."

"The strengths of Kotler and Armstrong are that the focus is on the customer, which is very important, and they define marketing in an understandable manner. I think they use excellent examples . . . I am impressed."

"Kotler and Armstrong have stayed contemporary with everything going on in the field."

"Segmentation is a key chapter in my course. Kotler and Armstrong are superior in their coverage of this material . . . I feel my students would be better off with Kotler and Armstrong's text."

"The authors offer appropriate organizations and marketing efforts as examples and illustrations, and they have done a superb job of accounting for the current and emerging trends in a discipline that is characterized by rapid change."

"The CRM topic is given better coverage than in our present text."

"I do applaud the authors' practice of clearly delineating chapter objectives up front, followed by a review of the objectives/concepts at the end of the chapter—I like this continuity."

"Kotler and Armstrong is quite refreshing, as it draws the reader into the fascinating areas of marketing via the use of real life examples right off the bat."

"I particularly think that Kotler and Armstrong's text is far superior relative to the 'What is Marketing?' section in the first chapter. . . . I love the diversity of products and companies chosen for the company examples and cases; examples of companies that all ages can relate to and that are of interest to young professionals."

Principles of Marketing

Eleventh Edition

Philip Kotler
Northwestern University

Gary Armstrong
University of North Carolina

PEARSON

Prentice Hall

Upper Saddle River, New Jersey 07458

Library of Congress Cataloging-in-Publication Data

Kotler, Philip.
    Principles of marketing / Philip Kotler, Gary Armstrong.—11th ed.
        p. cm.
    Includes bibliographical references and index.
    ISBN 0-13-146918-5
    1. Marketing.   I. Armstrong, Gary.   II. Title.

    HF5415.K636 2005
    658.8—dc22

                                    2004029593

Acquisitions Editor: Katie Stevens
Editor-in-Chief: Jeff Shelstad
Assistant Editor: Melissa Pellerano
Editorial Assitant: Rebecca Lembo
Media Project Manager: Peter Snell
Marketing Manager: Michelle O'Brien
Marketing Assistant: Joanna Sabella
Managing Editor (Production): Judith Leale
Production Editor: Cindy Durand
Permissions Coordinator: Charles Morris
Production Manager: Arnold Vila
Manufacturing Buyer: Diane Peirano
Design Manager: Maria Lange
Interior Design: Amanda Kavanagh and Brian Salisbury
Manager, Print Production: Christy Mahon
Composition: Carlisle Communications
Full-Service Project Management: Lynn Steines, Carlisle Communications
Printing/Binder: Courier-Kendallville
Cover Printer: Coral Graphics
Typeface: 9 pt. Melior

Credits and acknowledgments borrowed from other sources and reproduced, with permission, in this textbook appear on page C-1.

Copyright © 2006, 2004, 2001, 1999, and 1996 by Pearson Education, Inc., Upper Saddle River, New Jersey 07458. All rights reserved. Printed in the United States of America. This publication is protected by Copyright and permission should be obtained from the publisher prior to any prohibited reproduction, storage in a retrieval system, or transmission in any form or by any means, electronic, mechanical, photocopying, recording, or likewise. For information regarding permission(s), write to: Rights and Permissions Department.

Pearson Prentice Hall™ is a trademark of Pearson Education, Inc.
Pearson® is a registered trademark of Pearson plc
Prentice Hall® is a registered trademark of Pearson Education, Inc.

Pearson Education LTD.
Pearson Education Australia PTY, Limited
Pearson Education Singapore, Pte. Ltd.
Pearson Education North Asia Ltd.

Pearson Education Canada, Ltd.
Pearson Educacíon de Mexico, S.A. de C.V.
Pearson Education—Japan
Pearson Education Malaysia, Pte. Ltd.

10 9 8 7 6 5 4 3 2 1
ISBN: 0-13-146918-5

Dedication

To Kathy, Betty, KC, Keri, Delaney, Mandy, Matt, and Molly;
and Nancy, Amy, Melissa, and Jessica

About the Authors

As a team, Philip Kotler and Gary Armstrong provide a blend of skills uniquely suited to writing an introductory marketing text. Professor Kotler is one of the world's leading authorities on marketing. Professor Armstrong is an award-winning teacher of undergraduate business students. Together they make the complex world of marketing practical, approachable, and enjoyable.

PHILIP KOTLER | is one of the world's leading authorities on marketing. He is the S. C. Johnson & Son Distinguished Professor of International Marketing at the Kellogg School of Management, Northwestern University. He received his master's degree at the University of Chicago and his Ph.D. at MIT, both in economics. Dr. Kotler is author of *Marketing Management*, now in its twelfth edition and the most widely used marketing textbook in graduate schools of business. He has authored more than 20 other successful books and more than one hundred articles in leading journals. He is the only three-time winner of the coveted Alpha Kappa Psi award for the best annual article published in the *Journal of Marketing.* He was named the first recipient of two major awards: the *Distinguished Marketing Educator of the Year Award* given by the American Marketing Association and the *Philip Kotler Award for Excellence in Health Care Marketing* presented by the Academy for Health Care Services Marketing. Other major honors include the 1978 Paul Converse Award of the AMA, honoring his original contribution to marketing, the European Association of Marketing Consultants and Sales Trainers Prize for Marketing Excellence, the 1995 Sales and Marketing Executives International (SMEI) Marketer of the Year award, the 2002 Academy of Marketing Science Distinguished Educator Award, and honorary doctoral degrees from Stockholm University, the University of Zurich, Athens University of Economics and Business, DePaul University, the Cracow School of Business and Economics, Groupe H.E.C. in Paris, the Budapest School of Economic Science and Public Administration, and the University of Economics and Business Administration in Vienna.

Professor Kotler has been a consultant to many major U.S. and foreign companies in the areas of marketing strategy and planning, marketing organization, and international marketing. He has been Chairman of the College of Marketing of the Institute of Management Sciences, a Director of the American Marketing Association, a Trustee of the Marketing Science Institute, a Director of the MAC Group, a member of the Yankelovich Advisory Board, and a member of the Copernicus Advisory Board, and a member of the Advisory Board of the Drucker Foundation. He has traveled extensively throughout Europe, Asia, and South America, advising and lecturing to many companies about global marketing opportunities.

GARY ARMSTRONG | is Crist W. Blackwell Distinguished Professor of Undergraduate Education in the Kenan-Flagler Business School at the University of North Carolina at Chapel Hill. He holds undergraduate and masters degrees in business from Wayne State University in Detroit, and he received his Ph.D. in marketing from Northwestern University. Dr. Armstrong has contributed numerous articles to leading business journals. As a consultant and researcher, he has worked with many companies on marketing research, sales management, and marketing strategy. But Professor Armstrong's first love is teaching. His Blackwell Distinguished Professorship is the only permanent endowed professorship for distinguished undergraduate teaching at the University of North Carolina at Chapel Hill. He has been very active in the teaching and administration of Kenan-Flagler's undergraduate program. His recent administrative posts include Chair of the Marketing Faculty, Associate Director of the Undergraduate Business Program, Director of the Business Honors Program, and others. He works closely with business student groups and has received several campus-wide and Business School teaching awards. He is the only repeat recipient of the school's highly regarded Award for Excellence in Undergraduate Teaching, which he won three times. In 2004, Professor Armstrong received the UNC Board of Governors Award for Excellence in Teaching, the highest teaching honor bestowed at the University of North Carolina at Chapel Hill.

Brief Contents

Contents

Welcome to the Eleventh Edition!

Our goal with *Principles of Marketing* has always been to offer the most current, applied, resourceful, and exciting text for the introductory marketing course. That's why it continues to be the most widely used introductory marketing text around the world. That's what makes it stand out in a crowd.

We've poured over every book page, figure, table, exercise, illustration, example, and reference. We've included the latest concepts and practices to keep the text fresh and timely. And we've reviewed hundreds of pages of feedback from marketing instructors and students to make sure that this book responds to your needs.

We think you'll agree that the eleventh edition is the best edition yet!

What Makes This Book Stand Out in a Crowd?

NEW! An Integrative New Customer-Value Framework

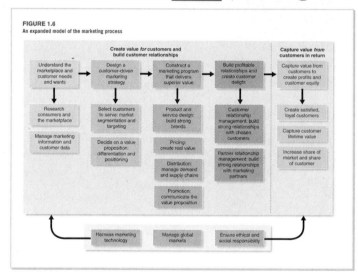

FIGURE 1.6
An expanded model of the marketing process

■ **Creating value *for* customers in order to capture value *from* customers in return:** This innovative customer value framework is introduced in a five-step marketing process model at the start of chapter 1, which details how marketing *creates* customer value and *captures* value in return. The framework is carefully explained in the first two chapters, providing students with a solid foundation. It is then integrated throughout the remainder of the text.

The Eleventh Edition Builds on Four Major Themes

■ **Building and managing profitable customer relationships:** Creating value *for* customers in order to capture value *from* customers in return. Today's marketers must be good at *creating customer value* and *managing customer relationships.* Leading marketing companies understand the marketplace and customer needs, design customer-driven marketing strategies that create customer value, develop marketing programs that deliver value and satisfaction, and build strong customer relationships. In return, they capture value from customers in the form of sales, profits, and customer equity.

Marketers must also excel at *partner relationship management.* They must work closely with partners inside and outside the company to jointly build profitable customer relationships. Successful marketers are now partnering effectively with other company departments to build strong company value chains. And they are joining with outside partners to build effective supply chains and effective customer-focused alliances.

■ **Building and managing strong brands to create brand equity:** Well-positioned brands with strong brand equity provide the basis upon which to build profitable customer relationships. Today's marketers must know how to position their brands and manage them well.

■ **Harnessing marketing technologies in this digital age:** Digital and high-tech marketing developments are dramatically changing both buyers and marketers. Today's marketers must know how to leverage new information, communication, and transportation technologies to connect more effectively with customers and marketing partners in this digital age.

■ **Marketing in a socially responsible way around the globe:** As technological developments make the world an increasingly smaller place, marketers must market their brands globally and in socially responsible ways.

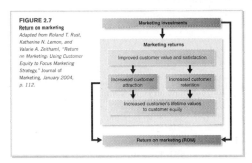

FIGURE 2.7
Return on marketing
Adapted from Roland T. Rust, Katherine N. Lemon, and Valarie A. Zeithaml, "Return on Marketing: Using Customer Equity to Focus Marketing Strategy," Journal of Marketing, January 2004, p. 112.

Other Important Changes and Additions

The Eleventh Edition includes new and expanded material on a wide range of topics, including:

■ Measuring and managing return on marketing ■ Managing customer relationships ■ Positioning and positioning maps ■ Value-based pricing ■ Database marketing ■ Buzz marketing and experiential marketing ■ Environmental sustainability ■ Supplier development and supply chain management ■ Marketing and diversity ■ Socially responsible marketing ■ New marketing technologies ■ Global marketing

Real Marketing

Principles of Marketing features real-world examples that show concepts in action and reveal the drama of modern marketing. In the Eleventh Edition, every chapter-opening vignette and Real Marketing highlight has been replaced or significantly updated to deliver on our promise of offering the most current and exciting text.

Learn how . . .

■ **NASCAR** creates high-octane, totally involving, very profitable customer relationships

■ **MTV** achieves phenomenal global success with its unique blend of global strategy and local programming

■ **McDonald's** reversed its fortunes by aligning itself with the new marketplace realties and now has customers and stockholders alike humming its catchy "I'm lovin' it" jingle

■ **RFID technology**—embedding tiny "smart chips" in the products you buy—gives us an exciting glimpse into the future of supply chain management

■ **Steinway** proves that when it comes to its pianos, price is nothing, the Steinway experience is everything

■ **Krispy Kreme** sells more than just a few ounces of flour and sugar with chocolate and sprinkles on top—it creates truly magical moments for customers

■ **Whole Foods Market** thrives by positioning away from behemoth Wal-Mart rather than trying to compete head to head

■ **Crispin Porter & Bogusky,** an award-winning ad agency, has made itself the agency of the moment by preaching that "anything and everything is an ad"

■ **Washington Mutual** (or WaMu to the faithful) applies an unusual relationship-building strategy in an effort to become the Wal-Mart of the banking industry

- **Burt's Bees** proves that small can be beautiful—business is buzzing for this small maker of earth-friendly natural products for natural people
- **Google** triumphs amid the dot-com meltdown by focusing heavily on simply helping users search the Internet
- *and much more!*

Supplements that Stand Out

For Instructors

NEW! **ANNOTATED INSTRUCTOR'S MEDIA EDITION:** The new Annotated Instructor's Media Edition includes an insert at the front of each chapter, which serves as a "Quick Reference" for the entire supplements package. Suggestions for using materials from the Instructor's Manual, PowerPoint slides, Test Item File, Video Library, and online materials are offered for each main section within every chapter.

INSTRUCTOR'S MANUAL IN PRINT: Contains chapter overviews and objectives, plus detailed lecture outlines—incorporating key terms and various pedagogy from the text. Also includes support for end-of-chapter material, along with additional student projects and assignments.

- *New feature:* "Outside Examples" offer instructors additional lecture material for each chapter. The examples may include extensions of concepts or company examples mentioned briefly in the chapter, or new material that further develops a key concept in the text.
- *New feature:* "Professors on the Go!" was created with the busy professor in mind. This helpful feature brings key material upfront in the manual, where instructors who are short on time can take a quick look and find key points and assignments to incorporate into a lecture without having to page through all the material provided for each chapter.

TEST ITEM FILE IN PRINT: Contains over **3,000 questions.** Each chapter consists of multiple-choice, true/false, essay, and short-answer questions, with page references and difficulty levels provided for each question.

- *New feature:* An entire section dedicated to application questions. This resource provides real-life situations that take students beyond basic chapter concepts and vocabulary and asks them to apply their newly-learned marketing skills.

PC/MAC TESTGEN: Prentice Hall's test generating software is available from the *Instructor's Resource Center (IRC) Online* (**www.prenhall.com/kotler**) or from the *IRC on CD-ROM.*

- PC/Mac compatible; preloaded with all of the Test Item File questions.
- Manually or randomly view test bank questions and drag-and-drop to create a test.
- Add or modify test bank questions using the built-in Question Editor.
- Print up to 25 variations of a single test and deliver the test on a local area network using the built-in QuizMaster feature.

Free customer support is available at media.support@pearsoned.com or 1-800-6-PROFESSOR between 8:00 A.M. and 5:00 P.M. CST.

NEW! **INSTRUCTOR'S RESOURCE CENTER:** All instructor resources are password protected and available for download via **www.prenhall.com/kotler.** For your convenience, these resources are also available on the Instructor's Resource CD-ROM.

- *Instructor's Manual:* View this resource chapter-by-chapter or download the entire manual as a .zip file.
- *Test Item File:* View chapter-by-chapter or download the entire test item file as a .zip file.
- *TestGen for PC/Mac:* Download this easy-to-use software; it's preloaded with the Eleventh Edition test questions and a user's manual.
- *Image bank (On CD only):* Access many of the images, ads, and illustrations featured in the text. Ideal for PowerPoint customization.

- *PowerPoints:* When it comes to PowerPoints, Prentice Hall knows one size does not fit all. That's why we offer instructors more than one option.

    - **PowerPoint BASIC:** This simple presentation includes only basic outlines and key points from each chapter. It integrates no animation or forms of rich media, which makes the total file size manageable and easier to share online or via email. BASIC was also designed for instructors who prefer to customize PowerPoints and who want to be spared from having to strip out animation, embedded files, or other media rich features.

    - **PowerPoint MEDIA RICH (On IRC-CD only):** This media rich alternative includes basic outlines and key points from each chapter, plus advertisements and art from the text, images from outside the text, discussion questions, Web links, and embedded video snippets from the accompanying video library. It's the best option if you want a complete presentation solution. Instructors can further customize this presentation using the image library featured on the IRC on CD-ROM.

    - **PowerPoints for CLASSROOM RESPONSE SYSTEMS (CRS):** These Q&A style slides are designed for classrooms using 'clickers' or classroom response systems. Instructors who are interested in making CRS a part of their course should contact their Prentice Hall representative for details and a demonstration. CRS is a fun and easy way to make your classroom more interactive.

COLOR OVERHEADS: Feature 15–20 color acetates per chapter selected from the Media Rich set of PowerPoints; includes images from text.

VIDEO: The video library features 20 exciting segments, *all new* to this edition and filmed in 2003 or 2004. All segments are available online, VHS, and on DVD. Here are the videos filmed in 2004:

- American Express and the modern marketing environment
- The NFL and the importance of social responsibility
- Song Airlines and smart pricing strategies
- Eaton's approach to B2B issues, including buyer behavior
- Hasbro and its views on distribution channels and logistics management
- Reebok's retailing and wholesaling policies
- Wild Planet's strategies in consumer markets

Reminder: The DVD can be shrink-wrapped FREE with student copies of this text. Ask your representative about special value-package ISBNs.

ONLINE COURSES: See OneKey below. Compatible with BlackBoard and WebCT.

ADCRITIC.COM: Prentice Hall and AdAge are bringing the most current ads and commentary from advertising experts into your classroom. Only Prentice Hall can offer students 16 weeks of access to a special AdCritic.com site that includes AdAge's encyclopedia of articles at a deeply discounted rate. An access code is available only when shrinkwrapped with a Prentice Hall text, so be sure and specify the appropriate package with your local bookstore in advance. Please visit **www.prenhall.com/marketing** for a tour of the AdCritic site.

For Students

ONEKEY: Available through CourseCompass, Blackboard, and WebCT, this site delivers all classroom resources for students in one place. Resources include:

- Additional quizzing for review
- Case Pilot to aid in analyzing cases
- Marketing Toolkit: Interactive modules to aid in review of understanding key concepts
- Marketing Updates: Bringing current articles to the classroom
- *Much more . . .*

For more information on using OneKey, please see **www.prenhall.com/onekey**.

OneKey requires an access code, which can be shrink-wrapped free with new copies of this text. Please contact your local sales representative for the correct ISBN. Codes may also be purchased separately at www.prenhall.com/marketing.

STUDY GUIDE: Includes detailed chapter outlines, student exercises, plus exercises correlated to award-winning print advertisements. This guide serves as a great review tool in preparing for exams.

COMPANION WEBSITE: This site contains two student quizzes per chapter. The Concept Check Quiz is administered prior to reviewing the chapter, in order to assess the students' initial understanding. The Concept Challenge Quiz is administered after reviewing the chapter to assess the student's comprehension. Also featured is the text glossary. You can reach the Companion Website by going to **www.prenhall.com/kotler**.

More Outstanding Resources

NEW! Announcing SafariX Textbooks Online—Where the Web meets textbooks for student savings!

Principles of Marketing, Eleventh Edition is also available as a WebBook! SafariX WebBooks offer study advantages no print textbook can match. With an Internet-enhanced SafariX WebBook, students can search the entire text for key concepts; navigate easily to a page number, reading assignment, or chapter; or bookmark important pages or sections for quick review at a later date. Some key features:

- *Digital Textbook Delivery* that saves students as much as 50 percent off the print edition suggested list price.
- *Internet-based Service* making textbook content available anytime, anywhere there is a Web connection.
- *Easy Navigation* which makes finding pages and completing assignments easy and efficient.
- *Search, Bookmark, and Note Taking Tools* that save study time and reduce frustration by making critical information immediately accessible. Organizing study notes has never been easier!
- *Ability to print pages on the fly* making critical content available for offline study and review.

Prentice Hall is pleased to be the first publisher to offer students a new choice in how they purchase and access required or recommended course textbooks. For details and a demonstration, visit **www.prenhall.com/safarix**

NEW! Classroom Response Systems (CRS)

This exciting new wireless polling technology makes classrooms, no matter how large or small, even more interactive because it enables instructors to pose questions to their students, record results, and display those results instantly. Students answer questions using compact remote control style transmitters, commonly known as "clickers." Prentice Hall has partnerships with leading classroom response systems providers and can show you everything you need to know about setting up and using a CRS system. We'll provide the classroom hardware, software and support, and show you how your students can save!

- Enhance interactivity with content specific PowerPoints located in the Instructor's Resource Center
- Capture attention
- Get instant feedback
- Assess comprehension
- Learn more at **www.prenhall.com/crs**

Acknowledgments

No book is the work only of its authors. We owe much to the pioneers of marketing who first identified its major issues and developed its concepts and techniques. Our thanks also go to our colleagues at the J. L. Kellogg Graduate School of Management, Northwestern University, and at the Kenan-Flagler Business School, University of North Carolina at Chapel Hill, for ideas and suggestions.

We owe special thanks to Mandy Roylance for her constant and invaluable advice, assistance, development work, video cases, and other involvement throughout every phase of this revision effort. Thanks also go to Lew Brown and Martha McEnally, both of the University of North Carolina at Greensboro, for preparing high-quality company cases; to Professor Robert Wheeler of the University of California, Irvine for his skillful development of end-of-chapter material; and to Andrea Meyer for her able development assistance. In addition, we thank Marian Wood for help in creating the marketing plan for this edition.

Many reviewers at other colleges provided valuable comments and suggestions. We are indebted to the following colleagues who reviewed for this edition:

Ron Adams, *University North Florida*

Mark Anderson, *Eastern Kentucky University*

Michael Ballif, *University of Utah*

Pat Bernson, *County College of Morris*

Amit Bhatnagar, *University of Wisconsin*

Fred Brunel, *Boston University*

Jeff Bryden, *Bowling Green University*

Mary Conran, *Temple University*

Kenny Herbst, *Saint Joseph's University*

Terry Holmes, *Murray State University*

Eileen Kearney, *Montgomery County Community College*

Tina Kiesler, *Cal State University at North Ridge*

Bruce Lammers, *California State University at North Ridge*

J. Ford Laumer, *Auburn University*

Kenneth Lawrence, *New Jersey Institute of Technology*

Mohan K. Menon, *University Southern Alabama*

William Mindak, *Tulane University*

Howard Olsen, *University of Nevada at Reno*

Betty Parker, *Western Michigan University*

Vanessa Perry, *George Washington University*

Abe Qastin, *Lakeland College*

Paul Redig, *Milwaukee Area Technical College*

Roberta Schultz, *Western Michigan University*

Karen Stone, *Southern New Hampshire University*

Ruth Taylor, *Texas State University*

Mark Wasserman, *University of Texas*

Alvin Williams, *University of Southern Mississippi*

We would also like to thank the many colleagues who reviewed previous editions of this book:

Sana Akili, *Iowa State University*

Mark Alpert, *University of Texas at Austin*

Allan L. Appell, *San Francisco State University*

Laurie Babin, *University of Southern Mississippi*

Thomas Brashear, *Isenberg School of Management, University of Massachusetts, Amherst*

David J. Burns, *Youngstown State University*

Sang T. Choe, *University of Southern Indiana*

Alicia Cooper, *Morgan State University*

Preyas Desai, *Purdue University*

J. Ford Laumer, Jr, *Auburn University*

Richard Leventhal, *Metropolitan State College, Denver*

Tamara Mangleburg, *Florida Atlantic University*

Patricia M. Manninen, *North Shore Community College*

H. Lee Meadow, *Northern Illinois University*

Martin Meyers, *University of Wisconsin, Stevens Point*

David M. Nemi, *Niagra County Community College*

Carl Obermiller, *Seattle University*

Howard W. Olsen, *University of Nevada, Reno*

Alan T. Shao, *University of North Carolina, Charlotte*

Martin St. John, *Westmoreland County Community College*

John Stovall, *University of Illinois, Chicago*

Jeff Streiter, *SUNY Brockport*

Donna Tillman, *California State Polytechnic University*

Simon Walls, *University of Tennessee*

Andrew Yap, *Florida International University*

Irvin A. Zaenglein, *Northern Michigan University*

We also owe a great deal to the people at Prentice Hall who helped develop this book. Editor, Katie Stevens provided energetic support and ably managed the many facets of this complex revision project. We also owe much thanks to Judy Leale and Cindy Durand, who helped shepherd the project smoothly through production. Additional thanks go to Executive Marketing Manager Michelle O'Brien, who provided many good ideas, a keen design eye, and a positive attitude. Keri Jean Miksza provided substantial help in acquiring text illustrations.

Finally, we owe many thanks to our families—Kathy, Betty, KC, Keri, Delaney, Mandy, Matt, and Molly; and Nancy, Amy, Melissa, and Jessica—for their constant support and encouragement. To them, we dedicate this book.

Philip Kotler
Gary Armstrong

Principles of Marketing

C H A P T E R **1**

> **After studying this chapter, you should be able to**

1. define marketing and outline the steps in the marketing process
2. explain the importance of understanding customers and the marketplace, and identify the five core marketplace concepts
3. identify the key elements of a customer-driven marketing strategy and discuss the marketing management orientations that guide marketing strategy
4. discuss customer relationship management, and identify strategies for creating value *for* customers and capturing value *from* customers in return
5. describe the major trends and forces that are changing the marketing landscape in this age of relationships

Marketing: Managing Profitable Customer Relationships

Previewing the Concepts

Welcome to the exciting world of marketing! In this chapter, to start you off, we will introduce you to the basic concepts. We'll start with a simple question: What *is* marketing? Simply put, marketing is managing profitable customer relationships. The aim of marketing is to create value for customers and to capture value in return. Chapter 1 is organized around five steps in the marketing process—from understanding customer needs, to designing customer-driven marketing strategies and programs, to building customer relationships and capturing value for the firm. Understanding these basic concepts, and forming your own ideas about what they really mean to you, will give you a solid foundation for all that follows.

To set the stage, let's first look at NASCAR. In only a few years, NASCAR has swiftly evolved from a pastime for beer-guzzling Bubbas into a national marketing phenomenon. How? By creating high-octane value for its millions of fans. In return, NASCAR captures value from these fans, both for itself and for its many sponsors. Read on and see how NASCAR does it.

When you think of NASCAR, do you think of tobacco-spitting rednecks and run-down racetracks? Think again! These days, NASCAR (the National Association for Stock Car Auto Racing) is much, much more. In fact, it's one great marketing organization. And for fans, NASCAR is a lot more than stock car races. It's a high-octane, totally involving experience.

As for the stereotypes, throw them away. NASCAR is now the second-highest rated regular season sport on TV—only the NFL draws more viewers. NASCAR fans are young, affluent, and decidedly family-oriented. What's more, they are 75 million strong—4 of every 10 people in the United States regularly watch or attend NASCAR events. Most important, fans are passionate about NASCAR. An ardent NASCAR fan spends nearly $700 a year on NASCAR-related clothing, collectibles, and other items. NASCAR has even become a cultural force, as politicians scramble to gain the favor of a powerful demographic dubbed "NASCAR dads."

What's NASCAR's secret? Its incredible success results from a single-minded focus: creating lasting customer relationships. For fans, the NASCAR relationship develops through a careful blend of live racing events, abundant media coverage, and compelling Web sites.

Each year, fans experience the adrenalin-charged, heart-stopping excitement of NASCAR racing first-hand by attending national tours to some two dozen tracks around the country. NASCAR races attract the largest crowds of any U.S. sporting event. About 200,000 people attended the recent Daytona 500, more than twice as many as attended the Super Bowl.

At these events, fans hold tailgate parties, camp and cook out, watch the cars roar around the track, meet the drivers, and swap stories with other NASCAR enthusiasts. Track facilities even include RV parks next to and right inside the racing oval.

Marvels one sponsor, "[In] what other sport can you drive your beat-up RV or camper into the stadium and sit on it to watch the race?" NASCAR really cares about its customers and goes out of its way to show them a good time. For example, rather than fleecing fans with overpriced food and beer, NASCAR tracks encourage fans to bring their own. Such actions mean that NASCAR might lose a sale today, but it will keep the customer tomorrow.

To further the customer relationship, NASCAR makes the sport a wholesome family affair. The environment is safe for kids—uniformed security guards patrol the track to keeps things in line. The family atmosphere extends to the drivers, too. Unlike the aloof and often distant athletes in other sports, NASCAR drivers seem like regular guys. They are friendly and readily available to mingle with fans and sign autographs. Fans view drivers as good role models, and the long NASCAR tradition of family involvement creates the next generation of loyal fans.

Can't make it to the track? No problem. NASCAR TV coverage reaches 20 million viewers weekly. Well-orchestrated coverage and in-car cameras put fans in the middle of the action, giving them vicarious thrills that keep them glued to the screen. "When the network gets it right, my surround-sound bothers my neighbors but makes my ears happy," says Angela Kotula, a 35-year old human resources professional.

NASCAR also delivers the NASCAR experience through its engaging Web sites. NASCAR.com serves up a glut of information and entertainment—in-depth news, driver bios, background information, online games, community discussions, and merchandise. True die-hard fans can subscribe to TrackPass to get up-to-the-minute standings, race video, streaming audio from the cars, and access to a host of archived audio and video highlights. TrackPass with PitCommand even delivers a real-time data feed, complete with the GPS locations of cars and data from drivers' dashboards.

But a big part of the NASCAR experience is the feeling that the sport, itself, is personally accessible. Anyone who knows how to drive feels that he or she, too, could be a champion NASCAR driver. As 48-year police officer Ed Sweat puts it: "Genetics did not bless me with the height of a basketball player, nor was I born to have the bulk of a lineman in the NFL. But . . . on any given Sunday, with a rich sponsor, the right car, and some practice, I could be draftin' and passin,' zooming to the finish line, trading paint with Tony Stewart. . . . Yup, despite my advancing age and waistline, taking Zocor, and driving by a gym. . . . I could be Dale Jarrett!"

Ultimately, all of this fan enthusiasm translates into financial success for NASCAR, and for its sponsors. Television networks pay some $2.8 billion per year for the rights to broadcast NASCAR events. The sport is third in licensed merchandise sales, behind only the NFL and the NCAA. And Marketing studies show that NASCAR's fans are more loyal to the sport's sponsors than fans of any other sport. They are three times as likely to purchase a sponsor's product rather than a nonsponsor's product.

Just ask dental hygienist Jenny German, an ardent fan of NASCAR driver Jeff Gordon. According to one account: "She actively seeks out any product he endorses. She drinks Pepsi instead of Coke, eats Edy's ice cream for dessert, and owns a pair of Ray-Ban sunglasses. 'If they sold underwear with the number 24 on it, I'd have it on,' German says."

Because of such loyal fan relationships, NASCAR has attracted more than 250 big-name sponsors, from Wal-Mart and Home Depot to Procter & Gamble, M&Ms, Wrangler, and the U.S. Army. In all, corporations spend more than $1 billion a year for NASCAR sponsorships and promotions. Nextel is shelling out $750 million over the next 10 years to be a NASCAR sponsor and to put its name on the Nextel Cup series. "I could pay you $1 million to try and not run into our name at a NASCAR race and you would lose," says a Nextel spokesperson. Other sponsors eagerly pay up to $15 million per year to sponsor a top car and to get their corporate colors and logos emblazoned on team uniforms and on the hoods or side panels of team cars. Or they pay $3 million to $5 million a year to become the "official" (fill-in-the-blank) of NASCAR racing.

So if you're still thinking of NASCAR as rednecks and moonshine, you'd better think again. NASCAR is a premier marketing organization that knows how to create customer value that translates into deep and lasting customer relationships. "Better than any other sport," says a leading sports marketing executive, "NASCAR listens to its fans and gives them what they want." In turn, fans reward NASCAR and its sponsors with deep loyalty and the promise of lasting profits.[1]

Today's successful companies have one thing in common: Like NASCAR, they are strongly customer focused and heavily committed to marketing. These companies share a passion for satisfying customer needs in well-defined target markets. They motivate everyone in the organization to help build lasting customer relationships through superior customer value and satisfaction. As co-founder Bernie Marcus of Home Depot asserted, "All of our people understand what the Holy Grail is. It's not the bottom line. It's an almost blind, passionate commitment to taking care of customers."

What Is Marketing?

Marketing, more than any other business function, deals with customers. Although we will soon explore more-detailed definitions of marketing, perhaps the simplest definition is this one: Marketing is managing profitable customer relationships. The twofold goal of marketing is to attract new customers by promising superior value and to keep and grow current customers by delivering satisfaction.

Wal-Mart has become the world's largest retailer, and the world's largest company, by delivering on its promise, "Always low prices. Always!" At Disney theme parks, "imagineers" work wonders in their quest to "make a dream come true today." Dell leads the personal computer industry by consistently making good on its promise to "be direct." Dell makes it easy for customers to custom-design their own computers and have them delivered quickly to their doorsteps or desktops. These and other highly successful companies know that if they take care of their customers, market share and profits will follow.

Sound marketing is critical to the success of every organization. Large for-profit firms such as Procter & Gamble, Sony, Wal-Mart, IBM, and Marriott use marketing. But so do not-for-profit organizations such as colleges, hospitals, museums, symphony orchestras, and even churches.

You already know a lot about marketing—it's all around you. You see the results of marketing in the abundance of products in your nearby shopping mall. You see marketing in the advertisements that fill your TV screen, spice up your magazines, stuff your mailbox, or enliven your Web pages. At home, at school, where you work, and where you play, you see marketing in almost everything you do. Yet, there is much more to marketing than meets the consumer's casual eye. Behind it all is a massive network of people and activities competing for your attention and purchases.

This book will give you a complete and formal introduction to the basic concepts and practices of today's marketing. In this chapter, we begin by defining marketing and the marketing process.

Marketing Defined

What *is* marketing? Many people think of marketing only as selling and advertising. And no wonder—every day we are bombarded with television commercials, direct-mail offers, sales calls, and Internet pitches. However, selling and advertising are only the tip of the marketing iceberg.

Today, marketing must be understood not in the old sense of making a sale—"telling and selling"—but in the new sense of *satisfying customer needs*. If the marketer does a good job of understanding consumer needs; develops products that provide superior value; and prices, distributes, and promotes them effectively, these products will sell very easily. Thus, selling and advertising are only part of a larger "marketing mix"—a set of marketing tools that work together to satisfy customer needs and build customer relationships.

Broadly defined, marketing is a social and managerial process by which individuals and groups obtain what they need and want through creating and exchanging value with others.[2] In a narrower business context, marketing involves building profitable, value-laden exchange relationships with customers. Hence, we define **marketing** as the process by which companies create value for customers and build strong customer relationships in order to capture value from customers in return.

Marketing
The process by which companies create value for customers and build strong customer relationships in order to capture value from customers in return.

The Marketing Process

Figure 1.1 presents a simple five-step model of the marketing process. In the first four steps, companies work to understand consumers, create customer value, and build strong customer relationships. In the final step, companies reap the rewards of creating superior customer value. By creating value *for* consumers, they in turn capture value *from* consumers in the form of sales, profits, and long-term customer equity.[3]

In this and the next chapter, we will examine the steps of this simple model of marketing. In this chapter, we will review each step but focus more on the customer relationship steps—understanding consumers, building customer relationships, and capturing value from customers. In Chapter 2, we'll look more deeply into the second and third steps—designing marketing strategies and constructing marketing programs.

FIGURE 1.1
A simple model of the marketing process

Create value *for* customers and build customer relationships				Capture value *from* customers in return
Understand the marketplace and customer needs and wants	Design a customer-driven marketing strategy	Construct a marketing program that delivers superior value	Build profitable relationships and create customer delight	Capture value from customers to create profits and customer quality

Understanding the Marketplace and Consumer Needs

As a first step, marketers need to understand customer needs and wants and the marketplace within which they operate. We now examine five core customer and marketplace concepts: *needs, wants, and demands*; *marketing offers (products, services, and experiences)*; *value and satisfaction*; *exchanges and relationships*; and *markets*.

Customer Needs, Wants, and Demands

Needs
States of felt deprivation.

The most basic concept underlying marketing is that of human needs. Human **needs** are states of felt deprivation. They include basic *physical* needs for food, clothing, warmth, and safety; *social* needs for belonging and affection; and *individual* needs for knowledge and self-expression. These needs were not created by marketers; they are a basic part of the human makeup.

Wants
The form human needs take as shaped by culture and individual personality.

Wants are the form human needs take as they are shaped by culture and individual personality. An American *needs* food but *wants* a Big Mac, french fries, and a soft drink. A person in Mauritius *needs* food but *wants* a mango, rice, lentils, and beans. Wants are shaped by one's society and are described in terms of objects that will satisfy needs. When backed by buying power, wants become **demands**. Given their wants and resources, people demand products with benefits that add up to the most value and satisfaction.

Demands
Human wants that are backed by buying power.

Outstanding marketing companies go to great lengths to learn about and understand their customers' needs, wants, and demands. They conduct consumer research and analyze mountains of customer data. Their people at all levels—including top management—stay close to customers. For example, top executives from Wal-Mart spend two days each week visiting stores and mingling with customers. Harley-Davidson's chairman and CEO regularly mounts his Harley and rides with customers to get feedback and ideas.

At consumer products giant Procter & Gamble, top executives even visit with ordinary consumers in their homes and on shopping trips. "We read the data and look at the charts," says one P&G executive, "but to shop [with consumers] and see how the woman is changing retailers to save 10 cents on a loaf of bread [so she can] spend it on things that are more important—that's important to us to keep front and center." Says P&G's CEO, "When the consumer is boss, when you try to win the consumer value equation, when you try to make the consumer's life better, then you're focused externally . . . and it's an absolutely huge difference."[4]

Marketing Offers—Products, Services, and Experiences

Marketing offer
Some combination of products, services, information, or experiences offered to a market to satisfy a need or want.

Consumers' needs and wants are fulfilled through a **marketing offer**—some combination of products, services, information, or experiences offered to a market to satisfy a need or want. Marketing offers are not limited to physical *products*. They also include *services*, activities or benefits offered for sale that are essentially intangible and do not result in the ownership of anything. Examples include banking, airline, hotel, tax preparation, and home repair services. More broadly, marketing offers also include other entities, such as *persons, places, organizations, information,* and *ideas*.

Many sellers make the mistake of paying more attention to the specific products they offer than to the benefits and experiences produced by these products. These sellers suffer from *"marketing myopia."* They are so taken with their products that they focus only on existing wants and lose sight of underlying customer needs.[5] They forget that a product is only a tool to solve a consumer problem. A manufacturer of quarter-inch drill bits may think that the customer needs a drill bit. But what the customer *really* needs is a quarter-inch hole. These sellers will have trouble if a new product comes along that serves the customer's need better or less expensively. The customer will have the same *need* but will *want* the new product.

Smart marketers look beyond the attributes of the products and services they sell. By orchestrating several services and products, they create *brand experiences* for consumers. For example, Disney World is an experience; so is a ride on a Harley-Davidson motorcycle. You experience a visit to Barnes & Noble or to Sony's playstation.com Web site. And you don't just watch a NASCAR race; you immerse yourself in the NASCAR experience. "What consumers really want [are offers] that dazzle their senses, touch their hearts, and stimulate their minds," declares one expert. "They want [offers] that deliver an experience."[6]

■ Products do not have to be physical objects, Here, the "product" is an idea: "how easy it is for you to help protect the prairies and the penguins and the planet."

Customer Value and Satisfaction

Consumers usually face a broad array of products and services that might satisfy a given need. How do they choose among these many marketing offers? Customers form expectations about the value and satisfaction that various marketing offers will deliver and buy accordingly. Satisfied customers buy again and tell others about their good experiences. Dissatisfied customers often switch to competitors and disparage the product to others.

Marketers must be careful to set the right level of expectations. If they set expectations too low, they may satisfy those who buy but fail to attract enough buyers. If they raise expectations too high, buyers will be disappointed. Customer value and customer satisfaction are key building blocks for developing and managing customer relationships. We will revisit these core concepts later in the chapter.

Exchanges and Relationships

Exchange
The act of obtaining a desired object from someone by offering something in return.

Marketing occurs when people decide to satisfy needs and wants through exchange relationships. **Exchange** is the act of obtaining a desired object from someone by offering something in return. In the broadest sense, the marketer tries to bring about a response to some marketing offer. The response may be more than simply buying or trading products and services. A political candidate, for instance, wants votes, a church wants membership, and a social action group wants idea acceptance.

Marketing consists of actions taken to build and maintain desirable exchange *relationships* with target audiences involving a product, service, idea, or other object. Beyond simply attracting new customers and creating transactions, the goal is to retain customers and grow their business with the company. Marketers want to build strong relationships by consistently delivering superior customer value. We will expand on the important concept of customer relationship management later in the chapter.

Markets

Market
The set of actual and potential buyers of a product or service.

The concepts of exchange and relationships lead to the concept of a market. A **market** is the set of actual and potential buyers of a product. These buyers share a particular need or want that can be satisfied through exchange relationships.

Marketing means managing markets to bring about profitable customer relationships. However, creating these relationships takes work. Sellers must search for buyers, identify

FIGURE 1.2

Elements of a modern marketing system

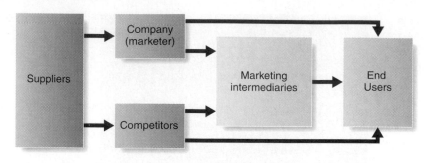

Environment

their needs, design good marketing offers, set prices for them, promote them, and store and deliver them. Activities such as product development, research, communication, distribution, pricing, and service are core marketing activities.

Although we normally think of marketing as being carried on by sellers, buyers also carry on marketing. Consumers do marketing when they search for the goods they need at prices they can afford. Company purchasing agents do marketing when they track down sellers and bargain for good terms.

Figure 1.2 shows the main elements in a modern marketing system. In the usual situation, marketing involves serving a market of final consumers in the face of competitors. The company and the competitors send their respective offers and messages to consumers, either directly or through marketing intermediaries. All of the actors in the system are affected by major environmental forces (demographic, economic, physical, technological, political/legal, social/cultural).

Each party in the system adds value for the next level. All of the arrows represent relationships that must be developed and managed. Thus, a company's success at building profitable relationships depends not only on its own actions but also on how well the entire system serves the needs of final consumers. Wal-Mart cannot fulfill its promise of low prices unless its suppliers provide merchandise at low costs. And Ford cannot deliver high quality to car buyers unless its dealers provide outstanding service.

Designing a Customer-Driven Marketing Strategy

Marketing management
The art and science of choosing target markets and building profitable relationships with them.

Once it fully understands consumers and the marketplace, marketing management can design a customer-driven marketing strategy. We define **marketing management** as the art and science of choosing target markets and building profitable relationships with them. The marketing manager's aim is to find, attract, keep, and grow target customers by creating, delivering, and communicating superior customer value.

To design a winning marketing strategy, the marketing manager must answer two important questions: *What customers will we serve (what's our target market)?* and *How can we serve these customers best (what's our value proposition)?* We will discuss these marketing strategy concepts briefly here, and then look at them in more detail in the next chapter.

Selecting Customers to Serve

The company must first decide *who* it will serve. It does this by dividing the market into segments of customers (*market segmentation*) and selecting which segments it will go after (*target marketing*). Some people think of marketing management as finding as many customers as possible and increasing demand. But marketing managers know that they cannot serve all customers in every way. By trying to serve all customers, they may not serve any customers well. Instead, the company wants to select only customers that it can serve well and profitably. For example, Nordstrom stores profitably target affluent professionals; Family Dollar stores profitably target families with more modest means.

Demarketing
Marketing to reduce demand temporarily or permanently; the aim is not to destroy demand but only to reduce or shift it.

Some marketers may even seek *fewer* customers and reduced demand. For example, many power companies have trouble meeting demand during peak usage periods. In these and other cases of excess demand, companies may practice **demarketing** to reduce the number of customers or to shift their demand temporarily or permanently. For instance, to reduce demand for space on congested expressways in Washington, D.C., the Metropolitan Washington Council of Governments has set up a Web site encouraging commuters to carpool and use mass transit.[7]

Thus, marketing managers must decide which customers they want to target, and on the level, timing, and nature of their demand. Simply put, marketing management is *customer management* and *demand management*.

Choosing a Value Proposition

The company must also decide how it will serve targeted customers—how it will *differentiate and position* itself in the marketplace. A company's *value proposition* is the set of benefits or values it promises to deliver to consumers to satisfy their needs. Porsche promises driving performance and excitement: "What a dog feels like when its leash breaks." Tide laundry detergent promises powerful, all-purpose cleaning, whereas Gain "cleans and freshens like sunshine." Altoids positions itself as "the curiously strong mint."

Such value propositions differentiate one brand from another. They answer the customer's question "Why should I buy your brand rather than a competitor's?" Companies must design strong value propositions that give them the greatest advantage in their target markets.

Marketing Management Orientations

Marketing management wants to design strategies that will build profitable relationships with target consumers. But what *philosophy* should guide these marketing strategies? What weight should be given to the interests of customers, the organization, and society? Very often, these interests conflict.

There are five alternative concepts under which organizations design and carry out their marketing strategies: the *production, product, selling, marketing,* and *societal marketing concepts.*

The Production Concept

Production concept
The idea that consumers will favor products that are available and highly affordable.

The **production concept** holds that consumers will favor products that are available and highly affordable. Therefore, management should focus on improving production and distribution efficiency. This concept is one of the oldest orientations that guides sellers.

The production concept is still a useful philosophy in two types of situations. The first occurs when the demand for a product exceeds the supply. Here, management should look for ways to increase production. The second situation occurs when the product's cost is too high and improved productivity is needed to bring it down. For example, Henry Ford's philosophy

■ Value propositions: Porsche targets affluent buyers with promises of driving excitement: "What a dog feels like when the leash breaks."

What a dog feels when the leash breaks.

Instant freedom, courtesy of the Boxster S. The 250 horsepower boxer engine launches you forward with its distinctive growl. Any memory of life on a leash evaporates in the wind rushing overhead. It's time to run free. Contact us at 1-800-PORSCHE or porsche.com.

PORSCHE

was to perfect the production of the Model T so that its cost could be reduced and more people could afford it. He joked about offering people a car of any color as long as it was black.

Although useful in some situations, the production concept can lead to marketing myopia. Companies adopting this orientation run a major risk of focusing too narrowly on their own operations and losing sight of the real objective—satisfying customer needs and building customer relationships.

The Product Concept

Product concept
The idea that consumers will favor products that offer the most in quality, performance, and features and that the organization should therefore devote its energy to making continuous product improvements.

The **product concept** holds that consumers will favor products that offer the most in quality, performance, and innovative features. Under this concept, marketing strategy focuses on making continuous product improvements. Some manufacturers believe that if they can build a better mousetrap, the world will beat a path to their door. But they are often rudely shocked. Buyers may well be looking for a better solution to a mouse problem but not necessarily for a better mousetrap. The solution might be a chemical spray, an exterminating service, or something that works better than a mousetrap. Furthermore, a better mousetrap will not sell unless the manufacturer designs, packages, and prices it attractively; places it in convenient distribution channels; brings it to the attention of people who need it; and convinces buyers that it is a better product.

Thus, the product concept also can lead to marketing myopia. For instance, railroad management once thought that users wanted *trains* rather than *transportation* and overlooked the growing challenge of airlines, buses, trucks, and automobiles. Kodak assumed that consumers wanted photographic film rather than a way to capture and share memories and at first overlooked the challenge of digital cameras. Although it now leads the digital camera market in sales, it has yet to make significant profits from this business.[8]

The Selling Concept

Selling concept
The idea that consumers will not buy enough of the firm's products unless it undertakes a large-scale selling and promotion effort.

Many companies follow the **selling concept**, which holds that consumers will not buy enough of the firm's products unless it undertakes a large-scale selling and promotion effort. The concept is typically practiced with unsought goods—those that buyers do not normally think of buying, such as insurance or blood donations. These industries must be good at tracking down prospects and selling them on product benefits.

Most firms practice the selling concept when they face overcapacity. Their aim is to sell what they make rather than make what the market wants. Such a marketing strategy carries high risks. It focuses on creating sales transactions rather than on building long-term, profitable customer relationships.

The Marketing Concept

Marketing concept
The marketing management philosophy that holds that achieving organizational goals depends on knowing the needs and wants of target markets and delivering the desired satisfactions better than competitors do.

The **marketing concept** holds that achieving organizational goals depends on knowing the needs and wants of target markets and delivering the desired satisfactions better than competitors do. Under the marketing concept, customer focus and value are the *paths* to sales and profits.

Instead of a product-centered "make and sell" philosophy, the marketing concept is a customer-centered "sense and respond" philosophy. It views marketing not as "hunting," but as "gardening." The job is not to find the right customers for your product, but to find the right products for your customers. As stated by famed direct marketer Lester Wunderman, "The chant of the Industrial Revolution was that of the manufacturer who said, 'This is what I make, won't you please buy it.' The call of the Information Age is the consumer asking, 'This is what I want, won't you please make it.'"[9]

Figure 1.3 contrasts the selling concept and the marketing concept. The selling concept takes an *inside-out* perspective. It starts with the factory, focuses on the company's existing products, and calls for heavy selling and promotion to obtain profitable sales. It focuses primarily on customer conquest—getting short-term sales with little concern about who buys or why.

In contrast, the marketing concept takes an *outside-in* perspective. As Herb Kelleher, Southwest Airlines's colorful CEO, puts it, "We don't have a Marketing Department; we have a Customer Department." And in the words of one Ford executive, "If we're not customer driven, our cars won't be either." The marketing concept starts with a well-defined market, focuses on customer needs, and integrates all the marketing activities that affect customers. In turn, it yields profits by creating lasting relationships with the right customers based on customer value and satisfaction.

Implementing the marketing concept often means more than simply responding to customers' stated desires and obvious needs. *Customer-driven* companies research current cus-

FIGURE 1.3
The selling and marketing concepts contrasted

The selling concept

The marketing concept

tomers deeply to learn about their desires, gather new product and service ideas, and test proposed product improvements. Such customer-driven marketing usually works well when a clear need exists and when customers know what they want.

In many cases, however, customers *don't* know what they want or even what is possible. For example, 20 years ago, how many consumers would have thought to ask for cell phones, fax machines, home copiers, 24-hour online buying, DVD players, satellite navigation systems in their cars, or wearable PCs? Such situations call for *customer-driving* marketing—understanding customer needs even better than customers themselves do and creating products and services that will meet existing and latent needs, now and in the future.

As Sony's visionary leader, Akio Morita, puts it: "Our plan is to lead the public with new products rather than ask them what kinds of products they want. The public does not know what is possible, but we do." And according to an executive at 3M, "Our goal is to lead customers where they want to go before *they* know where they want to go."[10]

The Societal Marketing Concept

Societal marketing concept
A principle of enlightened marketing that holds that a company should make good marketing decisions by considering consumers' wants, the company's requirements, consumers' long-run interests, and society's long run interests.

The **societal marketing concept** questions whether the pure marketing concept overlooks possible conflicts between consumer *short-run wants* and consumer *long-run welfare*. Is a firm that satisfies the immediate needs and wants of target markets always doing what's best for consumers in the long run? The societal marketing concept holds that marketing strategy should deliver value to customers in a way that maintains or improves both the consumer's *and the society's* well-being.

Consider the fast-food industry. You may see today's giant fast-food chains as offering tasty and convenient food at reasonable prices. Yet many consumer and environmental groups have voiced concerns. Critics point out that hamburgers, fried chicken, french fries, and most other fast-foods are high in fat and salt. Meals are now "super-sized," leading consumers to overeat and contributing to a national obesity epidemic. The products are wrapped in convenient packaging, but this leads to waste and pollution. Thus, in satisfying short-term consumer wants, the highly successful fast-food chains may be harming consumer health and causing environmental problems in the long run.[11]

As Figure 1.4 shows, companies should balance three considerations in setting their marketing strategies: company profits, consumer wants, *and* society's interests. Johnson & Johnson

FIGURE 1.4
Three considerations underlying the societal marketing concept

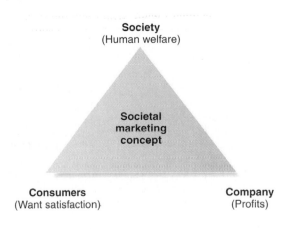

does this well. Its concern for societal interests is summarized in a company document called "Our Credo," which stresses honesty, integrity, and putting people before profits. Under this credo, Johnson & Johnson would rather take a big loss than ship a bad batch of one of its products.

Consider the tragic tampering case in which eight people died from swallowing cyanide-laced capsules of Tylenol, a Johnson & Johnson brand. Although Johnson & Johnson believed that the pills had been altered in only a few stores, not in the factory, it quickly recalled all of its product. The recall cost the company $240 million in earnings. In the long run, however, the company's swift recall of Tylenol strengthened consumer confidence and loyalty, and Tylenol remains one of the nation's leading brands of pain reliever.

Johnson & Johnson management has learned that doing what's right benefits both consumers and the company. Says Johnson & Johnson's chief executive, "The Credo should not be viewed as some kind of social welfare program . . . it's just plain good business. If we keep trying to do what's right, at the end of the day we believe the marketplace will reward us." Thus, over the years, Johnson & Johnson's dedication to consumers and community service has made it one of America's most-admired companies *and* one of the most profitable.[12]

Preparing a Marketing Plan and Program

The company's marketing strategy outlines which customers the company will serve and how it will create value for these customers. Next, the marketer constructs a marketing program that will actually deliver the intended value to target customers. The marketing program builds customer relationships by transforming the marketing strategy into action. It consists of the firm's *marketing mix*, the set of marketing tools the firm uses to implement its marketing strategy.

The major marketing mix tools are classified into four broad groups, called the *four Ps* of marketing: product, price, place, and promotion. To deliver on its value proposition, the firm

■ The societal marketing concept: Johnson & Johnson's Credo stresses putting people before profits. J&J's quick product recall following a tragic Tylenol tampering incident some years ago cost the company $240 million in earnings but strengthened consumer confidence and loyalty.

Our Credo

We believe our first responsibility is to the doctors, nurses and patients, to mothers and fathers and all others who use our products and services. In meeting their needs everything we do must be of high quality. We must constantly strive to reduce our costs in order to maintain reasonable prices. Customers' orders must be serviced promptly and accurately. Our suppliers and distributors must have an opportunity to make a fair profit.

We are responsible to our employees, the men and women who work with us throughout the world. Everyone must be considered as an individual. We must respect their dignity and recognize their merit. They must have a sense of security in their jobs. Compensation must be fair and adequate, and working conditions clean, orderly and safe. We must be mindful of ways to help our employees fulfill their family responsibilities. Employees must feel free to make suggestions and complaints. There must be equal opportunity for employment, development and advancement for those qualified. We must provide competent management, and their actions must be just and ethical.

We are responsible to the communities in which we live and work and to the world community as well. We must be good citizens — support good works and charities and bear our fair share of taxes. We must encourage civic improvements and better health and education. We must maintain in good order the property we are privileged to use, protecting the environment and natural resources.

Our final responsibility is to our stockholders. Business must make a sound profit. We must experiment with new ideas. Research must be carried on, innovative programs developed and mistakes paid for. New equipment must be purchased, new facilities provided and new products launched. Reserves must be created to provide for adverse times. When we operate according to these principles, the stockholders should realize a fair return.

Johnson & Johnson

must first create a need-satisfying marketing offer (product). It must decide how much it will charge for the offer (price) and how it will make the offer available to target consumers (place). Finally, it must communicate with target customers about the offer and persuade them of its merits (promotion). We will explore marketing programs and the marketing mix in much more detail in the next chapter.

Building Customer Relationships

The first three steps in the marketing process—understanding the marketplace and customer needs, designing a customer-driven marketing strategy, and constructing marketing programs—all lead up to the fourth and most important step: building profitable customer relationships.

Customer Relationship Management

Customer relationship management (CRM) is perhaps the most important concept of modern marketing. Until recently, CRM has been defined narrowly as a customer data management activity. By this definition, it involves managing detailed information about individual customers and carefully managing customer "touchpoints" in order to maximize customer loyalty. We will discuss this narrower CRM activity in Chapter 4 dealing with marketing information.

More recently, however, customer relationship management has taken on a broader meaning. In this broader sense, **customer relationship management** is the overall process of building and maintaining profitable customer relationships by delivering superior customer value and satisfaction. It deals with all aspects of acquiring, keeping, and growing customers.

Relationship Building Blocks: Customer Value and Satisfaction

The key to building lasting customer relationships is to create superior customer value and satisfaction. Satisfied customers are more likely to be loyal customers and to give the company a larger share of their business.

CUSTOMER VALUE Attracting and retaining customers can be a difficult task. Customers often face a bewildering array of products and services from which to choose. A customer buys from the firm that offers the highest **customer perceived value**—the customer's evaluation of the difference between all the benefits and all the costs of a marketing offer relative to those of competing offers.

For example, FedEx customers gain a number of benefits. The most obvious is fast and reliable package delivery. However, by using FedEx, customers also may receive some status and image values. Using FedEx usually makes both the package sender and the receiver feel more important. When deciding whether to send a package via FedEx, customers will weigh these and other perceived values against the money, effort, and psychic costs of using the service. Moreover, they will compare the value of using FedEx against the value of using other shippers—UPS, Airborne, the U.S. Postal Service. They will select the service that gives them the greatest perceived value.

Customers often do not judge product values and costs accurately or objectively. They act on *perceived* value. For example, does FedEx really provide faster, more reliable express delivery? If so, is this better service worth the higher prices that FedEx charges? The U.S. Postal Service argues that its express service is comparable, and its prices are much lower. However, judging by market share, most consumers perceive otherwise. Each day, they entrust FedEx with 3 million express packages, a 46 percent share of their next-day air shipping business, compared with the U.S. Postal Service's 6 percent share. The U.S. Postal Service's challenge is to change these customer value perceptions.[13]

CUSTOMER SATISFACTION **Customer satisfaction** depends on the product's perceived performance relative to a buyer's expectations. If the product's performance falls short of expectations, the customer is dissatisfied. If performance matches expectations, the customer is satisfied. If performance exceeds expectations, the customer is highly satisfied or delighted.

Outstanding marketing companies go out of their way to keep important customers satisfied. Highly satisfied customers make repeat purchases and tell others about their good experiences with the product. The key is to match customer expectations with company

Customer relationship management (CRM)
The overall process of building and maintaining profitable customer relationships by delivering superior customer value and satisfaction.

Customer perceived value
The difference between total customer value and total customer cost.

Customer satisfaction
The extent to which a product's perceived performance matches a buyer's expectations.

■ Is FedEx's service worth the higher price? FedEx thinks so. Its ads promise that if you need reliability, speed, and peace of mind, "Relax, it's FedEx."

performance. Smart companies aim to *delight* customers by promising only what they can deliver, then delivering *more* than they promise (see Real Marketing 1.1).[14]

However, although the customer-centered firm seeks to deliver high customer satisfaction relative to competitors, it does not attempt to *maximize* customer satisfaction. A company can always increase customer satisfaction by lowering its price or increasing its services. But this may result in lower profits. Thus, the purpose of marketing is to generate customer value profitably. This requires a very delicate balance: The marketer must continue to generate more customer value and satisfaction but not "give away the house."

Customer Relationship Levels and Tools

Companies can build customer relationships at many levels, depending on the nature of the target market. At one extreme, a company with many low-margin customers may seek to develop *basic relationships* with them. For example, Procter & Gamble does not phone or call on all of its Tide customers to get to know them personally. Instead, P&G creates relationships through brand-building advertising, sales promotions, a toll free customer response number, and its Tide FabricCare Network Web site (www.Tide.com).

At the other extreme, in markets with few customers and high margins, sellers want to create *full partnerships* with key customers. For example, P&G customer teams work closely with Wal-Mart, Safeway, and other large retailers. And Boeing partners with American Airlines, Delta, and other airlines in designing airplanes that fully satisfy their requirements. In between these two extreme situations, other levels of customer relationships are appropriate.

Today, most leading companies are developing customer loyalty and retention programs. Beyond offering consistently high value and satisfaction, marketers can use specific marketing tools to develop stronger bonds with consumers. For example, many companies now offer *frequency marketing programs* that reward customers who buy frequently or in large amounts. Airlines offer frequent-flier programs, hotels give room upgrades to their frequent guests, and supermarkets give patronage discounts to "very important customers."

Other companies sponsor *club marketing programs* that offer members special discounts and create member communities. For example:[15]

> Harley-Davidson sponsors the Harley Owners Group (H.O.G.), which gives Harley riders "an organized way to share their passion and show their pride." H.O.G membership benefits include two magazines (*Hog Tales* and *Enthusiast*), a *H.O.G. Touring Handbook,* a roadside assistance program, a specially designed insurance program, theft reward service, a travel center, and a "Fly & Ride" program enabling members to rent Harleys while on vacation. The company also maintains an extensive H.O.G. Web site, which offers information on H.O.G. chapters, rallies, events, and benefits. The worldwide club now numbers more than 1,300 local chapters and 800,000 members.

■ Building customer relationships: Harley-Davidson sponsors the Harley Owners Group (H.O.G.), which gives Harley owners "an organized way to share their passion and show their pride." The worldwide club now numbers more than 1,300 local chapters and 800,000 members.

To build customer relationships, companies can add structural ties as well as financial and social benefits. A business marketer might supply customers with special equipment or online linkages that help them manage their orders, payroll, or inventory. For example, McKesson Corporation, a leading pharmaceutical wholesaler, has set up an online system to help small pharmacies manage their inventories, their order entry, and their shelf space.

The Changing Nature of Customer Relationships

Dramatic changes are occurring in the ways in which companies are relating to their customers. Yesterday's companies focused on mass marketing to all customers at arm's length. Today's companies are building more direct and lasting relationships with more carefully selected customers. Here are some important trends in the way companies are relating to their customers.

Relating with More Carefully Selected Customers

Few firms today still practice true mass marketing—selling in a standardized way to any customer who comes along. Today, most marketers realize that they don't want relationships with every customer. Instead, companies now are targeting fewer, more profitable customers.

At the same time that companies are finding new ways to deliver more value *to* customers, they are also beginning to assess carefully the value *of* customers to the firm. Called *selective relationship management*, many companies now use customer profitability analysis to weed out losing customers and target winning ones for pampering. Once they identify profitable customers, firms can create attractive offers and special handling to capture these customers and earn their loyalty.

But what should the company do with unprofitable customers? If it can't turn them into profitable ones, it may even want to "fire" customers that are too unreasonable or that cost more to serve than they are worth. For example, the banking industry has led the way in assessing customer profitability. After decades of casting a wide net to lure as many customers

Real Marketing 1.1

Customer Relationships: Delighting Customers

Top-notch marketing companies know that delighting customers involves more than simply opening a complaint department, smiling a lot, and being nice. These companies set very high standards for customer satisfaction and often make seemingly outlandish efforts to achieve them. Consider the following example:

A man bought his first new Lexus—a $45,000 piece of machinery. He could afford a Mercedes, a Jaguar, or a Cadillac, but he bought the Lexus. He took delivery of his new honey and started to drive it home, luxuriating in the smell of the leather interior and the glorious handling. On the interstate, he put the pedal to the metal and felt the Gs in the pit of his stomach. The lights, the windshield washer, the gizmo cup holder that popped out of the center console, the seat heater that warmed his bottom on a cold winter morning—he tried all of these with mounting pleasure. On a whim, he turned on the radio. His favorite classical music station came on in splendid quadraphonic sound that ricocheted around the interior. He pushed the second button; it was his favorite news station. The third button brought his favorite talk station that kept him awake on long trips. The fourth button was set to his daughter's favorite rock station. In fact, every button was set to his specific tastes. The customer knew the car was smart, but was it psychic? No. The mechanic at Lexus had noted the radio settings on his trade-in and duplicated them on the new Lexus. The customer was delighted. This was his car now—through and through! No one told the mechanic to do it. It's just part of the Lexus philosophy: Delight a customer and continue to delight that customer, and you will have a customer for life. What the mechanic did cost Lexus nothing. Not one red cent. Yet it solidified the relationship that could be worth high six figures to Lexus in customer lifetime value. Such relationship-building passions in dealerships around the country have made Lexus the nation's top-selling luxury vehicle.

Studies show that going to extremes to keep customers happy, although sometimes costly, goes hand in hand with good financial performance. Delighted customers come back again and again. Thus, in today's highly competitive marketplace, companies can well afford to lose money on one transaction if it helps to cement a profitable long-term customer relationship.

For companies interested in delighting customers, exceptional value and service are more than a set of policies or actions—they are a companywide attitude, an important part of the overall company culture. Employees at the Cafe Un Deux Trois in Minneapolis learn about customer service from the restaurant's owner Michael Morse. Morse once overheard a customer raving about the egg rolls at the Chinese restaurant across the street. The next time the customer visited the café, Morse served him those very egg rolls.

Southwest Airlines is well known for its low fares and prompt arrivals. But its friendly and often funny flight staff goes to great lengths to delight customers. In one instance, after pushing away from the departure gate, a Southwest pilot spied an anguished passenger, sweat streaming from her face, racing down the jetway only to find that that she'd arrived too late. He returned to the gate to pick her up. Says Southwest's executive vice president for customers, "It

■ Delighting customers: Southwest Airline's friendly and often funny flight staff goes to great lengths to delight customers. Here a costumed Southwest attendant hands out candy on Halloween.

broke every rule in the book, but we congratulated the pilot on a job well done."

Four Seasons Hotels, long known for its outstanding service, tells its employees the story of Ron Dyment, a doorman in Toronto, who forgot to load a departing guest's briefcase into his taxi. The doorman called the guest, a lawyer in Washington, D.C., and learned that he desperately needed the briefcase for a meeting the following morning. Without first asking for approval from management, Dyment hopped on a plane and returned the briefcase. The company named Dyment Employee of the Year.

Similarly, the Nordstrom department store chain thrives on stories about its service heroics, such as employees dropping off orders at customers' homes or warming up cars while customers spend a little more time shopping. In one case, a salesclerk reportedly gave a customer a refund on a tire—Nordstrom doesn't carry tires, but the store prides itself on a no-questions-asked return policy. There's even a story about a man whose wife, a loyal Nordstrom customer, died with her Nordstrom account $1,000 in arrears. Not only did Nordstrom settle the account, it also sent flowers to the funeral.

There's no simple formula for taking care of customers, but neither is it a mystery. According to the CEO of L.L. Bean, "A lot of people have fancy things to say about customer service . . . but it's just a day-in, day-out, ongoing, never-ending, unremitting, persevering, compassionate kind of activity." For the companies that do it well, it's also very rewarding.

Sources: Examples and quotes are from Denny Hatch and Ernie Schell, "Delight Your Customers," *Target Marketing*, April 2002, pp. 32–39; Dana James, "Lighting the Way," *Marketing News*, April 1, 2002, pp. 1, 11; Patricia Sellers, "Companies That Serve You Best," *Fortune*, May 31, 1993, pp. 74–88; Chip R. Bell and Ron Zemke, "Service Magic," *Executive Excellence*, May 2003, p. 13; and Fiona Haley, "Fast Talk," *Fast Company*, December 2003, p. 57. Also see "Lexus Retains Best-Selling Luxury Brand Title for Fourth Year in a Row," January 5, 2004, accessed at www.lexus.com/about/press_releases/index.html; and "Lexus Awards and Accolades," accessed at www.lexus.com, June 2004.

■ Selective relationship management: BankOne in Louisiana lets its "Premier One" customers know that they are "special, exclusive, privileged, and valued." For example, after presenting a special gold card to the "concierge" near the front door, they are whisked away to a special teller window with no line or to the desk of a specially trained bank officer.

as possible, many banks are now mining their vast databases to identify winning customers and cut out losing ones.

Banks now routinely calculate customer value based on such factors as an account's average balances, account activity, services usage, branch visits, and other variables. A bank's customer service reps use such customer ratings when deciding how much—or how little—leeway to give a customer who wants, say, a lower credit-card interest rate or to escape the bank's bounced-check fee. Profitable customers often get what they want; for customers whose accounts lose money for the bank, the reps rarely budge.

This sorting-out process, of course, has many risks. For one, future profits are hard to predict. A high school student on his or her way to a Harvard MBA and a plum job on Wall Street might be unprofitable now but worth courting for the future. Still, most banks believe that the benefits outweigh the risks. For example, after First Chicago imposed a $3 teller fee some years ago on its money-losing customers, 30,000 of them—or close to 3 percent of the bank's customers—closed their accounts. However, many marginal customers became profitable by boosting their account balances high enough to avoid the fee or by visiting ATMs instead of tellers. On balance, imposing the fee improved the profitability of the bank's customer base.[16]

Relating for the Long-Term

Just as companies are being more selective about which customers they choose to serve, they are serving chosen customers in a deeper, more lasting way. Today's companies are going beyond designing strategies to *attract* new customers and create *transactions* with them. They are using customer relationship management to *retain* current customers and build profitable, long-term *relationships* with them. The new view is that marketing is the science and art of finding, retaining, *and* growing profitable customers.

Why the new emphasis on retaining and growing customers? In the past, growing markets and an upbeat economy meant a plentiful supply of new customers. However, companies today face some new marketing realities. Changing demographics, more sophisticated competitors, and overcapacity in many industries mean that there are fewer customers to go around. Many companies are now fighting for shares of flat or fading markets.

As a result, the costs of attracting new consumers are rising. In fact, on average, it costs 5 to 10 times as much to attract a new customer as it does to keep a current customer satisfied. Sears found that it costs 12 times more to attract a customer than to keep an existing one. Given these new realities, companies now go all out to keep profitable customers.[17]

Relating Directly

Beyond connecting more deeply with their customers, many companies are also connecting more *directly*. In fact, direct marketing is booming. Consumers can now buy virtually any product without going to a store—by telephone, mail-order catalogs, kiosks, and online. Business purchasing agents routinely shop on the Web for items ranging from standard office supplies to high-priced, high-tech computer equipment.

Some companies sell *only* via direct channels—firms such as Dell, Expedia, and Amazon.com, to name only a few. Other companies use direct connections to supplement their other communications and distribution channels. For example, Sony sells Playstation consoles and game cartridges through retailers, supported by millions of dollars of mass-media advertising. However, Sony uses its www.PlayStation.com Web site to build relationships with game players of all ages. The site offers information about the latest games, news about events and promotions, game guides and support, and even online forums in which game players can swap tips and stories.

Some marketers have hailed direct marketing as the "marketing model of the next century." They envision a day when all buying and selling will involve direct connections between companies and their customers. Others, although agreeing that direct marketing will play a growing and important role, see it as just one more way to approach the marketplace. We will take a closer look at the world of direct marketing in Chapters 16 and 17.

Partner Relationship Management

When it comes to creating customer value and building strong customer relationships, today's marketers know that they can't go it alone. They must work closely with a variety of marketing partners. In addition to being good at *customer relationship management*, marketers must also be good at **partner relationship management**. Major changes are occurring in how marketers partner with others inside and outside the company to jointly bring more value to customers.

Partner relationship management
Working closely with partners in other company departments and outside the company to jointly bring greater value to customers.

Partners Inside the Company

Traditionally, marketers have been charged with understanding customers and representing customer needs to different company departments. The old thinking was that marketing is done only by marketing, sales, and customer support people. However, in today's more connected world, marketing no longer has sole ownership of customer interactions. Every functional area can interact with customers, especially electronically. The new thinking is that every employee must be customer focused. David Packard, co-founder of Hewlett-Packard, wisely said, "Marketing is far too important to be left only to the marketing department."[18]

Today, rather than letting each department go its own way, firms are linking all departments in the cause of creating customer value. Rather than assigning only sales and marketing people to customers, they are forming cross-functional customer teams. For example, Procter & Gamble assigns "customer development teams" to each of its major retailer accounts. These teams—consisting of sales and marketing people, operations specialists, market and financial analysts, and others—coordinate the efforts of many P&G departments toward helping the retailer be more successful.

Marketing Partners Outside the Firm

Changes are also occurring in how marketers connect with their suppliers, channel partners, and even competitors. Most companies today are networked companies, relying heavily on partnerships with other firms.

Marketing channels consist of distributors, retailers, and others who connect the company to its buyers. The *supply chain* describes a longer channel, stretching from raw materials to components to final products that are carried to final buyers. For example, the supply chain for personal computers consists of suppliers of computer chips and other components, the computer manufacturer, and the distributors, retailers, and others who sell the computers.

Through *supply chain management*, many companies today are strengthening their connections with partners all along the supply chain. They know that their fortunes rest not just on how well they perform. Success at building customer relationships also rests on how well their entire supply chain performs against competitors' supply chains. These companies don't just treat suppliers as vendors and distributors as customers. They treat both as partners in delivering customer value. On the one hand, for example, Lexus works closely with carefully selected suppliers to improve quality and operations efficiency. On the other hand, it works with its franchise dealers to provide top-grade sales and service support that will bring customers in the door and keep them coming back.

Beyond managing the supply chain, today's companies are also discovering that they need *strategic* partners if they hope to be effective. In the new, more competitive global environment, going it alone is going out of style. *Strategic alliances* are booming across almost all industries and services. For example, Dell Computer recently ran advertisements telling how it partners with Microsoft and Intel to provide customized e-business solutions. And Volkswagen is working jointly with Archer Daniels Midland to develop biodiesel fuel. Sometimes, even competitors work together for mutual benefit:

> Hewlett-Packard (HP) recently partnered with Apple Computer to bring to market HP-branded iPods, manufactured by Apple, as part of HP's effort to broaden its presence in consumer electronics. "By partnering with Apple, we have the opportunity to add value by integrating the world's largest digital music offering into HP's larger digital entertainment strategy," says HP Chairman and CEO Carly Fiorina. Adds Apple CEO Steve Jobs, "Apple's goal is to get iPods and iTunes into the hands of every music lover around the world, and partnering with HP, an innovative consumer company, is going to help us do just that."[19]

As Jim Kelly, former CEO at UPS, puts it, "The old adage 'If you can't beat 'em, join 'em,' is being replaced by 'Join 'em and you can't be beat.'"[20]

Capturing Value from Customers

The first four steps in the marketing process involve building customer relationships by creating and delivering superior customer value. The final step involves capturing value in return, in the form of current and future sales, market share, and profits. By creating superior customer value, the firm creates highly satisfied customers who stay loyal and buy more. This, in turn, means greater long-run returns for the firm. Here, we discuss the outcomes of creating customer value: customer loyalty and retention, share of market and share of customer, and customer equity.

Creating Customer Loyalty and Retention

Good customer relationship management creates customer delight. In turn, delighted customers remain loyal and talk favorably to others about the company and its products. Studies show big differences in the loyalty of customers who are less satisfied, somewhat satisfied, and completely satisfied. Even a slight drop from complete satisfaction can create an enormous drop in loyalty. Thus, the aim of customer relationship management is to create not just customer satisfaction, but customer delight.[21]

Companies are realizing that losing a customer means losing more than a single sale. It means losing the entire stream of purchases that the customer would make over a lifetime of patronage. For example, here is a dramatic illustration of **customer lifetime value**:

Customer lifetime value
The value of the entire stream of purchases that the customer would make over a lifetime of patronage.

> Stew Leonard, who operates a highly profitable three-store supermarket, says that he sees $50,000 flying out of his store every time he sees a sulking customer. Why? Because his average customer spends about $100 a week, shops 50 weeks a year, and remains in the area for about 10 years. If this customer has an unhappy experience and switches to another supermarket, Stew Leonard's has lost $50,000 in revenue.

The loss can be much greater if the disappointed customer shares the bad experience with other customers and causes them to defect. To keep customers coming back, Stew Leonard's has created what the *New York Times* has dubbed the "Disneyland of Dairy Stores," complete with costumed characters, scheduled entertainment, a petting zoo, and animatronics throughout the store. From its humble beginnings as a small dairy store in 1969, Stew Leonard's has grown at an amazing pace. It's built 29 additions onto the original store, which now serves more than 250,000 customers each week. This legion of loyal shoppers is largely a result of the store's passionate approach to customer service. Rule #1 at Stew Leonard's—The customer is always right. Rule #2—If the customer is ever wrong, reread rule #1![22]

Stew Leonard is not alone in assessing customer lifetime value. Lexus estimates that a single satisfied and loyal customer is worth $600,000 in lifetime sales. The customer lifetime value of a Taco Bell customer exceeds $12,000.[23] Thus, working to retain and grow customers makes good economic sense. In fact, a company can lose money on a specific transaction but still benefit greatly from a long-term relationship.

This means that companies must aim high in building customer relationships. Customer delight creates an emotional relationship with a product or service, not just a rational preference. L.L. Bean, long known for its outstanding customer service and high customer loyalty, preaches the following "golden rule": Sell good merchandise, treat your customers like human beings, and they'll always come back for more." Hanging on to customers is "so basic, it's scary," claims one marketing executive. "We find out what our customers' needs and wants are, and then we overdeliver."[24]

Growing Share of Customer

Share of customer

The portion of the customer's purchasing that a company gets in its product categories.

Beyond simply retaining good customers to capture customer lifetime value, good customer relationship management can help marketers to increase their **share of customer**—the share they get of the customer's purchasing in their product categories. Many marketers are now spending less time figuring out how to increase share of market and more time trying to grow share of customer. Thus, banks want to increase "share of wallet." Supermarkets and restaurants want to get more "share of stomach." Car companies want to increase "share of garage" and airlines want greater "share of travel."

To increase share of customer, firms can leverage customer relationships by offering greater variety to current customers. Or they can train employees to cross-sell and up-sell in order to market more products and services to existing customers. For example, Amazon.com

■ Customer lifetime value: To keep customers coming back, Stew Leonard's has created the "Disneyland of dairy stores." Rule #1—the customer is always right. Rule #2—if the customer is ever wrong, reread rule #1!

is highly skilled at leveraging relationships with its 35 million customers to increase its share of each customer's purchases. Originally an online bookseller, Amazon now offers customers music, videos, gifts, toys, consumer electronics, office products, home improvement items, lawn and garden products, apparel and accessories, and an online auction. In addition, based on each customer's purchase history, the company recommends related books, CDs, or videos that might be of interest. In this way, Amazon.com captures a greater share of each customer's leisure and entertainment budget.

Building Customer Equity

We can now see the importance of not just acquiring customers, but of keeping and growing them as well. Customer relationship management takes a long-term view. Companies want not only to create profitable customers, but to "own" them for life, capture their customer lifetime value, and earn a greater share of their purchases.

What Is Customer Equity?

Customer equity

The total combined customer lifetime values of all of the company's customers.

The ultimate aim of customer relationship management is to produce high **customer equity**.[25] Customer equity is the combined discounted customer lifetime values of all of the company's current and potential customers. Clearly, the more loyal the firm's profitable customers, the higher the firm's customer equity. Customer equity may be a better measure of a firm's performance than current sales or market share. Whereas sales and market share reflect the past, customer equity suggests the future. Consider Cadillac:

> In the 1970s and 1980s, Cadillac had some of the most loyal customers in the industry. To an entire generation of car buyers, the name "Cadillac" defined American luxury. Cadillac's share of the luxury car market reached a whopping 51 percent in 1976. Based on market share and sales, the brand's future looked rosy. However, measures of customer equity would have painted a bleaker picture. Cadillac customers were getting older (average age 60) and average customer lifetime value was falling. Many Cadillac buyers were on their last car. Thus, although Cadillac's market share was good, its customer equity was not. Compare this with BMW. Its more youthful and vigorous image didn't win BMW the early market share war. However, it did win BMW younger customers with higher customer lifetime values. The result: Cadillac now captures only about a 15 percent market share, lower than BMW's. And BMW's customer equity remains much higher—it has more customers with a higher average customer lifetime value. Thus, market share is not the answer. We should care not just about current sales but also about future sales. Customer lifetime value and customer equity are the name of the game.[26]

■ To increase customer lifetime value and customer equity, Cadillac's highly successful Break Through ads target a younger generation of consumers.

FIGURE 1.5
Customer relationship groups
Source: Reprinted by permission of Harvard Business Review. *Adapted from "The Management of Customer Loyalty" by Werner Relnartz and V. Kumar, July 2002, p. 93. Copyright © by the president and fellow of Harvard College; all rights reserved.*

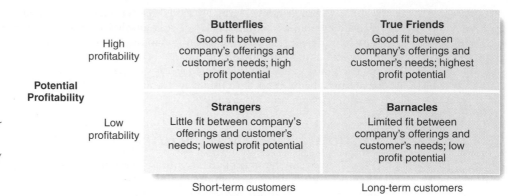

Building the Right Relationships with the Right Customers

Companies should manage customer equity carefully. They should view customers as assets that need to be managed and maximized. But not all customers, not even all loyal customers, are good investments. Surprisingly, some loyal customers can be unprofitable, and some disloyal customers can be profitable. Which customers should the company acquire and retain? "Up to a point, the choice is obvious: Keep the consistent big spenders and lose the erratic small spenders," says one expert. "But what about the erratic big spenders and the consistent small spenders? It's often unclear whether they should be acquired or retained, and at what cost."[27]

The company can classify customers according to their potential profitability and manage its relationships with them accordingly. Figure 1.5 classifies customers into one of four relationship groups, according to their profitability and projected loyalty.[28] Each group requires a different relationship management strategy. "Strangers" show low profitability and little projected loyalty. There is little fit between the company's offerings and their needs. The relationship management strategy for these customers is simple: don't invest anything in them.

"Butterflies" are profitable but not loyal. There is a good fit between the company's offerings and their needs. However, like real butterflies, we can enjoy them for only a short while and then they're gone. An example is stock market investors who trade shares often and in large amounts, but who enjoy hunting out the best deals without building a regular relationship with any single brokerage company. Efforts to convert butterflies into loyal customers are rarely successful. Instead, the company should enjoy the butterflies for the moment. It should use promotional blitzes to attract them, create satisfying and profitable transactions with them, and then cease investing in them until the next time around.

"True friends" are both profitable and loyal. There is a strong fit between their needs and the company's offerings. The firm wants to make continuous relationship investments to delight these customers and nurture, retain, and grow them. It wants to turn true friends into "true believers," who come back regularly and tell others about their good experiences with the company.

"Barnacles" are highly loyal but not very profitable. There is a limited fit between their needs and the company's offerings. An example is smaller bank customers who bank regularly but do not generate enough returns to cover the costs of maintaining their accounts. Like barnacles on the hull of a ship, they create drag. Barnacles are perhaps the most problematic customers. The company might be able to improve their profitability by selling them more, raising their fees, or reducing service to them. However, if they cannot be made profitable, they should be "fired."

The point here is an important one: Different types of customers require different relationship management strategies. The goal is to build the *right relationships* with the *right customers*.[29]

The New Marketing Landscape

As the world spins into the first decade of the twenty-first century, dramatic changes are occurring in the marketplace. Richard Love of Hewlett-Packard observes, "The pace of change is so rapid that the ability to change has now become a competitive advantage." Yogi Berra, the legendary New York Yankees catcher, summed it up more simply when he said, "The future ain't what it used to be." As the marketplace changes, so must those who serve it.

In this section, we examine the major trends and forces that are changing the marketing landscape and challenging marketing strategy. We look at four major developments: the new digital age, rapid globalization, the call for more ethics and social responsibility, and the growth in not-for-profit marketing.

The New Digital Age

The recent technology boom has created a new digital age. The explosive growth in computer, telecommunications, information, transportation, and other technologies has had a major impact on the ways companies bring value to their customers.

Now, more than ever before, we are all connected to each other and to things near and far in the world around us. Where it once took weeks or months to travel across the United States, we can now travel around the globe in only hours or days. Where it once took days or weeks to receive news about important world events, we now see them as they are occurring through live satellite broadcasts. Where it once took weeks to correspond with others in distant places, they are now only moments away by phone or the Internet.

The technology boom has created exciting new ways to learn about and track customers, and to create products and services tailored to individual customer needs. Technology is also helping companies to distribute products more efficiently and effectively. And it's helping them to communicate with customers in large groups or one-to-one.

Through videoconferencing, marketing researchers at a company's headquarters in New York can look in on focus groups in Chicago or Paris without ever stepping onto a plane. With only a few clicks of a mouse button, a direct marketer can tap into online data services to learn anything from what car you drive to what you read to what flavor of ice cream you prefer. Or, using today's powerful computers, marketers can create their own detailed customer databases and use them to target individual customers with offers designed to meet their specific needs.

Technology has also brought a new wave of communication and advertising tools—ranging from cell phones, fax machines, CD-ROM, and interactive TV to video kiosks at airports and shopping malls. Marketers can use these tools to zero in on selected customers with carefully targeted messages. Through e-commerce, customers can learn about, design, order, and pay for products and services—without ever leaving home. Then, through the marvels of express delivery, they can receive their purchases in less than 24 hours. From virtual reality displays that test new products to online virtual stores that sell them, the technology boom is affecting every aspect of marketing.

■ The New Digital Age: The recent technology boom has had a major impact on the ways marketers connect with and bring value to their customers.

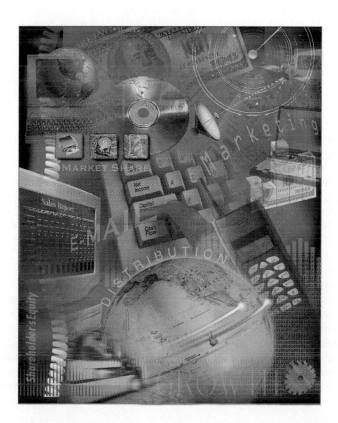

The Internet

Internet

A vast public web of computer networks, which connects users of all types all around the world to each other and to an amazingly large information repository.

Perhaps the most dramatic new technology is the **Internet**. Today, the Internet links individuals and businesses of all types to each other and to information all around the world. The Internet has been hailed as the technology behind a New Economy. It allows anytime, anywhere connections to information, entertainment, and communication. Companies are using the Internet to build closer relationships with customers and marketing partners. Beyond competing in traditional marketplaces, they now have access to exciting new market*spaces*.

Internet usage surged in the 1990s with the development of the user-friendly World Wide Web. Entering the twenty-first century, Internet penetration in the United States has reached 63 percent, with more than 186 million people accessing the Web in any given month. The Internet is truly a global phenomenon—the number of Internet users worldwide reached 719 million last year and is expected to approach 1.5 billion by 2007.[30] This growing and diverse Internet population means that all kinds of people are now going to the Web for information and to buy products and services.

These days, it's hard to find a company that doesn't use the Web in a significant way. Most traditional "brick-and-mortar" companies have now become "click-and-mortar" companies. They have ventured online to attract new customers and build stronger relationships with existing ones. The Internet also spawned an entirely new breed of "click-only" companies—the so-called "dot-coms." During the Web frenzy of the late 1990s, dot-coms popped up everywhere, selling anything from books, toys, and CDs to furniture, home mortgages, and 100-pound bags of dog food via the Internet. The frenzy cooled during the "dot-com meltdown" of 2000, when many poorly conceived e-tailers and other Web start-ups went out of business. Today, despite its turbulent start, online consumer buying is growing at a healthy rate, and many of the dot-com survivors face promising futures. More than half of the companies that survived the meltdown are now profitable.[31]

If consumer e-commerce looks promising, business-to-business e-commerce is just plain booming. Business-to-business transactions were projected to reach $4.3 trillion this year, compared with only $107 billion in consumer purchases. It seems that almost every business has set up shop on the Web. Giants such as GE, IBM, Dell, Cisco Systems, Microsoft, and many others have moved quickly to exploit the power of the Internet.[32]

Thus, the technology boom is providing exciting new opportunities for marketers. We will explore the impact of the new digital age in more detail in Chapter 18.

Rapid Globalization

As they are redefining their relationships with customers and partners, marketers are also taking a fresh look at the ways in which they connect with the broader world around them. In an increasingly smaller world, many marketers are now connected *globally* with their customers and marketing partners.

Today, almost every company, large or small, is touched in some way by global competition. A neighborhood florist buys its flowers from Mexican nurseries, while a large U.S. electronics manufacturer competes in its home markets with giant Japanese rivals. A fledgling Internet retailer finds itself receiving orders from all over the world at the same time that an American consumer-goods producer introduces new products into emerging markets abroad.

American firms have been challenged at home by the skillful marketing of European and Asian multinationals. Companies such as Toyota, Siemens, Nestlé, Sony, and Samsung have often outperformed their U.S. competitors in American markets. Similarly, U.S. companies in a wide range of industries have found new opportunities abroad. General Motors, ExxonMobil, IBM, General Electric, Microsoft, DuPont, and dozens of other American companies have developed truly global operations, making and selling their products worldwide. Coca-Cola offers a mind-boggling 300 different brands in more than 200 countries. Even MTV has joined the elite of global brands, delivering localized versions of its pulse-thumping fare to teens in 140 countries around the globe (see Real Marketing 1.2).

Today, companies are not only trying to sell more of their locally produced goods in international markets, they also are buying more supplies and components abroad. For example, Bill Blass, one of America's top fashion designers, may choose cloth woven from Australian wool with designs printed in Italy. He will design a dress and e-mail the drawing to a Hong Kong agent, who will place the order with a Chinese factory. Finished dresses will be air-freighted to New York, where they will be redistributed to department and specialty stores around the country.

Thus, managers in countries around the world are increasingly taking a global, not just local, view of the company's industry, competitors, and opportunities. They are asking: What

■ Many U.S. companies have developed truly global operations. Coca-Cola offers more than 300 different brands in more than 200 countries including BPM Energy drink in Ireland, Mare Rosso Bitter in Spain, Sprite Ice Cube in Belgium, Fanta in Chile, and NaturAqua in Hungary. "Coca-Cola," "BMP," "Fanta," "NaturAqua," "Bitter Mare Rosso," and accompanying trade dress are trademarks of The Coca-Cola Company. "Sprite Ice" is a trademark of Coca-Cola Ltd.

is global marketing? How does it differ from domestic marketing? How do global competitors and forces affect our business? To what extent should we "go global"? We will discuss the global marketplace in more detail in Chapter 19.

The Call for More Ethics and Social Responsibility

Marketers are reexamining their relationships with social values and responsibilities and with the very Earth that sustains us. As the worldwide consumerism and environmentalism movements mature, today's marketers are being called upon to take greater responsibility for the social and environmental impact of their actions. Corporate ethics and social responsibility have become hot topics for almost every business. And few companies can ignore the renewed and very demanding environmental movement.

The social-responsibility and environmental movements will place even stricter demands on companies in the future. Some companies resist these movements, budging only when forced by legislation or organized consumer outcries. More forward-looking companies, however, readily accept their responsibilities to the world around them. They view socially responsible actions as an opportunity to do well by doing good. They seek ways to profit by serving the best long-run interests of their customers and communities.

Some companies—such as Ben & Jerry's, Saturn, Honest Tea, and others—are practicing "caring capitalism" and distinguishing themselves by being more civic-minded and caring. They are building social responsibility and action into their company value and mission statements. For example, consider Ben & Jerry's, a division of Unilever. Its mission statement challenges all employees, from top management to the ice cream scoopers in each store, to include concern for individual and community welfare in their day-to-day decisions. We will revisit the relationship between marketing and social responsibility in greater detail in Chapter 20.[33]

The Growth of Not-for-Profit Marketing

In the past, marketing has been most widely applied in the for-profit business sector. In recent years, however, marketing also has become a major part of the strategies of many not-for-profit

Real Marketing 1.2

MTV Global: Music Is the Universal Language

Some say love is the universal language. But for MTV, the universal language is *music*. In 1981, MTV began offering its unique brand of programming for young music lovers across the United States. The channel's quirky but pulse-thumping lineup of shows soon attracted a large audience in its targeted 12-to-34 age group. MTV quickly established itself as the nation's youth-culture network, offering up "everything young people care about."

With success in the United States secured, MTV went global in 1986, and the network has experienced phenomenal global growth ever since. MTV now offers programming in 166 countries. It recently became the first U.S. cable network to provide round-the-clock programming in China. The result of this global expansion? Today, MTV reaches twice as many people around the world as CNN, and 80 percent of MTV viewers live outside of the United States. All together, MTV reaches into an astounding 384 million households in 19 different languages on 37 different channels and 17 Web sites.

What is the secret to MTV's roaring international success? Of course, it offers viewers around the globe plenty of what made it so popular in the United States. Tune in to the network anywhere in the world—Paris, or Beijing, or Moscow, or Tierra del Fuego, or anywhere else—and you'll see all of the elements that make it uniquely MTV. You'll feel right at home with the global MTV brand symbols, fast-paced format, veejays, rockumentaries, and music, music, music.

But rather than just offering a carbon copy of its U.S. programming to international viewers, MTV carefully localizes its fare. Each channel serves up a mix that includes 70 percent local programming tailored to the specific tastes on viewers in local markets. A *Business Week* analyst notes:

> [MTV is] shrewd enough to realize that while the world's teens want American music, they really want the local stuff, too. So, MTV's producers and veejays scour their local markets for the top talent. The result is an endless stream of overnight sensations that keep MTV's global offerings fresh. Just over a year ago, for example, Lena Katina and Yulia Volkova were no different than most Moscow schoolgirls. Today, Katina and Volkova make up Tatu, one of the hottest bands ever to come out of Russia.

> Tatu is just one of a slew of emerging local music groups gaining international exposure through MTV and a wider audience in the United States, too. Colombian rock singer Shakira was unknown outside Latin America until 1999, when she recorded an MTV Unplugged CD—the acoustic live concerts recorded by MTV. Her CD has now gone platinum, and she's won one U.S. Grammy and two Latin Grammy awards.

MTV's push for local content has resulted in some of the network's most creative shows. Another MTV analyst observes:

> MTV Russia now has a show called "12 Angry Viewers," in which intellectuals and others debate music videos. In Brazil, "Mochilao," a backpack travel show, is hosted by a popular Brazilian model. In China, MTV Mandarin broadcasts "Mei Mei Sees MTV," which features a "virtual video jockey." And MTV India screens "Silly Point," which is made up of short films poking fun at how cricket gear can be used in everyday life.

At the center of MTV's global growth machine is Bill Roedy, president of MTV Networks International. He's a nonstop ambassador on

■ MTV has joined the ranks of the global brand elite. It reaches into an astounding 384 million households in 19 different languages on 37 different channels and 17 Web sites. From Germany to China, "MTV's version of globalization rocks."

a mission to make MTV available in every last global nook and cranny. According to *Business Week*:

> To give kids their dose of rock, [Roedy] has breakfasted with former Israeli Prime Minister Shimon Peres, dined with Singapore founder Lee Kuan Yew, and chewed the fat with Chinese leader Jiang Zemin. [He] even met with El Caudillo himself—Cuban leader Fidel Castro—who wondered if MTV could teach Cuban kids English. Says Roedy: "We've had very little resistance once we explain that we're not in the business of exporting American culture."

MTV's unique blend of international and local programming is not only popular, it's also highly profitable. The network's hold on a young, increasingly wealthy population makes its programming especially popular with advertisers. Altogether, its mix of local and international content, combined with early entry in international markets, makes it tough to beat. "MTV Networks International makes buckets of money year after year from a potent combination of cable subscriber fees, advertising, and, increasingly, new media," concludes the analyst. Meanwhile, the competition struggles just to break even. VIVA, MTV's strongest competitor in Europe, has yet to turn a profit.

Thus, in only two decades, MTV has joined the ranks of the global brand elite, alongside such icons as Coke, Levi's, and Sony. Concludes the analyst: "MTV's version of globalization rocks."

Sources: Excerpts from Kerry Capell, "MTV's World: Mando-Pop. Mexican Hip Hop. Russian Rap. It's All Fueling the Biggest Global Channel," *Business Week*, February 18, 2002, pp. 81–84; and Charles Goldsmith, "MTV Seeks Global Appeal," *Wall Street Journal*, July 21, 2003, p. B1. Also see "MTV to Begin 24-Hour Service in Part of China," *New York Times*, March 27, 2003, p. C.13; the MTV Worldwide Web site, www.mtv.com/mtvinternational; information accessed at www.viacom.com, February 2004; and "MTV: Music Television: The Facts," accessed at www.viacom.com/prodbyunit1.tin?ixBusUnit-19, May 2004.

organizations, such as colleges, hospitals, museums, symphony orchestras, and even churches. Consider the following example:

> "Want to feed your soul?" implores a subway ad for Marble Collegiate Church in New York City. "We've got a great menu." Indeed, Marble Collegiate has something on its plate for almost every type of spiritual consumer. It has ministries targeting senior citizens; young singles; older singles; gays and lesbians; entrepreneurs; artists, actors, and writers; men; women; children; and people who love singing gospel music, to name a few. Like many other religious institutions working to maintain their shrinking flocks, Marble Collegiate is borrowing marketing tools and tactics from companies selling more worldly goods. It is tailoring its "brand" and "core product"—religion itself—to the needs of spiritually minded people who may be wary of conventional religious organizations. To get its message out, it anointed a Madison Avenue advertising agency as its missionary. The agency produced a slick marketing campaign with hip, youth-oriented messages. One ad urges potential parishioners to "Make a friend in a very high place." Exhorts another: "Our product really does perform miracles." All the marketing seems to be working. Marble Collegiate's Web site traffic has increased by 30 percent since its ad campaign launched, and the church has had its highest attendance in more than 30 years.[34]

Similarly, private colleges, facing declining enrollments and rising costs, are using marketing to compete for students and funds. Many performing arts groups—even the Lyric Opera Company of Chicago, which has seasonal sellouts—face huge operating deficits that they must cover by more aggressive donor marketing. Finally, many long-standing not-for-profit organizations—the YMCA, the Salvation Army, the Girl Scouts—have lost members and are now modernizing their missions and "products" to attract more members and donors.[35]

Make A Friend In A Very High Place.

Marble Collegiate Church
Where good things happen.

11:15 Service / Fifth Ave at 29th St./ www.marblechurch.org / 212-686-2770

Our Product Really Does Perform Miracles.

Marble Collegiate Church
Where good things happen.

Fifth Ave at 29th St. / 11:15 Service / 12:30 Coffee Hour / Dr. Arthur Caliandro, Minister
www.marblechurch.org

■ Not-for-profit marketing: Marble Collegiate Church's advertising agency has produced ads with hip, youth-oriented messages.

Government agencies have also shown an increased interest in marketing. For example, the U.S. Army has a marketing plan to attract recruits, and various government agencies are now designing *social marketing campaigns* to encourage energy conservation and concern for the environment or to discourage smoking, excessive drinking, and drug use. Even the once-stodgy U.S. Postal Service has developed innovative marketing to sell commemorative stamps, promote its priority mail services against those of its competitors, and lift its image. In all, the U.S. Government is the nation's twenty-fourth largest advertiser, with an annual advertising budget of more than $1 billion.[36]

So, What Is Marketing? Pulling It All Together

At the start of this chapter, Figure 1.1 presented a simple model of the marketing process. Now that we've discussed all of the steps in the model, Figure 1.6 presents an expanded model that will help you pull it all together. What is marketing? Simply put, marketing is the process building profitable customer relationships by creating value for customers and capturing value in return.

The first four steps of the marketing process focus on creating value for customers. The company first gains a full understanding of the marketplace by researching consumer needs and managing marketing information. It then designs a customer-driven marketing strategy based on the answers to two simple questions. The first question is "What consumers will we serve?" (market segmentation and targeting). Good marketing companies know that they cannot serve all customers in every way. Instead, they need to focus their resources on the cus-

FIGURE 1.6

An expanded model of the marketing process

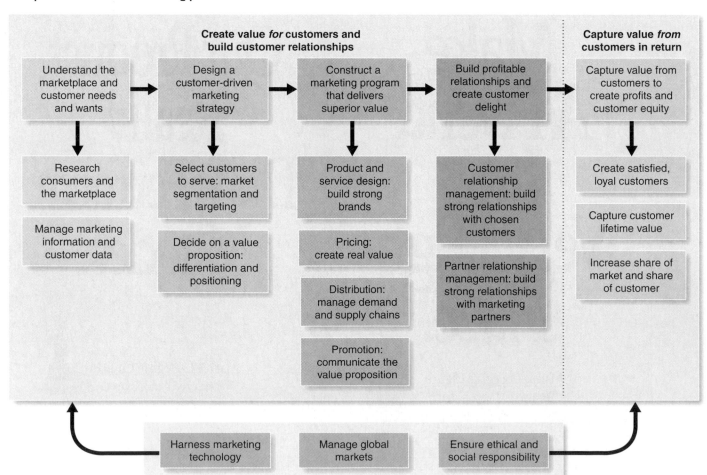

tomers they can serve best and most profitably. The second marketing strategy question is "How can we best serve targeted customers?" (differentiation and positioning). Here, the marketer outlines a value proposition that spells out what values the company will deliver in order to win target customers.

With its marketing strategy decided, the company now constructs a marketing program—consisting of the four marketing mix elements, or the four Ps—that transforms the marketing strategy into real value for customers. The company develops product offers and creates strong brand identities for them. It prices these offers to create real customer value and distributes the offers to make them available to target consumers. Finally, the company designs promotion programs that communicate the value proposition to target consumers and persuade them to act on the marketing offer.

Perhaps the most important step in the marketing process involves building value-laden, profitable relationships with target customers. Throughout the process, marketers practice customer relationship management to create customer satisfaction and delight. In creating customer value and relationships, however, the company cannot go it alone. It must work closely with marketing partners both inside the company and throughout the marketing system. Thus, beyond practicing good customer relationship management, firms must also practice good partner relationship management.

The first four steps in the marketing process create value *for* customers. In the final step, the company reaps the rewards of its strong customer relationships by capturing value *from* customers. Delivering superior customer value creates highly satisfied customers who will buy more and will buy again. This helps the company to capture customer lifetime value and greater share of customer. The result is increased long-term customer equity for the firm.

Finally, in the face of today's changing marketing landscape, companies must take into account three additional factors. In building customer and partner relationships, they must harness marketing technology, take advantage of global opportunities, and ensure that they act in an ethical and socially responsible way.

Figure 1.6 provides a good roadmap to future chapters of the text. Chapters 1 and 2 introduce the marketing process, with a focus on building customer relationships and capturing value from customers. Chapters 3, 4, 5, and 6 address the first step of the marketing process—understanding the marketing environment, managing marketing information, and understanding consumer behavior. In Chapter 7, we look more deeply into the two major marketing strategy decisions: selecting which customers to serve (segmentation and targeting) and deciding on a value proposition (differentiation and positioning). Chapters 8 through 16 discuss the marketing mix variables, one by one. Chapter 17 sums up on customer-driven marketing strategy and creating competitive advantage in the marketplace. Then, the final three chapters examine the special marketing factors: marketing technology in this new digital age, global marketing, and marketing ethics and social responsibility.

> Reviewing the Concepts <

Today's successful companies share a strong customer focus and a heavy commitment to marketing. The goal of marketing is to build and manage profitable customer relationships.

1. Define marketing and outline the steps in the marketing process.

Marketing is the process by which companies create value for customers and build strong customer relationships in order to capture value from customers in return.

The marketing process involves five steps. The first four steps create value *for* customers. First, marketers need to understand the marketplace and customer needs and wants. Next, marketers design a customer-driven marketing strategy with the goal of getting, keeping, and growing target customers. In the third step, marketers construct a marketing program that actually delivers superior value. All of these steps form the basis for the fourth step, building profitable customer relationships and creating customer delight. In the final step, the company reaps the rewards of strong customer relationships by capturing value *from* customers.

2. Explain the importance of understanding customers and the marketplace, and identify the five core marketplace concepts.

Outstanding marketing companies go to great lengths to learn about and understand their customers' needs, wants, and demands. This understanding helps them to design want-satisfying marketing offers and build value-laden customer relationships by which they can capture customer lifetime value and greater share of customer. The result is increased long-term customer equity for the firm.

The core marketplace concepts are *needs, wants,* and *demands; marketing offers (products, services, and experiences); value* and *satisfaction; exchange* and *relationships;* and *markets. Wants* are the form taken by human needs when shaped by culture and individual personality. When backed by buying power, wants become *demands.* Companies address needs by putting forth a *value proposition,* a set of benefits that they promise to consumers to satisfy their needs. The value proposition is fulfilled through a *marketing offer* that delivers customer value and satisfaction, resulting in long-term exchange relationships with customers.

3. **Identify the key elements of a customer-driven marketing strategy and discuss marketing management orientations that guide marketing strategy.**

To design a winning marketing strategy, the company must first decide *who* it will serve. It does this by dividing the market into segments of customers (*market segmentation*) and selecting which segments it will cultivate (*target marketing*). Next, the company must decide *how* it will serve targeted customers (how it will *differentiate and position* itself in the marketplace).

Marketing management can adopt one of five competing market orientations. The *production concept* holds that management's task is to improve production efficiency and bring down prices. The *product concept* holds that consumers favor products that offer the most in quality, performance, and innovative features; thus, little promotional effort is required. The *selling concept* holds that consumers will not buy enough of the organization's products unless it undertakes a large-scale selling and promotion effort. The *marketing concept* holds that achieving organizational goals depends on determining the needs and wants of target markets and delivering the desired satisfactions more effectively and efficiently than competitors do. The *societal marketing concept* holds that generating customer satisfaction *and* long-run societal well-being are the keys to both achieving the company's goals and fulfilling its responsibilities.

4. **Discuss customer relationship management, and identify strategies for creating value *for* customers and capturing value *from* customers in return.**

Broadly defined, *customer relationship management* is the process of building and maintaining profitable customer relationships by delivering superior customer value and satisfaction. The aim of customer relationship management is to produce high *customer equity*, the total combined customer lifetime values of all of the company's customers. The key to building lasting relationships is the creation of superior *customer value* and *satisfaction*.

Companies want not only to acquire profitable customers, but also to build relationships that will keep them and grow "share of customer." Different types of customer require different customer relationship management strategies. The marketer's aim is to build the *right relationships* with the *right customers*. In return for creating value *for* targeted customers, the company captures value *from* customers in the form of profits and customer equity.

In building customer relationships, good marketers realize that they cannot go it alone. They must work closely with marketing partners inside and outside the company. In addition to being good at customer relationship management, they must also be good at *partner relationship management.*

5. **Describe the major trends and forces that are changing the marketing landscape in this new age of relationships.**

As the world spins into the twenty-first century, dramatic changes are occurring in the marketing arena. The boom in computer, telecommunications, information, transportation, and other technologies has created exciting new ways to learn about and track customers, and to create products and services tailored to individual customer needs. In an increasingly smaller world, many marketers are now connected *globally* with their customers and marketing partners. Today, almost every company, large or small, is touched in some way by global competition. Today's marketers are also reexamining their ethical and societal responsibilities. Marketers are being called upon to take greater responsibility for the social and environmental impact of their actions. Finally, in the past, marketing has been most widely applied in the for-profit business sector. In recent years, however, marketing also has become a major part of the strategies of many not-for-profit organizations, such as colleges, hospitals, museums, symphony orchestras, and even churches.

As discussed throughout the chapter, the major new developments in marketing can be summed up in a single word: *relationships.* Today, marketers of all kinds are taking advantage of new opportunities for building relationships with their customers, their marketing partners, and the world around them.

> Reviewing the Key Terms <

Customer equity 21	Demands 6	Marketing concept 10	Product concept 10
Customer lifetime value 19	Demarketing 8	Marketing management 8	Production concept 9
Customer perceived value 13	Exchange 7	Marketing offer 6	Selling concept 10
Customer relationship	Internet 24	Needs 6	Share of customer 20
management 13	Market 7	Partner relationship	Societal marketing concept 11
Customer satisfaction 13	Marketing 5	management 18	Wants 6

> Discussing the Concepts <

1. "Customer value and satisfaction" is one unit of the five core marketplace concepts used in understanding the marketplace and consumer needs. What are the other four core marketplace concepts? Of the five core concepts is there one concept that stands out as being more important than any of the others? Support your answer.

2. Contrast the following two marketing management orientations: "The Selling Concept" and "The Marketing Concept." Can you name a market or market category where "The Selling Concept" is still the most popular marketing management orientation?

3. Customer loyalty and retention programs are important in building customer relationships and customer equity. Discuss why a national grocery chain such as Von's or Kroger's would choose a "club" program over a "frequency" program.

4. "Today, most marketers realize that they don't want to connect with just any customers." Do you agree with this statement? Why? Which company would be more likely to follow this creed, Wal-Mart or Porsche?

5. Does it make sense that working with other departments in an organization may bring greater value to customers? Create a short description of how working with your human resources department could generate increased customer value.

6. The fifth and final step in the marketing process is to capture value and generate profits and customer equity for the organization. Name the four customer value creation steps in this marketing process that result in creation of value for the organization. Is the marketing process iterative?

> Applying the Concepts <

1. This chapter discusses the concepts of customer value and satisfaction. Building on this knowledge, is it logical to assume that if you increase the perceived customer value for a product that there is a corresponding increase in customer satisfaction? Under what conditions might this not occur?

2. A cell phone company spends $148.50 in total costs to acquire a new user. On average, this new user spends $60 a month for calling and related services, and the cell-phone company generates an 18 percent profit margin in each of the 25 months that the user is expected to stay with the service. What is the customer lifetime value of this user to the cell phone company?

> Focus on Technology <

A CFO.com article by John Berry, eCFO, discusses the concept of Customer Lifetime Value (although in the article it is referred to as Lifetime Customer Value).* Berry describes how Convergys, a billing, customer and employee care solutions provider, developed technology that enabled a $2.1 billion-in-revenue company to report a 16% increase in operating income from its Customer Management Group. A large portion of this increase came from "winning new business from old customers" and was directly related to the "lifetime value modeling index" technology Convergys created. Bob Lento, VP of Sales for Convergys said, "This lifetime value modeling index is an empirical validation of our own instinctive belief that there is potential to grow existing client relationships significantly." The table shows the index that Convergys developed for their customer.

1. What is the basic premise on which CLV rests?
2. State your own opinion on the value of CLV.
3. The example includes nonoperation measures. Does this make sense? Why?

THE CLV RATING SYSTEM DEVELOPED BY CONVERGYS

Index	Measures	Weight
Average revenue score	Current and projected spending	15%
Revenue change score	Year-to-year actual spending	15%
Profitability score	Customer contribution margin	20%
Current relationship	Signed contract length, total years as client	10%
Technology entanglement	Systems integration, reporting, Convergys Web-assisted service, e-mail	20%
Share of client	Outsource potential	10%
Partnership	Level of contact, referenceable future value	10%

* See "Lifetime Customer Value," CFO.com, September 15, 2001, www.cfo.com/Article?article-4899

> Focus on Ethics <

As a brother, sister, aunt or uncle you know that a considerable amount of food advertising is directed at children from the ages of 6 to 11. A recent Kaiser Foundation report reviewed the findings of 40 studies on the role of the media in fuelling the rapid growth of childhood obesity in the United States. The report concluded that the majority of research finds a direct link between the amount of time children spend interacting with the media and their body weight. "The report cites studies showing that the typical American child sees about 40,000 ads a year on television, and that the majority of ads aimed at children are for sweets, cereal, soda and fast food."*

Place yourself in the role of a brand manager of a food product (sweet snack) with a primary target market of children aged 6 to 11. In a telephone interview, you are asked the following questions by a reporter from the Wall Street Journal in response to the Kaiser Foundation report. How would you respond?

1. Do food ads children are exposed to on TV influence them to make unhealthy food choices?
2. Do cross promotions between your product and popular TV and movie characters encourage children to buy and eat high-calorie foods?
3. Would you support government regulation directed at regulating food ads for children aged 6 to 11?

* See "Making a Meal of Couch Potatoes and Doughnuts," Marketing Week, March 25, 2004, p. 28; and www.kff.org/entmedia/7030.cfm.

◉ Video Case

Subaru of America

Building strong, profitable relationships with customers is the key to good marketing. Companies build brands by delighting customers and reinforcing good relationships with each interaction and through every touch point. But how do you maintain ties with customers who only make a purchase once every five or ten years? For Subaru, the answer is simple: by providing satisfying experiences with each service visit between purchases.

The goal of Subaru's Stellar Performer Dealers is to provide an exceptional dealer experience with every visit. Working with their customers, these dealers take an in-depth look at the way they do business, and what they can do to better serve their customers and improve their long-term relationships. Those relationships give Subaru an edge when the time comes for a customer to make the next car purchase decision.

After viewing the video featuring Subaru of America, answer the following questions about building profitable customer relationships.

1. How does Subaru's research help the company and its dealers build stronger customer relationships?
2. How has your experience with dealer service affected your satisfaction with your car? How could that experience be improved to enhance your relationship with the brand and the company? If you were in the market for new car, what impact would your relationship have on your purchase decision?
3. What is Subaru's value proposition?
4. How is Subaru's approach to creating relationships with customers similar to Lexus's approach? How is it different?

Company Case

Office Depot: "Thank You for Calling. . ."

"Thank you for calling Office Depot. All of our customer service representatives are busy serving other customers. Please stay on the line, and you will be connected to the next available agent."

"Thank you for calling Office Depot. Your call may be monitored and recorded for use in customer service representative training."

Steve Haine switched the telephone receiver to his right hand and glanced at his watch. He'd been on hold for almost ten minutes and had listened as the automated system repeated the pair of messages about every minute during that period.

Normally, Steve, a marketing professor at a well-known southern university, would have hung up long ago rather than spending his valuable time on hold just to register a complaint. However, he'd spent this Monday morning making a presentation on customer service to a group of middle and top managers at a major corporation's local manufacturing plant. As a part of the presentation, he'd discussed complaint handling. Now, he was interested in seeing how Office Depot would react to his story.

A BOTCHED DELIVERY

Steve's story had begun earlier in the afternoon. Upon returning from his presentation, he'd phoned his wife Dana to confirm their plans for the evening. Dana was an independent insurance salesperson who worked out of their home.

Steve noted that the phone rang more than the usual number of times before Dana picked up. "Hi," he began after she answered. "Just got back from the presentation and wanted to check in with you about tonight."

"Listen," Dana barked, and Steve immediately detected from the tone of her voice that he had called at a bad time. "I've got a delivery man stuck in the driveway and don't have time to talk now. I'm so mad. Call back later."

"Okay," Steve answered, realizing Dana had already hung up. He knew it was very unusual for Dana to be so upset, so something must have really gotten to her.

Steve wondered about Dana's statement that someone was stuck in the driveway. He and Dana lived in a neighborhood characterized by its rolling hills and trees. Their house sat on the side of a heavily wooded hill. Their driveway was about 120 feet long, curving to the left and rising about 12 feet from the street entrance to the parking area. From the parking area, there were 15 steps leading to a deck on the front of the house and to the front door. The left-hand turn and incline made the driveway appear steeper than it really was, and it was not unusual for delivery trucks to have some problems negotiating the driveway.

About an hour-and-a-half later, Steve called Dana again. "Hi," she responded after recognizing Steve's voice. "I'm sorry if I snapped at you earlier, but I was so mad."

"Who was the delivery from?" Steve asked.

"Office Depot. Two small packages for you."

"Oh. That must be my new pen and the refills. Wow, I just ordered them on Friday at the Office Depot Web site! You remember that I lost my good Cross pen at the conference I attended in Tampa last week. After I got back, I went to Office Max, Staples, and Office Depot to buy a new pen, but none of them had my pen. So I went to the Cross Web site to find the pen's model name and then ordered it from the Office Depot Web site. The pen only cost $25, and I also ordered two refills. The total bill was just over $30, and I paid an additional $5.95 for delivery. I just assumed Office Depot would mail the pen to me within the three to five business days its Web site indicates. Anyway, that's what the packages are, and I'm sorry I contributed to a bad time for you."

"Well, you don't know the half of it," Dana responded. "I was working in the office when the telephone rang. It was the delivery person. He announced that he was from Office Depot and had a delivery. He was at the bottom of the driveway and said he could not make it up the driveway. I couldn't imagine what we were getting from Office Depot, but I told him I would meet him at the driveway at the bottom of the stairs. When I got to the bottom of the stairs, I saw his truck. He was only a few feet into the driveway, at the curve. I looked at him and he looked at me. Then, he rolled down his window and stuck out his arm with the two small packages and a clipboard with a form for me to sign. I continued to look at him and realized that he was not going to get out of his truck. Finally, I understood that I was going to have to walk down the driveway and take the packages!"

"You mean he didn't get out of the truck?"

"No! He wasn't willing to get out of the truck and walk the 80 or 90 feet to bring me the packages, which must have weighed about eight ounces in total!"

"Well, I can understand your being upset. We've delivery people all the time who don't want to drive up the driveway. But, they always just walk the package up to the house and either give it to us or leave it at the door."

"Yes, but that's not all the story," Dana continued. "As I walked back up the driveway with the packages, I heard the truck backing out and then heard a scraping sound. I turned around and saw that the driver had backed at the wrong angle and the right-hand rear wheel had gone off the driveway. The truck had bottomed out on the driveway's edge. He was stuck."

"You're kidding!"

"No, I couldn't believe it. He wasn't far enough into the driveway to get stuck, but somehow he had. So, over the next hour I made several trips to and from the house to bring him boards from your shop and other things so he could try to get some leverage and get out. None of his attempts worked. Finally, I had to go back up to the office and get him a phone book so he could call a tow truck. I had to call three companies before I could find one that could come. The truck came finally and pulled him out."

"Why did you have to make the calls?" Steve asked.

"The driver didn't speak English very well, and I thought I could communicate our location better than he could."

"What a nightmare!" Steve exclaimed. "I know how busy you are and to have to spend an hour with this lazy guy and make trips for him up and down the driveway must have really gotten to you. I can understand you didn't have time to talk to me when I called."

"Well, just don't order anything else from Office Depot!"

THE CALLS

After his call to Dana, Steve thought about the situation. He had just spent the morning telling the managers that complaints were valuable. Despite being busy, he decided to share this story with Office Depot.

First, he'd gone to the Office Depot Web site. After some looking, he found a "contact us" link that contained a toll-free number to speak to a customer service representative. After a brief wait and several recorded messages, he got a representative. Steve told her the story, but realized during the conversation that her job was only to assist with orders. Steve told the representative that he wanted to share his story with someone who could deal with his complaint. The representative informed him that he would need to call corporate headquarters, and gave him the toll-free number.

When Steve called the number, the Office Depot operator answered, then transferred him to the customer service line, and the wait and recorded messages began.

THE COMPLAINT

Steve shifted his weight, switched hands again, and looked out his office window. He was just about to give up, despite his good intentions, when a real person finally answered his call.

"Hello, my name is Iris. Thank you for calling Office Depot. How may I help you?"

"Hello, Iris. My name's Steve Haine. I've a story I want to relate to you."

Iris asked Steve for his order number but he didn't have it. However, using his name and street address she found his order and the related information. Steve then told Iris his story, interrupted only by her asking incredulously: "You mean he didn't get out of the truck? He just rolled down the window and handed the packages out for your wife to come get them?"

"Yes, that's correct," Steve answered. He went on to complete recounting the event and then concluded: "Iris, I'm a marketing professor. I wanted to share this story with you, hoping that it will help you improve your customer service. I'm not asking for my money back, and I don't want to tell you how to run your business. But if I worked in customer service at Office Depot, I'd follow up on this situation and take some steps to keep this kind of thing from happening again."

"I've made notes on your call, Mr. Haine. Thank you for calling," Iris concluded.

Steve hung up the phone and wondered what, if anything, Office Depot would do with his complaint. He reflected on the topics he'd covered in his presentation that morning, topics like customer perceived value, customer satisfaction, customer relationship management, customer lifetime value, and customer equity. He hoped Iris had taken good notes; but, if she hadn't, he hoped his call had been recorded!

Questions for Discussion

1. How does Office Depot create value for its customers?

2. Are Steve and Dana Haine the "right" customers for Office Depot?

3. What customer satisfaction problems do you see in the case?

4. How do the concepts of customer lifetime value and customer equity come into play in this case?

5. If you were in charge of Office Depot's customer service operation and learned of Steve's story, what steps would you take?

CHAPTER 2

Company and Marketing Strategy: Partnering to Build Customer Relationships

> **After studying this chapter, you should be able to**

1. explain companywide strategic planning and its four steps
2. discuss how to design business portfolios and develop growth strategies
3. explain marketing's role in strategic planning and how marketing works with its partners to create and deliver customer value
4. describe the elements of a customer-driven marketing strategy and mix, and the forces that influence it
5. list the marketing management functions, including the elements of a marketing plan, and discuss the importance of measuring and managing return on marketing.

Previewing the Concepts

In the first chapter, we explored the marketing process by which companies create value for consumers in order to capture value in return. In this chapter, we'll dig more deeply into steps two and three of the marketing process—designing customer-driven marketing strategies and constructing marketing programs. But first we'll examine marketing's role in the broader organization. Marketing contributes to and is guided by the company's overall strategic plan. First, marketing urges a whole-company philosophy that puts customers at the center. Then, under the overall strategic plan, marketers work with other company functions to design marketing strategies for delivering value to carefully targeted customers. Finally, marketers develop "marketing mixes"—consisting of product, price, distribution, and promotion tactics—to carry out these strategies profitably.

Let's look first at the Walt Disney Company. When you hear the name Disney, you probably think of wholesome family entertainment. Most people do. For generations, with its theme parks and family films, the company has woven its special "Disney magic" to create and fulfill fantasies for people around the world. But what you may not know is that the Walt Disney Company has now grown to include much, much more than just theme parks and family films. As you read on, think about all the strategic planning challenges facing Disney's modern-day Magic Kingdom.

When you think of the Walt Disney Company, you probably think first of theme parks and animated films. And no wonder. Since the release of its first Mickey Mouse cartoon more than 75 years ago, Disney has grown to become the undisputed master of family entertainment. It perfected the art of movie animation. From pioneering films such as *Snow White and the Seven Dwarfs*, *Fantasia*, and *Pinocchio* to more recent features such as *The Lion King*, *Toy Story*, *Monsters, Inc.* and *Finding Nemo*, Disney has brought pure magic to the theaters, living rooms, and hearts and minds of audiences around the world.

But perhaps nowhere is the Disney magic more apparent than at the company's premier theme parks. Each year, more than 40 million people flock to the Disney World Resort alone—15 times more than visit Yellowstone National Park—making it the world's number one tourist attraction. What brings so many people to Walt Disney World? Part of the answer lies in its many attractions. The resort's four major theme parks—Magic Kingdom, Epcot, Disney-MGM Studios, and Disney's Animal Kingdom—brim with such attractions as Cinderella's Castle, Mission: Space, the Tower of Terror, Soarin' Over California, the Kilimanjaro Safari, and Big Thunder Mountain Railroad.

But these attractions reveal only part of the Disney World value proposition. In fact, what visitors like even more, they say, is the park's sparkling cleanliness and the friendliness of Disney World employees. As one observer notes, "In the Magic Kingdom, America still works the way it is supposed to. Everything is clean and safe, quality and service still matter, and the customer is always right." Thus, the real "Disney magic" lies in the company's obsessive dedication to its mission to "make people happy" and to "make a dream come true."

The company orients all of its people—from the executive in the corner office, to the monorail driver, to the ticket seller at the gate—around the customer's experience. On their first day, all new Disney World employees report for a 3-day motivational course at Disney University in Orlando, where they learn about the hard work of making fantasies come true. They learn that they are in the entertainment business—"cast members" in the Disney World "show." The job of each cast member is to enthusiastically serve Disney's "guests."

Before they receive their "theme costumes" and go "on stage," employees take courses titled Traditions I and Traditions II, in which they learn the Disney language, history, and culture. They are taught to be enthusiastic, helpful, and *always* friendly. They learn to do good deeds, such as volunteering to take pictures of guests, so that the whole family can be in the picture. Cast members are taught never to say, "It's not my job." When a guest asks a question—whether it's "Where's the nearest restroom?" or "What are the names of Snow White's seven dwarves?"—they need to know the answer. If they see a piece of trash on the ground, they pick it up.

Disney goes to extremes to fulfill guests' expectations and dreams. For example, to keep the Magic Kingdom feeling fresh and clean, five times a year the Main Street painters strip every painted rail in the park down to bare metal and apply a new coat of paint. Disney's customer-delight mission and marketing have become legendary. Its theme parks are so highly regarded for outstanding customer service that many of America's leading corporations send managers to Disney University to learn how Disney does it.

You might be surprised to learn, however, theme parks are only a small part of a much bigger Disney story. Parks and resorts account for only about 30 percent of today's Walt Disney Company empire. In recent years, Disney has become a real study in strategic planning. Throughout the 1990s, seeking growth, Disney diversified rapidly, transforming itself into a $27 billion international media and entertainment colossus. Beyond its theme parks, the Walt Disney Company now owns or has a major stake in all of the following:

- A major television and radio network—ABC—along with 10 company-owned television stations, 72 radio stations, and 13 international broadcast channels
- Nineteen cable networks (including the Disney Channel, Toon Disney, SOAPnet, ESPN, A&E, the History Channel, Lifetime Television, E! Entertainment, and ABC Family)
- Four television production companies, eight movie and theatrical production companies, and a distribution company (including Walt Disney Pictures, Touchstone Pictures, Hollywood Pictures, Miramax Films, Dimension Films, and Buena Vista Productions)
- Five publishing groups (including Hyperion Books, Disney Educational Productions, and Disney Press)
- Five music labels (Walt Disney Records, Hollywood Records, Buena Vista Records, Mammoth Records, and Lyric Street Records)

- Nineteen Internet groups (including Disney Online, Disney's Blast, ABC.com, ESPN.com, FamilyFun.com, NASCAR.com, NBA.com, and NFL.com)
- Disney Interactive (which develops and markets computer software, video games, and CD-ROMS)
- Disney Consumer Products Worldwide (Disney brand and character products ranging from toys, apparel, and books to breakfast foods, personal care items, stationery, home furnishings, interactive games, and electronics)
- The Disney Store—550 retail store locations carrying Disney-related merchandise
- Anaheim Sports (the Mighty Ducks of Anaheim National Hockey League team)
- Disney Cruise Lines

It's an impressive list. However, for Disney, managing this diverse portfolio of businesses has become a real *Monsters, Inc.* Although hurting recently because of the travel slump caused by a down economy and increased fears of terrorism, Disney's theme park and family movie operations have been wonderfully successful over the years. During the last half of the 1980s, the smaller, more focused Disney experienced soaring sales and profits. Revenues grew at an average rate of 23 percent annually; net income grew at 50 percent a year. In contrast, the new and more complex Disney has struggled for growth and profitability. Despite a recent uptick, during the past 8 years, the more diversified Disney's sales have grown at an average rate of only 2.8 percent annually, while income has fallen.

Thus, for Disney, bigger isn't necessarily better. Many critics assert that Disney has grown too large, too diverse, and too distant from the core strengths that made it so successful over the years. Others, however, believe that such diversification is essential for profitable long-term growth. Disagreements over long-term strategic direction have erupted into high-level boardroom brawls in recent years. One thing seems certain—creating just the right blend of businesses to make up the new Magic Kingdom won't be easy. It will take masterful strategic planning—along with some big doses of the famed "Disney magic"—to give the modern Disney story a happy-ever-after ending.[1]

Marketing strategies and programs operate within the context of broader, companywide strategic plans. Thus, to understand the role of marketing within an organization, we must first understand the organization's overall strategic planning process. Like Disney, all companies must look ahead and develop long-term strategies to meet the changing conditions in their industries and ensure long-term survival.

In this chapter, we look first at the organization's overall strategic planning. Next, we discuss how marketers, guided by the strategic plan, work closely with others inside and outside the firm to serve customers. We then examine marketing strategy and planning—how marketers choose target markets, position their marketing offers, develop a marketing mix, and manage their marketing programs. Finally, we look at the important step of measuring and managing return on marketing investment.

Companywide Strategic Planning: Defining Marketing's Role

Strategic planning

The process of developing and maintaining a strategic fit between the organization's goals and capabilities and its changing marketing opportunities. It involves defining a clear company mission, setting supporting objectives, designing a sound business portfolio, and coordinating functional strategies.

The hard task of selecting an overall company strategy for long-run survival and growth is called *strategic planning*. Each company must find the game plan that makes the most sense given its specific situation, opportunities, objectives, and resources. This is the focus of **strategic planning**—the process of developing and maintaining a strategic fit between the organization's goals and capabilities and its changing marketing opportunities.

Strategic planning sets the stage for the rest of the planning in the firm. Companies usually prepare annual plans, long-range plans, and strategic plans. The annual and long-range plans deal with the company's current businesses and how to keep them going. In contrast, the strategic plan involves adapting the firm to take advantage of opportunities in its constantly changing environment.

At the corporate level, the company starts the strategic planning process by defining its overall purpose and mission (see Figure 2.1). This mission then is turned into detailed supporting objectives that guide the whole company. Next, headquarters decides what portfolio of businesses and products is best for the company and how much support to give each one. In turn, each business and product develops detailed marketing and other departmental plans that support the companywide plan. Thus, marketing planning occurs at the business-unit, product, and market levels. It supports company strategic planning with more detailed plans for specific marketing opportunities.[2]

Defining a Market-Oriented Mission

An organization exists to accomplish something. At first, it has a clear purpose or mission, but over time its mission may become unclear as the organization grows, adds new products and markets, or faces new conditions in the environment. When management senses that the organization is drifting, it must renew its search for purpose. It is time to ask: What is our business? Who is the customer? What do consumers value? What should our business be? These simple-sounding questions are among the most difficult the company will ever have to answer. Successful companies continuously raise these questions and answer them carefully and completely.

Mission statement

A statement of the organization's purpose— what it wants to accomplish in the larger environment.

Many organizations develop formal mission statements that answer these questions. A **mission statement** is a statement of the organization's purpose—what it wants to accomplish in the larger environment. A clear mission statement acts as an "invisible hand" that guides people in the organization. Studies have shown that firms with well-crafted mission statements have better organizational and financial performance.[3]

Some companies define their missions myopically in product or technology terms ("We make and sell furniture" or "We are a chemical-processing firm"). But mission statements should be *market oriented* and defined in terms of customer needs. Products and technologies eventually become outdated, but basic market needs may last forever.

A market-oriented mission statement defines the business in terms of satisfying basic customer needs. For example, Charles Schwab isn't just a brokerage firm—it sees itself as the "guardian of our customers' financial dreams." Likewise, eBay's mission isn't simply to hold

FIGURE 2.1

Steps in strategic planning

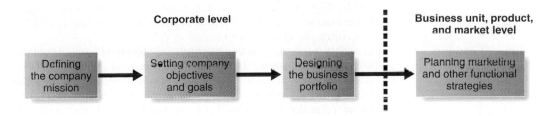

TABLE 2.1   Market-Oriented Business Definitions

Company	Product-Oriented Definition	Market-Oriented Definition
Amazon.com	We sell books, videos, CDs, toys, consumer electronics, hardware, housewares, and other products.	We make the Internet buying experience fast, easy, and enjoyable—we're the place where you can find and discover anything you want to buy online.
America Online	We provide online services.	We create customer connectivity, anytime, anywhere.
Disney	We run theme parks.	We create fantasies—a place where America still works the way it's supposed to.
eBay	We hold online auctions.	We connect individual buyers and sellers in the world's online marketplace, a unique Web community in which they can shop around, have fun, and get to know each other.
Home Depot	We sell tools and home repair and improvement items.	We provide advice and solutions that transform ham-handed homeowners into Mr. and Mrs. Fixits.
Nike	We sell shoes.	We help people experience the emotion of competition, winning, and crushing competitors.
Revlon	We make cosmetics.	We sell lifestyle and self-expression; success and status; memories, hopes, and dreams.
Ritz-Carlton Hotels	We rent rooms.	We create the Ritz-Carlton experience—one that enlivens the senses, instills well-being, and fulfills even the unexpressed wishes and needs of our guests.
Wal-Mart	We run discount stores.	We deliver low prices every day and give ordinary folks the chance to buy the same things as rich people.

online auctions. Instead, it connects individual buyers and sellers in "the world's online marketplace." Its mission is to be a unique Web community in which people can shop around, have fun, and get to know each other, for example, by chatting at the eBay Cafe. Table 2.1 provides several other examples of product-oriented versus market-oriented business definitions.

Management should avoid making its mission too narrow or too broad. A pencil manufacturer that says it is in the communication equipment business is stating its mission too broadly. Missions should be *realistic*. Singapore Airlines would be deluding itself if it adopted the mission to become the world's largest airline. Missions should also be *specific*. Many mission statements are written for public relations purposes and lack specific, workable guidelines. Such generic statements sound good but provide little real guidance or inspiration.

Missions should fit the *market environment*. The Girl Scouts of USA would not recruit successfully in today's environment with its former mission: "to prepare young girls for motherhood and wifely duties." Today, its mission is to be the place "where girls grow strong." The organization should base its mission on its *distinctive competencies*. Finally, mission statements should be *motivating*. A company's mission should not be stated as making more sales or profits—profits are only a reward for undertaking a useful activity. A company's employees need to feel that their work is significant and that it contributes to people's lives. For example, Walt Disney Company's aim is to "make people happy." Wal-Mart's mission is to "Give ordinary folks the chance to buy the same things as rich people."

Setting Company Objectives and Goals

The company's mission needs to be turned into detailed supporting objectives for each level of management. Each manager should have objectives and be responsible for reaching them. For example, Monsanto operates in many businesses, including agriculture, pharmaceuticals, and food products. The company defines its mission as creating "abundant food and a healthy environment." It seeks to help feed the world's exploding population while at the same time sustaining the environment.

This mission leads to a hierarchy of objectives, including business objectives and marketing objectives. Monsanto's overall objective is to build profitable customer relationships by creating environmentally better products and getting them to market faster at lower costs. For its part, the agricultural division's objective is to increase agricultural productivity and reduce chemical pollution. It does this by researching new pest- and disease-resistant crops that pro-

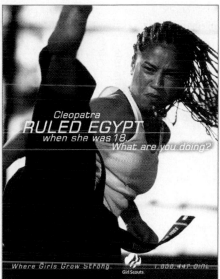
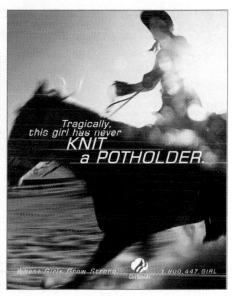

■ Mission statements: The Girl Scouts' mission is to be a place "Where Girls Grow Strong."

duce higher yields without chemical spraying. But research is expensive and requires improved profits to plow back into research programs. So improving profits becomes another major Monsanto objective. Profits can be improved by increasing sales or reducing costs. Sales can be increased by improving the company's share of the U.S. market, by entering new foreign markets, or both. These goals then become the company's current marketing objectives.

Marketing strategies and programs must be developed to support these marketing objectives. To increase its U.S. market share, Monsanto might increase its products' availability and promotion. To enter new foreign markets, the company may cut prices and target large farms abroad. These are its broad marketing strategies. Each broad marketing strategy must then be defined in greater detail. For example, increasing the product's promotion may require more salespeople and more advertising; if so, both requirements will have to be spelled out. In this way, the firm's mission is translated into a set of objectives for the current period.

Designing the Business Portfolio

Business portfolio
The collection of businesses and products that make up the company.

Guided by the company's mission statement and objectives, management now must plan its **business portfolio**—the collection of businesses and products that make up the company. The best business portfolio is the one that best fits the company's strengths and weaknesses to opportunities in the environment. Business portfolio planning involves two steps. First, the company must analyze its *current* business portfolio and decide which businesses should receive more, less, or no investment. Second, it must shape the *future* portfolio by developing strategies for growth and downsizing.

Analyzing the Current Business Portfolio

Portfolio analysis
The process by which management evaluates the products and businesses making up the company.

The major activity in strategic planning is business **portfolio analysis**, whereby management evaluates the products and businesses making up the company. The company will want to put strong resources into its more profitable businesses and phase down or drop its weaker ones.

Management's first step is to identify the key businesses making up the company. These can be called the strategic business units. A *strategic business unit* (SBU) is a unit of the company that has a separate mission and objectives and that can be planned independently from other company businesses. An SBU can be a company division, a product line within a division, or sometimes a single product or brand.

The next step in business portfolio analysis calls for management to assess the attractiveness of its various SBUs and decide how much support each deserves. Most companies are well advised to "stick to their knitting" when designing their business portfolios. It's usually a good idea to focus on adding products and businesses that fit closely with the firm's core philosophy and competencies.

The purpose of strategic planning is to find ways in which the company can best use its strengths to take advantage of attractive opportunities in the environment. So most standard

FIGURE 2.2
The BCG growth-share matrix

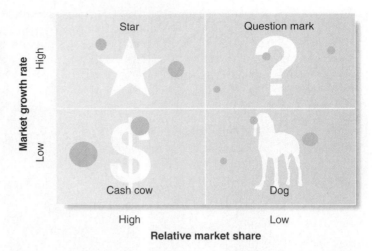

portfolio-analysis methods evaluate SBUs on two important dimensions—the attractiveness of the SBU's market or industry and the strength of the SBU's position in that market or industry. The best-known portfolio-planning method was developed by the Boston Consulting Group, a leading management consulting firm.[4]

THE BOSTON CONSULTING GROUP APPROACH Using the Boston Consulting Group (BCG) approach, a company classifies all its SBUs according to the **growth-share matrix** shown in Figure 2.2. On the vertical axis, *market growth rate* provides a measure of market attractiveness. On the horizontal axis, *relative market share* serves as a measure of company strength in the market. The growth-share matrix defines four types of SBUs:

Growth-share matrix

A portfolio-planning method that evaluates a company's strategic business units in terms of their market growth rate and relative market share. SBUs are classified as stars, cash cows, question marks, or dogs.

Stars. Stars are high-growth, high-share businesses or products. They often need heavy investment to finance their rapid growth. Eventually their growth will slow down, and they will turn into cash cows.

Cash cows. Cash cows are low-growth, high-share businesses or products. These established and successful SBUs need less investment to hold their market share. Thus, they produce a lot of cash that the company uses to pay its bills and to support other SBUs that need investment.

Question marks. Question marks are low-share business units in high-growth markets. They require a lot of cash to hold their share, let alone increase it. Management has to think hard about which question marks it should try to build into stars and which should be phased out.

Dogs. Dogs are low-growth, low-share businesses and products. They may generate enough cash to maintain themselves but do not promise to be large sources of cash.

The 10 circles in the growth-share matrix represent a company's 10 current SBUs. The company has 2 stars, 2 cash cows, 3 question marks, and 3 dogs. The areas of the circles are proportional to the SBU's dollar sales. This company is in fair shape, although not in good shape. It wants to invest in the more promising question marks to make them stars and to maintain the stars so that they will become cash cows as their markets mature. Fortunately, it has 2 good-sized cash cows. Income from these cash cows will help finance the company's question marks, stars, and dogs. The company should take some decisive action concerning its dogs and its question marks. The picture would be worse if the company had no stars, if it had too many dogs, or if it had only 1 weak cash cow.

Once it has classified its SBUs, the company must determine what role each will play in the future. One of four strategies can be pursued for each SBU. The company can invest more in the business unit in order to *build* its share. Or it can invest just enough to *hold* the SBU's share at the current level. It can *harvest* the SBU, milking its short-term cash flow regardless of the long-term effect. Finally, the company can *divest* the SBU by selling it or phasing it out and using the resources elsewhere.

As time passes, SBUs change their positions in the growth-share matrix. Each SBU has a life cycle. Many SBUs start out as question marks and move into the star category if they succeed. They later become cash cows as market growth falls, then finally die off or turn into dogs toward the end of their life cycle. The company needs to add new products and units continuously so that some of them will become stars and, eventually, cash cows that will help finance other SBUs.

PROBLEMS WITH MATRIX APPROACHES The BCG and other formal methods revolutionized strategic planning. However, such approaches have limitations. They can be difficult, time-consuming, and costly to implement. Management may find it difficult to define SBUs and measure market share and growth. In addition, these approaches focus on classifying *current* businesses but provide little advice for *future* planning.

Formal planning approaches can also place too much emphasis on market-share growth or growth through entry into attractive new markets. Using these approaches, many companies plunged into unrelated and new high-growth businesses that they did not know how to manage—with very bad results. At the same time, these companies were often too quick to abandon, sell, or milk to death their healthy mature businesses. As a result, many companies that diversified too broadly in the past now are narrowing their focus and getting back to the basics of serving one or a few industries that they know best.

Because of such problems, many companies have dropped formal matrix methods in favor of more customized approaches that are better suited to their specific situations. Unlike former strategic-planning efforts, which rested mostly in the hands of senior managers at company headquarters, today's strategic planning has been decentralized. Increasingly, companies are placing responsibility for strategic planning in the hands of cross-functional teams of managers who are close to their markets. Some teams even include customers and suppliers in their strategic-planning processes.

Developing Strategies for Growth and Downsizing

Beyond evaluating current businesses, designing the business portfolio involves finding businesses and products the company should consider in the future. Companies need growth if they are to compete more effectively, satisfy their stakeholders, and attract top talent. "Growth is pure oxygen," states one executive. "It creates a vital, enthusiastic corporation where people see genuine opportunity." At the same time, a firm must be careful not to make growth itself an objective. The company's objective must be "profitable growth."

Marketing has the main responsibility for achieving profitable growth for the company. Marketing must identify, evaluate, and select market opportunities and lay down strategies for capturing them. One useful device for identifying growth opportunities is the **product/market expansion grid**, shown in Figure 2.3.[5] We apply it here to Starbucks (see Real Marketing 2.1).

First, Starbucks management might consider whether the company can achieve deeper **market penetration**—making more sales to current customers without changing its products. It might add new stores in current market areas to make it easier for more customers to visit. In fact, Starbucks is adding an average of 26 stores a week, 52 weeks a year. Improvements in advertising, prices, service, menu selection, or store design might encourage customers to stop by more often, stay longer, or to buy more during each visit. For example, Starbucks recently added drive-through windows to many of its stores. And Starbucks has introduced a company debit card, which lets customers prepay for coffee and snacks or give the gift of Starbucks to family and friends.[6]

Second, Starbucks management might consider possibilities for **market development**—identifying and developing new markets for its current products. For instance, managers could review new *demographic markets*. Perhaps new groups—such as seniors or ethnic groups—could be encouraged to visit Starbucks coffee shops for the first time or to buy more from them. Managers also could review new *geographical markets*. Starbucks is now expanding swiftly into new U.S. markets, especially in the Southeast and Southwest.

Third, management could consider **product development**—offering modified or new products to current markets. For example, Starbucks has added hot breakfast sandwiches to its menu to steal some early-morning business from McDonald's and Burger King. And it recently added a line of iced shaken beverages to attract more customers during the hot summer season.

Fourth, Starbucks might consider **diversification**—starting up or buying businesses outside of its current products and markets. For example, in 1999, Starbucks purchased Hear Music and

---

Product/market expansion grid

A portfolio planning tool for identifying company growth opportunities through market penetration, market development, product development, or diversification.

Market penetration

A strategy for company growth by increasing sales of current products to current market segments without changing the product.

Market development

A strategy for company growth by identifying and developing new market segments for current company products.

Product development

A strategy for company growth by offering modified or new products to current market segments.

Diversification

A strategy for company growth through starting up or acquiring businesses outside the company's current products and markets.

FIGURE 2.3
The product/market expansion grid

	Existing products	New products
Existing markets	Market penetration	Product development
New markets	Market development	Diversification

Real Marketing 2.1

Starbucks Coffee: Where Things Are Really Perking

Back in 1983, Howard Schultz hit on the idea of bringing a European-style coffeehouse to America. People needed to slow down, he believed—to "smell the coffee" and enjoy life a little more. The result was Starbucks. This coffeehouse doesn't sell just coffee, it sells *The Starbucks Experience*. "There's the Starbucks ambience," notes an analyst, "The music. The comfy velvety chairs. The smells. The hissing steam." Says Starbucks CEO Schultz, "We aren't in the coffee business, serving people. We are in the people business, serving coffee."

Starbucks is now a powerhouse premium brand in a category in which only cheaper commodity products once existed. As the brand has perked, Starbucks's sales and profits have risen like steam off a mug of hot java. Some 25 million customers visit the company's more than 7,600 stores worldwide each week. During just the past 5 years, Starbucks's sales and earnings have both more than tripled, and revenues continue to grow at more than 20 percent each year. Since 1992, its stock has soared more than 3,028 percent.

■ To maintain its phenomenal growth in an increasingly overcaffeinated marketplace, Starbucks has brewed up an ambitious, multipronged growth strategy.

Starbucks's success, however, has drawn a full litter of copycats, ranging from direct competitors such as Caribou Coffee to fast-food merchants (such as McDonald's McCafe) and even discounters (Wal-Mart's Kicks Coffee). These days it seems that everyone is peddling their own brand of premium coffee. In the early 1990s, there were only 200 coffee houses in the United States. Today there are more than 14,000. To maintain its phenomenal growth in an increasingly overcaffeinated marketplace, Starbucks has brewed up an ambitious, multipronged growth strategy. Let's examine the key elements of this strategy:

More store growth: Almost 86 percent of Starbucks's sales comes from its stores. So, not surprisingly, Starbucks is opening new stores at a breakneck pace. Eight years ago, Starbucks had just 1,015 stores, total—that's 424 fewer than it built last year alone. Starbucks's strategy is to put stores *everywhere*. In Seattle, there's a Starbucks for every 9,400 people; in Manhattan, there's one for every 12,000. One three-block stretch in Chicago contains six of the trendy coffee bars. In fact, cramming so many stores close together caused one satirical publication to run this headline: "A New Starbucks Opens in the Restroom of Existing Starbucks." Although it may seem that there aren't many places left without a Starbucks, there's still plenty of room to expand. The company's ultimate goal is 25,000 stores worldwide.

Enhanced Starbucks experience: Beyond opening new shops, Starbucks is adding in-store products and features that get customers to stop in more often, stay longer, and buy more. Its beefed-up menu now includes hot breakfast sandwiches plus lunch and dinner items, increasing the average customer purchase. The chain has tested everything from Krispy Kreme doughnuts and Fresh Fields gourmet sandwiches to Greek pasta salads and assorted chips. And it recently added a new line of hand-shaken iced beverages.

To get customers to hang around longer, Starbucks now offers T-Mobile HotSpot wireless Internet access in 2,700 of its

began making compilation music CDs to play and sell in its stores. It is now installing Hear Music CD-burning kiosks, allowing customers to create their own custom CDs.[7]

In a more extreme diversification, Starbucks might consider leveraging its strong brand name by making and marketing a line of branded casual clothing consistent with the "Starbucks Experience." However, this would probably be unwise. Companies that diversify too broadly into unfamiliar products or industries can lose their market focus, something that some critics are already concerned about with Starbucks.

Companies must not only develop strategies for *growing* their business portfolios but also strategies for **downsizing** them. There are many reasons that a firm might want to abandon products or markets. The market environment might change, making some of the company's products or markets less profitable. The firm may have grown too fast or entered areas where it lacks experience. This can occur when a firm enters too many foreign markets without the proper research or when a company introduces new products that do not offer superior customer value. Finally, some products or business units simply age and die. One marketing expert summarizes the problem this way:

Downsizing
Reducing the business portfolio by eliminating products or business units that are not profitable or that no longer fit the company's overall strategy.

stores. The chain recently added in-store music downloads, letting customers burn their own CDs while sipping their lattes. Out of cash? No problem—just swipe your prepaid Starbucks card on the way out ("a Starbucks store in your wallet"). Or use your Starbucks Card Duetto Visa (a credit card that also serves as a gift, stored-value, and rewards card).

New retail channels: The vast majority of coffee in America is bought in retail stores and brewed at home. To capture this demand, Starbucks has also pushed into America's supermarket aisles. It has a co-branding deal with Kraft, under which Starbucks roasts and packages its coffee while Kraft markets and distributes it. Beyond supermarkets, Starbucks has forged an impressive set of new ways to bring its brand to market. Some examples: Host Marriott operates Starbucks kiosks in America's airports and several airlines serve Starbucks coffee to their passengers. Westin and Sheraton hotels offer packets of Starbucks brew in their rooms. Starbucks has installed coffee shops in most Borders Books and Target stores. Starbucks also sells gourmet coffee, tea, gifts, and related goods through business and consumer catalogs. And its Web site, www.starbucks.com, has become a kind of "lifestyle portal" on which it sells coffee, tea, coffeemaking equipment, compact discs, gifts, and collectibles.

New products and store concepts: Starbucks has partnered with several firms to extend its brand into new categories. For example, it joined with PepsiCo to stamp the Starbucks brand on bottled Frappuccino drinks and its DoubleShot espresso drink. Starbucks ice cream, marketed in a joint venture with Dreyer's, is now the leading brand of coffee ice cream. Starbucks has also examined a number of new store concepts. In San Francisco, for example, it's testing Circadia—a kind of bohemian coffeehouse concept with tattered rugs, high-speed Internet access, and live music as well as coffee specialties.

International growth: Finally, Starbucks has taken its American-brewed concept global. In 1996, the company had only 11 coffeehouses outside North America. By 2004, the num-

ber had grown to more than 2,000 stores in 34 international markets, from Paris to Osaka to Oman. Starbucks continues to open new international stores at a rate of close to 400 per year.

Although Starbucks's growth strategy so far has met with amazing success, some analysts express strong concerns. What's wrong with Starbucks's rapid expansion? Some critics worry that the company may be overextending the Starbucks brand name. "People pay $3.50 for a caffe latte because it's supposed to be a premium product," asserts one such critic. "When you see the Starbucks name on what an airline is pouring, you wonder." Others fear that, by pursuing such a broad-based growth strategy, Starbucks will stretch its resources too thin or lose its focus.

Still others, however, remain true believers. Some even see similarities between Starbucks and a young McDonald's, which rode the humble hamburger to such incredible success. In fact, Starbucks has more stores, greater revenues, and better stock returns than McDonald's did at the same point in its growth. And Starbucks still has a lot of growing to do before it gets as large as McDonald's is today.

Only time will tell whether Starbucks turns out to be the next McDonald's—it all depends how well the company manages growth. Says Schultz, "We are in the second inning of a nine-inning game. We are just beginning to tap into all sorts of new markets, new customers, and new products." For now, things are really perking. But Starbucks has to be careful that it doesn't boil over.

Sources: Quotes and other information from Cora Daniels, "Mr. Coffee," *Fortune,* April 14, 2003, pp. 139–140; Nelson D. Schwartz, "Still Perking After All These Years," *Fortune,* May 24, 1999, pp. 203–210; Stephane Fitch, "Latte Grande, Extra Froth," *Forbes,* March 19, 2001, p. 58; Andy Serwer, "Hot Starbucks to Go," *Fortune,* January 26, 2004, pp. 60–74; Jake Batsell, "Starbucks Steams Ahead with Aggressive Expansion Plans," *Knight Ridder Tribune Business News,* March 28, 2004, p. 1; and information accessed online at www.starbucks.com, November 2004.

Companies spend vast amounts of money and time launching new brands, leveraging existing ones, and acquiring rivals. They create line extensions and brand extensions, not to mention channel extensions and subbrands, to cater to the growing number of niche segments in every market. . . . Surprisingly, most businesses do not examine their brand portfolios from time to time to check if they might be selling too many brands, identify weak ones, and kill unprofitable ones. They tend to ignore loss-making brands rather than merge them with healthy brands, sell them off, or drop them. Consequently, most portfolios have become [jammed] with loss-making and marginally profitable brands. Moreover, the surprising truth is that most brands don't make money for companies. Many corporations generate fewer than 80 to 90 percent of their profits from fewer than 20 percent of the brands they sell, while they lose money or barely break even on many of the other brands in their portfolios.[9]

When a firm finds brands or businesses that are unprofitable or that no longer fit its overall strategy, it must carefully prune, harvest, or divest them. Weak businesses usually require a disproportionate amount of management attention. Managers should focus on promising growth opportunities, not fritter away energy trying to salvage fading ones.

Planning Marketing: Partnering to Build Customer Relationships

The company's strategic plan establishes what kinds of businesses the company will be in and its objectives for each. Then, within each business unit, more detailed planning takes place. The major functional departments in each unit—marketing, finance, accounting, purchasing, operations, information systems, human resources, and others—must work together to accomplish strategic objectives.

Marketing plays a key role in the company's strategic planning in several ways. First, marketing provides a guiding *philosophy*—the marketing concept—that suggests that company strategy should revolve around building profitable relationships with important consumer groups. Second, marketing provides *inputs* to strategic planners by helping to identify attractive market opportunities and by assessing the firm's potential to take advantage of them. Finally, within individual business units, marketing designs *strategies* for reaching the unit's objectives. Once the unit's objectives are set, marketing's task is to help carry them out profitably.

Customer value and satisfaction are important ingredients in the marketer's formula for success. However, as we noted in Chapter 1, marketers alone cannot produce superior value for customers. Although it plays a leading role, marketing can be only a partner in attracting, keeping, and growing customers. In addition to *customer relationship management*, marketers must also practice *partner relationship management*. They must work closely with partners in other company departments to form an effective *value chain* that serves the customer. Moreover, they must partner effectively with other companies in the marketing system to form a competitively superior *value-delivery network*. We now take a closer look at the concepts of a company value chain and value-delivery network.

Partnering with Other Company Departments

Value chain

The series of departments that carry out value-creating activities to design, produce, market, deliver, and support a firm's products.

Each company department can be thought of as a link in the company's **value chain**.[9] That is, each department carries out value-creating activities to design, produce, market, deliver, and support the firm's products. The firm's success depends not only on how well each department performs its work but also on how well the activities of various departments are coordinated.

For example, Wal-Mart's goal is to create customer value and satisfaction by providing shoppers with the products they want at the lowest possible prices. Marketers at Wal-Mart play an important role. They learn what customers need and stock the store's shelves with the desired products at unbeatable low prices. They prepare advertising and merchandising programs and assist shoppers with customer service. Through these and other activities, Wal-Mart's marketers help deliver value to customers.

However, the marketing department needs help from the company's other departments. Wal-Mart's ability to offer the right products at low prices depends on the purchasing department's skill in developing the needed suppliers and buying from them at low cost. Wal-Mart's information technology department must provide fast and accurate information about which products are selling in each store. And its operations people must provide effective, low-cost merchandise handling.

A company's value chain is only as strong as its weakest link. Success depends on how well each department performs its work of adding customer value and on how well the activities of various departments are coordinated. At Wal-Mart, if purchasing can't wring the lowest prices from suppliers, or if operations can't distribute merchandise at the lowest costs, then marketing can't deliver on its promise of lowest prices.

Ideally, then, a company's different functions should work in harmony to produce value for consumers. But, in practice, departmental relations are full of conflicts and misunderstandings. The marketing department takes the consumer's point of view. But when marketing tries to develop customer satisfaction, it can cause other departments to do a poorer job *in their terms*. Marketing department actions can increase purchasing costs, disrupt production schedules, increase inventories, and create budget headaches. Thus, the other departments may resist the marketing department's efforts.

- The value chain: Wal-Mart's ability to offer the right products at low prices depends on the contributions of people in all of the company's departments—marketing, purchasing, information systems, and operations.

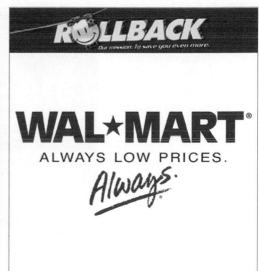

Yet marketers must find ways to get all departments to "think consumer" and to develop a smoothly functioning value chain. Marketing management can best gain support for its goal of customer satisfaction by working to understand the company's other departments. Marketing managers need to work closely with managers of other functions to develop a system of functional plans under which the different departments can work together to accomplish the company's overall strategic objectives.

Jack Welch, General Electric's highly regarded former CEO, told his employees: "Companies can't give job security. Only customers can!" He emphasized that all General Electric people, regardless of their department, have an impact on customer satisfaction and retention. His message: "If you are not thinking customer, you are not thinking."[10]

Partnering with Others in the Marketing System

In its quest to create customer value, the firm needs to look beyond its own value chain and into the value chains of its suppliers, distributors, and, ultimately, customers. Consider McDonald's. McDonald's 31,000 restaurants worldwide serve more than 47 million customers daily, capturing a 43 percent share of the burger market.[11] People do not swarm to McDonald's only because they love the chain's hamburgers. In fact, consumers typically rank McDonald's behind Burger King and Wendy's in taste. Consumers flock to the McDonald's *system*, not just to its food products. Throughout the world, McDonald's finely tuned system delivers a high standard of what the company calls QSCV—quality, service, cleanliness, and value. McDonald's is effective only to the extent that it successfully partners with its franchisees, suppliers, and others to jointly deliver exceptionally high customer value.

Value-delivery network

The network made up of the company, suppliers, distributors, and ultimately customers who "partner" with each other to improve the performance of the entire system.

More companies today are partnering with the other members of the supply chain to improve the performance of the customer **value-delivery network**. For example, Honda has designed a program for working closely with its suppliers to help them reduce their costs and improve quality. When Honda chose Magna Donnelly Corporation to supply all of the mirrors for its U.S.-made cars, it sent engineers swarming over the supplier's plants, looking for ways to improve its products and operations. This helped Magna Donnelly reduce its costs by 2 percent in the first year. As a result of its improved performance, its sales to Honda grew from $5 million annually to more than $60 million in less than 10 years. In turn, Honda gained an efficient, low-cost supplier of quality components. And Honda customers received greater value in the form of lower-cost, higher-quality cars.[12]

Increasingly in today's marketplace, competition no longer takes place between individual competitors. Rather, it takes place between the entire value-delivery networks created by these competitors. Thus, Honda's performance against Toyota depends on the quality of Honda's overall value-delivery network versus Toyota's. Even if Honda makes the best cars, it might lose in the marketplace if Toyota's dealer network provides more customer-satisfying sales and service.

■ The value-delivery network: Toyota and its dealers must work together to sell cars. Toyota makes good cars and builds the brand; dealerships like Modern Toyota bring value to customers and communities.

Marketing Strategy and the Marketing Mix

The strategic plan defines the company's overall mission and objectives. Marketing's role and activities are shown in Figure 2.4, which summarizes the major activities involved in managing marketing strategy and the marketing mix.

Consumers stand in the center. The goal is to build strong and profitable customer relationships. Next comes **marketing strategy**—the marketing logic by which the company hopes to achieve these profitable relationships. Through market segmentation, targeting, and positioning, the company decides which customers it will serve and how. It identifies the total market, then divides it into smaller segments, selects the most promising segments, and focuses on serving and satisfying customers in these segments.

Guided by marketing strategy, the company designs a marketing mix made up of factors under its control—product, price, place, and promotion. To find the best marketing strategy and mix, the company engages in marketing analysis, planning, implementation, and control. Through these activities, the company watches and adapts to the actors and forces in the marketing environment. We will now look briefly at each activity. Then, in later chapters, we will discuss each one in more depth.

Marketing strategy
The marketing logic by which the business unit hopes to achieve its marketing objectives.

Customer-Centered Marketing Strategy

As we emphasized throughout Chapter 1, to succeed in today's competitive marketplace, companies need to be customer centered. They must win customers from competitors, then keep and grow them by delivering greater value. But before it can satisfy consumers, a company must first understand their needs and wants. Thus, sound marketing requires a careful customer analysis.

Companies know that they cannot profitably serve all consumers in a given market—at least not all consumers in the same way. There are too many different kinds of consumers

FIGURE 2.4
Managing marketing strategy and the marketing mix

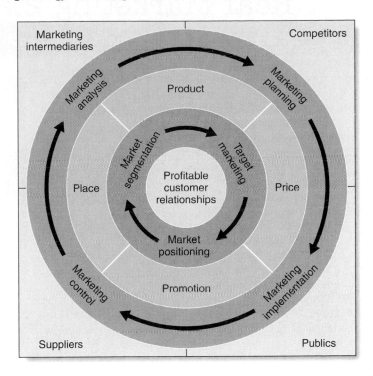

with too many different kinds of needs. And most companies are in a position to serve some segments better than others. Thus, each company must divide up the total market, choose the best segments, and design strategies for profitably serving chosen segments. This process involves three steps: *market segmentation, target marketing,* and *market positioning.*

Market Segmentation

The market consists of many types of customers, products, and needs. The marketer has to determine which segments offer the best opportunity for achieving company objectives. Consumers can be grouped and served in various ways based on geographic, demographic, psychographic, and behavioral factors. The process of dividing a market into distinct groups of buyers with different needs, characteristics, or behavior who might require separate products or marketing programs is called **market segmentation**.

Every market has segments, but not all ways of segmenting a market are equally useful. For example, Tylenol would gain little by distinguishing between male and female users of pain relievers if both respond the same way to marketing efforts. A **market segment** consists of consumers who respond in a similar way to a given set of marketing efforts. In the car market, for example, consumers who want the biggest, most comfortable car regardless of price make up one market segment. Customers who care mainly about price and operating economy make up another segment. It would be difficult to make one car model that was the first choice of consumers in both segments. Companies are wise to focus their efforts on meeting the distinct needs of individual market segments.

Target Marketing

After a company has defined market segments, it can enter one or many segments of a given market. **Target marketing** involves evaluating each market segment's attractiveness and selecting one or more segments to enter. A company should target segments in which it can profitably generate the greatest customer value and sustain it over time.

A company with limited resources might decide to serve only one or a few special segments or "market niches." Such "nichers" specialize in serving market segments that major competitors overlook or ignore. For example, Arm & Hammer has a lock on the baking soda corner of most consumer goods categories, including toothpaste, deodorizers, and others. Oshkosh Truck has found its niche as the world's largest producer of airport rescue trucks and front-loading concrete mixers. And in its niche, the Philippines, Jollibee proves that small can be beautiful. It captures 65 percent of the Filipino burger market, dominating McDonald's and other fast-food giants (see Real Marketing 2.2).

Market segmentation
Dividing a market into distinct groups of buyers who have distinct needs, characteristics, or behavior and who might require separate products or marketing mixes.

Market segment
A group of consumers who respond in a similar way to a given set of marketing efforts.

Target marketing
The process of evaluating each market segment's attractiveness and selecting one or more segments to enter.

Real Marketing 2.2

Jollibee vs. McDonald's: Small Can Be Beautiful

When someone says "fast-food restaurant," what's the first name that comes to mind? Chances are its McDonald's, the world's largest food service organization. McDonald's holds a 43 percent share of the U.S. fast-food burger market, many times the share of its nearest competitor. Ask the same question in the Philippines, however, and the first name uttered will likely be Jollibee. That's right, Jollibee. In the grand scheme of global commerce, Jollibee Foods Corporation isn't exactly a household name. But in its niche, the Philippines, it's king of the burger market. "If McDonald's is the Goliath of fast food," notes one industry analyst, "Jollibee is its Filipino David."

At first glance, the rivalry between Jollibee and McDonald's looks like no contest. McDonald's has more than 30,000 outlets in more than 100 countries, more than 3,000 of them in Asia alone, and more than $50 billion in annual systemwide sales. By comparison, Jollibee has only about 400 restaurants contributing about $516 million in annual revenues. Its sales equal less than half of the $1.3 billion or more that McDonald's spends annually just on U.S. advertising. When the first golden arches went up in Manila in 1981, everyone assumed that McDonald's would dominate in the Philippines as it has everywhere else.

But despite these lopsided numbers, in the Philippines, small Jollibee has humbled the global giant. Jollibee captures a 65 percent share of the Philippines' hamburger market, more than half of the fast-food market as a whole, and about twice McDonald's sales in the country. Its revenues are growing rapidly and profitably. What's Jollibee's secret? Smart niching. Whereas McDonald's exports largely standardized fare to consumers around the world, Jollibee is relentlessly local—it concentrates on serving the unique tastes of Filipino consumers.

In many ways, Jollibee's operations mirror those of McDonald's: Both offer cleanliness, fast service, and convenient locations. Jollibee's Champ burger competes with the Big Mac and its peach-mango pie replicates McDonald's apple version. However, in contrast to the fairly bland fare that McDonald's serves so successfully worldwide, Jollibee's menu and flavors are specially suited to Filipino tastes. The local chain cooks up sweet, spicy burgers and serves seasoned chicken and spaghetti with sweet sauce, the way Filipinos like it. It serves these meals with rice or noodles, not french fries. "We've designed these products, which are really all-American delights, to suit the Filipino palate," says Jollibee's marketing vice president. Some items, however, are uniquely Filipino. For example, Jollibee's Palabok Fiesta meal, featuring bihon noodles topped with pork-shrimp sauce and garnished with flaked smoked fish, is very popular in the Philippines. Most Americans wouldn't like it because it smells of fish.

Beyond its special understanding of the Filipino palate, Jollibee has also mastered the country's culture and lifestyle. "What happens in the normal Filipino family is that weekends are especially for children," notes a Philippine business analyst, "and parents try to ask their children where they want to eat." Jollibee lures kids with in-store play activities and a cast of captivating characters. Its hamburger-headed Champ, complete with boxing gloves, goes head-to-head with McDonald's Hamburglar. And its massive orange-jacketed Jolly Bee character and a blonde spaghetti-haired girl named Hetti are better known and loved in the Philippines than Ronald McDonald.

The well-known Jolly Bee character epitomizes the Filipino spirit of lighthearted, everyday happiness. Like Filipino working people,

■ Market nicher Jollibee is king of the burger market in the Philippines. The Jollibee burger is similar to "what a Filipino mother would cook at home."

explains Jollibee CEO Tony Tan, "the bee hops around and produces sweet things for life, and is happy even though it is busy." Indeed, the company's "jolliness is infectious," says the analyst. It's "as much a part of [the chain's] success as its recipes. Jollibee's staff outsmile McDonald's by a huge stretch. [They recently] started greeting customers with a gesture adopted from the sign language of the deaf—a vertical stroke for 'bee' and hands shoveling towards the heart for 'happy'—which kids have now started using on playgrounds. Jollibee staff call customers and one another 'sir' and 'mom,' which is at once casual and respectful in the Philippines . . . everyone at Jollibee projects fun."

Jollibee has some additional advantages in this seemingly unfair rivalry. Although much smaller in global terms than McDonald's, Jollibee concentrates most of its limited resources within the Philippines, where its restaurants outnumber McDonald's two to one. But its primary advantage comes from simply doing a better job of giving Filipino consumers what they want. Notes the analyst, "The Jollibee burger is similar to what a Filipino mother would cook at home."

So, small can be beautiful. Jollibee has shown that, through smart niching, small players can compete effectively against industry giants.

Sources: See "Happy Meals for McDonald's Rival," *Business Week,* July 29, 1996, p. 77; Cris Prystay and Sanjay Kumar, "Asia Bites Back," *Asian Business,* January 1997, pp. 58–60; Dominic Jones and Nicholas Bradbury, "Blue Chips of the Future," *Euromoney,* December 1998, pp. 99–102; "McDonald's Sales Momentum Continues," McDonald's press release, February 17, 2004, accessed at www.mcdonalds.com/corp/news/fnpr/fpr_03052004.html; Rizzarene S. Manrique, "Special Report: Industry Report (Hotels and Restaurants):[8]," *BusinessWorld,* March 3, 2004, p. 1; "Retail Brief—Jollibee Foods Corporation," *Wall Street Journal,* February 18, 2004, p. 1; "Good Food, Family and Happiness," *BusinessWorld,* February 24, 2004, p. 1; and "Our Company: The Jollibee Phenomenon," accessed online at www.jollibee.com.ph/corporate/phenomenon.htm, November 2004.

Alternatively, a company might choose to serve several related segments—perhaps those with different kinds of customers but with the same basic wants. Pottery Barn, for example, targets kids, teens, and adults with the same lifestyle-themed merchandise in different outlets: the original Pottery Barn, Pottery Barn Kids, and PB Teen. Or a large company might decide to offer a complete range of products to serve all market segments. Most companies enter a new market by serving a single segment, and if this proves successful, they add segments. Large companies eventually seek full market coverage. They want to be the General Motors of their industry. GM says that it makes a car for every "person, purse, and personality." The leading company normally has different products designed to meet the special needs of each segment.

Market Positioning

After a company has decided which market segments to enter, it must decide what positions it wants to occupy in those segments. A product's *position* is the place the product occupies relative to competitors in consumers' minds. Marketers want to develop unique market positions for their products. If a product is perceived to be exactly like others on the market, consumers would have no reason to buy it.

Market positioning
Arranging for a product to occupy a clear, distinctive, and desirable place relative to competing products in the minds of target consumers.

Market positioning is arranging for a product to occupy a clear, distinctive, and desirable place relative to competing products in the minds of target consumers. Thus, marketers plan positions that distinguish their products from competing brands and give them the greatest strategic advantage in their target markets. For example, Saturn is "a different kind of company, different kind of car"; the Hummer is "like nothing else"; and Toyota's hybrid Prius provides "a lifetime of fresh air with every purchase." The luxurious Bentley promises "18 hand-crafted feet of shameless luxury." Such deceptively simple statements form the backbone of a product's marketing strategy.

■ Positioning: Toyota's Prius is "a revelation brilliantly disguised as a car." The Hummer is "like nothing else—need is a very subjective word."

In positioning its product, the company first identifies possible competitive advantages upon which to build the position. To gain competitive advantage, the company must offer greater value to target consumers. It can do this either by charging lower prices than competitors do or by offering more benefits to justify higher prices. But if the company positions the product as *offering* greater value, it must then *deliver* that greater value. Thus, effective positioning begins with actually *differentiating* the company's marketing offer so that it gives consumers more value. Once the company has chosen a desired position, it must take strong steps to deliver and communicate that position to target consumers. The company's entire marketing program should support the chosen positioning strategy.

Developing the Marketing Mix

Marketing mix

The set of controllable tactical marketing tools— product, price, place, and promotion—that the firm blends to produce the response it wants in the target market.

Once the company has decided on its overall marketing strategy, it is ready to begin planning the details of the marketing mix, one of the major concepts in modern marketing. The **marketing mix** is the set of controllable, tactical marketing tools that the firm blends to produce the response it wants in the target market. The marketing mix consists of everything the firm can do to influence the demand for its product. The many possibilities can be collected into four groups of variables known as the "four *Ps*": *product, price, place,* and *promotion.* Figure 2.5 shows the particular marketing tools under each *P.*

Product means the goods-and-services combination the company offers to the target market. Thus, a Ford Taurus product consists of nuts and bolts, spark plugs, pistons, headlights, and thousands of other parts. Ford offers several Taurus styles and dozens of optional features. The car comes fully serviced and with a comprehensive warranty that is as much a part of the product as the tailpipe.

Price is the amount of money customers have to pay to obtain the product. Ford calculates suggested retail prices that its dealers might charge for each Taurus. But Ford dealers rarely charge the full sticker price. Instead, they negotiate the price with each customer, offering discounts, trade-in allowances, and credit terms. These actions adjust prices for the current competitive situation and bring them into line with the buyer's perception of the car's value.

Place includes company activities that make the product available to target consumers. Ford partners with a large body of independently owned dealerships that sell the company's many different models. Ford selects its dealers carefully and supports them strongly. The dealers keep an inventory of Ford automobiles, demonstrate them to potential buyers, negotiate prices, close sales, and service the cars after the sale.

Promotion means activities that communicate the merits of the product and persuade target customers to buy it. Ford spends more than $2.2 billion each year on advertising, just less than $755 per car sold, to tell consumers about the company and its many products.[13] Dealership salespeople assist potential buyers and persuade them that Ford is the best car for

FIGURE 2.5
The four *Ps* of the marketing mix

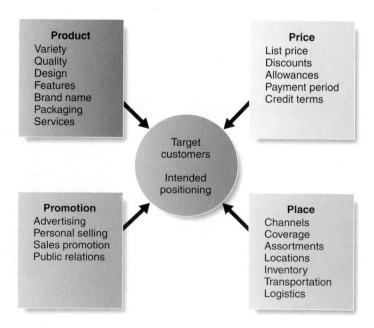

them. Ford and its dealers offer special promotions—sales, cash rebates, low financing rates—as added purchase incentives.

An effective marketing program blends all of the marketing mix elements into a coordinated program designed to achieve the company's marketing objectives by delivering value to consumers. The marketing mix constitutes the company's tactical tool kit for establishing strong positioning in target markets.

Some critics feel that the four Ps may omit or underemphasize certain important activities. For example, they ask, "Where are services?" Just because they don't start with a P doesn't justify omitting them. The answer is that services, such as banking, airline, and retailing services, are products too. We might call them *service products*. "Where is packaging?" the critics might ask. Marketers would answer that they include packaging as just one of many product decisions. All said, as Figure 2.5 suggests, many marketing activities that might appear to be left out of the marketing mix are subsumed under one of the four Ps. The issue is not whether there should be four, six, or ten Ps so much as what framework is most helpful in designing marketing programs.

There is another concern, however, that is valid. It holds that the four Ps concept takes the seller's view of the market, not the buyer's view. From the buyer's viewpoint, in this age of customer relationships, the four Ps might be better described as the four Cs:[14]

4Ps	4Cs
Product	Customer solution
Price	Customer cost
Place	Convenience
Promotion	Communication

Thus, while marketers see themselves as selling products, customers see themselves as buying value or solutions to their problems. And customers are interested in more than just the price; they are interested in the total costs of obtaining, using, and disposing of a product. Customers want the product and service to be as conveniently available as possible. Finally, they want two-way communication. Marketers would do well to think through the four Cs first and then build the four Ps on that platform.

Managing the Marketing Effort

In addition to being good at the *marketing* in marketing management, companies also need to pay attention to the *management*. Managing the marketing process requires the four marketing management functions shown in Figure 2.6—*analysis*, *planning*, *implementation*, and *control*. The company first develops companywide strategic plans, and then translates them into marketing and other plans for each division, product, and brand. Through implementation, the company turns the plans into actions. Control consists of measuring and evaluating the results of marketing activities and taking corrective action where needed. Finally, marketing analysis provides information and evaluations needed for all of the other marketing activities.

FIGURE 2.6
Marketing analysis, planning, implementation, and control

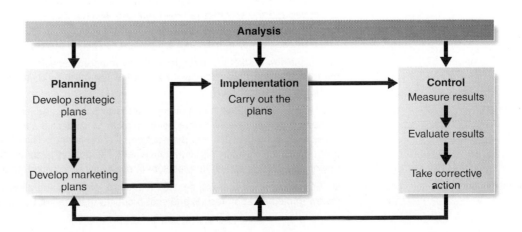

Marketing Analysis

Managing the marketing function begins with a complete analysis of the company's situation. The company must analyze its markets and marketing environment to find attractive opportunities and avoid environmental threats. It must analyze company strengths and weaknesses as well as current and possible marketing actions to determine which opportunities it can best pursue. Marketing provides input to each of the other marketing management functions. We discuss marketing analysis more fully in Chapter 3.

Marketing Planning

Through strategic planning, the company decides what it wants to do with each business unit. Marketing planning involves deciding on marketing strategies that will help the company attain its overall strategic objectives. A detailed marketing plan is needed for each business, product, or brand. What does a marketing plan look like? Our discussion focuses on product or brand plans.

Table 2.2 outlines the major sections of a typical product or brand plan. (See Appendix 2 for a sample marketing plan.) The plan begins with an executive summary, which quickly overviews major assessments, goals, and recommendations. The main section of the plan presents a detailed analysis of the current marketing situation as well as potential threats and

TABLE 2.2   **Contents of a Marketing Plan**

Section	Purpose
Executive summary	Presents a brief summary of the main goals and recommendations of the plan for management review, helping top management to find the plan's major points quickly. A table of contents should follow the executive summary.
Current marketing situation	Describes the target market and company's position in it, including information about the market, product performance, competition, and distribution. This section includes: • A *market description* that defines the market and major segments, then reviews customer needs and factors in the marketing environment that may affect customer purchasing. • A *product review,* that shows sales, prices, and gross margins of the major products in the product line. • A review of *competition,* which identifies major competitors and assesses their market positions and strategies for product quality, pricing, distribution, and promotion. • A review of *distribution,* which evaluates recent sales trends and other developments in major distribution channels.
Threats and opportunities analysis	Assesses major threats and opportunities that the product might face, helping management to anticipate important positive or negative developments that might have an impact on the firm and its strategies.
Objectives and issues	States the marketing objectives that the company would like to attain during the plan's term and discusses key issues that will affect their attainment. For example, if the goal is to achieve a 15 percent market share, this section looks at how this goal might be achieved.
Marketing strategy	Outlines the broad marketing logic by which the business unit hopes to achieve its marketing objectives and the specifics of target markets, positioning, and marketing expenditure levels. It outlines specific strategies for each marketing-mix element and explains how each responds to the threats, opportunities, and critical issues spelled out earlier in the plan.
Action programs	Spells out how marketing strategies will be turned into specific action programs that answer the following questions: *What* will be done? *When* will it be done? *Who* is responsible for doing it? *How* much will it cost?
Budgets	Details a supporting marketing budget that is essentially a projected profit-and-loss statement. It shows expected revenues (forecasted number of units sold and the average net price) and expected costs (of production, distribution, and marketing). The difference is the projected profit. Once approved by higher management, the budget becomes the basis for materials buying, production scheduling, personnel planning, and marketing operations.
Controls	Outlines the control that will be used to monitor progress and allow higher management to review implementation results and spot products that are not meeting their goals.

opportunities. It next states major objectives for the brand and outlines the specifics of a marketing strategy for achieving them.

A *marketing strategy* consists of specific strategies for target markets, positioning, the marketing mix, and marketing expenditure levels. In this section, the planner explains how each strategy responds to the threats, opportunities, and critical issues spelled out earlier in the plan. Additional sections of the marketing plan lay out an action program for implementing the marketing strategy along with the details of a supporting *marketing budget.* The last section outlines the controls that will be used to monitor progress and take corrective action.

Marketing Implementation

Marketing implementation

The process that turns marketing strategies and plans into marketing actions in order to accomplish strategic marketing objectives.

Planning good strategies is only a start toward successful marketing. A brilliant marketing strategy counts for little if the company fails to implement it properly. **Marketing implementation** is the process that turns marketing *plans* into marketing *actions* in order to accomplish strategic marketing objectives. Implementation involves day-to-day, month-to-month activities that effectively put the marketing plan to work. Whereas marketing planning addresses the *what* and *why* of marketing activities, implementation addresses the *who, where, when,* and *how.*

Many managers think that "doing things right" (implementation) is as important as, or even more important than, "doing the right things" (strategy). The fact is that both are critical to success, and companies can gain competitive advantages through effective implementation. One firm can have essentially the same strategy as another, yet win in the marketplace through faster or better execution. Still, implementation is difficult—it is often easier to think up good marketing strategies than it is to carry them out.

In an increasingly connected world, people at all levels of the marketing system must work together to implement marketing strategies and plans. At Black & Decker, for example, marketing implementation for the company's power tool products requires day-to-day decisions and actions by thousands of people both inside and outside the organization. Marketing managers make decisions about target segments, branding, packaging, pricing, promoting, and distributing. They talk with engineering about product design, with manufacturing about production and inventory levels, and with finance about funding and cash flows. They also connect with outside people, such as advertising agencies to plan ad campaigns and the media to obtain publicity support. The sales force urges Home Depot, Wal-Mart, and other retailers to advertise Black & Decker products, provide ample shelf space, and use company displays.

Successful marketing implementation depends on how well the company blends its people, organizational structure, decision and reward systems, and company culture into a cohesive action program that supports its strategies. At all levels, the company must be staffed by people who have the needed skills, motivation, and personal characteristics. The company's formal organization structure plays an important role in implementing marketing strategy; so do its decision and reward systems. For example, if a company's compensation system rewards managers for short-run profit results, they will have little incentive to work toward long-run market-building objectives.

Finally, to be successfully implemented, the firm's marketing strategies must fit with its company culture, the system of values and beliefs shared by people in the organization. A study of America's most successful companies found that these companies have almost cult-like cultures built around strong, market-oriented missions. At companies such as Wal-Mart, Dell, Microsoft, Nordstrom, Citicorp, Procter & Gamble, and Walt Disney, "employees share such a strong vision that they know in their hearts what's right for their company."[15]

Marketing Department Organization

The company must design a marketing organization that can carry out marketing strategies and plans. If the company is very small, one person might do all of the research, selling, advertising, customer service, and other marketing work. As the company expands, a marketing department emerges to plan and carry out marketing activities. In large companies, this department contains many specialists. Thus, General Electric and Microsoft have product and market managers, sales managers and salespeople, market researchers, advertising experts, and many other specialists.

Modern marketing departments can be arranged in several ways. The most common form of marketing organization is the *functional organization.* Under this organization, different marketing activities are headed by a functional specialist—a sales manager, advertising manager, marketing research manager, customer service manager, or new-product manager. A company that sells across the country or internationally often uses a *geographic organization.*

■ Marketers must continually plan their analysis, implementation, and control activities.

Its sales and marketing people are assigned to specific countries, regions, and districts. Geographic organization allows salespeople to settle into a territory, get to know their customers, and work with a minimum of travel time and cost.

Companies with many very different products or brands often create a *product management organization*. Using this approach, a product manager develops and implements a complete strategy and marketing program for a specific product or brand. Product management first appeared at Procter & Gamble in 1929. A new company soap, Camay, was not doing well, and a young P&G executive was assigned to give his exclusive attention to developing and promoting this product. He was successful, and the company soon added other product managers.[16] Since then, many firms, especially consumer products companies, have set up product management organizations.

For companies that sell one product line to many different types of markets and customers that have different needs and preferences, a *market* or *customer management organization* might be best. A market management organization is similar to the product management organization. Market managers are responsible for developing marketing strategies and plans for their specific markets or customers. This system's main advantage is that the company is organized around the needs of specific customer segments.

Large companies that produce many different products flowing into many different geographic and customer markets usually employ some *combination* of the functional, geographic, product, and market organization forms. This ensures that each function, product, and market receives its share of management attention. However, it can also add costly layers of management and reduce organizational flexibility. Still, the benefits of organizational specialization usually outweigh the drawbacks.

Marketing organization has become an increasingly important issue in recent years. As we discussed in Chapter 1, many companies are finding that today's marketing environment calls for less focus on products, brands, and territories and more focus on customers and customer relationships. More and more companies are shifting their brand management focus toward *customer management*—moving away from managing just product or brand profitability and toward managing customer profitability and customer equity.[17] And many companies now organize their marketing operations around major customers. For example, companies such as Procter & Gamble, Black & Decker, and Newell Rubbermaid have large teams, or even whole divisions, set up to serve large customers like Wal-Mart, Target, or Home Depot.

Marketing control
The process of measuring and evaluating the results of marketing strategies and plans, and taking corrective action to ensure that objectives are achieved.

Marketing Control

Because many surprises occur during the implementation of marketing plans, the marketing department must practice constant marketing control. **Marketing control** involves evaluating the results of marketing strategies and plans and taking corrective action to ensure that objectives are attained. Marketing control involves four steps. Management first sets specific marketing goals. It then measures its performance in the marketplace and evaluates the causes of any differences between expected and actual performance. Finally, management takes corrective action to close the gaps between its goals and its performance. This may require changing the action programs or even changing the goals.

Operating control involves checking ongoing performance against the annual plan and taking corrective action when necessary. Its purpose is to ensure that the company achieves the sales, profits, and other goals set out in its annual plan. It also involves determining the profitability of different products, territories, markets, and channels.

Strategic control involves looking at whether the company's basic strategies are well matched to its opportunities. Marketing strategies and programs can quickly become outdated, and each company should periodically reassess its overall approach to the marketplace. A major tool for such strategic control is a **marketing audit**. The marketing audit is a comprehensive, systematic, independent, and periodic examination of a company's environment, objectives, strategies, and activities to determine problem areas and opportunities. The audit provides good input for a plan of action to improve the company's marketing performance.[18]

The marketing audit covers *all* major marketing areas of a business, not just a few trouble spots. It assesses the marketing environment, marketing strategy, marketing organization, marketing systems, marketing mix, and marketing productivity and profitability. The audit is normally conducted by an objective and experienced outside party. The findings may come as a surprise—and sometimes as a shock—to management. Management then decides which actions make sense and how and when to implement them.

Marketing audit
A comprehensive, systematic, independent, and periodic examination of a company's environment, objectives, strategies, and activities to determine problem areas and opportunities and to recommend a plan of action to improve the company's marketing performance.

The Marketing Environment

Managing the marketing function would be hard enough if the marketer had to deal only with the controllable marketing mix variables. But the company operates in a complex marketing environment, consisting of uncontrollable forces to which the company must adapt. The environment produces both threats and opportunities. The company must carefully analyze its environment so that it can avoid the threats and take advantage of the opportunities.

The company's marketing environment includes forces close to the company that affect its ability to serve consumers, such as other company departments, channel members, suppliers, competitors, and publics. It also includes broader demographic and economic forces, political and legal forces, technological and ecological forces, and social and cultural forces. Marketers need to consider all of these forces in the process of building and maintaining profitable relationships with customers and marketing partners. We will examine the marketing environment more fully in Chapter 3.

Measuring and Managing Return on Marketing

Marketing managers must ensure that their marketing dollars are being well spent. In the past, many marketers spent freely on big advertising campaigns and other expensive marketing programs, often without thinking carefully about the financial returns on their spending. They believed that marketing produces intangible outcomes, which do not lend themselves readily to measures of productivity or return. "Many believe marketing is essentially creative and that, consequently, its financial returns are not measurable," notes one analyst. "Measuring and managing the effectiveness of marketing investments in generating profitable returns has long been a problem for corporations," says a marketing productivity consultant. "Marketing is perhaps the only remaining function within an organization not held to strict financial performance requirements."[19]

But all that is changing. Given today's tighter economy and shrinking budgets, marketers face growing pressures to show that they are adding value in line with their costs. Many companies now view marketing as an investment rather than an expense. They expect marketers to account for results, in terms of both market impact and profits. In response, marketers are developing better measures of *return on marketing*. **Return on marketing** (or *marketing ROI*) is the net return from a marketing investment divided by the costs of the marketing investment. It measures the profits generated by investments in marketing activities.

**Return on marketing
(or marketing ROI)**
The net return from a marketing investment divided by the costs of the marketing investment.

■ Measuring the sometimes intangible outcomes of marketing programs can be difficult. For example, how would you measure the "return on marketing" for an ad like this one?

GREEN GIANT VEGETABLES. NOW RESEALABLE.

It's true that marketing returns are difficult to measure. One recent study found that 68 percent of marketing executives have difficulty measuring the ROI of their marketing programs. In another study of marketing professionals, 73 percent of those surveyed felt there are no adequate return on marketing measurement tools available.[20] "There's a reason why companies aren't keeping closer tabs on their marketing ROI: It's tough to measure, more so than for other business expenses," says one analyst. "You can imagine buying a piece of equipment, . . . and then measuring the productivity gains that result from the purchase," he says. "But in marketing, benefits like advertising impact aren't easily put into dollar returns. It takes a leap of faith to come up with a number."[21]

A company can assess return on marketing in terms of standard marketing performance measures, such as brand awareness, sales, or market share. Increasingly, however, marketers are using customer-centered measures of marketing impact, such as customer acquisition, customer retention, and customer lifetime value. Figure 2.7 views marketing expenditures as investments that produce returns in the form of more profitable customer relationships.[22] Marketing investments result in improved customer value and satisfaction, which in turn increases customer attraction and retention. This increases individual customer lifetime values and the firm's overall customer equity. Increased customer equity, in relation to the cost of the marketing investments, determines return on marketing.

Regardless of how it's defined or measured, the return on marketing concept is here to stay. In a recent survey of marketing professionals, 70 percent asserted that marketing ROI represents a long-term change in how they do business. "All good marketers live and die by measurements of their results," states the marketing productivity consultant. "Projections are made, marketing is delivered, results are measured, and the knowledge is applied to guide future marketing. . . . The return on marketing investments is integral to strategic decisions at [all levels] of the business."[23]

FIGURE 2.7
Return on marketing
*Adapted from Roland T. Rust,
Katherine N. Lemon, and
Valarie A. Zeithaml, "Return
on Marketing: Using Customer
Equity to Focus Marketing
Strategy,"* Journal of
Marketing, *January 2004,
p. 112.*

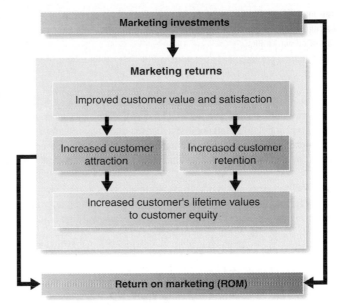

> **Reviewing the Concepts** <

In Chapter 1, we defined marketing and outlined the steps in the marketing process. In this chapter, we examined companywide strategic planning and marketing's role in the organization. Then, we looked more deeply into marketing strategy and the marketing mix, and reviewed the major marketing management functions. So you've had a pretty good overview of the fundamentals of modern marketing. In future chapters, we'll expand on these fundamentals.

1. Explain companywide strategic planning and its four steps.

Strategic planning sets the stage for the rest of the company's planning. Marketing contributes to strategic planning, and the overall plan defines marketing's role in the company. Although formal planning offers a variety of benefits to companies, not all companies use it or use it well.

Strategic planning involves developing a strategy for long-run survival and growth. It consists of four steps: defining the company's mission, setting objectives and goals, designing a business portfolio, and developing functional plans. *Defining a clear company mission* begins with drafting a formal mission statement, which should be market oriented, realistic, specific, motivating, and consistent with the market environment. The mission is then transformed into detailed *supporting goals and objectives* to guide the entire company. Based on those goals and objectives, headquarters designs a *business portfolio*, deciding which businesses and products should receive more or fewer resources. In turn, each business and product unit must develop *detailed marketing plans* in line with the companywide plan.

2. Discuss how to design business portfolios and develop strategies for growth and downsizing.

Guided by the company's mission statement and objectives, management plans its *business portfolio*, or the collection of businesses and products that make up the company. The firm wants to produce a business portfolio that best fits its strengths and weaknesses to opportunities in the environment. To do this, it must analyze and adjust its *current* business portfolio and develop growth and downsizing strategies for adjusting the *future* portfolio. The company might use a formal portfolio-planning method. But many

companies are now designing more-customized portfolio-planning approaches that better suit their unique situations. The *product/market expansion grid* suggests four possible growth paths: market penetration, market development, product development, and diversification.

3. Assess marketing's role in strategic planning and explain how marketers partner with others inside and outside the firm to build profitable customer relationships.

Under the strategic plan, the major functional departments—marketing, finance, accounting, purchasing, operations, information systems, human resources, and others—must work together to accomplish strategic objectives. Marketing plays a key role in the company's strategic planning by providing a *marketing-concept philosophy* and *inputs* regarding attractive market opportunities. Within individual business units, marketing designs *strategies* for reaching the unit's objectives and helps to carry them out profitably.

Marketers alone cannot produce superior value for customers. A company's success depends on how well each department performs its customer value-adding activities and how well the departments work together to serve the customer. Thus, marketers must practice *partner relationship management*. They must work closely with partners in other company departments to form an effective *value chain* that serves the customer. And they must partner effectively with other companies in the marketing system to form a competitively superior *value-delivery network*.

4. Describe the elements of a customer-driven marketing strategy and mix, and the forces that influence it.

Consumers' relationships are at the center of marketing strategy and programs. Through market segmentation, target marketing, and market positioning, the company divides the total market into smaller segments, selects segments it can best serve, and decides how it wants to bring value to target consumers. It then designs a *marketing mix* to produce the response it wants in the target market. The marketing mix consists of product, price, place, and promotion decisions.

5. List the marketing management functions, including the elements of a marketing plan, and discuss the importance of measuring and managing return on marketing.

To find the best strategy and mix and to put them into action, the company engages in marketing analysis, planning, implementation, and control. The main components of a *marketing plan* are the executive summary, current marketing situation, threats and opportunities, objectives and issues, marketing strategies, action programs, budgets, and controls. To plan good strategies is often easier than to carry them out. To be successful, companies must also be effective at *implementation*—turning marketing strategies into marketing actions.

Much of the responsibility for implementation goes to the company's marketing department. Marketing departments can be organized in one or a combination of ways: *functional marketing organiza-* *tion, geographic organization, product management organization,* or *market management organization*. In this age of customer relationships, more and more companies are now changing their organizational focus from product or territory management to customer relationship management. Marketing organizations carry out *marketing control*, both operating control and strategic control. They use *marketing audits* to determine marketing opportunities and problems and to recommend short-run and long-run actions to improve overall marketing performance.

Marketing managers must ensure that their marketing dollars are being well spent. Today's marketers face growing pressures to show that they are adding value in line with their costs. In response, marketers are developing better measures of *return on marketing* (or *marketing ROI*). Increasingly, they are using customer-centered measures of marketing impact as a key input into their strategic decision making.

> Reviewing the Key Terms <

Business portfolio 39
Diversification 41
Downsizing 42
Growth-share matrix 40
Market development 41
Market penetration 41
Market positioning 49

Market segment 47
Market segmentation 47
Marketing audit 55
Marketing control 54
Marketing implementation 53
Marketing mix 50

Marketing strategy 46
Mission statement 37
Portfolio analysis 39
Product development 41
Product/market expansion
  grid 41

Return on marketing 55
Strategic planning 37
Target marketing 47
Value chain 44
Value-delivery network 45

> Discussing the Concepts <

1. Which of the following two terms do you think best describes the process of developing and maintaining a fit between the organization's goals and capabilities and its changing marketing opportunities: strategic planning or corporate planning. Why?

2. The BCG growth-share matrix identifies four classifications of SBU's: Stars, Cash Cows, Question Marks, and Dogs. Briefly discuss why management may find it difficult to dispose of a "Question Mark."

3. Discuss each of the three steps that a company must perform in choosing the best market segments and designing strategies to maximize profitability in selected segments.

4. This chapter discusses a useful strategy tool for identifying growth opportunities. Discuss the differences between the four options that comprise the product/market expansion grid. Which option would a smaller company pursue if it decided to enter an existing market served by many large, well-known competitors? Assume the product being introduced by this smaller company is a new offering for the organization, but this new product offers a number of unique features.

5. Do you think that the "four Ps" marketing mix framework does an adequate job of describing marketer responsibilities in preparing and managing marketing programs? Why? Do you see any issues with this framework in relation to service products?

> Applying the Concepts <

1. In a small group, discuss whether the following statement from Burton Snowboards North America, manufacturer and marketer of a leading snowboard brand, meets the five criteria of a good mission statement:

   "Burton Snowboards is a rider-driven company solely dedicated to creating the best snowboarding equipment on the planet."

2. Ansoff's product/market expansion grid is a portfolio-planning tool used to identify potential growth opportunities for companies. The four opportunities defined by the grid are: market penetration, market development, product development, and diversification. Cite one example for each of these four possible growth opportunities that has occurred in the PC industry during the past few years.

3. During the past few years, Nike has successfully entered the golfing market with a line of clubs, balls, bags, footware, and apparel for men, women, and kids. Most visibly, Nike has enlisted the services of Tiger Woods to promote its golf products. Prepare a brief marketing plan for Nike's golfing products line for the coming year. In preparing the plan, consider who Nike is targeting and how it positions its golfing products in its target markets. For more information, visit www.nikegolf.com.

> Focus on Technology <

AT&T Natural Voices designs text-to-speech (T2S) software. These T2S software engines convert written language into speech that sounds amazingly real. AT&T has partnered with many companies to improve the customer value network and increase sales. One of the partner companies that sells AT&T Natural Voices directly to customers over the Internet is NextUp. If you have not used or experienced a T2S engine before, you can get a free demonstration at http://www.nextup.com/nvdemo.html. Just follow these simple directions: (A) paste any sentence of less than 30 words into the demonstration space provided, (B) select a language, (C) select a voice, and (D) click "Go."

Now suppose that you are a member of a new-product marketing team in a firm that has developed T2S technology. You have been asked by the company CEO to present some possible applications for the university undergraduate education market.

1. In a small team, brainstorm at least three applications for the university undergraduate education market.
2. The T2S engine that you demo'ed was developed by AT&T. Why, do you think, did AT&T seek out a partner (NextUp.com) to co-market this product, rather than marketing the product itself?
3. Are there other companies with which AT&T could have partnered? Which ones?

> Focus on Ethics <

Even new companies with revolutionary products fail if they do not develop a marketing strategy that is sound. One such company that failed was the original Napster. In 1999, Shawn Fanning developed peer-to-peer (P2P) software that allows users to share music, movies, and games with others over the Internet. Fanning went on to found Napster, a company that created a firestorm of controversy around the question, "What is fair use, and what is piracy?" Napster was at the center of major lawsuits between the P2P software enablers on one side and global recording companies on the other. Napster argued that its software only facilitates the private, noncommercial use of previously owned recorded musical works. The Recording Industry Association of America (RIAA) stated that Napster "launched a service that enables and facilitates the piracy of music on an unprecedented scale."*

1. Assuming that Napster knew its software was used to share copyrighted material on the Internet, possibly illegally, should it have proceeded with the P2P software?

2. While this Napster situation was unique, what should an organization do if it has a promising technology or product that potentially infringes on others' legal rights? Can you think of an organization that has recently experienced a similar situation?
3. In your opinion, has file sharing and downloading of music over the Internet decreased, remained the same, or increase in the 2 years following RIAA's legal action against Napster? Why?

*See Steven V. Brull, "Commentary: The Record Industry Can't Stop the Music," *BusinessWeek Online*, May 15, 2000, accessed at www.businessweek.com/2000/00-20/b3681181.htm.

Video Case

Starbucks

Today, with more than 7,500 stores, it might seem like there is a Starbucks on almost every street corner in every town across the United States and in many cities abroad. But less than 20 years ago, Starbucks was just getting started, boasting only 15 stores. Starbucks has achieved this phenomenal growth by sticking closely to its winning formula: the Starbucks experience. Plush armchairs, frothy lattes, soothing music, and indulgent treats encourage customers to return again and again.

Starbucks growth has not been limited to its stores. In addition, the coffee house has explored new retail channels, introduced new products, and sought opportunities for international growth. But without baristas, extending the Starbuck's experience to these new ventures can be tricky. As Starbucks expands its product line and global reach, the company will have to stay true to its original formula to keep things perking.

After watching the video featuring Starbucks, answer the following questions about strategic planning.

1. List several businesses and products that are included in Starbucks' business portfolio. Analyze the portfolio using the Boston Consulting Group Approach.
2. How does Starbucks' entry into the grocery market affect the company's relationships with its customers?
3. Is it possible to convey the "Starbuck's experience" through new retail channels?
4. How did Starbucks successfully transition from a nicher to a mainstream marketer? What can the company do to maintain its small company feel as it expands?

Company Case

Trap-Ease America: The Big Cheese of Mousetraps

CONVENTIONAL WISDOM

One April morning, Martha House, president of Trap-Ease America, entered her office in Costa Mesa, California. She paused for a moment to contemplate the Ralph Waldo Emerson quote that she had framed and hung near her desk:

> "If a man [can] . . . make a better mousetrap than his neighbor . . . the world will make a beaten path to his door."

Perhaps, she mused, Emerson knew something that she didn't. She *had* the better mousetrap—Trap-Ease—but the world didn't seem all that excited about it.

The National Hardware Show

Martha had just returned from the National Hardware Show in Chicago. Standing in the trade show display booth for long hours and answering the same questions hundreds of times had been tiring. Yet, all the hard work had paid off. Each year, National Hardware Show officials held a contest to select the best new product introduced at that year's show. The Trap-Ease had won the contest this year, beating out over 300 new products.

Such notoriety was not new for the Trap-Ease mousetrap, however. *People* magazine had run a feature article on the trap, and the trap had been the subject of numerous talk shows and articles in various popular press and trade publications.

Despite all of this attention, however, the expected demand for the trap had not materialized. Martha hoped that this award might stimulate increased interest and sales.

BACKGROUND

A group of investors had formed Trap-Ease America in January after it had obtained worldwide rights to market the innovative mousetrap. In return for marketing rights, the group agreed to pay the inventor and patent holder, a retired rancher, a royalty fee for each trap sold. The group then hired Martha to serve as president and to develop and manage the Trap-Ease America organization.

Trap-Ease America contracted with a plastics-manufacturing firm to produce the traps. The trap consisted of a square, plastic tube measuring about 6 inches long and 1-½ inches in diameter. The tube bent in the middle at a 30-degree angle, so that when the front part of the tube rested on a flat surface, the other end was elevated. The elevated end held a removable cap

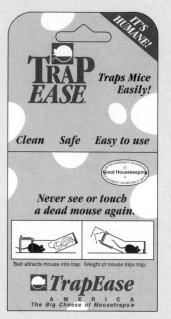

into which the user placed bait (cheese, dog food, or some other aromatic tidbit). The front end of the tube had a hinged door. When the trap was "open," this door rested on two narrow "stilts" attached to the two bottom corners of the door. (See Exhibit 1)

The simple trap worked very efficiently. A mouse, smelling the bait, entered the tube through the open end. As it walked up the angled bottom toward the bait, its weight made the elevated end of the trap drop downward. This action elevated the open end, allowing the hinged door to swing closed, trapping the mouse. Small teeth on the ends of the stilts caught in a groove on the bottom of the trap, locking the door closed. The user could then dispose of the mouse while it was still alive, or the user could leave it alone for a few hours to suffocate in the trap.

Martha believed the trap had many advantages for the consumer when compared with traditional spring-loaded traps or poisons. Consumers could use it safely and easily with no risk of catching their fingers while loading it. It posed no injury or poisoning threat to children or pets. Furthermore, with Trap-Ease, consumers avoided the unpleasant "mess" they often encountered with the violent spring-loaded traps. The Trap-Ease created no "clean-up" problem. Finally, the user could reuse the trap or simply throw it away.

Martha's early research suggested that women were the best target market for the Trap-Ease. Men, it seemed, were more willing to buy and use the traditional, spring-loaded trap. The targeted women, however, did not like the traditional trap. These women often stayed at home and took care of their children. Thus, they wanted a means of dealing with the mouse problem that avoided the unpleasantness and risks that the standard trap created in the home.

To reach this target market, Martha decided to distribute Trap-Ease through national grocery, hardware, and drug chains such as Safeway, Kmart, Hechingers, and CB Drug. She sold the trap directly to these large retailers, avoiding any wholesalers or other middlemen.

The traps sold in packages of two, with a suggested retail price of $2.49. Although this price made the Trap-Ease about five to ten times more expensive than smaller, standard traps, consumers appeared to offer little initial price resistance. The manufacturing cost for the Trap-Ease, including freight and packaging costs, was about 31 cents per unit. The company paid an additional 8.2 cents per unit in royalty fees. Martha priced the traps to retailers at 99 cents per unit (two units to a package) and estimated that, after sales and volume discounts, Trap-Ease would produce net revenue from retailers of 75 cents per unit.

To promote the product, Martha had budgeted approximately $60,000 for the first year. She planned to use $50,000 of this amount for travel costs to visit trade shows and to make sales calls on retailers. She planned to use the remaining $10,000 for advertising. So far, however, because the mousetrap had generated so much publicity, she had not felt that she needed to do much advertising. Still, she had placed advertising in *Good Housekeeping* (after all, the trap had earned the *Good Housekeeping* Seal of Approval) and in other "home and shelter" magazines. Martha was the company's only salesperson, but she intended to hire more salespeople soon.

Martha had initially forecasted Trap-Ease's first-year sales at five million units. Through April, however, the company had only sold several hundred thousand units. Martha wondered if most new products got off to such a slow start, or if she was doing something wrong. She had detected some problems, although none seemed overly serious. For one, there had not been enough repeat buying. For another, she had noted that many of the retailers upon whom she called kept their sample mousetraps on their desks as conversation pieces—she wanted the traps to be used and demonstrated. Martha wondered if consumers were also buying the traps as novelties rather than as solutions to their mouse problems.

Martha knew that the investor group believed that Trap-Ease America had a "once-in-a-lifetime chance" with its innovative mousetrap, and she sensed the group's impatience with the company's progress so far. She had budgeted approximately $250,000 in administrative and fixed costs for the first year (not including marketing costs). To keep the investors happy, the company needed to sell enough traps to cover those costs and make a reasonable profit.

BACK TO THE DRAWING BOARD

In these first few months, Martha had learned that marketing a new product was not an easy task. Some customers were very demanding. For example, one national retailer had placed a large order with instructions that Trap-Ease America was to deliver the order to the loading dock at one of the retailer's warehouses between 1:00 and 3:00 P.M. on a specified day. When the truck delivering the order arrived after 3 P.M., the retailer had refused to accept the shipment. The retailer had told Martha it would be a year before she got another chance.

As Martha sat down at her desk, she realized she needed to rethink her marketing strategy. Perhaps she had missed something or made some mistake that was causing sales to be so slow. Glancing at the quotation again, she thought that perhaps she should send the picky retailer and other customers a copy of Emerson's famous quote.

Questions for Discussion

1. Martha and the Trap-Ease America investors believe they face a once-in-a-lifetime opportunity. What information do they need to evaluate this opportunity? How do you think the group would write its mission statement? How would *you* write it?

2. Has Martha identified the best target market for Trap-Ease? What other market segments might the firm target?

3. How has the company positioned the Trap-Ease for the chosen target market? Could it position the product in other ways?

4. Describe the current marketing mix for Trap-Ease. Do you see any problems with this mix?

5. Who is Trap-Ease America's competition?

6. How would you change Trap-Ease's marketing strategy? What kinds of control procedures would you establish for this strategy?

> After studying this chapter, you should be able to

1. describe the environmental forces that affect the company's ability to serve its customers
2. explain how changes in the demographic and economic environments affect marketing decisions
3. identify the major trends in the firm's natural and technological environments
4. explain the key changes in the political and cultural environments
5. discuss how companies can react to the marketing environment

CHAPTER 3

The Marketing Environment

Previewing the Concepts

In Part I (Chapters 1 and 2), you learned about the basic concepts of marketing and the steps in the marketing process for building profitable relationships with targeted consumers. In Part II, we'll look more deeply into the first step of the marketing process—understanding the marketplace and customer needs and wants. In this chapter, you'll discover that marketing does not operate in a vacuum but rather in a complex and changing environment. Other *actors* in this environment—suppliers, intermediaries, customers, competitors, publics, and others—may work with or against the company. Major environmental *forces*—demographic, economic, natural, technological, political, and cultural—shape marketing opportunities, pose threats, and affect the company's ability to serve customers and develop lasting relationships with them. To understand marketing, and to develop effective marketing strategies, you must first understand the context in which marketing operates.

First, we'll look at an American icon, McDonald's. More than half a century ago, Ray Kroc spotted an important shift in U.S. consumer lifestyles and bought a small chain of restaurants. He built that chain into the vast McDonald's fast-food empire. But while the shifting marketing environment brought opportunities for McDonald's, it has also created challenges.

In 1955, Ray Kroc, a 52-year-old salesman of milk-shake mixing machines, discovered a string of seven restaurants owned by Richard and Maurice McDonald. Kroc saw the McDonald brothers' fast-food concept as a perfect fit for America's increasingly on-the-go, time-squeezed, family-oriented lifestyles. Kroc bought the small chain for $2.7 million, and the rest is history.

McDonald's grew quickly to become the world's largest fast-feeder. Its more than 31,000 restaurants worldwide now serve 47 million customers each day, racking up sales of more than $50 billion annually. The Golden Arches are one of the world's most familiar symbols, and other than Santa Claus, no character in the world is more recognizable than Ronald McDonald. "By making fast food respectable for middle-class families," says an industry analyst, "the Golden Arches did for greasy spoons what Holiday Inn did for roadside motels in the 1950's and what Sam Walton later did for the discount retail store."

But just as the changing marketplace has provided opportunities for McDonald's, it has also presented challenges. In fact, over the past decade, the once-shiny Golden Arches have lost some of their luster, as the company has struggled to address shifting consumer lifestyles. While McDonald's is still the nation's most-visited fast-food chain, its sales growth has slumped, and its market share has fallen by more than 3 percent since 1997. In 2002, the company posted its first-ever quarterly loss.

What happened? For one thing, McDonald's appears to have fumbled on the fundamentals. For years now, it has regularly rated rock-bottom in customer surveys on food and service quality. But perhaps more damaging, in this age of obesity lawsuits and $5 lattes, McDonald's has seemed a bit out of step with the times. "When I was a teenager, it was much more acceptable within my peer level to eat here," says one 26-year-old customer about his local McDonald's. "But now, it comes off as uncultured, unclassy, and uncool. . . . If you want to be chic, you eat sushi. Indian food is even more cutting edge. McDonald's is like white bread."

Today's consumers want more choices. They're looking for fresher, better tasting food and more upscale atmospheres. As a result, McDonald's has been losing share to what the industry calls "fast-casual" restaurants. New competitors such as Panera Bread, Baja Fresh, Pret a Manger, and Cosi offer more imaginative meals in more fashionable surroundings. And for busy consumers who'd rather "eat-out-in," even the local supermarket offers a full selection of preprepared, ready-to-serve gourmet meals to go.

Americans are also seeking healthier eating options. But in a recent survey, 63 percent of fast-food patrons complained there are too few healthy menu choices. Thirty-six percent said they don't eat at fast-food restaurants as much because they worry about their health. As the market leader, McDonald's often bears the brunt of such criticism. In a recent, unsuccessful lawsuit, the parents of two teenage girls even charged that McDonald's was responsible for their children's obesity and related health problems, including diabetes.

Reacting to these challenges, in early 2003, McDonald's announced a turnaround plan to better align the company with the new marketplace realities. The plan included the following initiatives:

Back to Basics—McDonald's is now refocusing on what made it successful: consistent products and reliable service. Management is pouring money back into existing stores, speeding up service, training employees, and monitoring restaurants to make sure they stay bright and clean.

If You Can't Lick 'Em, Join 'Em—To compete better with the likes of Starbucks and Panera, and to expand its customer base, McDonald's recently reintroduced *McCafe*, a chain of upscale coffee shops. McCafe offers leather seating, a knowledgeable staff, and espresso in porcelain cups, along with made-to-order drinks, gourmet sandwiches, and Internet access. McDonald's is also testing *Bistro Gourmet* stores in a dozen or more locations around the country. The McDonald's Bistro offers high-back leather chairs, a made-to-order omelet breakfast bar, and food served on real china. Kids can still get their Happy Meals, but parents can feast on more sophisticated fare, such as panini sandwiches, gourmet burgers, and crème brulée cheesecake.

What's On Your Plate—Working with American Academy of Pediatrics, the American Dietetic Association, and the Society for Nutrition Education, McDonald's has designed a children's nutrition education program called *What's On Your Plate*. The program features Willie Munchright, a purple clay animation character, who goes on television, online, and into the classroom to teach children how to maintain a balanced diet and enjoy a healthy lifestyle. Willie reminds kids that "it takes all different kinds of foods to build stronger dudes."

Improving the Fare—McDonald's is working to make its menu and its customers healthier. For example, it recently phased out its "supersize" option and introduced a "Go Active! Adult Happy Meal featuring an entrée salad, a bottle of Dasani water, and a "Stepometer," which measures physical activity by tracking daily steps. It now offers all-white-meat chicken in McNuggets, low-fat "milk jugs," and apple slices. The company also runs ads in such publications as *O, the Oprah Magazine* and *Marie Claire,* recommending its salads, milks, and juices along with exercise tips for women and children who care about nutrition. And McDonald's *Real Life Choices* campaign helps consumers fit the foods they love into any of three lifestyles: "watching calories," "watching fat," and "watching carbohydrates." Says a nationally renowned nutritionist who helped develop the program, "I teamed up with McDonald's to show consumers how to enjoy the McDonald's food they love, without compromising their diets." Even the harshest McDonald's critics, although still skeptical, applaud these actions.

McDonald's efforts to realign itself with the changing marketing environment appear to be paying off. By early 2004, the company was posting steady, even startling, sales and profit increases, and customers and stockholders alike were humming the chain's catchy new jingle, "I'm lovin' it." In the first quarter of 2004, McDonald's drew 2.3 million more customers each day than a year earlier, and earnings soared 56 percent. Former McDonald's CEO, Jim Cantalupo, summed it up this way: "Ray Kroc used to say he didn't know what we would be selling in the year 2000, but whatever it was we would be selling the most of it. He recognized early on that consumer needs change and we want to change with it.[1]

Marketing environment

The actors and forces outside marketing that affect marketing management's ability to build and maintain successful relationships with target customers.

Marketers need to be good at building relationships with customers, others in the company, and external partners. To do this effectively, they must understand the major environmental forces that surround all of these relationships. A company's **marketing environment** consists of the actors and forces outside marketing that affect marketing management's ability to build and maintain successful relationships with target customers. Successful companies know the vital importance of constantly watching and adapting to the changing environment.

As we move into the twenty-first century, both consumers and marketers wonder what the future will bring. The environment continues to change rapidly. More than any other group in the company, marketers must be the trend trackers and opportunity seekers. Although every manager in an organization needs to observe the outside environment, marketers have two special aptitudes. They have disciplined methods—marketing intelligence and marketing research—for collecting information about the marketing environment. They also spend more time in the customer and competitor environments. By carefully studying the environment, marketers can adapt their strategies to meet new marketplace challenges and opportunities.

The marketing environment is made up of a *microenvironment* and a *macroenvironment*. The **microenvironment** consists of the actors close to the company that affect its ability to serve its customers—the company, suppliers, marketing intermediaries, customer markets, competitors, and publics. The **macroenvironment** consists of the larger societal forces that affect the microenvironment—demographic, economic, natural, technological, political, and cultural forces. We look first at the company's microenvironment.

Microenvironment
The actors close to the company that affect its ability to serve its customers—the company, suppliers, marketing intermediaries, customer markets, competitors, and publics.

Macroenvironment
The larger societal forces that affect the microenvironment—demographic, economic, natural, technological, political, and cultural forces.

The Company's Microenvironment

Marketing management's job is to build relationships with customers by creating customer value and satisfaction. However, marketing managers cannot do this alone. Figure 3.1 shows the major actors in the marketer's microenvironment. Marketing success will require building relationships with other company departments, suppliers, marketing intermediaries, customers, competitors, and various publics, which combine to make up the company's value delivery network.

The Company

In designing marketing plans, marketing management takes other company groups into account—groups such as top management, finance, research and development (R&D), purchasing, operations, and accounting. All these interrelated groups form the internal environment. Top management sets the company's mission, objectives, broad strategies, and policies. Marketing managers make decisions within the strategies and plans made by top management.

Marketing managers must also work closely with other company departments. Finance is concerned with finding and using funds to carry out the marketing plan. The R&D department focuses on designing safe and attractive products. Purchasing worries about getting supplies and materials, whereas operations is responsible for producing and distributing the desired quality and quantity of products. Accounting has to measure revenues and costs to help marketing know how well it is achieving its objectives. Together, all of these departments have an impact on the marketing department's plans and actions. Under the marketing concept, all of these functions must "think consumer." They should work in harmony to provide superior customer value and satisfaction.

Suppliers

Suppliers form an important link in the company's overall customer value delivery system. They provide the resources needed by the company to produce its goods and services. Supplier problems can seriously affect marketing. Marketing managers must watch supply availability—supply shortages or delays, labor strikes, and other events can cost sales in the short run and damage customer satisfaction in the long run. Marketing managers also monitor

FIGURE 3.1
Actors in the microenvironment

the price trends of their key inputs. Rising supply costs may force price increases that can harm the company's sales volume.

Most marketers today treat their suppliers as partners in creating and delivering customer value. Wal-Mart goes to great lengths to work with its suppliers. For example, it helps them to test new products in its stores. And its Supplier Development Department publishes a Supplier Proposal Guide and maintains a supplier Web site, both of which help suppliers to navigate the complex Wal-Mart buying process. It knows that good partnership relationship management results in success for Wal-Mart, suppliers, and, ultimately, its customers.

Marketing Intermediaries

Marketing intermediaries

Firms that help the company to promote, sell, and distribute its goods to final buyers; they include resellers, physical distribution firms, marketing service agencies, and financial intermediaries.

Marketing intermediaries help the company to promote, sell, and distribute its goods to final buyers. They include resellers, physical distribution firms, marketing services agencies, and financial intermediaries. *Resellers* are distribution channel firms that help the company find customers or make sales to them. These include wholesalers and retailers, who buy and resell merchandise. Selecting and partnering with resellers is not easy. No longer do manufacturers have many small, independent resellers from which to choose. They now face large and growing reseller organizations such as Wal-Mart, Target, Home Depot, Costco, and Best Buy. These organizations frequently have enough power to dictate terms or even shut the manufacturer out of large markets.

Physical distribution firms help the company to stock and move goods from their points of origin to their destinations. Working with warehouse and transportation firms, a company must determine the best ways to store and ship goods, balancing factors such as cost, delivery, speed, and safety. *Marketing services agencies* are the marketing research firms, advertising agencies, media firms, and marketing consulting firms that help the company target and promote its products to the right markets. When the company decides to use one of these agencies, it must choose carefully because these firms vary in creativity, quality, service, and price. *Financial intermediaries* include banks, credit companies, insurance companies, and other businesses that help finance transactions or insure against the risks associated with the buying and selling of goods. Most firms and customers depend on financial intermediaries to finance their transactions.

Like suppliers, marketing intermediaries form an important component of the company's overall value delivery system. In its quest to create satisfying customer relationships, the company must do more than just optimize its own performance. It must partner effectively with marketing intermediaries to optimize the performance of the entire system.

Thus, today's marketers recognize the importance of working with their intermediaries as partners rather than simply as channels through which they sell their products. For example, Coca-Cola has a 10-year deal with Wendy's that makes it the fast-food chain's exclusive soft drink provider. In the deal, Coca-Cola provides Wendy's much more than just soft drinks. It also pledges powerful marketing support.

> Along with the soft drinks, Wendy's gets a cross-functional team of 50 Coke employees who are dedicated to understanding the finer points of Wendy's business. It also benefits from Coke dollars spent in joint marketing campaigns. Bigger still is the staggering amount of consumer research that Coca-Cola provides its partners. Coke . . . goes to great lengths to understand beverage drinkers—and to make sure its partners can use those insights. The company has also analyzed the demographics of every zip code in the country and used the information to create a software program called Solver. By answering questions about their target audience, Wendy's franchise owners can determine which Coke brands are preferred by the customers in their area. Coca-Cola also has even studied the design of drive-through menu boards to better understand which layouts, fonts, letter sizes, colors, and visuals induce consumers to order more food and drink. Such intense partnering efforts have earned Coca-Cola a 68 percent share of the U.S. fountain soft drink market, compared with a 22 percent share for Pepsi.[2]

Customers

The company needs to study five types of customer markets closely. *Consumer markets* consist of individuals and households that buy goods and services for personal consumption. *Business markets* buy goods and services for further processing or for use in their production

■ Partnering with marketing intermediaries: Coca-Cola provides Wendy's with much more than just soft drinks. It also pledges powerful marketing support.

process, whereas *reseller markets* buy goods and services to resell at a profit. *Government markets* are made up of government agencies that buy goods and services to produce public services or transfer the goods and services to others who need them. Finally, *international markets* consist of these buyers in other countries, including consumers, producers, resellers, and governments. Each market type has special characteristics that call for careful study by the seller.

Competitors

The marketing concept states that to be successful, a company must provide greater customer value and satisfaction than its competitors do. Thus, marketers must do more than simply adapt to the needs of target consumers. They also must gain strategic advantage by positioning their offerings strongly against competitors' offerings in the minds of consumers.

No single competitive marketing strategy is best for all companies. Each firm should consider its own size and industry position compared with those of its competitors. Large firms with dominant positions in an industry can use certain strategies that smaller firms cannot afford. But being large is not enough. There are winning strategies for large firms, but there are also losing ones. And small firms can develop strategies that give them better rates of return than large firms enjoy. We will look more deeply into competitor analysis and competitive marketing strategies in Chapter 17.

Publics

Public

Any group that has an actual or potential interest in or impact on an organization's ability to achieve its objectives.

The company's marketing environment also includes various publics. A **public** is any group that has an actual or potential interest in or impact on an organization's ability to achieve its objectives. We can identify seven types of publics.

■ *Financial publics* influence the company's ability to obtain funds. Banks, investment houses, and stockholders are the major financial publics.

■ *Media publics* carry news, features, and editorial opinion. They include newspapers, magazines, and radio and television stations.

■ Publics: Wal-Mart's Good.WORKS efforts, such as the Wal-Mart Teacher of the Year program, recognize the importance of community publics. "Supporting our communities is good for everyone," says this ad.

- *Government publics.* Management must take government developments into account. Marketers must often consult the company's lawyers on issues of product safety, truth in advertising, and other matters.
- *Citizen-action publics.* A company's marketing decisions may be questioned by consumer organizations, environmental groups, minority groups, and others. Its public relations department can help it stay in touch with consumer and citizen groups.
- *Local publics* include neighborhood residents and community organizations. Large companies usually appoint a community relations officer to deal with the community, attend meetings, answer questions, and contribute to worthwhile causes.
- *General public.* A company needs to be concerned about the general public's attitude toward its products and activities. The public's image of the company affects its buying.
- *Internal publics* include workers, managers, volunteers, and the board of directors. Large companies use newsletters and other means to inform and motivate their internal publics. When employees feel good about their company, this positive attitude spills over to external publics.

A company can prepare marketing plans for these major publics as well as for its customer markets. Suppose the company wants a specific response from a particular public, such as goodwill, favorable word of mouth, or donations of time or money. The company would have to design an offer to this public that is attractive enough to produce the desired response.

The Company's Macroenvironment

The company and all of the other actors operate in a larger macroenvironment of forces that shape opportunities and pose threats to the company. Figure 3.2 shows the six major forces in the company's macroenvironment. In the remaining sections of this chapter, we examine these forces and show how they affect marketing plans.

FIGURE 3.2
Major forces in the company's macroenvironment

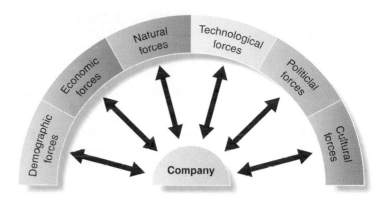

Demographic Environment

Demography
The study of human populations in terms of size, density, location, age, gender, race, occupation, and other statistics.

Demography is the study of human populations in terms of size, density, location, age, gender, race, occupation, and other statistics. The demographic environment is of major interest to marketers because it involves people, and people make up markets. The world population is growing at an explosive rate. It now totals more than 6.4 billion and will exceed 8.1 billion by the year 2030.[3] The world's large and highly diverse population poses both opportunities and challenges.

Changes in the world demographic environment have major implications for business. For example, consider China. Twenty-five years ago, to curb its skyrocketing population, the Chinese government passed regulations limiting families to one child each. As a result, Chinese children—known as "little emperors and empresses"—are being showered with attention and luxuries under what's known as the "six-pocket syndrome." As many as six adults—two parents and four doting grandparents—may be indulging the whims of each child. Parents in the average Beijing household now spend about 40 percent of their income on their cherished only child. Among other things, this trend has created huge market opportunities for children's educational products.

In China's increasingly competitive society, parents these days are desperate to give Junior an early edge. "Today's moms and dads are . . . looking to supplement a kid's education starting from Day Zero," says one marketer. That's creating opportunities for companies peddling educational offerings aimed at kids. Disney, for example, began in China in 1994 with Mandarin versions of Mickey Mouse and Donald Duck comic books. A year later, it introduced children's books. Today, with more than 10 million

■ Demographics and business: Chinese regulations limiting families to one child have resulted in what's known as the "six-pocket syndrome." Chinese children are being showered with attention and luxuries, creating opportunities for marketers.

comics and 2.7 million books sold, it's moving full speed into educational products. Magic English, a $225 Disney package that includes workbooks, flash cards, and 26 videodisks, has been phenomenally successful since it was introduced 2 years ago. This summer, Disney launched interactive educational CD-ROMs featuring the likes of Winnie the Pooh and 101 Dalmations' Cruella DeVille. In April, Disney plans to start selling Baby Einstein, a series of videos that bombard infants and toddlers with images and classical music that supposedly make them more receptive to learning later on. Disney isn't alone in catering to lucrative Chinese coddled-kiddies market. For example, Time Warner is testing the waters in Shanghai with an interactive language course called English Time. The 200-lesson, 40-CD set takes as long as 4 years for a child to complete. Time Warner is expecting strong sales, despite the $3,300 price tag.[4]

Thus, marketers keep close track of demographic trends and developments in their markets, both at home and abroad. They track changing age and family structures, geographic population shifts, educational characteristics, and population diversity. Here, we discuss the most important demographic trends in the United States.

Changing Age Structure of the Population

The U.S. population stood at more than 293 million in 2004 and may reach almost 364 million by the year 2030.[5] The single most important demographic trend in the United States is the changing age structure of the population. As shown in Figure 3.3, the U.S. population contains seven generational groups. Here, we discuss the three largest age groups—the baby boomers, Generation X, and Generation Y—and their impact on today's marketing strategies.

Baby boomers

The 78 million people born during the baby boom following World War II and lasting until the early 1960s.

THE BABY BOOMERS The post-World War II baby boom produced 78 million **baby boomers**, born between 1946 and 1964. Since then, the baby boomers have become one of the most powerful forces shaping the marketing environment. Today's baby boomers account for about 28 percent of the population but earn more than half of all personal income.

Marketers typically have paid the most attention to the smaller upper crust of the boomer generation—its more educated, mobile, and wealthy segments. These segments have gone by many names. In the 1980s, they were called "yuppies" (young urban professionals), "bumpies" (black upwardly mobile professionals), "yummies" (young upwardly mobile mommies), and "DINKs" (dual-income, no-kids couples). In the 1990s, yuppies and DINKs gave way to a new breed, with names such as "DEWKs" (dual-earners with kids) and "MOBYs" (mother older, baby younger). Now, to the chagrin of many in this generation, they are acquiring such titles as "WOOFs" (well-off older folks) or even "GRUMPIES" (just what the name suggests).

Although the more affluent boomers have grabbed most of the headlines, baby boomers cut across all walks of life, creating a diverse set of target segments for businesses. There are wealthy boomers but also boomers with more modest means. Boomers span a 20-year age range, and almost 25 percent of boomers belong to a racial or ethnic minority.[6]

The youngest boomers are now in their early 40s; the oldest are in their late-50s. Somewhere in America, seven boomers will turn 50 every minute from now until 2014. By 2025, there will be 64 million baby boomers aged 61 to 79, a 90 percent increase in the size of this population from today. Thus, the boomers have evolved from the "youthquake generation" to the "backache generation."

FIGURE 3.3

The seven U.S. generations

Source: Adapted from Alison Stein Wellner, "Generational Divide," American Demographics, *October 2000, pp. 53–58.*

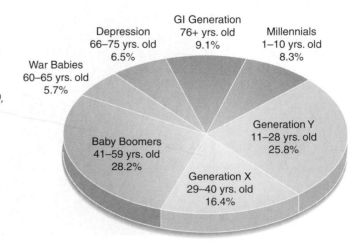

The maturing boomers are rethinking the purpose and value of their work, responsibilities, and relationships. They are approaching life with a new stability and reasonableness in the way they live, think, eat, and spend. The aging boomers are also reaching their peak earning and spending years. Thus, they constitute a lucrative market for new housing and home remodeling, financial services, travel and entertainment, eating out, health and fitness products, and high-priced cars and other luxuries. For example, more than half of all U.S. home remodeling expenditures last year were made by baby boomers.[7]

It would be a mistake to think of the boomers as aging, staid retirees. In fact, the boomers are spending $30 billion a year on *anti*-aging products and services. And unlike previous generations, boomers are likely to postpone retirement. Many boomers are rediscovering the excitement of life and have the means to play it out. For example, one-half of all U.S. adults took adventure vacations within the past 5 years. Some 56 percent of these travelers were boomers. The median age of a Harley-Davidson buyer is 46 years old, squarely within the boomer age range. And the personal watercraft industry has now virtually abandoned young adult consumers in favor of targeting middle-aged boomers and their kids.[8]

> Those one-man, stand-up Jet Skis that used to terrorize beachgoers, with ab-ribbed guys in shell necklaces vaulting over waves on their water hogs, now represent only about 1 percent of the market. New models have wider seats and room for three or even four people, with storage space for coolers and spray shields to keep legs dry. They're practically minivans. . . . The boomers want youthful lifestyle forever.

GENERATION X The baby boom was followed by a "birth dearth," creating another generation of 49 million people born between 1965 and 1976. Author Douglas Coupland calls them **Generation X**, because they lie in the shadow of the boomers and lack obvious distinguishing characteristics. Others call them the "baby busters," the "yiffies"—young, individualistic, freedom-minded few, or the "generation caught in the middle" (between the larger baby boomers and Generation Ys).

Generation X

The 45 million people born between 1965 and 1976 in the "birth dearth" following the baby boom.

The Generation Xers are defined as much by their shared experiences as by their age. Increasing divorce rates and higher employment for their mothers made them the first generation of latchkey kids. Having grown up during times of recession and corporate downsizing, they have developed a more cautious economic outlook. They care about the environment and respond favorably to socially responsible companies. Although they seek success, they are less materialistic; they prize experience, not acquisition. They are cautious romantics who want a better quality of life and are more interested in job satisfaction than in sacrificing personal happiness and growth for promotion.

As a result, the GenXers are a more skeptical bunch, cynical of frivolous marketing pitches that promise easy success. Says one marketer, "marketing to Gen Xers is difficult, and it's all about word of mouth. You can't tell them you're good, and they have zero interest in a

■ The baby boomers: It would be a mistake to think of the boomers as aging and staid. The personal watercraft industry has now virtually abandoned young adult consumers in favor of targeting middle-aged boomers.

slick brochure that says so. You have to rely on somebody they know and trust to give you instant credibility. They have a lot of 'filters' in place."[9]

Once labeled as "the MTV generation" and as body-piercing slackers who whined about "McJobs," the GenXers have now grown up and are beginning to take over. The GenXers are poised to displace the lifestyles, culture, and materialistic values of the baby boomers. They represent close to $1.4 trillion in annual purchasing power. By the year 2010, they will have overtaken the baby boomers as a primary market for almost every product category.[10]

With so much potential, many companies are focusing on GenXers. Consider the following example:

In a gritty Northside Chicago neighborhood, in a former grocery store here, under an L-train and next to a Trader Joe's, percolates CB2, the store where the definition of home for the next generation of consumers is being refined. Inside, the store pulses with techno-jazz and high-impact displays. The "CB" stands for Crate & Barrel, the "2" signals that the store is a spin-off, a cheekier cousin geared to price-and-design conscious customers in their 20s and 30s. Who are CB2's core consumers? GenXers. They're urban professionals, age 25 to 40, who are more likely to live in a loft, apartment, or townhouse than a house in the suburbs. They are skep-

Real Marketing 3.1

The Teen Market: Youth Will Be Served

Gone are the days when kids saved up their pennies for candy and ice cream at the corner soda fountain. Today's teens are big spenders. The average U.S. teen spends $103 each week; combined, the nation's 33 million 12- to 19-year-olds spend more than $175 billion a year. What's more, teens influence another $30 billion annually of their parents' spending. With so much cash to spend, teens represent a lucrative market for companies willing to cater to their often fickle, trend-driven tastes.

To tap into this vast market of potential new customers, all kinds of companies are targeting teens with new or modified products. Some of these products are naturals for the teen market, such as action movies, acne creams, teen magazines, and cell phones. Others are less expected, such as Avon products, cars, and hotels. Here are just a few examples of companies attempting to cash in on the hot teen market:

- *Wildseed:* Cell phone manufacturer Wildseed has spent years conducting research to develop cell phones for teens. The company regularly summons teenagers to focus groups, where it pays them $20 to lounge around, eat pizza, play video games, and give their thumbs up or thumbs down on various proposals. The research shows that for teenagers, a desirable cellphone is not about smaller, lighter, sleeker. What teens want from a cell phone ranges from the concrete (music, messaging, and games) to the abstract (style, personality, and individuality). As a result, Wildseed phones have "smart skins"—replaceable faceplates with computer chips that allow teens to individualize the phone's functions and appearance to match their personalities. For example, skateboarders can choose graffiti-splattered faceplates that come with edgy urban ringer tones and gritty icons. A Wildseed marketer quotes one 17-year-old customer as saying, "I want to be in charge of my wireless phone, change the screens, have new ringtones. That is what is so cool about skins. I can change my phone every day."

- *Teen Vogue:* After years of preliminary market testing, Vogue launched the first issue of the teen version of its popular women's magazine in early 2003. The publisher, Condé Nast, built an initial subscription base of more than 550,000 teens and expects the readership to expand to more than 750,000. In addition to including articles on fashion and stunning pictures, Condé Nast has decreased the size of the magazine, measuring only 6 3/4 inches by 9 1/8 inches, perfect for hiding in class.

- *Avon:* Avon recently launched a new beauty business called *mark,* in celebration of young women making their mark in the world today. The new brand targets young women 16–24. To sell *mark,* Avon has signed on a corps of young women as independent sales representatives (parental consent required), who market the brand to their peer group while at the same time creating their own entrepreneurial business opportunity. *mark* is sold through magalogs, the www.meetmark.com Web site, and "social beauty parties." Can a company known for its appeal to middle American-women sell successfully to young women? Avon thinks so. The new brand is distinctly more upscale and trendier than Avon's traditional look. "This is very much not just another brand," says Avon's chief executive, Andrea Jung.

- *BMW:* BMW offers a motorsports training program for young drivers, some of whom are too young to have licenses. As a part of its "Ultimate Driving Experience" tour, the Formula BMW USA program offers go-kart drivers between the ages of 15 and 23 an array of scholarships, training, and race experience to help develop their racing careers. "We are courting teenagers," says a BMW marketing executive. "BMW is the premier brand for youth, so we have a reason to work harder with the next generation."

- *Hot Topic:* Clothing retailer Hot Topic targets the 17 percent of American high school students who consider themselves

tical, impatient, and highly mobile. They like trends but not gimmicks, and they gravitate to the cool and casual. At CB2, it's taken 3 years to get the mix right. For example, while Crate & Barrel attracts cooks, CB2 discovered that its core customers spend more time at their computers than at the stove. So gourmet was scaled down and home office beefed up.[11]

Generation Y

The 72 million children of the baby boomers, born between 1977 and 1994.

GENERATION Y Both the baby boomers and GenXers will one day be passing the reins to the latest demographic group, **Generation Y** (also called echo boomers). Born between 1977 and 1994, these children of the baby boomers now number 72 million, dwarfing the GenXers and almost equal in size to the baby boomer segment.

The echo boom has created large teen and young adult market. With an average disposable income of $103 a week, the nation's teens spend $175 billion a year and influence another $30 billion in family spending (see Real Marketing 3.1). After years of bust, markets for teen's toys and games, clothes, furniture, and food have enjoyed a boom. Designers and retailers have created new lines, new products, and even new stores devoted to children and teens—Tommy Hilfiger, DKNY, Gap, Talbots, Pottery Barn, and Eddie Bauer, to name just a few. New media appeared that cater specifically to this market: *Time*, *Sports Illustrated*, and *People* have all started new editions for kids and teens. Banks have offered banking and investment services for young people, including investment camps.[12]

■ To target young women, Avon launched a new beauty business, *mark*, offering more upscale and trendier products through "social beauty parties" and *meet mark* magalogs like this one.

"alternative teens." The store carries an assortment of items you just won't find at Abercrombie & Fitch. The merchandise reflects a variety of music-related lifestyles, including street, retro-influenced lounge, punk, club, and gothic wear. Rather than khakis and tank tops, the store stocks pinstripe fishnet stockings, pink fur pants, feather boas, blue hair dye, black nail polish, and Morbid Makeup. Teens can buy T-shirts from TV shows such as "SpongeBobSquarePants," Kermit the Frog underwear, and licensed concert apparel from rockers such as Eminem, Marilyn Manson, Tool, and Linkin Park. Whereas Gap, American Eagle, and other teen retailers have recently reported flat or declining sales, Hot Topic's sales are, well, a hot topic. Sales have increased an average of more than 30 percent annually for the last 3 years.

Sources: Examples adapted from information found in "Teens Spent $175 Billion in 2003," press release, Teenage Research Unlimited, January 9, 2004, accessed at www.teenresearch.com; Leslie Earnest, "California: Hot Topic Results Suit It to a Tee," *The Los Angeles Times*, March 5, 2003, p. C2; Arlene Weintraub, "Hotter Than a Pair of Vinyl Jeans," *Business Week*, June 9, 2003, pp. 84–85; "California: Hot Topic's Earnings Climb 36%," *Los Angeles Times*," March 4, 2004, p. C2; Frand Washington, "Aim Young; No, Younger," *Advertising Age*, April 9, 2001; Aimee Deeken, "Startup of the Year," *Adweek*, March 1, 2004, pp. SR22–SR25; Leslie Earnest, Sally Beatty, "Avon Set to Sell to Teens," *Wall Street Journal*, October 17, 2002, p. B1; Deborah Netburn, "The New Avon Ladies," *Los Angeles Times*, March 21, 2004, p. E.4; Jennifer Lee, "Youth Will Be Served, Wirelessly," *New York Times*, May 30, 2002, p. G1; Brad Smith, "Personalization: Bigger than Games?" *Wireless Week*, January 15, 2004, p. 15; and Jean Halliday, "Automakers Mix It up to Chase Young Buyers," *Automotive News*, April 26, 2004, p. 28B.

Generation Y oldsters have now graduated from college and are moving up in their careers. Like the trailing edge of the Generation Xers ahead of them, one distinguishing characteristic of Generation Y is their utter fluency and comfort with computer, digital, and Internet technology. About 9 out of 10 teens have a home computer, 50 percent have Internet access, and more than 50 percent of teens 12 to 17 own a mobile phone. In all, they are an impatient, now-oriented bunch. "Blame it on the relentless and dizzying pace of the Internet, 240-hour cable news cycles, cell phones, and TiVo for creating the on-demand, gotta-get-it-now universe in which we live," says one observer. "Perhaps nowhere is the trend more pronounced than among the Gen Y set."[13]

Generation Y represents an attractive target for marketers. Even the automobile industry is aggressively targeting this generation of future car buyers.

> Automakers are using music, online contests, and racecars to lure Generation Y as they approach their key vehicle-buying years. For example, Honda's Civic Tour targets a core segment of 15- to 25-year-olds. It consists of a 38-stop music tour, featuring the band Dashboard Confessional. Honda will pay for the first 100,000 downloads at civictour.com of one of the band's songs, to be performed live at one of three concerts. In a similar effort, Audi kicked off an online contest at neverfollow.com in conjunction with its sponsorship of singer David Bowie's North American "Reality Tour." Visitors to the Web site are asked to "mash up" two of Bowie's songs into one to win an Audi TT coupe. Whereas, Audi's traditional buyers are in their late 30s to early 50s, the contest targets 20-somethings. The promotion's goals are to build brand awareness and "bring Audi to a whole new generation" says an Audi marketer.[14]

GENERATIONAL MARKETING Do marketers have to create separate products and marketing programs for each generation? Some experts caution that each generation spans decades of time and many socioeconomic levels. For example, marketers often split the baby boomers into three smaller groups—leading boomers, core boomers, and trailing boomers—each with its own beliefs and behaviors. Similarly, they split Generation Y into Gen Y adults, Gen Y teens, and Gen Y kids. Thus, marketers need to form more precise age-specific segments within each group. More important, defining people by their birth date may be less effective than segmenting them by their lifestyle or life stage.

Others warn that marketers have to be careful about turning off one generation each time they craft a product or message that appeals effectively to another. "The idea is to try to be broadly inclusive and at the same time offer each generation something specifically designed for it," notes one expert. "Tommy Hilfiger has big brand logos on his clothes for teenagers and little pocket polo logos on his shirts for baby boomers. It's a brand that has a more inclusive than exclusive strategy."[15]

■ To lure the Gen Y set as they approach their key vehicle-buying years, Honda's 38-stop Civic Tour features bands like Dashboard Confessional.

The Changing American Family

The "traditional household" consists of a husband, wife, and children (and sometimes grand-parents). Yet, the once American ideal of the two-child, two-car suburban family has lately been losing some of its luster. "Ward and June Cleaver used to represent the typical American household," says one demographer. "Today, marketers would be remiss in not incorporating the likes of Murphy Brown, Ally McBeal, and Will and Grace into their business plans."[16]

In the United States today, married couples with children now make up only about 34 percent the nation's 105 million households, and this percentage is falling. Married couples and people living with other relatives make up 22 percent; single parents comprise another 12 percent. A full 32 percent are nonfamily households—single live-alones or adult live-togethers of one or both sexes.[17] More people are divorcing or separating, choosing not to marry, marrying later, or marrying without intending to have children. Marketers must increasingly consider the special needs of nontraditional households, because they are now growing more rapidly than traditional households. Each group has distinctive needs and buying habits.

The number of working women has also increased greatly, growing from under 30 percent of the U.S. workforce in 1950 to just over 60 percent today.[18] However, that trend may be slowing. After increasing steadily for 25 years, the percentage of women with children under age 1 in the workforce has fallen during the past few years. Meanwhile, men are staying home with their children in record numbers. Last year, more than 1.7 million stay-at-home dads managed the household while their wives went to work.

The significant number of women in the workforce has spawned the child day care business and increased consumption of convenience foods and services, career-oriented women's clothing, financial services, and many other business opportunities. For example, new niche malls feature customized mixes of specialty shops with extended hours for working women who can find time to shop only before or after work. Stores in these malls feature targeted promotions and phone-in shopping. Busy shoppers can phone ahead with color choices and other preferences while store employees perform a "wardrobe consulting" service.[19]

■ The changing American family: Non-family households—single live-alones or adult live-togethers of one or both sexes—make up a full 32 percent of U.S. households. Today's marketers must incorporate "the likes of Murphy Brown, Ally McBeal, and Will and Grace into their business plans."

Geographic Shifts in Population

This a period of great migratory movements between and within countries. Americans, for example, are a mobile people with about 14 percent of all U.S. residents moving each year.[20] Over the past two decades, the U.S. population has shifted toward the Sunbelt states. The West and South have grown, while the Midwest and Northeast states have lost population. Such population shifts interest marketers because people in different regions buy differently. For example, research shows that people in Seattle buy more toothbrushes per capita than people in any other U.S. city; people in Salt Lake City eat more candy bars; people from New Orleans use more ketchup; and people in Miami drink more prune juice.

Also, for more than a century, Americans have been moving from rural to metropolitan areas. In the 1950s, they made a massive exit from the cities to the suburbs. Today, the migration to the suburbs continues. And more and more Americans are moving to "micropolitan areas," small cities located beyond congested metropolitan areas. These smaller micros offer many of the advantages of metro areas—jobs, restaurants, diversions, community organizations—but without the population crush, traffic jams, high crime rates, and high property taxes often associated with heavily urbanized areas.[21]

The shift in where people live has also caused a shift in where they work. For example, the migration toward micropolitan and suburban areas has resulted in a rapid increase in the number of people who "telecommute"—work at home or in a remote office and conduct their business by phone, fax, modem, or the Internet. This trend, in turn, has created a booming SOHO (small office/home office) market. One in every five Americans is now working out of the home with the help of electronic conveniences such as personal computers, cell phones, fax machines, and handheld organizers. Many marketers are actively courting the home office segment of this lucrative SOHO market. One example is FedEx Kinko's Office and Print Centers:

> Founded in the 1970s as a campus photocopying business, Kinko's was bought by FedEx in 2004. It's locations were renamed FedEx Kinko's Office and Print Centers. As the new name suggests, FedEx Kinko's is now much more than a self-service copy shop. Serving primarily small office/home office customers, it has reinvented itself as the well-appointed office outside the home. New ads proclaim, "Our office is your office." Where once there were once only copy machines, FedEx Kinko's 1,200 centers now offer a full range business services, including

■ Geographic shifts: To serve the burgeoning small office/home office market, FedEx Kinkos has reinvented itself as the well-appointed office outside the home. New ads proclaim, "Our office is your office."

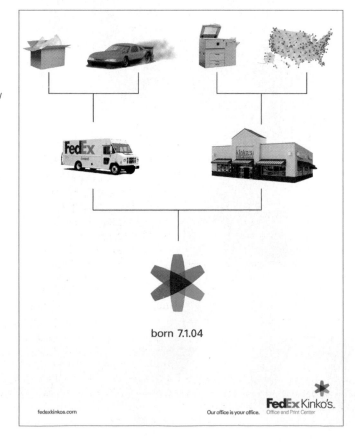

fedexkinkos.com   Our office is your office.   FedEx Kinko's. Office and Print Center

born 7.1.04

binding and finishing, color copying and printing, document management, shipping services, computer rental, T-Mobile HotSpot wireless Internet connections, and much more. People can come to a FedEx Kinko's store to do all their office jobs: They can copy, send and receive faxes, use various programs on the computer, go on the Internet, order stationery and other printed supplies, ship packages, and even rent a conference room or conduct a teleconference. As more and more people join the work-at-home trend, FedEx Kinko's offers an escape from the isolation of the home office.[22]

A Better-Educated and More White-Collar Population

The U.S. population is becoming better educated. For example, in 2002, 84 percent of the U.S. population over age 25 had completed high school and 27 percent had completed college, compared with 69 percent and 17 percent in 1980. Moreover, nearly two-thirds of high school graduates now enroll in college within 12 months of graduating.[23] The rising number of educated people will increase the demand for quality products, books, magazines, travel, personal computers, and Internet services.

The workforce also is becoming more white collar. Between 1950 and 1985, the proportion of white-collar workers rose from 41 percent to 54 percent, that of blue-collar workers declined from 47 percent to 33 percent, and that of service workers increased from 12 percent to 14 percent. Between 1983 and 1999, the proportion of managers and professionals in the workforce increased from 23 percent to more than 30 percent. These trends have continued into the new century.[24]

Increasing Diversity

Countries vary in their ethnic and racial makeup. At one extreme is Japan, where almost everyone is Japanese. At the other extreme is the United States, with people from virtually all nations. The United States has often been called a melting pot—diverse groups from many nations and cultures have melted into a single, more homogenous whole. Instead, the United States seems to have become more of a "salad bowl" in which various groups have mixed together but have maintained their diversity by retaining and valuing important ethnic and cultural differences.

Marketers are facing increasingly diverse markets, both at home and abroad as their operations become more international in scope. The U.S. population is 71 percent white, with African Americans and Hispanics each making up another 12 percent. The U.S. Asian American population now totals about 4 percent of the population, with the remaining 1 percent made up of American Indian, Eskimo, and Aleut. Moreover, nearly 26 million people living in the United States—more than 9 percent of the population—were born in another country. The nation's ethnic populations are expected to explode in coming decades. By 2050, Hispanics will comprise 24 percent of the U.S. population, with African Americans at 13 percent and Asians at 9 percent.[25]

Most large companies, from Procter & Gamble, Sears, Wal-Mart, and Bank of America to Levi Strauss and General Mills, now target specially designed products and promotions to one or more of these groups. General Mills targets the African American market with separate campaigns for its Big G cereals—Cheerios, Trix, Honey Nut Cheerios, and Cinnamon Toast Crunch. The campaigns consist of advertising, sponsorships, sampling, and community-based promotions that feature a strong family emphasis. For example, for the past several years, Honey Nut Cheerios has been the title sponsor of the Universal Circus, and for a "Soul Fest" music event that travels to 30 urban markets. Similarly, Bank of America's spent more than $50 million on multicultural marketing efforts in 2003. Based on customer research and careful study of cultural differences, it has developed different marketing programs and advertising messages for Hispanic, Asian, and African American markets.

Diversity goes beyond ethnic heritage. For example, many major companies have recently begun to explicitly target gay and lesbian consumers. A Simmons Research study of readers of the National Gay Newspaper Guild's 12 publications found that, compared with the average American, respondents are 12 times more likely to be in professional jobs, almost twice as likely to own a vacation home, 8 times more likely to own a notebook computer, and twice as likely to own individual stocks. They are twice as likely as the general population to have a household income between $60,000 and $250,000. More than two-thirds have graduated from college and 20 percent hold a master's degree.[26]

In addition, gays and lesbians tend to be early adopters with word of mouth clout in their communities. For example, according to one expert, "in the weeks following an episode of the Bravo/CBS hit show *Queer Eye for the Straight Guy*—in which five gay men, known as the Fab 5, make over a low-maintenance straight man—many businesses whose products are featured have seen a significant sales boost." Lucky Brand jeans saw a 17 percent sales jump for

■ Based on careful study of cultural differences, Bank of America has developed targeted advertising messages for different cultural subgroups, here Asians and Hispanics.

the 2 months following a mention on *Queer Eye*. And since an episode in which Thomasville Furniture was plugged as a shopping hot spot, sales of its Patchwork leather upholstery have jumped 50 percent.[27]

Companies in several industries are now waking up to the needs and potential of the gay and lesbian segment, a $450 billion market. For example, ad spending to reach gay and lesbian consumers is booming. Gay.com, a Web site that attracts more than 2 million unique visitors each month from more than 100 countries, has also attracted a diverse set of well-known advertisers, from IBM, eBay, Quicken Mortgage, Saturn, Absolut, and AT&T to American Airlines and Neiman Marcus. Here are examples of gay and lesbian marketing efforts:[28]

> American Express Financial Advisors launched print ads that depict same-sex couples planning their financial futures. The ads ran in *Out* and *The Advocate*, the two highest-circulation national gay publications. The company's director of segment marketing, Margaret Vergeyle, said: "We're targeting gay audiences with targeted ads and promotions that are relevant to them and say that we understand their specific needs. Often, gay couples are very concerned about issues like Social Security benefits and estate planning, since same-sex marriages often are not recognized under the law."
>
> IBM recently targeted the gay small-business community with an ad that ran in *The Advocate, Out,* and about 40 other gay-themed publications. The ad pictures a diverse group of men and women and links IBM's Armonk, N.Y., headquarters with well-known gay communities: "Chelsea/Provincetown/The Castro/Armonk." The six people shown in the ad are among the 1,100 IBM employees who make up the company's GLBT (Gay Lesbian Bisexual Transgender) Network. IBM launched the GLBT group 3 years ago when research showed that gay business owners are more likely to buy from gay salespeople.
>
> Last year, Avis, the rental car company, devoted about 5 percent of its advertising and marketing budget to the gay community. Its ad campaign highlights its pol-

icy for domestic partners to automatically be included as additional drivers. "It's a loyal group and an affluent group, and one that our research shows will respond to marketing that speaks to their consumer needs," says an Avis spokesperson. Avis' strategy also includes sponsorship of gay pride festivals and the placement of coupons noting that for every rental, Avis will donate a dollar to the nonprofit Gay and Lesbian Alliance Against Defamation.

Another attractive segment is the more than 54 million people with disabilities in the United States—a market larger than African Americans or Hispanics—representing almost $1 trillion in annual spending power. People with mobility challenges are an ideal target market for companies such as Peapod (www.peapod.com), which teams up with large supermarket chains in many heavily populated areas to offer online grocery shopping and home delivery. They also represent a growing market for travel, sports, and other leisure-oriented products and services. Consider the following example:[29]

In the past, Volkswagen has targeted people with disabilities who want to travel. For example, one recent marketing campaign for its EuroVan touted the vehicle's extra-wide doors, high ceilings, and overall roominess, features that accommodate most wheelchair lifts and make driving more fun for people with disabilities. Volkswagen even modified its catchy tag line "Drivers Wanted" to appeal to motorists with disabilities, coining the new slogan "All Drivers Wanted." Volkswagen also teams each year with nonprofit VSA arts to sponsor its "Driving Force" competition, designed to identify promising young artists with physical, cognitive, or mental disabilities. "America's love affair with the automobile extends beyond the visual cues of engines and sheet metal," proclaims a VW spokesperson. "Volkswagen believes that the 'heartware' is equally as important as the 'hardware.' For people with disabilities, the automobile provides both freedom of mobility and self-expression."

■ Volkswagon targets people with disabilities by teaming each year with nonprofit VSA arts to sponsor its "Driving Force" competition, designed to identify promising young artists with physical, cognitive, or mental disabilities.

As the population in the United States grows more diverse, successful marketers will continue to diversify their marketing programs to take advantage of opportunities in fast-growing segments. Says one expert, "diversity will be more than a buzzword—diversity will be the key to economic survival."[30]

Economic Environment

Economic environment
Factors that affect consumer buying power and spending patterns.

Markets require buying power as well as people. The **economic environment** consists of factors that affect consumer purchasing power and spending patterns. Nations vary greatly in their levels and distribution of income. Some countries have *subsistence economies*—they consume most of their own agricultural and industrial output. These countries offer few market opportunities. At the other extreme are *industrial economies*, which constitute rich markets for many different kinds of goods. Marketers must pay close attention to major trends and consumer spending patterns both across and within their world markets. Following are some of the major economic trends in the United States.

Changes in Income

Throughout the 1990s, American consumers fell into a consumption frenzy, fueled by income growth, a boom in the stock market, rapid increases in housing values, and other economic good fortune. They bought and bought, seemingly without caution, amassing record levels of debt. However, the free spending and high expectations of those days were dashed by the recent recession. In fact, we are now facing the age of the "squeezed consumer." Along with rising incomes in some segments has come increased financial burdens. Consumers now face repaying debts acquired during earlier spending splurges, increased household and family expenses, and saving ahead for college tuition payments and retirement.

These financially squeezed consumers have adjusted to their changing financial situations and are spending more carefully. *Value marketing* has become the watchword for many marketers. Rather than offering high quality at a high price, or lesser quality at very low prices, marketers are looking for ways to offer today's more financially cautious buyers greater value—just the right combination of product quality and good service at a fair price.

Marketers should pay attention to *income distribution* as well as average income. Income distribution in the United States is still very skewed. At the top are *upper-class* consumers, whose spending patterns are not affected by current economic events and who are a major market for luxury goods. There is a comfortable *middle class* that is somewhat careful about its spending but can still afford the good life some of the time. The *working class* must stick close to the basics of food, clothing, and shelter and must try hard to save. Finally, the *underclass* (persons on welfare and many retirees) must count their pennies when making even the most basic purchases.

Over the past three decades, the rich have grown richer, the middle class has shrunk, and the poor have remained poor. In 2003, 12 percent of American households had an annual income of $100,000 or more, compared with just 4 percent in the early 1990s. Meanwhile, the share of income captured by the bottom 20 percent of income-earning households decreased from 4 percent to 3.6 percent.[31] This distribution of income has created a two-tiered market. Many companies—such as Nordstrom and Nieman-Marcus department stores—aggressively target the affluent. Others—such as Dollar General and Family Dollar stores—target downscale. In fact, such dollar stores are now the fastest growing retailers in the nation. Still other companies tailor their marketing offers to two different markets—the affluent and the less affluent. For example, Walt Disney Company markets two distinct Winnie-the-Pooh bears:

> The original line-drawn figure appears on fine china, pewter spoons, and pricey kids' stationery found in upscale specialty and department stores such as Nordstrom and Bloomingdale's. The plump, cartoonlike Pooh, clad in a red shirt and a goofy smile, adorns plastic key chains, polyester bed sheets, and animated videos. It sells in Wal-Mart stores and five-and-dime shops. Except at Disney's own stores, the two Poohs do not share the same retail shelf. [Thus, Disney offers both] upstairs and downstairs Poohs, hoping to land customers on both sides of the [income] divide.[32]

Changing Consumer Spending Patterns

Table 3.1 shows the proportion of total expenditures made by U.S. households at different income levels for major categories of goods and services. Food, housing, and transportation use up most household income. However, consumers at different income levels have different

TABLE 3.1   Consumer Spending at Different Income Levels

Percent of Spending at Different Income Levels

Expenditure	$10,000–20,000	$20,000–30,000	$30,000–40,000	$70,000 and Over
Food	15.3	15.1	13.9	11.6
Housing	34.0	33.3	32.0	30.9
Utilities	8.6	8.0	7.2	4.9
Clothing	4.6	4.1	4.3	4.5
Transportation	18.9	18.3	20.1	17.6
Health care	8.7	7.9	6.8	4.2
Entertainment	4.1	4.1	4.4	5.8
Contributions	2.8	3.4	3.1	3.5
Insurance	3.9	6.5	8.3	14.8

Source: Consumer Expenditure Survey, 2002, U.S. Department of Labor, Bureau of Labor Statistics, accessed at www.bls.gov/cex/2002/Standard/income.pdf, November 2004.

Engel's laws

Differences noted over a century ago by Ernst Engel in how people shift their spending across food, housing, transportation, health care, and other goods and services categories as family income rises.

Natural environment

Natural resources that are needed as inputs by marketers or that are affected by marketing activities.

spending patterns. Some of these differences were noted over a century ago by Ernst Engel, who studied how people shifted their spending as their income rose (see Table 3.1). He found that as family income rises, the percentage spent on food declines, the percentage spent on housing remains about constant (except for such utilities as gas, electricity, and public services, which decrease), and both the percentage spent on most other categories and that devoted to savings increase. **Engel's laws** generally have been supported by later studies.

Changes in major economic variables such as income, cost of living, interest rates, and savings and borrowing patterns have a large impact on the marketplace. Companies watch these variables by using economic forecasting. Businesses do not have to be wiped out by an economic downturn or caught short in a boom. With adequate warning, they can take advantage of changes in the economic environment.

Natural Environment

The **natural environment** involves the natural resources that are needed as inputs by marketers or that are affected by marketing activities. Environmental concerns have grown steadily during the past three decades. In many cities around the world, air and water pollution have reached dangerous levels. World concern continues to mount about the possibilities of global warming, and many environmentalists fear that we soon will be buried in our own trash.

Marketers should be aware of several trends in the natural environment. The first involves growing *shortages of raw materials*. Air and water may seem to be infinite resources, but some groups see long-run dangers. Air pollution chokes many of the world's large cities, and water shortages are already a big problem in some parts of the United States and the world. Renewable resources, such as forests and food, also have to be used wisely. Nonrenewable resources, such as oil, coal, and various minerals, pose a serious problem. Firms making products that require these scarce resources face large cost increases, even if the materials do remain available.

A second environmental trend is *increased pollution*. Industry will almost always damage the quality of the natural environment. Consider the disposal of chemical and nuclear wastes; the dangerous mercury levels in the ocean; the quantity of chemical pollutants in the soil and food supply; and the littering of the environment with nonbiodegradable bottles, plastics, and other packaging materials.

A third trend is *increased government intervention* in natural resource management. The governments of different countries vary in their concern and efforts to promote a clean environment. Some, like the German government, vigorously pursue environmental quality. Others, especially many poorer nations, do little about pollution, largely because they lack the needed funds or political will. Even the richer nations lack the vast funds and political accord needed to mount a worldwide environmental effort. The general hope is that companies around the world will accept more social responsibility, and that less expensive devices can be found to control and reduce pollution.

In the United States, the Environmental Protection Agency (EPA) was created in 1970 to set and enforce pollution standards and to conduct pollution research. In the future, companies

■ Environmental responsibility: UPS's fleet of 70,000 boxy brown trucks now includes some 1,800 alternative-fuel vehicles, 2,500 low emissions vehicles, and a growing number of electric vehicles, including zero-emission Dodge fuel cell-powered vans like this one.

doing business in the United States can expect continued strong controls from government and pressure groups. Instead of opposing regulation, marketers should help develop solutions to the material and energy problems facing the world.

Concern for the natural environment has spawned the so-called green movement. Today, enlightened companies go beyond what government regulations dictate. They are developing *environmentally sustainable* strategies and practices in an effort to create a world economy that the planet can support indefinitely. They are responding to consumer demands with ecologically safer products, recyclable or biodegradable packaging, recycled materials and components, better pollution controls, and more energy-efficient operations.

3M runs a Pollution Prevention Pays program that helps prevent pollution at the source—in products and manufacturing processes. Between 1975 and 2002, the program prevented 857,282 tons of pollutants and saved $894 million. McDonald's has a long-standing rainforest policy and a commitment to purchasing recycled products and energy-efficient restaurant construction techniques. And UPS's fleet of 70,000 boxy brown trucks now includes some 1,800 alternative-fuel vehicles, 2,500 low-emissions vehicles, and a growing number of electric vehicles. More and more, companies are recognizing the link between a healthy economy and a healthy ecology.[33]

Technological Environment

Technological environment
Forces that create new technologies, creating new product and market opportunities.

The **technological environment** is perhaps the most dramatic force now shaping our destiny. Technology has released such wonders as antibiotics, organ transplants, laptop computers, and the Internet. It also has released such horrors as nuclear missiles, chemical weapons, and assault rifles. It has released such mixed blessings as the automobile, television, and credit cards. Our attitude toward technology depends on whether we are more impressed with its wonders or its blunders. For example, what would you think about having a tiny little transmitters implanted in all of the products you buy that would allow tracking products from their point of production though use and disposal? On the one hand, it would provide many advantages. On the other hand, it could be a bit scary. Either way, it's already happening (see Real Marketing 3.2).

The technological environment changes rapidly. Think of all of today's common products that were not available 100 years ago, or even 30 years ago. Abraham Lincoln did not know about automobiles, airplanes, radios, or the electric light. Woodrow Wilson did not know about television, aerosol cans, automatic dishwashers, air conditioners, antibiotics, or computers. Franklin Delano Roosevelt did not know about xerography, synthetic detergents, tape recorders, birth control pills, or earth satellites. John F. Kennedy did not know about personal computers, DVD players, or the Internet.

Real Marketing 3.2

Tiny Transmitters in Every Product. Is This Great Technology, or What?

Envision a world in which every product contains a tiny transmitter, loaded with information. Imagine a time when we could track every item electronically—anywhere in the world, at any time, automatically. Producers could track the precise flow of goods up and down the supply chain, ensuring timely deliveries and lowering inventory and distribution costs. Retailers could track real-time merchandise movements in their stores, helping them manage inventories, keep shelves full, and automatically reorder goods.

And picture the futuristic new world that such technology would create for consumers:

As you stroll through the aisles of your supermarket, you pluck a six-pack of your favorite beverage from the shelf. Shelf sensors detect your selection and beam an ad to the screen on your shopping cart, offering special deals on salty snacks that might go great with your beverage. When you reach the shampoo section, electronic readers scan your cart and note that you haven't made the usual monthly purchase of your favorite brand. "Did you forget the shampoo?" asks the screen. As your shopping cart fills, scanners detect that you might be buying for a dinner party; the screen suggests a wine that complements the meal you've planned. After shopping, you bag your groceries and leave the store. Exit scanners automatically total up your purchases and charge them

to your credit card. At home, readers track what goes into and out of your pantry, automatically updating your shopping list when stocks run low. To plan your Sunday dinner, you scan the Butterball turkey you just purchased. An embedded transmitter chip yields serving instructions and recipes for several side dishes. You pop the bird into your "smart oven," which follows instructions coded on the chip and cooks the turkey to perfection. Is this great technology, or what?

Seem far-fetched? Not really. In fact, it might soon become a reality with the backing of such marketing heavyweights as Wal-Mart, Home Depot, Target, Albertson's, Procter & Gamble, Coca-Cola, IBM, Gillette, and even the U.S. Department of Defense.

This futuristic technology is exploding onto today's marketing scene, boosted by the rapid development of tiny, affordable radio-frequency identification (RFID) transmitters—or smart chips—that can be embedded in all of the products you buy. The transmitters are so small that several would fit on the head of a pin. Yet they can be packed with coded information that can be read and rewritten at any point in the supply chain.

RFID technology (also called Auto-ID) provides producers and retailers with amazing new ways to track inventories, trends, and sales. They can use embedded chips to follow products—everything from ice cream and cat food to tires, insulation, and jet engines—

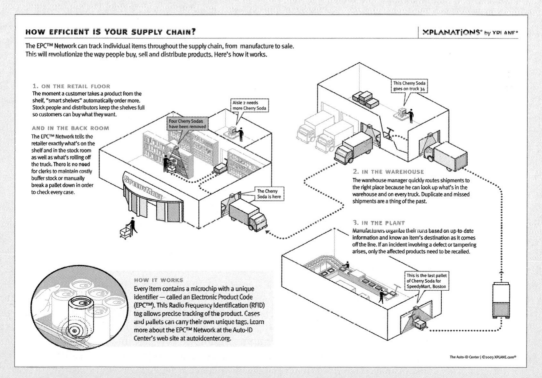

■ Imagine a time when we could track every item electronically—anywhere in the world, at any time, automatically. RFID technology might soon make this a reality.

(box continues)

step by step from factories, to warehouses, to retail shelves, to recycling centers.

The smart chips make today's bar code systems seem badly outmoded. Whereas bar codes must be visible to be read, embedded RFID chips can be read in any location. Bar codes identify only a product's manufacturer. In contrast, the chips can identify each individual product item and can carry codes that, when paired with a database containing the details, reveal an almost endless supply of information. Thus, beyond identifying an item as a gallon of Borden 2% skim milk, an embedded smart chip can identify that *specific* gallon of milk—its manufacture date, expiration date, location in the supply chain, and a storehouse of other product-specific information.

Although it may seem futuristic, Auto-ID technology is already in use. Every time consumers flash an ExxonMobil Speed-Pass card to purchase gas at the pump or breeze through an automated toll booth, they're using an RFID chip. In addition, Auto-ID technology is being tested and implemented by a number of big companies. For example, Gillette recently launched two RFID pilot projects. The first project uses embedded transmitters to track products from the factory to grocery store shelves. Gillette hopes that the technology will improve service to its retail customers while at the same time reducing its inventories from 5 percent to 25 percent. In the second project, Gillette has installed readers on shelves in selected Wal-Mart and Tesco stores. It claims that retailers lose more than $30 billion a year in sales because shelves aren't fully stocked. The shelf readers track Gillette's razors as they come and go, and prompt store staff to restock when quantities dwindle.

Other large manufacturers and retailers are adding fuel to the RFID fire. Procter & Gamble plans to have the chips on products in broad distribution as soon as 2008. By 2010, P&G will be able to link shopper loyalty card information with data about the products they buy. Mega-retailers such as Wal-Mart, Target, and Albertson's have ordered their top suppliers to be RFID-capable by as early as next year.

Even smaller retailers are putting smart chips to work. Fashion retailer Prada recently installed the chips in its store in New York City. Based on scans of items in customers' hands, video screens show personalized product demonstrations and designer sketches. In dressing rooms, readers identify each item of clothing a customer tries it on and offer additional size, color, and design information through interactive touch screens.

With innovations like these, you'd think most consumers would welcome the tiny transmitters. But many consumer advocates worry about invasion of privacy issues. If companies can link products to specific consumers and track consumer buying and usage, they fear, marketers would gain access to too much personal information. Says one analyst, "backers of the technology appear torn between the urge to hype its huge potential and fear that consumers will get spooked."

To counter these concerns, Auto-ID technology proponents point out that the transmitters have limited range, most under 20 feet. So reading chips inside consumers' homes or tracking them on the move would be nearly impossible. The Auto-ID industry is also working to address consumer privacy concerns. Among other things, it is drafting a privacy policy that includes giving customers the option of permanently disabling the chips at checkout. And according to an RFID consultant, the basic mission is not to spy on consumers. It's to serve them better. "It's not Orwellian. That is absolutely, positively not the vision of Auto-ID," she says. "The vision is for . . . brand manufacturers and retailers to be able to have right-time, right-promotion, real-time eye-to-eye [contact] with the consumer."

In coming years, as smart chips appear on more and more products, RFID technology will no doubt bring significant benefits to both marketers and the customers they serve. "The idea of someone using tiny radio transmitters to influence consumer purchase behavior was once only the stuff of paranoid delusions," says the analyst. "But in the not-so-distant future, it could become the basis of a new generation of marketing."

Sources: Jack Neff, "A Chip Over Your Shoulder?" *Advertising Age,* April 22, 2002, p. 4; "Business: The Best Thing Since the Bar-Code: The IT Revolution," *The Economist,* February 8, 2003, p. 57–58; "Gillette, Michelin Begin RFID Pilots," *Frontline Solutions,* March 2003, p. 8; "RFID Benefits Apparent," *Chain Store Age,* March 2003, p. 63; Faith Keenan, "If Supermarket Shelves Could Talk," *Business Week,* March 31, 2003, pp. 66–67; Jack Neff, "P&G Products to Wear Wire," *Advertising Age,* December 15, 2004, pp. 1, 32; Greg Lindsey, "Prada's High-Tech Misstep," *Business 2.0,* March 2004, pp. 72–75; Kevin Higgins "Brave New RFID World," *Food Engineering,* January 2004, p. 81; Robert Spiegel, "RFID Report," *Supply Chain Management Review,* April 2004, pp. 17–18; and information accessed online at www.autoidlabs.org, July 2004.

New technologies create new markets and opportunities. However, every new technology replaces an older technology. Transistors hurt the vacuum-tube industry, xerography hurt the carbon-paper business, the auto hurt the railroads, and compact discs hurt phonograph records. When old industries fought or ignored new technologies, their businesses declined. Thus, marketers should watch the technological environment closely. Companies that do not keep up with technological change soon will find their products outdated. And they will miss new product and market opportunities.

The United States leads the world in research and development spending. Total U.S. R&D spending reached an estimated $291 billion in 2004. The federal government was the largest R&D spender at about $90 billion.[34] Scientists today are researching a wide range of promising new products and services, ranging from practical solar energy, electric cars, and cancer cures to voice-controlled computers and genetically engineered food crops.

■ Technological environment: Technology is perhaps the most dramatic force shaping the marketing environment. Here, a herder makes a call on his cell phone.

Today's research usually is carried out by research teams rather than by lone inventors such as Thomas Edison, Samuel Morse, or Alexander Graham Bell. Many companies are adding marketing people to R&D teams to try to obtain a stronger marketing orientation. Scientists also speculate on fantasy products, such as flying cars, three-dimensional televisions, and space colonies. The challenge in each case is not only technical but also commercial—to make *practical, affordable* versions of these products.

As products and technology become more complex, the public needs to know that these are safe. Thus, government agencies investigate and ban potentially unsafe products. In the United States, the Food and Drug Administration (FDA) has set up complex regulations for testing new drugs. The Consumer Product Safety Commission sets safety standards for consumer products and penalizes companies that fail to meet them. Such regulations have resulted in much higher research costs and in longer times between new-product ideas and their introduction. Marketers should be aware of these regulations when applying new technologies and developing new products.

Political Environment

Political environment

Laws, government agencies, and pressure groups that influence and limit various organizations and individuals in a given society.

Marketing decisions are strongly affected by developments in the political environment. The **political environment** consists of laws, government agencies, and pressure groups that influence or limit various organizations and individuals in a given society.

Legislation Regulating Business

Even the most liberal advocates of free-market economies agree that the system works best with at least some regulation. Well-conceived regulation can encourage competition and ensure fair markets for goods and services. Thus, governments develop *public policy* to guide commerce—sets of laws and regulations that limit business for the good of society as a whole. Almost every marketing activity is subject to a wide range of laws and regulations.

INCREASING LEGISLATION Legislation affecting business around the world has increased steadily over the years. The United States has many laws covering issues such as competition, fair trade practices, environmental protection, product safety, truth in advertising, consumer privacy, packaging and labeling, pricing, and other important areas (see Table 3.2). The European Commission has been active in establishing a new framework of laws covering competitive behavior, product standards, product liability, and commercial transactions for the nations of the European Union.

Several countries have gone further than the United States in passing strong consumerism legislation. For example, Norway bans several forms of sales promotion—trading stamps, contests, premiums—as being inappropriate or unfair ways of promoting products.

TABLE 3.2   **Major U.S. Legislation Affcting Marketing**

Legislation	Purpose
Sherman Antitrust Act (1890)	Prohibits monopolies and activities (price fixing, predatory pricing) that restrain trade or competition in interstate commerce.
Federal Food and Drug Act (1906)	Forbids the manufacture or sale of adulterated or fraudulently labeled foods and drugs. Created the Food and Drug Administration.
Clayton Act (1914)	Supplements the Sherman Act by prohibiting certain types of price discrimination, exclusive dealing, and tying clauses (which require a dealer to take additional products in a seller's line).
Federal Trade Commission Act (1914)	Establishes a commission to monitor and remedy unfair trade methods.
Robinson-Patman Act (1936)	Amends Clayton Act to define price discrimination as unlawful. Empowers FTC to establish limits on quantity discounts, forbid some brokerage allowances, and prohibit promotional allowances except when made available on proportionately equal terms.
Wheeler-Lea Act (1938)	Makes deceptive, misleading, and unfair practices illegal regardless of injury to competition. Places advertising of food and drugs under FTC jurisdiction.
Lanham Trademark Act (1946)	Protects and regulates distinctive brand names and trademarks.
National Traffic and Safety Act (1958)	Provides for the creation of compulsory safety standards for automobiles and tires.
Fair Packaging and Labeling Act (1966)	Provides for the regulation of packaging and labeling of consumer goods. Requires that manufacturers state what the package contains, who made it, and how much it contains.
Child Protection Act (1966)	Bans sale of hazardous toys and articles. Sets standards for child-resistant packaging.
Federal Cigarette Labeling and Advertising Act (1967)	Requires that cigarette packages contain the following statement: "Warning: The Surgeon General Has Determined That Cigarette Smoking Is Dangerous to Your Health."
National Environmental Policy Act (1969)	Establishes a national policy on the environment. The 1970 Reorganization Plan established the Environmental Protection Agency.
Consumer Product Safety Act (1972)	Establishes the Consumer Product Safety Commission and authorizes it to set safety standards for consumer products as well as exact penalties for failure to uphold those standards.
Magnuson-Moss Warranty Act (1975)	Authorizes the FTC to determine rules and regulations for consumer warranties and provides consumer access to redress, such as the class-action suit.
Children's Television Act (1990)	Limits number of commercials aired during children's programs.
Nutrition Labeling and Education Act (1990)	Requires that food product labels provide detailed nutritional information.
Telephone Consumer Protection Act (1991)	Establishes procedures to avoid unwanted telephone solicitations. Limits marketers' use of automatic telephone dialing systems and artificial or prerecorded voices.
Americans with Disabilities Act (1991)	Makes discrimination against people with disabilities illegal in public accommodations, transportation, and telecommunications.
Children's Online Privacy Protection Act (2000)	Prohibits Web sites or online services operators from collecting personal information from children without obtaining consent from a parent and allowing parents to review information collected from their children.

Thailand requires food processors selling national brands to market low-price brands also, so that low-income consumers can find economy brands on the shelves. In India, food companies must obtain special approval to launch brands that duplicate those already existing on the market, such as additional cola drinks or new brands of rice.

Understanding the public policy implications of a particular marketing activity is not a simple matter. For example, in the United States, there are many laws created at the national, state, and local levels, and these regulations often overlap. Aspirins sold in Dallas are governed both by federal labeling laws and by Texas state advertising laws. Moreover, regulations are constantly changing—what was allowed last year may now be prohibited, and what was prohibited may now be allowed. Marketers must work hard to keep up with changes in regulations and their interpretations.

Business legislation has been enacted for a number of reasons. The first is to *protect companies* from each other. Although business executives may praise competition, they sometimes try to neutralize it when it threatens them. So laws are passed to define and prevent unfair competition. In the United States, such laws are enforced by the Federal Trade Commission and the Antitrust Division of the Attorney General's office.

The second purpose of government regulation is to *protect consumers* from unfair business practices. Some firms, if left alone, would make shoddy products, tell lies in their advertising, and deceive consumers through their packaging and pricing. Unfair business practices have been defined and are enforced by various agencies, such as the Federal Trade Commission and the Food and Drug Administration.

The third purpose of government regulation is to *protect the interests of society* against unrestrained business behavior. Profitable business activity does not always create a better quality of life. Regulation arises to ensure that firms take responsibility for the social costs of their production or products.

CHANGING GOVERNMENT AGENCY ENFORCEMENT International marketers will encounter dozens, or even hundreds, of agencies set up to enforce trade policies and regulations. In the United States, Congress has established federal regulatory agencies, such as the Federal Trade Commission, the Food and Drug Administration, the Federal Communications Commission, the Federal Energy Regulatory Commission, the Civil Aeronautics Board, the Consumer Product Safety Commission, and the Environmental Protection Agency. Because such government agencies have some discretion in enforcing the laws, they can have a major impact on a company's marketing performance. At times, the staffs of these agencies have appeared to be overly eager and unpredictable. Some of the agencies sometimes have been dominated by lawyers and economists who lacked a practical sense of how business and marketing work. In recent years, the Federal Trade Commission has added staff marketing experts, who can better understand complex business issues.

New laws and their enforcement will continue to increase. Business executives must watch these developments when planning their products and marketing programs. Marketers need to know about the major laws protecting competition, consumers, and society. They need to understand these laws at the local, state, national, and international levels.

Increased Emphasis on Ethics and Socially Responsible Actions

Written regulations cannot possibly cover all potential marketing abuses, and existing laws are often difficult to enforce. However, beyond written laws and regulations, business is also governed by social codes and rules of professional ethics.

SOCIALLY RESPONSIBLE BEHAVIORCHANGING GOVERNMENT AGENCY ENFORCEMENT Enlightened companies encourage their managers to look beyond what the regulatory system allows and simply "do the right thing." These socially responsible firms actively seek out ways to protect the long-run interests of their consumers and the environment.

The recent rash of business scandals and increased concerns about the environment have created fresh interest in the issues of ethics and social responsibility. Almost every aspect of marketing involves such issues. Unfortunately, because these issues usually involve conflicting interests, well-meaning people can honestly disagree about the right course of action in a given situation. Thus, many industrial and professional trade associations have suggested codes of ethics. And more companies are now developing policies, guidelines, and other responses to complex social responsibility issues. For example, 45 percent of Fortune 250 companies issued environmental, social, or sustainability reports in 2001, up from 35 percent in 1998.[35]

The boom in e-commerce and Internet marketing has created a new set of social and ethical issues. Online privacy issues are the primary concern. For example, Web site visitors often provide extensive personal information that might leave them open to abuse by unscrupulous marketers. Moreover, both Intel and Microsoft have been accused of covert, high-tech computer chip and software invasions of customers' personal computers to obtain information for marketing purposes.[36]

Throughout the text, we present Real Marketing exhibits that summarize the main public policy and social responsibility issues surrounding major marketing decisions. These exhibits discuss the legal issues that marketers should understand and the common ethical and societal concerns that marketers face. In Chapter 20, we discuss a broad range of societal marketing issues in greater depth.

CAUSE-RELATED MARKETING To exercise their social responsibility and build more positive images, many companies are now linking themselves to worthwhile causes. These days, every product seems to be tied to some cause: Buy Purina cat food and help the American Association of Zoological Parks and Aquariums save endangered big cat species. Drink Tang and earn money for Mothers Against Drunk Driving. Drive a Dollar rental car and help support the Special Olympics. Buy from EddieBauer.com and have a percentage of your purchase go to support your local grade school. Buy a pink mixer from KitchenAid and support breast cancer research. Or if you want to help the Leukemia Society of America, buy Helping Hand trash bags or toilet paper. Pay for these purchases with the right charge card and you can support a local cultural arts group or help fight cancer or heart disease.

Cause-related marketing has become a primary form of corporate giving. It lets companies "do well by doing good" by linking purchases of the company's products or services with fund-raising for worthwhile causes or charitable organizations. Companies now sponsor dozens of cause-related marketing campaigns each year. Many are backed by large budgets and a full complement of marketing activities. Consider this example:

In 1996, General Mills launched its Box Tops for Education program. The program offers schools nationwide a chance to earn as much as $60,000 each year to pay for everything from field trips, to computers, to play ground equipment. Box Tops for Education has really caught on. Today, more than 60 percent of the nation's elementary schools are enrolled. To participate, students and parents clip box tops and labels from any of more than 330 eligible products, including brands like Yoplait,

■ Cause-related marketing: KitchenAid donates $50 to breast cancer research for every pink mixer it sells and encourages consumers to host a "Cook for the Cure" dinner party.

Big G, Lloyd's, and Betty Crocker. General Mills then pays the school 10 cents for every box top redeemed. To date, the company has given nearly $70 million to local public, private, and parochial schools. Based on that success, General Mills has now teamed up with Visa to offer a Box Tops for Education credit card. Visa donates 1 percent of every purchase made to the cardholder's designated school. In addition, consumers who link to Web sites of any of 200 online retailers, ranging from EddieBauer.com and Gap.com to OfficeDepot.com and Hallmark.com, are guaranteed a donation to their schools of up to 12 percent of every purchase.[37]

Cause-related marketing has stirred some controversy. Critics worry that cause-related marketing is more a strategy for selling than a strategy for giving—that "cause-related" marketing is really "cause-exploitative" marketing. Thus, companies using cause-related marketing might find themselves walking a fine line between increased sales and an improved image, and facing charges of exploitation.

However, if handled well, cause-related marketing can greatly benefit both the company and the cause. The company gains an effective marketing tool while building a more positive public image. The charitable organization or cause gains greater visibility and important new sources of funding. Cause-related marketing programs generate more than $700 million from U.S. corporations each year for various causes.[38] Thus, when cause marketing works, everyone wins.

Cultural Environment

Cultural environment

Institutions and other forces that affect society's basic values, perceptions, preferences, and behaviors.

The **cultural environment** is made up of institutions and other forces that affect a society's basic values, perceptions, preferences, and behaviors. People grow up in a particular society that shapes their basic beliefs and values. They absorb a worldview that defines their relationships with others. The following cultural characteristics can affect marketing decision making.

Persistence of Cultural Values

People in a given society hold many beliefs and values. Their core beliefs and values have a high degree of persistence. For example, most Americans believe in working, getting married, giving to charity, and being honest. These beliefs shape more specific attitudes and behaviors found in everyday life. *Core* beliefs and values are passed on from parents to children and are reinforced by schools, churches, business, and government.

Secondary beliefs and values are more open to change. Believing in marriage is a core belief; believing that people should get married early in life is a secondary belief. Marketers have some chance of changing secondary values but little chance of changing core values. For example, family-planning marketers could argue more effectively that people should get married later than that they should not get married at all.

Shifts in Secondary Cultural Values

Although core values are fairly persistent, cultural swings do take place. Consider the impact of popular music groups, movie personalities, and other celebrities on young people's hairstyling and clothing norms. Marketers want to predict cultural shifts in order to spot new opportunities or threats. Several firms offer "futures" forecasts in this connection, such as the Yankelovich Monitor, Market Facts' BrainWaves Group, and the Trends Research Institute.

The Yankelovich Monitor has tracked consumer value trends for years. At the dawn of the twenty-first century, it looked back to capture lessons from the past decade that might offer insight into the 2000s.[39] Yankelovich maintains that the "decade drivers" for the 2000s will primarily come from the baby boomers and Generation Xers. The baby boomers will be driven by four factors in the 2000's: "adventure" (fueled by a sense of youthfulness), "smarts" (fueled by a sense of empowerment and willingness to accept change), "intergenerational support" (caring for younger and older, often in nontraditional arrangements), and "retreading" (embracing early retirement with second career or phase of their work life). Gen Xers will be driven by three factors: "redefining the good life" (being highly motivated to improve their economic well-being and remain in control), "new rituals" (returning to traditional values but with a tolerant mind-set and active lifestyle), and "cutting and pasting" (balancing work, play, sleep, family, and other aspects of their lives).

The major cultural values of a society are expressed in people's views of themselves and others, as well as in their views of organizations, society, nature, and the universe.

PEOPLE'S VIEWS OF THEMSELVES People vary in their emphasis on serving themselves versus serving others. Some people seek personal pleasure, wanting fun, change, and escape. Others seek self-realization through religion, recreation, or the avid pursuit of careers or other life goals. People use products, brands, and services as a means of self-expression, and they buy products and services that match their views of themselves.

Yankelovich Monitor recently discovered a conflicted consumer segment whose purchases are motivated by self-views of both duty and fun:[40]

> Yankelovich's Monitor has identified a paradoxical consumer segment motivated equally by duty and fun. Comprising more than one-third of the population, these folks want to have their cake and rely on it, too. "Duty and Fun" consumers agree that "duty should always come before pleasure" *and* say that they "try to have as much fun as they can now and let the future take care of itself." Their split personalities indicate an internal struggle that affects everyday life and buying. To reach these conflicted consumers, marketers must give them something that makes them smile at the register, while offering sound payment options, guarantees, testimonials, and other forms of assurance. For example, PetSmart permits shoppers to bring their pets shopping, allowing duty and fun to happily coexist. And with its hybrid Prius, Toyota merges a respected company brand (duty) and leading-edge technology (fun), turning what could have been a fuddy-duddy failure into a ride for those sold on dutiful fun.

PEOPLE'S VIEWS OF OTHERS Recently, observers have noted a shift from a "me society" to a "we society" in which more people want to be with and serve others.[41]

> After years of serious "nesting"—staying close to the security and creature comforts of home and hearth—Americans are finally starting to tiptoe out of their homes to hang out in the real world. The nesting instinct has gone in and out of fashion before. When the first big wave hit in the early '80s, trend watchers coined the term "cocooning" to describe the surge of boomers buying their first homes and filling them up with oversize furniture and fancy gadgets. The dot-com boom set off another round, partly fueled by cool home gizmos like plasma TVs and PlayStations. Though many expected 9/11 to send people even deeper into nesting mode, sociologists say it actually got people out looking for companionship. After being hunkered down through terror alerts and the war in Iraq, many people were naturally itching to get out. Marketers are beginning to address the shift. In Las Vegas, the Saks Fifth Avenue store is trying to ease folks back out of the house with a simulated living room, complete with sofas where shoppers can sit and mingle, or munch from bowls of candy and watch a giant TV. And no less a nesting icon than Home Depot is expanding its gardening business, testing out landscape-supply stores.

■ People's self-views: PetSmart serves the conflicted "Duty and Fun" segment by permitting customers to bring their pets shopping, allowing duty and fun to happily coexist.

More and more, people are wanting to get out of the house and be with others. This trend suggests a greater demand for "social support" products and services that improve direct communication between people, such as health clubs and family vacations.

PEOPLE'S VIEWS OF ORGANIZATIONS People vary in their attitudes toward corporations, government agencies, trade unions, universities, and other organizations. By and large, people are willing to work for major organizations and expect them, in turn, to carry out society's work.

The late 1980s saw a sharp decrease in confidence in and loyalty toward America's business and political organizations and institutions. In the workplace, there has been an overall decline in organizational loyalty. During the 1990s, waves of company downsizings bred cynicism and distrust. And recent corporate scandals at Enron, WorldCom, Tyco International, and other large companies have resulted in a further loss of confidence in big business. Many people today see work not as a source of satisfaction but as a required chore to earn money to enjoy their nonwork hours. This trend suggests that organizations need to find new ways to win consumer and employee confidence.

PEOPLE'S VIEWS OF SOCIETY People vary in their attitudes toward their society; patriots defend it, reformers want to change it, malcontents want to leave it. People's orientation to their society influences their consumption patterns and attitudes toward the marketplace. American patriotism has been increasing gradually for the past two decades. It surged, however, following the September 11 terrorist attacks and the Iraq war. For example, the summer following the Iraq war saw a surge of pumped-up Americans visiting U.S. historic sites, ranging from the Washington, D.C., monuments, Mount Rushmore, the Gettysburg battlefield, and the USS *Constitution* ("Old Ironsides") to Pearl Harbor and the Alamo.[42]

Marketers have responded with patriotic products and promotions, offering everything from floral bouquets to clothing with patriotic themes. For example, following the September 11 attacks, Mars introduced a new limited-edition patriotic package for its M&M brand, featuring red, white, and blue candy pieces. It donated 100 percent of the profits from the sale of those special packages to the American Red Cross.

Although most of these marketing efforts were tasteful and well received, waving the red, white, and blue proved tricky for some marketers. Following September 11, consumers quickly became wary of patriotic products and ads. Except in cases where companies tied product sales to charitable contributions, "patriotism as a marketing program was largely unwelcome," says one analyst. They were often "seen by consumers as attempts to cash in on the tragedy." Marketers must take care when responding to such national emotions.[43]

PEOPLE'S VIEWS OF NATURE People vary in their attitudes toward the natural world. Some feel ruled by it, others feel in harmony with it, and still others seek to master it. A long-term trend has been people's growing mastery over nature through technology and the belief that nature is bountiful. More recently, however, people have recognized that nature is finite and fragile, that it can be destroyed or spoiled by human activities.

This renewed love of things natural has created a sizable "lifestyles of health and sustainability" (LOHAS) market for everything from natural, organic, and nutritional products to renewable energy and alternative medicine. Business has responded by offering more products and services catering to these interests. For example, food producers have found fast-growing markets for natural and organic foods. Natural and organic products are now a $25 billion industry, growing at a rate of 20 percent annually. Niche marketers, such as Whole Foods Markets, have sprung up to serve this market, and traditional food chains such as Kroger and Safeway have added separate natural and organic food sections. Sales of White Wave's Silk soymilk, for example, have jumped from $4 million in 1998 to $270 million last year. Even McDonald's has joined the movement, recently replacing its milk offering with cartons of organic milk.[44]

PEOPLE'S VIEWS OF THE UNIVERSE Finally, people vary in their beliefs about the origin of the universe and their place in it. Although most Americans practice religion, religious conviction and practice have been dropping off gradually through the years. Some futurists, however, have noted a renewed interest in spirituality, perhaps as a part of a broader search for a new inner purpose. People have been moving away from materialism and dog-eat-dog ambition to seek more permanent values—family, community, earth, faith—and a more certain grasp of right and wrong.

"Americans are on a spiritual journey, increasingly concerned with the meaning of life and issues of the soul and spirit," observes one expert. "For the past five years, Americans have been feeling more spiritual," says another. People "say they are increasingly looking to

■ Marketers are responding to changes in people's view of the natural environment by offering more natural and organic products. White Wave's Silk soymilk has found success in the $25 billion industry.

May today bring more potential boyfriends and less potential annoyances

More job opportunities and less "call again in a few months"

More future and less saturated fat

A better breakfast starts with no cholesterol, more determination, less sugar and more possibilities.

Silk
Rise and Shine™

religion—Christianity, Judaism, Hinduism, Islam, and others—as a source of comfort in a chaotic world." This new spiritualism affects consumers in everything from the television shows they watch and the books they read to the products and services they buy. "Since consumers don't park their beliefs and values on the bench outside the marketplace," adds the expert, "they are bringing this awareness to the brands they buy. Tapping into this heightened sensitivity presents a unique marketing opportunity for brands."[45]

Responding to the Marketing Environment

Someone once observed, "There are three kinds of companies: those who make things happen, those who watch things happen, and those who wonder what's happened."[46] Many companies view the marketing environment as an uncontrollable element to which they must react and adapt. They passively accept the marketing environment and do not try to change it. They analyze the environmental forces and design strategies that will help the company avoid the threats and take advantage of the opportunities the environment provides.

Other companies take a *proactive* stance toward the marketing environment. Rather than simply watching and reacting, these firms take aggressive actions to affect the publics and forces in their marketing environment. Such companies hire lobbyists to influence legislation affecting their industries and stage media events to gain favorable press coverage. They run advertorials (ads expressing editorial points of view) to shape public opinion. They press lawsuits and file complaints with regulators to keep competitors in line, and they form contractual agreements to better control their distribution channels.

Often, companies can find positive ways to overcome seemingly uncontrollable environmental constraints. For example:

Cathay Pacific Airlines . . . determined that many travelers were avoiding Hong Kong because of lengthy delays at immigration. Rather than assuming that this was a problem they could not solve, Cathay's senior staff asked the Hong Kong government how to avoid these immigration delays. After lengthy discussions, the airline agreed to make an annual grant-in-aid to the government to hire more immigration inspectors—but these reinforcements would service primarily the Cathay Pacific gates. The reduced waiting period increased customer value and thus strengthened [Cathay's competitive advantage].[47]

Marketing management cannot always control environmental forces. In many cases, it must settle for simply watching and reacting to the environment. For example, a company would have little success trying to influence geographic population shifts, the economic environment, or major cultural values. But whenever possible, smart marketing managers will take a *proactive* rather than *reactive* approach to the marketing environment.

> Reviewing the Concepts <

In this chapter and the next three chapters, you'll examine the environments of marketing and how companies analyze these environments to better understand the marketplace and consumers. Companies must constantly watch and manage the *marketing environment* in order to seek opportunities and ward off threats. The marketing environment comprises all the actors and forces influencing the company's ability to transact business effectively with its target market.

1. Describe the environmental forces that affect the company's ability to serve its customers.

The company's *microenvironment* consists of other actors close to the company that combine to form the company's value delivery network or that affect its ability to serve its customers. It includes the company's *internal environment*—its several departments and management levels—as it influences marketing decision making. *Marketing-channel firms*—suppliers and marketing intermediaries, including resellers, physical distribution firms, marketing services agencies, and financial intermediaries—cooperate to create customer value. Five types of customer *markets* include consumer, business, reseller, government, and international markets. *Competitors* vie with the company in an effort to serve customers better. Finally, various *publics* have an actual or potential interest in or impact on the company's ability to meet its objectives.

The *macroenvironment* consists of larger societal forces that affect the entire microenvironment. The six forces making up the company's macroenvironment include demographic, economic, natural, technological, political, and cultural forces. These forces shape opportunities and pose threats to the company.

2. Explain how changes in the demographic and economic environments affect marketing decisions.

Demography is the study of the characteristics of human populations. Today's *demographic environment* shows a changing age structure, shifting family profiles, geographic population shifts, a better-educated and more white-collar population, and increasing diversity. The *economic environment* consists of factors that affect buying power and patterns. The economic environment is characterized by more consumer concern for value and shifting consumer spending patterns. Today's squeezed consumers are seeking greater value—just the right combination of good quality and service at a fair price. The distribution of income also is shifting. The rich have grown richer, the middle class has shrunk, and the poor have remained poor, leading to a two-tiered market. Many companies now tailor their marketing offers to two different markets—the affluent and the less affluent.

3. Identify the major trends in the firm's natural and technological environments.

The *natural environment* shows three major trends: shortages of certain raw materials, higher pollution levels, and more government intervention in natural resource management. Environmental concerns create marketing opportunities for alert companies. The marketer should watch for four major trends in the *technological environment*: the rapid pace of technological change, high R&D budgets, the concentration by companies on minor product improvements, and increased government regulation. Companies that fail to keep up with technological change will miss out on new product and marketing opportunities.

4. Explain the key changes in the political and cultural environments.

The *political environment* consists of laws, agencies, and groups that influence or limit marketing actions. The political environment has undergone three changes that affect marketing worldwide: increasing legislation regulating business, strong government agency enforcement, and greater emphasis on ethics and socially responsible actions. The *cultural environment* is made up of institutions and forces that affect a society's values, perceptions, preferences, and behaviors. The environment shows long-term trends toward a "we society," a lessening trust of institutions, increasing patriotism, greater appreciation for nature, a new spiritualism, and the search for more meaningful and enduring values.

5. Discuss how companies can react to the marketing environment.

Companies can passively accept the marketing environment as an uncontrollable element to which they must adapt, avoiding threats and taking advantage of opportunities as they arise. Or they can take a *proactive* stance, working to change the environment rather than simply reacting to it. Whenever possible, companies should try to be proactive rather than reactive.

> Reviewing the Key Terms <

Baby boomers 70
Cultural environment 89
Demography 69
Economic environment 80

Engel's laws 81
Generation X 71
Generation Y 73
Macroenvironment 65

Marketing environment 64
Marketing intermediaries 66
Microenvironment 65
Natural environment 81

Political environment 85
Public 67
Technological environment 82

> Discussing the Concepts <

1. List the six actors in the company's microenvironment. Next, go to the Wal-Mart Web site at www.walmart.com, scroll down to Investor Relations section, and click on the most recent annual report. In the annual report, how many of the six microenvironment actors can you find? Briefly describe each.

2. List the six larger macroenvironmental forces. Go to The Nature Conservancy home page at www.nature.org, click on the Financial Information link, and find the most recent annual report. In the annual report, find and briefly describe as many of the six macroenvironmental forces as you can.

3. The text list seven types of publics that may impact a company's ability to achieve its objectives. Assume you are a marketing manager for an automobile company. You have been charged with repositioning an SUV model that was once identified as a "fuel guzzler." The model has been redesigned with a superefficient, nonpolluting hybrid engine. Which of the seven types of publics would have the greatest impact on your establishing the new "fuel efficient" positioning?

4. A wag once said, "You can watch the size of the Cadillac market shrink by just reading the obituaries." In the context of the external environmental forces discussed in the chapter, what did this person mean? What has Cadillac done to counter this trend? From an environmental management perspective, are Cadillac's actions reactive or proactive? Why?

5. Discuss the primary reasons why a company would hire a lobbyist in Washington DC? Would it make sense for the same company to also hire lobbyist at the state level? Why?

6. There's an old saying that "two good marketing people can't make-up for one bad technology decision." Is it a certainty that a company will lose out on new opportunities if it does not keep-up with new technology? Explain your position. Can you think of an industry where technology may not play an important role?

> Applying the Concepts <

1. Manic Panic (www.manicpanic.com) is one of the more popular brands at Hot Topic (Real Marketing 3.1), Tish and Snooky, two sisters from the Bronx, opened their shop in New York's East Village business district because, "there was no other store or company that catered to . . . musicians, punks, Goths, club-kids, performers, dancers, models and just about anyone who likes a little wild style." Using the macroenvironmental forces and recent trends as the basis for your answer, explain why you believe Manic Panic has been successful. Would your answers be the same if you were explaining the success of Vera Wang, the New York City-based clothing designer/retailer? Why?

2. Most well-known cause-related marketing campaigns are launched by companies with substantial resources. In a small group, discuss how smaller companies with more limited resources can implement successful cause-related marketing efforts . How could such organizations benefit the charities they work with while successfully promoting their own products and services?

> Focus on Technology <

The FTC recently hosted a public workshop on Radio Frequency Identification (RFID) to discuss all of the technology's applications as well as its potential pitfalls. At the workshop, one speaker commented that RFID "promises to reform, if not revolutionize, many corners of the marketplace." As we discussed in the chapter, RFID is already a part of many consumers' daily lives. And, as companies like Wal-Mart and Gillette embrace the technology, RFID is truly changing the way suppliers and retailers work together.

At the FTC workshop, Simon Langford, Manager of RFID Strategy for Wal-Mart, offered his thoughts on the benefits of RFID. Review his presentation online at http://www.ftc.gov/bcp/workshops/rfid/langford.pdf and answer the following questions:

1. How does RFID help strengthen Wal-Mart's relationships with its many partners?

2. What are some of the benefits for Wal-Mart? For Wal-Mart's suppliers?

3. How does RFID technology increase value and satisfaction for Wal-Mart's customers?

4. How might consumer privacy concerns impact the widespread acceptance of RFID technology?

> Focus on Ethics <

In *Imperfect Alternatives: Choosing Institutions in Law, Economics and Public Policy,* Neil Komesar discusses who should make the rules governing major public policy, including environmental concerns, nonrenewable resource conservation, and information privacy. He asks who should decide when it comes to making the rules on these tough issues. Should we let the private sector (business) make the rules, and let it be sorted out in the market? Should we leave it to the courts who are charged with interpreting the laws? Or should government agencies be primarily responsible?

1. In small groups, choose one of the three issues above (environment concerns, non-renewable resources, or information privacy) and present three reasons that the private sector is the best institution to make the rules.

2. Have you heard these arguments used by business before? Are these good arguments?

3. Are you convinced that the private sector is suited to establish the rules? If not, which of the other institutions would you select?

Video Case

American Express

You might think that the explosion of media outlets—everything from cable channels and Internet sites to interactive retail stores and electronic billboards—has made it easier for marketers to reach consumers. But, in many cases, all of the new choices have resulted in fragmented market access with few good mainstream options for reaching the masses. Even more challenging for marketers, customers themselves are choosing when and how they want to interact with marketers and retailers. In this new marketing environment, marketers are seeking new ways to break through the clutter and build lasting relationships with consumers.

The marketers at American Express face a special challenge when trying to reach out to customers. Credit card companies are notorious for contributing to the marketing clutter by bombarding consumers with offers. Just stop and think—how many credit card offers did you receive in the mail last week? To break through, American Express first creates

credit cards that meet the differing needs of specific consumer groups based on income and spending habits. Then the credit card giant creates advertisements and promotions targeting each group.

After viewing the video featuring American Express, answer the following questions about the marketing environment.

1. Is American Express taking a proactive approach to managing its marketing environment? How?

2. Select one of the demographic trends detailed in the chapter and discuss how that trend impacts American Express's core customers and, in turn, the company's marketing efforts.

Company Case

Prius: Leading a Wave of Hybrids

Americans love their cars. In a country where SUVs sell briskly and the biggest sport is stockcar racing, you wouldn't expect a small, hybrid, sluggish vehicle to sell well. Despite such expectations, Toyota successfully introduced the Prius in 2000, and Honda introduced the Insight. The Prius, whose name means "to go before," literally flew out of dealer showrooms, even if consumers weren't quite sure how to pronounce it (it's PREE-us, not PRY-us). Given Toyota's success with the Prius and Honda's with the Insight, other automotive companies have plans to introduce hybrids of some sort.

Hybrid vehicles have both a gas engine and an electric motor. When starting up or at very low speeds (under 15 mph), the auto runs on the electric motor. At roughly 15 mph, the gas engine kicks in. This means that the auto gets power from only the battery at low speeds, and from both the gas engine and electric motor during heavy acceleration. Once up to speed, the gas engine sends power directly to the wheels and, through the generator, to the electric motor or battery. When braking, energy from the slowing wheels— energy that is wasted in a conventional car—is sent back through the electric motor to charge the battery. At a stop, the gas engine shuts off, saving fuel. When the driver presses the accelerator, the electric motor kicks in. When

starting up and operating at low speed speeds, the auto does not make noise, which seems eerie to some drivers and to pedestrians who don't hear it coming!

The original Prius was a small, cramped compact with a dull design. It had a four-cylinder gas engine and a 33-kilowatt electric motor. It went from 0 to 60 in a woeful 14.5 seconds. But it got 42 miles per gallon. The 2004 Prius is a much spiffier-looking car that can hit 60 mph in 10.5 seconds and get 55 mpg. Its top speed is 105 mph and it goes from 30 to 60 in 4.5 seconds. Although that sounds like a big improvement, in actual driving it isn't so exciting. One test driver referred to the Prius as laboring its way to 60 in 10.5 seconds; then taking another 10.5 seconds to get to 80, and then he didn't have enough time in the day to get to 100 mph. The car ran a quarter-mile track in 18 seconds at a 77 mph; so the test driver concluded that you could drag race any school bus, confident of victory. But you better watch out for SUVs—they can blow you off the road! A muscle car, the Prius isn't.

In a country where everyone was ecstatic when governments raised speed limits above 55 mph, why would the Prius be so successful? For the first model, the answer lies in Toyota's clever marketing campaign. To begin with, it wasn't aimed at the mass market. Instead, Toyota thought

(box continues)

that the first hybrid buyers would be "techies" and early adopters (people who are highly likely to buy something just because it's new). The company was right. Once Toyota identified the target market, it was able to educate the *right* consumers 2 years before introduction. The company established a Web site to distribute information and sent e-brochures to 40,000 likely buyers just before the introduction. The press was also excited about the technology. Auto magazines, and even general interest media, ran articles describing, enthusing, or belittling the hybrids. All of this coverage helped Toyota sell 1,800 cars immediately.

In all, Toyota spent $15 million in 2002 touting the Prius. There were print ads in magazines such as *Newsweek* and *Vanity Far*, but the bulk of the campaign was in television advertising on channels such as Discovery, the History Channel, the Learning Channel, and MSNBC. Ads running before the actual introduction used the tagline, "A car that sometimes runs on gas power and sometimes runs on electric power, from a company that always runs on brain power." These ads helped to position Toyota as an "environmentally concerned" company and more subtly stressed the technology aspect of the car. After all, Americans love technology and are quick adopters of it.

After introduction, the ads appealed more to emotion with taglines such as "When it sees red, it charges,"—a reference to the recharging of the battery at stoplights. Such ads are based on ambiguity where the headline attracts attention because its meaning is not clear. The consumer must process the information in the ad in order to interpret it. The result is higher ad impact and longer ad recall. Toyota also took advantage of the environmental appeal by sending out green seed cars shaped like Toyota's logo to prospective buyers on Earth Day. They also wrapped some Priuses in green and gave away cars at Earth Day events.

While $15 million in advertising may sound like a lot, it's really just a drop in the bucket compared with the $190 million that Toyota spent overall to market cars and trucks in 2002. For the first 6 months of introduction, Toyota sold close to 5,000 cars, which is quite good given the newness of the technology, the dull design, and the lack of muscle.

Much of the Prius's success is based on correct identification of the target market. Many early purchasers were attracted by the technology, began to modify cars, and shared their experiences through chat rooms such as Priusenvy.com. The object of attachment was the computer system. One owner in Philadelphia was able to add cruise control (an option not offered by Toyota) by wiring in a few switches in the car's computer system. The founder of the Priusenvy.com Web site figured out how to use the car's dashboard display screen to show files from his laptop, play video games, and look at images taken by a camera mounted on the rear of his car. One Austrian consumer installed a sniffer—a device on the car's computer network that monitors electronic messages. With the sniffer, he could hook up add-ons such as a MiniDisc Player, an MP3 player, a laptop computer, and a TV tuner.

Even though the Internet played a major part in the Prius launch, Toyota does not sell the car from its Web site. Buyers go to www.prius.toyota.com online to look at colors and decide on options such as CD players and floor mats. After that, the dealers get involved, but it takes specially trained salespeople to explain and promote the Prius. One of the most common questions dealers are asked is "Does it have to be plugged in?" The answer is no; you push a button and it starts. But if you want the high fuel efficiency of the car—nearly 60 mpg—you have to operate it correctly, and many Prius owners haven't done that. Therefore, Toyota is planning to launch an educational campaign aimed at salespeople and consumers. It will also put an operating manual in the glove compartment of each new car.

By 2004, Toyota had skimmed off the market of techies and adopters and needed to launch a new version of its car to appeal to a wider market. To launch the new Prius, Toyota spent more than $40 million dollars spread over media in more consumer-oriented magazines and TV. It seems to have worked, as Prius sales are up 120 percent and will likely reach 28,000 units this year.

The new Prius is a sleek, Asian-inspired design that comes in seven colors, such as salsa red pearl or tidal and pearl. The most popular color is silver metallic with a gray/burgundy interior. Once inside the Prius, you find a stubby switch to engage reverse or drive and a push button that turns everything on. A 7-inch energy monitor touch screen displays fuel consumption, outside temperature, and battery charge level. It also explains whether you're running on gas, electricity, regenerated energy, or a combination of these. There are also screens to show how much electricity you have stored and to arrange your air conditioning, audio, and satellite navigation system. The interior is roomy and practical, with plenty of rear legroom. There are many storage space cubbyholes and shelves in the front, as well as a deep dashboard which leaves ample space for maps, books, and even your lunch. The CD player holds six discs. In all, it's quite an improvement over the 2000 model.

Besides the improved styling and performance, higher gas efficiency, and "environmentally friendly" aspects of the car, there are also governmental breaks on the car. The federal government will give you a $1,500 tax deduction, and some states allow single-occupant hybrids in HOV (High Occupancy Vehicle) lanes. Although the federal deduction will be phased out in the near future, other bills are pending to extend the tax break based on greater fuel efficiency and lower emissions from vehicles.

In the summer of 2004, gasoline prices began to rise—going to over $2 a gallon in some locations. There were fears that this would not just be a summer spike in prices, but a permanent increase. As a result, buyers moved toward smaller SUVs, cars, and hybrids. Sales of full-sized SUVs such as the Ford Excursion and Expedition and the Lincoln Navigator fell during the first 4 months of the year followed by a sharp drop in April. Sales of GM's Hummer tanked 25 percent.

At the same time, demand for Priuses increased. By June 2004, waiting lists for the Prius often stretched to 6 months or more and some dealers had quit taking deposits. Spots on dealers' waiting lists were being auctioned on Ebay for $500 and some dealers tacked as much as $5,000 to the car's sticker price of $20,295 to $26,000. At the same time, automotive companies were trying to move the gas-guzzlers by offering incentives.

Until last December, Toyota's allocation scheme gave the U.S. and Japanese markets roughly the same number of cars, but late in 2003, Toyota allotted 47,000 Priuses to the U.S. market and 70,000 for the Japanese market. Frustrated dealers and customers besieged Toyota with letters and calls of complaint. As inventory levels dropped and waiting lists lengthened, Toyota increased monthly production from 7,500 vehicles per month to 10,000 and eventually to 15,000. Toyota President Fujio Cho announced that the increased production should alleviate the shortages. But he made it clear that Toyota has no plans at present to start production at a second plant.

Toyota and Honda are not the only companies in the hybrid market. While the Japanese have created new cars, Ford began production of a hybrid model of the Escape SUV, giving consumers a choice of a hybrid or regular model. To promote the hybrid, Ford began an environmental print campaign built around mileage, emissions, and other environmental concerns. Later in 2004, the campaign broadened to include TV. GM is following a similar strategy, putting hybrid technology in vehicles that use the most gas. GM claims that each of its hybrid buses (sold to cities) will provide the fuel savings of 8,000 hybrid cars. It has also developed a hybrid model of its Silverado truck that will hit the market in late 2004 or early 2005. By 2007, GM expects to be making 1 million hybrids of some sort. Analysts believe that U.S. automakers need to get into the hybrid market because of the internal learning curve—"the quicker you get into the game, the quicker you get the real-world experience at developing and marketing these vehicles."

Clearly Toyota is the leader in hybrid sales with the Prius, and its Lexus division planned to introduce a Lexus SUV hybrid in the fall of 2004, moving hybrids up to the luxury car level. The company began taking orders for it during the summer. Thus, Toyota has a big jump on U.S. automakers who have only dabbled in this market. If gas prices remain high or rise even higher, Toyota will be very well-placed to take advantage of the scramble for hybrid cars. Perhaps Mr. Cho would decide that a second plant is needed after all.

Questions for Discussion

1. What microenvironmental factors affected the introduction and re-launch of the Toyota Prius? How well has Toyota dealt with these factors?

2. Outline the major macroenvironmental factors—demographic, economic, natural, technological, political and cultural—that affected the introduction and re-launch of the Toyota Prius. How well has Toyota dealt with each of these factors?

3. Evaluate Toyota's marketing strategy so far. What has Toyota done well? How might it improve its strategy?

4. GM's marketing director for new ventures, Ken Stewart, says "If you want to get a lot of hybrids on the road, you put them in vehicles that people are buying now." This tends to summarize the U.S. automakers' approach to hybrids. Would you agree with Mr. Stewart? Why or why not?

Sources: Kevin Ransom, "Ford, GM Get Rolling on Hybrid Debuts," *Adweek*, August 2, 2004, p. 6; "Testing Toyota's Hybrid Car," *GP*, June 7, 2004; Kevin A. Wilson, "Hyped Hybrid," *Autoweek*, June 28, 2004; Norihiko Shirouzu and Jeffrey Ball, "Revolution Under the Hood," *Wall Street Journal*, May 12, 2004, p. B.1; and Sholnn Freeman, "Auto Watch: Hot for a Hybrid Car? Cool Your Engines," *Wall Street Journal*, June 13, 2004, p. 4.

CHAPTER 4

> **After reading this chapter, you should be able to**

1. explain the importance of information to the company and its understanding of the marketplace
2. define the marketing information system and discuss its parts
3. outline the steps in the marketing research process
4. explain how companies analyze and distribute marketing information
5. discuss the special issues some marketing researchers face, including public policy and ethics issues

Managing Marketing Information

Previewing the Concepts

In the last chapter, you learned about the complex and changing marketing environment. In this chapter, we'll continue our exploration of how marketers go about understanding the marketplace and consumers. We'll look at how companies develop and manage information about important marketplace elements—about customers, competitors, products, and marketing programs. We'll examine marketing information systems designed to give managers the right information, in the right form, at the right time to help them make better marketing decisions. We'll also take a close look at the marketing research process and at some special marketing research considerations. To succeed in today's marketplace, companies must know how to manage mountains of marketing information effectively.

We'll start the chapter with a look at a classic marketing blunder—Coca-Cola's ill-considered decision some years ago to introduce New Coke. The company based its decision on substantial marketing research, yet the new product fizzled badly. As you read on, ask yourself how a large and resourceful marketing company such as Coca-Cola could make such a huge research mistake. The moral: If it can happen to Coca-Cola, it can happen to any company.

In 1985, in what has now become an all-time classic marketing tale, the Coca-Cola Company made a major marketing blunder. After 99 successful years, it set aside its long-standing rule—"Don't mess with Mother Coke"—and dropped its original formula Coke! In its place came *New* Coke with a sweeter, smoother taste.

At first, amid the introductory flurry of advertising and publicity, New Coke sold well. But sales soon went flat, as a stunned public reacted. Coke began receiving sacks of mail and more than 1,500 phone calls each day from angry consumers. One angry consumer addressed his concerns in a letter sent to "Chief Dodo, The Coca-Cola Company." (Coke's CEO claimed that he was less concerned about the contents of the letter than about the fact that it was actually delivered to him!) Other consumers panicked, filling their basements with cases of the old tried-and-true. One man in Texas drove to a local bottler and bought $1,000 worth of the old Coca-Cola. A group called "Old Cola Drinkers" staged protests, handed out T-shirts, and threatened a class-action suit unless Coca-Cola brought back the old formula. Meanwhile, Pepsi was so delighted that it declared April 23, 1985, New Coke's debut day, a corporate holiday.

After only 3 months, the Coca-Cola Company brought old Coke back. That July day, virtually every major newspaper featured the return of the "old Coke" on the front page. Now called "Coke Classic," the old formula sold side-by side with New Coke on supermarket shelves. The company said that New Coke would remain its flagship brand, but consumers had a different idea. By the end of that year, Classic was outselling New Coke in supermarkets by two to one.

Quick reaction saved Coca-Cola from potential disaster. The company stepped up efforts for Coke Classic and slotted New Coke into a supporting role. Coke Classic again became the company's main brand and the country's leading soft drink. New Coke became the company's "attack brand"—its Pepsi stopper—and ads boldly compared New Coke's taste with Pepsi's. Still, New Coke managed only a 2 percent market share. In the spring of 1990, the company repackaged New Coke and relaunched it as a brand extension with a new name, Coke II. Today, Coke Classic captures almost 19 percent of the U.S. soft drink market; Coke II sells in only a few selected markets.

Why was New Coke introduced in the first place? What went wrong? Many analysts blame the blunder on poor marketing research.

In the early 1980s, although Coke was still the leading soft drink, it was slowly losing market share to Pepsi. For almost 15 years, Pepsi had successfully mounted the "Pepsi Challenge," a series of televised taste tests showing that consumers preferred the sweeter taste of Pepsi. By early 1985, although Coke led in the overall market, Pepsi led in share of supermarket sales by 2 percent. (That doesn't sound like much, but 2 percent of today's huge $64 billion U.S. soft drink market amounts to $1.28 billion in retail sales!) Coca-Cola had to do something to stop the loss of its market share, and the solution appeared to be a change in Coke's taste.

Coca-Cola began the largest new-product research project in the company's history. It spent more than 2 years and $4 million on research before settling on a new formula. It conducted some 200,000 taste tests—30,000 on the final formula alone. In blind tests, 60 percent of consumers chose the new Coke over the old, and 52 percent chose it over Pepsi. Research showed that New Coke would be a winner, and the company introduced it with confidence. So what happened?

Looking back, we can see that Coke defined its marketing research problem too narrowly. The research looked only at taste; it did not explore consumers' feelings about dropping the old Coke and replacing it with a new version. It took no account of the *intangibles*— Coke's name, history, packaging, cultural heritage, and image. However, to many people, Coke stands alongside baseball, hot dogs, and apple pie as an American institution; it represents the very fabric of America. Coke's symbolic meaning turned out to be more important to many consumers than its taste. Research addressing a broader set of issues would have detected these strong emotions.

Coke's managers may also have used poor judgment in interpreting the research and planning strategies around it. For example, they took the finding that 60 percent of consumers preferred New Coke's taste to mean that the new product would win in the marketplace, as when a political candidate wins with 60 percent of the vote. But it also meant that 40 percent still liked the original formula. By dropping the old Coke, the company trampled the taste buds of the large core of loyal Coke drinkers who didn't want a change. The company might have been wiser to leave the old Coke alone and introduce New Coke as a brand extension, as it later did successfully with Cherry Coke.

The Coca-Cola Company has one of the largest, best-managed, and most advanced marketing research operations in America. Good marketing research has kept the company atop the rough-and-tumble soft drink market for decades. But marketing research is far from an exact science. Consumers are full of surprises, and figuring them out can be awfully tough. If Coca-Cola can make a large marketing research mistake, any company can.[1]

In order to produce superior value and satisfaction for customers, companies need information at almost every turn. As the New Coke story highlights, good products and marketing programs begin with solid information on consumer needs and wants. Companies also need an abundance of information on competitors, resellers, and other actors and forces in the marketplace.

With the recent explosion of information technologies, companies can now generate information in great quantities. In fact, today's managers often receive too much information. One study found that with all the companies offering data, and with all the information now available through supermarket scanners, large retailers typically now have the equivalent of 320 miles of bookshelves of information on their products. Wal-Mart, the largest retailer of all, has more than three and a half times that much information in its data warehouse. Thus, running out of information is not a problem, but seeing through the "data smog" is. "In this oh-so-overwhelming Information age," comments one observer, "it's all too easy to be buried, burdened, and burned out by data overload."[2]

Despite this data glut, marketers frequently complain that they lack enough information of the *right* kind. One recent study found that although half of the managers surveyed said they couldn't cope with the volume of information coming at them, two-thirds wanted even more. The researcher concluded that, "despite the volume, they're still not getting what they want."[3] Thus, most marketing managers don't need *more* information, they need *better* information.

A former CEO at Unilever once said that if Unilever only knew what it knows, it would double its profits. The meaning is clear: Many companies sit on rich information but fail to manage and use it well.[4] Companies must design effective marketing information systems that give managers the right information, in the right form, at the right time to help them make better marketing decisions.

Marketing information system (MIS)

People, equipment, and procedures to gather, sort, analyze, evaluate, and distribute needed, timely, and accurate information to marketing decision makers.

A **marketing information system (MIS)** consists of people, equipment, and procedures to gather, sort, analyze, evaluate, and distribute needed, timely, and accurate information to

■ Information overload: "In this oh-so-overwhelming Information age, it's all too easy to be buried, burdened, and burned out by data overload."

marketing decision makers. Figure 4.1 shows that the MIS begins and ends with information users—marketing managers, internal and external partners, and others—who need marketing information. First, it interacts with these information users to *assess information needs*. Next, it *develops needed information* from internal company databases, marketing intelligence activities, and marketing research. Then it helps users to analyze information to put it in the right form for making marketing decisions and managing customer relationships. Finally, the MIS *distributes* the marketing information and helps managers *use* it in their decision making.

Assessing Marketing Information Needs

The marketing information system primarily serves the company's marketing and other managers. However, it may also provide information to external partners, such as suppliers, resellers, or marketing services agencies. For example, Wal-Mart gives Procter & Gamble and other key suppliers access to information on customer buying patterns and inventory levels. And Dell creates tailored Premium Pages for large customers, giving them access to product design, order status, and product support and service information. In designing an information system, the company must consider the needs of all of these users.

A good marketing information system balances the information users would *like* to have against what they really *need* and what is *feasible* to offer. The company begins by interviewing managers to find out what information they would like. Some managers will ask for whatever information they can get without thinking carefully about what they really need. Too much information can be as harmful as too little. Other managers may omit things they ought to know, or they may not know to ask for some types of information they should have. For example, managers might need to know that a competitor plans to introduce a new product during the coming year. Because they do not know about the new product, they do not think to ask about it. The MIS must monitor the marketing environment in order to provide decision makers with information they should have to make key marketing decisions.

FIGURE 4.1
The marketing information system

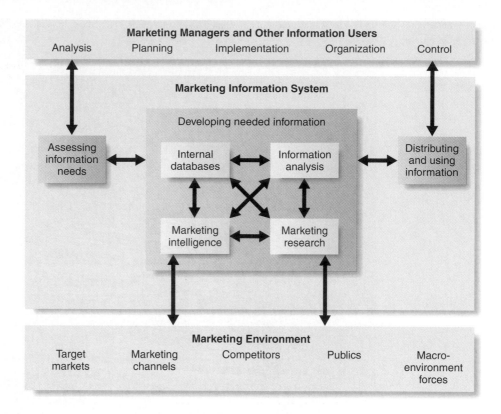

Sometimes the company cannot provide the needed information, either because it is not available or because of MIS limitations. For example, a brand manager might want to know how competitors will change their advertising budgets next year and how these changes will affect industry market shares. The information on planned budgets probably is not available. Even if it is, the company's MIS may not be advanced enough to forecast resulting changes in market shares.

Finally, the costs of obtaining, processing, storing, and delivering information can mount quickly. The company must decide whether the benefits of having additional information are worth the costs of providing it, and both value and cost are often hard to assess. By itself, information has no worth; its value comes from its *use*. In many cases, additional information will do little to change or improve a manager's decision, or the costs of the information may exceed the returns from the improved decision. Marketers should not assume that additional information will always be worth obtaining. Rather, they should weigh carefully the costs of getting more information against the benefits resulting from it.

Developing Marketing Information

Marketers can obtain the needed information from *internal data, marketing intelligence*, and *marketing research*.

Internal Data

Internal databases
Electronic collections of information obtained from data sources within the company.

Many companies build extensive **internal databases**, electronic collections of information obtained from data sources within the company. Marketing managers can readily access and work with information in the database to identify marketing opportunities and problems, plan programs, and evaluate performance.

Information in the database can come from many sources. The accounting department prepares financial statements and keeps detailed records of sales, costs, and cash flows. Operations reports on production schedules, shipments, and inventories. The sales force reports on reseller reactions and competitor activities. The marketing department furnishes information on customer demographics, psychographics, and buying behavior. And the customer service department keeps records of customer satisfaction or service problems. Research studies done for one department may provide useful information for several others.

Here is an example of how one company uses its internal database to make better marketing decisions:

> USAA, which provides financial services to U.S. military personnel and their families, maintains a customer database built from customer purchasing histories and from information collected directly from customers. To keep the database fresh, the organization regularly surveys its 5 million customers worldwide to learn such things as whether they have children (and if so, how old they are), if they have moved recently, and when they plan to retire. USAA uses the database to tailor marketing offers to the specific needs of individual customers. For example, if the family has college-age children, the USAA sends those children information on how to manage their credit cards. If the family has younger children, it sends booklets on things like financing a child's education. Or, for customers looking toward retirement, it sends information on estate planning. Through skillful use of its database, USAA serves each customer uniquely, resulting in high levels of customer loyalty and sales growth. The $10.5 billion company retains 97 percent of its customers and expects to double its membership by 2010.[5]

Internal databases usually can be accessed more quickly and cheaply than other information sources, but they also present some problems. Because internal information was collected for other purposes, it may be incomplete or in the wrong form for making marketing decisions. For example, sales and cost data used by the accounting department for preparing financial statements must be adapted for use in evaluating the value of specific customer segment, sales force, or channel performance. Data also ages quickly; keeping the database current requires a major effort. In addition, a large company produces mountains of information, which must be well integrated and readily accessible so that managers can find it easily and use it effectively.

■ Financial services provider USAA uses its extensive database to tailor marketing offers to the specific needs of individual customers, resulting in greater than 97 percent customer retention.

Marketing Intelligence

Marketing intelligence
The systematic collection and analysis of publicly available information about competitors and developments in the marketing environment.

Marketing intelligence is systematic collection and analysis of publicly available information about competitors and developments in the marketplace. The goal of marketing intelligence is to improve strategic decision making, assess and track competitors' actions, and provide early warning of opportunities and threats.

Competitive intelligence gathering has grown dramatically as more and more companies are now busily snooping on their competitors. Techniques range from quizzing the company's own employees and benchmarking competitors' products to researching the Internet, lurking around industry trade shows, and rooting through rivals' trash bins.

Much intelligence can be collected from people inside the company—executives, engineers and scientists, purchasing agents, and the sales force. The company can also obtain important intelligence information from suppliers, resellers, and key customers. Or it can get good information by observing competitors. It can buy and analyze competitors' products, monitor their sales, check for new patents, and examine various types of physical evidence. For example, one company regularly checks out competitors' parking lots—full lots might indicate plenty of work and prosperity; half-full lots might suggest hard times.

Some companies have even rifled their competitors' garbage, which is legally considered abandoned property once it leaves the premises. In one garbage snatching incident, Oracle was caught rifling through rival Microsoft's dumpsters. In another case, Procter & Gamble admitted to "dumpster diving" at rival Unilever's headquarters. The target was Unilever's hair-care products—including Salon Selectives, Finesse, Thermasilk, and Helene Curtis—which competed with P&G's own Pantene, Head & Shoulders, and Pert brands. "Apparently, the operation was a big success," notes an analyst. "P&G got its mitts on just about every iota of info there was to be had about Unilever's brands." However, when news of the questionable tactics reached top P&G managers, they were shocked. They immediately stopped the project, voluntarily informed Unilever, and set up negotiations to right whatever competitive wrongs had been done. Although P&G claims it broke no laws, the company reported that the dumpster raids "violated our strict guidelines regarding our business policies."[6]

Competitors may reveal intelligence information through their annual reports, business publications, trade show exhibits, press releases, advertisements, and Web pages. The Internet is proving to be a vast new source of competitor-supplied information. Most companies now place volumes of information on their Web sites, providing details to attract customers, partners, suppliers, or franchisees. Using Internet search engines, marketers can search specific competitor names, events, or trends and see what turns up.[7]

■ Marketing intelligence: Procter & Gamble admitted to "dumpster diving" at rival Unilever's Helene Curtis headquarters. When P&G's top management learned of the questionable practice, it stopped the project, voluntarily informed Unilever, and set up talks to right whatever competitive wrongs had been done.

Even companies with the most basic technology can use it to gather intelligence, advises a competitive intelligence consultant. Keep tabs on your rivals' Web sites, and check to see if they have updated or altered their copy on any product lines. Have they redesigned the site or shifted its focus? What do search engines turn up on rivals? How is the press covering them? Your industry? Often, publicly accessible bulletin boards offer additional clues: Investors may log on to discuss rumors and tidbits of information. And keep watch for off-duty employees. They post, too. "Clients are often surprised that there's so much out there to know," says the consultant. "They're busy with their day-to-day operations and they don't realize how much information can be obtained with a few strategic keystrokes."

Intelligence seekers can also pore through any of thousands of online databases. Some are free. For example, the U.S. Security and Exchange Commission's database provides a huge stockpile of financial information on public competitors, and the U.S. Patent Office database reveals patents competitors have filed. And for a fee, companies can subscribe to any of more than 3,000 online databases and information search services such as Dialog, DataStar, Lexis-Nexis, Dow Jones News Retrieval, UMI ProQuest, and Dun & Bradstreet's Online Access.

The intelligence game goes both ways. Facing determined marketing intelligence efforts by competitors, most companies are now taking steps to protect their own information. For example, Unilever has begun widespread competitive intelligence training. According to a former Unilever staffer, "We were told how to protect information, as well as how to get it from competitors. We were warned to always keep our mouths shut when traveling. . . . We were even warned that spies from competitors could be posing as drivers at the mini-cab company we used." Unilever even performs random checks on internal security. Says the former staffer, "At one [internal marketing] conference, we were set up when an actor was employed to infiltrate the group. The idea was to see who spoke to him, how much they told him, and how long it took to realize that no one knew him. He ended up being there for a long time."[8]

The growing use of marketing intelligence raises a number of ethical issues. Although most of the preceding techniques are legal, and some are considered to be shrewdly competitive, some may involve questionable ethics. Clearly, companies should take advantage of publicly available information. However, they should not stoop to snoop. With all the legitimate intelligence sources now available, a company does not have to break the law or accepted codes of ethics to get good intelligence.

Marketing Research

In addition to information about competitor and marketplace happenings, marketers often need formal studies of specific situations. For example, General Electric wants to know what appeals will be most effective in its corporate advertising campaign. Or Toshiba wants to know how many and what kinds of people or companies will buy its new superfast tablet PC. In such situations, marketing intelligence will not provide the detailed information needed. Managers will need marketing research.

Marketing research
The systematic design, collection, analysis, and reporting of data relevant to a specific marketing situation facing an organization.

Marketing research is the systematic design, collection, analysis, and reporting of data relevant to a specific marketing situation facing an organization. Companies use marketing research in a wide variety of situations. For example, marketing research can help marketers understand customer satisfaction and purchase behavior. It can help them assess market potential and market share, or to measure the effectiveness of pricing, product, distribution, and promotion activities.

Some large companies have their own research departments that work with marketing managers on marketing research projects. This is how Kraft, Citigroup, and many other corporate giants handle marketing research. In addition, these companies—like their smaller counterparts—frequently hire outside research specialists to consult with management on specific marketing problems and conduct marketing research studies. Sometimes firms simply purchase data collected by outside firms to aid in their decision making.

The marketing research process has four steps (see Figure 4.2): *defining the problem and research objectives, developing the research plan, implementing the research plan*, and *interpreting and reporting the findings.*

FIGURE 4.2
The marketing research process

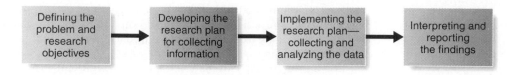

| Defining the problem and research objectives | → | Developing the research plan for collecting information | → | Implementing the research plan—collecting and analyzing the data | → | Interpreting and reporting the findings |

Defining the Problem and Research Objectives

Marketing managers and researchers must work closely together to define the problem and agree on research objectives. The manager best understands the decision for which information is needed; the researcher best understands marketing research and how to obtain the information.

Defining the problem and research objectives is often the hardest step in the research process. The manager may know that something is wrong, without knowing the specific causes. For example, in the New Coke case, Coca-Cola defined its research problem too narrowly, with disastrous results. Careful problem definition would have avoided the cost and delay of doing advertising research.

After the problem has been defined carefully, the manager and researcher must set the research objectives. A marketing research project might have one of three types of objectives. The objective of **exploratory research** is to gather preliminary information that will help define the problem and suggest hypotheses. The objective of **descriptive research** is to describe things, such as the market potential for a product or the demographics and attitudes of consumers who buy the product. The objective of **causal research** is to test hypotheses about cause-and-effect relationships. For example, would a 10 percent decrease in tuition at a private college result in an enrollment increase sufficient to offset the reduced tuition? Managers often start with exploratory research and later follow with descriptive or causal research.

The statement of the problem and research objectives guides the entire research process. The manager and researcher should put the statement in writing to be certain that they agree on the purpose and expected results of the research.

Exploratory research
Marketing research to gather preliminary information that will help define problems and suggest hypotheses.

Descriptive research
Marketing research to better describe marketing problems, situations, or markets, such as the market potential for a product or the demographics and attitudes of consumers.

Causal research
Marketing research to test hypotheses about cause-and-effect relationships.

Developing the Research Plan

Once the research problems and objectives have been defined, researchers must determine the exact information needed, develop a plan for gathering it efficiently, and present the plan to management. The research plan outlines sources of existing data and spells out the specific research approaches, contact methods, sampling plans, and instruments that researchers will use to gather new data.

Research objectives must be translated into specific information needs. For example, suppose Campbell decides to conduct research on how consumers would react to the introduction of new heat-and-go microwavable cups for its Franco-American Spaghetti and SpaghettiOs. Such packaging has been successful for Campbell's soups—the company promotes its Soup at Hand brands as "sippable soup, anytime, anywhere." The containers would cost more but would allow consumers to heat their SpaghettiOs in a microwave oven and to eat them without using dishes. This research might call for the following specific information:

- The demographic, economic, and lifestyle characteristics of current SpaghettiOs users. (Busy working couples might find the convenience of the new packaging worth the price; families with children might want to pay less and wash the bowls.)

- Consumer-usage patterns for SpaghettiOs and related products: how much they eat, where, and when. (The new packaging might be ideal for adults eating lunch on the go, but less convenient for parents feeding lunch to several children.)

- Retailer reactions to the new packaging. (Failure to get retailer support could hurt sales of the new package.)

- Forecasts of sales of both new and current packages. (Will the new packaging create new sales or simply take sales from the current packaging? Will the package increase Campbell's profits?)

Campbell managers will need these and many other types of information to decide whether to introduce the new packaging.

The research plan should be presented in a *written proposal*. A written proposal is especially important when the research project is large and complex or when an outside firm carries it out. The proposal should cover the management problems addressed and the research objectives, the information to be obtained, and the way the results will help management decision making. The proposal also should include research costs.

To meet the manager's information needs, the research plan can call for gathering secondary data, primary data, or both. **Secondary data** consist of information that already exists somewhere, having been collected for another purpose. **Primary data** consist of information collected for the specific purpose at hand.

Secondary data
Information that already exists somewhere, having been collected for another purpose.

Primary data
Information collected for the specific purpose at hand.

Gathering Secondary Data

Researchers usually start by gathering secondary data. The company's internal database provides a good starting point. However, the company can also tap a wide assortment of external information sources, including commercial data services and government sources (see Table 4.1).

TABLE 4.1   **Selected External Information Sources**

For business data:

AC Nielsen Corporation (www.acnielsen.com) provides supermarket scanner data on sales, market share, and retail prices; data on household purchasing; and data on television audiences.

Information Resources, Inc. (www.infores.com) provides supermarket scanner data for tracking grocery product movement and new product purchasing data.

Arbitron (www.arbitron.com) provides local-market and Internet radio audience and advertising expenditure information, among other media and ad spending data.

NDC Health Information Services (www.ndchealth.com) reports on the movement of drugs, laboratory supplies, animal health products, and personal care products.

Simmons Market Research Bureau (www.smrb.com) provides detailed analysis of consumer patterns in 400 product categories in selected markets.

Dun & Bradstreet (www.dnb.com) maintains a database containing information on more than 50 million individual companies around the globe.

ComScore Networks (www.comscore.com) provides consumer behavior information and geodemographic analysis of Internet and digital media users around the world.

Thomson Dialog (http://library.dialog.com) offers access to ABI/INFORM, a database of articles from 800+ publications and to reports, newsletters, and directories covering dozens of industries.

LEXIS-NEXIS (www.lexis-nexis.com) features articles from business, consumer, and marketing publications plus tracking of firms, industries, trends, and promotion techniques.

CompuServe (www.compuserve.com) provides access to databases of business and consumer demographics, government reports, and patent records, plus articles from newspapers, newsletters, and research reports.

Factiva (www.factiva.com) specializes in in-depth financial, historical, and operational information on public and private companies.

Hoovers Online (www.hoovers.com) provides business descriptions, financial overviews, and news about major companies around the world.

CNN (www.cnn.com) reports U.S. and global news and covers the markets and news-making companies in detail.

American Demographics (www.demographics.com) reports on demographic trends and their significance for businesses.

For government data:

Securities and Exchange Commission Edgar database (www.sec.gov) provides financial data on U.S. public corporations

Small Business Administration (www.sba.gov) features information and links for small business owners.

Federal Trade Commission (www.ftc.gov) shows regulations and decisions related to consumer protection and antitrust laws.

Stat-USA (www.stat-usa.gov), a Department of Commerce site, highlights statistics on U.S. business and international trade.

U.S. Census (www.census.gov) provides detailed statistics and trends about the U.S. population.

U.S. Patent and Trademark Office (www.uspto.gov) allows searches to determine who has filed for trademarks and patents.

For Internet data:

ClickZ Stats/CyberAtlas (www.clickz.com/stats) brings together a wealth of information about the Internet and its users, from consumers to e-commerce.

Interactive Advertising Bureau (www.iab.net) covers statistics about advertising on the Internet.

Jupiter Research (www.jupiterresearch.com) monitors Web traffic and ranks the most popular sites.

■ Online database services such as Dialog put an incredible wealth of information at the keyboards of marketing decision makers. Dialog puts "information to change the world, or your corner of it," at your fingertips.

Companies can buy secondary data reports from outside suppliers.[9] For example, Information Resources, Inc., sells supermarket scanner purchase data from a panel of 70,000 households nationally, with measures of trial and repeat purchasing, brand loyalty, and buyer demographics. The *Monitor* service by Yankelovich sells information on important social and lifestyle trends. These and other firms supply high-quality data to suit a wide variety of marketing information needs.[10]

Using commercial **online databases**, marketing researchers can conduct their own searches of secondary data sources. General database services such as Dialog and LEXIS-NEXIS put an incredible wealth of information at the keyboards of marketing decision makers. Beyond commercial Web sites offering information for a fee, almost every industry association, government agency, business publication, and news medium offers free information to those tenacious enough to find their Web sites. There are so many Web sites offering data that finding the right ones can become an almost overwhelming task.

Secondary data can usually be obtained more quickly and at a lower cost than primary data. Also, secondary sources can sometimes provide data an individual company cannot collect on its own—information that either is not directly available or would be too expensive to collect. For example, it would be too expensive for Kraft Foods to conduct a continuing retail store audit to find out about the market shares, prices, and displays of competitors' brands. But it can buy the InfoScan service from Information Resources, Inc., which provides this information from thousands of scanner-equipped supermarkets in dozens of U.S. markets.

Secondary data can also present problems. The needed information may not exist—researchers can rarely obtain all the data they need from secondary sources. For example, Campbell will not find existing information about consumer reactions to new packaging that it has not yet placed on the market. Even when data can be found, they might not be very usable. The researcher must evaluate secondary information carefully to make certain it is *relevant* (fits research project needs), *accurate* (reliably collected and reported), *current* (up-to-date enough for current decisions), and *impartial* (objectively collected and reported).

Online databases
Computerized collections of information available from online commercial sources or via the Internet.

TABLE 4.2   Planning Primary Data Collection

Research Approaches	Contact Methods	Sampling Plan	Research Instruments
Observation Survey Experiment	Mail Telephone Personal Online	Sampling unit Sample size Sampling procedure	Questionnaire Mechanical instruments

Primary Data Collection

Secondary data provide a good starting point for research and often help to define research problems and objectives. In most cases, however, the company must also collect primary data. Just as researchers must carefully evaluate the quality of secondary information, they also must take great care when collecting primary data. They need to make sure that it will be relevant, accurate, current, and unbiased. Table 4.2 shows that designing a plan for primary data collection calls for a number of decisions on *research approaches*, *contact methods*, *sampling plan*, and *research instruments*.

Research Approaches

Research approaches for gathering primary data include observation, surveys, and experiments. Here, we discuss each one in turn.

Observational research

The gathering of primary data by observing relevant people, actions, and situations.

OBSERVATIONAL RESEARCH **Observational research** involves gathering primary data by observing relevant people, actions, and situations. For example, a consumer packaged-goods marketer might visit supermarkets and observe shoppers as they browse the store, pick up and examine packages, and make buying decisions. Or a bank might evaluate possible new branch locations by checking traffic patterns, neighborhood conditions, and the location of competing branches. Fisher-Price even set up an observation lab in which it could observe the reactions of little tots to new toys:

> The Fisher-Price Play Lab is a sunny, toy-strewn space where, since 1961, lucky kids have tested Fisher-Price prototypes. Today three boys and three girls—all 4-year-olds—speed through the front door. Two boys tug quietly, but firmly, for the wheel of a new radio-controlled race set—a brand-new offering. The girls skid to a stop near a small subdevelopment of dollhouses. And from behind the one-way glass, toy designers study the action intently, occasionally stepping out to join the play. At the Play Lab, creation and (attempted) destruction happily coexist. Over an 8-week session with these kids, designers will test dozens of toy concepts, sending out crude models, then increasingly sophisticated revisions, to figure out what gets kids worked up into a new-toy frenzy.[11]

■ Observational research: Fisher-Price set up an observation lab in which it could observe the reactions of little tots to new toys.

Observational research can obtain information that people are unwilling or unable to provide. In some cases, observation may be the only way to obtain the needed information. In contrast, some things simply cannot be observed, such as feelings, attitudes and motives, or private behavior. Long-term or infrequent behavior is also difficult to observe. Because of these limitations, researchers often use observation along with other data collection methods.

A wide range of companies now use *ethnographic research.* Ethnographic research involves sending trained observers to watch:[12]

A girl walks into a bar and says to the bartender, "Give me a Diet Coke and a clear sight line to those guys drinking Miller Lite in the corner." No joke. The "girl" is Emma Gilding, corporate ethnographer at the Ogilvy & Mather ad agency. Her assignment is to hang out in bars across the country, watching guys in their native habitat as they knock back beers with their friends. As a videographer films the action, Gilding keeps tabs on how closely the guys stand to one another. She sees that high-living is out, fist-pounding is in. She eavesdrops on stories, and observes how the mantle is passed from one speaker to another, as in a tribe around a campfire. Back at the office, a team of trained anthropologists and psychologists pored over more than 70 hours of footage from five similar nights in bars from San Diego to Philadelphia. One key insight: Miller is favored by groups of drinkers, while its main competitor, Bud Lite, is a beer that sells to individuals. Miller drinkers felt more comfortable expressing affection for friends than did the Bud Lite boys. The result was a hilarious series of ads that cut from a Miller Lite drinker's weird experiences in the world—getting caught in the subway taking money from a blind musician's guitar case, or hitching a ride in the desert with a deranged trucker—to shots of him regaling friends with tales over a brew. The Miller Lite ads got high marks from audiences for their entertainment value and emotional resonance. Notes Miller's brand manager, "so much other research is done in isolation of social groups. But [ethnographic research] helped us to understand the Miller Lite drinker and his friends as genuine people."

Ethnographic research often yields the kinds of intimate details that just don't emerge from traditional focus groups. To glean greater insights into buying behavior, one company even went so far as to set up an actual retail store that serves as an ethnographic lab (see Real Marketing 4.1).

Survey research

The gathering of primary data by asking people questions about their knowledge, attitudes, preferences, and buying behavior.

Single-source data systems

Electronic monitoring systems that link consumers' exposure to television advertising and promotion (measured using television meters) with what they buy in stores (measured using store checkout scanners).

Experimental research

The gathering of primary data by selecting matched groups of subjects, giving them different treatments, controlling related factors, and checking for differences in group responses.

SURVEY RESEARCH **Survey research**, the most widely used method for primary data collection, is the approach best suited for gathering *descriptive* information. A company that wants to know about people's knowledge, attitudes, preferences, or buying behavior can often find out by asking them directly.

Some firms provide marketers with a more comprehensive look at buying patterns through **single-source data systems**. These systems start with surveys of huge consumer panels—carefully selected groups of consumers who agree to participate in ongoing research. Then, they electronically monitor survey respondents' purchases and exposure to various marketing activities. Combining the survey and monitoring information gives a better understanding of the link between consumer characteristics, attitudes, and purchase behavior.

The major advantage of survey research is its flexibility—it can be used to obtain many different kinds of information in many different situations. However, survey research also presents some problems. Sometimes people are unable to answer survey questions because they cannot remember or have never thought about what they do and why. People may be unwilling to respond to unknown interviewers or about things they consider private. Respondents may answer survey questions even when they do not know the answer in order to appear smarter or more informed. Or they may try to help the interviewer by giving pleasing answers. Finally, busy people may not take the time, or they might resent the intrusion into their privacy.

EXPERIMENTAL RESEARCH Whereas observation is best suited for exploratory research and surveys for descriptive research, **experimental research** is best suited for gathering *causal* information. Experiments involve selecting matched groups of subjects, giving them different treatments, controlling unrelated factors, and checking for differences in group responses. Thus, experimental research tries to explain cause-and-effect relationships.

For example, before adding a new sandwich to its menu, McDonald's might use experiments to test the effects on sales of two different prices it might charge. It could introduce the new sandwich at one price in one city and at another price in another city. If the cities are

Real Marketing 4.1

Once Famous: Watching Consumers in Their Natural Settings

Microphones capture every word while cameras record the action. Observers, posted at every turn, document each move. The run way at the Academy Awards? Or the paparazzi shadowing the royal family in London? No, this is a retail store called Once Famous, and the observers and microphones aren't focused on celebrities, they're scrutinizing consumers.

Once Famous is a unique ethnographic laboratory for studying consumer behavior in a natural setting. Although designed to look and feel like an ordinary retail store, this boutique is anything but ordinary. Surveillance is everywhere at Once Famous. Ethnographers watch from behind mirrored glass, while salespeople interview would-be buyers. Five cameras track consumers as they prowl the store, and store employees study their meanderings, whims, and buying behaviors. Sensitive hidden microphones catch every utterance, from shoppers' questions to snide comments between friends. Later, researchers pour over the tapes and analyze each shopper's behavior, looking for clues.

It all sounds like a massive invasion of consumer privacy. But there's no need to fear Big Brother here. The store posts a prominent sign, complete with flashing lights, to alert shoppers that the store is in "Testing Mode." Additional signs invite shoppers who don't wish to be observed to "kindly visit us when this sign has been removed." However, despite the prominent disclosures, researchers at Once Famous hope that, once inside, shoppers will quickly forget that they are under close scrutiny.

Once Famous is the work of FAME, a retail brand advertising agency located in Minneapolis. In late 2001, FAME opened its first observational research lab in a heavily trafficked downtown skyway. Stocked with fancy pillows, knickknacks, and hand-made arts and crafts, the store attracts a variety of shoppers. Mingled with the store's regular inventory is an ever-changing assortment of clients' test products. Rather than interrogate test subjects in an artificial environment, researchers at Once Famous watch shoppers in their natural surroundings. In fact, much of the time Once Famous is just a store like any other store—it doesn't stay in "test mode" all of the time and it even turns a profit on sales. Such ethnographic research often yields insights that just don't emerge from traditional survey or focus group studies.

For FAME and its clients, the store helps fill a big gap in everyone's understanding of that elusive species, the shopper. Retailers know from inventory records what is on the shelf, and they know from point-of-sale data what ends up in shopper's baskets. But they lack a true understanding of the mysterious, often fickle buying process that connects the shelf to the checkout counter. What causes a consumer to skip past one aisle but spend a half hour strolling down another? What leads a person to pick up a product, examine it, put it back, walk away, come back later, pick it up again, and then finally buy it? How do the off-hand or pointed comments of friends, spouses, or sales staff impact the buying decision?

The data FAME collects at Once Famous help marketers understand a bit more about consumers and how they interact with the wealth of sensory and social cues in a retail store. "Ninety percent of all purchases are made on impulse," says Jeri Quest, FAME's executive vice president for strategic development. "We can get really close to customers at the point of decision making."

To gain these valuable insights, manufacturers and retailers pay anywhere from $50,000 to $200,000 to have their products stocked at Once Famous. In addition to product tests, FAME uses the lab as a testing ground for a variety of retailing decisions, such as product placement and traffic flow. Although Once Famous is usually outfitted as an eclectic home furnishings and gift boutique, FAME can strip it to the walls and reconfigure it for other product categories in a matter of days.

Once Famous experiments have yielded interesting details on how people shop, including the different ways in which men and women decide what to buy. "Women find an object they like and visit it," Quest says. "Men look at how it's made, what's the construction." Men stand back and study things, but women can't wait to get their hands on merchandise.

These differences may go as far back as childhood shopping experiences. Mothers are more likely to tell their sons to keep their hands to themselves while shopping. When they are adults, men are

■ Watching consumers in their natural settings: OnceFamous is an actual retail store that serves as an ethnographic lab to yield greater insights into buying behavior.

(box continues)

considerably less likely to pick up a product and get a closer look unless explicitly invited to. In contrast, daughters who shop with mom more are likely to learn her approach to evaluating a product by experiencing it. As adults, women evaluate products based on the story they tell and what they may say about their owners.

Based on results like these, many retailers tailor their displays to appeal to men and women differently. Stores like Brookstone and Sharper Image that target men provide details about design and construction and post signs encouraging shoppers to push buttons, test out massage chairs, and ask questions. Pottery Barn, with its largely female audience, displays products in quaint groupings, allowing shoppers to visualize merchandise in their own homes, experience the products more intimately, and discover what those products might say about them.

Other in-store research has revealed that consumers react strongly to colors. Researchers at OnceFamous conducted an experiment by launching three separate sales, all on the same merchandise with the same signs and promotions. The only detail the researchers varied was the color of the signs. The sales that were promoted with signs colored blue and green failed while the event with red signs enticed shoppers to buy. The conclusion? Consumers associate warm colors, such as red and yellow, with low prices. They associate cool colors, including blue and green, with higher prices. Consumers are

so drawn to warm colors that red and yellow signs posted toward the rear of a store will draw shoppers in and through the aisles.

Once Famous may be the first research lab of its kind, but it won't be the last. Analysts predict a rise in the number of such detailed, "retail ethnography" labs as the retail world grows more and more competitive. To keep up with demand for consumer behavior insights, FAME plans to open a second retail shop at the ultimate retailing venue, the Mall of America. We'll be watching.

Sources: Keyla Kokmen, "The Company Store," *City Pages Media*, June 5, 2002, accessed at www.citypages.com/databank/23/1122/article10444.asp; Erik Baard, "Going Retail with Market Research," *Wired News*, August 8, 2002, p.1; Bruce Horovitz, "Shop, You're on Candid Camera," *USA Today*, November 5, 2002, p1B; Timothy Henderson, "Shopping Guinea Pigs," *Stores*, December 2002, accessed at www.stores.org/archives/archives02.html; Stephanie Simon, "Shopping with Big Brother," *Los Angeles Times*, May 2, 2002, accessed at www.chicagotribune.com/technology/chi-020502shopping.story; Lynda Gutierrez, "Spy and Buy," *Plain Talk*, accessed at www.plainvanillashell.com/archiveoped.asp?id5324, May 2004; and information gathered from www.fameretail.com, March 2004.

similar, and if all other marketing efforts for the sandwich are the same, then differences in sales in the two cities could be related to the price charged.

Contact Methods

Information can be collected by mail, telephone, personal interview, or online. Table 4.3 shows the strengths and weaknesses of each of these contact methods.

MAIL, TELEPHONE, AND PERSONAL INTERVIEWING *Mail questionnaires* can be used to collect large amounts of information at a low cost per respondent. Respondents may give more honest answers to more personal questions on a mail questionnaire than to an unknown interviewer in person or over the phone. Also, no interviewer is involved to bias the respondent's answers.

However, mail questionnaires are not very flexible—all respondents answer the same questions in a fixed order. Mail surveys usually take longer to complete, and the response rate—the number of people returning completed questionnaires—is often very low. Finally, the researcher often has little control over the mail questionnaire sample. Even with a good mailing list, it is hard to control *who* at the mailing address fills out the questionnaire.

Telephone interviewing is the one of the best methods for gathering information quickly, and it provides greater flexibility than mail questionnaires. Interviewers can explain difficult questions and, depending on the answers they receive, skip some questions or probe on others. Response rates tend to be higher than with mail questionnaires, and interviewers can ask to speak to respondents with the desired characteristics or even by name.

However, with telephone interviewing, the cost per respondent is higher than with mail questionnaires. Also, people may not want to discuss personal questions with an interviewer. The method introduces interviewer bias—the way interviewers talk, how they ask questions, and other differences may affect respondents' answers. Finally, different interviewers may interpret and record responses differently, and under time pressures some interviewers might even cheat by recording answers without asking questions.

Personal interviewing takes two forms—individual and group interviewing. *Individual interviewing* involves talking with people in their homes or offices, on the street, or in shopping malls. Such interviewing is flexible. Trained interviewers can guide interviews, explain difficult questions, and explore issues as the situation requires. They can show sub-

TABLE 4.3 Strengths and Weaknesses of Contact Methods

	Mail	Telephone	Personal	Online
Flexibility	Poor	Good	Excellent	Good
Quantity of data that can be collected	Good	Fair	Excellent	Good
Control of interviewer effects	Excellent	Fair	Poor	Fair
Control of sample	Fair	Excellent	Fair	Poor
Speed of data collection	Poor	Excellent	Good	Excellent
Response rate	Fair	Good	Good	Good
Cost	Good	Fair	Poor	Excellent

Source: Adapted with permission from *Marketing Research: Measurement and Method*, 7th ed., by Donald S. Tull and Del I. Hawkins. Copyright 1993 by Macmillan Publishing Company.

jects actual products, advertisements, or packages and observe reactions and behavior. However, individual personal interviews may cost three to four times as much as telephone interviews.

Group interviewing consists of inviting 6 to 10 people to talk with a trained moderator to talk about a product, service, or organization. Participants normally are paid a small sum for attending. The moderator encourages free and easy discussion, hoping that group interactions will bring out actual feelings and thoughts. At the same time, the moderator "focuses" the discussion—hence the name **focus group interviewing**. Researchers and marketers watch the focus group discussions from behind one-way glass and comments are recorded in writing or on videotape for later study.

Focus group interviewing
Personal interviewing that involves inviting 6 to 10 people to gather for a few hours with a trained interviewer to talk about a product, service, or organization. The interviewer "focuses" the group discussion on important issues.

Focus group interviewing has become one of the major marketing research tools for gaining insight into consumer thoughts and feelings. However, focus group studies usually employ small sample sizes to keep time and costs down, and it may be hard to generalize from the results. Because interviewers have more freedom in personal interviews, the problem of interviewer bias is greater.

Today, many researchers are changing the way they conduct focus groups. Some are employing videoconferencing technology to connect marketers in distant locations with live focus group action. Using cameras and two-way sound systems, marketing executives in a far-off boardroom can look in and listen, even using remote controls to zoom in on faces and pan the focus group at will. Other researchers are changing the environments in which they conduct focus groups. To help consumers relax and to elicit more authentic responses, they are using settings that are more comfortable and more relevant to the products being researched. For example, they might conduct focus groups for cooking products in a kitchen setting, or focus groups for home furnishings in a living room setting. One research firm offers facilities that look just like anything from a living room or play room to a bar or even a courtroom.

Some firms are now going on-site to conduct focus group sessions. Target did this before designing a new line of products for students entering college:

To hear firsthand from college-bound students about their concerns when shopping for their dorm rooms, and to get a sense from college students of what life in a dorm is like, Target hired research firm Jump Associates to conduct focus groups. But rather than inviting respondents to its research facilities, Jump sponsored a series of "game nights" at high school grads' homes, inviting incoming college freshman as well as students with a year of dorm living under their belts. To get teens talking about dorm life, Jump devised a board game that involved issues associated with going to college. The game naturally led to informal conversations—and questions— about college life. Jump researchers were on the sidelines to observe, while a video camera recorded the proceedings. The research paid off. Target launched the Todd Oldham Dorm Room product line designed for college freshman. Among the new offerings: Kitchen in a Box, which provides basic accessories for a budding college cook; Bath in a Box, which includes an extra-large bath towel to preserve modesty on the trek to and from the shower; and a laundry bag with instructions on how to actually do the laundry printed on the bag.[13]

■ Focus group technology: Today, many researchers are employing videoconferencing and Internet technology to connect marketers with live focus group action. The ActiveGroup research firm lets marketers eavesdrop on focus groups from any location, no matter how distant. Says the company, "no traveling, no scheduling, no problems."

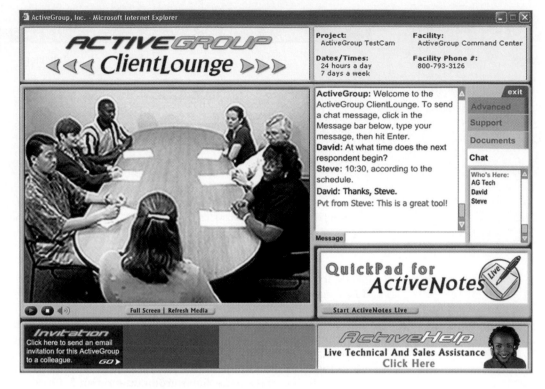

Online (Internet) marketing research

Collecting primary data through Internet surveys and online focus groups.

ONLINE MARKETING RESEARCH Advances in communication technologies have resulted in a number of new high-tech contact methods. One is *computer-assisted telephone interviewing (CATI),* in which interviewers sit at computers, read questions on the screen, and type in respondents' answers. Another is *completely automated telephone surveys (CATS),* in which respondents are dialed by computer and asked prerecorded questions. They enter responses by voice or through the phone's touchpad. Other high-tech contact methods include disks-by-mail and computer-based fax surveys.

The latest technology to hit marketing research is the Internet. Increasingly, marketing researchers are collecting primary data through **online (Internet) marketing research—** *Internet surveys, experiments,* and *online focus groups.*

Web research offers some real advantages over traditional surveys and focus groups. The most obvious advantages are speed and low costs. Online focus groups require some advance scheduling, but results are practically instantaneous. For example, one soft drink company recently conducted an online survey to test teenager opinions of new packaging ideas. The 10- to 15-minute Internet survey included dozens of questions along with 765 different images of labels and bottle shapes. Some 600 teenagers participated over a 3- to 4-day period. Detailed analysis from the survey was available just 5 days after all the responses had come in—lightning quick compared with offline efforts.[14]

Internet research is also relatively low in cost. Participants can dial in for a focus group from anywhere in the world, eliminating travel, lodging, and facility costs. For surveys, the Internet eliminates most of the postage, phone, labor, and printing costs associated with other approaches. "A survey on the Internet is only 10 or 20 percent as expensive as mail, telephone, or in-person surveys," says one researcher. Moreover, notes another, sample size has little influence on costs. "There's not a huge difference between 10 and 10,000 on the Web," he says.

Online surveys and focus groups are also excellent for reaching the hard-to-reach—the often-elusive teen, single, affluent, and well-educated audiences. It's also good for reaching working mothers and other people who lead busy lives. They respond to it in their own space and at their own convenience. The Internet also works well for bringing together people from different parts of the country, especially those in higher-income groups who can't spare the time to travel to a central site.

Using the Internet to conduct marketing research does have some drawbacks. For one, restricted Internet access can make it difficult to get a broad cross section of Americans. Another major problem is controlling who's in the sample. "If you can't see a person with whom you are communicating," says a research executive, "how do know who they really are?"

■ Companies are increasingly moving their research onto the Web. Greenfield online tells customers, "you get instant access to our robust panel of 1.7 million members that can help you keep your marketing strategies on track."

Even when you reach the right respondents, online surveys and focus groups can lack the dynamics of more personal approaches. The online world is devoid of the eye contact, body language, and direct personal interactions found in traditional focus group research. And the Internet format—running, typed commentary, and online "emoticons" (punctuation marks that express emotion, such as :-) to signify happiness)—greatly restricts respondent expressiveness. "You're missing all of the key things that make a focus group a viable method," says the executive. "You may get people online to talk to each other and play off each other, but it's very different to watch people get excited about a concept."

To overcome such sample and response problems, many online research firms use opt-in communities and respondent panels. Advances in technology—such as the integration of animation, streaming audio and video, and virtual environments—also help to overcome these limitations.

Perhaps the most explosive issue facing online researchers concerns consumer privacy. Some fear that unethical researchers will use the e-mail addresses and confidential responses gathered through surveys to sell products after the research is completed. They are concerned about the use of electronic agents (called Spambots or Spiders) that collect personal information without the respondents' consent. Failure to address such privacy issues could result in angry, less cooperative consumers and increased government intervention. Despite these concerns, online research now accounts for 8 percent of all spending on quantitative marketing research, and most industry insiders predict healthy growth.[15]

Sampling Plan

Sample
A segment of the population selected for marketing research to represent the population as a whole.

Marketing researchers usually draw conclusions about large groups of consumers by studying a small sample of the total consumer population. A **sample** is a segment of the population selected to represent the population as a whole. Ideally, the sample should be representative so that the researcher can make accurate estimates of the thoughts and behaviors of the larger population.

TABLE 4.4   **Types of Samples**

Probability Sample	
Simple random sample	Every member of the population has a known and equal chance of selection.
Stratified random sample	The population is divided into mutually exclusive groups (such as age groups), and random samples are drawn from each group.
Cluster (area) sample	The population is divided into mutually exclusive groups (such as blocks), and the researcher draws a sample of the groups to interview.
Nonprobability Sample	
Convenience sample	The researcher selects the easiest population members from which to obtain information.
Judgment sample	The researcher uses his or her judgment to select population members who are good prospects for accurate information.
Quota sample	The researcher finds and interviews a prescribed number of people in each of several categories.

Designing the sample requires three decisions. First, *who* is to be surveyed (what *sampling unit*)? The answer to this question is not always obvious. For example, to study the decision-making process for a family automobile purchase, should the researcher interview the husband, wife, other family members, dealership salespeople, or all of these? The researcher must determine what information is needed and who is most likely to have it.

Second, *how many* people should be surveyed (what *sample size*)? Large samples give more reliable results than small samples. It is not necessary to sample the entire target market or even a large portion to get reliable results, however. If well chosen, samples of less than 1 percent of a population can often give good reliability.

Third, *how* should the people in the sample be *chosen* (what *sampling procedure*)? Table 4.4 describes different kinds of samples. Using *probability samples*, each population member has a known chance of being included in the sample, and researchers can calculate confidence limits for sampling error. But when probability sampling costs too much or takes too much time, marketing researchers often take *nonprobability samples*, even though their sampling error cannot be measured. These varied ways of drawing samples have different costs and time limitations as well as different accuracy and statistical properties. Which method is best depends on the needs of the research project.

Research Instruments

In collecting primary data, marketing researchers have a choice of two main research instruments—the *questionnaire* and *mechanical devices*. The *questionnaire* is by far the most common instrument, whether administered in person, by phone, or online.

Questionnaires are very flexible—there are many ways to ask questions. *Closed-end questions* include all the possible answers, and subjects make choices among them. Examples include multiple-choice questions and scale questions. *Open-end questions* allow respondents to answer in their own words. In a survey of airline users, Southwest might simply ask, "What is your opinion of Southwest Airlines?" Or it might ask people to complete a sentence: "When I choose an airline, the most important consideration is. . . ." These and other kinds of open-end questions often reveal more than closed-end questions because respondents are not limited in their answers. Open-end questions are especially useful in exploratory research, when the researcher is trying to find out *what* people think but not measuring *how many* people think in a certain way. Closed-end questions, on the other hand, provide answers that are easier to interpret and tabulate.

Researchers should also use care in the *wording* and *ordering* of questions. They should use simple, direct, unbiased wording. Questions should be arranged in a logical order. The first question should create interest if possible, and difficult or personal questions should be asked last so that respondents do not become defensive. A carelessly prepared questionnaire usually contains many errors (see Table 4.5).

Although questionnaires are the most common research instrument, researchers also use *mechanical instruments* to monitor consumer behavior. Nielsen Media Research attaches

TABLE 4.5   **A "Questionable Questionnaire"**

Suppose that a summer camp director had prepared the following questionnaire to use in interviewing the parents of prospective campers. How would you assess each question?

1. What is your income to the nearest hundred dollars? *People don't usually know their income to the nearest hundred dollars, nor do they want to reveal their income that closely. Moreover, a researcher should never open a questionnaire with such a personal question.*
2. Are you a strong or weak supporter of overnight summer camping for your children? *What do "strong" and "weak" mean?*
3. Do your children behave themselves well at a summer camp? Yes ( ) No ( ) *"Behave" is a relative term. Furthermore, are yes and no the best response options for this question? Besides, will people answer this honestly and objectively? Why ask the question in the first place?*
4. How many camps mailed literature to you last year? This year? *Who can remember this?*
5. What are the most salient and determinant attributes in your evaluation of summer camps? *What are salient and determinant attributes? Don't use big words on me!*
6. Do you think it is right to deprive your child of the opportunity to grow into a mature person through the experience of summer camping? *A loaded question. Given the bias, how can any parent answer yes?*

people meters to television sets in selected homes to record who watches which programs. And retailers use *checkout scanners* to record shoppers' purchases.

Other mechanical devices measure subjects' physical responses. For example, eye cameras are used to study respondents' eye movements to determine at what points their eyes focus first and how long they linger on a given item. IBM is perfecting an "emotion mouse" that will figure out users' emotional states by measuring pulse, temperature, movement, and galvanic skin response. Using such inputs, an Internet marketer might offer a different screen display if it senses that the user is frustrated. Here's another new technology that captures information on consumers' emotional and physical responses:[16]

Machine response to facial expressions that indicate emotions will soon be a commercial reality. The technology discovers underlying emotions by capturing an image of a user's facial features and movements—especially around the eyes and mouth—and comparing the image against facial feature templates in a database. Hence, an elderly man squints at an ATM screen and the font size doubles almost instantly. A woman at a shopping center kiosk smiles at a travel ad, prompting the device to print out a travel discount coupon. Several users at another kiosk frown at a racy ad, leading a store to pull it.

Implementing the Research Plan

The researcher next puts the marketing research plan into action. This involves collecting, processing, and analyzing the information. Data collection can be carried out by the company's marketing research staff or by outside firms. The data collection phase of the marketing research process is generally the most expensive and the most subject to error. Researchers should watch closely to make sure that the plan is implemented correctly. They must guard against problems with contacting respondents, with respondents who refuse to cooperate or who give biased answers, and with interviewers who make mistakes or take shortcuts.

Researchers must process and analyze the collected data to isolate important information and findings. They need to check data for accuracy and completeness and code it for analysis. The researchers then tabulate the results and compute averages and other statistical measures.

Interpreting and Reporting the Findings

The market researcher must now interpret the findings, draw conclusions, and report them to management. The researcher should not try to overwhelm managers with numbers and fancy statistical techniques. Rather, the researcher should present important findings that are useful in the major decisions faced by management.

However, interpretation should not be left only to the researchers. They are often experts in research design and statistics, but the marketing manager knows more about the problem

■ Mechanical measures of consumer response: Devices are in the works that will allow marketers to measure facial expressions and adjust their offers or communications accordingly.

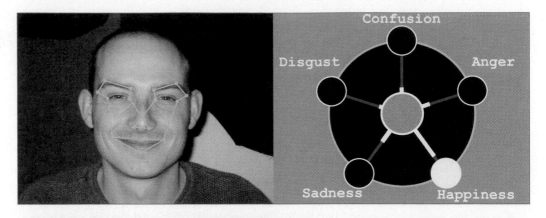

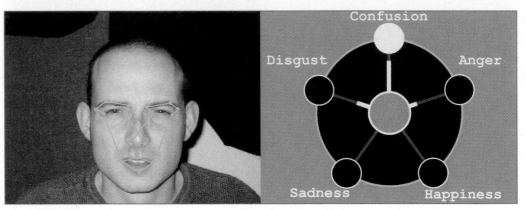

and the decisions that must be made. The best research is meaningless if the manager blindly accepts faulty interpretations from the researcher. Similarly, managers may be biased—they might tend to accept research results that show what they expected and to reject those that they did not expect or hope for. In many cases, findings can be interpreted in different ways, and discussions between researchers and managers will help point to the best interpretations. Thus, managers and researchers must work together closely when interpreting research results, and both must share responsibility for the research process and resulting decisions.[17]

Analyzing Marketing Information

Information gathered in internal databases and through marketing intelligence and marketing research usually requires more analysis. And managers may need help in applying the information to their marketing problems and decisions. This help may include advanced statistical analysis to learn more about both the relationships within a set of data and their statistical reliability. Such analysis allows managers to go beyond means and standard deviations in the data and to answer questions about markets, marketing activities, and outcomes.

Information analysis might also involve a collection of analytical models that will help marketers make better decisions. Each model represents some real system, process, or outcome. These models can help answer the questions of *what if* and *which is best*. Marketing scientists have developed numerous models to help marketing managers make better marketing mix decisions, design sales territories and sales call plans, select sites for retail outlets, develop optimal advertising mixes, and forecast new-product sales.

Customer Relationship Management (CRM)

The question of how best to analyze and use individual customer data presents special problems. Most companies are awash in information about their customers. In fact, smart companies capture information at every possible customer *touch point*. These touch points include customer purchases, sales force contacts, service and support calls, Web site visits, satisfaction surveys, credit and payment interactions, market research studies—every contact between the customer and the company.

■ CRM: SAS offers CRM software that provides "a complete view of your customers." So you'll understand their needs enhance their life-time value, and achieve greater competitive advantage.

Customer relationship management (CRM)
The overall process of building and maintaining profitable customer relationships by delivering superior customer value and satisfaction.

The trouble is that this information is usually scattered widely across the organization. It is buried deep in the separate databases and records of different company departments. To overcome such problems, many companies are now turning to **customer relationship management (CRM)** to manage detailed information about individual customers and carefully manage customer touch points in order to maximize customer loyalty. In recent years, there has been an explosion in the number of companies using CRM. U.S. companies spent an estimated $42.8 billion last year on CRM systems from companies such as Siebel Systems, Oracle, Microsoft, and SAS, and spending is expected to increase by 11.5 percent a year through 2007.[18]

CRM consists of sophisticated software and analytical tools that integrate customer information from all sources, analyze it in depth, and apply the results to build stronger customer relationships. CRM integrates everything that a company's sales, service, and marketing teams know about individual customers to provide a 360-degree view of the customer relationship.

CRM analysts develop *data warehouses* and use sophisticated *data mining* techniques to unearth the riches hidden in customer data. A data warehouse is a companywide electronic database of finely detailed customer information that needs to be sifted through for gems. The purpose of a data warehouse is not just to gather information, but to pull it together into a central, accessible location. Then, once the data warehouse brings the data together, the company uses high-powered data mining techniques to sift through the mounds of data and dig out interesting findings about customers. Such data systems can give a company a big competitive advantage (see Real Marketing 4.2).

By using CRM to understand customers better, companies can provide higher levels of customer service and develop deeper customer relationships. They can use CRM to pinpoint high-value customers, target them more effectively, cross-sell the company's products, and create offers tailored to specific customer requirements. Consider the following examples:[19]

■ FedEx's CRM system has helped to cut costs, improve customer support, and use customer data to cross-sell and up-sell services to customers. The system gives every member of FedEx's 3,300-person sales force a comprehensive view of every customer, detailing each

Real Marketing 4.2

BudNet: Making Customer Information the Lifeblood of the Organization

Every time a six-pack of Bud Light moves off the shelf at the Piggly Wiggly, Anheuser-Busch's top-secret BudNet nationwide data network knows it. The network will also likely record what the customer pays, when the beer was brewed, whether it was purchased warm or chilled, and whether the buyer could have gotten a better deal down the street. Anheuser-Busch (A-B) has made a deadly accurate science out of finding out what beer lovers are buying, as well as when, where, and why. "If Anheuser-Busch loses shelf space in a store in Clarksville, Tennessee, they know it right away," says an industry consultant. "They're better at [the information] game than anyone, even Coca-Cola."

Until recently, the beer industry lagged technologically. The major breweries had little information, and they made poor use of what data they had. But A-B changed the rules in 1997, when chairman August Busch III vowed to make his company a leader in mining its customers' buying patterns. The result was BudNet, an extensive, finely tuned consumer and market data network.

Anheuser-Busch now works hand-in-hand with its distributors to amass detailed store-level data. "Wholesaler and store-level data has become the lifeblood of our organization," says a high-level A-B executive. Distributor sales reps scour their territories, snapping up every scrap of useful information, such as how much shelf space their retailers devote to all beer brands, which ones have the most visible displays, and which ones are on deal.

Take Dereck Gurden, a rep for one of A-B's central California distributors. When Gurden pulls up at one of his customers' stores—7-Eleven, Buy N Save, or one of dozens of liquor marts and restaurants—thanks to BudNet, he's loaded with useful account information. And, of course, he's hungry for more. Toting a brick-size handheld PC, his constant companion and his window into BudNet, Gurden starts his routine. "First I'll scroll through and check the accounts receivable, make sure everything's current," he says. "Then it'll show me an inventory screen with a four-week history. I can get past sales, package placements—facts and numbers on how much of the sales they did when they had a display in a certain location."

After consulting with his customer, Gurden "walks the store, inputting what I see"—not just what he sees about his own brands, but also about competitors' products, prices, and displays, which go into the handheld, too. A few years ago, still toting around clipboards and invoices, Gurden didn't even bother keeping track of the Coors and Miller displays in his customers' stores. Today those are among the most important data fields in his handheld. "It's no extra work to get the competitive info," he says. "You always want to walk the store." All done, Gurden jacks the handheld into his cell phone and fires off new orders to the warehouse, along with the data he's gathered. "Honestly? I think I know more about these guys' businesses than they do," he says. "At least in the beer section."

Gurden and several thousand reps and drivers serve as the eyes and ears of the BudNet data network through which A-B distributors report, in excruciating detail, on sales, shelf stocks, and displays at thousands of outlets. But amassing the data is just the first step. "It's not just collecting data," says Harry Schuhmacher, editor of *Beer Business Daily*. "It depends on brainpower. Anheuser-Busch is the smartest in figuring out how to use it." And knowing how to use it gives A-B Wal-Mart-like clout in its markets.

Collecting the data in a nightly nationwide sweep of its distributors' servers, A-B can draw a picture each morning of what brands

■ BudNet: Every time a six-pack of Bud Light moves off a grocery store shelf, Anheuser-Busch's nationwide BudNet data network knows it. Anheuser has made a deadly accurate science out of finding out what beer lovers are buying, as well as when, where, and why.

are selling in which packages using which medley of displays, discounts, and promotions. Additional data from other sources helps to complete the picture. Today, A-B is the only major brewer to rely heavily on data from Information Resources, Inc.—which tracks every bar-coded product swiped at checkout and performs Nielsen-style consumer surveys. Anheuser-Busch also conducts its own monthly surveys to see what beer drinkers buy and why.

Anheuser-Busch uses the data to constantly change marketing strategies, to design promotions to suit the ethnic makeup of its markets, and as early warning radar that detects where rivals might have an edge. None of the other brewers approaches A-B's data-mining savvy. Mining the aggregate data tells A-B everything from what images or ideas to push in its ads to what new products to unveil—such as low-carb Michelob Ultra, A-B's most successful launch since Bud Light.

Crossing store-level data with U.S. Census figures on the ethnic and economic makeup of neighborhoods helps A-B tailor marketing campaigns with a local precision only dreamed of a few years ago. The data reveals trends by city (Tequiza may be hot in San Antonio, but Bud Light plays better in Peoria), by neighborhood (gay models appear on posters in San Francisco's Castro district, but not on those in the Mission), by holiday (the Fourth of July is a big seller in Atlanta, but St. Patrick's Day isn't), and by class (cans for blue-collar stores, bottles for white-collar). "They're drilling down to the level of the individual store," says the industry consultant. "They can pinpoint if customers are gay, Latino, 30-year-old, college-educated conservatives."

The BudNet data-mining operation is the King of Beers's little-known crown jewel. It's a primary reason that A-B's volume share of the $74.4 billion U.S. beer market stands at an astounding 50.1 percent, putting Coors, Miller, and other brewers on ice. Since August Busch III announced the company's high-tech data blitz, A-B has posted double-digit profit gains for 20 straight quarters, while the profits at Coors and Miller have flatlined.

Source: Adapted from Kevin Kelleher, "66,207,896 Bottles of Beer on the Wall," *Business 2.0*, January–February, 2004, pp. 47–50.

one's needs and helping the rep to sort through the company's more than 220 different services to find the best fit for each customer. For instance, if a customer who does a lot of international shipping calls to arrange a delivery, a sales rep will see a detailed customer history on his or her computer screen, assess the customer's needs, and determine the most appropriate offering on the spot. The CRM system will also help FedEx conduct promotions and qualify potential sales leads. The CRM software analyzes market segments, points out market "sweet spots," and calculates how profitable those segments will be to the company and to individual salespeople.

■ Marks & Spencer—Britain's "most trusted retailer"—has one of the richest customer databases of any retailer in the world. The database contains demographic and purchasing information on more than 3 million M&S charge account customers, point-of-sale information from 10 million store transactions per week, and a wealth of data from external sources. The CRM system organizes this wealth of data and analyzes it to help Marks & Spencer make better decisions on everything from corporate branding to targeted communications and sales promotions. "We have a much better idea of what kinds of offers to put in front of different customers and when, and what tone of voice to use, based on their individual tastes, preferences, and behavior," says Steven Bond, head of the retailer's Customer Insight Unit (CIU). For example, by identifying who shops and when—older customers tend to shop early to avoid the crowds, while younger male shoppers leave things until the last minute, for instance—M&S can align its product availability and marketing activity accordingly. Or a regular customer checking out of the store's food section might be enticed into the menswear department with a promotion personalized according to whether he or she is an "Egyptian cotton and silk tie" purchaser or has a lifestyle that demands no-iron shirts. CRM has put Marks & Spencer at the leading edge of customer analysis. This, in turn, creates more satisfied customers and more profitable customer relationships.

CRM benefits don't come without cost or risk, not only in collecting the original customer data but also in maintaining and mining it. An estimated half or more of all CRM efforts fail to meet their objectives. The most common cause of CRM failures is that companies mistakenly view CRM only as a technology and software solution.[20] But technology alone cannot build profitable customer relationships. "CRM is not a technology solution—you can't achieve . . . improved customer relationships by simply slapping in some software," says a CRM expert. Instead, CRM is just one part of an effective overall *customer relationship management strategy*. "Focus on the *R*," advises the expert. "Remember, a relationship is what CRM is all about."[21]

When it works, the benefits of CRM can far outweigh the costs and risks. Based on regular polls of its customers, Siebel Systems claims that customers using its CRM software

■ CRM: Marks & Spencer's Customer Insight Unit uses the retailer's rich customer database to make better decisions on everything from corporate branding to targeted communications and sales promotions.

report an average 16 percent increase in revenues and 21 percent increase in customer loyalty and staff efficiency. "No question that companies are getting tremendous value out of this," says a CRM consultant. "Companies [are] looking for ways to bring disparate sources of customer information together, then get it to all the customer touch points." The powerful new CRM techniques can unearth "a wealth of information to target that customer, to hit their hot button."[22]

Distributing and Using Marketing Information

Marketing information has no value until it is used to make better marketing decisions. Thus, the marketing information system must make the information available to the managers and others who make marketing decisions or deal with customers on a day-to-day basis. In some cases, this means providing managers with regular performance reports, intelligence updates, and reports on the results of research studies.

But marketing managers may also need nonroutine information for special situations and on-the-spot decisions. For example, a sales manager having trouble with a large customer may want a summary of the account's sales and profitability over the past year. Or a retail store manager who has run out of a best-selling product may want to know the current inventory levels in the chain's other stores. Increasingly, therefore, information distribution involves entering information into databases and making it available in a user-friendly and timely way.

Many firms use a company *intranet* to facilitate this process. The intranet provides ready access to research information, stored reports, shared work documents, contact information for employees and other stakeholders, and more. For example, iGo, a catalog and Web retailer, integrates incoming customer service calls with up-to-date database information about customers' Web purchases and e-mail inquiries. By accessing this information on the intranet while speaking with the customer, iGo's service representatives can get a well-rounded picture of each customer's purchasing history and previous contacts with the company.

In addition, companies are increasingly allowing key customers and value-network members to access account, product, and other data on demand through *extranets*. Suppliers, customers, resellers, and select other network members may access a company's extranet to update their accounts, arrange purchases, and check orders against inventories to improve customer service. For example, one insurance firm allows its 200 independent agents access to a Web-based database of claim information covering 1 million customers. This allows the agents to avoid high-risk customers and to compare claim data with their own customer databases. And Wal-Mart stores around the globe use the Retail Link system, which provides suppliers with up to 2 years worth of data on how their products have sold in Wal-Mart stores.[23]

Thanks to modern technology, today's marketing managers can gain direct access to the information system at any time and from virtually any location. They can tap into the system while working at a home office, from a hotel room, or from the local Starbuck's through a wireless network—anyplace where they can turn on a laptop and link up. Such systems allow managers to get the information they need directly and quickly and to tailor it to their own needs. From just about anywhere, they can obtain information from company or outside databases, analyze it using statistical software, prepare reports and presentations, and communicate directly with others in the network.

Other Marketing Information Considerations

This section discusses marketing information in two special contexts: marketing research in small businesses and nonprofit organizations, and international marketing research. Finally, we look at public policy and ethics issues in marketing research.

Marketing Research in Small Businesses and Nonprofit Organizations

Just like larger firms, small organizations need market information. Start-up businesses need information about their industries, competitors, potential customers, and reactions to new market offers. Existing small businesses must track changes in customer needs and wants, reactions to new products, and changes in the competitive environment.

Managers of small businesses and nonprofit organizations often think that marketing research can be done only by experts in large companies with big research budgets. True, large-scale research studies are beyond the budgets of most small businesses. However, many of the marketing research techniques discussed in this chapter also can be used by smaller organizations in a less formal manner and at little or no expense.

Managers of small businesses and nonprofit organizations can obtain good marketing information simply by *observing* things around them. For example, retailers can evaluate new locations by observing vehicle and pedestrian traffic. They can monitor competitor advertising by collecting ads from local media. They can evaluate their customer mix by recording how many and what kinds of customers shop in the store at different times. In addition, many small business managers routinely visit their rivals and socialize with competitors to gain insights. Tom Coohill, a chef who owns two Atlanta restaurants, gives managers a food allowance to dine out and bring back ideas. Atlanta jeweler Frank Maier Jr., who often visits out-of-town rivals, spotted and copied a dramatic way of lighting displays.[24]

Managers can conduct informal *surveys* using small convenience samples. The director of an art museum can learn what patrons think about new exhibits by conducting informal focus groups—inviting small groups to lunch and having discussions on topics of interest. Retail salespeople can talk with customers visiting the store; hospital officials can interview patients. Restaurant managers might make random phone calls during slack hours to interview consumers about where they eat out and what they think of various restaurants in the area. Bissell, a nicher in the carpet-cleaning industry, used a small convenience sample to quickly and cheaply test the market for its Steam Gun—a newly developed home-cleaning device that resembled a hand-held vacuum cleaner.

> Bissell had only 4 weeks and a tight budget to get a feel for how consumers would respond to the new product. Aware that women with children often purchase such products, Bissell made a $1,500 donation to a local Parent Teacher Association (PTA) for the chance to make a presentation. After the presentation, it gave 20 interested women the Steam Gun to take home. Following a 2-week trial period, Bissell's marketing research director visited the mothers in their homes to watch them use product. This "research on a shoestring" yielded several interesting discoveries. First, Bissell learned that the women weren't sold on the cleaning ability

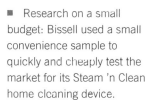

■ Research on a small budget: Bissell used a small convenience sample to quickly and cheaply test the market for its Steam 'n Clean home cleaning device.

of hot water used without chemicals. Second, it would have to change the product name. When roped into chores, children would arm themselves with the Steam Gun and take aim at their siblings. One child was quoted as saying, "Freeze, or I'll melt your face off!" Finally, Bissell found that the product had special appeal to those who were serious about cleaning. They used it to get into hard to reach places and blast off tough grime. Based on these findings, Bissell changed the name of the product to the Steam 'n Clean and focused on the cleaning power of super hot steam when promoting the product. The Steam 'n Clean was successfully launched through infomercials and in nationwide retail chains.[25]

Managers also can conduct their own simple *experiments.* For example, by changing the themes in regular fund-raising mailings and watching the results, a nonprofit manager can find out much about which marketing strategies work best. By varying newspaper advertisements, a store manager can learn the effects of things such as ad size and position, price coupons, and media used.

Small organizations can obtain most of the secondary data available to large businesses. In addition, many associations, local media, chambers of commerce, and government agencies provide special help to small organizations. The U.S. Small Business Administration offers dozens of free publications and a Web site (www.sbaonline.sba.gov) that give advice on topics ranging from starting, financing, and expanding a small business to ordering business cards. Other excellent Web resources for small businesses include the U.S. Census Bureau (www.census.gov) and the Bureau of Economic Analysis (www.bea.doc.gov).

The business sections at local libraries can also be a good source of information. Local newspapers often provide information on local shoppers and their buying patterns. Finally, small businesses can collect a considerable amount of information at very little cost on the Internet. They can scour competitor and customer Web sites and use Internet search engines to research specific companies and issues.

In summary, secondary data collection, observation, surveys, and experiments can all be used effectively by small organizations with small budgets. Although these informal research methods are less complex and less costly, they still must be conducted carefully. Managers must think carefully about the objectives of the research, formulate questions in advance, recognize the biases introduced by smaller samples and less skilled researchers, and conduct the research systematically.[26]

International Marketing Research

International marketing researchers follow the same steps as domestic researchers, from defining the research problem and developing a research plan to interpreting and reporting the results. However, these researchers often face more and different problems. Whereas domestic researchers deal with fairly homogenous markets within a single country, international researchers deal with differing markets in many different countries. These markets often vary greatly in their levels of economic development, cultures and customs, and buying patterns.

In many foreign markets, the international researcher sometimes has a difficult time finding good secondary data. Whereas U.S. marketing researchers can obtain reliable secondary data from dozens of domestic research services, many countries have almost no research services at all. Some of the largest international research services do operate in many countries. For example, AC Nielsen Corporation (owned by VNU NV, the world's largest marketing research company) has offices in more than 100 countries, from China to Chile. And 65 percent of the revenues of the world's 25 largest marketing research firms comes from outside their home countries.[27] However, most research firms operate in only a relative handful of countries. Thus, even when secondary information is available, it usually must be obtained from many different sources on a country-by-country basis, making the information difficult to combine or compare.

Because of the scarcity of good secondary data, international researchers often must collect their own primary data. Here again, researchers face problems not found domestically. For example, they may find it difficult simply to develop good samples. U.S. researchers can use current telephone directories, census tract data, and any of several sources of socioeconomic data to construct samples. However, such information is largely lacking in many countries.

Once the sample is drawn, the U.S. researcher usually can reach most respondents easily by telephone, by mail, on the Internet, or in person. Reaching respondents is often not so easy

■ Some of the largest
research services have large
international organizations.
AC Nielsen has offices in
more than 100 countries.

in other parts of the world. Researchers in Mexico cannot rely on telephone, Internet, and mail data collection—most data collection is door to door and concentrated in three or four of the largest cities. In some countries, few people have phones or personal computers (PCs). For example, whereas there are 668 phones and 554 PCs per 1,000 people in the United States, there are only 117 phones and 54 PCs per 1,000 in Mexico. In Ghana, the numbers drop to 11 phones and 3 PCs per 1,000 people. In some countries, the postal system is notoriously unreliable. In Brazil, for instance, an estimated 30 percent of the mail is never delivered. In many developing countries, poor roads and transportation systems make certain areas hard to reach, making personal interviews difficult and expensive.[28]

Cultural differences from country to country cause additional problems for international researchers. Language is the most obvious obstacle. For example, questionnaires must be prepared in one language and then translated into the languages of each country researched. Responses then must be translated back into the original language for analysis and interpretation. This adds to research costs and increases the risks of error.

Translating a questionnaire from one language to another is anything but easy. Many idioms, phrases, and statements mean different things in different cultures. For example, a Danish executive noted, "Check this out by having a different translator put back into English what you've translated from English. You'll get the shock of your life. I remember [an example in which] 'out of sight, out of mind' had become 'invisible things are insane.' "[29]

Consumers in different countries also vary in their attitudes toward marketing research. People in one country may be very willing to respond; in other countries, nonresponse can be a major problem. Customs in some countries may prohibit people from talking with strangers. In certain cultures, research questions often are considered too personal. For example, in many Latin American countries, people may feel embarrassed to talk with researchers about their choices of shampoo, deodorant, or other personal care products. Similarly, in most Muslim countries, mixed-gender focus groups are taboo, as is videotaping female-only focus groups.[30]

Even when respondents are *willing* to respond, they may not be *able* to because of high functional illiteracy rates. And middle-class people in developing countries often make false claims in order to appear well-off. For example, in a study of tea consumption in India, over 70 percent of middle-income respondents claimed that they used one of several national brands. However, the researchers had good reason to doubt these results—more than 60 percent of the tea sold in India is unbranded generic tea.

Despite these problems, the recent growth of international marketing has resulted in a rapid increase in the use of international marketing research. Global companies have little choice but to conduct such research. Although the costs and problems associated with international research may be high, the costs of not doing it—in terms of missed opportunities and mistakes—might be even higher. Once recognized, many of the problems associated with international marketing research can be overcome or avoided.

Public Policy and Ethics in Marketing Research

Most marketing research benefits both the sponsoring company and its consumers. Through marketing research, companies learn more about consumers' needs, resulting in more satisfying products and services and stronger customer relationships. However, the misuse of marketing research can also harm or annoy consumers. Two major public policy and ethics issues in marketing research are intrusions on consumer privacy and the misuse of research findings.

Intrusions on Consumer Privacy

Many consumers feel positively about marketing research and believe that it serves a useful purpose. Some actually enjoy being interviewed and giving their opinions. However, others strongly resent or even mistrust marketing research. A few consumers fear that researchers might use sophisticated techniques to probe our deepest feelings and then use this knowledge to manipulate our buying. Or they worry that marketers are building huge databases full of personal information about customers. For example, consider a company called Acxiom:

> Never heard of Acxiom? Chances are it's heard of you. Once upon a time in America, a savvy store clerk knew that you had, say, three kids, an old Ford, a pool, and a passion for golf and yellow sweaters. Today Acxiom is that store clerk. It's the world's largest processor of consumer data, collecting and massaging more than a billion records a day. Acxiom's 5-acre data center manages 20 billion customer records and has enough storage space to house all the information in the Library of Congress 50 times over. The company maintains a database on 96 percent of U.S. households that gives marketers a so-called real-time, 360-degree view of their customers. How? Acxiom provides a 13-digit code for every person, "so we can identify you wherever you go," says the company's demographics guru. Each person is placed into one of 70 lifestyle clusters, ranging from "Rolling Stones" and "Single City Struggles" to "Timeless Elders." Acxiom's catalog offers customers hundreds of lists, including a "pre-movers file," updated daily, of people preparing to change residences, as well as lists of people sorted by the frequency with which they use credit cards, the square footage of their homes, and their interest in the "strange and unusual." Its customers include 9 of the country's top 10 credit-card issuers, as well as nearly all the major retail banks, insurers, and automakers. Acxiom may even know things about you that you don't know yourself.[31]

Others consumers may have been taken in by previous "research surveys" that actually turned out to be attempts to sell them something. Still other consumers confuse legitimate marketing research studies with telemarketing efforts and say "no" before the interviewer can even begin. Most, however, simply resent the intrusion. They dislike mail, telephone, or Web surveys that are too long or too personal or that interrupt them at inconvenient times.

Increasing consumer resentment has become a major problem for the research industry. One recent survey found that 70 percent of Americans say that companies have too much of consumers' personal information, and 76 percent feel that their privacy has been compromised if a company uses the collected personal information to sell them products. These concerns have led to lower survey response rates in recent years.[32]

Another study found that 59 percent of consumers had refused to give information to a company because they thought it was not really needed or too personal, up from 42 percent 5 years earlier. "Some shoppers are unnerved by the idea of giving up any information at all," says an analyst. When asked for something as seemingly harmless as a Zip code, "one woman told me she always gives the Zip code for Guam, and another said she never surrenders any information, not even a Zip code, because "I don't get paid to help them with market research."[33]

The research industry is considering several options for responding to this problem. One example is the Council for Marketing and Opinion Research's "Your Opinion Counts" program to educate consumers about the benefits of marketing research and to distinguish it from telephone selling and database building. The industry also has considered adopting broad standards, perhaps based on The International Chamber of Commerce's International Code of Marketing and Social Research Practice. This code outlines researchers' responsibilities to respondents and to the general public. For example, it says that researchers should make their names and addresses available to participants, and it bans companies from representing activities such as database compilation or sales and promotional pitches as research.[34]

Many companies—including IBM, CitiGroup, American Express, Bank of America, DoubleClick, EarthLink, and Microsoft—have now appointed a "chief privacy officer (CPO)," whose job is to safeguard the privacy of consumers who do business with the company. The chief privacy officer for Microsoft says that his job is to come up with data policies for the company to follow, make certain that every program the company creates enhances customer privacy, and inform and educate company employees about privacy issues and concerns. Some 2,000 U.S. companies now employ such privacy chiefs and the number is expected to grow.[35]

American Express, which deals with a considerable volume of consumer information, has long taken privacy issues seriously. The company developed a set of formal privacy principles in 1991, and in 1998 it became one of the first companies to post privacy policies on its Web site. This penchant for customer privacy led American Express to introduce new services that protect consumers' privacy when they use an American Express card to buy items online. American Express views privacy as way to gain competitive advantage—as something that leads consumers to choose one company over another.[36]

In the end, if researchers provide value in exchange for information, customers will gladly provide it. For example, Amazon.com's customers do not mind if the firm builds a database of products they buy in order to provide future product recommendations. This saves time and provides value. Similarly, Bizrate users gladly complete surveys rating e-tail sites because they can view the overall ratings of others when making purchase decisions. The best approach is for researchers to ask only for the information they need, to use it responsibly to provide customer value, and to avoid sharing information without the customer's permission.

■ Consumer privacy: American Express was one of the first companies to post its privacy policies on the Web. "American Express respects your privacy and is committed to protecting it at all times."

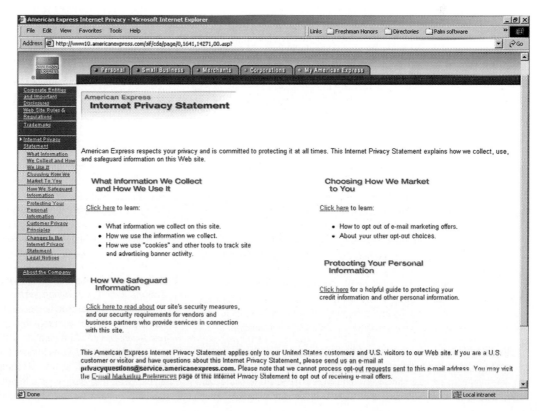

Misuse of Research Findings

Research studies can be powerful persuasion tools; companies often use study results as claims in their advertising and promotion. Today, however, many research studies appear to be little more than vehicles for pitching the sponsor's products. In fact, in some cases, the research surveys appear to have been designed just to produce the intended effect. Few advertisers openly rig their research designs or blatantly misrepresent the findings; most abuses tend to be subtle "stretches." Consider the following examples:[37]

- A study by Chrysler contends that Americans overwhelmingly prefer Chrysler to Toyota after test-driving both. However, the study included just 100 people in each of two tests. More importantly, none of the people surveyed owned a foreign car brand, so they appear to be favorably predisposed to U.S. brands.

- A Black Flag survey asked: "A roach disk . . . poisons a roach slowly. The dying roach returns to the nest and after it dies is eaten by other roaches. In turn these roaches become poisoned and die. How effective do you think this type of product would be in killing roaches?" Not surprisingly, 79 percent said effective.

- A poll sponsored by the disposable diaper industry asked: "It is estimated that disposable diapers account for less than 2 percent of the trash in today's landfills. In contrast, beverage containers, third-class mail, and yard waste are estimated to account for about 21 percent of the trash in landfills. Given this, in your opinion, would it be fair to ban disposable diapers?" Again, not surprisingly, 84 percent said no.

Thus, subtle manipulations of the study's sample or the choice or wording of questions can greatly affect the conclusions reached.

In others cases, so-called independent research studies are actually paid for by companies with an interest in the outcome. Small changes in study assumptions or in how results are interpreted can subtly affect the direction of the results. For example, at least four widely quoted studies compare the environmental effects of using disposable diapers with those of using cloth diapers. The two studies sponsored by the cloth diaper industry conclude that cloth diapers are more environmentally friendly. Not surprisingly, the other two studies, sponsored by the paper diaper industry, conclude just the opposite. Yet both appear to be correct *given* the underlying assumptions used.

Recognizing that surveys can be abused, several associations—including the American Marketing Association, Marketing Research Association, and the Council of American Survey Research Organizations (CASRO)—have developed codes of research ethics and standards of conduct. For example, the CASRO Code of Standards and Ethics for Survey Research outlines researcher responsibilities to respondents, including confidentiality, privacy, and avoidance of harassment. It also outlines major responsibilities in reporting results to clients and the public.[38] In the end, however, unethical or inappropriate actions cannot simply be regulated away. Each company must accept responsibility for policing the conduct and reporting of its own marketing research to protect consumers' best interests and its own.

> Reviewing the Concepts <

In today's complex and rapidly changing marketplace, marketing managers need more and better information to make effective and timely decisions. This greater need for information has been matched by the explosion of information technologies for supplying information. Using today's new technologies, companies can now obtain great quantities of information, sometimes even too much. Yet marketers often complain that they lack enough of the *right* kind of information or have an excess of the *wrong* kind. In response, many companies are now studying their managers' information needs and designing information systems to help managers develop and manage market and customer information.

1. Explain the importance of information to the company and its understanding of the marketplace.

The marketing process starts with a complete understanding of the marketplace and consumer needs and wants. Thus, the company needs sound information in order to produce superior value and satisfaction for customers. The company also requires information on competitors, resellers, and other actors and forces in the marketplace. Increasingly, marketers are viewing information not only as an input for making better decisions but also as an important strategic asset and marketing tool.

2. Define the marketing information system and discuss its parts.

The *marketing information system (MIS)* consists of people, equipment, and procedures to gather, sort, analyze, evaluate, and distribute needed, timely, and accurate information to marketing decision makers. A well-designed information system begins and ends with users.

The MIS first *assesses information needs*. The marketing information system primarily serves the company's marketing and other managers, but it may also provide information to external partners. Then, the MIS *develops information* from internal databases, marketing intelligence activities, and marketing research. *Internal databases* provide information on the company's own operations and departments. Such data can be obtained quickly and cheaply but often needs to be adapted for marketing decisions. *Marketing intelligence* activities supply everyday information about developments in the external marketing environment. *Market research* consists of collecting information relevant to a specific marketing problem faced by the company. Lastly, the MIS *distributes information* gathered from these sources to the right managers in the right form and at the right time.

3. Outline the steps in the marketing research process.

The first step in the marketing research process involves *defining the problem and setting the research objectives,* which may be exploratory, descriptive, or causal research. The second step consists of *developing a research plan* for collecting data from primary and secondary sources. The third step calls for *implementing the marketing research plan* by gathering, processing, and analyzing the information. The fourth step consists of *interpreting and reporting the findings.* Additional information analysis helps marketing managers apply the information and provides them with sophisticated statistical procedures and models from which to develop more rigorous findings.

Both *internal* and *external* secondary data sources often provide information more quickly and at a lower cost than primary data sources, and they can sometimes yield information that a company cannot collect by itself. However, needed information might not exist in secondary sources. Researchers must also evaluate secondary information to ensure that it is *relevant, accurate, current,* and *impartial.* Primary research must also be evaluated for these features. Each primary data collection method—*observational, survey,* and *experimental*—has its own advantages and disadvantages. Each of the various primary research contact methods—mail, telephone, personal interview, and online—also has its own advantages and drawbacks. Similarly, each contact method has its pluses and minuses.

4. Explain how companies analyze and distribute marketing information.

Information gathered in internal databases and through marketing intelligence and marketing research usually requires more analysis. This may include advanced statistical analysis or the application of analytical models that will help marketers make better decisions. To analyze individual customer data, many companies have now acquired or developed special software and analysis techniques—called *customer relationship management (CRM)*—that integrate, analyze, and apply the mountains of individual customer data contained in their databases.

Marketing information has no value until it is used to make better marketing decisions. Thus, the marketing information system must make the information available to the managers and others who make marketing decisions or deal with customers. In some cases, this means providing regular reports and updates; in other cases it means making nonroutine information available for special situations and on-the-spot decisions. Many firms use company intranets and extranets to facilitate this process. Thanks to modern technology, today's marketing managers can gain direct access to the information system at any time and from virtually any location.

5. Discuss the special issues some marketing researchers face, including public policy and ethics issues.

Some marketers face special marketing research situations, such as those conducting research in small business, nonprofit, or international situations. Marketing research can be conducted effectively by small businesses and nonprofit organizations with limited budgets. International marketing researchers follow the same steps as domestic researchers but often face more and different problems. All organizations need to respond responsibly to major public policy and ethical issues surrounding marketing research, including issues of intrusions on consumer privacy and misuse of research findings.

> Reviewing the Key Terms <

Causal research 106
Customer relationship
  management 119
Descriptive research 106
Experimental research 110
Exploratory research 106

Focus group interviewing 113
Internal databases 102
Marketing information
  system 100
Marketing intelligence 104
Marketing research 105

Observational research 109
Online databases 108
Online (Internet) marketing
  research 114
Primary data 107
Sample 115

Secondary data 107
Single-source data systems 110
Survey research 110

> Discussing the Concepts <

1. Assume that you are a regional marketing manager for a cellular phone company. List at least three potential sources of internal data and discuss how these data would help you create cellular services that provide greater customer value and satisfaction.

2. In this chapter we define primary data and secondary data. Once secondary data, such as customer usage, is gathered and analyzed with the express purpose of making a pricing decision, is it still called secondary data, or is it primary data? Why?

3. Marketing research over the Internet has increased significantly in the past decade. Outline the strengths and weaknesses of marketing research conducted online.

4. One of the most important sections of a marketing research report is the executive summary. It may be the only part that decision makers read. What essential elements must this summary include?

5. Small businesses and nonprofit organizations often lack the resources to conduct extensive market research. Assume that you are the director of fundraising for a small nonprofit that is focused on a social issue. List three ways, using limited resources, that you could gather information about your primary donor group.

6. Conducting international marketing research is imperative for global firms. What basic problems might a U.S. toy manufacturer of replica firearms and other military artifacts face in conducting research in Asia? How might those issues differ from country to country?

> Applying the Concepts <

1. The Internet is now the largest source of secondary data available to a marketer. More and more sites with hundreds or even thousands of pages of information are being added on a daily basis. In a small group count the number of clicks that it takes you to find the following items:

   - Microsoft net income for 2003

   - Number of WalMart stores (all types) at close of the fiscal year 2004

   - The corporate mission/vision statement for Leo Burnett advertising agency

   - The 10th largest radio market in the United States

   - Cost to run a one-page black and white ad in the Marketplace section of the full national addition of the *Wall Street Journal* (assume no existing contract)

2. Imagine you are the owner of a small children's clothing store that specializes in upscale girl's fashions from size 2 to 6. You have found a potential new clothing line, but you are unsure whether or not the line will generate the sales needed to be profitable. Which type of research methodology (exploratory, descriptive or causal) is best suited for answering your questions? Why?

3. Many consumer rights advocates argue that research data can be manipulated to support any conclusion. Assume you are attending a meeting where a car company's research for a fuel-efficient SUV is being presented. List five questions that you would ask that would test the interpretation and objectivity of the findings being presented.

> Focus on Technology <

If you were a Web marketer, you'd more than likely have heard of or used WebTrends analytic software. In mid-2004, NetIQ, a leading provider of systems management, security management, Windows administration, and web analytics solutions, introduced Version 7 of this popular product. WebTrends provides the marketer many valuable features. Go to www.netiq.com and read about the marketing benefits WebTrends.

1. From a marketing perspective what is the primary purpose of WebTrends?

2. List and explain four of the marketing benefits of WebTrends?

3. Is WebTrends a marketing intelligence or marketing research product?

4. Does WebTrends collect primary or secondary data?

> Focus on Ethics <

TiVo Inc., leading provider of digital video recorders and services, was founded on a single vision: "to create and continually enhance a new, easy, and much better, way to watch television." With over one million subscribers, TiVo leads in an increasingly competitive market through its continual improvement and introduction of new services. While providing services, TiVo collects a great amount of viewing behavior information, including each customer's recording and viewing history. In mid-2004, TiVo announced its intention to sell information about the viewing habits of its subscribers (excluding personal information) to advertisers and broadcasters.

1. Is TiVo acting ethically in selling this information? Is it acting legally?

2. Go to www.tivo.com and check out TiVo's privacy policy. What options does TiVo offer subscribers who are interested in protecting their privacy?

3. Consumer advocates assert that most TiVo subscribers are unaware of the information that the company collects. What steps, if any, would you recommend that TiVo take to inform subscribers about this practice?

⊙ Video Case

DDB Worldwide

DDB Worldwide, a global communications firm, has successfully mounted advertising campaigns for mega marketers including McDonald's, ExxonMobil, Johnson & Johnson, and Volkswagen. The agency strives to offer a unique approach to targeting, and communicating with a host of clients' consumers. As a result, DDB is one of the most decorated advertising agencies in the world.

The agency has also created some memorable campaigns. You may remember the humorous Rubberband Man commercials that aired for Office Max or the "Dude, You're Getting a Dell" series that DDB crafted for Dell. While both campaigns won awards for creativity and humor, those traits alone don't make a campaign successful. Advertising is meant to connect with the customer, build brand meaning, and, ultimately, drive sales. So, how does DDB ensure the success of its campaigns? Each campaign is based on extensive marketing research that helps DDB to understand each client's target customers.

After viewing the video featuring DDB Worldwide, answer the following questions about marketing research.

1. What marketing research techniques did DDB use to get to know JC Penney's core customer? Which technique uncovered the most useful information?

2. What other techniques might have helped DDB better understand JC Penney's target consumers?

3. How might DDB's marketing research approach differ if JC Penney was developing an online campaign to drive consumers to its website?

Company Case

Enterprise Rent-A-Car: Measuring Service Quality

SURVEYING CUSTOMERS

Kevin Kirkman wheeled his shiny blue BMW coupe into his driveway, put the gearshift into park, set the parking brake, and got out to check his mailbox as he did every day when he returned home. As he flipped through the deluge of catalogs and credit card offers, he noticed a letter from Enterprise Rent-A-Car. He wondered why Enterprise would be writing him.

THE WRECK

Then he remembered. Earlier that month, Kevin had been involved in a wreck. As he was driving to work one rainy morning, another car had been unable to stop on the slick pavement and had plowed into his car as he waited at a stoplight. Thankfully, neither he nor the other driver was hurt, but both cars had sustained considerable damage. In fact, he was not able to drive his car.

Kevin had used his cell phone to call the police, and while he was waiting for the officers to come, he had called his auto insurance agent. The agent had assured Kevin that his policy included coverage to pay for a rental car while he was having his car repaired. He told Kevin to have the car towed to a nearby auto repair shop and gave him the telephone number for the Enterprise Rent-A-Car office that served his area. The agent noted that his company recommended using Enterprise for replacement rentals and that Kevin's policy would cover up to $20 per day of the rental fee.

Once Kevin had checked his car in at the body shop and made the necessary arrangements, he telephoned the Enterprise office. Within 10 minutes, an Enterprise employee had driven to the repair shop and picked him up. They drove back to the Enterprise office, where Kevin completed the paperwork and rented a Ford Taurus. He drove the rental car for 12 days before the repair shop completed work on his car.

"Don't know why Enterprise would be writing me," Kevin thought. "The insurance company paid the $20 per day, and I paid the extra because the Taurus cost more than that. Wonder what the problem could be?"

TRACKING SATISFACTION

Kevin tossed the mail on the passenger's seat and drove up the driveway. Once inside his house, he opened the Enterprise letter to find that it was a survey to determine how satisfied he was with his rental. The survey itself was only one page long and consisted of 13 questions (see Exhibit 1).

Enterprise's executives believed that the company had become the largest rent-a-car company in the U.S. (in terms of number of cars, rental locations, and revenue) because of its laserlike focus on customer satisfaction and because of its concentration on serving the home-city replacement market. It aimed to serve customers like Kevin who were involved in wrecks and suddenly found themselves without a car. While the more well known companies like Hertz and Avis battled for business in the cutthroat airport market, Enterprise quietly built its business by cultivating insurance agents and body-shop managers as referral agents so that when one of their clients or customers needed a replacement vehicle, they would recommend Enterprise. Although such replacement rentals accounted for about 80 percent of the company's business, it also served the discretionary market (leisure/vacation rentals), and the business market (renting cars to businesses for their short-term needs). It had also begun to provide on-site and off-site service at some airports.

Throughout its history, Enterprise had followed founder Jack Taylor's advice. Taylor believed that if the company took care of its customers and employees first, profits would follow. So the company was careful to track customer satisfaction.

About one in 20 randomly selected customers received a letter like Kevin's. An independent company mailed the letter and a postage-paid return envelope to the selected customers. Customers who completed the survey used the envelope to return it to the independent company. That company compiled the results and provided them to Enterprise.

CONTINUOUS IMPROVEMENT

Meanwhile, back at Enterprise's St. Louis headquarters, the company's top managers were interested in taking the next steps in their customer satisfaction program. Enterprise had used the percentage of customers who were completely satisfied to develop its Enterprise Service Quality index (ESQi). It used the survey results to calculate an overall average ESQi score for the company and a score for each individual branch. The company's branch managers believed in and supported the process.

However, top management believed that to really "walk the walk" on customer satisfaction, it needed to make the ESQi a key factor in the promotion process. The company wanted to take the ESQi for the branch or branches a manager supervised into consideration when it evaluated that manager for a promotion. Top management believed that such a process would ensure that its managers and all its employees would focus on satisfying Enterprise's customers.

However, the top managers realized they had two problems in taking the next step. First, they wanted a better survey response rate. Although the company got a 25 percent response rate, which was good for this type of survey, it was concerned that it might still be missing important information. Second, it could take up to two months to get results back, and Enterprise believed it needed a process that would get the customer satisfaction information more quickly, at least on a monthly basis, so its branch managers could identify and take action on customer service problems quickly and efficiently.

Enterprise's managers wondered how they could improve the customer-satisfaction-tracking process.

(box continues)

SERVICE QUALITY SURVEY

Please mark the box that best reflects your response to each question.

1. Overall, how satisfied were you with your recent car rental from Enterprise on January 1, 2003?

Completely Satisfied	Somewhat Satisfied	Neither Satisfied Nor Dissatisfied	Somewhat Dissatisfied	Completely Dissatisfied
☐	☐	☐	☐	☐

2. What, if anything, could Enterprise have done better? *(Please be specific)* _____
_____
_____

3a. Did you experience any problems during the rental process?   Yes ☐   No ☐

3b. If you mentioned any problems to Enterprise, did they resolve them to your satisfaction?   Yes ☐   No ☐   Did not mention ☐

4. If you personally called Enterprise to reserve a vehicle, how would you rate the telephone reservation process?

Excellent	Good	Fair	Poor	N/A
☐	☐	☐	☐	☐

5. Did you go to the Enterprise office. . . .

Both at start and end of rental	Just at start of rental	Just at end of rental	Neither time
☐	☐	☐	☐

6. Did an Enterprise employee give you a ride to help with your transportation needs. . . .

Both at start and end of rental	Just at start of rental	Just at end of rental	Neither time
☐	☐	☐	☐

7. After you arrived at the Enterprise office, how long did it take you to:

	Less than 5 minutes	5–10 minutes	11–15 minutes	16–20 minutes	21–30 minutes	More than 30 minutes	N/A
♦ pick up your rental car?	☐	☐	☐	☐	☐	☐	☐
♦ return your rental car?	☐	☐	☐	☐	☐	☐	☐

8. How would you rate the . . .

	Excellent	Good	Fair	Poor	N/A
♦ timeliness with which you were either picked up at the start of the rental or dropped off afterwards?	☐	☐	☐	☐	☐
♦ timeliness with which the rental car was either brought to your location and left with you or picked up from your location afterwards?	☐	☐	☐	☐	☐
♦ Enterprise employee who handled your paperwork . . . at the START of the rental?	☐	☐	☐	☐	☐
at the END of the rental?	☐	☐	☐	☐	☐
♦ mechanical condition of the car?	☐	☐	☐	☐	☐
♦ cleanliness of the car interior/exterior?	☐	☐	☐	☐	☐

9. If you asked for a specific type or size of vehicle, was Enterprise able to meet your needs?

Yes	No	N/A
☐	☐	☐

10. For what reason did you rent this car?

Car repairs due to accident	All other car repairs/ maintenance	Car was stolen	Business	Leisure/ vacation	Some other reason
☐	☐	☐	☐	☐	☐

11. The next time you need to pick up a rental car in the city or area in which you live, how likely are you to call Enterprise?

Definitely will call	Probably will call	Might or might not call	Probably will not call	Definitely will not call
☐	☐	☐	☐	☐

12. Approximately how many times in total have you rented from Enterprise (including this rental)?

Once—this was first time	2 times	3–5 times	6–10 times	11 or more times
☐	☐	☐	☐	☐

13. Considering *all rental companies,* approximately how many times *within the past year* have you rented a car in the city or area in which you live (including this rental)?

0 times	1 time	2 times	3–5 times	6–10 times	11 or more times
☐	☐	☐	☐	☐	☐

Questions for Discussion

1. Analyze Enterprise's Service Quality Survey. What information is it trying to gather? What are its research objectives?

2. What decisions has Enterprise made with regard to primary data collection—research approach, contact methods, sampling plan, and research instruments?

3. In addition to or instead of the mail survey, what other means could Enterprise use to gather customer satisfaction information?

4. What specific recommendations would you make to Enterprise to improve the response rate and the timeliness of feedback from the process?

Source: Officials at Enterprise Rent-A-Car contributed to and supported development of this case. See also Company Case in Chapter 18 for more details on Enterprise Rent-A-Car.

5

> **After studying this chapter, you should be able to**

1. define the consumer market and construct a simple model of consumer buyer behavior
2. name the four major factors that influence consumer buyer behavior
3. list and understand the major types of buying decision behavior and the stages in the buyer decision process
4. describe the adoption and diffusion process for new products

Consumer Markets and Consumer Buyer Behavior

Previewing the Concepts

In the previous chapter, you studied how marketers obtain, analyze, and use information to identify marketing opportunities and to assess marketing programs. In this and the next chapter, we'll continue with a closer look at the most important element of the marketing environment—customers. The aim of marketing is to somehow affect how customers think about and behave toward the organization and its marketing offers. To affect the whats, whens, and hows of buying behavior, marketers must first understand the *whys*. In this chapter, we look at *final consumer* buying influences and processes. In the next chapter, we'll study the buying behavior of *business customers*. You'll see that understanding buying behavior is an essential but very difficult task.

To get a better sense of the importance of understanding consumer behavior, let's look first at Harley-Davidson, maker of the nation's top-selling heavyweight motorcycles. Who rides these big Harley "Hogs"? What moves them to tattoo their bodies with the Harley emblem, abandon home and hearth for the open road, and flock to Harley rallies by the hundreds of thousands? *You* might be surprised, but Harley-Davidson knows *very* well.

Few brands engender such intense loyalty as that found in the hearts of Harley-Davidson owners. Harley buyers are granitelike in their devotion to the brand. "You don't see people tattooing Yamaha on their bodies," observes the publisher of *American Iron*, an industry publication. And according to another industry insider, "For a lot of people, it's not that they want a motorcycle; it's that they want a Harley—the brand is that strong."

Each year, in early March, more than 500,000 Harley bikers rumble through the streets of Daytona Beach, Florida, to attend Harley-Davidson's Bike Week celebration. Bikers from across the nation lounge on their low-slung Harleys, swap biker tales, and sport T-shirts proclaiming "I'd rather push a Harley than drive a Honda."

Riding such intense emotions, Harley-Davidson has rumbled its way to the top of the heavyweight motorcycle market. Harley's "Hogs" capture 22 percent of all U.S. bike sales and 56 percent of the heavyweight segment. For

several years running, sales have outstripped supply, with customer waiting lists of up to 2 years for popular models and street prices running well above suggested list prices. During just the past 5 years, Harley sales have more than doubled, and earnings have tripled. By 2004, the company had experienced 18 straight years of record sales and income.

Harley-Davidson's marketers spend a great deal of time thinking about customers and their buying behavior. They want to know who their customers are, what they think and how they feel, and why they buy a Harley Fat Boy Softail rather than a Yamaha or a Kawasaki or a big Honda American Classic. What is it that makes Harley buyers so fiercely loyal? These are difficult questions; even Harley owners themselves don't know exactly what motivates their buying. But Harley management puts top priority on understanding customers and what makes them tick.

Who rides a Harley? You might be surprised. It's no longer the Hell's Angels crowd—the burly, black-leather-jacketed rebels and biker chicks who once made up Harley's core clientele. Motorcycles are attracting a new breed of riders—older, more affluent, and better educated. Harley now appeals more to "rubbies" (rich urban bikers) than to rebels. "While the outlaw bad-boy biker image is what we might typically associate with Harley riders," says an analyst, "they're just as likely to be CEOs and investment bankers." The average Harley customer is a 46-year-old husband with a median household income of $78,300.

Harley-Davidson makes good bikes, and to keep up with its shifting market, the company has upgraded its showrooms and sales approaches. But Harley customers are buying a lot more than just a quality bike and a smooth sales pitch. To gain a better understanding of customers' deeper motivations, Harley-Davidson conducted focus groups in which it invited bikers to make cut-and-paste collages of pictures that expressed their feelings about Harley-Davidsons. (Can't you just see a bunch of hard-core bikers doing this?) It then mailed out 16,000 surveys containing a typical battery of psychological, sociological, and demographic questions as well as subjective questions such as "Is Harley more typified by a brown bear or a lion?"

The research revealed seven core customer types: adventure-loving traditionalists, sensitive pragmatists, stylish status seekers, laid-back campers, classy capitalists, cool-headed loners, and cocky misfits. However, all owners appreciated their Harleys for the same basic reasons. "It didn't matter if you were the guy who swept the floors of the factory or if you were the CEO at that factory, the attraction to Harley was very similar," says a Harley executive. "Independence, freedom, and power were the universal Harley appeals."

"It's much more than a machine," says the analyst. "It is part of their own self expression and lifestyle." Another analyst suggests that owning a Harley makes you "the toughest, baddest guy on the block. Never mind that [you're] a dentist or an accountant. You [feel] wicked astride all that power." Your Harley renews your spirits and announces your independence. As the Harley Web site's home page announces, "Thumbing the starter of a Harley-Davidson does a lot more than fire the engine. It fires the imagination." Adds a Harley dealer: "We sell a dream here." The classic look, the throaty sound, the very idea of a Harley—all contribute to its mystique. Owning this "American legend" makes you a part of something bigger, a member of the Harley family.

Such strong emotions and motivations are captured in a classic Harley-Davidson advertisement. The ad shows a close-up of an arm, the bicep adorned with a Harley-Davidson tattoo. The headline asks, "When was the last time you felt this strongly about anything?" The ad copy outlines the problem and suggests a solution: "Wake up in the morning and life picks up where it left off. . . . What once seemed exciting has now become part of the numbing routine. It all begins to feel the same. Except when you've got a Harley-Davidson. Something strikes a nerve. The heartfelt thunder rises up, refusing to become part of the background. Suddenly things are different. Clearer. More real. As they should have been all along. Riding a Harley changes you from within. The effect is permanent. Maybe it's time you started feeling this strongly. Things are different on a Harley."[1]

The Harley-Davidson example shows that many different factors affect consumer buyer behavior. Buying behavior is never simple, yet understanding it is the essential task of marketing management. First we explore the dynamics of the consumer market and consumer buyer behavior. We then examine business markets and the business buying process.

Consumer buyer behavior

The buying behavior of final consumers—individuals and households who buy goods and services for personal consumption.

Consumer market

All the individuals and households who buy or acquire goods and services for personal consumption.

Consumer buyer behavior refers to the buying behavior of final consumers—individuals and households who buy goods and services for personal consumption. All of these final consumers combine to make up the **consumer market**. The American consumer market consists of more than 295 million people who consume many trillions of dollars' worth of goods and services each year, making it one of the most attractive consumer markets in the world. The world consumer market consists of almost 6.4 *billion* people.[2]

Consumers around the world vary tremendously in age, income, education level, and tastes. They also buy an incredible variety of goods and services. How these diverse consumers connect with each other and with other elements of the world around them impacts their choices among various products, services, and companies. Here we examine the fascinating array of factors that affect consumer behavior.

Model of Consumer Behavior

Consumers make many buying decisions every day. Most large companies research consumer buying decisions in great detail to answer questions about what consumers buy, where they buy, how and how much they buy, when they buy, and why they buy. Marketers can study actual consumer purchases to find out what they buy, where, and how much. But learning about the *whys* of consumer buyer behavior is not so easy—the answers are often locked deep within the consumer's head.

Penetrating the dark recesses of the consumer's mind is no easy task. Often, consumers themselves don't know exactly what influences their purchases. "Ninety-five percent of the thought, emotion, and learning [that drive our purchases] occur in the unconscious mind—that is, without our awareness," notes one consumer behavior expert.[3]

The central question for marketers is: How do consumers respond to various marketing efforts the company might use? The starting point is the stimulus-response model of buyer behavior shown in Figure 5.1. This figure shows that marketing and other stimuli enter the consumer's "black box" and produce certain responses. Marketers must figure out what is in the buyer's black box.

Marketing stimuli consist of the four *P*s: product, price, place, and promotion. Other stimuli include major forces and events in the buyer's environment: economic, technological, political, and cultural. All these inputs enter the buyer's black box, where they are turned into a set of observable buyer responses: product choice, brand choice, dealer choice, purchase timing, and purchase amount.

The marketer wants to understand how the stimuli are changed into responses inside the consumer's black box, which has two parts. First, the buyer's characteristics influence how he or she perceives and reacts to the stimuli. Second, the buyer's decision process itself affects the buyer's behavior. We look first at buyer characteristics as they affect buying behavior and then discuss the buyer decision process.

Characteristics Affecting Consumer Behavior

Consumer purchases are influenced strongly by cultural, social, personal, and psychological characteristics, as shown in Figure 5.2. For the most part, marketers cannot control such factors, but they must take them into account.

Cultural Factors

Cultural factors exert a broad and deep influence on consumer behavior. The marketer needs to understand the role played by the buyer's *culture*, *subculture*, and *social class*.

Culture
The set of basic values, perceptions, wants, and behaviors learned by a member of society from family and other important institutions.

Culture

Culture is the most basic cause of a person's wants and behavior. Human behavior is largely learned. Growing up in a society, a child learns basic values, perceptions, wants, and behaviors from the family and other important institutions. A child in the United States normally learns or is exposed to the following values: achievement and success, activity and involvement,

FIGURE 5.1
Model of buyer behavior

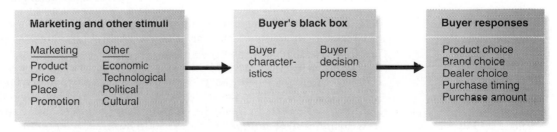

Marketing and other stimuli		Buyer's black box		Buyer responses
Marketing	Other	Buyer character-istics	Buyer decision process	Product choice
Product	Economic			Brand choice
Price	Technological			Dealer choice
Place	Political			Purchase timing
Promotion	Cultural			Purchase amount

FIGURE 5.2
Factors influencing
consumer behavior

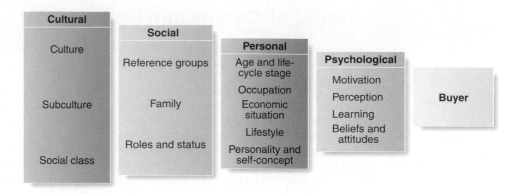

efficiency and practicality, progress, material comfort, individualism, freedom, humanitarianism, youthfulness, and fitness and health. Every group or society has a culture, and cultural influences on buying behavior may vary greatly from country to country. Failure to adjust to these differences can result in ineffective marketing or embarrassing mistakes.

Marketers are always trying to spot *cultural shifts* in order to discover new products that might be wanted. For example, the cultural shift toward greater concern about health and fitness has created a huge industry for health and fitness services, exercise equipment and clothing, more-natural foods, and a variety of diets. The shift toward informality has resulted in more demand for casual clothing and simpler home furnishings.

Subculture

Subculture

A group of people with shared value systems based on common life experiences and situations.

Each culture contains smaller **subcultures**, or groups of people with shared value systems based on common life experiences and situations. Subcultures include nationalities, religions, racial groups, and geographic regions. Many subcultures make up important market segments, and marketers often design products and marketing programs tailored to their needs. Examples of four such important subculture groups include Hispanic, African American, Asian, and mature consumers.

HISPANIC CONSUMERS The U.S. *Hispanic market*—Americans of Cuban, Mexican, Central American, South American, and Puerto Rican descent—consists of almost 39 million consumers. Last year, Hispanic consumers bought more than $580 billion worth of goods and services, up 25 percent from just 2 years earlier. Expected to almost double in the next 25 years, this group will make up more than 20 percent of the total U.S. population by 2030.[4]

Hispanic consumers tend to buy more branded, higher-quality products—generics don't sell well to this group. And they tend to make shopping a family affair, and children have a big say in what brands they buy. Perhaps more important, Hispanics are brand loyal, and they favor companies who show special interest in them.

Most marketers now produce products tailored to the Hispanic market and promote them using Spanish-language ads and media. For example, General Mills offers a line of Para su Familia (for your family) cereals for Hispanics and Mattel has opened a Spanish-language site for its Barbie dolls—BarbieLatina.com—targeting U.S. Hispanic girls. Last year, Procter & Gamble spent $90 million on advertising directed toward Hispanics, including 10 percent of its budget for megabrands such as Tide and Crest. And across the country, Kroger, the nation's largest grocery chain, recently expanded its private-label Buena Comida line from basic standard beans and rice to 105 different items. It also began converting stores in heavily Hispanic neighborhoods to all-Hispanic *Supermercados.*[5]

Sears makes a special effort to market to Hispanic American consumers, especially for the 20 percent of its stores that are located in heavily Hispanic neighborhoods:

Sears is widely considered one of the most successful marketers to the U.S. Hispanic population. Last year, it targeted more than one-fifth of its advertising budget to Hispanics—more than any other retailer. Sears neighborhoods receive regular visits from a Fiesta Mobile, a colorful Winnebago that plays music, gives out prizes, and promotes the Sears credit card. Sears also sponsors major Hispanic cultural festivals and concerts. The retailer's Spanish-language Web site—Sears En Espanol (Sears in Spanish)—features content and events carefully tailored to Hispanic consumers. One of Sears's most successful marketing efforts is its magazine *Nuestra Gente*—which means Our People—the nation's largest Spanish-language magazine. The magazine features articles about Hispanic celebrities alongside glossy spreads of Sears fashions. As a result of this careful cultivation of Hispanic consumers, although Sears has lost sales in recent years to discount retailers, the Hispanic segment has remained steadfastly loyal.[6]

AFRICAN AMERICAN CONSUMERS If the U.S. population of 39 million *African Americans* were a separate nation, its buying power of $630 billion annually would rank among the top 15 in the world. The black population in the United States is growing in affluence and sophistication. Although more price conscious than other segments, blacks are also strongly motivated by quality and selection. Brands are important. So is shopping—black consumers seem to enjoy shopping more than other groups, even for something as mundane as groceries. Black consumers are also the most fashion-conscious of the ethnic groups.[7]

In recent years, many companies have developed special products and services, packaging, and appeals to meet the needs of African Americans. For example, Hallmark launched its Afrocentric brand, Mahogany, with only 16 cards in 1987. Today the brand features more than 900 cards designed to celebrate African American culture, heritage, and traditions.[8] Other companies are moving away from creating separate products for African Americans. Instead, they are offering more inclusive product lines within the same brand that goes out to the general market. For example, Sara Lee discontinued its separate Color-Me-Natural line of L'eggs pantyhose for black women and now offers shades and sheer styles popular among black women as half of the company's general-focus subbrands.

A wide variety of magazines, television channels, and other media now target African American consumers. Marketers are also reaching out to the African American virtual community. Per capita, black consumers spend twice as much as white consumers for online services. African Americans are increasingly turning to Web sites such as BlackPlanet.com, an African American community site with 5.3 million registered users. BlackPlanet.com's mission is to enable members to "cultivate meaningful personal and professional relationships,

■ Hallmark launched its Afrocentric brand, Mahogany, with only 16 cards in 1987. Today the brand features more than 900 cards designed to celebrate African American culture, heritage, and traditions.

stay informed about the world, and gain access to goods and services that allow members to do more in life." Other popular sites include Afronet and Black Voices.[9]

ASIAN AMERICANS *Asian Americans*, the fastest-growing and most affluent U.S. demographic segment, now number more than 12 million, with disposable income of $296 billion annually. Chinese Americans constitute the largest group, followed by Filipinos, Japanese Americans, Asian Indians, and Korean Americans. The U.S. Asian American population is expected to more than double by 2050, when it will make up more than 9 percent of the U.S. population. Asian consumers may be the most tech savvy segment—more than a third made an Internet purchase last year. As a group, Asian consumers shop frequently and are the most brand-conscious of all the ethnic groups. Interestingly, they are also the least brand loyal—they change brands more often compared with the other groups.[10]

Because of the segment's rapidly growing buying power, many firms now target the Asian American market. For example, consider Wal-Mart. Today, in one Seattle store, where the Asian American population represents over 13 percent of the population, Wal-Mart stocks a large selection of CDs and videos from Asian artists, Asian-favored health and beauty products, and children's learning videos that feature multiple language tracks.

Financial services provider Charles Schwab also goes all out to court the lucrative Asian American investor market. Schwab has opened 14 Chinese-language offices in such places as New York's and San Francisco's Chinatowns and plans to add more. It employs more than 300 people who speak Chinese, Korean, or Vietnamese at call centers serving Asian American customers who prefer to speak their own languages. And Schwab's Chinese-language Web site racks up more than 5 million hits per month. The brokerage also maintains an online Chinese-language news service, where customers can check real-time market activity, news headlines, and earnings estimates. As a result of such efforts, Schwab's Asian American customers tend to be very loyal.[11]

MATURE CONSUMERS As the U.S. population ages, *mature consumers* are becoming a very attractive market. Now 75 million strong, the population of U.S. seniors will more than double during the next 25 years. The 65-and-over crowd alone numbers 36 million, more than 12 percent of the population. Mature consumers are better off financially than are younger consumer groups. Because mature consumers have more time and money, they are an ideal market for exotic travel, restaurants, high-tech home entertainment products, leisure goods and services, designer furniture and fashions, financial services, and health care services.[12]

Their desire to look as young as they feel also makes more-mature consumers good candidates for cosmetics and personal care products, health foods, fitness products, and other items that combat the effects of aging. The best strategy is to appeal to their active, multidimensional lives. For example, Kellogg aired a TV spot for All-Bran cereal in which individuals ranging in age from 53 to 81 are featured playing ice hockey, water skiing, running hurdles, and playing baseball, all to the tune of "Wild Thing." A recent Pepsi ad features a young

■ Financial services provider Charles Schwab goes all out to court the large and lucrative Chinese American market. It has opened 14 Chinese-language offices and its Chinese-language Web site racks up more than 5 million hits per month.

man in the middle of a mosh pit at a rock concert who turns around to see his father rocking out nearby. And an Aetna commercial portrays a senior who, after retiring from a career as a lawyer, fulfills a lifelong dream of becoming an archeologist.[13]

Social Class

Social classes

Relatively permanent and ordered divisions in a society whose members share similar values, interests, and behaviors.

Almost every society has some form of social class structure. **Social classes** are society's relatively permanent and ordered divisions whose members share similar values, interests, and behaviors. Social scientists have identified the seven American social classes shown in Figure 5.3.

Social class is not determined by a single factor, such as income, but is measured as a combination of occupation, income, education, wealth, and other variables. In some social systems, members of different classes are reared for certain roles and cannot change their social positions. In the United States, however, the lines between social classes are not fixed and rigid; people can move to a higher social class or drop into a lower one. Marketers are interested in social class because people within a given social class tend to exhibit similar buying behavior. Social classes show distinct product and brand preferences in areas such as clothing, home furnishings, leisure activity, and automobiles.[14]

Social Factors

A consumer's behavior also is influenced by social factors, such as the consumer's *small groups*, *family*, and *social roles* and *status*.

FIGURE 5.3
The major American social classes

Wealth · **Education** · **Occupation** · **Income**

Upper Class
Upper Uppers (1 percent) The social elite who live on inherited wealth. They give large sums to charity, own more than one home, and send their children to the finest schools.

Lower Uppers (2 percent) Americans who have earned high income or wealth through exceptional ability. They are active in social and civic affairs and buy expensive homes, educations, and cars.

Middle Class
Upper Middles (12 percent) Professionals, independent businesspersons, and corporate managers who possess neither family status nor unusual wealth. They believe in education, are joiners and highly civic minded, and want the "better things in life."

Middle Class (32 percent) Average-pay white- and blue-collar workers who live on "the better side of town." They buy popular products to keep up with trends. Better living means owning a nice home in a nice neighborhood with good schools.

Working Class
Working Class (38 percent) Those who lead a "working-class lifestyle," whatever their income, school background, or job. They depend heavily on relatives for economic and emotional support, for advice on purchases, and for assistance in times of trouble.

Lower Class
Upper Lowers (9 percent) The working poor. Although their living standard is just above poverty, they strive toward a higher class. However, they often lack education and are poorly paid for unskilled work.

Lower Lowers (7 percent) Visibly poor, often poorly educated unskilled laborers. They are often out of work and some depend on public assistance. They tend to live a day-to-day existence.

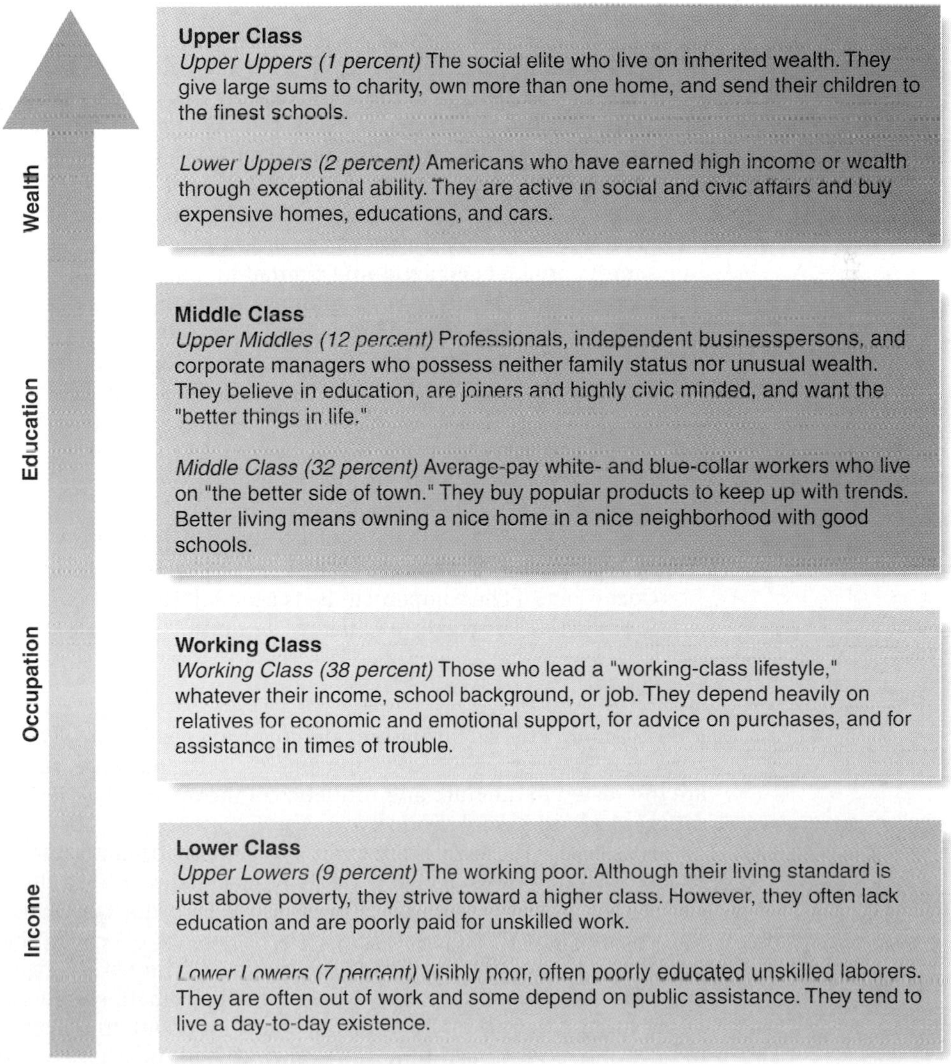

Groups

Group

Two or more people who interact to accomplish individual or mutual goals.

A person's behavior is influenced by many small **groups**. Groups that have a direct influence and to which a person belongs are called *membership groups*. In contrast, *reference groups* serve as direct (face-to-face) or indirect points of comparison or reference in forming a person's attitudes or behavior. People often are influenced by reference groups to which they do not belong. For example, an *aspirational group* is one to which the individual wishes to belong, as when a teenage basketball player hopes to play someday for the Los Angeles Lakers. Marketers try to identify the reference groups of their target markets. Reference groups expose a person to new behaviors and lifestyles, influence the person's attitudes and self-concept, and create pressures to conform that may affect the person's product and brand choices.

The importance of group influence varies across products and brands. It tends to be strongest when the product is visible to others whom the buyer respects. Manufacturers of products and brands subjected to strong group influence must figure out how to reach **opinion leaders**—people within a reference group who, because of special skills, knowledge, personality, or other characteristics, exert influence on others. One expert calls them *the influentials*. "They drive trends, influence mass opinion and, most importantly, sell a great many products," he says. "These are the early adopters who had a digital camera before everyone else and who were the first to fly again after September 11. They are the 10 percent of Americans who determine how the rest consume and live by chatting about their likes and dislikes."[15]

Opinion leader

Person within a reference group who, because of special skills, knowledge, personality, or other characteristics, exerts influence on others.

Many marketers try to identify opinion leaders for their products and direct marketing efforts toward them. They use *buzz marketing* by enlisting or even creating opinion leaders to spread the word about their brands. For example, one New York marketing firm, Big Fat Promotions, enlists bar "leaners" to talk casually with tavern patrons about merits of certain liquors, mothers to chat up new laundry products at their kids' little-league games, and commuters to play with new PDAs during the ride home.[16]

BzzAgent, a 2-year-old Boston marketing firm, takes a different approach to creating opinion leaders:

> BzzAgent has assembled a nationwide volunteer army of 25,000 natural-born buzzers, and will channel their chatter toward products and services they deem authentically worth talking about. "Our goal is to find a way to capture honest word of mouth," says David Baiter, BzzAgent's founder, "and to build a network that will turn passionate customers into brand evangelists." Once a client signs on, BzzAgent searches its database for "agents" matching the demographic and psychographic profile of target customers of the product or service. Selected volunteers receive a sample product and a training manual for buzz-creating strategies. These volunteers aren't just mall rats on cell phones. Some 65 percent are over 25, 60 percent are women, and two are Fortune 500 CEOs. They've buzzed products as diverse as Estee Lauder facial masks, Lee jeans, and Rock Bottom Restaurants. In Alabama, Bzzagent ArnoldGinger123 buttonholed her probation officer to chat up a tush-flattering new brand of jeans. In Illinois, Bzzagent GeminiDreams spent a family Christmas party extolling the features of Monster.com's new networking site. And, in an especially moving final tribute in New Jersey, Bzzagent Karnj buzzed her grandpa into the great beyond with a round of Anheuser World Select beer at the old gent's wake. The service's appeal is its authenticity. "What I like is that Bzzagents aren't scripted," says Steve Cook, vice president of worldwide strategic marketing at Coca-Cola. "[The company tells its agents,] 'Here's the information; if you believe in it, say whatever you think.' It's . . . genuine."[17]

Family

Family members can strongly influence buyer behavior. The family is the most important consumer buying organization in society, and it has been researched extensively. Marketers are interested in the roles and influence of the husband, wife, and children on the purchase of different products and services.

Husband-wife involvement varies widely by product category and by stage in the buying process. Buying roles change with evolving consumer lifestyles. In the United States, the wife traditionally has been the main purchasing agent for the family in the areas of food, household products, and clothing. But with 70 percent of women holding jobs outside the home and the willingness of husbands to do more of the family's purchasing, all this is changing. Whereas women make up just 40 percent of drivers, they now influence more than 80 percent of car-buying decisions. Men now account for about 40 percent of all food-shopping dollars. In all, women now make almost 85 percent of all purchases, spending $6 trillion each year.[18]

■ Opinion leaders: BzzAgent has assembled a nationwide volunteer army of 25,000 natural-born buzzers, and will channel their chatter toward products and services they deem authentically worth talking about.

Such changes suggest that marketers who've typically sold their products to only men or only women are now courting the opposite sex. For example, consider home improvement retailer Lowe's:

> War has broken out over your home-improvement dollar, and Lowe's has superpower Home Depot on the defensive. Its not-so-secret ploy: Lure women, because they'll drag their Tim Allen tool-guy husbands behind them. According to Lowe's research, women initiate 80 percent of all home-improvement purchase decisions, especially the big-ticket orders like kitchen cabinets, flooring, and bathrooms. And women appreciate Lowe's obsession with store aesthetics. Lowe's stores are bright and airy with wide, uncluttered aisles and supermarket-like signs that list what is in each aisle. Stack-outs, those pallets of merchandise set out on the floor in front of the main shelves, are banned. They add to revenue per square foot, but they also obstruct the aisles, triggering the dreaded "butt-brush" phenomenon: Female shoppers don't like to be touched by passersby. Pam and Shawn Panuline, a young North Carolina couple who just bought a three-bedroom home, have shopped the nearby Home Depot and Lowe's stores. For Pam, Lowe's felt friendlier and had far more choices in home decor, and she liked that it wasn't as contractor-oriented. "But it's not too froofy," says her husband. "We're always looking to improve the stores," says a spokeswoman, "and many of the changes have made a real difference in the way women see Lowe's."[19]

Children may also have a strong influence on family buying decisions. For example, children as young as age six may influence the family car purchase decision. Recognizing this fact, Toyota recently launched a new kid-focused ad campaign for its Sienna minivan. Whereas most other minivan ads have focused on soccer moms, the new Sienna ads show kids expressing what they want out of a minivan. In one spot, for example, engineers in Sienna's design center anxiously await what looks to be a shakedown by company big shots. Instead, in rush three little girls on bicycles who begin certain demanding features and offering other advice. "I want a hundred cup holders," says one. "Is 14 all right?" asks the engineer. The ad concludes: "Everything kids want. Everything you need."[20] The Sienna Web site adds: "Happiness is hereditary—you get it from your kids!"

Roles and Status

A person belongs to many groups—family, clubs, organizations. The person's position in each group can be defined in terms of both role and status. A *role* consists of the activities people are expected to perform according to the persons around them. Each role carries a *status* reflecting the general esteem given to it by society.

■ Family buying influences: Lowe's targets women shoppers, who initiate 80 percent of all home-improvement decisions. "Lure women, and they'll drag their Tim Allen tool guy husbands behind them."

People usually choose products appropriate to their roles and status. Consider the various roles a working mother plays. In her company, she plays the role of a brand manager; in her family, she plays the role of wife and mother; at her favorite sporting events, she plays the role of avid fan. As a brand manager, she will buy the kind of clothing that reflects her role and status in her company.

Personal Factors

A buyer's decisions also are influenced by personal characteristics such as the buyer's *age* and *life-cycle stage, occupation, economic situation, lifestyle,* and *personality* and *self-concept.*

Age and Life-Cycle Stage

People change the goods and services they buy over their lifetimes. Tastes in food, clothes, furniture, and recreation are often age related. Buying is also shaped by the stage of the *family life cycle*—the stages through which families might pass as they mature over time. Marketers often define their target markets in terms of life-cycle stage and develop appropriate products and marketing plans for each stage.

Traditional family life-cycle stages include young singles and married couples with children. Today, however, marketers are increasingly catering to a growing number of alternative, nontraditional stages such as unmarried couples, singles marrying later in life, childless couples, same-sex couples, single parents, extended parents (those with young adult children returning home), and others.

Sony recently overhauled its marketing approach in order to target products and services to consumers based on their life stages. It created a new unit called the Consumer Segment Marketing Division, which has identified seven life-stage segments. They include, among others, Gen Y (under 25), Young Professionals/D.I.N.K.s (double income no kids, 25 to 34), Families (35 to 54), and Zoomers (55 and over). A recent Sony ad aimed at Zoomers, people who have just retired or are close to doing so, shows a man living his dream by going into outer space. The ad deals not just with going into retirement, but with the psychological life-stage changes that go with it. "The goal is to get closer to consumers," says a Sony segment marketing executive.[21]

Occupation

A person's occupation affects the goods and services bought. Blue-collar workers tend to buy more rugged work clothes, whereas executives buy more business suits. Marketers try to identify the occupational groups that have an above-average interest in their products and services. A company can even specialize in making products needed by a given occupational group.

For example, Carhartt makes rugged, durable, no nonsense work clothes—what it calls "original equipment for the American worker. From coats to jackets, bibs to overalls . . . if the apparel carries the name Carhartt, the performance will be legendary." Its Web site carries real-life testimonials of hard-working Carhartt customers. One electrician, battling the cold in Canada's arctic region, reports wearing Carhartt's lined Arctic bib overalls, Arctic jacket, and other clothing for more than 2 years without a single "popped button, ripped pocket seam, or stuck zipper." And an animal trainer in California says of his favorite pair of Carhartt jeans: "Not only did they keep me warm but they stood up to one playful lion and her very sharp claws."[22]

Economic Situation

A person's economic situation will affect product choice. Marketers of income-sensitive goods watch trends in personal income, savings, and interest rates. If economic indicators point to a recession, marketers can take steps to redesign, reposition, and reprice their products closely. Some marketers target consumers who have lots of money and resources, charging prices to match. For example, Rolex positions it luxury watches as "a tribute to elegance, and object of passion, a symbol for all time." Other marketers target consumers with more modest means. Timex makes more affordable watches that "take a licking and keep on ticking."

■ Occupation: Carhartt makes rugged, durable, no nonsense work cloths—what it calls "original equipment for the American worker."

Lifestyle

Lifestyle
A person's pattern of living as expressed in his or her activities, interests, and opinions.

People coming from the same subculture, social class, and occupation may have quite different lifestyles. **Lifestyle** is a person's pattern of living as expressed in his or her *psychographics*. It involves measuring consumers' major *AIO dimensions—activities* (work, hobbies, shopping, sports, social events), *interests* (food, fashion, family, recreation), and *opinions* (about themselves, social issues, business, products). Lifestyle captures something more than the person's social class or personality. It profiles a person's whole pattern of acting and interacting in the world.

Several research firms have developed lifestyle classifications. The most widely used is the SRI Consulting's *Values and Lifestyles (VALS)* typology (see Figure 5.4). VALS classifies people according to how they spend their time and money. It divides consumers into eight groups based on two major dimensions: primary motivation and resources. *Primary motivations* include ideals, achievement, and self-expression. According to SRI Consulting, consumers who are primarily motivated by ideals are guided by knowledge and principles. Consumers who are primarily motivated by *achievement* look for products and services that demonstrate success to their peers. Consumers who are primarily motivated by *self-expression* desire social or physical activity, variety, and risk.

Consumers within each orientation are further classified into those with *high resources* and those with *low resources*, depending on whether they have high or low levels of income, education, health, self-confidence, energy, and other factors. Consumers with either very high or very low levels of resources are classified without regard to their primary motivations (Innovators, Survivors). Innovators are people with so many resources that they exhibit all three primary motivations in varying degrees. In contrast, Survivors are people with so few resources that they do not show a strong primary motivation. They must focus on meeting needs rather than fulfilling desires.

FIGURE 5.4
VALS™ lifestyle classifications

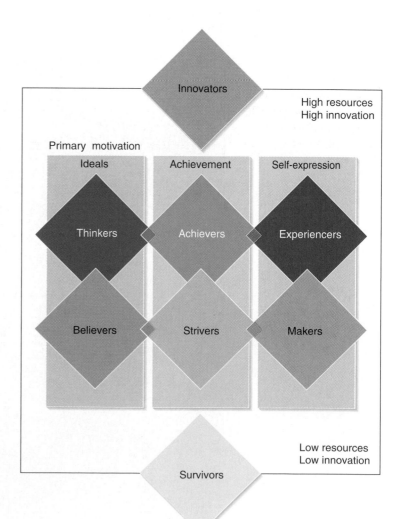

Iron City beer, a well-known brand in Pittsburgh, used VALS to update its image and improve sales. Iron City was losing sales—its aging core users were drinking less beer, and younger men weren't buying the brand. VALS research showed that one VALS segment, male Experiencers, drink the most beer, followed by Strivers. Men in these segments perceived Iron City drinkers as blue-collar steelworkers stopping off at the local bar. However, they saw themselves as more modern, hardworking, and fun loving. They strongly rejected the out-moded, heavy-industry image of Pittsburgh. Based on this research, Iron City created ads link-ing its beer to the new self-image of target consumers. The ads mingled images of the old Pittsburgh with those of the new, dynamic city and scenes of young Experiencers and strivers having fun and working hard. Within just 1 month of the start of the campaign, Iron City sales shot up by 26 percent.[23]

Lifestyle segmentation can also be used to understand how consumers use the Internet, computers, and other technology. Forrester developed its "Technographics" scheme, which segments consumers according to motivation, desire, and ability to invest in technology. The framework splits people into 10 categories, such as:[24]

- *Fast Forwards:* the biggest spenders on computer technology. Fast Forwards are career focused, time-strapped, driven, and top users of technology.
- *New Age Nurturers:* also big spenders. However, they are focused on technology for home uses, such as family education and entertainment.
- *Mouse Potatoes:* consumers who are dedicated to interactive entertainment and willing to spend for the latest in "technotainment."
- *Techno-Strivers:* consumers who are up-and-coming believers in technology for career advancement.
- *Traditionalists:* small-town folks, suspicious of technology beyond the basics.

- Lifestyles: To promote a new image, Iron City beer ads mingled images of the old Pittsburgh with those of the new, dynamic city and scenes of young Experiencers and Strivers having fun and working hard.

Delta Airlines used Technographics to better target online ticket sales. It created marketing campaigns for time-strapped Fast Forwards and New Age Nurturers, and eliminated Technology Pessimists (those skeptical of technology) from its list of targets. When used carefully, the lifestyle concept can help marketers understand changing consumer values and how they affect buying behavior.

Personality and Self-Concept

Personality

The unique psychological characteristics that lead to relatively consistent and lasting responses to one's own environment.

Each person's distinct personality influences his or her buying behavior. **Personality** refers to the unique psychological characteristics that lead to relatively consistent and lasting responses to one's own environment. Personality is usually described in terms of traits such as self-confidence, dominance, sociability, autonomy, defensiveness, adaptability, and aggressiveness. Personality can be useful in analyzing consumer behavior for certain product or brand choices. For example, coffee marketers have discovered that heavy coffee drinkers tend to be high on sociability. Thus, to attract customers, Starbucks and other coffeehouses create environments in which people can relax and socialize over a cup of steaming coffee.

The idea is that brands also have personalities, and that consumers are likely to choose brands whose personalities match their own. A *brand personality* is the specific mix of human traits that may be attributed to a particular brand. One researcher identified five brand personality traits:[25]

1. Sincerity (down-to-earth, honest, wholesome, and cheerful)
2. Excitement (daring, spirited, imaginative, and up-to-date)
3. Competence (reliable, intelligent, and successful)
4. Sophistication (upper class and charming)
5. Ruggedness (outdoorsy and tough)

The researcher found that a number of well-known brands tended to be strongly associated with one particular trait: Levi's with "ruggedness," MTV with "excitement," CNN with "competence," and Campbell's with "sincerity." Hence, these brands will attract persons who are high on the same personality traits.

Many marketers use a concept related to personality—a person's *self-concept* (also called *self-image*). The basic self-concept premise is that people's possessions contribute to and reflect their identities; that is, "we are what we have." Thus, in order to understand consumer behavior, the marketer must first understand the relationship between consumer self-concept and possessions.

Psychological Factors

A person's buying choices are further influenced by four major psychological factors: *motivation*, *perception*, *learning*, and *beliefs and attitudes*.

Motivation

Motive (drive)

A need that is sufficiently pressing to direct the person to seek satisfaction of the need.

A person has many needs at any given time. Some are *biological*, arising from states of tension such as hunger, thirst, or discomfort. Others are *psychological*, arising from the need for recognition, esteem, or belonging. A need becomes a *motive* when it is aroused to a sufficient level of intensity. A **motive** (or ***drive***) is a need that is sufficiently pressing to direct the person to seek satisfaction. Psychologists have developed theories of human motivation. Two of the most popular—the theories of Sigmund Freud and Abraham Maslow—have quite different meanings for consumer analysis and marketing.

Sigmund Freud assumed that people are largely unconscious about the real psychological forces shaping their behavior. He saw the person as growing up and repressing many urges. These urges are never eliminated or under perfect control; they emerge in dreams, in slips of the tongue, in neurotic and obsessive behavior, or ultimately in psychoses.

Freud's theory suggests that a person's buying decisions are affected by subconscious motives that even the buyer may not fully understand. Thus, an aging baby boomer who buys a sporty BMW 330Ci convertible might explain that he simply likes the feel of the wind in his thinning hair. At a deeper level, he may be trying to impress others with his success. At a still deeper level, he may be buying the car to feel young and independent again.

■ Brand personality: Well-known brands tend to be strongly associated with one particular trait: CNN stands for confidence and trust.

The term *motivation research* refers to qualitative research designed to probe consumers' hidden, subconscious motivations. Motivation researchers collect in-depth information from small samples of consumers to uncover the deeper motives for their product choices. The techniques range from sentence completion, word association, and inkblot or cartoon interpretation tests, to having consumers describe typical brand users or form daydreams and fantasies about brands or buying situations (see Real Marketing 5.1).

Many companies employ teams of psychologists, anthropologists, and other social scientists to carry out motivation research. One agency routinely conducts one-on-one, therapy-like interviews to delve into the inner workings of consumers. Another agency asks consumers to describe their favorite brands as animals or cars (say, Cadillacs versus Chevrolets) in order to assess the prestige associated with various brands. Still another agency has consumers draw figures of typical brand users. In one case, the agency asked 50 participants to sketch likely buyers of two different brands of cake mixes. Consistently, the group portrayed Pillsbury customers as apron-clad, grandmotherly types, whereas they pictured Duncan Hines purchasers as svelte, contemporary women.

Abraham Maslow sought to explain why people are driven by particular needs at particular times. Why does one person spend much time and energy on personal safety and another on gaining the esteem of others? Maslow's answer is that human needs are arranged in a hierarchy, as shown in Figure 5.5, from the most pressing at the bottom to the least pressing at the top. They include *physiological* needs, *safety* needs, *social* needs, *esteem* needs, and *self-actualization* needs.

A person tries to satisfy the most important need first. When that need is satisfied, it will stop being a motivator and the person will then try to satisfy the next most important need. For example, starving people (physiological need) will not take an interest in the latest happenings in the art world (self-actualization needs), nor in how they are seen or esteemed by others (social or esteem needs), nor even in whether they are breathing clean

Real Marketing 5.1

"Touchy-Feely" Research: Psyching Out Consumers

Consumers often don't know or can't describe just why they act as they do. Thus, motivation researchers use a variety of probing techniques to uncover underlying emotions and attitudes toward brands and buying situations. These sometimes bizarre techniques range from free association and inkblot interpretation tests to having consumers form daydreams and fantasies about brands or buying situations. One writer offers the following tongue-in-cheek summary of a motivation research session:

> Good morning, ladies and gentlemen. We've called you here today for a little consumer research. Now, lie down on the couch, toss your inhibitions out the window, and let's try a little free association. First, think about brands as if they were your *friends*. Imagine you could talk to your TV dinner. What would he say? And what would you say to him? . . . Now, think of your shampoo as an animal. Go on, don't be shy. Would it be a panda or a lion? A snake or a wooly worm? For our final exercise, let's all sit up and pull out our magic markers. Draw a picture of a typical cake-mix user. Would she wear an apron or a negligee? A business suit or a can-can dress?

Such projective techniques seem pretty goofy. But more and more, marketers are using such touchy-feely approaches to dig deeply into consumer psyches and develop better marketing strategies. For example, Shell Oil used motivation research in an attempt to uncover the real reasons behind a decade-long sales slump:

> The manager of corporate advertising for Shell Oil, Sixtus Oeschle, was at his wits' end. For months, he and his team of researchers had pumped the consumer psyche. For months, they'd come up empty. "We tried psychographic memory triggers," he recalls. "We tried dream therapy." All to no avail. At one point, respondents were even given mounds of wet clay and urged to mold figures that expressed their inner feelings about Shell.
>
> It was time, Oeschle decided, to try something radical. To craft a more potent appeal for its brand of gasoline, Shell would have to go deeper—much deeper. Oeschle called in a consumer researcher who specializes in focus groups conducted under hypnosis. The results, Oeschle says, wowed even the skeptics. "I've got to tell you, it was fascinating, fascinating stuff," he says. After dimming the lights, the researcher took respondents back, back—back all the way to their infancy. "He just kept taking them back and back," Oeschle says, "until . . . he's saying, 'Tell me about your first experience in a gas station.' And people were actually having memory flashbacks. I mean, they were going there. They were saying, 'I was three-and-a half years old. I was in the back of my dad's brand new Chevy.' It was like it was yesterday to them. I was stunned."
>
> The real breakthrough, however, came after the respondents awoke out of their trance. "When he brought them all back out, he asked them who'd they prefer as a gasoline purveyor," Oeschle says. "What staggered me was that, to a person, it was always linked to that experience in their youth." One woman volunteered that she always made a point of fill-

■ Motivation research: Shell designed new marketing approaches based on the insights gleaned from groups of mesmerized motorists, whose current feelings about gas stations spring from early childhood experiences.

ing up at Texaco. "We asked her why," Oeschle recalls. "And she said, 'I don't know, I guess I just feel good about Texaco.' Well, this was the little three-and-a-half-year-old in the back of her daddy's car speaking."

Shell is now designing new marketing approaches based on the insights gleaned from the groups of mesmerized motorists. Where Shell had gone wrong, it seems, was in reasoning that, since people don't start buying gas until at least age 16, there was no need to target the tiniest consumers. "They weren't even on Shell's radar," Oeschle laments. "It dawned on us . . . that we'd better figure out how to favorably impact people from an early age."

Some marketers dismiss such motivation research as mumbo jumbo. However, like Shell, many companies are now delving into the murky depths of the consumer unconscious. "Such tactics have been worshipfully embraced by even the no-nonsense, jut-jawed captains of industry," claims an analyst. "At companies like Kraft, Coca-Cola, Procter & Gamble, and DaimlerChrysler, the most sought-after consultants hail not from [traditional consulting firms like McKinsey. They come] from brand consultancies with names like Archetype Discoveries, PsychoLogics, and Semiotic Solutions."

Sources: Examples and quotes from Ruth Shalit, "The Return of the Hidden Persuaders," Salon Media, September 27, 1999, accessed online at www.salon.com; Annetta Miller and Dody Tsiantar, "Psyching Out Consumers," *Newsweek*, February 27, 1989, pp. 46–47; Alison Stein Wellner, "Research on a Shoestring," *American Demographics,* April 2001, pp. 38–39; and "Taste—Review & Outlook: Sweet 16," *Wall Street Journal,* January 24, 2003, p. W13. Also see Leon G. Schiffman and Leslie L. Kanuk, *Consumer Behavior,* 8th ed. (Upper Saddle River, NJ: 2004), chapter 4.

FIGURE 5.5
Maslow's hierarchy of needs
Source: From Motivation and
Personality *by Abraham
H. Maslow. Copyright © 1970
by Abraham H. Maslow.
Copyright 1954, 1987 by
Harper & Row Publishers, Inc.
Reprinted by permission of
Addison-Wesley Educational
Publishers Inc. Also see
Barbara Marx Hubbard,
"Seeking Our Future
Potentials,"* The Futurist, *May
1998, pp. 29–32.*

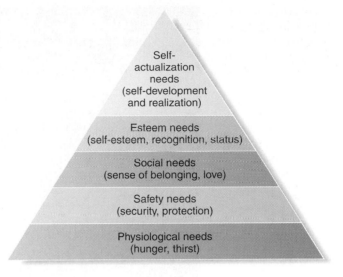

air (safety needs). But as each important need is satisfied, the next most important need will come into play.

Perception

A motivated person is ready to act. How the person acts is influenced by his or her own perception of the situation. All of us learn by the flow of information through our five senses: sight, hearing, smell, touch, and taste. However, each of us receives, organizes, and interprets this sensory information in an individual way. **Perception** is the process by which people select, organize, and interpret information to form a meaningful picture of the world.

Perception

The process by which people select, organize, and interpret information to form a meaningful picture of the world.

People can form different perceptions of the same stimulus because of three perceptual processes: selective attention, selective distortion, and selective retention. People are exposed to a great amount of stimuli every day. For example, one analyst estimates that people are exposed to about 5,000 ads every day.[26] It is impossible for a person to pay attention to all these stimuli. *Selective attention*—the tendency for people to screen out most of the information to which they are exposed—means that marketers have to work especially hard to attract the consumer's attention.

Even noticed stimuli do not always come across in the intended way. Each person fits incoming information into an existing mind-set. *Selective distortion* describes the tendency of people to interpret information in a way that will support what they already believe. For example, if you distrust a company, you might perceive even honest ads from the company as questionable. Selective distortion means that marketers must try to understand the mind-sets of consumers and how these will affect interpretations of advertising and sales information.

People also will forget much that they learn. They tend to retain information that supports their attitudes and beliefs. Because of *selective retention*, consumers are likely to remember good points made about a brand they favor and to forget good points made about competing brands. Because of selective exposure, distortion, and retention, marketers have to work hard to get their messages through. This fact explains why marketers use so much drama and repetition in sending messages to their market.

Interestingly, although most marketers worry about whether their offers will be perceived at all, some consumers worry that they will be affected by marketing messages without even knowing it—through *subliminal advertising*. In 1957, a researcher announced that he had flashed the phrases "Eat popcorn" and "Drink Coca-Cola" on a screen in a New Jersey movie theater every five seconds for 1/300th of a second. He reported that although viewers did not consciously recognize these messages, they absorbed them subconsciously and bought 58 percent more popcorn and 18 percent more Coke. Suddenly advertisers and consumer-protection groups became intensely interested in subliminal perception. People voiced fears of being brainwashed, and California and Canada declared the practice illegal. Although the researcher later admitted to making up the data, the issue has not died. Some consumers still fear that they are being manipulated by subliminal messages.

Numerous studies by psychologists and consumer researchers have found no link between subliminal messages and consumer behavior. It appears that subliminal advertising

■ Selective perception: It's impossible for people to pay attention to the thousands of ads they're exposed to every day, so they screen most of them out.

simply doesn't have the power attributed to it by its critics. Most advertisers scoff at the notion of an industry conspiracy to manipulate consumers through "invisible" messages. Says one industry insider: "[Some consumers believe we are] wizards who can manipulate them at will. Ha! Snort! Oh my sides! As we know, just between us, most of [us] have difficulty getting a 2 percent increase in sales with the help of $50 million in media and extremely liminal images of sex, money, power, and other [motivators] of human emotion. The very idea of [us] as puppeteers, cruelly pulling the strings of consumer marionettes, is almost too much to bear."[27]

Learning

Learning
Changes in an individual's behavior arising from experience.

When people act, they learn. **Learning** describes changes in an individual's behavior arising from experience. Learning theorists say that most human behavior is learned. Learning occurs through the interplay of *drives*, *stimuli*, *cues*, *responses*, and *reinforcement*.

A *drive* is a strong internal stimulus that calls for action. A drive becomes a motive when it is directed toward a particular *stimulus object*. For example, a person's drive for self-actualization might motivate him or her to look into buying a digital camera. The consumer's response to the idea of buying a camera is conditioned by the surrounding cues. *Cues* are minor stimuli that determine when, where, and how the person responds. For example, the person might spot several camera brands in a shop window, hearing of a special sale price, or discuss cameras with a friend. These are all cues that might influence a consumer's *response* to his or her interest in buying the product.

Suppose the consumer buys a Nikon digital camera. If the experience is rewarding, the consumer will probably use the camera more and more, and his or her response will be *reinforced*. Then, the next time the consumer shops for a camera, or for binoculars or some similar product, the probability is greater that he or she will buy a Nikon product. The practical significance of learning theory for marketers is that they can build up demand for a product by associating it with strong drives, using motivating cues, and providing positive reinforcement.

Beliefs and Attitudes

Belief
A descriptive thought that a person holds about something.

Through doing and learning, people acquire beliefs and attitudes. These, in turn, influence their buying behavior. A **belief** is a descriptive thought that a person has about something. Beliefs may be based on real knowledge, opinion, or faith, and may or may not carry an emotional charge. Marketers are interested in the beliefs that people formulate about specific products and services, because these beliefs make up product and brand images that affect buying behavior. If some of the beliefs are wrong and prevent purchase, the marketer will want to launch a campaign to correct them.

Attitude
A person's consistently favorable or unfavorable evaluations, feelings, and tendencies toward an object or idea.

People have attitudes regarding religion, politics, clothes, music, food, and almost everything else. **Attitude** describes a person's relatively consistent evaluations, feelings, and tendencies toward an object or idea. Attitudes put people into a frame of mind of liking or disliking things, of moving toward or away from them. Our digital camera buyer may hold attitudes such as "Buy the best," "The Japanese make the best electronics products in the world," and "Creativity and self-expression are among the most important things in life." If so, the Nikon camera would fit well into the consumer's existing attitudes.

Attitudes are difficult to change. A person's attitudes fit into a pattern, and to change one attitude may require difficult adjustments in many others. Thus, a company should usually try to fit its products into existing attitudes rather than attempt to change attitudes. Of course, there are exceptions in which the cost of trying to change attitudes may pay off handsomely:

> By 1994, milk consumption had been in decline for 20 years. The general perception was that milk was unhealthy, outdated, just for kids, or good only with cookies and cake. To counter these notions, the National Fluid Milk Processors Education Program (MilkPEP) began an ad campaign featuring milk be-mustached celebrities and the tag line Got Milk? The campaign has not only been wildly popular, it has been successful as well—not only did it stop the decline, milk consumption actually increased. The campaign is still running. Although initially the target market was women in their 20s, the campaign has been expanded to other target markets and has gained cult status with teens, much to their parents' delight. Teens collect the print ads featuring celebrities ranging from music stars Hanson and LeAnn Rimes, supermodel Tyra Banks, Kermit the Frog, and Garfield to sports idols such as Jeff Gordon, Mia Hamm, and Venus and Serena Williams. Building on this popularity with teens, the industry set up a Web site (www.whymilk.com) where young folks can make their own mustache, check out the latest Got Milk? ads, or get facts about "everything you ever need to know about milk." The industry also promotes milk to them through grass roots marketing efforts. It recently launched a traveling

■ Attitudes are difficult to change, but the National Fluid Milk Processor's wildly popular milk moustache campaign succeeded in changing attitudes toward milk.

promotion event searching for the best teen bands and dancers. The best band will receive a recording contract, and the most talented dancer will spend next summer at the MTV Beach House. Teens can also enter a contest to sport a milk mustache in *Rolling Stone* magazine alongside a famous musician, and then follow the celebrity for a day as a roadie.[28]

We can now appreciate the many forces acting on consumer behavior. The consumer's choice results from the complex interplay of cultural, social, personal, and psychological factors.

Types of Buying Decision Behavior

Buying behavior differs greatly for a tube of toothpaste, a tennis racket, financial services, and a new car. More complex decisions usually involve more buying participants and more buyer deliberation. Figure 5.6 shows types of consumer buyer behavior based on the degree of buyer involvement and the degree of differences among brands.[29]

Complex Buying Behavior

Complex buying behavior
Consumer buying behavior in situations characterized by high consumer involvement in a purchase and significant perceived differences among brands.

Consumers undertake **complex buying behavior** when they are highly involved in a purchase and perceive significant differences among brands. Consumers may be highly involved when the product is expensive, risky, purchased infrequently, and highly self-expressive. Typically, the consumer has much to learn about the product category. For example, a personal computer buyer may not know what attributes to consider. Many product features carry no real meaning: a "3.4GHz Pentium processor," "super VGA resolution," or "2GB SDRAM memory."

This buyer will pass through a learning process, first developing beliefs about the product, then attitudes, and then making a thoughtful purchase choice. Marketers of high-involvement products must understand the information-gathering and evaluation behavior of high-involvement consumers. They need to help buyers learn about product-class attributes and their relative importance. They need to differentiate their brand's features, perhaps by describing the brand's benefits using print media with long copy. They must motivate store salespeople and the buyer's acquaintances to influence the final brand choice.

Dissonance-Reducing Buying Behavior

Dissonance-reducing buying behavior
Consumer buying behavior in situations characterized by high involvement but few perceived differences among brands.

Dissonance-reducing buying behavior occurs when consumers are highly involved with an expensive, infrequent, or risky purchase, but see little difference among brands. For example, consumers buying carpeting may face a high-involvement decision because carpeting is expensive and self-expressive. Yet buyers may consider most carpet brands in a given price range to be the same. In this case, because perceived brand differences are not large, buyers may shop around to learn what is available, but buy relatively quickly. They may respond primarily to a good price or to purchase convenience.

After the purchase, consumers might experience *postpurchase dissonance* (after-sale discomfort) when they notice certain disadvantages of the purchased carpet brand or hear favor-

FIGURE 5.6
Four types of buying behavior
Source: Adapted from Henry Assael, Consumer Behavior and Marketing Action *(Boston: Kent Publishing Company, 1987), p.87. Copyright © 1987 by Wadsworth, Inc. Printed by permission of Kent Publishing Company, a division of Wadsworth, Inc.*

	High involvement	Low involvement
Significant differences between brands	Complex buying behavior	Variety-seeking buying behavior
Few differences between brands	Dissonance-reducing buying behavior	Habitual buying behavior

able things about brands not purchased. To counter such dissonance, the marketer's after-sale communications should provide evidence and support to help consumers feel good about their brand choices.

Habitual Buying Behavior

Habitual buying behavior
Consumer buying behavior in situations characterized by low consumer involvement and few significant perceived brand differences.

Habitual buying behavior occurs under conditions of low consumer involvement and little significant brand difference. For example, take salt. Consumers have little involvement in this product category—they simply go to the store and reach for a brand. If they keep reaching for the same brand, it is out of habit rather than strong brand loyalty. Consumers appear to have low involvement with most low-cost, frequently purchased products.

In such cases, consumer behavior does not pass through the usual belief-attitude-behavior sequence. Consumers do not search extensively for information about the brands, evaluate brand characteristics, and make weighty decisions about which brands to buy. Instead, they passively receive information as they watch television or read magazines. Ad repetition creates *brand familiarity* rather than *brand conviction*. Consumers do not form strong attitudes toward a brand; they select the brand because it is familiar. Because they are not highly involved with the product, consumers may not evaluate the choice even after purchase. Thus, the buying process involves brand beliefs formed by passive learning, followed by purchase behavior, which may or may not be followed by evaluation.

Because buyers are not highly committed to any brands, marketers of low-involvement products with few brand differences often use price and sales promotions to stimulate product trial. In advertising for a low-involvement product, ad copy should stress only a few key points. Visual symbols and imagery are important because they can be remembered easily and associated with the brand. Ad campaigns should include high repetition of short-duration messages. Television is usually more effective than print media because it is a low-involvement medium suitable for passive learning. Advertising planning should be based on classical conditioning theory, in which buyers learn to identify a certain product by a symbol repeatedly attached to it.

Variety-Seeking Buying Behavior

Variety-seeking buying behavior
Consumer buying behavior in situations characterized by low consumer involvement but significant perceived brand differences.

Consumers undertake **variety-seeking buying behavior** in situations characterized by low consumer involvement but significant perceived brand differences. In such cases, consumers often do a lot of brand switching. For example, when buying cookies, a consumer may hold some beliefs, choose a cookie brand without much evaluation, then evaluate that brand during consumption. But the next time, the consumer might pick another brand out of boredom or simply to try something different. Brand switching occurs for the sake of variety rather than because of dissatisfaction.

In such product categories, the marketing strategy may differ for the market leader and minor brands. The market leader will try to encourage habitual buying behavior by dominating shelf space, keeping shelves fully stocked, and running frequent reminder advertising. Challenger firms will encourage variety seeking by offering lower prices, special deals, coupons, free samples, and advertising that presents reasons for trying something new.

The Buyer Decision Process

Now that we have looked at the influences that affect buyers, we are ready to look at how consumers make buying decisions. Figure 5.7 shows that the buyer decision process consists of five stages: *need recognition, information search, evaluation of alternatives, purchase decision,* and *postpurchase behavior.* Clearly, the buying process starts long before actual purchase and continues long after. Marketers need to focus on the entire buying process rather than on just the purchase decision.

The figure suggests that consumers pass through all five stages with every purchase. But in more routine purchases, consumers often skip or reverse some of these stages. A woman buying her regular brand of toothpaste would recognize the need and go right to the purchase decision,

FIGURE 5.7
Buyer decision process

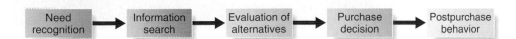

skipping information search and evaluation. However, we use the model in Figure 5.7 because it shows all the considerations that arise when a consumer faces a new and complex purchase situation.

① Need Recognition

Need recognition
The first stage of the buyer decision process, in which the consumer recognizes a problem or need.

The buying process starts with **need recognition**—the buyer recognizes a problem or need. The need can be triggered by *internal stimuli* when one of the person's normal needs—hunger, thirst, sex—rises to a level high enough to become a drive. A need can also be triggered by *external stimuli*. For example, an advertisement or a discussion with a friend might get you thinking about buying a new car. At this stage, the marketer should research consumers to find out what kinds of needs or problems arise, what brought them about, and how they led the consumer to this particular product.

② Information Search

Information search
The stage of the buyer decision process in which the consumer is aroused to search for more information; the consumer may simply have heightened attention or may go into active information search.

An interested consumer may or may not search for more information. If the consumer's drive is strong and a satisfying product is near at hand, the consumer is likely to buy it then. If not, the consumer may store the need in memory or undertake an **information search** related to the need. For example, once you've decided you need a new car, at the least, you will probably pay more attention to car ads, cars owned by friends, and car conversations. Or you may actively look for reading material, phone friends, and gather information in other ways. The amount of searching you do will depend on the strength of your drive, the amount of information you start with, the ease of obtaining more information, the value you place on additional information, and the satisfaction you get from searching.

■ Need recognition can be triggered by advertising. This ad from America's Dairy Farmers alerts consumers of their need for more dairy products to build strong bones.

Having three servings of dairy products a day is a deliciously simple way to get more calcium. And calcium, as we all know, helps make bones stronger. It's worth eating up.

www.3aday.org

Consumers can obtain information from any of several sources. These include *personal sources* (family, friends, neighbors, acquaintances), *commercial sources* (advertising, sales-people, dealers, packaging, displays), *public sources* (mass media, consumer-rating organizations), and *experiential sources* (handling, examining, using the product). The relative influence of these information sources varies with the product and the buyer. Generally, the consumer receives the most information about a product from commercial sources—those controlled by the marketer. The most effective sources, however, tend to be personal. Commercial sources normally *inform* the buyer, but personal sources *legitimize* or *evaluate* products for the buyer.

As more information is obtained, the consumer's awareness and knowledge of the available brands and features increase. In your car information search, you may learn about the several brands available. The information might also help you to drop certain brands from consideration. A company must design its marketing mix to make prospects aware of and knowledgeable about its brand. It should carefully identify consumers' sources of information and the importance of each source.

Evaluation of Alternatives

Alternative evaluation
The stage of the buyer decision process in which the consumer uses information to evaluate alternative brands in the choice set.

We have seen how the consumer uses information to arrive at a set of final brand choices. How does the consumer choose among the alternative brands? The marketer needs to know about **alternative evaluation**—that is, how the consumer processes information to arrive at brand choices. Unfortunately, consumers do not use a simple and single evaluation process in all buying situations. Instead, several evaluation processes are at work.

The consumer arrives at attitudes toward different brands through some evaluation procedure. How consumers go about evaluating purchase alternatives depends on the individual consumer and the specific buying situation. In some cases, consumers use careful calculations and logical thinking. At other times, the same consumers do little or no evaluating; instead they buy on impulse and rely on intuition. Sometimes consumers make buying decisions on their own; sometimes they turn to friends, consumer guides, or salespeople for buying advice.

Suppose you've narrowed your car choices to three brands. And suppose that you are primarily interested in four attributes—styling, operating economy, warranty, and price. By this time, you've probably formed beliefs about how each brand rates on each attribute. Clearly, if one car rated best on all the attributes, we could predict that you would choose it. However, the brands will no doubt vary in appeal. You might base your buying decision on only one attribute, and your choice would be easy to predict. If you wanted styling above everything else, you would buy the car that you think has the best styling. But most buyers consider several attributes, each with different importance. If we knew the importance weights that you assigned to each of the four attributes, we could predict your car choice more reliably.

Marketers should study buyers to find out how they actually evaluate brand alternatives. If they know what evaluative processes go on, marketers can take steps to influence the buyer's decision.

④ Purchase Decision

Purchase decision
The buyer's decision about which brand to purchase.

In the evaluation stage, the consumer ranks brands and forms purchase intentions. Generally, the consumer's **purchase decision** will be to buy the most preferred brand, but two factors can come between the purchase *intention* and the purchase *decision*. The first factor is the *attitudes of others*. If someone important to you thinks that you should buy the lowest-priced car, then the chances of your buying a more expensive car are reduced.

The second factor is *unexpected situational factors*. The consumer may form a purchase intention based on factors such as expected income, expected price, and expected product benefits. However, unexpected events may change the purchase intention. For example, the economy might take a turn for the worse, a close competitor might drop its price, or a friend might report being disappointed in your preferred car. Thus, preferences and even purchase intentions do not always result in actual purchase choice.

Postpurchase behavior
The stage of the buyer decision process in which consumers take further action after purchase, based on their satisfaction or dissatisfaction.

⑤ Postpurchase Behavior

The marketer's job does not end when the product is bought. After purchasing the product, the consumer will be satisfied or dissatisfied and will engage in **postpurchase behavior** of interest to the marketer. What determines whether the buyer is satisfied or dissatisfied with a purchase? The answer lies in the relationship between the *consumer's expectations* and the product's *perceived performance*. If the product falls short of expectations, the consumer is disappointed; if it meets expectations, the consumer is satisfied; if it exceeds expectations, the consumer is delighted.

The larger the gap between expectations and performance, the greater the consumer's dissatisfaction. This suggests that sellers should promise only what their brands can deliver so that buyers are satisfied. Some sellers might even understate product performance levels to boost later consumer satisfaction. For example, Boeing's salespeople tend to be conservative when they estimate the potential benefits of their aircraft. They almost always underestimate fuel efficiency—they promise a 5 percent savings that turns out to be 8 percent. Customers are delighted with better-than-expected performance; they buy again and tell other potential customers that Boeing lives up to its promises.

Cognitive dissonance
Buyer discomfort caused by postpurchase conflict.

Almost all major purchases result in **cognitive dissonance**, or discomfort caused by postpurchase conflict. After the purchase, consumers are satisfied with the benefits of the chosen brand and are glad to avoid the drawbacks of the brands not bought. However, every purchase involves compromise. Consumers feel uneasy about acquiring the drawbacks of the chosen brand and about losing the benefits of the brands not purchased. Thus, consumers feel at least some postpurchase dissonance for every purchase.[30]

Why is it so important to satisfy the customer? Customer satisfaction is a key to building profitable relationships with consumers—to keeping and growing consumers and reaping their customer lifetime value. Satisfied customers buy a product again, talk favorably to others about

Real Marketing 5.2

Lexus: Delighting Customers to Keep Them Coming Back

Close your eyes for a minute and picture a typical car dealership. Not impressed? Talk to a friend who owns a Lexus, and you'll no doubt get a very different picture. The typical Lexus dealership is . . . well, anything but typical.

In Plano, Texas, Lexus customers waiting for their cars to be serviced can lounge on an overstuffed sofa, watch a big-screen TV, surf the Internet, and sip lattes in the beverage area. The dealership is considering adding a manicure area. "We try to make it like a den would be in your own home," says the dealership's president.

In California, another Lexus dealer bought a $50,000 putting machine so customers can brush up on their golf while waiting for an oil change. Across the country, a dealer in Raleigh, North Carolina, provides a fully furnished business center for busy executives, complete with a fax machine and wireless Internet access. Less ambitious customers can relax at a café table in the nearby lounge, chatting over a cup of fresh-brewed Starbuck's coffee and a plate of still-warm chocolate chip cookies.

Why all the special amenities? Lexus knows that good marketing doesn't stop with making the sale. Keeping customers happy *after* the sale is the key to building lasting relationships. Dealers across the country have a common goal: to delight customers and keep them coming back. Lexus believes that if you "delight the customer, and continue to delight the customer, you will have a customer for life." And Lexus understands just how valuable a customer can be—it estimates that the average lifetime value of a Lexus customer is $600,000.

Despite the amenities, few Lexus customers spend much time hanging around the dealership. Lexus knows that the best dealership visit is the one that you don't have to make at all. So it builds customer-pleasing cars to start with—high-quality cars that need little servicing. In its "Lexus Covenant," the company vows that it will

■ Customer delight: Lexus pledges to create the most satisfying ownership experience the world has ever seen.

make "the finest cars ever built." In 2004, J.D. Power once again rated Lexus as the top brand for initial quality. The Lexus SC 430 model set the record for the fewest quality problems ever reported.

Still, when a car does need to be serviced, Lexus goes out of its way to make it easy and painless. Most dealers will even pick up the car, and then return it when the maintenance is finished. And the car comes back spotless, thanks to a complimentary cleaning to remove bugs and road grime from the exterior and smudges from the leather interior. You might even be surprised to find that they've touched up a door ding to help restore the car to its fresh-from-the-factory luster. "My wife will never buy another car except a Lexus," says one satisfied Lexus owner. "They come to our

the product, pay less attention to competing brands and advertising, and buy other products from the company. Many marketers go beyond merely *meeting* the expectations of customers—they aim to *delight* the customer (see Real Marketing 5.2).

A dissatisfied consumer responds differently. Bad word of mouth often travels farther and faster than good word of mouth. It can quickly damage consumer attitudes about a company and its products. But companies cannot simply rely on dissatisfied customers to volunteer their complaints when they are dissatisfied. Most unhappy customers never tell the company about their problem. Therefore, a company should measure customer satisfaction regularly. It should set up systems that *encourage* customers to complain. In this way, the company can learn how well it is doing and how it can improve.

But what should companies do about dissatisfied customers? At a minimum, most companies offer toll-free numbers and Web sites to handle complaints and inquiries. For example, over the past two decades, the Gerber help line (1-800-4-GERBER) has received more than 5 million calls. Help line staffers, most of them mothers or grandmothers themselves, handle customer concerns and provide baby care advice 24 hours a day, 365 days a year to more than 2,400 callers a day. Customers can also log onto the Gerber Web site and enter a phone number, and a staffer will call them.

By studying the overall buyer decision, marketers may be able to find ways to help consumers move through it. For example, if consumers are not buying a new product because they do not perceive a need for it, marketing might launch advertising messages that trigger the need and show how the product solves customers' problems. If customers

house, pick up the car, do an oil change, [spiff it up,] and bring it back. She's sold for life."

And when a customer does bring a car in, Lexus repairs it right the first time, on time. Dealers know that their well-heeled customers have money, "but what they don't have is time." So dealers like Mike Sullivan of California are testing a system that uses three technicians instead of one for 35,000-mile service checkups. The new system will cut a customer's wait in half. "I'm not in the car business," says one dealer. "I'm in the service business."

Beyond pampering customers with outstanding service, Lexus also creates special experiences that foster long-lasting relationships. Lexus Australia, for example, rewards loyal customers with VIP packages to the theater. It gives them an opportunity to buy the best seats at the Sydney Opera House. During intermission, customers can visit the exclusive Inner Circle VIP lounge and sip a complimentary glass of Domaine Chandon while opening their VIP gift pack of exclusive commemorative merchandise from the show.

According to its Web site, from the very start, Lexus set out to "revolutionize the automotive experience with a passionate commitment the finest products, supported by dealers who create the most satisfying ownership experience the world has ever seen. We vow to value the customer as an important individual. To do things right the first time. And to always exceed expectations."

At Lexus, exceeding customer expectations sometimes means fulfilling even seemingly outrageous customer requests. Dave Wilson, owner of several Lexus dealerships in Southern California, tells of an angry letter he received from a Lexus owner who spent $374 to repair her car at his dealership. She'd owned four prior Lexus vehicles without a single problem. She said in her letter that she resented paying to fix her current one. Turns out, she thought they were maintenance free—as in get in and drive . . . and drive and drive. "She didn't think she had to do anything to her Lexus," says Wilson. "She had 60,000 miles on it, and never had the oil changed." Wilson sent back her $374.

By all accounts, Lexus has lived up to its ambitious customer-satisfaction promise. It has created what appear to be the world's most satisfied car owners. Lexus regularly tops not just the J.D. Power quality ratings, but also its customer-satisfaction ratings, and not just in the United States, but worldwide. In 2004, in the UK, Lexus achieved the highest J.D. Power customer-satisfaction score ever in the rating's 11-year history. Customer satisfaction translates into sales and customer loyalty. Last year, for the fourth straight year, Lexus was this nation's number-one selling luxury car. And once a Lexus customer, always a Lexus customer—Lexus retains 84 percent of customers who've gone to the dealership for service.

Sources: Jean Halliday, "Dealers Improve Waiting Areas to Boost Loyalty," *Automotive News*, March 22, 2004, p. 38; Doron Levin, "Lexus Breaks the 'Rule' to Reign as Top Luxury Marque," *The Detroit News*, January 21, 2004; "J.D. Power and Associates and What Car? Report," press release, April 20, 2004; Steve Finlay, "At Least She Put Fuel in It," *Ward's Dealer Business*, August 1, 2003; "Lexus Roars for Loyal Customers," *B&T Magazine*, November 27, 2003; J.D. Power and Associates, "Lexus Dealers Repeat Top Ranking in Satisfaction with Vehicle Service," press release, October 25, 2001; "Keeping the Customer Satisfied," *The Derry Journal*, April 30, 2004, "Servco Lexus Customers Get a Sneak Peak at the All-New GX 470," *Servo Pacific*, April 2004; Mark Rechtin, "Lexus: Growth Won't Hurt Brand's Cachet," *Automotive News*, April 19, 2004, p. 49; "Lexus Sweeps Quality and Satisfaction Awards," Lexus press release, May 13, 2004; and "Lexus Covenant," accessed at www.lexus.com/about/corporate/covenant.html, January 2005.

know about the product but are not buying because they hold unfavorable attitudes toward it, the marketer must find ways either to change the product or change consumer perceptions.

The Buyer Decision Process for New Products

We have looked at the stages buyers go through in trying to satisfy a need. Buyers may pass quickly or slowly through these stages, and some of the stages may even be reversed. Much depends on the nature of the buyer, the product, and the buying situation.

We now look at how buyers approach the purchase of new products. A **new product** is a good, service, or idea that is perceived by some potential customers as new. It may have been around for a while, but our interest is in how consumers learn about products for the first time and make decisions on whether to adopt them. We define the **adoption process** as "the mental process through which an individual passes from first learning about an innovation to final adoption," and *adoption* as the decision by an individual to become a regular user of the product.[31]

New product
A good, service, or idea that is perceived by some potential customers as new.

Adoption process
The mental process through which an individual passes from first hearing about an innovation to final adoption.

Stages in the Adoption Process

Consumers go through five stages in the process of adopting a new product:

- *Awareness:* The consumer becomes aware of the new product, but lacks information about it.
- *Interest:* The consumer seeks information about the new product.
- *Evaluation:* The consumer considers whether trying the new product makes sense.
- *Trial:* The consumer tries the new product on a small scale to improve his or her estimate of its value.
- *Adoption:* The consumer decides to make full and regular use of the new product.

This model suggests that the new-product marketer should think about how to help consumers move through these stages. A manufacturer of HDTVs (high-density televisions) may discover that many consumers in the interest stage do not move to the trial stage because of uncertainty and the large investment. If these same consumers were willing to use HDTVs on a trial basis for a small fee, the manufacturer could consider offering a trial-use plan with an option to buy.

Individual Differences in Innovativeness

People differ greatly in their readiness to try new products. In each product area, there are "consumption pioneers" and early adopters. Other individuals adopt new products much later. People can be classified into the adopter categories shown in Figure 5.8. After a slow start, an increasing number of people adopt the new product. The number of adopters reaches a peak and then drops off as fewer nonadopters remain. Innovators are defined as the first 2.5 percent of the buyers to adopt a new idea (those beyond two standard deviations from mean adoption time); the early adopters are the next 13.5 percent (between one and two standard deviations); and so forth.

FIGURE 5.8
Adopter categorization on the basis of relative time of adoption of innovations
Source: Reprinted with the permission of The Free Press, a Division of Simon & Schuster, from Diffusion of Innovations, *Fifth Edition, by Everett M. Rogers. Copyright © 2003 by The Free Press.*

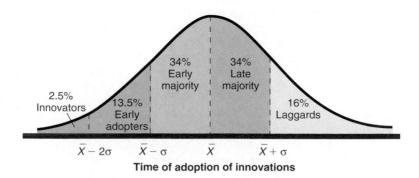

The five adopter groups have differing values. *Innovators* are venturesome—they try new ideas at some risk. *Early adopters* are guided by respect—they are opinion leaders in their communities and adopt new ideas early but carefully. The *early majority* are deliberate—although they rarely are leaders, they adopt new ideas before the average person. The *late majority* are skeptical—they adopt an innovation only after a majority of people have tried it. Finally, *laggards* are tradition bound—they are suspicious of changes and adopt the innovation only when it has become something of a tradition itself.

This adopter classification suggests that an innovating firm should research the characteristics of innovators and early adopters and should direct marketing efforts toward them. In general, innovators tend to be relatively younger, better educated, and higher in income than later adopters and nonadopters. They are more receptive to unfamiliar things, rely more on their own values and judgment, and are more willing to take risks. They are less brand loyal and more likely to take advantage of special promotions such as discounts, coupons, and samples.

Influence of Product Characteristics on Rate of Adoption

The characteristics of the new product affect its rate of adoption. Some products catch on almost overnight (Beanie Babies), whereas others take a long time to gain acceptance (HDTV). Five characteristics are especially important in influencing an innovation's rate of adoption. For example, consider the characteristics of HDTV in relation to the rate of adoption:

- *Relative advantage:* the degree to which the innovation appears superior to existing products. The greater the perceived relative advantage of using HDTV—say, in picture quality and ease of viewing—the sooner HDTVs will be adopted.

- *Compatibility:* the degree to which the innovation fits the values and experiences of potential consumers. HDTV, for example, is highly compatible with the lifestyles found in upper middle-class homes. However, it is not very compatible with the programming and broadcasting systems currently available to consumers.

■ The adoption process: This ad encourages trial by offering a coupon.

- *Complexity:* the degree to which the innovation is difficult to understand or use. HDTVs are not very complex and, therefore, once programming is available and prices come down, will take less time to penetrate U.S. homes than more complex innovations.

- *Divisibility:* the degree to which the innovation may be tried on a limited basis. HDTVs are still very expensive. To the extent that people can lease them with an option to buy, their rate of adoption will increase.

- *Communicability:* the degree to which the results of using the innovation can be observed or described to others. Because HDTV lends itself to demonstration and description, its use will spread faster among consumers.

Other characteristics influence the rate of adoption, such as initial and ongoing costs, risk and uncertainty, and social approval. The new-product marketer has to research all these factors when developing the new product and its marketing program.

Consumer Behavior Across International Borders

Understanding consumer behavior is difficult enough for companies marketing within the borders of a single country. For companies operating in many countries, however, understanding and serving the needs of consumers can be daunting. Although consumers in different countries may have some things in common, their values, attitudes, and behaviors often vary greatly. International marketers must understand such differences and adjust their products and marketing programs accordingly.

Sometimes the differences are obvious. For example, in the United States, where most people eat cereal regularly for breakfast, Kellogg focuses its marketing on persuading consumers to select a Kellogg brand rather than a competitor's brand. In France, however, where most people prefer croissants and coffee or no breakfast at all, Kellogg advertising simply attempts to convince people that they should eat cereal for breakfast. Its packaging includes step-by-step instructions on how to prepare cereal. In India, where many consumers eat heavy, fried breakfasts and many consumers skip the meal altogether, Kellogg's advertising attempts to convince buyers to switch to a lighter, more nutritious breakfast diet.

Often, differences across international markets are more subtle. They may result from physical differences in consumers and their environments. For example, Remington makes smaller electric shavers to fit the smaller hands of Japanese consumers and battery-powered shavers for the British market, where fewer bathrooms have electrical outlets. Other differences result from varying customs. In Japan, for example, where humility and deference are considered great virtues, pushy, hard-hitting sales approaches are considered offensive. Failing to understand such differences in customs and behaviors from one country to another can spell disaster for a marketer's international products and programs.

Marketers must decide on the degree to which they will adapt their products and marketing programs to meet the unique cultures and needs of consumers in various markets. On the one hand, they want to standardize their offerings in order to simplify operations and take advantage of cost economies. On the other hand, adapting marketing efforts within each country results in products and programs that better satisfy the needs of local consumers. The question of whether to adapt or standardize the marketing mix across international markets has created a lively debate in recent years.

> Reviewing the Concepts <

The American consumer market consists of more than 293 million people who consume many trillions of dollars worth of goods and services each year, making it one of the most attractive consumer markets in the world. The world consumer market consists of more than 6.4 *billion* people. Consumers around the world vary greatly in age, income, education level, and tastes. Understanding how these differences affect *consumer buyer behavior* is one of the biggest challenges marketers face.

1. Define the consumer market and construct a simple model of consumer buyer behavior.

The *consumer market* consists of all the individuals and households who buy or acquire goods and services for personal consumption. The simplest model of consumer buyer behavior is the stimulus–response

model. According to this model, marketing stimuli (the four Ps) and other major forces (economic, technological, political, cultural) enter the consumer's "black box" and produce certain responses. Once in the black box, these inputs produce observable buyer responses, such as product choice, brand choice, purchase timing, and purchase amount.

2. Name the four major factors that influence consumer buyer behavior.

Consumer buyer behavior is influenced by four key sets of buyer characteristics: cultural, social, personal, and psychological. Although many of these factors cannot be influenced by the marketer, they can be useful in identifying interested buyers and in shaping products and appeals to serve consumer needs better. *Culture* is the most basic determinant of a person's wants and behavior. It includes the basic values, perceptions, preferences, and behaviors that a person learns from family and other important institutions. *Subcultures* are "cultures within cultures" that have distinct values and lifestyles and can be based on anything from age to ethnicity. People with different cultural and subcultural characteristics have different product and brand preferences. As a result, marketers may want to focus their marketing programs on the special needs of certain groups.

Social factors also influence a buyer's behavior. A person's *reference groups*—family, friends, social organizations, professional associations—strongly affect product and brand choices. The buyer's age, life-cycle stage, occupation, economic circumstances, lifestyle, personality, and other *personal characteristics* influence his or her buying decisions. Consumer *lifestyles*—the whole pattern of acting and interacting in the world—are also an important influence on purchase decisions. Finally, consumer buyer behavior is influenced by four major *psychological factors*—motivation, perception, learning, and beliefs and attitudes. Each of these factors provides a different perspective for understanding the workings of the buyer's black box.

3. List and understand the major types of buying decision behavior and stages in the buyer decision process.

Buying behavior may vary greatly across different types of products and buying decisions. Consumers undertake *complex buying behavior* when they are highly involved in a purchase and perceive significant differences among brands. *Dissonance-reducing behavior* occurs when consumers are more highly involved but see little difference among brands. *Habitual buying behavior* occurs under conditions of low involvement and little significant brand difference. In situations characterized by low involvement but significant perceived brand differences, consumers engage in *variety-seeking buying behavior.*

When making a purchase, the buyer goes through a decision process consisting of *need recognition, information search, evaluation of alternatives, purchase decision,* and *postpurchase behavior.* The marketer's job is to understand the buyer's behavior at each stage and the influences that are operating. During *need recognition,* the consumer recognizes a problem or need that could be satisfied by a product or service in the market. Once the need is recognized, the consumer is aroused to seek more information and moves into the *information search* stage. With information in hand, the consumer proceeds to *alternative evaluation,* during which the information is used to evaluate brands in the choice set. From there, the consumer makes a *purchase decision* and actually buys the product. In the final stage of the buyer decision process, *postpurchase behavior,* the consumer takes action based on satisfaction or dissatisfaction.

4. Describe the adoption and diffusion process for new products.

The product adoption process is comprised of five stages: awareness, interest, evaluation, trial, and adoption. Initially, the consumer must become aware of the new product. *Awareness* leads to *interest,* and the consumer seeks information about the new product. Once information has been gathered, the consumer enters the *evaluation* stage and considers buying the new product. Next, in the *trial* stage, the consumer tries the product on a small scale to improve his or her estimate of its value. If the consumer is satisfied with the product, he or she enters the *adoption* stage, deciding to use the new product fully and regularly.

With regard to diffusion of new products, consumers respond at different rates, depending on the consumer's characteristics and the product's characteristics. Consumers may be innovators, early adopters, early majority, late majority, or laggards. *Innovators* are willing to try risky new ideas; *early adopters*—often community opinion leaders—accept new ideas early but carefully; the *early majority*—rarely leaders—decide deliberately to try new ideas, doing so before the average person does; the *late majority* try an innovation only after a majority of people have adopted it; whereas *laggards* adopt an innovation only after it has become a tradition itself. Manufacturers try to bring their new products to the attention of potential early adopters, especially those who are opinion leaders.

> Reviewing the Key Terms <

Adoption process 160	Consumer market 136	Learning 152	Personality 148
Alternative evaluation 157	Culture 137	Lifestyle 146	Postpurchase behavior 157
Attitude 153	Dissonance-reducing buying	Motive (or drive) 148	Purchase decision 157
Belief 152	behavior 154	Need recognition 156	Social classes 141
Cognitive dissonance 158	Group 142	New product 160	Subculture 138
Complex buying behavior 154	Habitual buying behavior 155	Opinion leader 142	Variety-seeking buying
Consumer buyer behavior 136	Information search 156	Perception 151	behavior 155

> Discussing the Concepts <

1. Which of the following general characteristics affecting consumer behavior would most influence the purchase of a new music CD: social class, age and life-cycle stage, or beliefs and attitudes?

2. A bank used SRI Consulting's Values and Lifestyles (VALS) research to profile customer segments that did not use any automated or electronic services. Based on your knowledge of the VALS classification system, speculate what might be the primary and secondary VALS types for this customer segment.

3. On a trip to Best Buy, suppose you overhear the following comment made in a conversation between two salespeople: "I think that the sales director really knows our products and the market, and I've thought so for years." Is the salesperson expressing a belief or an attitude? Explain?

4. The vice president of marketing for a regional doughnut retailer says, "We believe our customers exhibit high-involvement buying behaviors." Do you agree? Why or why not?

5. Compare and contrast the consumer decision process someone might use in purchasing a new notebook PC at Comp USA with that of purchasing a 16 oz. jar of Jif creamy style peanut butter at Wal-Mart.

6. In a small group, discuss the following question: Who would be the better opinion leader for a high technology cellular service, Bill Clinton or Bill Gates? Support your choice?

> Applying the Concepts <

1. You are the vice president of marketing for a small software company that has developed new and novel spam blocking software. You are charged with selecting a target market segment for the product launch. How would you use Roger's *Diffusion of Innovations* framework to help you with this choice? What are some of the likely characteristics of this customer group?

2. In a small group, discuss how the buyer decision process for a college student would differ from that of a snowboarder in purchasing a backpack. How would you use this knowledge to develop an advertising plan?

3. The chapter defines "alternative evaluation" as: "how the consumer processes information to arrive at brand choices." Suppose, as discussed in the chapter, that you have narrowed your choice of new cars to brand A, B, or C. You have finalized the four most important new car attributes and their weights, and have created and filled in the evaluation matrix below. Which new car alternative will you more than likely select?

		New Car Alternatives		
Attributes	**Importance Weight**	**Brand A**	**Brand B**	**Brand C**
Styling	0.5	3	7	4
Operating Economy	0.2	6	5	7
Warranty	0.1	5	5	6
Price	0.2	8	7	8

> Focus on Technology <

Biometric technology is emerging from the 9/11 tragedy as one of the most important and accurate systems of personal identification. Biometric systems discriminate based on measurement of a physical feature or repeatable behavior or action of the individual. They recognize individuals based on hand geometry, retinal scan, iris scan, fingerprint patterns, facial characteristics, DNA sequence characteristics, voice prints, and hand written signature.

1. Name five situations where biometric technology would help with an issue or problem at your university or college. How would this technology help you as a student or personally?

2. In what situations might this technology help marketers to understand consumer buying or decision processes better? Explain.

> Focus on Ethics <

You are the product manager of Red Zone, a financial services product that provides consumers with information on their personal financial situations. Marketed directly to consumers via the Internet and direct mail, Red Zone is sold in the form of an annual prepaid membership for $79.95, after a 30 day free trial. To help attract subscribers, the company provides a "Free Red Zone Score" report along with the trial membership. Promotion focuses on the "Free Red Zone Score" with little mention of the Red Zone "trial membership." All the promotional language, ads, and the order form have been approved by your legal department. The "Free Red Zone Score" offer has great impact on the evaluation stage of the consumer decision process—it provides a 50 percent lift in membership trials over the basic offer.

Your research shows that a significant proportion of the paid members do not realize that they have signed a $79.95 Red Zone annual membership agreement that will be charged to their credit cards at the end of the 30-day free trial. When these unaware Red Zone members receive their monthly credit card bill and see the $79.95 charge, they often file complaints for a fraudulent charge with the credit card company. Moreover,

they often followed up with a complaint to a state attorney general or the Better Business Bureau. Your boss, the marketing VP, has scheduled a meeting with you for tomorrow to ask what the company should do about the number of "complaint" letters that the company is receiving from customers, state attorney general's offices, and the BBB concerning how Red Zone is marketed.

1. Assess the consumer buying process for Red Zone. How do current promotion practices affect this buying process?

2. Is the current Red Zone promotion legal? Is it ethical? Is it good business practice?

3. What will you recommend tomorrow? Should the company redirect the focus of the promotion toward the value of the Red Zone membership and away from the "Free Red Zone Score," even if this will lead to profit erosion? Or should you tell the boss that it is all legal and recommend that the company continue selling Red Zone as it is presently configured and promoted?

◯ Video Case

Wild Planet

We've all heard about the community outreach efforts of retailers like Body Shop and Ben & Jerry's. But unlike the social activists of the past, today's values-led businesses are founded by well-trained business managers and company builders with a passion for a cause. The result is socially minded businesses with the know how needed to target and connect with customers. For example, to make money and follow their values at the same time, the folks at Wild Planet, based in San Francisco, have decided to market much more than just toys. They sell positive play experiences. Daniel Grossman started Wild Planet to create innovative products to "spark the imagination, promote creativity, and provide positive experiences without relying on violence."

Wild Planet appeals to consumers by pursuing its social mission of creating toys that do not rely on gender stereotypes or promote violence.

And by getting to know its customers and their buying characteristics, the small toy retailer competes alongside mega-retailers such as Toys 'R' Us.

After viewing the video featuring Wild Planet, answer the following questions about consumer buying behavior.

1. What characteristics of consumer behavior are likely to influence Wild Planet's customers? Which characteristic do you think is most likely to motivate customers' purchases?

2. Visit Wild Planet's Web site and browse the information about the company as well as the products it offers. What demographic segment of consumers is the company targeting?

3. How does Wild Planet learn more about its customers' characteristics and buying behavior?

▣ Company Case

READ CASE FOR DISCUSSION

Weight? I'm on Atkins

Check out these startling statistics: In 1980, 46 percent of the adult population was overweight or obese. By 1990, the figure had grown to 56 percent, and by 2000, it had jumped again to 64.5 percent. And that's just the adults. In 1960, 8.9 percent of U.S. children, aged 6 to 19, were overweight or obese. By 1980, it was up to 11.7 percent; by 2000, 30.8 percent. Moreover, overweight children are likely to grow up to be overweight adults. The "weight growth spurt" in children could result in as many as 90 percent of the adult population being overweight in the future. As a result, this generation of children may be the first to die before their parents. That's an incredibly grim prospect.

Obesity is becoming the #1 killer in the United States. More than 300,000 Americans died in 2003 because of some obesity-related ailment. These ailments range from heart attacks to 19 different kinds of cancer, kidney disease, and diabetes. Overweight people are also prone to depression, other emotional upsets, and job loss (physical inability to perform at work). One study showed that children thought being overweight was as bad as having cancer, because they suffer from poor social interactions, low school achievement, lack of athletic prowess, and troubled family relationships.

Overweight children stay home from school four times as much as other children; are teased mercilessly; and have physical problems such as sleep apnea, fatty liver, type 2 diabetes, or high cholesterol. The last two ailments were formerly associated mostly with middle-aged adults. Finally, a study at Duke University showed that while the overall well-being of American children had increased by 5 percent since 1975, most of that increase was due to a drop in crime. The children's health index would have risen by 15 percent if not for obesity-related problems.

What's causing this epidemic? Fast-food restaurants have a lot to answer for here. The movie, *Supersize Me*, reported one man's attempt to live on fast food for a month. The result? He gained more than 20 pounds. Every day, nearly one-third of U.S. children aged 4 to 19 eats fast food, likely packing on about 6 extra pounds per child per year. Other restaurants with "all-you-can eat" meals encourage Americans to gorge themselves, and portions served in the United States tend to be larger than they are in the rest of the world.

Besides overeating, we are becoming more sedentary. We have become a nation of office workers who spend a great deal of time sitting down, talking on telephones, and typing on computers. Instead of walking, Americans drive everywhere. My neighbors drive their bags of trash to the dumpster—a distance of 200 feet. Bill Bryson in his book, *I'm a Stranger Here Myself*, makes fun of folks who drive to exercise programs. Major food processors prepare frozen, canned, and dried foods that are frequently low in protein and high in salt and fat. They've introduced all sorts of desserts and snackables and made them so convenient that you can eat, drive, and talk on your cell phone at the same time. The bottom line is that food is easier come by (we don't have to kill it, grow it, or cook it), so that it's easy to overeat.

What are Americans doing about this? Currently, some 59 million U.S. adults follow some kind of low-carb program.

(box continues)

The favorites are the Atkins diet and the South Beach Diet. Who has not had a colleague or friend declare "I'm on Atkins," meaning don't serve me bread, potatoes, or pasta at your house. The essence of Atkins, South Beach, and other low-carb diets is that a calorie is not just a calorie. Atkins believed the body switched from a carbohydrate-burning mechanism to a fat-burning machine when the quantity of carbohydrates was reduced. In the first 2 weeks of the Atkins Diet, dieters ingest almost no carbohydrates in order to stimulate the fat-burning process. Therefore, Atkins allows you to eat protein (meat, even bacon), eggs, and butter. Over the centuries, our bodies have been programmed to store fat. As the body shifts to fat-burning, it begins to reduce our stored fat.

Of course, the Atkins diet flies in the face of conventional nutritional wisdom, which stresses low-fat diets. But is this diet really nonsense and pseudoscience, as one doctor called it? Doctors and nutritionists have to admit that people *do* lose weight on Atkins. An experiment at Harvard, in which participants were divided into low-fat diet groups, a low-carb group that got the same number of calories as the low-fat group, and a low-carb group that got 300 more calories per day. All participants were given their food for each day. At the end of a year, the low-fat group had lost 17 pounds, the low-carb group 23 pounds, and the low-carb group with the extra 300 calories 20 pounds. These counter-intuitive results contradict the theory that the best way to lose weight is to eat fewer calories and cut out fat. And they support Atkins' metabolic-advantage theory.

Atkins has had major effects on American businesses— some good and some not-so-good. First, there's Atkins Direct, a catalog company (founded by guess who?) that sells supplements and more than 100 approved foodstuffs, including bread. So, Atkins sells the book that stimulates the diet along with the foodstuffs and supplements to maintain the diet. Other businesses have jumped on the low-carb bandwagon. Publications such as *Low-Carb Living* and the *Low-Carb Energy* book have hit newsstands. Two California companies—Castus and Pure Foods—have developed low-carb supermarkets. Castus had 7 outlets by mid-2004 with an eventual goal of 5,000. It sells more than 1,600 low-carb foods. Companies such as Mission Foods, a major producer of tortillas, cannot keep up with demand as tortillas are substituted for bread in sandwiches.

American restaurants such as Carls Jr., Hardees, Burger King, McDonald's, T.G.I. Fridays, Blimpies, and Subway have put low-carb alternatives on their menus. Frequently low-carb or bunless burgers (burgers with more lettuce and tomato in a box) show up on other restaurant's menus. Anheuser Busch has been successful with Michelob Ultra and Heinz

has developed One Carb Ketchup. HVC Lizard sells a sugarless chocolate bar to 7-11 convenience stores. Pasta companies have introduced low-carb pasta. There are plenty of opportunities for companies to take advantage of the low-carb diet craze. That's just food processors and restaurants.

Besides Atkins and the low-carb craze, there are other businesses catering to the 50 million Americans who want to lose a little weight. A frequent choice is diet pills. Americans like pills—take one and problems disappear. This requires no real effort—the medicine does it for you. Americans spend more than $100 million a year on pills. The best-known are Acutrim and Dexatrim, but there's no evidence that they work. There are also commercial weight-loss centers such as Diet Center, Jenny Craig, and Weight Watchers, that sell consultations, programs, books, and foodstuffs. Meal-replacement shakes such as SlimFast and Shaklee often show up at work at lunchtime.

Prescription drugs are like diet pills in that the customer expects the pill to do the work. Diet pills frequently hit the headlines: first because they are hailed as miracles and second because they create scandals. Drugs such as Redux and phen-fen were well publicized as causing ailments such as pulmonary hypertension, heart valve disorders, and seizures. Last, there's surgery—bariatric surgery in which the stomach is stapled so that only a small amount of it is available for digestion. With smaller stomachs, people eat less. Such surgery is expensive and can lead to follow-up surgery for conditions such as abdominal hernias.

While Atkins has "created" new businesses, it has also hurt other, older businesses. Fast-food sales have dropped and makers of cereal and processed foods report lower sales and revenue. Sales of Unilever's SlimFast are down; Weight Watchers' slimming programs are down 6 percent. Bread makers such as Panera have lost revenues, and pasta makers have convened to discuss ploys to combat lower sales. In terms of helping people change their eating habits, this is good. But for employees and stockholders, it's bad.

Doctors and nutritionists have said for years that people should lose weight slowly and exercise. Most Americans, however, want something that works fast—like those pills. They have also resisted exercise, even though just a little bit of it can go a long way. Swedish researchers have demonstrated that older adults who exercised only once a week were 40 percent less likely to die during a 12-year study than those who did nothing. Other research shows that people who say that they "exercise only occasionally" still had a 28 percent lower risk of dying in a 12-year study. Studies have also shown that exercise by aging adults helps to improve brain function. Finally, a study of teens in Texas high schools using physical education classes reported that feelings of sadness and the risk of suicide were lowered. Exercise is not only good for you physically, but also mentally.

American business has also jumped on the exercise bandwagon. Exercise clinics and gyms are springing up in local communities, and it's becoming a social outing to work out. People talk about their "workouts" at work, on lunch breaks, and among friends. One of my friends has even figured out that Friday and Saturday nights are urban-professional-singles night at her exercise club. On *Seinfeld,* Elaine frequently worked out and several shows were built around experiences at the gym. Personal trainers and custom exercise programs have become more common. More exercise equipment is sold for home use. How many of you come from homes where there are used or (more likely) unused exercycles, tread mills, and weight stations.

Beyond the problem of real obesity, there's also another obesity-related problem, one which is imaginary. Eating disorders such as anorexia and bulimia are on the rise due to "perceived obesity." Anorexics starve themselves and bulimics binge eat and then purge themselves by vomiting. These two disorders affect 10 million women and 1 million men. The age of anorexics and bulimics is dropping to children 8 to 10 years old. Eating disorders are accompanied by stress and body image problems, and empowerment comes from being thin. Furthermore, psychological studies show that eating disorders lead to obsessiveness, dependency, overcontrolled hostility, assertiveness, locus of control, and lower self-esteem.

"Perceived obesity" is encouraged by cultural and social mores. Young women want to be as thin as Kate Moss, not heavy like Roseanne. Thanks to television, magazines, movies, and the Internet, rail-thin girls and steroid-built beef-boys are being shoved into the faces of everyone. Thin women get loved while heavy women get to mop the kitchen floor; beefed-up boys get the girl while puny men get sand kicked in their faces, as in the old Charles Atlas ads. Babe Paley, wife of a CBS executive, has been quoted for years as saying "A woman can never be too thin or too rich." If we follow that line of reasoning, then thin—even to the point of anorexia—is definitely beautiful. Models starve themselves and take drugs to stay incredibly thin. Obese people come to hate themselves because they don't meet society's expectations, and others regard them negatively. In *Shallow Hal,* the actor Jack Black could not deal with having an obese girlfriend—that's why he was shallow! "Perceived obesity" also leads to business opportunities such as counseling, mental health, and psychological programs.

Worse yet, obesity is not an equal opportunity ailment. Low-income Americans are more likely to be obese than the well-off. African Americans are more likely to be obese than whites, and Hispanics more so than African-Americans. Women are more likely to be obese than men. The relationship between education and obesity is very strong. While higher income, white Americans are extending their life spans, lower income racial and ethnic groups could be shortening theirs. But businesses such as weight loss programs and tony exercise clinics don't locate in low income neighborhoods—either white or ethnic.

Whether Atkins is a fad or permanent, it's clear that for the moment Americans are prone to jumping on the diet bandwagon. They know that they need to lose weight; they know they need to exercise and change their eating habits. However, instead, they go for the "latest popular thing."

Questions for Discussion

1. What social, cultural, and personal factors are associated with obesity? With eating disorders? What psychological factors?

2. How would obesity, diets, and exercise programs fit into VALS lifestyles? What groups are most likely to take advantage of which means of losing weight?

3. Why have so many consumers chosen Atkins or the South Beach Diet? How has the decision making process affected their choice?

4. How has American business capitalized on obesity and eating disorders? Is this desirable?

5. Americans spend more than $100 billion a year on ways to lose weight, but it doesn't happen. Next year, the same people will probably spend more. People appear not to care if they don't get the product they pay for. What social, cultural, and personal factors explain this? How does it benefit business?

Sources: Lori Widzinski, "Inside Out: Stories of Bulimia," *Library Journal,* June 1, 2003, p. 182; Susan McClelland, "Distorted Images," *Maclean's,* August 14, 2000, pp. 41–42; Rebecca L. Rogers and Trent A. Petrie, "Psychological Correlates of Anorexic and Bulimic Symptomatology," *Journal of Counseling and Development,* pp. 178–188; "Kids Say Being Fat Is as Bad as Having Cancer," *Medical Post,* May 6, 2003, Vol. 39, Iss. 18; Tara Parker-Pope, "Health Matters: When It Comes to Exercise, a Little Bit Goes a Long Way," *Wall Street Journal,* August 9, 2004, p. R.5; Louise Witt, "Why We're Losing the War Against Obesity," *American Demographics,* December 2004, p. 27; Rachel Lehmann-Haupt, "La Vida Low Carb," *Folio,* March 2004, p. 58; Ann Brocklehurst, "The Lowdown on the Low-Carb Diet Wars," *Maclean's,* February 23, 2004, pp 38–39.

CHAPTER

6

> After studying this chapter, you should be able to

1. define the business market and explain how business markets differ from consumer markets
2. identify the major factors that influence business buyer behavior
3. list and define the steps in the business buying-decision process
4. compare the institutional and government markets and explain how institutional and government buyers make their buying decisions

Business Markets and Business Buyer Behavior

Previewing the Concepts

In the previous chapter, you studied *final consumer* buying behavior and factors that influence it. In this chapter, we'll do the same for *business customers*—those that buy goods and services for use in producing their own products and services or for resale to others.

To start, let's look at UPS (United Parcel Service). You probably know UPS as a neighborhood small package delivery company. It turns out, however, that a majority of UPS's business comes not from residential consumers like you and me, but from large *business* customers. To succeed in its business-to-business markets, UPS must do more than just pick up and deliver packages. It must work closely and deeply with its business customers to become a strategic logistics partner.

"I've been using three different companies for international, overnight and ground. Now I just call Brown." It's all part of a simpler lifestyle I'm trying out."

Your world is complicated enough. Simplify it. Let Brown handle all your shipping. In return, we'll give you the peace of mind that comes from using just one, perfectly integrated shipping network. One company that can deliver international, overnight and ground shipments to your customers, on time. Guaranteed. It's as simple as that.

INTERNATIONAL. OVERNIGHT. GROUND. SYNCHRONIZED.

WHAT CAN BROWN DO FOR YOU?™

UPS.com® 1-800-PICK-UPS®
© 2003 United Parcel Service of America, Inc.

Mention UPS, and most people envision one of those familiar brown trucks with a friendly driver, rumbling around their neighborhood dropping off parcels. That makes sense. The company's 80,000 brown-clad drivers deliver more than 3.4 billion packages annually, an average of 13.6 million each day.

For most of us, seeing a brown UPS truck evokes fond memories of past package deliveries. If you close your eyes and listen, you can probably imagine the sound of the UPS truck pulling up in front of your home. Even the company's brown color has come to mean something special to customers. "We've been referred to for years as Big Brown," says a UPS marketing executive. "People love our drivers, they love our brown trucks, they love everything we do." Thus was born UPS's current "What Can Brown Do for You?" advertising theme.

For most residential customers, the answer to the question "What can Brown do for you?" is pretty simple: "Deliver my package as quickly as possible." But most of UPS's revenues come not from the residential customers who receive the packages, but from the *business* customers who send them. And for these business customers, UPS does more than just get Grandma's holiday package there on time. Whereas residential consumers might look to "Brown" simply for fast, friendly, low-cost package delivery, business customers usually have much more complex needs.

For businesses, package delivery is just part of a much more complex logistics process that involves purchase orders, inventory, order status checks, invoices, payments, returned merchandise, and fleets of delivery vehicles. Beyond the physical package flow, companies must also handle the accompanying information and money flows. They need timely information about packages— what's in them, where they're currently located, to whom they are going, when they will get there, how much has been paid, and how much is owed. UPS knows that for many companies, all these work-a-day logistical concerns can be a nightmare. Moreover, most companies don't see these activities as strategic competencies that provide competitive advantage.

That's where Big Brown comes in. These are exactly the things that UPS does best. Over the years, UPS has grown to become much more than a neighborhood small package delivery service. It is now a $35 billion corporate giant providing a broad range of logistics solutions. UPS handles the logistics, allowing customers to focus on what they do best. It offers everything from ground and air package distribution, freight delivery (air, ocean, rail, and road), and mail services to inventory management, third-party logistics, international trade management, logistics management software and e-commerce solutions, and even financing. If it has to do with logistics, at home or abroad, UPS can probably do it better than anyone can.

UPS has the resources to handle the logistics needs of just about any size business. It employs 360,000 people, some 88,000 vehicles (package cars, vans, tractors, and motorcycles), 600 aircraft, and more than 750 warehouse facilities in 120 countries. UPS now moves an astounding 6 percent of the gross domestic product in the United States, links 1.8 million sellers with 6 million buyers every day, and processes more than 460 million electronic transactions every week. It serves 90 percent of the world population and 99 percent of businesses in the Fortune 1000. UPS invests $1 billion a year in information technology to support its highly synchronized, by-the-clock logistics services and to provide customers with information at every point in the process.

Beyond moving their packages around the United States, UPS can also help business customers to navigate the complexities of international shipping, with some 800 international flights per day to or from 466 international destinations. For example, although most residential customers don't need next-day air service to or from China, many businesses do seek help shipping to and from the burgeoning Asian manufacturing zones. UPS helps ensure the timely flow of crucial business documents, prototypes, high-value goods (like semiconductors), and emergency repair parts that wing their way across the Pacific every day. UPS even offers expedited

U.S. Customs services, with fast inspection and clearance processes that help get goods into the country quickly.

In addition to shipping and receiving packages, UPS provides a wide range of financial services for its business customers. For example, its UPS Capital division will handle client's accounts receivable—UPS shippers can choose to be reimbursed immediately and have UPS collect payment from the recipient. Other financial services include credit cards for small businesses and programs to fund inventory, equipment leasing, and asset financing. UPS even bought a bank to underpin UPS Capital's operations.

At a deeper level, UPS can provide the advice and technical resources needed to help business customers large and small improve their own logistics operations. UPS Consulting advises companies on redesigning logistics systems to align them better with business strategies. UPS Supply Chain Solutions helps customers to synchronize the flow of goods, funds, and information up and down their supply chains. UPS Logistics Technologies supplies software that improves customers' distribution efficiency, including street-level route optimization, territory planning, mobile delivery execution, real-time wireless dispatch, and GPS tracking.

So, what can Brown do for you? As it turns out, the answer depends on who you are. For its residential consumers, UPS uses those familiar chugging brown trucks to provide simple and efficient package pickup and delivery services. But in its business-to-business markets, it develops deeper and more involved customer relationships. The company's "What Can Brown Do for You?" ads feature a variety of business professionals discussing how UPS's broad range of services makes their jobs easier. But such ad promises have little meaning if not reinforced by actions. Says former UPS CEO Jim Kelly, "A brand can be very hollow and lifeless . . . if the people and the organization . . . are not 100 percent dedicated to living out the brand promise every day."

For UPS, that means that employees around the world must do more than just deliver packages from point A to point B for their business customers. They must roll up their sleeves and work hand-in-hand with customers to help solve their complex logistics problems. More than just providing shipping services, they must become strategic logistics partners.[1]

In one way or another, most large companies sell to other organizations. Companies such as DuPont, Boeing, Cisco Systems, Caterpillar, and countless other firms, sell *most* of their products to other businesses. Even large consumer-products companies, which make products used by final consumers, must first sell their products to other businesses. For example, General Mills makes many familiar consumer brands—Big G cereals (Cheerios, Wheaties, Total, Golden Grahams), baking products (Pillsbury, Betty Crocker, Gold Medal flour), snacks (Nature Valley, Chex Mix, Pop Secret), Yoplait Yogurt, and others. But to sell these products to consumers, General Mills must first sell them to the wholesalers and retailers that serve the consumer market.

Business buyer behavior
The buying behavior of the organizations that buy goods and services for use in the production of other products and services or for the purpose of reselling or renting them to others at a profit.

Business buyer behavior refers to the buying behavior of the organizations that buy goods and services for use in the production of other products and services that are sold, rented, or supplied to others. It also includes the behavior of retailing and wholesaling firms that acquire goods for the purpose of reselling or renting them to others at a profit. In the **business buying process**, business buyers determine which products and services their organizations need to purchase, and then find, evaluate, and choose among alternative suppliers and brands. *Business-to-business (B-to-B) marketers* must do their best to understand business markets and business buyer behavior.

Business Markets

Business buying process
The decision process by which business buyers determine which products and services their organizations need to purchase, and then find, evaluate, and choose among alternative suppliers and brands.

The business market is *huge*. In fact, business markets involve far more dollars and items than do consumer markets. For example, think about the large number of business transactions involved in the production and sale of a single set of Goodyear tires. Various suppliers sell Goodyear the rubber, steel, equipment, and other goods that it needs to produce the tires. Goodyear then sells the finished tires to retailers, who in turn sell them to consumers. Thus, many sets of *business* purchases were made for only one set of *consumer* purchases. In addition, Goodyear sells tires as original equipment to manufacturers who install them on new vehicles, and as replacement tires to companies that maintain their own fleets of company cars, trucks, buses, or other vehicles.

Characteristics of Business Markets

In some ways, business markets are similar to consumer markets. Both involve people who assume buying roles and make purchase decisions to satisfy needs. However, business markets differ in many ways from consumer markets. The main differences, shown in Table 6.1 and discussed in the following sections, are in *market structure and demand*, the *nature of the buying unit*, and the *types of decisions and the decision process* involved.

① Market Structure and Demand

The business marketer normally deals with *far fewer but far larger buyers* than the consumer marketer does. Even in large business markets, a few buyers often account for most of the purchasing. For example, when Goodyear sells replacement tires to final consumers, its potential

TABLE 6.1   Characteristics of Business Markets

Marketing Structure and Demand
Business markets contain *fewer but larger buyers*.
Business customers are *more geographically concentrated*.
Business buyer demand is *derived* from final consumer demand.
Demand in many business markets is *more inelastic*—not affected as much in the short run by price changes.
Demand in business markets *fluctuates more,* and more quickly.

Nature of the Buying Unit
Business purchases involve *more buyers*.
Business buying involves a *more professional purchasing effort*.

Types of Decisions and the Decision Process
Business buyers usually face *more complex buying decisions*.
The business buying process is *more formalized*.
In business buying, buyers and sellers work more closely together and build close long-run *relationships*.

market includes the owners of the millions of cars currently in use in the United States and around the world. But Goodyear's fate in the business market depends on getting orders from one of only a handful of large automakers. Similarly, Black & Decker sells its power tools and outdoor equipment to tens of millions of consumers worldwide. However, it must sell these products through three huge retail customers—Home Depot, Lowe's, and Wal-Mart—which combined account for more than half its sales.

Business markets are also *more geographically concentrated*. More than half the nation's business buyers are concentrated in eight states: California, New York, Ohio, Illinois, Michigan, Texas, Pennsylvania, and New Jersey. Further, business demand is **derived demand**—it ultimately derives from the demand for consumer goods. IBM and Dell buy Intel microprocessor chips because consumers buy personal computers (PCs). If consumer demand for PCs drops, so will the demand for computer chips.

Derived demand
Business demand that ultimately comes from (derives from) the demand for consumer goods.

Therefore, B-to-B marketers sometimes promote their products directly to final consumers to increase business demand. For example, Intel's long-running "Intel Inside" advertising campaign sells PC buyers on the virtues of Intel microprocessors. The increased demand for Intel chips boosts demand for the PCs containing them, and both Intel and its business partners win.

Similarly, DuPont promotes Teflon directly to final consumers as a key branded ingredient in many products—from nonstick cookware to stain-repellent, wrinkle-free clothing. You see Teflon Fabric Protector hangtags on clothing lines such as Levi's Dockers, Donna Karan's menswear, and Ralph Lauren denim.[2] By making Teflon familiar and attractive to final buyers, DuPont also makes the products containing it more attractive.

Many business markets have *inelastic demand*; that is, total demand for many business products is not affected much by price changes, especially in the short run. A drop in the price of leather will not cause shoe manufacturers to buy much more leather unless it results in lower shoe prices that, in turn, will increase consumer demand for shoes.

Finally, business markets have more *fluctuating demand*. The demand for many business goods and services tends to change more—and more quickly—than the demand for consumer goods and services does. A small percentage increase in consumer demand can cause large increases in business demand. Sometimes a rise of only 10 percent in consumer demand can cause as much as a 200 percent rise in business demand during the next period.

Nature of the Buying Unit

Compared with consumer purchases, a business purchase usually involves *more decision participants* and a *more professional purchasing effort*. Often, business buying is done by trained purchasing agents who spend their working lives learning how to buy better. The

■ Derived demand: Intel's long-running "Intel Inside" logo advertising campaign boosts demand for Intel chips and for the PCs containing them. Now, most computer markets feature a logo like this one in their ads.

more complex the purchase, the more likely that several people will participate in the decision-making process. Buying committees made up of technical experts and top management are common in the buying of major goods.

Beyond this, many companies are now upgrading their purchasing functions to "supply management" or "supplier development" functions. B-to-B marketers now face a new breed of higher-level, better-trained supply managers. These supply managers sometimes seem to know more about the supplier company than it knows about itself. Therefore, business marketers must have well-trained marketers and salespeople to deal with these well-trained buyers.

③ Types of Decisions and the Decision Process

Business buyers usually face *more complex* buying decisions than do consumer buyers. Purchases often involve large sums of money, complex technical and economic considerations, and interactions among many people at many levels of the buyer's organization. Because the purchases are more complex, business buyers may take longer to make their decisions. The business buying process also tends to be *more formalized* than the consumer buying process. Large business purchases usually call for detailed product specifications, written purchase orders, careful supplier searches, and formal approval.

Finally, in the business buying process, buyer and seller are often much *more dependent* on each other. Consumer marketers are often at a distance from their customers. In contrast, B-to-B marketers may roll up their sleeves and work closely with their customers during all stages of the buying process—from helping customers define problems, to finding solutions, to supporting after-sale operation. They often customize their offerings to individual customer needs.

In the short run, sales go to suppliers who meet buyers' immediate product and service needs. In the long run, however, B-to-B marketers keep a customer's sales by meeting current needs *and* by partnering with customers to help them solve their problems. In recent years, relationships between customers and suppliers have been changing from downright adversarial to close and chummy. In fact, many customer companies are now practicing **supplier development**, systematically develop networks of supplier-partners to ensure an appropriate and dependable supply of products and materials that they will use in making their own products or resell to others. For example, Caterpillar no longer calls its buyers "purchasing agents"—they are managers of "purchasing and supplier development." And Wal-Mart

Supplier development
Systematic development of networks of supplier-partners to ensure an appropriate and dependable supply of products and materials that they will use in making their own products or resell to others.

■ Business marketers often roll up their sleeves and work closely with their customers throughout the buying and consuming process. In this award-winning business-to-business ad, Fujitsu promises more than just high-tech products: "Our technology helps keep you moving upward. And our people won't let you down."

Today, business uses technology to gain a strategic advantage. And the higher the technology, the greater the advantage. So long as the technology does what it's supposed to do, that is. At Fujitsu, ours does. ∞ We create, from the components up, computer, communications and microelectronic products of not only the highest technology, but the highest quality and reliability as well. ∞ And we support them in ways that few other companies do. With extended warranties. Liberal replacement policies. And superior technical support. ∞ Moreover, as part of a company at the forefront of today's emerging and converging computer and communications technologies, our systems support teams offer unique expertise. ∞ Fujitsu. Our technology helps keep you moving upward. And our people won't let you down. To learn more about Fujitsu, our products and support programs, see us at www.fujitsu.com.

THE HIGHER THE TECHNOLOGY, THE MORE IMPORTANT THE SUPPORT.

FUJITSU

COMPUTERS, COMMUNICATIONS, MICROELECTRONICS

doesn't have a "Purchasing Department," it has a "Supplier Development Department" (see Real Marketing 6.1). "Through appropriate supplier relationships management," says one manager, "both the buyer and supplier can . . . deliver [more] value throughout each of their supply chains. Suppliers are an extension of our capabilities."[3]

A Model of Business Buyer Behavior

At the most basic level, marketers want to know how business buyers will respond to various marketing stimuli. Figure 6.1 shows a model of business buyer behavior. In this model, marketing and other stimuli affect the buying organization and produce certain buyer responses. As with consumer buying, the marketing stimuli for business buying consist of the four *P*s: product, price, place, and promotion. Other stimuli include major forces in the environment: economic, technological, political, cultural, and competitive. These stimuli enter the organization and are turned into buyer responses: product or service choice; supplier choice; order quantities; and delivery, service, and payment terms. In order to design good marketing mix strategies, the marketer must understand what happens within the organization to turn stimuli into purchase responses.

Real Marketing 6.1

The Business Buying Process: Not Just "Purchasing," It's "Supplier Development"

Wal-Mart sells more than a quarter of a trillion dollars worth of goods each year. But before it can *sell* products to customers, it must first *purchase* them from suppliers. The giant retailer can't rely on spot purchases from suppliers who might be available when needed. Wal-Mart must systematically develop a robust network of supplier-partners who will efficiently and reliably provide the tremendous volume of goods that it sells.

Some critics argue that Wal-Mart uses its massive size and buying power to force suppliers to accept razor thin margins, sometimes even forcing them out of business. But if Wal-Mart were to do that to all of its suppliers, where would it obtain the huge supply of goods it needs to stock its store shelves around the world? Instead, for its own benefit, Wal-Mart must work with suppliers to make them more able.

These days, like Wal-Mart, most large businesses do more than "purchasing" in a narrow sense. Instead, they practice "supplier development," identifying, developing, and supporting suppliers to ensure a dependable supply of products and materials that they will use in making their own products or resell to others. They know that what's good for suppliers is also good for the company. So they partner with suppliers to help make them more effective.

Wal-Mart doesn't have a "Purchasing Department," it has a "Supplier Development Department," which seeks out qualified suppliers and helps guide them through the complex Wal-Mart buying process. The department offers a Supplier Proposal Guide and maintains a Web site providing advice to suppliers wishing to do business with Wal-Mart. The retailer supports its suppliers in other ways. For example, it works actively with suppliers to test new products and marketing programs in its stores. And it lets major suppliers use its voluminous point-of-sale databases to analyze customers' regional buying habits. Proctor & Gamble, for example, learned that its liquid Tide sells better at Wal-Mart stores in the North and Northeast, while Tide powder sells better in the South and Southwest. P&G uses such data to tailor its product availability to specific regions. By sharing information with suppli-

ers, Wal-Mart helps them sell more products which, in turn, brings in more sales for Wal-Mart.

Like Wal-Mart, buyers in a wide range of industries are evolving from "purchasing" to "supplier development." Consider the heavily supplier-dependent automobile industry. Honda of America purchases parts and materials from hundreds of suppliers. More than a decade ago, Honda established a rigorous supplier relations program, which provides extensive supplier development and support. Honda doesn't just buy from its suppliers—it helps to train them as well. It offers more than 160 training classes for suppliers, on topics ranging from improving quality and reducing costs to developing front-line leadership. Honda also hosts twice-a-year events in which quality teams from as many as 100 suppliers meet to share ideas on improving manufacturing processes. "Our intent is to strengthen supplier business operations," says one Honda supplier executive. "The whole family organization is only as strong as the weakest link," says another. "So we have to perform together."

Competitor Toyota also seeks out quality suppliers and helps to train them. For example, Toyota's Supplier Support Center spent 3 years teaching managers at supplier Ernie Green Industries about the Toyota Production System before issuing the first purchase order. Similarly, Toyota sent several consultants to supplier Summit Polymers' plant every day for 4 months to help Summit implement the Toyota system. Such supplier development activities have produced dramatic results. On average, Toyota has helped its suppliers increase productivity by 123 percent. Of course, Toyota expects to benefit in return. "We've grown quickly with . . . Toyota, and we're profitable," says Carl Code, a vice president at Ernie Green Industries. "But it's no gravy train. They want suppliers to make enough money to stay in business, grow, and bring them innovation."

What does the shift from purchasing to supplier development mean for business-to-business marketers? It means that major business buyers are no longer looking only for "suppliers" from which to purchase goods and services. They are seeking "supplier-partners" with which they can develop mutually beneficial supply relation-

Within the organization, buying activity consists of two major parts: the buying center, made up of all the people involved in the buying decision, and the buying-decision process. The model shows that the buying center and the buying-decision process are influenced by internal organizational, interpersonal, and individual factors as well as by external environmental factors.

Business Buyer Behavior

The model in Figure 6.1 suggests four questions about business buyer behavior: What buying decisions do business buyers make? Who participates in the buying process? What are the major influences on buyers? How do business buyers make their buying decisions?

Major Types of Buying Situations

There are three major types of buying situations.[4] At one extreme is the *straight rebuy*, which is a fairly routine decision. At the other extreme is the *new task*, which may call for thorough research. In the middle is the *modified rebuy*, which requires some research.

ships. But such relationships are a two-way street. Just as buyers are partnering with and supporting their suppliers, the suppliers must be worthy partners in return. They must work closely with the customers to better meet their supply needs.

For example, small industrial detergent maker ChemStation supplies thousands of products in hundreds of industries. ChemStation sells industrial cleaning chemicals to a wide variety of business customers, ranging from car washes to the U.S. Air Force. Whether a customer is washing down a fleet or a factory, a store or a restaurant, a distillery or an Army base, ChemStation comes up with the right cleaning solution every time.

But ChemStation does more than simply sell cleaning chemicals to its customers. It partners closely with them to custom-design solutions to their unique cleaning problems. First, ChemStation works with each individual customer to concoct a soap formula specially designed for that customer. It has brewed special formulas for cleaning hands, mufflers, flutes, feathers, perfume vats, cosmetic eye makeup containers, yacht-making molds, concrete trucks, oceangoing trawlers, and about anything else you can imagine. Next, ChemStation delivers the custom-made mixture to a tank installed at the customer's site. Finally, it maintains the tank by monitoring usage and automatically refilling the tank when supplies run low.

Partnering with an individual customer to find a full solution creates a lasting supplier-buyer relationship that helps ChemStation to lock out the competition. As noted in a recent issue of *Insights*, ChemStation's customer newsletter, "Our customers . . . oftentimes think of us as more of a partner than a supplier."

Sources: Katherine Zachary, "Honda Goes Beyond Philosophy in Supplier Efforts." *Ward's Auto World*, July 1, 2003, accessed at http://www.wardsauto.com/ar/auto_honda_goes_beyond_2/index.htm; Jeffrey H. Dyer and Nile W. Hatch, "Using Supplier Networks to Learn Faster," *MIT Sloan Management Review*, Spring 2004, pp. 77–84; "BJ's Knows . . . Our System Is Their Solution," *Insights*, March 2002, p. 1; Robert Sherefkin and Amy Wilson, "Why the Big 3 Can't be Japanese" *Automotive News*, February 10, 2003; David Hannon, "Suppliers: Friend or Foe?" *Purchasing*, February 6, 2003, pp. 25–30; "Delphi: Parts Maker Helps Suppliers Shape Up," *InformationWeek*, April 19, 2004; information accessed online at www.chemstation.com, January 2005; and "Supplier Information: Your Guide to Becoming a Wal-Mart Supplier," accessed at www.walmartstores.com, January 2005.

■ ChemStation does more than simply supply its customers with cleaning chemicals. "Our customers . . . think of us as more of a partner than a supplier."

FIGURE 6.1
Model of business buyer behavior

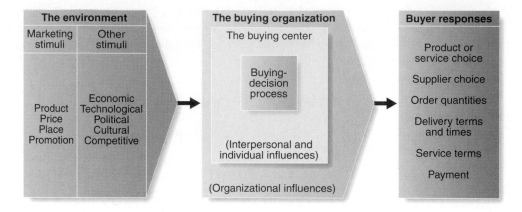

Straight rebuy
A business buying situation in which the buyer routinely reorders something without any modifications.

Modified rebuy
A business buying situation in which the buyer wants to modify product specifications, prices, terms, or suppliers.

New task
A business buying situation in which the buyer purchases a product or service for the first time.

Systems selling
Buying a packaged solution to a problem from a single seller, thus avoiding all the separate decisions involved in a complex buying situation.

In a **straight rebuy**, the buyer reorders something without any modifications. It is usually handled on a routine basis by the purchasing department. Based on past buying satisfaction, the buyer simply chooses from the various suppliers on its list. "In" suppliers try to maintain product and service quality. They often propose automatic reordering systems so that the purchasing agent will save reordering time. "Out" suppliers try to offer something new or exploit dissatisfaction so that the buyer will consider them.

In a **modified rebuy**, the buyer wants to modify product specifications, prices, terms, or suppliers. The modified rebuy usually involves more decision participants than does the straight rebuy. The in suppliers may become nervous and feel pressured to put their best foot forward to protect an account. Out suppliers may see the modified rebuy situation as an opportunity to make a better offer and gain new business.

A company buying a product or service for the first time faces a **new-task** situation. In such cases, the greater the cost or risk, the larger the number of decision participants and the greater their efforts to collect information will be. The new-task situation is the marketer's greatest opportunity and challenge. The marketer not only tries to reach as many key buying influences as possible but also provides help and information.

The buyer makes the fewest decisions in the straight rebuy and the most in the new-task decision. In the new-task situation, the buyer must decide on product specifications, suppliers, price limits, payment terms, order quantities, delivery times, and service terms. The order of these decisions varies with each situation, and different decision participants influence each choice.

Many business buyers prefer to buy a packaged solution to a problem from a single seller. Instead of buying and putting all the components together, the buyer may ask sellers to supply the components *and* assemble the package or system. The sale often goes to the firm that provides the most complete system meeting the customer's needs. Thus, **systems selling** is often a key business marketing strategy for winning and holding accounts.

Sellers increasingly have recognized that buyers like this method and have adopted systems selling as a marketing tool. Systems selling is a two-step process. First, the supplier sells a group of interlocking products. For example, the supplier sells not only glue, but also applicators and dryers. Second, the supplier sells a system of production, inventory control, distribution, and other services to meet the buyer's need for a smooth-running operation.

Systems selling is a key business marketing strategy for winning and holding accounts. The contract often goes to the firm that provides the most complete solution to the customer's needs. For example, the Indonesian government requested bids to build a cement factory near Jakarta. An American firm's proposal included choosing the site, designing the cement factory, hiring the construction crews, assembling the materials and equipment, and turning the finished factory over to the Indonesian government. A Japanese firm's proposal included all of these services, plus hiring and training workers to run the factory, exporting the cement through their trading companies, and using the cement to build some needed roads and new office buildings in Jakarta. Although the Japanese firm's proposal cost more, it won the contract. Clearly, the Japanese viewed the problem not as just building a cement factory (the narrow view of systems selling) but of running it in a way that would contribute to the country's economy. They took the broadest view of the customer's needs. This is true systems selling.[5]

■ Buying Center: Cardinal Health deals with a wide range of buying influences, from purchasing executives and hospital administrators to the surgeons who actually use its products.

Participants in the Business Buying Process

Who does the buying of the trillions of dollars' worth of goods and services needed by business organizations? The decision-making unit of a buying organization is called its **buying center**: all the individuals and units that participate in the business decision-making process. The buying center includes all members of the organization who play a role in the purchase decision process. This group includes the actual users of the product or service, those who make the buying decision, those who influence the buying decision, those who do the actual buying, and those who control buying information.

The buying center includes all members of the organization who play any of five roles in the purchase decision process.[6]

Buying center
All the individuals and units that participate in the business buying-decision process.

- **Users** are members of the organization who will use the product or service. In many cases, users initiate the buying proposal and help define product specifications.

Users
Members of the buying organization who will actually use the purchased product or service.

- **Influencers** often help define specifications and also provide information for evaluating alternatives. Technical personnel are particularly important influencers.

Influencers
People in an organization's buying center who affect the buying decision; they often help define specifications and also provide information for evaluating alternatives.

- **Buyers** have formal authority to select the supplier and arrange terms of purchase. Buyers may help shape product specifications, but their major role is in selecting vendors and negotiating. In more complex purchases, buyers might include high-level officers participating in the negotiations.

Buyers
The people who make an actual purchase.

- **Deciders** have formal or informal power to select or approve the final suppliers. In routine buying, the buyers are often the deciders, or at least the approvers.

Deciders
People in the organization's buying center who have formal or informal power to select or approve the final suppliers.

- **Gatekeepers** control the flow of information to others. For example, purchasing agents often have authority to prevent salespersons from seeing users or deciders. Other gatekeepers include technical personnel and even personal secretaries.

Gatekeepers
People in the organization's buying center who control the flow of information to others.

The buying center is not a fixed and formally identified unit within the buying organization. It is a set of buying roles assumed by different people for different purchases. Within the organization, the size and makeup of the buying center will vary for different products and for different buying situations. For some routine purchases, one person—say a purchasing agent—may assume all the buying center roles and serve as the only person involved in the buying decision. For more complex purchases, the buying center may include 20 or 30 people from different levels and departments in the organization.

The buying center concept presents a major marketing challenge. The business marketer must learn who participates in the decision, each participant's relative influence, and what evaluation criteria each decision participant uses. For example, the medical products and services group of Cardinal Health sells disposable surgical gowns to hospitals. It identifies the hospital personnel involved in this buying decision as the vice president of purchasing, the operating room administrator, and the surgeons. Each participant plays a different role. The vice president of purchasing analyzes whether the hospital should buy disposable gowns or reusable gowns. If analysis favors disposable gowns, then the operating room administrator compares competing products and prices and makes a choice. This administrator considers the gown's absorbency, antiseptic quality, design, and cost, and normally buys the brand that meets requirements at the lowest cost. Finally, surgeons affect the decision later by reporting their satisfaction or dissatisfaction with the brand.

The buying center usually includes some obvious participants who are involved formally in the buying decision. For example, the decision to buy a corporate jet will probably involve the company's CEO, chief pilot, a purchasing agent, some legal staff, a member of top management, and others formally charged with the buying decision. It may also involve less obvious, informal participants, some of whom may actually make or strongly affect the buying decision. Sometimes, even the people in the buying center are not aware of all the buying participants. For example, the decision about which corporate jet to buy may actually be made by a corporate board member who has an interest in flying and who knows a lot about airplanes. This board member may work behind the scenes to sway the decision. Many business buying decisions result from the complex interactions of ever-changing buying center participants.

Major Influences on Business Buyers

Business buyers are subject to many influences when they make their buying decisions. Some marketers assume that the major influences are economic. They think buyers will favor the supplier who offers the lowest price or the best product or the most service. They concentrate on offering strong economic benefits to buyers. However, business buyers actually respond to both economic and personal factors. Far from being cold, calculating, and impersonal, business buyers are human and social as well. They react to both reason and emotion.

Today, most B-to-B marketers recognize that emotion plays an important role in business buying decisions. For example, you might expect that an advertisement promoting large trucks to corporate fleet buyers would stress objective technical, performance, and economic factors. However, a recent ad for Volvo heavy-duty trucks shows two drivers arm-wrestling and claims, "It solves all your fleet problems. Except who gets to drive." It turns out that, in the face of an industrywide driver shortage, the type of truck a fleet provides can help it to attract qualified drivers. The Volvo ad stresses the raw beauty of the truck and its comfort and roominess, features that make it more appealing to drivers. The ad concludes that Volvo trucks are "built to make fleets more profitable and drivers a lot more possessive."

■ Emotions play an important role in business buying: This Volvo truck ad mentions objective factors, such as efficiency and ease of maintenance. But it stresses more emotional factors such as the raw beauty of the truck and its comfort and roominess, features that make "drivers a lot more possessive."

FIGURE 6.2
Major influences on
business buyer behavior

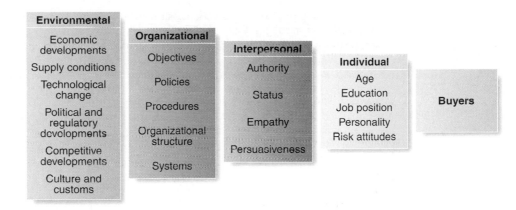

When suppliers' offers are very similar, business buyers have little basis for strictly rational choice. Because they can meet organizational goals with any supplier, buyers can allow personal factors to play a larger role in their decisions. However, when competing products differ greatly, business buyers are more accountable for their choice and tend to pay more attention to economic factors. Figure 6.2 lists various groups of influences on business buyers—environmental, organizational, interpersonal, and individual.[7]

Environmental Factors

Business buyers are influenced heavily by factors in the current and expected *economic environment*, such as the level of primary demand, the economic outlook, and the cost of money. As economic uncertainty rises, business buyers cut back on new investments and attempt to reduce their inventories.

An increasingly important environmental factor is shortages in key materials. Many companies now are more willing to buy and hold larger inventories of scarce materials to ensure adequate supply. Business buyers also are affected by technological, political, and competitive developments in the environment. Culture and customs can strongly influence business buyer reactions to the marketer's behavior and strategies, especially in the international marketing environment (see Real Marketing 6.2). The business marketer must watch these factors, determine how they will affect the buyer, and try to turn these challenges into opportunities.

Organizational Factors

Each buying organization has its own objectives, policies, procedures, structure, and systems, and the business marketer must understand these factors well. Questions such as these arise: How many people are involved in the buying decision? Who are they? What are their evaluative criteria? What are the company's policies and limits on its buyers?

Interpersonal Factors

The buying center usually includes many participants who influence each other, so *interpersonal factors* also influence the business buying process. However, it is often difficult to assess such interpersonal factors and group dynamics. Managers do not wear labels that identify them as important or unimportant buying center participants, and powerful influencers are often buried behind the scenes. Nor does the highest-ranking buying center participant always have the most influence. Participants may influence the buying decision because they control rewards and punishments, are well liked, have special expertise, or have a special relationship with other important participants. Interpersonal factors are often very subtle. Whenever possible, business marketers must try to understand these factors and design strategies that take them into account.

Individual Factors

Each participant in the business buying-decision process brings in personal motives, perceptions, and preferences. These individual factors are affected by personal characteristics such as age, income, education, professional identification, personality, and attitudes toward risk. Also, buyers have different buying styles. Some may be technical types who make in-depth analyses of competitive proposals before choosing a supplier. Other buyers may be intuitive negotiators who are adept at pitting the sellers against one another for the best deal.

AQUÍ

Real Marketing 6.2

International Marketing Manners: When In Rome, Do as the Romans Do

Picture this: Consolidated Amalgamation, Inc., thinks it's time that the rest of the world enjoyed the same fine products it has offered American consumers for two generations. It dispatches Vice President Harry E. Slicksmile to Europe, Africa, and Asia to explore the territory. Mr. Slicksmile stops first in London, where he makes short work of some bankers—he rings them up on the phone. He handles Parisians with similar ease: After securing a table at La Tour d'Argent, he greets his luncheon guest, the director of an industrial engineering firm, with the words, "Just call me Harry, Jacques."

In Germany, Mr. Slicksmile is a powerhouse. Whisking through a lavish, state-of-the-art marketing presentation, complete with flip charts and audiovisuals, he shows 'em that this Georgia boy *knows* how to make a buck. Heading on to Milan, Harry strikes up a conversation with the Japanese businessman sitting next to him on the plane. He flips his card onto the guy's tray and, when the two say good-bye, shakes hands warmly and clasps the man's right arm. Later, for his appointment with the owner of an Italian packaging design firm, our hero wears his comfy corduroy sport coat, khaki pants, and Topsiders. Everybody knows Italians are zany and laid back.

Mr. Slicksmile next swings through Saudi Arabia, where he coolly presents a potential client with a multimillion-dollar proposal in a classy pigskin binder. His final stop is Beijing, China, where he talks business over lunch with a group of Chinese executives. After completing the meal, he drops his chopsticks into his bowl of rice and presents each guest with an elegant Tiffany's clock as a reminder of his visit.

A great tour, sure to generate a pile of orders, right? Wrong. Six months later, Consolidated Amalgamation has nothing to show for the trip but a stack of bills. Abroad, they weren't wild about Harry.

This hypothetical case has been exaggerated for emphasis. Americans are seldom such dolts. But experts say success in international business has a lot to do with knowing the territory and its people. By learning English and extending themselves in other ways, the world's business leaders have met Americans more than halfway. In contrast, Americans too often do little except assume that others

■ American companies must help their managers understand international customers and cultures. For example, Japanese people revere the business card as an extension of self—they do not hand it out to others, they present it.

will march to their music. "We want things to be 'American' when we travel. Fast. Convenient. Easy. So we become 'ugly Americans' by demanding that others change," says one American world trade expert. "I think more business would be done if we tried harder."

The Business Buying Process

Figure 6.3 lists the eight stages of the business buying process.[8] Buyers who face a new-task buying situation usually go through all stages of the buying process. Buyers making modified or straight rebuys may skip some of the stages. We will examine these steps for the typical new-task buying situation.

Problem Recognition

Problem recognition
The first stage of the business buying process in which someone in the company recognizes a problem or need that can be met by acquiring a good or a service.

The buying process begins when someone in the company recognizes a problem or need that can be met by acquiring a specific product or service. **Problem recognition** can result from internal or external stimuli. Internally, the company may decide to launch a new product that requires new production equipment and materials. Or a machine may break down and need new parts. Perhaps a purchasing manager is unhappy with a current supplier's product quality, service, or prices. Externally, the buyer may get some new ideas at a trade show, see an ad, or receive a call from a salesperson who offers a better product or a lower price. In fact, in their advertising, business marketers often alert customers to potential problems and then show how their products provide solutions.

Poor Harry tried, all right, but in all the wrong ways. The British do not, as a rule, make deals over the phone as much as Americans do. It's not so much a "cultural" difference as a difference in approach. A proper Frenchman neither likes instant familiarity—questions about family, church, or alma mater—nor refers to strangers by their first names. "That poor fellow, Jacques, probably wouldn't show anything, but he'd recoil. He'd *not* be pleased," explains an expert on French business practices. "It's considered poor taste," he continues. "Even after months of business dealings, I'd wait for him or her to make the invitation [to use first names]. . . . You are always right, in Europe, to say 'Mister'."

Harry's flashy presentation would likely have been a flop with the Germans, who dislike overstatement and showiness. According to one German expert, however, German businessmen have become accustomed to dealing with Americans. Although differences in body language and customs remain, the past 20 years have softened them. "I hugged an American woman at a business meeting last night," he said. "That would be normal in France, but [older] Germans still have difficulty [with the custom]." He says that calling secretaries by their first names would still be considered rude: "They have a right to be called by the surname. You'd certainly ask—and get—permission first." In Germany, people address each other formally and correctly—someone with two doctorates (which is fairly common) must be referred to as "Herr Doktor Doktor."

When Harry Slicksmile grabbed his new Japanese acquaintance by the arm, the executive probably considered him disrespectful and presumptuous. Japan, like many Asian countries, is a "no-contact culture" in which even shaking hands is a strange experience. Harry made matters worse by tossing his business card. Japanese people revere the business card as an extension of self and as an indicator of rank. They do not *hand* it to people, they *present* it—with both hands. In addition, the Japanese are sticklers about rank. Unlike Americans, they don't heap praise on subordinates in a room; they will praise only the highest-ranking official present.

Hapless Harry also goofed when he assumed that Italians are like Hollywood's stereotypes of them. The flair for design and style

that has characterized Italian culture for centuries is embodied in the businesspeople of Milan and Rome. They dress beautifully and admire flair, but they blanch at garishness or impropriety in others' attire.

To the Saudi Arabians, the pigskin binder would have been considered vile. An American salesman who really did present such a binder was unceremoniously tossed out and his company was blacklisted from working with Saudi businesses. In China, Harry's casually dropping his chopsticks could have been misinterpreted as an act of aggression. Stabbing chopsticks into a bowl of rice and leaving them signifies death to the Chinese. The clocks Harry offered as gifts might have confirmed such dark intentions. To "give a clock" in Chinese sounds the same as "seeing someone off to his end."

Thus, to compete successfully in global markets, or even to deal effectively with international firms in their home markets, companies must help their managers to understand the needs, customs, and cultures of international business buyers. "When doing business in a foreign country and a foreign culture—particularly a non-Western culture—assume nothing," advises an international business specialist. "Take nothing for granted. Turn every stone. Ask every question. Dig into every detail. Because cultures really are different, and those differences can have a major impact." So the old advice is still good advice: When in Rome, do as the Romans do.

Sources: Portions adapted from Susan Harte, "When in Rome, You Should Learn to Do What the Romans Do," *The Atlanta Journal-Constitution*, January 22, 1990, pp. D1, D6. Additional examples can be found in David A. Ricks, *Blunders in International Business Around the World* (Malden, MA: Blackwell Publishing, 2000); Terri Morrison, Wayne A. Conway, and Joseph J. Douress, *Dun & Bradstreet's Guide to Doing Business* (Upper Saddle River, NJ: Prentice Hall, 2000); Jame K. Sebenius, "The Hidden Challenge of Cross-Border Negotiations," *Harvard Business Review*, March 2002, pp. 76–85; Daniel Joseph, "Dangerous Assumptions," *Ceramic Industry*, January 2003, p. 120; and information accessed at www.executiveplanet.com, January 2005.

General need description
The stage in the business buying process in which the company describes the general characteristics and quantity of a needed item.

General Need Description

Having recognized a need, the buyer next prepares a **general need description** that describes the characteristics and quantity of the needed item. For standard items, this process presents few problems. For complex items, however, the buyer may have to work with others—engineers, users, consultants—to define the item. The team may want to rank the importance of reliability, durability, price, and other attributes desired in the item. In

FIGURE 6.3
Stages of the business buying process

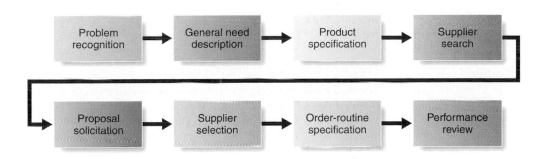

this phase, the alert business marketer can help the buyers define their needs and provide information about the value of different product characteristics.

Product Specification

Product specification
The stage of the business buying process in which the buying organization decides on and specifies the best technical product characteristics for a needed item.

The buying organization next develops the item's technical **product specifications**, often with the help of a value analysis engineering team. **Value analysis** is an approach to cost reduction in which components are studied carefully to determine if they can be redesigned, standardized, or made by less costly methods of production. The team decides on the best product characteristics and specifies them accordingly. Sellers, too, can use value analysis as a tool to help secure a new account. By showing buyers a better way to make an object, outside sellers can turn straight rebuy situations into new-task situations that give them a chance to obtain new business.

Value analysis
An approach to cost reduction in which components are studied carefully to determine if they can be redesigned, standardized, or made by less costly methods of production.

Supplier Search

The buyer now conducts a **supplier search** to find the best vendors. The buyer can compile a small list of qualified suppliers by reviewing trade directories, doing a computer search, or phoning other companies for recommendations. Today, more and more companies are turning to the Internet to find suppliers. For marketers, this has leveled the playing field—the Internet gives smaller suppliers many of the same advantages as larger competitors.

Supplier search
The stage of the business buying process in which the buyer tries to find the best vendors.

The newer the buying task, and the more complex and costly the item, the greater the amount of time the buyer will spend searching for suppliers. The supplier's task is to get listed in major directories and build a good reputation in the marketplace. Salespeople should watch for companies in the process of searching for suppliers and make certain that their firm is considered.

Proposal Solicitation

Proposal solicitation
The stage of the business buying process in which the buyer invites qualified suppliers to submit proposals.

In the **proposal solicitation** stage of the business buying process, the buyer invites qualified suppliers to submit proposals. In response, some suppliers will send only a catalog or a salesperson. However, when the item is complex or expensive, the buyer will usually require detailed written proposals or formal presentations from each potential supplier.

Business marketers must be skilled in researching, writing, and presenting proposals in response to buyer proposal solicitations. Proposals should be marketing documents, not just technical documents. Presentations should inspire confidence and should make the marketer's company stand out from the competition.

Supplier Selection

Supplier selection
The stage of the business buying process in which the buyer reviews proposals and selects a supplier or suppliers.

The members of the buying center now review the proposals and select a supplier or suppliers. During **supplier selection**, the buying center often will draw up a list of the desired supplier attributes and their relative importance. In one survey, purchasing executives listed the following attributes as most important in influencing the relationship between supplier and customer: quality products and services, on-time delivery, ethical corporate behavior, honest communication, and competitive prices. Other important factors include repair and servicing capabilities, technical aid and advice, geographic location, performance history, and reputation. The members of the buying center will rate suppliers against these attributes and identify the best suppliers.

Buyers may attempt to negotiate with preferred suppliers for better prices and terms before making the final selections. In the end, they may select a single supplier or a few suppliers. Many buyers prefer multiple sources of supplies to avoid being totally dependent on one supplier and to allow comparisons of prices and performance of several suppliers over time. Today's supplier development managers want to develop a full network of supplier-partners that can help the company bring more value to its customers.

Order-Routine Specification

Order-routine specification
The stage of the business buying process in which the buyer writes the final order with the chosen supplier(s).

The buyer now prepares an **order-routine specification**. It includes the final order with the chosen supplier or suppliers and lists items such as technical specifications, quantity needed, expected time of delivery, return policies, and warranties. In the case of maintenance, repair, and operating items, buyers may use *blanket contracts* rather than periodic purchase orders. A blanket contract creates a long-term relationship in which the supplier promises to resupply the buyer as needed at agreed prices for a set time period. A blanket order eliminates the expensive process of renegotiating a purchase each time that stock is required. It also allows buyers to write more, but smaller, purchase orders, resulting in lower inventory levels and carrying costs.

Blanket contracting leads to more single-source buying and to buying more items from that source. This practice locks the supplier in tighter with the buyer and makes it difficult for other suppliers to break in unless the buyer becomes dissatisfied with prices or service.

Performance Review

Performance review
The stage of the business buying process in which the buyer assesses the performance of the supplier and decides to continue, modify, or drop the arrangement.

In this stage, the buyer reviews supplier performance. The buyer may contact users and ask them to rate their satisfaction. The **performance review** may lead the buyer to continue, modify, or drop the arrangement. The seller's job is to monitor the same factors used by the buyer to make sure that the seller is giving the expected satisfaction.

We have described the stages that typically would occur in a new-task buying situation. The eight-stage model provides a simple view of the business buying-decision process. The actual process is usually much more complex. In the modified rebuy or straight rebuy situation, some of these stages would be compressed or bypassed. Each organization buys in its own way, and each buying situation has unique requirements.

Different buying center participants may be involved at different stages of the process. Although certain buying-process steps usually do occur, buyers do not always follow them in the same order, and they may add other steps. Often, buyers will repeat certain stages of the process. Finally, a customer relationship might involve many different types of purchases ongoing at a given time, all in different stages of the buying process. The seller must manage the total customer relationship, not just individual purchases.

Business Buying on the Internet

During the past few years, advances in information technology have changed the face of the business-to-business marketing process. Online purchasing, often called *e-procurement*, is growing rapidly. In a recent survey, almost 75 percent of business buyers indicated that they use the Internet to make at least some of their purchases. Another study estimates that e-procurement accounted for 13 percent of company total direct materials purchases last year, up from 2 percent in 2003.[9] In addition to their own Web pages on the Internet, companies are establishing extranets that link a company's communications and data with its regular suppliers and distributors.

Much online purchasing also takes place through online auctions and on public and private online trading exchanges (or e-marketplaces). For example, public trading exchanges like the auto industry's Covisint exchange offer a faster, more efficient way to buy, sell, trade, and exchange information B-to-B. The exchange handled more than $50 billion in auto parts orders last year. Similarly, the Global Exchange Services (GXS) network is one of the world's largest e-commerce networks. The GXS network was originally set up by General Electric as a central Web site through which all GE business units could make their purchases. Now operated independently, GXS processes 1 billion transactions annually, accounting for $1 trillion worth of goods and services. Customers include GE, Eastman Kodak, FedEx, DaimlerChrysler, JCPenney, Sara Lee, and Unilever Bestfoods.[10]

E-procurement gives buyers access to new suppliers, lowers purchasing costs, and hastens order processing and delivery. In turn, business marketers can connect with customers online to share marketing information, sell products and services, provide customer support services, and maintain ongoing customer relationships.

So far, most of the products bought online are MRO materials—maintenance, repair, and operations. For instance, Los Angeles County purchases everything from chickens to lightbulbs over the Internet. National Semiconductor has automated almost all of the company's 3,500 monthly requisitions to buy materials ranging from the sterile booties worn in its fabrication plants to state-of-the-art software. General Electric, one of the world's biggest purchasers, plans to be buying *all* of its general operating and industrial supplies online within the next few years.

The actual dollar amount spent on these types of MRO materials pales in comparison to the amount spent for items such as airplane parts, computer systems, and steel tubing. Yet, MRO materials make up 80 percent of all business orders and the transaction costs for order processing are high. Thus, companies have much to gain by streamlining the MRO buying process on the Web.

Business-to-business e-procurement yields many benefits. First, it shaves transaction costs and results in more efficient purchasing for both buyers and suppliers. A Web-powered

■ Online purchasing—or e-procurement: Public trading exchanges like the auto industry's Covisint exchange offer "a faster, more efficient way to communicate, collaborate, buy, sell, trade, and exchange information— business to business. The exchange handled more than $50 billion in auto-parts orders last year.

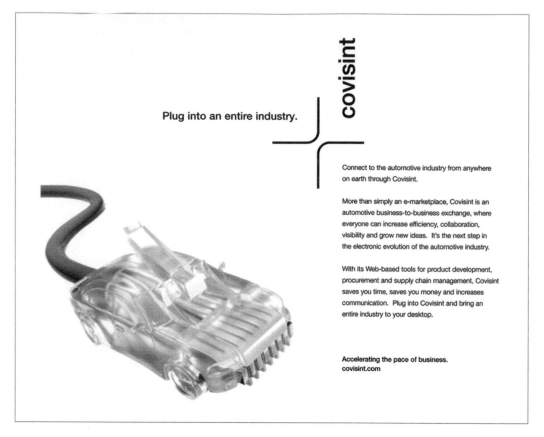

purchasing program eliminates the paperwork associated with traditional requisition and ordering procedures. On average, companies can trim the costs of purchased goods alone by 15 to 20 percent. For example, Owens Corning estimates that e-procurement has shaved 10 percent off its annual purchasing bill of $3.4 billion. And Microsoft recently reduced its purchasing costs by $700 million after implementing it MS Market e-procurement system.[11]

E-procurement reduces the time between order and delivery. Time savings are particularly dramatic for companies with many overseas suppliers. Adaptec, a leading supplier of computer storage, used an extranet to tie all of its Taiwanese chip suppliers together in a kind of virtual family. Now messages from Adaptec flow in seconds from its headquarters to its Asian partners, and Adaptec has reduced the time between the order and delivery of its chips from as long as 16 weeks to just 55 days—the same turnaround time for companies that build their own chips.

Finally, beyond the cost and time savings, e-procurement frees purchasing people to focus on more strategic issues. For many purchasing professionals, going online means reducing drudgery and paperwork and spending more time managing inventory and working creatively with suppliers. "That is the key," says the H-P executive. "You can now focus people on value-added activities. Procurement professionals can now find different sources and work with suppliers to reduce costs and to develop new products."

The rapidly expanding use of e-purchasing, however, also presents some problems. For example, at the same time that the Web makes it possible for suppliers and customers to share business data and even collaborate on product design, it can also erode decades-old customer-supplier relationships. Many firms are using the Web to search for better suppliers.

E-purchasing can also create potential security disasters. More than 80 percent of companies say security is the leading barrier to expanding electronic links with customers and partners. Although e-mail and home banking transactions can be protected through basic encryption, the secure environment that businesses need to carry out confidential interactions is still lacking. Companies are spending millions for research on defensive strategies to keep hackers at bay. Cisco Systems, for example, specifies the types of routers, firewalls, and security procedures that its partners must use to safeguard extranet connections. In fact, the company goes even further—it sends its own security engineers to examine a partner's defenses and holds the partner liable for any security breach that originates from its computer.

Institutional and Government Markets

So far, our discussion of organizational buying has focused largely on the buying behavior of business buyers. Much of this discussion also applies to the buying practices of institutional and government organizations. However, these two nonbusiness markets have additional characteristics and needs. In this final section, we address the special features of institutional and government markets.

Institutional Markets

Institutional market
Schools, hospitals, nursing homes, prisons, and other institutions that provide goods and services to people in their care.

The **institutional market** consists of schools, hospitals, nursing homes, prisons, and other institutions that provide goods and services to people in their care. Institutions differ from one another in their sponsors and in their objectives. For example, Humana hospitals are run for profit, whereas a not-for-profit Sisters of Charity Hospital provides health care to the poor, and a government-run hospital might provide special services to veterans.

Many institutional markets are characterized by low budgets and captive patrons. For example, hospital patients have little choice but to eat whatever food the hospital supplies. A hospital purchasing agent has to decide on the quality of food to buy for patients. Because the food is provided as a part of a total service package, the buying objective is not profit. Nor is strict cost minimization the goal—patients receiving poor-quality food will complain to others and damage the hospital's reputation. Thus, the hospital purchasing agent must search for institutional-food vendors whose quality meets or exceeds a certain minimum standard and whose prices are low.

Many marketers set up separate divisions to meet the special characteristics and needs of institutional buyers. For example, Heinz produces, packages, and prices its ketchup and other products differently to better serve the requirements of hospitals, colleges, and other institutional markets.

Government Markets

Government market
Governmental units—federal, state, and local—that purchase or rent goods and services for carrying out the main functions of government.

The **government market** offers large opportunities for many companies, both big and small. In most countries, government organizations are major buyers of goods and services. In the United States alone, federal, state, and local governments contain more than 82,000 buying units. Government buying and business buying are similar in many ways. But there are also differences that must be understood by companies that wish to sell products and services to governments. To succeed in the government market, sellers must locate key decision makers, identify the factors that affect buyer behavior, and understand the buying-decision process.

Government organizations typically require suppliers to submit bids, and normally they award the contract to the lowest bidder. In some cases, the government unit will make allowance for the supplier's superior quality or reputation for completing contracts on time. Governments will also buy on a negotiated contract basis, primarily in the case of complex projects involving major R&D costs and risks, and in cases where there is little competition.

Government organizations tend to favor domestic suppliers over foreign suppliers. A major complaint of multinationals operating in Europe is that each country shows favoritism toward its nationals in spite of superior offers that are made by foreign firms. The European Economic Commission is gradually removing this bias.

Like consumer and business buyers, government buyers are affected by environmental, organizational, interpersonal, and individual factors. One unique thing about government buying is that it is carefully watched by outside publics, ranging from Congress to a variety of private groups interested in how the government spends taxpayers' money. Because their spending decisions are subject to public review, government organizations require considerable paperwork from suppliers, who often complain about excessive paperwork, bureaucracy, regulations, decision-making delays, and frequent shifts in procurement personnel. Given all the red tape, why would any firm want to do business with the U.S. government? Here's how a consultant who has helped clients obtain more than $30 billion in government contracts answers that question:[12]

> When I hear that question, I tell the story of the businessman who buys a hardware store after moving to a small town. He asks his new employees who the biggest hardware customer in town is. He is surprised to learn that the customer isn't doing business with his store. When the owner asks why not, his employees say the customer is difficult to do business with and requires that a lot of forms be filled out. I point out that the same customer is probably very wealthy, doesn't bounce his

checks, and usually does repeat business when satisfied. That's the type of customer the federal government can be.

Most governments provide would-be suppliers with detailed guides describing how to sell to the government. For example, the U.S. Small Business Administration publishes a guide entitled *U.S. Government Purchasing, Specifications, and Sales Directory*, which lists products and services frequently bought by the federal government and the specific agencies most frequently buying them. The Government Printing Office issues the *Commerce Business Daily*, which lists major current and planned purchases and recent contract awards, both of which can provide leads to subcontracting markets. The U.S. Commerce Department publishes *Business America*, which provides interpretations of government policies and programs and gives concise information on potential worldwide trade opportunities.

In several major cities, the General Services Administration operates *Business Service Centers* with staffs to provide a complete education on the way government agencies buy, the steps that suppliers should follow, and the procurement opportunities available. Various trade magazines and associations provide information on how to reach schools, hospitals, highway departments, and other government agencies. And almost all of these government organizations and associations maintain Internet sites offering up-to-date information and advice.

Still, suppliers have to master the system and find ways to cut through the red tape. For example, the U.S. government has always been ADI Technology Corporation's most important client—federal contracts account for about 90 percent of its nearly $6 million in annual revenues. Yet managers at this small professional services company often shake their heads at all the work that goes into winning the coveted government contracts. A comprehensive bid proposal will run from 500 to 700 pages because of federal paperwork requirements. And the company's president estimates that the firm has spent as much as $20,000, mostly in worker hours, to prepare a single bid proposal. Fortunately, government buying reforms are being put in place that will simplify contracting procedures and make bidding more attractive, particularly to smaller vendors. These reforms include more emphasis on buying commercial off-the-shelf items instead of items built to the government's specs, online communication with vendors to eliminate the massive paperwork, and a "debriefing" from the appropriate government agency for vendors who lose a bid, enabling them to increase their chances of winning the next time around.[13]

Noneconomic criteria also play a growing role in government buying. Government buyers are asked to favor depressed business firms and areas; small business firms; minority-owned firms; and business firms that avoid race, gender, and age discrimination. Sellers need to keep these factors in mind when deciding to seek government business.

Many companies that sell to the government have not been marketing oriented for a number of reasons. Total government spending is determined by elected officials rather than by any marketing effort to develop this market. Government buying has emphasized price, making suppliers invest their effort in technology to bring costs down. When the product's characteristics are specified carefully, product differentiation is not a marketing factor. Nor do advertising or personal selling matter much in winning bids on an open-bid basis.

Several companies, however, have established separate government marketing departments, including General Electric, Rockwell, Kodak, and Goodyear. These companies anticipate government needs and projects, participate in the product specification phase, gather competitive intelligence, prepare bids carefully, and produce stronger communications to describe and enhance their companies' reputations. Other companies have set up customized marketing programs for government buyers. For example, Dell Computer has specific business units tailored to meet the needs of federal as well as state and local government buyers. Dell offers its customers tailor-made Premier Dell.com Web pages that include special pricing, online purchasing, and service and support for each city, state, and federal government entity.

During the past decade, some of the government's buying has gone online. For example, *Commerce Business Daily* is now online with its FedBizOpps/CBD site (http://cbd.cos.com). And the two federal agencies that act as purchasing agents for the rest of government have launched Web sites providing online access to government purchasing activity. The General Services Administration has set up a GSA Advantage! Web site (www.gsa.gov), and the Defense Logistics Agency (www.dla.mil) offers a Procurement Gateway. Such sites allow authorized defense and civilian agencies to buy everything from medical and office supplies to clothing through online purchasing. The GSA and DLA not only sell stocked merchandise through their Web sites but also create direct links between buyers and contract suppliers. For example, the branch of the DLA that sells 160,000 types of medical supplies to military forces transmits orders directly to vendors such as Bristol-Myers. Such Internet systems promise to eliminate much of the hassle sometimes found in dealing with government purchasing.[14]

■ The Federal government's buying has gone online. The GSA Advantage! Web site allows authorized defense and civilian agencies to buy everything from medical and office supplies to clothing through online purchasing.

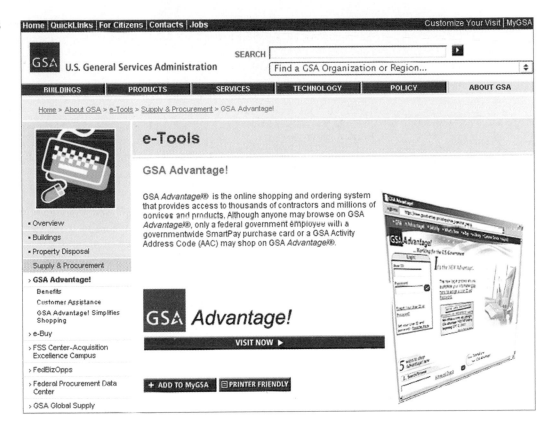

> Reviewing the Concepts <

Business markets and consumer markets are alike in some key ways. For example, both include people in buying roles who make purchase decisions to satisfy needs. But business markets also differ in many ways from consumer markets. For one thing, the business market is *enormous,* far larger than the consumer market. Within the United States alone, the business market includes organizations that annually purchase trillions of dollars' worth of goods and services.

1. Define the business market and explain how business markets differ from consumer markets.

Business buyer behavior refers to the buying behavior of the organizations that buy goods and services for use in the production of other products and services that are sold, rented, or supplied to others. It also includes the behavior of retailing and wholesaling firms that acquire goods for the purpose of reselling or renting them to others at a profit.

As compared with consumer markets, business markets usually have fewer, larger buyers who are more geographically concentrated. Business demand is *derived,* largely *inelastic,* and more *fluctuating.* More buyers are usually involved in the business buying decision, and business buyers are better trained and more professional than are consumer buyers. In general, business purchasing decisions are more complex, and the buying process is more formal than consumer buying.

2. Identify the major factors that influence business buyer behavior.

Business buyers make decisions that vary with the three types of buying situations: *straight rebuys, modified rebuys,* and *new tasks.* The buying center, which can consist of many different persons playing many different roles, is the decision-making unit of a buying organization. The business marketer needs to know the following: Who are the

major participants? In what decisions do they exercise influence? What is their relative degree of influence? What evaluation criteria does each decision participant use? The business marketer also needs to understand the major environmental, organizational, interpersonal, and individual influences on the buying process.

3. List and define the steps in the business buying-decision process.

The business–buying–decision process itself can be quite involved, with eight basic stages: (1) *problem recognition,* someone in the company recognizes a problem or need that can be met by acquiring a product or service; (2) *general need description,* the company determines the general characteristics and quantity of the needed item; (3) *product specification,* the buying organization decides on and specifies the best technical product characteristics for the needed item; (4) *supplier search,* the buyer seeks the best vendors; (5) *proposal solicitation,* the buyer invites qualified suppliers to submit proposals; (6) *supplier selection,* the buyer reviews proposals and selects a supplier or suppliers; (7) *order-routine specification,* the buyer writes the final order with the chosen supplier(s), listing the technical specifications, quantity needed, expected time of delivery, return policies, and warranties; and (8) *performance review,* the buyer rates its satisfaction with suppliers, deciding whether to continue, modify, or cancel them.

4. Compare the institutional and government markets and explain how institutional and government buyers make their buying decisions.

The *institutional market* comprises schools, hospitals, prisons, and other institutions that provide goods and services to people in their care. These markets are characterized by low budgets and captive patrons. The *government market,* which is vast, consists of government units—federal, state, and local—that purchase or rent goods and services for carrying out the main functions of government.

Government buyers purchase products and services for defense, education, public welfare, and other public needs. Government buying practices are highly specialized and specified, with open bidding or negotiated contracts characterizing most of the buying. Government buyers operate under the watchful eye of Congress and many private watchdog groups. Hence, they tend to require more forms and signatures, and to respond more slowly and deliberately when placing orders.

> Reviewing the Key Terms <

Business buyer behavior 171
Business buying process 171
Buyers 177
Buying center 177
Deciders 177
Derived demand 172
Gatekeepers 177

General need description 181
Government market 185
Influencers 177
Institutional market 185
Modified rebuy 176
New task 176

Order-routine specification 182
Performance review 183
Problem recognition 180
Product specification 182
Proposal solicitation 182
Straight rebuy 176

Supplier development 173
Supplier search 182
Supplier selection 182
Systems selling 176
Users 177
Value analysis 182

> Discussing the Concepts <

1. How do the market structure and demand of the business markets for Intel's microprocessor chips differ from those of final consumer markets?

2. In general, how are decisions and the decision processes for business markets similar to those of consumer markets? How are they different?

3. In a buying center purchasing process, which buying center participant is most likely to make each of the following statements—a buyer, decider, gatekeeper, influencer, user?

    ■ "This bonding agent better be good. I have to put this product together."

    ■ "I specified this bonding agent on another job, and it worked for them."

    ■ "Without an appointment, no sales rep gets in to see Mr. Johnson."

    ■ "OK, it's a deal—we'll buy it."

    ■ "I'll place the order first thing tomorrow."

4. The chapter claims that the eight-step business buying process is similar to the five-step consumer buying process. How would you group the eight steps in the business buying process into the five steps in the consumer buying process?

5. List and explain three benefits and three drawbacks of business-to-business e-commerce.

6. Suppose that you own a small printing firm and have the opportunity to bid on a federal government contract that could bring a considerable amount of new business to your company. List three advantages and three disadvantages of working under contract with the federal government.

> Applying the Concepts <

1. Burst-of-Energy is a food product positioned in the extreme sports market as a performance enhancer. A distributor of the product has seen a change in the demand for the product (depicted in the figure at the right). The manufacturer has done nothing to generate this demand, but there have been a couple of reports that two popular celebrities were photographed with the product. Could something like this happen? Based on the demand chart, how would you characterize the demand for the product? Is it elastic or inelastic? Would you call this an example of fluctuating demand? Support your answers.

2. Suppose that you own a small business that provides PC repair services to local businesses. In addition to the basic fix-it services you now provide, you are thinking about offering new services. Applying the "systems-selling" concept, what additional services could you offer that would make a complete package or systems solution for your customers?

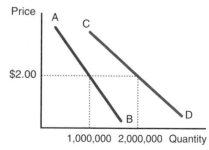

3. Form a small group and compare the similarities and differences between a buyer at a Veteran's Administration Hospital and a buyer at a for-profit hospital like Humana. Compare the buyers on the following four factors: environmental, organizational, interpersonal, and individual.

> Focus on Technology <

For small businesses, getting a contract with a division of the federal government can be both a blessing and a curse. The blessing comes in the form of welcome addition revenue. The curse comes with the unbelievable effort required to become a qualified federal government supplier. One of the better sites specifically developed to assist small businesses in becoming qualified suppliers to the federal government can be found at http://www10.americanexpress.com/sif/cda/page/0,1641,6279,00.asp#section2. At this site American Express provides the knowledge and tools necessary to start the process of bidding on government contracts. Suppose that you are a small manufacturing company that specializes in

the manufacturer of hand-print biometric security systems. Go to the site and do the following:

1. Obtain a copy of the SF 129 form (may not be on the American Express site) and fill it out as best you can.

2. What is your SIC or NAICS number and description? What's a Dunn's Number?

3. Find a federal bid that is open for a security system.

4. Was this a difficult task? Explain.

> Focus on Ethics <

You are the senior buyer for a growing technology company and an avid golfer. You have just opened an invitation to attend the Masters Golf Tournament in Augusta, Georgia this coming spring. The invitation is from a supplier company that has been trying to sell you its new line of products for the past year. They will pay for everything, travel, room, meals, and you'll even get an opportunity to play in the pro-am event on Wednesday before the match starts. You have read the newly released Employee Manual and there is no reference or rule that specifically states that an employee cannot accept a fully paid trip from a vendor; although there are some vague restrictions on lunches and dinners paid for by suppliers.

1. Do you accept or decline the invitation?

2. Just because it is not specifically mentioned in the Employee Manual would you be acting ethically if you accepted?

3. Do you think the supplier will expect "special" treatment in the next buying situation?

4. How would other company employees interpret your acceptance of this invitation?

Video Case

Eaton

You might not know about Eaton Corporation, but the company touches your life in many ways. Eaton's engine valves and torque converters are in your automobiles. More than three-quarters of new large commercial jets and all new military aircraft platforms rely on Eaton products to fly. And you'll find Eaton's products in the circuit breaker box in your home. So how come you've never heard of the company? Eaton is a business-to-business marketer, primarily selling its products to other businesses.

The company's success stems from its ability to create lasting relationships with its business customers. According to the company's Web site, Eaton works with customers and suppliers to "leverage collective strengths, capitalize on market positions, and provide an unparalleled combination of technologies and services." The company's rich understanding of its customers has made Eaton an $8 billion dollar company.

After viewing the video featuring Eaton Corporation, answer the following questions about business buyer behavior.

1. How do Eaton's business-to-business marketing efforts differ form those of companies targeting final customers?

2. Visit Eaton's Web site and review the pages detailing the products the company makes. How many products containing parts manufactured by Eaton play a role in your life? Do you think Eaton could or should market some of its products directly to final consumers to increase demand?

Company Case

Kodak: Changing the Picture

MEMORIES

"You press the button—we do the rest." With that simple slogan, George Eastman unveiled the first Kodak camera in 1888—yes, 1888, over 116 years ago. In 1900, Kodak launched its famous Brownie cameras, which it priced at $1.00, opening the photography market to millions. Throughout the 20th century, Kodak dominated the photography business. In the early 1960s, it introduced the first pocket camera, the Instamatic, and even smaller 110m cameras in the 1970s. In the 1990s, Kodak teamed with four other companies to develop and introduce the Advanced Photo System (APS), which allowed photographers to take three different-sized photos, including panoramic pictures, on one roll.

By 2000, Kodak was one of the most recognized and trusted brands in the world. Many people referred to the company as "Big Yellow." The company saw itself as being in the memory business, not in the photography business.

GOING NEGATIVE

Despite its storied past, however, when Kodak President Daniel Carp assumed the role of CEO in 2000, he knew the company faced many new challenges that would require it to rethink and perhaps redesign its business strategy. The company's stock price, which had reached a historic peak of $90 in 1997, had been plummeting. The company had begun to lay off workers.

Several factors were causing Kodak's problems. First, although Kodak had been the first company to produce a digital camera in 1976, it had been reluctant to develop the technology. Kodak, like many other companies, thought consumers would be slow to adopt digital technology. More importantly, however, it saw every digital camera consumers purchased as another nail in the coffin of its core business—making film, photo-developing chemicals, and light-sensitive paper. Second, despite Kodak's dominance in traditional photography, many competitors, especially Fuji, were exposing flaws in Kodak's marketing and stealing market share. Third, the September 11, 2001, tragedy severely depressed vacation travel and the associated picture taking. Fourth, competition from an unexpected source—cellular phone manufacturers—surprised Kodak. Nokia introduced the first cellular phone with a built-in camera in November 2001.

Although many people thought such phones would only be toys, consumers began snapping them up such that in 2003 sales of camera phones from all makers topped 84 million units—twice the sales of conventional digital cameras. Finally, consumers who owned digital cameras or cell-phone cameras were increasingly using their PCs to download and then print their own pictures on their printers, if they printed them at all. Analysts discovered that consumers printed only two percent of camera-phone pictures in the U.S. versus 10 percent in Japan. Further, analysts predicted that the number of cell phones with cameras would jump from six percent in 2003, to 19 percent in 2004, to 42 percent in 2005.

THE PROOF IS IN THE PICTURE—WALGREEN

Up through the 1980s, when consumers wanted to develop pictures, they took their film rolls to local drug stores, discount department stores, or photo shops. These stores sent to film to regional labs run by Kodak and others, which produced the prints and returned them to the store for pick up. This process took many days. Then, with the development of the self-contained photo lab, retailers could place a machine directly in their store that would do all the photo processing. These photo labs allowed the retailers to offer faster service—even one-hour service. As consumers demanded more one-hour photo developing, Kodak agreed to help Walgreen, the nation's largest drugstore chain, set up a national one-hour photo business. Kodak had been the exclusive supplier of photo-developing services to Walgreen for years. In response to the request, Kodak provided minilabs, which it bought from a Swiss manufacturer, that handled the photo developing on-site, collecting fees for leasing the equipment. Kodak even loaned Walgreen $31.6 million, interest free, to help it implement the system.

Problems developed, however, when the minilabs proved to be unreliable. They broke down up to 11 times a month due to paper jams and software glitches. It often took two to three days to get the machines serviced, and when they were, the customers' film was exposed to light when the service people opened the machine.

As a result, in 2001, Walgreen quietly began to install Fuji minilabs in some of its California stores. Fuji's machines, in addition to handling traditional film, also allowed consumers to make prints from their digital cameras memory devices, something Kodak's did not do. Kodak began selling kits to allow its minilabs to handle digital prints, but Walgreen officials believed Kodak's prints were lower quality. By early 2004, Fuji had 1,500 minilabs in Walgreen's almost 4,300 outlets.

Walgreen also approached Kodak about developing a Walgreen Internet site that would allow consumers to upload digital photos over the Web. Kodak would then store, and allow customers to order prints, which would then be mailed to them. Walgreen did not like Kodak's proposal as it minimized the Walgreen role and allowed Kodak to keep the pictures on its site, gaining an advantage in future customer orders. Despite these concerns, Walgreen was about to sign a deal with Kodak when two top officials, who favored Kodak, retired. The company then nixed the deal and started developing its own Web site with Fuji, which was comfortable with a less prominent role. Walgreen launched its Web service in 2003, with Fuji carrying out the photo developing.

A NEW DEVELOPMENT

Given all this, in early 2003, CEO Carp decided Kodak needed to reevaluate its strategy. He hired Antonio Perez, who oversaw Hewlett-Packard's rise to dominance in inkjet printers, to be Kodak's new COO. Perez believes that Kodak's future is in digital imaging for consumers, businesses, and healthcare providers. As a result, in September 2003, Carp announced that Kodak would make a historic shift in its strategy. The company would reduce its dependence on traditional film, boost investment in nonphotographic markets, and pursue digital markets, such as inkjet printers and high-end digital printing. These moves will put it in direct competition with entrenched competitors, such as H-P, Canon, Seiko Epson, and Xerox. Kodak indicated it would not make any long-term investments in traditional consumer film. At the time of this announcement, traditional film and photography accounted for 70 percent of Kodak's revenue and all of its operating profits. By 2006, the company says its traditional business will fall to 40 percent of revenues and one-half of earnings, while the digital business will provide 60 percent of revenue and one-half of earnings. As a part of the shift in strategy, Kodak announced in early 2004 that it would abandon its APS camera business and stop selling reloadable film cameras in the U.S., Canada, and Europe.

To grow Kodak's digital business, Carp and Perez will have to introduce new digital products and enter highly competitive new markets while maintaining its traditional film business, a highly profitable business it needs to fund its strategic changes. The company's goal is to increase revenues from $13.3 billion in 2003 to $16 billion in 2006 and $20 billion by 2010.

Questions for Discussion

1. How are the market structure and demand, the nature of the buying unit, and the types of decisions and decision process different as Kodak moves from its focus on the consumer market to an increased focus on the commercial and healthcare markets?

2. What examples of the major types of buying situations do you see in the case?

3. How might the buying process change as Kodak moves to new products and new markets?

4. What marketing recommendations would you make to Kodak as it responds to the digital revolution?

Sources: Ravi Chandiramani, "Can Kodak Thrive Amid the Digital Revolution?" *Marketing,* July 3, 2003, p. 13; James Bandler, "Kodak Shifts Focus From Film, Betting Future on Digital Lines," *Wall Street Journal*, September 25, 2003, p. A1; Gregory Zuckerman and James Bandler, "Investors Seek to Rewind Kodak," *Wall Street Journal*, October 21, 2003, p. C1; "Business: Has Kodak Missed the Moment?" *The Economist,* January 3, 2004, p. 46; James Bandler, "Ending Era, Kodak Will Stop Selling Most Film Cameras," *Wall Street Journal,* January 14, 2004; James Bandler, "Kodak to Cut Staff Up to 21%, Amid Digital Push," *Wall Street Journal*, January 22, 2004, p. A1; "Kodak Changes the Picture," *Economist.com*, January 23, 2004, p. 1; James Bandler, "Losing Focus: As Kodak Eyes Digital Future, A Big Partner Starts to Fade," *Wall Street Journal,* January 23, 2004; Andy Reinhardt, Hiroko Tashiro, and Ben Elgin, "The Camera Phone Revolution," *Business Week*, April 12, 2004, p. 52; Faith Arner and Rachael Tiplady, "'No Excuse Not to Succeed'; How COO Antonio Perez Is Hustling Kodak Into the Digital Age," *Business Week*, May 10, 2004, p. 96.

> After studying this chapter, you
should be able to

1. define the three steps of target
   marketing: market segmentation, target
   marketing, and market positioning
2. list and discuss the major bases for
   segmenting consumer and business
   markets
3. explain how companies identify
   attractive market segments and choose
   a target marketing strategy
4. discuss how companies position their
   products for maximum competitive
   advantage in the marketplace

CHAPTER 7

Segmentation, Targeting, and Positioning: Building the Right Relationships with the Right Customers

Previewing the Concepts

So far, you've learned what marketing is and about the importance of understanding consumers and the marketplace environment. With that as background, you're now ready to delve more deeply into marketing strategy and tactics. This chapter looks further into key marketing strategy decisions—how to divide up markets into meaningful customer groups (market segmentation), choose which customer groups to serve (target marketing), and create marketing offers that best serve targeted customers (positioning). Then, the chapters that follow explore the tactical marketing tools—the 4 *P*s—by which marketers bring these strategies to life.

As an opening example of segmentation, targeting, and position at work, let's look first at Procter & Gamble (P&G), one of the world's premier consumer goods companies. Some 99 percent of all U.S. households use at least one of P&G's more than 300 brands, and the typical household regularly buys and uses from one to two *dozen* P&G brands. But why does this superb marketer compete with itself on supermarket shelves by marketing seven different brands of laundry detergent? The P&G story provides a great example of how smart marketers use segmentation, targeting, and positioning.

P &G sells seven brands of laundry detergent in the United States (Tide, Cheer, Bold, Gain, Era, Dreft, Febreze, and Ivory Snow). It also sells six brands of hand soap (Ivory, Safeguard, Camay, Olay, Zest, and Old Spice); five brands of shampoo (Pantene, Head & Shoulders, Pert, Physique, and Vidal Sassoon); four brands of dishwashing detergent (Dawn, Ivory, Joy, and Cascade); three brands each of tissues and towels (Charmin, Bounty, Puffs), and deodorant (Secret, Sure, and Old Spice) ; and two brands each of fabric softener (Downy and Bounce), cosmetics (Cover Girl and Max Factor), skin care potions (Olay and Noxema), and disposable diapers (Pampers and Luvs). Moreover, P&G has many additional brands in each category for different international markets. For example, it sells 16 different laundry product brands in Latin America and 19 in Europe, the Middle East, and Africa. (See Procter &

Gamble's Web site at www.pg.com for a full glimpse of the company's impressive lineup of familiar brands.)

These P&G brands compete with one another on the same supermarket shelves. But why would P&G introduce several brands in one category instead of concentrating its resources on a single leading brand? The answer lies in the fact that different people want different *mixes of benefits* from the products they buy. Take laundry detergents as an example. People use laundry detergents to get their clothes clean. But they also want other things from their detergents—such as economy, bleaching power, fabric softening, fresh smell, strength or mildness, and lots of suds or only a few. We all want *some* of every one of these benefits from our detergent, but we may have different *priorities* for each benefit. To some people, cleaning and bleaching power are most important; to others, fabric softening matters most; still others want a mild, fresh-scented detergent. Thus, there are groups—or segments—of laundry detergent buyers, and each segment seeks a special combination of benefits.

P&G has identified at least seven important laundry detergent segments, along with numerous subsegments, and has developed a different brand designed to meet the special needs of each. The seven brands are positioned for different segments as follows:

- *Tide* provides "fabric cleaning and care at its best." It's the all-purpose family detergent that is "tough on greasy stains."
- *Cheer* is the "color expert." It helps protect against fading, color transfer, and fabric wear, with or without bleach. *Cheer Free* is "dermatologist tested . . . contains no irritating perfume or dye."
- *Bold* is the detergent with built-in fabric softener and pill/fuzz removal.
- *Gain*, originally P&G's "enzyme" detergent, was repositioned as the detergent that gives you clean, fresh-smelling clothes. It "cleans and freshens like sunshine. Great cleaning power and a smell that stays clean."
- *Era* is "the power tool for stain removal and pretreating." It contains advanced enzymes to fight a family's tough stains and help get the whole wash clean. *Era Max* has three types of active enzymes to help fight many stains that active families encounter.
- *Ivory Snow* is "Ninety-nine and forty-four one hundredths percent pure." It provides "mild cleansing benefits for a pure and simple clean."
- *Dreft* is a "specially formulated detergent that rinses out thoroughly, leaving clothes soft next to baby's skin." It is the #1 choice of pediatricians.

Within each segment, P&G has identified even *narrower* niches. For example, you can buy regular Tide (in powder or liquid form) or any of several formulations:

- *Tide with Bleach* helps to "clean even what's unseen." Available in regular, "clean breeze," or "mountain spring" scents.
- *Tide Liquid with Bleach Alternative* is the "smart alternative to chlorine bleach." It uses active enzymes in pretreating and washing to break down and remove the toughest stains while whitening whites.
- *Tide Rapid Action Tabs* offer portable cleaning power for a convenient way to get your clothes Tide clean.
- *Tide High Efficiency* "unlocks the cleaning power of high-efficiency top-loading machines"—it prevents oversudsing.
- *Tide Clean Breeze* gives the fresh scent of laundry line-dried in a clean breeze.
- *Tide Mountain Spring* lets you "bring the fresh clean scent of the great outdoors inside—the scent of crisp mountain air and fresh wildflowers."
- *Tide Free* "provides all the stain removal benefits without any dyes or perfumes."

By segmenting the market and having several detergent brands, P&G has an attractive offering for consumers in all important preference groups. As a result, P&G is really cleaning up in the $4 billion U.S. laundry detergent market. Tide, by itself, captures a whopping 38 percent market share. All P&G brands combined take a 60 percent share of the U.S. market—more than three times that of nearest rival Unilever and much more than any single brand could obtain by itself.[1]

Companies today recognize that they cannot appeal to all buyers in the marketplace, or at least not to all buyers in the same way. Buyers are too numerous, too widely scattered, and too varied in their needs and buying practices. Moreover, the companies themselves vary widely in their abilities to serve different segments of the market. Instead, a company must identify the parts of the market that it can serve best and most profitably. It needs to design strategies to build the *right* relationships with the *right* customers.

Thus, most companies have moved away from mass marketing and toward *market segmentation and targeting*—identifying market segments, selecting one or more of them, and developing products and marketing programs tailored to each. Instead of scattering their marketing efforts (the "shotgun" approach), firms are focusing on the buyers who have greater interest in the values they create best (the "rifle" approach).

Companies have not always practiced market segmentation and targeting. For most of the past century, major consumer products companies held fast to *mass marketing*—mass-producing, mass-distributing, and mass-promoting about the same product in about the same way to all consumers. Henry Ford typified this marketing strategy when he offered the Model T Ford to all buyers; they could have the car "in any color as long as it is black." Similarly, Coca-Cola at one time produced only one drink for the whole market, hoping it would appeal to everyone.

However, many factors now make mass marketing more difficult. For example, the world's mass markets have slowly splintered into a profusion of smaller segments—the baby boomers here, the Gen Xers there; here the Hispanic segment, there the African American seg-

FIGURE 7.1
Steps in market segmentation, targeting, and positioning

Market segmentation	Target marketing	Market positioning
Identify bases for segmenting the market	Develop measure of segment attractiveness	Develop positioning for target segments
Develop segment profiles	Select target segments	Develop a marketing mix for each segment

ment; here working women, there single parents; here the Sun Belt, there the Rust Belt. Today, marketers find it very hard to create a single product or program that appeals to all of these diverse groups.

Market segmentation
Dividing a market into smaller groups of buyers distinct needs, characteristics, or behavior who might require separate products or marketing mixes.

Figure 7.1 shows the three major steps in target marketing. The first is **market segmentation**—dividing a market into smaller groups of buyers with distinct needs, characteristics, or behaviors who might require separate products or marketing mixes. The company identifies different ways to segment the market and develops profiles of the resulting market segments. The second step is **target marketing**—evaluating each market segment's attractiveness and selecting one or more of the market segments to enter. The third step is **market positioning**—setting the competitive positioning for the product and creating a detailed marketing mix. We discuss each of these steps in turn.

Market Segmentation

Target marketing
The process of evaluating each market segment's attractiveness and selecting one or more segments to enter.

Market positioning
Arranging for a product to occupy a clear, distinctive, and desirable place relative to competing products in the minds of target consumers.

Markets consist of buyers, and buyers differ in one or more ways. They may differ in their wants, resources, locations, buying attitudes, and buying practices. Through market segmentation, companies divide large, heterogeneous markets into smaller segments that can be reached more efficiently and effectively with products and services that match their unique needs. In this section, we discuss four important segmentation topics: segmenting consumer markets, segmenting business markets, segmenting international markets, and requirements for effective segmentation.

Segmenting Consumer Markets

There is no single way to segment a market. A marketer has to try different segmentation variables, alone and in combination, to find the best way to view the market structure. Table 7.1 outlines the major variables that might be used in segmenting consumer markets. Here we look at the major *geographic*, *demographic*, *psychographic*, and *behavioral variables*.

Geographic Segmentation

Geographic segmentation
Dividing a market into different geographical units such as nations, states, regions, counties, cities, or neighborhoods.

Geographic segmentation calls for dividing the market into different geographical units such as nations, regions, states, counties, cities, or even neighborhoods. A company may decide to operate in one or a few geographical areas, or to operate in all areas but pay attention to geographical differences in needs and wants.

Many companies today are localizing their products, advertising, promotion, and sales efforts to fit the needs of individual regions, cities, and even neighborhoods. For example, Campbell sells Cajun gumbo soup in Louisiana and Mississippi and makes its nacho cheese soup spicier in Texas and California. Starbucks offers more desserts and larger, more comfortable coffee shops in the South, where customers tend to arrive later in the day and stay longer. And Parker Brothers offers localized versions of its popular Monopoly game for several major cities, including Chicago, New York, San Francisco, St. Louis, and Las Vegas. The Las Vegas version features a black board with The Strip rather than Boardwalk, hotel casinos, red Vegas dice, and custom pewter tokens including blackjack cards, a wedding chapel, and a roulette wheel.

Other companies are seeking to cultivate as-yet untapped geographic territory. For example, many large companies are fleeing the fiercely competitive major cities and suburbs to set up shop in small-town America. Hampton Inns has opened a chain of smaller-format motels in towns too small for its standard-size units. For example, Townsend, Tennessee, with a population of only 329, is small even by small-town standards. But looks can be deceiving. Situated on a heavily traveled and picturesque route between Knoxville and the Smoky Mountains, the village serves both business and vacation travelers. Hampton Inns opened a unit in Townsend and plans to open 100 more in small towns. It costs less to operate in these

TABLE 7.1   **Major Segmentation Variables for Consumer Markets**

Geographic	
World region or country	North America, Western Europe, Middle East, Pacific Rim, China, India, Canada, Mexico
Country region	Pacific, Mountain, West North Central, West South Central, East North Central, East South Central, South Atlantic, Middle Atlantic, New England
City or metro size	Under 5,000; 5,000–20,000, 20,000–50,000, 50,000–100,000; 100,000–250,000; 250,000–500,000; 500,000–1,000,000; 1,000,000–4,000,000; over 4,000,000
Density	Urban, suburban, rural
Climate	Northern, southern
Demographic	
Age	Under 6, 6–11, 12–19, 20–34, 35–49, 50–64, 65+
Gender	Male, female
Family size	1–2, 3–4, 5+
Family life-cycle	Young, single; young, married, no children; young, married with children; older, married with children; older, married, no children under 18; older, single; other
Income	Under $10,000; $10,000–$20,000; $20,000–$30,000; $30,000–$50,000; $50,000–$100,000; $100,000 and over
Occupation	Professional and technical; managers, officials, and proprietors; clerical; sales; craftspeople; supervisors; operatives; farmers; retired; students; homemakers; unemployed
Education	Grade school or less; some high school; high school graduate; some college; college graduate
Religion	Catholic, Protestant, Jewish, Muslim, Hindu, other
Race	Asian, Hispanic, black, white
Generation	Baby boomer, Generation X, Generation Y
Nationality	North American, South American, British, French, German, Italian, Japanese
Psychographic	
Social class	Lower lowers, upper lowers, working class, middle class, upper middles, lower uppers, upper uppers
Lifestyle	Achievers, strivers, survivors
Personality	Compulsive, gregarious, authoritarian, ambitious
Behavioral	
Occasions	Regular occasion; special occasion
Benefits	Quality, service, economy, convenience, speed
User status	Nonuser, ex-user, potential user, first-time user, regular user
User rates	Light user, medium user, heavy user
Loyalty status	None, medium, strong, absolute
Readiness stage	Unaware, aware, informed, interested, desirous, intending to buy
Attitude toward product	Enthusiastic, positive, indifferent, negative, hostile

towns, and the company builds smaller units to match lower volume. The Townsend Hampton Inn, for example, has 54 rooms instead of the usual 135.

In contrast, other retailers are developing new store concepts that will give them access to higher-density urban areas. For example, Home Depot is introducing neighborhood stores that look a lot like its traditional stores but at about two-thirds the size. It is placing these stores in high-density markets, such as Manhattan, where full-size stores are impractical. Similarly, Wal-Mart is testing Neighborhood Market grocery stores to complement its supercenters.[2]

Demographic Segmentation

Demographic segmentation

Dividing the market into groups based on demographic variables such as age, sex, family size, family life cycle, income, occupation, education, religion, race, and nationality.

Demographic segmentation divides the market into groups based on variables such as age, gender, family size, family life cycle, income, occupation, education, religion, race, generation, and nationality. Demographic factors are the most popular bases for segmenting customer groups. One reason is that consumer needs, wants, and usage rates often vary closely with demographic variables. Another is that demographic variables are easier to measure than most other types of variables. Even when market segments are first defined using other bases, such as benefits sought or behavior, their demographic characteristics must be known in order to assess the size of the target market and to reach it efficiently.

Age and life-cycle segmentation

Dividing a market into different age and life-cycle groups.

AGE AND LIFE-CYCLE STAGE Consumer needs and wants change with age. Some companies use **age and life-cycle segmentation**, offering different products or using different marketing approaches for different age and life-cycle groups. For example, for kids, Procter & Gamble sells Crest Spinbrushes featuring favorite children's characters. For adults, it sells more serious models, promising "a dentist-clean feeling twice a day." And Gap has branched out to target people at different life stages. In addition to its standard line of clothing, the retailer now offers baby Gap, Gap kids, and Gap Maternity.[3]

Marketers must be careful to guard against stereotypes when using age and life-cycle segmentation. For example, although some 70-year-olds require wheelchairs, others play tennis. Similarly, whereas some 40-year-old couples are sending their children off to college, others are just beginning new families. Thus, age is often a poor predictor of a person's life cycle, health, work or family status, needs, and buying power. Companies marketing to mature consumers usually employ positive images and appeals. For example, ads for Olay ProVital—designed to improve the elasticity and appearance the "maturing skin" of women over 50—feature attractive older spokeswomen and uplifting messages.

Gender segmentation

Dividing a market into different groups based on gender.

GENDER **Gender segmentation** has long been used in clothing, cosmetics, toiletries, and magazines. For example, Procter & Gamble was among the first with Secret, a brand of antiperspirant specially formulated for a woman's chemistry, packaged and advertised to reinforce the female image. More recently, other marketers have noticed opportunities for targeting women.

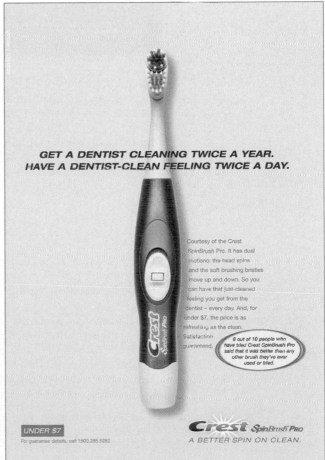

■ Age and life-cycle segmentation: For kids, Procter & Gamble sells Crest Spinbrushes featuring favorite children's characters. For adults, it sells more serious models, promising "a dentist-clean feeling twice a day."

■ Gender segmentation: Leatherman targets women with its "juice" tool in five vibrant colors, with ads like this one in *Cooking Light* magazine.

Citibank launched Women & Co., a financial program created around the distinct financial needs of women. Leatherman, which has traditionally targeted its multipurpose combination tool to men, now makes Leatherman Juice for women, hip and stylish tools offered in five vibrant colors. And after its research showed that women make 90 percent of all home improvement decisions, home improvement retailer Lowe's recently widened its isles, brightened its stores, expanded its housewares departments, and launched a family-oriented advertising campaign that reaches out to women buyers.[4]

A growing number of Web sites also target women, such as Oxygen, iVillage, Lifetime, and WE. For example, Oxygen Media runs a Web site "designed for women by women" (www.oxygen.com). It appeals 18- to 34-year-old women with fresh and hip information, features, and exchanges on a wide variety of topics—from health and fitness, money and work, and style and home to relationships and self-discovery. The leading women's online community, iVillage (www.iVillage.com), offers "real solutions for real women" and entreats visitors to "join our community of smart, compassionate, real women." Various iVillage channels cover topics ranging from babies, food, fitness, pets, and relationships to careers, finance, and travel.[5]

Income segmentation
Dividing a market into different income groups.

INCOME Income segmentation has long been used by the marketers of products and services such as automobiles, boats, clothing, cosmetics, financial services, and travel. Many companies target affluent consumers with luxury goods and convenience services. Stores such as Neiman Marcus pitch everything from expensive jewelry and fine fashions to glazed Australian apricots priced at $20 a pound. To cater to its best customers, Neiman Marcus created its InCircle Rewards program:

> InCircle members, who must spend $3,000 a year using their Neiman Marcus credit cards to be eligible, earn points with each purchase—one point for each dollar charged. They then cash in points for anything from champagne and long-stem tuxedo strawberries with a guest in a private gazebo at the top of the Lodge at Rancho Mirage (5000 points) or a Samsung Napster Digital Audio Player (15,000 points) to three nights in a premier room at the Lake Austin Spa Resort in Texas, including gourmet meals, monogrammed robes, and four spa treatments (50,000 points). For 500,000

■ Income segmentation: To thank its very best customers, Neiman Marcus created the InCircle Rewards Program. Last year, members could redeem 1.5 million points for a 13 night African safari, complete with luxury accommodations, visits with renowned conservationists, and a hot air balloon ride.

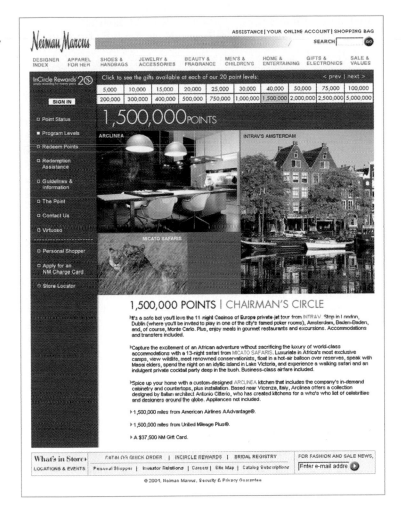

points, InCircle members can get $12,500 Nieman Marcus gift card and for 1.5 million points, a 13-night African safari, complete with luxury accommodations, visits with renowned conservationists, and a hot air balloon ride. The top prize (for 5 million points!) is a tour of Europe's finest golf courses in a private luxury jet with 15 close friends. The trip includes a personal golf professional to arrange tee times, create the pairings for a personal tournament, and clean the member's clubs between rounds.[8]

However, not all companies that use income segmentation target the affluent. For example, many retailers—such as the Dollar General, Family Dollar, and Dollar Tree store chains—successfully target lower income groups. More than half the sales in such stores come from shoppers with family incomes under $30,000. By comparison, the typical Wal-Mart shopper has an income over $40,000. When Family Dollar real estate experts scout locations for new stores, they look for lower-middle-class neighborhoods where people wear less expensive shoes and drive old cars that drip a lot of oil.

With their low-income strategies, the dollar stores are now the fastest growing retailers in the nation. They have been so successful that giant discounters such as Wal-Mart and Target are now taking notice. Wal-Mart is testing "Pennies-n-Cents" sections in 20 Supercenters, and Target is trying out "The 1 Spot" in 125 of its stores. "They are a major threat," says a retailing expert, "so much so that Wal-Mart will eventually have to buy one of these chains or start one."[7]

Psychographic Segmentation

Psychographic segmentation
Dividing a market into different groups based on social class, lifestyle, or personality characteristics.

Psychographic segmentation divides buyers into different groups based on social class, lifestyle, or personality characteristics. People in the same demographic group can have very different psychographic makeups.

In Chapter 5, we discussed how the products people buy reflect their *lifestyles*. As a result, marketers often segment their markets by consumer lifestyles. For example, Duck Head apparel targets a casual student lifestyle claiming "You can't get them old until you get them new." And Pottery Barn sells more than just home furnishings, it sells an entire lifestyle—all that its customers aspire to be (see Real Marketing 7.1). One forward-looking grocery store found that segmenting its self-service meat products by lifestyle had a big payoff:

> Walk by the refrigerated self-service meat cases of most grocery stores and you'll usually find the offering grouped by type of meat. Pork is in one case, lamb is another, and chicken is in a third. However, a Nashville, Tennessee, Kroger supermarket decided to experiment and offer groupings of different meats by lifestyle. For instance, the store had a section called "Meals in Minutes," one called "Cookin' Lite," another, filled with prepared products like hot dogs and ready-made hamburger patties, called "Kids Love This Stuff," and one called "I Like to Cook." By focusing on lifestyle needs and not on protein categories, Kroger's test store encouraged habitual beef and pork buyers to consider lamb and veal as well. As a result, the 16-foot service case has seen a substantial improvement in both sales and profits.[8]

Marketers also have used *personality* variables to segment markets. For example, marketing for Honda motor scooters *appears* to target hip and trendy 22-year-olds. But it is *actually* aimed at a much broader personality group. One ad, for example, showed a delighted child bouncing up and down on his bed while the announcer says, "You've been trying to get there all your life." The ad reminds viewers of the euphoric feelings they got when they broke away from authority and did things their parents told them not to do. Thus, Honda is appealing to the rebellious, independent kid in all of us. As Honda notes on its Web page, "Fresh air, freedom, and flair—on a Honda scooter, every day is independence day!" In fact, more than half of Honda's scooter sales are to young professionals and older buyers—15 percent are purchased by the over-50 group. "My most stable [base of] customers are white males over 60," says one dealer. "They remember riding [motor scooters] when they were young."[9]

Behavioral Segmentation

Behavioral segmentation divides buyers into groups based on their knowledge, attitudes, uses, or responses to a product. Many marketers believe that behavior variables are the best starting point for building market segments.

OCCASIONS Buyers can be grouped according to occasions when they get the idea to buy, actually make their purchase, or use the purchased item. **Occasion segmentation** can help firms build up product usage. For example, orange juice is most often consumed at breakfast, but orange growers have promoted drinking orange juice as a cool and refreshing drink at other times of the day. In contrast, Coca-Cola's "Coke in the Morning" advertising campaign attempts to increase Coke consumption by promoting the beverage as an early morning pick-me-up.

Behavioral segmentation
Dividing a market into groups based on consumer knowledge, attitude, use, or response to a product.

Occasion segmentation
Dividing the market into groups according to occasions when buyers get the idea to buy, actually make their purchase, or use the purchased item.

■ Psychographic segmentation: When Honda markets its Reflex and Elite scooters, it appeals to the rebellious, independent kid in all of us.

Real Marketing 7.1

Pottery Barn: Oh, What a Lifestyle!

Shortly after Hadley MacLean got married, she and her husband, Doug, agreed that their old bed had to go. It was a mattress and box spring on a cheap metal frame, a relic of Doug's Harvard days. But Hadley never anticipated how tough it would be to find a new bed. "We couldn't find anything we liked, even though we were willing to spend the money," says Hadley, a 31-year-old marketing director. It turned out to be much more than just finding a piece of furniture at the right price. It was a matter of emotion: They needed a bed that meshed with their lifestyle—with who they are and where they are going.

The couple finally ended up at the Pottery Barn on Boston's upscale Newbury Street, where Doug fell in love with a mahogany sleigh bed that Hadley had spotted in the store's catalog. The couple was so pleased with how great it looked in their Dutch Colonial home that they hurried back to the store for a set of end tables. And then they bought a quilt. And a mirror for the living room. And some stools for the dining room. "We got kind of addicted," Hadley confesses.

The MacLeans aren't alone. Pottery Barn's smart yet accessible product mix, seductive merchandising, and first-rate customer service have made it the front-runner in the fragmented home furnishings and housewares industry—not just because of the products that it sells, but also because of the connections that it makes with customers. Pottery Barn does more than just sell home furnishings. It sells an entire lifestyle.

Three-thousand miles away from Hadley MacLean's home in Massachusetts, Laura Alber is obsessed with a towel. A tall, slim blond with pale-blue eyes and no makeup, Alber could be the poster child for the Pottery Barn lifestyle. The 34-year-old California mother of two says that she enjoys entertaining, describes herself as living "holistically," and has just bought the company's Westport sectional sofa, with its kid-resistant twill slipcovers. She also happens to be Pottery Barn's president.

"Feel how great this is," says Alber, pulling a large white bath towel from a stack. "It's thick, it's got a beautiful dobby [the woven band a few inches from the towel's edge], it's highly absorbent, and it's $24. I can say with great confidence that you can't top this." To some merchants, a towel is just a towel. But to Alber, the towel is a fluffy icon of the lifestyle to which Pottery Barn customers aspire: upscale but casual, active but laid back, family- and friend-focused, affluent but sensibly so.

Everyone at Pottery Barn works obsessively to understand the store's customers—who they are, how they live, and what they want out of life. To create a powerful lifestyle brand, says Celia Tejada, head of Pottery Barn's design and product development, you must first have a life. So staffers are encouraged to go to restaurants and notice how the tables are set. To scavenge flea markets for interesting artifacts. To cruise real-estate open houses and model homes, looking for new architectural and design trends. To entertain friends and note what products they wish that they had: a bigger platter, a nicer serving utensil, a better bowl for salsa—anything that may be a good addition to the lifestyle line.

Staffers then use their deep personal insights to develop products and store concepts that deliver the Pottery Barn lifestyle to

■ Pottery Barn sells more than just home furnishings; it sells all that its customers aspire to be. It offers idyllic scenes of the perfect childhood at Pottery Barn Kids; trendy, fashion-forward self-expression at PB Teen; and an upscale yet casual, family- and friend-focused lifestyle at its flagship Pottery Barn stores.

customers. To pass muster, a potential new Pottery Barn product needs to pass the ultimate hurdle: "I ask my designers, 'Will you take it home or give it as a present to your best friends,'" Tejada says. "If they hesitate, I say, 'Throw it in the garbage.' Emotionally, it has to feel right."

Individual products or lines of merchandise aren't the only things inspired by the personal lives of Pottery Barn staffers. It's no coincidence that the first Pottery Barn Kids catalog debuted simultaneously with the birth of Laura Alber's first child. The company's president was frustrated at trying to put together a good-looking nursery. She and her team developed a business plan for extending the Pottery Barn lifestyle to the bedrooms of newborns and young children.

There are now 64 Pottery Barn Kids stores, with 16 more scheduled to open this year. As you might expect, Pottery Barn Kids delivers the ultimate kid lifestyle. Stores and catalogs create idyllic scenes of the perfect childhood, featuring themed bedrooms packed with accessories: fluttering curtains, cozy quilts, and stuffed animals. "My husband would tell you the furniture was for me and not the baby," says one mom. It's "a reflection of what I want her to be."

The latest Pottery Barn sibling is PBteen, which targets the lifestyles of tweens and teens. The PBteen concept seems like a

(box continues)

| Pottery Barn: Oh, What a Lifestyle! | *continued* |

natural extension, but Pottery Barn staffers spent months trying to get inside the heads of their teenage customers. "Our designers [were] going to concerts, hanging out at schools, and watching MTV," says one VP. A contest asking kids to mail in snapshots of their rooms generated photographs that gave PBteen staffers a view into the real life-spaces of teenagers. Staffers pored over them like CIA analysts.

The first PBteen catalog featured furry beanbag chairs, animal-print sheets, and desks that look like lockers. The core products consist of basic things a teenager's room needs: from shag rugs and CD stands to furniture, pillows, and frames. There are some fashion-forward offerings—a surfboard headboard, for instance—but the majority have timeless designs, in keeping with Pottery Barn's other lifestyle offerings. "We've got the stuff that fits your world," says the PBteen Web site. "Go to my room?" it concludes. "Gladly."

Regardless of which family member it targets, Pottery Barn gives customers an attainable and inspirational vision of what a really great lifestyle might look like. That may be the reason why, when Condé Nast magazine recently asked readers to name their favorite home-decorating magazine, an overwhelming number cited the Pottery Barn catalog.

The Pottery Barn lifestyle suits the company as well as its customers. Pottery Barn sales were up almost 12 percent last year; sales at Pottery Barn Kids increased by almost half. The chain's success has helped Pottery Barn's parent company, Williams-Sonoma, to achieve a sixfold increase in revenues during the past decade, and a tenfold increase in earnings. Last year, the PB chain generated almost 72 percent of Williams-Sonoma's gross sales. Pottery Barn's allure is no mystery to Tejada. "Our brand [embraces a lifestyle]. It's a state of mind. And customers can make it their own."

Sources: Adapted from Linda Tischler, "How Pottery Barn Wins with Style," *Fast Company*, June 2003, pp. 106–113. Additional information from Amy Merrick, "Child's Play for Furniture Retailers?—Amid Signs of a Baby Boom, the Big Chains Rush to Expand Offerings to Newborns, Kids," *Wall Street Journal*, September 25, 2002, p. B1; Charlyne Varkonyi Schaub, "Pottery Barn Tailoring Itself for Teens," *Sun-Sentinel*, May 9, 2003, accessed online at www.sun-sentinel.com; "William's Sonoma, Inc.," *Hoover's Company Profiles*, Austin, May 15, 2003; "'Barns' Big Part of Williams-Sonoma Cash," *Home Textiles Today*, May 3, 2004, p. 1; and information accessed at www.pbteen.com, January 2005.

Some holidays, such as Mother's Day and Father's Day, were originally promoted partly to increase the sale of candy, flowers, cards, and other gifts. And many marketers prepare special offers and ads for holiday occasions. For example, Altoids offers a special "Love Tin," the "curiously strong valentine." Beatrice Foods runs special Thanksgiving and Christmas ads for Reddi-wip during November and December, months that account for 30 percent of all whipped cream sales. Butterball, on the other hand, advertises "Happy Thanksgrilling" during the summer to increase the demand for turkeys on non-Thanksgiving occasions.

Kodak, Konica, Fuji, and other camera makers use occasion segmentation in designing and marketing their one-time-use cameras. By mixing lenses, film speeds, and accessories, they have developed special disposable cameras for about any picture-taking occasion, from underwater photography to taking baby pictures. The Kodak Water & Sport one-time-use camera is water resistant to 50 feet deep and features a shock-proof frame, a sunscreen and scratch resistant lens, and 800 speed film. "It survives where your regular camera won't!" claims Kodak. [10]

BENEFITS SOUGHT A powerful form of segmentation is to group buyers according to the different *benefits* that they seek from the product. **Benefit segmentation** requires finding the major benefits people look for in the product class, the kinds of people who look for each benefit, and the major brands that deliver each benefit. For example, our chapter-opening example pointed out that Procter & Gamble has identified several different laundry detergent segments. Each segment seeks a unique combination of benefits, from cleaning and bleaching to economy, fabric softening, fresh smell, strength or mildness, and lots of suds or only a few.

● **Benefit segmentation**
Dividing the market into groups according to the different benefits that consumers seek from the product.

The Champion athletic wear division of Sara Lee Corporation segments its markets according to benefits that different consumers seek from their activewear. For example, "fit and polish" consumers seek a balance between function and style—they exercise for results but want to look good doing it. "Serious sports competitors" exercise heavily and live in and love their activewear—they seek performance and function. By contrast, "value-seeking moms" have low sports interest and low activewear involvement—they buy for the family and seek durability and value. Thus, each segment seeks a different mix of benefits. Champion must target the benefit segment or segments that it can serve best and most profitably using appeals that match each segment's benefit preferences.

USER STATUS Markets can be segmented into groups of nonusers, ex-users, potential users, first-time users, and regular users of a product. For example, one study found that blood

■ Occasion segmentation: Altoids created a special "Love Tin"—a "curiously strong valentine."

donors are low in self-esteem, low risk takers, and more highly concerned about their health; nondonors tend to be the opposite on all three dimensions. This suggests that social agencies should use different marketing approaches for keeping current donors and attracting new ones. A company's market position also influences its focus. Market share leaders focus on attracting potential users, whereas smaller firms focus on attracting current users away from the market leader.

USAGE RATE Markets can also be segmented into light, medium, and heavy product users. Heavy users are often a small percentage of the market but account for a high percentage of total consumption. Marketers usually prefer to attract one heavy user to their product or service rather than several light users.

For example, in the fast-food industry, heavy users make up only 20 percent of patrons but eat up about 60 percent of all the food served. A single heavy user, typically a single male in his 20s or 30s who doesn't know how to cook, might spend as much as $40 in a day at fast-food restaurants and visit them more than 20 times a month. Despite claims by some consumers that the fast-food chains are damaging their health, these heavy users are extremely loyal. "They insist they don't need saving," says one analyst, "protesting that they are far from the clueless fatties anti-fast-food activists make them out to be." Even the heaviest users "would have to be stupid not to know that you can't eat only burgers and fries and not exercise," he says. [11]

Interestingly, although fast-food companies such as Burger King, McDonald's, and KFC depend a lot on heavy users and do all they can to keep them satisfied with every visit, these companies often target light users with their ads and promotions. The heavy users "are in our restaurants already," says a Burger King marketer. The company's marketing dollars are more often spent trying to convince light users that they want a burger in the first place.

LOYALTY STATUS A market can also be ~~segmented by consumer loyalty~~. Consumers can be loyal to brands (Tide), stores (Wal-Mart), and companies (Ford). Buyers can be divided into groups according to their degree of loyalty. Some consumers are completely loyal—they buy one brand all the time. Others are somewhat loyal—they are loyal to two or three brands of a given product or favor one brand while sometimes buying others. Still other buyers show no loyalty to any brand. They either want something different each time they buy or they buy whatever's on sale.

A company can learn a lot by analyzing loyalty patterns in its market. It should start by studying its own loyal customers. For example, to better understand the needs and behavior of its core soft drink consumers, Pepsi observed them in places where its products are consumed—in homes, in stores, in movie theaters, at sporting events, and at the beach. "We learned that there's a surprising amount of loyalty and passion for Pepsi's products," says Pepsi's director of consumer insights. "One fellow had four or five cases of Pepsi in his basement and he felt he was low on Pepsi and had to go replenish." The company used these and other study findings to pinpoint the Pepsi target market and develop marketing appeals. [12]

By studying its less loyal buyers, the company can detect which brands are most competitive with its own. If many Pepsi buyers also buy Coke, Pepsi can attempt to improve its positioning against Coke, possibly by using direct-comparison advertising. By looking at customers who are shifting away from its brand, the company can learn about its marketing weaknesses. As for nonloyals, the company may attract them by putting its brand on sale.

Using Multiple Segmentation Bases

Marketers rarely limit their segmentation analysis to only one or a few variables. Rather, they are increasingly using multiple segmentation bases in an effort to identify smaller, better-defined target groups. Thus, a bank may not only identify a group of wealthy retired adults but also, within that group, distinguish several segments based on their current income, assets, savings and risk preferences, housing, and lifestyles.

One good example of multivariable segmentation is "geodemographic" segmentation. Several business information services—such as such as Claritas, Experian, Acxiom, and MapInfo—have arisen to help marketing planners link U.S. Census and consumer transaction data with consumer lifestyle patterns to better segment their markets down to Zip codes, neighborhoods, and even city blocks.

One of the leading lifestyle segmentation systems is the PRIZM "You Are Where You Live" system by Claritas. The PRIZM system marries a host of demographic factors—such as age, educational level, income, occupation, family composition, ethnicity, and housing—with buying transaction data and lifestyle information taken from consumer surveys. Using PRIZM, marketers can use where you live to paint a surprisingly precise picture of who you are and what you might buy.

■ Customer loyalty: A company can learn a lot by analyzing loyalty patterns in its market. It should start by studying its own loyal customers.

You're a 36-year-old college graduate, and the price tag on your clothing testifies to your success. You drive a 3-year-old VW Jetta but have your eye on a new Honda Odyssey. You know your way around the gourmet section of your local market, buy fresh-ground coffee, and vacation at your time-share in Hilton Head Island, South Carolina. You're living out your own, individual version of the good life in the suburbs. You're unique—not some demographic cliché. Right? Wrong. You're a prime example of PRIZM's "Kids & Cul-de-Sacs" cluster. If you consume, you can't hide from Claritas. [13]

PRIZM classifies you and everyone else into one 62 unique neighborhood types or "clusters." PRIZM clusters carry such exotic names as "Kids & Cul-de-Sacs," "Blue Blood Estates," "Money & Brains," "Young Literati," "Shotguns & Pickups," "American Dreams," "New Ecotopias," "Mobility Blues," "Gray Power," and "Hard Scrabble." "Those image-triggered nicknames save a lot of time and geeky technical research terms explaining what you mean," says one marketer. "It's the names that bring the clusters to life," says another. [14]

Regardless of what you call the categories, such systems can help marketers to segment people and locations into marketable groups of like-minded consumers. Each cluster exhibits unique characteristics and buying behavior. For example, "Blue Blood Estates" neighborhoods are suburban areas populated by elite, super-rich families. People in this cluster are more likely to belong to health clubs, take expensive trips, buy classical music, and read *Architectural Digest*. In contrast, the "Shotguns & Pickups" cluster is populated by rural blue-collar workers and families. People in this group are more likely to go fishing, use chain saws, own a dog, drink RC Cola, watch ESPN2, and read *Motor Trend*. People in the "Hispanic Mix" cluster are highly brand conscious, quality conscious, and brand loyal. They have a strong family and home orientation.

Such segmentation provides a powerful tool for segmenting markets, refining demand estimates, selecting target markets, and shaping promotion messages. For example, in marketing its Suave shampoo, Unilever's Helene Curtis division uses PRIZM to identify neighborhoods with high concentrations of working women. Such women respond best to advertising messages suggesting that with Suave, looking great doesn't have to cost a fortune. Bookseller

■ In marketing its Suave shampoo, Helene Curtis uses PRIZM to identify neighborhoods with high concentrations of working women. Such women respond best to advertising messages that with Suave, looking great doesn't have to cost a fortune.

Volumizes hair as well as Matrix® Amplify? For one fifth of the price. **Suave**

Barnes & Noble locates its stores where there are concentrations of "Money & Brains" consumers, because they buy lots of books.

With the burgeoning availability of data and computer power, geodemographic marketers are continually refining their techniques. More than just tracking major demographic shifts and adding new clusters or adjusting old ones, they are slicing and dicing geographic segments into ever-smaller patches of real estate. What was previously defined for ZIP codes is now refined to smaller blocks of only a dozen or so households. Some companies, including Claritas, are taking the trend to its logical conclusion: geographic segmentation of individual households. Recognizing that the big 4-bedroom, 5-bath house on the corner may be different from the student rental housing in the middle of the block, these companies are looking to categorize every one of the nation's 110 million households.[15]

Segmenting Business Markets

Consumer and business marketers use many of the same variables to segment their markets. Business buyers can be segmented geographically, demographically (industry, company size), or by benefits sought, user status, usage rate, and loyalty status. Yet, business marketers also use some additional variables, such as customer *operating characteristics*, *purchasing approaches*, *situational factors*, and *personal characteristics*. By going after segments instead of the whole market, companies can deliver just the right value proposition to each segment served and capture more value in return.

Almost every company serves at least some business markets. For example, you probably know American Express as a company that offers personal credit cards to consumers. But American Express also targets businesses in three segments—merchants, corporations, and small businesses. It has developed distinct marketing programs for each segment. In the merchants segment, American Express focuses on convincing new merchants to accept the

■ Segmenting business markets: For small business customers, American Express has created the OPEN: Small Business Network, "the one place that's all about small business."

card and on managing relationships with those that already do. For larger corporate customers, the company offers a corporate card program, which includes extensive employee expense and travel management services. It also offers this segment a wide range of asset management, retirement planning, financial education services. Finally, for small business customers, American Express has created the OPEN: Small Business Network, "the one place that's all about small business." Small business cardholders can access the network for everything from account and expense management software to expert small-business management advice and connecting with other small business owners to share ideas and get recommendations.[16]

Many companies set up separate systems for dealing with larger or multiple-location customers. For example, Steelcase, a major producer of office furniture, first segments customers into 10 industries, including banking, insurance, and electronics. Next, company salespeople work with independent Steelcase dealers to handle smaller, local, or regional Steelcase customers in each segment. But many national, multiple-location customers, such as Exxon/Mobile or IBM, have special needs that may reach beyond the scope of individual dealers. So Steelcase uses national accounts managers to help its dealer networks handle its national accounts.

Within a given target industry and customer size, the company can segment by purchase approaches and criteria. As in consumer segmentation, many marketers believe that *buying behavior* and *benefits* provide the best basis for segmenting business markets.[17]

Segmenting International Markets

Few companies have either the resources or the will to operate in all, or even most, of the countries that dot the globe. Although some large companies, such as Coca-Cola or Sony, sell products in more than 200 countries, most international firms focus on a smaller set. Operating in many countries presents new challenges. Different countries, even those that are close together, can vary greatly in their economic, cultural, and political makeup. Thus, just as they do within their domestic markets, international firms need to group their world markets into segments with distinct buying needs and behaviors.

Companies can segment international markets using one or a combination of several variables. They can segment by _geographic location_, grouping countries by regions such as Western Europe, the Pacific Rim, the Middle East, or Africa. Geographic segmentation assumes that nations close to one another will have many common traits and behaviors. Although this is often the case, there are many exceptions. For example, although the United States and Canada have much in common, both differ culturally and economically from neighboring Mexico. Even within a region, consumers can differ widely. For example, some U.S. marketers lump all Central and South American countries together. However, the Dominican Republic is no more like Brazil than Italy is like Sweden. Many Latin Americans don't even speak Spanish, including 140 million Portuguese-speaking Brazilians and the millions in other countries who speak a variety of Indian dialects.

World markets can also be segmented on the basis of _economic factors_. For example, countries might be grouped by population income levels or by their overall level of economic development. A company's economic structure shapes its population's product and service needs and, therefore, the marketing opportunities it offers. Countries can be segmented by _political and legal factors_ such as the type and stability of government, receptivity to foreign firms, monetary regulations, and the amount of bureaucracy. Such factors can play a crucial role in a company's choice of which countries to enter and how. _Cultural factors_ can also be used, grouping markets according to common languages, religions, values and attitudes, customs, and behavioral patterns.

Intermarket segmentation

Forming segments of consumers who have similar needs and buying behavior even though they are located in different countries.

Segmenting international markets on the basis of geographic, economic, political, cultural, and other factors assumes that segments should consist of clusters of countries. However, many companies use a different approach called **intermarket segmentation**. Using this approach, they form segments of consumers who have similar needs and buying behavior even though they are located in different countries. For example, Mercedes-Benz targets the world's well-to-do, regardless of their country.

MTV targets the world's teenagers. The world's 560 million teens have a lot in common: They study, shop, and sleep. They are exposed to many of the same major issues: love, crime, homelessness, ecology, and working parents. In many ways, they have more in common with each other than with their parents. "Last year I was in 17 different countries," says one expert, "and it's pretty difficult to find anything that is different, other then language,

■ Intermarket segmentation: Teens show surprising similarity no matter where in the world they live. For instance, these two teens could live almost anywhere. Thus, many companies target teenagers with worldwide marketing campaigns.

among a teenager in Japan, a teenager in the UK, and a teenager in China." Says another, "Global teens in Buenos Aires, Beijing, and Bangalore swing to the beat of MTV while sipping Coke." MTV bridges the gap between cultures, appealing to what teens around the world have in common. Sony, Reebok, Nike, Swatch, and many other firms also actively target global teens. [18]

Requirements for Effective Segmentation

Clearly, there are many ways to segment a market, but not all segmentations are effective. For example, buyers of table salt could be divided into blond and brunette customers. But hair color obviously does not affect the purchase of salt. Furthermore, if all salt buyers bought the same amount of salt each month, believed that all salt is the same, and wanted to pay the same price, the company would not benefit from segmenting this market.

To be useful, market segments must be

■ *Measurable:* The size, purchasing power, and profiles of the segments can be measured. Certain segmentation variables are difficult to measure. For example, there are 32.5 million left-handed people in the United States—almost equaling the entire population of Canada. Yet few products are targeted toward this left-handed segment. The major problem may be that the segment is hard to identify and measure. There are no data on the demographics of lefties, and the U.S. Census Bureau does not keep track of left-handedness in its surveys. Private data companies keep reams of statistics on other demographic segments but not on left-handers.

■ *Accessible:* The market segments can be effectively reached and served. Suppose a fragrance company finds that heavy users of its brand are single men and women who stay out late and socialize a lot. Unless this group lives or shops at certain places and is exposed to certain media, its members will be difficult to reach.

■ *Substantial:* The market segments are large or profitable enough to serve. A segment should be the largest possible homogenous group worth pursuing with a tailored marketing program. It would not pay, for example, for an automobile manufacturer to develop cars especially for people whose height is greater than 7 feet.

■ *Differentiable:* The segments are conceptually distinguishable and respond differently to different marketing mix elements and programs. If married and unmarried women respond similarly to a sale on perfume, they do not constitute separate segments.

■ *Actionable:* Effective programs can be designed for attracting and serving the segments. For example, although one small airline identified seven market segments, its staff was too small to develop separate marketing programs for each segment.

■ The "Leftie" segment can be hard to identify and measure. As a result, few companies tailor their offers to left-handers. However, some nichers such as Anything Left-Handed in the UK target this segment.

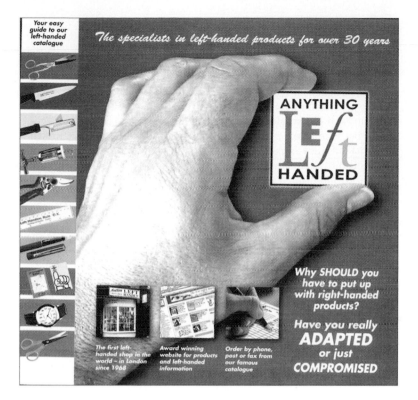

Target Marketing

Market segmentation reveals the firm's market segment opportunities. The firm now has to evaluate the various segments and decide how many and which segments it can serve best. We now look at how companies evaluate and select target segments.

Evaluating Market Segments

In evaluating different market segments, a firm must look at three factors: segment size and growth, segment structural attractiveness, and company objectives and resources. The company must first collect and analyze data on current segment sales, growth rates, and expected profitability for various segments. It will be interested in segments that have the right size and growth characteristics. But "right size and growth" is a relative matter. The largest, fastest-growing segments are not always the most attractive ones for every company. Smaller companies may lack the skills and resources needed to serve the larger segments. Or they may find these segments too competitive. Such companies may select segments that are smaller and less attractive, in an absolute sense, but that are potentially more profitable for them.

The company also needs to examine major structural factors that affect long-run segment attractiveness.[19] For example, a segment is less attractive if it already contains many strong and aggressive *competitors*. The existence of many actual or potential *substitute products* may limit prices and the profits that can be earned in a segment. The relative *power of buyers* also affects segment attractiveness. Buyers with strong bargaining power relative to sellers will try to force prices down, demand more services, and set competitors against one another—all at the expense of seller profitability. Finally, a segment may be less attractive if it contains *powerful suppliers* who can control prices or reduce the quality or quantity of ordered goods and services.

Even if a segment has the right size and growth and is structurally attractive, the company must consider its own objectives and resources. Some attractive segments can be dismissed quickly because they do not mesh with the company's long-run objectives. Or the company may lack the skills and resources needed to succeed in an attractive segment. The company should enter only segments in which it can offer superior value and gain advantages over competitors.

Selecting Target Market Segments

After evaluating different segments, the company must now decide which and how many segments it will target. A **target market** consists of a set of buyers who share common needs or characteristics that the company decides to serve.

Target market
A set of buyers sharing common needs or characteristics that the company decides to serve.

Because buyers have unique needs and wants, a seller could potentially view each buyer as a separate target market. Ideally, then, a seller might design a separate marketing program for each buyer. However, although some companies do attempt to serve buyers individually, most face larger numbers of smaller buyers and do not find individual targeting worthwhile. Instead, they look for broader segments of buyers. More generally, target marketing can be carried out at several different levels. Figure 7.2 shows that companies can target very broadly (undifferentiated marketing), very narrowly (micromarketing), or somewhere in between (differentiated or concentrated marketing).

Undifferentiated Marketing

Undifferentiated (mass) marketing
A market-coverage strategy in which a firm decides to ignore market segment differences and go after the whole market with one offer.

Using an **undifferentiated marketing** (or **mass marketing**) strategy, a firm might decide to ignore market segment differences and target the whole market with one offer. This mass-marketing strategy focuses on what is *common* in the needs of consumers rather than on what is *different*. The company designs a product and a marketing program that will appeal to the largest number of buyers.

As noted earlier in the chapter, most modern marketers have strong doubts about this strategy. Difficulties arise in developing a product or brand that will satisfy all consumers. Moreover, mass marketers often have trouble competing with more focused firms that do a better job of satisfying the needs of specific segments and niches.

Differentiated Marketing

Differentiated (segmented) marketing
A market-coverage strategy in which a firm decides to target several market segments and designs separate offers for each.

Using a **differentiated marketing** (or **segmented marketing**) strategy, a firm decides to target several market segments and designs separate offers for each. General Motors tries to produce a car for every "purse, purpose, and personality." Gap Inc. has created three different retail store formats—Gap, Banana Republic, and Old Navy—to serve the varied needs of different fashion segments. And American Express offers not only its traditional green cards but also gold cards, platinum cards, corporate cards, and even a black card, called the Centurian, with a $1,000 annual fee aimed at a segment of "superpremium customers."

Estée Lauder offers dozens of different products aimed at carefully defined segments:

> The four best-selling prestige perfumes in the United States belong to Estée Lauder. So do seven of the top ten prestige makeup products and eight of the ten best-selling prestige skin care products. Estée Lauder is an expert in creating differentiated brands that serve the tastes of different market segments. There's the original Estée Lauder brand, which appeals to older, Junior League types. Then there's Clinique, perfect for the middle-aged mom with a GMC Suburban and no time to waste. For the youthful hipster, there's the hip M.A.C. line. And, for the New Age type, there's upscale Aveda, with its aromatherapy line, and earthy Origins, which the company expects will become a $1 billion brand. The company even offers downscale brands, such as Jane by Sassaby, for teens at Wal-Mart and Rite Aid.[20]

By offering product and marketing variations to segments, companies hope for higher sales and a stronger position within each market segment. Developing a stronger position within several segments creates more total sales than undifferentiated marketing across all segments. Estée Lauder's combined brands give it a much greater market share than any single brand could. The Estée Lauder and Clinique brands alone reap a combined 40 percent share of the prestige cosmetics market.

FIGURE 7.2
Target marketing strategies

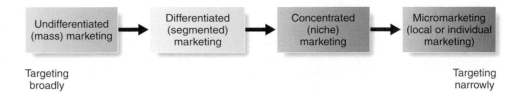

| Undifferentiated (mass) marketing | → | Differentiated (segmented) marketing | → | Concentrated (niche) marketing | → | Micromarketing (local or individual marketing) |

Targeting
broadly

Targeting
narrowly

■ Differentiated marketing: Gap has created three different retail store formats—Old Navy, GAP, and Banana Republic—to serve the varied needs of different fashion segments.

But differentiated marketing also increases the costs of doing business. A firm usually finds it more expensive to develop and produce, say, 10 units of 10 different products than 100 units of one product. Developing separate marketing plans for the separate segments requires extra marketing research, forecasting, sales analysis, promotion planning, and channel management. And trying to reach different market segments with different advertising increases promotion costs. Thus, the company must weigh increased sales against increased costs when deciding on a differentiated marketing strategy.

Concentrated Marketing

Concentrated (niche) marketing

A market-coverage strategy in which a firm goes after a large share of one or a few segments or niches.

A third market-coverage strategy, **concentrated marketing** (or **niche marketing**), is especially appealing when company resources are limited. Instead of going after a small share of a large market, the firm goes after a large share of one or a few segments or niches. For example, Oshkosh Truck is the world's largest producer of airport rescue trucks and front-loading concrete mixers. Tetra sells 80 percent of the world's tropical fish food, and Steiner Optical captures 80 percent of the world's military binoculars market.

Through concentrated marketing, the firm achieves a strong market position because of its greater knowledge of consumer needs in the niches it serves and the special reputation it acquires. It can market more *effectively* by fine-tuning its products, prices, and programs to the needs of carefully defined segments. It can also market more *efficiently*, targeting its products or services, channels, and communications programs toward only consumers that it can serve best and most profitably.

Whereas segments are fairly large and normally attract several competitors, niches are smaller and may attract only one or a few competitors. Niching offers smaller companies an opportunity to compete by focusing their limited resources on serving niches that may be unimportant to or overlooked by larger competitors. Consider Apple Computer. Although it once enjoyed a better than 13 percent market share, Apple is now a market nicher, capturing only about 3.5 percent of its market. Rather than competing head-on with other PC makers as they slash prices and focus on volume, Apple invests in research and development, making it the industry trendsetter. For example, when the company recently introduced iTunes, it captured more than 70 percent of the music download market. Such innovation has created a loyal base of consumers who are willing to pay more for Apple's cutting edge products.[21]

Many companies start as nichers to get a foothold against larger, more resourceful competitors, then grow into broader competitors. For example, Southwest Airlines began by serving intrastate, no-frills commuters in Texas but is now one of the nation's largest airlines. In contrast, as markets change, some mega-marketers develop niche markets to create sales growth. For example, in recent years, Pepsi has introduced several niche products, such as Sierra Mist, Pepsi Blue, Mountain Dew Code Red, and Mountain Dew LiveWire. Initially, these brands combined accounted for barely 5 percent of Pepsi's overall soft-drink sales. However, Sierra Mist has now blossomed into Pepsi's fastest-growing beverage brand, and Code Red and LiveWire have revitalized the Mountain Dew brand. Says Pepsi-Cola North America's chief marketing officer, "The era of the mass brand has been over for a long time."[22]

■ Some mega-marketers develop niche markets to create sales growth. For example, niche brands such as Code Red and LiveWire have revitalized Pepsi's Mountain Dew brand.

Today, the low cost of setting up shop on the Internet makes it even more profitable to serve seemingly minuscule niches. Small businesses, in particular, are realizing riches from serving small niches on the Web. Here is a "Webpreneur" who achieved astonishing results:

> Whereas Internet giants like Amazon.com have yet to even realize a consistent profit, Steve Warrington is earning a six-figure income selling ostriches—and every product derived from them—online (www.ostrichesonline.com). Launched for next to nothing on the Web in 1996, Ostrichesonline.com now boasts that it sends newsletters to 43,000 subscribers and sells 20,000 ostrich products to more than 25,000 satisfied clients in more than 125 countries. The site tells visitors everything they ever wanted to know about ostriches and much, much more—it supplies ostrich facts, ostrich pictures, an ostrich farm index, and a huge ostrich database and reference index. Visitors to the site can buy ostrich meat, feathers, leather jackets, videos, eggshells, and skin care products derived from ostrich body oil.[23]

Concentrated marketing can be highly profitable. At the same time, it involves higher-than-normal risks. Companies that rely on one or a few segments for all of their business will suffer greatly if the segment turns sour. Or larger competitors may decide to enter the same segment with greater resources. For these reasons, many companies prefer to diversify in several market segments.

Micromarketing

Differentiated and concentrated marketers tailor their offers and marketing programs to meet the needs of various market segments and niches. At the same time, however, they do not customize their offers to each individual customer. **Micromarketing** is the practice of tailoring products and marketing programs to suit the tastes of specific individuals and locations. Rather than seeing a customer in every individual, micromarketers see the individual in every customer. Micromarketing includes *local marketing* and *individual marketing*.

LOCAL MARKETING **Local marketing** involves tailoring brands and promotions to the needs and wants of local customer groups—cities, neighborhoods, and even specific stores. Citibank provides different mixes of banking services in each of its branches, depending on neighborhood demographics. Kraft helps supermarket chains identify the specific cheese assortments and shelf positioning that will optimize cheese sales in low-income, middle-income, and high-income stores and in different ethnic communities.

Local marketing has some drawbacks. It can drive up manufacturing and marketing costs by reducing economies of scale. It can also create logistics problems as companies try to meet the varied requirements of different regional and local markets. Further, a brand's overall image might be diluted if the product and message vary too much in different localities.

Still, as companies face increasingly fragmented markets, and as new supporting technologies develop, the advantages of local marketing often outweigh the drawbacks. Local

Micromarketing
The practice of tailoring products and marketing programs to the needs and wants of specific individuals and local customer groups—includes *local marketing* and *individual marketing*.

Local marketing
Tailoring brands and promotions to the needs and wants of local customer groups—cities, neighborhoods, and even specific stores.

marketing helps a company to market more effectively in the face of pronounced regional and local differences in demographics and lifestyles. It also meets the needs of the company's first-line customers—retailers—who prefer more fine-tuned product assortments for their neighborhoods.

Individual marketing

Tailoring products and marketing programs to the needs and preferences of individual customers—also labeled "markets-of-one marketing," "customized marketing," and "one-to-one marketing."

INDIVIDUAL MARKETING In the extreme, micromarketing becomes **individual marketing**—tailoring products and marketing programs to the needs and preferences of individual customers. Individual marketing has also been labeled *one-to-one marketing, mass customization,* and *markets-of-one marketing.*

The widespread use of mass marketing has obscured the fact that for centuries consumers were served as individuals: The tailor custom-made the suit, the cobbler designed shoes for the individual, the cabinetmaker made furniture to order. Today, however, new technologies are permitting many companies to return to customized marketing. More powerful computers, detailed databases, robotic production and flexible manufacturing, and interactive communication media such as e-mail and the Internet—all have combined to foster "mass customization." *Mass customization* is the process through which firms interact one-to-one with masses of customers to design products and services tailor-made to individual needs.[24]

Dell creates custom-configured computers, Reflect.com formulates customized beauty products, and Ford lets buyers "build a vehicle" from a palette of options. Hockey stick maker Branches Hockey lets customers choose from more than two-dozen options—including stick length, blade patterns, and blade curve—and turns out a customized stick in 5 days. Companies selling all kinds of products—from candy, clothing, and golf clubs to fire trucks—are customizing their offerings to the needs of individual buyers. Consider this example:

> Looking to sweeten up a party or special celebration? Try the Customized M&M's section at the M&M's Brand Store site (http://shop.mms.com), where you can special order the tasty little candies in whatever combination of colors suits your fancy. The site lets you pick from a palette of 21 colors and order in 8-ounce or 5-pound customized bags. Mix up a patriotic combo of red, white, and blue M&Ms for the chocolate lovers at your Fourth of July celebration. Or special order a blend of your school colors for the next tailgate party. Send customized promotional tins or gift bags featuring your company colors to special customers. You can even print your very own M&Ms with personalized messages tailored to a special occasion. How about "boo" on your Halloween M&Ms, or "HO HO HO" at Christmas? Want to see your name on a batch of aqua-green M&Ms? No problem. Customized M&Ms are a bit spendy—nearly three times the cost of regular M&Ms. But business is booming, with sales doubling every year.[25]

■ Individual marketing: At the Customized M&M's section of the M&M's Brand Store site, you can special order the tasty little candies in whatever combination of colors or letters suits your fancy.

Consumer goods marketers aren't the only ones going one-to-one. Business-to-business marketers are also finding new ways to customize their offerings. For example, BD, a major medical supplier, offers to customize almost anything for its hospital customers. It offers custom-designed labeling, individual packaging, customized quality control, customized computer software, and customized billing. And John Deere manufactures seeding equipment that can be configured in more than 2 million versions to individual customer specifications. The seeders are produced one at a time, in any sequence, on a single production line.

Particularly for small companies, mass customization provides a way to stand out against larger competitors:

> Oshkosh Truck specializes in making fire, garbage, cement, and military trucks. Oshkosh is small—a tenth the size of larger rivals such as Paccar and Navistar International—and the truck industry is slumping. Yet Oshkosh's have grown by 65 percent over the past 5 years; profits have more than doubled. What's the secret to Oshkosh's success? Mass customization—the ability to personalize its products and services to the needs of individual customers. For example, when firefighters order a truck from Oshkosh, it's an event. They travel to the plant to watch the vehicle, which may cost as much as $800,000, take shape. The firefighters can choose from 19,000 options. A stripped-down fire truck costs $130,000, but 75 percent of Oshkosh's customers order lots of extras, like hideaway stairs, ladders, special doors, compartments, and firefighting foam systems for those difficult-to-extinguish fires. Some bring along paint chips so they can customize the color of their fleet. Others are content just to admire the vehicles, down to the water tanks and hideaway ladders. "Some chiefs even bring their wives; we encourage it," says the president of Oshkosh's firefighting unit, Pierce Manufacturing. "Buying a fire truck is a very personal thing." Indeed, Pierce customers are in town so often the Holiday Inn renamed its lounge the Hook and Ladder. Through such customization and personalization, smaller Oshkosh has gained a big edge over its languishing larger rivals.[26]

Unlike mass production, which eliminates the need for human interaction, one-to-one has made relationships with customers more important than ever. Just as mass production was the marketing principle of the last century, mass customization is becoming a marketing principle for the twenty-first century. The world appears to be coming full circle—from the good old days when customers were treated as individuals, to mass marketing when nobody knew your name, and back again.

The move toward individual marketing mirrors the trend in consumer *self-marketing*. Increasingly, individual customers are taking more responsibility for determining which products and brands to buy. Consider two business buyers with two different purchasing styles. The first sees several salespeople, each trying to persuade him to buy his or her product. The second sees no salespeople but rather logs on to the Internet. She searches for information on available products; interacts electronically with various suppliers, users, and product analysts; and then makes up her own mind about the best offer. The second purchasing agent has taken more responsibility for the buying process, and the marketer has had less influence over her buying decision.

As the trend toward more interactive dialogue and less advertising monologue continues, self-marketing will grow in importance. As more buyers look up consumer reports, join Internet product discussion forums, and place orders via phone or online, marketers will have to influence the buying process in new ways. They will need to involve customers more in all phases of the product development and buying processes, increasing opportunities for buyers to practice self-marketing.

Choosing a Target Marketing Strategy

Companies need to consider many factors when choosing a target-marketing strategy. Which strategy is best depends on *company resources*. When the firm's resources are limited, concentrated marketing makes the most sense. The best strategy also depends on the degree of *product variability*. Undifferentiated marketing is more suited for uniform products such as grapefruit or steel. Products that can vary in design, such as cameras and automobiles, are more suited to differentiation or concentration. The *product's life-cycle stage* also must be considered. When a firm introduces a new product, it may be practical to launch only one version, and undifferentiated marketing or concentrated marketing may make the most sense. In the mature stage of the product life cycle, however, differentiated marketing begins to make more sense.

Another factor is *market variability*. If most buyers have the same tastes, buy the same amounts, and react the same way to marketing efforts, undifferentiated marketing is appropriate. Finally, *competitors' marketing strategies* are important. When competitors use differentiated or concentrated marketing, undifferentiated marketing can be suicidal. Conversely, when competitors use undifferentiated marketing, a firm can gain an advantage by using differentiated or concentrated marketing.

Socially Responsible Target Marketing

Smart targeting helps companies to be more efficient and effective by focusing on the segments that they can satisfy best and most profitably. Targeting also benefits consumers—companies reach specific groups of consumers with offers carefully tailored to satisfy their needs. However, target marketing sometimes generates controversy and concern. The biggest issues usually involve the targeting of vulnerable or disadvantaged consumers with controversial or potentially harmful products.

For example, over the years, the cereal industry has been heavily criticized for its marketing efforts directed toward children. Critics worry that premium offers and high-powered advertising appeals presented through the mouths of lovable animated characters will overwhelm children's defenses. The marketers of toys and other children's products have been similarly battered, often with good justification.

Other problems arise when the marketing of adult products spills over into the kid segment—intentionally or unintentionally. For example, the Federal Trade Commission and citizen action groups have accused tobacco companies of targeting underage smokers. And a recent FTC study found that 80 percent of R-rated movies and 70 percent of video games with a mature rating were targeted to children under 17. Some critics have even called for a complete ban on advertising to children.[27] To encourage responsible advertising, the Children's Advertising Review Unit, the advertising industry's self-regulatory agency, has published extensive children's advertising guidelines that recognize the special needs of child audiences.

Cigarette, beer, and fast-food marketers have also generated much controversy in recent years by their attempts to target inner-city minority consumers. For example, McDonald's and other chains have drawn criticism for pitching their high-fat, salt-laden fare to low-income, urban residents who are much more likely than are suburbanites to be heavy consumers. Similarly, R.J. Reynolds took heavy flak in the early 1990s when it announced plans to market Uptown, a menthol cigarette targeted toward low-income blacks. It quickly dropped the brand in the face of a loud public outcry and heavy pressure from black leaders.

The meteoric growth of the Internet and other carefully targeted direct media has raised fresh concerns about potential targeting abuses. The Internet allows increasing refinement of audiences and, in turn, more precise targeting. This might help makers of questionable products or deceptive advertisers to more readily victimize the most vulnerable audiences. Unscrupulous marketers can now send tailor-made deceptive messages directly to the computers of millions of unsuspecting consumers. For example, the FBI's Internet Fraud Complaint Center Web site alone received more than 75,000 complaints last year.[28]

■ Most target marketing benefits both the marketer and the consumer. Nacara Cosmetiques markets cosmetics for "ethnic women who have a thirst for the exotic."

Not all attempts to target children, minorities, or other special segments draw such criticism. In fact, most provide benefits to targeted consumers. For example, Colgate makes a large selection of toothbrushes and toothpaste flavors and packages for children—from Colgate Barbie Sparkling Bubble Fruit, Colgate Barnie Mild Bubble Fruit, and Colgate Looney Tunes Tazmanian Devil Wild Mint toothpastes to Colgate Pokemon and Disney Monsters, Inc. character toothbrushes. Such products help make tooth brushing more fun and get children to brush longer and more often. Golden Ribbon Playthings developed a highly acclaimed and very successful black character doll named "Huggy Bean" targeted toward minority consumers. Huggy comes with books and toys that connect her with her African heritage. And Nacara Cosmetiques markets cosmetics for "ethnic women who have a thirst for the exotic." The line is specially formulated to complement the darker skin tones of African American women and dark-skinned women of Latin American, Indian, and Caribbean origins.

Thus, in target marketing, the issue is not really *who* is targeted but rather *how* and for *what*. Controversies arise when marketers attempt to profit at the expense of targeted segments—when they unfairly target vulnerable segments or target them with questionable products or tactics. Socially responsible marketing calls for segmentation and targeting that serve not just the interests of the company but also the interests of those targeted.

Positioning for Competitive Advantage

Product position

The way the product is defined by consumers on important attributes—the place the product occupies in consumers' minds relative to competing products.

Beyond deciding which segments of the market it will target, the company must decide what positions it wants to occupy in those segments. A **product's position** is the way the product is *defined by consumers* on important attributes—the place the product occupies in consumers' minds relative to competing products. Positioning involves implanting the brand's unique benefits and differentiation in customers' minds.

Tide is positioned as a powerful, all-purpose family detergent; Ivory Snow is positioned as the gentle detergent for fine washables and baby clothes. At Subway restaurants, you "Eat

■ Positioning: At Olive Garden restaurants, "When You're Here, You're Family."

CAPPUCCINO & TIRAMISU

WE LOVE WHEN YOU HATE TO LEAVE.

When you're here, you're Family.

Fresh"; at Olive Garden restaurants, "When You're Here, You're Family." In the automobile market, the Toyota Echo and Ford Focus are positioned on economy, Mercedes and Cadillac on luxury, and Porsche and BMW on performance. Volvo positions powerfully on safety. And Toyota positions its fuel-efficient, hybrid Prius as a high-tech solution to the energy shortage. "How far will you go to save the planet?" it asks.

Consumers are overloaded with information about products and services. They cannot reevaluate products every time they make a buying decision. To simplify the buying process, consumers organize products, services, and companies into categories and "position" them in their minds. A product's position is the complex set of perceptions, impressions, and feelings that consumers have for the product compared with competing products.

Consumers position products with or without the help of marketers. But marketers do not want to leave their products' positions to chance. They must *plan* positions that will give their products the greatest advantage in selected target markets, and they must design marketing mixes to create these planned positions.

Positioning Maps

In planning their positioning strategies, marketers often prepare *perceptual positioning maps,* which show consumer perceptions of their brands versus competing products on important buying dimensions. Figure 7.3 shows a positioning map for the U.S. large luxury sport utility vehicle market. [29] The position of each circle on the map indicates the brand's perceived positioning on two dimensions—price and orientation (luxury versus performance). The size of each circle indicates the brand's relative market share. Thus, customers view the market-leading Cadillac Escalade as a moderately priced large luxury SUV with a balance of luxury and performance.

The original Hummer H1 is positioned as a very high performance SUV with a price tag to match. Hummer targets the H1 toward a small segment of well-off rugged individualists. According to the H1 Web site, "The H1 was built around one central philosophy: function. Every aspect of the H1 was created to allow it to go where cars and trucks just aren't supposed to go. [It] gives you an incredible sense of freedom and allows you to experience the world and your place in it."

By contrast, although also oriented toward performance, the Hummer H2 is positioned as a more luxury-oriented and more reasonably priced luxury SUV. The H2 is targeted toward a larger segment of urban and suburban professionals. "In a world where SUVs have begun to look like their owners, complete with love handles and mushy seats, the H2 proves that there is still one out there that can drop and give you twenty," says the H2 Web site. The H2 "strikes a perfect balance between interior comfort, on-the-road capability, and off-road capability."

FIGURE 7.3
Positioning map: Large luxury SUVs

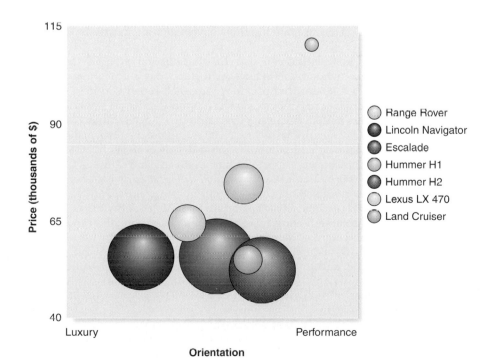

Choosing a Positioning Strategy

Some firms find it easy to choose their positioning strategy. For example, a firm well known for quality in certain segments will go for this position in a new segment if there are enough buyers seeking quality. But in many cases, two or more firms will go after the same position. Then, each will have to find other ways to set itself apart. Each firm must differentiate its offer by building a unique bundle of benefits that appeals to a substantial group within the segment.

The positioning task consists of three steps: identifying a set of possible competitive advantages upon which to build a position, choosing the right competitive advantages, and selecting an overall positioning strategy. The company must then effectively communicate and deliver the chosen position to the market.

Identifying Possible Competitive Advantages

Competitive advantage
An advantage over competitors gained by offering consumers greater value, either through lower prices or by providing more benefits that justify higher prices.

To build profitable relationships with target customers, marketers must understand customer needs better than competitors do and deliver more value. To the extent that a company can position itself as providing superior value, it gains **competitive advantage**. But solid positions cannot be built on empty promises. If a company positions its product as *offering* the best quality and service, it must then *deliver* the promised quality and service. Thus, positioning begins with actually *differentiating* the company's marketing offer so that it will give consumers superior value.

To find points of differentiation, marketers must think through the customer's entire experience with the company's product or service. An alert company can find ways to differentiate itself at every customer contact point. In what specific ways can a company differentiate itself or its market offer? It can differentiate along the lines of *product, services, channels, people,* or *image.*

Product differentiation takes place along a continuum. At one extreme we find physical products that allow little variation: chicken, steel, aspirin. Yet even here some meaningful differentiation is possible. For example, Perdue claims that its branded chickens are better—fresher and more tender—and gets a 10 percent price premium based on this differentiation. At the other extreme are products that can be highly differentiated, such as automobiles, clothing, and furniture. Such products can be differentiated on features, performance, or style and design. Thus, Volvo provides new and better safety features; Whirlpool designs its dishwasher to run more quietly; Bose positions its speakers on their striking design characteristics. Similarly, companies can differentiate their products on such attributes as consistency, durability, reliability, or repairability.

Beyond differentiating its physical product, a firm can also differentiate the services that accompany the product. Some companies gain *services differentiation* through speedy, convenient, or careful delivery. For example, BankOne has opened full-service branches in supermarkets to provide location convenience along with Saturday, Sunday, and weekday-evening hours.

Installation can also differentiate one company from another, as can repair services. Many an automobile buyer will gladly pay a little more and travel a little farther to buy a car from a dealer that provides top-notch repair services. Some companies differentiate their offers by providing customer training service or consulting services—data, information systems, and advising services that buyers need. McKesson Corporation, a major drug wholesaler, consults with its 12,000 independent pharmacists to help them set up accounting, inventory, and computerized ordering systems. By helping its customers compete better, McKesson gains greater customer loyalty and sales.

Firms that practice *channel differentiation* gain competitive advantage through the way they design their channel's coverage, expertise, and performance. Amazon.com, Dell, and Avon set themselves apart with their high-quality direct channels. Caterpillar's success in the construction-equipment industry is based on superior channels. Its dealers worldwide are renowned for their first-rate service.

Companies can gain a strong competitive advantage through *people differentiation*—hiring and training better people than their competitors do. Disney people are known to be friendly and upbeat. Singapore Airlines enjoys an excellent reputation largely because of the grace of its flight attendants. IBM offers people who make sure that the solution customers want is the solution they get: "People Who Get It. People Who Get It Done." People differentiation requires that a company select its customer-contact people carefully and train them well. For example, Disney trains its theme park people thoroughly to ensure that they are competent, courteous, and friendly—from the hotel check-in agents, to the monorail drivers,

■ People differentiation: Disney World people are known to be friendly and upbeat. Each employee is carefully trained to understand customers and to "make people happy."

to the ride attendants, to the people who sweep Main Street USA. Each employee is carefully trained to understand customers and to "make people happy."

Even when competing offers look the same, buyers may perceive a difference based on company or brand *image differentiation*. A company or brand image should convey the product's distinctive benefits and positioning. Developing a strong and distinctive image calls for creativity and hard work. A company cannot develop an image in the public's mind overnight using only a few advertisements. If Ritz-Carlton means quality, this image must be supported by everything the company says and does. Symbols—such as the McDonald's golden arches, the Prudential rock, the Nike swoosh, or Google's colorful logo—can provide strong company or brand recognition and image differentiation. The company might build a brand around a famous person, as Nike did with its Air Jordan basketball shoes and Tiger Woods golfing products. Some companies even become associated with colors, such as IBM (blue) or UPS (brown). The chosen symbols, characters, and other image elements must be communicated through advertising that conveys the company's or brand's personality.

Choosing the Right Competitive Advantages

Suppose a company is fortunate enough to discover several potential competitive advantages. It now must choose the ones on which it will build its positioning strategy. It must decide *how many* differences to promote and *which ones*.

HOW MANY DIFFERENCES TO PROMOTE? Many marketers think that companies should aggressively promote only one benefit to the target market. Ad man Rosser Reeves, for example, said a company should develop a *unique selling proposition* (USP) for each brand and stick to it. Each brand should pick an attribute and tout itself as "number one" on that attribute. Buyers tend to remember number one better, especially in an overcommunicated society. Thus, Crest toothpaste consistently promotes its anticavity protection and Wal-Mart promotes low prices. A company that hammers away at one of these positions and consistently delivers on it probably will become best known and remembered for it.

Other marketers think that companies should position themselves on more than one differentiator. This may be necessary if two or more firms are claiming to be best on the same attribute. Today, in a time when the mass market is fragmenting into many small segments, companies are trying to broaden their positioning strategies to appeal to more segments. For example, Unilever introduced the first three-in-one bar soap—Lever 2000—offering cleansing, deodorizing, *and* moisturizing benefits. Clearly, many buyers want all three benefits. The challenge was to convince them that one brand can deliver all three. Judging from Lever 2000's outstanding success, Unilever easily met the challenge. However, as companies increase the number of claims for their brands, they risk disbelief and a loss of clear positioning.

■ Unilever positioned its best-selling Lever 2000 soap on three benefits in one: cleansing, deodorizing, and moisturizing benefits. It's good "for all your 2000 parts."

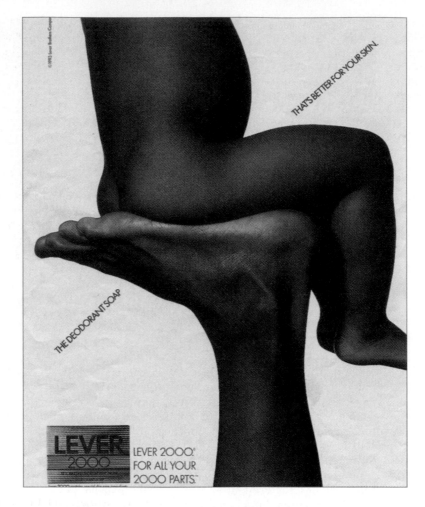

WHICH DIFFERENCES TO PROMOTE? Not all brand differences are meaningful or worthwhile; not every difference makes a good differentiator. Each difference has the potential to create company costs as well as customer benefits. Therefore, the company must carefully select the ways in which it will distinguish itself from competitors. A difference is worth establishing to the extent that it satisfies the following criteria:

■ *Important:* The difference delivers a highly valued benefit to target buyers.

■ *Distinctive:* Competitors do not offer the difference, or the company can offer it in a more distinctive way.

■ *Superior:* The difference is superior to other ways that customers might obtain the same benefit.

■ *Communicable:* The difference is communicable and visible to buyers.

■ *Preemptive:* Competitors cannot easily copy the difference.

■ *Affordable:* Buyers can afford to pay for the difference.

■ *Profitable:* The company can introduce the difference profitably.

Many companies have introduced differentiations that failed one or more of these tests. When Westin Stamford hotel in Singapore advertised that it is the world's tallest hotel, the distinction that was not important to most tourists—in fact, it turned many off. Polaroid's Polarvision, which produced instantly developed home movies, bombed too. Although Polarvision was distinctive and even preemptive, it was inferior to another way of capturing motion, namely, camcorders. Thus, choosing competitive advantages upon which to position a product or service can be difficult, yet such choices may be crucial to success.

 Selecting an Overall Positioning Strategy

Consumers typically choose products and services that give them the greatest value. Thus, marketers want to position their brands on the key benefits that they offer relative to compet-

FIGURE 7.4
Possible value propositions

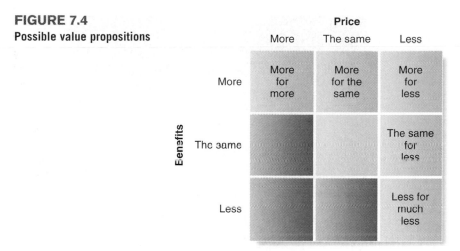

Value proposition

The full positioning of a brand—the full mix of benefits upon which it is positioned.

ing brands. The full positioning of a brand is called the brand's **value proposition**—the full mix of benefits upon which the brand is positioned. It is the answer to the customer's question "Why should I buy your brand?" Volvo's value proposition hinges on safety but also includes reliability, roominess, and styling, all for a price that is higher than average but seems fair for this mix of benefits.

Figure 7.4 shows possible value propositions upon which a company might position its products. In the figure, the five green cells represent winning value propositions—positioning that gives the company competitive advantage. The red cells, however, represent losing value propositions. The center yellow cell represents at best a marginal proposition. In the following sections, we discuss the five winning value propositions upon which companies can position their products: more for more, more for the same, the same for less, less for much less, and more for less.[30]

MORE FOR MORE "More for more" positioning involves providing the most upscale product or service and charging a higher price to cover the higher costs. Ritz-Carlton Hotels, Mont Blanc writing instruments, Mercedes-Benz automobiles—each claims superior quality, craftsmanship, durability, performance, or style and charges a price to match. Not only is the marketing offer high in quality, it also gives prestige to the buyer. It symbolizes status and a loftier lifestyle. Often, the price difference exceeds the actual increment in quality.

Sellers offering "only the best" can be found in every product and service category, from hotels, restaurants, food, and fashion to cars and kitchen appliances. Consumers are sometimes surprised, even delighted, when a new competitor enters a category with an unusually high-priced brand. Starbucks coffee entered as a very expensive brand in a largely commodity category; Häagen-Dazs came in as a premium ice cream brand at a price never before charged.

In general, companies should be on the lookout for opportunities to introduce a "much-more-for-much-more" brand in any underdeveloped product or service category. Yet "more-for-more" brands can be vulnerable. They often invite imitators who claim the same quality but at a lower price. Luxury goods that sell well during good times may be at risk during economic downturns when buyers become more cautious in their spending.

MORE FOR THE SAME Companies can attack a competitor's more-for-more positioning by introducing a brand offering comparable quality but at a lower price. For example, Toyota introduced its Lexus line with a "more-for-the-same" value proposition. Its headline read: "Perhaps the first time in history that trading a $72,000 car for a $36,000 car could be considered trading up." It communicated the high quality of its new Lexus through rave reviews in car magazines and through a widely distributed videotape showing side-by-side comparisons of Lexus and Mercedes automobiles. It published surveys showing that Lexus dealers were providing customers with better sales and service experiences than were Mercedes dealerships. Many Mercedes owners switched to Lexus, and the Lexus repurchase rate has been 60 percent, twice the industry average.

THE SAME FOR LESS Offering "the same for less" can be a powerful value proposition—everyone likes a good deal. For example, Dell offers equivalent quality computers at a lower "price for performance." Discounts stores such as Wal-Mart and "category killers" such as Best Buy,

■ "Much more for much more" value proposition: Häagen-Dazs offers its superpremium ice cream at a price never before charged.

Circuit City, and Sportmart also use this positioning. They don't claim to offer different or better products. Instead, they offer many of the same brands as department stores and specialty stores but at deep discounts based on superior purchasing power and lower-cost operations. Other companies develop imitative but lower-priced brands in an effort to lure customers away from the market leader. For example, AMD makes less expensive versions of Intel's market-leading microprocessor chips.

LESS FOR MUCH LESS A market almost always exists for products that offer less and therefore cost less. Few people need, want, or can afford "the very best" in everything they buy. In many cases, consumers will gladly settle for less than optimal performance or give up some of the bells and whistles in exchange for a lower price. For example, many travelers seeking lodgings prefer not to pay for what they consider unnecessary extras, such as a pool, attached restaurant, or mints on the pillow. Motel chains such as Motel 6 suspend some of these amenities and charge less accordingly.

"Less for much less" positioning involves meeting consumers' lower performance or quality requirements at a much lower price. For example, Family Dollar and Dollar General stores offer more affordable goods at very low prices. Sam's Club and Costco warehouse stores offer less merchandise selection and consistency, and much lower levels of service; as a result, they charge rock-bottom prices. Southwest Airlines, the nation's most profitable air carrier, also practices less for much less positioning. It charges incredibly low prices by not serving food, not assigning seats, and not using travel agents (see Real Marketing 7.2).

MORE FOR LESS Of course, the winning value proposition would be to offer "more for less." Many companies claim to do this. For example, Dell Computer to have better products *and* lower prices for a given level of performance. Procter & Gamble claims that its laundry detergents provide the best cleaning *and* everyday low prices. In the short run, some companies can actually achieve such lofty positions. For example, when it first opened for business, Home Depot had arguably the best product selection, the best service, *and* the lowest prices compared with local hardware stores and other home improvement chains.

Real Marketing 7.2

In an industry beset by hard times, Southwest Airlines soars above its competition. In the wake a global economic slump and the effects of increased terrorism, most airlines have suffered huge loses in recent years, or even declared bankruptcy. Yet even in these bleak times, Southwest has yet to suffer a loss in a single quarter. Amazingly, Southwest has experienced 31 straight years of profits. What's the secret? Southwest is the most strongly and clearly positioned airline in the world. It offers a classic "less-for-much-less" value proposition.

From the start, Southwest has positioned itself firmly as *the* no-frills, low-price airline. Its average flight time is just 1½ hours; its average one-way fare is less than $88. Southwest's passengers have learned to fly without the amenities. For example, the airline provides no meals—just peanuts and other snacks. It also offers no first-class section, only six-across seating in all of its planes. There's no in-flight entertainment, either, and there's no such thing as a reserved seat on a Southwest flight. Passengers are assigned to boarding groups when checking in and herded onto the plane in three groups. "Southwest will get you and your luggage where you're going," comments an industry analyst, "but we don't call their planes cattle cars for nothing."

Why, then, do so many passengers love Southwest? Perhaps most importantly, Southwest excels at the basics of getting passengers where they want to go on time. Every year, Southwest ranks among the industry's leaders in on-time performance, baggage handling, and customer service. All this makes Southwest passengers a satisfied bunch. For the past 13 consecutive years, Southwest has ranked number one in fewest customer complaints in the U.S. Department of Transportation's Air Travel Consumer Report. And for at least the last 10 years, it has rated number-one in the airline industry in customer satisfaction on the American Customer Satisfaction Index.

Beyond the basics, however, there are two key elements to Southwest's strong positioning. The analyst sums up Southwest's positioning this way: "It is not luxurious, . . . but it's cheap and it's fun." Southwest is a model of efficiency and low-cost operations. As a result, its prices are shockingly low. When it enters a new market, Southwest proclaims: "Southwest is coming to town, and airline prices are coming down." In fact, prices are so low that when Southwest enters a market, it actually increases total air traffic by attracting customers who might otherwise travel by car or bus. For example, when Southwest began its Louisville-Chicago flight at a one-way rate of $49 versus competitors' $250, total weekly air passenger traffic between the two cities increased from 8,000 to 26,000.

No frills and low prices, however, don't mean drudgery. To lighten things up, Southwest adds another key positioning ingredient—lots of good, clean fun. With its happy go lucky chairman and co-founder, Herb Kelleher, leading the charge, Southwest refuses to take itself seriously. Cheerful employees go out of their way to amuse, surprise, or somehow entertain passengers. According to one account:

> Southwest employees are apt to dress as leprechauns on St.
> Patrick's Day, rabbits on Easter, and almost anything on

■ Southwest offers a classic "less for much less" value proposition, with lots of zany fun. It all starts at the top with company founder and chairman Herb Kelleher.

> Halloween. I have heard flight attendants sing the safety lecture as country music, blues, and rap; I have heard them compare the pilot to Rocky Raccoon and insist that passengers introduce themselves to one another, then hug, then kiss, then propose marriage.

Kelleher himself has been known to dress up as Elvis Presley to greet passengers.

During delays at the gate, ticket agents will award prizes to the passenger with the largest hole in his or her sock. Flight attendants have been known to hide in overhead luggage bins and then pop out when passengers start filing on board. Veteran Southwest fliers have learned to listen up to announcements over the intercom. On a recent flight, the pilot suggested, "Flight attendants will please prepare their hair for departure." Safety instructions from the flight attendant included the advice: "In the unlikely event of a sudden loss of cabin pressure, oxygen masks will descend from the ceiling. Stop screaming, grab the mask, and pull it over your face. If you have small children traveling with you, secure your mask before assisting with theirs. If you are traveling with two small children, decide now which one you love more."

Even the company's headquarters reflect the airline's sense of humor.

> Pay a visit to Southwest's headquarters just off Love Field in
> Dallas, and you'll probably think you've wandered onto the
> set of Pee-Wee's Playhouse. The walls are festooned with

(box continues)

Southwest's Value Proposition: "Less for Much Less" | *continued*

more than ten thousand picture frames—no exaggeration—containing photos of employees' pets, of Herb dressed like Elvis or in drag, of stewardesses in miniskirts, and of Southwest planes gnawing on competitors' aircraft. Then there are the teddy bears, and jars of pickled hot peppers, and pink flamingos. There is . . . lots of chuckling and nary a necktie to be seen.

As a result of its strong positioning, Southwest has grown to become the nation's fourth-largest domestic carrier based on scheduled domestic departures. The company has successfully beaten off determined challenges from several major competitors who have tried to copy its winning formula, including Continental Lite, Delta Express, and Shuttle by United. Southwest now makes 2,900 flights a day, serving 59 cities in 31 states. Through good times and bad, Southwest has been the *only* airline to consistently turn a profit. Last year, the nation's three largest airlines lost almost $6 billion; Southwest *made* $442 million, more than all other U.S. airlines combined.

Simple, clear positioning has made Southwest *Fortune* magazine's most admired airline for the past 8 years running. And last year, Southwest was *Fortune's* number-three most admired company overall. Southwest not only promises an appealing value proposition, it delivers on the promise. It's not ritzy, but it gets you where you want to go, when you want to get there. You get low, low prices and lots of good fun. Just the ticket when you need a good lift!

Sources: Quotes and other information from Molly Ivins, "From Texas, with Love and Peanuts," *New York Times*, March 14, 1999, p. 11; Wendy Zellner, "Southwest: After Kelleher, More Blue Skies," *Business Week*, April 2, 2001, p. 45; Ron Suskind, "Humor Has Returned After 9/11 Hiatus," *Wall Street Journal*, January 13, 2003, p. A1; "Airline of the Year: Southwest Airlines," *Air Transport World*, February 2003, pp. 26–27; Andy Serwer, "Southwest Airlines: The Hottest Thing in the Sky," *Fortune*, March 8, 2004, p. 86; and *Southwest Airlines Fact Sheet*, November 5, 2004, accessed at www.southwest.com.

Yet in the long run, companies will find it very difficult to sustain such best-of-both positioning. Offering more usually costs more, making it difficult to deliver on the "for less" promise. Companies that try to deliver both may lose out to more focused competitors. For example, facing determined competition from Lowe's stores, Home Depot must now decide whether it wants to compete primarily on superior service or on lower prices.

All said, each brand must adopt a positioning strategy designed to serve the needs and wants of its target markets. "More for more" will draw one target market, "less for much less" will draw another, and so on. Thus, in any market, there is usually room for many different companies, each successfully occupying different positions.

The important thing is that each company must develop its own winning positioning strategy, one that makes it special to its target consumers. Offering only "the same for the same" provides no competitive advantage, leaving the firm in the middle of the pack. Companies offering one of the three losing value propositions—"the same for more," "less for more," and "less for the same"—will inevitably fail. Customers soon realize that they've been underserved, tell others, and abandon the brand.

Developing a Positioning Statement

Positioning statement
A statement that summarizes company or brand positioning—it takes this form: *To (target segment and need) our (brand) is (concept) that (point-of-difference).*

Company and brand positioning should be summed up in a **positioning statement**. The statement should follow the form: *To (target segment and need) our (brand) is (concept) that (point-of-difference).*[31] For example: "To *busy professionals who need to stay organized, Palm* is *an electronic organizer* that *allows you to backup files on your PC more easily and reliably than competitive products.*" Sometimes a positioning statement is more detailed:

To young, active soft-drink consumers who have little time for sleep, Mountain Dew is the soft drink that gives you more energy than any other brand because it has the highest level of caffeine. With Mountain Dew, you can stay alert and keep going even when you haven't been able to get a good night's sleep.

Note that the positioning first states the product's membership in a category (Mountain Dew is a soft drink) and then shows its point-of-difference from other members of the category (has more caffeine). Placing a brand in a specific category suggests similarities that it might share with other products in the category. But the case for the brand's superiority is made on its points of difference. Sometimes marketers put a brand in a surprisingly different category before indicating the points of difference:

DiGiorno's is a frozen pizza whose crust rises when the pizza is heated. Instead of putting it in the frozen pizza category, the marketers positioned it in the delivered pizza category. Their ad shows party guests asking which pizza delivery service the host used. But, says the host, "It's not delivery, its DiGiorno!" This helped highlight DiGiorno's fresh quality and superior taste over the normal frozen pizza.

Communicating and Delivering the Chosen Position

Once it has chosen a position, the company must take strong steps to deliver and communicate the desired position to target consumers. All the company's marketing mix efforts must support the positioning strategy.

Positioning the company calls for concrete action, not just talk. If the company decides to build a position on better quality and service, it must first *deliver* that position. Designing the marketing mix—product, price, place, and promotion—involves working out the tactical details of the positioning strategy. Thus, a firm that seizes on a more-for-more position knows that it must produce high-quality products, charge a high price, distribute through high-quality dealers, and advertise in high-quality media. It must hire and train more service people, find retailers who have a good reputation for service, and develop sales and advertising messages that broadcast its superior service. This is the only way to build a consistent and believable more-for-more position.

Companies often find it easier to come up with a good positioning strategy than to implement it. Establishing a position or changing one usually takes a long time. In contrast, positions that have taken years to build can quickly be lost. Once a company has built the desired position, it must take care to maintain the position through consistent performance and communication. It must closely monitor and adapt the position over time to match changes in consumer needs and competitors' strategies. However, the company should avoid abrupt changes that might confuse consumers. Instead, a product's position should evolve gradually as it adapts to the ever-changing marketing environment.

> Reviewing the Concepts <

In this chapter, you've learned about the major elements of marketing strategy: segmentation, targeting, and positioning. Marketers know that they cannot appeal to all buyers in their markets, or at least not to all buyers in the same way. Buyers are too numerous, too widely scattered, and too varied in their needs and buying practices. Therefore, most companies today practice *target marketing*—identifying market segments, selecting one or more of them, and developing products and marketing mixes tailored to each.

1. Define the three steps of target marketing: market segmentation, target marketing, and market positioning.

Targeting marketing involves designing strategies to build the *right relationships* with the *right customers*. *Market segmentation* is the act of dividing a market into distinct groups of buyers with different needs, characteristics, or behaviors who might require separate products or marketing mixes. Once the groups have been identified, *targeting marketing* evaluates each market segment's attractiveness and selecting one or more segments to serve. *Market positioning* consists of deciding how to best serve target customer—setting the competitive positioning for the product and creating a detailed marketing plan.

2. List and discuss the major bases for segmenting consumer and business markets.

There is no single way to segment a market. Therefore, the marketer tries different variables to see which give the best segmentation opportunities. For consumer marketing, the major segmentation variables are geographic, demographic, psychographic, and behavioral. In *geographic segmentation*, the market is divided into different geographical units such as nations, regions, states, counties, cities, or neighborhoods. In *demographic segmentation*, the market is divided into groups based on demographic variables, including age, gender, family size, family life cycle, income, occupation, education, religion,

race, generation, and nationality. In *psychographic segmentation*, the market is divided into different groups based on social class, lifestyle, or personality characteristics. In *behavioral segmentation*, the market is divided into groups based on consumers' knowledge, attitudes, uses, or responses to a product.

Business marketers use many of the same variables to segment their markets. But business markets also can be segmented by business consumer *demographics* (industry, company size), *operating characteristics, purchasing approaches, situational factors*, and *personal characteristics*. The effectiveness of segmentation analysis depends on finding segments that are *measurable, accessible, substantial, differentiable*, and *actionable*.

3. Explain how companies identify attractive market segments and choose a target marketing strategy.

To target the best market segments, the company first evaluates each segment's size and growth characteristics, structural attractiveness, and compatibility with company objectives and resources. It then chooses one of four target marketing strategies—ranging from very broad to very narrow targeting. The seller can ignore segment differences and target broadly using *undifferentiated (or mass) marketing*. This involves mass-producing, mass-distributing, and mass promoting about the same product in about the same way to all consumers. Or the seller can adopt *differentiated marketing*—developing different market offers for several segments. *Concentrated marketing* (or *niche marketing*) involves focusing on only one or a few market segments. Finally, *micromarketing* is the practice of tailoring products and marketing programs to suit the tastes of specific individuals and locations. Micromarketing includes *local marketing* and *individual marketing*. Which targeting strategy is best depends on company resources, product variability, product life-cycle stage, market variability, and competitive marketing strategies.

4. Discuss how companies position their products for maximum competitive advantage in the marketplace.

Once a company has decided which segments to enter, it must decide on its *market positioning* strategy—on which positions to occupy in its chosen segments. The positioning task consists of three steps: identifying a set of possible competitive advantages upon which to build a position, choosing the right competitive advantages, and selecting an overall positioning strategy. The brand's full positioning is called its *value proposition*—the full mix of benefits upon which the brand is positioned. In general, companies can choose from one of five winning value propositions upon which to position their products: more for more, more for the same, the same for less, less for much less, or more for less. Company and brand positioning are summarized in positioning statements that state the target segment and need, positioning concept, and specific points of difference. The company must then effectively communicate and deliver the chosen position to the market.

> Reviewing the Key Terms <

Age and life-cycle
    segmentation 197
Behavioral segmentation 200
Benefit segmentation 202
Competitive advantage 218
Concentrated (or niche)
    marketing 211

Demographic segmentation 196
Differentiated (or segmented)
    marketing 210
Gender segmentation 197
Geographic segmentation 195
Income segmentation 198
Individual marketing 213

Intermarket segmentation 207
Local marketing 212
Market positioning 195
Market segmentation 195
Micromarketing 212
Occasion segmentation 200
Positioning statement 224

Product position 216
Psychographic segmentation 199
Target market 210
Target marketing 195
Undifferentiated (or mass)
    marketing 210
Value proposition 221

> Discussing the Concepts <

1. The chapter states that once we divide large, heterogeneous markets into smaller segments we can reach them more efficiently and effectively. What does that statement mean? Why is this important to the marketer?

2. Briefly define each of the four sets of primary segmentation variables. If you could only use one of the four sets of variables to segment prospective students for the "part-time" MBA Program at your university or college, which would it be? Why did you choose this variable?

3. The chapter discusses five requirements for effective segmentation. Suppose you are a product manager in a regional fast-food restaurant company. You are listening to a presentation on a new sandwich wrap idea (chicken breast and okra), and it is your turn to ask questions. Write five questions that you would ask the person presenting this product idea. Each question should be directed at one of the five segmentation requirements.

4. Is it a good idea for a small company to adopt a differentiated segmentation strategy? Explain.

5. In the context of marketing, what does the term "product positioning" mean? Why is it so important?

6. Using the value propositions presented in Figure 7.4, describe the value proposition of Toys "R" Us. Is the Toys "R" Us value proposition clear? Is it appropriate?

> Applying the Concepts <

1. As discussed in the chapter, PRIZM is one of the leading lifestyle segmentation systems. Go to www.tetrad.com/pcensus/usa/prizmlst.html and review the 67 PRIZM clusters. Now identify a desirable cluster for each of the following retailers: Tiffany's, Macy's, and Wal-Mart.

2. You are the product manager of a financial services product that is being sold directly to consumers over the Internet. The most important metric to the company is customer acquisition cost. This is the cost associated with convincing a consumer to buy the service. You have been conducting tests with both a concentrated and undifferentiated segmentation strategy, and the results are presented below. Which strategy is the best? Why?

Concentrated segmentation outcome

- Purchased 10,000 very targeted exposures on Web sites such Yahoo Financial and keywords such as retirement, IRA, and ROTH.

- Paid $80 per thousand exposures

- Obtained 400 clicks to the site, 40 trials, and 20 repeat customers

Undifferentiated segmentation outcome

- Purchased 1,000,000 run-of-site exposures on Web sites

- Paid $1.60 per thousand exposures

- Obtained 2,000 clicks to the site, 100 trials, and 40 repeat customers

3. Assume that you are the marketing director for the school of business at your college or university, and that the dean has asked you to prepare a positioning statement for the business school. Write a positioning statement using the form presented in the chapter.

> Focus on Technology <

The chapter defines micromarketing as the practice of tailoring products and marketing programs to suit the tastes of specific individuals and locations. If you are a consumer-goods marketer, chances are good that you already have known the value of micromarketing in general and of SRC's Solocast in particular. Solocast is one of the many SRC desktop database engines that marketers can use to help them make better decisions. Suppose you are a women's clothing retailer, and based on buyer information that you have collected, you have a good idea of the personal lifestyle characteristics of your target market. According to SRC, Solocast will help you find more of your best target customers. You can get a better understanding of their habits—where they shop, what brands they prefer, and what types of communication would work best in reaching them.

Visit SRC's homepage at **www.extendthereach.com** and review the Solocast product. Now place yourself in the role of the women's clothing retailer.

1. Can you use Solocast to help find your next retail location?
2. Can you identify undetected segments of potential customers in your existing trade areas?
3. Can you use Solocast to reach your target more effectively?

> Focus on Ethics <

Electronic gaming continues to see rapid growth. A mid-summer 2004 report from the Consumer Electronics Association indicated that gaming systems are present in 38 percent of U.S. households. The Entertainment Software Rating Board oversees the rating system use by gaming software manufacturers. There are six rating categories: early childhood, everyone, teen (13 and older), mature (17 and older), adults (mature content not suitable for persons under 18), and rating pending. In its fourth update in July 2004 of the *Marketing Violent Entertainment to Children* report to Congress, the FTC indicated that most gaming software manufacturers are in compliance with the industry regulations for the rating codes and advertising. This is a significant change from the first report in September 2000 that found "these industries had engaged in marketing of . . . electronic games to children that was inconsistent with the cautionary messages and their own parental advisories. . . ."

1. What if anything, should be done to the gaming software manufacturers that do not comply with the industry regulations? What?
2. In general what do you think of the practice of targeting children?
3. Are there markets where targeting children is appropriate?

 **Video Case**

Procter & Gamble

With dozens of brands in the marketplace, Procter & Gamble offers an array of consumer products with dazzling success. In the United States alone, P&G offers seven brands of laundry detergent, three brands of deodorant, and two brands each of fabric softener, cosmetics, and disposable diapers. In each of these categories, P&G's products compete against each other, as well as with products offered by other companies, for share of the customer's wallet.

How does Procter and Gamble manage so many competing brands without cannibalizing its own profits? The company maximizes market penetration and sales by carefully segmenting markets, positioning products and brands, and targeting the right consumers. Together, P&G's portfolio of products meets the needs of a wide range of consumers. The result? Ninety-nine percent of all households in the United States use at least one P&G product.

After viewing the video featuring P&G, answer the following questions about segmentation, targeting, and positioning.

1. Visit P&G's Web site (www.PandG.com) and select two consumer products that compete in the same category. How are the two products positioned differently? Who is in the target market for each? List several P & G brands in other categories that target the same consumers.
2. What bases for segmentation does P&G use to differentiate the products you considered in the previous question?
3. According to the video, how does P&G position itself, as a company, in the marketplace?

Company Case

GM: Downsizing the Hummer

A LITTLE MILITARY HISTORY

If you've studied the 1991 Gulf War or the recent conflict in Iraq, kept up with Arnold Schwarzeneeger films, or watched any TV at all, you know what a Hummer is. You probably know that the Hummer derives from what soldiers informally call the "Humvee," which is an acronym for the formal designation, "High Mobility Multi-Purpose Wheeled Vehicle." In addition to seeing the TV ads, you've probably also seen the original nonmilitary Hummer, the H1, or its smaller offspring, the H2, around town. Well, you're going to see a lot more Hummers.

This Hummer story starts in 1979, when AM General, a specialty vehicle manufacturer, earned a contract from the U.S. Army to design the Humvee. The Army wanted a new

(box continues)

vehicle to replace its outdated Jeeps. AM General produced the big, boxy Humvee, which labored in relative obscurity until the Gulf War in 1991. TV coverage of the military build-up in advance of the short war and live broadcasts of the war itself introduced the public to the workhorse Humvee.

In 1992, AM General, responding to the Humvee's notoriety, decided to introduce the first *civilian* version of the Humvee—the Hummer. Weighing in at 7,100 pounds, the Hummer featured a huge, 6.5 liter V-8, turbo-diesel engine that produced 195 horsepower and propelled the Hummer from 0 to 60 miles per hour in a snail-like 18 seconds. However, the Hummer's purpose was not speed. AM General designed it, like its military parent, to take people off the beaten path—way off. The Hummer could plow through water to a depth of 30 inches and climb almost vertical, rocky surfaces. It even had a central tire inflation system that allowed the driver to inflate or deflate the vehicle's tires while on the move.

The advertising tag line dubbed the Hummer as "The world's most serious 4 x 4," and ad copy played up the vehicle's off-road capabilities and its military heritage. AM General targeted serious, elite road warriors who were willing to pay more than $100,000 to have the toughest vehicle in the carpool. These people wanted to tell the world that they had been successful. To help buyers learn how to handle the Hummer in extreme off-road situations, AM General even offered a Hummer Driving Academy, where drivers learned to handle 22 inch vertical walls, high water, 40 percent side slopes, and 60 percent inclines.

GM'S MARKET RESEARCH

In 1998, GM was conducting market research using a concept vehicle that it described as rugged and militaristic. When the vehicle bore the GMC brand name (GM's truck division), the company found that consumers had a lukewarm reaction. However, when GM put the Hummer name on the vehicle, researchers found that it had the highest, most widespread appeal of any vehicle GM had *ever* tested. Armed with this insight, GM signed a 1999 agreement with AM General, giving it rights to the Hummer Brand. AM General also signed a 7-year contract to produce the Hummer H2 sport utility vehicle for GM.

Based on its research, GM believed that the H2, a smaller version of the Hummer, would appeal to rugged individualists and wealthy baby-boomers who wanted the ability to go off-road and to "successful achievers," 30- and 40-something wealthy consumers who had jobs in investment banking and the like. GM believed that it could introduce the H2 in the luxury SUV market and compete successfully with brands such as the Lincoln Navigator or GM's own Cadillac Escalade. The company charted production plans that called for AM General to build a new $200 million manufacturing facility in Indiana and for GM to launch the H2 in July 2002 at a base sticker price of about $49,000. It predicted that it could sell 19,000 H2s in 2002 (the 2003 model year) and then ramp up production to sell 40,000 units per year thereafter—a number that would make the H2 the largest seller in the luxury SUV market.

These numbers compared with annual sales of only about 800 Hummers.

SOFTENING UP THE MARKET

During 2000, GM and AM General did not advertise the Hummer, but they mapped out a campaign for the year leading up to the H2's 2002 introduction that would raise the Hummer brand's awareness and serve as a bridge to the introduction. GM hired a marketing firm, Modernista, to develop the estimated $3 million campaign.

In mid-2001, GM launched the Modernista campaign using the tag line, "Hummer. Like nothing else." Placements in *The Wall Street Journal, Barron's, Spin, Business Week, Cigar Aficionado,* and *Esquire,* used four different headlines:

"How did my soul get way out here?"

"What good is the world at your finger-tips if you never actually touch it?"

"You can get fresh air lots of places, but this is the really good stuff."

"Out here you're nobody. Perfect."

Following each headline was the same copy: "Sometimes you find yourself in the middle of nowhere. And sometimes in the middle of nowhere you find yourself. The legendary H1." One agency official said the ads used journalistic-type photography to make them more believable and to play down the he-man imagery. "Authenticity is probably the most important word when it comes to branding," the official argued. Whereas previous Hummer ads had featured the tough SUV plowing through snow and streams, the new ads featured the Hummer with gorgeous Chilean vistas. The new ads, the agency suggested, were as much about the people who buy Hummers as they were about the vehicle. Hummer owners often believed they got a bum rap as show-offs, the representative suggested, but he argued that the new ads would show the owner's other side.

THE LAUNCH

Right on schedule in July 2002, GM introduced the 2003 Hummer 2. For the H2, GM targeted buyers with an average age of 42 and annual household incomes above $125,000 versus H1 owners' averages of about 50 years old and household incomes above $200,000.

GM and AM General designed and built the H2 in just 16 months, using GM's GMT 800 truck platform and a number of parts used in other GM models. The H2 was about the same size as the Chevy Tahoe, five inches narrower than the Hummer and about 700 pounds lighter. However, it was about 1,400 pounds heavier than other SUVs. It had a 316 horsepower engine that slurped a gallon of gasoline every 12 miles. It also featured a nine-speaker Bose stereo system. Buyers could upgrade the base model with a $2,575 luxury package that added heated leather front seats and a six-disc CD changer or with a $2,215 Adventure package that added air suspension, brush guards, and crossbars for the roof rack.

For promotion, GM stayed with the Modernista firm. Late in the summer of 2002, TV ads broke on shows such as

"CSI: Miami" that featured a well-dressed woman driving the H2 through an urban business district. The ad concluded with the line, "Threaten Men in a New Way." A later ad featured a young boy who builds a soap-box-derby-style racer that looks like a small Hummer. Although it was slower, he won the downhill race by going off-road and cutting across the paved, zig-zagged race course to edge out the typical race cars at the end.

THE ON-ROAD TEST

At the H2's launch, auto analysts noted that it had a surprisingly smooth ride, but some questioned the quality of the interior furnishings and criticized the lack of storage space. The H2 sat only five people unless the owner installed an optional sixth seat in the back beside the spare tire. Further, they wondered if consumers would really spend so much for an off-the-road vehicle that studies showed only 10 percent of owners would *ever* take off the road. In addition, analysts noted the increasingly crowded luxury SUV market with pending entries from Porsche, BMW, Volvo, and Infiniti.

Despite the criticism, H2s roared out of the showrooms. Some buyers waited months to take delivery and even paid up to a $10,000 price premium just to get one. GM was realizing profits of $20,000 per vehicle. It reached its first-year target by selling 18,861 H2s by mid-2003. For calendar 2003, GM sold 35,259 H2s. Then, demand slowed; and GM began to offer $2,000 dealer-cash incentives to try to reduce dealer inventories from an 80-day supply to a 45-day supply. Moreover, in early 2004, after 5 straight months of sales declines, increasing gas prices seemed to be taking their toll on Hummer sales and pushing it toward the bottom in J.D. Power customer satisfaction ratings. H2 owners were forking out $50 for gas every 320 miles! Analysts thought GM would have to reduce its annual sales target to 30,000 H2s.

These events, however, did not deter GM from pursuing its long-term plan to sell 100,000 Hummer-branded vehicles a year. In mid-2003, it introduced the H2 Sport Utility Truck (SUT), an H2 with a pickup-truck-style cargo area in back replacing the enclosed area in the standard H2. The basic SUT's price was about $1,000 more than the base SUV.

For mid-2005, GM planned to introduce an even smaller Hummer, the H3 SUV. Priced in the $28,000 to $35,000 range, the company wanted the smaller, less menacing H3 to target drivers under 40. It believed the H3 would be especially appealing to young males, including teenagers.

To get the process rolling, GM unveiled an H3T concept vehicle at the Los Angeles Auto Show in December 2003. The H3T was a smaller, pickup-truck version of the H2 SUT. GM worked with Nike, the athletic-shoe company, and BF Goodrich to design the H3T's tires, which were reversible to alter the tread pattern and featured the trademarked Nike swoosh. The H3T would also have a folding canvas top, drop-down rear window, and a TV camera mounted on the hood to record those off-road adventures!

The H3T would be similar in size to the H3 SUV, about 15 inches shorter and 7 inches narrower than the H2. It would feature a 5-cylinder, 350hp engine that would get between 19 and 24 miles per gallon.

The 167 Hummer dealers who wanted to sell the H3s would have to build Quonset-shaped showrooms with helicopter-style ceiling fans and a large steel sign in the shape of an "H" outside. They would also have to construct an off-road driving course on the dealership's grounds. The showrooms alone would cost about $3 million for a 20,000 square-foot store.

GM wants to show that the smaller Hummers can retain the gesture, stance, and attitude of the larger Hummer. GM officials indicate that the typical Hummer owner makes more than $200,000 a year and has two other vehicles he/she uses for routine driving. The Hummer is for fun. These officials believe that continued high gas prices will not affect Hummer sales. Hummer owners are proud and know that they will get attention. They own a Hummer because they want to and can afford it.

Some industry analysts, however, wonder if introducing more Hummers will dilute the brand's image and even steal sales from other GM vehicles. They argue that the decision to introduce smaller and lower-priced Hummers is a risky move, especially given the brand's aspirational nature.

Maybe so, but GM is already discussing the possibility of an H4.

Questions for Discussion

1. How has GM used the major segmentation variables for consumer markets in segmenting the SUV market?

2. What target-market decisions has GM made in selecting targets for the Hummer H2? How are those decisions different from AM General's target for the original Hummer?

3. How has GM attempted to position the H2?

4. Why do you think some consumers will pay $40,000 or more for an off-road vehicle that 90 percent of them will never take off road?

5. What segmentation, targeting, and positioning recommendations would you make to GM for the H3?

6. What other marketing recommendations would you make?

Sources: Rosemary Barnes, "Popularity of Hummer Remains Unfazed by High Gasoline Prices," *KnightRidder/Tribune News*, June 5, 2004; David Welch, "A Bummer for the Hummer; Sales Are Way Down," *Business Week,* February 23, 2004, p. 49; Rick Dranz, "How Will Hummer Get Smaller? Check out H3T," *Automotive News*, December 15, 2003, p. 20; Dave Guilford, "Would a Small Hummer be Dumber?" *Automotive News,* October 13, 2003; Melanie Wells, "Muscle Car," *Forbes*, July 22, 2002, p. 181; David Welch, "More Sport, Less Utility," *Business Week,* July 8, 2002, p. 110; Jean Halliday, "Of Hummers and Zen," *Advertising Age,* August 6, 2001, p. 29; Gregory L. White, "GM's New Baby Hummer Shares Its Toys With Chevy," *The Wall Street Journal*, April 10, 2001, p. B1.

> **After studying this chapter, you should be able to:**

1. define *product* and the major classifications of products and services
2. describe the decisions companies make regarding their individual products and services, product lines, and product mixes
3. discuss branding strategy—the decisions companies make in building and managing their brands
4. identify the four characteristics that affect the marketing of a service and the additional marketing considerations that services require
5. discuss two additional product issues: socially responsible product decisions and international product and services marketing

Product, Services, and Branding Strategy

Previewing the Concepts

Now that you've had a good look at marketing strategy, we'll take a deeper look at the marketing mix—the tactical tools that marketers use to implement their strategies. In this and the next chapter, we'll study how companies develop and manage products and brands. Then, in the chapters that follow, we'll look at pricing, distribution, and marketing communication tools. The product is usually the first and most basic marketing consideration. We'll start with a seemingly simple question: What *is* a product? As it turns out, however, the answer is not so simple.

To start things off, remember that seemingly simple question—what is a product? Well, what is a doughnut? That's right, a *doughnut?* As it turns out, to a Krispy Kreme customer, a doughnut is more than just a few ounces of flour and sugar with chocolate and sprinkles on top. It's a truly magical moment.

You're craving a doughnut—what's the first name that comes to mind? Five years ago, you probably would have said Dunkin' Donuts, still the world's largest coffee and doughnut chain. But today, thanks to the hot popularity of southern phenomenon Krispy Kreme Doughnuts, your answer might be different. The Krispy Kreme name and famous bowtie logo are cropping up throughout the country and around the world, bringing the company's delicious yeast-raised doughnuts to more and more satisfied customers.

To be sure, Krispy Kreme sells doughnuts—*lots* of doughnuts. The company and its franchisees now make 7.5 million doughnuts each day—2.7 *billion* doughnuts a year. In only one week, Krispy Kreme stores worldwide produce enough doughnuts to stretch from New York City to Los Angeles. In the process, each year they use 1.3 million pounds of sprinkles and enough chocolate to fill nearly five Olympic size swimming pools.

But to a true believer, a Krispy Kreme isn't just a doughnut. It's an *experience*. A magical moment. With every doughnut the company sells, it creates a happy customer. And each happy customer can't wait to tell others about the experience. If you haven't had a gooey, hot glazed Krispy Kreme, they'd say, you simply haven't lived. "If you've never sampled a Krispy Kreme, we should get one thing straight," says one analyst. "These doughnuts—particularly the original glazed version served hot—are amazingly good. (My older daughter says they taste like glazed fluffy clouds.)" Krispy Kreme magical moments seem to appeal to everyone. Says the analyst: "They are loved equally by 5 year-olds and 75-year-olds. By whites, blacks, Asians, and Hispanics. By New Englanders and Southerners. By Californians and New Yorkers."

Krispy Kreme is so focused on the magical moments it creates, that it actually *defines* its brand through the store experience. Its *Retail Environments* book, which details new store design, states "Our brand and how our customers experience Krispy Kreme is the platform that supports us all. Nothing can be more important than the preservation and nurturing of these valuable possessions." This passion for the consumer-brand relationship forms the foundation of Krispy Kreme's success.

The powerful Krispy Kreme brand experience has built a host of fervent followers that most competitors could only dream about. Says Ceres Wood, Krispy Kreme's Senior Vice President of Store Development, "people wait in line for hours to get into a new store opening and they have fun . . . they talk to each other, share their Krispy Kreme stories . . . amazing. I've never seen anything that even comes close to the passion people feel for this brand."

For many neighborhoods the arrival of a Krispy Kreme is an event to celebrate. Consumers in Clackamas, Oregon, greeted the groundbreaking for a new Krispy Kreme store with the local marching band and hordes of supporters. When a new store opened just outside of Seattle, eager customers camped out on the sidewalk overnight to be the first inside at 5:30 a.m. the next morning. When Krispy Kreme debuted in Denver, morning traffic was snarled for hours. According to one account:

> They begin lining up in the cold darkness, hours before the store opens. Some come wearing pajamas, some lug couches and TVs, others bring beer. And when dawn finally breaks and the ribbon is cut, the rabid customers bolt through the doors. Many of them, in what must be an anticipatory sugar rush, scream at the top of their lungs: "Krispy Kreme doughnuts, yowweeee!" Last year it happened in Fargo and Philadelphia and Amarillo and dozens of other cities in North America. This year it

will happen in Boston, Sydney, and elsewhere. All for a simple doughnut.

For those who have never heard of Krispy Kreme, word travels quickly. But to ensure that the message gets out, local franchisees often deliver several dozen glazed doughnuts to a local radio station, or to—you guessed it—the town's fire and police stations. When a new store opened in Phoenix, Sheriff Joe Arpaio, the infamous "toughest sheriff in America"—the lawman known for making prisoners wear pink underwear—was the first person to try a fresh Krispy Kreme doughnut. In front of a sea of television cameras, he uttered the perfect phrase: "These doughnuts are so good, they should be illegal." Such free promotion is the norm for Krispy Kreme. The delicious doughnuts have also played cameo roles in the movie *Primary Colors* and on such TV shows as "NYPD Blue" and "The Tonight Show" with Jay Leno.

Thus, Krispy Kreme does more than just sell doughnuts. It creates carefully crafted magical moments for its customers, moments that are gaining popularity with just about anyone within "aroma range" of a Krispy Kreme store. Notes marketing manager Jennifer Gardner, "I've seen a blue-collar worker, an expectant mother, a biker, a businessman, and a woman who was driven up in a Rolls Royce all standing in line inside a Krispy Kreme, and they were talking to each other like long-lost friends." Says Krispy Kreme fan Jamie Karn, "You have to experience one. You have to eat it to understand it!" More than a doughnut, Krispy Kreme is truly sweet customer experience. Creating magical moments for customers has also been a pretty sweet experience for Krispy Kreme. The company's sales have more than tripled in the past 5 years.[1]

Product
Anything that can be offered to a market for attention, acquisition, use, or consumption that might satisfy a want or need.

Clearly, donuts are more than just donuts when Krispy Kreme sells them. This chapter begins with a deceptively simple question: *What is a product?* After answering this question, we look at ways to classify products in consumer and business markets. Then we discuss the important decisions that marketers make regarding individual products, product lines, and product mixes. Next, we look into the critically important issue of how marketers build and manage brands. Finally, we examine the characteristics and marketing requirements of a special form of product—services.

What Is a Product?

A Sony DVD player, a Ford Taurus, a Costa Rican vacation, a Caffé Mocha at Starbucks, Fidelity online investment services, and advice from your family doctor—all are products. We define a **product** as anything that can be offered to a market for attention, acquisition, use, or consumption and that might satisfy a want or need. Products include more than just tangible goods. Broadly defined, products include physical objects, services, events, persons, places, organizations, ideas, or mixes of these entities. Thus, throughout this text, we use the term *product* broadly to include any or all of these entities.

Because of their importance in the world economy, we give special attention to services. **Services** are a form of product that consists of activities, benefits, or satisfactions offered for sale that are essentially intangible and do not result in the ownership of anything. Examples are banking, hotel, airline, retail, tax preparation, and home repair services. We will look at services more closely later in this chapter.

Products, Services, and Experiences

Product is a key element in the *market offering*. Marketing-mix planning begins with formulating an offering that brings value to target customers. This offering becomes the basis upon which the company builds profitable relationships with customers.

A company's market offering often includes both tangible goods and services. Each component can be a minor or a major part of the total offer. At one extreme, the offer may consist of a *pure tangible good,* such as soap, toothpaste, or salt—no services accompany the product. At the other extreme are *pure services,* for which the offer consists primarily of a service. Examples include a doctor's exam or financial services. Between these two extremes, however, many goods-and-services combinations are possible.

Today, as products and services become more and more commoditized, many companies are moving to a new level in creating value for their customers. To differentiate their offers, beyond simply making products and delivering services, companies are staging, marketing, and delivering memorable customer *experiences*.

Experiences have always been important in the entertainment industry—Disney has long manufactured memories through its movies and theme parks. Today, however, all kinds of firms are recasting their traditional goods and services to create experiences. For example, Starbucks patrons are paying for more than just coffee. The company treats customers to poetry on its wallpaper, apron-clad performers behind espresso machines, and a warm but modern interior ambience that leaves them feeling more affluent and fulfilled. And you don't just shop at the Toys "R" Us store on Times Square in New York City, you *experience* it.[2]

Step into Toys "R" Us Times Square to enjoy three levels of incredible fun right on Broadway! Take a ride on a 60 foot high Ferris Wheel with cool character-themed cabs. Feel like a celebrity in our amazing two-story Barbie Dollhouse. Take a stroll through our life-size Candy Land. Gaze up in wonder at our LEGO Empire State Building. And for a classic Jurassic experience, say hello to a larger than life, 20-foot tall, T-Rex with realistic moves and a mighty roar. You really have to see it to believe it!

Service
Any activity or benefit that one party can offer to another that is essentially intangible and does not result in the ownership of anything.

■ Marketing experiences: you don't just shop at the Toys "R" Us store on Times Square in New York City, you experience it.

FIGURE 8.1
Three levels of product

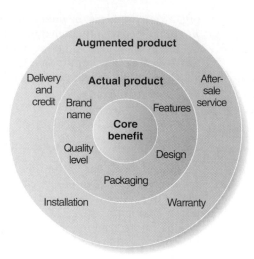

Companies that market experiences realize that customers are really buying much more than just products and services. They are buying what those offers will *do* for them.[3]

Levels of Product and Services

Product planners need to think about products and services on three levels (see Figure 8.1). Each level adds more customer value. The most basic level is the *core benefit*, which addresses the question *What is the buyer really buying?* When designing products, marketers must first define the core, problem-solving benefits or services that consumers seek. A woman buying lipstick buys more than lip color. Charles Revson of Revlon saw this early: "In the factory, we make cosmetics; in the store, we sell hope." Charles Schwab does more than sell financial services—it promises to fulfill customers' "financial dreams."

At the second level, product planners must turn the core benefit into an *actual product*. They need to develop product and service features, design, a quality level, a brand name, and packaging. For example, a Sony camcorder is an actual product. Its name, parts, styling, features, packaging, and other attributes have all been combined carefully to deliver the core benefit—a convenient, high-quality way to capture important moments.

Finally, product planners must build an *augmented product* around the core benefit and actual product by offering additional consumer services and benefits. Sony must offer more than just a camcorder. It must provide consumers with a complete solution to their picture-taking problems. Thus, when consumers buy a Sony camcorder, Sony and its dealers also might give buyers a warranty on parts and workmanship, instructions on how to use the camcorder, quick repair services when needed, and a toll-free telephone number to call if they have problems or questions.

Consumers see products as complex bundles of benefits that satisfy their needs. When developing products, marketers first must identify the *core* consumer needs the product will satisfy. They must then design the *actual* product and find ways to *augment* it in order to create the bundle of benefits that will provide the most satisfying customer experience.

Product and Service Classifications

Products and services fall into two broad classes based on the types of consumers that use them—*consumer products* and *industrial products*. Broadly defined, products also include other marketable entities such as experiences, organizations, persons, places, and ideas.

Consumer Products

Consumer product
Product bought by final consumer for personal consumption.

Consumer products are products and services bought by final consumers for personal consumption. Marketers usually classify these products and services further based on how consumers go about buying them. Consumer products include *convenience products*, *shopping products*, *specialty products*, and *unsought products*. These products differ in the ways consumers buy them and therefore in how they are marketed (see Table 8.1).

■ Core, actual, and augmented product: consumers perceive this Sony Handycam as a complex bundle of intangible features and services that deliver a core benefit—a convenient, high-quality way to capture important moments.

TABLE 8.1   Marketing Considerations for Consumer Productions

Marketing Considerations	Type of Consumer Product			
	Convenience	**Shopping**	**Specialty**	**Unsought**
Customer buying behavior	Frequent purchase, little planning, little comparison or shopping effort, low customer involvement	Less frequent purchase, much planning and shopping effort, comparison of brands on price, quality, style	Strong brand preference and loyalty, special purchase effort, little comparison of brands, low price sensitivity	Little product awareness, knowledge (or, if aware, little or even negative interest)
Price	Low Price	Higher price	High price	Varies
Distribution	Widespread distribution, convenient locations	Selective distribution in fewer outlets	Exclusive distribution in only one or a few outlets per market area	Varies
Promotion	Mass promotion by the producer	Advertising and personal selling by both producer and resellers	More carefully targeted promotion by both producer and resellers	Aggressive advertising and personal selling by producer and resellers
Examples	Toothpaste, magazines, laundry detergent	Major appliances, televisions, furniture, clothing	Luxury goods, such as Rolex watches or fine crystal	Life insurance, Red Cross blood donations

Convenience product
Consumer product that the customer usually buys frequently, immediately, and with a minimum of comparison and buying effort.

Shopping product
Consumer good that the customer, in the process of selection and purchase, characteristically compares on such bases as suitability, quality, price, and style.

Specialty product
Consumer product with unique characteristics or brand identification for which a significant group of buyers is willing to make a special purchase effort.

Unsought product
Consumer product that the consumer either does not know about or knows about but does not normally think of buying.

Industrial product
Product bought by individuals and organizations for further processing or for use in conducting a business.

Convenience products are consumer products and services that the customer usually buys frequently, immediately, and with a minimum of comparison and buying effort. Examples include soap, candy, newspapers, and fast food. Convenience products are usually low priced, and marketers place them in many locations to make them readily available when customers need them.

Shopping products are less frequently purchased consumer products and services that customers compare carefully on suitability, quality, price, and style. When buying shopping products and services, consumers spend much time and effort in gathering information and making comparisons. Examples include furniture, clothing, used cars, major appliances, and hotel and airline services. Shopping products marketers usually distribute their products through fewer outlets but provide deeper sales support to help customers in their comparison efforts.

Specialty products are consumer products and services with unique characteristics or brand identification for which a significant group of buyers is willing to make a special purchase effort. Examples include specific brands and types of cars, high-priced photographic equipment, designer clothes, and the services of medical or legal specialists. A Lamborghini automobile, for example, is a specialty product because buyers are usually willing to travel great distances to buy one. Buyers normally do not compare specialty products. They invest only the time needed to reach dealers carrying the wanted products.

Unsought products are consumer products that the consumer either does not know about or knows about but does not normally think of buying. Most major new innovations are unsought until the consumer becomes aware of them through advertising. Classic examples of known but unsought products and services are life insurance, preplanned funeral services, and blood donations to the Red Cross. By their very nature, unsought products require a lot of advertising, personal selling, and other marketing efforts.

Industrial Products TEST

Industrial products are those purchased for further processing or for use in conducting a business. Thus, the distinction between a consumer product and an industrial product is based on the *purpose* for which the product is bought. If a consumer buys a lawn mower for use around home, the lawn mower is a consumer product. If the same consumer buys the same lawn mower for use in a landscaping business, the lawn mower is an industrial product.

The three groups of industrial products and services include materials and parts, capital items, and supplies and services. *Materials and parts* include raw materials and manufactured materials and parts. Raw materials consist of farm products (wheat, cotton, livestock, fruits, vegetables) and natural products (fish, lumber, crude petroleum, iron ore). Manufactured materials and parts consist of component materials (iron, yarn, cement, wires) and component parts (small motors, tires, castings). Most manufactured materials and parts are sold directly to industrial users. Price and service are the major marketing factors; branding and advertising tend to be less important.

■ Business services: Aramark offers everything from food, housekeeping, laundry, office, and equipment maintenance services to facilities and supply chain management.

Capital items are industrial products that aid in the buyer's production or operations, including installations and accessory equipment. Installations consist of major purchases such as buildings (factories, offices) and fixed equipment (generators, drill presses, large computer systems, elevators). Accessory equipment includes portable factory equipment and tools (hand tools, lift trucks) and office equipment (computers, fax machines, desks). They have a shorter life than installations and simply aid in the production process.

The final group of business products is *supplies and services*. Supplies include operating supplies (lubricants, coal, paper, pencils) and repair and maintenance items (paint, nails, brooms). Supplies are the convenience products of the industrial field because they are usually purchased with a minimum of effort or comparison. Business services include maintenance and repair services (window cleaning, computer repair) and business advisory services (legal, management consulting, advertising). Such services are usually supplied under contract.

Organizations, Persons, Places, and Ideas

In addition to tangible products and services, in recent years marketers have broadened the concept of a product to include other market offerings—organizations, persons, places, and ideas.

Organizations often carry out activities to "sell" the organization itself. *Organization marketing* consists of activities undertaken to create, maintain, or change the attitudes and behavior of target consumers toward an organization. Both profit and not-for-profit organizations practice organization marketing. Business firms sponsor public relations or corporate advertising campaigns to polish their images. *Corporate image advertising* is a major tool companies use to market themselves to various publics. For example, BASF ads say "We don't make the products you buy, we make the products you buy better." And General Electric stands for "imagination at work." Similarly, not-for-profit organizations, such as churches, colleges, charities, museums, and performing arts groups, market their organizations in order to raise funds and attract members or patrons.

■ Organization marketing: Companies use corporate image advertising to market themselves to various publics. BASF says, "We don't make the products you buy, we make the products you buy better."

People can also be thought of as products. *Person marketing* consists of activities undertaken to create, maintain, or change attitudes or behavior toward particular people. People ranging from presidents, entertainers, and sports figures to professionals such as doctors, lawyers, and architects use person marketing to build their reputations and increase business. Businesses, charities, sports teams, and other organizations also use person marketing. Creating or associating with well-known personalities often helps these organizations achieve their goals better. That's why more than a dozen different companies—including Nike, Target, Buick, American Express, Disney, Accenture, and Titleist—combine to pay more than $70 million a year to link themselves with golf superstar Tiger Woods.[4]

The skillful use of person marketing can turn a person's name into a powerhouse brand. Michael Jordan has his own brand of Nike shoes and apparel, a chain of namesake restaurants, car dealerships, a brand of cologne, and more. The brand power of Oprah Winfrey's name has made her a billionaire: Oprah branded products include her television show; TV and feature movies; *O, The Oprah Magazine*; and Oprah's Book Club. And businessman Donald Trump has slapped his well-known name on everything from skyscrapers and casinos to bottled water, magazines, and reality TV programs:

> Donald Trump has made and lost fortunes as a real estate developer. But Trump's genius is in brand building, and he is the brand. Thanks to tireless self-promotion, "The Donald" has established the Trump brand as a symbol of quality, luxury, and success. In a recent survey, Trump was named as one of two of the most recognizable names in real estate. More than 25 buildings and five casinos bear Donald Trump's name, and he's erecting seven new skyscrapers and three lavish new golf courses. What's the value of the Trump brand? Plenty. In residential real estate in particular, Trump's name commands a premium. "I put my name on a building and I get $5,000 a square foot," says Trump. "That's twice what the guy gets across the street. I put my name on a golf course, Trump National in Briarcliff Manor, and I get $300,000 per member. Other guys only get $25,000. If I didn't put my name on it, I'd get nothing." In Chicago, Trump is planning a 90-story condo tower downtown—the Trump International Hotel & Tower. Even before the building now on the site has been razed, Trump has sold so many units at such high prices—from $575,000 to $15 million—that he single-handedly raised the average condo price for the entire city by 25 percent at the end of last year. Based on this real estate success, Trump's name now adorns everything from magazines and bottled water (Trump Ice) to beauty pageants and reality TV shows ("The Apprentice"). Trump does commercials for Verizon, was

■ People as brands: Businessman Donald Trump has put his well-known name on everything from skyscrapers and casinos to bottled water, magazines, and reality TV programs.

host of "Saturday Night Live," and recently unveiled Trump Visa, which rewards cardholders with casino discounts. "He's like P.T. Barnum on steroids," says a friend. "What's his greatest asset? It's his name. He's a skillful marketing person, and what he markets is his name."[5]

Place marketing involves activities undertaken to create, maintain, or change attitudes or behavior toward particular places. Cities, states, regions, and even entire nations compete to attract tourists, new residents, conventions, and company offices and factories. Texas advertises "It's Like a Whole Other Country" and New York State shouts, "I Love New York!"[6] Michigan says "Great Lakes, Great Times" to attract tourists, "Great Lakes, Great Jobs" to attract residents, and "Great Lakes, Great Location" to attract businesses. The Irish Development Agency has attracted more than 1,200 companies to locate their plants in Ireland. At the same time, the Irish Tourist Board has built a flourishing tourism business by advertising "Live a different life: friendly, beautiful, relaxing." And the Irish Export Board has created attractive markets for Irish exports.[7]

Ideas can also be marketed. In one sense, all marketing is the marketing of an idea, whether it be the general idea of brushing your teeth or the specific idea that Crest toothpastes "create smiles every day." Here, however, we narrow our focus to the marketing of *social ideas*. This area has been called **social marketing**, defined by the Social Marketing Institute as the use of commercial marketing concepts and tools in programs designed to influence individuals' behavior to improve their well-being and that of society.[8]

Social marketing programs include public health campaigns to reduce smoking, alcoholism, drug abuse, and overeating. Other social marketing efforts include environmental campaigns to promote wilderness protection, clean air, and conservation. Still others address issues such as family planning, human rights, and racial equality. The Ad Council of America has developed dozens of social advertising campaigns, involving issues ranging from preventive health, education, and personal safety to environmental preservation (see Real Marketing 8.1).

But social marketing involves much more than just advertising—the Social Marketing Institute encourages the use of a broad range of marketing tools. "Social marketing goes well beyond the promotional '*P*' of the marketing mix to include every other element to achieve its social change objectives," says the SMI's executive director.[9]

Social marketing

The design, implementation, and control of programs seeking to increase the acceptability of a social idea, cause, or practice among a target group.

Product and Service Decisions

Marketers make product and services decisions at three levels: individual product decisions, product line decisions, and product mix decisions. We discuss each in turn.

Individual Product and Service Decisions

Figure 8.2 shows the important decisions in the development and marketing of individual products and services. We will focus on decisions about *product attributes*, *branding*, *packaging*, *labeling*, and *product support services*.

Product and Service Attributes

Developing a product or service involves defining the benefits that it will offer. These benefits are communicated and delivered by product attributes such as *quality*, *features*, and *style and design*.

Product quality

The ability of a product to perform its functions; it includes the product's overall durability, reliability, precision, ease of operation and repair, and other valued attributes.

PRODUCT QUALITY **Product quality** is one of the marketer's major positioning tools. Quality has a direct impact on product or service performance; thus, it is closely linked to customer value and satisfaction. In the narrowest sense, quality can be defined as "freedom from defects." But most customer-centered companies go beyond this narrow definition. Instead, they define quality in terms of creating customer value and satisfaction. The American Society for Quality defines quality as the characteristics of a product or service that bear on its

FIGURE 8.2
Individual product and service decisions

Real Marketing 8.1

The Ad Council: Advertising for the Common Good

When it comes to creating positive social change through advertising, no organization grabs the headlines like the Ad Council. Consider these for familiar phrases: "Friends don't let friends drive drunk." "Only you can prevent forest fires." "Take A Bite Out of Crime®." "A mind is a terrible thing to waste." "I am an American." Or how about these familiar characters: Smokey Bear, Rosie the Riveter, the Crash Test Dummies, and McGruff the Crime Dog®. These are only a fraction of the phrases and icons created by Ad Council public service campaigns over the years.

The Ad Council was formed in 1942, at a time when people were especially cynical about advertising and all the money spent on it, to show the good that advertising can do. The Ad Council's mission is "to identify a select number of significant public issues and stimulate action on those issues through communications programs that make a measurable difference in our society." To that end, the Ad Council works to connect ad agencies (who donate their time), sponsors (who donate money), and media (who donate advertising time and space) with worthy not-for-profit organizations and governmental agencies that need a promotional voice.

Through this joint volunteer effort, the Ad Council has created thousands of public service campaigns on issues such as improving the quality of life for children, preventive health, education, community well being, environmental preservation, crime awareness and prevention, and strengthening families. These campaigns have produced more than just catchy slogans—they've created positive and lasting social change as well. Ad Council campaigns have achieved significant results on a wide range of issues:

- *Environment:* Launched in 1944, Smokey Bear has been urging children and adults not to play with matches, not to leave a campfire unattended, and to keep a bucket of water and a shovel nearby. Since the campaign began, the number of forest acres lost to fires annually has decreased from 22 million to 4 million.

- *Education:* The Ad Council teamed with Young & Rubicam advertising agency to create the campaign message, "A mind

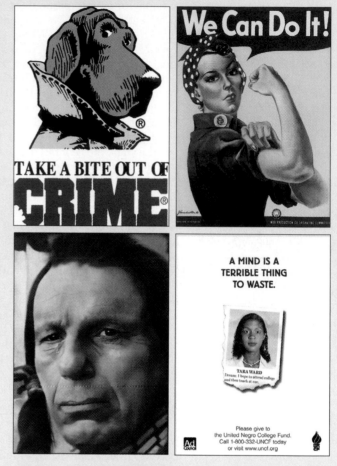

■ The Ad Council has created thousands of public service campaigns that have produced positive and lasting social change.

is a terrible thing to waste." Now in its 30th year, the campaign has helped raise more than $1.9 billion for the United

ability to satisfy stated or implied customer needs. Similarly, Siemans defines quality this way: "Quality is when our customers come back and our products don't."[10]

Total quality management (TQM) is an approach in which all the company's people are involved in constantly improving the quality of products, services, and business processes. During the past two decades, companies large and small have credited TQM with greatly improving their market shares and profits. Recently, however, the TQM movement has drawn criticism. Too many companies viewed TQM as a magic cure-all and created token total quality programs that applied quality principles only superficially. Still others became obsessed with narrowly defined TQM principles and lost sight of broader concerns for customer value and satisfaction. As a result, many such programs failed, causing a backlash against TQM.

When applied in the context of creating customer satisfaction, however, *total quality* principles remain a requirement for success. Although many firms don't use the TQM label anymore, for most top companies customer-driven quality has become a way of doing business. Today, companies are taking a "return on quality" approach, viewing quality as an investment and holding quality efforts accountable for bottom-line results.[11]

Negro College Fund and helped more than 300,000 minority students graduate college.

■ *Health:* In the 1940s, Ad Council campaigns urged Americans to get vaccinated against polio—not an easy sell at the time because the vaccination involved three sets of unpleasant shots. Today, polio is virtually unheard-of in this country.

■ *Crime awareness and prevention:* In 1979, the successful National Citizens' Crime Prevention Campaign was created and a year later McGruff the Crime Dog® and his slogan "Take A Bite Out of Crime®" were born. McGruff made his public debut in 1980, letting everyone know—children and adults alike—that each of us has a responsibility to prevent crime. In response to McGruffs incentive, people began to take charge of crime prevention themselves. Today, over 75% of Americans believe that they can personally take action to reduce crime, and that their neighborhoods and communities can act to prevent crime. As McGruff reminds us, crime prevention is everybody's business.

■ *Seat Belt Safety:* When Vince & Larry, the crash-test dummies, first flew through a windshield on network TV in 1985, seat-belt usage was at 21 percent and most states did not mandate seat belt usage by law. Since then, most states have adopted seat-belt laws and safety-belt usage has increased from 21 percent to 73 percent, saving an estimated 85,000 lives.

■ *Drunk Driving:* Since the Ad Council began its drunk-driving prevention campaign, the old saying "One more for the road" has been replaced with "Friends Don't Let Friends Drive Drunk." Some 68 percent of Americans say they have personally stopped someone from driving drunk.

■ *Social Issues:* More than 6,000 children were paired with a mentor in just the first 18 months of the Ad Council's mentoring campaign. And public awareness about child abuse has increased from just 10 percent in the mid-1970s to more than 90 percent today. According to the CEO of Prevent Child Abuse America, "When we first started our child abuse

prevention campaign, the public's understanding of the issue was very low. But our partnership with the Ad Council has brought child abuse and neglect out into the open."

The Ad Council has drawn widespread support for its social marketing mission. Made up largely of donations, the Ad Council's annual operating budget totals more than $35 million. Some 28,000 media outlets have contributed free ad space and time, and hundreds of socially conscious corporations, foundations, and individuals have provided crucial operating funds. Big ad agencies willingly donate their creative energies to create Ad Council campaigns. And the campaigns often turn out to be some of their very best work. For example, ad agency Marstellar's "People start pollution, people can stop it" campaign on behalf of Keep America Beautiful rates as one of the most memorable campaigns in history. The campaign ranked 50th on Advertising Age's list of top 100 ad campaigns of the century. And Foote, Cone & Belding's Smokey Bear and "Only you can prevent forest fires" campaign ranked 26th on the Ad Age top 100 list.

The Ad Council has proven that advertising can be used to do good, and its success has spawned other social marketing efforts. Not-for-profit groups such as Partnership for a Drug-Free America have followed suit with additional public service announcements. And TV networks now routinely use their stars to promote worthy causes (such as NBC's "The More You Know. . . ." series). "The Ad Council was a model that proved it could work," says former Ad Council president Ruth Wooden. Advertising no longer just pushes products—it improves, and even saves, human lives.

Sources: See Bob Garfield, "Inspiration and Urge-to-Serve Mark the Best of the Ad Council," *Advertising Age*, April 29, 2002, pp. c2–c20; MEDIAWEEK Special Advertising Section, June 10, 2002; and Ira Teinowitz, "Ad Council Seeks Partners for $50 Million Initiative," *Advertising Age*, March 1, 2004, p 2. Portions adapted from "The Advertising Council," accessed at www.adcouncil.org/about/, December 2004.

Product quality has two dimensions—level and consistency. In developing a product, the marketer must first choose a *quality level* that will support the product's position in the target market. Here, product quality means *performance quality*—the ability of a product to perform its functions. For example, a Rolls-Royce provides higher performance quality than a Chevrolet: It has a smoother ride, handles better, and lasts longer. Companies rarely try to offer the highest possible performance quality level—few customers want or can afford the high levels of quality offered in products such as a Rolls-Royce automobile, a Sub-Zero refrigerator, or a Rolex watch. Instead, companies choose a quality level that matches target market needs and the quality levels of competing products.

Beyond quality level, high quality also can mean high levels of quality *consistency*. Here, product quality means *conformance quality*—freedom from defects and *consistency* in delivering a targeted level of performance. All companies should strive for high levels of conformance quality. In this sense, a Chevrolet can have just as much quality as a Rolls-Royce. Although a Chevy doesn't perform as well as a Rolls, it can as consistently deliver the quality that customers pay for and expect.

Many companies today have turned customer-driven quality into a potent strategic weapon. They have created customer satisfaction and value by consistently and profitably meeting customers' needs and preferences for quality.

PRODUCT FEATURES A product can be offered with varying features. A stripped-down model, one without any extras, is the starting point. The company can create higher-level models by adding more features. Features are a competitive tool for differentiating the company's product from competitors' products. Being the first producer to introduce a needed and valued new feature is one of the most effective ways to compete.

How can a company identify new features and decide which ones to add to its product? The company should periodically survey buyers who have used the product and ask these questions: How do you like the product? Which specific features of the product do you like most? Which features could we add to improve the product? The answers provide the company with a rich list of feature ideas. The company can then assess each feature's *value* to customers versus its *cost* to the company. Features that customers value little in relation to costs should be dropped; those that customers value highly in relation to costs should be added.

PRODUCT STYLE AND DESIGN Another way to add customer value is through distinctive *product style and design.* Design is a larger concept than style. *Style* simply describes the appearance of a product. Styles can be eye-catching or yawn producing. A sensational style may grab attention and produce pleasing aesthetics, but it does not necessarily make the product *perform* better. Unlike style, *design* is more than skin deep—it goes to the very heart of a product. Good design contributes to a product's usefulness as well as to its looks.

Good design begins with a deep understanding of customer needs. More than simply creating product or service attributes, it involves shaping the customers product or service *experience.* For example Kaiser Permanente, the nation's largest health maintenance organization, has hundreds of medical offices and hospitals. It recently hired IDEO, a design firm, to help it design the next-generation medical building. Thanks to IDEO's novel design process, it turned out to be a fascinating journey of self-discovery:

> For starters, Kaiser nurses, doctors, and facilities managers teamed up with IDEO's social scientists, designers, architects, and engineers and observed patients as they made their way through Kaiser medical facilities. At times, they even played the role of patient themselves. Together they came up with some surprising insights. IDEO's architects revealed that patients and family often became annoyed well before seeing a doctor, because checking in was a nightmare and waiting rooms were uncomfortable. IDEO's cognitive psychologists pointed out that many people visit doctors with a parent or friend, but that second person is often not allowed to stay with the patient, leaving the afflicted alienated and anxious. IDEO's sociologists explained that patients hated Kaiser's examination rooms because they often had to wait alone for up to 20 minutes half-naked, with

■ IDEO helped Kaiser Permanente design the next generation medical facilities. It has also numerous helped other companies design products that not only look good but also reshape the customer's use, as with this shopping cart and PDA.

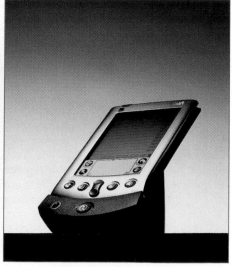

nothing to do, surrounded by threatening needles. IDEO and Kaiser concluded that, even when people leave treated and cured, the patient experience can be awful.

What to do? After working with IDEO, Kaiser realized that it didn't need lots of expensive new buildings. What it needed was to overhaul the patient *experience*. Kaiser learned that seeking medical care is much like shopping—it is a social experience shared with others. So Kaiser needed to offer more comfortable waiting rooms and a lobby with clear instructions on where to go. It needed larger exam rooms, with space for three or more people and curtains for privacy, to make patients comfortable. And it needed special corridors for medical staffers to meet and increase their efficiency. "IDEO showed us that we are designing human experiences, not buildings," says Kaiser's medical operations services manager. "[And] its recommendations didn't require big capital expenditures."[12]

In the same way, product designers should think less about product attributes and technical specifications and more about how customers will use and benefit from the product. Good design can improve product or service performance, cut costs, and create strong competitive advantage in the target market.

Branding TEST

Brand

A name, term, sign, symbol, or design, or a combination of these intended to identify the goods or services of one seller or group of sellers and to differentiate them from those of competitors.

Perhaps the most distinctive skill of professional marketers is their ability to build and manage their brands. A **brand** is a name, term, sign, symbol, or design, or a combination of these, that identifies the maker or seller of a product or service. Consumers view a brand as an important part of a product, and branding can add value to a product. For example, most consumers would perceive a bottle of White Linen perfume as a high-quality, expensive product. But the same perfume in an unmarked bottle would likely be viewed as lower in quality, even if the fragrance were identical.

Branding has become so strong that today hardly anything goes unbranded. Salt is packaged in branded containers, common nuts and bolts are packaged with a distributor's label, and automobile parts—spark plugs, tires, filters—bear brand names that differ from those of the automakers. Even fruits, vegetables, and poultry are branded—Sunkist oranges, Dole pineapples, Chiquita bananas, Fresh Express salad greens, and Perdue chickens.

Branding helps buyers in many ways. Brand names help consumers identify products that might benefit them. Brands also tell the buyer something about product quality. Buyers who always buy the same brand know that they will get the same features, benefits, and quality each time they buy. Branding also gives the seller several advantages. The

■ Branding has become so strong that hardly anything goes unbranded, even fruits and vegetables.

brand name becomes the basis on which a whole story can be built about a product's special qualities. The seller's brand name and trademark provide legal protection for unique product features that otherwise might be copied by competitors. And branding helps the seller to segment markets. For example, General Mills can offer Cheerios, Wheaties, Total, Kix, Golden Grahams, Trix, and many other cereal brands, not just one general product for all consumers.

Building and managing brands is perhaps the marketer's most important task. We will discuss branding strategy in more detail later in the chapter.

Packaging

Packaging

The activities of designing and producing the container or wrapper for a product.

Packaging involves designing and producing the container or wrapper for a product. The package includes a product's primary container (the tube holding Colgate Total toothpaste). It may also include a secondary package that is thrown away when the product is about to be used (the cardboard box containing the tube of Colgate). Finally, it can include a shipping package necessary to store, identify, and ship the product (a corrugated box carrying six dozen tubes of Colgate). Labeling, printed information appearing on or with the package, is also part of packaging.

Traditionally, the primary function of the package was to contain and protect the product. In recent times, however, numerous factors have made packaging an important marketing tool. Increased competition and clutter on retail store shelves means that packages must now perform many sales tasks—from attracting attention, to describing the product, to making the sale.

Companies are realizing the power of good packaging to create instant consumer recognition of the company or brand. For example, in an average supermarket, which stocks 15,000 to 17,000 items, the typical shopper passes by some 300 items per minute, and more than 60 percent of all purchases are made on impulse. In this highly competitive environment, the package may be the seller's last chance to influence buyers. "Not long ago, the package was merely the product's receptacle, and the brand message was elsewhere—usually on TV," says a packaging expert. But changes in the marketplace environment are now "making the package itself an increasingly important selling medium."[13]

Innovative packaging can give a company an advantage over competitors. Consumer packaged-goods firms have recently upped their investments in packaging research to develop package designs that grab more shelf attention or make life easier for customers. For example, Dutch Boy recently came up with a long overdue innovation—paint in plastic containers with twist-off caps:

> How did Dutch Boy Paint stir up the paint business? It's so simple, it's scary. Imagine a paint can that's easy to carry, doesn't take a screwdriver to pry open, doesn't dribble when pouring, and doesn't take a hammer to bang closed again. It's here—in the form of Dutch Boy's new Twist and Pour paint container. Touted as "a whole new way to carry, mix, open, pour, brush, and store paint," the new container is an all-plastic gallon container with a twist-off lid, side handle, and pour spout. It's lighter weight than a can and rust-proof, too. It kind of makes you wonder: Why did it take so long to come up with an idea like this? The new containers cost a dollar or two more than traditional cans, but consumers don't seem to mind. More than 50 percent of Dutch Boy's customers are now buying the plastic containers, and new stores, like Wal-Mart, are now carrying it. "It's an amazing innovation. Worth noticing," says one observer. "Not only did the new packaging increase sales, but it also got them more distribution at a higher retail price!"[14]

In contrast, poorly designed packages can cause headaches for consumers and lost sales for the company. For example, a few years ago, Planters Lifesavers Company attempted to use innovative packaging to create an association between fresh-roasted peanuts and fresh-roasted coffee. It packaged its Fresh Roast Salted Peanuts in vacuum-packed "Brik-Pacs," similar to those used for ground coffee. Unfortunately, the coffeelike packaging worked too well: Consumers mistook the peanuts for a new brand of flavored coffee and ran them through supermarket coffee-grinding machines, creating a gooey mess, disappointed customers, and lots of irate store managers.[15]

In recent years, product safety has also become a major packaging concern. We have all learned to deal with hard-to-open "childproof" packages. And after the rash of product tampering scares during the 1980s, most drug producers and food makers now put their products in tamper-resistant packages. In making packaging decisions, the company also must heed

■ Innovative packaging: Dutch Boy came up with a long overdue innovation—paint in plastic containers with twist-off caps. It created a paint can that's easy to carry, doesn't take a screwdriver to pry open, doesn't dribble when pouring, and doesn't take a hammer to bang closed again.

growing environmental concerns. Fortunately, many companies have gone "green" by reducing their packaging and using environmentally responsible packaging materials. For example, SC Johnson repackaged Agree Plus shampoo in a stand-up pouch using 80 percent less plastic. Procter & Gamble eliminated outer cartons from its Secret and Sure deodorants, saving 3.4 million pounds of paperboard per year.

Labeling

Labels may range from simple tags attached to products to complex graphics that are part of the package. They perform several functions. At the very least, the label *identifies* the product or brand, such as the name Sunkist stamped on oranges. The label might also *describe* several things about the product—who made it, where it was made, when it was made, its contents, how it is to be used, and how to use it safely. Finally, the label might *promote* the product through attractive graphics.

There has been a long history of legal concerns about packaging and labels. The Federal Trade Commission Act of 1914 held that false, misleading, or deceptive labels or packages constitute unfair competition. Labels can mislead customers, fail to describe important ingredients, or fail to include needed safety warnings. As a result, several federal and state laws regulate labeling. The most prominent is the Fair Packaging and Labeling Act of 1966, which set mandatory labeling requirements, encouraged voluntary industry packaging standards, and allowed federal agencies to set packaging regulations in specific industries.

Labeling has been affected in recent times by *unit pricing* (stating the price per unit of standard measure), *open dating* (stating the expected shelf life of the product), and *nutritional labeling* (stating the nutritional values in the product). The Nutritional Labeling and Educational Act of 1990 requires sellers to provide detailed nutritional information on food products, and recent sweeping actions by the Food and Drug Administration regulate the use of health-related terms such as *low-fat*, *light*, and *high-fiber*. Sellers must ensure that their labels contain all the required information.

■ Innovative labeling can help to promote a product.

Product Support Services

Customer service is another element of product strategy. A company's offer usually includes some support services, which can be a minor or a major part of the total offering. Later in the chapter, we will discuss services as products in themselves. Here, we discuss services that augment actual products.

The first step is to survey customers periodically to assess the value of current services and to obtain ideas for new ones. For example, Cadillac holds regular focus group interviews with owners and carefully watches complaints that come into its dealerships. From this careful monitoring, Cadillac has learned that buyers are very upset by repairs that are not done correctly the first time.

Once the company has assessed the value of various support services to customers, it must next assess the costs of providing these services. It can then develop a package of services that will both delight customers and yield profits to the company. Based on its consumer interviews, Cadillac has set up a system directly linking each dealership with a group of 10 engineers who can help walk mechanics through difficult repairs. Such actions helped Cadillac jump, in one year, from fourteenth to seventh in independent rankings of service. For the past several years, Cadillac has rated at or near the top of its industry on the American Customer Satisfaction Index.[16]

Many companies are now using a sophisticated mix of phone, e-mail, fax, Internet, and interactive voice and data technologies to provide support services that were not possible before. Consider the following example:

> Some online merchants are watching where you surf, then opening a chat window on your screen to askjust as they would in the storeif you have questions about the goods they see you eyeing. Last year, Hewlett-Packard began sending pop-up chat boxes to visitors who were shopping on HP.com's pages for digital-photography products. If a shopper loiters a few minutes over some gear, up pops a photo of an attractive woman with the words, "Hello, Need Information? An HP live chat representative is standing by to assist you." Click on "Go" and type a question, and a live sales agent responds immediately. SunTrust Banks, which has been inviting customers to chat about loan and bank products for about two years, is taking proactive chat one step further by experimenting with co-browsing. This feature essentially lets chat agents take control of a customer's computer screen, opening Web pages directly on their browser to help them find what they're looking for. In

the future, "call cams" will even let customers see an agent on their screen and talked directly through voice-over-Web capabilities.[17]

Product Line Decisions

Product line

A group of products that are closely related because they function in a similar manner, are sold to the same customer groups, are marketed through the same types of outlets, or fall within given price ranges.

Beyond decisions about individual products and services, product strategy also calls for building a product line. A **product line** is a group of products that are closely related because they function in a similar manner, are sold to the same customer groups, are marketed through the same types of outlets, or fall within given price ranges. For example, Nike produces several lines of athletic shoes and apparel, Nokia produces several lines of telecommunications products, and Charles Schwab produces several lines of financial services.

The major product line decision involves *product line length*—the number of items in the product line. The line is too short if the manager can increase profits by adding items; the line is too long if the manager can increase profits by dropping items. The company should manage its product lines carefully. Product lines tend to lengthen over time, and most companies eventually need to prune unnecessary or unprofitable items from their lines to increase overall profitability.

Product line length is influenced by company objectives and resources. For example, one objective might be to allow for upselling. Thus BMW wants to move customers up from it's 3-series models to 5- and 7-series models. Another objective might be to allow cross-selling: Hewlett-Packard sells printers as well as cartridges. Still another objective might be to protect against economic swings: Gap runs several clothing-store chains (Gap, Old Navy, Banana Republic) covering different price points.

A company can lengthen its product line in two ways: by *line stretching* or by *line filling*. *Product line stretching* occurs when a company lengthens its product line beyond its current range. The company can stretch its line downward, upward, or both ways.

Companies located at the upper end of the market can stretch their lines *downward*. A company may stretch downward to plug a market hole that otherwise would attract a new competitor or to respond to a competitor's attack on the upper end. Or it may add low-end products because it finds faster growth taking place in the low-end segments. DaimlerChrysler stretched its Mercedes line downward for all these reasons. Facing a slow-growth luxury car market and attacks by Japanese automakers on its high-end positioning, it successfully introduced its Mercedes C-Class cars. These models sell in the $30,000 range without harming the firm's ability to sell other Mercedes for $100,000 or more.

Companies at the lower end of a market can stretch their product lines *upward*. Sometimes, companies stretch upward in order to add prestige to their current products. Or they may be attracted by a faster growth rate or higher margins at the higher end. For example, each of the leading Japanese auto companies introduced an upmarket automobile: Toyota launched Lexus; Nissan launched Infinity; and Honda launched Acura. They used entirely new names rather than their own names.

Companies in the middle range of the market may decide to stretch their lines in *both directions*. Marriott did this with its hotel product line. Along with regular Marriott hotels, it has added new branded hotel lines to serve both the upper and lower ends of the market. Renaissance aims to attract and please top executives; Marriotts, upper and middle managers; Courtyards, salespeople and other "road warriors"; and Fairfield Inns, vacationers and business travelers on a tight travel budget. ExecuStay by Marriott provides temporary housing for those relocating or away on long-term assignments of 30 days or longer. Marriott's Residence Inn provides a relaxed, residential atmosphere—a home away from home for people who travel for a living. Marriott TownePlace Suites provide a comfortable atmosphere at a moderate price for extended-stay travelers.[18] The major risk with this strategy is that some travelers will trade down after finding that the lower-price hotels in the Marriott chain give them pretty much everything they want. However, Marriott would rather capture its customers who move downward than lose them to competitors.

An alternative to product line stretching is *product line filling*—adding more items within the present range of the line. There are several reasons for product line filling: reaching for extra profits, satisfying dealers, using excess capacity, being the leading full-line company, and plugging holes to keep out competitors. Sony filled its Walkman line by adding solar-powered and waterproof Walkmans, ultralight models for exercisers, the CD Walkman, and the Memory Stick Walkman, which enables users to download tracks straight from the Net. However, line filling is overdone if it results in cannibalization and customer confusion. The company should ensure that new items are noticeably different from existing ones.

■ Product line stretching: Marriott offers a full line of hotel brands, each aimed at a different target market.

Product Mix Decisions

Product mix (or product assortment)

The set of all product lines and items that a particular seller offers for sale.

An organization with several product lines has a product mix. A **product mix** (or **product assortment**) consists of all the product lines and items that a particular seller offers for sale. Avon's product mix consists of five major product lines: beauty products, wellness products, jewelry and accessories, gifts, and "inspirational" products (inspiring gifts, books, music, and home accents). Each product line consists of several sublines. For example, the beauty line breaks down into makeup, skin care, bath and beauty, fragrance, and outdoor protection products. Each line and subline has many individual items. Altogether, Avon's product mix includes 1,300 items. In contrast, a typical Kmart stocks 15,000 items, 3M markets more than 60,000 products, and General Electric manufactures as many as 250,000 items.

A company's product mix has four important dimensions: width, length, depth, and consistency. Product mix *width* refers to the number of different product lines the company carries. Procter & Gamble markets a fairly wide product mix consisting of 250 brands organized into five major product lines: personal and beauty, house and home, health and wellness, baby and family, and pet nutrition and care products. Product mix *length* refers to the total number of items the company carries within its product lines. P&G typically carries many brands within each line. For example, its house and home line includes seven laundry detergents, six hand soaps, five shampoos, and four dishwashing detergents.

Product line *depth* refers to the number of versions offered of each product in the line. P&G's Crest toothpaste comes in 16 varieties, ranging from Crest Multicare, Crest Cavity Protection, and Crest Tartar Protection to Crest Sensitivity Protection, Crest Dual Action Whitening, Crest Whitening Plus Scope, Kid's Cavity Protection, and Crest Baking Soda & Peroxide Whitening formulations.[19] (Talk about niche marketing! Remember our Chapter 7 discussion?)

Finally, the *consistency* of the product mix refers to how closely related the various product lines are in end use, production requirements, distribution channels, or some other way. P&G's product lines are consistent insofar as they are consumer products that go through the same distribution channels. The lines are less consistent insofar as they perform different functions for buyers.

These product mix dimensions provide the handles for defining the company's product strategy. The company can increase its business in four ways. It can add new product lines, widening its product mix. In this way, its new lines build on the company's reputation in its other lines. The company can lengthen its existing product lines to become a more full-line company. Or it can add more versions of each product and thus deepen its product mix. Finally, the company can pursue more product line consistency—or less—depending on whether it wants to have a strong reputation in a single field or in several fields.

Branding Strategy: Building Strong Brands

Some analysts see brands as *the* major enduring asset of a company, outlasting the company's specific products and facilities. John Stewart, co-founder of Quaker Oats, once said, "If this business were split up, I would give you the land and bricks and mortar, and I would keep the brands and trademarks, and I would fare better than you." A former CEO of McDonald's agrees:[20]

> A McDonald's board member who worked at Coca-Cola once talked to us about the value of our brand. He said if every asset we own, every building, and every piece of equipment were destroyed in a terrible natural disaster, we would be able to borrow all the money to replace it very quickly because of the value of our brand. And he's right. The brand is more valuable than the totality of all these assets.

Thus, brands are powerful assets that must be carefully developed and managed. In this section, we examine the key strategies for building and managing brands.

Brand Equity

Brands are more than just names and symbols. Brands represent consumers' perceptions and feelings about a product and its performance—everything that the product or service *means* to consumers. In the final analysis, brands exist in the minds of consumers. Thus, the real value of a strong brand is its power to capture consumer preference and loyalty.

Brands vary in the amount of power and value they have in the marketplace. Some brands—such as Coca-Cola, Tide, Nike, Harley-Davidson, Disney, and others—become larger-than-life icons that maintain their power in the market for years, even generations. "These brands win competitive battles not [just] because they deliver distinctive benefits, trustworthy service, or innovative technologies," notes a branding expert. "Rather, they succeed because they forge a deep connection with the culture."[21]

Brand equity

The positive differential effect that knowing the brand name has on customer response to the product or service.

A powerful brand has high *brand equity*. **Brand equity** is the positive differential effect that knowing the brand name has on customer response to the product or service. A measure of a brand's equity is the extent to which customers are willing to pay more for the brand. One study found that 72 percent of customers would pay a 20 percent premium for their brand of choice relative to the closest competing brand; 40 percent said they would pay a 50 percent premium.[22] Tide and Heinz lovers are willing to pay a 100 percent premium. Loyal Coke drinkers will pay a 50 percent premium and Volvo users a 40 percent premium.

■ A strong brand is a valuable asset. How many familiar brands and brand symbols can you find in this picture?

A brand with strong brand equity is a very valuable asset. *Brand valuation* is the process of estimating the total financial value of a brand. Measuring such value is difficult. However, according to one estimate, the brand value of Coca-Cola is almost $67 billion, Microsoft is $61 billion, and IBM is $54 billion. Other brands rating among the world's most valuable include General Electric, Intel, Nokia, Disney, McDonald's, Marlboro, and Mercedes.[23]

High brand equity provides a company with many competitive advantages. A powerful brand enjoys a high level of consumer brand awareness and loyalty. Because consumers expect stores to carry the brand, the company has more leverage in bargaining with resellers. Because the brand name carries high credibility, the company can more easily launch line and brand extensions, as when Coca-Cola used its well-known brand to introduce Diet Coke and Vanilla Coke, and when Procter & Gamble introduced Ivory dishwashing detergent. A powerful brand offers the company some defense against fierce price competition.

Above all, a powerful brand forms the basis for building strong and profitable customer relationships. Therefore, the fundamental asset underlying brand equity is *customer equity*—the value of the customer relationships that the brand creates. A powerful brand is important, but what it really represents is a profitable set of loyal customers. The proper focus of marketing is building customer equity, with brand management serving as a major marketing tool.[24]

Building Strong Brands

Branding poses challenging decisions to the marketer. Figure 8.3 shows that the major brand strategy decisions involve brand positioning, brand name selection, brand sponsorship, and brand development.

Brand Positioning

Marketers need to position their brands clearly in target customers' minds. They can position brands at any of three levels.[25] At the lowest level, they can position the brand on *product attributes*. Thus, marketers of Crest toothpaste can talk about the product's innovative ingredients and good taste. However, attributes are the least desirable level for brand positioning. Competitors can easily copy attributes. More important, customers are not interested in attributes as such; they are interested in what the attributes will do for them.

A brand can be better positioned by associating its name with a desirable *benefit*. Thus, Crest marketers can go beyond the brand's ingredients and talk about the resulting cavity prevention or teeth whitening benefits. Some successful brands positioned on benefits are Volvo (safety), Hallmark (caring), Harley-Davidson (adventure), FedEx (guaranteed on-time delivery), Nike (performance), and Lexus (quality).

The strongest brands go beyond attribute or benefit positioning. They are positioned on strong *beliefs and values*. These brands pack an emotional wallop. Thus, Crest's marketers can talk not just about ingredients and cavity-prevention benefits, but about how these give customers "healthy, beautiful smiles for life." Brand expert Marc Gobe argues that successful brands must engage customers on a deeper level, touching a universal emotion.[26] His brand design agency, which has worked on such brands as Starbucks, Victoria's Secret, Godiva, Versace, and Lancome, relies less on a product's tangible attributes and more on creating surprise, passion, and excitement surrounding a brand.

When positioning a brand, the marketer should establish a mission for the brand and a vision of what the brand must be and do. A brand is the company's promise to deliver a specific set of features, benefits, services, and experiences consistently to the buyers. It can be thought of as a contract to the customer regarding how the product or service will deliver value and satisfaction. The brand contract must be simple and honest. Motel 6, for example,

FIGURE 8.3

Major brand strategy decisions

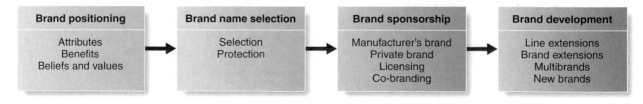

■ Brand positioning: The strongest brands go beyond attribute or benefit positioning. They engage customers on a deeper level, touching universal emotions.

offers clean rooms, low prices, and good service but does not promise expensive furniture or large bathrooms. In contrast, Ritz-Carlton offers luxurious rooms and a truly memorable experience but does not promise low prices.

Brand Name Selection

A good name can add greatly to a product's success. However, finding the best brand name is a difficult task. It begins with a careful review of the product and its benefits, the target market, and proposed marketing strategies.

Desirable qualities for a brand name include the following: (1) It should suggest something about the product's benefits and qualities. Examples: Beautyrest, Craftsman, Snuggles, Merrie Maids, OFF! bug spray. (2) It should be easy to pronounce, recognize, and remember. Short names help (Tide, Crest, Puffs). But longer ones are sometimes effective ("Love My Carpet" carpet cleaner, "I Can't Believe It's Not Butter" margarine). (3) The brand name should be distinctive (Lexus, Kodak, Oracle). (4) It should be extendable: Amazon.com began as an online bookseller but chose a name that would allow expansion into other categories. (5) The name should translate easily into foreign languages. Before spending $100 million to change its name to Exxon, Standard Oil of New Jersey tested several names in 54 languages in more than 150 foreign markets. It found that the name Enco referred to a stalled engine when pronounced in Japanese. (6) It should be capable of registration and legal protection. A brand name cannot be registered if it infringes on existing brand names.

Once chosen, the brand name must be protected. Many firms try to build a brand name that will eventually become identified with the product category. Brand names such as Kleenex, Levi's, Jell-O, Scotch Tape, Formica, Ziploc, and Fiberglas have succeeded in this way. However, their very success may threaten the company's rights to the name. Many originally protected brand names—such as cellophane, aspirin, nylon, kerosene, linoleum, yo-yo, trampoline, escalator, thermos, and shredded wheat—are now generic names that any seller can use.

Brand Sponsorship

A manufacturer has four sponsorship options. The product may be launched as a *manufacturer's brand* (or national brand), as when Kellogg and IBM sell their output under their own manufacturer's brand names. Or the manufacturer may sell to resellers who give it a *private brand* (also called a *store brand* or *distributor brand*). Although most manufacturers create their own brand names, others market *licensed brands*. Finally, two companies can join forces and *co-brand* a product.

Private brand (or store brand)

A brand created and owned by a reseller of a product or service.

MANUFACTURER'S BRANDS VERSUS PRIVATE BRANDS Manufacturers' brands have long dominated the retail scene. In recent times, however, an increasing number of retailers and wholesalers have created their own **private brands** (or **store brands**). And in many industries, these private brands are giving manufacturers' brands a real run for their money:

> Melanie Turner has forgotten her shopping list, but the 42-year-old pension consultant doesn't seem to mind. Entering her local Costco store, Turner knows right where she's going. In the dish detergent section, her hand goes past Procter & Gamble's Cascade to grab two 96-ounce bottles of Kirkland Signature, the in-store brand that Costco has plastered on everything from cashews to cross-trainer sneakers. Trolling for some fresh fish for dinner, she hauls in a 2 1/2-pound package of tilapia—it, too, emblazoned with the bold red, white, and black Kirkland logo. Then it's off to the paper aisle, where she picks up mammoth packs of Kirkland dinner napkins, Kirkland toilet paper, and . . . wait, where are the Kirkland paper towels? Her eyes scan the store's maze of hulking pallets—no sign of them—before coming to rest on a 12-pack of P&G's Bounty. A moment of decision. "I'll wait on this," she says finally.
>
> And there, in microcosm, is why Melanie Turner scares the pants off Procter & Gamble, Unilever, Kraft, and just about every consumer goods company out there.

■ An increasing number of retailers have created their own store brands. Costco's Kirkland brand adorns everything from baby wipes to barbeques.

Her shopping cart is headed for the checkout aisle, and there's hardly a national brand in it. . . . An almost imperceptible tectonic shift has been reshaping the world of brands. Retailers—once the lowly peddlers of brands that were made and marketed by big, important manufacturers—are now behaving like full-fledged marketers.[27]

It seems that almost every retailer now carries its own store brands. Wal-Mart offers Sam's Choice beverages and food products; Spring Valley nutritional products; and White Cloud brand toilet tissue, diapers, detergent, and fabric softener. Its Ol' Roy dog food (named for Sam Walton's Irish setter), has now passed Nestle's venerable Purina as the world's best-selling dog chow. More than half the products at your local Target are private brands, and grocery giant Kroger makes and markets some 4,300 food and drink items under its own brands. At the other end of the spectrum, upscale retailer Saks Fifth Avenue carries its own Platinum clothing line, which features $1,000 jackets and $500 cotton dress shirts.

In U.S. supermarkets, taken as a single brand, private-label products are the number-one, -two, or -three brand in over 40 percent of all grocery product categories. In all, they capture more than a 20 percent share of sales in U.S. supermarkets, drug chains, and mass merchandise stores. Private-label apparel captures a 36 percent share of all U.S. apparel sales.[28]

In the so-called *battle of the brands* between manufacturers' and private brands, retailers have many advantages. They control what products they stock, where they go on the shelf, what prices they charge, and which ones they will feature in local circulars. Most retailers also charge manufacturers *slotting fees*—payments from the manufacturers before the retailers will accept new products and find "slots" for them on their shelves. Slotting fees have recently received much scrutiny from the Federal Trade Commission, which worries that they might dampen competition by restricting retail shelf access for smaller manufacturers who can't afford the fees.[29]

Private brands can be hard to establish and costly to stock and promote. However, they also yield higher profit margins for the reseller. And they give resellers exclusive products that cannot be bought from competitors, resulting in greater store traffic and loyalty. Retailers price their store brands lower than comparable manufacturers' brands, thereby appealing to budget-conscious shoppers, especially in difficult economic times. And most shoppers believe that store brands are often made by one of the larger manufacturers anyway.

To fend off private brands, leading brand marketers will have to invest in R&D to bring out new brands, new features, and continuous quality improvements. They must design strong advertising programs to maintain high awareness and preference. They must find ways to "partner" with major distributors in a search for distribution economies and improved joint performance.

LICENSING Most manufacturers take years and spend millions to create their own brand names. However, some companies license names or symbols previously created by other manufacturers, names of well-known celebrities, or characters from popular movies and books. For a fee, any of these can provide an instant and proven brand name.

Apparel and accessories sellers pay large royalties to adorn their products—from blouses to ties, and linens to luggage—with the names or initials of well-known fashion innovators such as Calvin Klein, Tommy Hilfiger, Gucci, or Armani. Sellers of children's products attach an almost endless list of character names to clothing, toys, school supplies, linens, dolls, lunch boxes, cereals, and other items. Licensed character names range from classics such as *Sesame Street*, Disney, Peanuts, Winnie the Pooh, the Muppets, Scooby Doo, and Dr. Seuss characters to the more recent Teletubbies, Pokemon, Powerpuff Girls, Rugrats, Blue's Clues, and Harry Potter characters. Almost half of all retail toy sales come from products based on television shows and movies such as *Scooby Doo, SpongeBob SquarePants, The Rugrats Movie, The Lion King, Batman, Spider-Man, Men in Black, Lord of the Rings,* or *Harry Potter.*

Name and character licensing has grown rapidly in recent years. Annual retail sales of licensed products in the United States and Canada have grown from only $4 billion in 1977 to $55 billion in 1987 and more than $105 billion today. Licensing can be a highly profitable business for many companies. For example, Warner Brothers has turned Looney Tunes characters into one of the most sought-after licenses. More than 225 licensees generate billions of dollars in retail sales of products sporting Bugs Bunny, Daffy Duck, Foghorn Leghorn, or one of the more than 100 Looney Tunes characters. Similarly, Nickelodeon has developed a stable full of hugely popular characters—such as Dora the Explorer, the Rugrats clan, and SpongeBob SquarePants. Products sporting these characters generate more than $5 billion in annual retail sales. "When it comes to licensing its brands for consumer products, Nickelodeon has proved that it has the Midas touch," states a brand licensing expert.[30]

■ Character licensing: Warner Brothers has turned Looney Tunes characters into one of the world's most sought-after licenses.

The fastest-growing licensing category is corporate brand licensing, as more and more for-profit and not-for-profit organizations are licensing their names to generate additional revenues and brand recognition. Coca-Cola, for example, has some 320 licensees in 57 countries producing more than 10,000 products, ranging from baby clothes and boxer shorts to earrings, a Coca-Cola Barbie doll, and even a fishing lure shaped like a tiny Coke can. Each year, licensees sold more than $1 billion worth of licensed Coca-Cola products.[31]

Co-branding

The practice of using the established brand names of two different companies on the same product.

CO-BRANDING Although companies have been **co-branding** products for many years, there has been a recent resurgence in co-branded products. Co-branding occurs when two established brand names of different companies are used on the same product. For example, Nabisco joined forces with Pillsbury to create Pillsbury Oreo Bars baking mix, and Kellogg joined with ConAgra to co-brand Healthy Choice from Kellogg's cereals. Ford and Eddie Bauer co-branded a sport utility vehicle—the Ford Explorer, Eddie Bauer edition. General Electric worked with Culligan to develop its Water by Culligan Profile Performance refrigerator with a built-in Culligan water filtration system. In most co-branding situations, one company licenses another company's well-known brand to use in combination with its own.

Co-branding offers many advantages. Because each brand dominates in a different category, the combined brands create broader consumer appeal and greater brand equity. Co-branding also allows a company to expand its existing brand into a category it might otherwise have difficulty entering alone. For example, by licensing its Healthy Choice brand to Kellogg, ConAgra entered the breakfast segment with a solid product. In return, Kellogg could leverage the broad awareness of the Healthy Choice name in the cereal category.

Co-branding also has limitations. Such relationships usually involve complex legal contracts and licenses. Co-branding partners must carefully coordinate their advertising, sales promotion, and other marketing efforts. Finally, when co-branding, each partner must trust the other will take good care of its brand. For example, consider the marriage between Kmart and the Martha Stewart housewares brand. When Kmart declared bankruptcy, it cast a shadow on the Martha Stewart brand. In turn, when Martha Stewart was convicted of illegal financial dealings, it created negative associations for Kmart. As one Nabisco manager puts it, "Giving away your brand is a lot like giving away your child—you want to make sure everything is perfect."[32]

Brand Development

A company has four choices when it comes to developing brands (see Figure 8.4). It can introduce *line extensions* (existing brand names extended to new forms, sizes, and flavors of an existing product category), *brand extensions* (existing brand names extended to new product

FIGURE 8.4
Brand development strategies

Product Category

	Existing	New
Existing	Line extension	Brand extension
New	Multibrands	New brands

Brand Name

categories), *multibrands* (new brand names introduced in the same product category), or *new brands* (new brand names in new product categories).

Line extension

Using a successful brand name to introduce additional items in a given product category under the same brand name, such as new flavors, forms, colors, added ingredients, or package sizes.

1) **LINE EXTENSIONS** **Line extensions** occur when a company introduces additional items in a given product category under the same brand name, such as new flavors, forms, colors, ingredients, or package sizes. Thus, Dannon introduced several line extensions, including seven new yogurt flavors, a fat-free yogurt, and a large, economy-size yogurt. And Morton Salt has expanded its line to include regular iodized salt plus Morton Course Kosher Salt, Morton Lite Salt (low in sodium), Morton Popcorn Salt, and Morton Nature's Season seasoning blend. The vast majority of all new-product activity consists of line extensions.

A company might introduce line extensions as a low-cost, low-risk way to introduce new products. Or it might want to meet consumer desires for variety, to use excess capacity, or simply to command more shelf space from resellers. However, line extensions involve some risks. An overextended brand name might lose its specific meaning, or heavily extended brands can cause consumer confusion or frustration.

Another risk is that sales of an extension may come at the expense of other items in the line. For example, the original Nabisco Fig Newtons cookies have now morphed into a full line of Newtons Fruit Chewy Cookies, including Cranberry Newtons, Blueberry Newtons, and Apple Newtons. Although all are doing well, the original Fig Newton brand now seems like just another flavor. A line extension works best when it takes sales away from competing brands, not when it "cannibalizes" the company's other items.

Brand extension

Using a successful brand name to launch a new or modified product in a new category.

2) **BRAND EXTENSIONS** A **brand extension** involves the use of a successful brand name to launch new or modified products in a new category. Mattel has extended its enduring Barbie Doll brand into new categories ranging from Barbie home furnishings, Barbie cosmetics, and Barbie electronics to Barbie books, Barbie sporting goods, and even a Barbie band—Beyond

■ Line extensions: Morton sells an entire line of salts and seasonings for every occasion.

When it comes to salt, she's got it covered.

The Morton Salt girl.
Let her shake things up in your kitchen.
With salts and seasonings for every occasion,
she has that little something that makes a big difference.
For our entire line of salts and recipe ideas, see *mortonsalt.com*.

Pink. Swiss Army brand sunglasses, Disney Cruise Lines, Century 21 Home Improvements, and Brinks home security systems—all are brand extensions.

A brand extension gives a new product instant recognition and faster acceptance. It also saves the high advertising costs usually required to build a new brand name. At the same time, a brand extension strategy involves some risk. Brand extensions such as Bic pantyhose, Heinz pet food, LifeSavers gum, and Clorox laundry detergent met early deaths. The extension may confuse the image of the main brand. And if a brand extension fails, it may harm consumer attitudes toward the other products carrying the same brand name. Further, a brand name may not be appropriate to a particular new product, even if it is well made and satisfying—would you consider buying Texaco milk or Alpo chili? Companies that are tempted to transfer a brand name must research how well the brand's associations fit the new product.[33]

 MULTIBRANDS Companies often introduce additional brands in the same category. Thus, P&G markets many different brands in each of its product categories. *Multibranding* offers a way to establish different features and appeal to different buying motives. It also allows a company to lock up more reseller shelf space.

A major drawback of multibranding is that each brand might obtain only a small market share, and none may be very profitable. The company may end up spreading its resources over many brands instead of building a few brands to a highly profitable level. These companies should reduce the number of brands they sell in a given category and set up tighter screening procedures for new brands.

 NEW BRANDS A company might believe that the power of its existing brand name is waning and a new brand name is needed. Or a company may create a new brand name when it enters a new product category for which none of the company's current brand names is appropriate. For example, Honda created the Acura brand to differentiate its luxury car from the established Honda line. Toyota created the separate Scion automobile, targeted toward GenY consumers. Japan's Matsushita uses separate names for its different families of products: Technics, Panasonic, National, and Quasar.

As with multibranding, offering too many new brands can result in a company spreading its resources too thin. And in some industries, such as consumer packaged goods, consumers and retailers have become concerned that there are already too many brands, with too few differences between them. Thus, Procter & Gamble, Frito-Lay, and other large consumer-product marketers are now pursuing *megabrand* strategies—weeding out weaker brands and focusing their marketing dollars only on brands that can achieve the number one or number two market share positions in their categories.

Managing Brands

Companies must manage their brands carefully. First, the brand's positioning must be continuously communicated to consumers. Major brand marketers often spend huge amounts on advertising to create brand awareness and to build preference and loyalty. For example, Verizon spends more than a billion dollars annually to promote its brand. McDonald's spends more than $500 million.[34]

Such advertising campaigns can help to create name recognition, brand knowledge, and maybe even some brand preference. However, the fact is that brands are not maintained by advertising but by the *brand experience*. Today, customers come to know a brand through a wide range of contacts and touchpoints. These include advertising, but also personal experience with the brand, word of mouth, personal interactions with company people, telephone interactions, company Web pages, and many others. The company must put as much care into managing these touch points as it does into producing its ads.

The brand's positioning will not take hold fully unless everyone in the company lives the brand. Therefore the company needs to train its people to be customer-centered. Even better, the company should carry on internal brand building to help employees to understand and be enthusiastic about the brand promise. Many companies go even further by training and encouraging their distributors and dealers to serve their customers well.

All of this suggests that managing a company's brand assets can no longer be left only to brand managers. Brand managers do not have enough power or scope to do all the things necessary to build and enhance their brands. Moreover, brand managers often pursue short-term results, whereas managing brands as assets calls for longer-term strategy. Thus, some companies are now setting up brand asset management teams to manage their major brands. Canada Dry and Colgate-Palmolive have appointed *brand equity managers* to maintain and protect their brands' images, associations, and quality, and to prevent short-term actions by overeager brand managers from hurting the brand. Similarly, Hewlett-Packard has appointed a senior executive in charge of the customer experience in each of its two divisions, consumer and business-to-business (B2B). Their job is to track, measure, and improve the customer relationship with Hewlett-Packard products. They report directly to the presidents of their respective divisions.

Finally, companies need to periodically audit their brands' strengths and weaknesses.[35] They should ask: Does our brand excel at delivering benefits that consumers truly value? Is the brand properly positioned? Do all of our consumer touch points support the brand's positioning? Do the brand's managers understand what the brand means to consumers? Does the brand receive proper, sustained support?

The brand audit may turn up brands that need to be repositioned because of changing customer preferences or new competitors. Some cases may call for completely *rebranding* a product, service, or company. The recent wave of corporate mergers and acquisitions has set off a flurry of corporate rebranding campaigns.

A prime example is Verizon Communication, created by the merger of Bell Atlantic and GTE. The company decided that neither of the old names properly positioned the new company. "We needed a master brand to leave all our old names behind," says Verizon's senior vice president of brand management and marketing services. The old names created too much confusion, conjured up an image of old-fashioned phone companies, and "held us back from marketing in new areas of innovation—high speed Internet and wireless services." The new branding effort appears to have worked. Verizon Wireless is now the leading provider of wireless phone services, with better than a 24 percent market share. Number two is Cingular Wireless, another new brand created through a joint venture between Bell South and SBC Communications.[36]

However, building a new image and re-educating customers can be a huge undertaking. The cost of Verizon's brand overhaul included tens of millions of dollars just for a special 4-week advertising campaign to announce the new name, followed by considerable ongoing advertising expenses. And that was only beginning. The company had to repaint its fleet of 70,000 trucks along with its garages and service centers. The campaign also required relabeling 250,000 pay phones, redesigning 91 million customer billing statements, and producing videos and other in-house employee educational materials.

HASTA AQUÍ

Services Marketing

Services have grown dramatically in recent years. Services now account for 74 percent of U.S. gross domestic product and nearly 60 percent of personal consumption expenditures. Whereas service jobs accounted for 55 percent of all U.S. jobs in 1970, today they account for 82 percent of total employment. Services are growing even faster in the world economy, making up a quarter of the value of all international trade.[37]

Service industries vary greatly. *Governments* offer services through courts, employment services, hospitals, military services, police and fire departments, postal service, and schools. *Private not-for-profit organizations* offer services through museums, charities, churches, colleges, foundations, and hospitals. A large number of *business organizations* offer services—airlines, banks, hotels, insurance companies, consulting firms, medical and law practices, entertainment companies, real estate firms, retailers, and others.

Nature and Characteristics of a Service

A company must consider four special service characteristics when designing marketing programs: *intangibility, inseparability, variability,* and *perishability* (see Figure 8.5).

Service intangibility

A major characteristic of services—they cannot be seen, tasted, felt, heard, or smelled before they are bought.

Service intangibility means that services cannot be seen, tasted, felt, heard, or smelled before they are bought. For example, people undergoing cosmetic surgery cannot see the result before the purchase. Airline passengers have nothing but a ticket and the promise that they and their luggage will arrive safely at the intended destination, hopefully at the same time. To reduce uncertainty, buyers look for "signals" of service quality. They draw conclusions about quality from the place, people, price, equipment, and communications that they can see.

Therefore, the service provider's task is to make the service tangible in one or more ways and to send the right signals about quality. One analyst calls this *evidence management,* in which the service organization presents its customers with organized, honest evidence of its capabilities. The Mayo Clinic practices good evidence management:[38]

■ Service industries vary greatly: For example, governments offer services through courts, employment services, hospitals, military services, police and fire departments, schools, and the postal service.

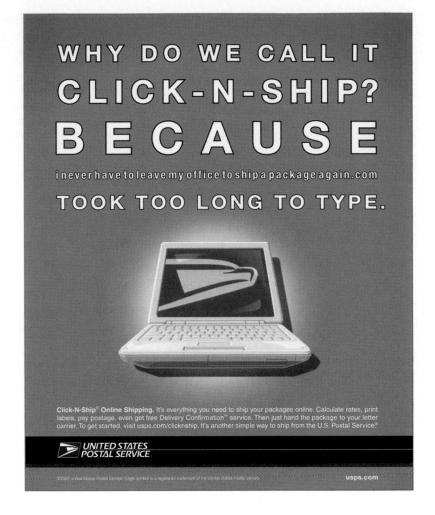

When it comes to hospitals, it's very hard for the average patient to judge the quality of the "product." You can't try it on, you can't return it if you don't like it, and you need an advanced degree to understand it. And so, when we're considering a medical facility, most of us unconsciously turn detective, looking for evidence of competence, caring, and integrity. The Mayo Clinic doesn't leave that evidence to chance. By carefully managing a set of visual and experiential clues, Mayo offers patients and their families concrete evidence of its strengths and values. For example, staff people at the clinic are trained to act in a way that clearly signals its patient-first focus. "My doctor calls me at home to check on how I am doing," marvels one patient. "She wants to work with what is best for my schedule." Mayo's physical facilities also send the right signals. They've been carefully designed to relieve stress, offer a place of refuge, create positive distractions, convey caring and respect, signal competence, accommodate families, and make it easy to find your

FIGURE 8.5
Four service characteristics

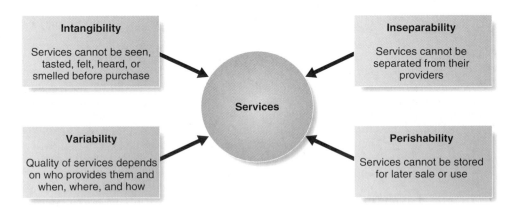

■ Signaling service quality: By carefully managing visual and experiential clues, Mayo Clinic offers patients concrete evidence of its strengths and values. It clearly signals that "The needs of the patient come first."

way around. The result? Exceptionally positive word-of-mouth and abiding customer loyalty, which have allowed Mayo Clinic to build what is arguably the most powerful brand in health care—with very little advertising.

Physical goods are produced, then stored, later sold, and still later consumed. In contrast, services are first sold, then produced and consumed at the same time. **Service inseparability** means that services cannot be separated from their providers, whether the providers are people or machines. If a service employee provides the service, then the employee is a part of the service. Because the customer is also present as the service is produced, *provider-customer interaction* is a special feature of services marketing. Both the provider and the customer affect the service outcome.

Service variability means that the quality of services depends on who provides them as well as when, where, and how they are provided. For example, some hotels—say, Marriott—have reputations for providing better service than others. Still, within a given Marriott hotel, one registration-desk employee may be cheerful and efficient, whereas another standing just a few feet away may be unpleasant and slow. Even the quality of a single Marriott employee's service varies according to his or her energy and frame of mind at the time of each customer encounter.

Service perishability means that services cannot be stored for later sale or use. Some doctors charge patients for missed appointments because the service value existed only at that point and disappeared when the patient did not show up. The perishability of services is not a problem when demand is steady. However, when demand fluctuates, service firms often have difficult problems. For example, because of rush-hour demand, public transportation companies have to own much more equipment than they would if demand were even throughout the day. Thus, service firms often design strategies for producing a better match between demand and supply. Hotels and resorts charge lower prices in the off-season to attract more guests. And restaurants hire part-time employees to serve during peak periods.

Service inseparability
A major characteristic of services—they are produced and consumed at the same time and cannot be separated from their providers.

Service variability
A major characteristic of services—their quality may vary greatly, depending on who provides them and when, where, and how.

Service perishability
A major characteristic of services—they cannot be stored for later sale or use.

Marketing Strategies for Service Firms

Just like manufacturing businesses, good service firms use marketing to position themselves strongly in chosen target markets. Wal-Mart promises "Always Low Prices, Always." Ritz-Carlton Hotels positions itself as offering a memorable experience that "enlivens the senses, instills well-being, and fulfills even the unexpressed wishes and needs of our guests." At the Mayo Clinic, "the needs of the patient come first." These and other service firms establish their positions through traditional marketing mix activities.

However, because services differ from tangible products, they often require additional marketing approaches. In a product business, products are fairly standardized and can sit on shelves waiting for customers. But in a service business, the customer and front-line service employee *interact* to create the service. Thus, service providers must interact effectively with customers to create superior value during service encounters. Effective interaction, in turn, depends on the skills of front-line service employees and on the support processes backing these employees.

The Service-Profit Chain

Service-profit chain

The chain that links service firm profits with employee and customer satisfaction.

Successful service companies focus their attention on *both* their customers and their employees. They understand the **service-profit chain**, which links service firm profits with employee and customer satisfaction. This chain consists of five links:[39]

■ *Internal service quality:* superior employee selection and training, a quality work environment, and strong support for those dealing with customers, which results in . . .

■ *Satisfied and productive service employees:* more satisfied, loyal, and hardworking employees, which results in . . .

■ *Greater service value:* more effective and efficient customer value creation and service delivery, which results in . . .

■ *Satisfied and loyal customers:* satisfied customers who remain loyal, repeat purchase, and refer other customers, which results in . . .

■ *Healthy service profits and growth:* superior service firm performance.

Therefore, reaching service profits and growth goals begins with taking care of those who take care of customers (see Real Marketing 8.2). In fact, Starbucks CEO Howard Schultz goes so far as to say that "customers always come in second—employees matter more." The idea is that happy employees will unleash their enthusiasm on customers, creating even greater customer satisfaction. "If the battle cry of the company [is] to exceed the expectations of our customers," says Schultz, "then as managers, we [must] first exceed the expectations of our people."[40]

Internal marketing

Marketing by a service firm to train and effectively motivate its customer-contact employees and all the supporting service people to work as a team to provide customer satisfaction.

Thus, service marketing requires more than just traditional external marketing using the four Ps. Figure 8.6 shows that service marketing also requires *internal marketing* and *interactive marketing*. **Internal marketing** means that the service firm must effectively train and motivate its customer-contact employees and supporting service people to work as a *team* to provide customer satisfaction. Marketers must get everyone in the organization to be customer-centered. In fact, internal marketing must *precede* external marketing. For example, Ritz-Carlton orients its employees carefully, instills in them a sense of pride, and motivates them by recognizing and rewarding outstanding service deeds.

Interactive marketing

Marketing by a service firm that recognizes that perceived service quality depends heavily on the quality of buyer–seller interaction.

Interactive marketing means that service quality depends heavily on the quality of the buyer-seller interaction during the service encounter. In product marketing, product quality often depends little on how the product is obtained. But in services marketing, service quality depends on both the service deliverer and the quality of the delivery. Service marketers, therefore, have to master interactive marketing skills. Thus, Ritz-Carlton selects only "people who care about people" and instructs them carefully in the fine art of interacting with customers to satisfy their every need.

In today's marketplace, companies must know how to deliver interactions that are not only "high-touch" but also "high-tech." For example, customers can log on to the Charles Schwab Web site and access account information, investment research, real-time quotes,

FIGURE 8.6
Three types of marketing in service industries

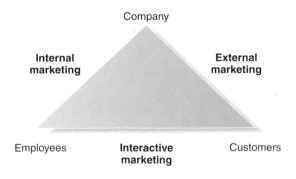

Real Marketing 8.2

Ritz-Carlton: Taking Care of Those Who Take Care of Customers

Ritz-Carlton, a chain of luxury hotels renowned for outstanding service, caters to the top 5 percent of corporate and leisure travelers. The company's Credo sets lofty customer service goals: "The Ritz-Carlton Hotel is a place where the genuine care and comfort of our guests is our highest mission. . . . The Ritz-Carlton experience enlivens the senses, instills well-being, and fulfills even the unexpressed wishes and needs of our guests."

The Credo is more than just words on paper—Ritz-Carlton delivers on its promises. In surveys of departing guests, some 95 percent report that they've had a truly memorable experience. In fact, at Ritz-Carlton, exceptional service encounters have become almost commonplace. Take the experiences of Nancy and Harvey Heffner of Manhattan, who stayed at the Ritz-Carlton Naples, in Naples, Florida (recently rated the best hotel in the United States, fourth best in the world, by *Travel & Leisure* magazine). As reported in the *New York Times*:

> "The hotel is elegant and beautiful," Mrs. Heffner said, "but more important is the beauty expressed by the staff. They can't do enough to please you." When the couple's son became sick last year in Naples, the hotel staff brought him hot tea with honey at all hours of the night, she said. When Mr. Heffner had to fly home on business for a day and his return flight was delayed, a driver for the hotel waited in the lobby most of the night.

Or how about this account: "An administrative assistant at Ritz-Carlton Philadelphia overheard a guest lamenting that he'd forgotten to pack a pair of formal shoes and would have to wear hiking boots to an important meeting. Early the next morning, she delivered to the awestruck man a new pair in his size and favorite color."

Such personal, high-quality service has also made the Ritz-Carlton a favorite among conventioneers. "They not only treat us like kings when we hold our top-level meetings in their hotels, but we just never get any complaints," comments one convention planner. Says another, who had recently held a meeting at The Ritz-Carlton at Half Moon Bay, "The . . . first-rate catering and service-oriented convention services staff [and] the Ritz-Carlton's ambiance and beauty—the elegant, Grand Dame-style lodge, nestled on a bluff between two championship golf courses overlooking the Pacific Ocean—makes a day's work there seem anything but."

Since its incorporation in 1983, Ritz-Carlton has received virtually every major award that the hospitality industry bestows. In addition, in 1992, it became the first hotel company ever to win the prestigious Malcolm Baldrige National Quality Award, which it won a *second* time in 1999. And it placed first in customer satisfaction among luxury hotels in the most recent J.D. Power & Associates hotel survey. More importantly, service quality has resulted in high customer retention. More than 90 percent of Ritz-Carlton customers return. And despite its hefty room rates, the chain enjoys a 70 percent occupancy rate, almost nine points above the industry average.

Most of the responsibility for keeping guests satisfied falls to Ritz-Carlton's customer-contact employees. Thus, the hotel chain takes great care in finding just the right personnel. "We don't hire or recruit, we select," says Ritz-Carlton's director of human resources. "We want only people who care about people," notes the company's vice president of quality. Once selected, employees are given intensive training in the art of coddling customers. New employees attend a 2-day orientation, in which top management drums into them the "20 Ritz Carlton Basics." Basic number one: "The Credo will be known, owned, and energized by all employees."

Employees are taught to do everything they can never to lose a guest. "There's no negotiating at Ritz-Carlton when it comes to solving customer problems," says the quality executive. Staff learn that *anyone* who receives a customer complaint *owns* that complaint

CREDO

The Ritz-Carlton Hotel is a place where the genuine care and comfort of our guests is our highest mission.

We pledge to provide the finest personal service and facilities for our guests who will always enjoy a warm, relaxed yet refined ambience.

The Ritz-Carlton experience enlivens the senses, instills well-being, and fulfills even the unexpressed wishes and needs of our guests.

THREE STEPS OF SERVICE

1
A warm and sincere greeting. Use the guest name, if and when possible.

2
Anticipation and compliance with guest needs.

3
Fond farewell. Give them a warm good-bye and use their name, if and when possible.

THE EMPLOYEE PROMISE

At The Ritz-Carlton, our Ladies and Gentlemen are the most important resource in our service commitment to our guests.

By applying the principles of trust, honesty, respect, integrity and commitment, we nurture and maximize talent to the benefit of each individual and the company.

The Ritz-Carlton fosters a work environment where diversity is valued, quality of life is enhanced, individual aspirations are fulfilled, and The Ritz-Carlton mystique is strengthened.

"We Are Ladies and Gentlemen Serving Ladies and Gentlemen"

■ The Credo and Employee Promise: Ritz-Carlton knows that to take care of customers, you must first take care of those who take care of customers.

(box continues)

| Ritz-Carlton: Taking Care of Those Who Take Care of Customers | *continued* |

until it's resolved (Ritz-Carlton Basic number eight). They are trained to drop whatever they're doing to help a customer—no matter what they're doing or what their department. Ritz-Carlton employees are empowered to handle problems on the spot, without consulting higher-ups. Each employee can spend up to $2,000 to redress a guest grievance. And each is allowed to break from his or her routine for as long as needed to make a guest happy. Thus, while competitors are still reading guest comment cards to learn about customer problems, Ritz-Carlton has already resolved them.

Ritz-Carlton instills a sense of pride in its employees. "You serve," they are told, "but you are not servants." The company motto states, "We are ladies and gentlemen serving ladies and gentlemen." Employees understand their role in Ritz-Carlton's success. "We might not be able to afford a hotel like this," says employee Tammy Patton, "but we can make it so people who can afford it will want to keep coming here." As the general manager of the Ritz-Carlton Naples puts it, "When you invite guests to your house, you want everything to be perfect."

Ritz-Carlton recognizes and rewards employees who perform feats of outstanding service. Under its 5-Star Awards program, outstanding performers are nominated by peers and managers, and winners receive plaques at dinners celebrating their achievements. For on-the-spot recognition, managers award Gold Standard Coupons, redeemable for items in the gift shop and free weekend stays at the hotel. Ritz-Carlton further motivates its employees with events such as Super Sports Day, an employee talent show, luncheons celebrating employment anniversaries and birthdays, a family picnic, and special themes in employee dining rooms. As a result, Ritz-Carlton's employees appear to be just as satisfied as its customers. Employee turnover is less than 25 percent a year, compared with 44 percent at other luxury hotels.

Ritz-Carlton's success is based on a simple philosophy: To take care of customers, you must first take care of those who take care of customers. Satisfied employees deliver high service value, which then creates satisfied customers. Satisfied customers, in turn, create sales and profits for the company.

Sources: Quotes and other information from Duff McDonald, "Roll Out the Blue Carpet," *Business 2.0,* May 2004, pp. 53–54; Edwin McDowell, "Ritz-Carlton's Keys to Good Service," *New York Times,* March 31, 1993, p. D1; "The Ritz-Carlton, Half Moon Bay," *Successful Meetings,* November 2001, p. 40; Scott Neuman, "Relax, Put Your Feet Up," *Far Eastern Economic Review,* April 17, 2003, p. 36; Terry R. Bacon and David G. Pugh, "Ritz-Carlton and EMC: The Gold Standards in Operational Behavior," *Journal of Organizational Excellence,* Spring 2004, pp. 61–77; and the Ritz-Carlton Web site at www.ritzcarlton.com, January 2005.

after-hours trading, and the Schwab learning center. They can also participate in live online events and chat online with customer service representatives. Customers seeking more-personal interactions can contact service reps by phone or visit a local Schwab branch office. Thus, Schwab has mastered interactive marketing at all three levels—calls, clicks, *and* visits.

Today, as competition and costs increase, and as productivity and quality decrease, more service marketing sophistication is needed. Service companies face three major marketing tasks: They want to increase their *competitive differentiation*, *service quality*, and *productivity*.

Managing Service Differentiation

In these days of intense price competition, service marketers often complain about the difficulty of differentiating their services from those of competitors. To the extent that customers view the services of different providers as similar, they care less about the provider than the price.

The solution to price competition is to develop a differentiated offer, delivery, and image. The *offer* can include innovative features that set one company's offer apart from competitors' offers. Some hotels offer car rental, banking, and business center services in their lobbies and high-speed Internet connections in their rooms. Airlines differentiate their offers though frequent flyer award programs and special services. For example, British Airways business and first cabins offers international travelers fully flat beds and private "demi-cabins," post-flight showers, and a la carte hot breakfasts.

Service companies can differentiate their service *delivery* by having more able and reliable customer-contact people, by developing a superior physical environment in which the service product is delivered, or by designing a superior delivery process. For example, many grocery chains now offer online shopping and home delivery as a better way to shop than having to drive, park, wait in line, and tote groceries home.

Finally, service companies also can work on differentiating their *images* through symbols and branding. The Harris Bank of Chicago adopted the lion as its symbol on its stationery, in its advertising, and even as stuffed animals offered to new depositors. The well-known Harris lion confers an image of strength on the bank. Other well-known service symbols include The Merrill Lynch's bull, MGM's lion, McDonald's Golden Arches, and Allstate's "good hands."

■ Service differentiation: British Airways offers international travelers fully flat beds and private "demi-cabins," post-flight showers, and a la carte hot breakfasts.

Managing Service Quality

One of the major ways a service firm can differentiate itself is by delivering consistently higher quality than its competitors do. Like manufacturers before them, most service industries have now joined the customer-driven quality movement. And like product marketers, service providers need to identify what target customers expect concerning service quality.

Unfortunately, service quality is harder to define and judge than is product quality. For instance, it is harder to agree on the quality of a haircut than on the quality of a hair dryer. Customer retention is perhaps the best measure of quality—a service firm's ability to hang onto its customers depends on how consistently it delivers value to them.[41]

Top service companies set high service quality standards. They watch service performance closely, both their own and that of competitors. They do not settle for merely good service; they aim for 100 percent defect-free service. A 98 percent performance standard may sound good, but using this standard, 64,000 FedEx packages would be lost each day, 10 words would be misspelled on each printed page, 400,000 prescriptions would be misfilled daily, and drinking water would be unsafe 8 days a year. [42]

Unlike product manufacturers who can adjust their machinery and inputs until everything is perfect, service quality will always vary, depending on the interactions between employees and customers. As hard as they try, even the best companies will have an occasional late delivery, burned steak, or grumpy employee. However, good *service recovery* can turn angry customers into loyal ones. In fact, good recovery can win more customer purchasing and loyalty than if things had gone well in the first place. Therefore, companies should take steps not only to provide good service every time but also to recover from service mistakes when they do occur.

The first step is to *empower* front-line service employees—to give them the authority, responsibility, and incentives they need to recognize, care about, and tend to customer needs. At Marriott, for example, well-trained employees are given the authority to do whatever it takes, on the spot, to keep guests happy. They are also expected to help management ferret out the cause of guests' problems and to inform managers of ways to improve overall hotel service and guests' comfort.

Managing Service Productivity

With their costs rising rapidly, service firms are under great pressure to increase service productivity. They can do so in several ways. They can train current employees better or hire new ones who will work harder or more skillfully. Or they can increase the quantity of their service by giving up some quality. The provider can "industrialize the service" by adding equipment and standardizing production, as in McDonald's assembly-line approach to fast-food retailing. Finally, the service provider can harness the power of technology. Although we often think of technology's power to save time and costs in manufacturing companies, it also has great—and often untapped—potential to make service workers more productive.

However, companies must avoid pushing productivity so hard that doing so reduces quality. Attempts to industrialize a service or to cut costs can make a service company more efficient in the short run. But they can also reduce its longer-run ability to innovate, maintain service quality, or respond to consumer needs and desires. In short, they can take the "service" out of service.

Additional Product Considerations

Here, we discuss two additional product policy considerations: social responsibility in product decisions and issues of international product and service marketing.

Product Decisions and Social Responsibility

Product decisions have attracted much public attention. Marketers should consider carefully public policy issues and regulations involving acquiring or dropping products, patent protection, product quality and safety, and product warranties.

Regarding new products, the government may prevent companies from adding products through acquisitions if the effect threatens to lessen competition. Companies dropping products must be aware that they have legal obligations, written or implied, to their suppliers, dealers, and customers who have a stake in the dropped product. Companies must also obey U.S. patent laws when developing new products. A company cannot make its product illegally similar to another company's established product.

Manufacturers must comply with specific laws regarding product quality and safety. The Federal Food, Drug, and Cosmetic Act protects consumers from unsafe and adulterated food, drugs, and cosmetics. Various acts provide for the inspection of sanitary conditions in the meat- and poultry-processing industries. Safety legislation has been passed to regulate fabrics, chemical substances, automobiles, toys, and drugs and poisons. The Consumer Product Safety Act of 1972 established a Consumer Product Safety Commission, which has the authority to ban or seize potentially harmful products and set severe penalties for violation of the law.

If consumers have been injured by a product that has been designed defectively, they can sue manufacturers or dealers. Product liability suits are now occurring in federal and state courts at the rate of almost 110,000 per year, with a median jury award of $1.8 million and individual awards often running into the tens or even hundreds of millions of dollars. For example, a jury recently ordered Ford to pay nearly $369 million to a women paralyzed in a rollover accident involving a Ford Explorer.[43]

This phenomenon has resulted in huge increases in product liability insurance premiums, causing big problems in some industries. Some companies pass these higher rates along to consumers by raising prices. Others are forced to discontinue high-risk product lines. Some companies are now appointing "product stewards," whose job is to protect consumers from harm and the company from liability by proactively ferreting out potential product problems.[44]

Many manufacturers offer written product warranties to convince customers of their products' quality. To protect consumers, Congress passed the Magnuson-Moss Warranty Act in 1975. The act requires that full warranties meet certain minimum standards, including repair "within a reasonable time and without charge" or a replacement or full refund if the product does not work "after a reasonable number of attempts" at repair. Otherwise, the company must make it clear that it is offering only a limited warranty. The law has led several manufacturers to switch from full to limited warranties and others to drop warranties altogether.

International Product and Services Marketing

International product and service marketers face special challenges. First, they must figure out what products and services to introduce and in which countries. Then, they must decide how much to standardize or adapt their products and services for world markets.

On the one hand, companies would like to standardize their offerings. Standardization helps a company to develop a consistent worldwide image. It also lowers manufacturing costs and eliminates duplication of research and development, advertising, and product design efforts. On the other hand, consumers around the world differ in their cultures, attitudes, and buying behaviors. And markets vary in their economic conditions, competition, legal requirements, and physical environments. Companies must usually respond to these differences by adapting their product offerings. Something as simple as an electrical outlet can create big product problems:

> Those who have traveled across Europe know the frustration of electrical plugs, different voltages, and other annoyances of international travel. . . . Philips, the electrical appliance manufacturer, has to produce 12 kinds of irons to serve just its European market. The problem is that Europe does not have a universal [electrical] standard. The ends of irons bristle with different plugs for different countries. Some have three prongs, others two; prongs protrude straight or angled, round or rectangular, fat, thin, and sometimes sheathed. There are circular plug faces, squares, pentagons, and hexagons. Some are perforated and some are notched. One French plug has a niche like a keyhole. Looking for a fix? One online travel service sells an elaborate 10-piece adapter plug set for international travelers for $65.00.[45]

Packaging also presents new challenges for international marketers. Packaging issues can be subtle. For example, names, labels, and colors may not translate easily from one country to another. A firm using yellow flowers in its logo might fare well in the United States but meet with disaster in Mexico, where a yellow flower symbolizes death or disrespect. Similarly, although Nature's Gift might be an appealing name for gourmet mushrooms in America, it would be deadly in Germany, where *gift* means poison. Packaging may also have to be tailored to meet the physical characteristics of consumers in various parts of the world. For instance, soft drinks are sold in smaller cans in Japan to fit the smaller Japanese hand better. Thus, although product and package standardization can produce benefits, companies must usually adapt their offerings to the unique needs of specific international markets.

Service marketers also face special challenges when going global. Some service industries have a long history of international operations. For example, the commercial banking industry was one of the first to grow internationally. Banks had to provide global services in order to meet the foreign exchange and credit needs of their home country clients wanting to sell overseas. In recent years, many banks have become truly global international. Germany's Deutsche Bank, for example, serves more than 12 million customers in 74 countries. For its clients around the world who wish to grow globally, Deutsche Bank can raise money not only in Frankfurt but also in Zurich, London, Paris, and Tokyo.[46]

Professional and business services industries such as accounting, management consulting, and advertising have only recently globalized. The international growth of these firms followed the globalization of the client companies they serve. For example, as their clients began to employ worldwide marketing and advertising strategies, advertising agencies responded by globalizing their own operations. McCann-Erickson Worldwide, a large U.S. advertising agency, operates in more than 130 countries. It serves international clients such as Coca-Cola, General Motors, ExxonMobile, Microsoft, Johnson & Johnson, and Unilever in markets ranging from the United States and Canada to Korea to Kazakhstan. Moreover, McCann-Erikson is one company in the Interpublic Group of Companies, an immense, worldwide network of advertising and marketing services companies.[47]

Retailers are among the latest service businesses to go global. As their home markets become saturated, American retailers such as Wal-Mart, Toys 'R' Us, Office Depot, and Saks Fifth Avenue are expanding into faster-growing markets abroad. For example, every year since 1995, Wal-Mart has entered a new country; its international division's sales grew more than 15 percent last year, skyrocketing to more than $40 billion. Foreign retailers are making similar moves. The Japanese retailer Yaohan now operates the largest shopping center in Asia, the 21-story Nextage Shanghai Tower in China, and Carrefour of France is the leading retailer in Brazil and Argentina. Asian shoppers now buy American products in Dutch-owned Makro stores, Southeast Asia's biggest store group with sales in the region of more than $2 billion.[48]

Service companies wanting to operate in other countries are not always welcomed with open arms. Whereas manufacturers usually face straightforward tariff, quota, or currency restrictions when attempting to sell their products in another country, service providers are likely to face more subtle barriers. In some cases, rules and regulations affecting international

■ Retailers are among the latest service businesses to go global. Here Asian shoppers buy American products in a Dutch-owned Makro store in Kuala Lumpur.

service firms reflect the host country's traditions. In others, they appear to protect the country's own fledgling service industries from large global competitors with greater resources. In still other cases, however, the restrictions seem to have little purpose other than to make entry difficult for foreign service firms.

Despite such difficulties, the trend toward growth of global service companies will continue, especially in banking, airlines, telecommunications, and professional services. Today service firms are no longer simply following their manufacturing customers. Instead, they are taking the lead in international expansion.

> Reviewing the Concepts <

A product is more than a simple set of tangible features. In fact, many marketing offers consist of combinations of both tangible goods and services, ranging from *pure tangible goods* at one extreme to *pure services* at the other. Each product or service offered to customers can be viewed on three levels. The *core product* consists of the core problem-solving benefits that consumers seek when they buy a product. The *actual product* exists around the core and includes the quality level, features, design, brand name, and packaging. The *augmented product* is the actual product plus the various services and benefits offered with it, such as warranty, free delivery, installation, and maintenance.

1. Define *product* and the major classifications of products and services.

Broadly defined, a *product* is anything that can be offered to a market for attention, acquisition, use, or consumption that might satisfy a want or need. Products include physical objects but also services, events, persons, places, organizations, ideas, or mixes of these entities. *Services* are products that consist of activities, benefits, or satisfactions offered for sale that are essentially intangible, such as banking, hotel, tax preparation, and home repair services.

Products and services fall into two broad classes based on the types of consumers that use them. *Consumer products*—those bought by final consumers—are usually classified according to consumer shopping habits (convenience products, shopping products, specialty products, and unsought products). *Industrial products*—purchased for further processing or for use in conducting a business—include materials and parts, capital items, and supplies and services. Other marketable entities—such as organizations, persons, places, and ideas—can also be thought of as products.

2. Describe the decisions companies make regarding their individual products and services, product lines, and product mixes.

Individual product decisions involve product attributes, branding, packaging, labeling, and product support services. *Product attribute* decisions involve product quality, features, and style and design. *Branding* decisions include selecting a brand name and developing a brand strategy. *Packaging* provides many key benefits, such as protection, economy, convenience, and promotion. Package decisions often include designing *labels,* which identify, describe, and possibly promote the product. Companies also develop *product support services* that enhance customer service and satisfaction and safeguard against competitors.

Most companies produce a product line rather than a single product. A *product line* is a group of products that are related in function, customer-purchase needs, or distribution channels. *Line stretching* involves extending a line downward, upward, or in both directions to occupy a gap that might otherwise be filled by a competitor. In contrast, *line filling* involves adding items within the present range of the line. All of product lines and items offered to customers by a particular seller make up the *product mix*. The mix can be described by four dimensions: width, length, depth, and consistency. These dimensions are the tools for developing the company's product strategy.

3. Discuss branding strategy—the decisions companies make in building and managing their brands.

Some analysts see brands as *the* major enduring asset of a company. Brands are more than just names and symbols—they embody everything that the product or service *means* to consumers. *Brand equity* is the positive differential effect that knowing the brand name has on customer response to the product or service. A brand with strong brand equity is a very valuable asset.

In building brands, companies need to make decisions about brand positioning, brand name selection, brand sponsorship, and brand development. The most powerful *brand positioning* builds around strong consumer beliefs and values. *Brand name selection* involves finding the best brand name based on a careful review of product benefits, the target market, and proposed marketing strategies. A manufacturer has four *brand sponsorship* options: it can launch a *manufacturer's brand* (or national brand), sell to resellers who use a *private brand*, market *licensed brands*, or join forces with another company to *co-brand* a product. A company also has four choices when it comes to developing brands. It can introduce *line extensions*, *brand extensions*, *multibrands*, or *new brands*.

Companies must build and manage their brands carefully. The brand's positioning must be continuously communicated to consumers. Advertising can help. However, brands are not maintained by advertising but by the *brand experience*. Customers come to know a brand through a wide range of contacts and interactions. The company must put as much care into managing these touchpoints as it does into producing its ads. Thus, managing a company's brand assets can no longer be left only to brand managers. Some companies are now setting up brand asset management teams to manage their major brands. Finally, companies must periodically audit their brands' strengths and weaknesses. In some cases, brands may need to be repositioned because of changing customer preferences or new competitors. Other cases may call for completely *rebranding* a product, service, or company.

4. Identify the four characteristics that affect the marketing of a service and the additional marketing considerations that services require.

Services are characterized by four key characteristics: they are *intangible*, *inseparable*, *variable*, and *perishable*. Each characteristic poses problems and marketing requirements. Marketers work to find ways to make the service more tangible, to increase the productivity of providers who are inseparable from their products, to standardize the quality in the face of variability, and to improve demand movements and supply capacities in the face of service perishability.

Good service companies focus attention on *both* customers and employees. They understand the *service-profit chain*, which links service firm profits with employee and customer satisfaction. Services marketing strategy calls not only for external marketing but also for *internal marketing* to motivate employees and *interactive marketing* to create service delivery skills among service providers. To succeed, service marketers must create *competitive differentiation*, offer high *service quality*, and find ways to increase *service productivity*.

5. Discuss two additional product issues: socially responsible product decisions and international product and services marketing.

Marketers must consider two additional product issues. The first is *social responsibility*. These include public policy issues and regulations involving acquiring or dropping products, patent protection, product quality and safety, and product warranties. The second involves the special challenges facing international product and service marketers. International marketers must decide how much to standardize or adapt their offerings for world markets.

> Reviewing the Key Terms <

> Discussing the Concepts <

1. Is Microsoft's Windows XP Professional operating software a product or a service? Describe the core, actual, and augmented levels of this software offering.

2. What is a brand? Describe the value of branding for both the buyer and seller.

3. Explain why brand equity is important to the seller. What is the difference between brand equity and brand value?

4. What are the three levels of brand positioning discussed in this chapter? In which level would you place the following ad headline: "The Few. The Proud. The Marines?" Why?

5. Merrill Lynch (ML) is one of the world's leading financial management and advisory companies (see www.ml.com). Do ML's financial advising activities meet the four special characteristics of a service? Explain.

6. What are the five links in the service-chain? Why is the service-profit concept so important to service firms?

> Applying the Concepts <

1. Products and services fall into two broad classifications: consumer and industrial. They are classified further by how customers go about buying them. Go to the five Web sites listed below and identify each product or service as either consumer or industrial and then by subtype.

   - www.electroluxusa.com/
   - http://looneytunes.warnerbros.com/web/homepage/homepage.jsp
   - www.leoburnett.com
   - www.army.mil/
   - www.google.com/

2. Using the six desirable qualities that a good brand name should possess, create a brand name for a personal care product that has the following positioning statement:

   "Intended for X-Games sports participants and enthusiasts, _____ is a deodorant that combines effective odor protection with an enduring and seductive fragrance that will enhance your romantic fortunes."

3. Assume you are the marketing director for a snowboard manufacturer that holds a 45 percent share of the men's 18- to 29-year-old segment. The company is thinking about extending the brand by developing a snowboard and related sports apparel line to be targeted toward women ages 18 to 29. Argue for or against such an extension.

> Focus on Technology <

According to its Web site, "eBay's mission is to provide a global trading platform where practically anyone can trade practically anything." Since it was founded in 1995, eBay has created the most visited Internet site in the world. On any given day, you can find millions of members reviewing, bidding on, and buying the hundreds of thousands of items listed on eBay. Members can purchase an item in an auction or at a fixed price. eBay focuses on a community of members, both buyers and sellers. It provides many features that enhance the trading experience. One of the more important ones is the eBay Feedback feature. This feature captures, in few words and symbols, the "reputation" of the members. Additional online services include convenient payment features and an assortment of tools for buyers, sellers, and developers. Go to www.ebay.com, take a tour of the site, and then respond to the following questions:

1. What is the service that eBay provides it members?
2. How has eBay differentiated itself from competitors?
3. Is the power of the eBay Feedback feature more fact or fiction?

> Focus on Ethics <

As an act of social responsibility and to avoid potential problems, many companies sponsor product advisory committees. Comprised of company personnel, consumer advocates, legislative and regulatory officials, and channel intermediaries, these groups meet frequently to review and comment on new products, services, and practices that their sponsoring firm's are exploring. A real benefit of these meetings is that the firm often gains valuable insights into important concerns and problems before making a significant investment or market launch.

1. Are such advisory committees important for a company? What are the important advantages and drawbacks?
2. Is such an activity more appropriate for a product firm than for a service firm?
3. What sponsoring company personnel should be assigned to such a committee? What noncompany people?

Video Case

Mayo Clinic

Founded as the first medical clinic where doctors worked together to diagnose and treat patients, people travel from all over the world seeking advice and treatment. The Clinic's patient-centered services ensure that every customer who walks through the door leaves feeling confident about her/his health care. A nonprofit organization, the Clinic's goal is to provide the best care to every patient every day through integrated clinical practice, education, and research.

As the Mayo Clinic expands into new markets, the key to maintaining the brand and building brand equity is providing the consistently high quality, patient-focused services consumers have come to expect. The payoff is exceptionally positive word-of-mouth and true customer loyalty, which allow the Mayo Clinic to build a powerful brand with very little advertising.

After watching the video featuring the Mayo Clinic, answer the following questions about product and service strategies.

1. How does branding a service differ from branding a product? How has the Mayo clinic taken these differences into account?

2. How does the Clinic manage the four service characteristics? How does the Clinic manage service quality?

3. How does the Mayo Clinic reinforce its brand image without advertising?

4. The Mayo Clinic has licensed its name for limited uses, including branded content on various Web sites. In addition, the Clinic has lent its name to several publications, including the *Mayo Clinic Williams-Sonoma Cookbook*. What are the risks the Mayo Clinic assumes with licensing and co-branding efforts? What are the benefits?

Company Case

Converse: We Love You, Chucks!

The first Olympic basketball team wore them; they dominated the basketball courts— amateur and professional—for more than 40 years; Dr. J made them famous; Kurt Cobain died in them. What are they? Converse All Stars—more particularly the famous Chuck Taylor All Stars, known around the world as Chucks.

Compared with today's marvels of performance engineering, Chucks are very basic shoes. Rubber covered toes, high-top canvas lace-ups in black, white and red with a blue strip on the back that read "Made in the U.S.A."—these were the major characteristics of Chucks. But then again, compared with the high-priced modern marvels, Chucks are downright affordable—about $35. That should warm the hearts and pocketbooks of parents everywhere.

Converse invented basketball shoes, and by the mid-1970s, 70 to 80 percent of basketball players still wore Converse. But today the company's market share dwindled has to only about 1.35 percent of the total athletic shoe market. In fact, Converse is no longer an independent company. It declared Chapter 11 bankruptcy, and Nike bought it in 2003 for $305 million. The question is: What will Nike do with Converse? Before dealing with that question, let's look at Converse's history.

Converse was founded in 1908 in North Reading, Massachusetts by Marquis. In 1917, the company introduced a canvas, high top called the All Star. By 1923, it was renamed the Chuck Taylor, after a semiprofessional basketball player from Akron, Ohio. After his basketball career ended, Charles "Chuck" Taylor became an aggressive member of the Converse sales force. He drove throughout the Midwest, stopping at playgrounds to sell the high tops to players. Some consider Taylor to be the original Phil Knight, Nike's CEO, who also started out selling his shoes at

track meets from the back of his van. Throughout the '30s, '40s, '50s and '60s, Chucks were *the* shoes to have.

By the early 1980s, with a secure on the basketball shoe market hold (it thought), Converse branched out into other athletic shoe lines. It introduced a tennis shoe endorsed by Jimmy Connors and Chris Evert Lloyd. It also introduced a running shoe. In 1984, Converse was the only sporting goods company sponsoring the Olympics.

These moves appeared to be successful. Sales in 1983 increased by 21 percent to $209 million; sales of tennis shoes went from $5 to $24 and sales of running shoes increased by 73 percent. Market observers attributed the success to new materials and designs. For example, the top-of-the-line running shoes featured stabilizing bars designed to reduce knee injuries. In addition, the company brought out its first biomechanically designed basketball shoe, which offered better support and flexibility.

By 1986, however, Converse's fortunes had taken a turn for the worse, and was acquired by consumer products maker and retailer Interco for approximately $132 million. By the late 1980s, Converse had been overtaken by a host of competitors. In 1989, the top four athletic shoe companies were Nike with a 26 percent market share, Reebok with 23 percent, L.A. Gear with 13 percent, and Converse with 5 percent. Nike and Reebok had jockeyed for several years over the #1 spot, with both claiming a performance positioning. While no one was really looking, L.A. Gear came into the market with a fashion appeal and scooped up sales. Attempting to meet the Air Jordan/Nike challenge head-on, Converse introduced The Magic line, named for L.A. Lakers guard, Magic Johnson. It's strategy revolved around price. Magics were $80, whereas some high-tech shoes sold for as much as $175. Marketing managers at

(box continues)

Converse thought that parents wouldn't pay that much. And kids would like the shoes because they were good enough for Magic Johnson. Strangely, while Nike was grabbing basketball shoe sales at a rapid clip, Converse was still the official shoe of the NBA, which gave it the right to use the NBA logo in its advertising.

Endorsement-wise, the '80s decade was a professional athlete's dream. Companies were signing up major stars and paying big, big bucks. Nike had the largest stable with players, including the likes of Bo Jackson, Charles Barkley, Shaquille O'Neal, and Michael Jordan. Reebok focused its ads on performance. Converse had Larry Bird (Boston Celtics), "Dr. J" Julius Irving (Philadelphia 76ers), Larry Johnson (Charlotte Hornets) and, of course, Magic. L.A. Gear also had athletic endorsers—prime among them Joe Montana (San Francisco 49ers). But there were others—Kareem Abdul-Jabar, Akeem Alajuwan, and Karl Malone.

By 1993, an ailing Converse had changed its positioning strategy. Instead of focusing on basketball and Chucks, it aimed at capitalizing on an image that was both sexy and streetwise. One ad showed a woman lying on a table while the camera panned down her body to show that she was wearing a pair of Converse shoes, with a Converse tattoo on her ankle. Another ad, entitled "Ugly," featured a mean-looking guy barking into the camera: "There are a lot more of what you call ugly people in the world than beautiful people. We don't have airbrushed bodies . . . and we don't want them. We don't want to live in a beer commercial. The point is to be beautiful . . . the point is to be you!" These ads were considered edgy and provocative, and they targeted to a new market segment that was more interested in fashion. Ad agency creative director, Rick Herstek, commented that the ads were what the target market was looking for; that they weren't supposed to appeal to the mainstream and that their customers (Converse types?) had a higher shock threshold.

In this campaign, nothing was sacred. Even the venerable Chuck Taylor All Star shoe was dissociated from basketball shoes and given new life as a fashion statement. Initially, the All Stars didn't need advertising to become fashionable. Candy Pratts, fashion director of shoes and accessories at Vogue, said "It's unbelievable. It's Converse's moment. It's the case of what is old is new. They work with today's fashion of loose-fitting, flowing dresses." She used high top canvas sneakers on models in numerous layouts. The best part,

according to Candy, was that this trend didn't come from advertising, but came from the kids on the street.

But Converse needed more. In 1992, it had sales of only $215 million and a meager 3.6 percent market share. In addition, it had a cost issue. For decades, Converse was "Made in the U.S.A." By the early 1990s, the cost of manufacturing the shoes in the United States was simply too great. Given its lower prices and higher costs, Converse's profit margins were too thin to support the brand advertising and marketing. With real sadness, Converse closed its U.S. plants and contracted for production of shoes with a sourcing firm in India. Management admitted that it had clung to the U.S. production statement for too long. It had believed for years that the U.S. claim gave it a competitive advantage over Nike and Reebok—especially when the scandals about labor conditions in Nike's Southeast Asian plants broke.

Things continued to worsen. In 1996, Converse had to restructure due to poor 1995 sales. The company cut 594 jobs from a little over 2,000 and reorganized its product into four categories: basketball, athletic-leisure, cross-training, and children's. (Notice that there are no tennis or running shoes, although Converse had once been big in those areas.) To boost its basketball shoes, Converse put the famous Chuck Taylor signature patch on a new line of performance wear—the All Star 2000 collection.

Encouraged by the successful re-launch of the All Star 2000, the company chose to launch another new line called Dr. J 2000. A remake of a '70s shoe, it was backed by heavy advertising. Dr. J was chosen because kids told Converse researchers that Dr. J. was cool enough to have a shoe. The campaign tagline was "Take the Soul to the Hole," and ads consisted of a cartoon Julius Irving performing his famous moves to a Stevie Wonder soundtrack. Unfortunately, the Dr. J. 2000 produced disappointing results.

At the turn of the century, nostalgia was in. Jimi Hendrix was on Rolling Stone and the VW bug was a hot selling car. Consumers were looking for "retro," so companies were redesigning classic products. And no athletic shoe was more classic than Chucks. So Converse introduced an updated black shoe, the EZ Chucks.

In 2000, Converse also introduced a line of shoes for skateboarders. Street kids had begun wearing Converse because of their affordability, and Converse picked up the counterculture market segment. The company became a favorite of the antiestablishment, anticorporate crowd for continuing to make its United States. It also appealed to the antiflash group, tired of polyester and synthetic, Michael Jordan-endorsed shoes. This segment wanted "antibrands" reflecting its antiglobalization perspective. Molly Ringwald's record-store clerk in "Pretty in Pink" wore Chucks, as did Kurt Cobain when he committed suicide.

Converse was hanging in, but only by there by the skin of its teeth. In 2001, the company had 180 employees and sales of $185 million. But Converse had global brand recognition and strong brand equity in the market; it was well-known. The question was, "Could the company make the products to back up its reputation?" Enter Nike and the buy-out.

Initially, Nike left Converse management alone to implement its own business strategy. But Nike did help them with advertising dollars. After nearly a decade-long absence from TV advertising, Converse produced ads with the tagline "The first school." The focus was on basketball, not famous players. The ads featured a basketball being dribbled and shot, but no player. They were "narrated" by Mos Def. "Before Mr. Taylor taught the world to play. Before fibreglass. Before parquet. Before the word 'doctor' was spelled with a J. And ballrooms were ball courts where renaissance played. Before the hype and before the dunk. After the rhythm, but before the funk. Before the money and before the fame. Before new and old school. Before school had a name. There was only the ball and the soul of the game." The ad ended with shots of the Converse logo or the Chuck Taylor All Star.

So, back to the original question. What Nike will do with Converse? Some observers believe that Converse should become a second-tier brand. Nike could use Converse to sell millions and millions of shoes in Wal-Mart and Target—a sort of "Sam Walton meets Chuck Taylor" scenario. Another option would be to position Converse as a fashion statement. The old school ad is working; sales are up. This could be a golden opportunity for Nike to get into the "classics" business, where it could do special make-ups in different colors and styles to continually refresh the line. People like retro shoes. A third possibility to position Converse as a perfor-

mance shoe. Nike has the technology, dollars, and market clout to try this.

But why take a classic brand with global recognition to Wal-Mart? Once there, it's not a Chuck any more. It's a discount shoe. And why take a basketball shoe and sell it short as a fashion statement. Fashions come and fashions go. Why take that chance? Finally, why would Nike create a competing in-house performance brand? Wouldn't Nike just be taking sales from itself?

What do you think Nike should do with the Converse brand?

Questions for Discussion

1. What are the core, actual, and augmented product benefits of the Converse Chuck?

2. When Converse sourced production of its shoes to India, it entered into a licensing arrangement. What are the benefits and negatives of that action? Do you think it has helped or hurt the company? The brand?

3. Converse and Chucks are great brands—known around the globe. What do these brands stand for today? What are the sources of their brand equity?

4. What should Nike do? Should it go second tier with Converse, position it as a fashion statement, develop it as a performance brand, or something else? Defend your position.

Sources: Brian Bagot, "Shoeboom!" *M&MD*, June 1990, p. 89; Kevin Goldman, "Converse Sneaker Seeks Statement of Fashion Instead of Foul Shots," *Wall Street Journal*, May 6, 1993, p. B8; Jennifer Laabs, "Converse Will Restructure and Cut Jobs," *Personnel Journal*, January 1996, p. 12; Bernhard Warner and David Gianatasio, "Erving Back on Air as Converse Rolls 'J 2000'," *Brandweek*, January 27, 1997, p. 9; Maureen Tkacik, "Leading the News: Nike to Swoosh Up Old-Line Converse for $305 Million," *Wall Street Journal*, July 10, 2003, p. A3; Lisa van der Pool and David Gianatasio, "Converse Hearkens Back to Roots in New Campaign," *Adweek*, August 4, 2003, p. 10; Hilary Cassidy, "Shoe Companies Use Body and Sole to Track Down Sales." *Brandweek*, June 21, 2004, p. S.50.

> **After studying this chapter, you should be able to**

1. explain how companies find and develop new-product ideas
2. list and define the steps in the new-product development process
3. describe the stages of the product life cycle
4. describe how marketing strategies change during the product's life cycle

CHAPTER 9

New-Product Development and Product Life-Cycle Strategies

Previewing the Concepts

In the previous chapter, you learned how marketers manage individual brands and entire product mixes. In this chapter, we'll look into two additional product topics: developing new products and managing products through their life cycles. New products are the lifeblood of an organization. However, new-product development is risky, and many new products fail. So, the first part of this chapter lays out a process for finding and growing successful new products. Once introduced, marketers want their products to enjoy a long and happy life. In the second part of the chapter, you'll see that every product passes through several life-cycle stages and that each stage poses new challenges requiring different marketing strategies and tactics.

For openers, consider Nokia. Nokia's prolific new-product development process has helped it to dominate the fiercely competitive mobile communications industry. But at Nokia, new-product development isn't something that happens just in the company's R&D labs. As you'll see, innovation is a part of Nokia's very culture—something Nokia calls "renewal."

The new organizer

NOKIA
6200

As workers quietly eat lunch in the cafeteria at Nokia House, a slide projector flips from pictures of summer cottages in Rauhalahti to snapshots of someone's favorite Finnish hound. Taken with camera phones by some of the 1,500 employees who work at Nokia's headquarters in Finland, the pictures are part of an internal corporate competition that rewards staff creativity.

These photographs won't ever grace the cover of National Geographic. But they do illustrate Nokia's sharpest insight: Creativity and innovative new products don't begin and end on an R&D lab bench. A long list of Nokia's innovative firsts came from the most unlikely of places. For example, the first user-changeable handset cover? Nokia engineer Aulis Perttula invented it after watching some of his colleagues customize their phones with car paint. Predictive text? Stephen Williams, a junior Nokia applications designer, suggested it after seeing disabled people make good use of it on their PCs.

Such firsts are why the 137-year-old Scandinavian giant, with annual sales of $36 billion across 130 countries, has been way out in front for most of the mobile phone industry's short history. Nokia sells five phones every second. Its global market share, 38 percent, is greater than that of its nearest three rivals combined. But Nokia isn't just the world's *biggest* mobile-phone company. It's also the most *innovative*. In an industry that's all about exciting new products, Nokia has created a culture where innovation is built into the way the company operates. Nokia even has a watchword for its culture of continuous innovation—renewal.

When it comes to new products, Nokia has its foot on the accelerator. It has almost tripled the launch of new products in the last 4 years. Why? Because peddling the same old goods to the same old customers simply doesn't work in this fast-changing, fiercely competitive business. Nokia has to keep churning out a steady stream of good new products. That means that the company's real business isn't phones, it's innovation.

At Nokia, innovation isn't an accident—it goes to the company's very core. Nokia is a company that refuses to grow big, grow old, or grow slow. Its new product development philosophy is simple: Small, nimble, creative units are much more likely to bubble up new ideas. So Nokia has organized itself into autonomous units, which are then backed with cost-effective central services. In other words, the company has built innovation into its organization.

For example, last year Nokia's Mobile Phone division splintered itself into nine smaller, independent business units, furthering its ability to explore completely new areas, such as entertainment and imaging. Each unit taps into Nokia's central research lab for basic technology and product design support and hands over end products to a shared operations and logistics group. But each independent team is a profit-and-loss center, with the autonomy to create its own business model, conduct its own advanced R&D and marketing, and draft its own product road maps. "Big companies lose sensitivity," says a senior Nokia executive. "People need to feel that they can make a difference. And they need to have the power to make their ideas happen. [By allowing teams the space they need to dig deeper into their area of interest,] we've created a small-company soul inside a big-company body."

The end goal is innovation, and Nokia creates new products at a head-spinning pace. In part, that's a result of the extraordinary intellectual and technical resources that Nokia invests in new product development. The

company boasts an annual R&D budget of $3 billion, and 40 percent of its 52,000 employees are involved in R&D. Most Nokia business units have at least three R&D sites.

But just as important is the emphasis that Nokia puts on continuous development. "It's a combination of putting people in the right environment to generate ideas and giving them the power to make those ideas happen," says the executive. Nokia makes a healthy habit of giving its people fresh challenges in completely new areas. Job rotation is routine, even for senior managers. Lawyers have become country managers. Network engineers have moved into handset design. The goal is to bring new thinking to familiar problems.

Beyond its prolific internal new product development activity, Nokia mines outside sources as well. For example, to find fresh outside thinking, Nokia has set up Insight & Foresight teams that seek out new technologies, new business models, and promising entrepreneurs beyond Nokia's walls. Innovent, its U.S. team, goes a step further. It identifies early-stage entrepreneurs, buys options on their work, and introduces them to people at Nokia headquarters.

To stay atop the heap in the mobile communications industry, Nokia will need a constant flow on innovative new products that serve the needs, preferences, and lifestyles of its customers. But the Finnish company has been practicing renewal for a lifetime: In its history, it has gone from manufacturing paper to making rubber boots, then raincoats, then hunting rifles, and then consumer electronics, until finally betting the farm on mobile phones. It's all part of an ongoing emphasis on renewal.[1]

New-product development
The development of original products, product improvements, product modifications, and new brands through the firm's own R&D efforts.

A company has to be good at developing and managing new products. Every product seems to go through a life cycle—it is born, goes through several phases, and eventually dies as newer products come along that better serve consumer needs. This product life cycle presents two major challenges: First, because all products eventually decline, a firm must be good at developing new products to replace aging ones (the challenge of *new-product development*). Second, the firm must be good at adapting its marketing strategies in the face of changing tastes, technologies, and competition as products pass through life-cycle stages (the challenge of *product life-cycle strategies*). We first look at the problem of finding and developing new products and then at the problem of managing them successfully over their life cycles.

New-Product Development Strategy

Given the rapid changes in consumer tastes, technology, and competition, companies must develop a steady stream of new products and services. A firm can obtain new products in two ways. One is through *acquisition*—by buying a whole company, a patent, or a license to produce someone else's product. The other is through **new-product development** in the company's own research-and-development department. By *new products* we mean original products, product improvements, product modifications, and new brands that the firm develops through its own research-and-development efforts. In this chapter, we concentrate on new-product development.

Innovation can be very risky. RCA lost $580 million on its SelectaVision videodisc player; Texas Instruments lost a staggering $660 million before withdrawing from the home computer business; and WebTV lost $725 million before it was shut down. Even these amounts pale in comparison to the failure of the $5 billion Iridium global satellite-based wireless telephone system. Other costly product failures from sophisticated companies include New Coke (Coca-Cola Company), Eagle Snacks (Anheuser-Busch), Zap Mail electronic mail (FedEx), Polarvision instant movies (Polaroid), Premier "smokeless" cigarettes (R.J. Reynolds), and Arch Deluxe sandwiches (McDonald's).[2]

New products continue to fail at a disturbing rate. One source estimates that more than 90 percent of all new products fail in within 2 years. Another study suggested that of the staggering 25,000 new consumer food, beverage, beauty, and health care products to hit the market each year, only 40 percent will be around 5 years later. Moreover, failure rates for new industrial products may be as high as 30 percent.[3]

Why do so many new products fail? There are several reasons. Although an idea may be good, the market size may have been overestimated. Perhaps the actual product was not designed as well as it should have been. Or maybe it was incorrectly positioned in the market, priced too high, or advertised poorly. A high-level executive might push a favorite idea despite poor marketing research findings. Sometimes the costs of product development are higher than expected, and sometimes competitors fight back harder than expected. However, the reasons behind some new-product failures seem pretty obvious. Try the following on for size:[4]

> Strolling the aisles at Robert McMath's New Product Showcase and Learning Center is like finding yourself in some nightmare version of a supermarket. There's Gerber food for adults (pureed sweet-and-sour pork and chicken Madeira), Hot Scoop microwaveable ice cream sundaes, Premier smokeless cigarettes, and Miller Clear Beer. How about Avert Virucidal Tissues or Richard Simmons Dijon Vinaigrette Salad Spray? Most of the 80,000 products on display were abject flops. Behind each of them are squandered dollars and hopes.
>
> McMath, the genial curator of this Smithsonian of consumerism, gets lots of laughs when he asks his favorite question, "What were they thinking?" Some companies failed because the attached trusted brand names to something totally out of character. For example, when you hear the name Ben-Gay, you immediately think of the way Ben-Gay cream sears and stimulates your skin. Can you imagine swallowing Ben-Gay aspirin? Or how would you feel about quaffing a can of Exxon fruit punch or Kodak quencher? Other misbegotten attempts to stretch a good name include Cracker Jack cereal, Smucker's premium ketchup, and Fruit of the

■ Visiting the New Product Showcase and Learning Center is like finding yourself in some nightmare version of a supermarket. Each product failure represents squandered dollars and hopes.

Loom laundry detergent. Looking back, what *were* they thinking? You can tell that some innovative products were doomed as soon as you hear their names: Toaster Eggs. Cucumber antiperspirant spray. Health-Sea sea sausage. Look of Buttermilk shampoo. Dr. Care Aerosol Toothpaste (many parents questioned the wisdom of arming their kids with something like this!) Really, what were they thinking?

So companies face a problem—they must develop new products, but the odds weigh heavily against success. In all, to create successful new products, a company must understand its consumers, markets, and competitors and develop products that deliver superior value to customers. It must carry out strong new-product planning and set up a systematic *new-product development process* for finding and growing new products. Figure 9.1 shows the eight major steps in this process.

Idea Generation

Idea generation

The systematic search for new-product ideas.

New-product development starts with **idea generation**—the systematic search for new-product ideas. A company typically has to generate many ideas in order to find a few good ones. According to one well-known management consultant, "For every 1,000 ideas, only 100 will have enough commercial promise to merit a small-scale experiment, only 10 of those will warrant substantial financial commitment, and of those, only a couple will turn out to be unqualified successes." His conclusion? "If you want to find a few ideas with the power to enthrall customers, foil competitors, and thrill investors, you must first generate hundreds and potentially thousands of unconventional strategic ideas."[5]

Major sources of new-product ideas include internal sources and external sources such as customers, competitors, distributors and suppliers, and others.

Internal Idea Sources

Using *internal sources*, the company can find new ideas through formal research and development. It can pick the brains of its executives, scientists, engineers, manufacturing staff, and salespeople. Some companies have developed successful "intrapreneurial" programs that encourage employees to think up and develop new-product ideas. For example, 3M's well-known "15 percent rule" allows employees to spend 15 percent of their time "bootlegging"—working on projects of personal interest, whether or not those projects directly benefit the company.

Companies sometimes look for creative innovation approaches that overcome barriers to the free flow of new product ideas. For example, firms like Eureka! Ranch—a well-known "new-product hatchery"—employ both "method" and "madness" in helping companies to jumpstart their new-product idea generation process (see Real Marketing 9.1).

External Idea Sources

Good new-product ideas also come from watching and listening to *customers*. The company can analyze customer questions and complaints to find new products that better solve consumer problems. Company engineers or salespeople can meet with and work

FIGURE 9.1

Major stages in new-product development

Real Marketing 9.1

Eureka! Ranch: Method and Madness in Finding New-Product Ideas

Having trouble thinking up the next hot new-product idea? Try a visit to Eureka! Ranch. For $75,000 to $150,000, you can send a dozen key marketing managers to loosen up, have some fun, and get the creative juices flowing. Located on 80 acres, with a sand volleyball court, a water sports lake, and a three-hole golf course, Eureka! Ranch seems more like an executive resort than a new-product hatchery. But Eureka! Ranch isn't just about relaxing and having fun. Instead, it's all about the very serious business of creating new product ideas.

Founded by Doug Hall, a former Procter & Gamble "Master Marketing Inventor," the Ranch seems at first to be sheer madness. Consider this account:

> Executives from Gardetto's, a Milwaukee-based snack foods company, stream through the doors of Eureka! Ranch. A two-man zydeco band cranks out early morning Cajun tunes. Amid the high-energy music, Doug Hall and his staff greet their visitors with laughs, handshakes, and platters of muffins, bagels, and other breakfast goodies. Hall, the opposite of Wall Street chic, in a blue Hawaiian shirt and faded jeans, soon gathers his clients in the center of the living room and welcomes everyone. A large blanket-covered mound lurks near his bare feet. After a brief introduction, in which he notes, "Today, reality isn't relevant," Hall rips the blanket off, revealing a pile of Nerf guns. With a commando yell, he grabs a foam assault rifle and starts firing away at the momentarily shocked participants. In an instant, however, they too join the battle, blasting away at one another in a frenzy of multicolored projectiles and screams. Let the games begin.

But there's method to the madness in Eureka! Ranch's intensive multiday sessions. Doug Hall, once described as "a combination of Bill Gates, Ben Franklin, and Bozo the Clown," is dedicated to helping participants throw off the self-imposed constraints that too often stifle creativity in a corporate conference room. The result: breakthrough ideas and strategies for new products and services.

Gardetto's—whose main product is called Snak-ens, a mixture of seasoned pretzels, rye crisps, and breadsticks—took 15 of its people to Eureka! Ranch's standard 2 1/2-day program. The agenda was serious and simple in concept. "I'm not looking for a line extension or just a good idea," said executive vice president Nan Gardetto. "I'm looking for something really breakthrough." But from day one, in execution, the program was freewheeling and action-packed. The majority of the first day was devoted to generating as many wild ideas as possible. Reality? Not relevant!

At Eureka! Ranch, fast-paced play and idea-generating zaniness open the flood gates for new ideas. It starts with brainstorming exercises that expand people's minds and generate new ideas around the client's problem. No idea is too far-fetched or impractical on the first day, and everything gets written down. By the time they sit down to a gourmet dinner at the ranch, clients have typically spawned some 1,500 to 2,000 ideas. Only after dinner do the participants start judging the fruits of their fun. For the Gardetto's team, ideas like Gar-Chia—a Chia-pet-like snack that expands in water—get tossed. But other ideas receive numerous votes of support. At 11 pm, after

"When Doug meets Disney, creativity never waits. Our team explodes when he jump starts our brains!"
Ellen Guidera, Vice President
The Walt Disney Company

"A rigorous, quantifiable process for inventing breakthrough ideas for clients. Unlike many creative gurus hustling ideation wares in the corporate marketplace, Eureka! inventing processes are quantified every step of the way."
CIO Magazine

"Eureka has developed more new products than any other organization in America."
New York Magazine

Need Growth? We Can Help!

"Former Procter & Gamble marketing whiz Doug Hall goes to any length to encourage a fresh perspective ... clients say it works."
The Wall Street Journal

"Eureka! Ranch's unconventional approach has won raves from some of the biggest corporations in the country."
CNN

"Doug Hall is THE idea man. The former P&G marketer has guided big corporation marketing team after big corporation marketing team to stunning new product breakthroughs."
Tom Peters

JUMP START YOUR BUSINESS BRAIN

WIN MORE • LOSE LESS and MAKE MORE MONEY
with your New Products, Services, Sales & Advertising

The Eureka! Ranch delivers OUTSTANDING client satisfaction. More than 00% of Eureka! Ranch business is REPEAT from such world class companies as The Ford Motor Company, Fidelity, Tenneco, Johnson & Johnson, Walt Disney, Frito-Lay, Compaq Computer, Procter & Gamble and American Express.

■ Generating new product ideas: Eureka! Ranch combines creative passion with a more systematic process and real-world data. But along with the scientific method, there's still a healthy portion of madness thrown into the brew.

the clients have retired for the night, Eureka! Ranch's tireless staff—its "Trained Brains"—debrief and refine the day's results.

Day 2 begins with a hearty breakfast and a stiff mug of Brain Brew coffee. Then the Gardetto's team gathers around a large board, to which Eureka! Ranch staffers have tacked the 12 most popular new product ideas and the 19 most popular new positioning ideas from the previous day. The team reviews the concepts, adds depth and refinement to the better ones, and votes again. They spend the rest of the day assessing each surviving idea in more detail. "After the previous day's anything-that-pops-up-in-your-head brainstorming," says one observer, "today is more focused; people sense that they're discussing ideas that may evolve into a completely new line of snacks."

Yet even as the group tackles the serious issues, the atmosphere remains lighthearted. "Just the fact that a Nerf ball comes whistling at your head [during an exercise] makes you think of something different. [It's] harnessed chaos," says one participant. When the day's session ends, the Gardetto's team heads out for a relaxing dinner at a local restaurant. Meanwhile, Doug Hall and his staff prepare for the final day. They whittle down the list of ideas and write concept statements for what they think are the most viable new-product options.

(box continues)

Eureka! Ranch: Method and Madness in Finding New-Product Ideas   *continued*

The final day: "Another foggy morning, another hearty breakfast, another mug of Brain Brew," notes the observer. Hall, dressed in a long purple robe and still barefoot, presents the results of the Gardetto's team's efforts—the best of the best. The team talks through each product idea. Some are sent packing—such as Saturday night Snack 'Ems (featuring Charlie's skillet corn bread) and Bistro Baguettes (sweet bread with raspberry-champagne and cream cheese). But other ideas garner enthusiastic support. Gardetto's leaves satisfied, with 16 new packaging ideas, 9 new logos, and several new snack food concepts for the R&D kitchens.

Gardetto's satisfying experience is typical. *Human Resource Executive* recently named Eureka! Ranch as one of the top 10 training programs in the country. Eighty-five percent of participants rate the program as the best training they've ever attended. And more than 80 percent of Eureka! Ranch sessions are repeat business from such world-class companies as Ford, Fidelity, Tenneco, Johnson & Johnson, Walt Disney, Nike, Frito-Lay, Procter & Gamble, and American Express. "When Doug meets Disney, creativity never wanes," says a Disney executive after a visit to Eureka! Ranch. "Our team explodes when he jumps starts our brains."

In working with more than 4,000 new products and 6,000 front-line development groups, Eureka! Ranch has learned a good many lessons on creativity itself. Interestingly, one lesson is that zany fun is only part of the process for generating creative ideas. In fact, in recent years, Eureka! Ranch sessions are becoming more serious and less chaotic. The Ranch now tackles the tough job of being creative by balancing the "madness" with a stronger mix of "method."

There's still plenty of fast-paced action and creative brainstorming (video games still line the walls), and the Ranch promises sessions that will "wake up and shake up" your thinking. But sessions are now supported by the heaps of qualitative and quantitative data gleaned from Eureka! Ranch's years of new-product development experience. Along with the brainstorming, refined product-development tools and more methodical processes now supplement the open-ended fun of previous days. For example, Eureka! Ranch has developed its Merwyn software, a scoring system for new ideas. The Merwyn software contains over one million data points that help it predict the likely market success of new products.

What has emerged is a more effective version of Eureka! Ranch. Under Hall's notions of "capitalist creativity," new-product success "is not random. . . . There are reproducible scientific lessons and laws that . . . can help you win more, lose less, and make more money." Eureka! Ranch now combines creative passion with a more systematic process and real-world data. But along with the scientific method, there's still a healthy portion of madness thrown into the brew.

Sources: Quotes and other information from Todd Datz, "Romper Ranch," *CIO* May 15, 1999; Lori Dahm, "Pursue Passion," *Stagnito's New Products Magazine*, Oct 2002, p. 58; Eva Kaplan-Leiserson, "Eureka!: This Little-Ranch-That-Could Teaches You to 'Win More, Lose Less, and Make More Money,'" *T&D*, December 2001, p. 50(14); Geoff Williams, "I've Got an Idea!" *Entrepreneur*, December 2001, p. 36; Monique Reece, "Expert Shares His Ideas to Jumpstart Businesses." *Denver Business Journal*, Sept 28, 2001, p. 33A; Doug Hall, *Jump Start Your Business Brain* (Whitehall, VA: Betterway Publications, 2002); John Eckberg, "New Radio Host Takes on Small Biz," *The Cincinnati Enquirer,* January 13, 2003, p. 7B; and www.eurekaranch.com, December 2004.

alongside customers to get suggestions and ideas. The company can conduct surveys or focus groups to learn about consumer needs and wants.

Heinz did just that when its researchers approached children, who consume more than half of the ketchup sold, to find out what would make ketchup more appealing to them. The answer: change the color. So, Heinz developed and launched EZ Squirt, green ketchup that comes in a squeezable bottle targeted at kids. Blastin' Green ketchup was a smash hit, so Heinz followed up with an entire rainbow of EZ Squirt colors, including Funky Purple, Passion Pink, Awesome Orange, Totally Teal, and Stellar Blue. The EZ Squirt bottle's special nozzle also emits a thin ketchup stream, "so tykes can autograph their burgers (or squirt someone across the table, though Heinz neglects to mention that)." In all, the new line earned the company a 5 percent increase in sales in the first year after hitting the grocery shelf.[6]

Consumers often create new products and uses on their own, and companies can benefit by putting them on the market. For example, for years customers were spreading the word that Skin-So-Soft bath oil and moisturizer was also a terrific bug repellent. Whereas some consumers were content simply to bathe in water scented with the fragrant oil, others carried it in their backpacks to mosquito-infested campsites or kept a bottle on the deck of their beach houses. Avon turned the idea into a complete line of Skin-So-Soft Bug Guard PLUS IR3535® products, including the Insect Repellent Gentle Breeze Moisturizing Sunblock Lotion SPF 30, a combination moisturizer, insect repellent, and sunscreen.[7]

Finally, some companies even give customers the tools and resources to design their own products. For example, Bush Boake Allen (BBA), a global supplier of specialty flavors to companies like Nestle, provides a tool kit that lets its customers develop their own flavors, which BBA then manufactures. Similarly, LSI Logic provides customers with do-it-yourself tools that let them design their own specialized chips and customized integrated circuits. Letting customers do the innovating has become a great new way to create value.[8]

■ New-product ideas from consumers: For years customers used Skin-So-Soft bath oil and moisturizer as a bug repellent. Avon turned the idea into a complete line of Skin-So-Soft Bug Guard PLUS IR3535® products.

Companies must be careful not to rely too heavily on customer input when developing new products. For some products, especially highly technical ones, customers may not know what they need. "Merely giving people what they want isn't always enough," says one innovation management consultant. "People want to be surprised; they want something that's better than they imagined, something that stretches them in what they like."[9]

Competitors are another good source of new-product ideas. Companies watch competitors' ads to get clues about their new products. They buy competing new products, take them apart to see how they work, analyze their sales, and decide whether they should bring out a new product of their own. *Distributors and suppliers* can also contribute many good new-product ideas. Resellers are close to the market and can pass along information about consumer problems and new-product possibilities. Suppliers can tell the company about new concepts, techniques, and materials that can be used to develop new products. Other idea sources include trade magazines, shows, and seminars; government agencies; new-product consultants; advertising agencies; marketing research firms; university and commercial laboratories; and inventors.

The search for new-product ideas should be systematic rather than haphazard. Otherwise, few new ideas will surface and many good ideas will sputter and die. Top management can avoid these problems by installing an *idea management system* that directs the flow of new ideas to a central point where they can be collected, reviewed, and evaluated. In setting up such a system, the company can do any or all of the following:[10]

✔ Appoint a respected senior person to be the company's idea manager.

✔ Create a cross-functional idea management committee consisting of people from R&D, engineering, purchasing, operations, finance, and sales and marketing to meet regularly and evaluate proposed new product and service ideas.

✔ Set up a toll-free number or Web site for anyone who wants to send a new idea to the idea manager.

✔ Encourage all company stakeholders—employees, suppliers, distributors, dealers—to send their ideas to the idea manager.

✔ Set up formal recognition programs to reward those who contribute the best new ideas.

The idea manager approach yields two favorable outcomes. First, it helps create an innovation-oriented company culture. It shows that top management supports, encourages, and rewards innovation. Second, it will yield a larger number of ideas, among which will be found some especially good ones. As the system matures, ideas will flow more freely. No longer will good ideas wither for the lack of a sounding board or a senior product advocate.

⟨?⟩ Idea Screening

Idea screening
Screening new-product ideas in order to spot good ideas and drop poor ones as soon as possible.

The purpose of idea generation is to create a large number of ideas. The purpose of the succeeding stages is to *reduce* that number. The first idea-reducing stage is **idea screening**, which helps spot good ideas and drop poor ones as soon as possible. Product development costs rise greatly in later stages, so the company wants to go ahead only with the product ideas that will turn into profitable products.

Many companies require their executives to write up new-product ideas on a standard form that can be reviewed by a new-product committee. The write-up describes the product, the target market, and the competition. It makes some rough estimates of market size, product price, development time and costs, manufacturing costs, and rate of return. The committee then evaluates the idea against a set of general criteria. For example, at Kao Company, the large Japanese consumer-products company, the committee asks questions such as these: Is the product truly useful to consumers and society? Is it good for our particular company? Does it mesh well with the company's objectives and strategies? Do we have the people, skills, and resources to make it succeed? Does it deliver more value to customers than do competing products? Is it easy to advertise and distribute? Many companies have well-designed systems for rating and screening new-product ideas.

⟨?⟩ Concept Development and Testing

Product concept
A detailed version of the new-product idea stated in meaningful consumer terms.

An attractive idea must be developed into a **product concept**. It is important to distinguish between a product idea, a product concept, and a product image. A *product idea* is an idea for a possible product that the company can see itself offering to the market. A *product concept* is a detailed version of the idea stated in meaningful consumer terms. A *product image* is the way consumers perceive an actual or potential product.

Concept Development

After 10 years of development, DaimlerChrysler is getting ready to commercialize its experimental fuel-cell-powered electric car. This car's nonpolluting fuel-cell system runs directly on methanol, which delivers hydrogen to the fuel cell with only water as a by-product. It is highly fuel efficient (75 percent more efficient than gasoline engines) and gives the new car an environmental advantage over standard internal combustion engine cars or even today's superefficient gasoline-electric hybrid cars.

Last year, DaimlerChrysler put 60 "F-Cell" cars on the road in Japan, Germany, and the United states to test their worth in everyday operation. Based on the tiny Mercedes A-Class, the car accelerates quickly, reaches speeds of 90 miles per hour, and has a 280-mile driving range, giving it a huge edge over battery-powered electric cars that travel only about 80 miles before needing 3 to 12 hours of recharging. Fuel cell systems are also being tested in busses, trucks, and other vehicles.[11]

Now DaimlerChrysler's task is to develop this new product into alternative product concepts, find out how attractive each concept is to customers, and choose the best one. It might create the following product concepts for the fuel-cell electric car:

Concept 1   A moderately priced subcompact designed as a second family car to be used around town. The car is ideal for running errands and visiting friends.

Concept 2   A medium-cost sporty compact appealing to young people.

Concept 3   An inexpensive subcompact "green" car appealing to environmentally conscious people who want practical transportation and low pollution.

Concept 4   A high-end SUV appealing to those who love the space SUVs provide but lament the poor gas mileage.

Concept testing
Testing new-product concepts with a group of target consumers to find out if the concepts have strong consumer appeal.

Concept Testing

Concept testing calls for testing new-product concepts with groups of target consumers. The concepts may be presented to consumers symbolically or physically. Here, in words, is concept 3:

■ DaimlerChrysler's task is to develop its fuel-cell-powered F-Cell car into alternative product concepts, find out how attractive each concept is to customers, and choose the best one.

An efficient, fun-to-drive, fuel-cell-powered electric subcompact car that seats four. This methanol-powered high-tech wonder provides practical and reliable transportation with virtually no pollution. It goes up to 90 miles per hour and, unlike battery-powered electric cars, it never needs recharging. It's priced, fully equipped, at $20,000.

For some concept tests, a word or picture description might be sufficient. However, a more concrete and physical presentation of the concept will increase the reliability of the concept test. Today, some marketers are finding innovative ways to make product concepts more real to consumer subjects. For example, some are using virtual reality to test product concepts. Virtual reality programs use computers and sensory devices (such as gloves or goggles) to simulate reality. A designer of kitchen cabinets might use a virtual reality program to help a customer "see" how his or her kitchen would look and work if remodeled with the company's products.

After being exposed to the concept, consumers then may be asked to react to it by answering questions such as those in Table 9.1. The answers will help the company decide which concept has the strongest appeal. For example, the last question asks about the consumer's intention to buy. Suppose 10 percent of the consumers said they "definitely" would buy and another 5 percent said "probably." The company could project these figures to the full population in this target group to estimate sales volume. Even then, the estimate is uncertain because people do not always carry out their stated intentions.

TABLE 9.1   **Questions for Fuel-Cell-Powered Electric Car Concept Test**

1. Do you understand the concept of a fuel-cell-powered electric car?
2. Do you believe the claims about the car's performance?
3. What are the major benefits of the fuel-cell-powered electric car compared with a conventional car?
4. What are its advantages compared with a battery-powered electric car?
5. What improvements in the car's features would you suggest?
6. For what uses would you prefer a fuel-cell-powered electric car to a conventional car?
7. What would be a reasonable price to charge for the car?
8. Who would be involved in your decision to buy such a car? Who would drive it?
9. Would you buy such a car (definitely, probably, probably not, definitely not)?

Many firms routinely test new-product concepts with consumers before attempting to turn them into actual new products. For example, AcuPOLL, a global brand building research company, tests thousands of new product concepts every year. In past polls, M&M Mini's, "teeny-tiny" M&M sold in a tube container, received a rare A+ concept rating, meaning that consumers thought it was an outstanding concept that they would try and buy. Other products such as Glad Stand & Zip Bags, CLOROX® Wipes, the Mead Inteli-Gear learning system, and Elmer's 3D Paint Pens were also big hits.

Other product concepts didn't fare so well. For example, Procter & Gamble's and Kimberly-Clark's moist toilet papers, tested after launch, received an F in AcuPOLL. Both companies spent millions to launch these products but have since withdrawn them from the market. Consumers saw wet toilet paper as unique but didn't find the benefit to be all that compelling. AcuPOLL has found that just being different doesn't lead to market success.

Nubrush Anti-Bacterial Toothbrush Spray disinfectant, from Applied Microdontics, also received an F. Consumers found Nubrush to be overpriced, and most don't think they have a problem with "infected" toothbrushes. Nor did consumers think much of Excedrin Tension Headache Cooling Pads. Another concept that fared poorly was Chef Williams 5 Minute Marinade, which comes with a syringe customers use to inject the marinade into meats. "I can't see that on grocery shelves," comments an AcuPOLL executive. Some consumers might find the thought of injecting something into meat a bit repulsive, and "it's just so politically incorrect to have this syringe on there."[12]

Hershey does its product concept testing on the Web. It uses online test subjects to gain insight to all aspects of its product concepts. Consumers might be shown pictures of proposed candy bars or baking mixes, quizzed about flavors, and asked about potential product names. Says one Hershey researcher, "You need to test maybe 100 concepts to get one good product that might make it to market." Putting concept testing online has cut the time Hershey spends on new-product development by two-thirds.[13]

■ AcuPOLL tests thousands of new-product concepts every year. Its polls correctly predicted that CLOROX® Wipes would be a big hit with consumers.

Marketing Strategy Development

Marketing strategy development

Designing an initial marketing strategy for a new product based on the product concept.

Suppose DaimlerChrysler finds that concept 3 for the fuel-cell-powered electric car tests is best. The next step is **marketing strategy development**, designing an initial marketing strategy for introducing this car to the market.

The *marketing strategy statement* consists of three parts. The first part describes the target market; the planned product positioning; and the sales, market share, and profit goals for the first few years. Thus:

> The target market is younger, well-educated, moderate-to-high-income individuals, couples, or small families seeking practical, environmentally responsible transportation. The car will be positioned as more economical to operate, more fun to drive, and less polluting than today's internal combustion engine or hybrid cars. It is also less restricting than battery-powered electric cars, which must be recharged regularly. The company will aim to sell 100,000 cars in the first year, at a loss of not more than $15 million. In the second year, the company will aim for sales of 120,000 cars and a profit of $25 million.

The second part of the marketing strategy statement outlines the product's planned price, distribution, and marketing budget for the first year:

> The fuel-cell-powered electric car will be offered in three colors—red, white, and blue—and will have optional air-conditioning and power-drive features. It will sell at a retail price of $20,000—with 15 percent off the list price to dealers. Dealers who sell more than 10 cars per month will get an additional discount of 5 percent on each car sold that month. An advertising budget of $50 million will be split 50-50 between a national media campaign and local advertising. Advertising will emphasize the car's fun spirit and low emissions. During the first year, $100,000 will be spent on marketing research to find out who is buying the car and their satisfaction levels.

The third part of the marketing strategy statement describes the planned long-run sales, profit goals, and marketing mix strategy:

> DaimlerChrysler intends to capture a 3 percent long-run share of the total auto market and realize an after-tax return on investment of 15 percent. To achieve this, product quality will start high and be improved over time. Price will be raised in the second and third years if competition permits. The total advertising budget will be raised each year by about 10 percent. Marketing research will be reduced to $60,000 per year after the first year.

Business Analysis

Business analysis

A review of the sales, costs, and profit projections for a new product to find out whether these factors satisfy the company's objectives.

Once management has decided on its product concept and marketing strategy, it can evaluate the business attractiveness of the proposal. **Business analysis** involves a review of the sales, costs, and profit projections for a new product to find out whether they satisfy the company's objectives. If they do, the product can move to the product development stage.

To estimate sales, the company might look at the sales history of similar products and conduct surveys of market opinion. It can then estimate minimum and maximum sales to assess the range of risk. After preparing the sales forecast, management can estimate the expected costs and profits for the product, including marketing, R&D, operations, accounting, and finance costs. The company then uses the sales and costs figures to analyze the new product's financial attractiveness.

Product Development

Product development

Developing the product concept into a physical product in order to ensure that the product idea can be turned into a workable product.

So far, for many new-product concepts, the product may have existed only as a word description, a drawing, or perhaps a crude mock-up. If the product concept passes the business test, it moves into **product development**. Here, R&D or engineering develops the product concept into a physical product. The product development step, however, now calls for a large jump in investment. It will show whether the product idea can be turned into a workable product.

The R&D department will develop and test one or more physical versions of the product concept. R&D hopes to design a prototype that will satisfy and excite consumers and that can be produced quickly and at budgeted costs. Developing a successful prototype can take days, weeks, months, or even years.

Often, products undergo rigorous tests to make sure that they perform safely and effectively, or that consumers will find value in them. Here are some examples of such product tests:[14]

Procter & Gamble (P&G) spends $150 million on 4,000 to 5,000 studies a year, testing everything from the ergonomics of picking up a shampoo bottle to how long women can keep their hands in sudsy water. On any given day, subjects meet in focus groups, sell their dirty laundry to researchers, put prototype diapers on their babies' bottoms, and rub mysterious creams on their faces. Last year, one elementary school raised $17,000 by having students and parents take part in P&G product tests. Students tested toothpaste and shampoo and ate brownies, while their mothers watched advertising for Tempo tissue, P&G's paper wipes packaged to fit in a car.

At Gillette, almost everyone gets involved in new-product testing. Every working day at Gillette, 200 volunteers from various departments come to work unshaven, troop to the second floor of the company's gritty South Boston plant, and enter small booths with a sink and mirror. There they take instructions from technicians on the other side of a small window as to which razor, shaving cream, or aftershave to use. The volunteers evaluate razors for sharpness of blade, smoothness of glide, and ease of handling. In a nearby shower room, women perform the same ritual on their legs, underarms, and what the company delicately refers to as the "bikini area." "We bleed so you'll get a good shave at home," says one Gillette employee.

Thunk. Thunk. Thunk. Behind a locked door in the basement of Louis Vuitton's elegant Paris headquarters, a mechanical arm hoists a brown-and-tan handbag a half-meter off the floor—then drops it. The bag, loaded with an 8-pound weight, will be lifted and dropped, over and over again, for 4 days. This is Vuitton's test laboratory, a high-tech torture chamber for its fabled luxury goods. Another piece of lab equipment bombards handbags with ultraviolet rays to test resistance to fading. Still another tests zippers by tugging them open and shutting them 5,000 times. There's even a mechanized mannequin hand, with a Vuitton charm bracelet around its wrist, being shaken vigorously to make sure none of the charms falls off.

A new-product must have the required functional features and also convey the intended psychological characteristics. The fuel-cell electric car, for example, should strike consumers as being well built, comfortable, and safe. Management must learn what makes consumers decide that a car is well built. To some consumers, this means that the car has "solid-sounding" doors. To others, it means that the car is able to withstand heavy impact in crash tests. Consumer tests are conducted in which consumers test-drive the car and rate its attributes.

■ Product testing: Gillette uses employee-volunteers to test new shaving products—"We bleed so you'll get a good shave at home," says a Gillette employee.

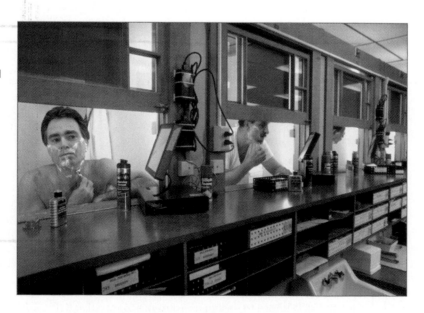

① Test Marketing

Test marketing
The stage of new-product development in which the product and marketing program are tested in more realistic market settings.

If the product passes functional and consumer tests, the next step is **test marketing**, the stage at which the product and marketing program are introduced into more realistic market settings. Test marketing gives the marketer experience with marketing the product before going to the great expense of full introduction. It lets the company test the product and its entire marketing program—positioning strategy, advertising, distribution, pricing, branding and packaging, and budget levels.

The amount of test marketing needed varies with each new product. Test marketing costs can be high, and it takes time that may allow competitors to gain advantages. When the costs of developing and introducing the product are low, or when management is already confident about the new product, the company may do little or no test marketing. In fact, test marketing by consumer package-goods firms has been declining in recent years. Companies often do not test-market simple line extensions or copies of successful competitor products. For example, P&G introduced its Folger's decaffeinated coffee crystals without test marketing, and Pillsbury rolled out Chewy granola bars and chocolate-covered Granola Dipps with no standard test market.

However, when introducing a new product requires a big investment, or when management is not sure of the product or marketing program, a company may do a lot of test marketing. For instance, Lever USA spent 2 years testing its highly successful Lever 2000 bar soap in Atlanta before introducing it internationally. Frito-Lay did 18 months of testing in three markets on at least five formulations before introducing its Baked Lays line of low-fat snacks. And Nokia test-marketed its N-Gage cell phone/mobile game player extensively in London before introducing it worldwide.[15]

Although test-marketing costs can be high, they are often small when compared with the costs of making a major mistake. For example, Nabisco's launch of one new product without testing had disastrous—and soggy—results:[16]

Nabisco hit a marketing home run with its Teddy Grahams, teddy-bear-shaped graham crackers in several different flavors. So, the company decided to extend Teddy Grahams into a new area. It introduced chocolate, cinnamon, and honey versions of Breakfast Bears Graham Cereal. When the product came out, however, consumers didn't like the taste enough, so the product developers went back to the kitchen and modified the formula. But they didn't test it. The result was a disaster. Although the cereal may have tasted better, it no longer stayed crunchy in milk, as the advertising on the box promised. Instead, it left a gooey mess of graham

■ Test marketing: Nokia test-marketed its N-Gage cell phone/mobile game player extensively before introducing it worldwide.

mush on the bottom of cereal bowls. Supermarket managers soon refused to restock the cereal, and Nabisco executives decided it was too late to reformulate the product again. So a promising new product was killed through haste to get it to market.

Still, test marketing doesn't guarantee success. For example, Procter & Gamble tested its new Fit produce rinse heavily for 5 years and Olay cosmetics for 3 years. Although market tests suggested the products would be successful, P&G had to pull the plug on both shortly after their introductions.[17]

When using test marketing, consumer products companies usually choose one of three approaches—standard test markets, controlled test markets, or simulated test markets.

Standard Test Markets

Using standard test markets, the company finds a small number of representative test cities, conducts a full marketing campaign in these cities, and uses store audits, consumer and distributor surveys, and other measures to gauge product performance. The results are used to forecast national sales and profits, discover potential product problems, and fine-tune the marketing program.

Standard test markets have some drawbacks. They can be very costly and they may take a long time—some last as long as 3 to 5 years. Moreover, competitors can monitor test market results or even interfere with them by cutting their prices in test cities, increasing their promotion, or even buying up the product being tested. Finally, test markets give competitors a look at the company's new product well before it is introduced nationally. Thus, competitors may have time to develop defensive strategies, and may even beat the company's product to the market. For example, while CLOROX® was still test marketing its new detergent with bleach in selected markets, P&G launched Tide with Bleach nationally. Tide with Bleach quickly became the segment leader; CLOROX® later withdrew its detergent.

Despite these disadvantages, standard test markets are still the most widely used approach for major in-market testing. However, many companies today are shifting toward quicker and cheaper controlled and simulated test marketing methods.

Controlled Test Markets

Several research firms keep controlled panels of stores that have agreed to carry new products for a fee. Controlled test marketing systems like ACNielsen's Scantrack and Information Resources, Inc.'s (IRI) BehaviorScan track individual consumer behavior for new products from the television set to the checkout counter.

In each BehaviorScan market, IRI maintains a panel of shoppers who report all of their purchases by showing an identification card at check-out in participating stores and by using a handheld scanner at home to record purchases at nonparticipating stores.[18] Within test stores, IRI controls such factors as shelf placement, price, and in-store promotions for the product being tested. IRI also measures TV viewing in each panel household and sends special commercials to panel member television sets. Direct mail promotions can also be tested.

■ Controlled Test Markets: IRI's BehaviorScan system tracks individual consumer behavior for new products from the television set to the checkout counter.

Detailed scanner information on each consumer's purchases is fed into a central computer, where it is combined with the consumer's demographic and TV viewing information and reported daily. Thus, BehaviorScan can provide store-by-store, week-by-week reports on the sales of tested products. Such panel purchasing data enables in-depth diagnostics not possible with retail point-of-sale data alone, including repeat purchase analysis, buyer demographics, and earlier, more accurate sales forecasts after just 12 to 24 weeks in market. Most importantly, the system allows companies to evaluate their specific marketing efforts.

Controlled test markets, such as BehaviorScan, usually cost less than standard test markets. Also, because retail distribution is "forced" in the first week of the test, controlled test markets can be completed much more quickly than standard test markets. As in standard test markets, controlled test markets allow competitors to get a look at the company's new product. And some companies are concerned that the limited number of controlled test markets used by the research services may not be representative of their products' markets or target consumers. However, the research firms are experienced in projecting test market results to broader markets and can usually account for biases in the test markets used.

Simulated Test Markets

Companies can also test new products in a simulated shopping environment. The company or research firm shows ads and promotions for a variety of products, including the new product being tested, to a sample of consumers. It gives consumers a small amount of money and invites them to a real or laboratory store where they may keep the money or use it to buy items. The researchers note how many consumers buy the new product and competing brands.

This simulation provides a measure of trial and the commercial's effectiveness against competing commercials. The researchers then ask consumers the reasons for their purchase or nonpurchase. Some weeks later, they interview the consumers by phone to determine product attitudes, usage, satisfaction, and repurchase intentions. Using sophisticated computer models, the researchers then project national sales from results of the simulated test market. Recently, some marketers have begun to use interesting new high-tech approaches to simulated test market research, such as virtual reality and the Internet.

Simulated test markets overcome some of the disadvantages of standard and controlled test markets. They usually cost much less, can be run in 8 weeks, and keep the new product out of competitors' view. Yet, because of their small samples and simulated shopping environments, many marketers do not think that simulated test markets are as accurate or reliable as larger, real-world tests. Still, simulated test markets are used widely, often as "pretest" markets. Because they are fast and inexpensive, they can be run to quickly assess a new product or its marketing program. If the pretest results are strongly positive, the product might be introduced without further testing. If the results are very poor, the product might be dropped or substantially redesigned and retested. If the results are promising but indefinite, the product and marketing program can be tested further in controlled or standard test markets.

Commercialization

Commercialization
Introducing a new product into the market.

Test marketing gives management the information needed to make a final decision about whether to launch the new product. If the company goes ahead with **commercialization**—introducing the new product into the market—it will face high costs. The company may have to build or rent a manufacturing facility. And it may have to spend, in the case of a new consumer packaged good, between $10 million and $200 million for advertising, sales promotion, and other marketing efforts in the first year.

The company launching a new product must first decide on introduction *timing*. If DaimlerChrysler's new fuel-cell electric car will eat into the sales of the company's other cars, its introduction may be delayed. If the car can be improved further, or if the economy is down, the company may wait until the following year to launch it.

Next, the company must decide *where* to launch the new product—in a single location, a region, the national market, or the international market. Few companies have the confidence, capital, and capacity to launch new products into full national or international distribution. They will develop a planned *market rollout* over time. In particular, small companies may enter attractive cities or regions one at a time. Larger companies, however, may quickly introduce new models into several regions or into the full national market.

Companies with international distribution systems may introduce new products through global rollouts. Colgate-Palmolive used to follow a "lead-country" strategy. For example, it launched its Palmolive Optima shampoo and conditioner first in Australia, the Philippines,

■ Colgate introduces new products, like its Actibrush toothbrush, in swift global assaults, solidifying the brand's market position before foreign competitors can react.

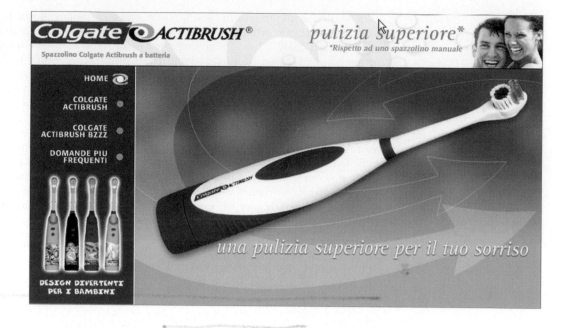

Hong Kong, and Mexico, then rapidly rolled it out into Europe, Asia, Latin America, and Africa. However, most international companies now introduce their new products in swift global assaults. More recently, in its fastest new-product rollout ever, Colgate introduced its Actibrush battery-powered toothbrush into 50 countries in a year, generating $115 million in sales. Such rapid worldwide expansion solidified the brand's market position before foreign competitors could react.[19]

Organizing for New-Product Development

Sequential product development

A new-product development approach in which one company department works to complete its stage of the process before passing the new product along to the next department and stage.

Simultaneous (or team-based) product development

An approach to developing new products in which various company departments work closely together, overlapping the steps in the product-development process to save time and increase effectiveness.

Many companies organize their new-product development process into the orderly sequence of steps shown in Figure 9.1, starting with idea generation and ending with commercialization. Under this **sequential product development** approach, one company department works individually to complete its stage of the process before passing the new product along to the next department and stage. This orderly, step-by-step process can help bring control to complex and risky projects. But it also can be dangerously slow. In fast-changing, highly competitive markets, such slow-but-sure product development can result in product failures, lost sales and profits, and crumbling market positions. "Speed to market" and reducing new-product development cycle time have become pressing concerns to companies in all industries.

In order to get their new products to market more quickly, many companies are adopting a faster, team-oriented approach called **simultaneous product development** (or **team-based** or **collaborative product development**). Under this approach, company departments work closely together through cross-functional teams, overlapping the steps in the product development process to save time and increase effectiveness. Instead of passing the new product from department to department, the company assembles a team of people from various departments that stays with the new product from start to finish. Such teams usually include people from the marketing, finance, design, manufacturing, and legal departments, and even supplier and customer companies.

Top management gives the product development team general strategic direction but no clear-cut product idea or work plan. It challenges the team with stiff and seemingly contradictory goals—"turn out carefully planned and superior new products, but do it quickly"—and then gives the team whatever freedom and resources it needs to meet the challenge. In the sequential process, a bottleneck at one phase can seriously slow the entire project. In the simultaneous approach, if one functional area hits snags, it works to resolve them while the team moves on.

The Allen-Bradley Company, a maker of industrial controls, realized tremendous benefits by using simultaneous development. Under its old sequential approach, the company's marketing department handed off a new-product idea to designers, who worked in isolation to prepare concepts that they then passed along to product engineers. The engineers, also working by themselves, developed expensive prototypes and handed them off to manufacturing, which tried to find a way to build the new product. Finally, after many years and dozens of costly design compromises and delays, marketing was asked to sell the new product, which it often found to be too high priced or sadly out of date. Now, all of Allen-Bradley's departments work together to develop new products. The results have been astonishing. For example, the company recently developed a new electrical control in just 2 years; under the old system, it would have taken 6 years.

The simultaneous team-based approach does have some limitations. Superfast product development can be riskier and more costly than the slower, more orderly sequential approach. Moreover, it often creates increased organizational tension and confusion. And the company must take care that rushing a product to market doesn't adversely affect its quality—the objective is not only to create products faster, but to create them *better* and faster.

Despite these drawbacks, in rapidly changing industries facing increasingly shorter product life cycles, the rewards of fast and flexible product development far exceed the risks. Companies that get new and improved products to the market faster than competitors often gain a big competitive edge. They can respond more quickly to emerging consumer tastes and charge higher prices for more advanced designs. As one auto industry executive states, "What we want to do is get the new car approved, built, and in the consumer's hands in the shortest time possible. . . . Whoever gets there first gets all the marbles."[20]

Thus, new-product success requires more than simply thinking up a few good ideas, turning them into products, and finding customers for them. It requires a systematic approach for finding new ways to create valued customer experiences, from generating and screening new-product ideas to creating and rolling out want-satisfying products to customers. More than this, successful new-product development requires a total-company commitment. At companies known for their new-product prowess—such as 3M, Gillette, Intel, and Nokia—the entire culture encourages, supports, and rewards innovation:

You see the headline in every 3M ad: "Innovation Working for You." But at 3M, innovation isn't just an advertising pitch. Throughout its history, 3M has been one of America's most innovative companies. The company markets more than 50,000 products, ranging from sandpaper, adhesives, and hundreds of sticky tapes to

■ Innovation: At 3M, new products don't just happen. The company's entire culture encourages, supports, and rewards innovation.

contact lenses, heart-lung machines, and futuristic synthetic ligaments. Each year 3M launches more than 200 new products. But these new products don't just happen. 3M works hard to create an entrepreneurial culture that fosters innovation. For more than a century, 3M's culture has encouraged employees to take risks and try new ideas. 3M knows that it must try thousands of new-product ideas to hit one big jackpot. Trying out lots of new ideas often means making mistakes, but 3M accepts blunders and dead ends as a normal part of creativity and innovation.

In fact, "blunders" have turned into some of 3M's most successful products. Old-timers at 3M love to tell the story about 3M scientist Spencer Silver. Silver started out to develop a superstrong adhesive; instead he came up with one that didn't stick very well at all. He sent the apparently useless substance on to other 3M researchers to see whether they could find something to do with it. Nothing happened for several years. Then Arthur Fry, another 3M scientist, had a problem—and an idea. As a choir member in a local church, Mr. Fry was having trouble marking places in his hymnal—the little scraps of paper he used kept falling out. He tried dabbing some of Mr. Silver's weak glue on one of the scraps. It stuck nicely and later peeled off without damaging the hymnal. Thus were born 3M's Post-It Notes, a product that is now one of the top selling office supply products in the world.[21]

START | **Product Life-Cycle Strategies**

After launching the new product, management wants the product to enjoy a long and happy life. Although it does not expect the product to sell forever, the company wants to earn a decent profit to cover all the effort and risk that went into launching it. Management is aware that each product will have a life cycle, although its exact shape and length is not known in advance.

Product life cycle (PLC)

The course of a product's sales and profits over its lifetime. It involves five distinct stages: product development, introduction, growth, maturity, and decline.

Figure 9.2 shows a typical **product life cycle (PLC)**, the course that a product's sales and profits take over its lifetime. The PLC has five distinct stages:

1. *Product development* begins when the company finds and develops a new-product idea. During product development, sales are zero and the company's investment costs mount.
2. *Introduction* is a period of slow sales growth as the product is introduced in the market. Profits are nonexistent in this stage because of the heavy expenses of product introduction.
3. *Growth* is a period of rapid market acceptance and increasing profits.
4. *Maturity* is a period of slowdown in sales growth because the product has achieved acceptance by most potential buyers. Profits level off or decline because of increased marketing outlays to defend the product against competition.
5. *Decline* is the period when sales fall off and profits drop.

Not all products follow this product life cycle. Some products are introduced and die quickly; others stay in the mature stage for a long, long time. Some enter the decline stage and are then cycled back into the growth stage through strong promotion or repositioning. As one analyst notes, "well-managed, a brand could live forever. American Express, Budweiser, Camel, Coca-Cola, Gillette, Western Union, and Wells-Fargo, for instance, are still going

FIGURE 9.2

Sales and profits over the product's life from inception to demise

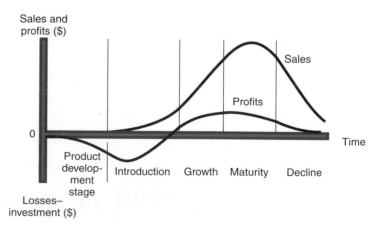

■ Product life cycle: Some products die quickly; others stay in the mature stage for a long, long time. For more than 300 years, TABASCO® Sauce "has stood as the ultimate test of courage."

strong in their respective categories after 100+ years. Even if a brand dies, it can rise again, though perhaps in more limited distribution. Take Pabst Blue Ribbon and PanAm Airlines."[22]

The PLC concept can describe a *product class* (gasoline-powered automobiles), a *product form* (SUVs), or a *brand* (the Ford Explorer). The PLC concept applies differently in each case. Product classes have the longest life cycles—the sales of many product classes stay in the mature stage for a long time. Product forms, in contrast, tend to have the standard PLC shape. Product forms such as "dial telephones" and "cassette tapes" passed through a regular history of introduction, rapid growth, maturity, and decline.

A specific brand's life cycle can change quickly because of changing competitive attacks and responses. For example, although laundry soaps (product class) and powdered detergents (product form) have enjoyed fairly long life cycles, the life cycles of specific brands have tended to be much shorter. Today's leading brands of powdered laundry soap are Tide and Cheer; the leading brands 75 years ago were Fels Naptha, Octagon, and Kirkman.[23]

The PLC concept also can be applied to what are known as styles, fashions, and fads. Their special life cycles are shown in Figure 9.3. A style is a basic and distinctive mode of expression. For example, styles appear in homes (colonial, ranch, transitional), clothing (formal, casual), and art (realist, surrealist, abstract). Once a style is invented, it may last for generations, passing in and out of vogue. A style has a cycle showing several periods of renewed interest. A fashion is a currently accepted or popular style in a given field. For example, the more formal "business attire" look of corporate dress of the 1980s and early 1990s gave way to the "business casual" look of today. Fashions tend to grow slowly, remain popular for a while, and then decline slowly.

Fads are temporary periods of unusually high sales driven by consumer enthusiasm and immediate product or brand popularity.[24] A fad may be part of an otherwise normal life cycle, as in the case of recent surges in the sales of scooters and yo-yos. Or the fad may comprise a brand's or product's entire life cycle. "Pet rocks" are a classic example. Upon hearing his

Style

A basic and distinctive mode of expression.

Fashion

A currently accepted or popular style in a given field.

Fad

A temporary period of unusually high sales driven by consumer enthusiasm and immediate product or brand popularity.

FIGURE 9.3
Styles, fashions, and fads

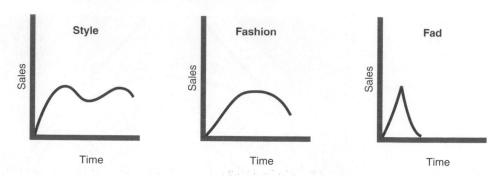

friends complain about how expensive it was to care for their dogs, advertising copywriter Gary Dahl joked about his pet rock. He soon wrote a spoof of a dog-training manual for it, titled "The Care and Training of Your Pet Rock." Soon Dahl was selling some 1.5 million ordinary beach pebbles at $4 a pop. Yet the fad, which broke one October, had sunk like a stone by the next February. Dahl's advice to those who want to succeed with a fad: "Enjoy it while it lasts." Other examples of such fads include Rubik's Cubes, lava lamps, and certain fad diets or hairstyles.[25]

The PLC concept can be applied by marketers as a useful framework for describing how products and markets work. But using the PLC concept for forecasting product performance or for developing marketing strategies presents some practical problems. For example, managers may have trouble identifying which stage of the PLC the product is in or pinpointing when the product moves into the next stage. They may also find it hard to determine the factors that affect the product's movement through the stages. In practice, it is difficult to forecast the sales level at each PLC stage, the length of each stage, and the shape of the PLC curve.

■ Fads: Pet rocks, introduced one October, had sunk like a stone by the next February.

Using the PLC concept to develop marketing strategy also can be difficult because strategy is both a cause and a result of the product's life cycle. The product's current PLC position suggests the best marketing strategies, and the resulting marketing strategies affect product performance in later life-cycle stages. Yet, when used carefully, the PLC concept can help in developing good marketing strategies for different stages of the product life cycle.

We looked at the product development stage of the product life cycle in the first part of the chapter. We now look at strategies for each of the other life-cycle stages.

Introduction Stage

Introduction stage
The product life-cycle stage in which the new product is first distributed and made available for purchase.

The introduction stage starts when the new product is first launched. Introduction takes time, and sales growth is apt to be slow. Well-known products such as instant coffee and frozen orange juice lingered for many years before they entered a stage of rapid growth.

In this stage, as compared with other stages, profits are negative or low because of the low sales and high distribution and promotion expenses. Much money is needed to attract distributors and build their inventories. Promotion spending is relatively high to inform consumers of the new product and get them to try it. Because the market is not generally ready for product refinements at this stage, the company and its few competitors produce basic versions of the product. These firms focus their selling on those buyers who are the most ready to buy.

A company, especially the *market pioneer*, must choose a launch strategy that is consistent with the intended product positioning. It should realize that the initial strategy is just the first step in a grander marketing plan for the product's entire life cycle. If the pioneer chooses its launch strategy to make a "killing," it may be sacrificing long-run revenue for the sake of short-run gain. As the pioneer moves through later stages of the life cycle, it will have to continuously formulate new pricing, promotion, and other marketing strategies. It has the best chance of building and retaining market leadership if it plays its cards correctly from the start.

Growth Stage

Growth stage
The product life-cycle stage in which a product's sales start climbing quickly.

If the new product satisfies the market, it will enter a **growth stage**, in which sales will start climbing quickly. The early adopters will continue to buy, and later buyers will start following their lead, especially if they hear favorable word of mouth. Attracted by the opportunities for profit, new competitors will enter the market. They will introduce new product features, and the market will expand. The increase in competitors leads to an increase in the number of distribution outlets, and sales jump just to build reseller inventories. Prices remain where they are or fall only slightly. Companies keep their promotion spending at the same or a slightly higher level. Educating the market remains a goal, but now the company must also meet the competition.

Profits increase during the growth stage, as promotion costs are spread over a large volume and as unit manufacturing costs fall. The firm uses several strategies to sustain rapid market growth as long as possible. It improves product quality and adds new product features and models. It enters new market segments and new distribution channels. It shifts some advertising from building product awareness to building product conviction and purchase, and it lowers prices at the right time to attract more buyers.

In the growth stage, the firm faces a trade-off between high market share and high current profit. By spending a lot of money on product improvement, promotion, and distribution, the company can capture a dominant position. In doing so, however, it gives up maximum current profit, which it hopes to make up in the next stage.

Maturity Stage

Maturity stage
The stage in the product life cycle in which sales growth slows or levels off.

At some point, a product's sales growth will slow down, and the product will enter a **maturity stage**. This maturity stage normally lasts longer than the previous stages, and it poses strong challenges to marketing management. Most products are in the maturity stage of the life cycle, and therefore most of marketing management deals with the mature product.

The slowdown in sales growth results in many producers with many products to sell. In turn, this overcapacity leads to greater competition. Competitors begin marking down prices, increasing their advertising and sales promotions, and upping their R&D budgets to find better versions of the product. These steps lead to a drop in profit. Some of the weaker competitors start dropping out, and the industry eventually contains only well-established competitors.

Real Marketing 9.2

Age-Defying Products or Just Skillful PLC Management?

Some products are born and die quickly. Others, however, seem to defy the product life cycle, enduring for decades, or even generations. Skillful product life-cycle management keeps them fresh, relevant, and appealing to customers. Here are examples of two long-term market winners with plenty of staying power.

Volkswagen Beetle

The original Volkswagen Beetle first sputtered into America in 1949. With its simple, buglike design, no-frills engineering, and economical operation, the Beetle was the antithesis of Detroit's chrome-laden gas guzzlers. During the 1960s, as young baby boomers by the thousands were buying their first cars, demand exploded and the anything-but-flashy Beetle blossomed. Bursting with personality, the understated Bug came to personify an era of rebellion against conventions. It became the most popular car in American history, with sales peaking at 423,000 in 1968. By the late 1970s, however, the boomers had moved on. Bug mania faded, and Volkswagen dropped Beetle production for the United States.

Still, decades later, the mere mention of these chugging oddities evoked smiles and strong emotions. So rather than letting the old Beetle die, Volkswagen decided to rekindle the life cycle of this little car that could. In 1998, it introduced a New Beetle. Outwardly, the reborn Beetle resembles the original, tapping the strong emotions and memories of times gone by. Beneath the skin, however, the New Beetle is packed with modern features. According to an industry analyst:

> With a familiar bubble shape that still makes people smile as it skitters by, the new Beetle offers a pull that is purely emotional. Built into the dashboard is a bud vase perfect for a daisy plucked straight from the 1960s. But [despite the warmly familiar look and touches, it's really not the same old Beetle.] Right next to [the bud vase] is a high-tech multi-speaker stereo—and options like power windows, cruise control, and a power sunroof make it a very different car than the rattly old Bug. The new version . . . comes with all the modern features car buyers demand, such as four air bags and power outlets for cell phones.

■ Some products seem to defy the product life cycle: Rather than acting like a 50 year old, the rejuvenated Volkswagen Beetle is behaving more like a frisky adolescent.

Initial advertising for the New Beetle played strongly on the car's former life, while at the same time refreshing the old Beetle heritage. "If you sold your soul in the '80s," tweaked one ad, "here's your chance to buy it back." Other ads read, "Less flower, more power," and "Comes with wonderful new features. Like heat." Still another ad declared "0 to 60? Yes."

Volkswagen invested $560 million to bring the Beetle back to life. But the investment paid big dividends as demand quickly outstripped supply. Rather than acting like a 50 year old, the rejuvenated brand behaved more like a frisky adolescent. Even before the

Although many products in the mature stage appear to remain unchanged for long periods, most successful ones are actually evolving to meet changing consumer needs (see Real Marketing 9.2). Product managers should do more than simply ride along with or defend their mature products—a good offense is the best defense. They should consider modifying the market, product, and marketing mix.

In *modifying the market,* the company tries to increase the consumption of the current product. It may look for new users and market segments, as when Johnson & Johnson targeted the adult market with its baby powder and shampoo. Or the company may reposition the brand to appeal to a larger or faster-growing segment, as Verizon did when it expanded into high speed Internet and wireless services. The manager may also look for ways to increase usage among present customers. Amazon.com does this by sending permission-based e-mails to regular customers letting them know when their favorite authors or performers publish new books or CDs. The WD-40 Company has shown a real knack for expanding the market by finding new uses for its popular substance.

first cars reached VW showrooms, dealers across the country had long waiting lists of people who'd paid for the car without ever seeing it, let alone driving it. Even kids too young to remember the original Bug loved this new one.

After only 9 months, New Beetle sales exceeded first-year sales projections by more than 25 percent. Sales are still sizzling—the New Beetle now accounts for more than a quarter of Volkswagen's U.S. sales and has helped win VW a fivefold increase in sales during the past decade. Says one trend analyst, the New Beetle "is different, yet deeply familiar—a car for the times."

Crayola Crayons

Over the past 100 years or so, Binney & Smith's Crayola crayons have become a household staple in more than 80 countries around the world. Few people can forget their first pack of "64s"—64 beauties neatly arranged in the familiar green and yellow flip-top box with a sharpener on the back. The aroma of a freshly opened Crayola box still drives kids into a frenzy and takes members of the older generation back to some of their fondest childhood memories.

In some ways, Crayola crayons haven't changed much since 1903, when they were sold in an eight-pack for a nickel. But a closer look reveals that Binney & Smith has made many adjustments to keep the brand out of decline. The company has added a steady stream of new colors, shapes, sizes, and packages. It has gradually increased the number of colors from the original eight in 1903 (red, yellow, blue, green, orange, black, brown, and white) to 120 in 2004.

Binney & Smith has also extended the Crayola brand to new markets, such as Crayola Markers, scissors, watercolor paints, gel pens, themed stamps and stickers, and activity kits. The company has licensed the Crayola brand for use on everything from camera outfits, backpacks, and bookends to cartoon cups and mousepads. Finally, the company has added several programs and services to help strengthen its relationships with Crayola customers. Its *Crayola Kids* magazine and Crayola Web site offer features for children along with interactive art and craft suggestions for parents and educators on helping develop reading skills and creativity.

Not all of Binney & Smith's life-cycle adjustments have been greeted favorably by consumers. For example, in 1990, to make room for more modern colors, it retired eight colors from the time-honored box of 64—raw umber, lemon yellow, maize, blue grey, orange yellow, orange red, green blue, and violet blue—into the Crayola Hall of Fame. The move unleashed a groundswell of protest from loyal Crayola users, who formed such organizations as the RUMPS—the Raw Umber and Maize Preservation Society—and the National Committee to Save Lemon Yellow. Company executives were flabbergasted—"We were aware of the loyalty and nostalgia surrounding Crayola crayons," a spokesperson says, "but we didn't know we [would] hit such a nerve." The company reissued the old standards in a special collector's tin—it sold all of the 2.5 million tins made.

Thus, Crayola continues its long and colorful life cycle. Through smart product life-cycle management, Binney & Smith, now a subsidiary of Hallmark, has dominated the crayon market for almost a century. The company now makes nearly 3 billion crayons a year, enough to circle the globe six times. By the age of 10 the average American child has worn down 730 crayons. Sixty-five percent of all American children between the ages of 2 and 7 pick up a crayon at least once a day and color for an average of 28 minutes. Nearly 80 percent of the time, they pick up a Crayola crayon.

Sources: Quotes and information from Theresa Howard, "Nostalgia Helps Beetle Score," *USA Today,* February 23, 2003, accessed online at www.usatoday.com; James R. Rosenfield, "Millennial Fever," *American Demographics,* December 1997, pp. 47–51; "A Top-Popping Good Time," *The Washington Post,* April 24, 2003, p. G18; Margaret O. Kirk, "Coloring Our Children's World Since '03," *Chicago Tribune,* October 29, 1986, sec. 5, p. 1; "Hue and Cry over Crayola May Revive Old Colors," *Wall Street Journal,* June 14, 1991, p. B1; Dennis Bruce and Philip Maynard, "Don't Sell Your Brand's Soul," *Marketing,* April 26, 2004, p. 17; and "Crayola Trivia," accessed at www.crayola.com, January 2005.

In 2000, the company launched a search to uncover 2,000 unique uses for WD-40. After receiving 300,000 individual submissions, it narrowed the list to the best 2,000 and posted it on the company's Web site. Some consumers suggest simple and practical uses. One teacher uses WD-40 to clean old chalkboards in her classroom. "Amazingly, the boards started coming to life again," she reports. "Not only were they restored, but years of masking and Scotch tape residue came off as well." Others, however, report some pretty unusual applications. One man uses WD-40 to polish his glass eye; another uses it to remove a prosthetic leg. And did you hear about the nude burglary suspect who had wedged himself in a vent at a cafe in Denver? The fire department extracted him with a large dose of WD-40. Or how about the Mississippi naval officer who used WD-40 to repel an angry bear? Then there's the college student who wrote to say that a friend's nightly amorous activities in the next room were causing everyone in his dorm to lose sleep—he solved the problem by treating the squeaky bedsprings with WD-40.[26]

■ The WD-40 Company's knack for finding new uses has made this popular substance one of the truly essential survival items in most American homes.

The company might also try *modifying the product*—changing characteristics such as quality, features, or style to attract new users and to inspire more usage. It might improve the product's quality and performance—its durability, reliability, speed, taste. It can improve the product's styling and attractiveness. Thus, car manufacturers restyle their cars to attract buyers who want a new look. The makers of consumer food and household products introduce new flavors, colors, ingredients, or packages to revitalize consumer buying. Heinz did this when it introduce ketchup in EZ Squirt packaging and the new Blastin' Green and Awesome Orange colors. Or the company might add new features that expand the product's usefulness, safety, or convenience. For example, Sony keeps adding new styles and features to its Walkman and Discman lines, and Volvo adds new safety features to its cars.

Finally, the company can try *modifying the marketing mix*—improving sales by changing one or more marketing mix elements. It can cut prices to attract new users and competitors' customers. It can launch a better advertising campaign or use aggressive sales promotions— trade deals, cents-off, premiums, and contests. Hormel, maker of Spam, recently launched a new advertising campaign and other promotions to reposition and revitalize its mature product, which has been around since the late 1930s.[27]

Joe Spam is the everyman that impresses crowds at barbecues, beach get-togethers, and breakfasts by offering basic-assembly Spam-centered recipes. The pitch is that the spicy smoked taste of Spam makes eggs, pizza—almost anything—better. And it's done with all the over the top fervor of "Monty Python's Flying Circus" famed Spam routine. In the spots, people literally eat up the stuff, and when there's none left, Joe Spam is able to clap his hands, yell out "More Spam!" and call up a Spammobile that crashes the party out of the clear blue to deliver up more of the "crazy tasty" stuff. The crowd, of course, barely notices the unusual delivery, as

■ Revitalizing a mature brand: Hormel, maker of Spam, recently launched a new "crazy tasty" advertising and promotion campaign, complete with the SPAMMOBILE, to reposition and revitalize its mature product, which has been around since the late 1930s.

they only have eyes for the little tins of love. The campaign tries to capture the American boldness of the brand. Last year, the company's three Spammobiles and their crews of SPAMbassadors doled out more than 1.5 million Spamburgers at 675 events around the country.

In addition to pricing and promotion, the company can also move into larger market channels, using mass merchandisers, if these channels are growing. Finally, the company can offer new or improved services to buyers.

Decline Stage

The sales of most product forms and brands eventually dip. The decline may be slow, as in the case of oatmeal cereal, or rapid, as in the case of phonograph records. Sales may plunge to zero, or they may drop to a low level where they continue for many years. This is the **decline stage**.

Decline stage
The product life-cycle stage in which a product's sales decline.

Sales decline for many reasons, including technological advances, shifts in consumer tastes, and increased competition. As sales and profits decline, some firms withdraw from the market. Those remaining may prune their product offerings. They may drop smaller market segments and marginal trade channels, or they may cut the promotion budget and reduce their prices further.

Carrying a weak product can be very costly to a firm, and not just in profit terms. There are many hidden costs. A weak product may take up too much of management's time. It often requires frequent price and inventory adjustments. It requires advertising and sales force attention that might be better used to make "healthy" products more profitable. A product's failing reputation can cause customer concerns about the company and its other products. The biggest cost may well lie in the future. Keeping weak products delays the search for replacements, creates a lopsided product mix, hurts current profits, and weakens the company's foothold on the future.

For these reasons, companies need to pay more attention to their aging products. The firm's first task is to identify those products in the decline stage by regularly reviewing sales, market shares, costs, and profit trends. Then, management must decide whether to maintain, harvest, or drop each of these declining products.

Management may decide to *maintain* its brand without change in the hope that competitors will leave the industry. For example, Procter & Gamble made good profits by remaining in the declining liquid soap business as others withdrew. Or management may decide to reposition or reformulate the brand in hopes of moving it back into the growth stage of the product life cycle. P&G did this with its Mr. Clean brand:

> Mr. Clean's share of the all-purpose household cleaner market had plunged more than 45 percent in just 10 years. But rather than abandon the 46-year-old iconic brand, P&G chose to modify and extend it. First, it reformulated the core Mr. Clean all-purpose liquid cleaner, adding antibacterial properties and several new scents. Then, it extended the brand to include two revolutionary new products. The first was Mr. Clean Magic Eraser, a soft, disposable self-cleaning pad that acts like an eraser to lift away tough dirt, including difficult scuff and crayon marks. The second was the Mr. Clean AutoDry Carwash system, which gives your car a spot-free clean and shine with no need to hand dry. P&G backed the new-product launches with $50 million in marketing support. Now, after a decade of playing the 98-pound weakling, P&G hopes that a revitalized Mr. Clean can muscle its way back to a market-leading position.[28]

Management may decide to *harvest* the product, which means reducing various costs (plant and equipment, maintenance, R&D, advertising, sales force) and hoping that sales hold up. If successful, harvesting will increase the company's profits in the short run. Or management may decide to *drop* the product from the line. It can sell it to another firm or simply liquidate it at salvage value. In recent years, P&G has sold off a number of lesser or declining brands such as Oxydol detergent and Jif peanut butter. If the company plans to find a buyer, it will not want to run down the product through harvesting.

Table 9.2 summarizes the key characteristics of each stage of the PLC. The table also lists the marketing objectives and strategies for each stage.[29]

■ Back into the growth stage: P&G revitalized the Mr. Clean brand in hopes that it can muscle its way back into a market-leading position.

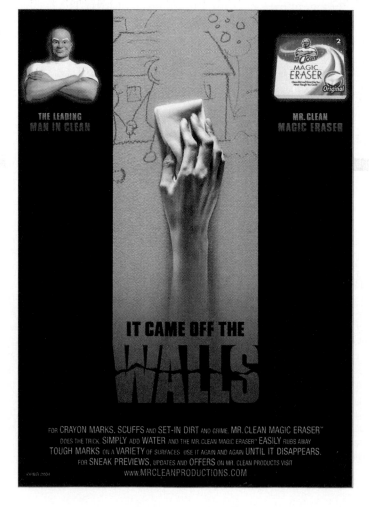

TABLE 9.2 Summary of Product Life-Cycle Characteristics, Objectives, and Strategies

Characteristics	Introduction	Growth	Maturity	Decline
Sales	Low sales	Rapidly rising sales	Peak sales	Declining sales
Costs	High cost per customer	Average cost per customer	Low cost per customer	Low cost per customer
Profits	Negative	Rising profits	High profits	Declining profits
Customers	Innovators	Early adopters	Middle majority	Laggards
Competitors	Few	Growing number	Stable number beginning to decline	Declining number
Marketing Objectives	Create product awareness and trial	Maximize market share	Maximize profit while defending market share	Reduce expenditure and milk the brand
Strategies				
Product	Offer a basic product	Offer product extensions, service, warranty	Diversify brand and models	Phase out weak items
Price	Use cost-plus	Price to penetrate market	Price to match or beat competitors	Cut price
Distribution	Build selective distribution	Build intensive distribution	Build more intensive distribution	Go selective: phase out unprofitable outlets
Advertising	Build product awareness among early adopters and dealers	Build awareness and interest in the mass market	Stress brand differences and benefits	Reduce to level needed to retain hard-core loyals
Sales Promotion	Use heavy sales promotion to entice trial	Reduce to take advantage of heavy consumer demand	Increase to encourage brand switching	Reduce to minimal level

Source: Philip Kotler, *Marketing Management*, 11th ed. (Upper Saddle River, N.J.: Prentice Hall, 2003), p. 340.

> Reviewing the Concepts <

A company's current products face limited life spans and must be replaced by newer products. But new products can fail—the risks of innovation are as great as the rewards. The key to successful innovation lies in a total-company effort, strong planning, and a systematic *new-product development* process.

1. Explain how companies find and develop new-product ideas.
Companies find and develop new-product ideas from a variety of sources. Many new-product ideas stem from *internal sources.* Companies conduct formal research and development, pick the brains of their employees, and brainstorm at executive meetings. Other ideas come from *external sources.* By conducting surveys and focus groups and analyzing *customer* questions and complaints, companies can generate new-product ideas that will meet specific consumer needs. Companies track *competitors'* offerings and inspect new products, dismantling them, analyzing their performance, and deciding whether to introduce a similar or improved product. *Distributors and suppliers* are close to the market and can pass along information about consumer problems and new-product possibilities.

2. List and define the steps in the new-product development process.
The new-product development process consists of eight sequential stages. The process starts with *idea generation.* Next comes *idea screening*, which reduces the number of ideas based on the com-

pany's own criteria. Ideas that pass the screening stage continue through *product concept development,* in which a detailed version of the new-product idea is stated in meaningful consumer terms. In the next stage, *concept testing,* new-product concepts are tested with a group of target consumers to determine whether the concepts have strong consumer appeal. Strong concepts proceed to *marketing strategy development,* in which an initial marketing strategy for the new product is developed from the product concept. In the *business analysis* stage, a review of the sales, costs, and profit projections for a new product is conducted to determine whether the new product is likely to satisfy the company's objectives. With positive results here, the ideas become more concrete through *product development* and *test marketing* and finally are launched during *commercialization.*

3. Describe the stages of the product life cycle.
Each product has a *life cycle* marked by a changing set of problems and opportunities. The sales of the typical product follow an S-shaped curve made up of five stages. The cycle begins with the *product development stage* when the company finds and develops a new-product idea. The *introduction stage* is marked by slow growth and low profits as the product is distributed to the market. If successful, the product enters a *growth stage,* which offers rapid sales growth and increasing profits. Next comes a *maturity stage* when sales growth slows down and profits stabilize. Finally, the product enters a *decline*

stage in which sales and profits dwindle. The company's task during this stage is to recognize the decline and to decide whether it should maintain, harvest, or drop the product.

4. Describe how marketing strategies change during the product's life cycle.
In the *introduction stage*, the company must choose a launch strategy consistent with its intended product positioning. Much money is needed to attract distributors and build their inventories and to inform consumers of the new product and achieve trial. In the *growth stage*, companies continue to educate potential consumers and distributors. In addition, the company works to stay ahead of the competition and sustain rapid market growth by improving product quality, adding new product features and models, entering new market segments and distribution channels, shifting advertising from building product awareness to building product conviction and purchase,

and lowering prices at the right time to attract new buyers. In the *maturity stage,* companies continue to invest in maturing products and consider modifying the market, the product, and the marketing mix. When *modifying the market,* the company attempts to increase the consumption of the current product. When *modifying the product,* the company changes some of the product's characteristics—such as quality, features, or style—to attract new users or inspire more usage. When *modifying the marketing mix,* the company works to improve sales by changing one or more of the marketing mix elements. Once the company recognizes that a product has entered the *decline stage*, management must decide whether to *maintain* the brand without change, hoping that competitors will drop out of the market; *harvest* the product, reducing costs and trying to maintain sales; or *drop* the product, selling it to another firm or liquidating it at salvage value.

> Reviewing the Key Terms <

> Discussing the Concepts <

1. Which is a better source of new-product ideas, the company's sales force or external sources?

2. Write a 100-word, three-part marketing strategy statement for a new music CD by your favorite recording artist.

3. Under what conditions would you consider not test marketing a product? Describe a product or service that meets these no-need-to-test criteria.

4. Compare the sequential and simultaneous product development approaches. Is one approach better than the other? Explain.

5. What major commercialization plan elements must a marketer address before launching a new product?

6. The chapter states that "In the growth stage [of the product life cycle], the firm faces a trade-off between high market share and high current profit." Explain this statement.

> Applying the Concepts <

1. You are a new-product manager and have been asked to design an idea screening process for your company. Prepare a 5-step process for screening consumer convenience good ideas.

2. Go to QuestionPro.com at www.questionpro.com/akira/showLibrary. Click on "New Product/Concept Testing (20)" under the "Marketing" header. Then click on the "Brief Product Concept Test" template (#9). Now prepare a concept test questionnaire for a new action toy figure with the following characteristics: middle-aged, stout, balding man; dressed in dark-gray suit, white shirt, dark tie; carries a brief case; and drives a 5-year-old Ford Crown Victoria.

3. You are a product manager in a firm that manufactures and markets a line of branded action figure toys. The branded toy line is 5 years

old. Annual sales and profits for this period are presented in the following chart. Prepare a one-sentence strategy for each of the four P's based on the brand's current product life cycle position.

Period	Sales	Profit
Year 1	$ 3,000,000	($ 100,000)
Year 2	$ 20,000,000	$ 1,500,000
Year 3	$ 50,000,000	$10,000,000
Year 4	$ 52,000,000	$ 8,000,000
Year 5	$ 31,000,000	$ 1,000,000

> Focus on Technology <

Many firms provide software and services to assist firms with product life cycle management. One of the more successful companies providing these services is Agile Software Corporation. According to the company, "Agile Product Lifecycle Management (Agile™ PLM) solutions help companies accelerate revenue, reduce costs, improve quality, ensure compliance, and drive innovation throughout the product lifecycle. . . . Agile helps companies get the most from their products." Go to Agile's Web site at www.agile.com/plm/plm_solutions.asp and review the PLM offering. Then respond to the following questions:

1. What are the PLM services that Agile provides?
2. On what portion of the product life cycle does Agile focus?
3. Based on what you have read at the Agile site, do you think Agile's PLM services would be a good or poor investment? Why?

> Focus on Ethics <

Concept testing is an invaluable part of the new-product development process. Time spent testing product concepts with consumers before developing them will reduce the number of false starts and conserve one of the most important resources in new-product development—money. Many companies shortcut the concept-testing stage and go direct to demand testing. They conduct what are called "dry tests." Dry testing occurs when you 'test the waters' for interest in a new product by placing an ad for the product before it actually exists.

1. Do you believe that such dry testing is ethical?
2. What does the Direct Marketing Association (DMA) say about the practice? (Do a Google search on "dry testing" [in quotes] and DMA.) What does the Federal Trade Commission (FTC) say?
3. Would you dry test a new-product concept? Under what conditions?

Video Case

eGo Bikes

When it hit the market in 2002, the eGO was the first vehicle of its kind: an environmentally friendly, compact electric moped. Although the concept seems simple, the design and development of the new product was anything but. And, although the new concept helped create buzz and generated interest for the electric moped, it also posed some challenges for eGO's marketers. For starters, eGO struggled with how to introduce and position the new product for potential customers who are unfamiliar with the technology and unaware of the need it fills. Perhaps most important, the moped was so different from already-available mopeds that there were no obvious channels for distribution.

Despite these setbacks, and with almost no advertising at all, eGO was selling nearly 1,000 mopeds each month just 3 months after introduction and sales were growing rapidly. Today the company is still working to promote the product and grow sales.

After viewing the video featuring eGO vehicles, answer the following questions about new product development:

1. How did design decisions impact the development and marketing of the eGO?
2. What strategies did eGO employ to successfully launch the eGO electric moped?
3. Identify the company's target markets. What other consumers might eGO target?
4. Develop two additional concepts for the eGO Cycle. Select one concept and list three questions marketers might ask consumers to test the concept.

Company Case

I Want My VOIP!!!!

One warm day in May, Rita Ramirez found two envelopes in the morning mail. One was a bill from the telephone company for nearly $50. The other was an introductory offer for digital telephone. When she looked at the bill, Rita was incensed—she had made no long distance calls and subscribed to a basic telephone package instead of adding all sorts of "extra" services. Her irritation with the phone bill caused her to pay more attention to the digital telephone offer.

Rita remembered someone talking to her several years ago about making telephone calls over the Internet, but she had gotten the impression that you had to pay for each call, that sound quality was poor, and that calls were frequently interrupted. However, the introductory offer claimed that digital telephone was the result of a new process, and that it could be purchased for only $29.95 for the first 6 months and $39.95 thereafter.

So Rita set out to learn more about digital telephone. She discovered that digital telephone uses VOIP—Voice Over Internet Protocol—based on soft switching technology. Soft switching uses a small box in the subscriber's home called an EMTA (Embedded Multimedia Terminal Adapter), which looks like a large cable modem. It brings in phone calls, converts them to digital signals, and then sends them over the coaxial cable and fiber links to the headend. There, a call is sent to either a telephone switch or a regional data service. Soft switching is a much less expensive technology than the traditional circuit switching used in the past to send cable telephone calls. It is also much less expensive to maintain.

Because VOIP converts phone calls into data, the integration of telephone, TV, and data is extensive. VOIP users will be able to access complete call lists on their PCs, send pictures from cell phones directly to set-top boxes, and easily manage computer-based telephone address books. All the regular services offered by telephone companies, such as caller id and call waiting can be offered with digital telephone.

The advantages do not end there. There are no long distance charges with digital telephone. All local and long distance calls in the United States and to Canada are covered by the same basic monthly charge. Furthermore, the physical location of equipment doesn't matter as long as it's connected to a broadband (DSL/cable) modem. This means that a California-based consumer with a broadband connection and a VOIP phone service could carry the broadband modem abroad, plug into the hotel's broadband connection, and call within the United States without paying an extra penny. Because VOIP systems allow for each user to have multiple phone numbers, families with kids in college can give them each a number with a local area code and the children can call home for free. It's the number and area code that matter, not where the caller or modem is physically located.

There will be even more features in the future, features that are out of the reach of the local telephone company to develop. There could be videophones, video e-mail, and integrating phone messages and e-mails on a Web page that can be retrieved from any computer with an Internet connection. Just imagine checking who's calling while you're watching TV!

What are some of the problems with digital telephone? The first is voice quality. According to one subscriber who had just switched to digital telephone, everyone she called said she sounded like she was talking underwater. The company sent technicians to work on the system and the voice quality improved, but it is still not as good as regular telephone service. Another problem is that loss of power means loss of telephone service, whereas regular telephone systems still operate when electricity is out. Companies such as Cox are working to develop batteries that provide temporary backup power, but there is nothing that would provide telephone service for extensive blackout periods.

The technology for digital telephone has been around for a couple of years but cable operators have been slow to introduce the service. They have been focusing on selling high-speed Internet service, but the growth of subscribers for that service is beginning to decline. Also, the telephone companies are taking away much of their business with satellite and DirectTV. Finally, residential telephone service is a big market—over $70 billion a year. For cable companies, it appears to be the next growth market.

In spite of all the current and potential advantages of digital telephone, companies are competing on the basis of cost, not services. They offer a basic package with standard features, such as call waiting and caller id, for one price. Usually the price is 30 percent below the telephone company's price. Cable operators have found that customers want packages, not a list of services with individual prices, and they like buying their video, high-speed Internet connection, and phone service from one company. Customers want one company and one bill. According to Cox President Jim Robbins, "bundled customers are more satisfied customers—we have lots of research to support that—and bundled customers churn (turn over) less." When companies offer the triple of video, Internet, and telephone, they find that normal churn of 20 percent drops by 40 to 50 percent. Of course, companies could offer packages of different bundles of services, just like current offers for cable TV. Then, it would be up to consumers to select the package of services that they want. But in this launch period, most companies are sticking to a basic package and making their pitch on price.

Given that there are still some problems with VOIP (voice quality and others), some companies are holding off on offering VOIP until they can offer more services, Others, however, are forging ahead. Cablevision in Bethpage, NY, was one of the first companies to offer VOIP service, identified as Optimum Voice. This service lacked operators and number portability, and subscribers could not transfer their existing phone number to Optimum Voice. It was offered as part of their "triple play" bundle of video, high-speed data, and telephone service. The three products at $30 each totaled $90 monthly, 32 percent below what Cablevision's video customers were paying.

Cox Communications, the fourth largest cable operator, was one of the first operator to offer digital telephone. Three years ago, it set up a "circuit-switched" service that runs on thin wires encased with the coax cable and managed to sign up 1 million of its 4.7 million consumers. Today, it is shifting to VOIP, which is much less expensive. Initially, Cox spent $700 to $900 in capital for each new phone customer. Today with VOIP, the cost is only about $300. Even though Cox prices are 20 to 30 percent less than the telephone company's, the average subscriber is paying $50 monthly. By 2005, telephone service will be 14 percent of Cox's profits but, more importantly, it will 27 percent of its profit growth.

Time Warner has also been very aggressive with digital telephony. It launched VOIP in late 2003 in Portland, Maine. Within 2 months, 25 percent of Time Warner cable subscribers had purchased VOIP service. Surprised and encouraged by the size of the response, Time Warner moved up its introduction timetable in order to offer VOIP to all of the 18 million households that subscribe to its cable system by the end of 2004. Time Warner, however, is not offering its service at the drastically reduced price of Cablevision because Time Warner executives believe that a pricing war would commoditize VOIP, which would mean little to no payoff for anyone. It would rather compete on the basis of service. If Time Warner can replicate its Portland experience, it will have reached the same level of penetration with VOIP in 2 years that it took 5 years to achieve with Internet service. Maybe product life-cycle time is declining.

Comcast, the largest U.S. cable company is moving much more slowly. It is offering VOIP to limited markets in 2004, to half of its subscribers in 2005, and to all 40 million of them in 2006. It plans to wait until it can offer more sophisticated services, such as videophones and video e-mail. Once Comcast enters the market and competition heats up, consumer awareness should increase, manufacturing costs of VOIP equipment should decline, and vendors will be motivated to develop new features.

Within 5 years, analysts expect 16 million subscribers to buy cable telephone services, which will generate up to $5 billion annually. More than 20 companies have entered the market so far. Startups like Vontage can launch their own Internet phone service that rides cable's lines without paying a toll.

Internet telephone service will change the way America communicates, and some companies, noticeably telephone providers, are crying "unfair." For now, the FCC has proposed only minimal regulation, but some members of Congress are mulling a 5-year moratorium on regulating VOIP carriers. States seem to be split on this issue. For now, Vontage and similar companies are classified as information service providers, which enables them to bypass local and international telecom laws. The ability to use equipment anywhere to dial a local number is also not what the North American Numbering Plan was set up to do. Eventually, there could be more tariffs on Internet telephony, raising its cost. If analysts are correct about the rapidly declining cost, however, customers will never notice the tariffs.

Rita's offer came from Time Warner—the company that calls its Internet service digital telephone. Her situation resembles the consumer scenario that cable companies expect. They realize that people like Rita aren't looking for an alternative means of making telephone calls. After all, she has a cell phone. Instead she wants to lower cost. She wants convenience and value but would be turned off by tech-speak; hence the name, digital telephone. It communicates what the service is and the introductory package hammered home lower price.

After finding out all about Internet telephony, Rita made a list of the pros and cons of accepting the Time Warner offer. What do you think she will do?

Questions for Discussion

1. What are the advantages and disadvantages to Rita of accepting the Time Warner offer? Think carefully through the process that Rita would have to go through to switch telephone services. What would you do in her place?

2. Write the first part of a marketing strategy statement for the Time Warner digital telephone offer? Include the target market and planned product positioning.

3. In what stage of the product life cycle is Internet telephony? Does the answer to this question vary across companies such as Vontage, Comcast, Time Warner, and Cox?

4. Why does bundling of services work so well for the cable companies? What are the advantages to both the consumer and the company?

5. In your opinion, is Comcast's strategy a big risk or a wise move? Is the aggressiveness of other companies appropriate?

Sources: John Higgins, "A Different Kind of Price War," *Broadcasting & Cable*, July 19, 2004, p. 14; "VOIP Is Getting Very Real," *America's Network*, September 15, 2003, p. 34; Peter Grant, "Cable Giants Vie to Improve Online Phoning," *Wall Street Journal*, January 8, 2004, p. A.15; John M. Higgins, "Cox Cable Plays Defense and Offense," *Broadcasting & Cable*, February 2, 2004, p. 38; John M. Higgins, "Cable Will Eat the Phone Company's Lunch . . ." *Broadcasting & Cable*, May 3, 2004, p. 1.

CHAPTER 10

> **After studying this chapter, you should be able to**
>
> 1. identify and define the internal factors affecting a firm's pricing decisions
> 2. identify and define the external factors affecting pricing decisions, including the impact of consumer perceptions of price and value
> 3. contrast the three general approaches to setting prices

Pricing Products: Pricing Considerations and Approaches

Previewing the Concepts

Next, we look at a second major marketing mix tool—pricing. According to one pricing expert, pricing involves "harvesting your profit potential."[1] If effective product development, promotion, and distribution sow the seeds of business success, effective pricing is the harvest. Firms successful at creating customer value with the other marketing mix activities must still capture some of this value in the prices they earn. Yet, despite its importance, many firms do not handle pricing well. In this chapter, we'll examine internal and external factors that affect pricing decisions and three general pricing approaches. In the next chapter, we dig into pricing strategies.

To start off, let's look at one of the most dramatic new developments in the fast-changing world of pricing—the impact of the Internet. Less than a decade ago, Priceline.com burst onto the Web with a simple but compelling new pricing concept—let consumers name their own prices! This radical new idea caught on, making Priceline one of today's few profitable dot-coms. Sound too good to be true? It could only happen on the Internet.

304

The headlines scream: *Name your own price deals! Best hotel prices guaranteed! Save a boatload on best-known cruise lines! Try our all-new airfare service and save! Low rates right now on home financing or refinancing!* Just the usual come-ons from fly-by-night operators? Too good to be true? Not at Priceline.com, at least not according to *Yahoo! Internet Life Magazine*, which proclaimed Priceline as the "Best Bargain Booker" on the Web. Priceline's byline: "I Think, Therefore I Save."

In 1998, founder Jay Walker launched Priceline as a radical new Internet service. It was based on an ingeniously simple concept—let consumers name their own prices, then dangle their offers in front of sellers and see who bites. Such transactions, he reasoned, benefited both buyers and sellers—buyers got lower prices; sellers turned excess inventory into profits. Although simple in concept, such "buyer-driven commerce" represented a dramatic departure from long-held pricing practices in

which sellers—not buyers—set prices. Still, the idea caught on. Priceline has now grown to become the leading name-your-own-price Internet service.

Priceline deals primarily in travel-related products—plane tickets, hotel rooms, rental cars, cruises, and vacation packages. Here's how it works—say, for a hotel room. First, you select your destination and desired dates. If it's a big city, you can scan Priceline's maps to narrow down the area in which you'd like to stay. You can also select the types of hotels you're willing to stay in—from one-star ("economy hotels that provide comfort with no frills") to five-star ("the best that money can buy"). Give Priceline the usual billing information and a credit card number—and decide how much you'd like to bid. Click on "Buy My Hotel Room," then sit back and wait for Priceline to broker the deal. Within 15 minutes, Priceline e-mails you with the news. If no suitable hotel is willing to accept your price, you can bid again later. If Priceline finds a taker, it immediately charges your credit card—no refunds, changes, or cancellations allowed—and lets you know where you'll be staying.

The concept of setting your own prices over the Internet has real appeal to many consumers. It starts with a good value proposition—getting really low prices. Beyond that, "name-your-price is a great hook," say a Priceline marketing executive. "If you get it, it's like 'I won!'" As a result, Priceline is attracting more and more customers. Its customer base has grown to almost 19 million users, and as many as 9 million people visit the Priceline site monthly. Last year, it booked more than $1.1 billion worth of travel through its Web site.

Despite accepting fire-sale prices, sellers also benefit from Priceline's services. It's especially attractive to those who sell "time sensitive" products. "If airlines or hotels don't sell seats on particular flights or rooms for certain nights, those assets become worthless," comments an analyst. "Such businesses are a natural fit for Priceline." Moreover, notes the analyst, "by requiring customers to commit to payment up front with their credit card, retailers face little risk in dumping excess inventory. It's particularly attractive in markets that have huge fixed costs from creating capacity and relatively small marginal costs, like air travel, cruise ships, and automobiles."

Priceline makes its money by buying up unsold rooms, seats, or vacation packages at heavily discounted rates, marking them up, and selling them to consumers for as much as a 12 percent return. So, on a $215 plane ticket, Priceline makes about $35, compared with the $10 gross profit made by a traditional travel agent.

Along with the successes and recent profitability, however, Priceline has encountered some major obstacles. For example, not all products lend themselves to Priceline's quirky business model. Although the Web seller currently takes bids in other categories, such as home financing products (home mortgages, refinancing, and home equity loans), selling products and services that aren't time sensitive has proven difficult. Priceline has tried its hand unsuccessfully at selling a variety of nontravel products, including new cars and long distance services.

Moreover, not all customers are thrilled with their Priceline experiences. Forcing customers to commit to purchases before they know the details—such as which hotel or airline, flight times, and hotel locations—can leave some customers feeling cheated. Those feelings are magnified by concerns that hotel ratings may be inconsis-

tent or even inaccurate. One frustrated user recently summed up his Priceline experience this way: "You don't get what you think you're gonna get." To better serve customers who worry about such things, Priceline recently launched an airlines ticket service that gives customers a choice. They can now select known flights, times, and airlines from a selection of low fares or choose the Name Your Own Price for deeper discounts. Customers can also search for lowest rates on known dates and providers at Priceline's companion site, www.lowestfare.com.

But for every disappointed customer, Priceline has hundreds or thousands of happy ones. Some 67 percent of those who now visit Priceline to name their own prices are repeat customers. You don't have to go far to get positive testimonials such as these:

> Using Priceline.com has worked out great! I remember the first time I used it. I'm not very technically savvy, but after navigating around the site, I set what I thought was a lowball price. It turns out that my offer was accepted and I saved more than 50 percent off the normal room rate. The hotel was great. In fact, I usually stay there when traveling, so I also knew I was getting it for a great price.
>
> I discovered Priceline.com and decided to try it out to visit my college roommate. She's in Albuquerque, New Mexico, and I'm in Hanover, Germany. The best price from the airlines was too high. After reading about Priceline.com, I decided I had nothing to lose by trying it to get a better deal. I offered a low price but was sure I wouldn't stand the slightest chance of an acceptance. To my amazement, within 20 minutes of logging in, I received a happy "congratulations" e-mail from Priceline. The visit was wonderful, my friend was amazed, and I've been telling everyone (lots of seasoned travelers who didn't believe my story at first) from Germany to the United States about this spectacular new way to travel.

More than just changing how people pay for travel services, Priceline is perhaps the best example of how the Internet is changing today's pricing practices. "Only through the Web could you match millions of bids with millions of products, all without a fixed price," says one analyst. "In the offline world, this would be a strange market indeed," says another. Try to imagine a real-world situation in which "buyers attach money to a board, along with a note stating what they want to buy for the sum. Later, sellers come along and have a look. If they like an offer, they take the money and deliver the goods." It couldn't happen anywhere but on the Web.[2]

Companies today face a fierce and fast-changing pricing environment. The recent economic downturn has put many companies in a "pricing vise." One analyst sums it up this way: "They have virtually no pricing power. It's impossible to raise prices, and often, the pressure to slash them continues unabated." "Businesspeople in all kinds of industries keep making the same complaint," says another analyst. "They can't raise prices, and its killing them." It seems that almost every company is slashing prices, and that is hurting their profits.[3]

Yet, cutting prices is often not the best answer. Reducing prices unnecessarily can lead to lost profits and damaging price wars. It can signal to customers that the price is more important than the brand. Instead, companies should sell value, not price. They should persuade customers that paying a higher price for the company's brand is justified by the greater value it delivers. The challenge is to find the price that will let the company make a fair profit by harvesting the customer value it creates. "Give people something of value," says Ronald Shaich, CEO of Panera Bread Company, "and they'll happily pay for it."[4]

In this chapter and the next, we focus on the process of setting prices. This chapter defines prices, looks at the factors marketers must consider when setting prices, and examines general pricing approaches. In the next chapter, we look at pricing strategies for new-product pricing, product mix pricing, price adjustments for buyer and situational factors, and price changes.

What Is a Price?

Price
The amount of money charged for a product or service, or the sum of the values that consumers exchange for the benefits of having or using the product or service.

In the narrowest sense, **price** is the amount of money charged for a product or service. More broadly, price is the sum of all the values that consumers exchange for the benefits of having or using the product or service. Historically, price has been the major factor affecting buyer choice. However, in recent decades, nonprice factors have become more important in buyer-choice behavior.

Today's New Pricing Environment

Dynamic pricing
Charging different prices depending on individual customers and situations.

Throughout most of history, prices were set by negotiation between buyers and sellers. *Fixed price* policies—setting one price for all buyers—is a relatively modern idea that arose with the development of large-scale retailing at the end of the nineteenth century. Today, most prices are set this way. However, some companies are now reversing fixed pricing trend. They are using **dynamic pricing**—charging different prices depending on individual customers and situations.

■ Pricing: The challenge is to harvest the customer value the company creates. Says Panera's CEO, pictured here, "Give people something of value, and they'll happily pay for it."

For example, think about how the Internet has affected pricing. From the mostly fixed pricing practices of the past century, the Web seems now to be taking us back—into a new age of fluid pricing. "Potentially, [the Internet] could push aside sticker prices and usher in an era of dynamic pricing," says one writer, "in which a wide range of goods would be priced according to what the market will bear—instantly, constantly."[5]

Dynamic pricing offers many advantages for marketers. For example, Internet sellers such as Amazon.com can mine their databases to gauge a specific shopper's desires, measure his or her means, instantaneously tailor products to fit that shopper's behavior, and price products accordingly. Catalog retailers such as L.L. Bean, Spiegel, or Fingerhut can change prices on the fly according to changes in demand or costs, changing prices for specific items on a day-by-day or even hour-by-hour basis. Online music retailer MusicRebellion.com lets consumer demand set the price for downloaded songs. Each song is initially available for download at 10 cents. As demand increases, however, prices may increase to as much as $1 per song.[6]

Many B2B marketers monitor inventories, costs, and demand at any given moment and adjust prices instantly. For example, IBM automatically adjusts prices on its servers based on customer demand and product life-cycle factors. As a result, customers will find that prices change dynamically when they visit the IBM Web site on any given day. Dell also uses dynamic online pricing. "If the price of memory or processors decreases, we pass those savings along to the customer almost in real time," says a Dell spokesperson.

Buyers also benefit from the Web and dynamic pricing. A wealth of Web sites—such as Froogle.com, Yahoo! Shopping, Bizrate.com, NexTag.com, PriceGrabber.com, CompareNet.com, and PriceScan.com—give instant product and price comparisons from thousands of vendors. Yahoo! Shopping, for instance, lets shoppers browse by category or search for specific products and brands. It then searches the Web and reports back links to sellers offering the best prices. In addition to simply finding the vendor with the best price, customers armed with price information can often negotiate lower prices.

Buyers can also negotiate prices at online auction sites and exchanges. Suddenly the centuries-old art of haggling is back in vogue. Want to sell that antique pickle jar that's been

■ A wealth of Web sites—such as Yahoo! Shopping—give instant product and price comparisons from online vendors.

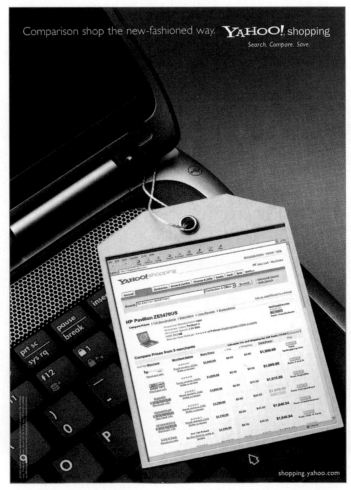

collecting dust for generations? Post it on eBay, the world's biggest online flea market. Want to purchase vintage baseball cards at a bargain price? Go to HeavyHitter.com. Want to name your own price for a hotel room or rental car? Visit Priceline.com or another reverse auction site.

Pricing: An Important but Difficult Decision

Price is the only element in the marketing mix that produces revenue; all other elements represent costs. Price is also one of the most flexible elements of the marketing mix. Unlike product features and channel commitments, price can be changed quickly.

At the same time, pricing is the number one problem facing many marketing executives. Yet many companies do not handle pricing well. One frequent problem is that companies are too quick to reduce prices in order to get a sale rather than convincing buyers that their products are worth a higher price. Other common mistakes include pricing that is too cost oriented rather than customer-value oriented and pricing that does not take the rest of the marketing mix into account.

START | # Factors to Consider When Setting Prices

A company's pricing decisions are affected by both internal company factors and external environmental factors (see Figure 10.1).[7]

Internal Factors Affecting Pricing Decisions

Internal factors affecting pricing include the company's marketing objectives, marketing mix strategy, costs, and organizational considerations.

Marketing Objectives

Before setting price, the company must decide on its strategy for the product. If the company has selected its target market and positioning carefully, then its marketing mix strategy, including price, will be fairly straightforward. For example, when Toyota developed its Lexus brands to compete with European luxury-performance cars in the higher-income segment, this required charging a high price. In contrast, when it introduced its "energetic but economical" Echo model, a car with "a sticker price that can really help you pursue your dreams," this positioning required charging a low price. Thus, pricing strategy is largely determined by decisions on market positioning.

At the same time, the company may seek additional general or specific objectives. General objectives include survival, current profit maximization, market share leadership, and product quality leadership. At a more specific level, a company can set prices low to prevent competition from entering the market or set prices at competitors' levels to stabilize the market. It can set prices to keep the loyalty and support of resellers or to avoid government intervention. Prices can be reduced temporarily to create excitement for a product or to draw more customers into a retail store. Or one product may be priced to help the sales of other products in the company's line. Thus, pricing may play an important role in helping to accomplish the company's objectives at many levels.

Many companies use *current profit maximization* as their pricing goal. They estimate what demand and costs will be at different prices and choose the price that will produce the maximum current profit, cash flow, or return on investment. Other companies want to obtain *market share leadership*. To become the market share leader, these firms set prices as low as possible.

FIGURE 10.1
Factors affecting price decisions

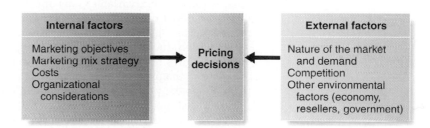

■ Product quality leadership: Caterpillar charges higher prices than competitors based on superior product and service quality. According to this ad, "Better service starts with better choices."

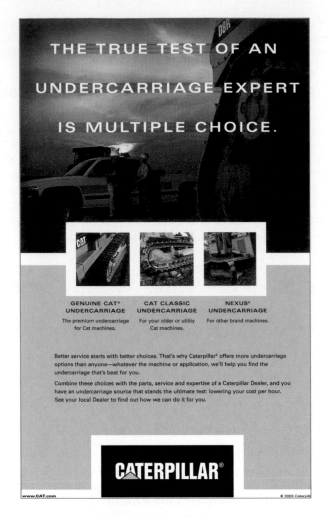

A company might decide that it wants to achieve *product quality leadership*. This normally calls for charging a high price to cover higher performance quality and the high cost of R&D. For example, Caterpillar charges 20 percent to 30 percent more than competitors for its heavy construction equipment based on superior product and service quality. A.T. Cross doesn't sell just ballpoint pens—you can get those from Bic. Instead, it sells "fine writing instruments" in models bearing names like Classic Century, Ion, Morph, Matrix, ATX, and Radiance, selling for prices as high as $400.

Not-for-profit and public organizations may adopt a number of other pricing objectives. A university aims for *partial cost recovery*, knowing that it must rely on private gifts and public grants to cover the remaining costs. A not-for-profit hospital may aim for *full cost recovery* in its pricing. A not-for-profit theater company may price its productions to fill the maximum number of theater seats. A social service agency may set a *social price* geared to accommodate the varying incomes of different clients.

Marketing Mix Strategy

Price is only one of the marketing mix tools that a company uses to achieve its marketing objectives. Price decisions must be coordinated with product design, distribution, and promotion decisions to form a consistent and effective marketing program. Decisions made for other marketing mix variables may affect pricing decisions. For example, a decision to position the product on high-performance quality will mean that the seller must charge a higher price to cover higher costs. And producers whose resellers are expected to support and promote their products may have to build larger reseller margins into their prices.

Target costing

Pricing that starts with an ideal selling price, then targets costs that will ensure that the price is met.

Companies often position their products on price and then tailor other marketing mix decisions to the prices they want to charge. Here, price is a crucial product-positioning factor that defines the product's market, competition, and design. Many firms support such price-positioning strategies with a technique called **target costing**, a potent strategic weapon. Target costing reverses the usual process of first designing a new product, determining its cost, and then asking, "Can we sell it for that?" Instead, it starts with an ideal selling price based on customer considerations, and then targets costs that will ensure that the price is met.

Procter & Gamble used target costing to price and develop its highly successful Crest SpinBrush electric toothbrush:

> P&G usually prices its goods at a premium. But with Crest SpinBrush, P&G reversed its usual thinking. It started with an attractive low market price, and then found a way to make a profit at that price. SpinBrush's inventors first came up with the idea of a low-priced electric toothbrush while walking through their local Wal-Mart, where they saw Sonicare, Interplak, and other electric toothbrushes priced at more than $50. These pricy brushes held only a fraction of the overall toothbrush market. A less expensive electric toothbrush, the designers reasoned, would have huge potential. They decided on a target price of just $5, batteries included—only $1 more than the most expensive manual brushes—and set out to design a brush they could sell at that price. Every design element was carefully considered with the targeted price in mind. To meet the low price, P&G passed on the usual lavish new-product launch campaign. Instead, to give SpinBrush more point-of-sale impact, it relied on "Try Me" packaging that allowed consumers to turn the brush on in stores. Target cost pricing has made Crest SpinBrush one of P&G's most successful new products ever. It has now become the nation's best-selling toothbrush, manual or electric, with a more than 40 percent share of the electric toothbrush market. Says brand manager Darin Yates, "It's hard for P&G's business models to conceive of a business growing as quickly as SpinBrush."[8]

Other companies deemphasize price and use other marketing mix tools to create *nonprice* positions. Often, the best strategy is not to charge the lowest price, but rather to differentiate the marketing offer to make it worth a higher price. For example, Sony builds more value into its consumer electronics products and charges a higher price than many competitors. Customers recognize Sony's higher quality and are willing to pay more to get it. Some marketers even *feature* high prices as part of their positioning. For example, Porsche

■ Positioning on high price: Porsche proudly advertises its Cayenne as "starting at $55,900."

**Unfold the road map.
Head for the squiggliest lines.**

There are roads out there just begging to be driven. And no SUV can oblige them like the Cayenne S. Permanent all-wheel drive. Porsche Stability Management. And exacting agility as ribbons of pavement unwind effortlessly before you. Porsche. There is no substitute.

The Cayenne S. Starting at $55,900.

PORSCHE

Real Marketing 10.1

Steinway: Price Is Nothing; The Steinway Experience Is Everything

A Steinway piano—any Steinway piano—costs a lot. But Steinway buyers aren't looking for bargains. In fact, it seems, the higher the prices, the better. High prices confirm that a Steinway is the very best that money can buy—the epitome of hand-crafted perfection. As important, the Steinway name is steeped in tradition. It evokes images of classical concert stages, sophisticated dinner parties, and the celebrities and performers who've owned and played Steinway pianos across more than 150 years. When it comes to Steinway, price is nothing, the Steinway experience is everything.

To be sure, Steinway & Sons makes very high quality pianos. With 120 patents to its credit, Steinway & Sons has done more than any other manufacturer to advance the art of piano building. Steinway pioneered the development of a one-piece piano rim produced out of 17 laminations of veneer. It invented a process for bending a single 22-foot long strip of these laminated sheets inside a massive piano-shaped vise. It's this strong frame that produces Steinway's distinctive clear tones. Steinway & Sons has continued perfecting this design, and today a Steinway piano's 243 tempered, hard-steel strings exert 35 tons of pressure—enough force to implode a three-bedroom house if the strings were strung between attic and cellar.

In addition to cutting edge technology, Steinway & Sons uses only the finest materials to construct each piano. Rock maple, spruce, birch, poplar, and four other species of wood each play a crucial functional role in the physical and acoustical beauty of a Steinway. The expansive wooden soundboard, which turns the string vibrations into sound, is made from select Alaskan Sitka spruce—one grade higher than aircraft grade. Through delicate hand craftsmanship, Steinway transforms these select materials into pianos of incomparable sound quality. From start to finish, it takes 300 skilled workers more than a year to handcraft and assemble a Steinway piano from its 12,000 component parts. Thus, Steinway is anything but mass market. Each year, Steinway's factories in Astoria,

A Steinway piano costs a lot, but buyers aren't looking for bargains. When it comes to Steinway, price is nothing, the Steinway experience is everything.

New York, and Hamburg, Germany, craft only 1,500 uprights and 3,000 grand pianos. (By comparison, Yamaha produces 100,000 pianos per year.)

proudly advertises its Cayenne as "starting at $55,900." And Steinway offers "the finest pianos in the world," with a price to match. Steinway's grand pianos can cost as much as $150,000 (see Real Marketing 10.1).

Thus, marketers must consider the total marketing mix when setting prices. If the product is positioned on nonprice factors, then decisions about quality, promotion, and distribution will strongly affect price. If price is a crucial positioning factor, then price will strongly affect decisions made about the other marketing mix elements. But even when featuring price, marketers need to remember that customers rarely buy on price alone. Instead, they seek products that give them the best value in terms of benefits received for the price paid.

Costs

Costs set the floor for the price that the company can charge. The company wants to charge a price that both covers all its costs for producing, distributing, and selling the product and delivers a fair rate of return for its effort and risk. A company's costs may be an important element in its pricing strategy. Many companies, such as Southwest Airlines, Wal-Mart, and Union Carbide, work to become the "low-cost producers" in their industries. Companies with lower costs can set lower prices that result in greater sales and profits.

Steinway's precision quality alone would command top dollar, but Steinway buyers get much more than just a well-made piano. They also get the Steinway mystique. Owning or playing a Steinway puts you in some very good company. Fully 98 percent of piano soloists with the world's major symphony orchestras prefer playing on a Steinway. More than 90 percent of the world's concert pianists, some 1,300 in all, bear the title of Steinway Artist—an elite club of Steinway-owning professional musicians. Steinway customers include composers and professional musicians (from Van Cliburn to Billy Joel), upscale customers (from Lamar Alexander to Paula Zahn), and heads of state (the 25,000th Steinway was sold to Czar Alexander of Russia and Piano No. 300,000 graces the East Room of the White House, replacing Piano No. 100,000, which is now in the Smithsonian).

Performers of all kinds sing Steinway's praises. "Steinway is the only piano on which the pianist can do everything he wants. And everything he dreams," declares premier pianist and conductor Vladimir Ashkenazy. At the other end of the performing spectrum, contemporary singer-songwriter Randy Newman puts it this way: "I have owned and played a Steinway all my life. It's the best Beethoven piano. The best Chopin piano. And the best Ray Charles piano. I like it, too." Whereas some people want a Porsche in the garage, others prefer a Steinway in the living room—both cost about the same, and both make a statement about their owners.

Even in the worst of times, Steinway & Sons has held true to its tradition and image—and to its premium prices. Although the Steinway family no longer owns the company, its current owners still prize and protect the brand's exclusivity. When they bought the troubled company in 1984, new management was burdened with 900 pianos of excess inventory. But rather than slashing prices to make a quick profit at the risk of tarnishing the brand, managers restored the company's health by holding the line on prices and renewing its commitment to quality. Through such actions, Steinway has retained its cult-like following and continues to dominate its market. Despite its very high prices—or more likely because of them—Steinway enjoys a 95 percent market share in concert halls.

So, you won't find any weekend sales on Steinway pianos. Charging significantly higher prices continues to be a cornerstone of the company's "much more for much more" value proposition. And high prices have been good for Steinway & Sons. "We have 2 percent of all keyboard unit sales in the U.S.," says Bruce Stevens, Steinway's president. "But we have 25 percent of the sales dollars and about 35 percent of the profits."

To customers, whatever a Steinway costs, it's a small price to pay for the experience of owning one. Just ask the collector who recently commissioned a 9-foot re-creation of the famous Steinway Alma-Tadema piano built in 1887. The price for his dream Steinway? An eye-popping $675,000! Classical pianist Krystian Zimerman sums up his Steinway experience this way: "My friendship with the Steinway piano is one of the most important and beautiful things in my life." Who can put a price on such feelings?

Sources: Andy Serwer, "Happy Birthday Steinway," *Fortune*, March 17, 2003, p. 94; "Books and Arts: Making the Sound of Music; Piano Manufacturers," *The Economist*, June 7, 2003, p. 102; Brian T. Majeski, "The Steinway Story," *Music Trades*, September 2003, p. 18; "The Most Famous Name in Music," *Music Trades*, September 2003, p. 118–130; "Today's Steinway," *Music Trades*, September 2003, p. 140–145; Stephan Wilkinson, "High-Strung. Powerful. Very Pricey," *Popular Science*, March 1, 2003, p. 32; "Steinway Musical Instruments, Inc.," *Hoover's Company Capsules*, Austin, March 15, 2004, p. 48052; Michael Z. Wise, "Piano Versus Piano," *New York Times*, May 9, 2004; and quotes and information found at www.steinway.com, January 2005.

Fixed costs

Costs that do not vary with production or sales level.

Variable costs

Costs that vary directly with the level of production.

Total costs

The sum of the fixed and variable costs for any given level of production.

TYPES OF COSTS A company's costs take two forms, fixed and variable. **Fixed costs** (also known as *overhead*) are costs that do not vary with production or sales level. For example, a company must pay each month's bills for rent, heat, interest, and executive salaries, whatever the company's output. **Variable costs** vary directly with the level of production. Each personal computer produced by Hewlett Packard involves a cost of computer chips, wires, plastic, packaging, and other inputs. These costs tend to be the same for each unit produced. They are called variable because their total varies with the number of units produced. **Total costs** are the sum of the fixed and variable costs for any given level of production. Management wants to charge a price that will at least cover the total production costs at a given level of production.

The company must watch its costs carefully. If it costs the company more than competitors to produce and sell its product, the company will have to charge a higher price or make less profit, putting it at a competitive disadvantage.

HASTA AQUI

COSTS AT DIFFERENT LEVELS OF PRODUCTION To price wisely, management needs to know how its costs vary with different levels of production. For example, suppose Texas Instruments (TI) has built a plant to produce 1,000 calculators per day. Figure 10.2A shows the typical short-run average cost curve (SRAC). It shows that the cost per calculator is high if TI's factory produces only a few per day. But as production moves up to 1,000 calculators per

FIGURE 10.2
Cost per unit at different levels of production per period

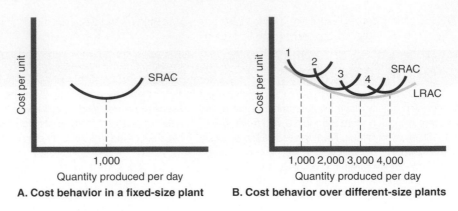

A. Cost behavior in a fixed-size plant   B. Cost behavior over different-size plants

day, average cost falls. This is because fixed costs are spread over more units, with each one bearing a smaller share of the fixed cost. TI can try to produce more than 1,000 calculators per day, but average costs will increase because the plant becomes inefficient. Workers have to wait for machines, the machines break down more often, and workers get in each other's way.

If TI believed it could sell 2,000 calculators a day, it should consider building a larger plant. The plant would use more efficient machinery and work arrangements. Also, the unit cost of producing 2,000 calculators per day would be lower than the unit cost of producing 1,000 units per day, as shown in the long-run average cost (LRAC) curve (Figure 10.2B). In fact, a 3,000-capacity plant would even be more efficient, according to Figure 10.2B. But a 4,000 daily production plant would be less efficient because of increasing diseconomies of scale—too many workers to manage, paperwork slowing things down, and so on. Figure 10.2B shows that a 3,000-daily production plant is the best size to build if demand is strong enough to support this level of production.

COSTS AS A FUNCTION OF PRODUCTION EXPERIENCE Suppose TI runs a plant that produces 3,000 calculators per day. As TI gains experience in producing calculators, it learns how to do it better. Workers learn shortcuts and become more familiar with their equipment. With practice, the work becomes better organized, and TI finds better equipment and production processes. With higher volume, TI becomes more efficient and gains economies of scale. As a result, average cost tends to fall with accumulated production experience. This is shown in Figure 10.3.[9] Thus, the average cost of producing the first 100,000 calculators is $10 per calculator. When the company has produced the first 200,000 calculators, the average cost has fallen to $9. After its accumulated production experience doubles again to 400,000, the average cost is $7. This drop in the average cost with accumulated production experience is called the **experience curve** (or the **learning curve**).

Experience curve (learning curve)

The drop in the average per-unit production cost that comes with accumulated production experience.

If a downward-sloping experience curve exists, this is highly significant for the company. Not only will the company's unit production cost fall, but it will fall faster if the company makes and sells more during a given time period. But the market has to stand ready to buy the higher output. And to take advantage of the experience curve, TI must get a large market share early in the product's life cycle. This suggests the following pricing strategy: TI should price its calculators low; its sales will then increase, and its costs will decrease through gaining more experience, and then it can lower its prices further.

Some companies have built successful strategies around the experience curve. For example, Bausch & Lomb solidified its position in the soft contact lens market by using computer-

FIGURE 10.3
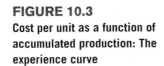
Cost per unit as a function of accumulated production: The experience curve

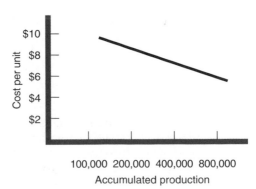

ized lens design and steadily expanding its one Soflens plant. As a result, its market share climbed steadily to 65 percent.

However, a single-minded focus on reducing costs and exploiting the experience curve will not always work. Experience-curve pricing carries some major risks. The aggressive pricing might give the product a cheap image. The strategy also assumes that competitors are weak and not willing to fight it out by meeting the company's price cuts. Finally, while the company is building volume under one technology, a competitor may find a lower-cost technology that lets it start at prices lower than those of the market leader, who still operates on the old experience curve.

Organizational Considerations

Management must decide who within the organization should set prices. Companies handle pricing in a variety of ways. In small companies, prices are often set by top management rather than by the marketing or sales departments. In large companies, pricing is typically handled by divisional or product line managers. In industrial markets, salespeople may be allowed to negotiate with customers within certain price ranges. Even so, top management sets the pricing objectives and policies, and it often approves the prices proposed by lower-level management or salespeople.

In industries in which pricing is a key factor (aerospace, steel, railroads, oil companies), companies often have a pricing department to set the best prices or to help others in setting them. This department reports to the marketing department or top management. Others who have an influence on pricing include sales managers, production managers, finance managers, and accountants.

External Factors Affecting Pricing Decisions

External factors that affect pricing decisions include the nature of the market and demand, competition, and other environmental elements.

The Market and Demand

Whereas costs set the lower limit of prices, the market and demand set the upper limit. Both consumer and industrial buyers balance the price of a product or service against the benefits of owning it. Thus, before setting prices, the marketer must understand the relationship between price and demand for its product. In this section, we explain how the price–demand relationship varies for different types of markets and how buyer perceptions of price affect the pricing decision. We then discuss methods for measuring the price–demand relationship.

PRICING IN DIFFERENT TYPES OF MARKETS The seller's pricing freedom varies with different types of markets. Economists recognize four types of markets, each presenting a different pricing challenge.

Under _pure competition_, the market consists of many buyers and sellers trading in a uniform commodity such as wheat, copper, or financial securities. No single buyer or seller has much effect on the going market price. A seller cannot charge more than the going price, because buyers can obtain as much as they need at the going price. Nor would sellers charge less than the market price, because they can sell all they want at this price. If price and profits rise, new sellers can easily enter the market. In a purely competitive market, marketing research, product development, pricing, advertising, and sales promotion play little or no role. Thus, sellers in these markets do not spend much time on marketing strategy.

Under _monopolistic competition_, the market consists of many buyers and sellers who trade over a range of prices rather than a single market price. A range of prices occurs because sellers can differentiate their offers to buyers. Either the physical product can be varied in quality, features, or style, or the accompanying services can be varied. Buyers see differences in sellers' products and will pay different prices for them. Sellers try to develop differentiated offers for different customer segments and, in addition to price, freely use branding, advertising, and personal selling to set their offers apart. Thus, Moen differentiates its faucets and other fixtures through strong branding and advertising, reducing the impact of price. Because there are many competitors in such markets, each firm is less affected by competitors' pricing strategies than in oligopolistic markets.

Under _oligopolistic competition_, the market consists of a few sellers who are highly sensitive to each other's pricing and marketing strategies. The product can be uniform (steel, aluminum) or nonuniform (cars, computers). There are few sellers because it is

■ Monopolistic competition: Moen sets its products apart though strong branding and advertising, reducing the impact of price.

difficult for new sellers to enter the market. Each seller is alert to competitors' strategies and moves. If a steel company slashes its price by 10 percent, buyers will quickly switch to this supplier. The other steelmakers must respond by lowering their prices or increasing their services.

In a *pure monopoly*, the market consists of one seller. The seller may be a government monopoly (the U.S. Postal Service), a private regulated monopoly (a power company), or a private nonregulated monopoly (DuPont when it introduced nylon). Pricing is handled differently in each case. In a regulated monopoly, the government permits the company to set rates that will yield a "fair return." Nonregulated monopolies are free to price at what the market will bear. However, they do not always charge the full price for a number of reasons: a desire not to attract competition, a desire to penetrate the market faster with a low price, or a fear of government regulation.

CONSUMER PERCEPTIONS OF PRICE AND VALUE In the end, the consumer will decide whether a product's price is right. Pricing decisions, like other marketing mix decisions, must be buyer oriented. When consumers buy a product, they exchange something of value (the price) to get something of value (the benefits of having or using the product). Effective, buyer-oriented pricing involves understanding how much value consumers place on the benefits they receive from the product and setting a price that fits this value.

A company often finds it hard to measure the values customers will attach to its product. For example, calculating the cost of ingredients in a meal at a fancy restaurant is relatively easy. But assigning a value to other satisfactions such as taste, environment, relaxation, conversation, and status is very hard. And these values will vary both for different consumers and different situations. Still, consumers will use these values to evaluate a product's price. If customers perceive that the price is greater than the product's value, they will not buy the product. If consumers perceive that the price is below the product's value, they will buy it, but the seller loses profit opportunities.

FIGURE 10.4
Demand curves

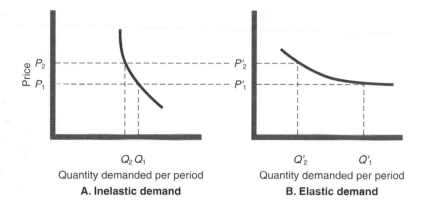

Q₂ Q₁
Quantity demanded per period
A. Inelastic demand

Q'₂   Q'₁
Quantity demanded per period
B. Elastic demand

Demand curve

A curve that shows the number of units the market will buy in a given time period, at different prices that might be charged.

ANALYZING THE PRICE–DEMAND RELATIONSHIP Each price the company might charge will lead to a different level of demand. The relationship between the price charged and the resulting demand level is shown in the **demand curve** in Figure 10.4. The demand curve shows the number of units the market will buy in a given time period at different prices that might be charged. In the normal case, demand and price are inversely related; that is, the higher the price, the lower the demand. Thus, the company would sell less if it raised its price from P_1 to P_2. In short, consumers with limited budgets probably will buy less of something if its price is too high.

In the case of prestige goods, the demand curve sometimes slopes upward. Consumers think that higher prices mean more quality. For example, a while back, Gibson Guitar Corporation toyed with the idea of lowering its prices to compete more effectively with Japanese rivals. To its surprise, Gibson found that its instruments didn't sell as well at lower prices. "We had an inverse [price–demand relationship]," noted Gibson's CEO. "The more we charged, the more product we sold." At a time when other guitar manufacturers are building their instruments more quickly, cheaply, and in greater numbers, Gibson still promises guitars that are made one-at-a-time, by hand. "Real pickers put Gibson Guitar on a pedestal," says an analyst. "Gibson builds instruments that are held in unparalleled esteem by many guitarists, including some of the world's top professional musicians." It turns out that low prices simply aren't consistent with such quality.[10] Still, if the company charges too high a price, the level of demand will be lower.

■ The demand curve sometimes slopes upward: Gibson was surprised to learn that its high-quality instruments didn't sell as well at lower prices.

Most companies try to measure their demand curves by estimating demand at different prices. The type of market makes a difference. In a monopoly, the demand curve shows the total market demand resulting from different prices. If the company faces competition, its demand at different prices will depend on whether competitors' prices stay constant or change with the company's own prices.

In measuring the price–demand relationship, the market researcher must not allow other factors affecting demand to vary. For example, if Sony increased its advertising at the same time that it lowered its television prices, we would not know how much of the increased demand was due to the lower prices and how much was due to the increased advertising. The same problem arises if a holiday weekend occurs when the lower price is set—more gift giving over the holidays causes people to buy more televisions. Economists show the impact of nonprice factors on demand through shifts in the demand curve rather than movements along it.

Price elasticity

A measure of the sensitivity of demand to changes in price.

PRICE ELASTICITY OF DEMAND Marketers also need to know **price elasticity**—how responsive demand will be to a change in price. Consider the two demand curves in Figure 10.4. In Figure 10.4A, a price increase from P_1 to P_2 leads to a relatively small drop in demand from Q_1 to Q_2. In Figure 10.4B, however, the same price increase leads to a large drop in demand from Q'_1 to Q'_2. If demand hardly changes with a small change in price, we say the demand is *inelastic*. If demand changes greatly, we say the demand is *elastic*. The price elasticity of demand is given by the following formula:

$$\text{Price Elasticity of Demand} = \frac{\%\ \text{Change in Quantity Demanded}}{\%\ \text{Change in Price}}$$

Suppose demand falls by 10 percent when a seller raises its price by 2 percent. Price elasticity of demand is therefore −5 (the minus sign confirms the inverse relation between price and demand) and demand is elastic. If demand falls by 2 percent with a 2 percent increase in price, then elasticity is −1. In this case, the seller's total revenue stays the same: The seller sells fewer items but at a higher price that preserves the same total revenue. If demand falls by 1 percent when price is increased by 2 percent, then elasticity is −1/2 and demand is inelastic. The less elastic the demand, the more it pays for the seller to raise the price.

What determines the price elasticity of demand? Buyers are less price sensitive when the product they are buying is unique or when it is high in quality, prestige, or exclusiveness. They are also less price sensitive when substitute products are hard to find or when they cannot easily compare the quality of substitutes. Finally, buyers are less price sensitive when the total expenditure for a product is low relative to their income or when the cost is shared by another party.[11]

If demand is elastic rather than inelastic, sellers will consider lowering their prices. A lower price will produce more total revenue. This practice makes sense as long as the extra costs of producing and selling more do not exceed the extra revenue. At the same time, most firms want to avoid pricing that turns their products into commodities. In recent years, forces such as deregulation and the instant price comparisons afforded by the Internet and other technologies have increased consumer price sensitivity, turning products ranging from telephones and computers to new automobiles into commodities in consumers' eyes.

Marketers need to work harder than ever to differentiate their offerings when a dozen competitors are selling virtually the same product at a comparable or lower price. More than ever, companies need to understand the price sensitivity of their customers and prospects and the trade-offs people are willing to make between price and product characteristics. In the words of marketing consultant Kevin Clancy, those who target only the price sensitive are "leaving money on the table."

Even in the energy marketplace, where you would think that a kilowatt is a kilowatt is a kilowatt, some utility companies are beginning to wake up to this fact. They are differentiating their power, branding it, and marketing it, even if it means higher prices. For example, Green Mountain Energy Company targets consumers who are not only concerned with the environment but are also willing to support their attitudes with dollars. Offering electricity made from cleaner sources such as water, wind, and natural gas, Green Mountain Energy Company positions itself as "the nation's leading brand of cleaner electricity." By providing energy from clean, renewable sources and developing products and services that help consumers protect the environment, GME completes successfully against "cheaper" brands that

■ By pledging leadership in providing clean, renewable energy sources and helping consumers protect the environment, GME completes successfully against "cheaper" brands that focused on more price-sensitive consumers.

Choose electricity that's 100% pollution-free

Want an easy way to help clean the air we breathe? Choose clean electricity from Green Mountain Energy Company. Green Mountain Energy® electricity is 100 percent pollution-free, because it's produced solely from wind and water.

In fact, by choosing *Green Mountain Energy* electricity, you can prevent as much carbon dioxide as your car makes in over 13,000 miles. This is a significant reduction in the average American household's share of CO_2 emissions!

And since all that's changing is how your electricity is generated, not how it comes to your home, your electric service will be just as reliable as always.

Make the choice for cleaner electricity. Sign up today.

1-888-749-5201

Green Mountain Energy®

www.greenmountain.com

focus on more price-sensitive consumers. "Is helping to clean the air worth the price of a movie?" the company asks. "That's about how much extra it costs each month when you choose cleaner, Green Mountain Energy electricity."[12]

Competitors' Costs, Prices, and Offers

In setting its prices, the company must also consider competitors' costs and prices and possible competitor reactions to the company's own pricing moves. A consumer who is considering the purchase of a Sony digital camera will evaluate Sony's price and value against the prices and values of comparable products made by Nikon, Kodak, Canon, Olympus, and others. In addition, the company's pricing strategy may affect the nature of the competition it faces. If Sony follows a high-price, high-margin strategy, it may attract competition. A low-price, low-margin strategy, however, may stop competitors or drive them out of the market. Sony needs to benchmark its costs and value against competitors' costs and value. It can then use these benchmarks as a starting point for its own pricing.

Other External Factors

When setting prices, the company also must consider a number of other factors in its external environment. *Economic conditions* can have a strong impact on the firm's pricing strategies. Economic factors such as boom or recession, inflation, and interest rates affect pricing decisions because they affect both the costs of producing a product and consumer perceptions of the product's price and value. The company must also consider what impact its prices will have on other parties in its environment. How will *resellers* react to various prices? The company should set prices that give resellers a fair profit, encourage their support, and help them to sell the product effectively. The *government* is another important external influence on pricing decisions. Finally, *social concerns* may have to be taken into account. In setting prices, a company's short-term sales, market share, and profit goals may have to be tempered by broader societal considerations.

AQUI
HASTA
FINAL

General Pricing Approaches

The price the company charges will be somewhere between one that is too low to produce a profit and one that is too high to produce any demand. Figure 10.5 summarizes the major considerations in setting price. Product costs set a floor to the price; consumer perceptions of the product's value set the ceiling. Between these two extremes, the company must consider competitors' prices and other external and internal factors to find the best price.

Companies set prices by selecting a general pricing approach that includes one or more of these three sets of factors. We will examine the following approaches: the *cost-based approach* (cost-plus pricing, break-even analysis, and target profit pricing), the *buyer-based approach* (value-based pricing), and the *competition-based approach* (going-rate and sealed-bid pricing).

Cost-Based Pricing

Cost-plus pricing
Adding a standard markup to the cost of the product.

The simplest pricing method is **cost-plus pricing**—adding a standard markup to the cost of the product. Construction companies, for example, submit job bids by estimating the total project cost and adding a standard markup for profit. Lawyers, accountants, and other professionals typically price by adding a standard markup to their costs. Some sellers tell their customers they will charge cost plus a specified markup; for example, aerospace companies price this way to the government.

To illustrate markup pricing, suppose a toaster manufacturer had the following costs and expected sales:

Variable cost	$10
Fixed costs	$300,000
Expected unit sales	50,000

Then the manufacturer's cost per toaster is given by:

$$\text{Unit Cost} = \text{Variable Cost} + \frac{\text{Fixed Costs}}{\text{Unit Sales}} = \$10 + \frac{\$300,000}{50,000} = \$16$$

Now suppose the manufacturer wants to earn a 20 percent markup on sales.
The manufacturer's markup price is given by:[13]

$$\text{Markup Price} = \frac{\text{Unit Cost}}{(1 - \text{Desired Return on Sales})} = \frac{\$16}{1 - .2} = \$20$$

The manufacturer would charge dealers $20 a toaster and make a profit of $4 per unit. The dealers, in turn, will mark up the toaster. If dealers want to earn 50 percent on sales price, they will mark up the toaster to $40 ($20 + 50% of $40). This number is equivalent to a *markup on cost* of 100 percent ($20/$20).

Does using standard markups to set prices make sense? Generally, no. Any pricing method that ignores demand and competitor prices is not likely to lead to the best price. Suppose the toaster manufacturer charged $20 but sold only 30,000 toasters instead of 50,000. Then the unit cost would have been higher because the fixed costs are spread over fewer units, and the realized percentage markup on sales would have been lower. Markup pricing works only if that price actually brings in the expected level of sales.

Still, markup pricing remains popular for many reasons. First, sellers are more certain about costs than about demand. By tying the price to cost, sellers simplify pricing—they do not have to make frequent adjustments as demand changes. Second, when all firms in the industry use this pricing method, prices tend to be similar and price competition is thus min-

FIGURE 10.5
Major considerations in setting price

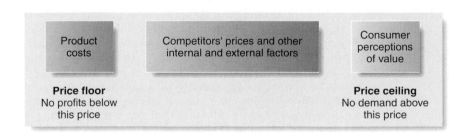

imized. Third, many people feel that cost-plus pricing is fairer to both buyers and sellers. Sellers earn a fair return on their investment but do not take advantage of buyers when buyers' demand becomes great.

Break-Even Analysis and Target Profit Pricing

Break-even pricing (target profit pricing)

Setting price to break even on the costs of making and marketing a product; or setting price to make a target profit.

Another cost-oriented pricing approach is **break-even pricing**, or a variation called **target profit pricing**. The firm tries to determine the price at which it will break even or make the target profit it is seeking. Such pricing is used by General Motors, which prices its automobiles to achieve a 15 to 20 percent profit on its investment. This pricing method is also used by public utilities, which are constrained to make a fair return on their investment.

Target pricing uses the concept of a *break-even chart*, which shows the total cost and total revenue expected at different sales volume levels. Figure 10.6 shows a break-even chart for the toaster manufacturer discussed here. Fixed costs are $300,000 regardless of sales volume. Variable costs are added to fixed costs to form total costs, which rise with volume. The total revenue curve starts at zero and rises with each unit sold. The slope of the total revenue curve reflects the price of $20 per unit.

The total revenue and total cost curves cross at 30,000 units. This is the *break-even volume*. At $20, the company must sell at least 30,000 units to break even; that is, for total revenue to cover total cost. Break-even volume can be calculated using the following formula:

$$\text{Break-Even Volume} = \frac{\text{Fixed Cost}}{\text{Price} - \text{Variable Cost}} = \frac{\$300,000}{\$20 - \$10} = 30,000$$

If the company wants to make a target profit, it must sell more than 30,000 units at $20 each. Suppose the toaster manufacturer has invested $1,000,000 in the business and wants to set price to earn a 20 percent return, or $200,000. In that case, it must sell at least 50,000 units at $20 each. If the company charges a higher price, it will not need to sell as many toasters to achieve its target return. But the market may not buy even this lower volume at the higher price. Much depends on the price elasticity and competitors' prices.

The manufacturer should consider different prices and estimate break-even volumes, probable demand, and profits for each. This is done in Table 10.1. The table shows that as price increases, break-even volume drops (column 2). But as price increases, demand for the toasters also falls off (column 3). At the $14 price, because the manufacturer clears only $4 per toaster ($14 less $10 in variable costs), it must sell a very high volume to break even. Even though the low price attracts many buyers, demand still falls below the high break-even point, and the manufacturer loses money. At the other extreme, with a $22 price the manufacturer clears $12 per toaster and must sell only 25,000 units to break even. But at this high price, consumers buy too few toasters, and profits are negative. The table shows that a price of $18 yields the highest profits. Note that none of the prices produce the manufacturer's target profit of $200,000. To achieve this target return, the manufacturer will have to search for ways to lower fixed or variable costs, thus lowering the break-even volume.

FIGURE 10.6
Break-even chart for determining target price

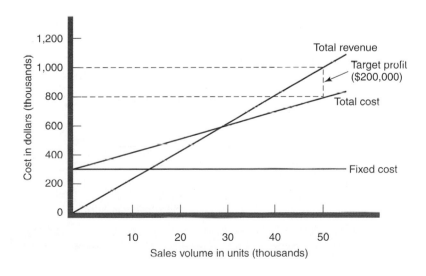

TABLE 10.1   Break-Even Volume and Profits at Different Prices

(1) Price	(2) Unit Demand Needed to Break Even	(3) Expected Unit Demand at Given Price	(4) Total Revenue (1) × (3)	(5) Total Costs*	(6) Profit (4) − (5)
$14	75,000	71,000	$ 994,000	$1,010,000	−$ 16,000
16	50,000	67,000	1,072,000	970,000	102,000
18	37,500	60,000	1,080,000	900,000	180,000
20	30,000	42,000	840,000	720,000	120,000
22	25,000	23,000	506,000	530,000	−24,000

* Assumes fixed costs of $300,000 and constant unit variable costs of $10.

 Value-Based Pricing

Value-based pricing

Setting price based on buyers' perceptions of value rather than on the seller's cost.

An increasing number of companies are basing their prices on the product's perceived value. **Value-based pricing** uses buyers' perceptions of value, not the seller's cost, as the key to pricing. Value-based pricing means that the marketer cannot design a product and marketing program and then set the price. Price is considered along with the other marketing mix variables *before* the marketing program is set.

Figure 10.7 compares cost-based pricing with value-based pricing. Cost-based pricing is product driven. The company designs what it considers to be a good product, totals the costs of making the product, and sets a price that covers costs plus a target profit. Marketing must then convince buyers that the product's value at that price justifies its purchase. If the price turns out to be too high, the company must settle for lower markups or lower sales, both resulting in disappointing profits.

Value-based pricing reverses this process. The company sets its target price based on customer perceptions of the product value. The targeted value and price then drive decisions about product design and what costs can be incurred. As a result, pricing begins with analyzing consumer needs and value perceptions, and price is set to match consumers' perceived value. It's important to remember that "good value" is not the same as "low price." For example, Montblanc pens sell for several hundred dollars or more. A less expensive pen might write as well, but some consumers place great value on the intangibles they receive from a "fine writing instrument."

A company using value-based pricing must find out what value buyers assign to different competitive offers. However, measuring perceived value can be difficult. Sometimes, companies ask consumers how much they would pay for a basic product and for each benefit added to the offer. Or a company might conduct experiments to test the perceived value of different product offers. According to an old Russian proverb, there are two fools in every market—one who asks too much and one who asks too little. If the seller charges more than the buyers' perceived value, the company's sales will suffer. If the seller charges less, its products sell very well. But they produce less revenue than they would if they were priced at the level of perceived value.

FIGURE 10.7

Cost-based versus value-based pricing

Source: Thomas T. Nagle and Reed K. Holden, The Strategy and Tactics of Pricing, *3rd ed. (Upper Saddle River, N.J.: Prentice Hall, 2002), p. 4.*

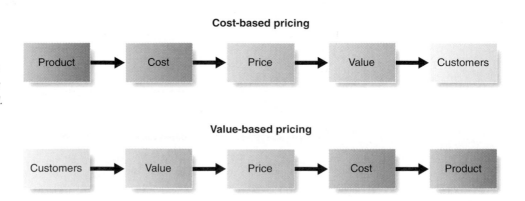

Cost-based pricing

Product → Cost → Price → Value → Customers

Value-based pricing

Customers → Value → Price → Cost → Product

■ Perceived value: A less expensive pen might write as well, but some consumers place great value on the intangibles they receive from a "fine writing instrument" such as a Montblanc.

Value Pricing

Value pricing
Offering just the right combination of quality and good service at a fair price.

During the past decade, marketers have noted a fundamental shift in consumer attitudes toward price and quality. Many companies have changed their pricing approaches to bring them into line with changing economic conditions and consumer price perceptions. More and more, marketers have adopted **value pricing** strategies—offering just the right combination of quality and good service at a fair price. In many cases, this has involved introducing less expensive versions of established, brand name products. Holiday Inn opened Holiday Express budget hotels, Revlon's Charles of the Ritz offered the Express Bar collection of affordable cosmetics, and fast-food restaurants such as Taco Bell and McDonald's offered "value menus." In other cases, value pricing has involved redesigning existing brands to offer more quality for a given price or the same quality for less.

An important type of value pricing at the retail level is *everyday low pricing (EDLP)*. EDLP involves charging a constant, everyday low price with few or no temporary price discounts. In contrast, *high-low pricing* involves charging higher prices on an everyday basis but running frequent promotions to lower prices temporarily on selected items. In recent years, high-low pricing has given way to EDLP in retail settings ranging from Saturn car dealerships to upscale department stores such as Nordstrom.

The king of EDLP is Wal-Mart, which practically defined the concept. Except for a few sale items every month, Wal-Mart promises everyday low prices on everything it sells. In contrast, Kmart's recent attempts to match Wal-Mart's EDLP strategy failed. To offer everyday low prices, a company must first have everyday low costs. However, because Kmart's costs are much higher than Wal-Mart's, it could not make money at the lower prices and quickly abandoned the attempt.[14]

Value-Added Marketing

In many business-to-business marketing situations, the challenge is to build the company's *pricing power*—its power to escape price competition and to justify higher prices and margins without losing market share. To retain pricing power, a firm must retain or build the value of

Real Marketing 10.2

Pricing Power: The Value of Value Added

When a company finds its major competitors offering a similar product at a lower price, the natural tendency is to try to match or beat that price. Although the idea of undercutting competitors' prices and watching customers flock to you is tempting, there are dangers. Successive rounds of price-cutting can lead to price wars that erode the profit margins of all competitors in an industry. Or worse, discounting a product can cheapen it in the minds of customers, greatly reducing the seller's power to maintain profitable prices in the long term. "It ends up being a losing battle," notes one marketing executive. "You focus away from quality, service, prestige—the things brands are all about."

So, how can a company keep its pricing power when a competitor undercuts its price? Often, the best strategy is not to price below the competitor, but rather to price above and convince customers that the product is worth it. The company should ask, "What is the value of the product to the customer?" then stand up for what the product is worth. In this way, the company shifts the focus from price to value.

But what if the company is operating in a "commodity" business, in which the products of all competitors seem pretty much alike? In such cases, the company must find ways to "decommoditize" its products—to create superior value for customers. It can do this by developing value-added features and services that differentiate its offer and justify higher prices and margins. Here are some examples of how suppliers are using value-added features and services to give them a competitive edge:

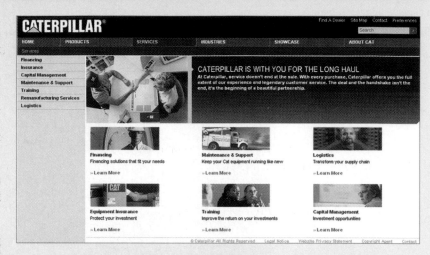

■ Value added: Caterpillar offers its dealers a wide range of value-added services—from guaranteed parts delivery to investment management advice and equipment training. Such added value supports a higher price.

■ *Caterpillar:* Caterpillar charges premium prices for its heavy construction and mining equipment by convincing customers that its products and service justify every additional cent—or, rather, the extra tens of thousands of dollars. Caterpillar typically reaps a 20 to 30 percent price premium over competitors—that can amount to an extra $200,000 or more on one of those huge yellow million-dollar dump trucks.

When a large potential customer says, "I can get it for less from a competitor," the Caterpillar dealer doesn't discount the price. Instead, the dealer explains that, even at the higher price, Cat offers the best value. Caterpillar equipment is designed with

its marketing offer. This is especially true for suppliers of commodity products, which are characterized by little differentiation and intense price competition.

In such cases, many companies adopt *value-added* strategies. Rather than cutting prices to match competitors, they attach value-added services to differentiate their offers and thus support higher margins (see Real Marketing 10.2). "Even in today's economic environment, it's not about price," says a pricing expert. "It's about keeping customers loyal by providing service they can't find anywhere else."[15]

 ## Competition-Based Pricing

Competition-based pricing

Setting prices based on the prices that competitors charge for similar products

Consumers will base their judgments of a product's value on the prices that competitors charge for similar products. One form of **competition-based pricing** is *going-rate pricing*, in which a firm bases its price largely on competitors' prices, with less attention paid to its own costs or to demand. The firm might charge the same as, more than, or less than its major competitors.

In oligopolistic industries that sell a commodity such as steel, paper, or fertilizer, firms normally charge the same price. The smaller firms follow the leader: They change their prices when the market leader's prices change, rather than when their own demand or costs change. Some firms may charge a bit more or less, but they hold the amount of difference constant. Thus, minor gasoline retailers usually charge a few cents less than the major oil companies, without letting the difference increase or decrease.

Going-rate pricing is quite popular. When demand elasticity is hard to measure, firms feel that the going price represents the collective wisdom of the industry concerning the price that

modular components that can be removed and repaired quickly, minimizing machine downtime. Caterpillar dealers carry an extensive parts inventory and guarantee delivery within 48 hours anywhere in the world, again minimizing downtime. Cat's products are designed to be rebuilt, providing a "second life" that competitors cannot match. As a result, Caterpillar used-equipment prices are often 20 percent to 30 percent higher.

In all, the dealer explains, even at the higher initial price, Caterpillar equipment delivers the lowest total cost per cubic yard of earth moved, ton of coal uncovered, or mile of road graded over the life of the product—guaranteed! Most customers seem to agree with Caterpillar's value proposition—the market-leading company dominates its markets with a more than 40 percent worldwide market share.

- *Pioneer Hi-Bred International:* A major supplier of corn seed and other agricultural products often thought of as commodities, DuPont subsidiary Pioneer Hi-Bred hardly acts like a commodity supplier. Its patented hybrid seeds yield 10 percent more corn than competitors' seeds. But beyond producing a superior product, Pioneer Hi-Bred provides a bundle of value-added services. For example, it equips its sales representatives with laptop computers that allow them to provide farmers with customized information and advice. The rep can plug in the type of hybrid that a farmer is using, along with information about pricing, acreage, and yield characteristics, then advise the farmer on how to do a better job of farm management. The reps can also supply farmers with everything from agricultural research reports to assistance in comparison shopping. Pioneer Hi-Bred also offers farmers crop insurance, financing, and marketing services.

Backing its claim "We believe in customer success" with superior products and value-added services gives Pioneer Hi-Bred plenty of pricing power. Despite charging a signifi-cant price premium—or perhaps because of it—the company's share of the North American corn market has grown from 35 percent during the mid-1980s to its current level of 44 percent.

- *Microsystems Engineering Company:* "The way we sell on value is by differentiating ourselves," says Mark Beckman, director of sales for Microsystems, a software company. "My product is twice as much as my nearest competitor's, but we sell as much as—if not more than   our competition." Rather than getting into price wars, Microsystems adds value to its products by adding new components and services. "[Customers] get more for their money," says Beckman. "We get the price because we understand what people want." When customers see the extra value, price becomes secondary. Ultimately, Beckman asserts, "let the customer decide whether the price you're charging is worth all the things they're getting." What if the answer is no? Beckman would suggest that dropping price is the last thing you want to do. Instead, look to the value of value added.

Sources: Erin Stout, "Keep Them Coming Back for More," *Sales & Marketing Management,* February 2002, pp. 51–52; "Pioneer Hi-Bred International, Inc.," *Hoover's Company Capsules,* Austin, March 15, 2004, p. 14440; and information accessed online at www.pioneer.com and www.caterpillar.com, December 2004. For other value-added pricing discussion and examples, see Stephanie N. Mehta, "How to Thrive when Prices Fall," *Fortune,* May 12, 2003, pp. 131–134; Alison Smith, "The Flip Side of Price," *Selling Power,* May 2003, pp. 28–30; and James C. Anderson and James A. Narus, *Business Market Management: Understanding, Creating, and Delivering Value* (Upper Saddle River, NJ: Prentice Hall, 2004) pp. 203–210 and elsewhere.

will yield a fair return. They also feel that holding to the going price will prevent harmful price wars.

Competition-based pricing is also used when firms *bid* for jobs. Using *sealed-bid pricing,* a firm bases its price on how it thinks competitors will price rather than on its own costs or on the demand. The firm wants to win a contract, and winning the contract requires pricing less than other firms. Yet the firm cannot set its price below a certain level. It cannot price below cost without harming its position. In contrast, the higher the company sets its price above its costs, the lower its chance of getting the contract.

> Reviewing the Concepts <

Price can be defined narrowly as the amount of money charged for a product or service. Or it can be defined more broadly as the sum of the values that consumers exchange for the benefits of having and using the product or service.

Despite the increased role of nonprice factors in the modern marketing process, price remains an important element in the marketing mix. It is the only element in the marketing mix that produces revenue; all other elements represent costs. Price is also one of the most flexible elements of the marketing mix. Unlike product features and channel commitments, price can be raised or lowered quickly.

Even so, many companies are not good at handling pricing—pricing decisions and price competition are major problems for many marketing executives. Pricing problems often arise because prices are too cost-oriented, not revised frequently enough to reflect market changes, and not consistent with the rest of the marketing mix.

1. Identify and define the internal factors affecting a firm's pricing decisions.
Many internal factors influence the company's pricing decisions, including the firm's *marketing objectives, marketing mix strategy, costs,* and *organization for pricing.* The pricing strategy is largely

determined by the company's *target market* and *positioning objectives*. Pricing decisions affect and are affected by product design, distribution, and promotion decisions. Therefore, pricing strategies must be carefully coordinated with the other marketing mix variables when designing the marketing program.

Costs set the floor for the company's price—the price must cover all the costs of making and selling the product, plus a fair rate of return. Common pricing objectives include survival, current profit maximization, market share leadership, and product quality leadership.

In order to coordinate pricing goals and decisions, management must decide who within the organization is responsible for setting price. In large companies, some pricing authority may be delegated to lower-level managers and salespeople, but top management usually sets pricing policies and approves proposed prices. Production, finance, and accounting managers also influence pricing decisions.

2. Identify and define the external factors affecting pricing decisions, including the impact of consumer perceptions of price and value.

External factors that influence pricing decisions include the nature of the *market and demand*; *competitors' prices and offers;* and factors such as the *economy, reseller needs,* and *government actions*. The seller's pricing freedom varies with different types of markets. Pricing is especially challenging in markets characterized by monopolistic competition or oligopoly.

Ultimately, the consumer decides whether the company has set the right price. The consumer weighs the price against the perceived values of using the product—if the price exceeds the sum of the values, consumers will not buy the product. The more *inelastic* the demand, the higher the company can set its price. Therefore, *demand* and *consumer value perceptions* set the ceiling for prices. Consumers differ in the values they assign to different product features, and marketers often vary their pricing strategies for different price segments. When assessing the market and demand, the company estimates the demand curve, which shows the probable quantity purchased per period at alternative price levels. Consumers also compare a product's price with the prices of *competitors'* products. As a result, a company must learn the price and quality of competitors' offers and use them as a starting point for its own pricing.

3. Contrast the three general approaches to setting prices.

A company can select one or a combination of three general pricing approaches: the *cost-based approach* (cost-plus pricing, break-even analysis, and target profit pricing), the *value-based approach*, and the *competition-based approach*. Cost-based pricing sets prices based on the seller's cost structure, whereas value-based pricing relies on consumer perceptions of value to drive pricing decisions. Competition-based pricing sets prices based on what competitors are charging.

> Reviewing the Key Terms <

Break-even pricing (target profit pricing) 321	Dynamic pricing 307	Fixed costs 313	Total costs 313
Competition-based pricing 324	Demand curve 317	Price 307	Value-based pricing 322
Cost-plus pricing 320	Experience curve (learning curve) 314	Price elasticity 318	Value pricing 323
		Target costing 310	Variable costs 313

> Discussing the Concepts <

1. The chapter points out that many companies do not handle pricing well. Beyond focusing too much on cost, what are some of the other difficulties that marketers have in setting prices?

2. What is target costing? For what product do you believe this approach would be most powerful?

3. Which three of the following external factors would have the greatest impact on setting the price for a 30-second commercial slot on Fox's "The OC"?

   ■ Perceived value
   ■ Competitors' prices
   ■ Economic conditions
   ■ Number of viewers

   ■ Government
   ■ Resellers
   ■ Social concerns
   ■ Viewer demographics

4. Explain why the elasticity of demand is such an important concept to marketers who market a "commodity"-type product?

5. Cost-plus-pricing and target-profit-pricing are two different types of cost-based pricing. Explain the differences between these two methods. Which of these methods is a better tool for marketers?

6. What pricing approach(es) does your college or university employ in setting tuition?

> Applying the Concepts <

1. What can you infer about the firm's marketing objectives, mix strategy, and costs based on the following positioning statement: "No one beats our prices. We crush the competition."

2. Go to a nearby Starbuck's and study its price list. Then, suppose that you are on the marketing team of Diedrich's Coffee (a Southwestern coffee house) and have been asked by Martin Diedrich to summarize Starbuck's pricing strategy in a few sentences. Based on the chapter's discussion of general pricing strategies, what would you report?

3. Given the following information, calculate the number of meals a restaurant would have to sell to break even:

   ■ Average meal price = $10.35
   ■ Meals sold = 8,560
   ■ Food = $27,653
   ■ Food labor = $18,386
   ■ Management = $4,855
   ■ Supplies = $3,133

   ■ Maintenance = $2,213
   ■ Marketing = $1,650
   ■ Insurance/legal = $1,904
   ■ Waste management = $988
   ■ Utilities = $3,159
   ■ Rent = $3,960

(For an online interactive break-even model, go to http://harvardbusinessonline.hbsp.harvard.edu/b01/en/academic/edu_tk_mkt_break_even.jhtml. Register and download the application. Use it as many times as you wish but be sure to read and observe the license restrictions.)

4. Burst-of-Energy is a food product positioned in the extreme sports market as a performance enhancer. A distributor of the product has seen an increase in demand for the product from 1 million units to 2 million units as depicted in the following chart. The manufacturer has done nothing to generate this increased demand, but there have been reports that two popular celebrities were photographed consuming the product. How could such a demand increase have happened? Based on the demand chart that follows, how would you characterize

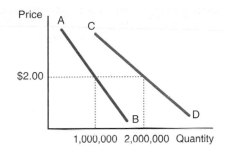

the demand for the product: Is it elastic or inelastic? Would you call this an example of fluctuating demand? Support your answers.

> Focus on Technology <

The Professional Pricing Society (PPS) is an association that supports price-decision makers and price-management personnel from a wide range of industries in more than 50 countries. Typical members of the PPS include pricing, marketing, and general management executives from Fortune 1000 and mid-sized firms. The PPS provides both strategic and information resources to its members through pricing conferences and workshops, monthly and quarterly publications, consulting services, pricing workbooks, and an active Internet site. Many sponsors of the PPS are high technology companies that provide the latest in pricing systems solution software. Setting market prices, revenue optimization, market measuring analytics, and answers designed to optimize difficult price decisions are just a few of the pricing issues tackled. Go to the PPS Web site at www.pricingsociety.com/tools.asp. Read the short PPS pricing systems sponsor descriptions and answer the following questions:

1. What products or services do the sponsoring companies provide?
2. What kinds of companies would use or not use such services? Explain.
3. Do you think that products and services such as these would be useful to smaller companies as well as larger ones?

> Focus on Ethics <

John Wenman, merchandising manager at Goodmark's stationery store, is setting the price for Craft fountain pens. The pens cost him $5 each. The store's usual markup is 50 percent over cost, which suggests that John should set the price at $7.50. However, to make this price seem like an unusually good bargain, John begins by offering the pen at $10. He realizes that he won't sell many pens at this inflated price, but he doesn't care. John holds the price at $10 for only a few days, and then cuts it to the usual level—$7.50—and advertises: "Terrific Bargain on Craft Pens. Were $10, Now Only $7.50!"

1. If consumers perceive Craft pens to be a good value at $10, is it fair for Goodmark's to sell the pen at that price?
2. Is John's price setting approach ethical? Is it legal? Explain.
3. How would you have set and advertised the Craft pen's price? Would you have used a cost-plus approach or some other method? Explain.

O| Video Case

Nextel

Last year, consumers across the world bought more than 500 million cell phones. And the market keeps growing both in the United States and abroad. So does the list of companies competing for cellular customers. In a market full of competitors, Nextel differentiates itself by tailoring its services to the needs of businesspeople. For example, Nextel offers easy conference calling, data management solutions, and global positioning services, including access to instant driving directions, programs to locate and deploy employees, and fleet and package tracking—all through its cell phone service.

Despite the company's range of targeted services, Nextel, like many cellular service providers, struggles to balance its marketing offers. In an industry so focused on pricing, how can a company build brand value through product and service benefits while offering competitive prices?

After viewing the video featuring Nextel, answer the following questions about pricing strategies.

1. How does Nextel's target market, business customers, affect its pricing decisions? How might the company's emphasis on service benefits and price differ if it targeted primarily leisure consumers?
2. If you have a cell phone, what factors led you to select your current provider? How important was price? If you do not have a cell phone, how did you select the service provider for your home phone?
3. Scan your local paper for ads offering cellular service. What strategies are service providers using to attract customers? Do you think these strategies are the most effective?

Company Case

Southwest Airlines: Waging War in Philly

BATTLE STATIONS!

In March 2004, US Airways CEO David Siegel addressed his employees via a Web-cast. "They're coming for one reason: They're coming to kill us. They beat us on the West Coast, they beat us in Baltimore, but if they beat us in Philadelphia they are going to kill us." Siegel exhorted his employees, emphasizing that US Airways had to repel Southwest Airlines when it joined the competition at the Philadelphia International Airport in May—or die.

On Sunday, May 9, 2004, at 5:05 A.M. (yes, A.M.), leisure passengers and some thrift-minded business people lined up to secure seats on Southwest's 7 A.M. flight from Philadelphia to Chicago—its inaugural flight from the new market. Other passengers scurried to get in line for a flight to Orlando—and why not? A family of six indicated it bought tickets for $49 each way, or $98 round trip. An equivalent round-trip ticket on US Air would have been $200.

Southwest employees, dressed in golf shirts and khaki pants or shorts, had decorated the ticket counters with lavender, red, and gold balloons and hustled to assist the throng of passengers. As the crowd blew noisemakers and hurled confetti, Herb Kelleher, Southwest's quirky CEO, shouted, "I hereby declare Philadelphia free from the tyranny of high fares!"

At 6:59 A.M., Southwest Flight 741 departed for Chicago.

THE WAR IS ON

You might wonder what's causing all this fuss. After all, isn't US Air firmly entrenched in Philadelphia, the nation's eighth-largest market, offering over 375 flights per day and controlling two-thirds of its 120 gates? Further, little Southwest, which only serves a total of 58 cities and 59 airports in 30 states, is offering only 14 flights a day from Philly and has only four gates. Even more, Southwest has a history of entering smaller, less expensive, more out-of-the-way airports where it didn't pose a direct threat to the major airlines, like US Air. Does Southwest really have a chance?

Thirty-three years ago, when Kelleher and a partner concocted a business plan on a cocktail napkin, most people didn't give Southwest much chance. It adopted a strategy completely in opposition to the industry's conventional wisdom. Its planes flew from "point-to-point" rather than using the "hub-and-spoke" pattern the major airlines have used. This gave it more flexibility to move planes around based on demand. Southwest served no meals, only snacks. It did not charge passengers a fee to change same-fare tickets. It had no assigned seats. It had no electronic entertainment, relying on comic flight attendants to entertain passengers. The airline did not offer a retirement plan; rather, it offered its employees a profit-sharing plan. [In 2003, that plan paid $126 million to the company's 31,000 employees.] Because of all this, Southwest had much lower costs than its competitors and was able to crush the competition with low fares.

Southwest has stuck with its strategy. In 2003, the company earned $442 million—more than all the other U.S. airlines *combined*. Over the last three years, Southwest earned $1.2 billion, while its competitors were *losing* a combined $22 billion. In May 2003, for the first time, it boarded more domestic customers than any other airline. From 1972 through 2002, *Money* magazine indicated that Southwest was the nation's best-performing stock—growing at a compound annual rate of 26 percent over the period! Moreover, while competing airlines laid off thousands of workers following the September 11 tragedy, Southwest didn't lay off a single employee and remained profitable every quarter—keeping its string of 31 straight profitable years intact! In 2004, its cost per average seat mile (CASM—the cost of flying one seat one mile) was 8.09 cents, as compared with between 9.42 and 11.18 for the big carriers.

LOW ON AMMUNITION

There are three problems for the major airlines, such as US Air, Delta, United, American, and Continental. First, "little" Southwest is not little any more. Second, many others, such as JetBlue, AirTran, ATA, and Virgin Atlantic, have adopted Southwest-like strategies. In fact, JetBlue and America West had CASMs of 5.90 and 7.72 cents, respectively. In 1990, discount airlines flew on just 159 of the nation's top 1,000 routes. In 2004, that number had risen to 754. As a result, the majors, who used to believe they could earn a 30 percent price premium, were lucky to get a 10 percent premium, if that. Third, and most importantly, the major (or legacy) airlines had high cost structures that were difficult to change. They had more long-service employees who earned higher pay and received expensive pension and health benefits. Many had unions, which worked hard to protect employee pay and benefits.

ATTACK AND COUNTERATTACK

US Air has experienced Southwest's attacks before. In the late 1980s, Southwest entered the California market, where US Air had a 58 percent market share on its routes. By the mid-90s, Southwest had forced US Air to abandon those routes. On the Oakland to Burbank route, average one-way fares fell from $104 to $42—and traffic tripled. In the early 90s, Southwest entered Baltimore Washington International Airport, where US Air had a significant hub and a 55 percent market share. By 2004, US Air had only 4.9 percent of BWI traffic, with Southwest ranking number one at 47 percent.

So, USAir knows it's in for a fight in Philly. Reluctantly, it has started to make changes. In preparation for Southwest's arrival, it began to re-shape its image as a high-fare, uncooperative carrier. It began to spread out its scheduling to reduce congestion and the resulting delays and to use two seldom-used runways to reduce bottlenecks. The company also lowered fares to match Southwest and dropped its requirement for a Saturday-night stay over on discounted flights.

US Air also began some new promotion tactics. It launched local TV spots on popular shows like "Friends," "American Idol," and "Frasier" to promote free massages, movie tickets, pizza, and flowers.

However, Herb Kelleher knows Philly won't be a cakewalk. The airport is known for its delays, congestion, bureaucracy, and baggage snafus—factors that work against Southwest's strategy of 20-minute turnarounds for its planes.

Therefore, Southwest has unveiled a new promotion plan for Philly. Kelleher ditched his tried-and-true, cookie-cutter approach. The airline held focus groups with local travelers to get their ideas on how it should promote its service—a first for Southwest. As a result, the airline developed a more intense ad campaign and assigned 50 percent more employees to the airport than it would in a customary launch. Southwest also recruited volunteers to stand on local street corners handing out free, inflatable airline hats, luggage tags, and antenna toppers. The airline is using billboards, TV, and radio to trumpet the accessibility of its low fares, pointing out that competitors make many fewer seats actually available at advertised low fares. The ads also note that frequent fliers earn free flights based on the number of Southwest flights, not based on mileage.

Southwest knows that Philadelphia passengers have other low-fare options, such as Frontier, AirTran, and America West. Further, some of the Southwest-wannabes are offering things like JetBlue's 24 channels of free TV and XM satellite radio at each seat in addition to low fares. Southwest will have to distinguish itself—just advertising low fares will not be enough anymore.

Questions for Discussion

1. How do Southwest Airlines' marketing objectives and its marketing mix strategy affect its pricing decisions?

2. What is the nature of costs in the airline industry? How does this affect pricing decisions?

3. How do the nature of the airline market and the demand for airline service affect Southwest's decisions?

4. What general pricing approaches have airlines pursued?

5. What pricing and other marketing recommendations would you make to Southwest as it enters the Philadelphia market?

Sources: "Let the Battle Begin," *Air Transport World*, May 2004, p. 9; Tom Belden, "Southwest Airlines Launches Low-Fare Service from Philadelphia's Airport," *Knight/Ridder/Tribune Business News*, May 11, 2004; Micheline Maynard, "Southwest Comes Calling, and a Race Begins," *The New York Times*, May 10, 2004; Tom Ramstack, "US Airways Faces Big Threat from Southwest Airlines in Philadelphia," *Knight Ridder/Tribune Business News*, May 8, 2004; Dan Fitzpatrick, "Southwest Airlines Challenges US Airways at Philadelphia Airport Hub," *Knight Ridder/Tribune Business News*, May 5, 2004; Melanie Trottman, "Destination: Philadelphia," *The Wall Street Journal*, May 4, 2004, p. B1; Eric Torbenson, "Rising Costs, Low-Fare Carriers Could Spell Doom for Big Airlines, Experts Say," *The Dallas Morning News*, April 8, 2004; Andy Serwer, Kate Bonamici, "Southwest Airlines: The Hottest Thing in the Sky," *Fortune*, March 8, 2004, p. 86.

11

> **After studying this chapter, you should be able to**

1. describe the major strategies for pricing imitative and new products
2. explain how companies find a set of prices that maximize the profits from the total product mix
3. discuss how companies adjust their prices to take into account different types of customers and situations
4. discuss the key issues related to initiating and responding to price changes

Pricing Products: Pricing Strategies

Previewing The Concepts

In the last chapter, you explored the many internal and external factors that affect a firm's pricing decisions and examined three general approaches to setting prices. In this chapter, we'll look at pricing strategies available to marketers—new-product pricing strategies, product mix pricing strategies, price adjustment strategies, and price reaction strategies.

Pricing decisions can make or break a company. For openers, consider Kmart, once the nation's most powerful discount retailers. Facing intense competition from the likes of Wal-Mart and Target, Kmart turned to price as its chief competitive weapon. It even rekindled its age-old BlueLight Specials, which had symbolized Kmart's early success. But in the end, BlueLight Specials meant lights out for Kmart.

Kmart was once the top discount retailer in the United States, with more stores and sales than any other chain in the country. Then came Wal-Mart. With its low-cost operations, efficient distribution, and "Always Low Prices, Always" positioning, Wal-Mart quickly left Kmart in its wake. Consumers soon learned that, day in and day out, without a doubt, Wal-Mart is the low-price leader—always. Throughout the 1980s and 1990s, Kmart struggled as Wal-Mart grew.

Then, in the 1990s, shoppers seeking a slightly classier discount store found Target, which offered an alternative to the bare-bones Wal-Mart atmosphere. Target positions itself strongly as the "upscale discounter." With its promise of "Expect More, Pay Less," Target delivers value with an upscale feel for those who are price conscious but not price obsessed.

The success of Wal-Mart and Target left Kmart in a positioning no-man's-land. With its prices higher than Wal-Mart's, and its stores less chic than Target's, Kmart could find no meaningful way to differentiate itself. So in early 2001, a desperate Kmart launched a repositioning campaign. It targeted family buyers and set out to establish itself as the place for moms to find great values every day on items ranging from clothing to cereal. However, rather than building the Kmart brand on value, the repositioning effort quickly—and tragically—degenerated into a focus on price.

For starters, Kmart slashed its everyday prices on more than 50,000 items in stores around the country to bring them within 2 percent of Wal-Mart's prices, as compared with 9 percent before the campaign. On top of this, rekindled its age-old BlueLight Specials, first offered years ago by an industrious store manager. For many consumers, the BlueLight Specials still symbolize Kmart's early success.

In December 1965, Earl Bartell, a 24-year-old Kmart store manager in Fort Wayne, Indiana, was having a problem getting rid of some holiday wrapping paper he had put on sale. Frankly, people were having trouble finding it. After thinking it over, he went to the sporting goods section and picked up a flashing lantern. He taped the lantern to the end of a two-by-four, which in turn he taped to a little stock cart. He rolled the cart to the sale aisle, turned on the flashing light, and made another announcement. This time, everyone went to the right place. Bartell continued to use this gimmick to feature other discounted items, and watched sales steadily improve. Within 6 months, the flashing lights were part of the landscape of every Kmart store in the country. The presence of BlueLight Specials in Kmart stores continued for more than 26 years. In 1991, a struggling Kmart officially killed the BlueLight Special in an effort to turn the chain around by cleaning house and getting rid of every reminder of the past. To this day, however, when many consumers think back to the good old days at Kmart, they remember those BlueLight Specials.

To kick off the repositioning campaign, Kmart launched a series of television ads featuring hip, animated blue spotlights dancing to Motown tunes and lowering everyday prices across the store. And, with hopes running high, Kmart introduced a new and improved version of its BlueLight Specials. The new program involved daylong discounts on certain items brought out in a cart every hour, flagged by sirens and a flashing blue light.

Despite the high hopes, the flashing blue lights signaled little more than "lights out" for Kmart. On the everyday-low-price front, Kmart simply could not outprice Wal-Mart. Its purchasing, distribution, and operating costs averaged 15 percent to 20 percent higher than Wal-Mart's. So in order to match Wal-Mart's prices, or even to come close, Kmart had to drop prices below cost.

To make matters worse, Kmart also failed to deliver consistently on the featured BlueLight Specials. As a result of disorganization and poor management, some stores carried the signage but didn't offer the specials. Accounts like the following were all too common:

> At one Chicago Kmart recently, a banner proclaims, "You are now entering the BlueLight Zone. Remain calm." Everyone does, because there is no BlueLight Special to be seen. A manager said one would be broadcast that day; pressed further, he promised it would happen within the hour. It didn't.

In addition, in too many cases, shoppers never had a chance to take advantage of BlueLight Always items, those supposedly offered at everyday low prices. Customers drawn to Kmart stores for advertised items often encountered only empty shelves.

At the height of the madness, Kmart launched a "Dare to Compare" campaign, in which it directly compared Kmart prices on specific products with those of other discounters, including Target and Wal-Mart. The campaign turned out to be a disaster. Kmart often got the comparisons wrong. In some cases, it quoted outdated or incorrect prices; in others, it compared products that other stores didn't even carry.

In the end, the BlueLight Specials and Dare to Compare campaigns kicked off a price war that Kmart had no chance of winning. Wal-Mart, the undisputed king of the discounters, responded in its usual ruthless way—by buckling down and cutting prices further. For Kmart, the results were disastrous—its losses mounted to more than $2.4 billion for the year. In early 2002, the once-dominant discount chain was forced into the largest bankruptcy in retail history, closing nearly a third of its stores and letting go more than 60,000 employees. Kmart's stock dropped by 68 percent in just 3 weeks. During that same time, sales at Target and Wal-Mart rose 8 percent.

Kmart emerged from bankruptcy in May of 2003 still searching for a tenable position. In late 2004, the once formidable retailer merged with Sears, and analysts speculated that the Kmart name would eventually be phased out altogether in favor of the stronger Sears name. Whatever happens from here, Kmart learned a hard pricing lesson. "To go head-to-head with a 10,000-pound gorilla is nonsense," asserts one retail consultant. "It's like Switzerland declaring war on the United States."[1]

As the Kmart example illustrates, pricing decisions are subject to an incredibly complex array of environmental and competitive forces. A company sets not a single price, but rather a pricing structure that covers different items in its line. This pricing structure changes over time as products move through their life cycles. The company adjusts product prices to reflect changes in costs and demand and to account for variations in buyers and situations. As the competitive environment changes, the company considers when to initiate price changes and when to respond to them.

This chapter examines the major dynamic pricing strategies available to marketers. In turn, we look at *new-product pricing strategies* for products in the introductory stage of the product life cycle, *product mix pricing strategies* for related products in the product mix, *price adjustment strategies* that account for customer differences and changing situations, and strategies for initiating and responding to *price changes*.[2]

AQUÍ

New-Product Pricing Strategies

Pricing strategies usually change as the product passes through its life cycle. The introductory stage is especially challenging. Companies bringing out a new product face the challenge of setting prices for the first time. They can choose between two broad strategies: *market-skimming pricing* and *market-penetration pricing*.

Market-Skimming Pricing

Market-skimming pricing

Setting a high price for a new product to skim maximum revenues layer by layer from the segments willing to pay the high price; the company makes fewer but more profitable sales.

Many companies that invent new products set high initial prices to "skim" revenues layer by layer from the market. Sony frequently uses this strategy, called **market-skimming pricing**. When Sony introduced the world's first high-definition television (HDTV) to the Japanese market in 1990, the high-tech sets cost $43,000. These televisions were purchased only by customers who could afford to pay a high price for the new technology. Sony rapidly reduced the price over the next several years to attract new buyers. By 1993 a 28-inch HDTV cost a Japanese buyer just over $6,000. In 2001, a Japanese consumer could buy a 40-inch HDTV for about $2,000, a price that many more customers could afford. An entry level HDTV set now sells for less than $1,000 in the United States, and prices continue to fall. In this way, Sony skimmed the maximum amount of revenue from the various segments of the market.[3]

Market skimming makes sense only under certain conditions. First, the product's quality and image must support its higher price, and enough buyers must want the product at that price. Second, the costs of producing a smaller volume cannot be so high that they cancel the advantage of charging more. Finally, competitors should not be able to enter the market easily and undercut the high price.

Market-Penetration Pricing

Market-penetration pricing

Setting a low price for a new product in order to attract a large number of buyers and a large market share.

Rather than setting a high initial price to skim off small but profitable market segments, some companies use **market-penetration pricing**. They set a low initial price in order to *penetrate* the market quickly and deeply—to attract a large number of buyers quickly and win a large market share. The high sales volume results in falling costs, allowing the company to cut its price even further. For example, Wal-Mart and other discount retailers use penetration pricing. And Dell used penetration pricing to enter the personal computer market, selling high-quality computer products through lower-cost direct channels. Its sales soared when IBM, Apple, and other competitors selling through retail stores could not match its prices.

Several conditions must be met for this low-price strategy to work. First, the market must be highly price sensitive so that a low price produces more market growth. Second, production and distribution costs must fall as sales volume increases. Finally, the low price must help keep out the competition, and the penetration pricer must maintain its low-price position—otherwise, the price advantage may be only temporary. For example, Dell faced difficult times when IBM and other competitors established their own direct distribution channels. However, through its dedication to low production and distribution costs, Dell has retained its price advantage and established itself as the industry's number one personal computer maker.

Product Mix Pricing Strategies

The strategy for setting a product's price often has to be changed when the product is part of a product mix. In this case, the firm looks for a set of prices that maximizes the profits on the total product mix. Pricing is difficult because the various products have related demand and costs and face different degrees of competition. We now take a closer look at the five product mix pricing situations summarized in Table 11.1: *product line pricing, optional-product pricing, captive-product pricing, by-product pricing,* and *product bundle pricing.*

Product Line Pricing

Companies usually develop product lines rather than single products. For example, Snapper makes many different lawn mowers, ranging from simple walk-behind versions priced at $259.95, $299.95, and $399.95, to elaborate "Yard Cruisers" and lawn tractors priced at

TABLE 11.1 **Product Mix Pricing Strategies**

Strategy	Description
Product line pricing	Setting price steps between product line items
Optional-product pricing	Pricing optional or accessory products sold with the main product
Captive-product pricing	Pricing products that must be used with the main product
By-product pricing	Pricing low-value by-products to get rid of them
Product bundle pricing	Pricing bundles of products sold together

Product line pricing

Setting the price steps between various products in a product line based on cost differences between the products, customer evaluations of different features, and competitors' prices.

$1,000 or more. Each successive lawn mower in the line offers more features. Sony offers not just one type of television, but several lines of televisions, each containing many models. It offers everything from Watchman portable color TVs starting at $99.99, to flat-screen Trinitrons ranging from $200 to $1,500, to its top-of-the-line plasma WEGA flat-panel sets running more than $5,000. In **product line pricing**, management must decide on the price steps to set between the various products in a line.

The price steps should take into account cost differences between the products in the line, customer evaluations of their different features, and competitors' prices. In many industries, sellers use well-established *price points* for the products in their line. Thus, men's clothing stores might carry men's suits at three price levels: $185, $325, and $495. The customer will probably associate low-, average-, and high-quality suits with the three price points. Even if the three prices are raised a little, men normally will buy suits at their own preferred price points. The seller's task is to establish perceived quality differences that support the price differences.

Optional-Product Pricing

Optional-product pricing

The pricing of optional or accessory products along with a main product.

Many companies use **optional-product pricing**—offering to sell optional or accessory products along with their main product. For example, a car buyer may choose to order power windows and a CD changer. Refrigerators come with optional ice makers.

Pricing these options is a sticky problem. Automobile companies have to decide which items to include in the base price and which to offer as options. Until recent years, General Motors' normal pricing strategy was to advertise a stripped-down model at a base price to pull people into showrooms and then to devote most of the showroom space to showing option-

■ Product line pricing: Gramophone makes a complete line of high quality sound systems, ranging in price from $5,000 to $120,000.

Mozart sacrificed his life to create beautiful music. Surely, you can afford $10,000.

There are two things you'll find only at Gramophone: The finest sound systems from $5,000 to $120,000. And a dedication to music that matches the passion of the people who created it.

GRAMOPHONE
VERY, VERY, VERY HI-FI
Lutherville 821-5690 • Ellicott City 465-5500

loaded cars at higher prices. The economy model was stripped of so many comforts and conveniences that most buyers rejected it. Then, GM and other U.S. car makers followed the example of the Japanese and German automakers and included in the sticker price many useful items previously sold only as options. Most advertised prices today represent a well-equipped car. However, during the recent economic downturn, the auto companies began to move some features back into the "options" category in order to reduce the prices of standard models.

Captive-Product Pricing

Captive-product pricing

Setting a price for products that must be used along with a main product, such as blades for a razor and film for a camera.

Companies that make products that must be used along with a main product are using **captive-product pricing**. Examples of captive products are razor blades, video games, and printer cartridges. Producers of the main products (razors, video game consoles, and printers) often price them low and set high markups on the supplies. Thus, Gillette sells low-priced razors but makes money on the replacement cartridges. U-Haul rents out trucks at low rates but commands high margins on accessories such as boxes, pads, insurance, and storage space rental. Hewlett-Packard (H-P) makes very low margins on its printers but very high margins on printer cartridges and other supplies.

Nintendo sells its game consoles at low prices and makes money on video games. In fact, whereas Nintendo's margins on its consoles run a mere 1 percent to 5 percent, margins on its game cartridges run close to 45 percent. Video game sales contribute more than half the company's profits. Similarly, Sony loses money on sales of its PlayStation two-game console. But the games themselves, while only accounting for 17 percent of sales, generate more than a third of Sony's profits.[4]

In the case of services, this strategy is called *two-part pricing*. The price of the service is broken into a *fixed fee* plus a *variable usage rate*. Thus, amusement parks charge admission plus fees for food, midway attractions, and rides over a minimum. Theaters charge admission, then generate additional revenues from concessions. And cell phone companies charge a flat rate for a basic calling plan, then charge for minutes over what the plan allows. The service firm must decide how much to charge for the basic service and how much for the variable usage. The fixed amount should be low enough to induce usage of the service; profit can be made on the variable fees.

By-Product Pricing

By-product pricing

Setting a price for by-products in order to make the main product's price more competitive.

In producing processed meats, petroleum products, chemicals, and other products, there are often by-products. If the by-products have no value and if getting rid of them is costly, this will affect the pricing of the main product. Using **by-product pricing**, the manufacturer will seek a market for these by-products and should accept any price that covers more than the cost of storing and delivering them.

By-products can even turn out to be profitable. For example, as a by-product of its candy-making process, Hershey Foods generates more than 10,000 tons of cocoa bean shells each year. Rather than paying to have the shells hauled away, Hershey packages them in 28-pound bags and sells them as mulch through landscape designers, home and garden centers, and grocery stores. Hershey claims that cocoa mulch is perfect for gardens and landscaping. It repels insects, adds protein to soil, and smells like chocolate. Cocoa mulch also makes an excellent soil for growing mushrooms—Hershey sells the fragrant by-product in 20-ton truckloads to the mushroom industry. Says the company's Web site: "Hershey's has the sweetest mulch!"[5]

Sometimes, companies don't realize how valuable their by-products are. For example, most zoos don't realize that one of their by-products—their occupants' manure—can be an excellent source of additional revenue. But the Zoo Doo Compost Company has helped many zoos understand the costs and opportunities involved with these by-products. Zoo Doo licenses its name to zoos and receives royalties on manure sales. So far, novelty sales have been the largest segment, with tiny containers of Zoo Doo (and even "Love, Love Me Doo" valentines) available in 160 zoo stores and 700 additional retail outlets. You can also buy Zoo Doo products online ("the easiest way to buy our crap," says Zoo Doo) or even send a friend (or perhaps a foe) a free Poopy Greeting via e-mail. Other zoos sell their by-products on their own. For example, the Woodland Park Zoo in Seattle sponsors annual Fecal Fests, selling processed manure by the trash can and truck load to lucky lottery winners. In all, the zoo creates 1 million pounds of compost each year, saving $60,000 a year in disposal costs.[6]

Product Bundle Pricing

Product bundle pricing
Combining several products and offering the bundle at a reduced price.

Using **product bundle pricing**, sellers often combine several of their products and offer the bundle at a reduced price. For example, fast-food restaurants bundle a burger, fries, and a soft drink at a combo price. Theaters and sports teams sell season tickets at less than the cost of single tickets. Resorts sell specially priced vacation packages that include airfare, accommodations, meals, and entertainment. And computer makers include attractive software packages with their personal computers. Price bundling can promote the sales of products consumers might not otherwise buy, but the combined price must be low enough to get them to buy the bundle.[7]

Price-Adjustment Strategies

Companies usually adjust their basic prices to account for various customer differences and changing situations. Here we examine the six price adjustment strategies summarized in Table 11.2: *discount and allowance pricing, segmented pricing, psychological pricing, promotional pricing, geographical pricing,* and *international pricing.*

Discount and Allowance Pricing

Most companies adjust their basic price to reward customers for certain responses, such as early payment of bills, volume purchases, and off-season buying. These price adjustments—called *discounts* and *allowances*—can take many forms.

Discount
A straight reduction in price on purchases during a stated period of time.

The many forms of **discounts** include a *cash discount,* a price reduction to buyers who pay their bills promptly. A typical example is "2/10, net 30," which means that although payment is due within 30 days, the buyer can deduct 2 percent if the bill is paid within 10 days. A *quantity discount* is a price reduction to buyers who buy large volumes. A typical example might be "$10 per unit for less than 100 units, $9 per unit for 100 or more units." Such discounts provide an incentive to the customer to buy more from one given seller, rather than from many different sources.

A *functional discount* (also called a *trade discount*) is offered by the seller to trade-channel members who perform certain functions, such as selling, storing, and record keeping. A *seasonal discount* is a price reduction to buyers who buy merchandise or services out of season. For example, lawn and garden equipment manufacturers offer seasonal discounts to retailers during the fall and winter months to encourage early ordering in anticipation of the

■ Product bundle pricing: cityPASS bundles tickets to many attractions at a low combined price.

TABLE 11.2   **Price Adjustment Strategies**

Strategy	Description
Discount and allowance pricing	Reducing prices to reward customer responses such as paying early or promoting the product
Segmented pricing	Adjusting prices to allow for differences in customers, products, or locations
Psychological pricing	Adjusting prices for psychological effect
Promotional pricing	Temporarily reducing prices to increase short-run sales
Geographical pricing	Adjusting prices to account for the geographic location of customers
International pricing	Adjusting prices for international markets

heavy spring and summer selling seasons. Seasonal discounts allow the seller to keep production steady during an entire year.

Allowance
Promotional money paid by manufacturers to retailers in return for an agreement to feature the manufacturer's products in some way.

Allowances are another type of reduction from the list price. For example, *trade-in allowances* are price reductions given for turning in an old item when buying a new one. Trade-in allowances are most common in the automobile industry but are also given for other durable goods. *Promotional allowances* are payments or price reductions to reward dealers for participating in advertising and sales support programs.

Segmented Pricing

Segmented pricing
Selling a product or service at two or more prices, where the difference in prices is not based on differences in costs.

Companies will often adjust their basic prices to allow for differences in customers, products, and locations. In **segmented pricing**, the company sells a product or service at two or more prices, even though the difference in prices is not based on differences in costs.

Segmented pricing takes several forms. Under *customer-segment* pricing, different customers pay different prices for the same product or service. Museums, for example, may charge a lower admission for students and senior citizens. Under *product-form pricing*, different versions of the product are priced differently but not according to differences in their costs. For instance, the most expensive Black & Decker iron is priced at $54.98, which is $12 more than the price of the next most expensive Black & Decker iron. The top model has a self-cleaning feature, yet this extra feature costs only a few more dollars to make.

Using *location pricing*, a company charges different prices for different locations, even though the cost of offering each location is the same. For instance, theaters vary their seat prices because of audience preferences for certain locations, and state universities charge higher tuition for out-of-state students. Finally, using *time pricing*, a firm varies its price by the season, the month, the day, and even the hour. Some public utilities vary their prices to commercial users by time of day and weekend versus weekday. Resorts give weekend and seasonal discounts.

Segmented pricing goes by many names. Robert Cross, a longtime consultant to the airlines, calls it *revenue management*. According to Cross, the practice ensures that "companies will sell the right product to the right consumer at the right time for the right price." Airlines, hotels, and restaurants call it *yield management* and practice it religiously. The airlines, for example, routinely set prices on an hour-by-hour—even minute-by-minute—basis, depending on seat availability, demand, and competitor price changes.

Continental Airlines launches about 2,000 flights every day. Each flight has between 10 and 20 prices. Continental starts booking flights 330 days in advance, and every flying day is different from every other flying day. As a result, at any given moment, Continental may have nearly 7 million prices in the market. It's a daunting marketing task—all of those prices need to be managed, all of the time. For Continental, setting prices is a complex process of balancing demand and customer satisfaction against company profitability.[8]

> The airlines know full well that we are puzzled by the frantic pricing and repricing that they do—puzzled, that is, when we aren't infuriated. "I do not set the prices," says Jim Compton, senior vice president of pricing and revenue management at Continental Airlines. "The market sets prices." That's point one. Point two: "I have a really perishable product. It's gone when the door of the plane closes. An empty seat is lost revenue." The most valuable airline seat is the one that somebody must

have an hour before takeoff and is willing to pay almost any price for. An airline seat gets more profitable with time—right up to the moment it goes from being worth $1,000 one-way to being worth $0.

Here's how Compton and his colleagues think about this: You want to sell every seat on the plane, except that you also want to have a handful left at the very end, for your most profitable (not to mention most grateful) customers. The airlines could easily sell out every seat, every flight, every day. They'd price 'em pretty low, book 'em up, and wait for takeoff. But that would mean there'd never be any seats available 2 or 3 weeks before a flight took off. How exasperated would customers be to call and find no seats 3 days out? When you understand that dilemma, all of a sudden, airline prices don't seem so exploitive. Although all of the seats on that New York–Miami flight are going to the same place, they aren't the same product. You pay less when you commit to a ticket 4 weeks in advance; Continental assumes a risk for holding a seat until the end—and wants to be paid a lot to balance the times when saving that last seat for you means that the seat flies empty.

Segmented pricing and yield management aren't really new ideas. For instance, Marriott Corporation used seat-of-the-pants yield-management approaches long before it installed its current sophisticated system.

Back when Bill Marriott was a young man working at the family's first hotel, the Twin Bridges in Washington, D.C., he sold rooms from a drive-up window. As Bill tells it, the hotel charged a flat rate for a single occupant, with an extra charge for each additional person staying in the room. When room availability got tight on some nights, Bill would lean out the drive-up window and assess the cars waiting in line. If some of the cars were filled with passengers, Bill would turn away vehicles with just a single passenger to sell his last rooms to those farther back in line who would be paying for multiple occupants. He might have accomplished the same result by charging a higher rate at peak times, regardless of the number of room occupants.[9]

For segmented pricing to be an effective strategy, certain conditions must exist. The market must be segmentable, and the segments must show different degrees of demand. The costs of segmenting and watching the market cannot exceed the extra revenue obtained from the price difference. Of course, the segmented pricing must also be legal. Most importantly, segmented prices should reflect real differences in customers' perceived value. Otherwise, in the long run, the practice will lead to customer resentment and ill will.

■ Segmented pricing: At any given moment, Continental may have nearly 7 million prices in the market. All of those prices need to be managed, all of the time.

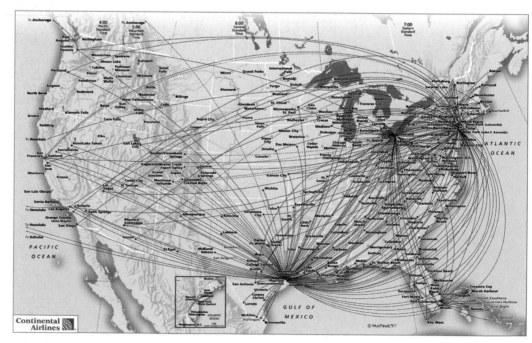

Psychological Pricing

Price says something about the product. For example, many consumers use price to judge quality. A $100 bottle of perfume may contain only $3 worth of scent, but some people are willing to pay the $100 because this price indicates something special.

In using **psychological pricing**, sellers consider the psychology of prices and not simply the economics. For example, consumers usually perceive higher-priced products as having higher quality. When they can judge the quality of a product by examining it or by calling on past experience with it, they use price less to judge quality. But when they cannot judge quality because they lack the information or skill, price becomes an important quality signal:

> Heublein produces Smirnoff, America's leading vodka brand. Some years ago, Smirnoff was attacked by another brand. Wolfschmidt, priced at one dollar less per bottle, claimed to have the same quality as Smirnoff. To hold on to market share, Heublein considered either lowering Smirnoff's price by one dollar or holding Smirnoff's price but increasing advertising and promotion expenditures. Either strategy would lead to lower profits and it seemed that Heublein faced a no-win situation. At this point, however, Heublein's marketers thought of a third strategy. They *raised* the price of Smirnoff by one dollar! Heublein then introduced a new brand, Relska, to compete with Wolfschmidt. Moreover, it introduced yet another brand, Popov, priced even *lower* than Wolfschmidt. This clever strategy positioned Smirnoff as the elite brand and Wolfschmidt as an ordinary brand, producing a large increase in Heublein's overall profits. The irony is that Heublein's three brands are pretty much the same in taste and manufacturing costs. Heublein knew that a product's price signals its quality. Using price as a signal, Heublein sells roughly the same product at three different quality positions.

Another aspect of psychological pricing is **reference prices**—prices that buyers carry in their minds and refer to when looking at a given product. The reference price might be formed by noting current prices, remembering past prices, or assessing the buying situation. Sellers

Psychological pricing
A pricing approach that considers the psychology of prices and not simply the economics; the price is used to say something about the product.

Reference prices
Prices that buyers carry in their minds and refer to when they look at a given product.

■ Psychological pricing: What do the prices marked on this tag suggest about the product and buying situation?

Real Marketing 11.1

It's Saturday morning and you stop by your local supermarket to pick up a few items for tonight's backyard barbeque. Cruising the aisles, you're bombarded with price signs, all suggesting that you just can't beat this store's deals. A 10-lb. bag of Kingsford Charcoal Briquets goes for only $3.99 with your frequent shopper card ($4.39 without the card). Cans of Van Camps Pork & Beans are 4 for $1.00 (4 for $2.16 without the card). An aisle display hawks big bags of Utz potato chips at an "everyday low price" of just $1.99. And a sign atop a huge mass of Coke 12-packs advertises 2 for $7.

These sure look like good prices, but *are* they? If you're like most shoppers, you don't really know. In a recent *Harvard Business Review* article, two pricing researchers conclude, "for most of the items they buy, consumers don't have an accurate sense of what the price should be." In fact, customers often don't even know what prices they're actually paying. In one recent study, researchers asked supermarket shoppers the price of an item just as they were putting it into their shopping carts. Less than half the shoppers gave the right answer.

To know for sure if you're paying the best price, you'd have to compare the marked price with past prices, prices of competing brands, and prices in other stores. For most purchases, consumers just don't bother. Instead, they rely on a most unlikely source. "Remarkably, . . . they rely on the retailer to tell them if they're getting a good price," say the researchers. "In subtle and not-so-subtle ways, retailers send signals [or pricing cues] to customers, telling them whether a given price is relatively high or low." In their article, the researchers outline the following common retailer pricing cues.

- *Sale Signs.* The most straightforward retail pricing cue is a sale sign. It might take any of several familiar forms: "Sale!" "Reduced!" "New low price!" "Price after rebate!" or "Now 2 for only . . . !" Such signs can be very effective in signaling low prices to consumers and increasing sales for the retailer. The researchers' studies in retail stores and mail-order catalogs reveal that using the word "sale" beside a price (even without actually varying the price) can increase demand by more than 50 percent.

  While sales signs can be effective, overuse or misuse can damage both the seller's credibility and its sales. Unfortunately, some retailers do not always use such signs truthfully. Still, consumers trust sale signs. Why? "Because

■ Pricing cues such as sales signs and prices ending in 9 can be effective in signaling low prices to consumers and increasing sales for the retailer.

they are accurate most of the time," say the researchers. "And besides, customers are not that easily fooled." They quickly become suspicious when sale signs are used improperly.

- *Prices Ending in 9.* Just like a sale sign, a 9 at the end of a price often signals a bargain. You see such prices everywhere. For example, browse the Web sites of discounters such as Target, Best Buy, or PetsMart: it's almost impossible to find even one price that *doesn't* end in 9 (really, try it!). "In fact, this pricing tactic is so common," say the researchers, "you'd think customers would ignore it. Think again. Response to this pricing cue is remarkable." Normally, you'd expect that demand for an item will fall as the price goes up. Yet in one study involving women's clothing, raising the price of a dress from $34 to $39 *increased* demand by a third. By comparison, raising the price from $34 to $44 yielded no difference in demand.

  But are prices ending in 9 accurate as pricing cues? "The answer varies," report the researchers. "Some retailers do reserve prices that end in 9 for their discounted items. For

can influence or use these consumers' reference prices when setting price. For example, a company could display its product next to more expensive ones in order to imply that it belongs in the same class. Department stores often sell women's clothing in separate departments differentiated by price: Clothing found in the more expensive department is assumed to be of better quality.

For most purchases, consumers don't have all the skill or information they need to figure out whether they are paying a good price. They don't have the time, ability, or inclination to research different brands or stores, compare prices, and get the best deals. Instead, the may rely on certain cues that signal whether a price is high or low. For example, the fact that a product is sold in a prestigious department store might signal that it's worth a higher price. Interestingly, such pricing cues are often provided by sellers. A retailer might show a high manufacturer's suggested price next to the marked price, indicating that the product was orig-

instance, J. Crew and Ralph Lauren generally use 00-cent endings on regularly priced merchandise and 99-cent endings on discounted items. Comparisons of prices at major department stores reveal that this is common, particularly for apparel. But at some stores, prices that end in 9 are a miscue—they are used on all products regardless of whether the items are discounted."

■ *Signpost Pricing (or Loss-Leader Pricing).* Unlike sale signs or prices that end in 9, signpost pricing is used on frequently purchased products about which consumers tend to have accurate price knowledge. For example, you probably know a good price on a 12-pack of Coke when you see one. New parents usually know how much they should expect to pay for disposable diapers. Research suggests that customers use the prices of such "signpost" items to gauge a store's overall prices. If a store has a good price on Coke or Pampers or Tide, they reason, it probably also has good prices on other items.

Retailers have long known the importance of signpost pricing, often called "loss-leader pricing." They offer selected signpost items at or below cost to pull customers into the store, hoping to make money on the shopper's other purchases. For instance, Best Buy often sells recently released DVDs at several dollars below wholesale price. Customers get a really good deal. And although Best Buy loses money on every DVD sold, the low DVD prices increase store traffic and purchases of higher-margin complementary products, such as DVD players.

■ *Pricing-Matching Guarantees.* Another widely used retail pricing cue is *price matching,* whereby stores promise to meet or beat any competitor's price. Best Buy, for example, says "we'll meet or beat any local competitor's price, guaranteed!" If you find a better price within 30 days on something you bought at Best Buy, the retailer will refund the difference plus 10 percent. Tweeter, a New England consumer electronics retailer, even offers at self-enforced price-matching policy. When Tweeter finds a competitor advertising a lower advertised price, it mails a check for the difference to any customers who paid a higher price at Tweeter in the previous 30 days.

Evidence suggests that customers perceive that stores offering price-matching guarantees have overall lower prices than competing stores, especially in markets where they perceive price comparisons to be relatively easy. But are such perceptions accurate? "The evidence is mixed," say the researchers. Consumers can usually be confident that they'll pay the lowest price on eligible items. However, some manufacturers make it hard to take advantage of price-matching policies by introducing "branded variants"—slightly different versions of products with different model numbers for different retailers. "When Tweeter introduced its highly effective automatic price-matching policy," the researchers note, "only 6 percent of its transactions were actually eligible for refunds." At a broader level, some pricing experts argue that price-matching policies are not really targeted at customers. Rather, they may serve as a warning to competitors: "If you cut your prices, we will, too." If this is true, price-matching policies might actually reduce price competition, leading to higher overall prices.

Watch Your Pricing Cues!

Used properly, pricing cues can help consumers. Careful buyers really can take advantage of signals such as sale signs, 9-endings, loss-leaders, and price guarantees to locate good deals. Used improperly, however, these pricing cues can mislead consumers, tarnishing a brand and damaging customer relationships.

The researchers conclude: "Customers need price information, just as they need products. They look to retailers to provide both. Retailers must manage pricing cues in the same way that they manage quality. . . . No retailer . . . interested in [building profitable long-term relationships with customers] would purposely offer a defective product. Similarly, no retailer who [values customers] would deceive them with inaccurate pricing cues. By reliably signaling which prices are low, companies can retain customers' trust—and [build more solid relationships]."

Sources: Quotes and other information from Eric Anderson and Duncan Simester, "Mind Your Pricing Cues," *Harvard Business Review,* September 2003, pp. 96–103. Also see Joydeep Srivastava and Nicholas Lurie, "Price-Matching Guarantees as Signals of Low Store Prices: Survey and Experimental Evidence," *Journal of Retailing,* 2004.

inally priced much higher. Or the retailer might sell a selection of familiar products for which consumers have accurate price knowledge at very low prices, suggesting that the store's prices on other, less familiar products are low as well. The use of such pricing cues has become a common marketing practice (see Real Marketing 11.1).

Even small differences in price can signal product differences. Consider a stereo priced at $300 compared with one priced at $299.95. The actual price difference is only 5 cents, but the psychological difference can be much greater. For example, some consumers will see the $299.95 as a price in the $200 range rather than the $300 range. The $299.95 will more likely be seen as a bargain price, whereas the $300 price suggests more quality. Some psychologists argue that each digit has symbolic and visual qualities that should be considered in pricing. Thus, 8 is round and even and creates a soothing effect, whereas 7 is angular and creates a jarring effect.[10]

■ Promotional pricing: Companies offer promotional prices to create buying excitement and urgency.

Promotional Pricing

Promotional pricing

Temporarily pricing products below the list price, and sometimes even below cost, to increase short-run sales.

With **promotional pricing**, companies will temporarily price their products below list price and sometimes even below cost to create buying excitement and urgency. Promotional pricing takes several forms. Supermarkets and department stores will price a few products as _loss leaders_ to attract customers to the store in the hope that they will buy other items at normal markups. For example, supermarkets often sell disposable diapers at less than cost in order to attract family buyers who make larger average purchases per trip. Sellers will also use _special-event pricing_ in certain seasons to draw more customers. Thus, linens are promotionally priced every January to attract weary Christmas shoppers back into stores.

Manufacturers sometimes offer _cash rebates_ to consumers who buy the product from dealers within a specified time; the manufacturer sends the rebate directly to the customer. Rebates have been popular with automakers and producers of durable goods and small appliances, but they are also used with consumer packaged goods. Some manufacturers offer _low-interest financing_, _longer warranties_, or _free maintenance_ to reduce the consumer's "price." This practice has become a favorite of the auto industry. Or, the seller may simply offer _discounts_ from normal prices to increase sales and reduce inventories.

Promotional pricing, however, can have adverse effects. Used too frequently and copied by competitors, price promotions can create "deal-prone" customers who wait until brands go on sale before buying them. Or, constantly reduced prices can erode a brand's value in the eyes of customers. Marketers sometimes use price promotions as a quick fix instead of sweating through the difficult process of developing effective longer-term strategies for building their brands. In fact, one observer notes that price promotions can be downright addicting to both the company and the customer: "Price promotions are the brand equivalent of heroin: easy to get into but hard to get out of. Once the brand and its customers are addicted to the short-term high of a price cut it is hard to wean them away to real brand building. . . . But continue and the brand dies by 1,000 cuts."[11]

The frequent use of promotional pricing can also lead to industry price wars. Such price wars usually play into the hands of only one or a few competitors—those with the most efficient operations. For example, until recently, the computer industry avoided price wars. Computer companies, including IBM, H-P, and Gateway, showed strong profits as their new technologies were snapped up by eager consumers. When the market cooled, however, many competitors began to unload PCs at discounted prices. In response, Dell, the industry's undisputed low-cost leader, started a price war that only it could win.

In mid-2000, Dell declared a brutal price war just as the industry slipped into its worst slump ever. The result was nothing short of a rout. While Dell chalked up $361 million in profits the following year, the rest of the industry logged $1.1 billion in losses. Dell's edge starts with its direct-selling approach. By taking orders straight from customers and building machines to order, Dell avoids paying retailer markups, getting stuck with unsold PCs, and keeping costly inventories. For example, at any given moment, Dell's warehouses hold just 4 days of stock, compared with 24 days for competitors. That gives it a gigantic edge in a market where the price of chips, drives, and other parts typically falls 1 percent a week. Moreover, Dell has mastered supply chain management. Last year, it required suppliers to use sophisticated software that wires them straight into Dell's factory floor, allowing Dell's plants to replenish supplies only as needed throughout the day. That software alone saved Dell $50 million in the first 6 months of use. Since launching the price war, the price of a Dell computer has dropped more than 18 percent, leaving competitors with few effective weapons. IBM has responded by outsourcing its PC production and sales. And H-P and Compaq merged in hopes of finding strength in numbers. Still locked in a brutal price war with Dell, H-P is now selling more PCs than Dell but making much less profit from PC sales. Says Michael Dell, "When we sell these products, we make money. When our competitors sell them, they lose money."[12]

The point is that promotional pricing can be an effective means of generating sales for some companies in certain circumstances. But it can be damaging for other companies or if taken as a steady diet.

Geographical Pricing

A company also must decide how to price its products for customers located in different parts of the country or world. Should the company risk losing the business of more-distant customers by charging them higher prices to cover the higher shipping costs? Or should the company charge all customers the same prices regardless of location? We will look at five geographical pricing strategies for the following hypothetical situation:

> The Peerless Paper Company is located in Atlanta, Georgia, and sells paper products to customers all over the United States. The cost of freight is high and affects the companies from whom customers buy their paper. Peerless wants to establish a geographical pricing policy. It is trying to determine how to price a $100 order to three specific customers: Customer A (Atlanta), Customer B (Bloomington, Indiana), and Customer C (Compton, California).

One option is for Peerless to ask each customer to pay the shipping cost from the Atlanta factory to the customer's location. All three customers would pay the same factory price of $100, with Customer A paying, say, $10 for shipping; Customer B, $15; and Customer C, $25. Called **FOB-origin pricing**, this practice means that the goods are placed *free on board* (hence, *FOB*) a carrier. At that point the title and responsibility pass to the customer, who pays the freight from the factory to the destination. Because each customer picks up its own cost, supporters of FOB pricing feel that this is the fairest way to assess freight charges. The disadvantage, however, is that Peerless will be a high-cost firm to distant customers.

Uniform-delivered pricing is the opposite of FOB pricing. Here, the company charges the same price plus freight to all customers, regardless of their location. The freight charge is set at the average freight cost. Suppose this is $15. Uniform-delivered pricing therefore results in a higher charge to the Atlanta customer (who pays $15 freight instead of $10) and a lower charge to the Compton customer (who pays $15 instead of $25). Although the Atlanta customer would prefer to buy paper from another local paper company that uses FOB-origin pricing, Peerless has a better chance of winning over the California customer. Other advantages of uniform-delivered pricing are that it is fairly easy to administer and it lets the firm advertise its price nationally.

Zone pricing falls between FOB-origin pricing and uniform-delivered pricing. The company sets up two or more zones. All customers within a given zone pay a single total price; the more distant the zone, the higher the price. For example, Peerless might set up an East Zone and charge $10 freight to all customers in this zone, a Midwest Zone in which it charges $15, and a West Zone in which it charges $25. In this way, the customers within a given price zone receive no price advantage from the company. For example, customers in Atlanta and Boston pay the same total price to Peerless. The complaint, however, is that the Atlanta customer is paying part of the Boston customer's freight cost.

Using **basing-point pricing**, the seller selects a given city as a "basing point" and charges all customers the freight cost from that city to the customer location, regardless of the city from which the goods are actually shipped. For example, Peerless might set Chicago as the basing point and charge all customers $100 plus the freight from Chicago to their locations. This means that an Atlanta customer pays the freight cost from Chicago to Atlanta, even though the goods may be shipped from Atlanta. If all sellers used the same basing-point city, delivered prices would be the same for all customers and price competition would be eliminated. Industries such as sugar, cement, steel, and automobiles used basing-point pricing for years, but this method has become less popular today. Some companies set up multiple basing points to create more flexibility: They quote freight charges from the basing-point city nearest to the customer.

FOB-origin pricing
A geographical pricing strategy in which goods are placed free on board a carrier; the customer pays the freight from the factory to the destination.

Uniform-delivered pricing
A geographical pricing strategy in which the company charges the same price plus freight to all customers, regardless of their location.

Zone pricing
A geographical pricing strategy in which the company sets up two or more zones. All customers within a zone pay the same total price; the more distant the zone, the higher the price.

Basing-point pricing
A geographical pricing strategy in which the seller designates some city as a basing point and charges all customers the freight cost from that city to the customer.

Freight-absorption pricing

A geographical pricing strategy in which the seller absorbs all or part of the freight charges in order to get the desired business.

Finally, the seller who is anxious to do business with a certain customer or geographical area might use **freight-absorption pricing**. Using this strategy, the seller absorbs all or part of the actual freight charges in order to get the desired business. The seller might reason that if it can get more business, its average costs will fall and more than compensate for its extra freight cost. Freight-absorption pricing is used for market penetration and to hold on to increasingly competitive markets.

International Pricing

Companies that market their products internationally must decide what prices to charge in the different countries in which they operate. In some cases, a company can set a uniform worldwide price. For example, Boeing sells its jetliners at about the same price everywhere, whether in the United States, Europe, or a third-world country. However, most companies adjust their prices to reflect local market conditions and cost considerations.

The price that a company should charge in a specific country depends on many factors, including economic conditions, competitive situations, laws and regulations, and development of the wholesaling and retailing system. Consumer perceptions and preferences also may vary from country to country, calling for different prices. Or the company may have different marketing objectives in various world markets, which require changes in pricing strategy. For example, Panasonic might introduce a new product into mature markets in highly developed countries with the goal of quickly gaining mass-market share—this would call for a penetration-pricing strategy. In contrast, it might enter a less developed market by targeting smaller, less price-sensitive segments; in this case, market-skimming pricing makes sense.

Costs play an important role in setting international prices. Travelers abroad are often surprised to find that goods that are relatively inexpensive at home may carry outrageously higher price tags in other countries. A pair of Levi's selling for $30 in the United States might go for $63 in Tokyo and $88 in Paris. A McDonald's Big Mac selling for a modest $2.25 here might cost $5.75 in Moscow, and an Oral-B toothbrush selling for $2.49 at home may cost $10 in China. Conversely, a Gucci handbag going for only $60 in Milan, Italy, might fetch $240 in the United States. In some cases, such *price escalation* may result from differences in selling strategies or market conditions. In most instances, however, it is simply a result of the higher costs of selling in another country—the additional costs of product modifications, shipping and insurance, import tariffs and taxes, exchange-rate fluctuations, and physical distribution.

For example, Campbell found that distribution in the United Kingdom cost 30 percent more than in the United States. U.S. retailers typically purchase soup in large quantities—48-

■ Companies that market products internationally must decide what prices to charge in the different countries.

can cases of a single soup by the dozens, hundreds, or carloads. In contrast, English grocers purchase soup in small quantities—typically in 24-can cases of *assorted* soups. Each case must be hand-packed for shipment. To handle these small orders, Campbell had to add a costly extra wholesale level to its European channel. The smaller orders also mean that English retailers order two or three times as often as their U.S. counterparts, bumping up billing and order costs. These and other factors caused Campbell to charge much higher prices for its soups in the United Kingdom.[13]

Thus, international pricing presents some special problems and complexities. We discuss international pricing issues in more detail in Chapter 19.

Price Changes

After developing their pricing structures and strategies, companies often face situations in which they must initiate price changes or respond to price changes by competitors.

Initiating Price Changes

In some cases, the company may find it desirable to initiate either a price cut or a price increase. In both cases, it must anticipate possible buyer and competitor reactions.

Initiating Price Cuts

Several situations may lead a firm to consider cutting its price. One such circumstance is excess capacity. In this case, the firm needs more business and cannot get it through increased sales effort, product improvement, or other measures. It may drop its "follow-the-leader pricing"—charging about the same price as its leading competitor—and aggressively cut prices to boost sales. But as the airline, construction equipment, fast-food, and other industries have learned in recent years, cutting prices in an industry loaded with excess capacity may lead to price wars as competitors try to hold on to market share.

Another situation leading to price changes is falling market share in the face of strong price competition. Several American industries—automobiles, consumer electronics, cameras, watches, and steel, for example—lost market share to Japanese competitors whose high-quality products carried lower prices than did their American counterparts. In response, American companies resorted to more-aggressive pricing action.

A company may also cut prices in a drive to dominate the market through lower costs. Either the company starts with lower costs than its competitors, or it cuts prices in the hope of gaining market share that will further cut costs through larger volume. Bausch & Lomb used an aggressive low-cost, low-price strategy to become an early leader in the competitive soft contact lens market. And Dell used this strategy in the PC market.

Initiating Price Increases

A successful price increase can greatly increase profits. For example, if the company's profit margin is 3 percent of sales, a 1 percent price increase will increase profits by 33 percent if sales volume is unaffected. A major factor in price increases is cost inflation. Rising costs squeeze profit margins and lead companies to pass cost increases along to customers. Another factor leading to price increases is overdemand: When a company cannot supply all that its customers need, it can raise its prices, ration products to customers, or both.

Companies can increase their prices in a number of ways to keep up with rising costs. Prices can be raised almost invisibly by dropping discounts and adding higher-priced units to the line. Or prices can be pushed up openly. In passing price increases on to customers, the company must avoid being perceived as a price gouger. Companies also need to think of who will bear the brunt of increased prices. Customers have long memories, and they will eventually turn away from companies or even whole industries that they perceive as charging excessive prices.

This happened to the cereal industry in the 1990s. Industry leader Kellogg covered rising costs and preserved profits by steadily raising prices without also increasing customer value. Eventually, frustrated consumers retaliated with a quiet fury by shifting away from branded cereals toward cheaper private-label brands. Worse, many consumers switched to less expensive, more portable handheld breakfast foods, such as bagels, muffins, and breakfast bars. As a result, total American cereal sales began falling off by 3 to 4 percent a year.

Moreover, by the end of the 1990s, private brands were capturing almost 20 percent of the U.S. cereal market, and Kellogg's market share had slumped to about 33 percent, down from more than 42 percent less than a decade earlier. Thus, customers paid the price in the short run but Kellogg paid the price in the long run. Kellogg's cereal business has only recently rebounded.[14]

There are some techniques for avoiding this problem. One is to maintain a sense of fairness surrounding any price increase. Price increases should be supported by company communications telling customers why prices are being increased. Making low-visibility price moves first is also a good technique: Some examples include eliminating discounts, increasing minimum order sizes, and curtailing production of low-margin products. The company sales force should help business customers find ways to economize.

Wherever possible, the company should consider ways to meet higher costs or demand without raising prices. For example, it can consider more cost-effective ways to produce or distribute its products. It can shrink the product instead of raising the price, as candy bar manufacturers often do. It can substitute less expensive ingredients or remove certain product features, packaging, or services. Or it can "unbundle" its products and services, removing and separately pricing elements that were formerly part of the offer. IBM, for example, now offers training and consulting as separately priced services.

Buyer Reactions to Price Changes

Whether the price is raised or lowered, the action will affect buyers, competitors, distributors, and suppliers and may interest government as well. Customers do not always interpret prices in a straightforward way. They may view a price *cut* in several ways. For example, what would you think if Joy perfume, "the costliest fragrance in the world," were to cut its price in half? Or what if Sony suddenly cut its PC prices drastically? You might think that the computers are about to be replaced by newer models or that they have some fault and are not selling well. You might think that Sony is abandoning the computer business and may not stay in this business long enough to supply future parts. You might believe that quality has been reduced. Or you might think that the price will come down even further and that it will pay to wait and see.

■ Buyer reactions to price changes: What would you think if the price of Joy was suddenly cut in half?

TEN PERFECTLY RATIONAL REASONS FOR WEARING THE COSTLIEST FRAGRANCE IN THE WORLD.

Similarly, a price *increase*, which would normally lower sales, may have some positive meanings for buyers. What would you think if Sony *raised* the price of its latest personal computer model? On the one hand, you might think that the item is very "hot" and may be unobtainable unless you buy it soon. Or you might think that the computer is an unusually good performer. On the other hand, you might think that Sony is greedy and charging what the traffic will bear.

Competitor Reactions to Price Changes

A firm considering a price change has to worry about the reactions of its competitors as well as those of its customers. Competitors are most likely to react when the number of firms involved is small, when the product is uniform, and when the buyers are well informed.

How can the firm anticipate the likely reactions of its competitors? The problem is complex because, like the customer, the competitor can interpret a company price cut in many ways. It might think the company is trying to grab a larger market share, or that it's doing poorly and trying to boost its sales. Or it might think that the company wants the whole industry to cut prices to increase total demand.

The company must guess each competitor's likely reaction. If all competitors behave alike, this amounts to analyzing only a typical competitor. In contrast, if the competitors do not behave alike—perhaps because of differences in size, market shares, or policies—then separate analyses are necessary. However, if some competitors will match the price change, there is good reason to expect that the rest will also match it.

Responding to Price Changes

Here we reverse the question and ask how a firm should respond to a price change by a competitor. The firm needs to consider several issues: Why did the competitor change the price? Was it to take more market share, to use excess capacity, to meet changing cost conditions, or to lead an industrywide price change? Is the price change temporary or permanent? What will happen to the company's market share and profits if it does not respond? Are other companies going to respond? And what are the competitor's and other firms' responses to each possible reaction likely to be?

Besides these issues, the company must make a broader analysis. It has to consider its own product's stage in the life cycle, the product's importance in the company's product mix, the intentions and resources of the competitor, and the possible consumer reactions to price changes. The company cannot always make an extended analysis of its alternatives at the time of a price change, however. The competitor may have spent much time preparing this decision, but the company may have to react within hours or days. About the only way to cut down reaction time is to plan ahead for both possible competitor's price changes and possible responses.

Figure 11.1 shows the ways a company might assess and respond to a competitor's price cut. Suppose the company learns that a competitor has cut its price and decides that

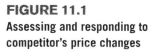

FIGURE 11.1

Assessing and responding to competitor's price changes

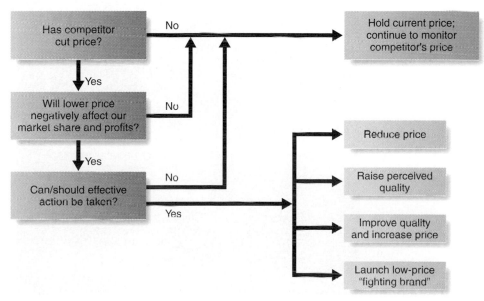

this price cut is likely to harm company sales and profits. It might simply decide to hold its current price and profit margin. The company might believe that it will not lose too much market share, or that it would lose too much profit if it reduced its own price. Or it might decide that it should wait and respond when it has more information on the effects of the competitor's price change. The argument against this holding strategy, however, is that the competitor may get stronger and more confident as its sales increase and that the company might wait too long to act.

If the company decides that effective action can and should be taken, it might make any of four responses. First, it could *reduce its price* to match the competitor's price. It may decide that the market is price sensitive and that it would lose too much market share to the lower-priced competitor. Or it might worry that recapturing lost market share later would be too hard. Cutting the price will reduce the company's profits in the short run. Some companies might also reduce their product quality, services, and marketing communications to retain profit margins, but this will ultimately hurt long-run market share. The company should try to maintain its quality as it cuts prices.

Alternatively, the company might maintain its price but *raise the perceived value* of its offer. It could improve its communications, stressing the relative quality of its product over that of the lower-price competitor. The firm may find it cheaper to maintain price and spend money to improve its perceived value than to cut price and operate at a lower margin.

Or, the company might *improve quality and increase price*, moving its brand into a higher-price position. The higher quality justifies the higher price, which in turn preserves the company's higher margins. Or the company can hold price on the current product and introduce a new brand at a higher-price position.

Finally, the company might *launch a low-price "fighting brand"*—adding a lower-price item to the line or creating a separate lower-price brand. This is necessary if the particular market segment being lost is price sensitive and will not respond to arguments of higher quality. Thus, when challenged on price by store brands and other low-price entrants, Procter & Gamble turned a number of its brands into fighting brands, including Luvs disposable diapers, Joy dishwashing detergent, and Camay beauty soap. In turn, P&G competitor Kimberly-Clark positions its value-priced Scott Towels brand as "the Bounty killer." It advertises Scott

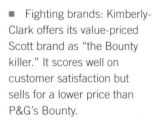

■ Fighting brands: Kimberly-Clark offers its value-priced Scott brand as "the Bounty killer." It scores well on customer satisfaction but sells for a lower price than P&G's Bounty.

Towels as "Common Sense on a Roll." The brand scores well on customer satisfaction measures but sells for a lower price than P&G's Bounty brand. "Scott Towels provide ample quantity and reliable quality and performance in every roll," says the company, "without the costly, unnecessary extras."[15]

Public Policy and Pricing

Price competition is a core element of our free-market economy. In setting prices, companies are not usually free to charge whatever prices they wish. Many federal, state, and even local laws govern the rules of fair play in pricing. In addition, companies must consider broader societal pricing concerns (see Real Marketing 11.2). The most important pieces of legislation affecting pricing are the Sherman, Clayton, and Robinson-Patman acts, initially adopted to curb the formation of monopolies and to regulate business practices that might unfairly restrain trade. Because these federal statutes can be applied only to interstate commerce, some states have adopted similar provisions for companies that operate locally.

Figure 11.2 shows the major public policy issues in pricing. These include potentially damaging pricing practices within a given level of the channel (price-fixing and predatory pricing) and across levels of the channel (retail price maintenance, discriminatory pricing, and deceptive pricing).[16]

Pricing Within Channel Levels

Federal legislation on *price-fixing* states that sellers must set prices without talking to competitors. Otherwise, price collusion is suspected. Price-fixing is illegal per se—that is, the government does not accept any excuses for price-fixing. Companies found guilty of such practices can receive heavy fines. For example, when the U.S. Justice Department found that Archer Daniels Midland Company and three of its competitors had met regularly in the early 1990s to illegally fix prices, the four companies paid more than $100 million to settle the charges. Similarly, Sotheby's and Christie's, two auction houses that for years have dominated the market for high end sales, were recently convicted of collusion and price-fixing. The collusion reportedly saved the companies in excess of $33 million a year, but they ended paying more than $512 million in fines and settlements.[17] Recently, governments at the state and national levels have been aggressively enforcing price-fixing regulations in industries ranging from tobacco, gasoline, and vitamins to diamonds and compact discs.[18]

Sellers are also prohibited from using *predatory pricing*—selling below cost with the intention of punishing a competitor or gaining higher long-run profits by putting competitors out of business. This protects small sellers from larger ones who might sell items below cost temporarily or in a specific locale to drive them out of business. The biggest problem is determining just what constitutes predatory pricing behavior. Selling below cost to sell off excess

FIGURE 11.2

Public policy issues in pricing

Source: Adapted from Dhruv Grewel and Larry D. Compeau, "Pricing and Public Policy: A Research Agenda and Overview of Special Issue," Journal of Marketing and Public Policy, *Spring 1999, pp. 3–10. Also see Michael V. Marn, Eric V. Roegner, and Craig C. Zawada,* The Price Advantage *(Hoboken, NJ: John Wiley & Sons, 2004), Appendix 2.*

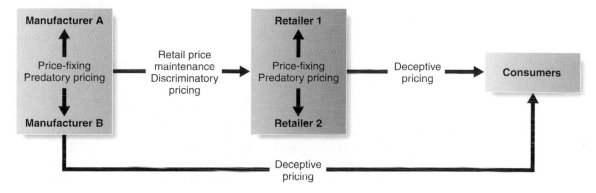

Real Marketing 11.2

Pricing Pharmaceutical Products: It Should Be More than Sales and Profits

The U.S. pharmaceutical industry has historically been one of the nation's most profitable industries. However, critics claim that this success has come at the expense of consumers. The United States and Canada together spent more than $230 billion on prescription medications last year, nearly half of worldwide spending. In the United States alone, spending is expected to exceed $360 billion by 2010.

Prescription prices have risen rapidly over the years, at a rate much higher than the overall inflation rate. The prices of many of the most important drugs are skyrocketing. For example, last year, Pfizer raised the price of its cholesterol-fighting Lipitor, the world's largest selling drug, by 11 percent. Similarly, Wyeth boosted the price of its flagship drug, Premarin, by 17 percent and Merck raised the price of asthma remedy Singulair by 11 percent. Abbott Laboratories recently quintupled the U.S. price of its crucial AIDS drug Norvir. High drug prices have sent many consumers, especially seniors with limited budgets and fixed-income, to Mexico and Canada in search of cheaper alternatives, including copycat versions of popular drugs like Zocor and Celebrex. Says one senior after a visit to Mexico, "If we couldn't get cheap meds, I wouldn't live."

The critics claim that competitive forces don't operate well in the pharmaceutical market, allowing companies to charge excessive prices. Unlike purchases of other consumer products, drug purchases cannot be postponed. Consumers don't usually shop for the best deal on medicines—they simply take what the doctor orders. Because physicians who write the prescriptions don't pay for the medicines they recommend, they have little incentive to be price conscious. Moreover, because of patents and FDA approvals, few competing brands exist to force lower prices, and existing brands don't go on sale. Finally, drug companies pour $20 billion a year into advertising and promotion, about as much as they spend on research and development. These efforts dictate higher prices at the same time that they build demand for more expensive remedies.

These market factors leave pharmaceutical companies free to practice monopoly pricing, the critics claim, resulting in seemingly outlandish cases of price gouging. One classic case involved the drug levamisole. Forty years ago, Johnson & Johnson introduced levamisole as a drug used to deworm sheep. When farmers using the drug noticed that dewormed sheep also suffered fewer cases of shipping fever, researchers began investigating the drug for human use. They found that levamisole, in combination with another drug, proved effective for patients with advanced colon cancer, reducing recurrence of the disease by 40 percent and cutting deaths by a third.

The FDA quickly approved levamisole for human use, and the Janssen division of Johnson & Johnson introduced the drug under the brand name Ergamisol. All went well until an Illinois farm woman noticed that her cancer pills contained the same active ingredient as

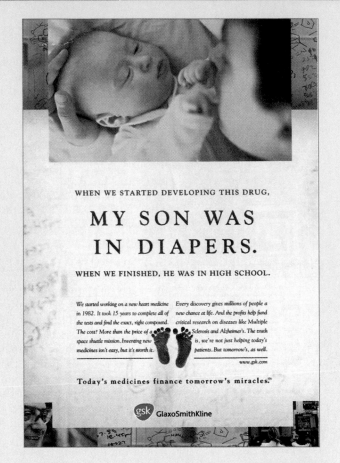

WHEN WE STARTED DEVELOPING THIS DRUG,

MY SON WAS IN DIAPERS.

WHEN WE FINISHED, HE WAS IN HIGH SCHOOL.

We started working on a new heart medicine in 1982. It took 15 years to complete all of the tests and find the exact, right compound. The cost? More than the price of a space shuttle mission. Inventing new medicines isn't easy, but it's worth it.

Every discovery gives millions of people a new chance at life. And the profits help fund critical research on diseases like Multiple Sclerosis and Alzheimer's. The truth is, we're not just helping today's patients. But tomorrow's, as well.

www.gsk.com

Today's medicines finance tomorrow's miracles.®

gsk GlaxoSmithKline

■ In defense of current prescription drug prices: This ad notes the costs of developing new drugs, and that profits help fund critical research on diseases like Multiple Sclerosis and Alzheimer's. "Today's medicines finance tomorrow's miracles."

the medicine she used to deworm her sheep. It wasn't the fact that both humans and sheep were using the drug that disturbed her. What really rankled her was that the sheep medicine sold for pennies a pill, whereas the human medicine sold for $5 to $6 per tablet. In a year's time, humans had to spend $1,250 to $3,000 for Ergamisol; the cost for treating sheep was only about $14.95.

The price discrepancy caused quite a stir. One consumer even filed suit against Janssen, claiming that he was forced to pay "an outrageous, unconscionable, and extortionate price for a lifesaving drug" that is sold at a fraction of the cost for treating sheep. Janssen replied that the price reflected decades of costly research and testing conducted to determine if levamisole could be used to treat humans.

inventory is not considered predatory; selling below cost to drive out competitors is. Thus, the same action may or may not be predatory depending on intent, and intent can be very difficult to determine or prove.

In recent years, several large and powerful companies have been accused of predatory pricing. For example, Wal-Mart has been sued by dozens of small competitors charging that it lowered prices in their specific areas to drive them out of business. In fact, the State

The company said it had conducted over 1,400 studies with 40,000 subjects. Critics disagreed, claiming that the National Cancer Institute, funded by the American taxpayer, had sponsored the levamisole studies. Further, they asserted, Janssen had had 25 years to recoup its investment before it ever sold the drug to humans.

The levamisole case may be extreme, but at one time or another we've all gulped at the prices we've had to pay for prescription drugs. Even when doctors or pharmacists recommend less expensive generic drugs, consumers may pay substantial markups. Pharmacies may look like good guys when they encourage the use of generics to save consumers money, but they also pocket a handsome profit. One recent study found that drugstores and pharmacies are marking up the price of some generics by more than 1,000 percent.

These examples highlight many important drug-pricing issues. Most consumers appreciate the steady stream of beneficial drugs produced by the U.S. pharmaceutical industry. And there is no question that developing new drugs is a risky endeavor, involving legions of scientists, expensive technology, and often years of effort with no certainty of success. A recent ad from GlaxoSmithKline notes that it took 15 years to complete all the tests and to find the exact right compound for a new heart medicine, at a cost of more than the price of a spaceshuttle mission. Profits from the heart drug help to fund critical research on diseases like Multiple Sclerosis and Alzheimer's. The ad concludes, "Inventing new medicines isn't easy, but it's worth it. . . . Today's medicines finance tomorrow's miracles."

However, there is still much concern that the industry may be taking advantage of its monopoly-pricing power. Perhaps the most serious concern is that high drug prices may have life-and-death consequences. Without levamisole, for example, many of the 22,000 patients diagnosed with advanced colon cancer each year would die. Thus, some critics claim that drug company profits may come at the expense of human life.

As a result of recent soaring prices, the industry is facing pressure from the federal government, insurance companies, managed care providers, and consumer advocates to exercise restraint in setting prices. Rather than waiting for tougher legislation on prices—or simply because it's the right thing to do—some forward-thinking drug companies have taken action on their own. Some voluntarily provide discounts to agencies such as the U.S. Public Health Service and to federally funded drug- and alcohol-treatment centers. Still other companies make drugs available free or at low prices to people who cannot afford them. Consider the following example:

Abbott Laboratories CEO Miles White returned from a recent eye-opening visit to Tanzania—where the HIV/AIDS epidemic rages almost unabated—with a new mission for his company. Among other things, he learned firsthand that

when local doctors decide whether or not to use a drug, the biggest consideration is its price, not whether it is the right drug. "I found out how much the price of drugs matters," says White. As a result, within days, he decided to reduce the price of Abbott's AIDS drugs to below cost for poor African nations. White also learned that the cost of the company's "rapid" AIDS detection test was the main reason it wasn't being used as a crucial tool in helping prevent the spread of the virus from infected pregnant women to their unborn children. Once detected, virus transmission can be blocked with the one-time use of a drug being given away by a competitor. But without an easy-to-use detection test, many expectant mothers are unaware they are infected. White now plans to give away 20 million test kits during the next five years. Asked how he can explain taking money out of the company coffers to fund such price cuts and give-aways, he says he'll tell shareholders that Abbott is doing "our part because we can." But, in a refreshing bit of honesty, he adds, "There is a practical business reason. If we don't lower prices and provide other help, we'll find governments [stepping in]."

In fact, the outrage generated by Abbott's recent fivefold increase in U.S. Norvir prices made the drug the centerpiece of federal hearings, in which consumer advocates argued that the government should begin allowing the import of cheaper drugs or the reimportation of drugs like Norvir (Americans who use Norvir now pay 10 times the price in Europe, where drug prices are regulated under national healthcare plans). Thus, Abbott and other companies must recognize that in setting prices, their short-term sales, market share, and profit goals must be tempered by broader societal considerations. In the long run, socially responsible pricing will benefit both the consumer and the company.

Sources: Abbott example adapted from Michael Waldholz, "Abbott Labs Improves Its Effort to Combat AIDS in Africa," *Wall Street Journal*, June 27, 2002, p. D4. Also see Marilyn Chase, "Doctor Assails J&J Price Tag on Cancer Drug," *Wall Street Journal*, May 20, 1992, p. B1; "Cancer Patient Sues Johnson & Johnson over Drug Pricing," *Wall Street Journal*, August 13, 1992, p. B6; Mike King, "Colon Cancer Drug: 5 Cents for an Animal, $5 for Humans," *Atlanta Constitution*, March 11, 1991, p. E1; Joel Millman, "Not Your Generic Smugglers—American Seniors Flock to Border Town for Cheap Prescriptions," *Wall Street Journal*, March 20, 2003, p. D.3; Scott Hensley, "Follow the Money: Drug Prices Rise at a Faster Clip, Placing Burden on Consumers," *Wall Street Journal*, April 15, 2003, p. D4; Ceci Connolly, "2003 Drug Spending Up Despite Pressure to Cut Costs," *The Washington Post*, March 16, 2004, p. A.04; and John Carey, "Drug Prices: A New Covenant?" *Business Week*, May 10, 2004, pp. 46–48.

of New York recently passed a bill requiring companies to price gas at or above 98 percent of cost to "address the more extreme cases of predatory pricing by big-box stores" like Wal-Mart.[19]

In another case, the Justice Department sued American Airlines for allegedly using predatory pricing to muscle three small competitors—Vanguard Airlines, Sun Jet, and Western Pacific—out of its huge Dallas-Fort Worth hub.

Every time a fledgling airline tried to get a toehold in the Dallas market, for example, American met its fares and added flights. As soon as the rival retreated, American jacked fares back up. Between Dallas and Kansas City, for instance, American's average one-way ticket was $108 before low-cost startup Vanguard Airlines entered the market. That prompted American to cut fares to $80 and almost double the number of daily flights, to 14. When Vanguard gave up [less than a year later], American jacked up prices to $147 and scaled back the number of flights. Justice lawyers even had memos from American execs plotting the upstarts' demise.

Despite such evidence, the case against American was dismissed. American had consistently priced flights higher than variable costs, thus avoiding predatory pricing. American won by arguing that it was just being a tough competitor.[20]

Pricing Across Channel Levels

The Robinson-Patman Act seeks to prevent unfair *price discrimination* by ensuring that sellers offer the same price terms to customers at a given level of trade. For example, every retailer is entitled to the same price terms from a given manufacturer, whether the retailer is Sears or the local bicycle shop. However, price discrimination is allowed if the seller can prove that its costs are different when selling to different retailers—for example, that it costs less per unit to sell a large volume of bicycles to Sears than to sell a few bicycles to a local dealer. Or the seller can discriminate in its pricing if the seller manufactures different qualities of the same product for different retailers. The seller has to prove that these differences are proportional. Price differentials may also be used to "match competition" in "good faith," provided the price discrimination is temporary, localized, and defensive rather than offensive.

Retail price maintenance is also prohibited—a manufacturer cannot require dealers to charge a specified retail price for its product. Although the seller can propose a manufacturer's *suggested* retail price to dealers, it cannot refuse to sell to a dealer who takes independent pricing action, nor can it punish the dealer by shipping late or denying advertising allowances. For example, the Florida attorney general's office recently investigated Nike for allegedly fixing the retail price of its shoes and clothing. It was concerned that Nike might be withholding items from retailers who were not selling its most expensive shoes—like the Air Jordan and Shox lines—at prices the company considered suitable.[21]

Deceptive pricing occurs when a seller states prices or price savings that mislead consumers or are not actually available to consumers. This might involve bogus reference or comparison prices, as when a retailer sets artificially high "regular" prices then announces "sale" prices close to its previous everyday prices. For example, Overstock.com recently came under scrutiny for inaccurately listing manufacturer's suggested retail prices, often quoting them higher than the actual price. Such comparison pricing is widespread:

> Open any Sunday newspaper and find hundreds of such promotions being offered by a variety of retailers, such as supermarkets, office supply stores, furniture stores, computer stores, appliance stores, pharmacies and drugstores, car dealers, department stores, and others. Surf the Internet and see similar price promotions. Watch the shopping channels on television and find more of the same. It seems that, today, selling prices rarely stand alone. Instead retailers are using an advertised reference price (e.g., regular price, original price, manufacturer's suggested price) to suggest that buyers will save money if they take advantage of the "deal" being offered.[22]

Such claims are legal if they are truthful. However, the FTC's *Guides Against Deceptive Pricing* warns sellers not to advertise a price reduction unless it is a saving from the usual retail price, not to advertise "factory" or "wholesale" prices unless such prices are what they are claimed to be, and not to advertise comparable value prices on imperfect goods.[23]

Other deceptive pricing issues include *scanner fraud* and price confusion. The widespread use of scanner-based computer checkouts has led to increasing complaints of retailers overcharging their customers. Most of these overcharges result from poor management—from a failure to enter current or sale prices into the system. Other cases, however, involve intentional overcharges. *Price confusion* results when firms employ pricing methods that make it difficult for consumers to understand just what price they are really paying. For example, consumers are sometimes misled regarding the real price of a home mortgage or car leasing agreement. In other cases, important pricing details may be buried in the "fine print." Many federal and state statutes regulate against deceptive pricing practices. For

■ Deceptive pricing concerns: The widespread use of checkout scanners has led to increasing complaints of retailers overcharging their customers.

example, the Automobile Information Disclosure Act requires automakers to attach a statement to new-car windows stating the manufacturer's suggested retail price, the prices of optional equipment, and the dealer's transportation charges. However, reputable sellers go beyond what is required by law. Treating customers fairly and making certain that they fully understand prices and pricing terms is an important part of building strong and lasting customer relationships.

> Reviewing the Concepts <

Pricing decisions are subject to an incredibly complex array of environmental and competitive forces. A company sets not a single price, but rather a *pricing structure* that covers different items in its line. This pricing structure changes over time as products move through their life cycles. The company adjusts product prices to reflect changes in costs and demand and to account for variations in buyers and situations. As the competitive environment changes, the company considers when to initiate price changes and when to respond to them.

1. Describe the major strategies for pricing imitative and new products.

Pricing is a dynamic process. Companies design a *pricing structure* that covers all their products. They change this structure over time and adjust it to account for different customers and situations. Pricing strategies usually change as a product passes through its life cycle. The company can decide on one of several price-quality strategies for introducing an imitative product, including premium pricing, economy pricing, good value, or overcharging. In pricing innovative new products, it can follow a *skimming policy* by initially setting high prices to "skim" the maximum amount of revenue from various segments of the market. Or it can use *penetration pricing* by setting a low initial price to penetrate the market deeply and win a large market share.

2. Explain how companies find a set of prices that maximize the profits from the total product mix.

When the product is part of a product mix, the firm searches for a set of prices that will maximize the profits from the total mix. In *product line pricing*, the company decides on price steps for the entire set of products it offers. In addition, the company must set prices for *optional products* (optional or accessory products included with the main product), *captive products* (products that are required for use of the main product), *by-products* (waste or residual products produced when making the main product), and *product bundles* (combinations of products at a reduced price).

3. Discuss how companies adjust their prices to take into account different types of customers and situations.

Companies apply a variety of *price adjustment strategies* to account for differences in consumer segments and situations. One is *discount and allowance pricing*, whereby the company establishes cash, quantity, functional, or seasonal discounts, or varying types of allowances. A second strategy is *segmented pricing*, where the company sells a product at two or more prices to accommodate different customers, product forms, locations, or times. Sometimes companies consider more than economics in their pricing decisions, using *psychological pricing* to better communicate a product's intended position. In *promotional pricing*, a company offers discounts or temporarily sells a product below list price as a special event, sometimes even selling below cost as a loss leader. Another approach is *geographical pricing*, whereby the company decides how to price to distant customers, choosing from such alternatives as FOB pricing, uniform-delivered pricing, zone pricing, basing-point pricing, and freight-absorption pricing. Finally, *international pricing* means that the company adjusts its price to meet different conditions and expectations in different world markets.

4. Discuss the key issues related to initiating and responding to price changes.

When a firm considers initiating a *price change*, it must consider customers' and competitors' reactions. There are different implications to *initiating price cuts* and *initiating price increases*. Buyer reactions to price changes are influenced by the meaning customers see in the price change. Competitors' reactions flow from a set reaction policy or a fresh analysis of each situation.

There are also many factors to consider in responding to a competitor's price changes. The company that faces a price change initiated by a competitor must try to understand the competitor's intent as well as the likely duration and impact of the change. If a swift reaction is desirable, the firm should preplan its reactions to different possible price actions by competitors. When facing a competitor's price change, the company might sit tight, reduce its own price, raise perceived quality, improve quality and raise price, or launch a fighting brand.

> Reviewing the Key Terms <

Allowance 337
Basing-point pricing 343
By-product pricing 335
Captive-product pricing 335
Discount 336

FOB-origin pricing 343
Freight-absorption pricing 344
Market-penetration pricing 333
Market-skimming pricing 333
Optional-product pricing 334

Product bundle pricing 336
Product line pricing 334
Promotional pricing 342
Psychological pricing 339
Reference prices 339

Segmented pricing 337
Uniform-delivered pricing 343
Zone pricing 343

> Discussing the Concepts <

1. What market conditions would discourage a company from using a penetration-pricing strategy to enter a market?

2. Automobile companies use optional-product pricing. In what other product categories do companies use this pricing strategy?

3. The chapter mentions "2/10, net 30" as an example of a cash discount given to reward customers for prompt payment, and "$10 per unit for less than 100 units, $9 per unit for 100 or more units" as an example of a quantity discount. Name and explain five other discounts or allowances commonly given in buyers.

4. Psychological pricing is a price-adjustment strategy often used by retailers. Explain this pricing strategy. How it is tied to the concept of reference prices?

5. Discuss the difficulties an international company would encounter if it set a uniform worldwide price for a commodity-type product.

6. Lawful price discrimination by sellers is a common practice. Discuss the conditions under which price discrimination becomes unlawful.

> Applying the Concepts <

1. Cell phone companies use a two-part pricing. From a consumer's perspective, is there a better pricing strategy? What is it? Explain.

2. Promotional pricing generates a sense of urgency and excitement. However, recognizing the dangers of this pricing approach, your boss has asked you to design an alternative pricing strategy that will generate the greater long-term sales and customer loyalty. What pricing strategy do you recommend? Will this strategy work as well as promotional pricing in the short term? Explain.

3. You are an owner of a small independent chain of coffeehouses competing head-to-head with Starbuck's. The retail price your customers pay for coffee is exactly the same as at Starbuck's. The wholesale price you pay for roasted coffee beans has increased by 25 percent. You understand that you cannot absorb this increase and that it must be passed on to your customers. However, you are concerned about the consequences of an open price increase. Discuss three alternative price-increase strategies that address your concerns.

> Focus on Technology <

From the consumer's perspective, the most-often-asked question is "Where can we get the best price?" In response to that question came "shopping bots." These software agents search through millions of online sites to find the best prices. The more popular shopping bots include Bizrate, mySimon, Nextag, PriceGrabber.com, PriceScan.com, and Shopping.com. These sites do a fine job providing the potential buyer with comparative price information. But what about sellers? How do they know if the online selling prices they feature are competitive? Are their prices too high? Too low? How can these online sellers manage their pricing? The answer, of course, is "pricing bots." Pricing bots are software agents that adjust prices automatically for the seller in response to changing market conditions. For example, suppose Barnes & Noble (B&N) at their online site (www.barnesandnoble.com) wishes to price the current top 10 hard cover and paperback fiction and nonfiction best sellers, at 10 cents below the price quoted by Amazon.com. Thousands of times a day, the B&N pricing bot would search each title at Amazon.com, record the competitor's price, and adjust B&N's prices accordingly.

1. What do you think about this type of pricing-setting technology? Do you see it as a help or hindrance to the seller? To the buyer?

2. What type of pricing strategy would a company be employing if it used a pricing bot to adjust prices to always have the lowest price on any given product?

3. Do you see any dangers with this pricing strategy?

> Focus on Ethics <

Segmented pricing is common. Most people understand and accept situations in which children or seniors get breaks on meal prices or movie tickets. But what do you say to an entire country full of consumers who want better prices on prescription drugs? The following excerpts from a *CBS Evening News* story capture the essence of the debate. "It may come as no surprise that the pharmaceutical industry is the most profitable business in the country. Americans pay far more for their prescription drugs than citizens of any place on Earth. It will also come as no surprise that as a political issue, the high price of drugs has united both Republicans and Democrats. More than a million Americans now buy their medications for much lower prices in Canada. And it's no longer just older people taking buses across the border. Mayors and governors from Minnesota to Alabama are helping Americans get Canadian drugs by mail. According to the FDA such purchases are technically illegal. So far, the government has declined to prosecute individual customers or the cities and states involved."

1. What pricing objectives do U.S. pharmaceutical companies pursue?

2. U.S pharmaceutical companies sell most drugs at significantly lower prices to Canadian drug outlets than they do to U.S. drug outlets. Is this a fair pricing policy? To whom?

3. What does the FDA say about U.S. citizens buying prescription drugs in Canada? What should it say?

 # Video Case

Song Airlines

To compete with phenomenally successful carriers such as Southwest, Delta Airlines recently launched Song, its own low-fare service. With new planes and a new approach to customer service, Song debuted in 2003. The airline promises to take the mystery out of ticket prices by keeping one-way fares between $79 and $299. In addition to low fares, Song offers every passenger 24 channels of DISH Network Satellite TV, streaming digital radio, and video games they can play against other passengers in real time. And, rather than the typical airline food, Song provides an array of tasty, body-smart breakfast, lunch, and dinner options to choose from during a flight. By promising low fares and offering passengers perks such as leather seating and satellite television, Song hopes to attract frequent flyers looking for more from their low-price carriers.

After viewing the video featuring Song Airlines, answer the following questions about pricing strategies.

1. What pricing strategies does Song employ to differentiate itself from other airlines?

2. Are Song's pricing strategies consistent with the rest of the airline's marketing mix?

3. Would you be interested in flying on Song Airlines? Should Song consider targeting students? Why or why not?

Company Case

Southeast Bank: Free Checking?

CHECKING INTO CHECKING

Kelly James, Director of Strategic Planning at Southeast Bank*, looked up from her conference table as Bonnie Summers, Manager of Retail Deposits, and Paul Bridges, Retail Product Manager, knocked at her office door.

"Come on in," Kelly exclaimed as she waved them in. "I'm ready to hear what you've determined on the issue of whether we should start offering free checking. I know there are a lot of pros and cons, and the issue's generated a lot of heated discussion around the bank. As you know, the Executive Committee's asked me to look into the issue and make a recommendation."

"Well, I've found some interesting information from a recent national study," Bonnie began. "Every six months, researchers at Bankrate.com conduct a national survey of checking accounts, looking at things like fees, minimum balances, service charges, and so on. It recently reported the results of its Fall survey that included 1,276 different accounts at 350 institutions.

"The survey found that the interest rate paid on checking account balances fell from a 1.17 percent annual rate to .97 percent. The average minimum balance required to open an account and earn interest was $695, a six percent increase in just one year. On the other hand, to open a non-interest-bearing checking account required just $76.30 on average, an amount that's barely changed in three years.

"To avoid monthly service fees on an interest-bearing account, you need an average minimum balance of $2,434.50, up 5.6 percent in the last couple of years. The average minimum balance in non-interest bearing accounts is just $408.16. If you don't want to keep a high balance in an interest-bearing account, the average monthly service fee is $10.85, up four percent per year for the last three years. The average monthly fee on non-interest-bearing accounts actually dropped to $6.19.

"About one-fourth of the checking accounts also charge per-item fees for various transactions, like check writing or deposits. The average interest-paying account allows 17 "freebies," while the average non-interest paying account allows 12 before fees kick in. I also found that ATM fees for non-customers who use a bank's ATM system have become almost universal and now average about $1.32 per transaction."

* The name of the bank and the names of people in this case have been disguised. Certain data on the bank's operations have also been adjusted but are indicative of reality.

"Are there any true free checking accounts with no minimum balance, no monthly service charges, and no per-item fees?" Kelly asked.

"The study showed that about 7.5 percent of the accounts surveyed were free, as you describe it, an all-time high," Bonnie answered. I also found that the number of banks offering free non-interest checking accounts jumped more than 15 percentage points to 45.3 percent. This move was especially true among large banks, like Southeast.

"What about insufficient funds charges (NSFs)?" Paul asked.

"The survey showed that they were at an all-time high, also, Paul, averaging $24.85," Bonnie noted. "So, it's very expensive to bounce a check. Many banks offer overdraft protection—often for a fee, of course. Some banks charge an annual fee, such as $10, for overdraft protection and then add a $5 charge each time the customer uses the service."

SOUTHEAST'S SITUATION

"That's very helpful, Bonnie. Paul, how would you summarize our situation?" Kelly asked.

"Competitors have not yet offered completely free checking in our markets, although some are promoting no-fee checking accounts that require that the account holder use direct deposit of payroll checks. These accounts often limit access to tellers. Some banks have used free checking as their number-one weapon in entering new markets and as a result have enjoyed significant gains in demand-deposit accounts (DDA). These banks promote their free checking on an ongoing basis.

"From a defensive standpoint, we should be prepared for a competitor to launch a completely free checking product in our markets. From an offensive standpoint, we have the opportunity to be the first in our markets with our own free-checking product. I believe we could realize significant DDA share gains if we advertised the product."

"What experience have we had with these products?" Kelly asked.

"Well, we've acquired some small banks that had no-fee products, and we've experimented with some limited promotional campaigns in limited market areas," Paul replied. Our free accounts have typically required a minimum balance of $500 or there was a $9.95 per month fee. The account holder also had to pay $.35 per item for all checks or debits in excess of 20 per month."

"Are these accounts profitable for the bank?" Kelly asked.

"Profitability depends on several variables," Paul answered. First, there's the account's cash balance during

---

Handwritten margin notes:

mkte segment
– people who want low balance in account
– Free checking to students

Focus on customer reactions
Psychological pricing
Market is shifting to free checking

the month. Then, we earn income through fees like NSF charges and ATM fees. We give certain credits to the branch that opened the account, which we treat as revenue. Then, we have allocated expenses, non-interest expenses we allocate to every account. If, however, the account has direct deposit, the allocated expenses are about 25 percent lower as it is less expensive for us to handle direct-deposits. That is why so many free-checking products require direct deposits. The savings help offset the lost fees.

"Given all that, our study shows that the free-checking accounts we have experimented with had average balances of $1,262. Our annual revenue per account from all sources was about $274 and our fully allocated expenses were about $237, giving us an annual profit of about $37. The average account had about four NSF or overdraft charges a year, producing the largest source of account revenue."

"I should add," Bonnie interjected, "that for our 10 different types of checking accounts, including accounts for students and seniors, the lower the average balance the greater the number of NSF charges, except for our student accounts. Students had _less_ than one-half of the average number of overdrafts."

"Okay, what's the bottom line in terms of the impact on our revenue if we offered a free-checking product just in our home state?" Kelly asked.

"Our analysis focused on just our home state and estimated that varying percentages of customers from each type of checking account would move to the new product," Paul began. "If we offered the account in all 282 branches in the state for all 522,000 accounts, and if our switching estimates are correct, we could lose about $4.5 million in various fees (revenue) per year that those accounts are now paying. That is, we would lose this money as our current customers switched from fee-paying accounts to the free accounts. But, of course, we would hope that the new product would draw in new customers to offset those losses, and that those customers would also use other bank products, like home-equity loans or car loans."

"Speaking of 'drawing in,' what'll it cost us to promote this program?" Kelly asked.

"Our best estimate for an eight-week promotional program is about $127,000," Paul answered.

WHAT TO DO?

"Thanks for your good work," Kelly responded. "This information is helpful. I've got to decide what to recommend to the Executive Committee.

"I know that free checking is the 'in' thing now in banking with people believing that free checking gets people in the door. I also know that we make money on lower-income customers' accounts due to fee income and on higher-income customers' accounts due to higher balances. Further, although our total dollar balance in our checking accounts has been growing, our total number of accounts has been declining somewhat.

"One concern I have is whether or not free checking fits the bank's positioning. We've tried to position ourselves as a relationship bank, differentiating ourselves based on service versus price. We build and value long-term customer relationships. For that reason, we've not tried to pay the highest interest rates or charge the lowest fees because we didn't want customers who were focused only on price. I'm not sure free checking fits our image. Further, we've not traditionally advertised products. Rather, we've used corporate advertising that focused on the bank's relationships with its customers.

"This certainly isn't as easy a decision as it might appear," Bonnie noted.

"You can say that again!" Kelly responded. "I'll just have to ponder all this information and decide what to recommend. Thanks for your help."

Questions for Discussion

1. What type of new-product pricing strategy would be involved in considering a new free-checking product for the bank?

2. What types of product mix pricing considerations do you see in bank's pricing for checking accounts?

3. What types of price-adjustment considerations do you see in the pricing strategies for checking accounts?

4. What strategy would your recommend that Southeast Bank pursue on the free-checking account issue? What options does it have? How can break-even analysis (presented in Chapter 10) assist you in your analysis of the various options?

Sources: Officials at Southeast Bank cooperated in development of this case. See also: Tim Henderson, "More ATM Fees, Free Checking," *American* Banker, June 17, 2002, p. 24; Laura Bruce, "Checking Accounts Keep Climbing in Price," Bankrate.com, posted September 28, 2001.

1) Market-penetration pricing → Bank focused on customer relationships but they were losing mkt share / Psychological pricing. /

2) Product Mix considerations → customers reactions & types of consumers / potential loss of revenue / draw people in but focus on long term value. / product line pricing & pdct Bundle pricing. / higher % rates attract # customers from free checking segments.

CHAPTER

12

Marketing Channels and Supply Chain Management

> **After studying this chapter, you should be able to**
>
> 1. explain why companies use marketing channels and discuss the functions these channels perform
> 2. discuss how channel members interact and how they organize to perform the work of the channel
> 3. identify the major channel alternatives open to a company
> 4. explain how companies select, motivate, and evaluate channel members
> 5. discuss the nature and importance of marketing logistics and integrated supply chain management

Previewing the Concepts

Let's look now at the third marketing mix tool—distribution. Firms rarely work alone in creating value for customers and building profitable customer relationships. Instead, most are only a single link in a larger supply chain and distribution channel. As such, an individual firm's success depends not only on how well *it* performs but also on how well its *entire distribution channel* competes with competitors' channels. To be good at customer relationship management, a company must also be good at partner relationship management. The first part of this chapter explores the nature of distribution channels and the marketer's channel design and management decisions. We then examine physical distribution—or logistics—an area that is growing dramatically in importance and sophistication. In the next chapter, we'll look more closely at two major channel intermediaries—retailers and wholesalers.

We'll start with a look at Caterpillar. You might think that Caterpillar's success, and its ability to charge premium prices, rests on the quality of the heavy construction and mining equipment that it produces. But Caterpillar sees things differently. The company's dominance, it claims, results from its unparalleled distribution and customer support system—from the strong and caring partnerships that it has built with independent Caterpillar dealers. Read on and see why.

358

For more than seven decades, Caterpillar has dominated the world's markets for heavy construction, mining, and logging equipment. Its familiar yellow tractors, crawlers, loaders, bulldozers, and trucks are a common sight at any construction area. Caterpillar sells more than 300 products in nearly 200 companies, generating sales of almost $23 billion annually. It captures 27 percent of the worldwide construction-equipment business, more than double that of number two Komatsu. Its share of the North American market is more than twice that of competitors Komatsu and Deere combined.

Many factors contribute to Caterpillar's enduring success—high-quality products, flexible and efficient manufacturing, and a steady stream of innovative new products. Yet these are not the most important reasons for Caterpillar's dominance. Instead, Caterpillar credits its focus on customers and its corps of 220 outstanding independent dealers worldwide, who do a superb job of taking care of every customer need. According to former Caterpillar CEO Donald Fites:

> After the product leaves our door, the dealers take over. They are the ones on the front line. They're the ones who live with the product for its lifetime. They're the ones customers see. . . . They're out there making sure that when a machine is delivered, it's in the condition it's supposed to be in. They're out there training a customer's operators. They service a product frequently throughout its life, carefully monitoring a machine's health and scheduling repairs to prevent costly downtime. The customer . . . knows that there is a $20-billion-plus company called Caterpillar. But the dealers create the image of a company that doesn't just stand *behind* its products but *with* its products, anywhere in the world. Our dealers are the reason that our motto—Buy the Iron, Get the Company—is not an empty slogan.

"Buy the Iron, Get the Company"—that's a powerful value proposition. It means that when you buy Cat equipment, you become a member of the Caterpillar family. Caterpillar and its dealers work in close harmony to find better ways to bring value to customers. Dealers play a vital role in almost every aspect of Caterpillar's operations, from product design and delivery, to product service and support, to market intelligence and customer feedback.

In the heavy-equipment industry, in which equipment downtime can mean big losses, Caterpillar's exceptional service gives it a huge advantage in winning and keeping customers. Consider Freeport-McMoRan, a Cat customer that operates one of the world's largest copper and gold mines, 24 hours a day, 365 days a year. High in the mountains of Indonesia, the mine is accessible only by aerial cableway or helicopter. Freeport-McMoRan relies on more than 500 pieces of Caterpillar mining and construction equipment—worth several hundred million dollars—including loaders, tractors, and mammoth 240-ton, 2,000-plus-horsepower trucks. Many of these machines cost well over $1 million apiece. When equipment breaks down, Freeport-McMoRan loses money fast. Freeport-McMoRan gladly pays a premium price for machines and service it can count on. It knows that it can count on Caterpillar and its outstanding distribution network for superb support.

The close working relationship between Caterpillar and its dealers comes down to more than just formal contracts and business agreements. The powerful partnership rests on a handful of basic principles and practices:

- *Dealer profitability:* Caterpillar's rule: "Share the gain as well as the pain." When times are good, Caterpillar shares the bounty with its dealers rather than trying to grab all the riches for itself. When times are bad, Caterpillar protects its dealers. In the mid-1980s, facing a depressed global construction-equipment market and cutthroat competition, Caterpillar sheltered its dealers by absorbing much of the economic damage. It lost almost $1 billion dollars in just 3 years but didn't lose a single dealer. In contrast, competitors' dealers struggled and many failed. As a result, Caterpillar emerged with its distribution system intact and its competitive position stronger than ever.

- *Extraordinary dealer support:* Nowhere is this support more apparent than in the company's parts delivery system, the fastest and most reliable in the industry. Caterpillar maintains 36 distribution centers and 1,500 service facilities around the world, which stock 320,000 different parts and ship 84,000 items per day, every day of the year. In turn, dealers have made huge investments in inventory, warehouses, fleets of trucks, service bays, diagnostic and service equipment, and information technology. Together, Caterpillar and its dealers guarantee parts delivery within 48 hours anywhere in the world. The company ships 80 percent of parts orders immediately and 99 percent on the same day

the order is received. In contrast, it's not unusual for competitors' customers to wait 4 or 5 days for a part.

- *Communications:* Caterpillar communicates with its dealers—fully, frequently, and honestly. According to Fites, "There are no secrets between us and our dealers. We have the financial statements and key operating data of every dealer in the world. . . . In addition, virtually all Caterpillar and dealer employees have real-time access to continually updated databases of service information, sales trends and forecasts, customer satisfaction surveys, and other critical data."

- *Dealer performance:* Caterpillar does all it can to ensure that its dealerships are run well. It closely monitors each dealership's sales, market position, service capability, financial situation, and other performance measures. It genuinely wants each dealer to succeed, and when it sees a problem, it jumps in to help. As a result, Caterpillar dealerships, many of which are family businesses, tend to be stable and profitable.

- *Personal relationships:* In addition to more formal business ties, Cat forms close personal ties with its dealers in a kind of family relationship. One Caterpillar executive relates the following example: "When I see Chappy Chapman, a retired executive vice-president . . . , out on the golf course, he always asks about particular dealers or about their children, who may be running the business now. And every time I see those dealers, they inquire, 'How's Chappy?' That's the sort of relationship we have. . . . I consider the majority of dealers personal friends."

Thus, Caterpillar's superb distribution system serves as a major source of competitive advantage. The system is built on a firm base of mutual trust and shared dreams. Caterpillar and its dealers feel a deep pride in what they are accomplishing together. As Fites puts it, "There's a camaraderie among our dealers around the world that really makes it more than just a financial arrangement. They feel that what they're doing is good for the world because they are part of an organization that makes, sells, and tends to the machines that make the world work."[1]

Most firms cannot bring value to customers by themselves. Instead, they must work closely with other firms in a larger value delivery network.

Supply Chains and the Value Delivery Network

Producing a product or service and making it available to buyers requires building relationships not just with customers, but also with key suppliers and resellers in the company's *supply chain*. This supply chain consists of "upstream" and "downstream" partners. Upstream from the company is the set of firms that supply the raw materials, components, parts, information, finances, and expertise needed to create a product or service. Marketers, however, have traditionally focused on the "downstream" side of the supply chain—on the *marketing channels* or *distribution channels* that look forward toward the customer. Downstream marketing channel partners, such as wholesalers and retailers, form a vital connection between the firm and its customers.

Both upstream and downstream partners may also be part of other firms' supply chains. But it is the unique design of each company's supply chain that enables it to deliver superior value to customers. An individual firm's success depends not only on how well *it* performs, but also on how well its entire supply chain and marketing channel competes with competitors' channels.

The term *supply chain* may be too limited—it takes a *make-and-sell* view of the business. It suggests that raw materials, productive inputs, and factory capacity should serve as the starting point for market planning. A better term would be *demand chain* because it suggests a *sense-and-respond* view of the market. Under this view, planning starts with the needs of target customers, to which the company responds by organizing a chain of resources and activities with the goal of creating customer value.

Even a demand-chain view of a business may be too limited, because it takes a step-by-step, linear view of purchase-production-consumption activities. With the advent of the Internet and other technologies, however, companies are forming more numerous and complex relationships with other firms. For example, Ford manages numerous supply chains. It also sponsors or transacts on many business-to-business (B2B) Web sites and online purchasing exchanges as needs arise. Like Ford, most large companies today are engaged in building and managing a continuously evolving *value delivery network*.

Companies today are increasingly taking a full-value-delivery-network view of their businesses. As defined in Chapter 2, a **value delivery network** is made up of the company, suppliers, distributors, and ultimately customers who "partner" with each other to improve the performance of the entire system. For example, Palm, the leading manufacturer of handheld devices, manages a whole community of suppliers and assemblers of semiconductor components, plastic cases, LCD displays, and accessories. Its network also includes offline and

Value delivery network
The network made up of the company, suppliers, distributors, and ultimately customers who "partner" with each other to improve the performance of the entire system.

■ Value delivery network: Palm manages a whole community of suppliers, assemblers, resellers, and complementors who must work effectively together to make life easier from Palm's customers.

online resellers, and 45,000 complementors who have created over 5,000 applications for the Palm operating systems. All of these diverse partners must work effectively together to bring superior value to Palm's customers.

This chapter focuses on marketing channels—on the downstream side of the value delivery network. However, it is important to remember that this is only part of the full value network. To bring value to customers, companies need upstream supplier partners just as they need downstream channel partners. Increasingly, marketers are participating in and influencing their company's upstream activities as well as its downstream activities. More than marketing channel managers, they are becoming full network managers.

The chapter examines four major questions concerning marketing channels: What is the nature of marketing channels and why are they important? How do channel firms interact and organize to do the work of the channel? What problems do companies face in designing and managing their channels? What role do physical distribution and supply chain management play in attracting and satisfying customers? In Chapter 13, we will look at marketing channel issues from the viewpoint of retailers and wholesalers.

start Here ✎

The Nature and Importance of Marketing Channels

Marketing channel (or distribution channel)
A set of interdependent organizations involved in the process of making a product or service available for use or consumption by the consumer or business user.

Few producers sell their goods directly to the final users. Instead, most use intermediaries to bring their products to market. They try to forge a **marketing channel** (or **distribution channel**)—a set of interdependent organizations involved in the process of making a product or service available for use or consumption by the consumer or business user.[2]

A company's channel decisions directly affect every other marketing decision. The company's pricing depends on whether it works with national discount chains, uses high-quality specialty stores, or sells directly to consumers via the Web. The firm's sales force and communications decisions depend on how much persuasion, training, motivation, and support

■ FedEx's creative and imposing distribution system made it a market leader in express delivery. "Relax, it's FedEx."

its channel partners need. Whether a company develops or acquires certain new products may depend on how well those products fit the capabilities of its channel members.

Companies often pay too little attention to their distribution channels, sometimes with damaging results. In contrast, many companies have used imaginative distribution systems to *gain* a competitive advantage. It's creative and imposing distribution system has made FedEx a leader in the express delivery industry. Dell Computer revolutionized its industry by selling personal computers directly to consumers rather than through retail stores. And Amazon.com pioneered the sales of books and a wide range of other goods via the Internet.

Distribution channel decisions often involve long-term commitments to other firms. For example, companies such as Ford, IBM, or McDonald's can easily change their advertising, pricing, or promotion programs. They can scrap old products and introduce new ones as market tastes demand. But when they set up distribution channels through contracts with franchisees, independent dealers, or large retailers, they cannot readily replace these channels with company-owned stores or Web sites if conditions change. Therefore, management must design its channels carefully, with an eye on tomorrow's likely selling environment as well as today's.

How Channel Members Add Value

Why do producers give some of the selling job to channel partners? After all, doing so means giving up some control over how and to whom the products are sold. The use of intermediaries results from their greater efficiency in making goods available to target markets. Through their contacts, experience, specialization, and scale of operation, intermediaries usually offer the firm more than it can achieve on its own.

Figure 12.1 shows how using intermediaries can provide economies. Figure 12.1A shows three manufacturers, each using direct marketing to reach three customers. This system requires nine different contacts. Figure 12.1B shows the three manufacturers working through one distributor, which contacts the three customers. This system requires only six contacts. In this way, intermediaries reduce the amount of work that must be done by both producers and consumers.

From the economic system's point of view, the role of marketing intermediaries is to transform the assortments of products made by producers into the assortments wanted by consumers. Producers make narrow assortments of products in large quantities, but consumers want broad assortments of products in small quantities. In the marketing channels, intermediaries buy large quantities from many producers and break them down into the smaller quantities and broader assortments wanted by consumers. Thus, intermediaries play an important role in matching supply and demand.

In making products and services available to consumers, channel members add value by bridging the major time, place, and possession gaps that separate goods and services from

FIGURE 12.1

How a marketing intermediary reduces the number of channel transactions

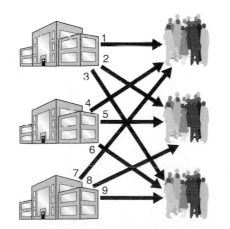

A. Number of contacts without a distributor
$M \times C = 3 \times 3 = 9$

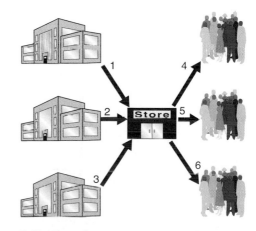

B. Number of contacts with a distributor
$M + C = 3 + 3 = 6$

 = Manufacturer   = Customer    = Distributor

those who would use them. Members of the marketing channel perform many key functions. Some help to complete transactions:

- *Information:* Gathering and distributing marketing research and intelligence information about actors and forces in the marketing environment needed for planning and aiding exchange.
- *Promotion:* Developing and spreading persuasive communications about an offer.
- *Contact:* Finding and communicating with prospective buyers.
- *Matching:* Shaping and fitting the offer to the buyer's needs, including activities such as manufacturing, grading, assembling, and packaging.
- *Negotiation:* Reaching an agreement on price and other terms of the offer so that ownership or possession can be transferred.

Others help to fulfill the completed transactions:

- *Physical distribution:* Transporting and storing goods.
- *Financing:* Acquiring and using funds to cover the costs of the channel work.
- *Risk taking:* Assuming the risks of carrying out the channel work.

The question is not *whether* these functions need to be performed—they must be—but rather *who* will perform them. To the extent that the manufacturer performs these functions, its costs go up and its prices have to be higher. When some of these functions are shifted to intermediaries, the producer's costs and prices may be lower, but the intermediaries must charge more to cover the costs of their work. In dividing the work of the channel, the various functions should be assigned to the channel members who can add the most value for the cost.

Number of Channel Levels

Channel level

A layer of intermediaries that performs some work in bringing the product and its ownership closer to the final buyer.

Direct marketing channel

A marketing channel that has no intermediary levels.

Indirect marketing channel

A channel containing one or more intermediary levels.

Companies can design their distribution channels to make products and services available to customers in different ways. Each layer of marketing intermediaries that performs some work in bringing the product and its ownership closer to the final buyer is a **channel level**. Because the producer and the final consumer both perform some work, they are part of every channel.

The *number of intermediary levels* indicates the *length* of a channel. Figure 12.2A shows several consumer distribution channels of different lengths. Channel 1, called a **direct marketing channel**, has no intermediary levels; the company sells directly to consumers. For example, Avon and Amway sell their products door-to-door, through home and office sales parties, and on the Web; L.L. Bean sells clothing direct through mail catalogs, by telephone, and online; and a university sells education on its campus or through distance learning. The remaining channels in Figure 12.2A are **indirect marketing channels**, containing one or more intermediaries.

FIGURE 12.2
Customer and business marketing channels

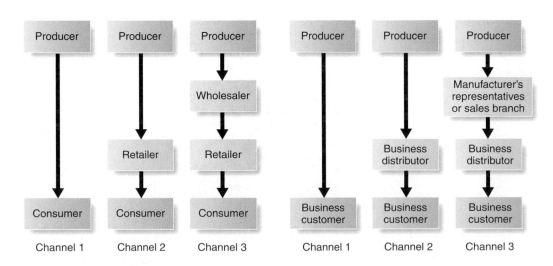

Channel 1   Channel 2   Channel 3   Channel 1   Channel 2   Channel 3

A. Consumer marketing channels   B. Business marketing channels

Figure 12.2B shows some common business distribution channels. The business marketer can use its own sales force to sell directly to business customers. Or it can sell to various types of intermediaries, who in turn sell to these customers. Consumer and business marketing channels with even more levels are sometimes found, but less often. From the producer's point of view, a greater number of levels means less control and greater channel complexity. Moreover, all of the institutions in the channel are connected by several types of *flows*. These include the *physical flow* of products, the *flow of ownership*, the *payment flow*, the *information flow*, and the *promotion flow*. These flows can make even channels with only one or a few levels very complex.

Channel Behavior and Organization

Distribution channels are more than simple collections of firms tied together by various flows. They are complex behavioral systems in which people and companies interact to accomplish individual, company, and channel goals. Some channel systems consist only of informal interactions among loosely organized firms. Others consist of formal interactions guided by strong organizational structures. Moreover, channel systems do not stand still—new types of intermediaries emerge and whole new channel systems evolve. Here we look at channel behavior and at how members organize to do the work of the channel.

Channel Behavior

A marketing channel consists of firms that have partnered for their common good. Each channel member depends on the others. For example, a Ford dealer depends on Ford to design cars that meet consumer needs. In turn, Ford depends on the dealer to attract consumers, persuade them to buy Ford cars, and service cars after the sale. Each Ford dealer also depends on other dealers to provide good sales and service that will uphold the brand's reputation. In fact, the success of individual Ford dealers depends on how well the entire Ford marketing channel competes with the channels of other auto manufacturers.

Each channel member plays a specialized role in the channel. For example, Sony's role is to produce consumer electronics products that consumers will like and to create demand through national advertising. Best Buy's role is to display these Sony products in convenient locations, to answer buyers' questions, and to complete sales. The channel will be most effective when each member is assigned the tasks it can do best.

Ideally, because the success of individual channel members depends on overall channel success, all channel firms should work together smoothly. They should understand and accept their roles, coordinate their activities, and cooperate to attain overall channel goals. However, individual channel members rarely take such a broad view. Cooperating to achieve overall channel goals sometimes means giving up individual company goals. Although channel members depend on one another, they often act alone in their own short-run best interests. They often disagree on who should do what and for what rewards. Such disagreements over goals, roles, and rewards generate **channel conflict**.

Channel conflict

Disagreement among marketing channel members on goals and roles—who should do what and for what rewards.

Horizontal conflict occurs among firms at the same level of the channel. For instance, some Ford dealers in Chicago might complain the other dealers in the city steal sales from them by pricing too low or by advertising outside their assigned territories. Or Holiday Inn franchisees might complain about other Holiday Inn operators overcharging guests or giving poor service, hurting the overall Holiday Inn image.

Vertical conflict, conflicts between different levels of the same channel, is even more common. For example, office furniture maker Herman Miller created conflict with its dealers when it opened an online store—www.hmstore.com—and began selling its products directly to customers. Although Herman Miller believed that the Web site was reaching only smaller customers who weren't being served by current channels, dealers complained loudly. As a result, the company closed down its online sales operations. Tupperware faced similar conflicts with its independent sales consultants when it decided to sell its familiar plastic food-storage containers through Target stores.

Tupperware decided to supplement its army of in-home sales consultants by placing its products in Target's 1,148 stores. The sales consultants—who bring in more than 90 percent of Tupperware's sales—typically sell the company's products through in-home and at-work sales parties. To avoid conflict, Tupperware invited consultants into the stores to demonstrate products. It looked like the answer to a

■ Channel conflict: Tupperware's decision to sell its familiar containers at retail through Target stores created conflict with the company's army of in-home sales consultants. Sales and profits plunged.

chronic problem: how to sell face-to-face in an era when shoppers don't have time for a home sales pitch. But moving into Target turned out to be one of the worst disasters ever at Tupperware. It became so easy to find the company's products at Target that interest in its parties plummeted, creating conflict between Tupperware and its sales consultants. Fewer parties meant fewer chances to land other parties and new salespeople. Existing salespeople, who get a share of the commissions their recruits earn, grew frustrated at the dwindling party and recruiting numbers. Some stopped volunteering to work at Target. Others quit selling Tupperware entirely. Target "was competition for us," says a former Tupperware salesperson. Tupperware soon yanked its merchandise out of Target stores, but the damage was done. After 3 straight years of increases, Tupperware sales in North America fell 17 percent to a 3-year low and profit plunged 47 percent.[3]

Some conflict in the channel takes the form of healthy competition. Such competition can be good for the channel—without it, the channel could become passive and noninnovative. But severe or prolonged conflict can disrupt channel effectiveness and cause lasting harm to channel relationships. Companies should manage channel conflict to keep it from getting out of hand.

Vertical Marketing Systems

For the channel as a whole to perform well, each channel member's role must be specified and channel conflict must be managed. The channel will perform better if it includes a firm, agency, or mechanism that provides leadership and has the power to assign roles and manage conflict.

Historically, *conventional distribution channels* have lacked such leadership and power, often resulting in damaging conflict and poor performance. One of the biggest channel developments over the years has been the emergence of *vertical marketing systems* that provide channel leadership. Figure 12.3 contrasts the two types of channel arrangements.

A **conventional distribution channel** consists of one or more independent producers, wholesalers, and retailers. Each is a separate business seeking to maximize its own profits, even at the expense of the system as a whole. No channel member has much control over the other members, and no formal means exists for assigning roles and resolving channel conflict. In contrast, a **vertical marketing system (VMS)** consists of producers, wholesalers, and retailers acting as a unified system. One channel member owns the others, has contracts with them, or wields so much power that they must all cooperate. The VMS can be dominated by the producer, wholesaler, or retailer.

We look now at three major types of VMSs: *corporate, contractual,* and *administered.* Each uses a different means for setting up leadership and power in the channel.

Conventional distribution channel
A channel consisting of one or more independent producers, wholesalers, and retailers, each a separate business seeking to maximize its own profits even at the expense of profits for the system as a whole.

Vertical marketing system (VMS)
A distribution channel structure in which producers, wholesalers, and retailers act as a unified system. One channel member owns the others, has contracts with them, or has so much power that they all cooperate.

FIGURE 12.3
A conventional marketing channel versus a vertical marketing system

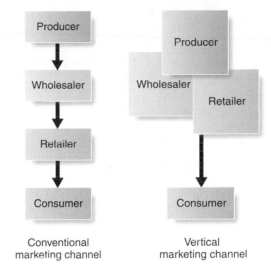

Conventional
marketing channel

Vertical
marketing channel

Corporate VMS

Corporate VMS

A vertical marketing system that combines successive stages of production and distribution under single ownership—channel leadership is established through common ownership.

A **corporate VMS** integrates successive stages of production and distribution under single ownership. Coordination and conflict management are attained through regular organizational channels. For example, grocery giant Kroger owns and operates 42 factories that crank out more than 4,300 of the food and drink items found on its store shelves. Giant Food Stores operates an ice-cube processing facility, a soft drink bottling operation, its own diary, an ice cream plant, and a bakery that supplies Giant stores with everything from bagels to birthday cakes. And little-known Italian eyewear maker Luxottica produces many famous eyewear brands—including Ray-Ban, Vogue, Anne Klein, Ferragamo, and Armani. It then sells these brands through two of the world's largest optical chains, LensCrafters and Sunglass Hut, which it also owns.[4]

Controlling the entire distribution chain has turned Spanish clothing chain Zara into the world's fastest-growing fashion retailer.

> The secret to Zara's success is its control over almost every aspect of the supply chain, from design and production to its own worldwide distribution network. Zara makes 40 percent of its own fabrics and produces more than half of its own clothes, rather than relying on a hodgepodge of slow-moving suppliers. New styles take shape in Zara's own design centers, supported by real-time sales data. New designs feed into Zara manufacturing centers, which ship finished products directly to 652 Zara stores in 48 countries, saving time, eliminating the need for warehouses, and keeping inventories low. Effective vertical integration makes Zara faster, more flexible, and more efficient than international competitors such as Gap, Benetton, and

■ Corporate VMS: Little-known Italian eyewear maker Luxottica produces many famous eyewear brands—including RayBan—then sells them through two of the world's largest optical chains, LensCrafters and Sunglass Hut, which it also owns.

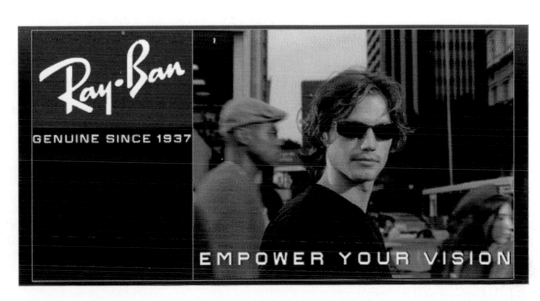

Sweden's H&M. Its finely tuned distribution systems makes Zara seem more like Dell or Wal-Mart than Gucci or Louis Vuitton. Zara can make a new line from start to finish in less than 15 days, so a look seen on MTV can be in Zara stores within a month, versus an industry average of 9 months. And Zara's low costs let it offer midmarket chic at downmarket prices. The company's stylish but affordable offerings have attracted a cult following, and the company's sales have more than doubled to $3.1 billion in the past 5 years.[5]

Contractual VMS

Contractual VMS

A vertical marketing system in which independent firms at different levels of production and distribution join together through contracts to obtain more economies or sales impact than they could achieve alone.

A **contractual VMS** consists of independent firms at different levels of production and distribution who join together through contracts to obtain more economies or sales impact than each could achieve alone. Coordination and conflict management are attained through contractual agreements among channel members.

Franchise organization

A contractual vertical marketing system in which a channel member, called a franchiser, links several stages in the production-distribution process.

The **franchise organization** is the most common type of contractual relationship—a channel member called a *franchisor* links several stages in the production-distribution process. In the United States alone, an estimated 760,000 franchise outlets account for more than $1.5 trillion in annual sales. Industry analysts estimate the a new franchise outlet opens somewhere in the United States every 8 minutes and that about 1 out of every 12 retail business outlets is a franchised business.[6] Almost every kind of business has been franchised—from motels and fast-food restaurants to dental centers and dating services, from wedding consultants and maid services to fitness centers and funeral homes.

There are three types of franchises. The first type is the *manufacturer-sponsored retailer franchise system*—for example, Ford and its network of independent franchised dealers. The second type is the *manufacturer-sponsored wholesaler franchise system*—Coca-Cola licenses bottlers (wholesalers) in various markets who buy Coca-Cola syrup concentrate and then bottle and sell the finished product to retailers in local markets. The third type is the *service-firm-sponsored retailer franchise system*—examples are found in the auto-rental business (Hertz, Avis), the fast-food service business (McDonald's, Burger King), and the motel business (Holiday Inn, Ramada Inn).

The fact that most consumers cannot tell the difference between contractual and corporate VMSs shows how successfully the contractual organizations compete with corporate chains. Chapter 13 presents a fuller discussion of the various contractual VMSs.

Administered VMS

Administered VMS

A vertical marketing system that coordinates successive stages of production and distribution, not through common ownership or contractual ties, but through the size and power of one of the parties.

In an **administered VMS**, leadership is assumed not through common ownership or contractual ties but through the size and power of one or a few dominant channel members. Manufacturers of a top brand can obtain strong trade cooperation and support from resellers. For example, General Electric, Procter & Gamble, and Kraft can command unusual cooperation from resellers regarding displays, shelf space, promotions, and price policies. Large retailers such as Wal-Mart, Home Depot, and Barnes & Noble can exert strong influence on the manufacturers that supply the products they sell.

Horizontal Marketing Systems

Horizontal marketing system

A channel arrangement in which two or more companies at one level join together to follow a new marketing opportunity.

Another channel development is the **horizontal marketing system**, in which two or more companies at one level join together to follow a new marketing opportunity. By working together, companies can combine their financial, production, or marketing resources to accomplish more than any one company could alone.

Companies might join forces with competitors or noncompetitors. They might work with each other on a temporary or permanent basis, or they may create a separate company. For example, the Lamar Savings Bank of Texas arranged to locate its savings offices and automated teller machines in Safeway stores. Lamar gained quicker market entry at a low cost, and Safeway was able to offer in-store banking convenience to its customers. Similarly, McDonald's now places "express" versions of its restaurants in Wal-Mart stores. McDonald's benefits from Wal-Mart's heavy store traffic, while Wal-Mart keeps hungry shoppers from having to go elsewhere to eat.

Such channel arrangements also work well globally. For example, because of its excellent coverage of international markets, Nestlé jointly sells General Mills's cereal brands in 80 countries outside North America. Similarly, Coca-Cola and Nestlé formed a joint venture to market ready-to-drink coffee and tea worldwide. Coke provides worldwide experience in marketing and distributing beverages, and Nestlé contributes two established brand names—Nescafé and Nestea.[7]

■ Horizontal marketing systems: Nestle jointly sells General Mills cereal brands in markets outside North America.

The perfect handful for your little handful.

Made from four healthy whole grains - corn, oats, rice and wheat - Cheerios are the perfect choice for growing families. Small and round, they make ideal finger food for toddlers too. **There's a whole lot of good in those little 'o's.**

Multichannel Distribution Systems

Multichannel distribution system (or hybrid marketing channel)

A distribution system in which a single firm sets up two or more marketing channels to reach one or more customer segments.

In the past, many companies used a single channel to sell to a single market or market segment. Today, with the proliferation of customer segments and channel possibilities, more and more companies have adopted **multichannel distribution systems**—often called **hybrid marketing channels**. Such multichannel marketing occurs when a single firm sets up two or more marketing channels to reach one or more customer segments. The use of multichannel systems has increased greatly in recent years.

Figure 12.4 shows a hybrid channel. In the figure, the producer sells directly to consumer segment 1 using direct-mail catalogs, telemarketing, and the Internet and reaches consumer

FIGURE 12.4
Multichannel distribution system

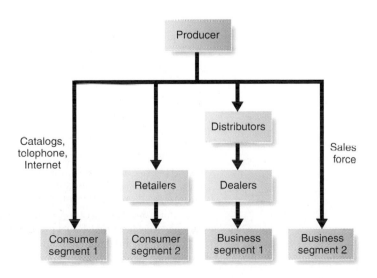

segment 2 through retailers. It sells indirectly to business segment 1 through distributors and dealers and to business segment 2 through its own sales force.

These days, almost every large company and many small ones distribute through multiple channels. Fidelity Investments reaches customers by telephone, over the Internet, and through its branch offices. It invites its customer to "call, click, or visit" Fidelity. Staples markets through its traditional retail outlets, a direct-response Internet site, virtual malls, and 30,000 links on affiliated sites.

IBM uses multiple channels to serve dozens of segments and niches, ranging from large corporate buyers to small businesses to home office buyers. In addition to selling through its vaunted sales force, IBM also sells through a full network of distributors and value-added resellers, which sell IBM computers, systems, and services to a variety of special business segments. Final consumers can buy IBM PCs from specialty computer stores or any of several large retailers. IBM uses telemarketing to service the needs of small and medium-size business. And both business and final consumers can buy online from the company's Web site (www.ibm.com).

Multichannel distribution systems offer many advantages to companies facing large and complex markets. With each new channel, the company expands its sales and market coverage and gains opportunities to tailor its products and services to the specific needs of diverse customer segments. But such multichannel channel systems are harder to control, and they generate conflict as more channels compete for customers and sales. For example, when IBM began selling directly to customers through telemarketing and its own Web site, many of its retail dealers cried "unfair competition" and threatened to drop the IBM line or to give it less emphasis. Many outside salespeople felt that they were being undercut by the new "inside channels."

Changing Channel Organization

Disintermediation

The displacement of traditional resellers from a marketing channel by radical new types of intermediaries.

Changes in technology and the explosive growth of direct and online marketing are having a profound impact on the nature and design of marketing channels. One major trend is toward **disintermediation**—a big term with a clear message and important consequences. Disintermediation means that more and more, product and service producers are bypassing intermediaries and going directly to final buyers, or that radically new types of channel intermediaries are emerging to displace traditional ones.

Thus, in many industries, traditional intermediaries are dropping by the wayside. For example, companies such as Dell and American Airlines are selling directly to final buyers, eliminating retailers from their marketing channels. E-commerce is growing rapidly, taking business from traditional brick-and-mortar retailers. Consumers can buy Flowers from 1-800-Flowers.com; books, videos, toys, jewelry, consumer electronics, and other goods from Amazon.com; and clothes from llbean.com or gap.com, all without ever visiting a store.

Disintermediation presents problems and opportunities for both producers and intermediaries. To avoid being swept aside, traditional intermediaries must find new ways to add value in the supply chain (see Real Marketing 12.1). To remain competitive, product and service producers must develop new channel opportunities, such as Internet and other direct channels. However, developing these new channels often brings them into direct competition with their established channels, resulting in conflict.

To ease this problem, companies often look for ways to make going direct a plus for both the company and its channel partners. For example, to trim costs and add business, Hewlett-Packard opened three direct-sales Web sites—Shopping Village (for consumers), H-P Commerce Center (for businesses buying from authorized resellers), and Electronic Solutions Now (for existing contract customers). However, to avoid conflicts with its established reseller channels, H-P forwards all its Web orders to resellers, who complete the orders, ship the products, and get the commissions. In this way, H-P gains the advantages of direct selling but also boosts business for resellers.

Channel Design Decisions

We now look at several channel decisions manufacturers face. In designing marketing channels, manufacturers struggle between what is ideal and what is practical. A new firm with limited capital usually starts by selling in a limited market area. Deciding on the best channels might not be a problem: The problem might simply be how to convince one or a few good intermediaries to handle the line.

If successful, the new firm might branch out to new markets through the existing intermediaries. In smaller markets, the firm might sell directly to retailers; in larger markets, it

Real Marketing 12.1

Disintermediation: A Fancy Word but a Clear Message

Buying music can be a pretty frustrating experience. Perhaps you can identify with the following scenario:

> You whistle a happy tune as you stroll into Tower Records to do a little music shopping. But when you pick up *The Essential Bruce Springsteen*, your temperature starts to rise. You should be ecstatic at the discovery of 12 new releases by the Boss, but instead you're furious: You can't buy them unless you shell out $25.99 for the entire three-CD set that includes 30 "career-spanning classics" that you already own from his other hit records. You shove Bruce back into his display case and pick up *The Ragpicker's Dream*, by Mark Knopfler. It has one funny, tender tune that you love, called "Devil Baby"—but what about those other 16 songs? It'll cost you $23.99 to find out. Suddenly, everything seems like a crapshoot. Why do they keep insisting that you buy an entire CD when you can just go online and get only the tunes you really want from iTunes or Musicmatch for 99 cents each—or through Kazaa or Grokster for free? Fed up, you walk away without buying anything.

Experiences like these, coupled with revolutionary changes in the way music is being distributed and purchased, have thrown the music industry into turmoil. Today, online music download services, such as BuyMusic.com, MusicMatch.com, MusicNow.com, and Apple's iTunes.com, offer an attractive alternative to buying over-priced standard CDs from the limited assortments of traditional music retailers. Instead, you can go online, choose from tens of thousands of individual tracks, digitally download one or a dozen in any of several formats, burn them onto a CD or dump them into your iPod, and listen to them wherever and whenever you please.

It seems like everyone is getting into the music download business these days. Coffee chain Starbucks opened an in-store music service—Hear Music—letting customers burn downloaded tracks onto CDs while sipping their lattes. T-Mobile announced that it will soon unveil a mobile phone-based music download service. And fearsome competitors like Dell, Microsoft, and Sony have announced their own online music stores. Even Coca-Cola launched mycokemusic.com, selling 50,000 tracks in its first week.

These new distribution options are great for consumers. But the new channel forms threaten the very existence of traditional music retailers. There's even a fancy word to describe this phenomenon—*disintermediation*. Strictly speaking, disintermediation means the elimination of a layer of intermediaries from a marketing channel—skipping a step between the source of a product or service and its consumers. For example, when Dell began selling personal computers directly to consumers, it eliminated—or disintermediated—retailers from the traditional PC distribution channel.

More broadly, disintermediation includes not only the elimination of channel levels through direct marketing but also the displacement of traditional resellers by radically new types of intermediaries. For example, only a few decades ago, most recorded music was sold through independent music retailers or small chains. Many of these smaller retailers were later disintermediated by large specialty music superstores, such as Tower Records, Virgin Records, and

■ Disintermediation: Online music download services, such as Apple's iTunes.com, are threatening to make traditional CD sellers obsolete.

Musicland. The superstores, in turn, have faced growing competition from broadline discount retailers such as Wal-Mart and Best Buy. In fact, Wal-Mart is currently the world's No. 1 CD seller.

Now, the surge of new online music sellers is threatening to make traditional CD sellers obsolete. "Tower Records and the other music-store chains are in a dizzying tailspin," comments one industry expert. Retail CD sales have dropped nearly 20 percent since 1999—the year Napster (the original music download site) was launched. Last year Tower Records declared bankruptcy and No. 2 music retailer Musicland shuttered 260 of its 1,230 stores. Smaller chains like National Record Mart have disappeared altogether. And things will likely get worse before they get better. One study suggests that in the next 5 years, one-fifth to one-third of music sales will shift from CDs to digital downloads, and that eventually, "CDs, DVDs, and other forms of physical media will become obsolete." One retail consultant predicts that half of today's music stores will be out of business within 5 years.

How are the traditional retailers responding to the disintermediation threat? Some are following the "if you can't beat them, join them" principle by creating their own downloading services. Several of the top chains—Best Buy, Borders, Hastings, Tower, Virgin, and Wherehouse—formed Echo, a consortium to offer music downloads. Wal-Mart offers in-store and online downloads for only 88 cents a song.

And music stores still have several advantages over their online counterparts. First, the stores have a larger base of existing customers. The Echo consortium encompasses some 3,500 retail outlets with 2 billion customer visits per year. Second, the physical store provides a shopping experience for customers that's difficult to duplicate online. Retailers can morph their stores into comfortable, sociable gathering spots were people hang out, chat with

(box continues)

friends, listen to music, go to album signings, and perhaps attend a live performance.

But the traditional store retailers also face daunting economics. Store rents are rising while CD prices are falling. And running stores generates considerable inventory and store operating costs. New online entrants face none of those traditional distribution costs. And whereas store retailers can physically stock only a limited number of in-print titles, the music download sites can provide millions of selections and offer out-of-print songs.

What's more, whereas music stores are stuck selling precompiled CDs at high album prices, music download sites let customers buy only the songs they want at low per-song rates. Finally, the old retailing model of selling CDs like they were LP vinyl records doesn't work so well anymore. That was fine in an era when people had one stereo in the living room and maybe one in the kids' room. But now consumers want music in a variety of formats that they can play anywhere, anytime: on Walkmans, boomboxes, car stereos, computers, and MP3 players like Apple's iPod,

which can store thousands of songs in a nifty credit-card-sized device.

Thus, disintermediation is a big word but the meaning is clear. Disintermediation occurs only when a new channel form succeeds in serving customers better than the old channels. Marketers who continually seek new ways to create real value for customers have little to fear. However, those who fall behind in adding value risk being swept aside. Will today's specialty music retailers survive? Stay iTuned.

Sources: Opening extract adapted from Paul Keegan, "Is the Music Store Over?" *Business 2.0*, March 2004, pp. 114–118. Other quotes and information from Lorin Cipolla, "Music's on the Menu." *Promo*, May 1, 2004; Sarah E. Lockyer, "Full Steam Ahead," *Nation's Restaurant News*, May 3, 2004, p. 4; Peter Lewis, "Drop a Quarter in the Internet." *Fortune*, March 22, 2004, p. 56; and Walter Mossberg, "Boss Talk: The Music Man," *Wall Street Journal*, June 14, 2004, p. B.1.

might sell through distributors. In one part of the country, it might grant exclusive franchises; in another, it might sell through all available outlets. Then, it might add a Web store that sells directly to hard-to-reach customers. In this way, channel systems often evolve to meet market opportunities and conditions.

For maximum effectiveness, however, channel analysis and decision making should be more purposeful. Designing a channel system calls for analyzing consumer needs, setting channel objectives, identifying major channel alternatives, and evaluating them.

Analyzing Consumer Needs

As noted previously, marketing channels are part of the overall *customer value delivery network*. Each channel member adds value for the customer. Thus, designing the marketing channel starts with finding out what target consumers want from the channel. Do consumers want to buy from nearby locations or are they willing to travel to more distant centralized locations? Would they rather buy in person, over the phone, through the mail, or via the Internet? Do they value breadth of assortment or do they prefer specialization? Do consumers want many add-on services (delivery, credit, repairs, installation), or will they obtain these elsewhere? The faster the delivery, the greater the assortment provided, and the more add-on services supplied, the greater the channel's service level.

Providing the fastest delivery, greatest assortment, and most services may not be possible or practical. The company and its channel members may not have the resources or skills needed to provide all the desired services. Also, providing higher levels of service results in higher costs for the channel and higher prices for consumers. The company must balance consumer needs not only against the feasibility and costs of meeting these needs but also against customer price preferences. The success of discount retailing shows that consumers will often accept lower service levels in exchange for lower prices.

Setting Channel Objectives

Companies should state their marketing channel objectives in terms of targeted levels of customer service. Usually, a company can identify several segments wanting different levels of service. The company should decide which segments to serve and the best channels to use in each case. In each segment, the company wants to minimize the total channel cost of meeting customer service requirements.

The company's channel objectives are also influenced by the nature of the company, its products, its marketing intermediaries, its competitors, and the environment. For example,

■ Channel objectives: Mary Kay Cosmetics sells direct to consumers through its corps of Independent Beauty Consultants.

the company's size and financial situation determine which marketing functions it can handle itself and which it must give to intermediaries. Companies selling perishable products may require more direct marketing to avoid delays and too much handling.

In some cases, a company may want to compete in or near the same outlets that carry competitors' products. In other cases, producers may avoid the channels used by competitors. Mary Kay Cosmetics, for example, sells direct to customers through its corps of more than 1 million independent beauty consultants in 34 markets worldwide, rather than going head-to-head with other cosmetics makers for scarce positions in retail stores. And GEICO Direct markets auto and homeowner's insurance directly to consumers via the telephone and Web rather than through agents.

Finally, environmental factors such as economic conditions and legal constraints may affect channel objectives and design. For example, in a depressed economy, producers want to distribute their goods in the most economical way, using shorter channels and dropping unneeded services that add to the final price of the goods.

Identifying Major Alternatives

When the company has defined its channel objectives, it should next identify its major channel alternatives in terms of *types* of intermediaries, the *number* of intermediaries, and the *responsibilities* of each channel member.

Types of Intermediaries

A firm should identify the types of channel members available to carry out its channel work. For example, suppose a manufacturer of test equipment has developed an audio device that detects poor mechanical connections in machines with moving parts. Company executives think this product would have a market in all industries in which electric, combustion, or steam engines are made or used. The company's current sales force is small, and

■ Channel objectives: GEICO markets auto insurance via the telephone and Web for those looking to save money and do business directly with the company. "Call now," says the ad, "or visit geico.com."

the problem is how best to reach these different industries. The following channel alternatives might emerge:

Company sales force: Expand the company's direct sales force. Assign outside salespeople to territories and have them contact all prospects in the area, or develop separate company sales forces for different industries. Or, add an inside telesales operation in which telephone salespeople handle small or midsize companies.

Manufacturer's agency: Hire manufacturer's agents—independent firms whose sales forces handle related products from many companies—in different regions or industries to sell the new test equipment.

Industrial distributors: Find distributors in the different regions or industries who will buy and carry the new line. Give them exclusive distribution, good margins, product training, and promotional support.

Number of Marketing Intermediaries

Companies must also determine the number of channel members to use at each level. Three strategies are available: intensive distribution, exclusive distribution, and selective distribution. Producers of convenience products and common raw materials typically seek **intensive distribution**—a strategy in which they stock their products in as many outlets as possible. These products must be available where and when consumers want them. For example, toothpaste, candy, and other similar items are sold in millions of outlets to provide maximum brand exposure and consumer convenience. Kraft, Coca-Cola, Kimberly-Clark, and other consumer goods companies distribute their products in this way.

By contrast, some producers purposely limit the number of intermediaries handling their products. The extreme form of this practice is **exclusive distribution**, in which the producer gives only a limited number of dealers the exclusive right to distribute its products in their territories. Exclusive distribution is often found in the distribution of luxury automobiles and prestige women's clothing. For example, Bentley dealers are few and far between—even large

Intensive distribution
Stocking the product in as many outlets as possible.

Exclusive distribution
Giving a limited number of dealers the exclusive right to distribute the company's products in their territories.

■ Exclusive distribution: Luxury car makers such as Bentley sell exclusively through a limited number of retailers. Such limited distribution enhances the car's image and generates stronger retailer support.

cities may have only one dealer. By granting exclusive distribution, Bentley gains stronger distributor selling support and more control over dealer prices, promotion, credit, and services. Exclusive distribution also enhances the car's image and allows for higher markups.

Selective distribution
The use of more than one, but fewer than all, of the intermediaries who are willing to carry the company's products.

Between intensive and exclusive distribution lies **selective distribution**—the use of more than one, but fewer than all, of the intermediaries who are willing to carry a company's products. Most television, furniture, and home appliance brands are distributed in this manner. For example, KitchenAid, Maytag, Whirlpool, and General Electric sell their major appliances through dealer networks and selected large retailers. By using selective distribution, they can develop good working relationships with selected channel members and expect a better-than-average selling effort. Selective distribution gives producers good market coverage with more control and less cost than does intensive distribution.

Responsibilities of Channel Members

The producer and intermediaries need to agree on the terms and responsibilities of each channel member. They should agree on price policies, conditions of sale, territorial rights, and specific services to be performed by each party. The producer should establish a list price and a fair set of discounts for intermediaries. It must define each channel member's territory, and it should be careful about where it places new resellers.

Mutual services and duties need to be spelled out carefully, especially in franchise and exclusive distribution channels. For example, McDonald's provides franchisees with promotional support, a record-keeping system, training at Hamburger University, and general management assistance. In turn, franchisees must meet company standards for physical facilities, cooperate with new promotion programs, provide requested information, and buy specified food products.

Evaluating the Major Alternatives

Suppose a company has identified several channel alternatives and wants to select the one that will best satisfy its long-run objectives. Each alternative should be evaluated against economic, control, and adaptive criteria.

Using *economic criteria*, a company compares the likely sales, costs, and profitability of different channel alternatives. What will be the investment required by each channel alternative, and what returns will result? The company must also consider *control issues*. Using intermediaries usually means giving them some control over the marketing of the product, and some intermediaries take more control than others. Other things being equal, the company prefers to keep as much control as possible. Finally, the company must apply *adaptive criteria*. Channels often involve long-term commitments, yet the company wants to keep the channel flexible so that it can adapt to environmental changes. Thus, to be considered, a channel involving long-term commitments should be greatly superior on economic and control grounds.

Designing International Distribution Channels

International marketers face many additional complexities in designing their channels. Each country has its own unique distribution system that has evolved over time and changes very slowly. These channel systems can vary widely from country to country. Thus, global marketers must usually adapt their channel strategies to the existing structures within each country.

In some markets, the distribution system is complex and hard to penetrate, consisting of many layers and large numbers of intermediaries. Consider Japan:

> The Japanese distribution system stems from the early seventeenth century when cottage industries and a [quickly growing] urban population spawned a merchant class. . . . Despite Japan's economic achievements, the distribution system has remained remarkably faithful to its antique pattern. . . . [It] encompasses a wide range of wholesalers and other agents, brokers, and retailers, differing more in number than in function from their American counterparts. There are myriad tiny retail shops. An even greater number of wholesalers supplies goods to them, layered tier upon tier, many more than most U.S. executives would think necessary. For example, soap may move through three wholesalers plus a sales company after it leaves the manufacturer before it ever reaches the retail outlet. A steak goes from rancher to consumers in a process that often involves a dozen middle agents. . . . The distribution network . . . reflects the traditionally close ties among many Japanese companies . . . [and places] much greater emphasis on personal relationships with users. . . . Although [these channels appear] inefficient and cumbersome, they seem to serve the Japanese customer well. . . . Lacking much storage space in their small homes, most Japanese homemakers shop several times a week and prefer convenient [and more personal] neighborhood shops.[8]

Many Western firms have had great difficulty breaking into the closely knit, tradition-bound Japanese distribution network.

■ The Japanese distribution system has remained remarkably traditional. A profusion of tiny retail shops are supplied by an even greater number of small wholesalers.

At the other extreme, distribution systems in developing countries may be scattered and inefficient, or altogether lacking. For example, China and India would appear to be huge markets, each with populations over 1 billion. In reality, however, these markets are much smaller than the population numbers suggest. Because of inadequate distribution systems in both countries, most companies can profitably access only a small portion of the population located in each country's most affluent cities. China's distribution system is so fragmented that logistics costs amount to 15 percent of the nation's GDP, far higher than in most other countries. After 10 years of effort, even Wal-Mart executives admit that they have been unable to assemble an efficient supply chain in the China.[9]

Thus, international marketers face a wide range of channel alternatives. Designing efficient and effective channel systems between and within various country markets poses a difficult challenge. We discuss international distribution decisions further in Chapter 19.

START HERE | # Channel Management Decisions

Once the company has reviewed its channel alternatives and decided on the best channel design, it must implement and manage the chosen channel. Channel management calls for selecting, managing, and motivating individual channel members and evaluating their performance over time.

Selecting Channel Members

Producers vary in their ability to attract qualified marketing intermediaries. Some producers have no trouble signing up channel members. For example, when Toyota first introduced its Lexus line in the United States, it had no trouble attracting new dealers. In fact, it had to turn down many would-be resellers.

At the other extreme are producers who have to work hard to line up enough qualified intermediaries. When Polaroid started, for example, it could not get photography stores to carry its new cameras, and it had to go to mass-merchandising outlets. Similarly, when the U.S. Time Company first tried to sell its inexpensive Timex watches through regular jewelry stores, most jewelry stores refused to carry them. The company then managed to get its watches into mass-merchandise outlets. This turned out to be a wise decision because of the rapid growth of mass merchandising.

When selecting intermediaries, the company should determine what characteristics distinguish the better ones. It will want to evaluate each channel member's years in business, other lines carried, growth and profit record, cooperativeness, and reputation. If the intermediaries are sales agents, the company will want to evaluate the number and character of other lines carried and the size and quality of the sales force. If the intermediary is a retail store that wants exclusive or selective distribution, the company will want to evaluate the store's customers, location, and future growth potential.

Managing and Motivating Channel Members

Once selected, channel members must be continuously managed and motivated to do their best. The company must sell not only *through* the intermediaries but *to* and *with* them. Most companies see their intermediaries as first-line customers and partners. They practice strong *partner relationship management (PRM)* to forge long-term partnerships with channel members. This creates a marketing system that meets the needs of both the company *and* its marketing partners.

In managing its channels, a company must convince distributors that they can succeed better by working together as a part of a cohesive value delivery system.[10] Thus, P&G and Wal-Mart work together to create superior value for final consumers. They jointly plan merchandising goals and strategies, inventory levels, and advertising and promotion plans. Similarly, GE Appliances has created an alternative distribution system called *CustomerNet* to coordinate, support, and motivate its dealers.

> GE CustomerNet gives dealers instant online access to GE Appliances' distribution and order-processing system, 24 hours a day, 7 days a week. By logging on to the GE CustomerNet Web site, dealers can obtain product specifications, photos, feature lists, and side-by-side model comparisons for hundreds of GE appliance models.

■ Creating dealer satisfaction and profitability: Using GE's CustomerNet system, dealers have instant online access to GE Appliances' distribution system, 24 hours a day, 7 days a week to check on product availability and prices, place orders, and review order status. "Simply put, it's an electronic one-stop shopping breakthrough that can help you sell."

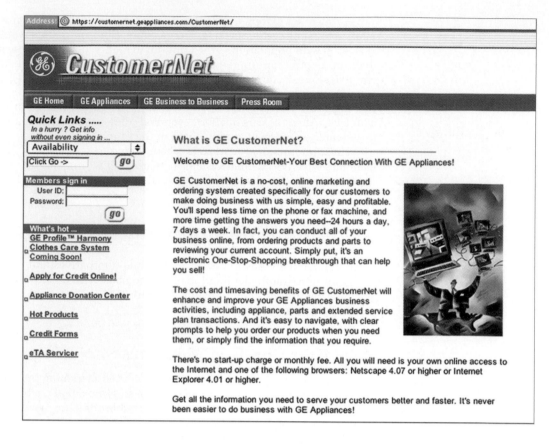

They can check on product availability and prices, place orders, and review order status. They can even create custom brochures, order point-of-purchase materials, or download "advertising slicks"—professionally prepared GE appliance ads ready for insertion in local media. GE promises next-day delivery on most appliance models, so dealers need carry only display models in their stores. This greatly reduces inventory costs, making even small dealers more price competitive. GE CustomerNet also helps dealers to sell GE appliances more easily and effectively. A dealer can put a computer terminal on the showroom floor, where salespeople and customers together can use the system to dig through detailed product descriptions and check availability for GE's entire line of appliances. Perhaps the biggest benefit to GE Appliances, however, is that the system builds strong bonds between the company and its dealers and motivates dealers to put more push behind the company's products.[11]

Many companies are now installing integrated high-tech partner relationship management systems to coordinate their whole-channel marketing efforts. Just as they use customer relationship management (CRM) software systems to help manage relationships with important customers, companies can now use PRM software to help recruit, train, organize, manage, motivate, and evaluate relationships with channel partners.

Evaluating Channel Members

The producer must regularly check channel member performance against standards such as sales quotas, average inventory levels, customer delivery time, treatment of damaged and lost goods, cooperation in company promotion and training programs, and services to the customer. The company should recognize and reward intermediaries who are performing well and adding good value for consumers. Those who are performing poorly should be assisted or, as a last resort, replaced. A company may periodically "requalify" its intermediaries and prune the weaker ones.

Finally, manufacturers need to be sensitive to their dealers. Those who treat their dealers poorly risk not only losing dealer support but also causing some legal problems. The next section describes various rights and duties pertaining to manufacturers and their channel members.

Public Policy and Distribution Decisions

For the most part, companies are legally free to develop whatever channel arrangements suit them. In fact, the laws affecting channels seek to prevent the exclusionary tactics of some companies that might keep another company from using a desired channel. Most channel law deals with the mutual rights and duties of the channel members once they have formed a relationship.

Many producers and wholesalers like to develop exclusive channels for their products. When the seller allows only certain outlets to carry its products, this strategy is called *exclusive distribution*. When the seller requires that these dealers not handle competitors' products, its strategy is called *exclusive dealing*. Both parties can benefit from exclusive arrangements: The seller obtains more loyal and dependable outlets, and the dealers obtain a steady source of supply and stronger seller support. But exclusive arrangements also exclude other producers from selling to these dealers. This situation brings exclusive dealing contracts under the scope of the Clayton Act of 1914. They are legal as long as they do not substantially lessen competition or tend to create a monopoly and as long as both parties enter into the agreement voluntarily.

Exclusive dealing often includes *exclusive territorial agreements*. The producer may agree not to sell to other dealers in a given area, or the buyer may agree to sell only in its own territory. The first practice is normal under franchise systems as a way to increase dealer enthusiasm and commitment. It is also perfectly legal—a seller has no legal obligation to sell through more outlets than it wishes. The second practice, whereby the producer tries to keep a dealer from selling outside its territory, has become a major legal issue.

Producers of a strong brand sometimes sell it to dealers only if the dealers will take some or all of the rest of the line. This is called full-line forcing. Such *tying agreements* are not necessarily illegal, but they do violate the Clayton Act if they tend to lessen competition substantially. The practice may prevent consumers from freely choosing among competing suppliers of these other brands.

Finally, producers are free to select their dealers, but their right to terminate dealers is somewhat restricted. In general, sellers can drop dealers "for cause." However, they cannot drop dealers if, for example, the dealers refuse to cooperate in a doubtful legal arrangement, such as exclusive dealing or tying agreements.[12]

Marketing Logistics and Supply Chain Management

In today's global marketplace, selling a product is sometimes easier than getting it to customers. Companies must decide on the best way to store, handle, and move their products and services so that they are available to customers in the right assortments, at the right time, and in the right place. Physical distribution and logistics effectiveness has a major impact on both customer satisfaction and company costs. Here we consider the nature and importance of logistics management in the supply chain, goals of the logistics system, major logistics functions, and the need for integrated supply chain management.

Nature and Importance of Marketing Logistics

To some managers, marketing logistics means only trucks and warehouses. But modern logistics is much more than this. **Marketing logistics**—also called **physical distribution**—involves planning, implementing, and controlling the physical flow of goods, services, and related information from points of origin to points of consumption to meet customer requirements at a profit. In short, it involves getting the right product to the right customer in the right place at the right time.

In the past, physical distribution typically started with products at the plant and then tried to find low-cost solutions to get them to customers. However, today's marketers prefer customer-centered logistics thinking, which starts with the marketplace and works backward to the factory, or even to sources of supply. Marketing logistics involves not only *outbound distribution* (moving products from the factory to resellers and ultimately to customers) but also *inbound distribution* (moving products and materials from suppliers to the factory) and *reverse distribution* (moving broken, unwanted, or excess products returned by consumers or resellers). That is, it involves entire **supply chain management**—managing upstream and

Marketing logistics (physical distribution)
The tasks involved in planning, implementing, and controlling the physical flow of materials, final goods, and related information from points of origin to points of consumption to meet customer requirements at a profit.

Supply chain management
Managing upstream and downstream value-added flows of materials, final goods, and related information among suppliers, the company, resellers, and final consumers.

FIGURE 12.5
Supply chain management

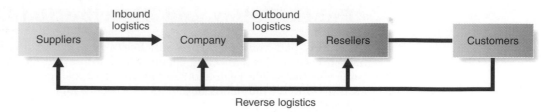

downstream value-added flows of materials, final goods, and related information among suppliers, the company, resellers, and final consumers, as shown in Figure 12.5.

Thus, the logistics manager's task is to coordinate activities of suppliers, purchasing agents, marketers, channel members, and customers. These activities include forecasting, information systems, purchasing, production planning, order processing, inventory, warehousing, and transportation planning.

Companies today are placing greater emphasis on logistics for several reasons. First, companies can gain a powerful competitive advantage by using improved logistics to give customers better service or lower prices. Second, improved logistics can yield tremendous cost savings to both the company and its customers. As much as 20 percent of an average product's price is accounted for by shipping and transport alone. Last year, American companies spent more than $930 billion—about 8.5 percent of gross domestic product—to wrap, bundle, load, unload, sort, reload, and transport goods. By itself, Ford has more than 500 million tons of finished vehicles, production parts, and aftermarket parts in transit at any given time, running up an annual logistics bill of around $4 billion.[13] Shaving off even a small fraction of these costs can mean substantial savings.

Third, the explosion in product variety has created a need for improved logistics management. For example, in 1911 the typical A&P grocery store carried only 270 items. The store manager could keep track of this inventory on about 10 pages of notebook paper stuffed in a shirt pocket. Today, the average A&P carries a bewildering stock of more than 16,700 items. A Wal-Mart Supercenter stores carry more than 100,000 products, 30,000 of which are grocery products.[14] Ordering, shipping, stocking, and controlling such a variety of products presents a sizable logistics challenge.

Finally, improvements in information technology have created opportunities for major gains in distribution efficiency. Today's companies are using sophisticated supply chain management software, Web-based logistics systems, point-of-sale scanners, uniform product

■ The importance of logistics: At any given time, Ford has more than 500 million tons of finished vehicles, production parts, and aftermarket parts in transit, running up an annual logistics bill of around $4 billion.

codes, satellite tracking, and electronic transfer of order and payment data. Such technology lets them quickly and efficiently manage the flow of goods, information, and finances through the supply chain.

Goals of the Logistics System

Some companies state their logistics objective as providing maximum customer service at the least cost. Unfortunately, no logistics system can *both* maximize customer service *and* minimize distribution costs. Maximum customer service implies rapid delivery, large inventories, flexible assortments, liberal returns policies, and other services—all of which raise distribution costs. In contrast, minimum distribution costs imply slower delivery, smaller inventories, and larger shipping lots—which represent a lower level of overall customer service.

The goal of marketing logistics should be to provide a *targeted* level of customer service at the least cost. A company must first research the importance of various distribution services to customers and then set desired service levels for each segment. The objective is to maximize *profits*, not sales. Therefore, the company must weigh the benefits of providing higher levels of service against the costs. Some companies offer less service than their competitors and charge a lower price. Other companies offer more service and charge higher prices to cover higher costs.

Major Logistics Functions

Given a set of logistics objectives, the company is ready to design a logistics system that will minimize the cost of attaining these objectives. The major logistics functions include *warehousing, inventory management, transportation*, and *logistics information management*.

Warehousing

Production and consumption cycles rarely match. So most companies must store their tangible goods while they wait to be sold. For example, Snapper, Toro, and other lawn mower manufacturers run their factories all year long and store up products for the heavy spring and summer buying seasons. The storage function overcomes differences in needed quantities and timing, ensuring that products are available when customers are ready to buy them.

Distribution center

A large, highly automated warehouse designed to receive goods from various plants and suppliers, take orders, fill them efficiently, and deliver goods to customers as quickly as possible.

A company must decide on *how many* and *what types* of warehouses it needs and *where* they will be located. The company might use either *storage warehouses* or *distribution centers*. Storage warehouses store goods for moderate to long periods. **Distribution centers** are designed to move goods rather than just store them. They are large and highly automated warehouses designed to receive goods from various plants and suppliers, take orders, fill them efficiently, and deliver goods to customers as quickly as possible.

For example, Wal-Mart operates a network of 78 huge U.S. distribution centers and another 37 around the globe. A single center, which might serve the daily needs of 165 Wal-Mart stores, typically contains more than a million square feet of space (about 24 football fields) under a single roof. One huge center near Williamsburg, Virginia contains more than 3 million square feet. At a typical center, laser scanners route as many as 190,000 cases of goods per day along 11 miles of conveyer belts, and the center's 1,000 workers load or unload some 500 trucks daily. Wal-Mart's Monroe, Georgia, distribution center contains a 127,000-square-foot freezer that can hold 10,000 pallets—room enough for 58 million Popsicles.[15]

Like almost everything else these days, warehousing has seen dramatic changes in technology in recent years. Older, multistoried warehouses with outdated materials-handling methods are steadily being replaced by newer, single-storied *automated warehouses* with advanced, computer-controlled materials-handling systems requiring few employees. Computers and scanners read orders and direct lift trucks, electric hoists, or robots to gather goods, move them to loading docks, and issue invoices.

Inventory Management

Inventory management also affects customer satisfaction. Here, managers must maintain the delicate balance between carrying too little inventory and carrying too much. With too little stock, the firm risks not having products when customers want to buy. To remedy this, the firm may need costly emergency shipments or production. Carrying too much inventory results in higher-than-necessary inventory-carrying costs and stock obsolescence. Thus, in managing inventory, firms must balance the costs of carrying larger inventories against resulting sales and profits.

Many companies have greatly reduced their inventories and related costs through *just-in-time* logistics systems. With such systems, producers and retailers carry only small inventories of parts or merchandise, often only enough for a few days of operations. For example, Dell, a master just-in-time producer, carries just 3 to 5 days of inventory, whereas competitors might carry 40 days or even 60.[16] New stock arrives exactly when needed, rather than being stored in inventory until being used. Just-in-time systems require accurate forecasting along with fast, frequent, and flexible delivery so that new supplies will be available when needed. However, these systems result in substantial savings in inventory-carrying and handling costs.

Marketers are always looking for new ways to make inventory management more efficient. In the not-too-distant future, handling inventory might even become fully automated. For example, in Chapter 3, we discussed RFID or "smart tag" technology, by which small transmitter chips are embedded in products and packaging on everything from flowers and razors to tires. "Smart" products could make the entire supply chain—which accounts for nearly 75 percent of a product's cost—intelligent and automated. Companies would know, at any time, exactly where a product is located physically within the supply chain. "Smart shelves" would not only tell them when it's time to reorder, but would also place the order automatically with their suppliers. Such exciting new information technology applications will revolutionize distribution as we know it.[17]

Transportation

The choice of transportation carriers affects the pricing of products, delivery performance, and condition of the goods when they arrive—all of which will affect customer satisfaction. In shipping goods to its warehouses, dealers, and customers, the company can choose among five main transportation modes: truck, rail, water, pipeline, and air, along with an alternative mode for digital products: the Internet.

Trucks have increased their share of transportation steadily and now account for nearly 41 percent of total cargo ton-miles (more than 65 percent of actual tonnage). Each year in the

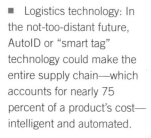

■ Logistics technology: In the not-too-distant future, AutoID or "smart tag" technology could make the entire supply chain—which accounts for nearly 75 percent of a product's cost—intelligent and automated.

United States, trucks travel more than 600 billion miles—equal to nearly 1.3 million round trips to the moon—carrying 7.7 billion tons of freight. Trucks are highly flexible in their routing and time schedules, and they can usually offer faster service than railroads. They are efficient for short hauls of high-value merchandise. Trucking firms have added many services in recent years. For example, Roadway Express and most other major carriers now offer satellite tracking of shipments and sleeper tractors that move freight around the clock.

Railroads account for 37 percent of total cargo ton-miles moved. They are one of the most cost-effective modes for shipping large amounts of bulk products—coal, sand, minerals, and farm and forest products—over long distances. In recent years, railroads have increased their customer services by designing new equipment to handle special categories of goods, providing flatcars for carrying truck trailers by rail (piggyback), and providing in-transit services such as the diversion of shipped goods to other destinations en route and the processing of goods en route.

Water carriers, which account for about 10 percent of cargo ton-miles, transport large amounts of goods by ships and barges on U.S. coastal and inland waterways. Although the cost of water transportation is very low for shipping bulky, low-value, nonperishable products such as sand, coal, grain, oil, and metallic ores, water transportation is the slowest mode and may be affected by the weather. *Pipelines* are a specialized means of shipping petroleum, natural gas, and chemicals from sources to markets. Most pipelines are used by their owners to ship their own products.

Although *air* carriers transport less than 1 percent of the nation's goods, they are an important transportation mode. Airfreight rates are much higher than rail or truck rates, but airfreight is ideal when speed is needed or distant markets have to be reached. Among the most frequently airfreighted products are perishables (fresh fish, cut flowers) and high-value, low-bulk items (technical instruments, jewelry). Companies find that airfreight also reduces inventory levels, packaging costs, and the number of warehouses needed.

The *Internet* carries digital products from producer to customer via satellite, cable modem, or telephone wire. Software firms, the media, music companies, and education all make use of the Internet to transport digital products. While these firms primarily use traditional transporta-

■ Roadway Express and other trucking firms have added many services in recent years, such as satellite tracking of shipments and sleeper tractors that keep freight moving around the clock.

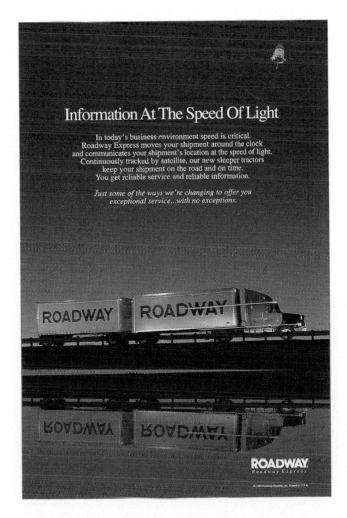

Information At The Speed Of Light

In today's business environment speed is critical. Roadway Express moves your shipment around the clock and communicates your shipment's location at the speed of light. Continuously tracked by satellite, our new sleeper tractors keep your shipment on the road and on time. You get reliable service and reliable information.

Just some of the ways we're changing to offer you exceptional service...with no exceptions.

ROADWAY.
Roadway Express

tion to distribute CDs, newspapers, and more, the Internet holds the potential for lower product distribution costs. Whereas planes, trucks, and trains move freight and packages, digital technology moves information bits.

Intermodal transportation
Combining two or more modes of transportation.

Shippers also use **intermodal transportation**—combining two or more modes of transportation. *Piggyback* describes the use of rail and trucks; *fishyback*, water and trucks; *trainship*, water and rail; and *airtruck*, air and trucks. Combining modes provides advantages that no single mode can deliver. Each combination offers advantages to the shipper. For example, not only is piggyback cheaper than trucking alone but it also provides flexibility and convenience.

In choosing a transportation mode for a product, shippers must balance many considerations: speed, dependability, availability, cost, and others. Thus, if a shipper needs speed, air and truck are the prime choices. If the goal is low cost, then water or pipeline might be best.

Logistics Information Management

Companies manage their supply chains through information. Channel partners often link up to share information and to make better joint logistics decisions. From a logistics perspective, information flows such as customer orders, billing, inventory levels, and even customer data are closely linked channel performance.

Information can be shared and managed in many ways—by mail or telephone, through salespeople, via the Internet, or through *electronic data interchange (EDI),* the computerized exchange of data between organizations. Wal-Mart, for example, maintains EDI links with 20 percent of its 91,000 suppliers. And in one month alone, JC Penney relies on EDI to share more than 5.5 million documents with its partners.[18] The company wants to design a simple, accessible, fast, and accurate process for capturing, processing, and sharing channel information.

In some cases, suppliers might actually be asked to generate orders and arrange deliveries for their customers. Many large retailers—such as Wal-Mart and Home Depot—work closely with major suppliers such as Procter & Gamble or Black & Decker to set up *vendor-managed inventory* (VMI) systems or *continuous inventory replenishment* systems. Using VMI, the customer shares real-time data on sales and current inventory levels with the supplier. The supplier then takes full responsibility for managing inventories and deliveries. Some retailers even go so far as to shift inventory and delivery costs to the supplier. Such systems require close cooperation between the buyer and seller.

Here is an example of how two channel partners—Sara Lee and Target Corporation—share information and coordinate their logistics functions:

> The Branded Apparel division of giant Sara Lee Corporation says that retailer Target Corporation's willingness to share information with suppliers separates this company from its competitors. Target's Global Merchandising System (GMS), its supply chain management system, consists of more than 60 applications, including forecasting, ordering, and trend analysis. Target stores can use GMS to order a certain number of sweatshirts from Sara Lee Branded Apparel without specifying more than style. As the delivery date draws near, Target analyzes trends for colors and sizes. Based on those forecasts, Sara Lee makes trial lots and Target starts to sell them. If customers buy more navy sweatshirts than initially predicted, Target adjusts its order. The result: Both Sara Lee and Target have fewer goods in inventory while at the same time doing a better job of meeting customer preferences, which in turn results in fewer markdowns.[19]

Integrated Logistics Management

Integrated logistics management
The logistics concept that emphasizes teamwork, both inside the company and among all the marketing channel organizations, to maximize the performance of the entire distribution system.

Today, more and more companies are adopting the concept of **integrated logistics management**. This concept recognizes that providing better customer service and trimming distribution costs require *teamwork*, both inside the company and among all the marketing channel organizations. Inside, the company's various departments must work closely together to maximize the company's own logistics performance. Outside, the company must integrate its logistics system with those of its suppliers and customers to maximize the performance of the entire distribution system.

Cross-Functional Teamwork Inside the Company

In most companies, responsibility for various logistics activities is assigned to many different functional units—marketing, sales, finance, operations, purchasing. Too often, each function tries to optimize its own logistics performance without regard for the activities of the other functions. However, transportation, inventory, warehousing, and order-processing activities interact, often in an inverse way. Lower inventory levels reduce inventory-carrying costs. But they may also reduce customer service and increase costs from stock outs, back orders, special production runs, and costly fast-freight shipments. Because distribution activities involve strong trade-offs, decisions by different functions must be coordinated to achieve better overall logistics performance.

The goal of integrated supply chain management is to harmonize all of the company's logistics decisions. Close working relationships among functions can be achieved in several ways. Some companies have created permanent logistics committees, made up of managers responsible for different physical distribution activities. Companies can also create management positions that link the logistics activities of functional areas. For example, Procter & Gamble has created supply managers, who manage all of the supply chain activities for each of its product categories. Many companies have a vice president of logistics with cross-functional authority. Finally, companies can employ sophisticated, systemwide supply chain management software, now available from wide range of suppliers.[20] The important thing is that the company must coordinate its logistics and marketing activities to create high market satisfaction at a reasonable cost.

Building Logistics Partnerships

Companies must do more than improve their own logistics. They must also work with other channel partners to improve whole-channel distribution. The members of a distribution channel are linked closely in creating customer value and building customer relationships. One company's distribution system is another company's supply system. The success of each channel member depends on the performance of the entire supply chain. For example, Wal-Mart can charge the lowest prices at retail only if its entire supply chain—consisting of thousands of merchandise suppliers, transport companies, warehouses, and service providers—operates at maximum efficiency.

■ Supply chain management: Many companies use sophisticated, systemwide supply chain management software, such as that available from Oracle and other software providers.

Smart companies coordinate their logistics strategies and forge strong partnerships with suppliers and customers to improve customer service and reduce channel costs. Many companies have created *cross-functional, cross-company teams*. For example, Procter & Gamble has a team of almost 100 people working in Bentonville, Arkansas, home of Wal-Mart. The P&Gers work jointly with their counterparts at Wal-Mart to find ways to squeeze costs out of their distribution system. Working together benefits not only P&G and Wal-Mart but also their final consumers.

Other companies partner through *shared projects*. For example, many large retailers are working closely with suppliers on in-store programs. Home Depot allows key suppliers to use its stores as a testing ground for new merchandising programs. The suppliers spend time at Home Depot stores watching how their product sells and how customers relate to it. They then create programs specially tailored to Home Depot and its customers. Clearly, both the supplier and the customer benefit from such partnerships. The point is that all supply chain members must work together in the cause of serving final consumers.

Real Marketing 12.2

Third-Party Logistics: Tightening Up Sluggish, Overstuffed Supply Chains

Most big companies love to make and sell their products. But many loathe the associated logistics "grunt work." They detest the bundling, loading, unloading, sorting, storing, reloading, transporting, customs-clearing, and tracking required to supply their factories and to get products out to customers.

They hate it so much that some 83 percent of the nation's largest manufacturing companies are now handing over some or all of their logistics to third-party logistics (3PL) suppliers, up from only 38 percent a decade ago. These 3PLs help companies to tighten up sluggish, overstuffed supply chains, slash inventories, and get products to customers more quickly and reliably. Below are some examples:

Ford: For years, the bane of most Ford dealers was the auto maker's antiquated system for getting cars from factory to showroom. Cars could take as long as a month to arrive—that is, when they weren't lost along the way. And Ford was not always able to tell its dealers exactly what was coming, or even what was in inventory at the nearest rail yards. "We'd lose track of whole trainloads of cars," recalls Jerry Reynolds, owner of Prestige Ford in Garland, Texas. "It was crazy."

But three years ago, Ford handed its tortuous distribution network to an unlikely source: UPS. In a joint venture with the carmaker, UPS redesigned Ford's entire North American delivery network. Ultimately, UPS deployed a tracking system similar to the one it uses to monitor its own 13.8 million packages daily—right down to slapping bar codes on the windshields of the 4 million cars rolling out of Ford's North American plants each year and onto railcars. The result: UPS has cut the time it takes autos to arrive at dealer lots by 40 percent, to 10 days on average. In the first year alone, that trimmed Ford's inventory carrying costs by $125 million. And the new system makes it easy for dealers to track down the models most in demand. "It was the most amazing transformation I had ever seen," marvels dealer Reynolds. "My last comment to UPS was: 'Can you get us spare parts like this?'"

Sony: Sony knows logistics. In fact, the company considers logistics to be one of its competitive advantages. So you might

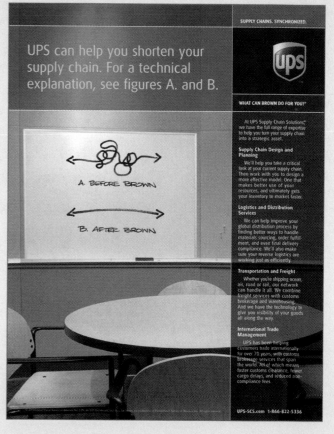

■ Third-party logistics: UPS's Supply Chain Solutions group can help a company shorten its supply chains and turn it into a strategic asset.

wonder why an industry leader would outsource half of its distribution requirements in Mexico to Redwood Systems, a 3PL provider with headquarters in Atlanta. The reasons are growth and speed to market. "In Mexico, logistics is challenging because of a lack of infrastructure," says Carlos Rojas,

Third-Party Logistics

Third-party logistics (3PL) provider

An independent logistics provider that performs any or all of the functions required to get its client's product to market.

Most businesses perform their own logistics functions. However, a growing number of firms now outsource some or all of their logistics to **third-party logistics (3PL) providers** such as UPS Supply Chain Services, Ryder Systems, FedEx Logistics, Roadway Logistics Services, or Emory Global Logistics (see Real Marketing 12.2). Such integrated logistics companies perform any or all of the functions required to get their clients' product to market.

For example, UPS's Supply Chain Services unit provides clients with a wide range of logistics services, from inventory control, warehousing, and transportation management to customer service and fulfillment:

UPS is leveraging decades of experience managing its own global delivery network to serve as the traffic manager for corporate America's sprawling distribution networks—doing everything from scheduling the planes, trains, and ships on which goods move to owning and managing companies' distribution centers and

logistics division manager for Sony Electronicas, Mexico. "Given those limitations, we couldn't take advantage of a growing market without a 3PL partner who could quickly expand our operations." Today, Redwood manages more than 500 different products and another 15,000 different parts for Sony. Products are received from all over the world, in quantities ranging from parcel shipments to full containers. Redwood ships an estimated 200 orders per day, with an average of 10 line items per order. "By relying on Redwood to manage the day-to-day details of our Mexico-based distribution," says Rojas, "we can concentrate on marketing and sales instead of logistics."

National Semiconductor: In the early 1990s, National Semiconductor—whose chips end up inside everything from cars and computers to telecommunications gear—faced a logistics nightmare. National produced and assembled chips at 13 plants located in the United States, Britain, Israel, and Southeast Asia. Finished products were then shipped to an array of large customers—IBM, Toshiba, Ford, Siemens—each with factories scattered around the globe. On their way to customers, chips traveled any of 20,000 direct routes, mostly in the cargo holds of planes flown by 12 airlines, stopping along the way at 10 different warehouses. National's logistics performance left much to be desired: 95 percent of its products were delivered within 45 days of the order. The other 5 percent took as long as 90 days. Because customers never knew which 5 percent would be late, they demanded 90 days' worth of inventory in everything. "The whole system was awash in inventory," comments a National executive.

Whereas National knew a lot about making chips, it knew little about how to fix its logistics. So rather than hiring its own specialists, National hired UPS to handle its global distribution. The results have been startling. By outsourcing logistics, National saves as much as 20 percent on distribution costs. At the same time, customer service and delivery performance have improved dramatically. National can now move prod-

ucts from the factory to global customers in an average of 48 hours, not 45 days.

Saturn: Saturn's just-in-time production system allows for almost no parts inventory at the plant. Instead, it relies on a world-class logistics system to keep parts flowing into the factory at precisely the times they're needed. Saturn is so good in managing its supply chain that in 4 years it has had to halt production just once—for only 18 minutes—because the right part failed to arrive at the right time. Most of the credit, however, goes to Ryder Integrated Logistics. Ryder, best known for renting trucks, manages Saturn's far-ranging supply chain, moving the automaker's materials, parts, and products efficiently and reliably from supplier to factory to dealer showroom.

To keep Saturn's assembly lines humming, Ryder transports thousands of preinspected and presorted parts—more than 2,200 receiving-dock transactions every day—hitting delivery windows as narrow as 5 minutes. Ryder keeps its parts, people, and trucks in a nearly constant blur of high-tech motion. For example, according to one account, when delivering service parts to Saturn dealerships, Ryder's long-haul drivers "plug a plastic key, loaded with electronic data, into an onboard computer. The screen tells them exactly where to go, which route to take, and how much time to spend getting there." Ryder's effective supply chain management results in lower costs, improved operations, more productive dealers, and—in the end—more satisfied customers.

Sources: Examples and other information found in or adapted from "Chipmaker Expands Its Relationship with 3PL into New Markets," *Purchasing,* March 20, 2003, pp. S11–S12; Ronald Henkoff, "Delivering the Goods," *Fortune,* November 28, 1994, pp. 64–77; "Even a Logistics Leader Needs Help Some of the Time," *Modern Materials Management,* December 2000, p. S15; "Add Value to Your Supply Chain—Hire a 3PL," *Materials Management and Distribution,* January–February 2004, p. A3; and Dean Foust, "Big Brown's New Bag," *Business Week,* July 19, 2004, pp. 54–56.

warehouses. UPS will undertake just about any logistics task for customers, anything from fixing busted electronics to answering customer phone calls to issuing corporate credit cards. For Jockey International, UPS not only manages a warehouse but also handles Internet order fulfillment. Apparel bought on the Jockey Web site is boxed for shipping by UPS warehouse staffers and delivered by UPS drivers. And if there's a problem, calls are handled by UPS phone reps. Big Brown also handles laptop repairs for Toshiba America, installs X-ray machines in Europe for Philips Medical Systems, and dresses Teddy bears for TeddyCrafters.[21]

According to a recent survey of chief logistics executives at Fortune 500 companies, 83 percent of these companies use third-party logistics (also called *outsourced logistics,* or *contract logistics*) services.[22]

Companies use third-party logistics providers for several reasons. First, because getting the product to market is their main focus, these providers can often do it more efficiently and at lower cost. According to one study, outsourcing typically results in 15 percent to 30 percent cost savings.[23] Second, outsourcing logistics frees a company to focus more intensely on its core business. Finally, integrated logistics companies understand increasingly complex logistics environments. This can be especially helpful to companies attempting to expand their global market coverage. For example, companies distributing their products across Europe face a bewildering array of environmental restrictions that affect logistics, including packaging standards, truck size and weight limits, and noise and emissions pollution controls. By outsourcing its logistics, a company can gain a complete pan-European distribution system without incurring the costs, delays, and risks associated with setting up its own system.

> Reviewing the Concepts <

Marketing channel decisions are among the most important decisions that management faces. A company's channel decisions directly affect every other marketing decision. Management must make channel decisions carefully, incorporating today's needs with tomorrow's likely selling environment. Some companies pay too little attention to their distribution channels, but others have used imaginative distribution systems to gain competitive advantage.

1. Explain why companies use marketing channels and discuss the functions these channels perform.

Most producers use intermediaries to bring their products to market. They try to forge a *marketing channel* (or *distribution channel*)—a set of interdependent organizations involved in the process of making a product or service available for use or consumption by the consumer or business user. Through their contacts, experience, specialization, and scale of operation, intermediaries usually offer the firm more than it can achieve on its own.

Marketing channels perform many key functions. Some help *complete* transactions by gathering and distributing *information* needed for planning and aiding exchange; by developing and spreading persuasive *communications* about an offer; by performing *contact* work—finding and communicating with prospective buyers; by *matching*—shaping and fitting the offer to the buyer's needs; and by entering into *negotiation* to reach an agreement on price and other terms of the offer so that ownership can be transferred. Other functions help to *fulfill* the completed transactions by offering *physical distribution*—transporting and storing goods; *financing*—acquiring and using funds to cover the costs of the channel work; and *risk taking*—assuming the risks of carrying out the channel work.

2. Discuss how channel members interact and how they organize to perform the work of the channel.

The channel will be most effective when each member is assigned the tasks it can do best. Ideally, because the success of individual channel members depends on overall channel success, all channel firms should work together smoothly. They should understand and accept their roles, coordinate their goals and activities, and cooperate to attain overall channel goals. By cooperating, they can more effectively sense, serve, and satisfy the target market. In a large company, the formal organization structure assigns roles and provides needed leadership. But in a distribution channel made up of independent firms, leadership and power are not formally set. Traditionally, distribution channels have lacked the leadership needed to assign roles and manage conflict. In recent years, however, new types of channel organizations have appeared that provide stronger leadership and improved performance.

3. Identify the major channel alternatives open to a company.

Each firm identifies alternative ways to reach its market. Available means vary from direct selling to using one, two, three, or more intermediary *channel levels*. Marketing channels face continuous and sometimes dramatic change. Three of the most important trends are the growth of *vertical, horizontal,* and *multichannel marketing systems.* These trends affect channel cooperation, conflict, and competition. *Channel design* begins with assessing customer channel service needs and company channel objectives and constraints. The company then identifies the major channel alternatives in terms of the *types* of intermediaries, the *number* of intermediaries, and the *channel responsibilities* of each. Each channel alternative must be evaluated according to economic, control, and adaptive criteria. Channel management calls for selecting qualified intermediaries and motivating them. Individual channel members must be evaluated regularly.

4. Explain how companies select, motivate, and evaluate channel members.

Producers vary in their ability to attract qualified marketing intermediaries. Some producers have no trouble signing up channel members. Others have to work hard to line up enough qualified intermediaries. When selecting intermediaries, the company should evaluate each channel member's qualifications and select those who best fit its channel objectives. Once selected, channel members must be continuously motivated to do their best. The company must sell not only *through* the intermediaries but *to* them. It should work to forge long-term partnerships with their channel partners to create a marketing system that meets the needs of both the manufacturer *and* the partners. The company must also regularly check channel member performance against established performance standards, rewarding intermediaries who are performing well and assisting or replacing weaker ones.

5. **Discuss the nature and importance of marketing logistics and integrated supply chain management.**

Just as firms are giving the marketing concept increased recognition, more business firms are paying attention to *marketing logistics* (or *physical distribution*). Logistics is an area of potentially high cost savings and improved customer satisfaction. Marketing logistics addresses not only *outbound distribution* but also *inbound distribution* and *reverse distribution*. That is, it involves entire *supply chain management*—managing value-added flows between suppliers, the

company, resellers, and final users. No logistics system can both maximize customer service and minimize distribution costs. Instead, the goal of logistics management is to provide a *targeted* level of service at the least cost. The major logistics functions include *order processing, warehousing, inventory management,* and *transportation*.

The *integrated supply chain management concept* recognizes that improved logistics requires teamwork in the form of close working relationships across functional areas inside the company and across various organizations in the supply chain. Companies can achieve logistics harmony among functions by creating cross-functional logistics teams, integrative supply manager positions, and senior-level logistics executives with cross-functional authority. Channel partnerships can take the form of cross-company teams, shared projects, and information sharing systems. Today, some companies are outsourcing their logistics functions to third-party logistics (3PL) providers to save costs, increase efficiency, and gain faster and more effective access to global markets.

> Reviewing the Key Terms <

Administered VMS 368
Channel conflict 365
Channel level 364
Contractual VMS 368
Conventional distribution channel 366
Corporate VMS 367
Direct marketing channel 364
Disintermediation 370

Distribution center 381
Exclusive distribution 374
Franchise organization 368
Horizontal marketing system 368
Indirect marketing channel 364
Integrated logistics management 384
Intensive distribution 374

Intermodal transportation 384
Marketing channel (or distribution channel) 362
Marketing logistics (or physical distribution) 379
Multichannel distribution system (or hybrid marketing channel) 369

Selective distribution 375
Supply chain management 379
Third-party logistics (3PL) provider 387
Value delivery network 361
Vertical marketing system (VMS) 366

> Discussing the Concepts <

1. Describe at least three different marketing channels a new textbook might take to get from the publisher to the student-consumer?

2. The chapter cites IBM and Schwab as examples of multichannel distribution. Discuss the pros and cons of choosing hybrid marketing channels.

3. Selecting channel members is often a difficult task, but once completed, the focus turns to managing and motivating the channel partner relationship. Identify the primary challenges an organization faces in managing its channel members. What are some of the methods companies use to motivate channel partners?

4. Provide three reasons why supply chain management is an important part of the value delivery network.

5. Why would a company consider outsourcing its own logistics functions?

6. What are the overall goals of integrated supply chain management? What can a company do to achieve the close working relationships necessary for effective supply chain management?

> Applying the Concepts <

1. Imagine you are a salesperson for an advertising media sales organization representing four noncompeting business publications. Answer the following questions asked by the marketing vice president of a potential advertiser: "Can't I go directly to the magazine publisher's home office and get what I want? How are you going to add value in this relationship?"

2. You have been asked by Steve Saleen, President of Saleen, Inc., to draft a short memo detailing your recommendations for expanding Saleen's distribution to Asia. Go to www.saleen.com, and tour the

Web site. Include in your recommendation the types, numbers, and responsibilities of proposed channel intermediaries.

3. PeopleSoft is one of the leading supply chain management software companies. Go to www.peoplesoft.com/corp/en/products/ent/scm/resource_library.jsp#demos and work your way through the four page demo on "Supply Chain Analytics." Explain how this software would help a company better manage its supply chain.

> Focus on Technology <

What does just-in-time inventory management have to do with the Carle Heart Center in Urbana, Illinois? The Carle Heart Center is one of the most sophisticated cardiac-care facilities in the Midwest. Integral to the success of Carle are three separate cardiac catheterization labs that are miles apart. These cath labs have pioneered techniques and technologies ranging from intravascular brachytherapy to digital cardiovascular imaging. The latest addition to this forward-thinking heart care center is a department-wide networking system from General Electric Medical Systems called CardioLink. Part of the CardioLink is a just-in-time inventory system. According to Carle's Cath Lab Manager Alan Kettelkamp, "Department-wide access to our Lab Management Tools not only eliminates the need for maintaining individual inventory systems for each lab, it also allows us to apply just-in-time techniques. We simply push a button to see which sup-

plies are below our par levels, by vendor. Our inventory specialists can then print out replenishment orders and fax them out for next-day shipment. We're even able to enter the replenishments into our system with a bar-code reader. This system has perfected our order-management process, and it has allowed us to reduce our total inventory significantly."

1. What are the benefits of the just-in-time inventory management system to Carle's Cath Lab?

2. What do you think would be a "safe" inventory level for Carle's Cath Lab? Is it 3 or 4 days as with Dell, or is it longer?

3. In what other critical service areas besides health care would a just-in-time inventory management system prove beneficial?

> Focus on Ethics <

In response to a request from a federal judge in Atlanta, the FTC prepared comments on a proposed North Carolina act entitled, "An Act to Amend the Wine Franchise Law to Provide for Exclusive Territories." Go to the Web site www.ftc.gov/be/v990003.htm and read the FTC's comments. Then, respond to the following questions:

1. Why would the North Carolina State Legislature propose this legislation?

2. Do you agree or disagree with the FTC position? Explain.

3. Under what circumstances would you expect exclusive territories to be lawful? Can you cite examples?

◎ Video Case

Federated Direct

Planning a wedding—it's the most exciting time in a young couple's life. And it's perhaps the best opportunity for a retailer to begin a relationship with consumers that will last a lifetime. So retailers, ranging from department stores to specialty boutiques, reach out to young people who are starting their lives together by offering in-store and online wedding registries. Facing competition from a retailers as varied as Williams-Sonoma, Target, and Linens 'N Things, Federated Direct (the company that owns Macy's and Bloomingdales) decided to lay the foundation for long-term relationships by offering a bridal registry of its own. To do so, the company worked with its supply-chain partners to offer consumers just the right assortment of products. The result? A new

approach to attracting young customers and building life-long relationships with consumers.

After viewing the video featuring Federated Direct, answer the following questions about distribution channels.

1. Does the explosion of retail channels benefit the average consumer?

2. How does Federated Direct act as a marketing intermediary?

3. List your three favorite retail stores. Are any of them department stores? If not, why not?

4. Do you think that Federated's approach will attract the target consumers the company is seeking?

Company Case

Staples, Inc.: Revising the Strategy

TAKING OVER

Back in January 2002, Ronald Sargent assumed the reins of office supply superstore Staples from founder Thomas Stemberg. At that time, Sargent and Staples faced many challenges. The office supply market seemed to be maturing—industry sales in 2001 actually shrank three percent after years of double-digit growth. Further, although Staples had significantly more stores than its two major competitors—Office Depot and Office Max—it trailed Office Depot in sales revenue (see Exhibit 1).

There were bright spots for Staples—whereas both Office Depot's and Office Max's sales had declined 5.6 percent and 9.7 percent, respectively, in 2001, Staples' sales had inched up .7 percent; and its profits had soared from just $59.7 million in 2000 to $265 million in 2001. Yet, analysts noted that Staples' return on net assets (RONA) was below its weighted-average cost of capital (WACC) and argued that the firm needed to improve its profitability. Sargent knew he had his work cut out for him.

TAKING STOCK

Sargent began by questioning one of the company's basic strategic assumptions—build a store with lots of inventory and the lowest prices in town and customers will beat a path to your door. Under this philosophy, Staples operated 400 more stores than Office Max and 541 more than Office Depot. Staples' stores typically stocked its stores from floor to ceiling, warehouse style, with all sorts of products. Yet, Staples' sales revenue per store was well below Office Depot's.

Sargent therefore decided to slow the company's store expansion. He also closed 32 under-performing stores, the largest store closing in the company's 16-year history. Moreover, the company planned to open only 115 new stores in 2002, down from 160 in 2001. It would also open most of these new stores in existing markets rather than new market areas in order to take advantage of operating efficiencies.

Further, focus groups with Staple's target market of small business customers indicated that those customers did not like the warehouse look. Customers wanted to be able to see across a store and to determine quickly from signage where items were located. Staples responded by experimenting with a smaller store (20,000 square feet versus about 24,000) with lower shelving and a more open atmosphere. This meant that it had to reduce inventory. As a result, the company removed many items that it found were not necessary, such as child-oriented computer games and educational software. Based on customer feedback, it also stopped offering some business services, like health insurance or prepaid legal services, so that it could focus on consumable products. Customers, it found, did not want to shop at Staples for these services.

The results with this new store format proved promising, with sales increasing up to 10 percent with about 10 percent less inventory. Sargent noted that, "We're doing the same sales volume with two printers selling for more than $100 than we did selling five printers at the different price points." As a result, Sargent decided to roll out the new format and reconfigure 280 stores in 2002 in hopes of improving both sales and inventory turnover. Staples' inventory turnover ratio was about 5.1 times as compared with Office Depot's 6.3 times.

As a second part of his strategy, Sargent turned to what the company calls its "North American Delivery" segment. This segment includes the company's Internet, catalog, and corporate contracts operations—all of its operations that *bypass* its stores. In 2001, this segment accounted for 28 percent of sales and 40 percent of profits. Competitor Office Depot got 34 percent of its sales and 33 percent of its profits from similar operations. In a Home Furnishing Network survey of Web-site traffic for the first four months of 2002, Office Depot had the highest number of unique Web-site visits, over 24 million, of the top 20 retail Web sites, ahead of Best Buy, Wal-Mart, Target, and others. Staples' site, www.staples.com, came in seventh with just under 14 million visits, while OfficeMax finished 10th with just under 10 million visits. *Forbes* magazine named Staple's site as the "Best of the Web Pick for Entrepreneurs" for the third year in a row based on its ability to assist smaller businesses to run as smoothly as larger organizations.

EXHIBIT 1: OFFICE SUPPLY DATA FOR FISCAL 2001

Company	Number of Stores	Sales Revenue ($B)	Net Income ($M)	Revenue per Store ($M)*	Employees
Staples	1,400	$10.74	$265	$5.7	53,000
Office Depot	859	$11.15	$201	$6.7	48,000
OfficeMax	1,000	$4.64	($296)	$4.6	30,000

*Revenue per store does not include revenue from Internet or catalog sales.
Source: *Westchester County Business Journal*, April 1, 2002, p. 14.

(box continues)

To handle its catalog operations, Staples has a subsidiary, Quill.com. A survey ranked Quill.com as highest in terms of its online sales conversion rate of 30.3 percent versus the average site's rate of eight percent or lower. Quills offered 35 percent of its products as private label brands as compared to seven percent for Staples. Sargent saw this as an opportunity for Staples to offer more of it own private-label brands that carried higher margins.

Although Staples built its business by targeting small businesses, while OfficeMax had targeted household consumers, it also developed programs for businesses with more than 100 employees. Its StaplesLink program allowed companies to link their internal procurement systems with Staples' computer systems. This allowed users to place their orders directly with Staples, which then prepared the order and delivered it to the business the next day.

For both its catalog and contract businesses, Sargent believed that Staples should beat a path to customers' doors. He ordered the doubling, to 400, of Staple's special sales force, which worked with customers to get them to order through its catalog or its Web site. He also added 100 staff members to the 600-person sales force that worked exclusively with corporate and small-business accounts.

To help get small-business customers into the stores, Staples entered a test with FleetBoston Financial Corp. to open 10 offices in select Staples stores in the Northeast. These 150-foot, in-store offices would have two Fleet staff members who would work with business owners to open specially designed business checking accounts, get debit cards, and make small business loan applications. The offices would not dispense cash or take deposits and would be open six or seven days a week. Fleet had more than 100 nontraditional branches, mostly in supermarkets.

Next, Sargent planned to continue Staples' international expansion. The retailer already operated 180 stores in the United Kingdom, Germany, the Netherlands, and Portugal. It planned to add 20 new stores in Europe and to open in one more country. European operations accounted for about $796 million of 2001's sales.

Finally, Sargent focused on customer retention. He understood that getting a customer was expensive. The company estimated that a customer doing business for three years was 4.5 times more profitable than a new customer. Staples' managers estimated that the company had a 30 percent share of their customers' office supply purchases, and they wanted to increase that share.

TAKING THE CHALLENGE

Sargent knew Staples' 53,000 employees would have to execute all of these strategic moves for the company to reach its target of $12 billion in sales and $440 million in net income by 2003. And, he knew that competition was only going to intensify. The struggling OfficeMax was trying to capture more of Staples' small-business customers. These customers were often willing to buy higher-margin items, thus leading to Staples' higher-than-average margins. In an industry with lots of stores, catalogs, and Internet sites offering similar merchandise at similar prices, maintaining a competitive advantage would not be easy. Further, Sargent worried about offering the same products and services to the same customers through multiple channels. Would this strategy generate channel conflict within the company?

Questions for Discussion

1. How are store, catalog, and Internet-based distribution channels alike or different in terms of the channel functions they perform?

2. Do you see any potential for conflict among Staples' different channels? Why or why not?

3. Is the Staples/FleetBoston horizontal marketing effort a good idea? Why or why not?

4. What are the advantages of more intensive development of individual market areas versus the advantages of putting more stores in new markets?

5. How can Staples develop a competitive advantage in a commodity market? What marketing recommendations would you make to Staples?

6. Once you have answered the questions above, you can conduct research to see how Staples' multi-channel distribution channel worked. You can begin your research to see how Staples had done through mid-2004 by using the *additional sources* cited below.

Sources: Alissa Swchmelkin, "Fleet to Open Offices in Staples," *American Banker*, July 11, 2002, p. 20; Alex Philippidis, "Wither the Warehouse Look: Can Staples, OfficeMax Raise Profits by Lowering Shelves," *Westchester County Business Journal*, April 1, 2002, p. 14; Joseph Pereira, "Staples Inc. Pulls Back on Its Store-Expansion Plans, *The Wall Street Journal*, March 13, 2002, p. B4; A. H. Rubinson, "Staples," UBS Warburg, December 10, 2001.

Additional Sources: Frank Byrt, "Staples Posts 39% Profit Jump," *The Wall Street Journal*, August 18, 2004, p. B7; W. C. Symmonds, "Thinking Outside the Big Box," *Business Week*, August 11, 2003; Jim Bodor, "Shopping On All Channels," *Telegram & Gazette*, Worcester, Mass., December 22, 2002, p. E1.

> **After studying this chapter, you should be able to**

1. explain the roles of retailers and wholesalers in the distribution channel
2. describe the major types of retailers and give examples of each
3. identify the major types of wholesalers and give examples of each
4. explain the marketing decisions facing retailers and wholesalers

Retailing and Wholesaling

Previewing the Concepts

In the previous chapter, you learned the basics of distribution channel design and management. Now, we'll look more deeply into the two major intermediary channel functions, retailing and wholesaling. You already know something about retailing—you're served every day by retailers of all shapes and sizes. However, you probably know much less about the hoard of wholesalers that work behind the scenes. In this chapter, we'll examine the characteristics of different kinds of retailers and wholesalers, the marketing decisions they make, and trends for the future.

To start, we'll look at Wal-Mart, the ultimate retailer. This megaretailer's phenomenal success has resulted from an unrelenting focus bringing value to its customers. Day in and day out, Wal-Mart lives up to its promise: Always low prices—*Always*. That focus on customer value has made Wal-Mart not just the world's largest retailer, but also the world's largest company.

In 1962, Sam Walton and his brother opened the first Wal-Mart discount store in small-town Rogers, Arkansas. It was a big, flat, warehouselike store that sold everything from apparel to automotive supplies to small appliances at very low prices. Experts gave the fledgling retailer little chance—conventional wisdom suggested that discount stores could succeed only in large cities.

Yet, from these modest beginnings, the chain exploded onto the national retailing scene. Incredibly, Wal-Mart's annual sales now approach $260 billion more than one and one-half times the sales of Target, Sears, J.C. Penney, and Costco combined—making it the world's largest company. Wal-Mart is the number-one seller in multiple categories of consumer products, including groceries, toys, CDs, and pet-care products. It sells more clothes than the Gap and Limited combined. Incredibly, Wal-Mart sells 30 percent of the disposable diapers purchased in the United States each year, 30 per-

cent of the hair-care products, 26 percent of the toothpaste, and 20 percent of the pet food.

Wal-Mart's sales of $1.42 billion on one day last fall were larger than the GDPs of 36 countries. The company is now well established in larger cities and is expanding rapidly into international markets. For example, Wal-Mart is now the largest private employer in Mexico. The giant retailer has had a substantial impact on the U.S. economy. One out of every 213 men, women, and children in the United States is a Wal-Mart associate. According to one study, Wal-Mart was responsible for some 25 percent of the nation's astonishing productivity gains during the 1990s.

What are the secrets behind this spectacular success? First and foremost, Wal-Mart is passionately dedicated to its value proposition of "Always Low Prices, *Always!*" Its mission is to "lower the world's cost of living." To deliver on this promise, it listens to and takes care of its customers, treats employees as partners, and keeps a tight rein on costs.

Wal-Mart knows its customers well and takes good care of them. As one analyst puts it, "The company gospel . . . is relatively simple: Be an agent for customers, find out what they want, and sell it to them for the lowest possible price." The company stays close to customers—for example, each top Wal-Mart executive spends at least 2 days a week visiting stores, talking directly with customers and getting a firsthand look at operations. Then, Wal-Mart delivers what customers want: a broad selection of carefully selected goods at unbeatable prices. Concludes Wal-Mart's current president and chief executive, "We're obsessed with delivering value to customers."

Beyond listening to and taking care of customers, Wal-Mart also takes good care of employees. It believes that, in the final accounting, the company's people are what really make it better. Wal-Mart was first to call employees "associates," a practice now widely copied by competitors. The associates work as partners, become deeply involved in operations, and share rewards for good performance.

> Everyone at Wal-Mart [is] an associate—from [the CEO] . . . to a cashier named Janet at the Wal-Mart on Highway 50 in Ocoee, Florida. "We," "us," and "our" are the operative words. Wal-Mart department heads, hourly associates who look after one or more of 30-some departments ranging from sporting goods to electronics, see figures that many companies never show general managers: costs, freight charges, profit margins. The company sets a profit margin for each store, and if the store exceeds it, then the hourly associates share part of the additional profit.

Finally, Wal-Mart delivers real value by keeping a sharp eye on costs. Wal-Mart is a lean, mean, distribution machine—it has the lowest cost structure in the industry. This lets the giant retailer charge lower prices but still reap higher profits. For example, grocery prices drop an average or 10 to 15 percent in markets Wal-Mart has entered, and Wal-Mart's food prices average 20 percent less then those of its grocery store rivals. Wal-Mart's lower prices attract more shoppers, producing more sales, making the company more efficient, and enabling it to lower prices even more.

Wal-Mart's low costs result in part from superior management and more sophisticated technology. Its Bentonville, Arkansas, headquarters contains a computer communications system that the Defense Department would envy, giving managers around the country instant access to sales and operating information. And its huge, fully automated distribution centers employ the latest technology to supply stores efficiently. Wal-Mart also spends less than competitors on advertising as a percentage of sales. Because Wal-Mart has what customers want at the prices they'll pay, its reputation has spread rapidly by word of mouth. It has not needed more advertising.

Finally, Wal-Mart keeps costs down through good old "tough buying." Whereas the company is known for the warm way it treats customers, it is equally well known for the cold, calculated way it wrings low prices from suppliers. The following passage describes a visit to Wal-Mart's buying offices:

> Don't expect a greeter and don't expect friendly. . . . Once you are ushered into one of the spartan little buyers' rooms, expect a steely eye across the table and be prepared to cut your price. "They are very, very focused people, and they use their buying power more forcefully than anyone else in America," says the marketing vice president of a major vendor. "They talk softly, but they have piranha hearts, and if you aren't totally prepared when you go in there, you'll have your [head] handed to you."

Some critics argue that Wal-Mart squeezes its suppliers too hard, driving some out of business. Wal-Mart proponents counter, however, that is simply acting in its customers' interests by forcing suppliers to be more efficient. "Wal-Mart is tough, but totally honest and straightforward in its dealings with vendors," says an industry consultant. "Wal-Mart has forced manufacturers to get their act together."

Some observers wonder whether Wal-Mart can be so big and still retain its focus and positioning. They wonder if an ever-larger Wal-Mart can stay close to its customers and employees. The company's managers are betting on it. No matter where it operates, Wal-Mart's announced policy is to take care of customers "one store at a time." Says one top executive: "We'll be fine as long as we never lose our responsiveness to the consumer."[1]

The Wal-Mart story provides many insights into the workings of one of today's most successful retailers. This chapter looks at *retailing* and *wholesaling*. In the first section, we look at the nature and importance of retailing, major types of store and nonstore retailers, the decisions retailers make, and the future of retailing. In the second section, we discuss these same topics as they relate to wholesalers.

Retailing

What is retailing? We all know that Wal-Mart, Home Depot, and Target are retailers, but so are Avon representatives, Amazon.com, the local Holiday Inn, and a doctor seeing patients. **Retailing** includes all the activities involved in selling products or services directly to final consumers for their personal, nonbusiness use. Many institutions—manufacturers, wholesalers, and retailers—do retailing. But most retailing is done by **retailers**: businesses whose sales come *primarily* from retailing.

Although most retailing is done in retail stores, in recent years *nonstore retailing* has been growing much faster than has store retailing. Nonstore retailing includes selling to final consumers through direct mail, catalogs, telephone, the Internet, TV home shopping shows, home and office parties, door-to-door contact, vending machines, and other direct selling approaches. We discuss such direct-marketing approaches in detail in Chapter 16. In this chapter, we focus on store retailing.

Retailing

All activities involved in selling goods or services directly to final consumers for their personal, nonbusiness use.

Retailer

A business whose sales come *primarily* from retailing.

Types of Retailers

Retail stores come in all shapes and sizes, and new retail types keep emerging. The most important types of retail stores are described in Table 13.1 and discussed in the following sections. They can be classified in terms of several characteristics, including the *amount of service* they offer, the breadth and depth of their *product lines*, the *relative prices* they charge, and how they are *organized*.

Amount of Service

Different products require different amounts of service, and customer service preferences vary. Retailers may offer one of three levels of service—self-service, limited service, and full service.

Self-service retailers serve customers who are willing to perform their own "locate-compare-select" process to save money. Self-service is the basis of all discount operations and is typically used by sellers of convenience goods (such as supermarkets) and nationally branded, fast-moving shopping goods (such as Best Buy).

Limited-service retailers, such as Sears or J.C. Penney, provide more sales assistance because they carry more shopping goods about which customers need information. Their

TABLE 13.1   Major Store Retailer Types

Specialty Stores: Carry a narrow product line with a deep assortment, such as apparel stores, sporting-goods stores, furniture stores, florists, and bookstores. A clothing store would be a *single-line* store, a men's clothing store would be a *limited-line store,* and a men's custom-shirt store would be a *superspecialty* store. Examples: The Body Shop, Gap, The Athlete's Foot.

Department Stores: Carry several product lines—typically clothing, home furnishings, and household goods—with each line operated as a separate department managed by specialist buyers or merchandisers. Examples: Sears, Macy's, Marshall Field's.

Supermarkets: A relatively large, low-cost, low-margin, high-volume, self-service operation designed to serve the consumer's total needs for food and household products. Examples: Kroger, Vons, A&P, Food Lion.

Convenience Stores: Relatively small stores located near residential areas, open long hours seven days a week, and carrying a limited line of high-turnover convenience products at slightly higher prices. Examples: 7-Eleven, Stop-N-Go, Circle K.

Discount Stores: Carry standard merchandise sold at lower prices with lower margins and higher volumes. Examples: General—Wal-Mart, Target, Kmart, Specialty—Circuit City.

Off-Price Retailers: Sell merchandise bought at less-than-regular wholesale prices and sold at less than retail: often leftover goods, overruns, and irregulars obtained at reduced prices from manufacturers or other retailers. These include *factory outlets* owned and operated by manufacturers (example: Mikasa); *independent off-price retailers* owned and run by entrepreneurs or by divisions of larger retail corporations (example: TJ Maxx); and *warehouse (or wholesale) clubs* selling a limited selection of brand-name groceries, appliances, clothing, and other goods at deep discounts to consumers who pay membership fees (examples: Costco, Sam's, BJ's Wholesale Club).

Superstores: Very large stores traditionally aimed at meeting consumers' total needs for routinely purchased food and nonfood items. Includes *category killers*, which carry a deep assortment in a particular category and have a knowledgeable staff (examples: Circuit City, Petsmart, Staples); *supercenters,* combined supermarket and discount stores (examples: Wal-Mart Supercenters, SuperTarget, Super Kmart Center); and *hypermarkets* with up to 220,000 square feet of space combining supermarket, discount, and warehouse retailing (examples: Carrefour [France], Pyrca [Spain]).

increased operating costs result in higher prices. In *full-service retailers*, such as specialty stores and first-class department stores, salespeople assist customers in every phase of the shopping process. Full-service stores usually carry more specialty goods for which customers like to be "waited on." They provide more services resulting in much higher operating costs, which are passed along to customers as higher prices.

Product Line

Retailers also can be classified by the length and breadth of their product assortments. Some retailers, such as **specialty stores**, carry narrow product lines with deep assortments within those lines. Today, specialty stores are flourishing. The increasing use of market segmentation, market targeting, and product specialization has resulted in a greater need for stores that focus on specific products and segments.

In contrast, **department stores** carry a wide variety of product lines. In recent years, department stores have been squeezed between more focused and flexible specialty stores on the one hand, and more efficient, lower-priced discounters on the other. In response, many have added promotional pricing to meet the discount threat. Others have stepped up the use of store brands and single-brand "designer shops" to compete with specialty stores. Still others are trying mail-order, telephone, and Web selling. Service remains the key differentiating factor. Department stores such as Nordstrom, Saks, Neiman Marcus, and other high-end department stores are doing well by emphasizing high-quality service.

Supermarkets are the most frequently shopped type of retail store. Today, however, they are facing slow sales growth because of slower population growth and an increase in competition from convenience stores, discount food stores, and superstores. Supermarkets also have been hit hard by the rapid growth of out-of-home eating.

Thus, most supermarkets are making improvements to attract more customers. In the battle for "share of stomachs," many large supermarkets have moved upscale, providing from-scratch bakeries, gourmet deli counters, and fresh seafood departments. Others are cutting costs, establishing more efficient operations, and lowering prices in order to compete more effectively with food discounters. Finally, a few have added Web-based sales. Today, one quarter of all grocery stores sell their goods online. Forrester Research estimates that 18 percent of the nation's household will be good prospects for online grocery buying and that the market will grow to $17.4 billion by 2008.[2]

Convenience stores are small stores that carry a limited line of high-turnover convenience goods. Some 132,000 U.S. convenience stores posted sales last year of $337 billion.

Specialty store
A retail store that carries a narrow product line with a deep assortment within that line.

Department store
A retail organization that carries a wide variety of product lines—typically clothing, home furnishings, and household goods; each line is operated as a separate department managed by specialist buyers or merchandisers.

Supermarket
Large, low-cost, low-margin, high-volume, self-service store that carries a wide variety of food, laundry, and household products.

Convenience store
A small store, located near a residential area, that is open long hours 7 days a week and carries a limited line of high-turnover convenience goods.

■ In the battle for "share of stomachs," Safeway and many large supermarkets have added Web-based sales. Today, one quarter of all grocery stores sell their goods online.

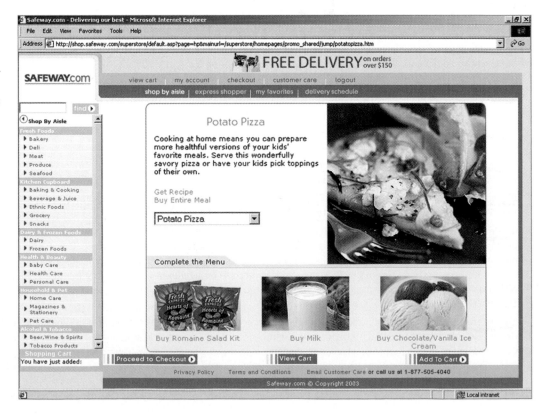

More than 60 percent of convenience store revenues come from sales of gasoline; more the 50 percent of in-store revenues are from cigarette and beverage sales.[3]

In recent years, the convenience store industry has suffered from overcapacity as its primary market of young, blue-collar men has shrunk. As a result, many chains are redesigning their stores to attract female shoppers. They are shedding the image of a "truck stop" where men go to buy beer, cigarettes, and magazines, and instead offer fresh prepared foods and cleaner, safer environments. Many are also applying micromarketing—tailoring each store's merchandise to the specific needs of its surrounding neighborhood. For example, a Stop-N-Go in an affluent neighborhood carries fresh produce, gourmet pasta sauces, chilled Evian water, and expensive wines. Stop-N-Go stores in Hispanic neighborhoods carry Spanish-language magazines and other goods catering to the specific needs of Hispanic consumers.

Superstores are much larger than regular supermarkets and offer a large assortment of routinely purchased food products, nonfood items, and services. Wal-Mart, Kmart, Target, and other discount retailers offer *supercenters*, combination food and discount stores that emphasize cross-merchandising. Toasters are above the fresh-baked bread, kitchen gadgets are across from produce, and infant centers carry everything from baby food to clothing. Supercenters are growing in the United States at an annual rate of 25 percent, compared with a supermarket industry growth rate of only 1 percent. Wal-Mart, which opened its first supercenter in 1988, now has more than 1,700, capturing more than 70 percent of all supercenter volume.[4]

Recent years have also seen the explosive growth of superstores that are actually giant specialty stores, the so-called **category killers**. They feature stores the size of airplane hangars that carry a very deep assortment of a particular line with a knowledgeable staff. Category killers are prevalent in a wide range of categories, including books, baby gear, toys, electronics, home improvement products, linens and towels, party goods, sporting goods, even pet supplies. Another superstore variation, *hypermarkets,* are huge superstores, perhaps as large as *six* football fields. Although hypermarkets have been very successful in Europe and other world markets, they have met with little success in the United States.

Finally, for some retailers, the product line is actually a service. Service retailers include hotels and motels, banks, airlines, colleges, hospitals, movie theaters, tennis clubs, bowling alleys, restaurants, repair services, hair care shops, and dry cleaners. Service retailers in the United States are growing faster than product retailers.

Relative Prices

Retailers can also be classified according to the prices they charge (see Table 13.1). Most retailers charge regular prices and offer normal-quality goods and customer service. Others offer higher-quality goods and service at higher prices. The retailers that feature low prices are discount stores and "off-price" retailers.

DISCOUNT STORES A **discount store** sells standard merchandise at lower prices by accepting lower margins and selling higher volume. The early discount stores cut expenses by offering few services and operating in warehouselike facilities in low-rent, heavily traveled districts. In recent years, facing intense competition from other discounters and department stores, many discount retailers have "traded up." They have improved décor, added new lines and services, and expanded regionally and nationally, leading to higher costs and prices.

OFF-PRICE RETAILERS When the major discount stores traded up, a new wave of **off-price retailers** moved in to fill the low-price, high-volume gap. Ordinary discounters buy at regular wholesale prices and accept lower margins to keep prices down. In contrast, off-price retailers buy at less-than-regular wholesale prices and charge consumers less than retail. Off-price retailers can be found in all areas, from food, clothing, and electronics to no-frills banking and discount brokerages.

The three main types of off-price retailers are *independents, factory outlets*, and *warehouse clubs*. **Independent off-price retailers** either are owned and run by entrepreneurs or are divisions of larger retail corporations. Although many off-price operations are run by smaller independents, most large off-price retailer operations are owned by bigger retail chains. Examples include store retailers such as TJ Maxx and Marshall's, owned by TJX Companies, and Web sellers such as RetailExchange.com, Redtag.com, and CloseOutNow.com.

Factory outlets such as the Manhattan's Brand Name Fashion Outlet and the factory outlets of Liz Claiborne, Carters, Levi Strauss, and other manufacturers—sometimes group together in *factory outlet malls* and *value-retail centers*, where dozens of outlet stores offer prices as low as 50 percent below retail on a wide range of items. Whereas outlet malls consist

---

Superstore
A store much larger than a regular supermarket that carries a large assortment of routinely purchased food products, nonfood items, and services.

Category killer
Giant specialty store that carries a very deep assortment of a particular line and is staffed by knowledgeable employees.

Discount store
A retail institution that sells standard merchandise at lower prices by accepting lower margins and selling at higher volume.

Off-price retailer
Retailer that buys at less-than-regular wholesale prices and sells at less than retail. Examples are factory outlets, independents, and warehouse clubs.

Independent off-price retailer
An off-price retailer that is either owned and run by an entrepreneur or is a division of a larger retail corporation.

Factory outlet
An off-price retailing operation that is owned and operated by a manufacturer and that normally carries the manufacturer's surplus, discontinued, or irregular goods.

primarily of manufacturers' outlets, value-retail centers combine manufacturers' outlets with off-price retail stores and department store clearance outlets. Factory outlet malls have become one of the hottest growth areas in retailing.

The malls now are moving upscale—and even dropping "factory" from their descriptions—narrowing the gap between factory outlet and more traditional forms of retailers. As the gap narrows, the discounts offered by outlets are getting smaller. However, a growing number of outlet malls now feature brands such as Coach, Polo, Ralph Lauren, Dolce & Gabbana, Giorgio Armani, Gucci, and Versace, causing department stores to protest to the manufacturers of these brands. Given their higher costs, the department stores have to charge more than the off-price outlets. Manufacturers counter that they send last year's merchandise and seconds to the factory outlet malls, not the new merchandise that they supply to the department stores. The malls are also located far from urban areas, making travel to them more difficult. Still, the department stores are concerned about the growing number of shoppers willing to make weekend trips to stock up on branded merchandise at substantial savings.[5]

Warehouse club

An off-price retailer that sells a limited selection of brand name grocery items, appliances, clothing, and a hodgepodge of other goods at deep discounts to members who pay annual membership fees.

Warehouse clubs (or *wholesale clubs* or *membership warehouses*), such as Sam's Club, Costco, and BJ's, operate in huge, drafty, warehouselike facilities and offer few frills. Customers themselves must wrestle furniture, heavy appliances, and other large items to the checkout line. Such clubs make no home deliveries and often accept no credit cards. However, they do offer ultralow prices and surprise deals on selected branded merchandise.

Although they account for only about 4 percent of total U.S. retail sales, warehouse clubs have grown rapidly in recent years. These retailers appeal not just to low-income consumers seeking bargains on bare-bones products. They appeal to all kinds of customers shopping for a wide range of goods, from necessities to extravagances. Consider Costco, the nation's largest warehouse retailer:

> What Costco has come to stand for is a retail segment where high-end products meet deep-discount prices. It's the United States' biggest seller of fine wines (including the likes of a Chateau Cheval-Blanc Bordeaux for $229.99 a bottle) and baster of poultry (55,000 rotisserie chickens a day). Last year it sold 45 million hot dogs at $1.50 each and 60,000 carats of diamonds at up to $100,000. Chef Julia Child buys meat at Costco. Yuppies seek the latest gadgets there. Even people who don't have to pinch pennies shop at Costco.
>
> Time was when only the great unwashed shopped at off-price stores. But warehouse clubs attract a breed of urban sophisticates attuned to what one retail consultant calls the "new luxury." These shoppers shun Seiko watches for TAG Heuer; Jack Nicklaus golf clubs for Callaway; Maxwell House coffee (it goes without saying) for Starbucks. They "trade up," eagerly spending more for items that make their hearts

■ Off-price retailers: Shoppers at warehouse clubs such as Costco "trade up," getting good prices on items that make their hearts pound. At the same time, they "trade down" to private labels for things like paper towels, detergent, and vitamins.

pound and for which they don't have to pay full price. Then they "trade down" to private labels for things like paper towels, detergent, and vitamins. Catering to this fast-growing segment, Costco has exploded too. "It's the ultimate concept in trading up and trading down," says the consultant. "It's a brilliant innovation for the new luxury."[6]

Organizational Approach

Although many retail stores are independently owned, an increasing number are banding together under some form of corporate or contractual organization. The major types of retail organizations—*corporate chains, voluntary chains* and *retailer cooperatives, franchise organizations*, and *merchandising conglomerates*—are described in Table 13.2.

Chain stores are two or more outlets that are commonly owned and controlled. They have many advantages over independents. Their size allows them to buy in large quantities at lower prices and gain promotional economies. They can hire specialists to deal with areas such as pricing, promotion, merchandising, inventory control, and sales forecasting.

The great success of corporate chains caused many independents to band together in one of two forms of contractual associations. One is the *voluntary chain*—a wholesaler-sponsored group of independent retailers that engages in group buying and common merchandising—which we discussed in Chapter 12. Examples include Western Auto and Do it Best hardware stores. The other form of contractual association is the *retailer cooperative*—a group of independent retailers that bands together to set up a jointly owned, central wholesale operation and conducts joint merchandising and promotion efforts. Examples are Associated Grocers and Ace Hardware. These organizations give independents the buying and promotion economies they need to meet the prices of corporate chains.

Another form of contractual retail organization is a **franchise**. The main difference between franchise organizations and other contractual systems (voluntary chains and retail cooperatives) is that franchise systems are normally based on some unique product or service; on a method of doing business; or on the trade name, goodwill, or patent that the franchiser has developed. Franchising has been prominent in fast foods, video stores, health and fitness centers, haircutting, auto rentals, motels, travel agencies, real estate, and dozens of other product and service areas.

Chain stores
Two or more outlets that are owned and controlled in common, have central buying and merchandising, and sell similar lines of merchandise.

Franchise
A contractual association between a manufacturer, wholesaler, or service organization (a franchiser) and independent businesspeople (franchisees) who buy the right to own and operate one or more units in the franchise system.

TABLE 13.2 **Major Types of Retail Organizations**

Type	Description	Examples
Corporate chain stores	Two or more outlets that are commonly owned and controlled, employ central buying and merchandising, and sell similar lines of merchandise. Corporate chains appear in all types of retailing, but they are strongest in department stores, variety stores, food stores, drugstores, shoe stores, and women's clothing stores.	Tower Records, Fayva (shoes), Pottery Barn (dinnerware and home furnishings)
Voluntary chains	Wholesaler-sponsored groups of independent retailers engaged in bulk buying and common merchandising.	Independent Grocers Alliance (IGA), Sentry Hardwares, Western Auto, True Value
Retailer cooperatives	Groups of independent retailers who set up a central buying organization and conduct joint promotion efforts.	Associated Grocers (groceries), Ace (hardware)
Franchise organizations	Contractual association between a franchiser (a manufacturer, wholesaler, or service organization) and franchisees (independent businesspeople who buy the right to own and operate one or more units in the franchise system). Franchise organizations are normally based on some unique product, service, or method of doing business, or on a tradename or patent, or on goodwill that the franchiser had developed.	McDonald's, Subway, Pizza Hut, Jiffy Lube, Meineke Mufflers, 7-Eleven
Merchandising conglomerates	A free-form corporation that combines several diversified retailing lines and forms under central ownership, along with some integration of their distribution and management functions.	Target Corporation

■ Franchises have sprung up to meet about any need—from familiar fast-feeders like McDonald's and Subway to computer consulting service Geeks on Call.

But franchising covers a lot more than just burger joints and fitness centers. Franchises have sprung up to meet about any need. Franchiser Geeks on Call provides computer consulting services to small businesses, and Mad Science Group franchisees put on science programs for schools, scout troops, and birthday parties. Mr. Handyman provides repair services for homeowners while Merry Maids tidies up their houses.

Once considered upstarts among independent businesses, franchises now command 35 percent of all retail sales in the United States. These days, it's nearly impossible to stroll down a city block or drive on a suburban street without seeing a McDonald's, Subway, Jiffy Lube, or Holiday Inn. One of the best-known and most successful franchisers, McDonald's, now has more than 31,000 stores in 119 countries. It serves more than 47 million customers a day and racks up more than $41 billion in annual systemwide sales. More than 70 percent of McDonald's restaurants worldwide are owned and operated by franchisees. Gaining fast is Subway Sandwiches and Salads, one of the fastest-growing franchises, with more than 21,795 shops in 74 countries, including some 17,500 in the United States.[7]

Finally, _merchandising conglomerates_ are corporations that combine several different retailing forms under central ownership. An example is Target Corporation, which operates Marshall Fields (upscale department stores), Target (upscale discount stores), Mervyn's (middle-market apparel and home soft goods), and Target.direct (online retailing and direct marketing). Such diversified retailing, similar to a multibranding strategy, provides superior management systems and economies that benefit all the separate retail operations.

Retailer Marketing Decisions

Retailers are always searching for new marketing strategies to attract and hold customers. In the past, retailers attracted customers with unique products, more or better services than their competitors offered, or credit cards. Today, national-brand manufacturers, in their drive for volume, have placed their branded goods everywhere. National brands are found not only in department stores but also in mass-merchandise discount stores, off-price discount stores, and on the Web. As a result, retail assortments are looking more and more alike.

Service differentiation among retailers has also eroded. Many department stores have trimmed their services, whereas discounters have increased theirs. Customers have become

FIGURE 13.1
Retailer marketing decisions

smarter and more price sensitive. They see no reason to pay more for identical brands, especially when service differences are shrinking. For all these reasons, many retailers today are rethinking their marketing strategies.

As shown in Figure 13.1, retailers face major marketing decisions about their *target market and positioning, product assortment and services, price, promotion,* and *place.*

Target Market and Positioning Decision

Retailers first must define their target markets and then decide how they will position themselves in these markets. Should the store focus on upscale, midscale, or downscale shoppers? Do target shoppers want variety, depth of assortment, convenience, or low prices? Until they define and profile their markets, retailers cannot make consistent decisions about product assortment, services, pricing, advertising, store décor, or any of the other decisions that must support their positions.

Too many retailers fail to define their target markets and positions clearly. They try to have "something for everyone" and end up satisfying no market well. In contrast, successful retailers define their target markets well and position themselves strongly. For example, thanks to strong targeting and positioning, upscale grocer Whole Foods has become one of the nation's most successful food retailers (see Real Marketing 13.1).

At the start of the chapter, we saw that giant Wal-Mart has become the world's largest company by positioning itself on the promise, "Always low prices. *Always!*" How can any discounter hope to compete with the likes of huge and dominating Wal-Mart? Again, the answer is good targeting and positioning. For example, rather than facing Wal-Mart head-on, Target—or Tar-*zhay* as many fans call it—thrives by aiming at a seemingly oxymoronic "upscale discount" niche. It offers discount prices but rises above the discount fray with upmarket style and design and higher-grade service. Target's "expect more, pay less" positioning sets it apart and helps insulate it from Wal-Mart.

In the same way, pet-supply chain Petco competes effectively with low-priced competitors Wal-Mart and Petsmart by positioning upscale:

> To avoid dog-eat-dog competition with Wal-Mart and cost-focused market leader Petsmart, Petco has transformed itself into an emporium of luxury pet supplies. With Gen Xers postponing child rearing and baby boomers coping with empty nests, more Americans are treating pets like spoiled kids with fur. "The way people view animals in the household has changed dramatically" in recent years, says a Petco executive, noting that 55 percent of pet canines now sleep in their owners' beds. People are now spending "more on what could be considered frivolous products," adds an industry consultant, "such as things to coddle their pets."
>
> This trend has been a boon for pets everywhere, but Sparky's not the only one wagging his tail. It's also been good for Petco, which remade its business model to cash in on the trend. Ten years ago Petco made most of its money selling food. Today two-thirds of its revenue comes from services like grooming and training, and from specialty goods like $7.50 beef-flavored toothpaste and $30 pheromone-emitting stress reducers. This shift to pricier offerings has helped Petco avoid a catfight with Wal-Mart, a growing pet-supply power. Of Petco's 10,000 offerings, only 40 overlap with Wal-Mart's. And going upscale has given Petco higher operating margins than the more warehouse-focused Petsmart, the industry's top dog. Such smart targeting and positioning have earned Petco more than 10 consecutive years of double-digit income growth.[8]

■ Retail positioning: To avoid dog-eat-dog competition with Wal-Mart and cost-focused market leader Petsmart, Petco has transformed itself into an emporium of luxury pet supplies.

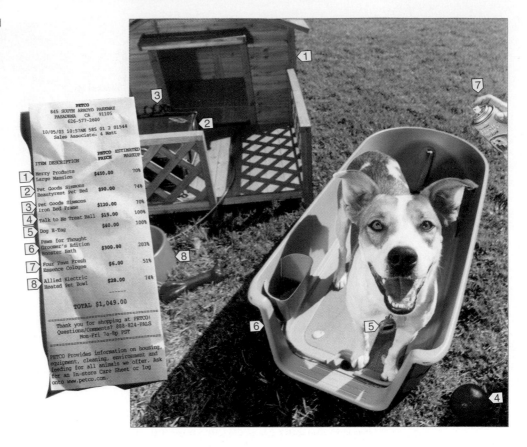

Product Assortment and Services Decision

Retailers must decide on three major product variables: *product assortment*, *services mix*, and *store atmosphere*.

The retailer's *product assortment* should differentiate the retailer while matching target shoppers' expectations. One strategy is to offer merchandise that no other competitor carries, such as private brands or national brands on which it holds exclusives. For example, Saks gets exclusive rights to carry a well-known designer's labels. The retailer can feature blockbuster merchandising events—Bloomingdale's is known for running spectacular shows featuring goods from a certain country, such as India or China. Or the retailer can offer surprise merchandise, as when Costco offers surprise assortments of seconds, overstocks, and closeouts. Finally, the retailer can differentiate itself by offering a highly targeted product assortment—Lane Bryant carries plus-size clothing; Brookstone offers an unusual assortment of gadgets in what amounts to an adult toy store.

The *services mix* can also help set one retailer apart from another. For example, some retailers invite customers to ask questions or consult service representatives in person or via phone or keyboard. Home Depot offers a diverse mix of services to do-it-yourselfers, from "how-to" classes to a proprietary credit card.

The *store's atmosphere* is another element in the reseller's product arsenal. Every store has a physical layout that makes moving around in it either hard or easy. Each store has a "feel"; one store is cluttered, another cheerful, a third plush, a fourth somber. The store must plan an atmosphere that suits the target market and moves customers to buy.

For example, many retailers are practicing "experiential retailing." At an REI store, consumers can try out climbing equipment on a huge wall in the store, and they can test Gore-tex raincoats by going under a simulated rain shower. Similarly, Maytag is now setting up "try-before-you-buy" stores in which products are displayed in realistic home kitchen and laundry room settings, beckoning customers to test drive products before making a choice. "Potential buyers of washers and dryers can do a load of laundry," notes an analyst. "Or if the need is a new range, consumers can bake a sheet of cookies first. They can listen to a dishwasher to see whether it's really quiet."[9]

Increasingly, retailers are turning their stores into theaters that transport customers into unusual, exciting shopping environments. For example, Barnes & Noble uses atmospherics to turn shopping for books into entertainment. It has found that "to consumers, shopping is a

Real Marketing 13.1

Whole Foods: Positioning Away from Wal-Mart

These days, Wal-Mart sells just about everything. That means that it competes ruthlessly with just about every other retailer, no matter what the product category. Wal-Mart outsells Toys 'R' Us in the toy market and sells half again as many groceries as the leading groceries-only retailer, Kroger. It gives Blockbuster big headaches in DVD and video sales and rentals, and puts a big dent in Best Buy's consumer electronics business. Almost every retailer, large or small, has its hands full devising strategies by which it can compete with Wal-Mart and survive.

So, how *do* you compete with a behemoth like Wal-Mart? The best answer: You don't—at least not directly. Perhaps the worst strategy is trying to out-Wal-Mart Wal-Mart. Instead of competing head-to-head, smart competitors choose their turf carefully.

Take Whole Foods Market, the small, upscale grocery chain. Whole Foods has only 160 stores worldwide versus Wal-Mart's more than 5,000, and its annual sales total little more than $3 billion, compared with Wal-Mart's $260 billion. Although it may not seem like a fair fight, Whole Foods is thriving. It succeeds through careful positioning—specifically, by positioning *away* from Wal-Mart. Rather than pursuing mass-market sales volume and razor thin margins, Whole Foods targets a select group of upscale customers and offers them "organic, natural, and gourmet foods, all swaddled in Earth Day politics." As one analyst puts it, "While other grocers are looking over their shoulder, watching and worrying about Wal-Mart, Whole Foods is going about business as usual. The tofu is still selling; the organic eggs are fresh in the back dairy cooler; and meats are still hormone free."

Whole Foods' strong positioning is summed up in its motto: "Whole Foods, Whole People, Whole Planet." Step into your local Whole Foods market and you'll quickly see that it's not your typical food store. In place of the sugary mass-market colas that fill whole aisles in a traditional grocery store, Whole Foods carries organic sodas and Odwalla juices. In the produce department, you'll find blue potatoes, dinner-plate-sized portabello mushrooms, taro root, and edamame (green Japanese soybeans). Natural soaps and toilet papers displace the usual national brands. Or pick up some meat-less moussaka and herbal tea for your post-meditation snack. In keeping with the company's positioning, most of the store's goods carry labels proclaiming "organic," "100% natural," and "contains no additives."

The Whole Foods Web site, bathed in earth-tones, reinforces the company's positioning. The site offers up recipes for healthy eating, such as "Sweet Potato Pancakes with Creamy Dill Sauce," "Baked Basmati & Currant Stuffed Trout," and "Beginner's Tips for Tofu, Tempeh, and Other Soy Foods." The site bursts at the seams with information on a wide range of health and wellness issues, from sources such as WholeHealthMD and the American Botanical Council. You'll find all you ever wanted to know about topics ranging from the potential medical uses of over 100 herbs to alternative therapies such as acupuncture, reflexology, and homeopathy.

Both online and in the flesh, a visit to Whole Foods is more than just a shopping trip, it's an experience. And the experience is any-thing but what you'd find at Wal-Mart. "We create store environ-

■ Whole Foods Market—the small, upscale grocery chain—thrives by giving carefully targeted customers an experience that is anything but what you'd find at Wal-Mart. It offers them "organic, natural, and gourmet foods, all swaddled in Earth Day politics."

ments that are inviting, fun, unique, informal, comfortable, attrac-tive, nurturing, and educational," the company claims. "We want our stores to become community meeting places where our cus-tomers come to join their friends and to make new ones."

By design, Whole Foods is not for everyone—the upscale retailer caters to a carefully selected segment of consumers. Whole Foods customers are affluent, liberal, educated people living in university towns like Austin, Texas, Boulder, Colorado, and Ann Arbor, Michigan. Their median annual household income exceeds the U.S. average by almost $8,000. Whole Foods customers live a health-conscious lifestyle, care about the food they eat, and worry about the environment. They tend to be social do-gooders who abhor soulless corporate greed. Whole Foods doesn't really have to compete with mass merchandisers like Wal-Mart for these customers. In fact, a Whole Foods customer is more likely to boycott the local Wal-Mart than to shop at it.

Whole Foods customers like the fact that the store's commitment to quality reaches far beyond what's on its shelves. In its "Declaration of Interdependence," the company recognizes that liv-ing up to its "Whole Foods, Whole People, Whole Planet" motto means doing more than simply selling food. It means caring about the well-being and quality of life of everyone associated with the business, from customers and employees, to suppliers, to the broader communities in which it operates.

Its concern for customers runs deep. "We go to extraordinary lengths to satisfy and delight our customers," says a company spokesperson. "We want to meet or exceed their expectations on every shopping trip." Whole Foods also cares about its employees—for the past 7 years, it's been listed among *Fortune* magazine's "Top 100 Companies to Work for in America." Whole Foods cares about its suppliers. The Declaration of Interdependence states, "We view our trade partners as allies in serving our stakeholders. We treat

(box continues)

them with respect, fairness, and integrity, and expect the same in return." To back this up, the company supports sustainable, environmentally friendly agriculture practices, offering organically grown foods almost exclusively.

Whole Foods also cares about its communities. It provides financial support for employees doing voluntary community service. And it invests in the local environment. One store in Berkeley, California gets most of its electrical power from roof-top solar panels. A special electrical system and energy-conserving features make the most of the sun. Perhaps most telling of Whole Foods broad community commitment: it donates 5 percent of its after-tax profits to not-for-profit organizations.

Such commitment, along with strong targeting and positioning, have made Whole Foods one of the nation's fastest growing and most profitable food retailers. It's now the world's number-one natural food chain. Its upscale stores ring up an average of $689 in sales per square foot, 75 percent greater than a traditional grocer. And the chain reaps 2.9 percent profit margins, more than double the grocery industry average. Whereas other grocers have faced limited growth, Whole Foods' sales have more than doubled in just the past 4 years.

So, Whole Foods can't compete directly with the Wal-Marts of the world. It can't match Wal-Mart's massive economies of scale, incredible volume purchasing power, ultra-efficient logistics, wide selection, and hard-to-beat prices. But then again, it doesn't even try. Instead, it targets customers that Wal-Mart can't serve, offering them value that Wal-Mart can't deliver. By positioning away from Wal-Mart and other mainstream grocers, Whole Foods has found its own very profitable place in the world.

Sources: Aliya Sternstein, "Green Grocer," *Forbes,* March 31, 2003, p. 40; Michael Thuresson, "Hot Food," *Los Angeles Business Journal*, February 24, 2003, p. 4; "Whole Foods Pushing for Organic Profit Growth," *Money Digest*, February 2003, p. 14; Galina Espinoza and Alicia Dennis, "The Natural," *People Weekly*, November 4, 2002, p. 137; Vilma Barr, "Sunshine Supermarket," *Progressive Grocer*, March 1, 2003, p. 94; "Whole Foods Market Inc.," *Hoover's Company Profiles,* Austin, June 15, 2003; "Whole Foods Market, Inc," *Hoover's Company Capsules*, March 15, 2004, p. 10952; Samantha Thompson Smith, "Grocer's Success Seems Entirely Natural," *The News & Observer*, May 21, 2004, p. D1; and www.wholefoods.com, January 2005.

social activity. They do it to mingle with others in a prosperous-feeling crowd, to see what's new, to enjoy the theatrical dazzle of the display, to treat themselves to something interesting or unexpected." Thus, Barnes & Noble stores are designed with "enough woody, traditional, soft-colored library to please book lovers; enough sophisticated modern architecture and graphics, sweeping vistas, and stylish displays to satisfy fans of the theater of consumption. And for everyone, plenty of space, where they can meet other people and feel at home." As one Barnes & Noble executive notes: "The feel-good part of the store, the quality-of-life contribution, is a big part of the success."[10]

Perhaps the most dramatic conversion of stores into theater is the Mall of America near Minneapolis. Containing more than 520 specialty stores and 50 restaurants, the mall is a veritable playground that attracts as many as 42 million visitors each year. Under a single roof, it shelters a seven-acre Camp Snoopy amusement park featuring 25 rides and attractions, an ice-skating rink, an aquarium, Underwater Adventures that features hundreds of marine specimens and a dolphin show, and a two-story miniature golf course. One of the stores, Oshman Supersports USA, features a basketball court, a boxing gym, a baseball batting cage, a 50-foot archery range, and a simulated ski slope.[11]

All of this confirms that retail stores are much more than simply assortments of goods. They are environments to be experienced by the people who shop in them. Store atmospheres offer a powerful tool by which retailers can differentiate their stores from those of competitors.

Price Decision

A retailer's price policy must fit its target market and positioning, product and service assortment, and competition. All retailers would like to charge high markups and achieve high volume, but the two seldom go together. Most retailers seek *either* high markups on lower volume (most specialty stores) *or* low markups on higher volume (mass merchandisers and discount stores).

Thus, Bijan's boutique on Rodeo Drive in Beverly Hills sells "the most expensive menswear in the world." Its million dollar wardrobes include $375 silk ties and $19,000 ostrich-skin vests. Its "by appointment only" policy is designed to make its wealthy, high-profile clients comfortable with these prices. Says Mr. Bijan, "If a man is going to spend $400,000 on his visit, don't you think it's only fair that he have my full attention?"[12] Bijan's sells a low volume but makes hefty profits on each sale. At the other extreme, T.J. Maxx sells brand-name clothing at discount prices, settling for a lower margin on each sale but selling at a much higher volume.

■ Bijan's boutique on Rodeo Drive in Beverly Hills sells $375 silk ties and $19,000 ostrich-skin vests. Its "by appointment only" policy makes wealthy, high-profile clients comfortable with these prices.

Promotion Decision

Retailers use any or all of the promotion tools—advertising, personal selling, sales promotion, public relations, and direct marketing—to reach consumers. They advertise in newspapers, magazines, radio, television, and on the Internet. Advertising may be supported by newspaper inserts and direct mail. Personal selling requires careful training of salespeople in how to greet customers, meet their needs, and handle their complaints. Sales promotions may include in-store demonstrations, displays, contests, and visiting celebrities. Public relations activities, such as press conferences and speeches, store openings, special events, newsletters, magazines, and public service activities, are always available to retailers. Most retailers have also set up Web sites, offering customers information and other features and often selling merchandise directly.

Place Decision

Retailers often point to three critical factors in retailing success: *location, location,* and *location!* It's very important that retailers select locations that are accessible to the target market in areas that are consistent with the retailer's positioning. Small retailers may have to settle for whatever locations they can find or afford. Large retailers, however, usually employ specialists who select locations using advanced methods.

Most stores today cluster together to increase their customer pulling power and to give consumers the convenience of one-stop shopping. *Central business districts* were the main form of retail cluster until the 1950s. Every large city and town had a central business district with department stores, specialty stores, banks, and movie theaters. When people began to move to the suburbs, however, these central business districts, with their traffic, parking, and crime problems, began to lose business. Downtown merchants opened branches in suburban shopping centers, and the decline of the central business districts continued. In recent years, many cities have joined with merchants to try to revive downtown shopping areas by building malls and providing underground parking.

Shopping center
A group of retail businesses planned, developed, owned, and managed as a unit.

A **shopping center** is a group of retail businesses planned, developed, owned, and managed as a unit. A *regional shopping center,* or *regional shopping mall,* the largest and most dramatic shopping center, contains from 40 to over 200 stores. It is like a covered mini-downtown and attracts customers from a wide area. A *community shopping center* contains between 15 and 40 retail stores. It normally contains a branch of a department store or variety store, a supermarket, specialty stores, professional offices, and sometimes a bank. Most shopping centers are *neighborhood shopping centers* or *strip malls* that generally contain between 5 and 15 stores. They are close and convenient for consumers. They usually contain a supermarket, perhaps a discount store, and several service stores—dry cleaner, self-service laundry, drugstore, video-rental outlet, barber or beauty shop, hardware store, or other stores.

A recent addition to the shopping center scene is the so-called *power center*. These huge unenclosed shopping centers consist of a long strip of retail stores, including large, freestanding anchors such as Wal-Mart, Home Depot, Best Buy, Michaels, OfficeMax, and CompUSA. Each store has its own entrance with parking directly in front for shoppers who wish to visit only one store. Power centers have increased rapidly during the past few years to challenge traditional indoor malls.

Combined, the nation's nearly 47,000 shopping centers now account for about one-third of all retail sales. The average American makes 3.2 trips to the mall per month, shopping for an average of 78 minutes per trip and spending about $58. However, many experts suggest that America is now "over-malled." During the 1990s, mall shopping space grew at about twice the rate of population growth. As a result, as many as 20 percent of America's regional malls are in danger of going out of business. There "is a glut of retail space," says one insider. "There's going to have to be a shakeout."[13]

Thus, despite the recent development of many new "megamalls," such as the spectacular Mall of America, the current trend is toward value-oriented outlet malls and power centers on the one hand, and smaller malls on the other. Many shoppers now prefer to shop at "lifestyle centers," smaller malls with upscale stores, convenient locations, and expensive atmospheres. "Think of lifestyle centers as part Main Street and part Fifth Avenue," comments an industry observer. "The idea is to combine the hominess and community of an old-time village square with the cachet of fashionable urban stores; the smell and feel of a neighborhood park with the brute convenience of a strip center." The future of malls "will be all about creating places to be rather than just places to buy."[14]

The Future of Retailing

Retailers operate in a harsh and fast-changing environment, which offers threats as well as opportunities. For example, the industry suffers from chronic overcapacity, resulting in fierce competition for customer dollars. Consumer demographics, lifestyles, and shopping patterns are changing rapidly, as are retailing technologies. To be successful, then, retailers will have to choose target segments carefully and position themselves strongly. They will have to take the following retailing developments into account as they plan and execute their competitive strategies.

■ Shopping centers: The spectacular Mall of America contains more than 520 specialty stores, 50 restaurants, and a 7-acre indoor theme park, an Underwater World featuring hundreds of marine specimens and a dolphin show, and a two story miniature gold course.

New Retail Forms and Shortening Retail Life Cycles

New retail forms continue to emerge to meet new situations and consumer needs, but the life cycle of new retail forms is getting shorter. Department stores took about 100 years to reach the mature stage of the life cycle; more recent forms, such as warehouse stores, reached maturity in about 10 years. In such an environment, seemingly solid retail positions can crumble quickly. Of the top 10 discount retailers in 1962 (the year that Wal-Mart and Kmart began), not one still exists today.

Consider the Price Club, the original warehouse store chain. When Sol Price pioneered his first warehouse store outside San Diego in 1976, he launched a retailing revolution. Selling everything from tires and office supplies to 5-pound tubs of peanut butter at superlow prices, his store chain was generating $2.6 billion a year in sales within 10 years. But Price refused to expand beyond its California base. And as the industry quickly matured, Price ran headlong into wholesale clubs run by such retail giants as Wal-Mart and Kmart. (In his autobiography, Sam Walton confesses: "I guess I've stolen—I actually prefer the word 'borrowed'—as many ideas from Sol Price as from anybody else in the business.") Only 17 years later, in a stunning reversal of fortune, a faltering Price sold out to competitor Costco. Price's rapid rise and fall shows that even the most successful retailers can't sit back with a winning formula. To remain successful, they must keep adapting.[15]

Many retailing innovations are partially explained by the **wheel-of-retailing concept**.[16] According to this concept, many new types of retailing forms begin as low-margin, low-price, low-status operations. They challenge established retailers that have become "fat" by letting their costs and margins increase. The new retailers' success leads them to upgrade their facilities and offer more services. In turn, their costs increase, forcing them to increase their prices. Eventually, the new retailers become like the conventional retailers they replaced. The cycle begins again when still newer types of retailers evolve with lower costs and prices. The wheel-of-retailing concept seems to explain the initial success and later troubles of department stores, supermarkets, and discount stores, and the recent success of off-price retailers.

Wheel-of-retailing concept
A concept of retailing that states that new types of retailers usually begin as low-margin, low-price, low-status operations but later evolve into higher-priced, higher-service operations, eventually becoming like the conventional retailers they replaced.

Growth of Nonstore Retailing

Most of us still make most of our purchases the old-fashioned way: We go to the store, find what we want, wait patiently in line to plunk down our cash or credit card, and bring home the goods. However, consumers now have an array of alternatives, including mail-order, television, phone, and online shopping. Americans are increasingly avoiding the hassles and crowds at malls by doing more of their shopping by phone or computer. Although such retailing advances may threaten some traditional retailers, they offer exciting opportunities for others. Most store retailers have now developed direct retailing channels. In fact, more online retailing is conducted by "click-and-brick" retailers than by "click-only" retailers.

Online retailing is the newest form of nonstore retailing. Only a few years ago, prospects for online retailing were soaring. As more and more consumers flocked to the Web, some experts even saw a day when consumers would bypass stodgy "old economy" store retailers and do almost all of their shopping via the Internet. However, the dot-com meltdown of 2000 dashed these overblown expectations. Many once-brash Web sellers such as eToys.com, Pets.com, Webvan.com, and Garden.com crashed and burned. After the shakeout, expectations reversed almost overnight. The experts began to predict that e-tailing was destined to be little more than a tag-on to in-store retailing.

However, although the pace has slowed, today's online retailing is alive, well, and growing. With easier-to-use Web sites, improved online service, and the demise of so many early competitors, business is booming for the survivors. In fact, online buying is growing at a much brisker pace than retail buying as a whole. By 2006, online retailing is expected to rival catalogs, capturing some 5 percent of total retail sales.

Although the dramatic dot-com collapses grabbed most of the headlines, some click-only retailers are now making it big on the Web. Heading this group is online auction site eBay, which has been consistently profitable since its inception. Click-only e-tailers account for a majority of online sales in several other categories as well, including books, music and video; foods and beverages; and collectibles. Business is also booming for online travel companies such as Travelocity and Expedia, which use the Web to sell airline tickets, hotel rooms, and discount travel packages to consumers.

Still, much of the anticipated growth in online sales will go to multichannel retailers—the click-and-brick marketers who can successfully merge the virtual and physical worlds. Such retailers accounted for 67 percent of total online sales last year. Consider Staples, the

- Online retailing: Today's e-tailing is alive, well, and growing, especially for click-and-brick competitors such as Staples. Its online sales have averaged double-digit quarterly growth for more than three years. Business is also booming for click-only e-tailers such as Travelocity.

$13 billion office-supply retailer. After just 6 years on the Web, Staples captures annual online sales of more than $2.1 billion. Its online sales have averaged double-digit quarterly growth for more than 3 years. But it's not robbing from store sales in the process. The average yearly spending of small-business customers jumps from $600 when they shop in Staples stores to $2,800 when they shop online. As a result, although Staples has slowed new store openings recently, it plans to keep expanding its Web presence. "We're still going whole hog," says CEO Thomas Stemberg. "The payoffs are just very high."[17]

Retail Convergence

Today's retailers are increasingly selling the same products at the same prices to the same consumers in competition with a wider variety of other retailers. For example, you can buy books at outlets ranging from independent local bookstores to discount stores such as Wal-Mart, superstores such as Barnes & Noble or Borders, or Web sites such as Amazon.com. And when it comes to brand-name appliances, department stores, discount stores, home improvement stores, off-price retailers, electronics superstores, and a slew of Web sites all compete for the same customers. So if you can't find the microwave oven you want at Sears, just step across the street and find one for a better price at Lowe's or Home Depot—or order one online.

This merging of consumers, products, prices, and retailers is called *retail convergence*:[18]

Retail convergence is the coming together of shoppers, goods, and prices. Customers of all income levels are shopping at the same stores, often for the same goods. Old distinctions such as discount store, specialty store, and department store are losing significance: The successful store must match a host of rivals on selection, service, and price.

The American consumer's road map for where products can be found has shifted from a segmented approach to a consolidation that is almost a throwback to the 1800s, when a general store was the place to shop for everything from coffee to a coffeepot. In the 1900s, shoppers migrated from the Sears catalog to the department store, and then to the shopping mall and specialty stores. A few years ago, the coffee pot customer may have gone to Williams-Sonoma or even Starbucks. Today, it could be Target or Wal-Mart.

Where you go for what you want—that has created the biggest challenge facing retailers. Consider fashion. Once the exclusive of the wealthy, fashion now moves just as quickly from the runways of New York and Paris to retailers at all levels. Ralph Lauren sells in department stores and in the Marshall's at the strip mall. Designer Stephen Sprouse, fresh off a limited edition of Louis Vuitton handbags and luggage, has designed a summer line of clothing and other products for Target.

Such convergence means greater competition for retailers and greater difficulty in differentiating offerings. The competition between chain superstores and smaller, independently owned stores has become particularly heated. Because of their bulk-buying power and high sales volume, chains can buy at lower costs and thrive on smaller margins. The arrival of a superstore can quickly force nearby independents out of business. For example, the decision by electronics superstore Best Buy to sell CDs as loss leaders at rock-bottom prices pushed a number of specialty record store chains into bankruptcy. And Wal-Mart has been accused of destroying independents in countless small towns around the country.

Yet the news is not all bad for smaller companies. Many small, independent retailers are thriving. They are finding that sheer size and marketing muscle are often no match for the personal touch small stores can provide or the specialty niches that small stores fill for a devoted customer base.

The Rise of Megaretailers

The rise of huge mass merchandisers and specialty superstores, the formation of vertical marketing systems, and a rash of retail mergers and acquisitions have created a core of superpower megaretailers. Through their superior information systems and buying power, these giant retailers can offer better merchandise selections, good service, and strong price savings to consumers. As a result, they grow even larger by squeezing out their smaller, weaker competitors.

The megaretailers are also shifting the balance of power between retailers and producers. A relative handful of retailers now controls access to enormous numbers of consumers, giving them the upper hand in their dealings with manufacturers. For example, in the United States, Wal-Mart's revenues are more than six times those of Procter & Gamble, and Wal-Mart generates almost 20 percent of P&G's revenues. Wal-Mart can, and often does, use this power to wring concessions from P&G and other suppliers.[19]

Growing Importance of Retail Technology

Retail technologies are becoming critically important as competitive tools. Progressive retailers are using advanced information technology and software systems to produce better forecasts, control inventory costs, order electronically from suppliers, send e-mail between stores, and even sell to customers within stores. They are adopting checkout scanning systems, online transaction processing, electronic data interchange, in-store television, and improved merchandise-handling systems.

Perhaps the most startling advances in retailing technology concern the ways in which today's retailers are connecting with customers. Many retailers now routinely use technologies such as touch screen kiosks, electronic shelf labels and signs, handheld shopping assistants, smart cards, self-scanning systems, and virtual reality displays. For example, in its new pilot store—Bloom—Southeastern grocery chain Food Lion is using technology to make shopping easier for its customers:

> Ever stood in the wine aisle at the grocery store and felt intimidated? You think that bottle of Shiraz looks pretty good but you're not sure what it goes with. It's the sort of problem the creators of Food Lion's new concept store—Bloom—thought about, and one they will use technology to solve. The store relies on technology to enhance the shopping experience and to help customers find products, get information, and check out with greater ease. A computerized kiosk in the wine section lets you scan a bottle and get serving suggestions. The kiosk, and a second one in the meat section, lets you print recipes off the screen. Eight stations with touch screens and scanners around the store let you check an item's price or locate it on the map. To make it easier to keep track of purchases and check out, you can pick up a personal hand-held scanner as you walk in the door, then scan and bag items as you shop. Checkout then is just a simple matter of paying as you leave. The personal scanners also give you a running total of the items you've selected as you shop, helping you stay within your budget and avoid surprises at the checkout. And if you drop off a prescription, the pharmacy can send a message to your scanner when your order is ready.[20]

Global Expansion of Major Retailers

Retailers with unique formats and strong brand positioning are increasingly moving into other countries. Many are expanding internationally to escape mature and saturated home markets. Over the years, several giant U.S. retailers—McDonald's, Gap, Toys "R" Us—have become globally prominent as a result of their great marketing prowess. Others, such as Wal-Mart, are rapidly establishing a global presence. Wal-Mart, which now operates more than 1,300 stores in nine countries abroad, sees exciting global potential. Its international division last year racked up sales of more than $40 billion, an increase of 15 percent over the previous year. Profits from international operations increased more than 55 percent last year. Here's what happened when it opened two new stores in Shenzhen, China:[21]

> [Customers came] by the hundreds of thousands—up to 175,000 on Saturdays alone—to China's first Wal-Mart Supercenter and Sam's Club. They broke the display glass to snatch out chickens at one store and carted off all the big-screen TVs before the other store had been open an hour. The two outlets . . . were packed on Day One and have been bustling ever since.

However, U.S retailers are still significantly behind Europe and Asia when it comes to global expansion. Only 18 percent of the top U.S. retailers operate globally, compared with 40 percent of European retailers and 31 percent of Asian retailers. Among foreign retailers that have gone global are France's Carrefour, Britain's Marks and Spencer, Italy's Benetton, Sweden's IKEA home furnishings stores, and Japan's Yaohan supermarkets.[22]

Marks and Spencer, which started out as a penny bazaar in 1884, grew into a chain of variety stores over the decades and now has a thriving string of 150 franchised stores around the world, which sell mainly its private-label clothes, including Brooks Brothers. It also runs a major food business. IKEA's well-constructed but fairly inexpensive furniture has proven very popular in the United States, where shoppers often spend an entire day in an IKEA store. And French discount retailer Carrefour, the world's second largest retailer after Wal-Mart, has embarked on an aggressive mission to extend its role as a leading international retailer:

> Carrefour now operates more than 9,600 discount stores in 30 countries in Europe, Asia, and the Americas, including 657 hypermarkets. In the European market, it now claims retail dominance in four leading markets: France, Spain, Belgium, and Greece; it's the No. 2 retailer in Italy. Outside Europe, in the all-important emerging markets of China, South America, and the Pacific Rim, Carrefour outpaces Wal-

■ Many retailers are expanding internationally to escape mature and saturated home markets. French discount retailer Carrefour, the world's second largest retailer after Wal-Mart, has embarked on an aggressive mission to extend its role as a leading international retailer.

Mart five-to-one in actual revenue. In South America, Carrefour is the market leader in Brazil and Argentina, where it operates more than 300 stores. By comparison, Wal-Mart has only 25 units in those two countries. In China, Carrefour operates 22 hypermarkets to Wal-Mart's 5 supercenters and 1 Sam's Club. In the Pacific Rim, excluding China, Carrefour operates 33 hypermarkets in five countries to Wal-Mart's 5 units in South Korea alone. In short, Carrefour is bounding ahead of Wal-Mart in most markets outside North America. The only question: Can the French titan hold its lead? While no one retailer can rightly claim to be in the same league with Wal-Mart as an overall retail presence, Carrefour stands a better chance than most to dominate global retailing.[23]

Retail Stores as "Communities" or "Hangouts"

With the rise in the number of people living alone, working at home, or living in isolated and sprawling suburbs, there has been a resurgence of establishments that, regardless of the product or service they offer, also provide a place for people to get together. These places include cafes, tea shops, juice bars, bookshops, superstores, children's play spaces, brew pubs, and urban greenmarkets. Brew pubs such as New York's Zip City Brewing and Seattle's Trolleyman Pub (run by Red Hook Brewery) offer tastings and a place to pass the time. And today's bookstores have become part bookstore, part library, and part living room.

> Welcome to today's bookstore. The one featuring not only shelves and cash registers but also cushy chairs and coffee bars. It's where backpack-toting high school students come to do homework, where retirees thumb through the gardening books, and parents read aloud to their toddlers. If no one actually buys books, that's just fine, say bookstore owners and managers. They're offering something grander than ink and paper, anyway. They're selling comfort, relaxation, community.[24]

Brick-and-mortar retailers are not the only ones creating community. Others have also built virtual communities on the Internet.

> Sony actively builds community among its Playstation customers. Its recent Playstation.com campaign created message boards where its game players could post messages to one another. The boards are incredibly active, discussing techie topics but also providing the opportunity for members, fiercely competitive and opinionated, to vote on lifestyle issues, such as music and personal taste, no matter how trivial. Although Sony is laissez-faire about the boards and does not feed them messages, the company sees the value in having its customers' adamant conversations occur directly on its site. "Our customers are our evangelists. They are a very vocal and loyal fan base," says a Sony spokesperson. "There are things we can learn from them."[25]

Wholesaling

Wholesaling
All activities involved in selling goods and services to those buying for resale or business use.

Wholesaler
A firm engaged *primarily* in wholesaling activity.

Wholesaling includes all activities involved in selling goods and services to those buying for resale or business use. We call **wholesalers** those firms engaged *primarily* in wholesaling activity.

Wholesalers buy mostly from producers and sell mostly to retailers, industrial consumers, and other wholesalers. As a result, many of the nation's largest and most important wholesalers are largely unknown to final consumers. For example, you may never have heard of SuperValu, even though it's a $20 billion company and the nation's largest food wholesaler. Or how about Grainger, the leading wholesaler of maintenance, repair, and operating (MRO) supplies? It's possibly the biggest market leader you've never heard of (see Real Marketing 13.2).

But why are wholesalers used at all? For example, why would a producer use wholesalers rather than selling directly to retailers or consumers? Simply put, wholesalers add value by performing one or more of the following channel functions:

- *Selling and promoting:* Wholesalers' sales forces help manufacturers reach many small customers at a low cost. The wholesaler has more contacts and is often more trusted by the buyer than the distant manufacturer.

- *Buying and assortment building:* Wholesalers can select items and build assortments needed by their customers, thereby saving the consumers much work.

- *Bulk-breaking:* Wholesalers save their customers money by buying in carload lots and breaking bulk (breaking large lots into small quantities).

Real Marketing 13.2

Grainger: The Biggest Market Leader You've Never Heard Of?

Grainger may be the biggest market leader you've never heard of. It's a $4.7 billion business that offers more than 500,000 products and parts to more than 1.6 million customers. Its more than 575 North American branches, more than 15,000 employees, and innovative Web site handle more than 100,000 transactions a day. Grainger's customers include organizations ranging from factories, garages, and grocers to military bases and schools. Most American businesses are located within 20 minutes of a Grainger branch. Customers include notables such as Abbott Laboratories, General Motors, Campbell Soup, American Airlines, Mercedes-Benz, and the U.S. Postal Service. Grainger also operates one of the highest-volume business-to-business sites on the Web.

So, how come you've never heard of Grainger? Most likely it's because Grainger is a wholesaler. And like most wholesalers, it operates behind the scenes, selling only to other businesses. Moreover, Grainger operates in the not-so-glamorous world of maintenance, repair, and operating (MRO) supplies.

But whereas you might know little about Grainger, to its customers the company is very well known and much valued. Through its branch network, service centers, sales reps, catalog, and Web site, Grainger links customers with the supplies they need to keep their facilities running smoothly—everything from lightbulbs, cleaners, and display cases to nuts and bolts, motors, valves, power tools, and test equipment. Grainger is by far the nation's largest MRO wholesaler. Notes one industry reporter, "If industrial America is an engine, Grainger is its lubricant."

Grainger serves as an important link between thousands of MRO supplies manufacturers on one side and millions of industrial and commercial customers on the other. It operates on a simple value proposition: to make it easier and less costly for customers to find and buy MRO supplies. It starts by acting as a one-stop shop for products to maintain facilities. Most customers will tell you that Grainger sells everything—*everything*—from the ordinary to the out-of-the-ordinary. For example, it stocks thousands of lightbulbs—about every lightbulb known to mankind. If you don't believe it, go to www.grainger.com and search "lightbulbs"! As for the not-so-ordinary:

> Grainger sells 19 different models of floor-cleaning machines, has 49 catalog pages of socket wrenches, and offers 9 different sizes of hydraulic service jacks, an assortment of NFL-licensed hard hats bearing team logos, and item No. 6AV22, a $36.90 dispenser rack for two 1 gallon contain-

■ Although you may never have heard it, Grainger is by far the world's leading wholesaler of maintenance, repair, and operating supplies.

ers of Gatorade. According to corporate legend, [Grainger] is the only place that workers on the Alaskan Pipeline have been able to find repellent to cope with arctic bears during their mating season.

Beyond making it easier for customers to find the products they need, Grainger also helps them streamline their acquisition processes. For most companies, acquiring MRO supplies is a very costly process. In fact, 40 percent of the cost of MRO supplies stems from the purchase process, including finding a supplier, negotiating the best deal, placing the order, receiving the order, and paying the invoice. Grainger constantly seeks ways to reduce the costs associated with MRO supplies acquisition, both internally and externally. Says one analyst, "Grainger will reduce your search and your process costs for items, instead of your having to order 10 things from 10 different companies, and you'll get one invoice. That's pretty powerful."

- *Warehousing:* Wholesalers hold inventories, thereby reducing the inventory costs and risks of suppliers and customers.
- *Transportation:* Wholesalers can provide quicker delivery to buyers because they are closer than the producers.
- *Financing:* Wholesalers finance their customers by giving credit, and they finance their suppliers by ordering early and paying bills on time.
- *Risk bearing:* Wholesalers absorb risk by taking title and bearing the cost of theft, damage, spoilage, and obsolescence.
- *Market information:* Wholesalers give information to suppliers and customers about competitors, new products, and price developments.

One company found that working with Grainger cut MRO requisition time by more than 60 percent; lead times went from days to hours. Its supply chain dropped from 12,000 suppliers to 560—significantly reducing expenses. Similarly, a large timber and paper-products company has come to appreciate the value of Grainger's selection and streamlined ordering process. It orders two-thirds of its supplies from Grainger's Web site at an annual acquisition cost of only $300,000. By comparison, for the remainder of its needs, this company deals with more than 1,300 small distributors at an acquisition cost of $2.4 million each year—eight times the cost of dealing with Grainger for half of the volume. As a result, the company is now looking for ways to buy all of its MRO supplies from Grainger.

You might think that helping customers find what they need easily and efficiently would be enough to keep Grainger atop of the MRO mountain. But Grainger goes even further. On a broader level, it builds lasting relationships with customers by helping them find *solutions* to their overall MRO problems. Acting as consultants, Grainger sales reps help buyers with everything from improving their supply chain management to reducing inventories and streamlining warehousing operations.

> Branches . . . serve as the base for Grainger territory managers who provide on-site help to big facilities. . . . [Reps can] tour a factory or an office complex or even a hotel and suggest to its managers exactly what supplies they really need to keep the place up to snuff, right down to how many gallons of carpet cleaner they'll require each week. That's how Grainger knows, for example, that one Biltmore Hotel has 7,000 light-bulbs. . . . "Our reps can pretty much stand outside a building and get a general feel for what kinds of products the customer needs," [says James Ryan, Grainger's executive vice president of marketing, sales, and service].

Grainger has launched a series of programs designed to add value to its commodity business. For example, through its "Click & Sell" program, Grainger uses information collected about customers, such as industry data and purchase histories, to help sales reps find solutions for customer needs. If, for example, a customer places an order for a pump to use with caustic chemicals, the Grainger rep might also suggest gloves and safety glasses. If an item is unavailable, the database identifies alternative products to get the job done.

Grainger also offers value to customers through its links to and clout with suppliers:

Jason Eastin is facilities operations director for JRV Management, a . . . company that runs community and private sports facilities in metropolitan Detroit. He relies on Grainger in part because of its clout with factory reps. When his company was opening up its newest complex, he asked Chris Clemons, a Grainger territory manager, for help figuring out the number and kinds of fixtures that would be required. Clemens summoned a rep from Rubbermaid, the household-products maker, who showed up with a laptop and a software program that churned out a reasonable supply chain within 20 minutes. Similarly, Clemons worked with a General Electric salesperson who figured out how Eastin could stretch out "relamping" his facilities to every 2 years, instead of annually, and cut costs significantly as well by switching to a different kind of metal-halide bulb as the primary kind of illumination for his ice arenas. "To have General Electric provide that service to me at no charge would never happen," Eastin says. "But Grainger has that buying-power structure. They open up those kinds of opportunities to me."

So now you've heard of Grainger, a wholesaler that succeeds by making life easier and more efficient for commercial and industrial buyers and sellers. Although a market leader, Grainger still captures only 4 percent of the highly fragmented U.S. market for MRO goods. That leaves a lot of room for growth. But to take advantage of the opportunities, Grainger must continue to find innovative ways to add value. "Our system makes our business partners and suppliers more efficient," says Fred Loepp, vice president of product management at Grainger, "and that benefits the entire supply chain." Says Theresa Dubiel, branch manager at Grainger's Romulus, Michigan branch, "If we don't save [customers] time and money every time they come [to us], they won't come back."

Sources: Excerpts from Dale Buss, "The New Deal," *Sales & Marketing Management*, June 2002, pp. 25–30; and Colleen Gourley, "Redefining Distribution," *Warehousing Management*, October 2000, pp. 28–30. Also see Steve Konicki and Eileen Colkin, "Attitude Adjustment," *Informationweek*, March 25, 2002, pp. 20–22; "W.W. Grainger, Inc.," *Hoover's Company Profiles*, Austin, July 15, 2003, p. 11593; "Grainger to Add, Relocate and Expand Branches," *Industrial Distribution*, June 2004, p. 20; and information accessed at www.grainger.com, December 2004.

■ *Management services and advice:* Wholesalers often help retailers train their salesclerks, improve store layouts and displays, and set up accounting and inventory control systems.

Types of Wholesalers

Merchant wholesaler

Independently owned business that takes title to the merchandise it handles.

Wholesalers fall into three major groups (see Table 13.3): *merchant wholesalers, agents and brokers,* and *manufacturers' sales branches and offices.* **Merchant wholesalers** are the largest single group of wholesalers, accounting for roughly 50 percent of all wholesaling. Merchant wholesalers include two broad types: full-service wholesalers and limited-service wholesalers. *Full-service wholesalers* provide a full set of services, whereas the various *limited-service wholesalers* offer fewer services to their suppliers and customers. The several different

TABLE 13.3 **Major Types of Wholesalers**

Type	Description
Merchant wholesalers	Independently owned businesses that take title to the merchandise they handle. In different trades they are called *jobbers, distributors,* or *mill supply houses.* Include full-service wholesalers and limited-service wholesalers:
Full-service wholesalers	Provide a full line of services: carrying stock, maintaining a sales force, offering credit, making deliveries, and providing management assistance. There are two types:
Wholesale merchants	Sell primarily to retailers and provide a full range of services, *General merchandise wholesalers* carry several merchandise lines, whereas *general line wholesalers* carry one or two lines in great depth. *Specialty wholesalers* specialize in carrying only part of a line. Examples: health food wholesalers, seafood wholesalers.
Industrial distributors	Sell to manufacturers rather than to retailers. Provide several services, such as carrying stock, offering credit, and providing delivery. May carry a broad range of merchandise, a general line, or a specialty line.
Limited-service wholesalers	Offer fewer services than full-service wholesalers. Limited-service wholesalers are of several types:
Cash-and-carry wholesalers	Carry a limited line of fast-moving goods and sell to small retailers for cash. Normally do not deliver. Example: A small fish store retailer may drive to a cash-and-carry fish wholesaler, buy fish for cash, and bring the merchandise back to the store.
Truck wholesalers (or truck jobbers)	Perform primarily a selling and delivery function. Carry limited line of semiperishable merchandise (such as milk, bread, snack foods), which they sell for cash as they make their rounds to supermarkets, small groceries, hospitals, restaurants, factory cafeterias, and hotels.
Drop shippers	Do not carry inventory or handle the product. On receiving an order, they select a manufacturer, who ships the merchandise directly to the customer. The drop shipper assumes title and risk from the time the order is accepted to its delivery to the customer. They operate in bulk industries, such as coal, lumber, and heavy equipment.
Rack jobbers	Serve grocery and drug retailers, mostly in nonfood items. They send delivery trucks to stores, where the delivery people set up toys, paperbacks, hardware items, health and beauty aids, or other items. They price the goods, keep them fresh, set up point-of-purchase displays, and keep inventory records. Rack jobbers retain title to the goods and bill the retailers only for the goods sold to consumers.
Producers' cooperatives	Are owned by farmer members and assemble farm produce to sell in local markets. The co-op's profits are distributed to members at the end of the year. They often attempt to improve product quality and promote a co-op brand name, such as Sun Maid raisins, Sunkist oranges, or Diamond walnuts.
Mail-order wholesalers	Send catalogs to retail, industrial, and institutional customers featuring jewelry, cosmetics, specialty foods, and other small items. Maintain no outside sales force. Main customers are businesses in small outlying areas. Orders are filled and sent by mail, truck, or other transportation.
Brokers and agents	Do not take title to goods. Main function is to facilitate buying and selling, for which they earn a commission on the selling price. Generally specialize by product line or customer type.
Brokers	Chief function is bringing buyers and sellers together and assisting in negotiation. They are paid by the party who hired them and do not carry inventory, get involved in financing, or assume risk. Examples: food brokers, real estate brokers, insurance brokers, and security brokers.
Agents	Represent either buyers or sellers on a more permanent basis than brokers do. There are several types:
Manufacturers' agents	Represent two or more manufacturers of complementary lines. A formal written agreement with each manufacturer covers pricing, territories, order-handling, delivery service and warranties, and commission rates. Often used in such lines as apparel, furniture, and electrical goods. Most manufacturers' agents are small businesses, with only a few skilled salespeople as employees. They are hired by small manufacturers who cannot afford their own field sales forces and by large manufacturers who use agents to open new territories or to cover territories that cannot support full-time salespeople.

(continued)

study Table.

TABLE 13.3   Continued

Type	Description
Selling agents	Have contractual authority to sell a manufacturer's entire output. The manufacturer either is not interested in the selling function or feels unqualified. The selling agent serves as a sales department and has significant influence over prices, terms, and conditions of sale. Found in product areas such as textiles, industrial machinery and equipment, coal and coke, chemicals, and metals.
Purchasing agents	Generally have a long-term relationship with buyers and make purchases for them, often receiving, inspecting, warehousing, and shipping the merchandise to the buyers. They provide helpful market information to clients and help them obtain the best goods and prices available.
Commission merchants	Take physical possession of products and negotiate sales. Normally, they are not employed on a long-term basis. Used most often in agricultural marketing by farmers who do not want to sell their own output and do not belong to producers' cooperatives. The commission merchant takes a truckload of commodities to a central market, sells it for the best price, deducts a commission and expenses, and remits the balance to the producers.
Manufacturers' and retailers' branches and offices	Wholesaling operations conducted by sellers or buyers themselves rather than through independent wholesalers. Separate branches and offices can be dedicated to either sales or purchasing.
Sales branches and offices	Set up by manufacturers to improve inventory control, selling, and promotion. *Sales branches* carry inventory and are found in industries such as lumber and automotive equipment and parts. *Sales offices* do not carry inventory and are most prominent in dry-goods and notions industries.
Purchasing officers	Perform a role similar to that of brokers or agents but are part of the buyer's organization. Many retailers set up purchasing offices in major market centers such as New York and Chicago.

types of limited-service wholesalers perform varied specialized functions in the distribution channel.

Brokers and *agents* differ from merchant wholesalers in two ways: They do not take title to goods, and they perform only a few functions. Like merchant wholesalers, they generally specialize by product line or customer type. A **broker** brings buyers and sellers together and assists in negotiation. **Agents** represent buyers or sellers on a more permanent basis. *Manufacturers' agents* (also called manufacturers' representatives) are the most common type of agent wholesaler. The third major type of wholesaling is that done in **manufacturers' sales branches and offices** by sellers or buyers themselves rather than through independent wholesalers.

HASTA
AQUI

Broker
A wholesaler who does not take title to goods and whose function is to bring buyers and sellers together and assist in negotiation.

Agent
A wholesaler who represents buyers or sellers on a relatively permanent basis, performs only a few functions, and does not take title to goods.

Manufacturers' sales branches and offices
Wholesaling by sellers or buyers themselves rather than through independent wholesalers.

Wholesaler Marketing Decisions

Wholesalers now face growing competitive pressures, more demanding customers, new technologies, and more direct-buying programs on the part of large industrial, institutional, and retail buyers. As a result, they have had to take a fresh look at their marketing strategies. As with retailers, their marketing decisions include choices of target markets, positioning, and the marketing mix—product assortments and services, price, promotion, and place (see Figure 13.2).

Target Market and Positioning Decision

Like retailers, wholesalers must define their target markets and position themselves effectively—they cannot serve everyone. They can choose a target group by size of customer (only large retailers), type of customer (convenience stores only), need for service (customers who need credit), or other factors. Within the target group, they can identify the more profitable customers, design stronger offers, and build better relationships with them. They can propose automatic reordering systems, set up management-training and advising systems, or even sponsor a voluntary chain. They can discourage less profitable customers by requiring larger orders or adding service charges to smaller ones.

FIGURE 13.2
Wholesaler marketing
decisions

Marketing Mix Decisions

Like retailers, wholesalers must decide on product assortment and services, prices, promotion, and place. The wholesaler's "product" is the assortment of *products and services* that it offers. Wholesalers are under great pressure to carry a full line and to stock enough for immediate delivery. But this practice can damage profits. Wholesalers today are cutting down on the number of lines they carry, choosing to carry only the more profitable ones. Wholesalers are also rethinking which services count most in building strong customer relationships and which should be dropped or charged for. The key is to find the mix of services most valued by their target customers.

Price is also an important wholesaler decision. Wholesalers usually mark up the cost of goods by a standard percentage—say, 20 percent. Expenses may run 17 percent of the gross margin, leaving a profit margin of 3 percent. In grocery wholesaling, the average profit margin is often less than 2 percent. Wholesalers are trying new pricing approaches. They may cut their margin on some lines in order to win important new customers. They may ask suppliers for special price breaks when they can turn them into an increase in the supplier's sales.

Although *promotion* can be critical to wholesaler success, most wholesalers are not promotion minded. Their use of trade advertising, sales promotion, personal selling, and public relations is largely scattered and unplanned. Many are behind the times in personal selling—they still see selling as a single salesperson talking to a single customer instead of as a team effort to sell, build, and service major accounts. Wholesalers also need to adopt some of the nonpersonal promotion techniques used by retailers. They need to develop an overall promotion strategy and to make greater use of supplier promotion materials and programs.

Finally, *place* is important—wholesalers must choose their locations, facilities, and Web locations carefully. Wholesalers typically locate in low-rent, low-tax areas and tend to invest little money in their buildings, equipment, and systems. As a result, their materials-handling and order-processing systems are often outdated. In recent years, however, large and progressive wholesalers are reacting to rising costs by investing in automated warehouses and online ordering systems. Orders are fed from the retailer's system directly into the wholesaler's computer, and the items are picked up by mechanical devices and automatically taken to a shipping platform where they are assembled. Most large wholesalers are using technology to carry out accounting, billing, inventory control, and forecasting. Modern wholesalers are adapting their services to the needs of target customers and finding cost-reducing methods of doing business.

Trends in Wholesaling

As the wholesaling industry moves into the twenty-first century, it faces considerable challenges. The industry remains vulnerable to one of the most enduring trends of the last decade—fierce resistance to price increases and the winnowing out of suppliers who are not adding value based on cost and quality. Progressive wholesalers constantly watch for better ways to meet the changing needs of their suppliers and target customers. They recognize that, in the long run, their only reason for existence comes from adding value by increasing the efficiency and effectiveness of the entire marketing channel. To achieve this goal, they must constantly improve their services and reduce their costs.

McKesson HBOC, the nation's leading wholesaler of pharmaceuticals, health and beauty care, and home health care products, provides an example of progressive wholesaling. To survive, McKesson HBOC has to remain more cost-effective than manufacturers' sales branches. Thus, the company has built efficient automated warehouses, established direct computer links with drug manufacturers, and set up extensive online supply management and accounts-receivable systems for customers. It offers retail pharmacists a wide

■ To improve efficiency and service, McKesson set up an extensive online supply management system by which customers can order, track, and manage their pharmaceutical and medical-surgical supplies. Retailers can even use the McKesson system to maintain medical profiles on their customers.

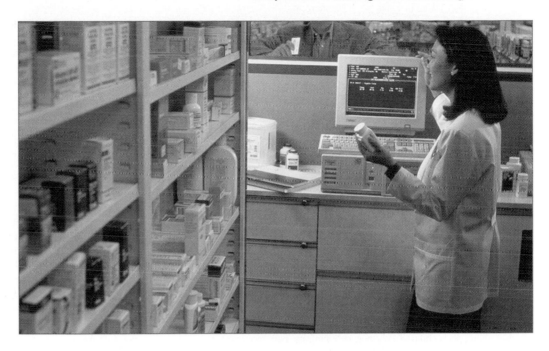

range of online resources, including supply management assistance, catalog searches, real-time order tracking, and account management system. Retailers can even use the McKesson system to maintain medical profiles on their customers. McKesson's medical-surgical supply and equipment customers receive a rich assortment of online solutions and supply management tools, including an online order-management system and real-time information on products and pricing, inventory availability, and order status. According to McKesson, it adds value in the channel by providing "supply, information, and health care management products and services designed to reduce costs and improve quality across healthcare."[26]

The distinction between large retailers and large wholesalers continues to blur. Many retailers now operate formats such as wholesale clubs and hypermarkets that perform many wholesale functions. In return, many large wholesalers are setting up their own retailing operations. For example, SuperValu, the nation's largest food wholesaling company, is also the country's eighth largest food retailer. Almost half of the company's $20 billion in sales comes from its Bigg's, Cub Foods, Save-A-Lot, Farm Fresh, Hornbacher's, Laneco, Metro, Scott's Foods, Shop 'n Save, and Shoppers Food Warehouse stores.[27]

Wholesalers will continue to increase the services they provide to retailers—retail pricing, cooperative advertising, marketing and management information reports, accounting services, online transactions, and others. Rising costs on the one hand, and the demand for increased services on the other, will put the squeeze on wholesaler profits. Wholesalers who do not find efficient ways to deliver value to their customers will soon drop by the wayside. However, the increased use of computerized, automated, and Web-based systems will help wholesalers to contain the costs of ordering, shipping, and inventory holding, boosting their productivity.

Finally, facing slow growth in their domestic markets and such developments as the North American Free Trade Agreement, many large wholesalers are now going global. For example, in 1991, McKesson bought out its Canadian partner, Provigo. The company now receives about 3 percent of its total revenues from Canada. Its Information Solutions group operates widely throughout North America, the United Kingdom, and other European countries.

> Reviewing the Concepts <

In this chapter, we first looked at the nature and importance of retailing, major types of retailers, the decisions retailers make, and the future of retailing. We then examined these same topics for wholesalers. Although most retailing is conducted in retail stores, in recent years, nonstore retailing has increased rapidly. In addition, although many retail stores are independently owned, an increasing number are now banding together under some form of corporate or contractual organization. Wholesalers, too, have experienced recent environmental changes, most notably mounting competitive pressures. They have faced new sources of competition, more demanding customers, new technologies, and more direct-buying programs on the part of large industrial, institutional, and retail buyers.

1. **Explain the roles of retailers and wholesalers in the distribution channel.**
   Retailing and wholesaling consist of many organizations bringing goods and services from the point of production to the point of use. *Retailing* includes all activities involved in selling goods or services directly to final consumers for their personal, nonbusiness use. *Wholesaling* includes all the activities involved in selling goods or services to those who are buying for the purpose of resale or for business use. Wholesalers perform many functions, including selling and promoting, buying and assortment building, bulk-breaking, warehousing, transporting, financing, risk bearing, supplying market information, and providing management services and advice.

2. **Describe the major types of retailers and give examples of each.**
   Retailers can be classified as *store retailers* and *nonstore retailers*. Although most goods and services are sold through stores, nonstore retailing has been growing much faster than has store retailing. Store retailers can be further classified by the *amount of service* they provide (self-service, limited service, or full service), *product line sold* (specialty stores, department stores, supermarkets, convenience stores, superstores, and service businesses), and *relative prices* (discount stores and off-price retailers). Today, many retailers are banding together in corporate and contractual *retail organizations* (corporate chains, voluntary chains and retailer cooperatives, franchise organizations, and merchandising conglomerates).

3. **Identify the major types of wholesalers and give examples of each.**
   Wholesalers fall into three groups. First, *merchant wholesalers* take possession of the goods. They include *full-service wholesalers* (wholesale merchants, industrial distributors) and *limited-service wholesalers* (cash-and-carry wholesalers, truck wholesalers, drop shippers, rack jobbers, producers' cooperatives, and mail-order wholesalers). Second, *brokers* and *agents* do not take possession of the goods but are paid a commission for aiding buying and selling. Finally, *manufacturers' sales branches and offices* are wholesaling operations conducted by nonwholesalers to bypass the wholesalers.

4. **Explain the marketing decisions facing retailers and wholesalers.**
   Each retailer must make decisions about its target markets and positioning, product assortment and services, price, promotion, and place. Retailers need to choose target markets carefully and position themselves strongly. Today, wholesaling is holding its own in the economy. Progressive wholesalers are adapting their services to the needs of target customers and are seeking cost-reducing methods of doing business. Faced with slow growth in their domestic markets and developments such as the North American Free Trade Association, many large wholesalers are also now going global.

> Reviewing the Key Terms <

> Discussing the Concepts <

1. There are retailers and there are retailers. What are the four major characteristics used in the chapter to classify retailers? What are the seven major store retailer types? Give an example of each type.

2. Describe the similarities and differences between chain stores and franchise organizations.

3. Explain why it is important for retailers to define their target markets and to decide how they will position themselves in these markets. Give an example of a national specialty retailer who has done this well.

4. Consider this statement made by a retailing insider: "The mall represents a point in time in the evolution of retailing.... We are reaching the end of one era and entering something new." What is the "something new" that is being suggested? Where will Americans be shopping if not at today's malls?

5. The chapter states that "the life cycle of new retail forms is getting shorter." What does this mean? Cite an example?

6. What is the primary challenge facing a wholesaler who wishes to remain a viable part of the marketing channel? Explain.

> Applying the Concepts <

1. Find a retail store "hangout" near campus, such as a coffee shop or bookstore, and visit it eight times (twice at 8 A.M., 12 noon, 4 P.M. and 10 P.M.) over the course of a week. On each visit record your observations regarding the number of people in the location, what they are doing, what they look like, how long they stay, and whether they are alone or with someone. Did you notice differences in patrons at different hours of the day? Did you see any repeat customers? What is the retailer doing to build community?

2. In a small group, discuss the pros and cons of locating an off-price retailer like Costco in a power center location?

3. Suppose that you are a manufacturer's agent for three lines of complementary women's apparel. Discuss what types of marketing mix decisions you will be making.

> Focus on Technology <

Retail site selection is a difficult job, and the consequences of a mistake can be very costly. However, new technology designed to assist marketers in retail location selection is becoming readily available. One site selection tool is MapInfo's AnySite. Says MapInfo: "Designed for both site selection analysts and executive decision makers, AnySite is the essential tool for leaders in the retail, hotel, restaurant, real estate, and financial services industries to analyze existing store locations and potential new sites. Dedicated to site selection, AnySite's features and functions are optimized to support the site selection process. [Use it to] create ring studies,

drive-times, custom polygons. Analyze and report on multiple existing and potential sites. Easily create detailed, eye-opening market and demographic maps." Go to the AnySite Web site (www.anysite.com/ info_analyzer.htm), learn as much as you can, and answer the following questions:

1. What do you think of this technology?

2. Would this technology be helpful in making a site selection decision?

3. Is this a tool only for large retailers, or can smaller one- or two-location retailers afford and use this technology?

> Focus on Ethics <

Large discount stores and superstores can wield enormous power and impact on a local community. When a megaretailer like Wal-Mart enters a town, especially a smaller one, it often drives nearby small retailers out of business and sends downtown business districts into a nosedive. Wal-Mart has been the target of much criticism for this. When Wal-Mart founder Sam Walton was alive, he responded as follows: "Quite a few smaller stores have gone out of business during the time of Wal-Mart's growth. Some people have tried to turn it into this big controversy, sort of a "Save the Small Town Merchants" deal, like they were whales or whooping cranes or something that has the right to be protected. Of all the notions I've heard about Wal-Mart, none has ever baffled me more than this idea that we are somehow the enemy of small-town America. Nothing could be further from the truth. Wal-Mart has actually kept quite a number of small towns from becoming extinct by saving literally billions of dollars for the people who live in them, as well as by creating hundreds of thousands of jobs in our stores. I believe millions of people are better off

today than they would have been if Wal-Mart had never existed. I don't want to be too critical of small-town merchants, but the truth is that a lot of these folks just weren't doing a very good job of taking care of their customers. Whenever we put a Wal-Mart store into a town, customers would just flock to us from the variety stores. With our low prices, we ended an era of 45 percent markups and limited selection. We shut the door on variety store thinking."*

1. What is your assessment of Sam Walton's remarks?

2. Does Wal-Mart have a responsibility to the small retailers it puts out of business? Why?

3. What does the future look like for small retailers in America? How can they compete with retailing giants like Wal-Mart?

*See www.emich.edu/public/geo/557book/c313.impactwalmart.html.

Video Case

Reebok

Today, Reebok is more than just aerobics shoes. The company sells everything from shoes and shorts to treadmills and sunglasses. To promote these products, Reebok infuses its fashions with pop culture. It's all part of an effort to position itself as an edgy, fresh company with products that appeal to young people. Reebok even developed a new brand, RBK, to better appeal to its newly defined target market. The goal? To reach young people before they establish a substantial preference for an athletic brand.

To reach these new consumers, Reebok builds programs with individual retailers, relying heavily on such partnerships to help differentiate the brand. Many of those partnerships include exclusive rights to carry particular Reebok products. So Footlocker and Sears, for example, carry different assortments of Reebok shoes and gear. As a result, Reebok and its

retail partners provide the continually evolving, fresh set of options that young consumers demand.

After viewing the video featuring Reebok, answer the following questions about retailing and wholesaling.

1. Visit Reebok's Web site and search for retailers near you. What types of retailers does Reebok rely on to sell its products? Are there any additional retailers with whom Reebok should consider working?

2. What consumers does Reebok target? How does the company reach these target consumers to build relationships?

3. Do you think that Reebok's chosen retail outlets are the most effective places to reach the company's targeted consumers?

Company Case

Sears: Visions of Grandeur?

In the 1970s, Sears was the nation's largest retailer. Positioned as a middle-line retailer, between low-priced, discount houses and higher-end department stores, Sears was indeed where America shopped—especially for hardware and appliances. Craftsman and Kenmore have consis-

tently been among the most highly praised brand names in the country. Americans still wash clothes and dishes with Kenmores, and mow lawns and drive nails with Craftsmen. Reliance on the hard lines, however, has not allowed Sears to keep pace with the American retailing scene.

(box continues)

The last 30 years have brought major changes to American retailing. The most dramatic development was the explosion of Wal-Mart. Sam Walton's original idea was to rely on low prices, stand-alone stores, and locations in small towns that were underserved by the retailing system. To maintain growth, Wal-Mart eventually moved to larger towns and cities and even outside the country. Today, it dominates both American and global retailing. Although Wal-Mart is a fierce competitor, it is not the primary source of Sears's market woes. While Wal-Mart has undoubtedly siphoned off some of Sears customers, the two retailers don't compete with each other on their individual strengths. Wal-Mart sells soft goods and Sears sells hardware. In some ways, they almost complement each other.

While Wal-Mart was gobbling up sales outside the mall, other retailers were changing their strategies within the mall. JC Penney, the company most closely resembling Sears in the 1970s, eliminated its hardware and appliance lines, beefed up soft goods—especially women's and children's clothing—and located *in* the mall, where 75 percent of women's clothing is sold. This strategy worked well for Penney's, which is now positioned below the major department stores but above the lower-priced specialty outlets.

Sears, in contrast, kept the appliances and hardware, tried to beef up the soft goods, and located stores both in and adjacent to malls. It also diversified into financial services. While other retailers focused on expanding their clothing lines and developing exciting in-store clothing sections, Sears spread itself too thin. From its beginnings 118 years ago, Sears always carried some women's clothing, household items, and toys at Christmas in order to make shopping a family experience. However, the predominant ambiance at Sears stores into the 1950s was that of a hardware store in which the tools and hard goods were the champs.

This image of a "hardware store" has been hard for Sears to change, and the retailer has not always shown a real willingness to do so. While saying that it would improve its clothing lines, and while signing contracts with Cheryl Tiegs and Stefani Powers, Sears left the position of women's fashion director unfilled for 9 years. Even when new, more-upscale lines were introduced, they were displayed next to neon-flowered tops and stretch pants. Clothing racks were a mess—overcrowded, sloppy, and utilitarian. There was no organization within the womens' clothing department. A shopper might find $20 sweaters next to $80 sweaters. If the two looked alike, guess which the consumer bought.

Not only were the clothing departments shabby and uninviting, there were not enough mirrors and dressing rooms—without which a store can't sell to women. Marketing research in the early 1990s showed that the woman who bought her clothes at Sears was almost 50, had an income of less than $30,000, and was there to buy $6.99 stretch pants. The company's 1990 ad slogan "You gotta be puttin' me on" admitted to the consumer that fashion had not been Sears' strength.

To change that, during the 1990s Sears threw out most of the cheap, polyester pants and brought in recognized brand lines such as Chaus and Village. Unfortunately, all the merchandising problems persisted. Goods were jumbled together, there were not enough mirrors, and the departments were still shabby and uninviting. Ugly red signs remained in place to remind consumers that goods were "as advertised" or "on sale." The clean-up of Sears's image was not complete and the introduction of "the softer side of Sears" was not a success.

In 2002, to specifically address its fashion image shortcomings, Sears purchased Lands' End for $1.86 billion and immediately put Lands' End management in charge of Sears fashion apparel. Unfortunately, the two companies are quite dissimilar. Lands' End is an upscale catalog company appealing to white baby boomers. It sells mostly casual wear supplemented with some professional wear. It is a "folksy" company located in Dodgeville, Wisconsin, that prides itself on the casualness of its work place, the completeness of catalog descriptions, and the helpfulness of telephone operators. Important decisions were often made over a frosty mug of beer.

Contrast that with Sears' many layers of management and hodgepodge of bureaucracy. Sears had even built one of the world's tallest buildings (at the time) as a monument to the company, and it once had a corporate guidelines book with 29,000 pages. Sears executives dress for success and use the latest business jargon while Lands' End managers ride bicycles to work. For example, at a recent meeting, a Sears manager was quoted as saying "We've been out interfacing with stakeholders to obtain consensus." A Lands' End manager responded with "Do you know what you just said? Normal people don't talk like that!"

Besides the corporate culture clash, Lands' End managers were under the gun to roll out their brand in Sears 870 stores in just 10 months. These managers did not have much experience with in-store retailing. The end result was overstocks of Lands' End merchandise that had to be discounted at the end of the season. Lands' End management realized that it had a lot to learn about in-store retailing. After 2 years, Lands' End has still not determined the appropriate level of merchandise for stores and is still plagued with overstocks.

The clash between the two groups emphasizes the difficulty that Sears faces in determining an appropriate positioning for the company. Lands' End executives claim that their first concern is the consumer while Sears' first concern is the stockholder—a claim that Sears denies.

A major issue at Sears is this: Just who *is* the consumer? Lands' End sells clothing to the market that frequently buys appliances and hardware at Sears, which might indicate that this could be a good fit. But market research shows that women are still uncomfortable shopping at Sears and prefer to go elsewhere. In addition, one of three customers at Sears is either African-American or Hispanic—market segments that Sears has nurtured. Among Sears' 872 stores are 97 MAC (Multicultural Aspirational Concept) stores, which carry ethnic-inspired lines. Most of these are located in urban areas such as Los Angeles and Miami and are scheduled in 2004 to get new ethnic lines—Russell Kemp for African Americans and Azucar Bella for Hispanics. At the same time, Sears will also introduce cookware catering to Mexican and Caribbean shoppers' tastes. These urban and inner-city locations might be a major opportunity for Sears, as inner-city areas especially are underserved by chain retailers and dominated by higher-priced, Mom 'n Pop stores. Studies show that inner-city locations do not have higher incidences of crime, shoplifting, or employee turnover. But that's a very different market from the Lands' End market and from the current, typical Sears' female customer.

Not only is it difficult to determine who Sears' customers are, it's also difficult to determine what Sears is. In the last 20 years, its financial business, especially the credit card operation, was so successful that some analysts dubbed Sears a financial company with a retail unit on the side. In 2001, retail sales were 76 percent of revenue with operating income of 2.2 percent. In contrast, credit card operations were 12.6 percent of sales, but 60.8 percent of operating income. In late 2003, Sears sold its credit card operation to Citigroup. This transaction left Sears free to concentrate on improving its retail operations and also generated some $32 billion, which Sears can use to renovate stores. It also means that Sears *must* increase operating income from retail sales.

What has Sears chosen to do? In addition to shoring up its fashion image through the Lands' End purchase, Sears has introduced a three-tier collection of home fashions, labeled Whole Home, which was enthusiastically received by industry people and which initially generated better than expected sales. Sears is also spending hundreds of millions of dollars to renovate stores. So far, this has not been enough. In the second quarter of 2004, Sears' revenue declined by 14 percent, sales declined by 2.9 percent, and net income dropped by a whopping 83 percent. As a result, analysts such as Standard & Poor's dropped Sears credit rating and Sears share prices declined.

Sears realizes that it has lost market share to Wal-Mart, Target, and Best Buy, and that it must find some means of competing with those retailers. Even the CEO of Sears has commented that "shoppers have to drive by these big-box category killers in order to get to the mall. We need to find a way to get closer to customers." Taking these comments to heart, Sears management is launching Sears Grand stores. These stores will be located away from malls in freestanding locations. Sears has already purchased 54 old Kmart stores and subleased 7 Wal-Mart stores, which could potentially be 61 Sears Grand stores.

The Sears Grand stores will be 250,000 square feet, considerably larger than traditional 90,000 square foot Sears stores. They will contain new departments such as music, movies, books and magazines, dry grocery, health and beauty aids, cleaning products, pet supplies, toys and games, a seasonal garden center, an automotive center, and home maintenance tools such as plumbing parts and furnace filters. Stores will be open from 8 A.M. to 10 P.M. on weekdays and from 10 A.M. to 9 P.M. on weekends. Instead of individual department checkouts, Sears Grand stores will include shopping carts and checkout lanes at the front of the store.

Apparel will be in the center of the store, prominently featured along the "boulevard"—an 18-foot wide aisle running through the center of the store. The boulevard is the only aisle that will contain product displays. Other aisles will also be wider and less cluttered. This might sound like a typical discount store format, but Sears maintains that the Grand stores will really be full-line Sears stores, located away from malls with a positioning of better quality merchandise at a good value. They maintain that Sears is not and will not be a discounter.

Given the company's previous difficulties with in-store layout and merchandising, the first five "Grands" will be pilot stores, with each one testing different things. Size and merchandise assortments will vary and customer reactions will be closely monitored in order to design a prototype store that best meets customer needs.

So far, there are three Sears Grand stores—one near Jordan Landing Shopping Center in Salt Lake City; one in Gurnee, Illinois, a suburb of Chicago; and one outside Las Vegas. The next two stores will be in Rancho Cucamonga, California, and Austin, Texas. After that, there will be 61 new stores in a hybrid format as well as renovations of 100 stores each year.

While the Grand stores are an exciting concept that offers customers many benefits, some observers claim that they will not be enough to save Sears. One analyst commented that "Sears has not fixed its core business. What they've done is play musical chairs with the management and worked on financial engineering—buying back shares, selling the credit portfolio, cutting costs like crazy—but not dealing with the core problem." Defenders of the Grand stores retort "[Critics] haven't been to one, so they don't know what we're trying to do. We're trying to grow this company so that we can bring Sears to places we haven't been before." Who is right? Customers will make that decision with their dollars.

Questions for Discussion

1. List Sears strengths and weaknesses. Then assess how well each of the proposed changes in Sears strategy will build on the strengths and work to eliminate the weaknesses.

2. Develop a positioning statement for the new Sears that would be broad enough to cover all the types of Sears stores.

3. In your opinion, is the claim "Sears is not a discounter" valid? Why or why not?

4. How successful do you think the Grand stores will be? Explain. Who is its competition?

Sources: Amy Merrick, "Sears's Earnings Plummet 83 Percent," *Wall Street Journal,* July 23, 2004, p. C4; "Sears Buys Kmart Sites, Leases Wal-Mart Stores," *Home Channel News,* July 19, 2004, Vol. 30, Iss. 13; "Sears' Grand Entrance," *Home Channel News,* October 6, 2003, Vol. 29, Iss. 18; Francine Schwadel, "Fashion Statement: Its Earnings Sagging, Sears Upgrades Line of Women's Apparel," *Wall Street Journal,* May 9, 1990, p. A1; Amy Merrick, "New Outfit: Sears Orders Fashion Makeover From the Lands' End Catalog," *Wall Street Journal,* January 28, 2004, p. A1; Debbie Howell, "Retail Experiments in Cities Starting to Pay Off," *DSN Retailing Today,* August 2, 2004, p. 17–18.

CHAPTER 14

WHIPTASTIC HANDLING

> **After studying this chapter you should be able to**
>
> 1. name and define the tools of the marketing communications mix
> 2. discuss the process and advantages of integrated marketing communications
> 3. outline the steps in developing effective marketing communications
> 4. explain the methods for setting the promotion budget and factors that affect the design of the promotion mix

Integrated Marketing Communications Strategy

Previewing the Concepts

In this and the next two chapters, we'll examine the last of the marketing mix tools—promotion. Promotion is not a single tool but rather a mix of several tools. Ideally, under the concept of *integrated marketing communications,* the company will carefully coordinate these promotion elements to deliver a clear, consistent, and compelling message about the organization and its products. We'll begin by introducing you to the various promotion mix tools, the importance of integrated marketing communications, the steps in developing marketing communication, and the promotion budgeting process. In the next two chapters, we'll visit the specific marketing communications tools.

To start, let's look at an award-winning integrated marketing communications campaign. When the BMW Group acquired the British-made MINI car brand a few years ago, hardly anyone in the United States had even heard of the brand. Marketing the quirky little car presented some big challenges for MINI USA and its ad agency, Crispin Porter + Bogusky. To introduce this anything-but-ordinary car, the MINI marketing team broke with automotive advertising tradition and created its anything-but-ordinary *LET'S MOTOR* campaign. What makes this campaign so special? Let's take a closer look.

424

In early 2002, BMW of North America's MINI USA unit and its ad agency, Crispin Porter + Bogusky (CP+B), faced a stiff challenge. A few years earlier, BMW had acquired the British-made MINI automobile brand. Now, inspired by the success of nostalgia-mobiles such as the VW New Beetle and the PT Cruiser, BMW wanted to introduce a souped-up, modernized version of the MINI Cooper into the U.S. market.

The car itself was a dramatic departure from anything American car buyers had seen—it was potent but tiny (a foot shorter than the new Beetle), and it had a funky two-tone, retro-60s look. To add to the challenge, BMW assigned the MINI unit had a paltry marketing budget of about $20 million (versus, say, $50 million for the PT Cruiser introduction) and a staff just big enough to fill, well, a MINI. The challenge: At a time when big-budget SUVs and monster trucks ruled the road, how could the company get consumers interested in the quirky little MINI? The answer: a very creative integrated marketing and promotion campaign.

MINI USA and CP+B decided to position the diminutive MINI as an anything-but-ordinary kind of car. Rather than trying to mask the car's small size, the company featured it as a lifestyle choice, as a key part of the brand's personality. "The SUV backlash officially starts now," declared one early MINI billboard. The MINI was more than just a hunk of metal—it represented an alternative driving culture. "It was not just a car to get you here to there, but an experience, or a way of living," explains CP+B executive Jim Poh. The marketing team summarized the MINI brand experience under a simple campaign theme: "LET'S MOTOR!"

To develop this anything-but-ordinary positioning, MINI USA and CP+B needed an anything-but-ordinary communications campaign. Whereas the major automakers typically relied on big-budget, mass-media campaigns, the MINI marketers ruled against these media from the start. Instead, they assembled a rich mix of unconventional media, carefully integrated to create personality for the car and a tremendous buzz of excitement among consumers.

"To prove to people that this was an out-of-the-ordinary vehicle, we agreed that we would use unique ways of communicating our message," said Alex Bogusky, executive creative director at Crispin Porter + Bogusky. MINI's marketers discovered that the little car's physical presence elicits a stronger emotional reaction than images on television or in print. Before the car was officially released, the agency placed hidden cameras near parked MINIs to watch as people got their first glimpse of the car. "Almost always they smiled," says Bogusky. "The reaction wasn't the same when we showed them photos of the car." As a result, the communications campaign focused on media and tactics that let consumers experience the car firsthand.

Kerri Martin, MINI USA's "Guardian of Brand Soul" (also known as marketing director) knew that her potential buyers would be people who see themselves as risk takers, nonconformists, and adventure seekers. "From the beginning, I told everyone involved that I did not want a single traditional piece of advertising for this campaign," she says. Instead of TV and splashy magazine spreads, MINI would rely on guerrilla marketing and introduce select non-traditional magazine print and outdoor advertising only as the car hit the market.

The *LET'S MOTOR* campaign exploded onto the scene several months before the MINI was actually introduced. "The car wasn't even on the road yet," Martin says. "But we had to get people talking about it." To create buzz, CP+B put MINIs in all kinds of imaginative places. It mounted them atop Ford Excursion SUVs and drove them around 22 major cities, celebrating the car's sensible size and the fact that the fun stuff always generally goes on top, such as skis, camping gear, and bikes. It ripped out seating sections of sports stadiums in New Orleans and Oakland, California, and sat MINI Coopers as "spectators" alongside other fans at fall NFL and MLB games.

CP+B set up "MINI Ride" displays outside department stores, featuring an actual MINI that looked like a children's ride. "Rides $16,850. Quarters only," the sign said. Displays in airport terminals and other public places featured extremely oversized waste baskets, newspaper vending machines, and pay phones next to billboards showing the undersized MINI and proclaiming, "Makes everything else seem a little too big." The car was also promoted on the Internet, in ads painted on city buildings, and on baseball-type trading cards handed out at auto shows. In addition, MINI USA created MINI games, MINI booklets, MINI suitcases, and MINI placements in movies.

As the *LET'S MOTOR* campaign progressed, CP+B worked closely with selected magazines to create memorable print ads. For example, an ad in the center spread of *Rolling Stone* showed a MINI slaloming through day-glo orange staples acting as traffic cones (*Rolling Stone* actually changed its staples for that issue to accommodate the ad). Ads in *Wired* magazine contained a cardboard fold-out of a MINI, suggesting that readers assemble it and drive it around their desks making "putt-putt" noises. CP+B bought the 1-inch margin around news stories in several magazines and designed the space to look like a road with a sharp corner, with a little MINI zooming around it and the words "Nothing corners like a MINI. LET'S MOTOR." *Playboy* came up with the idea of a six-page "centerfold" complete with the car's likes and

dislikes, such as: "The end to a perfect day: A hand-washing with warm, sudsy water and a nice wax."

Outdoor advertising has also played an important roll. Clever billboards presented the wee MINI as high performance in a small package, an exciting alternative to today's automotive excesses. "Napoleon was only 5'2", declares one outdoor ad. "Bruce Lee. Only 135 pounds," states another. "Popeye. 5'3", tops," says a third. One creative billboard shows a chili red MINI with a glossy white top whizzing by, with real-looking palm trees beside the billboard bending into its slipstream. But perhaps no billboard summarizes MINI's counter-positioning better than one that shows a solitary yellow MINI Cooper and proclaims, "Let's sip not guzzle. Let's leave the off-road vehicles off road. Let's not use the size of our vehicle to make up for other shortcomings. Let's reclaim our garage space. Let's be nimble. Let's be quick. Let's be honest. LET'S MOTOR!"

The MINI *LET'S MOTOR* campaign has been a smashing success, creating an almost cult-like following for the personable little car. By the time the car was introduced in spring 2002, the buyer waiting list was approximately 10 months long. (MINI created a "Where's My Baby?" program on the Internet, so customers could check on their cars' progress as it moved through the production line at the Oxford manufacturing plant.) In less than a year, awareness of the MINI brand among U.S. consumers grew to 53 percent—3 years earlier, only 2 percent of Americans had even heard of the car. MINI sales are now running better than 80 percent above the company's original projections. And the inexpensive, offbeat communications campaign has become one of the most celebrated marketing efforts in recent years, scooping up numerous advertising industry awards.

Thus, the MINI communications campaign has been impressive both for what it *does* and for what it *doesn't do*. First, it breaks with automotive advertising tradition—it doesn't use the flashy, expensive network TV and glossy magazine placements favored by the major automakers. As a result, like the car, the MINI campaign has gotten a lot of mileage out of a modest budget. Second, it does use a dazzling array of unconventional media and tactics to create innovative customer experiences with the MINI brand. As impressive, it carefully integrates this rich variety of unusual media to create a unified brand personality. Whether it's an outdoor ad, an airport display, their Website MINIUSA.com, each message has the same distinctive MINI look and feel. "Every consumer 'touchpoint' (a term Bogusky likes) conveys the same message as the ad campaign," says one advertising analyst. "The campaign fits the brand personality perfectly," says another.[1]

Modern marketing calls for more than just developing a good product, pricing it attractively, and making it available to target customers. Companies must also *communicate* with current and prospective customers, and what they communicate should not be left to chance. All of their communications efforts must be blended into a consistent and coordinated communications program. Just as good communication is important in building and maintaining any kind of relationship, it is a crucial element in a company's efforts to build profitable customer relationships.

The Marketing Communications Mix

Marketing communications mix (promotion mix)
The specific mix of advertising, personal selling, sales promotion, and public relations a company uses.

Advertising
Any paid form of nonpersonal presentation and promotion of ideas, goods, or services by an identified sponsor.

Sales promotion
Short-term incentives to encourage the purchase or sale of a product or service.

Public relations
Building good relations with the company's various publics by obtaining favorable publicity, building up a good "corporate image," and handling or heading off unfavorable rumors, stories, and events.

Personal selling
Personal presentation by the firm's sales force for the purpose of making sales and building customer relationships.

Direct marketing
Direct communications with carefully targeted individual consumers—the use of telephone, mail, fax, e-mail, the Internet, and other tools to communicate directly with specific consumers.

A company's total **marketing communications mix**—also called its **promotion mix**—consists of the specific blend of advertising, sales promotion, public relations, personal selling, and direct-marketing tools that the company uses to pursue its advertising and marketing objectives. Definitions of the five major promotion tools follow:[2]

- **Advertising**: Any paid form of nonpersonal presentation and promotion of ideas, goods, or services by an identified sponsor.
- **Sales promotion**: Short-term incentives to encourage the purchase or sale of a product or service.
- **Public relations**: Building good relations with the company's various publics by obtaining favorable publicity, building up a good corporate image, and handling or heading off unfavorable rumors, stories, and events.
- **Personal selling**: Personal presentation by the firm's sales force for the purpose of making sales and building customer relationships.
- **Direct marketing**: Direct connections with carefully targeted individual consumers to both obtain an immediate response and cultivate lasting customer relationships—the use of telephone, mail, fax, e-mail, the Internet, and other tools to communicate directly with specific consumers.

Each category involves specific tools. For example, advertising includes print, broadcast, Internet, outdoor, and other forms. Sales promotion includes point-of-purchase displays, premiums, discounts, coupons, specialty advertising, and demonstrations. Public relations includes press releases, sponsorships, and special events. Personal selling includes sales presentations, trade shows, and incentive programs. Direct marketing includes catalogs, telephone marketing, kiosks, the Internet, and more. Thanks to technological breakthroughs, people can now communicate through a wide variety of media, including newspapers, radio, telephone, television, fax, cell phones, and the Internet.

At the same time, communication goes beyond these specific promotion tools. The product's design, its price, the shape and color of its package, and the stores that sell it—*all* communicate something to buyers. Thus, although the promotion mix is the company's primary communication activity, the entire marketing mix—promotion *and* product, price, and place—must be coordinated for greatest communication impact.

In this chapter, we begin by examining the rapidly changing marketing communications environment, the concept of integrated marketing communications, and the marketing communication process. Next, we discuss the factors that marketing communicators must consider in shaping an overall communication mix. We then summarize the legal, ethical, and social responsibility issues in marketing communications. In Chapter 15, we look at *mass-communication tools*—advertising, sales promotion, and public relations. Finally, Chapter 16 examines the *sales force* and *direct marketing* as communication and promotion tools.

Integrated Marketing Communications

During the past several decades, companies around the world have perfected the art of mass marketing—selling highly standardized products to masses of customers. In the process, they have developed effective mass-media advertising techniques to support their mass-marketing strategies. These companies routinely invest millions of dollars in the mass media, reaching tens of millions of customers with a single ad. However, as we move into the twenty-first century, marketing managers face some new marketing communications realities.

The Changing Communications Environment

Two major factors are changing the face of today's marketing communications. First, as mass markets have fragmented, marketers are shifting away from mass marketing. More and more, they are developing focused marketing programs designed to build closer relationships with customers in more narrowly defined micromarkets. Second, vast improvements in information technology are speeding the movement toward segmented marketing. Today's information technology helps marketers to keep closer track of customer needs—more information about consumers at the individual and household levels is available than ever before. New technologies also provide new communications avenues for reaching smaller customer segments with more-tailored messages.

The shift from mass marketing to segmented marketing has had a dramatic impact on marketing communications. Just as mass marketing gave rise to a new generation of mass-media communications, the shift toward one-to-one marketing is spawning a new generation of more specialized and highly targeted communications efforts.

Given this new communications environment, marketers must rethink the roles of various media and promotion mix tools. Mass-media advertising has long dominated the promotion mixes of consumer product companies. However, although television, magazines, and other mass media remain very important, their dominance is now declining. *Market* fragmentation has resulted in *media* fragmentation—in an explosion of more focused media that better match today's targeting strategies. Beyond the traditional mass-media channels, advertisers are making increased use of new, highly targeted media, ranging from highly focused specialty magazines and cable television channels to Internet catalogs and Web coupon promotions, to airport kiosks and floor decals in supermarket aisles. In all, companies are doing less *broadcasting* and more *narrowcasting*.

The Need for Integrated Marketing Communications

The shift from mass marketing to targeted marketing, and the corresponding use of a larger, richer mix of communication channels and promotion tools, poses a problem for marketers. Customers don't distinguish between message sources the way marketers do. In the con-

■ The new media environment: The relatively few mass magazines of past decades have been replaced by thousands of magazines targeting special-interest audiences. Hearst Magazines alone publishes 18 titles, ranging from *Cosmopolitan* and *Good Housekeeping* to *Smart Money* and *Popular Mechanics*.

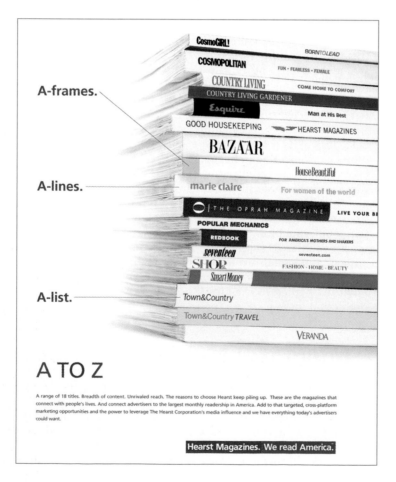

sumer's mind, advertising messages from different media and different promotional approaches all become part of a single message about the company. Conflicting messages from these different sources can result in confused company images and brand positions.

All too often, companies fail to integrate their various communications channels. The result is a hodgepodge of communications to consumers. Mass-media advertisements say one thing, while a price promotion sends a different signal and a product label creates still another message. Company sales literature says something altogether different and the company's Web site seems out of sync with everything else.

The problem is that these communications often come from different company sources. Advertising messages are planned and implemented by the advertising department or advertising agency. Personal selling communications are developed by sales management. Other functional specialists are responsible for public relations, sales promotion, direct marketing, Web sites, and other forms of marketing communications.

Recently, such functional separation has been a major problem for companies and their Internet communications. Many companies first organized their new Web and other digital communications operations into separate groups or divisions, isolating them from mainstream marketing activities. However, whereas some companies have compartmentalized the new communications tools, customers won't. According to one IMC expert:[3]

> The truth is, most [consumers] won't compartmentalize their use of the new systems. They won't say, "Hey, I'm going off to do a bit of Web surfing. Burn my TV, throw out all my radios, cancel all my magazine subscriptions and, by the way, take out my telephone and don't deliver any mail anymore." It's not that kind of world for consumers, and it shouldn't be that kind of world for marketers either.

Thus, if treated as a special case, the Internet—or any other marketing communication tool—can be a *dis*integrating force in marketing communications. Instead, all the communication tools must be carefully integrated into the broader marketing communications mix. Today, the best bet is to wed the emotional pitch and impact of traditional brand marketing with the interactivity and real service offered online. For example, print and television ads for Jeep build consumer preference for the brand. But the ads also point viewers to the company's Web site, which offers lots of help and very little hype. The site helps serious car buyers build and price a model, find a dealer online, and learn more about "the Jeep life."

■ Today, all the marketing communication tools must be carefully integrated. For example, this jeep print ad points consumers to the company's Web site, where serious car buyers build and price a model, find a dealer online, and learn more about "the Jeep life."

Integrated marketing communications (IMC)
The concept under which a company carefully integrates and coordinates its many communications channels to deliver a clear, consistent, and compelling message about the organization and its products.

In the past, no one person or department was responsible for thinking through the communication roles of the various promotion tools and coordinating the promotion mix. Today, however, more companies are adopting the concept of **integrated marketing communications (IMC)**. Under this concept, as illustrated in Figure 14.1, the company carefully integrates and coordinates its many communications channels to deliver a clear, consistent, and compelling message about the organization and its brands.[4]

IMC builds brand identity and strong customer relationships by tying together all of the company's messages and images. Brand messages and positioning are coordinated across all communication activities and media. IMC means that the company's advertising and personal selling communications have the same message, look, and feel as its Web site. And its public relations materials say the same thing as its direct mail campaign.[5]

IMC calls for recognizing all contact points where the customer may encounter the company, its products, and its brands. Each *brand contact* will deliver a message, whether good, bad, or indifferent. The company must strive to deliver a consistent and positive message with each contact. To help implement integrated marketing communications, some companies appoint a marketing communications director who has overall responsibility for the company's communications efforts.

Integrated marketing communications produces better communications consistency and greater sales impact. It places the responsibility in someone's hands—where none existed before—to unify the company's image as it is shaped by thousands of company activities. It leads to a total marketing communication strategy aimed at showing how the company and its products can help customers solve their problems.

A View of the Communication Process

Integrated marketing communications involves identifying the target audience and shaping a well-coordinated promotional program to obtain the desired audience response. Too often, marketing communications focus on immediate awareness, image, or preference goals in the target market. But this approach to communication is too shortsighted. Today, marketers are moving toward viewing communications as *managing the customer relationship over time.*

Because customers differ, communications programs need to be developed for specific segments, niches, and even individuals. And, given the new interactive communications technologies, companies must ask not only, "How can we reach our customers?" but also, "How can we find ways to let our customers reach us?"

FIGURE 14.1
Integrated marketing communications

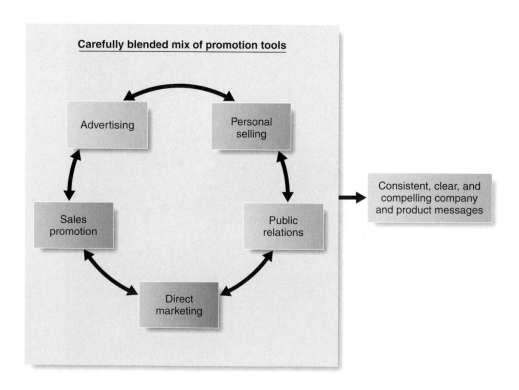

Thus, the communications process should start with an audit of all the potential contacts target customers may have with the company and its brands. For example, someone purchasing a new kitchen appliance may talk to others, see television ads, read articles and ads in newspapers and magazines, visit various Web sites, and check out appliances in one or more stores. The marketer needs to assess what influence each of these communications experiences will have at different stages of the buying process. This understanding will help marketers allocate their communication dollars more efficiently and effectively.

To communicate effectively, marketers need to understand how communication works. Communication involves the nine elements shown in Figure 14.2. Two of these elements are the major parties in a communication—the *sender* and the *receiver*. Another two are the major communication tools—the *message* and the *media*. Four more are major communication functions—*encoding*, *decoding*, *response*, and *feedback*. The last element is *noise* in the system. Definitions of these elements follow and are applied to an ad for Hewlett-Packard (H-P) color copiers.

- *Sender:* The *party sending the message* to another party—here, H-P.
- *Encoding:* The process of *putting thought into symbolic form*—H-P's advertising agency assembles words and illustrations into an advertisement that will convey the intended message.
- *Message:* The *set of symbols* that the sender transmits—the actual H-P copier ad.
- *Media:* The *communication channels* through which the message moves from sender to receiver—in this case, the specific magazines that H-P selects.
- *Decoding:* The process by which the receiver *assigns meaning to the symbols* encoded by the sender—a consumer reads the H-P copier ad and interprets the words and illustrations it contains.
- *Receiver:* The *party receiving the message* sent by another party—the home office or business customer who reads the H-P copier ad.
- *Response:* The *reactions of the receiver* after being exposed to the message—any of hundreds of possible responses, such as the consumer is more aware of the attributes of H-P copiers, actually buys an H-P copier, or does nothing.
- *Feedback:* The part of the *receiver's response communicated back to the sender*—H-P research shows that consumers are struck by and remember the ad, or consumers write or call H-P praising or criticizing the ad or H-P's products.
- *Noise:* The *unplanned static or distortion* during the communication process, which results in the receiver's getting a different message than the one the sender sent—the consumer it distracted while reading the magazine and misses the H-P ad or its key points.

FIGURE 14.2

Elements in the communication process

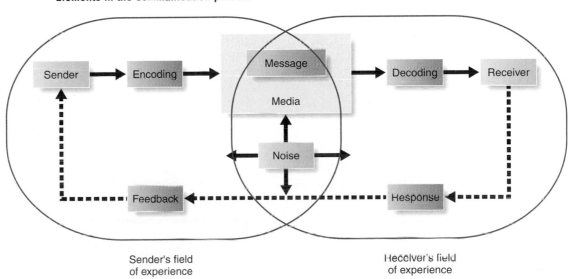

Sender's field of experience

Receiver's field of experience

For a message to be effective, the sender's encoding process must mesh with the receiver's decoding process. Thus, the best messages consist of words and other symbols that are familiar to the receiver. The more the sender's field of experience overlaps with that of the receiver, the more effective the message is likely to be. Marketing communicators may not always *share* their consumer's field of experience. For example, an advertising copywriter from one social stratum might create ads for consumers from another stratum—say, wealthy business owners. However, to communicate effectively, the marketing communicator must *understand* the consumer's field of experience.

This model points out several key factors in good communication. Senders need to know what audiences they wish to reach and what responses they want. They must be good at encoding messages that take into account how the target audience decodes them. They must send messages through media that reach target audiences, and they must develop feedback channels so that they can assess the audience's response to the message.

Steps in Developing Effective Communication

We now examine the steps in developing an effective integrated communications and promotion program. The marketing communicator must do the following: Identify the target audience, determine the communication objectives, design a message, choose the media through which to send the message, select the message source, and collect feedback.

Identifying the Target Audience

A marketing communicator starts with a clear target audience in mind. The audience may be potential buyers or current users, those who make the buying decision or those who influence it. The audience may be individuals, groups, special publics, or the general public. The target audience will heavily affect the communicator's decisions on *what* will be said, *how* it will be said, *when* it will be said, *where* it will be said, and *who* will say it.

Determining the Communication Objectives

Buyer-readiness stages
The stages consumers normally pass through on their way to purchase, including awareness, knowledge, liking, preference, conviction, and purchase.

Once the target audience has been defined, the marketing communicator must decide what response is sought. Of course, in many cases, the final response is *purchase*. But purchase is the result of a long process of consumer decision making. The marketing communicator needs to know where the target audience now stands and to what stage it needs to be moved. The target audience may be in any of six **buyer-readiness stages**, the stages consumers normally pass through on their way to making a purchase. These stages include *awareness*, *knowledge*, *liking*, *preference*, *conviction*, and *purchase* (see Figure 14.3).

The marketing communicator's target market may be totally unaware of the product, know only its name, or know only a few things about it. The communicator must first build *awareness* and *knowledge*. For example, when Nissan introduced its Infiniti automobile line, it began with an extensive "teaser" advertising campaign to create name familiarity. Initial ads for the Infiniti created curiosity and awareness by showing the car's name but not the car. Later ads created knowledge by informing potential buyers of the car's high quality and its many innovative features. Chrysler recently ran similar teaser ads when introducing its new Chrysler 300 model.

FIGURE 14.3
Buyer-readiness stages

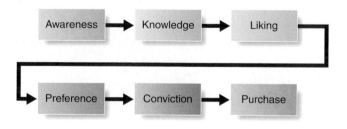

■ Moving consumers toward purchase: Chrysler used teaser ads to create initial curiosity and awareness for its new Chrysler 300 model.

TheMysteryCar.com

Assuming target consumers *know* about the product, how do they *feel* about it? Once potential buyers knew about the Infiniti, Nissan's marketers wanted to move them through successively stronger stages of feelings toward the car. These stages included *liking* (feeling favorable about the Infiniti), *preference* (preferring Infiniti to other car brands), and *conviction* (believing that Infiniti is the best car for them). Infiniti marketers used a combination of the promotion mix tools to create positive feelings and conviction. Advertising extolled the Infiniti's advantages over competing brands and established its "Accelerating the Future" positioning. Press releases and other public relations activities stressed the car's innovative features and performance. Dealer salespeople told buyers about options, value for the price, and after-sale service.

Finally, some members of the target market might be convinced about the product, but not quite get around to making the *purchase*. Potential Infiniti buyers might have decided to wait for more information or for the economy to improve. The communicator must lead these consumers to take the final step. Actions might include offering special promotional prices, rebates, or premiums. Salespeople might call or write to selected customers, inviting them to visit the dealership for a special showing. The Infiniti Web site (www.infiniti.com) tells potential buyers that "There is no substitute for a test drive," explains various financing options, and invites them to visit the local dealer's showroom.

Of course, marketing communications alone cannot create positive feelings and purchases for Infiniti. The car itself must provide superior value for the customer. In fact, outstanding marketing communications can actually speed the demise of a poor product. The more quickly potential buyers learn about the poor product, the more quickly they become aware of its faults. Thus, good marketing communication calls for "good deeds followed by good words."

Designing a Message

Having defined the desired audience response, the communicator turns to developing an effective message. Ideally, the message should get *Attention*, hold *Interest*, arouse *Desire*, and obtain *Action* (a framework known as the *AIDA model*). In practice, few messages take the consumer all the way from awareness to purchase, but the AIDA framework suggests the desirable qualities of a good message.

In putting the message together, the marketing communicator must decide what to say (*message content*) and how to say it (*message structure* and *format*).

Message Content

The communicator has to figure out an appeal or theme that will produce the desired response. There are three types of appeals: rational, emotional, and moral. *Rational appeals* relate to the audience's self-interest. They show that the product will produce the desired benefits. Examples are messages showing a product's quality, economy, value, or performance. Thus, in its ads, Mercedes offers automobiles that are "engineered like no other car in the world," stressing engineering design, performance, and safety.

Emotional appeals attempt to stir up either negative or positive emotions that can motivate purchase. Communicators may use positive emotional appeals such as love, pride, joy, and humor. For example, advocates for humorous messages claim that they attract more attention and create more liking and belief in the sponsor. In a recent RoperASW survey, Americans picked humor as their favorite ad approach, with 85 percent saying they like ads with humorous themes. Other favorite emotional themes in the post-September 11, 2001, era include such reassuring ones as "safety and security" (77 percent), "family closeness" (76 percent), "giving to others" (74 percent), "patriotism" (74 percent), and "optimism" (64 percent).[6]

These days, it seems as though every company is using humor in its advertising, from consumer product firms such as Anheuser-Busch to the scholarly American Heritage Dictionary. Advertising in recent Super Bowls appears to reflect consumers' preferences for humor. For example, all of the top 10 most popular ads in *USA Today*'s ad meter consumer rankings of 2004 Super advertisements used humor. Anheuser-Busch used humor to claim six of the top 10 ad spots. Its ads Budweiser and Bud Light featured everything from a Clydesdale wanna-be donkey who wears furry hoof extensions and brays in an effort to become part of the Budweiser Clydesdales team to Cedric the Entertainer mistakenly undergoing and bikini-wax treatment at a spa.

Properly used, humor can capture attention, make people feel good, and give a brand personality. Anheuser-Busch has used humor effectively for years, helping consumers relate to its brands. However, advertisers must be careful when using humor. Used poorly, it can detract from comprehension, wear out its welcome fast, overshadow the product, or even irritate consumers. For example, many consumers and ad critics took exception to some of the humor used in last year's Super Bowl ads, including Anheuser-Busch ads.

In a recent poll, advertising professionals agreed that the quality of Super Bowl ads last year had declined, mostly from the use of "toilet bowl" humor that insulted view-

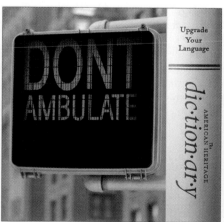

■ Humor in advertising: These days, it seems as though almost every company is using humor in its advertising, even the scholarly American Heritage Dictionary.

ers' intelligence. They pointed to Budweiser ads featuring a crotch-biting dog, a male monkey wooing a human female, and a gas-passing horse that spoiled a sleigh-ride date. Many critics and consumers complained that such ads showed that Budweiser was "reaching for the lowest common denominator in commercials aimed at the most frequent beer drinkers—men from 21 to 25 years old—resulting in a race to the bottom to fill commercials with bathroom humor, double entendres, crude sight gags and vulgarisms." As a result of such criticism, Anheuser-Busch is rethinking the tone and content of its ads for future Super Bowls. We are taking a more cautious approach to our creative," says Anheuser-Busch president August Busch IV. "[Bud Light] is about fun, being with friends, and good times," says a senior Budweiser ad agency executive, "and we can do that within the boundaries of good taste."[7]

Communicators can also use negative emotional appeals, such as fear, guilt, and shame that get people to do things they should (brush their teeth, buy new tires) or to stop doing things they shouldn't (smoke, drink too much, eat unhealthy foods). For example, a Crest ad invokes mild fear when it claims, "There are some things you just can't afford to gamble with" (cavities). And Etonic ads ask, "What would you do if you couldn't run?" They go on to note that Etonic athletic shoes are designed to avoid injuries—they're "built so you can last."

Moral appeals are directed to the audience's sense of what is "right" and "proper." They are often used to urge people to support social causes such as a cleaner environment, better race relations, equal rights for women, and aid to the disadvantaged. An example of a moral appeal is the Salvation Army, "While you're trying to figure out what to get the man who has everything, don't forget the man who has nothing."

Message Structure

The communicator must also decide how to handle three message structure issues. The first is whether to draw a conclusion or leave it to the audience. Recent research suggests that in many cases, rather than drawing a conclusion, the advertiser is better off asking questions and letting buyers come to their own conclusions. The second message structure issue is whether to present the strongest arguments first or last. Presenting them first gets strong attention but may lead to an anticlimactic ending. The third message structure issue is whether to present a one-sided argument (mentioning only the product's strengths) or a two-sided argument (touting the product's strengths while also admitting its shortcomings). Usually, a one-sided argument is more effective in sales presentations—except when audiences are highly educated or likely to hear opposing claims, or when the communicator has a negative association to overcome. In this spirit, Heinz ran the message "Heinz Ketchup is slow good" and Listerine ran the message "Listerine tastes bad twice a day." In such cases, two-sided messages can enhance the advertiser's credibility and make buyers more resistant to competitor attacks.

■ Moral appeals: The Salvation Army says "While you're trying to figure out what to get the man who has everything, don't forget the man who has nothing."

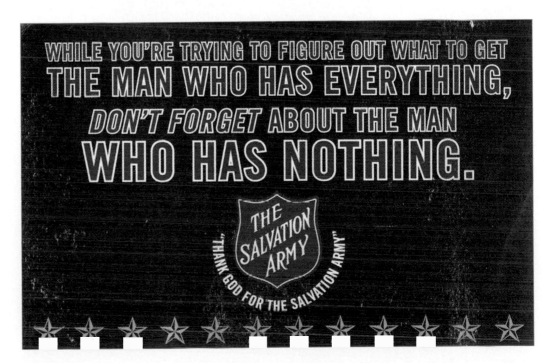

Message Format

The marketing communicator also needs a strong *format* for the message. In a print ad, the communicator has to decide on the headline, copy, illustration, and color. To attract attention, advertisers can use novelty and contrast; eye-catching pictures and headlines; distinctive formats; message size and position; and color, shape, and movement. If the message is to be carried over the radio, the communicator has to choose words, sounds, and voices. The "sound" of an announcer promoting banking services should be different from one promoting quality furniture.

If the message is to be carried on television or in person, then all these elements plus body language have to be planned. Presenters plan their facial expressions, gestures, dress, posture, and hairstyles. If the message is carried on the product or its package, the communicator has to watch texture, scent, color, size, and shape. For example, age and other demographics affect the way in which consumers perceive and react to color. Here are examples:

> How do you sell margarine—stodgy, wholesome margarine—to today's kids? One answer: color. "We knew we wanted to introduce a color product. It's been a big trend with kids since the blue M&M," says a Parkay spokesperson. So Parkay tried out margarine in blue, pink, green, and purple. "When we tested four different colors in focus groups, kids had a blast." Electric blue and shocking pink margarine emerged as clear favorites. In contrast, as we get older, our eyes mature and our vision takes on a yellow cast. Color looks less bright to older people, so they gravitate to white and other bright tones. A recent survey found 10 percent of people 55 years and older want the brightness of a white car, compared with 4 percent of 21- to 34-year-olds and 2 percent of teens. Lexus, which skews toward older buyers, makes sure that 60 percent of its cars are light in color.[8]

Thus, in designing effective marketing communications, marketers must consider color and other seemingly unimportant details carefully.

Choosing Media

The communicator now must select *channels of communication*. There are two broad types of communication channels—*personal* and *nonpersonal*.

■ Message format: To attract attention, advertisers can use novelty and contrast, eye-catching pictures and headlines, and distinctive formats, as in this Volkswagen New Beetle ad.

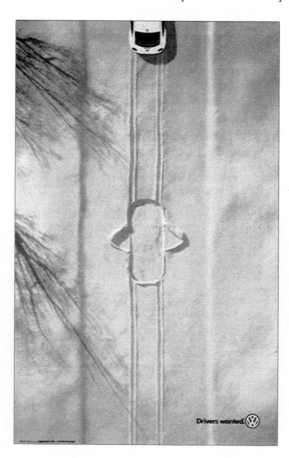

Personal Communication Channels

Personal communication channels

Channels through which two or more people communicate directly with each other, including face to face, person to audience, over the telephone, or through the mail.

In **personal communication channels**, two or more people communicate directly with each other. They might communicate face to face, over the telephone, through the mail, or even through an Internet "chat." Personal communication channels are effective because they allow for personal addressing and feedback.

Some personal communication channels are controlled directly by the company. For example, company salespeople contact buyers in the target market. But other personal communications about the product may reach buyers through channels not directly controlled by the company. These might include independent experts—consumer advocates, consumer buying guides, and others—making statements to target buyers. Or they might be neighbors, friends, family members, and associates talking to target buyers. This last channel, known as **word-of-mouth influence**, has considerable effect in many product areas.

Word-of-mouth influence

Personal communication about a product between target buyers and neighbors, friends, family members, and associates.

Personal influence carries great weight for products that are expensive, risky, or highly visible. For example, buyers of automobiles and major appliances often go beyond mass-media sources to seek the opinions of knowledgeable people.

Companies can take steps to put personal communication channels to work for them. For example, they can create marketing programs that will generate favorable word-of-mouth communications about their brands. Virgin Mobile created its "Share the Love" advertising campaign to promote word of mouth among young consumers of wireless services:

> Virgin Mobile USA, which targets 16- to 24-year-olds, stokes word of mouth through creative ad messages for its wireless service. One 30-second TV spot, part of its national "Share the Love" campaign, opens with the view of a car's back window that's all steamed up. In the condensation are the words: "Hello lovers: Get a hot Virgin Mobile cell phone for as low as $59." A kissing sound and the appearance of a woman's foot thrust out the window suggest backseat action. The ad mentions that anyone who gets a friend to sign up for the service receives a $20 bonus. Word of mouth is key to this campaign, suggest Virgin Mobile's chief marketing executive. "Kids this age still find out about most things through their friends," he says.[9]

Buzz marketing

Cultivating opinion leaders and getting them to spread information about a product or service to others in their communities.

Other companies create *opinion leaders*—people whose opinions are sought by others—by supplying influencer with the product on attractive terms or by educating them so that they can inform others. **Buzz marketing** involves cultivating opinion leaders and getting them to spread information about a product or service to others in their communities (see Real Marketing 14.1).

Nonpersonal Communication Channels

Nonpersonal communication channels

Media that carry messages without personal contact or feedback, including major media, atmospheres, and events.

Nonpersonal communication channels are media that carry messages without personal contact or feedback. They include major media, atmospheres, and events. Major *media* include print media (newspapers, magazines, direct mail), broadcast media (radio, television), display media (billboards, signs, posters), and online media (e-mail, Web sites). *Atmospheres* are designed environments that create or reinforce the buyer's leanings toward buying a product. Thus, lawyers' offices and banks are designed to communicate confidence and other qualities that might be valued by their clients. *Events* are staged occurrences that communicate messages to target audiences. For example, public relations departments arrange press conferences, grand openings, shows and exhibits, public tours, and other events.

Nonpersonal communication affects buyers directly. In addition, using mass media often affects buyers indirectly by causing more personal communication. Communications first flow from television, magazines, and other mass media to opinion leaders and then from these opinion leaders to others. Thus, opinion leaders step between the mass media and their audiences and carry messages to people who are less exposed to media. This suggests that mass communicators should aim their messages directly at opinion leaders, letting them carry the message to others.

Selecting the Message Source

In either personal or nonpersonal communication, the message's impact on the target audience is also affected by how the audience views the communicator. Messages delivered by highly credible sources are more persuasive. Thus, many food companies promote to doctors, dentists, and other health care providers to motivate these professionals to recommend their products to patients. And marketers hire celebrity endorsers—well-known athletes, actors,

Marketing at Work 14.1

Buzz Marketing: A Powerful New Way to Spread the Word

These days, buzz marketing is all the rage. Buzz marketing involves getting consumers themselves to spread information about a product or service to others in their communities. "In a successful buzz-marketing campaign, each carefully cultivated recipient of the brand message becomes a powerful carrier, spreading the word to yet more carriers, much as a virus rampages through a given population," says one expert.

Why the new trend? For starters, buzz marketing is cheap. It's a great way to extend brand exposure without blowing out the marketing budget. Buzz marketing's increasing popularity can also be attributed the growing ranks of skeptical consumers—such as teens and twenty-somethings—who are notoriously disdainful of mass-media advertising. Instead of the usual ad pitches, buzz marketing spreads the word through grassroots opinion leaders.

Perhaps the single most important reason that marketers are employing buzz marketing is that it really works. Consider the following examples.

Lee Dungarees: In recent years, VF had managed to reenergize the image of its stodgy Lee jeans brand among younger target consumers—mostly young males 17 to 22. But it needed to do more to convert that cooler image into sales at teen-toxic retailers like J.C. Penney and Sears Roebuck, its biggest outlets. So VF came up with one of the most free-wheeling and influential buzz-marketing campaigns to date. The campaign played on target consumers' weakness for video games and computers. First, VF developed a list of 200,000 "influential" guys from a list of Web surfers. It then zapped them a trio of grainy video clips that were hilarious in their apparent stupidity. The videos appeared to be ultra-low-budget flicks meant to draw visitors to the Web game sites of amateur filmmakers, such as open-shirted Curry, a 23-year-old race car driver. To the young Web surfers who received them, the clips seemed like delicious examples of the oddball digital debris that litters the Web. So not many of the recipients who eagerly forwarded the flicks to their friends would have guessed that they actually were abetting in a marketing campaign orchestrated by Lee.

According to VF research, the "stupid little films" were so intriguing that, on average, recipients forwarded them to six friends apiece. Despite virtually no advertising, some 100,000 visitors stormed the fictional filmmakers' Web sites the week

■ Tremor, an arm of Porter & Gamble, has a huge stealth teenage sales force-some 280,000 strong. Tremorites help companies spread the word about their brands among teens.

they went live, crashing the server. The marketing connection only became clear a few months later, after a TV and radio ad blitz finally revealed the three characters to be fictional antagonists developed as part of an online computer game. And that was a key to the program: To play the game at an advanced level, participants had to snag the product identification numbers—the "secret code"—off Lee items, which of course required a visit to a store. Ultimately, the effort drove thousands of kids age 17 to 22 into the stores and helped propel Lee sales upward by 20 percent.

Burger King TenderCrisps: The Web site, www.subservientchicken. com, opens up on the Burger King logo, with the words "Contacting the Chicken" underneath it. Then it dissolves to a living room, where the subservient chicken—someone in a

and even cartoon characters—to deliver their messages. Golfer Tiger Woods speaks for Nike, Buick, and a dozen other brands. Basketball pro LeBron James vouches for Nike and Coca-Cola's Powerade and Sprite brands. NASCAR superstar Jeff Gordon pitches everything from Ray-Ban sun glasses to Pepsi and Edy's ice cream. And soccer star Mia Hamm stands behind Gatorade, Nike, Disney, and Wheaties.

But companies must be careful when selecting celebrities to represent their brands. Picking the wrong spokesperson can result in embarrassment and a tarnished image. Hertz found this out when it entrusted its good name to the care of O. J. Simpson. Pepsi and Kodak faced similar embarrassment when their spokesperson, boxer Mike Tyson, was accused of beating his wife and was later jailed for rape. More recently, Kobe Bryant lost his sponsorship contracts with McDonald's and other companies after being accused of sexual assault.

giant chicken suit and a garter belt—awaits your bidding. The room has the look of one of those Web-cam sites, complete with tacky furniture and bare walls that make it somehow seedy and suggestive. Type in commands, and the chicken does exactly what you ask. It will flap its wings, roll over, or jump up and down. It will also moon the viewer, dance the Electric Slide, or die. In other words, you can have your way with the chicken. Get it? Have it your way! The site promotes Burger King's new TenderCrisp chicken and ties the new product into Burger King's successful "Have It Your Way" marketing campaign.

The funky subservient chicken is a really clever buzz-marketing idea. "As viral marketing goes, subservientchicken.com is a colossal success," says an advertising expert. "There is great overlap between Web habitués and Burger King's core audience." If nothing more, the site gets consumers to interact with the brand. And it gets them buzzing about Burger King's edgy new positioning. Hit the "tell a friend" button, and the site automatically announces itself to a designated friend. According to the chain, the site received more than 46 million hits in the week following its launch. By now it's probably received a billion hits.

Procter & Gamble's Tremor: Gina Lavagna is the ideal pitch gal. After receiving a $2 minidisc for Sony's Net MD and six $10-off coupons, she rushed four of her chums to a mall near her home in Carlstadt, New Jersey to show them the digital music player, which sells for $99 and up. "I've probably told 20 people about it," she says, adding, "At least 10 are extremely interested in getting one." Her parents got her one for Christmas.

Gina is a member of Procter & Gamble's huge stealth teenage sales force. Some 280,000 strong—roughly 1 percent of the U.S. teen population—all of them have been enlisted by an arm of Procter & Gamble called Tremor. Their mission is to help companies spread the word about their brands among teens, who are maddeningly difficult to reach and influence through advertising. They deliver endorsements in school cafeterias, at sleepovers, by cell phone, and by e-mail—and they do it for free. Initially focused only on P&G brands, Tremor's forces are now being tapped to talk up just about any brand, from Sony, Coca-Cola, and Kraft to Toyota and Valvoline motor oil.

Tremor recruits teens with a wide social circle and a gift of gab. (Tremorites have an average 170 names on their buddy lists; a typical teen has 30.) While P&G screens the kids it taps, it doesn't coach them beyond encouraging them to feel free to talk to friends. The kids, natural talkers, do the work without pay, not counting the coupons, product samples, and the thrill of being something of an "insider." "It's cool to know about stuff before other people," says one Tremorite.

More than just talk, such buzz can give a real lift to a brand's sales. Last May CoverGirl sent groups of Tremor gals in three cities a booklet of makeup tips in a thin round tin with some $1-off coupons. Nothing fancy, but CoverGirl wanted to see if it would give its lipstick, mascara, and foundation a boost. It did. Purchases rose 10 percent among teens in the targeted cities.

The International Dairy Foods Association, the group behind the "Got Milk?" ads, is also a believer. Last spring P&G worked with association member Shamrock Farms of Phoenix on its launch of a new chocolate-malt-flavored milk. The dairy monitored sales of the new product in Phoenix and Tucson where the plan and expenditures were the same, with one exception: In Phoenix, 2,100 Tremorites received product information, coupons, and stickers. After 23 weeks, Shamrock says, sales of the drink were 18 percent higher in Phoenix than in Tucson. Coupon redemption was an impressive 21 percent, the highest the dairy has ever seen.

P&G's buzz-marketing effort has been so successful that the packaged-goods giant is now building a new network of equal or greater size, one that will focus on moms—a much bigger and more affluent target than teens. Says P&G's marketing chief: "The possibilities are almost limitless."

Sources: Excerpts adapted from Gerry Khermouch and Jeff Green, "Buzz Marketing, *Business Week*, July 30, 2001, pp. 50–56; Melanie Wells, "Nabbing Teens," *Forbes,* February 2, 2004, pp. 85–88; Bob Garfield, "War & Peace and Subservient Chicken," April 26, 2004, accessed at www.adage.com; and Gregg Cebrzynski, "Burger King Says It's OK to Have Your Way with the Chicken," *Nation's Restaurant News,* May 10, 2004, p. 16.

Collecting Feedback

After sending the message, the communicator must research its effect on the target audience. This involves asking the target audience members whether they remember the message, how many times they saw it, what points they recall, how they felt about the message, and their past and present attitudes toward the product and company. The communicator would also like to measure behavior resulting from the message—how many people bought a product, talked to others about it, or visited the store.

Feedback on marketing communications may suggest changes in the promotion program or in the product offer itself. For example, JetBlue Airways uses television and newspaper advertising to inform area consumers about the airline, its routes, and its fares. Suppose

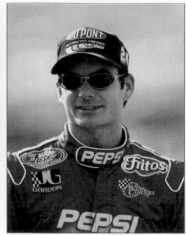

■ Marketers hire celebrity endorsers to deliver their messages. Mia Hamm and Tiger Woods speak for Nike. NASCAR superstar Jeff Gordon pitches everything from Ray-Ban sun glasses to Pepsi and Edy's ice cream.

feedback research shows that 80 percent of all fliers in an area recall seeing the airline's ads and are aware of its flights and prices. Sixty percent of these aware fliers have flown JetBlue, but only 20 percent of those who tried it were satisfied. These results suggest that although promotion is creating *awareness*, the airline isn't giving consumers the *satisfaction* they expect. Therefore, JetBlue needs to improve its service while staying with the successful communication program. In contrast, suppose the research shows that only 40 percent of area consumers are aware of the airline, only 30 percent of those aware have tried it, but 80 percent of those who have tried it return. In this case, JetBlue needs to strengthen its promotion program to take advantage of its power to create customer satisfaction.

Setting the Total Promotion Budget and Mix

We have looked at the steps in planning and sending communications to a target audience. But how does the company decide on the total *promotion budget* and its division among the major promotional tools to create the *promotion mix*? By what process does it blend the tools to create integrated marketing communications? We now look at these questions.

Setting the Total Promotion Budget

One of the hardest marketing decisions facing a company is how much to spend on promotion. John Wanamaker, the department store magnate, once said, "I know that half of my advertising is wasted, but I don't know which half. I spent $2 million for advertising, and I don't know if that is half enough or twice too much." Thus, it is not surprising that industries and companies vary widely in how much they spend on promotion. Promotion spending may be 20 to 30 percent of sales in the cosmetics industry and only 2 or 3 percent in the industrial machinery industry. Within a given industry, both low and high spenders can be found.[10]

How does a company decide on its promotion budget? We look at four common methods used to set the total budget for advertising: the *affordable method*, the *percentage-of-sales method*, the *competitive-parity method*, and the *objective-and-task method.*[11]

Affordable Method

Affordable method

Setting the promotion budget at the level management thinks the company can afford.

Some companies use the **affordable method**: They set the promotion budget at the level they think the company can afford. Small businesses often use this method, reasoning that the company cannot spend more on advertising than it has. They start with total revenues, deduct operating expenses and capital outlays, and then devote some portion of the remaining funds to advertising.

Unfortunately, this method of setting budgets completely ignores the effects of promotion on sales. It tends to place advertising last among spending priorities, even in situations in which advertising is critical to the firm's success. It leads to an uncertain annual promotion budget, which makes long-range market planning difficult. Although the affordable method can result in overspending on advertising, it more often results in underspending.

Percentage-of-Sales Method

Percentage-of-sales method
Setting the promotion budget at a certain percentage of current or forecasted sales or as a percentage of the unit sales price.

Other companies use the **percentage-of-sales method**, setting their promotion budget at a certain percentage of current or forecasted sales. Or they budget a percentage of the unit sales price. The percentage-of-sales method has advantages. It is simple to use and helps management think about the relationships between promotion spending, selling price, and profit per unit.

Despite these claimed advantages, however, the percentage-of-sales method has little to justify it. It wrongly views sales as the *cause* of promotion rather than as the *result*. Although studies have found a positive correlation between promotional spending and brand strength, this relationship often turns out to be effect and cause, not cause and effect. Stronger brands with higher sales can afford the biggest ad budgets.

Thus, the percentage-of-sales budget is based on availability of funds rather than on opportunities. It may prevent the increased spending sometimes needed to turn around falling sales. Because the budget varies with year-to-year sales, long-range planning is difficult. Finally, the method does not provide any basis for choosing a *specific* percentage, except what has been done in the past or what competitors are doing.

Competitive-Parity Method

Competitive-parity method
Setting the promotion budget to match competitors' outlays.

Still other companies use the **competitive-parity method**, setting their promotion budgets to match competitors' outlays. They monitor competitors' advertising or get industry promotion spending estimates from publications or trade associations, and then set their budgets based on the industry average.

Two arguments support this method. First, competitors' budgets represent the collective wisdom of the industry. Second, spending what competitors spend helps prevent promotion wars. Unfortunately, neither argument is valid. There are no grounds for believing that the competition has a better idea of what a company should be spending on promotion than does the company itself. Companies differ greatly, and each has its own special promotion needs. Finally, there is no evidence that budgets based on competitive parity prevent promotion wars.

Objective-and-Task Method

Objective-and-task method
Developing the promotion budget by (1) defining specific objectives; (2) determining the tasks that must be performed to achieve these objectives; and (3) estimating the costs of performing these tasks. The sum of these costs is the proposed promotion budget.

The most logical budget-setting method is the **objective-and-task method**, whereby the company sets its promotion budget based on what it wants to accomplish with promotion. This budgeting method entails (1) defining specific promotion objectives, (2) determining the tasks needed to achieve these objectives, and (3) estimating the costs of performing these tasks. The sum of these costs is the proposed promotion budget.

The advantage of the objective-and-task method is that it forces management to spell out its assumptions about the relationship between dollars spent and promotion results. But it is also the most difficult method to use. Often, it is hard to figure out which specific tasks will achieve stated objectives. For example, suppose Sony wants 95 percent awareness for its latest camcorder model during the 6-month introductory period. What specific advertising messages and media schedules should Sony use to attain this objective? How much would these messages and media schedules cost? Sony management must consider such questions, even though they are hard to answer.

Setting the Overall Communication Mix

The concept of integrated marketing communications suggests that the company must blend the promotion tools carefully into a coordinated *promotion mix*. But how does the company determine what mix of promotion tools it will use? Companies within the same industry differ greatly in the design of their promotion mixes. For example, Avon spends most of its promotion funds on personal selling and direct marketing, whereas Cover Girl spends heavily on consumer advertising. Hewlett-Packard relies on advertising and promotion to retailers, whereas Dell Computer uses only direct marketing. We now look at factors that influence the marketer's choice of promotion tools.

The Nature of Each Promotion Tool

Each promotion tool has unique characteristics and costs. Marketers must understand these characteristics in selecting their mix of tools.

■ Promotion mix: Companies within the same industry may use different mixes. Avon relies heavily on personal selling and direct marketing; Covergirl devotes significant resources to advertising.

ADVERTISING Advertising can reach masses of geographically dispersed buyers at a low cost per exposure, and it enables the seller to repeat a message many times. For example, television advertising can reach huge audiences. An estimated 143 million Americans tuned in to at least part of the most recent Super Bowl, more than 43 million people watched at least part of the last Academy Awards broadcast, and 51 million fans tuned in to watch the final episode of *Friends*. "If you want to get to the mass audience," says a media services executive, "broadcast TV is where you have to be." He adds, "For anybody introducing anything who has to lasso audience in a hurry—a new product, a new campaign, a new movie—the networks are still the biggest show in town." [12]

Beyond its reach, large-scale advertising says something positive about the seller's size, popularity, and success. Because of advertising's public nature, consumers tend to view advertised products as more legitimate. Advertising is also very expressive—it allows the company to dramatize its products through the artful use of visuals, print, sound, and color. On the one hand, advertising can be used to build up a long-term image for a product (such as Coca-Cola ads). On the other hand, advertising can trigger quick sales (as when Kohl's advertises its weekend specials).

Advertising also has some shortcomings. Although it reaches many people quickly, advertising is impersonal and cannot be as directly persuasive as can company salespeople. For the most part, advertising can carry on only a one-way communication with the audience, and the audience does not feel that it has to pay attention or respond. In addition, advertising can be very costly. Although some advertising forms, such as newspaper and radio advertising, can be done on smaller budgets, other forms, such as network TV advertising, require very large budgets.

PERSONAL SELLING Personal selling is the most effective tool at certain stages of the buying process, particularly in building up buyers' preferences, convictions, and actions. It involves personal interaction between two or more people, so each person can observe the other's needs and characteristics and make quick adjustments. Personal selling also allows all kinds of relationships to spring up, ranging from matter-of-fact selling relationships to personal friendships. The effective salesperson keeps the customer's interests at heart in order to build a long-term relationship. Finally, with personal selling, the buyer usually feels a greater need to listen and respond, even if the response is a polite "No thank you."

These unique qualities come at a cost, however. A sales force requires a longer-term commitment than does advertising—advertising can be turned on and off, but sales force size is harder to change. Personal selling is also the company's most expensive promotion tool, costing companies $170 on average per sales call. In some industries, the average cost of a sales call reaches $340. [13] U.S. firms spend up to three times as much on personal selling as they do on advertising.

SALES PROMOTION Sales promotion includes a wide assortment of tools—coupons, contests, cents-off deals, premiums, and others—all of which have many unique qualities. They attract consumer attention, offer strong incentives to purchase, and can be used to dramatize product offers and to boost sagging sales. Sales promotions invite and reward quick response—whereas advertising says, "Buy our product," sales promotion says, "Buy it now." Sales promotion effects are often short-lived, however, and often are not as effective as advertising or personal selling in building long-run brand preference.

PUBLIC RELATIONS Public relations is very believable—news stories, features, sponsorships, and events seem more real and believable to readers than ads do. Public relations can also reach many prospects who avoid salespeople and advertisements—the message gets to the buyers as "news" rather than as a sales-directed communication. And, as with advertising, public relations can dramatize a company or product. Marketers tend to underuse public relations or to use it as an afterthought. Yet a well-thought-out public relations campaign used with other promotion mix elements can be very effective and economical.

DIRECT MARKETING Although there are many forms of direct marketing—telephone marketing, direct mail, online marketing, and others—they all share four distinctive characteristics. Direct marketing is *nonpublic*: The message is normally directed to a specific person. Direct marketing is *immediate* and *customized*: Messages can be prepared very quickly and can be tailored to appeal to specific consumers. Finally, direct marketing is *interactive*: It allows a dialogue between the marketing team and the consumer, and messages can be altered depending on the consumer's response. Thus, direct marketing is well suited to highly targeted marketing efforts and to building one-to-one customer relationships.

Promotion Mix Strategies

Marketers can choose from two basic promotion mix strategies—*push* promotion or *pull* promotion. Figure 14.4 contrasts the two strategies. The relative emphasis on the specific promotion tools differs for push and pull strategies. A **push strategy** involves "pushing" the product through distribution channels to final consumers. The producer directs its marketing activities (primarily personal selling and trade promotion) toward channel members to induce them to carry the product and to promote it to final consumers.

Push strategy
A promotion strategy that calls for using the sales force and trade promotion to push the product through channels. The producer promotes the product to wholesalers, the wholesalers promote to retailers, and the retailers promote to consumers.

■ With personal selling, the customer feels a greater need to listen and respond, even if the response is a polite "No thank you."

FIGURE 14.4
Push versus pull promotion strategy

Pull strategy

A promotion strategy that calls for spending a lot on advertising and consumer promotion to build up consumer demand. If the strategy is successful, consumers will ask their retailers for the product, the retailers will ask the wholesalers, and the wholesalers will ask the producers.

Using a **pull strategy**, the producer directs its marketing activities (primarily advertising and consumer promotion) toward final consumers to induce them to buy the product. If the pull strategy is effective, consumers will then demand the product from channel members, who will in turn demand it from producers. Thus, under a pull strategy, consumer demand "pulls" the product through the channels.

Some industrial goods companies use only push strategies; some direct-marketing companies use only pull. However, most large companies use some combination of both. For example, Kraft uses mass-media advertising and consumer promotions to pull its products and a large sales force and trade promotions to push its products through the channels. In recent years, consumer goods companies have been decreasing the pull portions of their mixes in favor of more push. This has caused concern that they may be driving short-run sales at the expense of long-term brand equity (see Real Marketing 14.2).

Companies consider many factors when designing their promotion mix strategies, including *type of product/market* and the *product life-cycle stage*. For example, the importance of different promotion tools varies between consumer and business markets. Business-to-consumer (B2C) companies usually "pull" more, putting more of their funds into advertising, followed by sales promotion, personal selling, and then public relations. In contrast, business-to-business (B2B) marketers tend to "push" more, putting more of their funds into personal selling, followed by sales promotion, advertising, and public relations. In general, personal selling is used more heavily with expensive and risky goods and in markets with fewer and larger sellers.

The effects of different promotion tools also vary with stages of the product life cycle. In the introduction stage, advertising and public relations are good for producing high awareness, and sales promotion is useful in promoting early trial. Personal selling must be used to get the trade to carry the product. In the growth stage, advertising and public relations continue to be powerful influences, whereas sales promotion can be reduced because fewer incentives are needed. In the mature stage, sales promotion again becomes important relative to advertising. Buyers know the brands, and advertising is needed only to remind them of the product. In the decline stage, advertising is kept at a reminder level, public relations is dropped, and salespeople give the product only a little attention. Sales promotion, however, might continue strong.

Integrating the Promotion Mix

Having set the promotion budget and mix, the company must now take steps to see that all of the promotion mix elements are smoothly integrated. Here is a checklist for integrating the firm's marketing communications.[14]

- *Analyze trends—internal and external—that can affect the company's ability to do business.* Look for areas where communications can help the most. Determine the strengths and weaknesses of each communications function. Develop a combination of promotional tactics based on these strengths and weaknesses.

Real Marketing 14.2

Are Consumer Goods Companies Getting Too Pushy?

Consumer packaged-goods companies such as Kraft, Procter & Gamble, Kellogg, General Mills, and Gillette grew into giants by using mostly pull promotion strategies. They used massive doses of national advertising to differentiate their products, gain market share, and build brand equity and customer loyalty. But during the past few decades, these companies have gotten more "pushy," deemphasizing national advertising and putting more of their marketing budgets into trade and consumer sales promotions.

General trade promotions (trade allowances, displays, cooperative advertising, slotting fees) now account for 49 percent of total marketing spending by consumer product companies. Another 10 percent of the marketing budget goes to the trade in the form of "account-specific" marketing expenditures—promotional spending personalized to the local needs of a specific retail chain that backs both the brand and the retailer. The total of 59 percent represents a 7-percentage-point increase in trade spending in just the past 5 years. Consumer promotions (coupons, cents-off deals, premiums) account for another 17 percent of the typical marketing budget. That leaves less than 24 percent of total marketing spending for mass-media advertising, down from 42 percent 20 years ago.

Why have these companies shifted so heavily toward push strategies? One reason is that mass-media campaigns have become more expensive and less effective in recent years. Network television costs have risen sharply while audiences have fallen off, making national advertising less cost-effective. Companies have also increased their market segmentation efforts and are now tailoring their marketing programs more narrowly, making national advertising less suitable than localized retailer promotions. And in these days of brand extensions and me-too products, companies sometimes have trouble finding meaningful product differences to feature in advertising. So they have differentiated their products through price reductions, premium offers, coupons, and other push techniques.

Another factor speeding the shift from pull to push has been the growing strength of retailers. Retail giants such as Wal-Mart, Kroger, Safeway, and A&P, now have the power to demand and get what they want—and what they want is more push. Whereas national advertising bypasses them on its way to the masses, push promotion benefits them directly. Consumer promotions give retailers an immediate sales boost, and cash from trade allowances and other trade promotions pads retailer profits. Thus, producers must often use push just to obtain good shelf space and other support from important retailers.

However, many marketers are concerned that the reckless use of push will lead to fierce price competition and a never-ending spiral of price slashing and deal making. If used improperly, push promotion can mortgage a brand's future for short-term gains. Sales promotion buys short-run reseller support and consumer sales, but advertising builds long-run brand equity and consumer preference. By robbing the media advertising budget to pay for more sales promotion, companies might win the battle for short-run earnings but lose the war for long-run brand equity, consumer loyalty, and market share. In fact, some analysts blame the shift away from advertising

■ Today's food marketers are using more and more push promotion, including consumer price promotions. But they must be careful that they don't win the battle for short-run sales at the expense of long-run brand equity.

dollars for a recent two-decade long drop in the percentage of consumers who buy only well-known brands.

Of special concern is the overuse of price promotions. The regular use of price as a selling tool can destroy brand equity by encouraging consumers to seek value though price rather than through the benefits of the brand. Many marketers are too quick to drive short-term sales by reducing prices rather than building long-term build brand equity through advertising. In fact, studies show that almost 60 percent of consumers now go to the store to make a purchase without a specific brand in mind. Once they get to the store, shoppers are often more swayed by special prices, sales, and coupons than by brand.

In cases where price is a key part of the brand's positioning, featuring price makes sense. But for brands where price does not underlie value, "price promotions are really desperate acts by brands that have their backs against the wall," says one marketing executive. "Generally speaking, it is better to stick to your guns with price and invest in advertising to drive sales."

Jack Trout, a well-known marketing consultant, cautions that some categories tend to self-destruct by always being on sale. Discount pricing has become routine for a surprising number of companies. Furniture, automobile tires, and many other categories of goods are rarely sold at anything near list price, and when automakers get rebate happy, the market just sits back and waits for a deal. Even Coca-Cola and Pepsi, two of the world's most popular brands, engage in regular price wars that ultimately tarnish their brand equity. Trout offers several "Commandments of Discounting," such as

(box continues)

"Thou shalt not offer discounts because everyone else does," "Thou shalt be creative with your discounting," "Thou shalt put time limits on the deal," and "Thou shalt stop discounting as soon as you can."

Many consumer companies now are rethinking their promotion strategies and reversing the trend by shifting their promotion budgets back toward advertising. They have realized that it's not a question of sales promotion versus advertising, or of push versus pull. Success lies in finding the best mix of the two: consistent advertising to build long-run brand value and consumer preference, and sales promotion to create short-run trade support and consumer excitement. The company needs to blend both push and pull elements into an integrated promotion program that meets immediate consumer and retailer needs as well as long-run strategic needs.

Sources: Promotion spending statistics from *2002 Trade Promotion Spending & Merchandising Industry Study* (Cannondale Associates, Wilton, CT, May 2002), p. 13; and *Trade Promotion Spending & Merchandising 2003 Industry Study* (Wilton, CT: Cannondale Associates, 2003), p. 7. Other information from Jack Trout, "Prices: Simple Guidelines to Get Them Right," *Journal of Business Strategy*, November–December 1998, pp. 13–16; Tim Ambler, "Kicking Price Promotion Habit Is Like Getting Off Heroin—Hard," *Marketing*, May 27, 1999, p. 24; Alan Mitchell, "When Push Comes to Shove, It's All About Pull," *Marketing Week*, January 9, 2003, pp. 26–27; "Promotions and Incentives: Offers You Can't Refuse," *Marketing Week,* April 15, 2004, p. 31; and E. Craig Stacey, "Abandon TV at Your Own Risk," *Advertising Age*, June 7, 2004, p. 32.

- *Audit the pockets of communications spending throughout the organization.* Itemize the communications budgets and tasks and consolidate these into a single budgeting process. Reassess all communications expenditures by product, promotional tool, stage of the life cycle, and observed effect.

- *Identify all contact points for the company and its brands.* Work to ensure that communications at each point are consistent with the overall communications strategy and that communications efforts are occurring when, where, and how *customers* want them.

- *Team up in communications planning.* Engage all communications functions in joint planning. Include customers, suppliers, and other stakeholders at every stage of communications planning.

- *Create compatible themes, tones, and quality across all communications media.* Make sure each element carries the company's unique primary messages and selling points. This consistency achieves greater impact and prevents the unnecessary duplication of work across functions.

- *Create performance measures that are shared by all communications elements.* Develop systems to evaluate the combined impact of all communications activities.

- *Appoint a director responsible for the company's persuasive communications efforts.* This move encourages efficiency by centralizing planning and creating shared performance measures.

Socially Responsible Marketing Communication

In shaping its promotion mix, a company must be aware of the large body of legal and ethical issues surrounding marketing communications. Most marketers work hard to communicate openly and honestly with consumers and resellers. Still, abuses may occur, and public policy makers have developed a substantial body of laws and regulations to govern advertising, sales promotion, personal selling, and direct-marketing activities. In this section, we discuss issues regarding advertising, sales promotion, and personal selling. Issues regarding direct marketing are addressed in Chapter 16.

Advertising and Sales Promotion

By law, companies must avoid false or deceptive advertising. Advertisers must not make false claims, such as suggesting that a product cures something when it does not. They must avoid ads that have the capacity to deceive, even though no one actually may be deceived. An automobile cannot be advertised as getting 32 miles per gallon unless it does so under typical conditions, and a diet bread cannot be advertised as having fewer calories simply because its slices are thinner.

Sellers must avoid bait-and-switch advertising that attracts buyers under false pretenses. For example, a large retailer advertised a sewing machine at $179. However, when consumers tried to buy the advertised machine, the seller downplayed its features, placed faulty machines on showroom floors, understated the machine's performance, and took other actions in an attempt to switch buyers to a more expensive machine. Such actions are both unethical and illegal.

A company's trade promotion activities also are closely regulated. For example, under the Robinson-Patman Act, sellers cannot favor certain customers through their use of trade promotions. They must make promotional allowances and services available to all resellers on proportionately equal terms.

Beyond simply avoiding legal pitfalls, such as deceptive or bait-and-switch advertising, companies can use advertising and other forms of promotion to encourage and promote socially responsible programs and actions. For example, Caterpillar is one of several companies and environmental groups forming the Tropical Forest Foundation, which is working to save the great Amazon rain forest. It uses advertising to promote the cause and its involvement. Similarly, State Farm supports the National Service-Learning Partnership in its efforts to integrate community-service projects into local school curriculums. It's ads state: "When you're learning about life, the world is your classroom." And for more than a decade, Avon has sponsored the Avon Breast Cancer Crusade, dedicated to funding access to care and finding a cure for breast cancer. Through advertising and though a variety of promotions—such as the Avon Walk for Breast Cancer, charity cruises, the sale of pink ribbon products—Avon's crusade has raised more the $300 million for this worthwhile cause.[15]

Personal Selling

A company's salespeople must follow the rules of "fair competition." Most states have enacted deceptive sales acts that spell out what is not allowed. For example, salespeople may not lie to consumers or mislead them about the advantages of buying a product. To avoid bait-and-switch practices, salespeople's statements must match advertising claims.

■ State Farm uses ads like this one to support the National Service-Learning Partnership: "When you're learning about life, the world is your classroom."

Different rules apply to consumers who are called on at home versus those who go to a store in search of a product. Because people called on at home may be taken by surprise and may be especially vulnerable to high-pressure selling techniques, the Federal Trade Commission (FTC) has adopted a *three-day cooling-off rule* to give special protection to customers who are not seeking products. Under this rule, customers who agree in their own homes to buy something costing more than $25 have 72 hours in which to cancel a contract or return merchandise and get their money back, no questions asked.

Much personal selling involves B2B trade. In selling to businesses, salespeople may not offer bribes to purchasing agents or to others who can influence a sale. They may not obtain or use technical or trade secrets of competitors through bribery or industrial espionage. Finally, salespeople must not disparage competitors or competing products by suggesting things that are not true.[16]

> Reviewing the Concepts <

Modern marketing calls for more than just developing a good product, pricing it attractively, and making it available to target customers. Companies also must *communicate* with current and prospective customers, and what they communicate should not be left to chance.

1. Name and define the tools of the marketing communications mix.

A company's total *marketing communications mix*—also called its *promotion mix*—consists of the specific blend of *advertising, personal selling, sales promotion, public relations,* and *direct-marketing* tools that the company uses to pursue its advertising and marketing objectives. Advertising includes any paid form of nonpersonal presentation and promotion of ideas, goods, or services by an identified sponsor. Personal selling is any form of personal presentation by the firm's sales force for the purpose of making sales and building customer relationships. Firms use sales promotion to provide short-term incentives to encourage the purchase or sale of a product or service. Public relations focuses on building good relations with the company's various publics by obtaining favorable publicity. Finally, firms seeking immediate response from targeted individual customers use nonpersonal direct-marketing tools to communicate with customers.

2. Discuss the process and advantages of integrated marketing communications.

Recent shifts in marketing strategy from mass marketing to targeted or one-to-one marketing, coupled with advances in information technology, have had a dramatic impact on marketing communications. Although still important, the mass media are giving way to a profusion of smaller, more focused media. Companies are doing less *broadcasting* and more *narrowcasting*. As marketing communicators adopt richer but more fragmented media and promotion mixes to reach their diverse markets, they risk creating a communications hodgepodge for consumers. To prevent this, more companies are adopting the concept of *integrated marketing communications*, which calls for carefully integrating all sources of company communication to deliver a clear and consistent message to target markets.

To integrate its external communications effectively, the company must first integrate its internal communications activities. The company then works out the roles that the various promotional tools will play and the extent to which each will be used. It carefully coordinates the promotional activities and the timing of when major campaigns take place. Finally, to help implement its integrated marketing strategy, the company appoints a marketing communications director who has overall responsibility for the company's communications efforts.

3. Outline the steps in developing effective marketing communications.

In preparing marketing communications, the communicator's first task is to *identify the target audience* and its characteristics. Next, the communicator has to determine the *communication objectives* and define the response sought, whether it be *awareness, knowledge, liking, preference, conviction,* or *purchase*. Then a *message* should be constructed with an effective content and structure. *Media* must be selected, both for personal and nonpersonal communication. The communicator must find highly credible sources to deliver messages. Finally, the communicator must collect *feedback* by watching how much of the market becomes aware, tries the product, and is satisfied in the process.

4. Explain the methods for setting the promotion budget and factors that affect the design of the promotion mix.

The company has to decide how much to spend for promotion. The most popular approaches are to spend what the company can afford, to use a percentage of sales, to base promotion on competitors' spending, or to base it on an analysis and costing of the communication objectives and tasks.

The company has to divide the *promotion budget* among the major tools to create the *promotion mix*. Companies can pursue a *push* or a *pull* promotional strategy, or a combination of the two. The best specific blend of promotion tools depends on the type of product/market, the buyer's readiness stage, and the product life-cycle stage.

People at all levels of the organization must be aware of the many legal and ethical issues surrounding marketing communications. Companies must work hard and proactively at communicating openly, honestly, and agreeably with their customers and resellers.

> Reviewing the Key Terms <

Advertising 427
Affordable method 440
Buzz marketing 437
Buyer-readiness stages 432
Competitive-parity method 441
Direct marketing 427

Integrated marketing
communications (IMC) 430
Marketing communications mix
(promotion mix) 427
Nonpersonal communication
channels 437

Objective-and-task method 441
Percentage-of-sales method 441
Personal communication
channels 437
Personal selling 427
Public relations 427

Pull strategy 444
Push strategy 443
Sales promotion 427
Word-of-mouth influence 437

> Discussing the Concepts <

1. Many companies are adopting the integrated marketing communication concept. Discuss two major problems that this marketing communications philosophy is designed to remedy.

2. Why does the marketing communicator need to know the target market's readiness stage? Give an example of an ad targeting each stage.

3. Compare and contrast personal and nonpersonal communication channels.

4. What is the major advantage of the objective-and-task method for setting the promotional budget? What is the major drawback?

5. Suppose you are an advertising coordinator and your boss asks you to recommend a message appeal for the next series of print ads for a new scanner software product directed at small clothing retailers. What would you recommendation? Explain.

6. Name at least five types of sales that are exempt from the FTC's three-day-cooling-off rule.

> Applying the Concepts <

1. In your judgment who would be the best and the worst celebrity endorser for each of these products/services:

   - MADD
   - Dell
   - Internal Revenue Service
   - Weight Watchers
   - Lamborghini
   - Microsoft
   - Cosmopolitan
   - Lego
   - Reddi-Wip
   - Norwegian Cruise Lines

2. In a small group, prepare a chart comparing the five promotion mix tools on five different characteristics.

3. Outline a domestic U.S. promotion mix strategy for sports apparel manufacturer Quicksilver (www.quiksilver.com/?pageID=10). Include both push and pull promotion mix strategies.

> Focus on Technology <

Once you have identified the target audience, determined the communication objective, designed a message, chosen media, set the budget, established the overall communication mix, and checked to see if the promotional mix is integrated properly with other marketing communication efforts, it's time to put it all into a written document. Fortunately, some software tools exist to help you with this task. Advertising Plan Pro is one such software tool. It guides you through the creation of a comprehensive integrated marketing communications document, from strategy to implementation and evaluation. First, go to www.paloalto.com/ps/ap/index.cfm and tour the application. Next go to www.paloalto.com/sampleplans/protected/app4/boulderstop-app.pdf, download a free sample of a complete advertising plan, and review it. Now, respond to the following.

1. Assess Advertising Plan Pro as a tool for communications professionals.

2. Does the Advertising Plan Pro tool do all of the work for an advertiser? Explain.

3. Is this a tool designed only for large companies?

> Focus on Ethics <

Is it puffery or is it deceptive advertising? This is a question many communication professionals can't answer. Advertising puffery is legal but deceptive advertising isn't. So how do you tell the difference? Fortunately, the Federal Trade Commission (FTC), the agency most responsible for consumer protection, has established standards. The FTC says an advertising claim is puffery if (1) reasonable people do not believe it to be true, and (2) it can be proved either true or false. The FTC says an ad is deceptive if: (1) there is a representation, omission, act, or practice that (2) is likely to mislead consumers acting reasonably under the circumstances, and that (3) the representation, omission, or practice is material. Still not clear? Some practice may help. Read the advertising claims below and state whether they are most likely deceptive or just plain puffery. Explain your reasoning.

- There's a smile in every Hershey bar.
- I lost 95 pounds in just over 6 months. And I've kept the weight off for nearly 1 year!
- 93 percent Fat Free Frozen Dessert with chocolate flavored coating

Sources: http://advertising.utexas.edu/research/law/;
www.adlawbyrequest.com/; and www.ftc.gov.

Video Case

Dunkin' Donuts

Its restaurants seem so commonplace today that it may be difficult to imagine a time when Dunkin' Donuts wasn't a national icon. More than 50 years ago, the chain opened its first store. Five years later, the first franchise opened. Now the largest coffee and doughnut chain in the world, Dunkin' Donuts serves more than two million customers each day at more than 5,500 restaurants in the United States and abroad. Why the success? According to Dunkin' Donuts, it's all in the details. Dunkin' Donuts offers a consistent experience—the same donuts, the same coffee, the same store décor—each time a customer drops in.

Along with providing a consistent product and experience, Dunkin' Donuts marketers work to deliver a consistent marketing message to current and potential customers. But communicating the details of the Dunkin' Donuts experience to so many potential customers is a challenge. So, everything from print ads and television commercials to the company's

Web site to the in-store experience work together to engage customers and keep them coming back.

After viewing the video featuring Dunkin' Donuts, answer the following questions about integrated marketing communications.

1. How does Dunkin' Donuts insure that consumers have a consistent experience in restaurants across the country and the world?

2. Based on your experience and the information presented in the video, which communications tools does Dunkin' Donuts use to reach consumers? Do the tools, together, consistently communicate Dunkin' Donuts product mix and benefits?

3. Visit Dunkin' Donuts Web site (www.dunkindonuts.com). Are the messages and images there consistent with your impressions of Dunkin' Donuts? How do they differ?

Company Case

Burger King: Promoting a Food Fight

PASS THE MUSTARD

In early 2004, as Burger King's CEO Brad Blum reviewed the company's 2003 performance, he decided once again that he had to do something to spice up BK's bland performance. Industry leader McDonald's had just reported a 9 percent sales jump in 2003 to a total of $22.1 billion, while number-two BK's U.S. sales had slipped about five percent to $7.9 billion. Further, number-three Wendy's sales had spiked 11 percent to $7.4 billion, putting it in position to overtake BK.

Blum surprised the fast-food industry by abruptly firing the firm's advertising agency, Young & Rubicam (Y&R), and awarding its global creative account to a small, Miami-based, upstart firm Crispin Porter + Bogusky (CBP). The switch marked the fifth time in four years that BK had moved its account!

Ad agency Y&R had gotten the $350 million BK account only 10 months earlier. To help revive BK's sales, it had developed a campaign with the theme "The Fire's Ready," which focused on BK's flame-broiled versus frying cooking method. However, observers found the message to be flat and uninspiring, and the sales decline sealed Y&R's fate.

CHALLENGING CONVENTIONAL WISDOM

In announcing the CPB selection, Blum indicated he had challenged the firm to develop "groundbreaking, next-level, results-oriented, and innovative advertising that strongly connects with our core customers." BK automatically became the small firm's largest customer, but CPB was not without an impressive track record.

Chuck Porter joined Crispin Advertising in 1988. A middle-aged windsurfer, he wanted to be near the water. Alex Bogusky joined the firm later as a 24-year-old art director who raced motorbikes. The Porter-Bogusky combination

clicked, and CPB racked up local awards for its ad campaigns. A Sunglass Hut billboard featured a huge pair of sunglasses with the headline "What to Wear to a Nude Beach." Because its clients often had little money for advertising, CPB found inexpensive ways to gain attention. For a local homeless shelter, it placed ads on shopping carts, trash dumpsters, and park benches.

In 1997, with Bogusky serving as creative director, CPB finally got national attention with its "Truth" campaign aimed at convincing Florida teens to stop smoking. CPB started with street-level research, actually talking to teens in order to "get inside their heads." CPB found that cigarettes allowed teens to establish identities, associate with brand names, and take risks. To counter this, CPB created the "Truth" logo and turned it into a brand. It plastered the logo on everything from posters to t-shirts, developed a "Truth" Web site, and staged impromptu live "Truth" parties around the state. Between 1998 and 2002, teenage smoking in Florida declined 38 percent. The American Legacy Foundation picked up the "Truth" campaign and turned it into a national promotion, leading to a big-budget ad at the Super Bowl—the "Shards O'Glass Freeze Pop."

CPB followed with an award-winning, low-budget campaign for the BMW Mini Cooper auto. It decided to violate conventional wisdom and launch the U.S. campaign without TV advertising. It placed the Minis inside sports stadiums as seats and on top of SUVs driving around town. It got the car included in centerfold pictures in *Playboy* and in movies like "The Italian Job." It also created street props such as a coin-operated children's ride as well as Mini games, Mini booklets, and Mini suitcases. When BMW finally introduced the Mini in spring 2002, the waiting list was six months long.

Similar success with IKEA furniture and Virgin Atlantic Airways forged CPB's reputation as an out-of-the-box, results-oriented agency. Along the way, it developed some loose "rules." Among them were: zero in on the product, kick the TV commercial habit, find the sweet spot (the overlap between product characteristics and customer needs), surprise = buzz = exposure, don't be timid, and think of advertising as a product rather than a service.

BACK TO THE FUTURE

Within a month of getting BK's account, rather than recommending some kinky new idea, CPB recommended going back to the firm's "Have It Your Way" tagline, developed by BK's second advertising agency, BBDO, in 1974. CPB argued that it could take that old phrase and make it relevant to today's customers.

Uncharacteristically, CBP kicked of the new campaign with TV commercials that were a takeoff on a British comedy series, "The Office." In a series of off-beat office workers compete and compare their "made my way" BK burgers, reinforcing the message that each customer can have a burger just as he or she wants it—no matter how unusual that might be. CPB planned an entire package of promotions around the new-old theme, including everything from in-store signage to messages on cups.

Then, however, the real CPB approach emerged. To promote BK's TenderCrisp chicken, CPB launched a Web site, www.subservientchicken.com. When people visited the site, they saw what appeared to be a Web camera focused on a somewhat seedy living room. In the room was a man dressed like a chicken (except for the lady's garter belt he is wearing). The site invited the visitor to "Get chicken just the way you like it. Type in your command here." The visitor could type in a command, such as "stand on your head" or "do jumping jacks" and the chicken would respond. If someone typed in a risqué request, the chicken would wave a wing at the camera, as if to say "no-no."

Below the chicken video area were five other icons. "Subservient TV" featured three video clips with various people "having their way" with the chicken. "Photos" presented five "glamour" shots of the chicken. The "Chicken Mask" icon produced a printable chicken mask that one could print, cut out, and wear. The mask's instructions were to "cut along dotted line, put on chicken face, be subservient." A fourth icon, "Tell a friend," pulled up an Outlook Express email document that invited you to send an email to a friend with the text: "Finally, somebody in a chicken costume who will do whatever you want. Check it

out. www.subservientchicken.com." Finally, an icon marked "BK Tendercrisp" took the visitor to the Burger King home page. This was the only indication of BK's sponsorship on the site, reflecting CPB's desire to avoid seeming too commercial and "uncool." Unless a visitor clicked on that last icon, he or she would have no indication that the site had anything to do with Burger King.

When CPB launched the site, it told only 20 people—all of whom were friends of people who worked at the agency. Within the first 10 *days*, 20 million people visited the site, with the average visitor spending over seven minutes. Many visitors apparently selected the "tell a friend" icon, sending emails flying like feathers.

FOOD FOR THOUGHT

CPB clearly demonstrated with the subservient chicken that it was a master at viral marketing—using unusual methods to get attention and generate buzz and word-of-mouth. Despite its success, however, many analysts wonder if the campaign will produce increased sales for BK.

Further, what new feather-brained promotional ideas will CPB conceive in its campaign to keep BK going strong in the fast-food fights?

Questions for Discussion

1. Who is BK's target audience and what are its communication objectives for that audience?

2. Why is viral or buzz marketing effective? Analyze the design of the subservient chicken site's message, including content, structure, and format. What can you conclude from this analysis?

3. Do the TV and viral elements of the Burger King campaign work well together? What additional elements and media might CPB add to the integrated marketing communications campaign?

4. What other recommendations would you make to Burger King and CPB to help them improve the integration of BK's promotion mix?

Sources: Bob Garfield, "Garfield's Ad Review," *Advertising* Age, April 26, 2004, p. 103; Catharine P. Taylor, "Playing Chicken," Adweek, April 19, 2004, p. 19; Brian Steinberg and Suzanne Vranica, "Burger King Seeks Some Web Heat," *The Wall Street Journal*, April 15, 2004, p. B3; Warren Berger, "Dare-Devils: The Ad World's Most Buzzed-About Agency is Miami's Crispin Porter & Bogusky," *Business 2.0*, April 2004, p. 110; Kate McArthur, "Burger King's Big Idea: Have It Your Way, Again," *Advertising Age*, February 16, 2004, p. 1.

> After reading this chapter, you
should be able to

1. define the roles of advertising, sales
promotion, and public relations in the
promotion mix
2. describe the major decisions involved in
developing an advertising program
3. explain how sales-promotion campaigns
are developed and implemented
4. explain how companies use public
relations to communicate with their
publics

CHAPTER

15

Advertising, Sales Promotion, and Public Relations

Previewing the Concepts

Now that we've looked at overall integrated marketing communications planning, let's dig more deeply into the specific marketing communications tools. In this chapter, we'll explore the mass-communications tools—advertising, sales promotion, and public relations.

At the start of the previous chapter, we examined the highly successful integrated marketing campaign for the BMW's British-made MINI automobile. To start this chapter, let's look behind the scenes at the award-winning advertising agency that created the MINI campaign—Crispin Porter + Bogusky (CP+B). As it turns out, CP+B's success reflects all the current trends in the fast-changing world of modern advertising. As one advertising insider puts it: "CP+B is right where it's at in today's advertising."

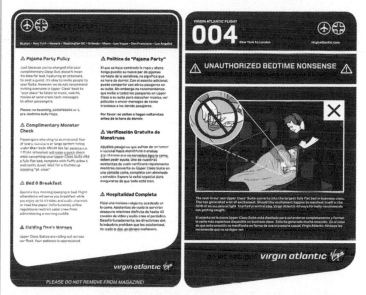

nside its sparkling steel-and-granite Miami headquarters, ad agency Crispin Porter + Bogusky (CP+B) was unveiling pieces of the campaign for new client Virgin Atlantic Airways. At presentations like this, agency executives typically hold up TV commercial storyboards and explain why everyone is going to love this particular dancing cat or flatulent horse. This morning, however, the presenters from CP+B—led by a pregnant woman, a young dude with a flop of unruly blond curls, and a guy with Elvis sideburns—had no TV storyboards. But they sure had a lot of other stuff, and it came flying from all sides at the three Virgin clients.

There were ads designed to look like those flight safety cards found in airplane seat backs. There were samples of a newspaper comic strip called "The Jet Set," as well as a mock-up for a lifestyle magazine titled *Jetrosexual*. Both played off the Virgin campaign's theme, "Go Jet Set, Go!" There was something titled *Night-Night Jet Set, Night-Night* that resembled an illustrated children's book, though it actually contained bedtime ditties for adult busi-

ness flyers—something that flight attendants would leave on pillows in Virgin's sleeping cabins.

And speaking of those flight attendants? CP+B wouldn't mind hiring a high-fashion designer to spruce up the uniforms. And how about staging "concert flights"? And wouldn't it be cool to hire celebrities to work as "guest flight attendants"? And by the way, could the pilots fly at a higher altitude so Virgin can claim it soars above the competition? And there's one more thing—well, no, actually there were 160 more, because that was how many far-flung ideas CP+B had come up with since starting work on the campaign.

Welcome to advertising as practiced by Crispin Porter + Bogusky, the agency of the moment. CP+B is as hot as South Beach on a Saturday night, and it's at the epicenter of all that's current in today's advertising world. The agency has snapped up every top advertising creative award lately while reeling in prime accounts including MINI cars, Ikea furniture stores, Virgin Atlantic Airways, Molson beer, and most recently Burger King—a $300 million-plus account.

Working with modest ad budgets, CP+B has riveted customers' attention with startling guerrilla tactics, unconventional uses of media, and holistic marketing strategies that tie together everything from product design to packaging to event marketing to stuff that can't even be categorized. "Anything and everything is an ad," preaches CP+B's 40-year-old creative director, Alex Bogusky. What the agency uses sparingly, however, is the traditional TV commercial. This is very close to heresy in a business that grew fat on those million-dollar 30-second spots. There's no good buzzword for what CP+B does (the term "integrated marketing communication" comes closest), but here are some appropriate adjectives: fresh, radical, street-smart, mischievous, all-over-the-lot, maybe-the-next-big-thing. In other words, it's extreme, dude.

Crispin Porter + Bogusky's Coconut Grove offices are far removed from mainstream Madison Avenue. Being far away from big agencies and big media has allowed CP+B to evolve as an independent species. "They're not breathing the same air as everybody else in advertising," observes the creative director of a competing New York agency. "Instead of being surrounded by ad people, they're surrounded by artists, music people, and the whole Cuban/Latin/European/gay/South Beach culture." Alex Bogusky is a homegrown product of that culture, and he looks it. He wears loose polo shirts over athletic shoulders, with long hair coming out from under a skullcap. He has an easy smile, calls people "bud," and politely asks if you "need a pee-pee break." But beneath Bogusky's sunny demeanor, "Alex plays advertising like an extreme sport," says a former creative director. "He is fearless."

During the early 1990s, CP+B produced ads that swept local award shows. Locals still admiringly recall a Sunglass Hut billboard featuring a gigantic pair of shades and the headline "What to Wear to a Nude Beach." To promote a local homeless shelter, CP+B put ads in the darndest places: on shopping carts, trash dumpsters, park benches. The agency's reputation grew, and in 1997 CP+B finally got hold of a project that could draw national attention—the Florida teen antismoking campaign "Truth."

Through street-level research with local teenagers, CP+B learned that conventional antismoking appeals—"This will kill you"—made rebellious kids want to smoke even more. So instead of using conventional marketing, such as slick TV commercials, CP+B used guerrilla-ambush tactics to create an "anti-brand" that kids could latch on to. Bogusky named the brand "Truth." The agency scattered the "Truth" logo across Florida on posters, leaflets, T-shirts, stickers, and other gear. It rented trucks and trains to traverse the state, staging impromptu live events and parties where "Truth" swag was disseminated. The "Truth" Web site served as information central for the whole campaign.

The "Truth" campaign worked: Between 1998 and 2002, smoking among middle and high school students in Florida declined an average of 38 percent. The American Legacy Foundation eventually took the "Truth" campaign national, complete with big-budget Super Bowl commercials. But the beauty of "Truth" was its grassroots origin—which showed that CP+B could build a popular movement around an unknown brand, using any and all available means. "Truth" begat the celebrated MINI campaign, and suddenly everyone—from Ikea, Molson, and Virgin Atlantic to big old Burger King—wanted a piece of CP+B.

How does CP+B do it? For starters, the agency swings for the fences on each new brand assignment, going beyond cute slogans to try to start a consumer movement behind the brand. "Truth" was a mobilizing idea, as were "motoring" in a MINI and joining "the jet set" on Virgin. Once a central theme is in place, the ad making begins—and this is where CP+B really turns the process upside down. Most copywriters and art directors instinctively start by sketching ideas for print ads and TV commercials. But CP+B begins with a blank slate. "What if there were no TV and no magazines—how would we make this brand famous?" Bogusky demands. The goal is to figure out the best places to reach the target audience and the most interesting vehicles to carry the message, even if those vehicles have to be invented. For Molson, the agency wanted to trigger conversation among men in bars. CP+B did it by stamping individualized barroom pickup lines on the labels of the beer bottles; each label became a new kind of billboard.

This leads to another CP+B difference: The agency often sticks its nose into things unrelated to advertising. Molson, for example, had to revamp its bottling process to accommodate those custom labels. Similarly, the agency persuaded MINI to rewrite its lease agreement to match the tone of the overall MINI campaign. What does CP+B know about car leases? "Nothing," Bogusky admits, but that doesn't stop him from trying to ensure that every consumer "touchpoint" conveys the same message as the ad campaign.

Although unconventional, Crispin Porter + Bogusky just keeps winning awards, including top honors at last year's International Advertising Festival. The industry's titans are watching CP+B closely. "They've turned guerrilla into an art form, and it's working," admits one of advertising's most revered creative stars, Dan Wieden of ad agency Wieden & Kennedy. "Did I mention I hate them?"[1]

Companies must do more than make good products—they must inform consumers about product benefits and carefully position products in consumers' minds. To do this, they must skillfully use the mass-promotion tools of *advertising*, *sales promotion*, and *public relations*. In this chapter, we take a closer look at each of these tools.

Advertising | START HERE

Advertising
Any paid form of nonpersonal presentation and promotion of ideas, goods, or services by an identified sponsor.

Advertising can be traced back to the very beginnings of recorded history. Archaeologists working in the countries around the Mediterranean Sea have dug up signs announcing various events and offers. The Romans painted walls to announce gladiator fights, and the Phoenicians painted pictures promoting their wares on large rocks along parade routes. Modern advertising, however, is a far cry from these early efforts. U.S. advertisers now run up an estimated annual advertising bill of more than $245 billion; worldwide ad spending approaches an estimated $498 billion. General Motors, the nation's largest advertiser, last year spent more than $3.4 billion on U.S. advertising.[2]

Although advertising is used mostly by business firms, it also is used by a wide range of not-for-profit organizations, professionals, and social agencies that advertise their causes to various target publics. In fact, the twenty-eighth largest advertising spender is a not-for-profit organization—the U.S. government. Advertising is a good way to inform and persuade, whether the purpose is to sell Coca-Cola worldwide or to get consumers in a developing nation to use birth control.

Marketing management must make four important decisions when developing an advertising program (see Figure 15.1): *setting advertising objectives, setting the advertising budget, developing advertising strategy* (*message decisions* and *media decisions*), and *evaluating advertising campaigns*.

Setting Advertising Objectives

The first step is to set *advertising objectives*. These objectives should be based on past decisions about the target market, positioning, and marketing mix, which define the job that advertising must do in the total marketing program.

Advertising objective
A specific communication *task* to be accomplished with a specific *target* audience during a specific period of *time*.

An **advertising objective** is a specific communication *task* to be accomplished with a specific *target* audience during a specific period of *time*. Advertising objectives can be classified by primary purpose—whether the aim is to *inform*, *persuade*, or *remind*. Table 15.1 lists examples of each of these objectives.

Informative advertising is used heavily when introducing a new product category. In this case, the objective is to build primary demand. Thus, early producers of DVD players first had to inform consumers of the image quality and convenience benefits of the new product. *Persuasive advertising* becomes more important as competition increases. Here, the company's objective is to build selective demand. For example, once DVD players became established, Sony began trying to persuade consumers that *its* brand offered the best quality for their money.

FIGURE 15.1
Major advertising decisions

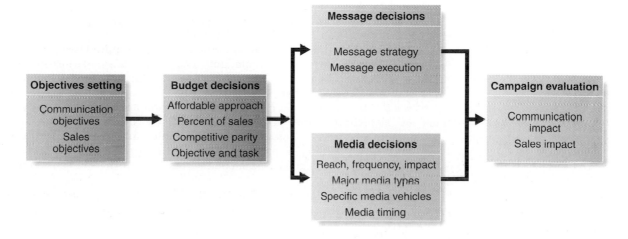

TABLE 15.1   Possible Advertising Objectives

Informative Advertising	
Telling the market about a new product	Describing available services
Suggesting new uses for a product	Correcting false impressions
Informing the market of a price change	Reducing consumers' fears
Explaining how the product works	Building a company image

Persuasive Advertising	
Building brand preference	Persuading customer to purchase now
Encouraging switching to your brand	Persuading customer to receive a sales call
Changing customer's perception of product attributes	

Reminder Advertising	
Reminding consumer that the product may be needed in the near future	Keeping it in customer's mind during off-seasons
Reminding consumer where to buy it	Maintaining its top-of-mind awareness

Some persuasive advertising has become *comparative advertising,* in which a company directly or indirectly compares its brand with one or more other brands. Comparative advertising has been used for products ranging from soft drinks, beer, and pain relievers to computers, batteries, car rentals, and credit cards. For example, in its classic comparative campaign, Avis positioned itself against market-leading Hertz by claiming, "We're number two, so we try harder."

More recently, Progresso ran ads showing side-by-side comparisons of its soups versus Campbell's condensed soups, inviting consumers to "Enjoy a better soup . . . with a more adult taste." And Procter & Gamble ran an ad comparing its Tide with Bleach to Oxy10. In the ad, consumers spread iodine, tomato sauce, mud, and grass on a white t-shirt that was then cut in half and treated with the two detergents. All the while, "Anything You Can Do I Can Do Better" played in the background. Of course, Tide did a better job of removing stains. Advertisers should use comparative advertising with caution. All too often, such ads invite competitor responses, resulting in an advertising war that neither competitor can win.

Reminder advertising is important for mature products—it keeps consumers thinking about the product. Expensive Coca-Cola television ads primarily remind people about Coca-Cola rather than informing or persuading them.

Setting the Advertising Budget

After determining its advertising objectives, the company next sets its *advertising budget* for each product. Four commonly used methods for setting promotion budgets were discussed in Chapter 14. Here we discuss some specific factors that should be considered when setting the advertising budget.

A brand's advertising budget often depends on its *stage in the product life cycle.* For example, new products typically need large advertising budgets to build awareness and to gain consumer trial. In contrast, mature brands usually require lower budgets as a ratio to sales. *Market share* also impacts the amount advertising needed: Because building the market or taking share from competitors requires larger advertising spending than does simply maintaining current share, low-share brands usually need more advertising spending as a percentage of sales. Also, brands in a market with many competitors and high advertising clutter must be advertised more heavily to be noticed above the noise in the market. Undifferentiated brands—those that closely resemble other brands in their product class (beer, soft drinks, laundry detergents)—may require heavy advertising to set them apart. When the product differs greatly from competitors, advertising can be used to point out the differences to consumers.

No matter what method is used, setting the advertising budget is no easy task. How does a company know if it is spending the right amount? Some critics charge that large consumer

■ Comparative advertising: Progresso makes side-by-side comparisons of its soup versus Campbell's, inviting consumers to "Enjoy a better soup . . . with a more adult taste."

packaged-goods firms tend to spend too much on advertising and business-to-business marketers generally underspend on advertising. They claim that, on the one hand, the large consumer companies use lots of image advertising without really knowing its effects. They overspend as a form of "insurance" against not spending enough. On the other hand, business advertisers tend to rely too heavily on their sales forces to bring in orders. They underestimate the power of company and product image in preselling industrial customers. Thus, they do not spend enough on advertising to build customer awareness and knowledge.

Companies such as Coca-Cola and Kraft have built sophisticated statistical models to determine the relationship between promotional spending and brand sales, and to help determine the "optimal investment" across various media. Still, because so many factors affect advertising effectiveness, some controllable and others not, measuring the results of advertising spending remains an inexact science. In most cases, managers must rely on large doses of judgment along with more quantitative analysis when setting advertising budgets.[3]

Developing Advertising Strategy

Advertising strategy consists of two major elements: creating advertising *messages* and selecting advertising *media*. In the past, companies often viewed media planning as secondary to the message-creation process. The creative department first created good advertisements, and then the media department selected the best media for carrying these advertisements to desired target audiences. This often caused friction between creatives and media planners.

Today, however, media fragmentation, soaring media costs, and more-focused target marketing strategies have promoted the importance of the media-planning function. More and more, advertisers are orchestrating a closer harmony between their messages and the media that deliver them. In some cases, an advertising campaign might start with a great message idea, followed by the choice of appropriate media. In other cases, however, a campaign might begin with a good media opportunity, followed by advertisements designed to take advantage of that opportunity.

Among the more noteworthy ad campaigns based on tight media-creative partnerships is the pioneering campaign for Absolut vodka, made by V&S Absolut Spirits:

The Absolut team and its ad agency meet once each year with a slew of magazines to set Absolut's media schedule. The schedule consists of up to 100 magazines, ranging from consumer and business magazines to theater playbills. The agency's creative department then creates media-specific ads. The result is a wonderful assortment of very creative ads for Absolut, tightly targeted to audiences of the media in which they appear. For example, an "Absolut Bravo" ad in playbills has roses adorning a clear bottle, while business magazines contain an "Absolut Merger" foldout. In New York-area magazines, "Absolut Manhattan" ads feature a satellite photo of Manhattan, with Central Park assuming the distinctive outline of an Absolut bottle. In Chicago, the windy city, ads show an Absolut bottle with the letters on the label blown askew. An "Absolut Primary" ad run during the political season featured the well-known bottle spattered with mud. In some cases, the creatives even developed ads for magazines not yet on the schedule, such as a clever "Absolut Centerfold" ad for *Playboy* magazine. The ad portrayed a clear, unadorned playmate bottle ("11-inch bust, 11-inch waist, 11-inch hips"). In all, Absolut has developed more than 1,000 ads for the more than two-decades-old campaign. At a time of soaring media costs and cluttered communication channels, a closer cooperation between creative and media people has paid off handsomely for Absolut. Largely as a result of its breakthrough advertising, in the United States, Absolut is the number-three liquor brand. It's the nation's number-one imported vodka and captures a 63 percent share of the imported vodka market. The Absolut ads have developed a kind of cult following, and Absolut is one of only three original brands to be inducted into the American Advertising Hall of Fame.[4]

Creating the Advertising Message

No matter how big the budget, advertising can succeed only if advertisements gain attention and communicate well. Good advertising messages are especially important in today's costly

■ Media planners for Absolut vodka work with creatives to design ads targeted to specific media audiences. "Absolut Bravo" appears in theater playbills. "Absolut Chicago" targets the Windy City.

and cluttered advertising environment. The average number of receivable television channels per U.S. household has skyrocketed from 3 in 1950 to more than 100 today, and consumers have more than 23,900 magazines from which to choose.[5] Add the countless radio stations and a continuous barrage of catalogs, direct-mail and e-mail ads, and out-of-home media, and consumers are being bombarded with ads at home, at work, and at all points in between. One expert estimates that the average person is exposed to some 1,600 ad messages a day. Another puts the number at an eye-popping 5,000 ads a day.[6]

BREAKING THROUGH THE CLUTTER If all this advertising clutter bothers some consumers, it also causes big problems for advertisers. Take the situation facing network television advertisers. They regularly pay $200,000 or more for 30 seconds of advertising time during a popular prime-time program, even more if it's an especially popular program such as *ER* ($479,000), *Survivor* ($412,000), *Will & Grace* ($360,000 per spot), or a mega-event such as the final episode of *Friends* (spots averaged $2 million) or the Super Bowl (as much as $2.4 million!).[7]

Then, their ads are sandwiched in with a clutter of other commercials, announcements, and network promotions, totaling more than 15 minutes of nonprogram material per prime-time hour, more than 21 minutes per daytime hour. Such clutter in television and other ad media has created an increasingly hostile advertising environment. According to one recent poll, 65 percent of Americans say they are "constantly bombarded with too much" advertising; 61 percent say that the quantity of marketing and advertising "is out of control"; and 60 percent say that their view of advertising is "much more negative than just a few years ago."[8]

Until recently, television viewers were pretty much a captive audience for advertisers. Viewers had only a few channels from which to choose. But with the growth in cable and satellite TV, VCRs, remote-controls, today's viewers have many more options. They can avoid ads by watching commercial-free cable channels. They can "zap" commercials by pushing the fast-forward button during taped programs. With remote control, they can instantly turn off the sound during a commercial or "zip" around the channels to see what else is on. A recent study found that nearly half of all television viewers now switch channels when the commercial break starts.

Adding to the problem is the new wave of digital video recorders (DVRs) and personal television services—such as TiVo and ReplayTV—that have armed viewers with an arsenal of new-age zipping and zapping weapons. DVRs are expected to occupy more than 20 percent of American homes by 2007. A recent study of TiVo and other DVR system users found that these users skip commercials 77 percent of the time, a much higher rate than for those watching live television or using VCRs. One ad agency executive calls TiVo and Replay "electronic weedwhackers." "These machines will rock the foundation of network advertising," he declares. "In time, the number of people using them to obliterate commercials will totally erode faith in the 30-second commercial."[9]

Just to gain and hold attention, today's advertising messages must be better planned, more imaginative, more entertaining, and more rewarding to consumers. Many advertisers

■ A new advertising challenge: The new wave of personal video recorder services, such as TiVo, have armed viewers with an arsenal of new-age zipping and zapping weapons. One ad agency executive calls TiVo an "electronic weedwhacker."

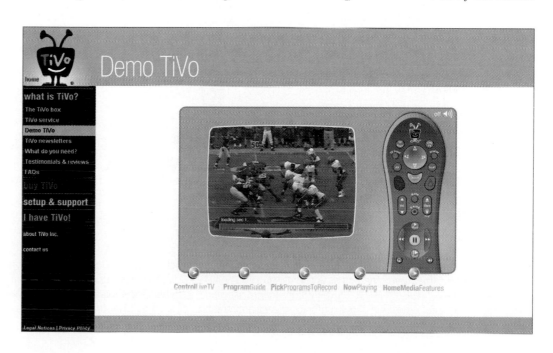

now see themselves as creating "advertainment"—ads that are both persuasive and entertaining. "Today we have to entertain and not just sell, because if you try to sell directly and come off as boring or obnoxious, people are going to press the remote on you," points out one advertising executive. "A commercial has to cut through the clutter and seize the viewers in one to three seconds, or they're gone," comments another.[10] Some advertisers even create intentionally controversial ads to break through the clutter and gain attention for their products (see Real Marketing 15.1).

Many advertisers are trying to counter the TiVo trend or even turn it into an opportunity. Some companies are developing 6-second ad spots that run in the time it takes a consumer to fast forward through a commercial break. Others, like Porsche, Best Buy, and Universal Music, have sponsored "advertainment showcases" on TiVo. For example, when Porsche launched its Cayenne SUV, it targeted TiVo's half million customers with an opt-in ad that allowed them to pause the program and visit a branded showcase. Once there, consumers were offered additional product information, encouraged to visit the Web site, and given the opportunity to receive additional information. Similarly, Best Buy ran a branded showcase on TiVo in which it offered subscribers the chance to access two exclusive videos, win a CD, and opt in to six entertaining product vignettes. Sixty-three percent of TiVo subscribers opted-in to the Best Buy showcase, staying an average of 3.36 minutes.[11]

MESSAGE STRATEGY   The first step in creating effective advertising messages is to plan a *message strategy*—to decide what general message will be communicated to consumers. The purpose of advertising is to get consumers to think about or react to the product or company in a certain way. People will react only if they believe that they will benefit from doing so.

Real Marketing 15.1

Advertising on the Edge: You Either Hate 'Em or Love 'Em

You either love 'em or you hate 'em. Today's cluttered advertising environment has spawned a new genre of "gross-out" ads that go to extremes to get attention. These irreverent, cutting-edge ads intentionally create controversy, even if it means turning off some potential customers. "It's the age-old question of breaking through the clutter," says an ad agency creative director. You turn to "anything you can to get noticed," he says.

You see these controversial ads almost everywhere. While flipping through your favorite magazine, you might encounter a Toyota ad targeting Gen Ys with the headline "Attention nose pickers." Next comes an Altoids ad in which a man peers down the front of his boxer shorts: "Shrinkage may occur," proclaims the ad's headline. "The curiously strong mints." The headline for an Altoids Sours ad screams "One bad motherpucker!" Other Altoids ads feature a women in a seductively devilish outfit, complete with horns, and headlines such as "Hot and bothered?" "Frigid?" and "Taste like hell!"

On television, an Orange Slice "twisted taste" commercial opens with the camera panning across a row of squeamish students in a science class, frog legs dangling from their dissection trays. As the teacher drones on about ruptured spleens and green

■ To be truly cutting-edge, advertising must do more than just capture attention. Altoids' irreverent ads fit the brand's "curious, strong, original" positioning and appeal to its cutting-edge target customers.

discharges, one kid lunches on his lab project. During the Super Bowl, a Dodge Truck ad features a man choking on a piece of beef jerky lodged in his throat. The solution: The driver puts the truck through its testosterone-charged paces, then stops abruptly. The

Thus, developing an effective message strategy begins with identifying customer *benefits* that can be used as advertising appeals. Ideally, advertising message strategy will follow directly from the company's broader positioning strategy.

Message strategy statements tend to be plain, straightforward outlines of benefits and positioning points that the advertiser wants to stress. The advertiser must next develop a compelling *creative concept* or *"big idea"*—that will bring the message strategy to life in a distinctive and memorable way. At this stage, simple message ideas become great ad campaigns. Usually, a copywriter and art director will team up to generate many creative concepts, hoping that one of these concepts will turn out to be the big idea. The creative concept may emerge as a visualization, a phrase, or a combination of the two.

The creative concept will guide the choice of specific appeals to be used in an advertising campaign. *Advertising appeals* should have three characteristics: First, they should be *meaningful,* pointing out benefits that make the product more desirable or interesting to consumers. Second, appeals must be *believable*—consumers must believe that the product or service will deliver the promised benefits.

However, the most meaningful and believable benefits may not be the best ones to feature. Appeals should also be *distinctive*—they should tell how the product is better than the competing brands. For example, the most meaningful benefit of owning a wristwatch is that it keeps accurate time, yet few watch ads feature this benefit. Instead, based on the distinctive benefits they offer, watch advertisers might select any of a number of advertising themes. For years, Timex has been the affordable watch that "Takes a lickin' and keeps on tickin'." In contrast, Swatch has featured style and fashion, whereas Rolex stresses luxury and status.

choking passenger hawks up the offending piece of meat, which splats against the windshield in a gooey mess. "Repulsive," says ad critic Bob Garfield.

Then, there's the "Blind Date" spot from SmartBeep, the retail paging-services provider. The spot, which generated enormous response, was part of a wacky five-part campaign that contrasted smart versus not-so-smart behavior to promote SmartBeep's free pagers and low rates on paging services. In it, a woman climbs into the front seat of her blind date's car. While he's crossing around to the other side, thinking she is alone, she leans to one side and lets rip a frat-house blast of gas. When her date hops in the car, she hesitates then turns red with embarrassment as he introduces her to another couple in the back seat. "You guys meet? Gregg, Janice?" he asks, to which Janice in the backseat responds, "We sure did." The announcer concludes, "That was stupid. . . . This is smart. A beeper service for just $1.99 a month." The ad closes: "We've got chemistry here. You feel it?" says the blind-date guy. "I felt it!" says Janice from the backseat. The ad became an immediate Internet cult item.

For pure gross-out value, few ads top the recent ad from FreshDirect, the online food retailer that delivers groceries directly to your home. In the ad, a woman with a cold and sniffles blows her nose and sneezes as she picks through a supermarket display of cheese and olives. As she sniffs an open bin of olives, one gets stuck in her right nostril. After checking to see that no one is watching, she closes off her left nostril with her index finger, exhales through her nose, and fires the offending olive back into the bin with a sploosh. "Where's *your* food been?" asks the ad.

Such outrageous ads can grab attention, create word-of-mouth, and even win awards. However, such techniques often attract more attention to the ad itself than to the brand's selling proposition. If used improperly, controversial ads can boost viewer attention but actually *distract* from the selling message. For example, the Dodge Truck Super Bowl ad drew much attention, but most of it was bad. According to one expert, "it was the only commercial to be unanimously, roundly, and thoroughly bashed." To be effective, advertising must do more than just capture attention. It must support and enhance the brand and its positioning.

If used properly, cutting edge humor can help do that, as proved by Altoids and its "Curiously Strong" campaign. The campaign's irreverent, sometimes controversial ads fit the brand's "curious, strong, original" positioning. They also appeal to the tastes as well as the taste buds of Altoids' cutting-edge target consumers. "We're allowed to poke fun at people," says an Altoids executive, "so we take advantage of it when we can." As a result, in only 2 years, the small-budget but high-impact ad campaign propelled Altoids past longtime strong-mint market leader Tic Tac. "Altoids is now—improbably—the boss of the mint world," says an analyst. What's the power behind this cheeky campaign? The analyst confirms that "Everything links back to [the brand's] 'curiously strong' and 'original' [positioning]."

Sources: Tim Nudd and Jack Feuer, "Everyone's an Ad Critic," *Adweek,* February 3, 2003, p. 44; Tom Kurtz, "Unsettling TV Commercials: And Now, a Gross-Out from Our Sponsor," *New York Times,* July 25, 1999, p. 7; Stefano Hatfield, "Opinion: Olive Nose," accessed at www.adcritic.com/news/op/detail/?q=36945; Mae Anderson, "The Fine Print," *Adweek,* June 7, 2004, p. 24; and information accessed online at About Altoids at www.altoids.com, January 2005.

MESSAGE EXECUTION The advertiser now has to turn the big idea into an actual ad execution that will capture the target market's attention and interest. The creative people must find the best style, tone, words, and format for executing the message. Any message can be presented in different *execution styles*, such as the following:

- *Slice of life:* This style shows one or more "typical" people using the product in a normal setting. For example, two mothers at a picnic discuss the nutritional benefits of Jif peanut butter.

- *Lifestyle:* This style shows how a product fits in with a particular lifestyle. For example, an ad for Mongoose mountain bikes shows a serious biker traversing remote and rugged but beautiful terrain and states, "There are places that are so awesome and so killer that you'd like to tell the whole world about them. But please, *don't.*"

- *Fantasy:* This style creates a fantasy around the product or its use. For instance, many ads are built around dream themes. Gap even introduced a perfume named Dream. Ads show a woman sleeping blissfully and suggests that the scent is "the stuff that clouds are made of."

- *Mood or image:* This style builds a mood or image around the product, such as beauty, love, or serenity. No claim is made about the product except through suggestion. Bermuda tourism ads create such moods.

- *Musical:* This style shows one or more people or cartoon characters singing about the product. For example, one of the most famous ads in history was a Coca-Cola ad built around the song "I'd Like to Teach the World to Sing." Similarly, Oscar-Meyer has long run ads showing children singing its now famous classic, "Oh, I wish I were an Oscar-Meyer weiner . . ." jingle.

- *Personality symbol:* This style creates a character that represents the product. The character might be *animated* (the Jolly Green Giant, Cap'n Crunch, Garfield the Cat) or *real* (the Marlboro man, Ol' Lonely the Maytag repairman, Morris the 9-Lives Cat, or the AFLAC duck).

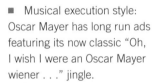

■ Musical execution style: Oscar Mayer has long run ads featuring its now classic "Oh, I wish I were an Oscar Mayer wiener . . ." jingle.

- *Technical expertise:* This style shows the company's expertise in making the product. Thus, Maxwell House shows one of its buyers carefully selecting coffee beans, and Gallo tells about its many years of wine-making experience.

- *Scientific evidence:* This style presents survey or scientific evidence that the brand is better or better liked than one or more other brands. For years, Crest toothpaste has used scientific evidence to convince buyers that Crest is better than other brands at fighting cavities.

- *Testimonial evidence or endorsement:* This style features a highly believable or likable source endorsing the product. It could be ordinary people saying how much they like a given product or a celebrity presenting the product. For example, Apple recently ran ads featuring real people who'd recently switched from Microsoft Windows-based PCs to Macs. And many companies use actors or sports celebrities as product endorsers.

The advertiser also must choose a *tone* for the ad. Procter & Gamble always uses a positive tone: Its ads say something very positive about its products. P&G usually avoids humor that might take attention away from the message. In contrast, many advertisers now use edgy humor to break through the commercial clutter.

The advertiser must use memorable and attention-getting *words* in the ad. For example, rather than claiming simply that "a BMW is a well-engineered automobile," BMW uses more creative and higher-impact phrasing: "The ultimate driving machine." Instead of stating plainly that Hanes socks last longer than less expensive ones, Hanes suggests, "Buy cheap socks and you'll pay through the toes." It's not Häagen-Dazs is "a good-tasting luxury ice cream," it's "Our passport to indulgence: passion in a touch, perfection in a cup, summer in a spoon, one perfect moment."

Finally, *format* elements make a difference in an ad's impact as well as in its cost. A small change in ad design can make a big difference in its effect. The *illustration* is the first thing the reader notices—it must be strong enough to draw attention. Next, the *headline* must effectively entice the right people to read the copy. Finally, the *copy*—the main block of text in the ad—must be simple but strong and convincing. Moreover, these three elements must effectively work *together*.

Selecting Advertising Media

The major steps in media selection are (1) deciding on *reach, frequency,* and *impact*; (2) choosing among major *media types*; (3) selecting specific *media vehicles*; and (4) deciding on *media timing*.

DECIDING ON REACH, FREQUENCY, AND IMPACT To select media, the advertiser must decide on the reach and frequency needed to achieve advertising objectives. *Reach* is a measure of the *percentage* of people in the target market who are exposed to the ad campaign during a given period of time. For example, the advertiser might try to reach 70 percent of the target market during the first 3 months of the campaign. *Frequency* is a measure of how many *times* the average person in the target market is exposed to the message. For example, the advertiser might want an average exposure frequency of three.

The advertiser also must decide on the desired *media impact*—the *qualitative value* of a message exposure through a given medium. For example, for products that need to be demonstrated, messages on television may have more impact than messages on radio because television uses sight *and* sound. The same message in one magazine (say, *Newsweek*) may be more believable than in another (say, *The National Enquirer*). In general, the more reach, frequency, and impact the advertiser seeks, the higher the advertising budget will have to be.

CHOOSING AMONG MAJOR MEDIA TYPES The media planner has to know the reach, frequency, and impact of each of the major media types. As summarized in Table 15.2, the major media types are newspapers, television, direct mail, radio, magazines, outdoor, and the Internet. Each medium has advantages and limitations.

Media planners consider many factors when making their media choices. The *media habits of target consumers* will affect media choice—advertisers look for media that reach target consumers effectively. So will the *nature of the product*—for example, fashions are best advertised in color magazines, and automobile performance is best demonstrated on television. Different *types of messages* may require different media. A message announcing a major sale tomorrow will require radio or newspapers; a message with a lot of technical data might require magazines, direct mailings, or an online ad and Web site. *Cost* is another major factor in media choice. For example, network television is very expensive, whereas newspaper or radio advertising costs much less but also reaches fewer consumers. The media planner looks

TABLE 15.2   Profiles of Major Media Types

Medium	Advantages	Limitations
Newspapers	Flexibility; timeliness; good local market coverage; broad acceptability; high believability	Short life; poor reproduction quality; small pass-along audience
Television	Good mass-market coverage; low cost per exposure; combines sight, sound, and motion; appealing to the senses	High absolute costs; high clutter; fleeting exposure; less audience selectivity
Direct mail	High audience selectivity; flexibility; no ad competition within the same medium; allows personalization	Relatively high cost per exposure, "junk mail" image
Radio	Good local acceptance; high geographic and demographic selectivity; low cost	Audio only, fleeting exposure; low attention ("the half-heard" medium); fragmented audiences
Magazines	High geographic and demographic selectivity; credibility and prestige; high-quality reproduction; long life and good pass-along readership	Long ad purchase lead time; high cost; no guarantee of position
Outdoor	Flexibility; high repeat exposure; low cost; low message competition; good positional selectivity	Little audience selectivity; creative limitations
Internet	High selectivity; low cost; immediacy; interactive capabilities	Small, demographically skewed audience; relatively low impact; audience controls exposure

both at the total cost of using a medium and at the cost per exposure of reaching specific target customers.

Media impact and cost must be reexamined regularly. For a long time, television and magazines have dominated in the media mixes of national advertisers, with other media often neglected. Recently, however, as network television costs soar and audiences shrink, many advertisers are looking for new ways to reach consumers. The move toward micromarketing strategies, focused more narrowly on specific consumer groups, has also fueled the search for new media to replace or supplement network television. As a result, advertisers are increasingly shifting larger portions of their budgets to media that cost less and target more effectively.

Three media benefiting greatly from the shift are outdoor advertising, cable television, and digital satellite television systems. Billboards have undergone a resurgence in recent years. Gone are the ugly eyesores of the past; in their place we now see cleverly designed, colorful attention grabbers. Outdoor advertising provides an excellent way to reach important local consumer segments at a fraction of the cost per exposure of other major media. Cable television and satellite systems are also booming. Such systems allow narrow programming formats such as all sports, all news, nutrition, arts, gardening, cooking, travel, history, and others that target select groups. Advertisers can take advantage of such "narrowcasting" to "rifle in" on special market segments rather than use the "shotgun" approach offered by network broadcasting.

Outdoor, cable, and satellite media seem to make good sense. But, increasingly, ads are popping up in far less likely places. In their efforts to find less costly and more highly targeted ways to reach consumers, advertisers have discovered a dazzling collection of "alternative media" (see Real Marketing 15.2).

Another important trend affecting media selection is the rapid growth in the number of "media multi-taskers," people who absorb more than one medium at a time:

It looks like people who aren't satisfied with "just watching TV" are in good company. According to a [recent] survey, . . . three-fourths of U.S. TV viewers read the newspaper while they watch TV, and two-thirds of them go online during their TV time. Of those who are waiting for downloads from the Internet, 61.8 percent watch TV, 52.1 percent listen to the radio, and 20.2 percent read the newspaper. According to the study, 70 percent of media users say they at one time or another try to absorb two or more forms of media at once.[12]

Real Marketing 15.2

Advertisers Seek Alternative Media

As consumers, we're used to ads on television, in magazines and newspapers, on the radio, and along the roadways. But these days, no matter where you go or what you do, you probably will run into some new form of advertising.

Tiny billboards attached to shopping carts, ads on shopping bags, and even advertising decals on supermarket floors urge you to buy Jell-O Pudding Pops or Pampers. Signs atop parking meters hawk everything from Jeeps to Minolta cameras to Recipe dog food. A city bus rolls by, fully wrapped for Trix cereal. You escape to the ballpark, only to find billboard-size video screens running Budweiser ads while a blimp with an electronic message board circles lazily overhead. How about a quiet trip in the country? Sorry—you find an enterprising farmer using his milk cows as four-legged billboards mounted with ads for Ben & Jerry's ice cream.

You pay to see a movie at your local theater, only to learn that the movie is full of not-so-subtle promotional plugs for Pepsi, Domino's Pizza, MasterCard, Fritos, Mercedes, Ray Ban sunglasses, Rockport shoes, or any of a dozen other products. You head home for a little TV to find your favorite sitcom full of "virtual placements" of Coca-Cola, Sony, or M&M/Mars products digitally inserted into the program. You pop in the latest video game and find that your action character is jumping into a Jeep on the way to the skateboarding park.

At the local rail station, it's the Commuter Channel; at the airport, you're treated to the CNN Airport Network. Shortly after your plane lifts off the runway, you look out the window and spot a 500-foot diameter crop circle carved into a farmer's field depicting Monster.com's mascot and corporate logo. As you wait to pick up your luggage, ads for Kenneth Cole baggage roll by on the luggage carousel conveyor belt.

These days, you're likely to find ads—well, anywhere. Boats cruise along public beaches flashing advertising messages for Sundown Sunscreen as sunbathers spread their towels over ads for Snapple pressed into the sand. Ad space is being sold on video cases, parking-lot tickets, golf scorecards, delivery trucks, gas pumps, ATMs, municipal garbage cans, police cars, and church bulletins. One agency even rents space on the foreheads of college students for temporary advertising tattoos.

The following accounts take a humorous look ahead at what might be in store for the future:

Tomorrow your alarm clock will buzz at 6 A.M., as usual. Then the digital readout will morph into an ad for Burger King's breakfast special. Hungry for a Croissan'wich, you settle for a bagel that you plop into the toaster. The coils burn a Toastmaster brand onto the sides. Biting into your embossed bread, you pour a cup of coffee as the familiar green-and-white Starbucks logo forms on the side. Sipping the brew, you slide on your Nikes to go grab the newspaper. The pressure sensitive shoes leave a temporary trail of swooshes behind them wherever you step. Walking outside, you pick up the *Times* and gaze at your lawn, where the fertilizer you put down last month time-releases ads for Scotts Turf Builder, Toro lawn mowers, Weber grills. . . .

Even some of the current alternative media seem a bit far-fetched, and they sometimes irritate consumers who resent it all as "ad nauseam." But for many marketers, these media can save money and provide a way to hit selected consumers where they live, shop, work, and play. "We like to call it the captive pause," says an

■ Marketers have discovered a dazzling array of "alternative media."

(box continues)

executive of an alternative-media firm, where consumers "really have nothing else to do but either look at the person in front of them or look at some engaging content as well as 15-second commercials"—the average person waits in line about 30 minutes a day. Many spend even more time on mass transit. So, companies like Target, Snapple, Calvin Klein, and American Express are testing new technologies to reach captive consumers. Riders on Manhattan's subway system now see a series of light boxes speed by that create a moving commercial in the subway car's windows.

Of course, this may leave you wondering if there are any commercial-free havens remaining for ad-weary consumers. The back seat of a taxi, perhaps, or public elevators, or stalls in a public restroom? Forget it! Each has already been invaded by innovative marketers.

Sources: See Cara Beardi, "From Elevators to Gas Stations, Ads Multiplying," *Advertising Age,* November 13, 2000, pp. 40–42; Charles Pappas, "Ad Nauseam," *Advertising Age,* July 10, 2000, pp. 16–18; Beardi, "Airport Powerhouses Make Connection," *Advertising Age,* October 2, 2000, p. 8; Wayne Friedman, "Eagle-Eye Marketers Find Right Spot," *Advertising Age,* January 22, 2001, pp. S2–S3; Jean Halliday, "Mercedes Ties Car to 'Men in Black II,'" *Advertising Age,* May 27, 2002, p. 4; and Cara Griffin, "Rockport, Ray-Ban Back in Black," *Sporting Goods Business,* April 2002, p. 14; Stephanie Mehta, "Ads Invade Video Games," *Fortune,* May 26, 2003, p. 46; Brian Hindo, "Getting a Head," *Business Week,* January 12, 2004, p. 14; and Sam Jaffe, "Easy Riders," *American Demographics,* March 2004, pp. 20–23.

Media planners need to take such media interactions into account when selecting the types of media they will use.

SELECTING SPECIFIC MEDIA VEHICLES The media planner now must choose the best *media vehicles*—specific media within each general media type. For example, television vehicles include *Scrubs* and *ABC World News Tonight*. Magazine vehicles include *Newsweek*, *People*, *In Style*, and *Sports Illustrated*.

Media planners must compute the cost per thousand persons reached by a vehicle. For example, if a full-page, four-color advertisement in *Newsweek* costs $200,000 and *Newsweek's* readership is 3.1 million people, the cost of reaching each group of 1,000 persons is about $64. The same advertisement in *Business Week* may cost only $103,320 but reach only 970,000 persons—at a cost per thousand of about $106. The media planner ranks each magazine by cost per thousand and favors those magazines with the lower cost per thousand for reaching target consumers.[13]

The media planner must also consider the costs of producing ads for different media. Whereas newspaper ads may cost very little to produce, flashy television ads may cost millions. On average, U.S. advertisers pay $358,000 to produce a single 30-second television commercial. A few years ago, Nike paid a cool $2 million to make a single ad called "The Wall."[14] In selecting media vehicles, the media planner must balance media cost measures against several media impact factors. First, the planner should balance costs against the media vehicle's *audience quality*. For a Huggies disposable diapers advertisement, for example, *Parenting* magazine would have a high exposure value; *Gentlemen's Quarterly* would have a low-exposure value. Second, the media planner should consider *audience attention*. Readers of *Vogue*, for example, typically pay more attention to ads than do *Newsweek* readers. Third, the planner should assess the vehicle's *editorial quality*—*Time* and the *Wall Street Journal* are more believable and prestigious than *The National Enquirer*.

DECIDING ON MEDIA TIMING The advertiser must also decide how to schedule the advertising over the course of a year. Suppose sales of a product peak in December and drop in March. The firm can vary its advertising to follow the seasonal pattern, to oppose the seasonal pattern, or to be the same all year. Most firms do some seasonal advertising. For example, The Picture People, Hallmark's national chain of family portrait studios, advertises more heavily before major holidays such as Christmas, Easter, Valentine's Day, and Fourth of July. Some marketers do *only* seasonal advertising: For example, Hallmark advertises its greeting cards only before major holidays.

Finally, the advertiser has to choose the pattern of the ads. *Continuity* means scheduling ads evenly within a given period. *Pulsing* means scheduling ads unevenly over a given time period. Thus, 52 ads could either be scheduled at one per week during the year or pulsed in several bursts. The idea behind pulsing is to advertise heavily for a short period to build awareness that carries over to the next advertising period. Those who favor pulsing feel that it can be used to achieve the same impact as a steady schedule but at a much lower cost. However, some media planners believe that although pulsing achieves minimal awareness, it sacrifices depth of advertising communications.

■ Media timing: The Picture People, Hallmark's national chain of family portrait studios, advertises more heavily before special holidays.

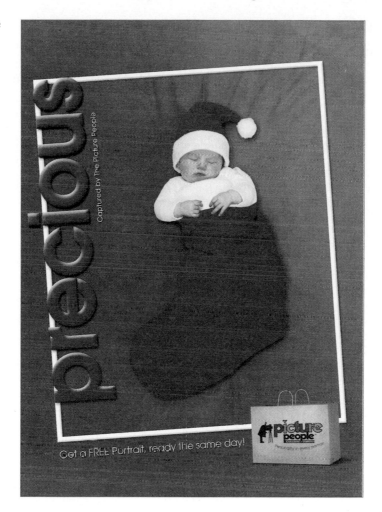

Recent advances in technology have had a substantial impact on the media planning and buying functions. Today, for example, computer software applications called *media optimizers* allow media planners to evaluate vast combinations of television programs and prices. Such programs help advertisers to make better decisions about which mix of networks, programs, and day parts will yield the highest reach per ad dollar.

Evaluating Advertising

The advertising program should evaluate both the communication effects and the sales effects of advertising regularly. Measuring the *communication effects* of an ad—*copy testing*—tells whether the ad is communicating well. Copy testing can be done before or after an ad is printed or broadcast. Before the ad is placed, the advertiser can show it to consumers, ask how they like it, and measure message recall or attitude changes resulting from it. After the ad is run, the advertiser can measure how the ad affected consumer recall or product awareness, knowledge, and preference.

But what *sales* are caused by an ad that increases brand awareness by 20 percent and brand preference by 10 percent? The *sales effects* of advertising are often harder to measure than the communication effects. Sales are affected by many factors besides advertising—such as product features, price, and availability.

One way to measure the sales effect of advertising is to compare past sales with past advertising expenditures. Another way is through experiments. For example, to test the effects of different advertising spending levels, Coca-Cola could vary the amount it spends on advertising in different market areas and measure the differences in the resulting sales levels. It could spend the normal amount in one market area, half the normal amount in another area, and twice the normal amount in a third area. If the three market areas are similar, and if all other marketing efforts in the area are the same, then differences in sales in the three areas could be related to advertising level. More complex experiments could be designed to include other variables, such as difference in the ads or media used.

STOPS HERE

Other Advertising Considerations

In developing advertising strategies and programs, the company must address two additional questions. First, how will the company organize its advertising function—who will perform which advertising tasks? Second, how will the company adapt its advertising strategies and programs to the complexities of international markets?

Organizing for Advertising

Different companies organize in different ways to handle advertising. In small companies, advertising might be handled by someone in the sales department. Large companies set up advertising departments whose job it is to set the advertising budget, work with the ad agency, and handle other advertising not done by the agency. Most large companies use outside advertising agencies because they offer several advantages.

Advertising agency

A marketing services firm that assists companies in planning, preparing, implementing, and evaluating all or portions of their advertising programs.

How does an **advertising agency** work? Advertising agencies were started in the mid-to-late 1800s by salespeople and brokers who worked for the media and received a commission for selling advertising space to companies. As time passed, the salespeople began to help customers prepare their ads. Eventually, they formed agencies and grew closer to the advertisers than to the media.

Today's agencies employ specialists who can often perform advertising tasks better than the company's own staff. Agencies also bring an outside point of view to solving the company's problems, along with lots of experience from working with different clients and situations. So, today, even companies with strong advertising departments of their own use advertising agencies.

Some ad agencies are huge—the largest U.S. agency, BBDO Worldwide, has worldwide annual revenues of more than $1.2 billion. In recent years, many agencies have grown by gobbling up other agencies, thus creating huge agency holding companies. The largest of these agency "megagroups," Omincon Group, includes several large advertising, public relations, and promotion agencies with combined worldwide revenues of $8.6 billion.[15] Most large advertising agencies have the staff and resources to handle all phases of an advertising campaign for their clients, from creating a marketing plan to developing ad campaigns and preparing, placing, and evaluating ads.

Many agencies have sought growth by diversifying into related marketing services. These new diversified agencies offer a complete list of integrated marketing and promotion services under one roof, including advertising, sales promotion, marketing research, public relations, and direct and online marketing. Some have even added marketing consulting, television production, and sales training units in an effort to become full "marketing partners" to their clients.

However, agencies are finding that most advertisers don't want much more from them than traditional media advertising services plus direct marketing, sales promotion, and sometimes public relations. Thus, many agencies have recently limited their diversification efforts in order to focus more on traditional services. Some have even started their own "creative boutiques," smaller and more independent agencies that can develop creative campaigns for clients free of large-agency bureaucracy.

International Advertising Decisions

International advertisers face many complexities not encountered by domestic advertisers. The most basic issue concerns the degree to which global advertising should be adapted to the unique characteristics of various country markets. Some large advertisers have attempted to support their global brands with highly standardized worldwide advertising, with campaigns that work as well in Bangkok as they do in Baltimore. For example, Jeep has created a worldwide brand image of ruggedness and reliability; Coca-Cola's Sprite brand uses standardized appeals to target the world's youth. Gillette's ads for its Gillette for Women Venus razor are almost identical worldwide, with only minor adjustments to suit the local culture.

Standardization produces many benefits—lower advertising costs, greater global advertising coordination, and a more consistent worldwide image. But it also has drawbacks. Most importantly, it ignores the fact that country markets differ greatly in their cultures, demographics, and economic conditions. Thus, most international advertisers "think globally but act locally." They develop global advertising *strategies* that make their worldwide advertising efforts more efficient and consistent. Then they adapt their advertising *programs* to make them more responsive to consumer needs and expectations within local markets. For example, Coca-Cola has a pool of different commercials that can be used in or adapted to several different international markets. Some can be used with only minor

  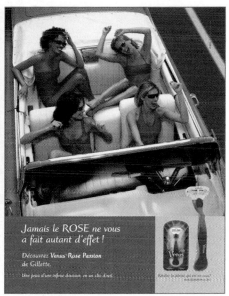

■ Standardized worldwide advertising: Gillette's ads for its Gillette for Women Venus razors are almost identical worldwide, with only minor adjustments to suit the local culture.

changes—such as language—in several different countries. Local and regional managers decide which commercials work best for which markets.

Global advertisers face several special problems. For instance, advertising media costs and availability differ vastly from country to country. Countries also differ in the extent to which they regulate advertising practices. Many countries have extensive systems of laws restricting how much a company can spend on advertising, the media used, the nature of advertising claims, and other aspects of the advertising program. Such restrictions often require advertisers to adapt their campaigns from country to country.

For example, alcoholic products cannot be advertised or sold in Muslim countries. In many countries, Sweden, for example, no TV ads may be directed at children under 12. Moreover, Sweden is lobbying to extend that ban to all European Union member countries. To play it safe, McDonald's advertises itself as a family restaurant in Sweden. Comparative ads, while acceptable and even common in the United States and Canada, are less commonly used in the United Kingdom, unacceptable in Japan, and illegal in India and Brazil. China has restrictive censorship rules for TV and radio advertising; for example, the words *the best* are banned, as are ads that "violate social customs" or present women in "improper ways." Coca-Cola's Indian subsidiary was forced to end a promotion that offered prizes, such as a trip to Hollywood, because it violated India's established trade practices by encouraging customers to buy in order to "gamble."[16]

Thus, although advertisers may develop global strategies to guide their overall advertising efforts, specific advertising programs must usually be adapted to meet local cultures and customs, media characteristics, and advertising regulations.

Sales Promotion | START HERE

Sales promotion
Short-term incentives to encourage the purchase or sale of a product or service.

Advertising often works closely with another promotion tool, sales promotion. **Sales promotion** consists of short-term incentives to encourage purchase or sales of a product or service. Whereas advertising offers reasons to buy a product or service, sales promotion offers reasons to buy *now*.

Examples of sales promotions are found everywhere. A freestanding insert in the Sunday newspaper contains a coupon offering $1 off Folgers coffee. An e-mail from Amazon.com offers free shipping on your next purchase over $35. The end-of-the-aisle display in the local supermarket tempts impulse buyers with a wall of Coke cartons. An executive buys a new Sony laptop and gets a free carrying case, or a family buys a new Taurus and receives a factory rebate of $500. A hardware store chain receives a 10 percent discount on selected Black & Decker portable power tools if it agrees to advertise them in local newspapers. Sales promotion includes a wide variety of promotion tools designed to stimulate earlier or stronger market response.

Rapid Growth of Sales Promotion

Sales promotion tools are used by most organizations, including manufacturers, distributors, retailers, and not-for-profit institutions. They are targeted toward final buyers (*consumer promotions*), retailers and wholesalers (*trade promotions*), business customers (*business promotions*), and members of the sales force (*sales force promotions*). Today, in the average consumer packaged-goods company, sales promotion accounts for 76 percent of all marketing expenditures.[17]

Several factors have contributed to the rapid growth of sales promotion, particularly in consumer markets. First, inside the company, product managers face greater pressures to increase their current sales, and promotion is viewed as an effective short-run sales tool. Second, externally, the company faces more competition and competing brands are less differentiated. Increasingly, competitors are using sales promotion to help differentiate their offers. Third, advertising efficiency has declined because of rising costs, media clutter, and legal restraints. Finally, consumers have become more deal oriented, and ever-larger retailers are demanding more deals from manufacturers.

The growing use of sales promotion has resulted in *promotion clutter*, similar to advertising clutter. Consumers are increasingly tuning out promotions, weakening their ability to trigger immediate purchase. Manufacturers are now searching for ways to rise above the clutter, such as offering larger coupon values or creating more dramatic point-of-purchase displays.

In developing a sales promotion program, a company must first set sales promotion objectives and then select the best tools for accomplishing these objectives.

Sales Promotion Objectives

Sales promotion objectives vary widely. Sellers may use *consumer promotions* to increase short-term sales or to help build long-term market share. Objectives for *trade promotions* include getting retailers to carry new items and more inventory, getting them to advertise the product and give it more shelf space, and getting them to buy ahead. For the *sales force*, objectives include getting more sales force support for current or new products or getting salespeople to sign up new accounts. Sales promotions are usually used together with advertising, personal selling, or other promotion mix tools. Consumer promotions must usually be advertised and can add excitement and pulling power to ads. Trade and sales force promotions support the firm's personal selling process.

In general, rather than creating only short-term sales or temporary brand switching, sales promotions should help to reinforce the product's position and build long-term *customer relationships*. Increasingly, marketers are avoiding "quick fix," price-only promotions in favor of promotions designed to build brand equity.

Even price promotions can be designed to help build customer relationships. Examples include all of the "frequency marketing programs" and loyalty clubs that have mushroomed in recent years. For example, most supermarkets, hotels, and airlines now offer frequent-buyer/flyer/guest programs offering discounts to regular customers. Lladró, maker of fine porcelain figurines, sponsors the Lladró Privilege Society. Members receive a subscription to the *Lladró Privilege Magazine*, access to exclusive Lladró sculptures, invitations to attend a variety of prestigious social gatherings and cultural events, as well as other relationship benefits. Similarly, Norwegian Cruise Lines sponsors a loyalty program called Latitudes. Latitudes members receive exclusive deals and promotions; an up to $200 on-board credit; the services of a special person assigned to answer their questions at sea; savings on future sailings; invitations to an exclusive captain's reception and escorted tours of the ship's bridge and galley; and *Latitudes* magazine, which contains special articles on NCL's fleet and ports. If properly designed, every sales promotion tool has the potential to build consumer relationships.

Major Sales Promotion Tools

Many tools can be used to accomplish sales promotion objectives. Descriptions of the main consumer, trade, and business promotion tools follow.

Consumer Promotion Tools

The main *consumer promotion tools* include samples; coupons; cash refunds; price packs; premiums; advertising specialties; patronage rewards; point-of-purchase displays and demonstrations; and contests, sweepstakes, and games.

■ Consumer relationship building promotions: Benefits of the Lladró Privilege Society include a subscription to the *Lladró Privilege Magazine,* access to exclusive Lladro sculptures, invitations to attend a variety of prestigious social gatherings and cultural events, and other relationship benefits.

Sample
A small amount of a product offered to customers for trial.

Samples are offers of a trial amount of a product. Sampling is the most effective—but most expensive—way to introduce a new product. For example, to launch Vanilla Coke, Coca-Cola distributed more than 1.3 million samples of the beverage. But the soft drink marketer didn't just hand out the samples. Instead, Coke's "experiential sampling teams" stopped targeted teen consumers at hangouts like malls, skate parks, concerts, and fairs, then delivered live commercials with messages like "Satisfy your curiosity, try a free Vanilla Coke." Says the president of Coca Cola's promotion agency, "We wanted to get Vanilla Coke's target audience with a memorable live experience for the brand." Based on the success of the Vanilla Coke sampling effort, Coca-Cola recently used its sampling teams to distribute more than 4 million samples of its new low-carb alternative, C2.[18]

Some samples are free; for others, the company charges a small amount to offset its cost. The sample might be delivered door-to-door, sent by mail, handed out in a store, attached to another product, or featured in an ad. Sometimes, samples are combined into sample packs, which can then be used to promote other products and services. Health food brand, Eat Natural, distributed samples via the Internet by encouraging customers to log on and send free products to their friends and families. Procter & Gamble also distributed samples via the Web:[19]

When Procter & Gamble decided to relaunch Pert Plus shampoo, it extended its $20 million ad campaign by constructing a new Web site (www.pertplus.com). P&G had three objectives for the Web site: to create awareness for reformulated Pert Plus, get consumers to try the product, and gather data about Web users. The site's first page invited visitors to place their heads against the computer screen in a mock attempt to measure the cleanliness of their hair. After "tabulating the results," the site told visitors that they "need immediate help." The solution: "How about a free sample of new Pert Plus?" Visitors obtained the sample by filling out a short demographic form. The site offered other interesting features as well. For example, clicking "get a friend in a lather" produced a template that sent an e-mail to a friend with an invitation to visit the site and receive a free sample. How did the sampling promotion work out? Even P&G was shocked by the turnout. Within just 2 months of launching the site, 170,000 people visited and 83,000 requested samples. More surprising, given that the site was only 10 pages deep, the average person visited the site 1.9 times and spent a total of 7.5 minutes each visit.

Coupon
Certificate that gives buyers a saving when they purchase a specified product.

Coupons are certificates that give buyers a saving when they purchase specified products. Most consumers love coupons. Manufacturers distribute 248 billion coupons a year. Consumers clip some 3.6 billion of them, with an average face value of 82 cents, for a total savings of $3 billion.[20] Coupons can promote early trial of a new brand or stimulate sales of a mature brand. However, as a result of coupon clutter, redemption rates have been declining in recent years. Thus, most major consumer goods companies are issuing fewer coupons and targeting them more carefully.

Marketers are also cultivating new outlets for distributing coupons, such as supermarket shelf dispensers, electronic point-of-sale coupon printers, or "paperless coupon systems." An example is Catalina Marketing Network's Checkout Direct system, which dispenses personalized discounts to targeted buyers at the checkout counter in stores, based on current and past purchasing behavior. Redemption rates for such coupons range from 8 to 11 percent, six to eight times that of traditional coupons. Some companies also offer coupons on their Web sites or through online coupon services such as coolsavings.com, valupage.com, hotcoupons.com, valpak.com, and directcoupons.com. Last year, as a result of sites like these, the number of coupons distributed online more than doubled.[21]

Cash refund offer (rebate)
Offer to refund part of the purchase price of a product to consumers who send a "proof of purchase" to the manufacturer.

Cash refund offers (or **rebates**) are like coupons except that the price reduction occurs after the purchase rather than at the retail outlet. The consumer sends a "proof of purchase" to the manufacturer, who then refunds part of the purchase price by mail. For example, Toro ran a clever preseason promotion on some of its snowblower models, offering a rebate if the snowfall in the buyer's market area turned out to be below average. Competitors were not able to match this offer on such short notice, and the promotion was very successful.

Price pack (cents-off deal)
Reduced price that is marked by the producer directly on the label or package.

Price packs (also called **cents-off deals**) offer consumers savings off the regular price of a product. The reduced prices are marked by the producer directly on the label or package. Price packs can be single packages sold at a reduced price (such as two for the price of one), or two related products banded together (such as a toothbrush and toothpaste). Price packs are very effective—even more so than coupons—in stimulating short-term sales.

Premium
Good offered either free or at low cost as an incentive to buy a product.

Premiums are goods offered either free or at low cost as an incentive to buy a product, ranging from toys included with kids' products to phone cards and CDs. A premium may come inside the package (in-pack), outside the package (on-pack), or through the mail. In its "Treasure Hunt" promotion, for example, Quaker Oats inserted $5 million worth of gold and

■ Coupons: Most consumers love coupons. Manufacturers distribute 248 billion of them a year, for a total savings of $3 billion.

silver coins in Ken-I. Ration dog food packages. United Airlines rewarded Chicago-area 75,000 Mileage Plus frequent-flier club members with a custom CD. The 10-song, Chicago-themed compilation disk, entitled "Chicago—Our Kind of Town," was widely played on local radio stations. It became so popular that United ended up selling it at record stores.[22]

Advertising specialties, also called *promotional products*, are useful articles imprinted with an advertiser's name, logo, or message that are given as gifts to consumers. Typical items include T-shirts and other apparel, pens, coffee mugs, calendars, key rings, mouse pads, matches, tote bags, coolers, golf balls, and caps. Such items can be very effective. In a recent study, 63 percent of all consumers surveyed were either carrying or wearing an ad specialty item. More than three-quarters of those who had an item could recall the advertiser's name or message before showing the item to the interviewer.[23]

Patronage rewards are cash or other awards offered for the regular use of a certain company's products or services. For example, airlines offer frequent flier plans, awarding points for miles traveled that can be turned in for free airline trips. Hotels have adopted honored-guest plans that award points to users of their hotels. And supermarkets issue frequent shopper cards that dole out a wealth of discounts at the checkout. Baskin-Robbins offers frequent-purchase awards—for every 10 purchases, customers receive a free quart of ice cream.

Point-of-purchase (POP) promotions include displays and demonstrations that take place at the point of purchase or sale. An example is a five-foot-high cardboard display of Cap'n Crunch next to Cap'n Crunch cereal boxes. Unfortunately, many retailers do not like to handle the hundreds of displays, signs, and posters they receive from manufacturers each year. Manufacturers have responded by offering better POP materials, tying them in with television or print messages, and offering to set them up.

Contests, sweepstakes, and games give consumers the chance to win something, such as cash, trips, or goods, by luck or through extra effort. A *contest* calls for consumers to submit an entry—a jingle, guess, suggestion—to be judged by a panel that will select the best entries. A *sweepstakes* calls for consumers to submit their names for a drawing. A *game* presents consumers with something—bingo numbers, missing letters—every time they buy, which may or may not help them win a prize. A sales contest urges dealers or the sales force to increase their efforts, with prizes going to the top performers.

Trade Promotion Tools

Manufacturers direct more sales promotion dollars toward retailers and wholesalers (78 percent) than to consumers (22 percent). Trade promotion can persuade resellers to carry a brand, give it shelf space, promote it in advertising, and push it to consumers. Shelf space is so scarce these days that manufacturers often have to offer price-offs, allowances, buy-back guarantees, or free goods to retailers and wholesalers to get products on the shelf and, once there, to stay on it.

Manufacturers use several trade promotion tools. Many of the tools used for consumer promotions—contests, premiums, displays—can also be used as trade promotions. Or the manufacturer may offer a straight **discount** off the list price on each case purchased during a stated period of time (also called a *price-off, off-invoice,* or *off list*). Manufacturers also may offer an **allowance** (usually so much off per case) in return for the retailer's agreement to feature the manufacturer's products in some way. An *advertising allowance* compensates retailers for advertising the product. A *display allowance* compensates them for using special displays.

Manufacturers may offer *free goods,* which are extra cases of merchandise, to resellers who buy a certain quantity or who feature a certain flavor or size. They may offer *push money*—cash or gifts to dealers or their sales forces to "push" the manufacturer's goods. Manufacturers may give retailers free *specialty advertising* items that carry the company's name, such as pens, pencils, calendars, paperweights, matchbooks, memo pads, and yardsticks.

STOPS HERE

Business Promotion Tools

Companies spend billions of dollars each year on promotion to industrial customers. These *business promotion tools* are used to generate business leads, stimulate purchases, reward customers, and motivate salespeople. Business promotion includes many of the same tools used for consumer or trade promotions. Here, we focus on two additional major business promotion tools—conventions and trade shows, and sales contests.

Many companies and trade associations organize *conventions and trade shows* to promote their products. Firms selling to the industry show their products at the trade show. Vendors receive many benefits, such as opportunities to find new sales leads, contact customers, introduce new products, meet new customers, sell more to present customers, and educate customers with publications and audiovisual materials. Trade shows also help companies reach

Advertising specialty
Useful article imprinted with an advertiser's name, given as a gift to consumers.

Patronage reward
Cash or other award for the regular use of a certain company's products or services.

Point-of-purchase (POP) promotion
Display and demonstration that takes place at the point of purchase or sale.

Contests, sweepstakes, games
Promotional events that give consumers the chance to win something—such as cash, trips, or goods—by luck or through extra effort.

Discount
A straight reduction in price on purchases during a stated period of time.

Allowance
Promotional money paid by manufacturers to retailers in return for an agreement to feature the manufacturer's products in some way.

■ Some trade shows are huge. At this year's International Consumer Electronics Show, 2,400 exhibitors attracted more than 130,000 professional visitors.

many prospects not reached through their sales forces. Some trade shows are huge. For example, at this year's International Consumer Electronics Show, 2,400 exhibitors attracted more than 130,000 professional visitors. Even more impressive, at the BAUMA mining and construction equipment trade show in Munich, Germany, some 2,800 exhibitors from 47 countries presented their latest product innovations to more than 400,000 attendees from 171 countries.[24]

A *sales contest* is a contest for salespeople or dealers to motivate them to increase their sales performance over a given period. Sales contests motivate and recognize good company performers, who may receive trips, cash prizes, or other gifts. Some companies award points for performance, which the receiver can turn in for any of a variety of prizes. Sales contests work best when they are tied to measurable and achievable sales objectives (such as finding new accounts, reviving old accounts, or increasing account profitability).

Developing the Sales Promotion Program

The marketer must make several other decisions in order to define the full sales promotion program. First, the marketer must decide on the *size of the incentive*. A certain minimum incentive is necessary if the promotion is to succeed; a larger incentive will produce more sales response. The marketer also must set *conditions for participation*. Incentives might be offered to everyone or only to select groups.

The marketer must then decide how to *promote and distribute the promotion* program itself. A 50-cents-off coupon could be given out in a package, at the store, by mail, or in an advertisement. Each distribution method involves a different level of reach and cost. Increasingly, marketers are blending several media into a total campaign concept. The *length of the promotion* is also important. If the sales promotion period is too short, many prospects (who may not be buying during that time) will miss it. If the promotion runs too long, the deal will lose some of its "act now" force.

Evaluation is also very important. Yet many companies fail to evaluate their sales promotion programs, and others evaluate them only superficially. The most common evaluation method is to compare sales before, during, and after a promotion. Suppose a company has a 6 percent market share before the promotion, which jumps to 10 percent during the promotion, falls to 5 percent right after, and rises to 7 percent later on. The promotion seems to have attracted new triers and stimulated more buying by current customers. After the promotion, sales fell as consumers used up their inventories. The long-run rise to 7 percent means that the company gained some new users. If the brand's share had returned to the old level, then the promotion would have changed only the *timing* of demand rather than the *total* demand.

Consumer research would also show the kinds of people who responded to the promotion and what they did after it ended. *Surveys* can provide information on how many consumers recall the promotion, what they thought of it, how many took advantage of it, and how it affected their buying. Sales promotions also can be evaluated through *experiments* that vary factors such as incentive value, length, and distribution method.

Clearly, sales promotion plays an important role in the total promotion mix. To use it well, the marketer must define the sales promotion objectives, select the best tools, design the sales promotion program, implement the program, and evaluate the results. Moreover, sales promotion must be coordinated carefully with other promotion mix elements within the integrated marketing communications program.

Public Relations START HERE

Public relations

Building good relations with the company's various publics by obtaining favorable publicity, building up a good "corporate image," and handling or heading off unfavorable rumors, stories, and events.

Another major mass-promotion tool is **public relations**—building good relations with the company's various publics by obtaining favorable publicity, building up a good corporate image, and handling or heading off unfavorable rumors, stories, and events. Public relations departments may perform any or all of the following functions:[25]

- *Press relations or press agency:* Creating and placing newsworthy information in the news media to attract attention to a person, product, or service.
- *Product publicity:* Publicizing specific products.
- *Public affairs:* Building and maintaining national or local community relations.
- *Lobbying:* Building and maintaining relations with legislators and government officials to influence legislation and regulation.
- *Investor relations:* Maintaining relationships with shareholders and others in the financial community.
- *Development:* Public relations with donors or members of not-for-profit organizations to gain financial or volunteer support.

■ Public relations is used to promote products, people, places, ideas, activities, organizations, and even nations. The state of New York turned its image around when its "I ♥ New York!" campaign took root, bringing in millions more tourists.

Public relations is used to promote products, people, places, ideas, activities, organizations, and even nations. Companies use public relations to build good relations with consumers, investors, the media, and their communities. Trade associations have used PR to rebuild interest in declining commodities such as eggs, apples, milk, and potatoes. The state of New York turned its image around when its "I ♥ New York!" publicity and advertising campaign took root, bringing in millions more tourists. Johnson & Johnson's masterly use of public relations played a major role in saving Tylenol from extinction after its product-tampering scare. Nations have used public relations to attract more tourists, foreign investment, and international support.

The Role and Impact of Public Relations

Public relations can have a strong impact on public awareness at a much lower cost than advertising can. The company does not pay for the space or time in the media. Rather, it pays for a staff to develop and circulate information and to manage events. If the company develops an interesting story, it could be picked up by several different media, having the same effect as advertising that would cost millions of dollars. And it would have more credibility than advertising.

Public relations results can sometimes be spectacular. Here's how publisher Scholastic, Inc., used public relations to turn a simple, new book introduction into a major international event, all on a very small budget:

> Secret codes. A fiercely guarded text. Huddled masses lined up in funny hats at the witching hour. Welcome to one of the biggest and oddest literary events in history. As the clock crept past midnight, kids worldwide rushed to buy the next installment of the Harry Potter series. It was the fastest-shrinking book pile in history—with nearly 3 million copies selling in 48 hours in the United States alone. The spellbinding plots, written by Scottish welfare-mom-turned-millionaire J. K. Rowling, captivated kids everywhere, but the hidden hand of [public relations] played a role, too. With contests, theme parties, and giveaways, conditions were hot for Harry. How do you whip up a consumer frenzy with a mere $1.8 million promotion budget? Scholastic mixed in-store promotions with a few carefully placed ads [and a heap of public relations hype] to create a sense of celebration. It heightened the tension by keeping the title and book jacket under wraps almost until the last minute, even forcing booksellers to sign secrecy agreements.[26]

Despite its potential strengths, public relations is sometimes described as a marketing stepchild because of its often limited and scattered use. The PR department is usually located at corporate headquarters. Its staff is so busy dealing with various publics—stockholders, employees, legislators, city officials—that public relations programs to support product marketing objectives may be ignored. Marketing managers and public relations practitioners do not always talk the same language. Many PR practitioners see their job as simply communicating. In contrast, marketing managers tend to be much more interested in how advertising and public relations affect brand building, sales, and profits.

This situation is changing, however. Although public relations still captures only a small portion of the overall marketing budgets of most firms, PR is playing an increasingly important brand-building role. Public relations can be a powerful brand-building tool. Consider how Procter & Gamble used PR to launch Crest Whitestrips:

> Just before the product launch, to spread the word about Whitestrips, Procter & Gamble first identified key "influencer groups" to target: bridal consultants, salon and spa owners, and national and local sorority leaders. These influencers were considered image "experts." P&G held special conferences for these image experts to introduce them to Whitestrips. It also hired Joan and Melissa Rivers for Whitestrips launch-day celebrations. These celebrities, along with the permission slips they distributed and a giant billboard in Times Square, assured consumers that it is "Okay to Wear White after Labor Day." P&G also created an "Uppers Challenge" encouraging skeptics to use Whitestrips on only their upper teeth to reveal the real difference. Spokespeople who'd taken this challenge worked the crowds, showing the "uppers" difference. In all, the PR campaign brought 240 million media impressions, including broadcast coverage on the "Today" show and

■ Public relations results can sometimes be spectacular. Scholastic sponsored low-cost sleepovers, games, and costume contests to whip up consumer frenzy for the fifth installment of its Harry Potter series.

print coverage in *Good Housekeeping, Family Circle, Glamour, InStyle,* and *Elle.* And when Procter & Gamble launched its highly successful White Strips, prelaunch efforts generated $23 million in sales prior to retail availability. Of those sales, one-third were directly linked to public relations. P&G now holds a substantial lead in the whitening segment of the $500 million a year oral care market.[27]

Two well-known marketing consultants even go so far as to conclude that advertising doesn't build brands, PR does. In their book *The Fall of Advertising & the Rise of PR,* the consultants proclaim that the era of advertising is over, and that public relations is quietly becoming the most powerful marketing communications tools.

The birth of a brand is usually accomplished with [public relations], not advertising. Our general rule is [PR] first, advertising second. [Public relations] is the nail, advertising the hammer. [PR] creates the credentials that provide the credibility for advertising. . . . Anita Roddick built the Body Shop into a major brand with no advertising at all. Instead, she traveled the world on a relentless quest for publicity. . . . Until recently Starbucks Coffee Co. didn't spend a hill of beans on advertising, either. In 10 years, the company spent less than $10 million on advertising, a trivial amount for a brand that delivers annual sales of $1.3 billion. Wal-Mart Stores became the world's largest retailer . . . with very little advertising. . . . On the Internet, Amazon.com became a powerhouse brand with virtually no advertising.[28]

Although the book created much controversy, and most advertisers wouldn't agree about the "fall of advertising" part of the title, the point is a good one. Advertising and public relations should work hand in hand to build and maintain brands.

Major Public Relations Tools

Public relations professionals use several tools. One of the major tools is *news*. PR professionals find or create favorable news about the company and its products or people. Sometimes news stories occur naturally, and sometimes the PR person can suggest events or activities that would create news. *Speeches* can also create product and company publicity. Increasingly, company executives must field questions from the media or give talks at trade associations or sales meetings, and these events can either build or hurt the company's image.

Another common PR tool is *special events*, ranging from news conferences, press tours, grand openings, and fireworks displays to laser shows, hot air balloon releases, multimedia presentations, star-studded spectaculars, or educational programs designed to reach and interest target publics. And as we discussed in Chapter 14, many marketers are now designing *buzz marketing* campaigns that create excitement and generate favorable word-of-mouth communication for their brands. Buzz marketing creates publicity by getting consumers themselves to spread the brand message.

Recently, *mobile marketing*—traveling promotional tours that bring the brand to consumers—has emerged as an effective way to build one-to-one relationships with targeted consumers.[29]

These days, it seems that almost every company is putting its show on the road. Not only are tours relatively cheap, they offer an irresistible opportunity to build brands while attracting additional sponsorship dollars and promotional relationships with retailers and other marketing partners. Home Depot recently brought do-it-yourself home project workshops and demonstrations to 26 NASCAR racetracks. Court TV launched a tour that visited malls in 20 cities, challenging consumers to solve a crime by visiting six "forensic labs" and interviewing a computerized virtual witness. Mattel's Matchbox Toys launched its first-ever tour last year, hitting store parking lots in 25 cities with events like interactive games, historic displays, free gifts, and an obstacle course for kids riding battery-powered vehicles. And Microsoft now teams with local partners to field Across America Mobile Solutions Centers, 27-foot techie dream vans, each complete with a server, two work stations, three laptops, and a 48-inch plasma screen. The vans visit information technology workers in offices around the country to demonstrate Microsoft's latest software products. According to a Microsoft executive, "The idea is to bring Microsoft's newest technology out to small and mid-size businesses that don't have time to visit every trade show, as well as to meet with customers."

Public relations people also prepare *written materials* to reach and influence their target markets. These materials include annual reports, brochures, articles, and company newsletters and magazines. *Audiovisual materials*, such as films, slide-and-sound programs, and video and audio CDs, are being used increasingly as communication tools. *Corporate identity materials* can also help create a corporate identity that the public immediately recognizes. Logos, stationery, brochures, signs, business forms, business cards, buildings, uniforms, and company cars and trucks—all become marketing tools when they are attractive, distinctive, and memorable. Finally, companies can improve public goodwill by contributing money and time to *public service activities*.

A company's Web site can be a good public relations vehicle. Consumers and members of other publics can visit the site for information and entertainment. Such sites can be extremely popular. For example, Butterball's site (www.butterball.com), which features cooking and carving tips, received 550,000 visitors in one day during Thanksgiving week last year. The

■ Mobile marketing: Microsoft teams with local partners to field Across America Mobile Solutions Centers, 27-foot techie dream vans, each complete with a server, two work stations, three laptops, and a 48-inch plasma screen.

Web site supplements the Butterball Turkey Talk-Line (1-800-BUTTERBALL)—called by some the "granddaddy of all help lines"—staffed by 50 home economists and nutritionists who respond to more than 100,000 questions each November and December.[30]

Web sites can also be ideal for handling crisis situations. For example, when several bottles of Odwalla apple juice sold on the West Coast were found to contain *E. coli* bacteria, Odwalla initiated a massive product recall. Within only 3 hours, it set up a Web site laden with information about the crisis and Odwalla's response. Company staffers also combed the Internet looking for newsgroups discussing Odwalla and posted links to the site. In another example, American Home Products quickly set up a Web site to distribute accurate information and advice after a model died reportedly after inhaling its Primatene Mist. The Primatene site, up less than 12 hours after the crisis broke, remains in place today (www.primatene.com). In all, notes one analyst, "Today, public relations is reshaping the Internet and the Internet, in turn, is redefining the practice of public relations." Says another, "People look to the Net for information, not salesmanship, and that's the real opportunity for public relations."[31]

As with the other promotion tools, in considering when and how to use product public relations, management should set PR objectives, choose the PR messages and vehicles, implement the PR plan, and evaluate the results. The firm's public relations should be blended smoothly with other promotion activities within the company's overall integrated marketing communications effort.

END.

> Reviewing the Concepts <

Companies must do more than make good products—they have to inform consumers about product benefits and carefully position products in consumers' minds. To do this, they must master three mass-promotion tools: *advertising, sales promotion,* and *public relations.*

1. Define the roles of advertising, sales promotion, and public relations in the promotion mix.

Advertising—the use of paid media by a seller to inform, persuade, and remind about its products or organization—is a strong promotion tool. American marketers spend more than $245 billion each year on advertising, and it takes many forms and has many uses. *Sales promotion* covers a wide variety of short-term incentive tools—coupons, premiums, contests, buying allowances—designed to stimulate final and business consumers, the trade, and the company's own sales force. Sales-promotion spending has been growing faster than advertising spending in recent years. *Public relations (PR)*—gaining favorable publicity and creating a favorable company image—is the least used of the major promotion tools, although it has great potential for building consumer awareness and preference.

2. Describe the major decisions involved in developing an advertising program.

Advertising decision making involves decisions about the objectives, the budget, the message, the media, and, finally, the evaluation of results. Advertisers should set clear *objectives* as to whether the advertising is supposed to inform, persuade, or remind buyers. The advertising *budget* can be based on sales, on competitors' spending, or on the objectives and tasks. The *message decision* calls for plan-

ning a message strategy and executing it effectively. The *media decision* involves defining reach, frequency, and impact goals; choosing major media types; selecting media vehicles; and deciding on media timing. Message and media decisions must be closely coordinated for maximum campaign effectiveness. Finally, *evaluation* calls for evaluating the communication and sales effects of advertising before, during, and after the advertising is placed.

3. Explain how sales promotion campaigns are developed and implemented.

Sales promotion campaigns call for setting sales promotions objectives (in general, sales promotions should be *consumer relationship building*); selecting tools; developing and implementing the sales promotion program by using trade promotion tools (*discounts, allowances, free goods, push money*) and business promotion tools (*conventions, trade shows, sales contests*) as well as deciding on such things as the size of the incentive, the conditions for participation, how to promote and distribute the promotion package, and the length of the promotion. After this process is completed, the company evaluates the results.

4. Explain how companies use public relations to communicate with their publics.

Companies use public relations to communicate with their publics by setting PR objectives, choosing PR messages and vehicles, implementing the PR plan, and evaluating PR results. To accomplish these goals, PR professionals use several tools such as *news, speeches,* and *special events.* They also prepare *written, audiovisual,* and *corporate identity materials* and contribute money and time to *public service activities.*

> Reviewing the Key Terms <

> Discussing the Concepts <

1. Discuss why it is important for an organization to set advertising objectives.

2. A number of factors make management's task of setting advertising budgets difficult. What are they?

3. What is advertising clutter and why is it a problem? How can an advertiser break through it?

4. Discuss three potential problems facing a pharmaceutical manufacturer who decides to advertise in Europe? Are these problems different from those the manufacturer would face when advertising in Asia?

5. Compare the major tools used in consumer sales promotion with those used in trade promotion and business promotion.

6. Public relations is sometimes referred to as a marketing stepchild. What is the basis for this comment, and what can be done to correct this problem?

> Applying the Concepts <

1. Prepare an advertising objective for a PC solutions provider who is entering a new business-to-business market in which the buying decision is made by a business buyer.

2. In a small group, choose three appropriate advertising media for an advertising campaign to introduce a new line of men's personal care products from Cedric the Entertainer.

3. Suppose you are the marketing coordinator responsible for recommending the sales promotion plan for the market launch of a new brand of Boba tea sold in supermarkets. What promotional tools would you consider for this task? Explain.

> Focus on Technology <

Coupons can play a major role in promoting trials of new brands and in reviving sales of mature brands. The delivery of coupons over the Internet has increased significantly over the years. One survey found that 19 percent of all Internet users have redeemed Internet coupons. Many organizations, including Yahoo, provide technology for sellers to create, post, and track coupons on the Internet. Advantages of Internet coupons for consumers include ease of use, convenience, relevance, and a targeted offer. For merchants, the advantages of using online coupon delivery over traditional mail or newspaper delivery are many. They are easy to prepare, quickly delivered, and cost effective. They can be used to target high-income and hard to reach markets and individuals with customized offers, and redemption is easy to track and measure. However, there are risks associated with Internet coupons. First is the risk of copying of coupons for multiple use. Second, Internet coupons are vulnerable to alteration,

increasing the redemption value or extending the time period. Finally, coupon print quality cannot be controlled and printed coupons may not scan properly. This may lead to unhappy customers or line slow-downs.

1. Do the advantages of Internet coupons outweigh the risks? Explain.

2. Beyond the risks discussed above, are there any other disadvantages in using Internet coupons?

3. What products or categories are good candidates for Internet coupons?

4. Can Internet coupons be integrated with other promotional tools? Explain.

Sources: See www.santella.com/Internet%20Coupon%20Guidelines.pdf; and www.imediaconnection.com/news/989.asp.

> Focus on Ethics <

Based on the chapter's definitions of advertising and public relations, there are big differences in these communications methods. However, both are susceptible to deception. The same standards used to gauge advertising deception are used to measure deception in pubic relations. A case in point is Nike vs. Kasky. The nature of the issue is captured in the lead paragraph of a Web article filed in mid-2003. "Today the U.S. Supreme Court dismissed an appeal by Nike Inc. on technical grounds. The shoe and apparel giant was appealing a California state Supreme Court decision that it can be sued for false advertising over a publicity campaign it used to defend itself against accusations that its footwear was made in Asian sweatshops." Go to www.law.duke.edu/publiclaw/supremecourtonline/certgrants/2002/nikvkas.

html and read the description of the suit. Then respond to the following questions.

1. What are your thoughts on this claim of deception in a publicity program?

2. Which standard did Nike violate?

3. Does this ruling support or undermine a need for integrated marketing communications?

Sources: See www.srimedia.com/artman/publish/article_642.shtml; and www.law.duke.edu/publiclaw/supremecourtonline/certgrants/2002/nikvkas.html.

Video Case

AFLAC

Quick, name a supplemental insurance company! The chances are good that you thought of AFLAC, even if you're not entirely certain what supplemental insurance is. The highly successful $9.7 billion insurer is now by far the best-known firm in the supplemental insurance industry, which offers policies that kick in to pay expenses not covered by the standard health, life, and disability policies provided by most employers.

But AFLAC hasn't always enjoyed such high levels of recognition. Until recently, about the only people who'd ever heard of AFLAC lived either in Columbus, Georgia (where the company was founded) or in Japan (where it does more than 70 percent of its business, commands 85 percent of the supplemental insurance market, and serves 95 percent of the companies listed on the Tokyo Stock Exchange). Just a few years ago, only 13 percent of Americans even recognized the company's name. But now, thanks to an unorthodox advertising campaign—featuring an improbable squawking white duck—practically every American knows about AFLAC.

After viewing the video featuring AFLAC, answer the following questions about advertising, sales promotion, and public relations.

1. What key attributes of AFLAC's ads make them so successful? Now that the insurance company is so widely known, should it consider changing its advertising approach or stick with the spokesduck?

2. How did the advertising media that AFLAC marketers selected for communicating with consumers affect the success of the campaign?

3. Could AFLAC supplement its advertising campaign with public relations? List two possible public relations activities that would help AFLAC publicize its products.

Company Case

Pepsi: Promoting Nothing

WATER WARS

Everyone's familiar with the cola wars—the epic battles between Pepsi Cola and Coca-Cola in the soft-drink market. The war has featured numerous taste tests and mostly friendly, but sometimes not-so-friendly, television ads featuring Pepsi and Coke delivery-truck drivers, each trying to outdo the other.

The major problem that Pepsi and Coke face is that the cola market is mature and not growing very rapidly. Thus, to generate new sales and new customers, the companies have to look for new fronts.

In the early 1990s, the bottled-water market was just a drop in huge U.S. beverage market bucket. The Evian and Perrier brands dominated the tiny niche and helped establish bottled spring water's clean, healthy image. Pepsi took an early interest in the water market. It tried several different ways to attack this market, with both spring water and sparkling water, but each failed. Then it hit on the idea of taking advantage of a built-in resource—its existing bottlers.

Pepsi's bottlers already had their own water treatment facilities to purify municipal tap water used in making soft drinks. Municipal tap water was already pure and had to pass constant monitoring and rigorous quarterly EPA prescribed tests. Still, cola bottlers filtered it again before using it in the production process.

Pepsi decided that it would *really* filter the tap water. It experimented with a reverse osmosis process, pushing already-filtered tap water at high pressure through fiberglass membranes to remove even the tiniest particles. Then, carbon filters removed chlorine and any other particles that might give the water any taste or smell. However, all this filtering removed even good particles that killed bacteria, so

Pepsi had to add ozone to the water to keep bacteria from growing. The result? Aquafina—a water with no taste or odor—that Pepsi believed could compete with the spring waters already on the market. Further, Pepsi could license its bottlers to use the Aquafina name and sell them the filtration equipment. Because the process used tap water that was relatively inexpensive, Pepsi's Aquafina would also compete well on price with the spring waters.

The marketing strategy was relatively simple. Whereas Evian and the other early entrants targeted women and high-end consumers, Pepsi wanted consumers to see Aquafina as a "unisex, mainstream" water with an everyday price. When the company launched the product in 1994, it was content just to build distribution using its established system and spend very little money on promotion. Pepsi believed that soft-drink advertising should be for soft drinks, not water.

COME ON IN—THE WATER'S FINE

By 1999, what had been a minor trickle in the beverage market had turned into a geyser—bottled water had become the fastest-growing beverage category, and Pepsi had a big head start. Coca-Cola decided it was time to take the plunge. Like Pepsi, Coca-Cola realized its bottlers were already set up to handle a filtered-water process. Unlike Pepsi, however, rather than taking everything out of the tap water, it wanted to put something in.

Coca-Cola's researchers analyzed tap waters and bottled waters and concocted a combination of minerals they believed would give filtered tap water a fresh, clean taste. The formula included magnesium sulfate, potassium chloride, and salt. Coca-Cola guarded the new water formula just

(box continues)

as it had the original Coke recipe. Thus, it could sell the formula to its bottlers, as it does Coke concentrate, and let them make the water. Like Pepsi, Coca-Cola was content initially just to get its water, which it called Dasani, into distribution.

HOW TO PROMOTE WATER

By 2001, however, the bottled-water category had over 800 competitors and had grown to $3.53 billion in U.S. sales. Analysts predicted bottled water would become the second largest beverage category by 2004.

Given the rapid market growth rate and all the competition, Pepsi and Coca-Cola decided they had better promote their products, just as they did their soft drinks. In 2001, Pepsi launched a $14 million campaign showing how water was a part of real people's lives. Coca-Cola countered with a $20 million campaign that targeted women and used the tagline: "Treat yourself well. Everyday."

Not to be outdone, Pepsi responded by more than doubling it *promotion* budget to $40 million in 2002. Included in the advertising was a spot featuring "Friends" star Lisa Kudrow. Lisa described how refreshing and mouthwatering Aquafina was—emphasizing that it made no promises it couldn't keep. She described Aquafina as "Pure nothing." The ads featured the tagline: "We promise nothing."

By 2003, the U.S. wholesale bottled-water market had surged to $8.3 billion, up 6.7 percent from 2002. In the same period, wholesale sales of carbonated beverages inched up only 1.5 percent to $45.7 billion. During 2003, Pepsi spent $24 million on Aquafina's *advertising*, while Coke spent $19 million on Dasani's. Although these two brands were number one and number two, respectively, with 17.7 and 13 percent market shares, all private-label brands combined took third place with a 10.4 percent market share.

One Aquafina 2003 ad featured black-and-white images of an artist, skier, and guitar player drinking the water and carried the tagline "Aquafina. Purity Guaranteed." In mid-2004, Pepsi introduced a new tagline, "Drink more water," to promote sales of all water. One ad showed people partying at an English pub and a German beer garden. Instead of drinking beer, however, they were chugging Aquafina. Coke also had an ad showing young people sipping Dasani at a nightclub.

HAVE ANOTHER ROUND

Pepsi, however, is not satisfied with its water advertising and plans to juice up what it sees as generally lackluster advertising and promotion throughout the industry. A problem with the category, a Pepsi marketing officer notes, is that many consumers shop based on price. This is especially true in a product category where the products are so similar. Analysts note that such similarity makes it difficult to build a brand or brand loyalty.

Further, even in such a category, the companies keep introducing new products. Pepsi already has Aquafina Essentials on the market, a water fortified with vitamins and minerals that comes in four fruit flavors. It has also applied for a trademark for Aquafina Sparkling water and is test marketing H2Oh!, a lower-priced bottled water.

So, Pepsi and Coca-cola have drawn new battle lines—this time for the water wars. Can Pepsi convince consumers to prefer a water that offered nothing versus Coca-Cola's water that offered something—although both products were colorless, odorless, and tasteless? Further, can Pepsi develop a promotion mix that builds brand loyalty across several products in a market characterized by price-conscious shoppers?

Questions for Discussion

1. What markets should Pepsi target for Aquafina?

2. What advertising objectives should Pepsi set for Aquafina?

3. What message strategy and message execution recommendations would you make for Aquafina?

4. What advertising media recommendations would you make for Aquafina, and how would you evaluate the effectiveness of those media and your advertising?

5. What sales promotion and public relations recommendations would you make for Aquafina?

6. What promotion recommendations would you make for Aquafina Essentials, Aquafina Sparkling Water, and H2Oh!?

Sources: Suzanne Vranica, "Partyers Knock Back a Few . . . Aquafinas," *The Wall Street Journal*, July 13, 2004, p. B4; "No Slowdown In Sight for Bottled Water," *Beverage Industry*, September 2003, pg. 22; Betsy McKay, "In a Water Fight, Coke and Pepsi Try Opposite Tacks," *The Wall Street Journal*, April 18, 2002, p. A1; Bob Garfield, "The Product Is Questionable, But Aquafina's Ads Hold Water," *Advertising* Age, July 9, 2001, p. 39; Kenneth Hein, "Coke, Pepsi Mull Jump Into 'Aquaceuticals'," *Brandweek*, June 25, 2001, p. 8; Betsy McKay, "Coke and Pepsi Escalate Their Water Fight, *The Wall Street Journal*, May 18, 2001, p. B8.

---

1) TARGET MARKET
   - Lower priced
   - Women
   - Unisex
   - Health conscious

2) Gain market share
   Grow the market for bottled water
   A water with no taste or odor

3) Lifestyle
   Slice of life
   Personality
   Testimonial

4) Races - marathons - fairs - sport events

> **After studying this chapter, you should be able to**

1. discuss the role of a company's salespeople in creating value for customers and building customer relationships
2. identify and explain the six major sales force management steps
3. discuss the personal selling process, distinguishing between transaction-oriented marketing and relationship marketing
4. define direct marketing and discuss its benefits to customers and companies
5. identify and discuss the major forms of direct marketing

Personal Selling and Direct Marketing

Previewing the Concepts

In the previous two chapters, you learned about integrated marketing communication (IMC) and three specific elements of the marketing communications mix—advertising, sales promotion, and publicity. In this chapter, we'll learn about the final two IMC elements—personal selling and direct marketing. Personal selling is the interpersonal arm of marketing communications in which the sales force interacts with customers and prospects to make sales and build relationships. Direct marketing consists of direct connections with carefully targeted consumers to both obtain an immediate response and cultivate lasting customer relationships. As you read on, remember that although this chapter examines personal selling and direct marketing as separate tools, they must be carefully integrated with other elements of the marketing communications mix.

When someone says "salesperson," what image comes to mind? Or how about "direct marketing"? Perhaps you think about a stereotypical glad-hander who's out to lighten your wallet by selling you something you don't really need, or about a high-pressure telemarketing call that interrupts your dinner. Think again. Today, for most companies, personal selling and direct marketing play an important role in building profitable customer relationships. Consider CDW Corporation, whose customer-focused "clicks and people" direct marketing strategy has helped it grow rapidly while competitors have faltered.

> **10:45 pm.** Account Manager Erin Bliss finishes Advanced Linux Volume IX. Meanwhile, husband Gary begins XP For Dummies.

CDW The Right Technology. Right Away.

They undergo continuous training and provide expert advice on over 1,200 leading technology brands. That's your dedicated account manager. Someone who knows technology and you.

800.800.4CDW

CDW.com

Perhaps no industry felt the recent economic slow-down more than the technology sector—total information technology spending has been relatively flat for several years. But despite the slump, CDW Corporation, the nation's largest direct marketer of multi-brand technology products and services, is thriving. Even as the tech world has collapsed, since 2000 CDW has managed to increase its sales 23 percent, to $4.7 billion annually. Profits are up 21 percent, and the company now serves some 415,000 active commercial accounts, up 35 percent from just three years ago.

How has CDW managed to grow while other tech companies have faltered? The company owes its success to its highly effective "clicks and people" direct marketing strategy. CDW's direct model combines good old fashioned high-touch personal selling with a modern high-tech Web presence to build lasting one-to-one customer relationships. The strategy is fueled by a genuine passion for solving customer problems. Under CDW's "Circle of Service" philosophy, "everything revolves around the customer."

CDW sells a complex assortment of more than 100,000 technology products and services—computers, software, accessories, and networking products—including top name brands such as APC, Apple, Cisco, HP, IBM, Microsoft, Sony, Symantec, Toshiba, and ViewSonic. Many of CDW's competitors chase after a relative handful of very large customers. However, while CDW serves customers of all sizes, one of the company's core customer segments is small and midsize businesses (SMBs). These smaller customers often need lots of advice and support. "Many of our clients don't have IT departments," says one CDW executive, "so they look to us for expertise."

That's where the "people" part of CDW's "clicks and people" strategy comes in. The major responsibility for building and managing customer relationships falls to CDW's sales force of nearly 2,000 account managers. Each customer is assigned an account manager, who helps the customer select the right products and technologies and keep them running smoothly.

Account managers do more than just sell technology products and services. They work closely with customers to find solutions to their technology problems. "This is a big deal to us," says Jim Grass, senior director of sales at CDW. "We want to go beyond fulfilling the order and become the trusted adviser for them. We [want to] talk . . . about what a customer is trying to accomplish and really add value to the sale, as opposed to just sending out a box."

To become trusted advisors and effective customer-relationship builders, CDW account managers really have to know their stuff. And CDW boasts some of the most knowledgeable salespeople in the industry. New account managers complete a six-week training program followed by six months of just-in-time training, courtesy of CDW University. They receive intensive schooling in the science behind the company's products and in the art of consultative selling. But that's just the beginning—the training never ends. Tenured account managers receive ongoing training to enhance their relationship-selling skills. Each year, CDW's sales force completes a whopping 339,000 hours of sales-specific training.

To further support salespeople's customer problem-solving efforts, CDW has also created nine technology teams consisting of more than 150 certified specialists. Account managers can draw on these teams to design customer-specific solutions in technology areas such as mobility/wireless, networking, security, and storage.

Customers who want to access CDW's products and expertise without going through their account manager can do so easily at any of several CDW Web sites—the "clicks" side of CDW's "clicks and people" strategy. Better yet, CDW will create a free personalized CDW@work extranet site that reflects a given customer's pricing, order status, account history, and special considerations. The extranet site serves as a 24-hour extension of the customer's account manager. CDW has set up more than 170,000 such sites, resulting in direct Web sales of more than $1 billion last year. But even here, the ever-present account managers are likely to add personal guidance. Account managers receive immediate notification of their customers'

online activities. So if a blurry-eyed SMB manager makes a mistake on an emergency order placed in the middle of the night, chances are good that the account manager will find and correct the error first thing in the morning.

Beyond being knowledgeable and ever-present, CDW's account managers are energetic and passionately customer-focused. Much of the energy has passed down from CDW founder and former chairman and CEO Michael Krasny. Selling has always been a top priority for Krasny, not surprising given that he began testing his direct marketing model by selling used personal computers out of his home through classified ads. During his nearly 20-year reign as head of CDW, Krasny created a hard-working and dedicated sales force. One favorite Krasny tale involves a windstorm that ripped off a chunk of the CDW building's roof. Within minutes, Krasny himself was up on the roof, nailing a tarp over the hole. When startled employees inside looked up, Krasny shouted down to them to get back to selling.

However, Krasny's most important legacy is the "Circle of Service" culture that he created—a culture that focuses on taking care of customers, and on the CDW employees who serve them (he calls them "co-workers"). "Whenever he made a decision, he'd always ask two questions," says current chairman and CEO John Edwardson: "'What will the reaction of the co-workers be?' and 'What will the response of the customers be?'"

When someone says "salesperson," you may still think of the stereotypical "traveling salesman"—the fast-talking, ever-smiling peddler who travels his territory foisting his wares on reluctant customers. Such stereotypes, however, are sadly out of date. Today, like CDW's account managers, most professional salespeople are well-educated, well-trained men and women who work to build valued customer relationships. They succeed not by taking customers in, but by helping them out—by assessing customer needs and solving customer problems.

CDW's high-touch, high-tech clicks and people direct marketing strategy instills loyalty in what are traditionally very price-conscious SMB customers. The company wants to create customer satisfaction at every touch point."[1]

In this chapter, we examine two more marketing communication and promotion tools—*personal selling* and *direct marketing*. Both involve direct connections with customers aimed at building customer-unique value and lasting relationships

Personal Selling | START HERE

Robert Louis Stevenson once noted that "everyone lives by selling something." We are all familiar with the sales forces used by business organizations to sell products and services to customers around the world. But sales forces are also found in many other kinds of organizations. For example, colleges use recruiters to attract new students, and churches use membership committees to attract new members. Museums and fine arts organizations use fund raisers to contact donors and raise money. Even governments use sales forces. The U.S. Postal Service, for instance, uses a sales force to sell Express Mail and other services to corporate customers. In the first part of this chapter, we examine the role of personal selling in the organization, sales force management decisions, and the personal selling process.

The Nature of Personal Selling

Selling is one of the oldest professions in the world. The people who do the selling go by many names: *salespeople, sales representatives, account executives, sales consultants, sales engineers, agents, district managers*, and *account development reps* to name just a few.

People hold many stereotypes of salespeople—including some unfavorable ones. "Salesman" may bring to mind the image of Arthur Miller's pitiable Willy Loman in *Death of a Salesman* or Meredith Willson's cigar-smoking, backslapping, joke-telling Harold Hill in *The Music Man*. Or you might think of Jim Carrey's portrayal of the pushy, psychologically unbalanced Cable Guy. These examples depict salespeople as loners, traveling their territories, trying to foist their wares on unsuspecting or unwilling buyers.

However, modern salespeople are a far cry from these unfortunate stereotypes. Today, most salespeople are well-educated, well-trained professionals who work to build and maintain long term customer relationships. They listen to their customers, assess customer needs, and organize the company's efforts to solve customer problems. Consider Boeing, the aerospace giant competing in the rough-and-tumble worldwide commercial aircraft market. It takes more than fast talk and a warm smile to sell expensive airplanes:

> Selling high-tech aircraft at $100 million or more a copy is complex and challenging. A single big sale can easily run into billions of dollars. Boeing salespeople head up an extensive team of company specialists—sales and service technicians, financial analysts, planners, engineers—all dedicated to finding ways to satisfy airline customer needs. The selling process is nerve-rackingly slow—it can take 2 or 3 years from the first sales presentation to the day the sale is announced. After getting the order, salespeople then must stay in almost constant touch to keep track of the account's equipment needs and to make certain the customer stays satisfied. Success depends on building solid, long-term relationships with customers, based on performance and trust. "When you buy an airplane, it is like getting married," says the head of Boeing's commercial airplane division. "It is a long-term relationship."[2]

Salesperson

An individual acting for a company by performing one or more of the following activities: prospecting, communicating, servicing, and information gathering.

The term **salesperson** covers a wide range of positions. At one extreme, a salesperson might be largely an *order taker*, such as the department store salesperson standing behind the counter. At the other extreme are *order getters*, whose positions demand *creative selling* and *relationship building* for products and services ranging from appliances, industrial equipment, and airplanes to insurance and information technology services. Here, we focus on the more creative types of selling and on the process of building and managing an effective sales force.

The Role of the Sales Force

Personal selling is the interpersonal arm of the promotion mix. Advertising consists of one-way, nonpersonal communication with target consumer groups. In contrast, personal selling involves two-way, personal communication between salespeople and individual customers—whether face-to-face, by telephone, through video or Web conferences, or by other means.

■ Professional selling: It takes more than fast talk and a warm smile to sell high-tech aircraft at $100 million or more a copy. Success depends on building solid, long-term relationships with customers.

Personal selling can be more effective than advertising in more complex selling situations. Salespeople can probe customers to learn more about their problems, then adjust the marketing offer and presentation to fit the special needs of each customer.

The role of personal selling varies from company to company. Some firms have no salespeople at all—for example, companies that sell only online or through catalogs, or companies that sell through manufacturer's reps, sales agents, or brokers. In most firms, however, the sales force plays a major role. In companies that sell business products and services, such as IBM or DuPont, the company's salespeople work directly with customers. In consumer product companies such as Procter & Gamble and Nike, the sales force plays an important behind-the-scenes role. It works with wholesalers and retailers to gain their support and to help them be more effective in selling the company's products.

The sales force serves as a critical link between a company and its customers. In many cases, salespeople serve both masters—the seller and the buyer. First, they *represent the company to customers*. They find and develop new customers and communicate information about the company's products and services. They sell products by approaching customers, presenting their products, answering objections, negotiating prices and terms, and closing sales. In addition, salespeople provide customer service and carry out market research and intelligence work.

At the same time, salespeople *represent customers to the company*, acting inside the firm as "champions" of customers' interests and managing the buyer–seller relationship. Salespeople relay customer concerns about company products and actions back inside to those who can handle them. They learn about customer needs and work with other marketing and nonmarketing people in the company to develop greater customer value. The old view was that salespeople should worry about sales and the company should worry about profit. However, the current view holds that salespeople should be concerned with more than just producing *sales*—they should work with others in the company to produce *customer satisfaction* and *company profit*.

Sales force management
The analysis, planning, implementation, and control of sales force activities. It includes setting and designing sales force strategy; and recruiting, selecting, training, supervising, compensating, and evaluating the firm's salespeople.

Managing the Sales Force

We define **sales force management** as the analysis, planning, implementation, and control of sales force activities. It includes designing sales force strategy and structure and recruiting, selecting, training, compensating, supervising, and evaluating the firm's salespeople. These major sales force management decisions are shown in Figure 16.1 and are discussed in the following sections.

Designing sales force strategy and structure	→	Recruiting and selecting salespeople	→	Training salespeople	→	Compensating salespeople	→	Supervising salespeople	→	Evaluating salespeople

FIGURE 16.1
Major steps in sales force management

Designing Sales Force Strategy and Structure

Marketing managers face several sales force strategy and design questions. How should salespeople and their tasks be structured? How big should the sales force be? Should salespeople sell alone or work in teams with other people in the company? Should they sell in the field or by telephone? We address these issues below.

Sales Force Structure

A company can divide up sales responsibilities along any of several lines. The decision is simple if the company sells only one product line to one industry with customers in many locations. In that case the company would use a *territorial sales force structure*. However, if the company sells many products to many types of customers, it might need either a , a *customer sales force structure*, or a combination of the two.

Territorial sales force structure

A sales force organization that assigns each salesperson to an exclusive geographic territory in which that salesperson sells the company's full line

TERRITORIAL SALES FORCE STRUCTURE In the **territorial sales force structure**, each salesperson is assigned to an exclusive geographic area and sells the company's full line of products or services to all customers in that territory. This organization clearly defines each salesperson's job and fixes accountability. It also increases the salesperson's desire to build local business relationships that, in turn, improve selling effectiveness. Finally, because each salesperson travels within a limited geographic area, travel expenses are relatively small.

A territorial sales organization is often supported by many levels of sales management positions. For example, Campbell Soup uses a territorial structure in which each salesperson is responsible for selling all Campbell Soup products. Starting at the bottom of the organization, *sales merchandisers* report to *sales representatives*, who report to *retail supervisors*, who report to *directors of retail sales operations*, who report to 1 of 22 *regional sales managers*. Regional sales managers, in turn, report to 1 of 4 *general sales managers* (West, Central, South, and East), who report to a *vice president* and *general sales manager*.

Product sales force structure

A sales force organization under which salespeople specialize in selling only a portion of the company's products or lines.

PRODUCT SALES FORCE STRUCTURE Salespeople must know their products—especially when the products are numerous and complex. This need, together with the growth of product management, has led many companies to adopt a **product sales force structure**, in which the sales force sells along product lines. For example, Kodak uses different sales forces for its film products than for its industrial products. The film products sales force deals with simple products that are distributed intensively, whereas the industrial products sales force deals with complex products that require technical understanding.

The product structure can lead to problems, however, if a single large customer buys many different company products. For example, Cardinal Health, the large health care products and services company, has several product divisions, each with a separate sales force. Several Cardinal salespeople might end up calling on the same hospital on the same day. This means that they travel over the same routes and wait to see the same customer's purchasing agents. These extra costs must be compared with the benefits of better product knowledge and attention to individual products.

Customer sales force structure

A sales force organization under which salespeople specialize in selling only to certain customers or industries.

CUSTOMER SALES FORCE STRUCTURE More and more companies are now using a **customer sales force structure**, in which they organize the sales force along customer or industry lines. Separate sales forces may be set up for different industries, for serving current customers versus finding new ones, and for major accounts versus regular accounts.

Organizing the sales force around customers can help a company build closer relationships with important customers. For example, IBM recently shifted from a product-based structure to a customer-based one. Before the shift, droves of salespeople representing different IBM software, hardware, and services divisions might call on a single large client, creating confusion and frustration. Such large customers wanted a "single face," one point of contact for all of IBM's vast array of products and services. Following the restructuring, a single IBM "client executive" works with each large customer and manages a team of IBMers who work with the customer. One client executive describes his role this way: "I am the owner of the business relationship with the client. If the client has a problem, I'm the one who pulls together software or hardware specialists or consultants." According to a sales organization expert, "This structure puts salespeople in the position of being advisors to clients, and it also allows them to offer holistic solutions to clients' business problems."[3] Such an intense focus on customers is widely credited for IBM's dramatic turnaround in recent years.

COMPLEX SALES FORCE STRUCTURES When a company sells a wide variety of products to many types of customers over a broad geographic area, it often combines several types of sales force structures. Salespeople can be specialized by customer and territory; by product and territory; by product and customer; or by territory, product, and customer. No single structure is best for all companies and situations. Each company should select a sales force structure that best serves the needs of its customers and fits its overall marketing strategy.

Sales Force Size

Once the company has set its structure, it is ready to consider *sales force size*. Sales force may range in size from only a few salespeople to many tens of thousands. Some sales forces are huge—for example, Microsoft employs 23,000 salespeople, PepsiCo 36,000, and Conseco 130,000.[4] Salespeople constitute one of the company's most productive—and most expensive—assets. Therefore, increasing their number will increase both sales and costs.

Many companies use some form of *workload approach* to set sales force size. Using this approach, a company first groups accounts into different classes according to size, account status, or other factors related to the amount of effort required to maintain them. It then determines the number of salespeople needed to call on each class of accounts the desired number of times. The company might think as follows: Suppose we have 1,000 Type-A accounts and 2,000 Type-B accounts. Type-A accounts require 36 calls a year and Type-B accounts require 12 calls a year. In this case, the sales force's *workload*—the number of calls it must make per year—is 60,000 calls [(1,000 × 36) + (2,000 × 12) = 36,000 + 24,000 = 60,000]. Suppose our average salesperson can make 1,000 calls a year. Thus, the company needs 60 salespeople (60,000 ÷ 1,000).[5]

Other Sales Force Strategy and Structure Issues

Sales management must also decide who will be involved in the selling effort and how various sales and sales support people will work together.

■ Some sales forces are huge—for example, Microsoft employs 22,500 salespeople, PepsiCo 36,000, IBM 10,000, and Hartford Financial Services 111,000.

Outside sales force (or field sales force)
Outside salespeople who travel to call on customers.

Inside sales force
Inside salespeople who conduct business from their offices via telephone or visits from prospective buyers.

OUTSIDE AND INSIDE SALES FORCES The company may have an **outside sales force** (or *field sales force*), an **inside sales force**, or both. Outside salespeople travel to call on customers. Inside salespeople conduct business from their offices via telephone or visits from prospective buyers.

To reduce time demands on their outside sales forces, many companies have increased the size of their inside sales forces. Inside salespeople include technical support people, sales assistants, and telemarketers. *Technical support people* provide technical information and answers to customers' questions. *Sales assistants* provide clerical backup for outside salespeople. They call ahead and confirm appointments, conduct credit checks, follow up on deliveries, and answer customers' questions when outside salespeople cannot be reached. *Telemarketers* use the phone to find new leads and qualify prospects for the field sales force, or to sell and service accounts directly.

The inside sales force frees outside salespeople to spend more time selling to major accounts and finding major new prospects. Depending on the complexity of the product and customer, a telemarketer can make from 20 to 33 decision-maker contacts a day, compared with the average of 4 that an outside salesperson can make. And for many types of products and selling situations, telemarketing can be as effective as a personal call but much less expensive. Whereas the average business-to-business personal sales call costs about $295, a routine industrial telemarketing call costs only about $5 and a complex call about $20.[6] Notes a DuPont telemarketer: "I'm more effective on the phone. [When you're in the field], if some guy's not in his office, you lose an hour. On the phone, you lose 15 seconds. . . . Through my phone calls, I'm in the field as much as the rep is." There are other advantages. "Customers can't throw things at you," quips the rep, "and you don't have to outrun dogs."[7]

Telephone marketing can be used successfully by both large and small companies:

IBM's traditional image has long been symbolized by the outside salesman in the blue suit, crisp white shirt, and red tie. Now, to sell its technology solutions to small businesses, IBM is boosting emphasis on its telemarketing effort. Stroll through IBM's Atlanta Sales Center and a new image of the IBM salesperson emerges: men and women, many recent college grads, sporting golf shirts and khakis or—gasp!—blue jeans. They wear headsets and talk on the phone with customers they'll likely never meet in person. IBM's roughly 1,200 phone reps now generate 30 percent of IBM's revenues from small and midsize businesses. The reps focus on specific industries and each calls on as many as 300 accounts. They nurture client relationships, pitch IBM solutions, and, when needed, refer customers to product and service specialists.[8]

Climax Portable Machine Tools has proven that a small company can use telemarketing to save money and still lavish attention on buyers. Under the old system,

■ Experienced telemarketers sell complex chemical products by telephone at DuPont's Customer Telecontact Center. Quips one, "I'm more effective on the phone . . . and you don't have to outrun dogs."

Climax sales engineers spent one-third of their time on the road and could make about 4 calls a day. Now, each of 5 sales engineers on Climax's telemarketing team calls about 30 prospects a day, following up on leads generated by ads and direct mail. The sales engineers update a prospect's computer file after each contact, noting the degree of commitment, requirements, next call date, and personal comments. "If anyone mentions he's going on a fishing trip, our sales engineer enters that in the computer and uses it to personalize the next phone call," says Climax's president, noting that's just one way to build good relations. Another is that the first mailing to a prospect includes the sales engineer's business card with his or her picture on it. Of course, it takes more than friendliness to sell $15,000 machine tools over the phone (special orders may run $200,000), but the telemarketing approach is working well. When Climax customers were asked, "Do you see the sales engineer often enough?" the response was overwhelmingly positive. Obviously, many people didn't realize that the only contact they'd had with Climax had been on the phone.[9]

Inside salespeople may perform a wide range of functions, from direct selling and account service to customer analysis and acting as liaisons between outside salespeople and

Real Marketing 16.1

Point, Click, and Sell: Welcome to the Web-Based Sales Force

There are few rules at Fisher Scientific International's sales training sessions. The chemical company's salespeople are allowed to show up for new workshops in their pajamas. And no one flinches if they stroll in at midnight for their first class, take a dozen breaks to call clients, or invite the family cat to sleep in their laps while they take an exam. Sound unorthodox? It would be if Fisher's salespeople were trained in a regular classroom. But for the past few years, the company has been using the Internet to teach the majority of its salespeople in the privacy of their homes, cars, hotel rooms, or wherever else they bring their laptops.

To get updates on Fisher's pricing or refresh themselves on one of the company's highly technical products, all salespeople have to do is log on to the Web site and select from the lengthy index. Any time of the day or night, they can get information on a new product, take an exam, or post messages for product experts—all without ever entering a corporate classroom. Welcome to the world of the Web-based sales force.

In the past few years, sales organizations around the world have begun saving money and time by using a host of new Web approaches to train reps, hold sales meetings, and even conduct live sales presentations. Fisher Scientific's reps can dial up the Web site at their leisure, and whereas newer reps might spend hours online going through each session in order, more seasoned sellers might just log on for a quick refresher on a specific product before a sales call. "It allows them to manage their time better, because they're only getting training when they need it, in the doses they need it in," says John Pavlik, director of the company's training department. If salespeople are spending less time on training, Pavlik says, they're able to spend more time on what they do best: selling.

Training is only one of the ways sales organizations are using the Internet. Many companies are using the Web to make sales presentations and service accounts. For example, computer and communications equipment maker NEC Corporation has adopted Web-based selling as an essential marketing tool.

■ Internet selling support: Sales organizations around the world are now using a host of new Web approaches to train reps, hold sales meetings, and even conduct live sales presentations.

After launching a new line of servers on September 11, 2001, NEC had to rethink its sales approach. Following 9/11 terrorist attacks, the company began looking for ways to cut down on sales force travel. According to Dick Csaplar, marketing manager for the new server line, NEC's old sales approach—traveling to customer sites to pitch NEC products—became unworkable literally overnight. Instead, NEC adopted a new Web-based sales approach. While the initial goal was to keep people off airplanes, however, Web selling has now grown into an intrinsic part of NEC's sales efforts. Web selling reduces travel time and costs. Whereas the average daily cost of salesperson travel is $663, an hour-long Web conference costs just $60. More importantly, Web selling lets sales reps meet with more prospective customers than ever before, creating a more efficient and effective sales organization. Csaplar estimates that he's doing 10 customer

customers. And they now have a broader range of tools at their disposal. According to one observer, "today's . . . representatives are just as likely to answer e-mails or add to their employer's Frequently Asked Questions list as they are to answer the phones."[10]

Just as telemarketing is changing the way that many companies go to market, the Internet offers explosive potential for restructuring sales forces and conducting sales operations. More and more companies are now using the Internet to support their personal selling efforts—not just for selling, but for everything from training salespeople to conducting sales meetings and servicing accounts (see Real Marketing 16.1).

Team selling

Using teams of people from sales, marketing, engineering, finance, technical support, and even upper management to service large, complex accounts.

TEAM SELLING As products become more complex, and as customers grow larger and more demanding, a single salesperson simply can't handle all of a large customer's needs. Instead, most companies now are using **team selling** to service large, complex accounts. Companies are finding that sales teams can unearth problems, solutions, and sales opportunities that no individual salesperson could. Such teams might include experts from any area or level of the selling firm—sales, marketing, technical and support services, R&D, engineering, operations, finance, and others. In team selling situations, the salesperson shifts from "soloist" to "orchestrator."

In many cases, the move to team selling mirrors similar changes in customers' buying organizations. "Today, we're calling on teams of buying people, and that requires more firepower on

Web conferences a week, during which he and his sales team show prospects product features and benefits. Customers love it because they get a clear understanding of NEC's technology without having to host the NEC team on-site. And Csaplar was pleased to find that Web based selling is an effective way to interact with customers and to build customer relationships. "By the time we're done with the Webcast, the customer understands the technology, the pricing, and the competition, and we understand the customer's business and needs," he says. Without Web-casts, "we'd be lost on how to communicate with the customer without spending a lot of money," says Csaplar. "I don't see us ever going back to the heavy travel thing."

The Internet can also be a handy way to hold sales strategy meetings. Consider Cisco Systems, which provides networking solutions for the Internet. Sales meetings used to take an enormous bite out of Cisco's travel budget. Now the company saves about $1 million per month by conducting many of those sessions on the Web using PlaceWare Web conferencing software. Whenever Cisco introduces a new product, it holds a Web meeting to update salespeople, in groups of 100 or more, on the product's marketing and sales strategy.

Usually led by the product manager or a vice president of sales, the meetings typically begin with a 10-minute slide presentation that spells out the planned strategy. Then, salespeople spend the next 50 or so minutes asking questions via teleconference. The meeting's leader can direct attendees' browsers to competitors' Web sites or ask them to vote on certain issues by using the software's instant polling feature. "Our salespeople are actually meeting more online then they ever were face-to-face," says Mike Mitchell, Cisco's distance learning manager, adding that some salespeople who used to meet with other reps and managers only a few times a quarter are meeting online nearly every day. "That's very empowering for the sales force, because they're able to make suggestions at every step

of the way about where we're going with our sales and marketing strategies."

Thus, Web-based technologies can produce big organizational benefits for sales forces. They help conserve salespeople's valuable time, save travel dollars, and give salespeople a new vehicle for selling and servicing accounts. But the technologies also have some drawbacks. For starters, they're not cheap. Setting up a Web-based system can cost up to several hundred thousand dollars. And such systems can intimidate low-tech salespeople or clients. "You must have a culture that is comfortable using computers," says one marketing communications manager. "As simple as it is, if your salespeople or clients aren't comfortable using the Web, you're wasting your money." Also, Web tools are susceptible to server crashes and other network difficulties, not a happy event when you're in the midst of an important sales meeting or presentation.

For these reasons, some high-tech experts recommend that sales executives use Web technologies for training, sales meetings, and preliminary client sales presentations, but resort to old-fashioned, face-to-face meetings when the time draws near to close the deal. "When push comes to shove, if you've got an account worth closing, you're still going to get on that plane and see the client in person," says sales consultant Sloane. "Your client is going to want to look you in the eye before buying anything from you, and that's still one thing you just can't do online."

Sources: Portions adapted from Melinda Ligos, "Point, Click, and Sell," *Sales & Marketing Management,* May 1999, pp. 51–55; and Tom Kontzer, "Web Conferencing Embraced," *Information Week,* May 26, 2003, pp. 68–70. Also see Julia Chang, "No Instructor Required," *Sales & Marketing Management,* May 2003, p. 26; Nicole Ridgeway, "A Safer Place to Meet," *Forbes,* April 28, 2003, p. 97; Andy Cohen, "Virtual Sales Meetings on the Rise," *Sales & Marketing Management,* August 2003, p. 12; and Daniel Tynan, "Next Best Thing to Being There," *Sales & Marketing Management,* April 2004, p. 22.

our side," says one sales vice president. "One salesperson just can't do it all—can't be an expert in everything we're bringing to the customer. We have strategic account teams, led by customer business managers, who basically are our quarterbacks."[11]

Some companies, such as IBM, Xerox, and Procter & Gamble, have used teams for a long time. P&G sales reps are organized into "customer business development (CBD) teams." Each CBD team is assigned to a major P&G customer, such as Wal-Mart, Safeway, or CVS Pharmacy. Teams consist of a customer business development manager, several account executives (each responsible for a specific category of P&G products), and specialists in marketing strategy, operations, information systems, logistics, and finance. This organization places the focus on serving the complete needs of each important customer. It lets P&G "grow business by working as a 'strategic partner' with our accounts, not just as a supplier. Our goal: to grow their business, which also results in growing ours."[12]

Team selling does have some pitfalls. For example, selling teams can confuse or overwhelm customers who are used to working with only one salesperson. Salespeople who are used to having customers all to themselves may have trouble learning to work with and trust others on a team. Finally, difficulties in evaluating individual contributions to the team selling effort can create some sticky compensation issues.

Recruiting and Selecting Salespeople

At the heart of any successful sales force operation is the recruitment and selection of good salespeople. The performance difference between an average salesperson and a top salesperson can be substantial. In a typical sales force, the top 30 percent of the salespeople might bring in 60 percent of the sales. Thus, careful salesperson selection can greatly increase overall sales force performance. Beyond the differences in sales performance, poor selection results in costly turnover. When a salesperson quits, the costs of finding and training a new salesperson—plus the costs of lost sales—can be very high. Also, a sales force with many new people is less productive, and turnover disrupts customer relationships.

What sets great salespeople apart from all the rest? In an effort to profile top sales performers, Gallup Management Consulting Group, a division of the well-known Gallup polling organization, has interviewed as many as half a million salespeople. Its research suggests that the best salespeople possess four key talents: intrinsic motivation, disciplined work style, the ability to close a sale, and perhaps most important, the ability to build relationships with customers.[13]

Super salespeople are motivated from within. "Different things drive different people—pride, happiness, money, you name it," says one expert. "But all great salespeople have one

■ This Procter & Gamble "customer business development team" serves a major southeastern grocery retailer. It consists of a customer business development manager and five account executives (shown here), along with specialists from other functional areas.

■ Great salespeople: The best salespeople possess intrinsic motivation, disciplined work style, the ability to close a sale, and perhaps most important, the ability to build relationships with customers.

thing in common: an unrelenting drive to excel." Some salespeople are driven by money, a hunger for recognition, or the satisfaction of competing and winning. Others are driven by the desire to provide service and to build relationships. The best salespeople possess some of each of these motivations. "A competitor with a strong sense of service will probably bring in a lot of business while doing a great job of taking care of customers," observes the managing director of the Gallup Management Consulting Group. "Who could ask for any thing more?"

Whatever their motivations, salespeople must also have a disciplined work style. If salespeople aren't organized and focused, and if they don't work hard, they can't meet the ever-increasing demands customers make these days. Great salespeople are tenacious about laying out detailed, organized plans, then following through in a timely, disciplined way. Says one sales trainer, "Some people say it's all technique or luck. But luck happens to the best salespeople when they get up early, work late, stay up till two in the morning working on a proposal, or keep making calls when everyone is leaving at the end of the day."

Other skills mean little if a salesperson can't close the sale. So what makes for a great closer? For one thing, it takes unyielding persistence. "Great closers are like great athletes," says one sales trainer. "They're not afraid to fail, and they don't give up until they close." Great closers also have a high level of self-confidence and believe that they are doing the right thing.

Perhaps most important in today's relationship-marketing environment, top salespeople are customer problem solvers and relationship builders. They have an instinctive understanding of their customers' needs. Talk to sales executives and they'll describe top performers in these terms: Empathetic. Patient. Caring. Responsive. Good listeners. Honest. Top performers can put themselves on the buyer's side of the desk and see the world through their customers' eyes. They don't want just to be liked, they want to add value for their customers.

When recruiting, companies should analyze the sales job itself and the characteristics of its most successful salespeople to identify the traits needed by a successful salesperson in their industry. Then, it must recruit the right salespeople. The human resources department looks for applicants by getting names from current salespeople, using employment agencies, placing classified ads, searching the Web, and working through college placement services. Another source is to attract top salespeople from other companies. Proven salespeople need less training and can be immediately productive.

Recruiting will attract many applicants from whom the company must select the best. The selection procedure can vary from a single informal interview to lengthy testing and interviewing. Many companies give formal tests to sales applicants. Tests typically measure sales aptitude, analytical and organizational skills, personality traits, and other characteristics. But test scores provide only one piece of information in a set that includes personal characteristics, references, past employment history, and interviewer reactions.

Training Salespeople

New salespeople may spend anywhere from a few weeks or months to a year or more in training. Then, most companies provide continuing sales training via seminars, sales meetings, and the Web throughout the salesperson's career. In all, U.S. companies spend more than $7 billion annually on training salespeople. Although training can be expensive, it can also yield dramatic returns. For example, one recent study showed that sales training conducted by a major telecommunications firm paid for itself in 16 days and resulted in a 6-month return on investment of 812 percent. Similarly, Nabisco analyzed the return on its 2-day Professional Selling Program, which teaches sales reps how to plan for and make professional presentations. Although it cost about $1,000 to put each sales rep through the program, the training resulted in additional sales of more than $122,000 per rep and yielded almost $21,000 of additional profit per rep.[14]

Training programs have several goals. Salespeople need to know and identify with the company and its products, so most training programs begin by describing the company's objectives, organization, financial structure, facilities, and chief products and markets. They also need to know about customers and competitors. So the training program teaches them about competitors' strategies and about different types of customers and their needs, buying motives, and buying habits. Finally, because salespeople must know how to sell effectively, they are also trained in the basics of the selling process.

Today, many companies are adding Web-based training to their sales training programs. In fact, the industry for online training is expected to more than triple to $23.7 billion by 2006.[15] Such training may range from simple text-based product information to Internet-based sales exercises that build sales skills to sophisticated simulations that re-create the dynamics of real-life sales calls. Networking equipment and software maker Cisco Systems has learned that using the Internet to train salespeople offers many advantages:

> Keeping a large sales force up to speed on hundreds of complex, fast-changing products can be a daunting task. Under the old training process, newly hired Cisco salespeople traveled to a central location for several 5-day training sessions each year. "We used to fly people in and put them through a week of death-by-PowerPoint," says a Cisco training executive. This approach involved huge program-development and travel costs. Perhaps worse, it cost salespeople precious lost-opportunity time spent away from their customers. To address these issues, Cisco launched its Field E-Learning Connection—an internal learning portal through which Cisco's salespeople around the world can plan, track, develop, and measure their skills and knowledge. The site links salespeople to tens of thousands of Web-based learning aids. Learning involves the blending of audio and video, live broadcasts of classes, and straight content. Content can be turned into an MP3 file, viewed on-screen, downloaded to the computer, even printed out in magazine form. Under the new system, Cisco can conduct a single training session that reaches up to 3,000 people at once, worldwide, by broadcasting it over the company's global intranet. Live events can then be archived as video-on-demand modules for viewers who missed the live broadcast. The system also provides electronic access to Cisco experts or "e-mentors," who can respond via e-mail or phone, or meet learners in a virtual lab, connect to their screens, and walk them through exercises. The Field E-Learning Connection has improved training by giving Cisco salespeople anywhere, anytime access to a vast system of training resources. At the same time, it has cut field training costs by 40 percent to 60 percent while boosting salesperson "face time" with customers by 40 percent.[16]

Compensating Salespeople   *Starts Here*

To attract good salespeople, a company must have an appealing compensation plan. Compensation is made up of several elements—a fixed amount, a variable amount, expenses, and fringe benefits. The fixed amount, usually a salary, gives the salesperson some stable income. The variable amount, which might be commissions or bonuses based on sales performance, rewards the salesperson for greater effort and success. Expense allowances, which repay salespeople for job-related expenses, let salespeople undertake needed and desirable selling efforts. Fringe benefits, such as paid vacations, sickness or accident benefits, pensions, and life insurance, provide job security and satisfaction.

Management must decide what *mix* of these compensation elements makes the most sense for each sales job. Different combinations of fixed and variable compensation give rise to four basic types of compensation plans—straight salary, straight commission, salary plus bonus, and salary plus commission. A study of sales force compensation plans showed that 70 percent of all companies surveyed use a combination of base salary and incentives. The average plan consisted of about 60 percent salary and 40 percent incentive pay.[17]

The sales force compensation plan can both motivate salespeople and direct their activities. Compensation should direct the sales force toward activities that are consistent with overall marketing objectives. Table 16.1 illustrates how a company's compensation plan should reflect its overall marketing strategy. For example, if the strategy is to grow rapidly and gain market share, the compensation plan might include a larger commission component coupled with a new-account bonus to encourage high sales performance and new-account development. In contrast, if the goal is to maximize current account profitability, the compensation plan might contain a larger base-salary component with additional incentives for current account sales or customer satisfaction.

In fact, more and more companies are moving away from high commission plans that may drive salespeople to make short-term grabs for business. They worry that a salesperson who is pushing too hard to close a deal may ruin the customer relationship. Instead, companies are designing compensation plans that reward salespeople for building customer relationships and growing the long-run value of each customer.

Supervising Salespeople

New salespeople need more than a territory, compensation, and training—they need *supervision*. Through supervision, the company *directs* and *motivates* the sales force to do a better job.

Companies vary in how closely they supervise their salespeople. Many help their salespeople in identifying customer targets and setting call norms. Some may also specify how much time the sales force should spend prospecting for new accounts and set other time management priorities. One tool is the *annual call plan* that shows which customers and prospects to call on in which months and which activities to carry out. Activities include taking part in trade shows, attending sales meetings, and carrying out marketing research. Another tool is *time-and-duty analysis*. In addition to time spent selling, the salesperson spends time traveling, waiting, eating, taking breaks, and doing administrative chores.

Figure 16.2 shows how salespeople spend their time. On average, actual face-to-face selling time accounts for less than 30 percent of total working time! If selling time could be raised from 30 percent to 40 percent, this would be a 33 percent increase in the time spent

TABLE 16.1 **The Relationship between Overall Marketing Strategy and Sales Force Compensation**

	Strategic Goal		
	To Gain Market Share Rapidly	*To Solidify Market Leadership*	*To Maximize Profitability*
Ideal salesperson	• An independent self-starter	• A competitive problem solver	• A team player • A relationship manager
Sales focus	• Deal making • Sustained high effort	• Consultative selling	• Account penetration
Compensation role	• To capture accounts • To reward high performance	• To reward new and existing account sales	• To manage the product mix • To encourage team selling • To reward account management

Source: Adapted from Sam T. Johnson, "Sales Compensation: In Search of a Better Solution," *Compensation & Benefits Review,* November–December 1993, pp. 53–60. Copyright © 1998 American Management Association, NY, www.amanet.org. All rights reserved, used with permission.

FIGURE 16.2
How salespeople spend their time
Source: Dartnell Corporation; 30th Sales Force Compensation Survey. © 1999 Dartnell Corporation.

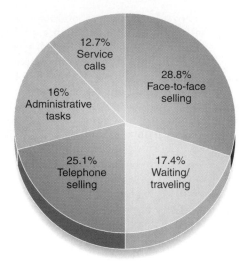

12.7% Service calls

28.8% Face-to-face selling

16% Administrative tasks

25.1% Telephone selling

17.4% Waiting/ traveling

selling. Companies always are looking for ways to save time—using phones instead of traveling, simplifying record-keeping forms, finding better call and routing plans, and supplying more and better customer information. Consider the changes GE made to support its sales force:[18]

> When Jeff Immelt became General Electric's new chairman, he was dismayed to find that members of the sales team were spending far more time on deskbound administrative chores than in face-to-face meetings with customers and prospects. "He said we needed to turn that around," recalls Venki Rao, an IT leader in global sales and marketing at GE Power Systems, a division focused on energy systems and products. "[We need] to spend four days a week in front of the customer and one day for all the admin stuff." GE Power's salespeople spent much of their time at their desks because they had to go to many sources for the information needed to sell multimillion-dollar turbines, turbine parts, and services to energy companies worldwide. To fix the problem, GE created a new sales portal, a kind of "one-stop shop" for just about everything they need. The sales portal connects the vast array of existing GE databases, providing everything from sales tracking and customer data to parts pricing and information on planned outages. GE also added external data, such as news feeds. "Before, you were randomly searching for things," says Bill Snook, a GE sales manager. Now, he says, "I have the sales portal as my home page, and I use it as the gateway to all the applications that I have." The sales portal has freed Snook and 2,500 other users around the globe from once time-consuming administrative tasks, greatly increasing their face time with customers.

Many firms have adopted *sales force automation systems*, computerized sales force operations for more efficient order-entry transactions, improved customer service, and better salesperson decision-making support. Salespeople use laptops, handheld computing devices, and Web technologies, coupled with customer-contact software and customer relationship management (CRM) software, to profile customers and prospects, analyze and forecast sales, manage account relationships, schedule sales calls, make presentations, enter orders, check inventories and order status, prepare sales and expense reports, process correspondence, and carry out many other activities. Sales force automation not only lowers sales force costs and improves productivity, it also improves the quality of sales management decisions. Here is an example of successful sales force automation:[19]

> Owens-Corning has put its sales force online with FSA—its Field Sales Advantage system. FSA gives Owens-Corning salespeople a constant supply of information about their company and the people they're dealing with. Using laptop computers, each salesperson can access three types of programs. First, FSA gives them a set of *generic tools*, everything from word processing to fax and e-mail transmission to creating presentations online. Second, it provides *product information*—tech bulletins, customer specifications, pricing information, and other data that can help close a sale. Finally, it offers up a wealth of *customer information*—buying history, types of products

■ Owens-Corning's Field Sales Advantage system gives salespeople a constant supply of information about their company and the people with whom they're dealing.

ordered, and preferred payment terms. Before FSA, reps stored such information in loose-leaf books, calendars, and account cards. Now, FSA makes working directly with customers easier than ever. Salespeople can prime themselves on backgrounds of clients; call up prewritten sales letters; transmit orders and resolve customer-service issues on the spot during customer calls; and have samples, pamphlets, brochures, and other materials sent to clients with a few keystrokes. With FSA, "salespeople automatically become more empowered," says Charley Causey, regional general manager. "They become the real managers of their own business and their own territories."

Perhaps the fastest-growing sales force technology tool is the Internet. The most common uses include gathering competitive information, monitoring customer Web sites, and researching industries and specific customers. As more and more companies provide their salespeople with Web access, experts expect continued growth in sales force Internet usage.[20]

Beyond directing salespeople, sales managers must also motivate them. Some salespeople will do their best without any special urging from management. To them, selling may be the most fascinating job in the world. But selling can also be frustrating. Salespeople often work alone and they must sometimes travel away from home. They may face aggressive competing salespeople and difficult customers. Therefore, salespeople often need special encouragement to do their best.

Management can boost sales force morale and performance through its organizational climate, sales quotas, and positive incentives. *Organizational climate* describes the feeling that salespeople have about their opportunities, value, and rewards for a good performance. Some companies treat salespeople as if they are not very important, and performance suffers accordingly. Other companies treat their salespeople as valued contributors and allow virtually unlimited opportunity for income and promotion. Not surprisingly, these companies enjoy higher sales force performance and less turnover.

Sales quota

A standard that states the amount a salesperson should sell and how sales should be divided among the company's products.

Many companies motivate their salespeople by setting **sales quotas**—standards stating the amount they should sell and how sales should be divided among the company's products. Compensation is often related to how well salespeople meet their quotas. Companies also use various *positive incentives* to increase sales force effort. *Sales meetings* provide social occasions, breaks from routine, chances to meet and talk with "company brass," and opportunities to air feelings and to identify with a larger group. Companies also sponsor *sales contests* to spur the sales force to make a selling effort above what would normally be expected. Other incentives include honors, merchandise and cash awards, trips, and profit-sharing plans. In all, American companies spend some $27 billion a year on incentives to motivate and reward sales-force performance.[21]

HASTA AQUÍ

■ Sales force incentives: Many companies offer cash, trips, or merchandise as incentives. Marriott suggests that companies reward outstanding sales performers by letting them "spread their wings and reenergize" at the fabulous Marriott resorts worldwide.

Selling process
The steps that the salesperson follows when selling, which include prospecting and qualifying, preapproach, approach, presentation and demonstration, handling objections, closing, and follow-up.

Evaluating Salespeople

We have thus far described how management communicates what salespeople should be doing and how it motivates them to do it. This process requires good feedback. And good feedback means getting regular information about salespeople to evaluate their performance.

Management gets information about its salespeople in several ways. The most important source is *sales reports,* including weekly or monthly work plans and longer-term territory marketing plans. Salespeople also write up their completed activities on *call reports* and turn in *expense reports* for which they are partly or wholly repaid. Additional information comes from personal observation, customer surveys, and talks with other salespeople.

Using various sales force reports and other information, sales management evaluates members of the sales force. It evaluates salespeople on their ability to "plan their work and work their plan." Formal evaluation forces management to develop and communicate clear standards for judging performance. It also provides salespeople with constructive feedback and motivates them to perform well.

The Personal Selling Process

We now turn from designing and managing a sales force to the actual personal selling process. The **selling process** consists of several steps that the salesperson must master. These steps focus on the goal of getting new customers and obtaining orders from them. However, most salespeople spend much of their time maintaining existing accounts and building long-term customer *relationships*. We discuss the relationship aspect of the personal selling process in a later section.

FIGURE 16.3
Major steps in effective selling

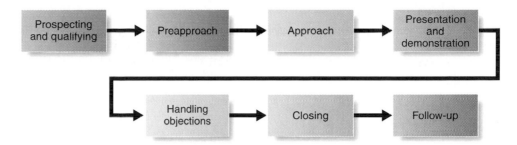

Steps in the Selling Process

As shown in Figure 16.3, the selling process consists of seven steps: prospecting and qualifying, preapproach, approach, presentation and demonstration, handling objections, closing, and follow-up.

Prospecting and Qualifying

Prospecting

The step in the selling process in which the salesperson identifies qualified potential customers.

The first step in the selling process is **prospecting**—identifying qualified potential customers. Approaching the right potential customers is crucial to selling success. As one expert puts it: "If the sales force starts chasing anyone who is breathing and seems to have a budget, you risk accumulating a roster of expensive-to-serve, hard-to-satisfy customers who never respond to whatever value proposition you have." He continues, "The solution to this isn't rocket science. [You must] train salespeople to actively scout the right prospects. If necessary, create an incentive program to reward proper scouting." Another expert concludes: "Increasing your prospecting effectiveness is the fastest single way to boost your sales."[22]

The salesperson must often approach many prospects to get just a few sales. Although the company supplies some leads, salespeople need skill in finding their own. They can ask current customers for referrals. They can cultivate referral sources, such as suppliers, dealers, noncompeting salespeople, and bankers. They can search for prospects in directories or on the Web and track down leads using the telephone and direct mail. Or they can drop in unannounced on various offices (a practice known as "cold calling").

Salespeople also need to know how to *qualify* leads—that is, how to identify the good ones and screen out the poor ones. Prospects can be qualified by looking at their financial ability, volume of business, special needs, location, and possibilities for growth.

Preapproach

Preapproach

The step in the selling process in which the salesperson learns as much as possible about a prospective customer before making a sales call.

Before calling on a prospect, the salesperson should learn as much as possible about the organization (what it needs, who is involved in the buying) and its buyers (their characteristics and buying styles). This step is known as the **preapproach**. The salesperson can consult standard industry and online sources, acquaintances, and others to learn about the company. The salesperson should set *call objectives*, which may be to qualify the prospect, to gather information, or to make an immediate sale. Another task is to decide on the best approach, which might be a personal visit, a phone call, or a letter. The best timing should be considered carefully because many prospects are busiest at certain times. Finally, the salesperson should give thought to an overall sales strategy for the account.

Approach

Approach

The step in the selling process in which the salesperson meets the customer for the first time.

During the **approach** step, the salesperson should know how to meet and greet the buyer and get the relationship off to a good start. This step involves the salesperson's appearance, opening lines, and the follow-up remarks. The opening lines should be positive to build goodwill from the beginning of the relationship. This opening might be followed by some key questions to learn more about the customer's needs or by showing a display or sample to attract the buyer's attention and curiosity. As in all stages of the selling process, listening to the customer is crucial.

Presentation and Demonstration

Presentation

The step in the selling process in which the salesperson tells the "product story" to the buyer, highlighting customer benefits.

During the **presentation** step of the selling process, the salesperson tells the product "story" to the buyer, presenting customer benefits and showing how the product solves the customer's problems. The problem-solver salesperson fits better with today's marketing concept than does a hard-sell salesperson or the glad-handing extrovert. Buyers today want solutions, not smiles; results, not razzle-dazzle. They want salespeople who listen to their concerns, understand their needs, and respond with the right products and services.

This *need-satisfaction approach* calls for good listening and problem-solving skills. "I think of myself more as a . . . well, psychologist," notes one experienced salesperson. "I listen to customers. I listen to their wishes and needs and problems, and I try to figure out a solution. If you're not a good listener, you're not going to get the order." Another salesperson suggests, "It's no longer enough to have a good relationship with a client. You have to understand their problems. You have to feel their pain." One sales manager suggests that salespeople need to put themselves in their customers' shoes: "Make yourself a customer and see first-hand how it feels," he says.[23]

The qualities that buyers *dislike most* in salespeople include being pushy, late, deceitful, and unprepared or disorganized. The qualities they *value most* include empathy, good listening, honesty, dependability, thoroughness, and follow-through. Great salespeople know how to sell, but more importantly they know how to listen and to build strong customer relationships.

Today, advanced presentation technologies allow for full multimedia presentations to only one or a few people. CDs and DVDs, online presentation technologies, and handheld and laptop computers with presentation software have replaced the flip chart. Here's an example:[24]

> Until 6 months ago, Credant Technologies, a firm that sells security software programs for handhelds, used standard presentation equipment—laptops and LCD projectors—to showcase its products to potential clients. That's no longer the case. Each member of the company's sales team is now equipped with Presenter-to-Go, a credit card-sized device that slips into handheld PDAs or pocket PCs to make them compatible with projectors. The $200 device reads PowerPoint, Microsoft Word, and Excel files, as well as Web pages, allowing salespeople to create presentations on computers, then transfer them to a PDA. It also lets reps add notes to presentations instantaneously by transmitting handwriting on their pocket PC to the screen. And it includes a wireless remote control, so sales reps can move freely throughout the presentation room, unattached to their laptop or projector-advancing button. When Credant Regional Account Executive Tom Gore met recently with an important prospect, he wowed buying executives with a feature that enabled him to type some of their comments into his PDA. Within seconds, their comments appeared on screen. "It makes each presentation more personal and interactive," Gore says.

Handling Objections

Customers almost always have objections during the presentation or when asked to place an order. The problem can be either logical or psychological, and objections are often unspoken. In **handling objections**, the salesperson should use a positive approach, seek out hidden

Handling objections
The step in the selling process in which the salesperson seeks out, clarifies, and overcomes customer objections to buying.

■ New presentation technologies: The old-fashioned flip chart has been replaced by CDs, online presentation technologies, and hand-held and laptop computers. Each member of Credant Technologies' sales team is equipped with Presenter-to-Go, a credit card-sized device that slips into hand-held PDAs or pocket PCs to make them compatible with projectors.

objections, ask the buyer to clarify any objections, take objections as opportunities to provide more information, and turn the objections into reasons for buying. Every salesperson needs training in the skills of handling objections.

Closing

Closing

The step in the selling process in which the salesperson asks the customer for an order.

After handling the prospect's objections, the salesperson now tries to close the sale. Some salespeople do not get around to **closing** or do not handle it well. They may lack confidence, feel guilty about asking for the order, or fail to recognize the right moment to close the sale. Salespeople should know how to recognize closing signals from the buyer, including physical actions, comments, and questions. For example, the customer might sit forward and nod approvingly or ask about prices and credit terms. Salespeople can use one of several closing techniques: They can ask for the order, review points of agreement, offer to help write up the order, ask whether the buyer wants this model or that one, or note that the buyer will lose out if the order is not placed now. The salesperson may offer the buyer special reasons to close, such as a lower price or an extra quantity at no charge.

Follow-Up

Follow-up

The last step in the selling process in which the salesperson follows up after the sale to ensure customer satisfaction and repeat business.

The last step in the selling process—**follow-up**—is necessary if the salesperson wants to ensure customer satisfaction and repeat business. Right after closing, the salesperson should complete any details on delivery time, purchase terms, and other matters. The salesperson then should schedule a follow-up call when the initial order is received, to make sure there is proper installation, instruction, and servicing. This visit would reveal any problems, assure the buyer of the salesperson's interest, and reduce any buyer concerns that might have arisen since the sale.

STARTS HERE

Personal Selling and Customer Relationship Management

The principles of personal selling as just described are *transaction oriented*—their aim is to help salespeople close a specific sale with a customer. But in many cases, the company is not seeking simply a sale: It has targeted a major customer that it would like to win and keep. The company would like to show that it has the capabilities to serve the customer over the long haul in a mutually profitable *relationship*. The sales force usually plays an important role in building and managing profitable customer relationships. "My company is selling something intangible," says one salesperson. "What we are really selling is 'Hey, when the time comes, we'll be there.' It all comes down to trust."[25]

Today's large customers favor suppliers who can sell and deliver a coordinated set of products and services to many locations, and who can work closely with customer teams to improve products and processes. For these customers, the first sale is only the beginning of the relationship. Unfortunately, some companies ignore these new realities. They sell their products through separate sales forces, each working independently to close sales. Their technical people may not be willing to lend time to educate a customer. Their engineering, design, and manufacturing people may have the attitude that "it's our job to make good products and the salesperson's to sell them to customers." Their salespeople focus on pushing products toward customers rather than listening to customers and providing solutions. Other companies, however, recognize that winning and keeping accounts requires more than making good products and directing the sales force to close lots of sales. It requires listening to customers, understanding their needs, and carefully coordinating the whole company's efforts to create customer value and to build lasting relationships with important customers.

Direct Marketing

Many of the marketing and promotion tools that we've examined in previous chapters were developed in the context of *mass marketing:* targeting broad markets with standardized messages and offers distributed through intermediaries. Today, however, with the trend toward more narrowly targeted or one-to-one marketing, many companies are adopting *direct marketing,* either as a primary marketing approach or as a supplement to other approaches. In this section, we explore the exploding world of direct marketing.

■ Building customer relationships: Smart companies listen to customers, understand their needs, and carefully coordinate the whole company's efforts toward creating customer value.

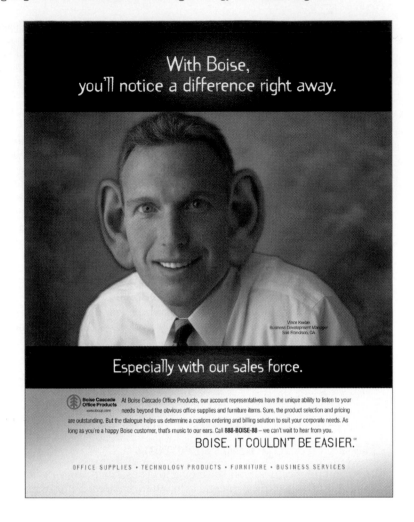

Direct marketing
Direct communications with carefully targeted individual consumers—the use of telephone, mail, fax, e-mail, the Internet, and other tools to communicate directly with specific consumers.

Direct marketing consists of direct connections with carefully targeted individual consumers to both obtain an immediate response and cultivate lasting customer relationships. Direct marketers communicate directly with customers, often on a one-to-one, interactive basis. Using detailed databases, they tailor their marketing offers and communications to the needs of narrowly defined segments or even individual buyers.

Beyond brand and image building, direct marketers usually seek a direct, immediate, and measurable consumer response. For example, Dell Computer interacts directly with customers, by telephone or through its Web site, to design built-to-order systems that meet customers' individual needs. Buyers order directly from Dell, and Dell quickly and efficiently delivers the new computers to their homes or offices.

The New Direct-Marketing Model

Early direct marketers—catalog companies, direct mailers, and telemarketers—gathered customer names and sold goods mainly by mail and telephone. Today, however, fired by rapid advances in database technologies and new marketing media—especially the Internet—direct marketing has undergone a dramatic transformation.

In previous chapters, we've discussed direct marketing as direct distribution—as marketing channels that contain no intermediaries. We also include direct marketing as one element of the marketing communications mix—as an approach for communicating directly with consumers. In actuality, direct marketing is both of these things.

Most companies still use direct marketing as a supplementary channel or medium for marketing their goods. Thus, Lexus markets mostly through mass-media advertising and its high-quality dealer network but also supplements these channels with direct marketing. Its direct marketing includes promotional CDs and other materials mailed directly to prospective buyers and a Web page (www.lexus.com) that provides consumers with information about various models, competitive comparisons, financing, and dealer locations. Similarly, most department stores sell the majority of their merchandise off their store shelves but also sell through direct mail and online catalogs.

However, for many companies today, direct marketing is more than just a supplementary channel or medium. For these companies, direct marketing—especially in its newest transformation, Internet marketing and e-commerce—constitutes a new and complete model for doing business. More than just another marketing channel or advertising medium, this new *direct model* is rapidly changing the way companies think about building relationships with customers.

Whereas most companies use direct marketing and the Internet as supplemental approaches, firms employing the direct model use it as the *only* approach. Some of these companies, such as Dell Computer, Amazon.com, and eBay, began as only direct marketers. Other companies—such as Cisco Systems, Charles Schwab, IBM, and many others—are rapidly transforming themselves into direct-marketing superstars. The company that perhaps best exemplifies this new direct-marketing model is Dell Computer (see Real Marketing 16.2). Dell has built its entire approach to the marketplace around direct marketing.

Benefits and Growth of Direct Marketing

Whether employed as a complete business model or as a supplement to a broader integrated marketing mix, direct marketing brings many benefits to both buyers and sellers. As a result, direct marketing is growing very rapidly.

For buyers, direct marketing is convenient, easy to use, and private. From the comfort of their homes or offices, they can browse mail catalogs or company Web sites at any time of the day or night. Direct marketing gives buyers ready access to a wealth of products and information, at home and around the globe. Finally, direct marketing is immediate and interactive—buyers can interact with sellers by phone or on the seller's Web site to create exactly the configuration of information, products, or services they desire, then order them on the spot.

For sellers, direct marketing is a powerful tool for building customer relationships. Using database marketing, today's marketers can target small groups or individual consumers, tailor offers to individual needs, and promote these offers through personalized communications. Direct marketing can also be timed to reach prospects at just the right moment. Because of its one-to-one, interactive nature, the Internet is an especially potent direct-marketing tool. Direct marketing also gives sellers access to buyers that they could not reach through other channels. For example, the Internet provides access to *global* markets that might otherwise be out of reach.

Finally, direct marketing can offer sellers a low-cost, efficient alternative for reaching their markets. For example, direct marketing has grown rapidly in B2B marketing, partly in response to the ever-increasing costs of marketing through the sales force. When personal sales calls cost $295 per contact, they should be made only when necessary and to high-potential customers and prospects. Lower cost-per-contact media—such as telemarketing, direct mail, and company Web sites—often prove more cost effective in reaching and selling to more prospects and customers.

As a result of these advantages to both buyers and sellers, direct marketing has become the fastest growing form of marketing. Sales through traditional direct-marketing channels (telephone marketing, direct mail, catalogs, direct-response television, and others) have been growing rapidly. According to the Direct Marketing Association, direct sales to consumers and businesses in the United States last year reached more than $2 trillion, about 9 percent of the economy. Moreover, whereas total U.S. sales over the next 5 years will grow at an estimated 5.5 percent annually, direct-marketing sales will grow at an estimated 8.5 percent annually, reaching $3 billion by 2007.[26]

Customer Databases and Direct Marketing

Customer database
An organized collection of comprehensive data about individual customers or prospects, including geographic, demographic, psychographic, and behavioral data.

Effective direct marketing begins with a good customer database. A **customer database** is an organized collection of comprehensive data about individual customers or prospects, including geographic, demographic, psychographic, and behavioral data. The database can be used to locate good potential customers, tailor products and services to the special needs of targeted consumers, and maintain long-term customer relationships. "If there's been any change in the past decade it's the knowledge we now can have about our customers," says one expert. "Strategically, the most essential tool is our customer database. A company is no better than what it knows."[27]

Real Marketing 16.2

Dell: Be Direct!

When 19-year-old Michael Dell began selling personal computers out of his college dorm room in 1984, competitors and industry insiders scoffed at the concept of mail-order computer marketing. Yet young Michael proved the skeptics wrong—way wrong. In little more than two decades, he has turned his dorm-room mail-order business into a burgeoning, $41 billion computer empire.

Dell is now the world's largest direct marketer of computer systems and the number-one PC maker worldwide. In the United States, Dell is number-one in desktop PC sales, number-one in laptops, number-one in servers, and number-two (and gaining) in printers. Over the past 10 years, despite the recent tech slump, Dell has experienced a more than 12-fold increase in sales and a 14-fold increase in profits. Dell's stock was the number-one performer of the 1990s, yielding an incredible 97 percent average annual return. Last year, while number-two Hewlett-Packard's PC sales fell 6 percent, Dell's grew 20 percent.

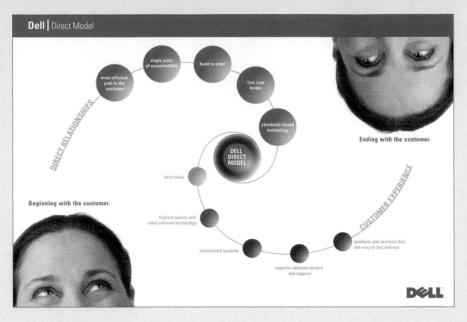

■ The Dell Direct Model: Dell's direct-marketing approach delivers greater customer value through an unbeatable combination of product customization, low prices, fast deliver, and award-winning customer service.

What's the secret to Dell's stunning success? Anyone at Dell can tell you without hesitation: It's the company's radically different business model—the *direct model*. "We have a tremendously clear business model," says Michael Dell, the 39-year-old founder. "There's no confusion about what the value proposition is, what the company offers, and why it's great for customers." An industry analyst agrees: "There's no better way to make, sell, and deliver PCs than the way Dell does it, and nobody executes that model better than Dell."

Dell's direct-marketing approach delivers greater customer value through an unbeatable combination of product customization, low prices, fast delivery, and award-winning customer service.

A customer can talk by phone with a Dell representative or log onto www.dell.com on Monday morning; order a fully customized, state-of-the-art PC to suit his or her special needs; and have the machine delivered to his or her doorstep or desktop by Wednesday—all at a price that's 10 to 15 percent below competitors' prices for a comparably performing PC. Dell backs its products with high-quality service and support. As a result, Dell consistently ranks among the industry leaders in product reliability and service, and its customers are routinely among the industry's most satisfied.

Dell customers get exactly the machines they need. Michael Dell's initial idea was to serve individual buyers by letting them customize machines with the special features they wanted at low prices.

Many companies confuse a customer mailing list with a customer database. A customer mailing list is simply a set of names, addresses, and telephone numbers. A customer database contains much more information. In business-to-business marketing, the salesperson's customer profile might contain the products and services the customer has bought; past volumes and prices; key contacts (and their ages, birthdays, hobbies, and favorite foods); competitive suppliers; status of current contracts; estimated customer spending for the next few years; and assessments of competitive strengths and weaknesses in selling and servicing the account.

In consumer marketing, the customer database might contain a customer's demographics (age, income, family members, birthdays), psychographics (activities, interests, and opinions), buying behavior (past purchases, buying preferences), and other relevant information. Some of these databases are huge. For example, Ford's customer database contains information on more than 33 million customers, including warranty information, survey results, retail sales input, finance records, and more. Internet portal Yahoo! records every click made by every visitor, adding some 400 billion bytes of data per day to its database—the equivalent of 800,000 books. And Wal-Mart's database contains more than 100 terabytes of data—that's 100 trillion bytes, equivalent to 16,000 bytes for every one of the world's 6 billion people.[28]

However, this one-to-one approach also appeals strongly to corporate buyers, because Dell can so easily preconfigure each computer to precise requirements. Dell routinely preloads machines with a company's own software and even undertakes tedious tasks such as pasting inventory tags onto each machine so that computers can be delivered directly to a given employee's desk. As a result, more than 70 percent of Dell's sales now come from large corporate, government, and educational buyers.

The direct model results in more efficient selling and lower costs, which translate into lower prices for customers. "Nobody, but nobody, makes [and markets] computer hardware more efficiently than Dell," says another analyst. "No unnecessary costs: This is an all-but-sacred mandate of the famous Dell direct business model." Because Dell builds machines to order, it carries barely any inventory—less than 3 day's worth by some accounts. Dealing one to one with customers helps the company react immediately to shifts in demand, so Dell doesn't get stuck with PCs no one wants. Finally, by selling directly, Dell has no dealers to pay. As a result, on average, Dell's costs are 12 percent lower than those of its leading PC competitor.

Dell knows that time is money, and the company is obsessed with "speed." According to one account, Dell squeezes "time out of every step in the process—from the moment an order is taken to collecting the cash. [By selling direct, manufacturing to order, and] tapping credit cards and electronic payment, Dell converts the average sale to cash in less than 24 hours." By contrast, competitors selling through dealers might take 35 days or longer.

Such blazing speed results in more satisfied customers and still lower costs. For example, customers are often delighted to find their new computers arriving within as few as 36 hours of placing an order. And because Dell doesn't order parts until an order is booked, it can take advantage of ever-falling component costs. On average, its parts are 60 days newer than those in competing machines, and, hence, 60 days farther down the price curve. This gives Dell a 6 percent profit advantage from parts costs alone.

The Internet is a perfect extension of Dell's direct-marketing model. It gives customers who were already comfortable buying direct from Dell an even more powerful way to do so. By simply clicking the "Buy a Dell" icon at Dell's Web site (www.dell.com), customers can design and price customized computer systems electronically. The direct-marketing pioneer now sells computers on some 80 country-specific Web sites, accounting for more than 50 percent of revenues. "The Internet is like a booster rocket on our sales and growth," proclaims Dell. "Our vision is to have *all* customers conduct *all* transactions on the Internet, globally."

As you might imagine, competitors are no longer scoffing at Michael Dell's vision of the future. In fact, competing and noncompeting companies alike are studying the Dell model closely. "Somehow Dell has been able to take flexibility and speed and build it into their DNA. It's almost like drinking water," says the CEO of another Fortune 500 company, who visited recently to absorb some of the Dell magic to apply to his own company. "I'm trying to drink as much water here as I can."

It's hard to argue with success, and Michael Dell has been very successful. By following his hunches, at the tender age of 39 he has built one of the world's hottest companies. In the process, he's become the world's richest man under 40, amassing a personal fortune of more than $17 billion.

Sources: Quotes, performance statistics, and other information from Kathryn Jones, "The Dell Way," *Business 2.0*, February 2003, pp. 60–66; "The InternetWeek Interview—Michael Dell," *InternetWeek*, April 13, 1999, p. 8, Andy Serwer, "Dell Does Domination," *Fortune*, January 21, 2002, pp. 71–75; Mark Boslet, "PC Market Posts Fresh Growth as Dell Regains No. 1 Ranking," *Wall Street Journal*, April 18, 2003, p. B3; "Dell Computer Corporation," *Hoover's Company Profiles*, Austin, March 15, 2004, p. 13193; Telis Demos, Richard Morgan, and Christopher Tkaczyk, "40 Under 40," *Fortune*, September 20, 2004, p. 72; Bob Keefe, "Dell Quickly Becomes Threat to HP Dominance in Printers," *Knight Ridder Tribune Business News*, June 13, 2004, p. 1; and www.dell.com/us/en/gen/corporate/access_company direct_model.htm, January 2005.

Armed with the information in their databases, these companies can identify small groups of customers to receive fine-tuned marketing offers and communications. Kraft Foods has amassed a list of more than 30 million users of its products who have responded to coupons or other Kraft promotions. Based on their interests, the company sends these customers tips on issues such as nutrition and exercise, as well as recipes and coupons for specific Kraft brands. FedEx uses its sophisticated database to create 100 highly targeted, customized direct-mail and telemarketing campaigns each year to its nearly 5 million customers shipping to 212 countries. By analyzing customers carefully and reaching the right customers at the right time with the right promotions, FedEx achieves response rates of 20 to 25 percent and earns an 8-to-1 return on its direct-marketing dollars.[29]

Companies use their databases in many ways. They can use a database to identify prospects and generate sales leads by advertising products or offers. Companies can use a database to deepen customer loyalty—they can build customers' interest and enthusiasm by remembering buyer preferences and sending appropriate information, gifts, or other materials. Or they can use the database to profile customers based on previous purchasing and to decide which customers should receive particular offers.

For example, Harrah's uses its sizable database to design different levels of service and rewards for its patrons. Through player cards and other means, Harrah's tracks individual customer activity in its casinos. It enters this data into a database containing millions of transactional data points about customers and their individual gambling preferences and spending. Harrah's then uses the database to tailor its messages and services to meet individual needs and to offer special rewards to loyal customers, including free flights on its privately chartered planes. As a result, the casino has the most devoted customers in the industry.[30]

Mars, a market leader in pet food as well as candy, maintains an exhaustive pet database. In Germany, the company has compiled the names of virtually every German family that owns a cat. It has obtained these names by contacting veterinarians, via its Katzen-Online.de Web site, and by offering the public a free booklet titled "How to Take Care of Your Cat." People who request the booklet fill out a questionnaire, providing their cat's name, age, birthday, and other information. Mars then sends a birthday card to each cat in Germany each year, along with a cat food sample and money-saving coupons for Mars brands. The result is a lasting relationship with the cat's owner.

Like many other marketing tools, database marketing requires a special investment. Companies must invest in computer hardware, database software, analytical programs, communication links, and skilled personnel. The database system must be user-friendly and available to various marketing groups, including those in product and brand management, new-product development, advertising and promotion, direct mail, telemarketing, Web marketing, field sales, order fulfillment, and customer service. A well-managed database should lead to sales gains that will more than cover its costs.

Forms of Direct Marketing

The major forms of direct marketing—as shown in Figure 16.4—include *personal selling, telephone marketing, direct-mail marketing, catalog marketing, direct-response television marketing, kiosk marketing,* and *online marketing*. We examined personal selling in depth earlier in this chapter and will look closely at online marketing in Chapter 17. Here, we examine the other direct-marketing forms.

■ In Germany, Mars has compiled a database containing information on virtually every family that owns a pet. To build lasting relationships, it sends free kitten starter packs to cat owners in Germany who register online.

FIGURE 16.4
Forms of direct marketing

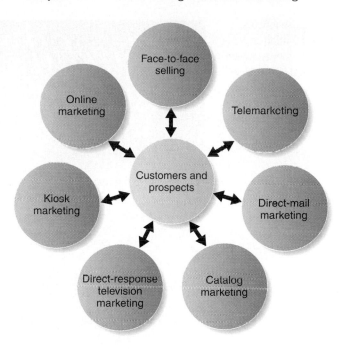

Telephone Marketing

Telephone marketing

Using the telephone to sell
directly to customers.

Telephone marketing—using the telephone to sell directly to consumers and business customers—has become the major direct-marketing communication tool. Telephone marketing now accounts for more than 39 percent of all direct-marketing media expenditures and 35 percent of direct-marketing sales. We're all familiar with telephone marketing directed toward consumers, but B2B marketers also use telephone marketing extensively, accounting for 59 percent of all telephone marketing sales.[31]

Marketers use *outbound* telephone marketing to sell directly to consumers and businesses. *Inbound* toll-free 800 numbers are used to receive orders from television and print ads, direct mail, or catalogs. The use of 800 numbers has taken off in recent years as more and more companies have begun using them, and as current users have added new features such as toll-free fax numbers. Residential use has also grown. To accommodate this rapid growth, new toll-free area codes, such as 888, 877, and 866, have been added. After the 800 area code was established in 1967, it took almost 30 years before its 8 million numbers were used up. In contrast, 888 area code numbers, established in 1996, were used up in only 2 years.[32]

Properly designed and targeted telemarketing provides many benefits, including purchasing convenience and increased product and service information. However, the explosion in unsolicited telephone marketing has annoyed many consumers, who object to the almost daily "junk phone calls" that pull them away from the dinner table or fill the answering machine. Lawmakers around the country have responded with legislation ranging from banning unsolicited telemarketing calls during certain hours to letting households sign up for "Do Not Call" lists. Consumers are responding enthusiastically. When the FTC opened registration for its "Do Not Call List" in mid-2003, nearly 10 million consumers registered more than 13 million phone numbers in just the first 3 days. To date, more than 57 million consumers have added their names to the list.

The depth of negative public feeling toward telemarketing abuses was evident in reader responses to a newspaper column written by humorist Dave Barry. In the column, Barry explained the do-not-call registry and noted that several telemarketing organizations had filed lawsuits to block the registry. Barry published the telephone number of one of the telemarketing organizations and suggested that readers give the organization a dose of its own medicine. They responded by the thousands:

> I've *never* touched a nerve like the one I touched when I wrote about telemarketers. [The do-not-call registry] displeases the telemarketing industry, which believes it has a constitutional right to call people who do not want to be called. . . . So in my column, I printed the toll-free telephone number of one of these groups, the American Teleservices Association. My thinking was: Hey, if the ATA feels its members have a constitutional right to call you, then surely the ATA feels that you have an equally constitutional right to call the ATA. Well, it turned out that a *lot* of you were eager to

■ Marketers use inbound toll-free 800 numbers to receive orders from television and print ads, direct mail, or catalogs. Here, the Carolina Cookie Company urges, "Don't wait another day. Call now to place an order or request a catalog."

Careful...you might sprain a taste bud.

Don't wait another day! Call now to place an order or request a catalog. Also, go on line at **www.carolinacookie.com** to place an order, request a catalog or view our entire selection of products.

1-800-447-5797

CAROLINA COOKIE COMPANY · JUST BAKED

call up the telemarketing industry. Thousands and thousands of you called the ATA. I found out about this when I saw an article in a direct-marketing newspaper, the *DM News*, which quoted the executive director of the ATA, Tim Searcy. Here's an excerpt from the article: "The ATA received no warning about the article from Barry or anyone connected with him," Searcy said. ". . . the Barry column has had harmful consequences for the ATA. An ATA staffer has spent about five hours a day for the past six days monitoring the voice mail and clearing out messages." That's correct: The ATA received NO WARNING that it was going to get unwanted calls! Not only that, but these unwanted calls were an INCONVENIENCE for the ATA, and WASTED THE ATA'S TIME! I just hope nobody interrupted the ATA's dinner. [33]

Most telemarketers are recognizing such negative reactions and support some action against random and poorly targeted telemarketing. As a Direct Marketing Association executive notes, "We want to target people who want to be targeted."

Direct-Mail Marketing

Direct-mail marketing
Sending an offer, announcement, reminder, or other item to a person at a particular address.

Direct-mail marketing involves sending an offer, announcement, reminder, or other item to a person at a particular address. Using highly selective mailing lists, direct marketers send out millions of mail pieces each year—letters, ads, brochures, samples, video- and audiotapes, CDs, and other "salespeople with wings." Direct mail accounts for nearly 24 percent of all direct-marketing media expenditures and more than 32 percent of direct-marketing sales. Together, telemarketing and direct-mail marketing account for some 64 percent of direct-marketing expenditures and 67 percent of direct-marketing sales.

Direct mail is well suited to direct, one-to-one communication. It permits high target-market selectivity, can be personalized, is flexible, and allows easy measurement of results. Although the cost per thousand people reached is higher than with mass media such as television or magazines, the people who are reached are much better prospects. Direct mail has proved successful in promoting all kinds of products, from books, magazine subscriptions, and insurance to gift items, clothing, gourmet foods, and industrial products. Direct mail is also used heavily by charities to raise billions of dollars each year.

The direct-mail industry constantly seeks new methods and approaches. For example, CDs are now among the fastest-growing direct-mail media. America Online has mailed out CDs by the hundreds of millions in one of the most successful direct mail campaigns in history. Now other marketers, especially those in technology or e-commerce, are using CDs in their direct mail offers. Used in conjunction with the Internet, CDs offer an affordable way to drive traffic to Web pages personalized for a specific market segment or a specific promotion. They can also be used to demonstrate computer-related products. For example, Sony sent out a CD that allowed PC users to demo its VAIO portable notebook on their own computers.

Until recently, all mail was paper based and handled by the U.S. Post Office or delivery services such as FedEx, UPS, DHL, or Airborne Express. Recently, however, three new forms of mail delivery have become popular:

- *Fax mail:* Marketers now routinely send fax mail announcing special offers, sales, and other events to prospects and customers with fax machines. Fax mail messages can be sent and received almost instantaneously. However, some prospects and customers resent receiving unsolicited fax mail, which ties up their machines and consumes their paper. And fax mail is subject to the same do-not-call restrictions as telemarketing.

- *E-mail:* Many marketers now send sales announcements, offers, product information, and other messages to e-mail addresses—sometimes to a few individuals, sometimes to large groups. Today's e-mail messages have moved far beyond the drab text-only messages of old. The new breed of e-mail ad uses animation, interactive links, streaming video, and personalized audio messages to reach out and grab attention. However, as people receive more and more e-mail, they resent the intrusion of unrequested messages. Smart marketers are using permission-based programs, sending e-mail ads only to those who want to receive them.

- *Voice mail:* Some marketers have set up automated programs that exclusively target voice mailboxes and answering machines with prerecorded messages. These systems target homes between 10 A.M. and 4 P.M. and businesses between 7 P.M. and 9 P.M. when people are least likely to answer. If the automated dialer hears a live voice, it disconnects. Such systems thwart hang-ups by annoyed potential customers. However, they can also create substantial ill will.

These new forms deliver direct mail at incredible speeds compared with the post office's "snail mail" pace. Yet, much like mail delivered through traditional channels, they may be resented as "junk mail" if sent to people who have no interest in them. For this reason, marketers must carefully identify appropriate targets so as not waste the company's money and recipients' time.

Catalog Marketing

Catalog marketing
Direct marketing through print, video, or electronic catalogs that are mailed to select customers, made available in stores, or presented online.

Advances in technology, along with the move toward personalized, one-to-one marketing have resulted in exciting changes in **catalog marketing**. *Catalog Age* magazine used to define a *catalog* as "a printed, bound piece of at least eight pages, selling multiple products, and offering a direct ordering mechanism." Today, only a few years later, this definition is sadly out of date.

With the stampede to the Internet, more and more catalogs are going electronic. Most print catalogers have added Web-based catalogs to their marketing mixes, and a variety of new Web-only catalogers have emerged. Still, the Internet has not yet killed off printed catalogs—far from it. Web catalogs currently generate only about 13 percent of all catalog sales. Although the Internet has provided a new avenue for catalog sales, printed catalogs remain the primary medium. Most catalogers use the Internet as an added sales tool to augment their printed catalogs.[34]

Catalog marketing has grown explosively during the past 25 years. Annual catalog sales amounted to about $133 billion last year and are expected to grow to top $175 billion by 2008.[35] Some large general-merchandise retailers—such as J.C. Penney and Spiegel—sell a full line of merchandise through catalogs. In recent years, these giants have been challenged by thousands of specialty catalogs that serve highly specialized market niches. According to one study, some 10,000 companies now produce 14,000 unique catalog titles in the United States.[36]

Consumers can buy just about anything from a catalog. Sharper Image catalogs hawk everything from $300 robot vacuum cleaners to $2,400 jet-propelled surfboards. Each year Lillian Vernon sends out 23 editions of its 6 catalogs with total circulation of 102 million copies to its 20-million-person database, selling more than 6,000 different items, ranging from shoes to decorative lawn birds and monogrammed oven mitts.[37] Specialty department stores,

■ Catalog marketing has grown explosively during the past 25 years. Some 10,000 companies now produce 14,000 unique catalog titles in the United States.

such as Neiman Marcus, Bloomingdale's, and Saks Fifth Avenue, use catalogs to cultivate upper-middle-class markets for high-priced, often exotic, merchandise. Several major corporations have also developed or acquired catalog divisions. For example, Avon now issues 10 women's fashion catalogs along with catalogs for children's and men's clothes. Walt Disney Company mails out over 6 million catalogs each year featuring videos, stuffed animals, and other Disney items.

Ninety-seven percent of all catalog companies now present merchandise and take orders over the Internet. Web-based catalogs present a number of benefits over printed catalogs. They save on production, printing, and mailing costs. Whereas print-catalog space is limited, online catalogs can offer an almost unlimited amount of merchandise. Web catalogs also allow real-time merchandising: products and features can be added or removed as needed, and prices can be adjusted instantly to match demand. Finally, online catalogs can be spiced up with interactive entertainment and promotional features, such as games, contests, and daily specials.

Along with the benefits, however, Web-based catalogs also present challenges. Whereas a print catalog is intrusive and creates its own attention, Web catalogs are passive and must be marketed. Attracting new customers is much more difficult for a Web catalog than for a print catalog. Thus, even catalogers who are sold on the Web are not likely to abandon their print catalogs.

Direct-Response Television Marketing

Direct-response television marketing

Direct marketing via television, including *direct-response television advertising* or *infomercials* and *home shopping channels*.

Direct-response television marketing takes one of two major forms. The first is *direct-response advertising*. Direct marketers air television spots, often 60 or 120 seconds long, that persuasively describe a product and give customers a toll-free number for ordering. Television viewers often encounter 30-minute advertising programs, or *infomercials*, for a single product.

Some successful direct-response ads run for years and become classics. For example, Dial Media's ads for Ginsu knives ran for 7 years and sold almost 3 million sets of knives worth more than $40 million in sales; its Armourcote cookware ads generated more than twice that much. And over the past 40 years, infomercial czar Ron Popeil's company, Ronco, has sold more than $1 billion worth of TV-marketed gadgets, including the original Veg-O-Matic, the Pocket Fisherman, Mr. Microphone, the Giant Food Dehydrator and Beef Jerky Machine, and the Showtime Rotisserie & BBQ.[38]

For years, infomercials have been associated with somewhat questionable pitches for juicers and other kitchen gadgets, get-rich-quick schemes, and nifty ways to stay in shape without working very hard at it. Traditionally, they have "almost been the Wild West of advertising, where people make rules for themselves as they go along," says Jack Kirby, chairman of the Electronic Retailing Association.[39] In recent years, however, a number of large companies—GTE, Johnson & Johnson, MCA Universal, Sears, Procter & Gamble, Revlon, IBM, Pontiac, Land Rover, Anheuser-Busch, even the U.S. Navy—have begun using infomercials to sell their wares over the phone, refer customers to retailers, send out coupons and product information, or attract buyers to their Web sites (see Real Marketing 16.3). According to Kirby, it's "time to really set some standards and move forward."

Direct response TV commercials are usually cheaper to make and the media purchase is less costly. Moreover, results are easily measured. Unlike most media campaigns, direct-response ads always include a toll-free number or Web address, making it easier for marketers to measure the impact of their pitches.

Home shopping channels, another form of direct-response television marketing, are television programs or entire channels dedicated to selling goods and services. Some home shopping channels, such as the Quality Value Channel (QVC), Home Shopping Network (HSN), and ValueVision, broadcast 24 hours a day. On QVC, the program's hosts offer bargain prices on products ranging from jewelry, lamps, collectible dolls, and clothing to power tools and consumer electronics—usually obtained by the home shopping channel at closeout prices. Viewers call a toll-free number to order goods from one of six QVC call centers.

With widespread distribution on cable and satellite television, the top three shopping networks combined now reach 248 million homes worldwide, selling more than $4 billion of goods each year. They are now combining direct-response television marketing with online and on-land selling. For example, QVC, which offers more than 1,700 items each week, recently launched a feature called "61st Minute," in which QVC viewers are urged to go online immediately after a given product showcase. Once there, viewers find a Webcast continuation of the product pitch. Those who miss out on a deal on the tube or online can now visit one of six QVC outlet stores or the company's QVC's full-line store at the Mall of America.[40]

Kiosk Marketing

Some companies place information and ordering machines—called *kiosks* (in contrast to vending machines, which dispense actual products)—in stores, airports, and other locations. Hallmark and American Greetings use kiosks to help customers create and purchase personalized greeting cards. In store Kodak kiosks let customers transfer pictures from a mobile phone, edit them, and make high-quality color prints. REI uses in-store, Web-enabled interactive kiosks that give customers access to the REI Web site and lets them purchase items that are out of stock or not available in the store. At Car Max, the used-car superstore, customers use a

■ Kiosks: REI uses in-store kiosks that give customers access to the REI Web site and lets them purchase items that are out of stock or not available in the store.

Real Marketing 16.3

Infomercials: But Wait, There's More!

It's late at night and you can't get to sleep. So you grab the TV remote, surf channels, and chance upon a fast-talking announcer, breathlessly pitching some new must-have kitchen gadget. A grinning blonde co-announcer fawns over the gadget's every feature, and the studio audience roars its approval. After putting the gadget through its paces, the announcer asks, "How much would you expect to pay? Three hundred dollars? Two hundred? Well, think again! This amazing gadget can be yours for just four easy payments of $19.95 plus shipping and handling!" "Oooooh!" the audience screams. "But wait! There's more," declares the announcer. "If you act now, you will also receive an additional gadget, absolutely free. That's two for the price of one." With operators standing by, you don't have a minute to lose.

Sound familiar? We've all seen countless infomercials like this, hawking everything from kitchen gadgets, cleaning solutions, and exercise equipment to psychic advice and get-rich-quick schemes. Traditionally, such pitches have had a kind of fly-by-night feel about them. And in the cold light of day, such a purchase may not seem like such a good deal after all. Such is the reputation of direct-response TV advertising. Yet, behind the hype is a powerful approach to marketing that is becoming more mainstream every day.

Ron Popeil pioneered direct-response product sales. Whether you realize it or not, you've probably been exposed to dozens of Popeil's inventions over the years, and his direct-marketing model has become the standard for the infomercial industry. His company, Ronco, has brought us such classics as the Veg-O-Matic, the Electric Food Dehydrator, the Showtime Rotisserie Oven, the GLH Formula Hair System, the Automatic 5-Minute Pasta and Sausage Maker, the Popeil Pocket Fisherman, the Inside the Egg Shell Electric Egg Scrambler, and the Dial-O-Matic Food Slicer.

Infomercials do work—two-thirds of Americans have seen the ads and one-third of viewers have bought goods they've "seen on TV." Since its beginning, Ronco has sold more than $1 billion worth of merchandise—that's millions of easy payments of just $14.95 each.

■ Ronco and Ron Popeil, with his Veg-o-Matics, food dehydrators, and electric egg scramblers, paved the way for a host of mainstream marketers who now use direct-response ads.

The success of Ronco and its countless imitators hasn't gone unnoticed among the big hitters in corporate America. Direct-response television marketing is rapidly becoming a mainstay weapon in the marketing arsenals of even the most reputable companies.

Ronco's revenues aren't the only reason for the expansion of direct-response TV. The explosion of cable and digital channels that reach a wide range of demographically targeted markets has cre-

kiosk with a touch-screen computer to get information about its vast inventory of as many as 1,000 cars and trucks. Customers can choose a handful and print out photos, prices, features, and location on the store's lot. The use of such kiosks is expected to increase fivefold during the next 3 years and generate more than $6.5 billion in annual sales by 2006.[41]

Business marketers also use kiosks. For example, Dow Plastics places kiosks at trade shows to collect sales leads and to provide information on its 700 products. The kiosk system reads customer data from encoded registration badges and produces technical data sheets that can be printed at the kiosk or faxed or mailed to the customer. The system has resulted in a 400 percent increase in qualified sales leads.[42]

Like about everything else these days, kiosks are also going online, as many companies merge the powers of the real and virtual worlds. For example, at the local Disney Store, kiosk guests can buy merchandise online, purchase theme-park passes, and learn more about Disney vacations and entertainment products. Gap has installed interactive kiosks, called Web lounges, in some of its stores that provide gift ideas or let customers match up outfits without trying them in dressing rooms. Kiosks in Virgin stores allow customers to download and purchase individual songs or entire albums online. Outdoor equipment retailer REI has at least four Web-enabled kiosks in each of its 63 stores that provide customers with product information and let them place orders online.[43]

ated a glut of airtime, which can be snapped up at attractive rates. Changing retailer reactions to direct response TV products have also given infomercials a boost. Mass retailers are now embracing such direct-response staples OxiClean, Roll-A-Hose, or George Foreman's Mean Lean Grilling Machine. Some, such as drug-chain heavyweight Walgreens, devote entire front-of-store sections to such goods. Whereas it used to take years to get retail distribution for "As seen on TV" products, many now make it to store shelves within a month of going on TV.

All this makes direct-response television advertising both attractive and cost-effective for an expanding range of companies and products, including the marketing heavyweights. Dell, Procter & Gamble (P&G), General Motors, Johnson & Johnson, Sears, Sharper Image, and many other mainstream marketers now use direct-response TV to peddle specific products and promotions, and to draw new customers into their other direct-to-consumer channels. Today's infomercials have evolved with the times—most now include highly professional pitches and Web sites to go along with the ever-present toll-free phone number.

Procter & Gamble, one of the nation's premier marketing companies, now routinely uses infomercials to sell products like the Swiffer WetJet and Dryel. A series of infomercials helped to propel the WetJet past rival Clorox's ReadyMop when other marketing efforts alone failed to do the trick. P&G launched its Swiffer Dusters product with a campaign that included direct-response ads and a tie-in to the DVD release of the Jennifer Lopez film *Maid in Manhattan*. Consumers contacting the 1-800 number got coupons for both the new Swiffer Duster and the DVD.

Beyond the usual domestic personal-care and home-care goods, interest in direct-response has now expanded to more serious products. Pharmacia, which makes Celebrex, used infomercials to help introduce the drug to arthritis sufferers. It plans another infomercial-style marketing campaign to highlight how the drug improves the quality of life. Although consumers can't order the medicine directly from the company, they can request informative literature and receive coupons that defray the costs of required doctor visits or first pill purchases.

Some retailers also use infomercials. Since 1998, retailer Sharper Image has employed 2-minute infomercials to sell products ranging from vacuum cleaners and scooters to air purifiers. The company buys time on a variety of major cable networks and runs the ads at all hours of the day and night. One Sharper Image VP boasts the retailer's direct-response TV effort generates "a fairly good-size piece of our business! It pays for itself even without accounting for the advertising's impact on our stores. And we typically see sales in stores go up when we run the infomercials." By last year, infomercials accounted for about 32 percent of Sharper Image's total advertising budget.

So, direct-response TV ads are no longer just the province of Ron Popeil and his Veg-O-Matics, food dehydrators, and electric egg scramblers. While Popeil and his imitators paved the way, their success now has mainstream marketers tuning in to direct-response ads. In fact, last year marketers spent $12.4 billion on direct-response television advertising, reaping $154 billion in revenues in return. What does the future hold for the direct-response industry? Wait, there's more!

Sources: Jack Neff, "Direct Response Getting Respect," *Advertising Age*, January 20, 2003, p. 4; Paul Miller, "Sharper Image Tunes in to Infomercials," *Catalog Age*, February 2001, p. 12; Bridget McCrea, "Removing the Blemishes," *Response*, March 2003, p. 32–34; "Nearly Two-Thirds of Americans Are Exposed to Direct-Response TV," *Research Alert*, March 21, 2003, p. 9; Millie Takaki, "Now Available," *SHOOT*, April 25, 2003, p. 11; "Pharmaceutical Infomercial," *Back Stage*, April 18, 2003, p. 37; Dean Tomasula, "Sharper Image Shares Soar on Ionic Breeze," July 18, 2003, accessed online at www.zephyr-media.com; Nat Ives, "Infomercials Clean Up Their Pitch," *New York Times*, April 12, 2004, p. C1; and Robert Yallen, "Marketers: DRTV Can Be Your Friend," *Brandweek*, May 10, 2004, p. 24.

Integrated Direct Marketing

Too often, a company's individual direct-marketing efforts are not well integrated with one another or with other elements of its marketing and promotion mixes. For example, a firm's media advertising may be handled by the advertising department working with a traditional advertising agency. Meanwhile, its direct-mail and catalog business may be handled by direct-marketing specialists, while its Web site is developed and operated by an outside Internet firm. Even within a given direct-marketing campaign, too many companies use only a "one-shot" effort to reach and sell a prospect or a single vehicle in multiple stages to trigger purchases.

Integrated direct marketing
Direct-marketing campaigns that use multiple vehicles and multiple stages to improve response rates and profits.

A more powerful approach is **integrated direct marketing**, which involves using carefully coordinated multiple-media, multiple-stage campaigns. Such campaigns can greatly improve response. Whereas a direct-mail piece alone might generate a 2 percent response, adding a Web site and toll-free phone number might raise the response rate by 50 percent. Then, a well-designed outbound telemarketing effort might lift response by an additional 500 percent. Suddenly, a 2 percent response has grown to 15 percent or more by adding interactive marketing channels to a regular mailing.

More elaborate integrated direct-marketing campaigns can be used. Consider the multimedia, multistage campaign shown in Figure 16.5. Here, the paid ad creates product awareness

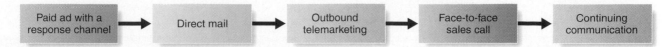

FIGURE 16.5
An integrated direct-marketing campaign

and stimulates phone, mail, or Web inquiries. The company immediately sends direct mail or e-mail responses to those who inquire. Within a few days, the company follows up with a phone call seeking an order. Some prospects will order by phone or the company's Web site; others might request a face-to-face sales call. In such a campaign, the marketer seeks to improve response rates and profits by adding media and stages that contribute more to additional sales than to additional costs.

HASTA AQUÍ

Public Policy and Ethical Issues in Direct Marketing

Direct marketers and their customers usually enjoy mutually rewarding relationships. Occasionally, however, a darker side emerges. The aggressive and sometimes shady tactics of a few direct marketers can bother or harm consumers, giving the entire industry a black eye. Abuses range from simple excesses that irritate consumers to instances of unfair practices or even outright deception and fraud. The direct-marketing industry has also faced growing concerns about invasion-of-privacy issues.

Irritation, Unfairness, Deception, and Fraud

Direct-marketing excesses sometimes annoy or offend consumers. Most of us dislike direct-response TV commercials that are too loud, too long, and too insistent. Especially bothersome are dinnertime or late-night phone calls. Beyond irritating consumers, some direct marketers have been accused of taking unfair advantage of impulsive or less sophisticated buyers. TV shopping channels and program-long "infomercials" targeting television-addicted shoppers seem to be the worst culprits. They feature smooth-talking hosts, elaborately staged demonstrations, claims of drastic price reductions, "while they last" time limitations, and unequaled ease of purchase to inflame buyers who have low sales resistance.

Worse yet, so-called heat merchants design mailers and write copy intended to mislead buyers. Even well-known direct mailers have been accused of deceiving consumers. Sweepstakes promoter Publishers Clearing House recently paid $52 million to settle accusations that its high-pressure mailings confused or misled consumers, especially the elderly, into believing that they had won prizes or would win if they bought the company's magazines.[44]

Other direct marketers pretend to be conducting research surveys when they are actually asking leading questions to screen or persuade consumers. Fraudulent schemes, such as investment scams or phony collections for charity, have also multiplied in recent years. Crooked direct marketers can be hard to catch: Direct-marketing customers often respond quickly, do not interact personally with the seller, and usually expect to wait for delivery. By the time buyers realize that they have been bilked, the thieves are usually somewhere else plotting new schemes.

Invasion of Privacy

Invasion of privacy is perhaps the toughest public policy issue now confronting the direct-marketing industry. These days, it seems that almost every time consumers enter a sweepstakes, apply for a credit card, take out a magazine subscription, or order products by mail, telephone, or the Internet, their names are entered into some company's already bulging database. Using sophisticated computer technologies, direct marketers can use these databases to "microtarget" their selling efforts.

Consumers often benefit from such database marketing—they receive more offers that are closely matched to their interests. However, many critics worry that marketers may know *too* much about consumers' lives and that they may use this knowledge to take unfair advantage of consumers. At some point, they claim, the extensive use of databases intrudes on consumer privacy.

For example, they ask, should AT&T be allowed to sell marketers the names of customers who frequently call the toll-free numbers of catalog companies? Should a company such as American Express be allowed to make data on its millions of cardholders worldwide available to merchants who accept AmEx cards? Is it right for credit bureaus to compile and sell lists of people who have recently applied for credit cards—people who are considered prime direct-marketing targets because of their spending behavior? Or is it right for states to sell the names and addresses of driver's license holders, along with height, weight, and gender information, allowing apparel retailers to target tall or overweight people with special clothing offers?

In their drives to build databases, companies sometimes get carried away. For example, when first introduced, Intel's Pentium III chip contained an embedded serial number that allowed the company to trace users' equipment. When privacy advocates screamed, Intel disabled the feature. Similarly, Microsoft caused substantial privacy concerns when one version of its Windows software used a "Registration Wizard" that snooped into users computers. When users went online to register, without their knowledge, Microsoft "read" the configurations of their PCs to learn about the major software products they were running. Users protested loudly and Microsoft abandoned the practice.

These days, it's not only the large companies that can access such private information. The explosion of information technology has put these capabilities into the hands of almost any business. For example, one bar owner discovered the power of information technology after he acquired a simple, inexpensive device to check IDs.

> About 10,000 people a week go to The Rack, a bar in Boston. . . . One by one, they hand over their driver's licenses to a doorman, who swipes them through a sleek black machine. If a license is valid and its holder is over 21, a red light blinks and the patron is waved through. But most of the customers are not aware that it also pulls up the name, address, birth date, and other personal details from a data strip on the back of the license. Even height, eye color, and sometimes Social Security number are registered. "You swipe the license, and all of a sudden someone's whole life as we know it pops up in front of you," said Paul Barclay, the bar's owner. "It's almost voyeuristic." Mr. Barclay soon found that he could build a database of personal information, providing an intimate perspective on his clientele that can be useful in marketing. Now, for any given night or hour, he can break down his clientele by sex, age, ZIP code, or other characteristics. If he wanted to, he could find out how many blond women named Karen over 5 feet 2 inches came in over a weekend, or how many of his customers have the middle initial M. More practically, he can build mailing lists based on all that data—and keep track of who comes back.[45]

Such access to and use of information has caused much concern and debate among companies, consumers, and public policy makers. Consumer privacy has become a major regulatory issue.

■ Privacy: The explosion of information technology has put sometimes frightening capabilities into the hands almost any business. One bar owner discovered the power of information technology after he acquired a simple, inexpensive device to check IDs.

■ The DMA's "Privacy Promise to American Consumers" attempts to build customer confidence by requiring that all DMA members adhere to certain carefully developed consumer privacy rules.

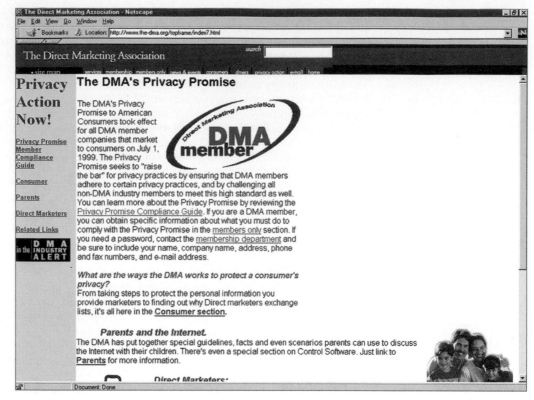

The direct-marketing industry is addressing issues of ethics and public policy. For example, in an effort to build consumer confidence in shopping direct, the Direct Marketing Association (DMA)—the largest association for businesses practicing direct, database, and interactive marketing, with more than 4,700 member companies—launched a "Privacy Promise to American Consumers." The Privacy Promise requires that all DMA members adhere to a carefully developed set of consumer privacy rules. Members must agree to notify customers when any personal information is rented, sold, or exchanged with others. They must also honor consumer requests to "opt out" of receiving further solicitations or having their contact information transferred to other marketers. Finally, they must abide by the DMA's Preference Service by removing the names of consumers who wish not to receive mail, telephone, or e-mail offers.[46]

Direct marketers know that, left untended, such problems will lead to increasingly negative consumer attitudes, lower response rates, and calls for more restrictive state and federal legislation. "Privacy and customer permission have become the cornerstones of customer trust, [and] trust has become the cornerstone to a continuing relationship," says one expert. Companies must "become the custodians of customer trust and protect the privacy of their customers."[47]

Most direct marketers want the same things that consumers want: honest and well-designed marketing offers targeted only toward consumers who will appreciate and respond to them. Direct marketing is just too expensive to waste on consumers who don't want it.

> Reviewing the Concepts <

Personal selling and direct marketing are both direct tools for communicating with and persuading current and prospective customers. Selling is the interpersonal arm of the communications mix. To be successful in personal selling, a company must first build and then manage an effective sales force. Firms must also be good at direct marketing, the process of forming one-to-one connections with customers. Today, many companies are turning to direct marketing in an effort to reach carefully targeted customers more efficiently and to build stronger, more personal, one-to-one relationships with them.

1. Discuss the role of a company's salespeople in creating value for customers and building customer relationships.

Most companies use salespeople, and many companies assign them an important role in the marketing mix. For companies selling business products, the firm's salespeople work directly with customers. Often, the sales force is the customer's only direct contact with the company and therefore may be viewed by customers as representing the company itself. In contrast, for consumer product companies that sell through intermediaries, consumers usually do not meet salespeople or even know about them. The sales force works behind the scenes, dealing with wholesalers and retailers to obtain their support and helping them become effective in selling the firm's products.

As an element of the promotion mix, the sales force is very effective in achieving certain marketing objectives and carrying out such activities as prospecting, communicating, selling and servicing, and information gathering. But with companies becoming more market oriented, a market-focused sales force also works to produce both *customer satisfaction* and *company profit*. To accomplish these goals, the sales force needs skills in marketing analysis and planning in addition to the traditional selling skills.

2. Identify and explain the six major sales force management steps.

High sales force costs necessitate an effective *sales management process* consisting of six steps: *designing sales force strategy and structure, recruiting and selecting, training, compensating, supervising,* and *evaluating* salespeople.

In designing a sales force, sales management must address strategy issues such as what type of sales force structure will work best (territorial, product, customer, or complex structure); how large the sales force should be; who will be involved in the selling effort; and how its various sales and sales support people will work together (inside or outside sales forces and team selling).

To hold down the high costs of hiring the wrong people, salespeople must be *recruited* and *selected* carefully. In recruiting salespeople, a company may look to job duties and the characteristics of its most successful salespeople to suggest the traits it wants in its salespeople and then look for applicants through recommendations of current salespeople, employment agencies, classified ads, and the Internet and by contacting college students. In the selection process, the procedure can vary from a single informal interview to lengthy testing and interviewing. After the selection process is complete, *training* programs familiarize new salespeople not only with the art of selling but also with the company's history, its products and policies, and the characteristics of its market and competitors.

The sales force *compensation* system helps to reward, motivate, and direct salespeople. In compensating salespeople, companies try to have an appealing plan, usually close to the going rate for the type of sales job and needed skills. In addition to compensation, all salespeople need *supervision*, and many need continuous encouragement because they must make many decisions and face many frustrations. Periodically, the company must *evaluate* their performance to help them do a better job. In evaluating salespeople, the company relies on getting regular information gathered through sales reports, personal observations, customers' letters and complaints, customer surveys, and conversations with other salespeople.

3. Discuss the personal selling process, distinguishing between transaction-oriented marketing and relationship marketing.

The art of selling involves a seven-step *selling process: prospecting and qualifying, preapproach, approach, presentation and demonstration, handling objections, closing,* and *follow-up*. These steps help marketers close a specific sale and as such are *transaction oriented*. However, a seller's dealings with customers should be guided by the larger concept of *relationship marketing*. The company's sales force should help to orchestrate a whole-company effort to develop profitable long-term relationships with key customers based on superior customer value and satisfaction.

4. Define direct marketing and discuss its benefits to customers and companies.

Direct marketing consists of direct connections with carefully targeted individual consumers to both obtain an immediate response and cultivate lasting customer relationships. Using detailed databases, direct marketers tailor their offers and communications to the needs of narrowly defined segments or even individual buyers.

For buyers, direct marketing is convenient, easy to use, and private. It gives them ready access to a wealth of products and information, at home and around the globe. Direct marketing is also immediate and interactive, allowing buyers to create exactly the configuration of information, products, or services they desire, then order them on the spot. For sellers, direct marketing is a powerful tool for building customer relationships. Using database marketing, today's marketers can target small groups or individual consumers, tailor offers to individual needs, and promote these offers through personalized communications. It also offers them a low-cost, efficient alternative for reaching their markets. As a result of these advantages to both buyers and sellers, direct marketing has become the fastest growing form of marketing.

5. Identify and discuss the major forms of direct marketing.

The main forms of direct marketing include *personal selling, telephone marketing, direct-mail marketing, catalog marketing, direct-response television marketing, kiosk marketing,* and *online marketing*. We discuss personal selling in the first part of this chapter and will examine online marketing in detail in Chapter 17.

Telephone marketing consists of using the telephone to sell directly to consumers. *Direct-mail marketing* consists of the company sending an offer, announcement, reminder, or other item to a person at a specific address. Recently, three new forms of mail delivery have become popular—*fax mail, e-mail,* and *voice mail*. Some marketers rely on *catalog marketing*, or selling through catalogs mailed to a select list of customers or made available in stores. *Direct response television marketing* has two forms: *direct-response advertising* or *infomercials* and *home shopping channels*. *Kiosks* are information and ordering machines that direct marketers place in stores, airports, and other locations. *Online marketing* involves online channels and e-commerce, which electronically link consumers with sellers.

> Reviewing the Key Terms <

> Discussing the Concepts <

1. According to the chapter, salespeople to serve "two masters." What does this mean? Is it a good or bad thing?

2. The chapter states that the ability to build relationships with customers is the most important of a salesperson's key talents. Do you agree? Explain.

3. What is a trial close? How can a rejected trial close further the personal selling process?

4. The text emphasizes the link between personal selling and customer relationship management. Why is this such an important concept?

5. How does direct marketing differ from personal selling?

6. Write a description of the most irritating, unfair, deceptive, or fraudulent experience you've had with a direct marketing company. Is the company still in business?

> Applying the Concepts <

1. Suppose your grade in one of your classes is hovering between an A and B. How would you apply the seven steps in the personal selling process to convince your professor that you deserve an A?

2. Suppose that you are a sales information technology consultant who has been asked to design a sales automation system for the Black &

Decker sales force. What hardware would you include in this system? What software? What input information would the system require and what outputs would it provide?

3. In a small group, prepare a list of the pros and cons from the seller's perspective of a "Do Not E-mail" list.

> Focus on Technology <

Database marketing has emerged as a major weapon in the marketer's arsenal. Over the past 15 years, database marketing technology has improved significantly. One of the better organizations in this area is DataFlux. In a whitepaper on database marketing, the company states, "The goal of a marketing database is to provide consistent, accurate, and reliable data that can be used to build and maintain mutually rewarding customer relationships." Visit the DataFlux Web site at www.dataflux.com. Find and explore the database marketing product area and associated links. Then respond to the following questions.

1. What are some of the challenges cited by DataFlux that require implementation of a database marketing system?

2. What services would DataFlux be able to provide a company interested in database marketing?

3. What are the potential benefits to the buyer of implementing a database marketing system? Are these benefits realistic?

Sources: See www.dataflux.com/Resources/resource.asp?rid=21.

> Focus on Ethics <

According to the FTC and many privacy advocates, consumer information privacy is a growing public policy concern. One area of special concern is the sharing of consumer financial information with affiliates of the same company. Visit http://about.nordstrom.com/popup/shopwithconfidence/protect-nbank.asp and read about the retailer's privacy policy. Then respond to the following questions.

1. What are the important issues concerning the sharing of personal financial information with affiliates and other third parties?

2. How might the retailer use such database marketing information?

3. Is such information sharing fair to the consumer? Explain.

Sources: See www.ftc.gov/speeches/beales/040112patriotact.pdf; www.privacyrights.org/financial.htm; and http://about.nordstrom.com/popup/shopwithconfidence/protect-nbank.asp.

O Video Case

Motorola

In the midst of the thousands of marketing messages consumers receive each day, how can a company break through the clutter to reach target customers? The answer is consistent messages that convey the real value of products and services. That's how Motorola built its global brand. The company's current campaign offers consumers a simple way to identify with Motorola and its product and service offerings. The entire campaign is based on simple tagline—Moto—that Motorola hopes consumers will associate with edgy innovation.

To firmly establish the brand worldwide, Motorola adapted the campaign for each local market, changing advertising images and media to effectively convey the same brand attributes across the globe. Connecting with consumers requires Motorola to use a variety of communications tools.

After viewing the video featuring Motorola, answer the following questions about personal selling and direct marketing.

1. How did Ogilvy & Mather apply the concepts of integrated marketing communications to build Motorola's communications strategy? What was the goal of the campaign that resulted?

2. How does Motorola use direct marketing, in addition to the advertising featured in the video, to communicate and promote the new brand concept? What other forms of direct marketing could Motorola use to communicate with consumers?

Company Case

Jefferson-Pilot Financial: Growing the Sales Force

AFTER THE MEETING

On a hot Friday afternoon in July, Bob Powell and John Knowles walked across a parking lot towards Bob's car. They had just finished a two-day strategic planning meeting with other members of Jefferson-Pilot Financial's (JPF) Independent Marketing channel at the Grandover Resort and Conference Hotel just outside Greensboro, North Carolina. The group had gathered to develop the sales goals it wanted to achieve in the next two and a half years, to identify strategic projects it needed to accomplish to meet those goals, and to assign responsibility for each project.

"Wow, it's going to be hot in your car," John noted. John served as Vice President for Independent Marketing and Bob was Senior Vice President.

"Especially after sitting in that air-conditioned room for two days," Bob responded. "But, I'm glad we're riding together. This'll give us a few minutes to talk about the sales force strategy project the group assigned us."

JEFFERSON-PILOT FINANCIAL

Jefferson-Pilot Corporation (JP), a holding company, was one of the nation's largest shareholder-owned life insurance companies. Jefferson-Pilot's life insurance and annuity businesses, known collectively as Jefferson Pilot Financial (JPF), was comprised principally of Jefferson-Pilot Life Insurance Company, Jefferson Pilot Financial Insurance Company, and Jefferson Pilot LifeAmerica Insurance Company. JPF offered full lines of individual and group life insurance products as well as annuity and investment products. Jefferson-Pilot Communications Company, which operated three network television stations and 17 radio stations, produced and syndicated sports programming.

In the previous year, the company amassed $3.33 billion in revenues and $513 million in net income. JP's insurance and investment products produced about 84 percent of its net income. JP took pride in its excellent financial ratings, having earned the highest possible financial ratings from A.M. Best, Standard and Poors, and Fitch.

Historically, the company generated its individual life insurance sales using a career sales force. The company employed managers to recruit and train life insurance agents, paying the managers commissions based on the insurance premiums their agents generated and an expense allowance to cover their overhead costs. The agents became "captive" Jefferson Pilot employees who sold *only* JP's policies.

Like most life insurance companies, the company paid agents on a commission-only basis. The agent earned a commission of 50 to 60 percent of the *first-year* premium paid by the policyholder. In the following years, the agent earned a much lower commission on annual renewal premiums, usually in the range of three percent. In addition to paying commission, the company provided the career agents with a full range of fringe benefits, such as health insurance, vacation, and sick leave. The individual agent had to pay his/her own business expenses.

A NEW STRATEGY

In 1993, JP was a conservative, well-run company. However, the Board of Directors wanted the company to grow more rapidly. The Board brought in a new top-management team and charged the team with speeding up the company's growth. The new team immediately examined the company's sales-force strategy. It concluded that although the career sales force had been a valuable asset, the company was not capable of meeting its growth goals using only a career force. It simply took too long to hire and train new agents and bring them up to the necessary productivity levels. Further, industry wide, only about one of every seven or eight recruits actually succeeded in the insurance business.

In addition to career agents, JPF had used some independent agents all along. Independent agents worked for themselves or for independent companies. They, like captive agents, sold life insurance; but they could sell policies offered by a variety of companies. JPF decided to expand it sales force by focusing on the independent agents. It began to recruit these established, experienced independent salespeople, licensing them to sell JPF's policies and encouraging them to do so. Because the agents remained independent, JPF did not have to provide them with typical employee benefits. However, because the independent agents still had to cover these expenses, the company had to pay a higher percentage of first-year premium, usually about 80 percent. The average first-year premium in the independent channel was about $5,000. Because there were independent agents located throughout the United States, the company was able to expand more rapidly outside of its traditional Southeastern market area and have agents offering its policies nationwide.

The new focus was extremely successful, and by 1999, the independent channel had become JPF's primary distribution channel, although the company retained its career agents. In 1999, JPF hired Bob Powell to head the Independent Marketing channel.

JPF had begun to recruit not only individual independent agents but also so-called Independent Marketing Organizations (IMOs). An IMO was in the business of serving life insurance agents. IMOs did not produce or "manufacture" life-insurance policies; they just served independent life insurance agents. Thus, the insurance company was the "manufacturer;" the IMO a "wholesaler;" and the independent agent the "retailer." The IMO represented multiple insurance companies and often had a large staff that helped agents develop customized policies to serve special customer needs.

IMOs dealt with the insurance companies, talked with underwriters and medical directors, and helped secure the needed life insurance on behalf of the agent's client. This allowed the agents to sell policies without having to worry about the massive amounts of paperwork and administrative details that someone had to perform after an agent

(box continues)

made a sale. As a result, the IMO earned an additional fee from the insurance company on policies sold by the agents who worked through it. The insurance company was able to pay this additional fee because the IMOs performed some functions that the insurance company would have to perform if it sold directly through the agent.

By recruiting IMOs, JPF was able to bring on more agents more rapidly than it could by having to recruit individual agents. There were also some IMOs that were "recruiting only," that is, they recruited agents but did not provide any of the administrative support for the agents.

Powell and Knowles realized that there was no way JPF could recruit and serve the thousands of IMOs in the United States from the Greensboro home office. Thus, they began to put together a field sales team. They divided the country into five multi-state regions and, with the help of an Executive Search firm, recruited a Sales Vice President (SVP) for each region.

The SVPs JPF recruited had many years of industry experience with other insurance companies, and several had held similar sales positions with other companies. The SVPs typically spent several days a week traveling to recruit new IMOs or to provide training and support for IMOs with whom JPF had a relationship. They also worked with the IMOs to resolve policy issuance or customer service problems the IMOs might have with the home office. The SVPs were relationship builders. They saw themselves as "premium gatherers" who wanted to get more "shelf space" for JPF's products with each IMO. They wanted to get the IMO's, their staff, and agents into the JPF "culture," make them comfortable doing business with JPF, and make it convenient to do so.

Like the career agents, the SVPs were JPF employees to whom it paid a small percentage of all the first-year premium dollars generated by JPF policies sold in their territory. Even though the percentage was small, because of the size of their territories, SVPs could earn a substantial income.

Because the SVPs put more "feet on the street" for JPF, and because JPF had very competitive products, policy sales had taken off in the previous year. By the time of this mid-year sales meeting, the IM channel was well ahead of its annual sales targets.

BACK IN THE CAR

"The problem we have," Bob Powell noted, "is that we are too successful. We are way ahead of this year's targets and you know top management is going to want us to exceed what we do this year next year. And, all of us are working as hard as we can. We can't do more by working any harder. You know that means we will have to add more SVPs."

"That's right," John Knowles observed, "but you saw in the meeting how the five SVPs reacted when we brought this up. They want to protect and keep all of their territory."

"Yes, but we all know that an SVP can't possibly cover eight to twelve states and develop the kinds of IMO relationships we need," Bob answered. "I don't think an SVP can work with more than 30 or so IMOs. What are we going to do when an SVP gets a full client load? How do we bring on more SVPs without upsetting the apple cart?"

"Well," John continued, "that brings up the issue of productivity. We have three marketing coordinators now based in Greensboro who work with the SVPs. However, we don't have a formal job description for them, and the SVPs are unhappy that they don't each have their own coordinator. But you know that in these economic times the company's reluctant to add more people, more overhead."

"I can see that some of our discussions may get as hot as this July weather," Bob laughed.

"When I get home," John said, "I'm going to dig out the old Kotler/Armstrong marketing textbook I had at Auburn and look back over the chapter on personal selling to see if it'll remind me of any issues we ought to be considering."

"We have a September 30 deadline for our sales force strategy proposals, so we'd better get to work," Bob concluded.

Questions for Discussion

1. What are the advantages and disadvantages of using a career sales force versus an independent sales force?

2. What are the advantages and disadvantages of commission-only compensation versus salary-only compensation?

3. What problems do you see with JPF's sales force strategy and structure decisions?

4. What recommendations would you make to JPF to help it deal with these problems?

Source: Officials at Jefferson-Pilot Financial cooperated in development of this case.

> After studying this chapter, you should be able to

1. discuss the need to understand competitors as well as customers through competitor analysis
2. explain the fundamentals of competitive marketing strategies based on creating value for customers
3. illustrate the need for balancing customer and competitor orientations in becoming a truly market-centered organization

CHAPTER 17

Creating Competitive Advantage

Previewing the Concepts

In previous chapters, you explored the basics of marketing. You learned that good marketing companies win, keep, and grow customers by creating superior value for customers in order to capture value from customers in return. In this chapter, we pull all of these basics together. Understanding customers is an important first step in developing profitable customer relationships, but it's not enough. To gain competitive advantage, companies must use this understanding to design market offers that deliver more value than the offers of *competitors* seeking to win the same customers. Thus, beyond understanding consumers, firms must also understand their competitors. In this chapter, we look first at competitor analysis, the process companies use to identify and analyze competitors. Then, we examine competitive marketing strategies by which companies position themselves against competitors to gain the greatest possible competitive advantage.

First let's examine Washington Mutual, a very successful financial services company with an unusual formula for building profitable relationships with its middle-American customers. As you read about Washington Mutual, ask yourself: Just what *is* it about this company's marketing strategy that has made it the nation's sixth largest banking company and one of the leading mortgage lenders? Pursuing this strategy, can "WaMu" become the Wal-Mart of the banking industry?

When you walk into a Washington Mutual branch for the first time, you'll probably do a double-take. This just isn't your usual bank. There are no teller windows or desks, no velvet ropes, and no marble counters. Instead, you'll find a warm and inviting retail environment, complete with a concierge area where WaMulians (that's what employees call themselves) meet and greet customers. According to Washington Mutual, the idea is to create a place where bank customers want to go rather than have to go. In many respects, a Washington Mutual branch is more like a retail store than a bank.

This is the bank of the future, Washington Mutual style (WaMu, to the faithful). Sales associates are dressed in Gap-like gear: blue shirts, khaki pants, and navy sweaters. But there's not a rack of cargo pants in sight, and denim shirts are in short supply. If you want a mutual fund, however, a young woman is eager to help. If it's a checking account you need, step right up to the concierge station,

and a friendly young man will direct you to the right nook. If your kids get fussy while you're chatting about overdraft protection, send them over to the kids corner, called WaMu Kids, where they can amuse themselves with games, books, and other activities.

The bank's look and feel are intended to put the 'retail' back in retail banking. Known internally as Occasio (Latin for "favorable opportunity"), the format grew out of 18 months of intense market research that investigated every customer touch point in a branch. One of the primary innovations of the bank's design is teller towers, pedestals where sales associates stand in front of screens fielding transactions. They handle no money. Customers who need cash back are given a slip, which they take over to a cash-dispensing machine. This is central to the bank's true goal: cross-selling products by helping customers to find additional products and services they might value. Since they aren't tethered to a cash drawer, tellers who discover that a customer's kid just got into college can march that person over to an education-loan officer. Or they can steer newlyweds to the mortgage desk.

This format might seem unusual for a bank, but it's working for Washington Mutual. The company's more than 1,850 branches around the country are pulling in new accounts hand over fist. WaMu's more than $18 billion in yearly revenues makes it the nation's 6th largest banking company and one of the largest mortgage companies. In the most recent *Fortune* rankings of America's most admired companies, WaMu topped the mortgage services industry, rating number-one or number-two in all eight of the ranking's key-attribute categories.

Washington Mutual's stunning success has resulted from its relentless dedication to a simple competitive marketing strategy: operational excellence. Some companies, like Ritz-Carlton hotels, create value through customer intimacy—by coddling customers and reaping high prices and margins. Others, like Microsoft or Intel, create value through product leadership—by offering a continuous stream of leading-edge products. In contrast, Washington Mutual creates value through a Wal-Mart-like strategy of offering convenience and competitive prices.

WaMu's high-tech, innovative retail stores provide customer convenience but cost much less to staff and operate than a typical bank branch. "Their inexpensive branch design allows WaMu to make use of existing retail space and keep personnel costs low, notes a banking analyst." Leveraging this low cost, WaMu can offer more affordable banking services, which in turn lets it profitably serve the mass market of moderate-income consumers that other banks now overlook. In fact, Washington Mutual wants to be the Wal-Mart of the banking industry:

WaMu's strategy is simple: Deliver great value and convenient service for the everyday Joe. "The blue-collar, lower white-collar end of the market is either underserved or overcharged," says one analyst who has followed WaMu for nearly two decades. The Home Depots, Targets, and Wal-Marts have built empires by focusing on those customers. Now WaMu's CEO, Kerry Killinger, aims to join their ranks. Killinger wants nothing less than to reinvent how people think about banking. "In every retailing industry there are category killers who figure out how to have a very low cost structure and pass those advantages on to customers, day in and day out, with better pricing," he says. "I think we have a

shot at doing that in this segment." His goal is to have his company mentioned in the same breath as Wal-Mart and Southwest Airlines. "We want to be put into a different category, as a high-growth retailer of consumer financial services," he says, without a trace of doubt. "We'll even start losing the banking label."

WaMu's strategy focuses on building full customer relationships. It begins with offering what the company considers to be its core relationship products: home mortgages and free checking with no minimum balance requirement to avoid a monthly fee. Pretty soon, customers are happily hooked on WaMu's entire range of banking services. According to one account:

"Checking accounts and mortgages are two of the most important products for Main Street America. WaMu can offer a package of products at better value than you could get by offering those products independently. When you team the convenience and the price value, it's a very powerful combination for the consumer."

WaMu's cross-selling, relationship-building formula is a powerful one. Five years after starting with free checking as their initial relationship, Washington Mutual's households on average maintain more than $23,000 in deposit, investment, and home and consumer loan balances.

WaMu's focus on customer relationships is a primary reason for the bank's success. But the company knows that to build strong customer relationships, it must also take good care of the employees who maintain those relationships. So WaMu has also created an exuberant corporate culture that motivates and supports the WaMulians. "In fact, some people feel that WaMu's culture lingers on the edge of cultism," suggests one observer. "The company has even held brand 'rallies' where employees sing catchy jingles, complete with accompanying hand motions. All of that enthusiasm translates into customer service, satisfaction, and value."

Will Washington Mutual's competitive marketing strategy of bringing value and convenience to middle-Americans make it the Wal-Mart of the banking industry? WaMu is certainly well on its way. "You can have a lucky streak for a few quarters, but you can't accomplish what they've done with just a lucky streak," says an analyst. "They have good people; they have scale; they are very focused on their customers. For WaMu, the best is still to come."[1]

Competitive advantage
An advantage over competitors gained by offering consumers greater value, either through lower prices or by providing more benefits that justify higher prices.

Competitor analysis
The process of identifying key competitors; assessing their objectives, strategies, strengths and weaknesses, and reaction patterns; and selecting which competitors to attack or avoid.

Competitive marketing strategies
Strategies that strongly position the company against competitors and that give the company the strongest possible strategic advantage.

Today's companies face their toughest competition ever. In previous chapters, we argued that to succeed in today's fiercely competitive marketplace, companies will have to move from a product-and-selling philosophy to a customer-and-marketing philosophy. John Chambers, CEO of Cisco Systems put it well: "Make your customer the center of your culture."

This chapter spells out in more detail how companies can go about outperforming competitors in order to win, keep, and grow customers. To win in today's marketplace, companies must become adept not just in *managing products*, but in *managing customer relationships* in the face of determined competition. Understanding customers is crucial, but it's not enough. Building profitable customer relationships and gaining **competitive advantage** requires delivering *more* value and satisfaction to target consumers than *competitors* do.

In this chapter, we examine *competitive marketing strategies*—how companies analyze their competitors and develop successful, value-based strategies for building and maintaining profitable customer relationships. The first step is **competitor analysis**, the process of identifying, assessing, and selecting key competitors. The second step is developing **competitive marketing strategies** that strongly position the company against competitors and give it the greatest possible competitive advantage.

Competitor Analysis

To plan effective marketing strategies, the company needs to find out all it can about its competitors. It must constantly compare its marketing strategies, products, prices, channels, and promotion with those of close competitors. In this way the company can find areas of potential competitive advantage and disadvantage. As shown in Figure 17.1, competitor analysis involves first identifying and assessing competitors and then selecting which competitors to attack or avoid.

Identifying Competitors

Normally, identifying competitors would seem a simple task. At the narrowest level, a company can define its competitors as other companies offering similar products and services to the same customers at similar prices. Thus, Coca-Cola might view Pepsi as a major competitor, but not Budweiser or Gatorade. Bookseller Barnes & Noble might see Borders as a major competitor, but not Wal-Mart or Costco. Buick might see Ford as a major competitor, but not Mercedes or Hyundai.

But companies actually face a much wider range of competitors. The company might define competitors as all firms making the same product or class of products. Thus, Buick would see itself as competing against all other automobile makers. Even more broadly, competitors might include all companies making products that supply the same service. Here Buick would see itself competing not only against other automobile makers but also against companies that make trucks, motorcycles, or even bicycles. Finally, and still more broadly, competitors might include all companies that compete for the same consumer dollars. Here Buick would see itself competing with companies that sell major consumer durables, new homes, or vacations abroad.

Companies must avoid "competitor myopia." A company is more likely to be "buried" by its latent competitors than its current ones. For example, for many years, Kodak held a comfortable lead in the photographic film business. It saw Fuji as its major competitor in this market. However, in recent years, Kodak's major new competition has not come from Fuji and other film producers. It has come from Sony, Canon, and other makers of digital cameras, which don't even use film. Because of its myopic focus on film, Kodak was late to enter the digital camera market. Now, digital cameras outsell film cameras, and Kodak finds itself in second place in the digital segment behind Sony, a company that it didn't even consider a competitor only a decade ago.[2]

FIGURE 17.1
Steps in analyzing competitors

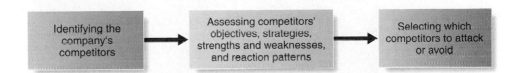

Similarly, 230-year-old Encyclopaedia Britannica viewed itself as competing mostly with other publishers of printed encyclopedia sets selling for as much as $2,200 per set. However, by the early to mid-1990s, computer-savvy kids were finding information online or on CD-ROMs such as Microsoft's Encarta, which sold for only $50. Although Encyclopaedia Britannica had begun publishing its encyclopedia in digital media in the early 1980s, it failed to treat online and CD-ROM versions as a serious competitive threat. Instead, it continued to emphasize door-to-door sales of the printed sets that had traditionally produced most of its revenues. It was a hard lesson for the traditional publisher. In 1996, it began a difficult transition by closing down its entire 2,300-person door-to-door sales force and making major adjustments in its product line and distribution methods. Today the company looks very different from the way it did 15 years ago, selling a high volume of digital products at lower prices instead of a low volume of one high-priced product, the printed encyclopedia.[3]

Companies can identify their competitors from the *industry* point of view. They might see themselves as being in the oil industry, the pharmaceutical industry, or the beverage industry. A company must understand the competitive patterns in its industry if it hopes to be an effective "player" in that industry. Companies can also identify competitors from a *market* point of view. Here they define competitors as companies that are trying to satisfy the same customer need or build relationships with the same customer group.

From an industry point of view, Coca-Cola might see its competition as Pepsi, Dr Pepper, 7UP, and other softdrink makers. From a market point of view, however, the customer really wants "thirst quenching." This need can be satisfied by iced tea, fruit juice, bottled water, or many other fluids. Similarly, Hallmark's Binney & Smith, maker of Crayola crayons, might define its competitors as other makers of crayons and children's drawing supplies. But from a market point of view, it would include all firms making recreational products for children.

In general, the market concept of competition opens the company's eyes to a broader set of actual and potential competitors. One approach is to profile the company's direct and indirect competitors by mapping the steps buyers take in obtaining and using the product. Figure 17.2 illustrates their *competitor map* of Eastman Kodak in the film business.[4] In the center is a list of consumer activities: buying a camera, buying film, taking pictures, and others. The first outer ring lists Kodak's main competitors with respect to each consumer activ-

■ Identifying competitors: Encyclopedia Britannica's real competitors were the computer and the Internet. It now offers online and DVD/CD versions.

FIGURE 17.2
Competitor map
Source: Jeffrey F. Rayport and Bernard J. Jaworski, e-Commerce (New York: McGraw-Hill, 2001), p. 53.

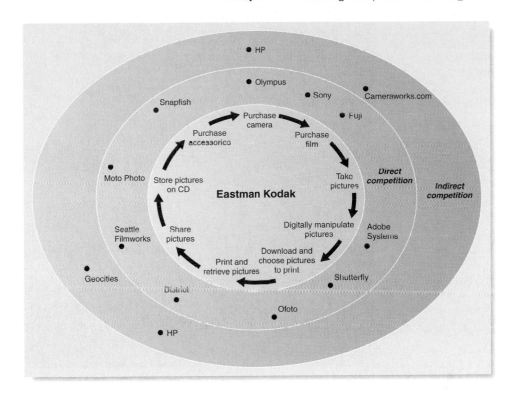

ity: Olympus and Sony for buying a camera, Fuji for purchasing film, and so on. The second outer ring lists indirect competitors—HP, cameraworks.com, and others—who may become direct competitors. This type of analysis highlights both the competitive opportunities and the challenges a company faces.

Assessing Competitors

Having identified the main competitors, marketing management now asks: What are competitors' objectives—what does each seek in the marketplace? What is each competitor's strategy? What are various competitor's strengths and weaknesses, and how will each react to actions the company might take?

Determining Competitors' Objectives

Each competitor has a mix of objectives. The company wants to know the relative importance that a competitor places on current profitability, market share growth, cash flow, technological leadership, service leadership, and other goals. Knowing a competitor's mix of objectives reveals whether the competitor is satisfied with its current situation and how it might react to different competitive actions. For example, a company that pursues low-cost leadership will react much more strongly to a competitor's cost-reducing manufacturing breakthrough than to the same competitor's advertising increase.

A company also must monitor its competitors' objectives for various segments. If the company finds that a competitor has discovered a new segment, this might be an opportunity. If it finds that competitors plan new moves into segments now served by the company, it will be forewarned and, hopefully, forearmed.

Identifying Competitors' Strategies

The more that one firm's strategy resembles another firm's strategy, the more the two firms compete. In most industries, the competitors can be sorted into groups that pursue different strategies. A **strategic group** is a group of firms in an industry following the same or a similar strategy in a given target market. For example, in the major appliance industry, General Electric, Whirlpool, and Maytag all belong to the same strategic group. Each produces a full line of medium-price appliances supported by good service. In contrast, Sub-Zero and Viking belong to a different strategic group. They produce a narrower line of higher-quality appliances, offer a higher level of service, and charge a premium price.

Strategic group
A group of firms in an industry following the same or a similar strategy.

■ Strategic groups: Sub-Zero belongs to the appliance industry strategic group offering a narrower line of higher-quality appliances supported by good service.

Some important insights emerge from identifying strategic groups. For example, if a company enters one of the groups, the members of that group become its key competitors. Thus, if the company enters the first group, against General Electric, Whirlpool, and Maytag, it can succeed only if it develops strategic advantages over these competitors.

Although competition is most intense within a strategic group, there is also rivalry among groups. First, some of the strategic groups may appeal to overlapping customer segments. For example, no matter what their strategy, all major appliance manufacturers will go after the apartment and home builders segment. Second, the customers may not see much difference in the offers of different groups—they may see little difference in quality between Whirlpool and KitchenAid. Finally, members of one strategic group might expand into new strategy segments. Thus, General Electric's Monogram line of appliances competes in the premium quality, premium-price line with Viking and Sub-Zero.

The company needs to look at all of the dimensions that identify strategic groups within the industry. It needs to know each competitor's product quality, features, and mix; customer services; pricing policy; distribution coverage; sales force strategy; and advertising and sales promotion programs. And it must study the details of each competitor's R&D, manufacturing, purchasing, financial, and other strategies.

Assessing Competitors' Strengths and Weaknesses

Benchmarking
The process of comparing the company's products and processes to those of competitors or leading firms in other industries to find ways to improve quality and performance.

Marketers need to assess each competitor's strengths and weaknesses carefully in order to answer the critical question: What *can* our competitors do? As a first step, companies can gather data on each competitor's goals, strategies, and performance over the last few years. Admittedly, some of this information will be hard to obtain. For example, business-to-business marketers find it hard to estimate competitors' market shares because they do not have the same syndicated data services that are available to consumer packaged-goods companies.

Companies normally learn about their competitors' strengths and weaknesses through secondary data, personal experience, and word of mouth. They also can conduct primary marketing research with customers, suppliers, and dealers. Or they can **benchmark** themselves against other firms, comparing the company's products and processes to those of competitors or leading firms in other industries to find ways to improve quality and performance. Benchmarking has become a powerful tool for increasing a company's competitiveness.

Estimating Competitors' Reactions

Next, the company wants to know: What *will* our competitors do? A competitor's objectives, strategies, and strengths and weaknesses go a long way toward explaining its likely actions. They also suggest its likely reactions to company moves such as price cuts, promotion increases, or new-product introductions. In addition, each competitor has a certain philosophy of doing business, a certain internal culture and guiding beliefs. Marketing managers need a deep understanding of a given competitor's mentality if they want to anticipate how the competitor will act or react.

Each competitor reacts differently. Some do not react quickly or strongly to a competitor's move. They may feel their customers are loyal; they may be slow in noticing the move; they may lack the funds to react. Some competitors react only to certain types of moves and not to others. Other competitors react swiftly and strongly to any action. Thus, Procter & Gamble does not let a new detergent come easily into the market. Many firms avoid direct competition with P&G and look for easier prey, knowing that P&G will react fiercely if challenged.

In some industries, competitors live in relative harmony; in others, they fight constantly. Knowing how major competitors react gives the company clues on how best to attack competitors or how best to defend the company's current positions.

Selecting Competitors to Attack and Avoid

A company has already largely selected its major competitors through prior decisions on customer targets, distribution channels, and marketing-mix strategy. Management now must decide which competitors to compete against most vigorously.

Strong or Weak Competitors

The company can focus on one of several classes of competitors. Most companies prefer to compete against *weak competitors*. This requires fewer resources and less time. But in the process, the firm may gain little. You could argue that the firm also should compete with *strong competitors* in order to sharpen its abilities. Moreover, even strong competitors have some weaknesses, and succeeding against them often provides greater returns.

A useful tool for assessing competitor strengths and weaknesses is **customer value analysis**. The aim of customer value analysis is to determine the benefits that target customers value and how customers rate the relative value of various competitors' offers. In conducting a customer value analysis, the company first identifies the major attributes that customers value and the importance customers place on these attributes. Next, it assesses the company's and competitors' performance on the valued attributes.

The key to gaining competitive advantage is to take each customer segment and examine how the company's offer compares to that of its major competitor. If the company's offer exceeds the competitor's offer on all important attributes, the company can charge a higher price and earn higher profits, or it can charge the same price and gain more market share. But if the company is seen as performing at a lower level than its major competitor on some important attributes, it must invest in strengthening those attributes or finding other important attributes where it can build a lead on the competitor.

Close or Distant Competitors

Most companies will compete with *close competitors*—those that resemble them most—rather than *distant competitors*. Thus, Chevrolet competes more against Ford than against Lexus. And Target competes with Wal-Mart and Kmart rather than against Neiman Marcus or Nordstrom.

At the same time, the company may want to avoid trying to "destroy" a close competitor. For example, in the late 1970s, Bausch & Lomb moved aggressively against other soft lens manufacturers with great success. However, this forced weak competitors to sell out to larger firms such as Johnson & Johnson. As a result, Bausch & Lomb now faced much larger competitors—and it suffered the consequences. Johnson & Johnson acquired Vistakon, a small nicher with only $20 million in annual sales. Backed by Johnson & Johnson's deep pockets,

Customer value analysis
Analysis conducted to determine what benefits target customers value and how they rate the relative value of various competitors' offers.

■ After driving smaller competitors from the market, Bausch & Lomb faces larger, more resourceful ones, such as Johnson & Johnson's Vistakon division. With Vistakon's Acuvue lenses leading the way, J&J is now the top U.S. contact lens maker.

however, the small but nimble Vistakon developed and introduced its innovative Acuvue disposable lenses. With Vistakon leading the way, Johnson & Johnson is now the top U.S. contact lens maker, with a 34 percent market share, while Bausch & Lomb lags in third place with a 15 percent share.[5] In this case, success in hurting a close rival brought in tougher competitors.

"Good" or "Bad" Competitors

A company really needs and benefits from competitors. The existence of competitors results in several strategic benefits. Competitors may help increase total demand. They may share the costs of market and product development and help to legitimize new technologies. They may serve less-attractive segments or lead to more product differentiation. Finally, they lower the antitrust risk and improve bargaining power versus labor or regulators. For example, Intel's recent aggressive pricing on low-end computer chips has sent smaller rivals like AMD and 3Com reeling. However, Intel may want to be careful not to knock these competitors completely out. "If for no other reason than to keep the feds at bay," notes one analyst, "Intel needs AMD, 3Com, and other rivals to stick around." Says another: "Intel may have put the squeeze on a little too hard. If AMD collapsed, the FTC would surely react."[6]

However, a company may not view all of its competitors as beneficial. An industry often contains *"good" competitors* and *"bad" competitors*.[7] Good competitors play by the rules of the industry. Bad competitors, in contrast, break the rules. They try to buy share rather than earn it, take large risks, and in general shake up the industry. For example, American Airlines finds Delta and United to be good competitors because they play by the rules and attempt to set their fares sensibly. But American finds Continental and America West bad competitors because they destabilize the airline industry through continual heavy price discounting and wild promotional schemes.

The implication is that "good" companies would like to shape an industry that consists of only well-behaved competitors. A company might be smart to support good competitors, aiming its attacks at bad competitors. Thus, some analysts claim that American Airlines has from time to time used huge fare discounts intentionally designed to teach disruptive airlines a lesson or to drive them out of business altogether.

Designing a Competitive Intelligence System

We have described the main types of information that companies need about their competitors. This information must be collected, interpreted, distributed, and used. The cost in money and time of gathering competitive intelligence is high, and the company must design its competitive intelligence system in a cost-effective way.

The competitive intelligence system first identifies the vital types of competitive information and the best sources of this information. Then, the system continuously collects information from the field (sales force, channels, suppliers, market research firms, trade associations, Web sites) and from published data (government publications, speeches, articles). Next the system checks the information for validity and reliability, interprets it, and organizes it in an appropriate way. Finally, it sends key information to relevant decision makers and responds to inquiries from managers about competitors.

With this system, company managers will receive timely information about competitors in the form of phone calls, e-mails, bulletins, newsletters, and reports. In addition, managers can connect with the system when they need an interpretation of a competitor's sudden move, or when they want to know a competitor's weaknesses and strengths, or when they need to know how a competitor will respond to a planned company move.

Smaller companies that cannot afford to set up formal competitive intelligence offices can assign specific executives to watch specific competitors. Thus, a manager who used to work for a competitor might follow that competitor closely; he or she would be the "in-house expert" on that competitor. Any manager needing to know the thinking of a given competitor could contact the assigned in-house expert.

Competitive Strategies

Having identified and evaluated its major competitors, the company now must design broad competitive marketing strategies by which it can gain competitive advantage by offering superior customer value. But what broad marketing strategies might the company use? Which ones are best for a particular company, or for the company's different divisions and products?

Approaches to Marketing Strategy

No one strategy is best for all companies. Each company must determine what makes the most sense given its position in the industry and its objectives, opportunities, and resources. Even within a company, different strategies may be required for different businesses or products. Johnson & Johnson uses one marketing strategy for its leading brands in stable consumer markets and a different marketing strategy for its new high-tech health-care businesses and products.

Companies also differ in how they approach the strategy-planning process. Many large firms develop formal competitive marketing strategies and implement them religiously. However, other companies develop strategy in a less formal and orderly fashion. Some companies, such as Harley-Davidson, Virgin Atlantic Airways, and BMW's Mini unit succeed by breaking many of the "rules" of marketing strategy. Such companies don't operate large marketing departments, conduct expensive marketing research, spell out elaborate competitive strategies, and spend huge sums on advertising. Instead, they sketch out strategies on the fly, stretch their limited resources, live close to their customers, and create more satisfying solutions to customer needs. They form buyer's clubs, use buzz marketing, and focus on winning customer loyalty. It seems that not all marketing must follow in the footsteps of marketing giants such as IBM and Procter & Gamble.

In fact, approaches to marketing strategy and practice often pass through three stages: entrepreneurial marketing, formulated marketing, and intrepreneurial marketing.[8]

- *Entrepreneurial marketing:* Most companies are started by individuals who live by their wits. They visualize an opportunity, construct flexible strategies on the backs of envelopes, and knock on every door to gain attention. Jim Koch, founder of Boston Beer Company, whose Samuel Adams beer has become a top-selling microbrewery beer, started out in 1984 carrying bottles of Samuel Adams from bar to bar to persuade bartenders to carry it. He would coax them into adding Samuel Adams beer to their menus. For 10 years, he couldn't afford advertising; he sold his beer through direct selling and grassroots public relations. Today, however, his business pulls in more than $230 million, making it the leader over more than 1000 competitors in the microbrewery market.

- *Formulated marketing:* As small companies achieve success, they inevitably move toward more-formulated marketing. They develop formal marketing strategies and adhere to them closely. Boston Beer now employs more than 175 salespeople and has a marketing department that carries out market research and plans strategy. Although Boston Beer is far less formal and sophisticated in its strategy than mega-competitor Anheuser-Busch, it has adopted some of the tools used in professionally run marketing companies.

- *Intrepreneurial marketing:* Many large and mature companies get stuck in formulated marketing. They pore over the latest Nielsen numbers, scan market research reports, and try to fine-tune their competitive strategies and programs. These companies sometimes lose the marketing creativity and passion that they had at the start. They now need to reestablish within their companies the entrepreneurial spirit and actions that made them successful in the first place. They need to encourage more initiative and "intrepreneurship" at the local level. They need to refresh their marketing strategies and try new approaches. Their brand and product managers need to get out of the office, start living with their customers, and visualize new and creative ways to add value to their customers' lives.

The bottom line is that there are many approaches to developing effective competitive marketing strategy. There will be a constant tension between the formulated side of marketing and the creative side. It is easier to learn the formulated side of marketing, which has occupied most of our attention in this book. But we have also seen how marketing creativity and passion in the strategies of many of the company's we've studied—whether small or large, new or mature—have helped to build and maintain success in the marketplace. With this in mind, we now look at broad competitive marketing strategies companies can use.

Basic Competitive Strategies

More than two decades ago, Michael Porter suggested four basic competitive positioning strategies that companies can follow—three winning strategies and one losing one.[9] The three winning strategies include:

- *Overall cost leadership:* Here the company works hard to achieve the lowest production and distribution costs. Low costs let it price lower than its competitors and win a large market share. Texas Instruments, Dell, and Wal-Mart are leading practitioners of this strategy.

- *Differentiation:* Here the company concentrates on creating a highly differentiated product line and marketing program so that it comes across as the class leader in the industry. Most customers would prefer to own this brand if its price is not too high. IBM and Caterpillar follow this strategy in information technology products and services and heavy construction equipment, respectively.

- *Focus:* Here the company focuses its effort on serving a few market segments well rather than going after the whole market. For example, Ritz-Carlton focuses on the top 5 percent of corporate and leisure travelers. Glassmaker AFG Industries focuses on users of tempered and colored glass. It makes 70 percent of the glass for microwave oven doors and 75 percent of the glass for shower doors and patio tabletops. Similarly, Hohner owns a stunning 85 percent of the harmonica market.

Companies that pursue a clear strategy—one of the above—will likely perform well. The firm that carries out that strategy best will make the most profits. But firms that do not pursue a clear strategy—*middle-of-the-roaders*—do the worst. Sears, Holiday Inn, and Kmart encountered difficult times because they did not stand out as the lowest in cost, highest in perceived value, or best in serving some market segment. Middle-of-the-roaders try to be good on all strategic counts, but end up being not very good at anything.

More recently, two marketing consultants, Michael Treacy and Fred Wiersema, offered a new classification of competitive marketing strategies.[10] They suggest that companies gain leadership positions by delivering superior value to their customers. Companies can pursue any of three strategies—called *value disciplines*—for delivering superior customer value. These are:

- *Operational excellence:* The company provides superior value by leading its industry in price and convenience. It works to reduce costs and to create a lean and efficient value-delivery system. It serves customers who want reliable, good-quality products or services, but who want them cheaply and easily. Examples include Wal-Mart, Washington Mutual, Southwest Airlines, and Dell.

- *Customer intimacy:* The company provides superior value by precisely segmenting its markets and tailoring its products or services to match exactly the needs of targeted customers.

■ Focus: Small but profitable Hohner owns a stunning 85 percent of the harmonica market.

It specializes in satisfying unique customer needs through a close relationship with and intimate knowledge of the customer. It builds detailed customer databases for segmenting and targeting, and empowers its marketing people to respond quickly to customer needs. Customer-intimate companies serve customers who are willing to pay a premium to get precisely what they want. They will do almost anything to build long-term customer loyalty and to capture customer lifetime value. Examples include Nordstrom, Ritz-Carlton, Sony, Lexus, American Express, and British Airways (see Real Marketing 17.1).

■ *Product leadership:* The company provides superior value by offering a continuous stream of leading-edge products or services. It aims to make its own and competing products obsolete. Product leaders are open to new ideas, relentlessly pursue new solutions, and work to get new products to market quickly. They serve customers who want state-of-the-art products and services, regardless of the costs in terms of price or inconvenience. Examples include Intel and Microsoft.

Some companies successfully pursue more than one value discipline at the same time. For example, FedEx excels at both operational excellence and customer intimacy. However, such companies are rare—few firms can be the best at more than one of these disciplines. By trying to be *good at all* of the value disciplines, a company usually ends up being *best at none.*

Treacy and Wiersema have found that leading companies focus on and excel at a single value discipline, while meeting industry standards on the other two. Such companies design their entire value delivery network to single mindedly support the chosen discipline. For example, Wal-Mart knows that customer intimacy and product leadership are important. Compared with other discounters, such as Kmart, it offers very good customer service and an excellent product assortment. Still, it offers less customer service and less product depth than do Nordstrom or Eddie Bauer, which pursue customer intimacy. Instead, Wal-Mart focuses obsessively on operational excellence—on reducing costs and streamlining its order-to-delivery process in order to make it convenient for customers to buy just the right products at the lowest prices.

Real Marketing 17.1

Marketing Upscale: Creating Customer Intimacy

Some companies go to extremes to coddle their customers, particularly when those customers are big spenders. These days, building relationships with high-end consumers often means providing extraordinary service. From department stores like Nordstrom, to carmakers like Lexus and BMW, to hotels like Ritz-Carlton and Four Seasons, customer-intimate companies give their customers exactly what they need—and even more.

For example, concierge services are no longer the sole province of five-star hotels and fancy credit cards. They are starting to show up at airlines, retailers, and even electronic-goods makers. Sony Electronics, for instance, offers a service for its richest customers, called Cierge, that provides a free personal shopper and early access to new gadgets, as well as "white-glove" help with the installation. (Translation: They will send someone over to set up the new gear.) Here are two more examples of customer-intimate companies:

British Airways:

The British Airways' *At Your Service* program really takes care of the company's best customers. There's almost nothing that the service won't do for members—tracking down hard-to-get Wimbledon tickets, for example, or running errands around town, sitting in a member's home to wait for the plumber or cable guy, or even planning your wedding, right down to the cake. But At Your Service isn't available to just anyone: Only a small hand picked circle of British Airways frequent-flyer programme members have access. The program includes only a fraction of BA's gold-level elite.

Where does BA's At Your Service concierge service draw the line on what it will do for its exclusive membership? Member Roderick Stevens has yet to find the limit. The Chicago resident recently asked if BA would help plan his wedding in a castle in the United Kingdom. To his surprise, the airline

■ Customer intimacy: The British Airways' *At Your Service* program—there's almost nothing that the service won't do for members.

readily agreed. "I thought it would be too big," says Stevens, a 36-year-old information technology consultant. He found the castle himself but the airline is handling the hotel accom-

Similarly, Ritz-Carlton Hotels want to be efficient and to employ the latest technologies. But what really sets the luxury hotel chain apart is its customer intimacy. Ritz-Carlton creates custom-designed experiences to coddle its customers:

Check into any Ritz-Carlton hotel around the world, and you'll be amazed at how well the hotel's employees anticipate your slightest need. Without ever asking, they seem to know that you want a nonsmoking room with a king-size bed, a nonallergenic pillow, and breakfast with decaffeinated coffee in your room. How does Ritz-Carlton work this magic? At the heart of the system is a huge customer database, which contains information gathered through the observations of hotel employees. Each day, hotel staffers—from those at the front desk to those in maintenance and housekeeping—discreetly record the unique habits, likes, and dislikes of each guest on small "guest preference pads." These observations are then transferred to a corporate-wide "guest preference database." Every morning, a "guest historian" at each hotel reviews the files of all new arrivals who have previously stayed at a Ritz-Carlton and prepares a list of suggested extra touches that might delight each guest. Guests have responded strongly to such markets-of-one service. Since inaugurating the guest-history system, Ritz-Carlton has boosted guest retention by 23 percent. An amazing 95 percent of departing guests report that their stay has been a truly memorable experience.

modations. More, the At Your Service concierge in charge of his account, Emily Brodsky, has also made suggestions about wedding cakes, flowers, and other details. Of course, there is a payoff for BA: The airline will also make the travel arrangements for Mr. Stevens's 100 guests, who will be flying in from Australia, Germany, the United States, and elsewhere.

American Express:

Long known for its premium services, American Express recently marked the five year anniversary of its most elite card: the Centurion Card, better known as "the Black Card." The Card comes dripping with perks, from a personal travel agent to a fleet of concierges on call 24 hours a day. Want that hard-to-get Mombasa handbag? They'll track one down and ship it to your suite at the Four Seasons (room upgrade courtesy of the Centunion Card). First-class seats on some airlines are also part of the deal. If the flight is to Europe, they'll even throw in a loaner cell phone.

For frequent travelers, the benefits of the Centunion Card can sometimes pay for themselves in travel perks. Besides the better rooms at the Four Seasons and Ritz-Carlton, the card offers bonus miles on Continental, Delta, and USAirways, plus enrollment in the elite level of the frequent-guest programs at Hilton, Hyatt, Inter-Continental, and Starwood.

The elusive plastic, with its elegant matte finish, is coveted by big spenders. But the card's success stems from its exclusivity. Although American Express won't say how many are in circulation, analysts estimate roughly 5,000 people in the United States have them. (American Express describes the Card as "invitation only" but denies the rumor that people calling to request one are automatically rejected.) Although American Express is discreet about the requirements, it confirms the basics: $150,000 in annual spending on an existing

American Express card, plus a $2,500 annual fee. Also, it can't hurt to have a large balance in an account managed by an American Express Financial Planner.

Byron Watson was so desperate to get a Black Card that he rounded up friends to run up his bill so that he could hit the spending target. He simply asked the company to issue additional cards on his existing Platinum account, and then handed them out. "I paid their annual fees, and they got the benefits that come from having the Platinum Card," says Watson, a Denver executive. "Everyone thinks I'm crazy." But it worked—he finally qualified.

Then there's Richard Mannion, of Swindon, England. He discovered that the domain name www.amexcenturion.co.uk was available. So he set up a Web site there and posted everything he knew about the qualification requirements. "I did it to annoy them, just because they were giving me the runaround," he says. He finally got a Centurion card, after charging up a storm while working as a consultant for a large technology company. Now, his site automatically redirects people to the official Amex Centurion page. Still, he receives at least five e-mails each week from people wanting to know how he pulled it off. "Sometimes, I get very shocked reactions when I use it," says the young consultant. "People think I've stolen it."

Sources: Examples adapted from Ron Lieber, "The Credit Card That You Can't Get—Invitation-Only 'Black Card' Offers Concierge, Hotel Suites; But Is It Worth a $1,000 Fee?" *Wall Street Journal*, April 9, 2002, p. D1; Eleena de Lisser, "How to Get an Airline to Wait for Your Plumber—In Battle for Biggest Spenders, British Airways, Sony Roll Out Hotel-Style 'Concierge' Service," *Wall Street Journal*, July 2, 2002, p. D1; and Lieber, "The Black Card Gets a Challenger," *Wall Street Journal*, April 6, 2004, p. D.1.

Market leader
The firm in an industry with the largest market share.

Market challenger
A runner-up firm that is fighting hard to increase its market share in an industry.

Market follower
A runner-up firm that wants to hold its share in an industry without rocking the boat.

Market nicher
A firm that serves small segments that the other firms in an industry overlook or ignore.

Classifying competitive strategies as value disciplines is appealing. It defines marketing strategy in terms of the single-minded pursuit of delivering superior value to customers. Each value discipline defines a specific way to build lasting customer relationships.

Competitive Positions

Firms competing in a given target market, at any point in time, differ in their objectives and resources. Some firms are large, others small. Some have many resources, others are strapped for funds. Some are old and established, others new and fresh. Some strive for rapid market share growth, others for long-term profits. And the firms occupy different competitive positions in the target market.

We now examine competitive strategies based on the roles firms play in the target market—leader, challenger, follower, or nicher. Suppose that an industry contains the firms shown in Figure 17.3. Forty percent of the market is in the hands of the **market leader**, the firm with the largest market share. Another 30 percent is in the hands of **market challengers**, runner-up firms that are fighting hard to increase their market share. Another 20 percent is in the hands of **market followers**, other runner-up firms that want to hold their share without rocking the boat. The remaining 10 percent is in the hands of **market nichers**, firms that serve small segments not being pursued by other firms.

■ Customer intimacy: Ritz-Carlton creates custom-designed experiences to coddle its customers.

Table 17.1 shows specific marketing strategies that are available to market leaders, challengers, followers, and nichers.[11] Remember, however, that these classifications often do not apply to a whole company, but only to its position in a specific industry. Large companies such as IBM, Microsoft, Procter & Gamble, or Disney might be leaders in some markets and nichers in others. For example, Procter & Gamble leads in many segments, such as dishwashing and laundry detergents, disposable diapers, and shampoo. But it challenges Lever in the hand soaps and Kimberly-Clark in facial tissues. Such companies often use different strategies for different business units or products, depending on the competitive situations of each.

Market Leader Strategies

Most industries contain an acknowledged market leader. The leader has the largest market share and usually leads the other firms in price changes, new-product introductions, distribution coverage, and promotion spending. The leader may or may not be admired or respected, but other firms concede its dominance. Competitors focus on the leader as a company to challenge, imitate, or avoid. Some of the best-known market leaders are Wal-Mart (retailing), General Motors (autos), IBM (computers and information technology services), Caterpillar (earth-moving equipment), Anheuser-Busch (beer), Coca-Cola (soft drinks), McDonald's (fast food), Nike (athletic footwear), and Gillette (razors and blades).

FIGURE 17.3
Hypothetical market structure

Market leader	Market challengers	Market followers	Market nichers
40%	30%	20%	10%

TABLE 17.1   **Strategies for Market Leaders, Challengers, Followers, and Nichers**

Market Leader Strategies	Market Challenger Strategies	Market Follower Strategies	Market Nicher Strategies
Expand total market Protect market share Expand market share	Full frontal attack Indirect attack	Follow closely Follow at a distance	By customer, market, quality-price, service Multiple niching

A leader's life is not easy. It must maintain a constant watch. Other firms keep challenging its strengths or trying to take advantage of its weaknesses. The market leader can easily miss a turn in the market and plunge into second or third place. A product innovation may come along and hurt the leader (as when Nokia's and Ericsson's digital phones took the lead from Motorola's analog models). The leader might grow arrogant or complacent and misjudge the competition (as when Sears lost its lead to Wal-Mart). Or the leader might look old-fashioned against new and peppier rivals (as when Levi's lost serious ground to more current or stylish brands like Gap, Tommy Hilfiger, DKNY, or Guess).

To remain number one, leading firms can take any of three actions. First, they can find ways to expand total demand. Second, they can protect their current market share through good defensive and offensive actions. Third, they can try to expand their market share further, even if market size remains constant.

Expanding the Total Demand

The leading firm normally gains the most when the total market expands. If Americans take more digital pictures, Sony stands to gain the most because it sells the nation's largest share of digital cameras. If Sony can convince more Americans to take digital pictures, or to take them on more occasions, or to take more pictures on each occasion, it will benefit more than its competitors.

Market leaders can expand the market by developing new users, new uses, and more usage of its products. They usually can find *new users* in many places. For example, Revlon might find new perfume users in its current markets by convincing women who do not use perfume to try it. It might find users in new demographic segments, such as by producing fragrances for men. Or it might expand into new geographic segments, perhaps by selling its fragrances in other countries.

Marketers can expand markets by discovering and promoting *new uses* for the product. For example, Intel invests heavily to develop new PC, networking, and telecommunications applications, which in turn increases the demand for microprocessors. Given its more than 80 percent microprocessor market share, it knows that it will get a lion's share of the new business. Another example of new-use expansion is Arm & Hammer baking soda, whose sales had flattened after 125 years. Then the company discovered that consumers were using baking soda as a refrigerator deodorizer. It launched a heavy advertising and publicity campaign focusing on this use and persuaded consumers in half of America's homes to place an open box of baking soda in their refrigerators and to replace it every few months. Today, its Web site (www.armandhammer.com) features new uses—"Solutions for my home, my family, my body"—ranging from removing residue left behind by hair-styling products and sweetening garbage disposals, laundry hampers, refrigerators, and trash cans to creating a home spa in your bathroom.

Finally, market leaders can encourage *more usage* by convincing people to use the product more often or to use more per occasion. For example, Campbell urges people to eat soup more often by running ads containing new recipes. It also offers a toll-free hot line (1-888-MM-MM-GOOD), staffed by live "recipe representatives" who offer recipes to last-minute cooks at a loss for meal ideas. And the Campbell's Kitchen section of the company's Web site (www.campbellsoup.com) lets visitors search for or exchange recipes, set up their own personal recipe box, and even sign up for a daily or weekly Meal Mail program.

Protecting Market Share

While trying to expand total market size, the leading firm also must protect its current business against competitors' attacks. Coca-Cola must also constantly guard against Pepsi; Gillette against Bic; Wal-Mart against Target; and McDonald's against Wendy's.

■ Creating new uses: The Arm & Hammer Web site features lots of new uses—"Solutions for my home, my family, my body."

What can the market leader do to protect its position? First, it must prevent or fix weaknesses that provide opportunities for competitors. It must always fulfill its value promise. Its prices must remain consistent with the value that customers see in the brand. It must work tirelessly to keep strong relationships with valued customers. The leader should "plug holes" so that competitors do not jump in.

But the best defense is a good offense, and the best response is *continuous innovation*. The leader refuses to be content with the way things are and leads the industry in new products, customer services, distribution effectiveness, and cost cutting. It keeps increasing its competitive effectiveness and value to customers. And when attacked by challengers, the market leader reacts decisively. For example, consider Frito-Lay's reaction to a challenge by a large competitor:

> In the early 1990s, Anheuser-Busch attacked Frito-Lay's leadership in salty snacks. The big brewer had noticed that Frito-Lay, a division of PepsiCo, had been distracted by its expansion into cookies and crackers. So Anheuser-Busch began to slip its new Eagle brand salty snacks onto the shelves of its traditional beer outlets—supermarkets and liquor stores—where Frito-Lay was comparatively weak. Frito-Lay reacted ruthlessly. First, to get itself into fighting shape, the salty-snacks leader cut the number of offerings in its product line by half—no more cookies, no more crackers—and invested in product quality, which had slipped below Eagle's. Then, Frito-Lay concentrated its energy, not to mention its 10,000 route drivers, on America's salty-snack aisles. Frito-Lay's strong brands and huge size gave it a clear economic advantage over Anheuser-Busch in the salty-snack business. Armed with a superior offering—better chips, better service, and lower prices—Frito-Lay began to put pressure on one of Eagle's strongholds: potato chips in supermarkets. It sent its salespeople streaming into supermarkets; some even stayed at the largest supermarkets full time, continually restocking the Frito-Lay products. When the dust had settled in 1996, Anheuser-Busch had shuttered its Eagle snack business. In the end, Frito-Lay even bought four of Eagle's plants—at very attractive prices.[12]

EXPANDING MARKET SHARE Market leaders also can grow by increasing their market shares further. In many markets, small market share increases mean very large sales increases. For example, in the U.S. digital camera market, a 1 percent increase in market share is worth $60 million; in carbonated soft drinks, $640 million![13]

Studies have shown that, on average, profitability rises with increasing market share. Because of these findings, many companies have sought expanded market shares to improve profitability. General Electric, for example, declared that it wants to be at least number one or two in each of its markets or else get out. GE shed its computer, air-conditioning, small appliances, and television businesses because it could not achieve top-dog position in these industries.

However, some studies have found that many industries contain one or a few highly profitable large firms, several profitable and more focused firms, and a large number of medium-sized firms with poorer profit performance. It appears that profitability increases as a business gains share relative to competitors in its *served market*. For example, Lexus holds only a small share of the total car market, but it earns high profit because it is a high-share company in its luxury-performance car segment. And it has achieved this high share in its served market because it does other things right, such as producing high quality, giving good service, and building close customer relationships.

Companies must not think, however, that gaining increased market share will improve profitability automatically. Much depends on their strategy for gaining increased share. There are many high-share companies with low profitability and many low-share companies with high profitability. The cost of buying higher market share may far exceed the returns. Higher shares tend to produce higher profits only when unit costs fall with increased market share, or when the company offers a superior-quality product and charges a premium price that more than covers the cost of offering higher quality.

Market Challenger Strategies

Firms that are second, third, or lower in an industry are sometimes quite large, such as Colgate, Ford, Target, Avis, and Pepsi. These runner-up firms can adopt one of two competitive strategies: They can challenge the leader and other competitors in an aggressive bid for more market share (market challengers). Or they can play along with competitors and not rock the boat (market followers).

A market challenger must first define which competitors to challenge and its strategic objective. The challenger can attack the market leader, a high-risk but potentially high-gain strategy. Its goal might be to take over market leadership. Wal-Mart began as a nicher in small towns in the Southwest, grew rapidly to challenge market leader Sears, and finally assumed market leadership, all within a span of less than 25 years.

Or the challenger's objective may simply be to wrest more market share. Miller knows that it's not likely to topple Anheuser-Busch in the beer market. But Miller recently mounted a direct challenge to Anheuser's brands. Miller Lite ads pointed out that the brand had a lower carb count than Bud Light. And Miller's "President of Beers" ads ("A better beer for a better tomorrow") poked fun at Budweiser's "King of Beers" positioning. The direct challenge gained market share for Miller in the short-run. However, it also risked provoking the wrath of Anheuser-Busch. In fact, Anheuser quickly retaliated with "Queen of Carbs" ads and lower Bud Light prices in some markets. According to one industry analyst, Anheuser-Busch "could pound Miller if it goes further."[14]

Alternatively, the challenger can avoid the leader and instead challenge firms its own size, or smaller local and regional firms. These smaller firms may be underfinanced and not serving their customers well. Several of the major beer companies grew to their present size not by challenging large competitors, but by gobbling up small local or regional competitors. If the company goes after a small local company, its objective may be to put that company out of business. The important point remains: The challenger must choose its opponents carefully and have a clearly defined and attainable objective.

How can the market challenger best attack the chosen competitor and achieve its strategic objectives? It may launch a full *frontal attack*, matching the competitor's product, advertising, price, and distribution efforts. It attacks the competitor's strengths rather than its weaknesses. The outcome depends on who has the greater strength and endurance. If the market challenger has fewer resources than the competitor, a frontal attack makes little sense. For example, the runner-up razor manufacturer in Brazil attacked Gillette, the market leader. The attacker was asked if it offered the consumer a better razor. "No," was the reply. "A lower price?" "No." "A clever advertising campaign?" "No." "Better allowances to the trade?" "No." "Then how do you expect to take share away from Gillette?" "Sheer determination" was the reply. Needless to say, the offensive failed. Even great size and strength may not be enough to challenge a firmly entrenched, resourceful competitor successfully.

Rather than challenging head-on, the challenger can make an *indirect attack* on the competitor's weaknesses or on gaps in the competitor's market coverage. For example, Dell found a foothold against giant IBM in the personal computer market by selling directly to consumers. Southwest Airlines challenged American and other large carriers by serving the overlooked short-haul, no-frills commuter segment at smaller, out-of-the-way airports. Such indirect challenges make good sense when the company has fewer resources than the competitor.

Market Follower Strategies

Not all runner-up companies want to challenge the market leader. Challenges are never taken lightly by the leader. If the challenger's lure is lower prices, improved service, or additional product features, the leader can quickly match these to defuse the attack. The leader probably has more staying power in an all-out battle for customers. For example, when Kmart launched its renewed low-price "bluelight special" campaign challenging Wal-Mart's everyday low prices, Wal-Mart had little trouble fending off Kmart's challenge, leaving Kmart worse off for the attempt. Thus, many firms prefer to follow rather than challenge the leader.

Similarly, after years of challenging Procter & Gamble unsuccessfully in the U.S. laundry detergent market, Unilever recently decided to throw in the towel and become a follower instead. P&G, which captures a 57 percent share of the market versus Unilever's 17 percent share, has outmuscled competitors on every front. For example, it spends more than $75 million a year on advertising for Tide alone, and has battered competitors with a relentless stream of new and improved products. Unilever cut prices and promotion on its detergents to focus on profit rather than market share.[15]

A follower can gain many advantages. The market leader often bears the huge expenses of developing new products and markets, expanding distribution, and educating the market. By contrast, the market follower can learn from the leader's experience. It can copy or improve on the leader's products and programs, usually with much less investment. Although the follower will probably not overtake the leader, it often can be as profitable.

Following is not the same as being passive or a carbon copy of the leader. A market follower must know how to hold current customers and win a fair share of new ones. It must find the right balance between following closely enough to win customers from the market leader but following at enough of a distance to avoid retaliation. Each follower tries to bring distinctive advantages to its target market—location, services, financing. The follower is often a major target of attack by challengers. Therefore, the market follower must keep its manufacturing costs low and its product quality and services high. It must also enter new markets as they open up.

Market Nicher Strategies

Almost every industry includes firms that specialize in serving market niches. Instead of pursuing the whole market, or even large segments, these firms target subsegments. Nichers are often smaller firms with limited resources. But smaller divisions of larger firms also may pursue niching strategies. Firms with low shares of the total market can be highly successful and profitable through smart niching. For example, natural personal-products nicher Burt's Bees is tiny compared with cosmetics mega-competitors like Esteé Lauder or L'Oreal, but its business is profitable and growing (see Real Marketing 17.2).

Why is niching profitable? The main reason is that the market nicher ends up knowing the target customer group so well that it meets their needs better than other firms that casually sell to this niche. As a result, the nicher can charge a substantial markup over costs because of the added value. Whereas the mass marketer achieves *high volume*, the nicher achieves *high margins*.

Nichers try to find one or more market niches that are safe and profitable. An ideal market niche is big enough to be profitable and has growth potential. It is one that the firm can serve effectively. Perhaps most importantly, the niche is of little interest to major competitors. And the firm can build the skills and customer goodwill to defend itself against a major competitor as the niche grows and becomes more attractive. Here's an example of a profitable nicher:

> Logitech has become a $1.3 billion global success story by focusing on human interface devices—computer mice, game controllers, keyboards, PC video cameras, and others. It makes every variation of computer mouse imaginable. Over the years, Logitech has flooded the world with more than 500 million computer mice of all varieties, mice for left- and right-handed people, wireless mice, travel mice, mini mice, mice shaped like real mice for children, and 3-D mice that let the user appear to move behind screen objects. Breeding mice has been so successful that Logitech

■ Profitable niching:
Breeding mice has been so
successful for Logitech that it
dominates the world mouse
market, with giant Microsoft
as its runner-up.

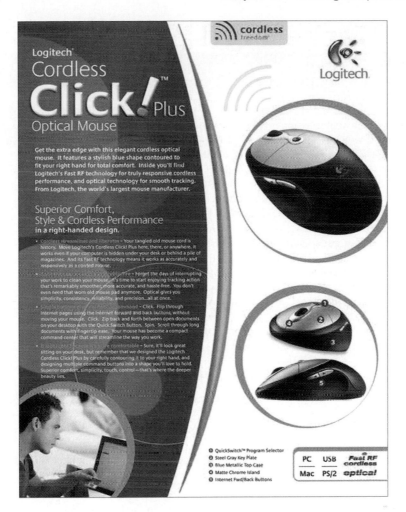

dominates the world mouse market, with giant Microsoft as its runner-up. Niching has been very good for Logitech. Its sales and profits have more than doubled in just the past four years.[16]

The key idea in niching is specialization. A market nicher can specialize along any of several market, customer, product, or marketing mix lines. For example, it can specialize in serving one type of *end user*, as when a law firm specializes in the criminal, civil, or business law markets. The nicher can specialize in serving a given *customer size* group. Many nichers specialize in serving small and mid-size customers who are neglected by the majors.

Some nichers focus on one or a few *specific customers*, selling their entire output to a single company, such as Wal-Mart or General Motors. Still other nichers specialize by *geographic market*, selling only in a certain locality, region, or area of the world. *Quality-price* nichers operate at the low or high end of the market. For example, Hewlett-Packard specializes in the high-quality, high-price end of the hand-calculator market. Finally, *service nichers* offer services not available from other firms. An example is a bank that takes loan requests over the phone and hand delivers the money to the customer.

Niching carries some major risks. For example, the market niche may dry up, or it might grow to the point that it attracts larger competitors. That is why many companies practice *multiple niching*. By developing two or more niches, a company increases its chances for survival. Even some large firms prefer a multiple niche strategy to serving the total market. For example, Alberto Culver is a $3 billion company that has used a multiple niching strategy to grow profitably without incurring the wrath of a market leader. The company, known mainly for its Alberto VO5 hair products, has focused its marketing muscle on acquiring a stable of smaller niche brands. It niches in hair, skin, and personal care products (Alberto VO5, St. Ives, TRESemme, and Consort men's hair spray), seasonings and sweeteners (Molly McButter, Mrs. Dash, SugarTwin), and home products (static-cling fighter Static Guard). Most of its brands are number one in their niches. CEO Howard Bernick explains the Alberto Culver philosophy this way: "We know who we are and, perhaps more importantly, we know who we are not. We know that if we try to out-Procter Procter, we will fall flat on our face."[17]

Real Marketing 17.2

Burt's Bees: This Nicher's Business Is Buzzing

When is a bushy-bearded beekeeper the perfect image symbol for a women's cosmetics line? When you're a small market nicher called Burt's Bees. Burt's Bees targets a narrow segment of consumers looking for an alternative to the glitzy image statements made by larger cosmetics makers. The company is small, only $50 million in sales. But Burt's business formula—earth-friendly natural products for natural people—is a winner. And business is buzzing.

Burt's Bees got its start in 1984 in Maine, when cofounder Roxanne Quimby met reclusive beekeeper Burt Shavitz and they began making lip balm and candles from his beeswax (that's Burt's image on the packaging). In the beginning, Burt's Bees was a very small operation. The company's first location, an old rented school house, housed the two cofounders and a pot-bellied wood stove, a kerosene lamp, and Burt's 30 beehives. For 5 years, Quimby and Shavitz pedaled their few products at local craft fairs, driving an old pickup truck back and forth every day to avoid the cost of motels.

From these simple beginnings, Burt's Bees began to grow. In 1990, the cofounders marshaled their resources and spent the extravagant sum of $3000 for a booth at the New York International Gift Fair. That was the turning point: greater exposure brought greater sales, and greater sales gave the company the resources to grow and diversify its product line. Now, using beeswax, nut oils, and other natural ingredients, Burt's Bees makes about 150 personal-care products, including the likes of Burt's Beeswax Lip Balm ("the world's best lip balm!"), Milk & Honey Body Lotion, Beeswax & Banana Hand Crème, Apricot Baby Oil, Peppermint Breath Drops, Lemon Butter Cuticle Crème, and Beeswax Moisturizing Crème.

How can tiny Burt's Bees survive in a world dominated by cosmetics mega-corporations, with their hundreds of millions of marketing dollars? Unlike its oversized competitors, Burt's Bees is firmly focused on the natural personal-products niche. Like most successful nichers, the company thrives by serving a small, focused market that larger competitors aren't interested in or can't serve as well. The company's use of Burt's wild-man beekeeper

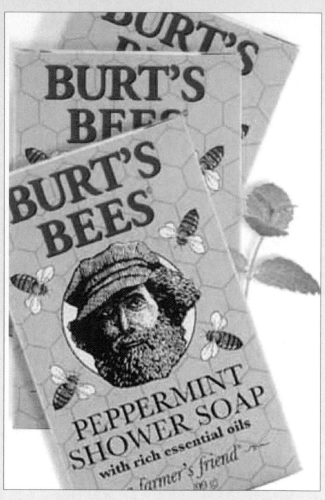

■ Market nichers: Burt's Bees targets a narrow segment of natural personal-products consumers looking for an alternative to the glitzy image statements made by larger cosmetics makers.

Balancing Customer and Competitor Orientations

Whether a company is a market leader, challenger, follower, or nicher, it must watch its competitors closely and find the competitive marketing strategy that positions it most effectively. And it must continually adapt its strategies to the fast-changing competitive environment. This question now arises: Can the company spend too much time and energy tracking competitors, damaging its customer orientation? The answer is yes! A company can become so competitor centered that it loses its even more important focus on maintaining profitable customer relationships.

A **competitor-centered company** is one that spends most of its time tracking competitors' moves and market shares and trying to find strategies to counter them. This approach has some pluses and minuses. On the positive side, the company develops a fighter orientation, watches for weaknesses in its own position and searches out competitors' weaknesses. On the

Competitor-centered company

A company whose moves are mainly based on competitors' actions and reactions.

image mocks the slick corporate style that Burt's customers disdain. And Burt's Bees models (one is a 38-year-old restaurant manager from Maine) look more likely to partake of yoga and yogurt than to be seen hanging on the arm of a millionaire playboy. "I see Burt's Bees for all the folks," Quimby says. "You don't have to be sophisticated to use it, though many of our customers are sophisticated."

Whereas the major cosmetics companies tout ingredients like alpha-hydroxy acids and their scientific battle against aging, Burt's touts natural remedies like avocado butter and citrus as a gentler way to achieve timeless beauty. And whereas most competitors' "natural products" may contain only a smattering of some natural ingredient, Burt's products are almost entirely natural. Further, Burt's lists the percentage of natural ingredients for each product. For example, Baby Bee Dusting Powder is a 99.63 percent natural blend of cornstarch, baking soda, French pink clay, bentonite (natural clay), powdered rosebuds, powdered myrrh, powdered slippery elm bark, and fragrance.

Like its carefully-selected ingredients, Burt's Bees' marketing mix includes carefully-selected distribution channels. True to its niche, the company has avoided the glitzy cosmetics counters of large department stores. Instead, Burt's has concentrated the sale of its products through boutiques and natural food stores that serve its niche, as well as through its Web site. It supports these channels with a modest, focused marketing effort. "We do a lot of grassroots-level marketing, like [giving away samples]," Quimby says. "Once people try one of our products, they'll see that it's better." Such demand-building creates shelf space that keeps Burt's Bees growing.

And Burt's Bees *is* growing. Although still a tiny player next to the giants of the industry, the company has experienced dizzying growth. Sales increased to $50 million last year, an almost four-fold increase in just the last three years. That might not amount to much for competitors like Estee Lauder or Procter & Gamble, who rack up billions of dollars in cosmetics sales each year. But it's profitable business for a nicher like Burt's Bees.

Such success has proven attractive to investors, reaping a hefty return for cofounder Quimby, who bought out Burt Shavitz in 1999. Quimby recently sold an 80 percent stake in Burt's Bees to AEA Investors for $179 million. AEA wants to give the brand more mass-market appeal, hoping to grow sales to more than $500 million in less than five years. It might work. Burt's Bees has "done a tremendous job creating a brand that's trusted by consumers [in its natural-products niche]," says a health and wellness industry expert. "They have that folksy, no-nonsense image I think will translate well with consumers in mainstream stores."

But being small and looking small has served Burt's Bees well. Past success came from serving a well-defined, focused market in a special way. Growing too fast or too large could change all of that. In broadening its appeal, the company must stay true to its niching roots. Failing to mind its own beeswax could take the sting out of Burt's Bees' success.

Sources: Quotes and other information from Vicki Lee Parker, "Buyers Aren't Swarming," *News & Observer*, August 26, 2003, pp.1D, 2D; "Natural Body-care Products and Their Down-home Grassroots Founders," *In Business*, January/February 2003, p. 9; Kim Nilsen, "$500M Bees-ness?" *Triangle Business Journal*, September 26, 2003; "The Buzz on Burt's Bees," *Business Week Online*, May 1, 2002, accessed at www.burtsbees.com; Loch Adamson, "Roxanne Quimby for Governor," *Fast Company*, December 2003, p. 112; "In Depth: Largest Triangle Deals of 2003," *Triangle Business Journal*, February 6, 2004; and information from www.burtsbees.com, December 2004.

Customer-centered company

A company that focuses on customer developments in designing its marketing strategies and on delivering superior value to its target customers.

Market-centered company

A company that pays balanced attention to both customers and competitors in designing its marketing strategies.

negative side, the company becomes too reactive. Rather than carrying out its own customer relationship strategy, it bases its own moves on competitors' moves. As a result, it may end up simply matching or extending industry practices rather than seeking innovative new ways to create more value for customers.

A **customer-centered company**, by contrast, focuses more on customer developments in designing its strategies. Clearly, the customer-centered company is in a better position to identify new opportunities and set long-run strategies that make sense. By watching customer needs evolve, it can decide what customer groups and what emerging needs are the most important to serve. Then it can concentrate its resources on delivering superior value to target customers. In practice, today's companies must be **market-centered companies**, watching both their customers and their competitors. But they must not let competitor watching blind them to customer focusing.

Figure 17.4 shows that companies have moved through four orientations over the years. In the first stage, they were product oriented, paying little attention to either customers or competitors. In the second stage, they became customer oriented and started to pay attention

FIGURE 17.4
Evolving company orientations

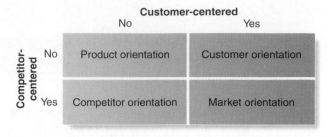

to customers. In the third stage, when they started to pay attention to competitors, they became competitor oriented. Today, companies need to be market oriented, paying balanced attention to both customers and competitors. Rather than simply watching competitors and trying to beat them on current ways of doing business, they need to watch customers and find innovative ways to build profitable customer relationships by delivering more value than competitors do.

> Reviewing the Concepts <

Today's companies face their toughest competition ever. Understanding customers is an important first step in developing strong customer relationships, but it's not enough. To gain competitive advantage, companies must use this understanding to design market offers that deliver more value than the offers of *competitors* seeking to win over the same customers. This chapter examines how firms analyze their competitors and design effective competitive marketing strategies.

1. Discuss the need to understand competitors as well as customers through competitor analysis.

In order to prepare an effective marketing strategy, a company must consider its competitors as well as its customers. Building profitable customer relationships requires satisfying target consumer needs *better than competitors do.* A company must continuously analyze competitors and develop *competitive marketing strategies* that position it effectively against competitors and give it the strongest possible *competitive advantage*.

Competitor analysis first involves identifying the company's major competitors, using both an industry-based and a market-based analysis. The company then gathers information on competitors' objectives, strategies, strengths and weaknesses, and reaction patterns. With this information in hand, it can select competitors to attack or avoid. Competitive intelligence must be collected, interpreted, and distributed continuously. Company marketing managers should be able to obtain full and reliable information about any competitor affecting their decisions.

2. Explain the fundamentals of competitive marketing strategies based on creating value for customers.

Which *competitive marketing strategy* makes the most sense depends on the company's industry, and on whether it is a market leader, challenger, follower, or nicher. A *market leader* has to mount strategies to expand the total market, protect market share, and expand market share. A *market challenger* is a firm that tries aggressively to expand its market share by attacking the leader, other runner-up companies, or smaller firms in the industry. The challenger can select from a variety of direct or indirect attack strategies. A *market follower* is a runner-up firm that chooses not to rock the boat, usually from fear that it stands to lose more than it might gain. But the follower is not without a strategy and seeks to use its particular skills to gain market growth. Some followers enjoy a higher rate of return than the leaders in their industry. A *market nicher* is a smaller firm that is unlikely to attract the attention of larger firms. Market nichers often become specialists in some end use, customer size, specific customer, geographic area, or service.

3. Illustrate the need for balancing customer and competitor orientations in becoming a truly market-centered organization.

A competitive orientation is important in today's markets, but companies should not overdo their focus on competitors. Companies are more likely to be hurt by emerging consumer needs and new competitors than by existing competitors. *Market-centered companies* that balance consumer and competitor considerations are practicing a true market orientation.

> Reviewing the Key Terms <

Benchmarking 530
Competitive advantage 527
Competitive marketing
    strategy 527

Competitor analysis 527
Competitor-centered
    company 544
Customer-centered company 545

Customer value analysis 531
Market-centered company 545
Market challenger 537
Market follower 537

Market leader 537
Market nicher 537
Strategic group 529

> Discussing the Concepts <

1. The first step in creating a competitive advantage is to identify the competition. Prepare a list of quick-service restaurant competitors (that is, fast-casual and fast food) close to your college or university. Make two columns, one for industry-level competitors and one for market-level competitors.

2. The chapter defines good and bad competitors. From Kmart's perspective, identify good and bad competitors in the discount store retailing industry.

3. Compare and contrast the two classifications of competitive strategies (Porter's competitive positioning strategies and Treacy and

Wiersema's value disciplines) presented in the text. Are they more similar than dissimilar?

4. If competitive intelligence systems are so important, then why do so few smaller companies use them?

5. What are the advantages and disadvantages of a market-nicher competitive strategy?

6. Why is it important for a company to maintain a balance between customer and competitor orientations?

> Applying the Concepts <

1. Using the customer value analysis chart below, interpret the findings from company A's perspective.

PORTABLE LAPTOP KEYBOARD

Keyboard Attribute	Customer Value Placed on Attribute	A	B	C	D
Travel	10%	5	6	4	6
Tactile Feedback	10%	4	6	8	4
Audibility	5%	5	8	3	7
Activation Force	10%	6	7	5	7
Feel	20%	6	6	7	5
Durability	15%	8	5	5	5
Cost	30%	7	5	6	4

Company Rating (1=Low to 10=High)

2. Tiffany & Co. is a high profile firm in the luxury retail jewelry market. Visit www.tiffany.com/about/timeline.asp? and review the Tiffany historical timeline for important events. What is Tiffany & Co.'s competitive marketing strategy? Explain.

3. Assume that your company is the overall cost leader in the manufacture of hard disk drives for PC's, capturing a 35 percent market share. In a group, prepare a series of recommendations designed to maintain your market leadership position.

> Focus on Technology <

For the next bit of competitive intelligence, should you contact James Bond or the team from Law and Order? Neither. You can contact Cipher Systems. This suburban Washington D.C. company offers a variety of products, including Knowledge.Works, a competitive intelligence database system. Visit www.cipher-sys.com/products.asp and download the Cipher Products.pdf found at the bottom of the page. Read the Knowledge.Works datasheet. If you are really interested in seeing how the Cipher system works, go to www.cipher-sys.com/index.asp, click on "auto summarize any text here," and follow the instructions. Then respond to the following questions.

1. What competitive intelligence activities can this technology help a company to perform better? Are there limitations? Explain.

2. Are companies acting ethically when they employ these systems?

3. What are your thoughts about these competitive intelligence systems?

> Focus on Ethics <

Competitive intelligence gathering can have disastrous consequences if done illegally. The Society of Competitive Intelligence Professionals (SCIP), founded in 1986, is a nonprofit organization dedicated to the training and enhancement of the business intelligence gathering skills that help organizations gain and maintain a competitive advantage. Listed at SCIP's site (www.scip.org/index.asp) is a reference to the following "The Ten Commandments of Legal and Ethical Intelligence Gathering," created by Leonard Fuld, a founder of the Fuld-Gilad-Herring Academy of Competitive Intelligence. Read the "10 Commandments" and respond to the questions that follow.

■ Thou shalt not lie when representing thyself.
■ Thou shalt observe thy company's legal guidelines as set forth by the legal department.
■ Thou shalt not tape-record a conversation.
■ Thou shalt not bribe.
■ Thou shalt not plant eavesdropping devices.

■ Thou shalt not deliberately mislead anyone in an interview.
■ Thou shalt neither obtain from nor give price information to thy competitor.
■ Thou shalt not swap misinformation.
■ Thou shalt not steal a trade secret (or steal employees away in hopes of learning a trade secret).
■ Thou shalt not knowingly press someone for information if it may jeopardize that person's job or reputation.

1. Are the "10 Commandments" appropriate? Are they realistic?

2. Do you think most companies practice the 10 Commandments?

3. What are the advantages and disadvantages for a company of following the 10 Commandments?

4. Would "dumpster diving" pass the 10 Commandments test? Explain.

Sources: See www.scip.org/index.asp; and www.academyci.com/HomePage.html.

◎ Video Case

Nike

The "swoosh"—it's everywhere! As a result, the swoosh has come to stand for all of the things that Nike means to those who wear it all around the world. The company was built on a genuine passion for sports, a maverick disregard for convention, and a belief in hard work and serious sports performance. Nike knows, however, that good marketing is more than promotional hype and promises—it means consistently building strong relationships with customers based on real value.

Nike's initial success resulted from the technical superiority of its running and basketball shoes, pitched to serious athletes who were frustrated by the lack of innovation in athletic equipment. To this day, Nike leads the industry in research-and-development spending. But, today, Nike markets it products to everyone, not just serious athletes. Nike succeeds by staying true to its core values and delivering consistently high quality, cutting-edge products that appeal to the athlete in all of us. Focusing on innovation, developing new product lines, creating sub-

brands, and connecting with customers of all kinds has helped the company dominate the athletic shoe market. Nike now captures a 42 percent market share in the United States and more than 25 percent abroad.

After viewing the video featuring Nike, answer the following questions about competitive advantage.

1. When you think of Nike, what are your impressions of the brand and how the company's products differ from those offered by other athletic companies?

2. Does Nike's broad definition of an athlete make it more difficult to focus on its core values and strengths? How does the definition impact Nike's identification and assessment of competitors?

3. Identify the market challengers, followers, and nichers in Nike's industry. What strategies is Nike using to maintain its place as a market leader?

▣ Company Case

Amazon.com: Strategic Evolution

THE BEGINNING OF TIME

In the beginning, there was the Internet. In the mid-1990s, visionary entrepreneurs began to see the birth of an entirely new marketplace—the online marketplace. They believed that the Internet would allow consumers and businesses the opportunity to search for, find, and purchase goods and services online. Internet shopping would bring buyers increased selection and convenience. Further, because the Internet-based companies would not have traditional store locations, they could pass these savings along in the form of lower prices.

Jeff Bezos was one of those visionaries. With degrees in electrical engineering and computer science from Princeton, the 28-year-old Wall Street whiz began looking for Internet-based business possibilities. After much research, Bezos settled on books. His strategy was simple. He'd create a "virtual" bookstore—a bookstore without a store. Even more, there'd be no books! Bezos envisioned an Internet-based business that would essentially be a clearinghouse. The company would create a Web site at which consumers could search for and purchase books. Bezos would then transfer the book orders to independent book wholesalers who would have the book in stock or have the ability to get it. The booksellers would then package and ship the order to the customer, with Bezos' company making money on the difference between the retail price it charged customers and the wholesale price the booksellers charged, and perhaps on the shipping.

In July 1995, Bezos was present at the birth of his baby, naming it Amazon.com—a "river of books."

GROWING PAINS

The rest, however, is not just history. Millions of investors poured billions of dollars into Internet start-ups like

Amazon. Intoxicated by the logic of e-commerce and the lure of huge profits, thousands of entrepreneurs took investors' money and launched online businesses offering everything from pet food and groceries to diamonds.

At first, everything worked well. Soon, twenty-something Web pioneers were becoming overnight millionaires, or even billionaires, based on the promise of future earnings. Amazon.com went public in 1997. In 1999, its stock price soared to over $100 a share and *Time* Magazine crowned Jeff Bezos as its "Man of the Year."

Then, the Internet bubble burst as market realities punctured the illusion of profits. Companies found that many consumers were reluctant to place orders and give credit card numbers online. Some customers still wanted the ability to see, touch, and try some items before purchasing. Others wanted the experience of going into a store and having clerks coddle them. Some online companies found out that shipping costs ate up their profits.

FINDING A REMEDY

Like the others, Bezos and Amazon.com learned things. They learned the value of an easy-to-navigate Web site and the importance of convenient "add-to-cart" purchasing and checkout procedures. However, they realized that although not physically owning the inventory of books did save money, it also meant that they could not guarantee delivery times to customers or assure accurate order fulfillment. Customer satisfaction suffered.

So Amazon, unlike some other Web start-ups, made a fundamental change in its strategy—it began to build massive warehouses in which it could store and manage its own inventory of books and CDs. It also put systems in place to guarantee delivery times and to make sure that it filled orders correctly. These changes allowed Amazon.com to control its transactions from beginning to end.

However, the warehouses, inventory, and staffing brought high infrastructure and fixed costs that Amazon.com needed to cover. Because it doubted that it could cover those costs just selling books and CDs, especially with increasing competition from other online booksellers, it began to expand its product selection and to offer free shipping on orders over $49 to encourage purchases.

The expanded product selection, however, brought new problems. Although Amazon.com understood how to run an online business, it did not understand the ins and outs of particular product categories, such as toys. So, in 2000, it executed an agreement with Toys "R" Us, making that company its exclusive source for toys sold on its Web site. This arrangement had the advantage of letting Toys "R" Us worry about what toys to buy and when to buy them, while Amazon.com managed the Toys "R" Us Web site, which the toy seller had struggled to do itself.

This led Amazon.com to develop two new programs. First, Merchants@Amazon allows established retailers in search of incremental sales, like Gap or Nordstrom's, access to Amazon.com's customers. The retailer is the seller of record and handles order fulfillment, with Amazon.com earning a commission on each sale. Second, Merchant.com allows a retailer, like Target, to control the "look and feel" of its Web site while letting Amazon.com handle technology services, fulfillment, and customer service.

Amazon.com realized the possibilities in these arrangements and began its Amazon Web Services (AWS) operation. AWS allows any qualified seller to create its own Web applications and use Amazon.com's database. Amazon.com takes a 15 percent commission on merchants' AWS sales. Amazon.com also started an Amazon Services subsidiary that sells a turnkey, outsourced e-commerce product incorporating Amazon.com's shopping features and technology, allowing small businesses to launch their own e-commerce platforms, which Amazon.com runs for them, taking a commission of 10 percent or more on sales.

During this period, Amazon.com stayed true to its philosophy of "start with the customer and work backward." It realized that some of its customers wanted used, not new, products. So, it began allowing individuals to list used goods for sale on its site. Thus, if you go to Amazon.com looking for a particular book, you may find Amazon.com's price for a new copy, but you may also find several other sellers who are offering used copies. By clicking on each seller, you will find that seller's price, the condition of the book, and other customers' ratings of that seller.

THE END OF EVOLUTION?

By the end of 2003, Amazon.com reported its first-ever, GAAP-based profit of $35 million on $5.3 billion in sales, 75 percent of which came from its ten warehouses located worldwide. Forty percent of its sales came from outside the United States. Amazon.com's stock price had zoomed from an Internet-meltdown low of $6 in late 2001 to $58 in early 2004. The online pioneer had 39 million active customer accounts and an inventory turnover ratio of 20 versus about 7.5 for typical store-based retailers. Moreover, Amazon.com had established one of the most widely recognized brands and superior customer satisfaction ratings.

Amazon has achieved its success by focusing on and enhancing the customer's experience and offering selection, convenience, and price. Jeff Bezos envisioned a place where customers can find and buy anything they want online.

Yet, even as Jeff Bezos and his management team celebrate their successful evolution, they know they face many challenges. Some analysts are still not convinced that Amazon can sustain profitability, even questioning the accounting decisions that led to 2003's reported profit. Others question whether it can continue its policy of offering free shipping on sales over $25. Others argue that it should consider taking the next step and opening Amazon retail stores to take advantage of its brand name and reputation.

Some analysts also suggest that increased competition from Yahoo, Google, MSN, and others will challenge Amazon.com., especially as it launches its new Internet search service, A9. Others wonder about the potential impact on all of these companies of a change in Internet tax policies. Finally, others argue that allowing almost anybody to sell almost anything on Amazon.com will dilute the value of Amazon.com's brand, while crowding and complicating its Web site.

Amazon.com has made many course corrections in its brief 10-year history. What strategic changes should it make as it enters its next phase?

Questions for Discussion

1. How does Amazon.com create value for its customers? How has its approach to creating value changed since its founding?

2. Who are Amazon.com's competitors and how has it created its competitive advantage?

3. Which of Porter's and Treacy and Wiersema's competitive strategies has Amazon pursued? What is its competitive position?

4. What marketing strategy recommendations would you make to Amazon.com?

Sources: Denise Hamilton, "Amazon.com: It's More Than Just Books (and Always Has Been!), *Searcher*, June 2004, p. 42; "Amazon.com, Inc. at Goldman Sachs Fifth Annual Conference—Final," *The America's Intelligence Wire*, May 27, 2004; Russ Banham, "Amazon Finally Clicks," *CFO, The Magazine for Senior Financial Executives*," April 2004, p. 20; Mary E. Behr, "Will Amazon.com's Growth Strategy Work," *eWeek*, December 4, 2003.

1. identify the major forces shaping the new digital age
2. explain how companies have responded to the Internet and other powerful new technologies with e-business strategies, and how these strategies have resulted in benefits to both buyers and sellers
3. describe the four major e-commerce domains
4. discuss how companies go about conducting e-commerce to profitably deliver more value to customers
5. overview the promise and challenges that e-commerce presents for the future

Marketing in the Digital Age

Previewing the Concepts

In previous chapters, you've learned that the aim of marketing is to create value *for* customers in order to capture value *from* consumers in return. In the final three chapters, we'll extend this concept to three special areas—marketing in the digital age, global marketing, and marketing ethics and social responsibility. Although we've visited these topics regularly in each previous chapter, because of their special importance, we will focus exclusively on them here.

In this chapter, we look into marketing in the new digital environment. Marketing strategy and practice have undergone dramatic changes during the past decade. Major technological advances, including the explosion of the Internet, have had a major impact on buyers and the marketers who serve them. To thrive in this new digital age—even to survive—marketers must rethink their strategies and adapt them to today's new environment.

To set the stage, let's first look at Amazon.com. In little more than a decade, Amazon.com has blossomed from an obscure dot-com upstart into one of the best-known names on the Internet. It pioneered the use of Web technology to build strong, one-to-one customer relationships based on creating genuine customer value. The only problem: This seemingly successful company has yet to prove that it can turn long-term profit. As you read on, ask yourself: Will Amazon.com eventually become the Wal-Mart of the Internet? Or will it become just another Internet catalog company?

Chances are, when you think of shopping on the Web, you think of Amazon.com. Amazon.com first opened its virtual doors in mid-July 1995, selling books out of founder Jeff Bezos's garage in suburban Seattle. It still sells books—by the millions. But it now sells products in a dozen other categories as well: from music, videos, consumer electronics, and computers to tools and hardware, kitchen and housewares, apparel, jewelry, and toys and baby products. "We have the Earth's Biggest Selection," declares the company's Web site.

In less than a decade, Amazon.com has become one of the best-known names on the Web. In perfecting the art of online selling, it has also rewritten the rules of marketing. Its most ardent fans view Amazon.com as *the* model for businesses in the new digital age.

But not everything has clicked smoothly for Amazon.com. Attracting customers and sales hasn't been the problem. Over the past 6 years, Amazon.com's customer base has grown rapidly to more than 39 million customers in more than 220 countries. Sales have rocketed from a modest $15 million a year in 1996 to more than $5.2 billion today, and they are growing by more than 33 percent per year. Some analysts confidently predict that sales will reach $8 billion by 2007. So, what *is* the problem? Profits—or a lack thereof. Amazon.com didn't turn its first full-year profit until just last year, and those profits were modest. Doubters say that Amazon.com's Web-only model can never be truly profitable.

No matter what your view on its future, there's little doubt that Amazon.com is an outstanding marketing company. To its core, the company is relentlessly customer driven. "The thing that drives everything is creating genuine value for customers," says founder Jeff Bezos. "If you focus on what customers want and build a relationship, they will allow you to make money."

Anyone at Amazon.com will tell you that the company wants to do much more than just sell books or DVDs or digital cameras. It wants to deliver a special *experience* to every customer. "The customer experience really matters," says Bezos. "We've focused on just having a better store, where it's easier to shop, where you can learn more about the products, where you have a bigger selection, and where you have the lowest prices. You combine all of that stuff together and people say, 'Hey, these guys really get it.'"

And they do get it. Most Amazon.com regulars feel a surprisingly strong and personal relationship with the company, especially given the almost complete lack of actual human interaction. For each the last 2 years, the American Customer Satisfaction Index has rated Amazon the highest ever in customer satisfaction for a service company, regardless of industry. Analyst Geoffrey Colvin comments:

> I travel a lot and talk with all kinds of people, and I'm struck by how many of them speak passionately about their retail experience with Amazon.com. . . . How can people get so cranked up about an experience in which they don't see, touch, or hear another soul? The answer is that Amazon.com creates a more human relationship than most people realize. . . . The experience has been crafted so carefully that most of us actually enjoy it.

Amazon.com obsesses over making each customer's experience uniquely personal. For example, the site's "Your Recommendations" feature prepares personalized product recommendations, and its "New for You" feature links customers through to their own personalized home pages. Amazon.com was first to use "collaborative filtering" technology, which sifts through each customer's past purchases and the purchasing patterns of customers with similar profiles to come up with personalized site content. "We want Amazon.com to be the right store for you as an individual," says Bezos. "If we have 39 million customers, we should have 39 million stores."

Visitors to Amazon.com's Web site receive a unique blend of benefits: huge selection, good value, convenience, and what Amazon vice president Jason Kilar calls "discovery." In books alone, for example, Amazon.com offers an easily searchable virtual selection of more than 3 million titles, 15 times more than in any physical bookstore. Good value comes in the form of reasonable prices. And at Amazon.com, it's irresistibly convenient to buy. You can log on, find what you want, and order with a single mouse click, all in less time than it takes to find a parking space at the local mall.

But it's the "discovery" factor that makes the Amazon.com experience really special. Once on the Web site, you're compelled to stay for a while—looking, learning, and discovering. Amazon.com has become a kind of online community, in which customers can browse for products, research purchase alternatives, share opinions and reviews with other visitors, and chat online with authors and experts. In this way, Amazon.com does much more than just sell goods on the Web. It creates customer relationships and satisfying online experiences.

In fact, Amazon.com has become so good at managing online relationships that many traditional "brick-and-mortar" retailers are turning to Amazon for help in adding more "clicks" to their "bricks." For example, Amazon.com now partners with well-known retailers such as Target, Toys 'R' Us, Circuit City, and Borders to help them run their Web interfaces. The brick-and-mortar partners handle purchasing and inventory; Amazon.com oversees the customer experience—maintaining the Web site, attracting customers, and managing customer service. Amazon.com has also formed alliances with hundreds of other retailers who sell their wares through the Amazon site. For example, Amazon's "apparel store" is more of a mall, featuring the products of partners such as Gap, Old Navy, Eddie Bauer, Spiegel, Foot Locker, Nordstrom, and Sears-owned Lands' End.

So, what do you think? Will Amazon eventually become the Wal-Mart of the Web? Or will it end up as just another Internet catalog company? Despite its successes and improving financials, until Amazon proves that it can be consistently profitable, the debate will continue. But whatever its fate, Amazon.com has forever changed the face of marketing. "No matter what becomes of Amazon," says the analyst, "it has taught us something new."[1]

Recent technological advances have created a new digital age. Widespread use of the Internet and other powerful new technologies are having a dramatic impact on marketers and buyers. Many standard marketing strategies and practices of the past—mass marketing, product standardization, media advertising, store retailing, and others—were well suited to the old economy. These strategies and practices will continue to be important in the new digital age. However, marketers will also have to develop new strategies and practices better suited to today's new environment.

In this chapter, we first describe the key forces shaping the new digital age. Then we examine how marketing strategy and practice are changing to take advantage of today's new technologies.

Major Forces Shaping the Digital Age   START HERE

Many forces are playing a major role in reshaping the world economy, including technology, globalization, environmentalism, and others. Here we discuss four specific forces that underlie the new digital age (see Figure 18.1): digitalization and connectivity, the explosion of the Internet, new types of intermediaries, and customization.

Digitalization and Connectivity

Many appliances and systems in the past—ranging from telephone systems, wristwatches, and musical recordings to industrial gauges and controls—operated on analog information. Analog information is continuously variable in response to physical stimuli. Today a growing number of appliances and systems operate on *digital information,* which comes as streams of zeros and ones, or *bits.* Text, data, sound, and images can be converted into *bitstreams.* A laptop computer manipulates bits in its thousands of applications. Software consists of digital content for operating systems, games, information storage, and other applications.

For bits to flow from one appliance or location to another requires *connectivity,* a telecommunications network. Much of the world's business today is carried out over networks that connect people and companies. **Intranets** are networks that connect people within a company to each other and to the company network. **Extranets** connect a company with its suppliers, distributors, and other outside partners. And the **Internet,** a vast public web of computer networks, connects users of all types all around the world to each other and to an amazingly large "information repository." The Internet makes up one big "information highway" that can dispatch bits at incredible speeds from one location to another.

Intranet
A network that connects people within a company to each other and to the company network.

Extranet
A network that connects a company with its suppliers and distributors.

Internet
A vast public web of computer networks, which connects users of all types all around the world to each other and to an amazingly large information repository.

The Internet Explosion

With the creation of the World Wide Web and Web browsers in 1990s, the Internet was transformed from a mere communication tool into a certifiably revolutionary technology. The Internet continues to grow explosively. Last year, Internet penetration in the United States had reached 63 percent, with more than 185 million people now using the Internet. Two million more Americans access the Internet for the first time each month.[2]

Although the dot-com crash in 2000 led to cutbacks in technology spending, research suggests that the growth of Internet access among the world's citizens will continue to explode, reaching 1.5 billion by 2007. Not only are more people using the Web, they are increasingly moving faster when they get there. A recent study found that 35 percent of U.S. households with Internet access now go online through high-speed broadband connections.[3]

This explosive worldwide growth in Internet usage forms the heart of the new digital age. The Internet has been *the* revolutionary technology of the new millennium, empowering

FIGURE 18.1

Forces shaping the digital age

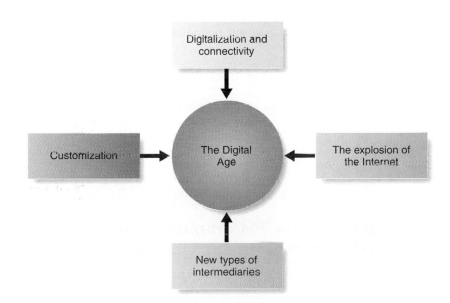

consumers and businesses alike with blessings of connectivity. The Internet enables consumers and companies to access and share huge amounts of information with just a few mouse clicks.

Recent studies have shown that consumers are accessing information on the Internet before making major life decisions. One in three consumers relies heavily on the Internet to gather information about choosing a school, buying a car, finding a job, dealing with a major illness, or making investment decisions. The average U.S. Internet user visits the Web 30 times a month at home and 66 times a month at work, spending more the 30 minutes per visit. As a result, to be competitive in today's new marketplace, companies must adopt Internet technology or risk being left behind.[4]

New Types of Intermediaries

New technologies have led thousands of entrepreneurs to launch Internet companies—the so-called dot-coms—in hopes of striking gold. The amazing success of early Internet-only companies, such as Amazon.com, Expedia, Priceline, eBay, and dozens of others, struck terror in the hearts of many established manufacturers and retailers. Established store-based retailers of all kinds—from bookstores, music stores, and florists to travel agents, stockbrokers, and car dealers—feared being cut out by these new types of intermediaries.

The new intermediaries and new forms of channel relationships caused existing firms to reexamine how they served their markets. At first, the established *brick-and-mortar* firms—such as Staples, Barnes & Noble, and Merrill Lynch—dragged their feet hoping that the aggressive *click-only* firms would falter or disappear. Then they wised up and started their own online sales channels, becoming *click-and-mortar* competitors. Ironically, many click-and-mortar competitors have become stronger than the click-only competitors that pushed them reluctantly onto the Internet. Still, many click-only competitors are surviving and even prospering in today's marketplace.

Customization

The old economy revolved around *manufacturing companies* that mainly focused on standardizing their production, products, and business processes. They invested large sums in brand building to tout the advantages of their standardized market offerings. In contrast, the today's economy revolves around *information businesses*. Information has the advantages of being easy to differentiate, customize, personalize, and send at incredible speeds over networks. With rapid advances in Internet and other information technologies, companies have grown skilled in gathering information about individual customers and business partners (suppliers, distributors, retailers). In turn, they have become more adept at individualizing their products and services, messages, and media.

Customization involves more than simply taking the initiative to customize the market offering. It also means giving customers the opportunity to design their own offerings. Dell, for example, lets customers specify exactly what they want in their computers and delivers customer-designed units in only a few days. On its Reflect.com Web site, Procter & Gamble allows people to reflect their needs for, say, a shampoo by answering a set of questions. It then formulates a unique shampoo for each person.

Marketing Strategy in the Digital Age

Conducting business in the new digital age will call for a new model for marketing strategy and practice. The Internet is revolutionizing how companies create value for customers and build customer relationships. The digital age has fundamentally changed customers' notions of convenience, speed, price, product information, and service. Thus, today's marketing requires new thinking and action. Companies need to retain most of the skills and practices that have worked in the past. But they will also need to add major new competencies and practices if they hope to grow and prosper in the new environment.

E-business

The use of electronic platforms—intranets, extranets, and the Internet—to conduct a company's business.

E-Business, E-Commerce, and E-Marketing in the Digital Age

E-business involves the use of electronic platforms—intranets, extranets, and the Internet—to conduct a company's business. Almost every company has set up a Web site to inform about

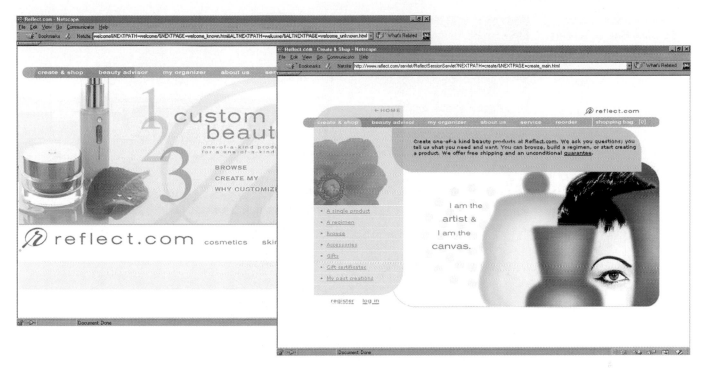

■ Customization: At reflect.com, people formulate their own beauty products—it offers "one-of-a-kind beauty products for a one-of-a-kind you."

and promote its products and services. Others use Web sites simply to build stronger customer relationships.

Most companies have also created intranets to help employees communicate with each other and to access information found in the company's computers. For example, some 14,000 employees regularly log on to P&G intranet, mNet, to receive training and to research marketing news from around the world. And the Cheesecake Factory, a national restaurant chain, uses its intranet to offer training tips and help employees communicate during preshift meetings.[5] Companies also set up extranets with their major suppliers and distributors to enable information exchange, orders, transactions, and payments.

E-commerce is more specific than e-business. E-business includes all electronics-based information exchanges within or between companies and customers. In contrast, e-commerce involves buying and selling processes supported by electronic means, primarily the Internet. *E-markets* are "market*spaces*," rather than physical market*places*. Sellers use e-markets to offer their products and services online. Buyers use them to search for information, identify what they want, and place orders using credit or other means of electronic payment.

E-commerce includes *e-marketing* and *e-purchasing* (*e-procurement*). **E-marketing** is the marketing side of e-commerce. It consists of company efforts to communicate about, promote, and sell products and services over the Internet. Thus, Amazon.com, LLBean.com, and Dell.com conduct e-marketing at their Web sites. The flip side of e-marketing is e-purchasing, the buying side of e-commerce. It consists of companies purchasing goods, services, and information from online suppliers. In business-to-business buying, e-marketers and e-purchasers come together in huge e-commerce networks.

E-commerce and the Internet bring many benefits to both buyers and sellers. Let's review some of these major benefits.

Benefits to Buyers

Internet buying benefits both final buyers and business buyers in many ways. It can be *convenient*: Customers don't have to battle traffic, find parking spaces, and trek through stores and aisles to find and examine products. They can do comparative shopping by surfing Web sites. Web marketers never close their doors. Buying is *easy* and *private*: Customers encounter fewer buying hassles and don't have to face salespeople or open themselves up to persuasion and emotional pitches. Business buyers can learn about and buy products and services without waiting for and tying up time with salespeople.

E-commerce

Buying and selling processes supported by electronic means, primarily the Internet.

E-marketing

The marketing side of e-commerce—company efforts to communicate about, promote, and sell products and services over the Internet.

■ Internet buying is easy and private: Final consumers can shop the world from home with few hassles; business buyers can learn about and obtain products and information without tying up time with salespeople.

In addition, the Internet often provides buyers with greater *product access and selection.* Unrestrained by physical boundaries, cybersellers can offer an almost unlimited selection to consumers almost anywhere in the world. Just compare the incredible selections offered by many Web merchants to the more meager assortments of their brick-and-mortar counterparts. For example, log onto Bulbs.com, "the Web's no. 1 light bulb superstore," and you'll have instant access to every imaginable kind of light bulb or lamp—incandescent bulbs, fluorescent bulbs, projection bulbs, surgical bulbs, automotive bulbs—you name it. No physical store could offer handy access to such a vast selection.

E-commerce channels also give buyers access to a wealth of comparative *information* about companies, products, and competitors. Good sites often provide more information in more useful forms than even the most solicitous salesperson can. For example, Amazon.com offers top-10 product lists, extensive product descriptions, expert and user product reviews, and recommendations based on customers' previous purchases.

Finally, online buying is *interactive* and *immediate*. Buyers often can interact with the seller's site to create exactly the configuration of information, products, or services they desire, then order or download them on the spot. Moreover, the Internet gives consumers a greater measure of control. Like nothing else before it, the Internet has empowered consumers. These days, for example, 60 percent of car buyers bargain hunt online before visiting a dealership, arming themselves with car and cost information. This is the new reality of consumer control.[6]

Benefits to Sellers

E-commerce also yields many benefits to sellers. First, the Internet is a powerful tool for *customer relationship building*. Because of its one-to-one, interactive nature, companies can interact online with customers to learn more about specific needs and wants. In turn, online customers can ask questions and volunteer feedback. Based on this ongoing interaction, companies can increase customer value and satisfaction through product and service refinements.

The Internet and other electronic channels can also *reduce costs* and *increase speed and efficiency*. By using the Internet to link directly to suppliers, factories, distributors, and customers, businesses can cut costs and pass savings on to customers. E-marketers avoid the expense of maintaining a store and the related costs of rent, insurance, and utilities. Because customers deal directly with sellers, online selling often results in lower costs and improved efficiencies for channel and logistics functions such as order processing, inventory handling, delivery, and trade promotion. Finally, communicating electronically often costs less than communicating on paper through the mail. For instance, a company can produce digital catalogs for much less than the cost of printing and mailing paper ones.

■ The Internet is a truly *global* medium. A Web surfer from Paris or Istanbul can access an online L.L. Bean catalog as easily as someone living in Freeport, Maine, the direct retailer's hometown.

E-marketing can also offer greater *flexibility*, allowing the marketer to make ongoing adjustments to its offers and programs. For example, once a paper catalog is mailed to final consumer or business customers, the products, prices, and other catalog features are fixed until the next catalog is sent. However, an online catalog can be adjusted daily or even hourly, adapting product assortments, prices, and promotions to match changing market conditions.

Finally, the Internet is a truly *global* medium that allows buyers and sellers to click from one country to another in seconds. A Web surfer from Paris or Istanbul can access an online L.L. Bean catalog as easily as someone living in Freeport, Maine, the direct retailer's hometown. Even small e-marketers find that they have ready access to global markets.

E-Marketing Domains

The four major e-marketing domains are shown in Figure 18.2 and discussed below. They include B2C (business to consumer), B2B (business to business), C2C (consumer to consumer), and C2B (consumer to business).

B2C (Business-to-Consumer)

B2C (business-to-consumer) e-commerce
The online selling of goods and services to final consumers.

The popular press has paid the most attention to **B2C (business-to-consumer) e-commerce**—the online selling of goods and services to final consumers. Despite some gloomy predictions, online consumer buying continues to grow at a healthy rate. Last year, consumers worldwide spent more than $167 billion online. In the United States alone, consumer spending online is

FIGURE 18.2
E-marketing domains

	Targeted to consumers	Targeted to businesses
Initiated by business	B2C (business to consumer)	B2B (business to business)
Initiated by consumer	C2C (consumer to consumer)	C2B (consumer to business)

expected to exceed $316 billion by 2010, accounting for 12 percent of total retail sales. The largest categories of consumer online spending include travel services, clothing, computer hardware and software, consumer electronics, books, music and video, health and beauty, home and garden, flowers and gifts, sports and fitness equipment, and toys.[7]

Online Consumers

In its early days, the Internet was populated largely by pasty-faced computer nerds or young, techy, upscale male professionals. As the Web has matured, however, Internet demographics have changed significantly. Today, almost two-thirds of U.S. households surf the Internet. And each year, more than 13 million Americans access the Internet for the first time. As more and more people find their way onto the Web, the cyberspace population is becoming more mainstream and diverse.

Thus, increasingly, the Internet provides e-marketers with access to a broad range of demographic segments. For example, one recent study found that consumers who have been buying online for more than 6 years have an average income exceeding $79,000. Thirty-four percent are women and 57 percent have college degrees. In contrast, consumers who've shopped less than 1 year online have an average income of $52,000. About 57 percent are women and 39 percent have college degrees.[8] These days, it seems, just about everybody is logging on:

> Doral Main, a 51-year-old mother of two and office manager of a low-income property company in Oakland, CA, saves precious time by shopping the Internet for greeting cards and getaways. Her Net-newbie father, Charles, 73, goes online to buy supplies for his wood-carving hobby. Even niece Katrina, 11, finds excitement on the Web, picking gifts she wants from the Disney.com site. "It's addictive," Main says of the Internet. [Indeed,] the Web isn't mostly a hangout for techno-nerds anymore.[9]

■ Online consumers: As more and more people find their way onto the Web, the online population is becoming more mainstream and diverse. The Web now offers marketers a palette of different kinds of consumers seeking different kinds of online experiences.

Growing Internet diversity continues to open new e-commerce targeting opportunities for marketers. For example, the Web now reaches consumers in all age groups. Children and teens are going online more than any other age group. Sixty-five percent of 10- to 14-year-olds and 75 percent of 14- to 17-year-olds now use the Internet. Some 59 percent of younger teen girls go online every day.[10] These "net kids" and teen segments have attracted a host of e-marketers.

At the other end of the age spectrum, consumers aged 50 and older make up almost 20 percent of the online population. And more than 22 million Americans over the age of 65 are expected to by online by 2009. Whereas younger groups are more likely to use the Internet for entertainment and socializing, older Websters go online for more serious matters. For example, 24 percent of people in this age group use the Internet for investment purposes, compared with only 3 percent of those 25 to 29. Thus, older Internet users make an attractive market for many Web businesses, ranging from florists and automotive retailers to travel sites and financial services providers.[11]

Internet consumers differ from traditional offline consumers in their approaches to buying and in their responses to marketing. The exchange process via the Internet has become more customer initiated and customer controlled. People who use the Internet place greater value on information and tend to respond negatively to messages aimed only at selling. Traditional marketing targets a somewhat passive audience. In contrast, e-marketing targets people who actively select which Web sites they will visit and what marketing information they will receive about which products and under what conditions. Thus, the new world of e-commerce requires new marketing approaches.

B2C Web Sites

Consumers can find a Web site for buying almost anything. The Internet is most useful for products and services when the shopper seeks greater ordering convenience or lower costs. The Internet also provides great value to buyers looking for information about differences in product features and value. However, consumers find the Internet less useful when buying products that must be touched or examined in advance. Still, even here there are exceptions. For example, who would have thought that tens of thousands of people would order automobiles online each year without seeing and trying them first?

People now go online to order a wide range of goods— clothing from Gap or L.L. Bean, books or electronics from Amazon.com, furniture from Ethan Allen, major appliances from Sears, flowers from Calyx & Corolla, or even home mortgages from Quicken Loans.[12]

> At Quicken Loans (www.quickenloans.com), prospective borrowers receive a high-tech, high-touch, one-stop mortgage shopping experience. At the site, customers can research a wide variety of home-financing and refinancing options, apply for a mortgage, and receive quick loan approval—all without leaving the comfort and security of their homes. The site provides useful interactive tools that help borrowers decide how much house they can afford, whether to rent or buy, whether to refinance a current mortgage, the economics of fixing up their current homes rather than moving, and much more. Customers can receive advice by phone or by chatting online with one of 2,100 mortgage experts and sign up for later e-mail rate updates. Quicken Loans closed more than $12 billion in mortgage loans in 2003.

B2B (Business-to-Business)

B2B (business-to-business) e-commerce
Using B2B trading networks, auction sites, spot exchanges, online product catalogs, barter sites, and other online resources to reach new customers, serve current customers more effectively, and obtain buying efficiencies and better prices.

Although the popular press has given the most attention to business-to-consumer (B2C) Web sites, consumer goods sales via the Web are dwarfed by **B2B (business-to-business) e-commerce**. In 2003, worldwide B2B e-commerce reached almost $4 trillion, compared with just $282 billion in 2000. One study estimates that as much as one-third of all U.S. B2B spending will occur online by 2006.[13] These firms are using B2B trading networks, auction sites, spot exchanges, online product catalogs, barter sites, and other online resources to reach new customers, serve current customers more effectively, and obtain buying efficiencies and better prices.

Most major B2B marketers now offer product information, customer purchasing, and customer support services online. For example, corporate buyers can visit Sun Microsystems' Web site (www.sun.com), select detailed descriptions of Sun's products and solutions, request sales and service information, and interact with staff members. Some

■ B2C Web sites: People now go online to order a wide range of goods and services, even home mortgages.

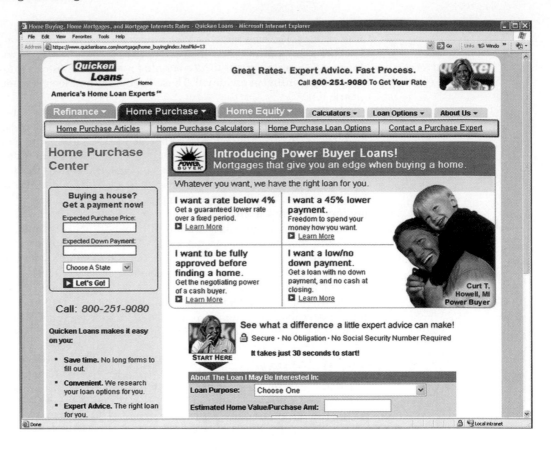

major companies conduct almost all of their business on the Web. Networking equipment and software maker Cisco Systems takes more than 80 percent of its orders over the Internet.

Open trading exchanges
Huge e-marketspaces in which B2B buyers and sellers find each other online, share information, and complete transactions efficiently.

Private trading exchanges
B2B trading networks that link a particular seller with its own trading partners.

Some B2B e-commerce takes place in **open trading exchanges**—huge e-marketspaces in which buyers and sellers find each other online, share information, and complete transactions efficiently. For example, PlasticsNet.com, an Internet marketplace for the plastics product industry, connects more than 90,000 monthly visitors with more than 200 suppliers. However, despite the use of such e-marketspaces, one Internet research firm estimates that 93 percent of all B2B e-commerce is conducted through private sites. Increasingly, online sellers are setting up their own **private trading exchanges**. Open trading exchanges facilitate transactions between a wide range of online buyers and sellers. In contrast, a private trading exchange links a particular seller with its own trading partners.

Rather than simply completing transactions, private exchanges give sellers greater control over product presentation and allow them to build deeper relationships with buyers and sellers by providing value-added services. As an example, take Trane Company, a maker of air-conditioning and heating systems:

> Since last autumn, Trane . . . has been red-hot with the business-to-business [B2B] Internet crowd. Each of the horde of B2B [open trading] exchanges targeting the construction industry wants Trane to join. "Construction.com, MyPlant.com, MyFacility.com—we get up to five calls a week," says James A. Bierkamp, head of Trane's e-business unit. But after some consideration, Bierkamp did not see what any of those [third-party] e-marketplaces could offer that his company couldn't do itself. So Trane rolled out its own private exchange, which allows its 5,000 dealers to browse, buy equipment, schedule deliveries, and process warranties. The site lets Trane operate with greater efficiency and trim processing costs—without losing control of the presentation of its brand name or running the risks of rubbing elbows with competitors in an open exchange. "Why let another party get between us and our customers?'" asks Bierkamp.[14]

C2C (Consumer-to-Consumer)

C2C (consumer-to-consumer) e-commerce
Online exchanges of goods and information between final consumers.

Much **C2C (consumer-to-consumer) e-commerce** and communication occurs on the Web between interested parties over a wide range of products and subjects. In some cases, the Internet provides an excellent means by which consumers can buy or exchange goods or information directly with one another. For example, eBay, Amazon.com Auctions, and other auction sites offer popular marketspaces for displaying and selling almost anything, from art and antiques, coins and stamps, and jewelry to computers and consumer electronics.

EBay's C2C online trading community of more than 95 million registered users worldwide transacted nearly $24 billion in trades last year, or almost 90 percent of all Internet auction business. On any given day, the company's Web site lists more than 16 million items up for auction in more than 27,000 categories. Such C2C sites give people access to much larger audiences than the local flea market or newspaper classifieds (which, by the way, are now also going online). Interestingly, based on its huge success in the C2C market, eBay has now attracted a large number of B2C sellers, ranging from small businesses peddling their regular wares to large businesses liquidating excess inventory at auction.[15]

In other cases, C2C involves interchanges of information through Internet forums that appeal to specific special-interest groups. Such activities may be organized for commercial or noncommercial purposes. An example is Web logs, or *blogs*, which are growing in popularity and offer opportunities for individuals to exchange information on any almost topic.

Not that long ago, blogs were one of those annoying buzz words that you could safely get away with ignoring. A blog, short for Web log, is a Web site where you can post daily scribblings, journal-style, about whatever you like. Bloggers usually focus their efforts on narrow topics, often rising to become de facto watchdogs and self-proclaimed experts. Blogs can be about anything: politics, sex, baseball, haiku, car repair. There are even blogs about blogs. Big whoop, right? But it turns out that some of the better blogs are drawing sizable audiences. They're free. They catch people at work, at their desks, when they're alert and thinking and making decisions. Blogs are fresh and often seem to be miles ahead of the mainstream news. Bloggers put up new stuff every day, all day, and there are thousands of them. Blogs have voice and personality. They're human. They come to us not from some media-genic anchorbot on an air-conditioned sound stage, but from an individual. They

■ Open trading exchanges: PlasticsNet.com, an Internet marketplace for the plastics product industry, connects more than 90,000 monthly visitors with more than 200 suppliers.

■ ·Web logs: Nike recently created an "Art of Speed" microsite on blog site Gawker.com, giving it high-quality exposure within a small, select audience.

are the voice of the little guy. In a way, blogs represent everything the Web was always supposed to be: a mass medium controlled by the masses, in which getting heard depends solely on having something to say and the moxie to say it.[16]

Many marketers are now tapping into blogs as a medium for reaching carefully targeted consumers. For example, Oxygen Media launched a blog to promote its new show "Good Girls Don't." And Web-savvy Nike recently created an "Art of Speed" microsite on blog site Gawker.com. The Art of Speed showcases the work of 15 innovative filmmakers who interpret the idea of speed. The showcase gave Nike high-quality exposure within a small audience. "Gawker is a very influential site among a community that appreciates creativity, film, and interesting projects and who are going to dig deeper and find out the back story," said Nike's communications manager. "In some circles, Gawker has more authenticity than Nike," says an online communications analyst. "That's why blogs really work for advertisers, because of the credibility of the blog."[17]

C2C means that online visitors don't just consume product information—increasingly, they create it. They join Internet interest groups to share information, with the result that "word of Web" is joining "word of mouth" as an important buying influence. Word about good companies and products travels fast. Word about bad companies and products travels even faster. Many sites, including eComplaints.com, ConsumerReview.com, and BadDealings.com, have cropped up to provide consumers a forum in which to air complaints and share information about product and service experiences.

C2B (consumer-to-business) e-commerce

Online exchanges in which consumers search out sellers, learn about their offers, and initiate purchases, sometimes even driving transaction terms.

C2B (Consumer-to-Business)

The final e-commerce domain is **C2B (consumer-to-business) e-commerce**. Thanks to the Internet, today's consumers are finding it easier to communicate with companies. Most companies now invite prospects and customers to send in suggestions and questions via company

Web sites. Beyond this, rather than waiting for an invitation, consumers can search out sellers on the Web, learn about their offers, initiate purchases, and give feedback. Using the Web, consumers can even drive transactions with businesses, rather than the other way around. For example, using Priceline.com, would-be buyers bid for airline tickets, hotel rooms, rental cars, and even home mortgages, leaving the sellers to decide whether to accept their offers.

Consumers can also use Web sites such as PlanetFeedback.com to ask questions, offer suggestions, lodge complaints, ask questions, or deliver compliments to companies. The site provides letter templates for consumers to use based on their moods and reasons for contacting the company. The site then forwards the letters to the customer service manager at each company and helps to obtain a response. Last year, PlanetFeedback.com forwarded 67,000 e-mails to 15,000 companies. "About 80 percent of the companies respond to complaints, some within an hour," says a PlanetFeedback spokesperson.[18]

Conducting E-Commerce

Companies of all types are now engaged in e-commerce. In this section, we first discuss different types of e-marketers shown in Figure 18.3. Then, we examine how companies go about conducting marketing online.

Click-Only Versus Click-and-Mortar E-Marketers

The Internet gave birth to a new species of e-marketers—the *click-only* dot-coms—that operate only online without any brick-and-mortar market presence. In addition, most traditional *brick-and-mortar* companies have now added e-marketing operations, transforming themselves into *click-and-mortar* competitors.

Click-Only Companies

Click-only companies
The so-called dot-coms, which operate only online without any brick-and-mortar market presence.

Click-only companies come in many shapes and sizes. They include *e-tailers*, dot-coms that sell products and services directly to final buyers via the Internet. Familiar e-tailers include Amazon.com, Expedia, and Wine.com. The click-only group also includes *search engines and portals* such as Yahoo, Google, and Excite, which began as search engines and later added services such as news, weather, stock reports, entertainment, and storefronts hoping to become the first port of entry to the Internet.

Internets service providers (ISPs) such as AOL and Earthlink are click-only companies that provide Internet and e-mail connections for a fee. *Transaction sites,* such as auction site eBay, take commissions for transactions conducted on their sites. Various *content sites,* such as *New York Times* on the Web (www.nytimes.com), ESPN.com, and Encyclopedia Britannica

■ C2B e-commerce: Consumers can use Web sites such as PlanetFeedback.com to ask questions, offer suggestions, lodge complaints, ask questions, or deliver compliments to companies.

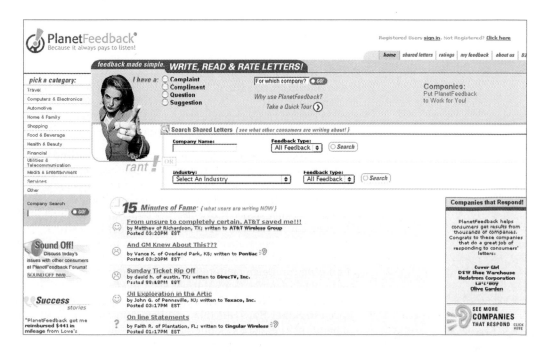

FIGURE 18.3
Types of e-marketers

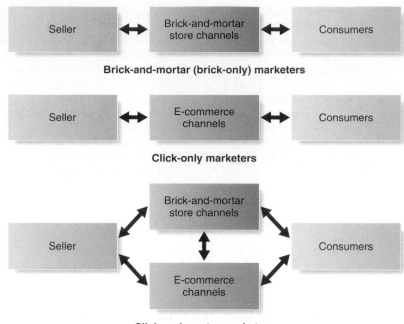

Brick-and-mortar (brick-only) marketers

Click-only marketers

Click-and-mortar marketers

Online, provide financial, research, and other information. Finally, *enabler sites* provide the hardware and software that enable Internet communication and commerce.

The hype surrounding such click-only Web businesses reached astronomical levels during the "dot-com gold rush" of the late 1990s, when avid investors drove dot-com stock prices to dizzying heights. However, the investing frenzy collapsed in the year 2000, and many high-flying, overvalued dot-coms came crashing back to Earth. Even some of the strongest and most attractive e-tailers—eToys.com, Pets.com, Furniture.com, Mothernature.com, Garden.com, Living.com, ValueAmerica.com—filed for bankruptcy. Survivors such as Amazon.com and Priceline.com saw their stock values plunge. Notes one analyst, "Once teeming with thousands of vibrant new ideas, the consumer Net [began] to look like the mall at midnight."[19]

Dot-coms failed for many reasons. Some rushed into the market without proper research or planning. Often, their primary goal was simply to launch an initial public offering (IPO) while the market was hot. Many relied too heavily on spin and hype instead of developing sound marketing strategies. Flush with investors' cash, the dot-coms spent lavishly offline on mass marketing in an effort to establish brand identities and attract customers to their sites. For example, during the fourth quarter of 1999, the average e-tailer spent an astounding 109 percent of sales on marketing and advertising.[20]

The dot-coms tended to devote too much effort to acquiring new customers instead of building loyalty and purchase frequency among current customers. As one industry watcher concluded, many dot-coms failed because they "had dumb-as-dirt business models, not because the Internet lacks the power to enchant and delight customers in ways hitherto unimaginable."[21]

Pets.com, the now defunct online pet store, provides a good example of how many dot-coms failed to understand their marketplaces.

From the start, Pets.com tried to force its way to online success with unbeatable low prices and heavy marketing hype. In the end, however, neither worked. During its first year of operation, Pets.com lost $61.8 million on a meager $5.8 million in sales. During that time, it paid $13.4 million for the goods it sold for just $5.8 million. Thus, for every dollar that Pets.com paid suppliers such as Purina for dog food and United Parcel Service for shipping, it collected only 43 cents from its customers. Moreover, by early spring of 1999, Pets.com had burned more than $21 million on marketing and advertising to create an identity and entice pet owners to its site. Its branding campaign centered the wildly popular Sock Puppet character, a white dog with black patches. Sock Puppet even made an appearance in Macy's Thanksgiving Day Parade in New York as a 36-foot-high balloon. The singing mascot was also featured in Super Bowl ads that cost Pets.com more than $2 million. At first, investors bought into Pet.com's "landgrab" strategy—investing more than $82 million to stake

■ Like many other dot-coms, Pets.com never did figure out how to make money on the Web. Following the "dot-com meltdown," the once-bold e-tailer retired its popular Sock Puppet spokesdog and quietly closed its cyberdoors.

out an early share, and then finding ways later to make a profit. However, even though it attracted 570,000 customers, Pets.com never did figure out how to make money in a low-margin business with high shipping costs. Its stock price slid from a February 1999 high of $14 to a dismal 22 cents by the end of 2000. In early 2001, the once-bold e-tailer retired Sock Puppet and quietly closed its cyberdoors.[22]

At the same time, many click-only dot-coms are surviving and even prospering in today's marketspace. Of those that survived the crash, 50 percent were profitable by the end of last year. However, for many dot-coms, including some Internet giants, the Web is still not a highly profitable proposition. Companies engaging in e-commerce need to describe to their investors how they will eventually make profits. They need to define a revenue and profit model. Table 18.1 shows that a dot-com's revenues may come from any of several sources.

Click-and-Mortar Companies

At first, many established companies moved quickly to open Web sites providing information about their companies and products. However, most resisted adding e-commerce to their sites. They worried that this would produce *channel conflict*—that selling their products or services online would be competing with their offline retailers and agents. For example, Hewlett-Packard feared that its retailers would drop HP's computers if the company sold the same computers directly online. Merrill Lynch hesitated to introduce online stock trading fearing that its own brokers would rebel. Even store-based bookseller Barnes & Noble delayed opening its online site to challenge Amazon.com.

These companies struggled with the question of how to conduct online sales without cannibalizing the sales of their own stores, resellers, or agents. However, they soon realized that the risks of losing business to online competitors were even greater than the risks of angering channel partners. If they didn't cannibalize these sales, online competitors soon would. Thus, most established brick-and-mortar companies are now prospering as **click-and-mortar companies**. For example, Office Depot's more than 1,000 office-supply superstores rack up annual sales of $12 billion in more than 20 countries. But you might be surprised to learn that most of Office Depot's recent growth was not from its traditional "brick-and-mortar" channels, but from the Internet.

Click-and-mortar companies
Traditional brick-and-mortar companies that have added e-marketing to their operations.

Whereas Office Depot's store sales have flattened recently, its online sales have soared, now accounting for 18.5 percent of total sales. Office Depot is now the third largest e-tailer in the world—behind Amazon.com and Dell. Selling on the Web lets Office Depot build deeper, more personalized relationships with customers large and small. "Contract customers"—the 80,000 or so larger businesses that have negotiated

TABLE 18.1   **Sources of E-Commerce Revenue**

Product and service sales income	Many e-commerce companies draw a good portion of their revenues from markups on goods and services they sell online.
Advertising income	Sales of online ad space can provide a major source of revenue. At one point, Buy.com received so much advertising revenue that it was able to sell products at cost.
Sponsorship income	A dot-com can solicit sponsors for some of its content and collect sponsorship fees to help cover its costs.
Alliance income	Online companies can invite business partners to share costs in setting up a Web site and offer them free advertising on the site.
Membership and subscription income	Web marketers can charge subscription fees for use of their site. Many online newspapers (*Wall Street Journal* and *Financial Times*) require subscription fees for their online services. Auto-By-Tel receives income from selling subscriptions to auto dealers who want to receive hot car buyer leads.
Profile income	Web sites that have built databases containing the profiles of particular target groups may be able to sell these profiles if they get permission first. However, ethical and legal codes govern the use and sale of such customer information.
Transaction commissions and fees	Some dot-coms charge commission fees on transactions between other parties who exchange goods on their Web sites. For example, eBay puts buyers in touch with sellers and takes from a 1.25 percent to a 5 percent commission on each transaction.
Market research and information fees	Companies can charge for special market information or intelligence. For example, NewsLibrary charges a dollar or two to download copies of archived news stories. LifeQuote provides insurance buyers with price comparisons from approximately 50 different life insurance companies, then collects a commission of 50 percent of the first year's premium from the company chosen by the consumer.
Referral income	Companies can collect revenue by referring customers to others. Edmunds receives a "finder's fee" every time a customer fills out an Auto-By-Tel form at its Edmunds.com Web site, regardless of whether a deal is completed.

relationships with Office Depot—enjoy customized online ordering that includes company-specific product lists and pricing. For example, General Electric or Procter & Gamble can create lists of approved office products at discount prices, and then let company departments or even individuals do their own purchasing. This reduces ordering costs, cuts through the red tape, and speeds up the ordering process for customers. At the same time, it encourages companies to use Office Depot as a sole source for office supplies. Even the smallest companies find 24-hour-a-day online ordering easier and more efficient. Importantly, Office Depot's Web operations don't steal from store sales. Instead, the OfficeDepot.com site actually builds store traffic by helping customers find a local store and check stock. In return, the local store promotes the Web site through in-store kiosks. If customers don't find what they need on the shelves, they can quickly order it via the Web from the kiosk. Thus, Office Depot now offers a full range of contact points and delivery modes—online, by phone or fax, and in the store. No click-only or brick-only seller can match the call, click, or visit convenience and support afforded by Office Depot's click-and-mortar model.[23]

Most click-and-mortar marketers have found ways to resolve channel conflicts. For example, Gibson Guitars found that although its dealers were outraged when it tried to sell guitars directly to consumers, the dealers didn't object to direct sales of accessories such as guitar strings and parts. Avon worried that direct online sales might cannibalize the business of its Avon ladies, who had developed close relationships with their customers. Fortunately, Avon's research showed little overlap between existing customers and potential Web customers. Avon shared this finding with the reps and then moved into online marketing. As an added bonus for the reps, Avon also offered to help them set up their own Web sites.

Despite potential channel conflict issues, many click-and-mortar companies are now having more online success than their click-only competitors. In fact, in one study of the top 50 retail sites, ranked by the number of unique visitors, 56 percent were click-and-mortar retailers, whereas 44 percent were Internet-only retailers.[24]

What gives the click-and-mortar companies an advantage? Established companies such as Office Depot, Williams Sonoma, Fidelity, and Gap have known and trusted brand names

■ Click-and-mortar marketing: No click-only or brick-only seller can match the call, click, or visit convenience and support afforded by Office Depot's click-and-mortar model.

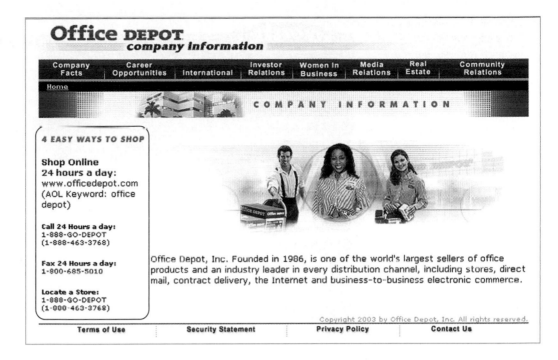

and greater financial resources. They have large customer bases, deeper industry knowledge and experience, and good relationships with key suppliers. By combining online marketing and established brick-and-mortar operations, they can offer customers more options. For example, consumers can choose the convenience and assortment of 24-hour-a-day online shopping, the more personal and hands-on experience of in-store shopping, or both. Customers can buy merchandise online, then easily return unwanted goods to a nearby store. For example, those wanting to do business with Fidelity Investments can call a Fidelity agent on the phone, go online to the company's Web site, or visit the local Fidelity branch office. This lets Fidelity issue a powerful invitation in its advertising: "Call, click, or visit Fidelity Investments."

Setting Up an E-Marketing Presence

Clearly all companies need to consider moving into e-marketing. Companies can conduct e-marketing in any of the four ways shown in Figure 18.4: creating a Web site, placing ads online, setting up or participating in Web communities, or using e-mail.

Creating a Web Site

For most companies, the first step in conducting e-marketing is to create a Web site. However, beyond simply creating a Web site, marketers must design an attractive site and find ways to get consumers to visit the site, stay around, and come back often.

Corporate Web site
A Web site designed to build customer goodwill and to supplement other sales channels, rather than to sell the company's products directly.

TYPES OF WEB SITES Web sites vary greatly in purpose and content. The most basic type is a **corporate Web site**. These sites are designed to build customer goodwill and to supplement other sales channels, rather than to sell the company's products directly. For example, you

FIGURE 18.4
Setting up for e-marketing

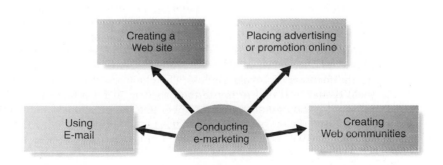

■ Corporate Web site: You can't buy ice cream at the Ben&Jerry's Web site, but you can learn all about Ben & Jerry's company and do lots of "fun-related stuff."

can't buy ice cream at benjerrys.com, but you can learn all about Ben & Jerry's company philosophy, products, and locations. Or you can visit the Fun Stuff area and send a free E-card to a friend, subscribe to the Chunk Mail newsletter, or while away time playing Scooper Challenge or Virtual Checkers.

Corporate Web sites typically offer a rich variety of information and other features in an effort to answer customer questions, build closer customer relationships, and generate excitement about the company. They generally provide information about the company's history, its mission and philosophy, and the products and services that it offers. They might also tell about current events, company personnel, financial performance, and employment opportunities. Most corporate Web sites also provide entertainment features to attract and hold visitors. Finally, the site might also provide opportunities for customers to ask questions or make comments through e-mail before leaving the site.

Marketing Web site
A Web site that engages consumers in interactions that will move them closer to a direct purchase or other marketing outcome.

Other companies create a **marketing Web site**. These sites engage consumers in an interaction that will move them closer to a direct purchase or other marketing outcome. Such sites might include a catalog, shopping tips, and promotional features such as coupons, sales events, or contests. For example, visitors to SonyStyle.com can search through dozens of categories of Sony products, review detailed features and specifications lists for specific items, read expert product reviews, and check out the latest hot deals. They can place an order for the desired Sony products online and pay by credit card, all with a few mouse clicks. Companies aggressively promote their marketing Web sites in offline print and broadcast advertising and through "banner-to-site" ads that pop up on other Web sites.

Toyota operates a marketing Web site at www.toyota.com. Once a potential customer clicks in, the carmaker wastes no time trying to turn the inquiry into a sale. The site offers plenty of useful information and a garage full of interactive selling features, such as detailed descriptions of current Toyota models and information on dealer locations and services, complete with maps and dealer Web links. Visitors who want to go further can use the Shop@Toyota feature to choose a Toyota, select equipment, and price it, then contact a dealer and even apply for credit. Or they fill out an online order form (supplying name, address, phone number, and e-mail address) for brochures and a free, interactive CD-ROM that shows off the features of Toyota models. The chances are good that before the CD-ROM arrives, a local dealer will call to invite the prospect in for a test drive. Toyota's Web site has now replaced its 800 number as the number one source of customer leads.

B2B marketers also make good use of marketing Web sites. For example, customers visiting GE Plastics' Web site can draw on more than 1,500 pages of information to get answers about the company's products anytime and from anywhere in the world. FedEx's Web site allows customers to schedule their own shipments, request package pickup, and track their packages in transit.

DESIGNING EFFECTIVE WEB SITES Creating a Web site is one thing; getting people to *visit* the site is another. The key is to create enough value and excitement to get consumers to come to the site, stick around, and come back again. Today's Web users are quick to abandon any Web site that doesn't measure up. "Whether people are online for work reasons or for personal reasons," says a Web design expert, "if a Web site doesn't meet their expectations, two-thirds say they don't return—now or ever. They'll visit you and leave and you'll never know. We call it the Internet death penalty."[25] This means that companies must constantly update their sites to keep them current, fresh, and useful. Doing so involves time and expense, but the expense is necessary if the e-marketer wishes to cut through the increasing online clutter.

In addition, many online marketers spend heavily on good old-fashioned advertising and other offline marketing avenues to attract visitors to their sites. For example, Mitsubishi recently ran an expensive Super Bowl ad to draw visitors to its Galant Web site. The ad featured a cliffhanger of a crash-avoidance test comparing the maneuverability of a Galant GTS versus a Toyota Camry—to find out what happened, viewers had to go to the Web site. The ad attracted 1.6 million site visits.[26]

For some types of products, attracting visitors is easy. Consumers buying new cars, computers, or financial services will be open to information and marketing initiatives from sellers. Marketers of lower-involvement products, however, may face a difficult challenge in attracting Web site visitors. As one veteran notes, "If you're shopping for a computer and you see a banner that says, 'We've ranked the top 12 computers to purchase,' you're going to click on the banner. [But] what kind of banner could encourage any consumer to visit dentalfloss.com?"[27]

For such low-interest products, the company can create a corporate Web site to answer customer questions, build goodwill and excitement, supplement selling efforts through other channels, and collect customer feedback. For example, although Kraft Food's LifeSavers Candystand Web site doesn't sell candy, it does generate a great deal of consumer excitement and sales support:

> The highly entertaining LifeSavers Candystand.com Web site, teeming with free videogames, endless sweepstakes, and sampling offers, has cast a fresh face on a brand that kid consumers once perceived as a stodgy adult confection. Visitors to the site—mostly children and teenagers—are not just passing through. They're clicking the mouse for an average 27-minute stay playing Foul Shot Shootout, Stingin' Red Ants Run, Arctic 3D Racer, and dozens of other arcade-style games. All the while, they're soaking in a LifeSavers aura swirling with information about products. "Our philosophy is to create an exciting online experience that reflects the fun and quality associated with the LifeSavers brands," says the company's manager of new media. "For the production cost of about two television spots we have a marketing vehicle that lives 24 hours a day, 7 days a week, 365 days a year."
>
> While Candystand.com has not directly sold a single roll of candy, the buzz generated by the site makes it an ideal vehicle for offering consumers their first glimpse of a new product, usually with an offer to get free samples by mail. In addition, LifeSavers reps use the site as sales leverage to help seal distribution deals when they talk with retailers. And the site offers LifeSavers an efficient channel for gathering customer feedback. Its "What Do You Think?" feature has generated hundreds of thousands of responses since the site launched 6 years ago. "It's instant communication that we pass along directly to our brand people," says the manager. Comments collected from the Web site have resulted in improved packaging of one LifeSavers product and the resurrection of the abandoned flavor of another. Candystand is now the number-one consumer packaged goods Web site, attracting more than twice the traffic of the number-two site.[28]

A key challenge is designing a Web site that is attractive on first view and interesting enough to encourage repeat visits. The early text-based Web sites have largely been replaced in recent years by graphically sophisticated Web sites that provide text, sound, and animation (for examples, see www.sonystyle.com or www.nike.com). To attract new visitors and to encourage revisits, suggests one expert, e-marketers should pay close attention to the seven *C*s of effective Web site design:[29]

- *Context:* the site's layout and design
- *Content:* the text, pictures, sound, and video that the Web site contains
- *Community:* the ways that the site enables user-to-user communication
- *Customization:* the site's ability to tailor itself to different users or to allow users to personalize the site
- *Communication:* the ways the site enables site-to-user, user-to-site, or two-way communication
- *Connection:* the degree that the site is linked to other sites
- *Commerce:* the site's capabilities to enable commercial transactions

At the very least, a Web site should be easy to use and physically attractive. Ultimately, however, Web sites must also be *useful.* "The bottom line: People seek substance over style, usefulness over flash," says one analyst. "They want to get what they want quickly. Surfers should know almost immediately upon accessing your site why they should stick around, what's in it for them."[30] Thus, effective Web sites contain deep and useful information, interactive tools that help buyers find and evaluate products of interest, links to other related sites, changing promotional offers, and entertaining features that lend relevant excitement.

For example, in addition to convenient online purchasing, Clinique.com offers in-depth information about cosmetics, a library of beauty tips, a computer for determining the buyer's skin type, advice from visiting experts, a bulletin board, a bridal guide, a directory of new products, and pricing information. Burpee.com provides aspiring gardeners with everything they need to make this year's garden the best ever. Besides selling seeds and plants by the thousands, the site offers an incredible wealth of information resources, including a Garden

■ Effective Web sites: Applying the 7Cs of effective Web site design, is this a good site (see http://www.altoids.com)?

Wizard (to help new gardeners pick the best plants for specific sun and soil conditions), the Burpee Garden School (online classes about plants and plant care), an archive of relevant service articles, and a chance to subscribe to an e-mail newsletter containing timely tips and gardening secrets.

From time to time, a company needs to reassess its Web site's attractiveness and usefulness. One way is to invite the opinion of site-design experts. But a better way is to have users themselves evaluate what they like and dislike about the site. For example, Otis Elevator Company's Web site serves 20,000 registered customers, among them architects, general contractors, building managers, and others interested in elevators. The site, offered in 52 countries and 26 languages, provides a wealth of helpful information, from modernization, maintenance, and safety information to drawings of various Otis models. To gauge user satisfaction with its complex site, Otis conducts quarterly phone surveys with 200 customers each in half the countries in which it does business. Such customer satisfaction tracking has resulted in many site improvements. For example, Otis found that some customers were finding it hard to locate a local Otis office, so the company added an Office Locator feature.[31]

Placing Ads and Promotions Online   *STARTS HERE*

Online advertising
Advertising that appears while consumers are surfing the Web, including banner and ticker ads, interstitials, skyscrapers, and other forms.

E-marketers can use **online advertising** to build their Internet brands or to attract visitors to their Web sites. Here, we discuss forms of online advertising and promotion and their future.

FORMS OF ONLINE ADVERTISING AND PROMOTION Online ads pop up while Internet users are surfing online. Such ads include *banner ads* and *tickers* (banners that move across the screen). A Web user or America Online subscriber who is looking up airline schedules or fares might find a flashing banner on the screen exclaiming, "Rent a car from Alamo and get up to 2 days free!" To attract visitors to its own Web site, Toyota sponsors Web banner ads on other sites, ranging from ESPN SportZone (www.espn.com) to Parent Soup (www.parentsoup.com). Advertisers pay as much as $100,000 to post a banner ad atop ESPN.com's homepage for 24 hours.[32]

Other online ad formats include *skyscrapers* (tall, skinny ads at the side of a Web page) and *rectangles* (boxes that are much larger than a banner). *Interstitials* are online ads that pop up between changes on a Web site. Visitors to www.msnbc.com who visit the site's sports area might suddenly be viewing a separate window hawking wireless video cameras. Ads for Johnson & Johnson's Tylenol headache reliever pop up on brokers' Web sites whenever the stock market falls by 100 points or more.

Content sponsorships are another form of Internet promotion. Many companies gain name exposure on the Internet by sponsoring special content on various Web sites, such as news or financial information. For example, Advil sponsors ESPN SportZone's Injury Report and General Mills sponsors an area on AOL called Quick Meals for Kids. The sponsor pays for showing the content and, in turn, receives recognition as the provider of the particular service on the Web site. Sponsorships are best placed in carefully targeted sites where they can offer relevant information or service to the audience.

E-marketers can also go online with *microsites,* limited areas on the Web managed and paid for by an external company. For example, an insurance company might create a microsite on a car-buying site, offering insurance advice for car buyers and at the same time offering good insurance deals. Internet companies can also develop alliances and affiliate programs in which they work with other online companies to "advertise" each other. AOL has created many successful alliances with other companies and mentions their names on its site. Amazon.com has more than 350,000 affiliates who post Amazon.com banners on their Web sites.

Viral marketing
The Internet version of word-of-mouth marketing—e-mail messages or other marketing events that are so infectious that customers will want to pass them along to friends.

Finally, online marketers use **viral marketing**, the Internet version of word-of-mouth marketing. As one observer puts it, viral marketing is "an extension of the oldest form of advertising in the world—word of mouth—on the newest platform, the Internet." Viral marketing involves creating an e-mail message or other marketing event that is so infectious that customers will want to pass it along to their friends. Because customers pass the message or promotion along to others, viral marketing can be very inexpensive. And when the information comes from a friend, the recipient is much more likely to open and read it. "The idea is to get your customers to do your marketing for you," notes a viral marketing expert. Consider this example:[33]

Gillette used viral marketing to introduce the three-bladed Venus razor for women. To reach college students, Gillette designed a truck that traveled around the Florida spring-break circuit, parking daily near a beach. Women were invited to come in and get some aromatherapy, learn about Venus, enter a "Celebrate the Goddess in You" sweepstakes, and make a digital greeting card with a picture of themselves enjoying the beach. The viral part came when they e-mailed the digital cards to friends. The e-mailed messages automatically included a chance for friends to enter the sweepstakes themselves. If e-mail recipients entered the contest, they saw a pitch for the Venus razor. Some 20 percent of the entries came from the viral-marketing cards, greatly expanding the audience reached by the beach-site promotions.

Viral marketing can also work well for B2B marketers. For example, to improve customer relationships, Hewlett-Packard sent tailored e-mail newsletters to customers who registered online. The newsletters contained information about optimizing the performance of H-P products and services. Now that was good, but here's the best part: The newsletters also featured a button that let customers forward the newsletters to friends or colleagues. By clicking the button, customers entered a Web site where they could type in the friend's e-mail address and a comment, then hit Send. The system inserted the message above the newsletter and e-mailed the whole thing to the friend. New recipients were then asked if they'd like to receive future H-P newsletters themselves. In this textbook case of viral marketing, Hewlett-Packard inexpensively met its goal of driving consumers to its Web site and ultimately increasing sales. "For those on our original e-mail list, the click-through rate was 10 to 15 percent," says an H-P executive. "For those who received it from a friend or colleague, it was between 25 and 40 percent."[34]

THE FUTURE OF ONLINE ADVERTISING Online advertising serves a useful purpose, especially as a supplement to other marketing efforts. However, the Internet will not soon rival the major television and print media. Costs are reasonable compared with those of other advertising media, but Web surfers can easily ignore such advertising and often do. As a result, Web advertising plays only a minor role in most promotion mixes. Last year, online advertising spending amounted to just $7 billion, about 3 percent of the total spent offline.[35]

Still, online advertising is playing an increasingly important role in the marketing mixes of many advertisers. Based on recent studies, the Interactive Advertising Bureau suggests that online advertising should be as much as 10 to 15 percent of the overall media mix in low-involvement product categories such as packaged goods. Kimberly-Clark found that increasing the levels of online advertising boosted the impact of the ad campaign for its Kleenex SoftPack line:[36]

Kimberly-Clark was spending 75 percent of its SoftPack budget on TV, 23 percent on print, and just 2 percent online. However, TV ads only reach about 42 percent of Kleenex's target audience. By boosting its online spending to more than 10 percent, Kimberly supplemented the light reach of TV and complemented its magazine advertising. The combination of print and online advertising helped raise brand awareness for SoftPack among its target audience from 34.7 percent to 42.7 percent; brand image from 35 percent to 41.8 percent; trial intent from 43.9 percent to 55.7 percent, and purchase intent from 24.2 to 34.0 percent. "It was surprising how impactful the lift on some of the brand [measures] were," says one Kimberly-Clark advertising executive.

Some Web sites, such as Google, have been very successful in creating effective online advertising processes and environments (see Real Marketing 18.1). Companies, themselves, are also finding more effective forms and uses for Web advertising. They are taking advantage of new technologies to create bolder, higher-impact online ads. For example, the use of rich-media ads—ads that move across the screen or appear with full motion video and audio—is soaring. Delta Airlines recently showcased one such ad on several sports sites. The ad featured a baseball player, who appeared in the corner of the screen hitting a baseball. A pop-up appears on the screen with the sound and image of the ball breaking through a window. The ad ends with the message: "That ball's outta here. And so are you." It turns out to be an ad inviting fans to win a trip to see their favorite team play in another city.

Some advertisers are now creating entertaining TV-like commercials that are being shown only on the Internet.

LOOK! Down on the PC. It's a banner ad. No, it's a pop-up ad. No, it's Web-only advertising for American Express that teams Jerry Seinfeld with Superman. In the entertaining 5-minute American Express "Webisode," Seinfeld and Superman stroll through New York talking about, well, nothing. All of a sudden a street hood steals Seinfeld's new DVD player. The Man of Steel leaps into action and nabs the crook,

Real Marketing 18.1

"We Love You, Google Users"—and Advertisers, Too!

The early dot-com boom was rife with brash, fast-growing startups led by off-beat, young entrepreneurs offering unique work environments to attract creative and talented employees. Google, the Web-search services provider, was no different. Founded in late 1998 by Sergey Brin and Larry Page, then 25 and 29 years old, Google got its start in a rented garage, complete with a washer, dryer, and hot tub.

Since then, Google has grown from 3 employees to more than 1,900. But it still offers a dot-com kind of environment. Working at the Googleplex (the company's headquarters) comes complete with backrubs from a company masseuse, meals from Google's resident chef, a self-playing ebony grand piano with Muppet-theme sheet music, and even baking bread from scratch if the mood strikes you.

However, although this start-up story mirrors that of previous dot-coms, for Google there is one big difference.

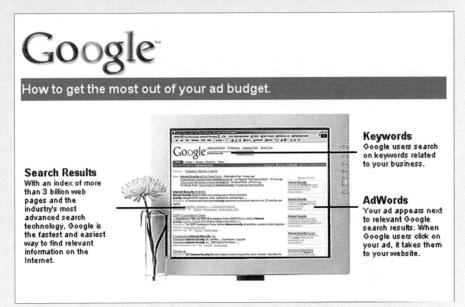

With the world's largest online search audience, Google has become a very attractive advertising medium. Its highly targeted ads reach users when they are already searching for related information.

Whereas other dot-coms have struggled, Google has grown at a phenomenal rate. Google is now by far the world's largest search engine, powering almost half of all Web searches. More than 82 million unique visitors use Google's search engine each month, making more than 3,000 queries every second, some 259 million searches per day. Even more amazing, most of these searches are answered within a quarter of a second. Finally, unlike many other dot-coms, Google turns a profit. In fact, Google is three times more profitable than eBay was at the same stage in its development.

What's behind this incredible success? Google's technology is an important part of the equation. The company's PageRank search technology revolutionized Internet searching. But beyond its revolutionary search engine technology, Google has triumphed by focusing heavily on simply helping users search. Unlike Yahoo! and other competitors, Google opted not to offer news, shopping, and other services. Its Web site promises "a laser-like focus on finding the right answer for each and every inquiry." In fact, the name of the company is a play on the word *googol*, a mathematical term for a 1 followed by 100 zeros. It's a very large number. Google chose the name to reflect its mission to organize and make accessible the immense amount of information available on the Web. Users rave about Google's accurate and easy to use, search-only home page, uncluttered with news reports or banner ads.

The best part is that Google's extraordinary services are free to users. But how, then, does Google make money? Some of Google's revenues come from contracts with corporate partners to provide search services for their own Internet and intranet sites. Today, more than 130 companies in 30 different countries rely on Google's WebSearch and SiteSearch technologies to power the search services on their Web sites. These partners include companies such as the Washington Post, Cisco, Red Hat, Palm, Nextel, Virgin, Netscape, Sony, and Cingular Wireless.

But most of Google's revenues come from advertising sales. In fact, last year Google generated more than $916 million in ad revenues, and that figure will likely double this year. By attracting the largest online search audience in the world, Google has made itself a very attractive advertising medium.

Here's how it works. Through constant data mining, Google determines which search terms are most popular. It then approaches companies who sell in those categories and offers them space for sponsored ad messages and links for a fee. Advertisers then bid on a search term, and the highest bidder gets the highest position on the page. Then, when someone searches Google for a topic related to the sponsor's product or service, a tasteful ad box appears at the top or side of the Google results page, with a short ad message and links to the sponsor's Web site.

Try it yourself. Go to the Google site (www.google.com), "google" a search word or phrase, and see what advertiser messages and links appear. For example, if you search "Disneyland," you'll see ads and links at the top of the search list for Expedia and other online travel services, promising deals on hotels and resort tickets. Search "barbeque grills" and you're greeted with "Shop Sears for brand name grills and all your barbeque needs" and a link to www.sears.com. Side sponsor boxes link you to a half-dozen other merchants, including GasGrillsDirect.com, grillstuff.com, woodstoves.com, flaminggrills.com, and Amazon.com. A search of "outdoor gear" yields "Find the best selection at REI.com" with side boxes for five other outfitters. You get the idea.

(box continues)

This "contextual advertising" on Google is subtle, not like the pop-up ads that make Web-viewing on other sites like swatting flies. In fact, the ads are actually useful. Google "wants everything that appears on the page to be related to your search," says one reporter, "so a car company can't buy an ad to appear with your search for 'perfume.'" Sheryl Sandberg, one of Google's top advertising executives, loves it when people tell her that they didn't even realize that Google runs ads. "It means their advertising experience is not encroaching on their search experience," she says. "The goal is to make the ads as useful as the search results."

Whereas other forms of online advertising may produce questionable results for advertisers, advertising on Google delivers. Google's highly targeted ads reach relevant users when they are already searching for information. According to another Google advertising executive, Google is reaching the person "who is actually sticking a hand up and is interested in your product or service." Moreover, Google's matching process lets advertisers tailor their ad messages or sites closely to users' search inquiries. Last year, Google added local advertising, breaking the United States into 210 regions to further tailor advertising messages to inquiries. As a result, "click-through" rates for the typical ad on Google average 4 to 6 percent, versus less than one-half percent for traditional banner ads.

Google works hard to make advertising on its site effective. It proactively monitors ads to ensure their success. "Advertisers are looking for results," says a Google marketer. "When you spend money with us you can actually measure what the return is on investment by measuring the response on our site." Google even lets advertisers know when their ads *aren't* working. One small business owner was shocked when he received an e-mail from Google suggesting that he pull his ads. "Google sent me an e-mail telling me what I was already thinking—that advertising with them was a waste of my money," he says.

This unique approach to selling advertising space has resulted in loyalty and satisfaction among the Google clients who do stay. Online advertisers, such as Acura, Expedia, Eddie Bauer, Ernst & Young, and REI, number more than 150,000 worldwide and regularly rank Google as their top online advertising choice. This, in turn, has fueled the company's financial success.

Almost from its first day, Google has been something of a cultural phenomenon. Google's success stems from its fervent passion to bring value to both the users who flock to its site and the advertisers wanting to reach them. In the company's lobby in Mountain View, California, a 6-foot trophy case brims with awards, including a 2000 Webby (the Internet's equivalent of an Oscar), which cofounders Brin and Page accepted wearing hockey uniforms and rollerblades. Their shared acceptance speech was simply, "We love you, Google users." They might have added, "And you, too, Google advertisers."

Sources: Quotes and other information from Betsy Cummings, "Beating the Odds," *Sales and Marketing Management*, March 2002, pp. 24–28; David Kirkpatrick, "In the Hands of Geeks, Web Advertising Actually Works," *Fortune*, April 14, 2003, p. 388; Kris Oser, "Google Challenge: Growth Without Sacrificing Brand," *Advertising Age*, May 10, 2004, pp. 4–5; Michael Krauss, "Google Changes the Context of Advertising," *Marketing News*, June 1, 2004, p. 6; Ben Elgin, "Why the World's Hottest Tech Company Will Have to Struggle to Keep Its Edge," *Business Week*, May 3, 2004, pp. 82–90; Melanie Warner, "What Your Company Can Learn from Google," *Business 2.0*, June 2004, pp. 100–106; and information gathered from www.google.com, January 2005.

but damages the DVD player in the process. Luckily, Seinfeld bought it with his Amex card so the damage is covered. In sponsoring such a commercial, American Express joins a lengthening list of marketers creating ads that can be seen only by computer users. The ads seek to avoid being perceived as hard-selling hucksterism while appealing to busy, educated, affluent, media-savvy consumers like—well, Jerry Seinfeld—who are watching less TV these days in favor of going online. "We're trying to reach consumers where they're going today, on the Internet," says an American Express marketing executive. "We're trying to create media content where people actually opt in to watch." And opt in they did. The creative and engaging Web ad garnered 1.1 million unique visitors in just its first 2 weeks.[37]

Creating or Participating in Web Communities

Web communities

Web sites upon which members can congregate online and exchange views on issues of common interest.

The popularity of forums and newsgroups has resulted in a rash of commercially sponsored Web sites called **Web communities**, which take advantage of the C2C properties of the Internet. Such sites allow members to congregate online and exchange views on issues of common interest. They are the cyberspace equivalent to a Starbucks coffeehouse, a place where everybody knows your e-mail address.

For example, iVillage.com is a Web community in which women can exchange views and obtain information, support, and solutions on families, food, fitness, relationships, relaxation, home and garden, news and issues, or just about any other topic. The site draws more than 16 million unique visitors a month, putting it in a league above magazines such as *Cosmopolitan*, *Glamour*, and *Vogue*. Another example is MyFamily.com, which aspires to be the largest and most active online community in the world for families. It provides free, private family Web sites upon which family members can connect online to hold family discus-

- Web communities: iVillage.com, a Web community for women, provides an ideal environment for Web ads of companies such as Procter & Gamble, Kimberly Clark, Avon, Hallmark, and others.

sions, share family news, create online family photo albums, maintain a calendar of family events, share family history information, jointly build family trees, and buy gifts for family members quickly and easily.[38]

Visitors to these Internet neighborhoods develop a strong sense of community. Such communities are attractive to advertisers because they draw frequent, lengthy visits from consumers with common interests and well-defined demographics. For example, iVillage provides an ideal environment for the Web ads of companies such as Procter & Gamble, Kimberly-Clark, Avon, Clairol, Hallmark, and others who target women consumers. And MyFamily.com hosts The Shops@MyFamily, in which such companies as Disney, Kodak, Hallmark, Compaq, Hewlett-Packard, and Microsoft advertise and sell their family-oriented products.

Web communities can be either social or work related. One successful work-related community is @griculture Online. This site offers commodity prices, recent farm news, and chat rooms of all types. Rural surfers can visit the Electronic Coffee Shop and pick up the latest down-on-the-farm joke or join a hot discussion on controlling soybean cyst nematodes. @griculture Online has been highly successful, attracting as many as 5 million hits per month. As such, it provides an excellent advertising environment for such companies as John Deere, Chevy Truck, and Farm Bureau, all of which sponsor featured areas on the site.[39]

Using E-Mail

E-mail has exploded onto the scene as an important e-marketing tool. A recent study of ad, brand, and marketing managers found that nearly half of all the B2B and B2C companies surveyed use e-mail marketing to reach consumers. Another study found that almost 80 percent of consumers with Internet access see ads in e-mails at least once a day. Jupiter Media Metrix estimates that companies will be spending $6.1 billion annually on e-mail marketing by 2008, up from just $164 million in 1999.[40]

To compete effectively in this ever-more-cluttered e-mail environment, marketers are designing "enriched" e-mail messages—animated, interactive, and personalized messages full of streaming audio and video. Then, they are targeting these attention-grabbers more carefully to those who want them and will act upon them. Consider Nintendo, a natural for e-mail based marketing:

> Young computer-savvy gaming fans actually look forward to Nintendo's monthly e-mail newsletter for gaming tips and for announcements of exciting new games. When the company launched its Star Fox Adventure game in 2002, it created an intensive e-mail campaign in the weeks before and after the product launch. The campaign included a variety of messages targeting potential customers. "Each message has a different look and feel, and . . . that builds excitement for Nintendo," notes an executive working on the account. The response? More than a third of all recipients opened the e-mails. And they did more than just glance at the messages: click-through rates averaged more than 10 percent. Nearly two-thirds of those opening the message watched its 30-second streaming video in its entirety. Nintendo also gathered insightful customer data from the 20 percent of people who completed an embedded survey. Although the company feared that the barrage of messages might create "list fatigue" and irritate customers, the campaign received very few negative responses. The unsubscribe rate was under 1 percent.[41]

Spam
Unsolicited, unwanted commercial e-mail messages.

As with other types of online marketing, companies must be careful that they don't cause resentment among Internet users who are already overloaded with "junk e-mail." The recent explosion of **spam**—unsolicited, unwanted commercial e-mail messages that clog up our e-mailboxes—has produced consumer frustration and anger. E-mail marketers walk a fine line between adding value for consumers and being intrusive (see Real Marketing 18.2).

Companies must beware of irritating consumers by sending unwanted e-mail to promote their products. Netiquette, the unwritten rules that guide Internet etiquette, suggests that marketers should ask customers for permission to e-mail marketing pitches. They should also tell recipients how to "opt in" or "opt out" of e-mail promotions at any time. This approach, known as permission-based marketing, has become a standard model for e-mail marketing.

The Promise and Challenges of E-Commerce

E-commerce continues to offer both great promise and many challenges for the future. We now look at both the promises of e-commerce and the "darker side" of the Web.

The Continuing Promise of E-Commerce

Its most ardent apostles still envision a time when the Internet and e-commerce will replace magazines, newspapers, and even stores as sources for information and buying. Most marketers, however, hold a more realistic view. To be sure, online marketing will become a successful business model for some companies, Internet firms such as Amazon.com, eBay, Expedia, and Google and direct-marketing companies such as Dell. Michael Dell's goal is one day "to have *all* customers conduct *all* transactions on the Internet, globally." However, for most companies, online marketing will remain just one important approach to the marketplace that works alongside other approaches in a fully integrated marketing mix.

Eventually, as companies become more adept at integrating e-commerce with their everyday strategy and tactics, the "e" will fall away from e-business or e-marketing. "The key question is not whether to deploy Internet technology—companies have no choice if they want to stay competitive—but how to deploy it," says business strategist Michael Porter. He continues: "We need to move away from the rhetoric about 'Internet industries,' 'e-business strategies,' and a 'new economy,' and see the Internet for what it is . . . a powerful set of tools that can be used, wisely or unwisely, in almost any industry and as part of almost any strategy."[42]

The Web's Darker Side

Along with its considerable promise, there is a "darker side" to Internet marketing. Here we examine two major sets of concerns: Internet profitability and legal and ethical issues.

Real Marketing 18.2

E-Mail Marketing: The Hot New Marketing Medium? Or Pestering Millions for Profit?

E-mail is *the* hot new marketing medium. In ever-larger numbers, e-mail ads are popping onto our computer screens and filling up our e-mailboxes. And they're no longer just the quiet, plain-text messages of old. The new breed of in-your-face e-mail ad is designed to command your attention—loaded with glitzy features such as animation, interactive links, color photos, streaming video, and personalized audio messages.

But there's a dark side to the exploding use of e-mail marketing. The biggest problem? *Spam*—the deluge of unsolicited, unwanted commercial messages that now clutter up our e-mailboxes and our lives. Various studies show that spam now accounts for an inbox-clogging 60 to 85 percent of e-mails sent daily throughout the world, up from only 7 percent in 2002. One recent study found that the average company employee now receives 29 spam messages per day, up from 13 a year ago. America Online blocks some 2 billion spam messages sent to its subscribers each day.

Despite these dismal statistics, when used properly, e-mail can be the ultimate direct marketing medium. Blue-chip marketers such as Amazon.com, Dell, L.L. Bean, Office Depot, and others use it regularly, and with great success. E-mail lets these marketers send highly targeted, tightly personalized, relationship-building messages to consumers who actually *want* to receive them, at a cost of only a few cents per contact. E-mail ads really can command attention and get customer to act. According to one estimate, well-designed e-mail campaigns typically achieve 10 percent to 15 percent click-through rates. That's pretty good when compared with the .5 percent to 2 percent average response rates for traditional direct mail.

However, while carefully designed e-mails may be effective, and may even be welcomed by selected consumers, critics argue that most commercial e-mail messages amount to little more than annoying "junk mail" to the rest of us. Too many bulk e-mailers blast out lowest-common denominator mailings to anyone with an e-mail address. There is no customization—no relationship building. Everyone gets the same hyperventilated messages. Moreover, too often, the spam comes from shady sources and pitches objectionable products—everything from Viagra and body enhancement products to pornography and questionable investments. And the messages are often sent from less-than-reputable marketers. Of the 11 million spam messages studied recently by the Federal Trade Commission, 44 percent came from phony addresses.

At least in part, it's e-mail economics that are to blame for our overflowing inboxes. Sending e-mail is so easy and so inexpensive that almost anyone can afford to do it, even at paltry response rates. For example, Data Resource Consulting, Inc. pumps out 720 million e-mails every year. That makes the company sound like a big-city direct marketing behemoth. But in reality, it's a home-based business run by a 41-year-old single mother, Laura Betterly, in Dunedin, Florida. Dubbed the Spam Queen by the *Wall Street Journal,* Betterly provides a good example of why spam is multiplying so quickly.

The sun was setting on . . . Betterly's six-bedroom house as she reviewed a pair of outgoing e-mail messages one last time. Satisfied, she moved her cursor to the "send" line icon

YOU CAN E-MAIL.

BUT

CAN YOU BLOCK %!#@*% JUNK MAIL?

High-Speed Spam Haters MEET Premeditated Spamicide.

Add AOL. for Broadband on top of your basic high-speed Internet connection, and get a whole lot more from your online experience. AOL's advanced spam filter automatically moves junk mail into your spam folder, and helps to keep it out of your inbox. Also, e-mail anti-virus protection scans every attachment for known viruses, then automatically repairs files. So high-speed Internet users

MEET

AOL.
FOR **BROADBAND**

To sign up, call 1-888-AOL-4-YOU or visit aol.com

■ E-mail is *the* hot new marketing medium, but there's a dark side. AOL and other companies are now offering solutions—"premeditated spamicide."

and clicked. "It's that simple," [she] said triumphantly, swiping her palms. She had just dispatched e-mail messages to 500,000 strangers. Half saw the subject line: "Don't miss your chance to win a Lexus RX300." The other half saw: "Win a trip to NASCAR!" The company [Betterly] runs from her home sends out as many as 60 million such messages a month. [This e-mass mail captured only a 0.013 percent response rate—only 65 responses—generating $40 in revenue for her company.] But Betterly has discovered that she can make a profit [on] as few as 100 responses for every 10 million messages sent. She figures her income will be $200,000 this year.

The problem, of course, it that it's far easier for Betterly to hit the "send" button on an e-mail to a million strangers than it is for the beleaguered recipients to hit the delete key on all those messages. One analyst calculated that the *recipient* cost of Betterly's e-mails far exceeded the $40 in revenue that it produced for her.

(box continues)

Assume that the average time getting rid of the junk was 2 seconds, and that the average recipient values his time at the mean wage paid in the U.S., which is around $14 per hour, or $0.0039 per second. This implies a total cost, incurred by uninterested recipients, of 500,000 times 2 seconds times $.0039 per second, which gives $3,900. And such dollar calculations don't begin to account for the shear frustration of having to deal with all those many junk messages.

The impact of spam on consumers and businesses is alarming. One recent study places the average yearly company cost of spam at $1,934 per employee, costing U.S. organizations $13 billion a year. AOL and other Internet service providers are being inundated with complaints from subscribers. And spam is ruining the rich potential of e-mail for companies that want to use it as a legitimate marketing tool.

So, what's a marketer to do? Permission-based e-mail is one solution. Companies can send e-mails only to customers who "opt in"—those who grant permission in advance. They can let consumers specify what types of messages they'd like to receive. Financial services firms such as Charles Schwab use configurable e-mail systems that let customers choose what they want to get. Others, such as Yahoo or Amazon.com, include long lists of opt-in boxes for different categories of marketing material. Although such companies also send targeted promotions, they limit the volume of such e-mails. Moreover, every message gives customers an easy way to "opt out" of future messages.

Permission-based marketing ensures that e-mails are sent only to customers who want them. Still, marketers must be careful not to abuse the privilege. There's a fine line between legitimate e-mail marketing and spam. Companies that cross the line will quickly learn that "opting out" is only a click away for disgruntled consumers.

If marketers themselves don't deal with the spam issues, others will. For example, more than two dozen states have banned spam in some fashion. And Congress recently passed the CAN-SPAM Act (the Controlling the Assault of Non-Solicited Pornography and Marketing Act) which called for the FTC to establish a national do-not-e-mail registry. Anti-spam software makers and Internet service providers have also taken steps to help consumers to automatically filter out spam. Unfortunately, such solutions too often filter out the good e-mails with the bad.

Most legitimate e-mail marketers welcome such controls. Left unchecked, they reason, spam will make legitimate e-mail marketing less effective, or even impossible. "Long term, if the industry cannot deal with spam," says Joe Barrett, AOL's senior vice-president for network operations, "it's going to destroy e-mail."

Sources: Excerpts and other information from Saul Hansell, "Internet Is Losing Ground in Battle Against Spam," *New York Times*, April 22, 2003, p. A1; Matt Haig, Mylene Mangalindan "Spam Queen: For Bulk E-Mailer, Pestering Millions Offers Path to Profit," *Wall Street Journal*, November 13, 2002, p. A1; Nikki Swartz, "Spam Costs Businesses $13 Billion Annually," *Information Management Journal*, March/April 2003, p. 9; Lorraine Woellert, "Slamming Spam," *Business Week*, May 12, 2003, p. 40; "Spam Makes up Two-Thirds of All E-mail Worldwide," *New Media Age*, March 11, 2004, p. P.12; Kevin G. DeMarrais, "Federal Trade Commission Says There's Just No Easy Way to Put a Lid on Spam," *Knight Ridder Tribune Business News,* June 16, 2004, p. 1; Jennifer Wolcott, "You Call It Spam, They Call It a Living," *Christian Science Monitor,* March 22, 2004, p. 12; and "Spam Costs," *The Controller's Report,* August 2004, p. 7.

Internet Profitability

One major concern is profitability, especially for B2C dot-coms. Surprisingly few B2C Internet companies are profitable. Of the 456 Internet companies that went public since 1994, only 11 percent are still in business and profitable. Of those still in business and not acquired by another company, only about 40 percent are profitable. One analyst calls this "the Web's pretty little secret."[43]

One problem is that, although expanding rapidly, online marketing still reaches only a limited marketspace. The Web audience is becoming more mainstream, but online users still tend to be somewhat more upscale and better educated than the general population. This makes the Internet ideal for marketing financial services, travel services, computer hardware and software, and certain other classes of products. However, it makes online marketing less effective for selling mainstream products. Moreover, in most product categories, users still do more window browsing and product research than actual buying.

Finally, the Internet offers millions of Web sites and a staggering volume of information. Thus, navigating the Internet can be frustrating, confusing, and time consuming for consumers. In this chaotic and cluttered environment, many Web ads and sites go unnoticed or unopened. Even when noticed, marketers will find it difficult to hold consumer attention. One study found that a site must capture Web surfers' attention within 8 seconds or lose them to another site. That leaves very little time for marketers to promote and sell their goods.

Legal and Ethical Issues

From a broader societal viewpoint, Internet marketing practices have raised a number of ethical and legal questions. In previous sections, we've touched on some of the negatives associated with the Internet, such as unwanted e-mail and the annoyance of pop-up ads. Here we examine concerns about consumer online privacy and security and other legal and ethical issues.

ONLINE PRIVACY AND SECURITY *Online privacy* is perhaps the number one e-commerce concern. Most online marketers have become skilled at collecting and analyzing detailed consumer information. Marketers can easily track Web site visitors, and many consumers who participate in Web site activities provide extensive personal information. This may leave consumers open to information abuse if companies make unauthorized use of the information in marketing their products or exchanging databases with other companies.

Many consumers and policy makers worry that marketers have stepped over the line and are violating consumers' right to privacy. A recent survey found that 69 percent of Americans agree that "consumers have lost all control over how personal information is collected and used by companies." Another study found that 7 out of 10 consumers are concerned about online privacy.[44]

Many consumers also worry about *online security*. They fear that unscrupulous snoopers will eavesdrop on their online transactions or intercept their credit card numbers and make unauthorized purchases. In turn, companies doing business online fear that others will use the Internet to invade their computer systems for the purposes of commercial espionage or even sabotage. There appears to be an ongoing competition between the technology of Internet security systems and the sophistication of those seeking to break them.

In response to such online privacy and security concerns, the federal government has considered numerous legislative actions to regulate how Web operators obtain and use consumer information. Such legislation would require online service providers and commercial Web sites to get customers' permission before they disclose important personal information. California recently enacted the California Online Privacy Protection Act (COPPA), under which any online business that collects personally identifiable information from California residents must take steps such as posting its privacy policy and notifying consumers about what data will be gathered and how it will be used.[45]

Of special concern are the privacy rights of children. In 1998, the Federal Trade Commission surveyed 212 Web sites directed toward children. It found that 89 percent of the sites collected personal information from children. However, 46 percent of them did not include any disclosure of their collection and use of such information. As a result, Congress passed the Children's Online Privacy Protection Act, which requires Web site operators targeting children to post privacy policies on their sites. They must also notify parents about the information they're gathering and obtain parental consent before collecting personal information from children under age 13. Under this act, Interstate Bakeries was recently required to rework its Planet Twinkie Web site after the Children's Advertising Review Unit found that the site allowed children under 13 to submit their full name and phone number without parental consent.[46]

Many companies have responded to consumer privacy and security concerns with actions of their own. Companies such as Expedia and E-Loan have conducted voluntary audits of their privacy and security policies. Other companies have taken similar and other steps, sometimes going even further.

> As a company that relies on client trust to build long-term relationships, Royal Bank of Canada (RBC) has used progressive privacy practices to strengthen its client-focused strategies. For the past 2 years, the company has taken a number of internal methods (such as privacy risk self assessments and internal audit reviews of privacy protection practices) to ensure its customers are protected and has used a variety of programs to show customers that it strives to meet or exceed government-mandated privacy regulations in relevant jurisdictions. The latter includes providing clients with a one-year subscription, at no cost, to security and privacy software to help them feel more comfortable with their general online experiences and to promote safe computing practices. RBC also provides its clients with relevant information about its privacy and security practices on its public Web site.[47]

Still others are taking a broad, industrywide approach. Founded in 1996, TRUSTe is a nonprofit, self-regulatory organization that works with a number of large corporate sponsors, including Microsoft, AT&T, and Intuit, to audit companies' privacy and security measures and help consumers navigate the Web safely. According to the company's Web site, "TRUSTe believes that an environment of mutual trust and openness will help make and keep the Internet a free, comfortable, and richly diverse community for everyone." To reassure consumers, the company lends it "trustmark" stamp of approval to Web sites that meet its privacy and security standards.[48]

Still, examples of companies aggressively protecting their customers' personal information are too few and far between. The costs of inaction could be great. Jupiter Media Metrix forecasts that in 2006 almost $25 billion in revenues will be lost as a result of consumers' privacy concerns. Moreover, they predict, online sales that year would be as much as 25 percent higher if consumers' concerns were adequately addressed.[49] Finally, if Web marketers don't act to curb privacy abuses, legislators most probably will.

OTHER LEGAL AND ETHICAL ISSUES Beyond issues of online privacy and security, consumers are also concerned about *Internet fraud*, including identity theft, investment fraud, and financial scams. Last year alone, the FTC received 166,000 online fraud complaints and the Federal Internet Fraud Complaint Center (IFCC) received nearly 50,000 complaints related to Internet fraud. Such fraud costs businesses and consumers more than $22 billion each year. The IFCC reports that nearly 43 percent of reported incidents involve online auctions. Fraudulent activities are most often conducted through Web pages and e-mail, with 70 percent involving e-mail transactions.[50]

There are also concerns about *segmentation and discrimination* on the Internet. Some social critics and policy makers worry about the so-called *digital divide*—the gap between those who have access to the latest Internet and information technologies and those who don't. They are concerned that in this information age, not having equal access to information can be an economic and social handicap. They point out that 80 percent of American families with annual household incomes over $75,000 are online, compared with only 25 percent of the poorest U.S. families. Internationally, in most African countries, less than 1 percent of the population is online. "The ideal of the Internet was to be free," says one critic. "The reality is that not everyone can afford a computer or Internet access."[51] This leaves poorer consumers less informed about products, services, and prices. Some people consider the digital divide to be a national crisis; others see it as an overstated nonissue.

A final Internet marketing concern is that of *access by vulnerable or unauthorized groups*. For example, marketers of adult-oriented materials have found it difficult to restrict access by minors. In a more specific example, a while back, sellers using eBay.com found themselves the victims of a 14-year-old boy who'd bid on and purchased more than $3 million worth of high-priced antiques and rare artworks on the site. eBay has a strict policy against bidding by anyone under age 18 but works largely on the honor system. Unfortunately, this honor system did little to prevent the teenager from taking a cyberspace joyride.[52]

Despite these challenges, companies large and small are quickly integrating online marketing into their marketing strategies and mixes. As it continues to grow, online marketing will prove to be a powerful tool for building customer relationships, improving sales, communicating company and product information, and delivering products and services more efficiently and effectively.

> Reviewing the Concepts <

Recent technological advances have created a new digital age. To thrive in this new environment, marketers will have to add some Internet thinking to their strategies and tactics. This chapter introduces the forces shaping the new Internet environment and how marketers are adapting.

1. Identify the major forces shaping the digital age.

Four major forces underlie the digital age: digitalization and connectivity, the explosion of the Internet, new types of intermediaries, and customization. Much of today's business operates on digital information, which flows through connected networks. Intranets, extranets, and the Internet now connect people and companies with each other and with important information. The Internet has grown explosively to become *the* revolutionary technology of the new millennium, empowering consumers and businesses alike with the blessings of connectivity.

The Internet and other new technologies have changed the ways that companies serve their markets. New Internet marketers and channel relationships have arisen to replace some types of traditional marketers. The new technologies are also helping marketers to tailor their offers effectively to targeted customers or even to help customers customize their own marketing offers. Finally, the New Economy technologies are blurring the boundaries between industries, allowing companies to pursue opportunities that lie at the convergence of two or more industries.

2. Explain how companies have responded to the Internet and other powerful new technologies with e-business strategies, and how these strategies have resulted in benefits to both buyers and sellers.

Conducting business in the new digital age will call for a new model of marketing strategy and practice. Companies need to retain most of the skills and practices that have worked in the past. However, they must also add major new competencies and practices if they hope to grow and prosper in the digital environment. E-business is the use of electronic platforms to conduct a company's business. E-commerce involves buying and selling processes supported by electronic means, primarily the Internet. It includes e-marketing (the selling side of e-commerce) and e-purchasing (the buying side of e-commerce).

E-commerce benefits both buyers and sellers. For buyers, e-commerce makes buying convenient and private, provides greater product access and selection, and makes available a wealth of product and buying information. It is interactive and immediate and gives the consumer a greater measure of control over the buying process. For sellers, e-commerce is a powerful tool for building customer relationships. It also increases the sellers' speed and efficiency, helping to reduce selling costs. E-commerce also offers great flexibility and better access to global markets.

3. Describe the four major e-commerce domains.

Companies can practice e-commerce in any or all of four domains. B2C (business-to-consumer) e-commerce is initiated by businesses and targets final consumers. Despite recent setbacks following the "dot-com gold rush" of the late 1990s, B2C e-commerce continues to grow at a healthy rate. Although online consumers are still somewhat higher in income and more technology oriented than traditional buyers, the cyberspace population is becoming much more mainstream and diverse. This growing diversity opens up new e-commerce targeting opportunities for marketers. Today, consumers can buy almost anything on the Web.

B2B (business-to-business) e-commerce dwarfs B2C e-commerce. Most businesses today operate Web sites or use B2B trading networks, auction sites, spot exchanges, online product catalogs, barter sites, or other online resources to reach new customers, serve current customers more effectively, and obtain buying efficiencies and better prices. Business buyers and sellers meet in huge marketspaces—or open trading networks—to share information and complete transactions efficiently. Or, they set up private trading networks that link them with their own trading partners.

Through C2C (consumer-to-consumer) e-commerce, consumers can buy or exchange goods and information directly from or with one another. Examples include online auction sites, forums, and Weblogs (blogs). Finally, through C2B (consumer-to-business) e-commerce, consumers are now finding it easier to search out sellers on the Web, learn about their products and services, and initiate purchases. Using the Web, customers can even drive transactions with business, rather than the other way around.

4. Discuss how companies can go about conducting e-commerce to profitably deliver more value to customers.

Companies of all types are now engaged in e-commerce. The Internet gave birth to the *click-only* dot-coms, which operate only online. In addition, many traditional brick-and-mortar companies have now added e-marketing operations, transforming themselves into *click-and-mortar* competitors. Many click-and-mortar companies are now having more online success than their click-only competitors.

Companies can conduct e-marketing in any of the four ways: creating a Web site, placing ads and promotions online, setting up or participating in Web communities, or using online e-mail or Webcasting. The first step typically is to set up a Web site. Beyond simply setting up a site, however, companies must make their sites engaging, easy to use, and useful in order to attract visitors, hold them, and bring them back again.

E-marketers can use various forms of online advertising to build their Internet brands or to attract visitors to their Web sites. Beyond online advertising, other forms of online marketing include content sponsorships, microsites, and viral marketing, the Internet version of word-of-mouth marketing. Online marketers can also participate in Web communities, which take advantage of the C2C properties of the Web. Finally, e-mail marketing has become a hot new e-marketing tool for both B2C and B2B marketers.

5. Overview the promise and challenges that e-commerce presents for the future.

E-commerce continues to offer great promise for the future. For most companies, online marketing will become an important part of a fully integrated marketing mix. For others, it will be the major means by which they serve the market. Eventually, the "e" will fall away from e-business or e-marketing as companies become more adept at integrating e-commerce with their everyday strategy and tactics. However, e-commerce also faces many challenges. One challenge is Web profitability—surprisingly few companies are using the Web profitably. The other challenge concerns legal and ethical issues—issues of online privacy and security, Internet fraud, and the *digital divide*. Despite these challenges, companies large and small are quickly integrating online marketing into their marketing strategies and mixes.

> Reviewing the Key Terms <

B2B (business-to-business) e-commerce 559

B2C (business-to-consumer) e-commerce 557

C2B (consumer-to-business) e-commerce 562

C2C (consumer-to-consumer) e-commerce 561

Click-and-mortar companies 565

Click-only companies 563

Corporate Web site 567

E-business 554

E-commerce 555

E-marketing 555

Extranet 553

Internet 553

Intranet 553

Marketing Web site 568

Online advertising 571

Open trading exchanges 560

Private trading exchanges 560

Spam 576

Viral marketing 571

Web communities 574

> Discussing the Concepts <

1. The chapter discusses how today's economy revolves around information businesses. Compare two new-economy information companies and how they have differentiated, customized, personalized, and delivered information to their customers over the Internet.

2. The Internet benefits both buyers and sellers in a number of ways. Using eBay as an example, describe the potential benefits gained by both the buyer and seller.

3. What are the primary differences between private trading exchanges and public trading exchanges in B2B e-commerce? What are the advantages of each type of exchange?

4. Many traditional brick-and-mortar companies have now become click-and-mortar companies. Has the reverse been true (can you name many click-only companies that are now click-and-mortar companies)? Explain?

5. What is a blog? Are blogs usually social or work-related? How are blogs the same as or different from Web communities? Explain.

6. What are the basic Internet security fears of consumers? Are these fears usually justified? Identify five actions a consumer can take to reduce the risk of security problems?

> Applying the Concepts <

1. Visit two Internet sites, one you like and one you don't like. Evaluate and compare each site using the seven C's of effective Web design. Based on the evaluation, which site is better designed?

2. Assume that you are a member of a marketing department for a click-only provider of financial services. Your company exchanges very personal and sensitive financial information with each customer over the Internet on a weekly basis. You have been asked by your boss to come up with a security idea that will be communicated in an ad. What primary message would you like to communicate to your customers in this ad?

3. Based on all that you have read and studied about e-business, what would you say to a friend who wanted to start a click-only business in a highly competitive sector of the market, such as resale of used text books?

> Focus on Technology <

Most consumers have tired of uninvited pop-up ads that interrupt their Web sessions. Many Internet users have installed the latest "pop-up blocker" software but are still not completely satisfied. But that's just one side of the story. Suppose that you are an Internet merchant who wants to run pop-up ads because you have heard they are effective and efficient. What do you do? You go to a company like Falk eSolutions. Falk is a full-service provider of interactive advertising campaigns. One of its many products is AdSolutions, a full-featured ad service offering everything a company needs to conduct interactive advertising campaigns. Visit www.falkag.com and respond to the following questions.

1. What would some of your concerns be about using this type of ad-serving technology?

2. If pop-up ads were effective and efficient, would you stop using them if your target segment disliked them? Why or why not?

3. What "rules of the road" should a pop-up advertiser observe to gain as much from this ad technique as possible?

Source: See www.cipher-sys.com/index.asp.

> Focus on Ethics <

Online privacy statements are a requirement of the Gramm-Leach-Bliley Act (GLBA) and the Children's Online Privacy Policy Act (COPPA). Most companies doing business on the Internet provide these privacy statements. However, a common problem with such statements is readability. Most are written at a level exceeding the average reading ability of those who visit the site. Visit your favorite Internet site. Find the site's privacy policy, copy it, paste it on a blank page in Microsoft Word, and run a spelling and grammar check on it (click on Tools, then Spelling and Grammar, making sure that the grammar option is checked at the bottom of the page). Respond to the following:

1. What Flesch-Kincaid (F-K) grade readability score did your favorite site's policy statement receive? The recommended reading grade level for privacy policies is grade 8.

2. Review the language of the statement and make changes you believe will make it more readable without changing the meaning. What is the F-K score on your reworked document?

3. What do you recommend be done to resolve the readability issues with privacy policy statements? Should sites be made to comply with the FTC readability recommendation?

Sources: For background, see www.ftc.gov/bcp/workshops/glb/presentations/faley.pdf; and www.ftc.gov/os/comments/glbaltprivacynotices/03-31992-0003.pdf.

⦿ Video Case

iWon

Want to win $10,000 just for surfing the Web? Visit iWon.com. There, members use iWon as a portal to search the Internet, clicking on links and browsing for news and entertainment information. But unlike other search engines, including Yahoo and Google, every time iWon members follow a sponsored link they are entered in a daily sweepstakes for a chance to win $10,000. To date, iWon has given away almost $61 million to more than 265,000 members.

Why the daily giveaways? iWon uses the incentive to attract a large group of loyal, responsive users. To become members, those users fill out demographic and psychographic profiles that iWon uses to attract advertisers who are interested in tailoring messages and offers to online consumers. And advertisers, from Amazon.com and Dell to Kraft and Wal-Mart, are lining up for their shot at iWon's members.

After viewing the video featuring iWon.com, answer the following questions about marketing in the digital age.

1. What product or service does iWon.com offer consumers? How does iWon.com's approach differ from that of Publishers Clearing House?

2. What edge does iWon offer advertisers? Why might a company choose to advertise with iWon rather than Google?

3. Visit the iWon Web site (iWon.com). How does iWon address concerns about privacy? As a consumer, would you be comfortable giving iWon the personal information required to become a member? Does the possibility of winning $10,000 change your feelings about giving iWon such personal information?

Company Case

eBay: Connecting Internationally

A RARE SUCCESS

Legend has it that Pierre Omidyar, a young engineer, concocted the idea for eBay in 1995 so that his girlfriend would have an easy way to meet and trade with fellow Pez dispenser collectors. Omidyar envisioned eBay's Internet site as becoming a place where a network of buyers and sellers could connect, forming a community. Bill Cobb, the company's global marketing director, calls eBay a step towards "the first worldwide economic democracy."

eBay is just a step in one sense. The company pales in comparison to, for example, Wal-Mart. Wal-Mart raked in about $258 billion in sales in 2003 from its network of 3,551 stores, 1.5 million workers, and countless warehouses. By comparison, eBay generated only $2.16 billion in revenue from sales fees and advertising on the $24 billion in goods sold through 170 million transactions using its system—less than 10 percent of Wal-Mart's sales. However, eBay has no stores or warehouses or inventory and accomplished its results with fewer than 6,000 employees. Further, unlike most of the dot-coms that sprouted in the late 1990s, eBay is profitable, having produced a net profit of $441 million in 2003.

eBay, however, is no flash-in-the-pan. Analysts predict that its revenues will double to about $4.25 billion by the end of 2005 and profits would continue to grow at the rate of 40 percent per year. Investors seemed to believe the predictions, as eBay's stock was trading at an astounding 94 times earnings in mid-2004, despite the stock market's depressed condition.

HOW EBAY WORKS

The idea for eBay's business model is simple—and old. Residents in rural and urban communities have for centuries gathered in town squares and marketplaces to buy, sell, and exchange goods and services. The modern-day "flea market" is a throwback to these markets.

eBay simply took this old idea and removed the need for a physical meeting between buyer and seller. The Internet provided the cyberspace where the marketing exchange could take place. eBay simply created the software programs to enable the transactions. The eBay system, however, improves on the old market system in that the seller can "display" his/her items to a huge number of potential customers at the same time. Given that there may be more than one person interested in the item, the seller can hold a virtual auction, hoping that demand for the item will produce a higher price than a typical market where the number of potential buyers would be more limited or even nonexistent. Obviously, the process also depends on modern transportation and payment systems that allow the buyers and sellers to arrange for the product's physical delivery as eBay plays no role in closing the transaction.

eBay charges the sellers insertion fees for listing an item, picture services fees, final value fees upon a sale, and listing upgrade fees. The following table presents the impact of the final value fee structure at various closing values:

Auction's Gross Closing Value	Final Value Fee
$0–$25	5.25% of the closing value
$25–$1,000	$1.31 + 2.75% of the amount above $25
$10,000	$26.81 + 1.5% of the amount above $1,000

Source: eBay Web site.

Because eBay does not take title to anything sold over its system, it has a gross margin of about 81 percent! Even with eBay's projected growth, analysts predicted that its sales and marketing expense would hold at 30 percent of revenues.

eBay's average auction lasted 6.55 days as of the first quarter of 2002, and the average gross value per auction was $22.50. As of early 2002, the average seller sponsored 3 auctions and produced $1.72 in net revenue for eBay per auction. EBay classified its offerings into 18,000 categories, with high-priced merchandise, like cars and computers, continuing to grow as a percent of total sales value. In fact, eBay Motors was the company's fastest-growing category. Collectibles, like the Pez dispensers, accounted for only about one-third of eBay's items.

eBay's members, or users (never called customers), would tell you that one reason the system has been successful is that they feel like "winners" whenever they are successful at an auction. The members police themselves, providing feedback points to each other so that disreputable buyers and sellers are quickly identified. Members also communicate directly with eBay's staff to point out problems and suggest solutions. And, it is very easy for members to use eBay's system.

A NEW CEO

In 1997, eBay recruited Meg Whitman to become the company's CEO. Whitman had worked at Disney and Hasbro, but was not an Internet junkie. She had degrees from Princeton and Harvard and brought with her a marketing background built on a commitment to customer satisfaction. When Whitman took over, the company had only $49 million in merchandise sales. She helped the company go public in 1998.

Whitman has led eBay through many changes. Recently, the company instituted a "buy-it-now" pricing system that

(box continues)

lets a seller set a fixed price at which a buyer can purchase the item without going through the traditional auction process. Whitman estimates that this type of purchase will increase from 20 percent to 33 percent of eBay's sales.

Although the company began as a way for individuals to buy and sell, many people have realized that it is a perfect vehicle for their own businesses. As a result, analysts estimate there are over 430,000 businesses that exist only on eBay.

NEW FRONTIERS

eBay has announced that its goal is to achieve sales of $4 billion by 2005. To reach this lofty target, Whitman realizes that eBay must develop international markets—especially in light of analysts' suggestions that the company's core U.S. market growth rate is slowing and advertising revenues are down due to the economic slowdown.

eBay has already ventured into international markets. It has operations in Australia, Austria, Canada, France, Germany, Ireland, Italy, New Zealand, Switzerland, the United Kingdom and other countries. In the first quarter of 2002, international revenues accounted for 21 percent of eBay's revenues, up from 18 percent in the last quarter of 2001; and its 2001 international revenue reached $115 million, up from $34 million a year earlier.

Despite eBay's progress in international markets, all has not gone well. Yahoo! Japan beat eBay to the punch by offering online auctions in Japan in September 1999. eBay entered Japan five months later, but those five months were critical. eBay charged a fee for each transaction, which Yahoo! did not, and required users to provide a credit card number. Many young Japanese do not use credit cards, preferring to pay by cash or bank draft. Further, although many observers thought online auctions would not work in Japan

due to Japanese reluctance to buy used goods from strangers, its economic recession and the emergence of environmental awareness helped to overcome this reluctance. Plus, Yahoo! users could adopt Internet nicknames for their transactions, removing some of the stigma. Then, observers suggested, eBay was slow to adopt local touches, like horoscopes and newsletters, that it needed to attract users. eBay compounded all this by taking a low-key approach to promotion, while Yahoo! bought billboards and opened an Internet café with Starbucks.

All these missteps, analysts argue, resulted in the "network effect." Sellers want to go where there are buyers, and buyers want to go where there is a large selection, i.e., sellers. Once this network reaches critical mass, it becomes very difficult for a competitor to succeed. Sellers and buyers flocked to Yahoo!; and by mid-2001, Yahoo! had captured 95 percent of the $1.6 billion online market—eBay had only three percent. By early 2002, eBay threw in the towel and announced its withdrawal from Japan.

Within weeks, however, eBay announced it had purchased 33 percent of a China Internet auction site, EachNet, for $30 million. Two young entrepreneurs who met at Harvard Business School started EachNet in 1999. Shao Yibo and Tan Haiyin studied Internet businesses as part of a class project and decided that the eBay model was the only one that would work in Asia. With support from Asian venture capitalists, they launched their site, which by 2002 had 3.5 million registered users and 50,000 items listed for sale.

Although eBay executives argue that the eBay model has universal application, the company's experience in Japan and China highlight key differences as companies move from one national market to another. In China, for example,

EachNet's customers hurried to the site to trade practical items like apparel or cellular phones, not the collectibles that fueled growth in the U.S. market. Rather than use the postal or courier systems to make payment, as one might do in the United States, Chinese traders mostly sell within their own cities. Although transportation systems are improving, they are still creaky by U.S. standards; so shipping items is not easy or reliable. Many Chinese still don't feel comfortable doing business online, especially when they are dealing with other individuals rather than companies. Moreover, e-commerce companies have also been concerned about regulation by the Chinese government. In early 2002, the government blocked access to foreign-based news and information sites.

China represents the world's fifth largest online economy with 47 million Internet users. Of these, some 32 percent indicate they made purchases online in the past year. Yet 30 percent of users say they rarely visit an e-commerce site. With a population of over one billion people, however, there certainly is plenty of room for growth. In recognition of this potential, eBay purchased the remainder of Eachnet.com in mid-2003, although the company was still not profitable. However, Yahoo also sees China's potential. In early 2004, it announced that it was purchasing another Chinese online auction business, Sino.com, signaling that it would battle eBay.

Moreover, in mid 2004, eBay announced that it would enter India, following a strategy similar to the one it followed in China. eBay indicated that it would acquire the country's largest online auction site, Baazee.com, Inc. for $50 million. Even though India ranks just behind China in population, it lags far behind the U.S. and other nations in Internet usage, with only 17 million users.

Meg Whitman and eBay's other executives know that to meet their sales and revenue targets, they must be successful in international markets—especially in China and India. eBay is the world's largest person-to-person trading community. Whitman hopes that China and India, with the world's two largest populations, will be perfect fits for eBay's business model.

Questions for Discussion

1. What are the forces shaping the development of Internet businesses like eBay in the United States? How are these forces similar or different in other countries, such as Japan, China, or India?

2. How do the text's terms "customization" and "customerization" apply to eBay's marketing strategy?

3. How does eBay create value for the members of its community?

4. What marketing recommendations would you make to eBay to help it be successful as it enters the Chinese and Indian markets?

Sources: Nick Wingfield, "Auctionner to the World," *The Wall Street Journal*, August 5, 2004, p. B1; Nick Wingfield, "EBay Sets Sights On Indian Market with Acquisition," *The Wall Street Journal*, June 23, 2004, p. A3; Jerry Adler, "The eBay Way of Life," *Newsweek*, June 17, 2002, pp. 51-59; Brad Stone, "eBay in China," *China E-Business*, April 1, 2002, p. 4; Nick Wingfield and Connie Ling, "Unbowed by Its Failure in Japan, eBay Will Try Its Hand in China," *The Wall Street Journal*, March 18, 2002, p. B1; Ina Steiner, "eBay Regroups in Asia: Goodbye Japan, Hello China"; Ken Belson, Rob Hoff, and Ben Elgin, "How Yahoo! Japan Beat eBay at Its Own Game, *BusinessWeek online*, June 4, 2001.

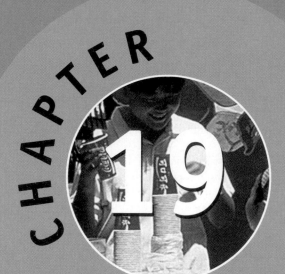
The Global Marketplace

> **After studying this chapter, you should be able to**

1. discuss how the international trade system, economic, political-legal, and cultural environments affect a company's international marketing decisions
2. describe three key approaches to entering international markets
3. explain how companies adapt their marketing mixes for international markets
4. identify the three major forms of international marketing organization

Previewing the Concepts

You've now learned the fundamentals of how companies develop competitive marketing strategies to create customer value and to build lasting customer relationships. In the final two chapters, we'll extend these fundamentals to two special areas—global marketing, and social responsibility and marketing ethics. Although we visited these topics regularly in each previous chapter, because of their special importance, we will focus exclusively on them here. We'll look first at special considerations in global marketing. As we move into the twenty-first century, advances in communication, transportation, and other technologies have made the world a much smaller place. Today, almost every firm, large or small, faces international marketing issues. In this chapter, we will examine six major decisions marketers make in going global.

Our first stop is Coca-Cola—America's soft drink. Or *is* it just America's brand? Read on and see how finding the right balance between global standardization and local adaptation has made Coca-Cola the number-one brand worldwide.

What could be more American than Coca-Cola—right? The brand is as American as baseball and apple pie. Coke got its start in an Atlanta pharmacy in 1893, where it sold for five cents a glass. From there, the company's first president, savvy businessman Asa Candler, set out to convince America that Coca-Cola really was "the pause that refreshes." The beverage quickly became an all-American phenomenon.

But from the get-go, Coke was destined to be more than just America's soft drink. By 1900, Coca-Cola had already ventured beyond America's borders into numerous countries, including Cuba, Puerto Rico, and France. By the 1920s, Coca-Cola was slapping its logo on everything from dogsleds in Canada to the walls of bullfighting arenas in Spain. During World War II, Coca-Cola built bottling plants in Europe and Asia to supply American soldiers in the field.

Strong marketing abroad fueled Coke's popularity throughout the world. In 1971, the company ran its legendary "I'd like to buy the world a Coke" television spot, in which a crowd of children sang the song from atop a hill in Italy. More recently, Coca-Cola's increased focus on emerging markets such as China, India, and Indonesia—home to 2.4 billion people, half the world's population—has bolstered the brand's global success.

Coca-Cola is now arguably the best-known and most admired brand in the world.

Coca-Cola's worldwide success results from a skillful balancing of global standardization and brand building with local adaptation. For years, the company has adhered to the mantra "Think globally, act locally." Coca-Cola spends lavishly on global Coke advertising—some $1.2 billion a year—to create a consistent overall positioning for the brand across the 200 countries it serves. In addition, Coke's taste and packaging are largely standardized around the world—the bottle of Coke you'd drink in New York or Philadelphia looks and tastes much the same as one you might order in Paris, Hong Kong, Moscow, Sidney, or Abu Dhabi. As one ad agency executive asserts, "There are about two products that lend themselves to global marketing—and one of them is Coca-Cola."

Although Coke's taste and positioning are fairly consistent worldwide, in other ways Coca-Cola's marketing is relentlessly local. The company carefully adapts its mix of brands and flavors, promotions, price, and distribution to local customs and preferences in each market. For example, beyond its core Coca-Cola brand, the company makes nearly 300 different beverage brands, created especially for the taste buds of local consumers. It sells a pear flavored drink in Turkey, a berry-flavored Fanta for

Germany, a honey-flavored green tea in China, Sprite with a hint of mint in Canada, and a sports drink called Aquarius in Belgium and the Netherlands.

Consistent with this local focus, within the framework of its broader global positioning, Coca-Cola adapts specific ads to individual country markets. For example, a localized Chinese New Year television ad features a dragon in a holiday parade, adorned from head to tail with red Coke cans. The spot concludes, "For many centuries, the color red has been the color for good luck and prosperity."

In India, Coca-Cola uses local promotions to aggressively cultivate a local image. It claimed official sponsorship for World Cup cricket, a favorite national sport, and used Indian cricket fans rather than actors to promote Coke products. Coca-Cola markets effectively in India to both retailers and imbibers. Observes one Coke watcher, "The company hosts massive gatherings of up to 15,000 retailers to showcase everything from the latest coolers and refrigerators, which Coke has for loan, to advertising displays. And its salespeople go house-to-house in their quest for new customers. In New Delhi alone, workers handed out more than 100,000 free bottles of Coke and Fanta last year."

Nothing better illustrates Coca-Cola's skill in balancing standardized global brand building with local adaptation than the explosive global growth of Sprite. Sprite's advertising uniformly targets the world's young people with the tag line "Image is nothing. Thirst is everything. Obey your thirst." The campaign taps into the rebellious side of teenagers and into their need to form individual identities.

According to Sprite's director of brand marketing, "The meaning of [Sprite] and what we stand for is exactly the same globally. Teens tell us it's incredibly relevant in nearly every market we go into." However, as always, Coca-Cola tailors its message to local consumers. In China, for example, the campaign was given a softer edge: "You can't be irreverent in China, because it's not acceptable in that society. It's all about being relevant [to the specific audience]," notes the marketer. As a result of such smart targeting and powerful positioning, Sprite's worldwide sales surged 35 percent within 3 years of the start of the campaign, making it the world's number-four soft drink brand.

As a result of its international marketing prowess, Coca-Cola dominates the global soft drink market. More than 70 percent of the company's sales and 75 percent of its profits come from abroad. In the United States, Coca-Cola captures an impressive 44 percent market share versus Pepsi's 32 percent. Overseas, however, it outsells Pepsi 2.5 to 1 and boasts four of the world's six leading soft drink brands: Coca-Cola, Diet Coke, Sprite, and Fanta.

Thus, Coca-Cola is truly an all-world brand. No matter where in the world you are, you'll find Coke "within an arm's length of desire." Yet, Coca-Cola also has a very personal meaning to consumers in different parts of the globe. Coca-Cola *is* as American as baseball and apple pie. But it's also as English as Big Ben and afternoon tea, as German as bratwurst and beer, as Japanese as sumo and sushi, and as Chinese as Ping-Pong and the Great Wall. Consumers in more than 200 countries think of Coke as *their* beverage. In Spain, Coke has been used as a mixer with wine; in Italy, Coke is served with meals in place of wine or cappuccino; in China, the beverage is served at special government occasions.

Says the company's Web site, "Our local strategy enables us to listen to all the voices around the world asking for beverages that span the entire spectrum of tastes and occasions. What people want in a beverage is a reflection of who they are, where they live, how they work and play, and how they relax and recharge. Whether you're a student in the United States enjoying a refreshing Coca-Cola, a woman in Italy taking a tea break, a child in Peru asking for a juice drink, or a couple in Korea buying bottled water after a run together, we're there for you. . . . It's a special thing to have billions of friends around the world, and we never forget it."[1]

In the past, U.S. companies paid little attention to international trade. If they could pick up some extra sales through exporting, that was fine. But the big market was at home, and it teemed with opportunities. The home market was also much safer. Managers did not need to learn other languages, deal with strange and changing currencies, face political and legal uncertainties, or adapt their products to different customer needs and expectations. Today, however, the situation is much different.

Global Marketing in the Twenty-First Century

The world is shrinking rapidly with the advent of faster communication, transportation, and financial flows. Products developed in one country—Gucci purses, Sony electronics, McDonald's hamburgers, Japanese sushi, German BMWs—are finding enthusiastic acceptance in other countries. We would not be surprised to hear about a German businessman wearing an Italian suit meeting an English friend at a Japanese restaurant who later returns home to drink Russian vodka and watch *West Wing* on TV.

International trade is booming. Since 1969, the number of multinational corporations in the world has grown from 7,000 to more than 63,000. Some of these multinationals are true giants. In fact, of the largest 100 "economies" in the world, only 47 are countries. The remaining 53 are multinational corporations. Exxon Mobil, the world's largest company, has annual revenues greater than the gross domestic product of all but the world's 20 largest countries.[2]

Imports of goods and services now account for 24 percent of gross domestic product worldwide, twice the level of 40 years ago. International trade now accounts for a quarter of the United States's GDP, and between 1996 and 2006, U.S. exports are expected to increase 51 percent. World trade now accounts for 29 percent of world GDP, a 10 percent increase from 1990.[3]

Many U.S. companies have long been successful at international marketing: Coca-Cola, General Electric, IBM, Gillette, Colgate, Caterpillar, Ford, Boeing, McDonald's, and dozens of other American firms have made the world their market. And in the United States, names such as Sony, Toyota, BP, Nestlé, Nokia, Nestle, and Prudential have become household words. Other products and services that appear to be American are in fact produced or owned by foreign companies: Bantam books, Baskin-Robbins ice cream, GE and RCA televisions, Carnation milk, Pillsbury food products, Universal Studios, and Motel 6, to name just a few. "Already two-thirds of all industry either operates globally or is in the process of doing so," notes one analyst. "Michelin, the oh-so-French tire manufacturer, now makes 35 percent of its money in the United States, while Johnson & Johnson does 43 percent of its business abroad. . . .The scope of every manager is the world."[4]

But today global competition is intensifying. Foreign firms are expanding aggressively into new international markets, and home markets are no longer as rich in opportunity. Few industries are now safe from foreign competition. If companies delay taking steps toward

■ Many American companies have made the world their market.

FIGURE 19.1
Major decisions in international marketing

internationalizing, they risk being shut out of growing markets in Western and Eastern Europe, China and the Pacific Rim, Russia, and elsewhere. Firms that stay at home to play it safe not only might lose their chances to enter other markets but also risk losing their home markets. Domestic companies that never thought about foreign competitors suddenly find these competitors in their own backyards.

Ironically, although the need for companies to go abroad is greater today than in the past, so are the risks. Companies that go global may face highly unstable governments and currencies, restrictive government policies and regulations, and high trade barriers. Corruption is also an increasing problem—officials in several countries often award business not to the best bidder but to the highest briber.

A **global firm** is one that, by operating in more than one country, gains marketing, production, R&D, and financial advantages that are not available to purely domestic competitors. The global company sees the world as one market. It minimizes the importance of national boundaries and develops "transnational" brands. It raises capital, obtains materials and components, and manufactures and markets its goods wherever it can do the best job. For example, Otis Elevator gets its elevators' door systems from France, small geared parts from Spain, electronics from Germany, and special motor drives from Japan. It uses the United States only for systems integration. "Borders are so 20th century," says one global marketing expert. "Transnationals take 'stateless' to the next level."[5]

This does not mean that small and medium-size firms must operate in a dozen countries to succeed. These firms can practice global niching. But the world is becoming smaller, and every company operating in a global industry—whether large or small—must assess and establish its place in world markets.

The rapid move toward globalization means that all companies will have to answer some basic questions: What market position should we try to establish in our country, in our economic region, and globally? Who will our global competitors be, and what are their strategies and resources? Where should we produce or source our products? What strategic alliances should we form with other firms around the world?

As shown in Figure 19.1, a company faces six major decisions in international marketing. Each decision will be discussed in detail in this chapter.

Looking at the Global Marketing Environment

Before deciding whether to operate internationally, a company must understand the international marketing environment. That environment has changed a great deal in the last two decades, creating both new opportunities and new problems.

The International Trade System

U.S. companies looking abroad must start by understanding the international *trade system*. When selling to another country, a U.S. firm faces various trade restrictions. The most common is the **tariff**, a tax levied by a foreign government against certain imported products. The tariff may be designed either to raise revenue or to protect domestic firms. The exporter also may face a **quota**, which sets limits on the amount of goods the importing country will accept in certain product categories. The purpose of the quota is to conserve on foreign exchange and to protect local industry and employment. An **embargo**, or boycott, which totally bans some kinds of imports, is the strongest form of quota.

American firms may face **exchange controls** that limit the amount of foreign exchange and the exchange rate against other currencies. The company also may face **nontariff trade barriers**, such as biases against U.S. company bids or restrictive product standards or other rules that go against American product features:

Global firm
A firm that, by operating in more than one country, gains R&D, production, marketing, and financial advantages in its costs and reputation that are not available to purely domestic competitors.

Tariff
A tax levied by a government against certain imported, designed to raise revenue or to protect domestic firms.

Quota
A limit on the amount of goods that an importing country will accept in certain product categories.

Embargo
A ban on the import of a certain product.

Exchange controls
Government limits on the amount of foreign exchange with other countries and on the exchange rate against other currencies.

Nontariff trade barriers
Nonmonetary barriers to foreign products, such as biases against a foreign company's bids, or product standards that go against a foreign company's product features.

One of the cleverest ways the Japanese have found to keep foreign manufacturers out of their domestic market is to plead "uniqueness." Japanese skin is different, the government argues, so foreign cosmetics companies must test their products in Japan before selling there. The Japanese say their stomachs are small and have room for only the *mikan*, the local tangerine, so imports of U.S. oranges are limited. Now the Japanese have come up with what may be the flakiest argument yet: Their snow is different, so ski equipment should be too.[6]

At the same time, certain forces *help* trade between nations. Examples include the General Agreement on Tariffs and Trade (GATT) and various regional free trade agreements.

The World Trade Organization and GATT

The General Agreement on Tariffs and Trade (GATT) is a 57-year-old treaty designed to promote world trade by reducing tariffs and other international trade barriers. Since the treaty's inception in 1948, member nations (currently numbering 146) have met in eight rounds of GATT negotiations to reassess trade barriers and set new rules for international trade. The first seven rounds of negotiations reduced the average worldwide tariffs on manufactured goods from 45 percent to just 5 percent.[7]

The most recently completed GATT negotiations, dubbed the Uruguay Round, dragged on for 7 long years before concluding in 1993. The benefits of the Uruguay Round will be felt for many years as the accord promotes long-term global trade growth. It reduced the world's remaining merchandise tariffs by 30 percent, boosting global merchandise trade by as much as 10 percent, or $270 billion in current dollars, by 2002. The agreement also extended GATT to cover trade in agriculture and a wide range of services, and it toughened international protection of copyrights, patents, trademarks, and other intellectual property.[8]

Beyond reducing trade barriers and setting global standards for trade, the Uruguay Round set up the World Trade Organization (WTO) to enforce GATT rules. In general, the WTO acts as an umbrella organization, overseeing GATT, mediating global disputes, and imposing trade sanctions. The previous GATT organization never possessed such authorities. A new round of GATT negotiations, the Doha round, began in Doha, Qatar, in late 2001 and was expected to conclude in January 2005.[9]

■ The WTO and GATT: The General Agreement on Tariffs and Trade (GATT) promotes world trade by reducing tariffs and other international trade barriers. The WTO, which oversees GATT, began a new round of negotiations in Doha, Qatar, in late 2001.

Regional Free Trade Zones

Economic community
A group of nations organized to work toward common goals in the regulation of international trade.

Certain countries have formed *free trade zones* or **economic communities**. These are groups of nations organized to work toward common goals in the regulation of international trade. One such community is the *European Union (EU)*. Formed in 1957, the EU set out to create a single European market by reducing barriers to the free flow of products, services, finances, and labor among member countries and developing policies on trade with nonmember nations. Today, the European Union represents one of the world's single largest markets. Its current 25 member countries contain some 448 million consumers and account for more than 20 percent of the world's exports.[10]

European unification offers tremendous trade opportunities for U.S. and other non-European firms. However, it also poses threats. As a result of increased unification, European companies will grow bigger and more competitive. Perhaps an even greater concern, however, is that lower barriers *inside* Europe will create only thicker *outside* walls. Some observers envision a "Fortress Europe" that heaps favors on firms from EU countries but hinders outsiders by imposing obstacles.

Progress toward European unification has been slow—many doubt that complete unification will ever be achieved. However, in recent years, 12 member nations have taken a significant step toward unification by adopting the euro as a common currency. Widespread adoption of the euro will decrease much of the currency risk associated with doing business in Europe, making member countries with previously weak currencies more attractive markets.[11]

Even with the adoption of the euro, it is unlikely that the EU will ever go against 2,000 years of tradition and become the "United States of Europe." As one observer asks, "Can a community that speaks at least a dozen languages and has two dozen different cultures effectively come together and operate as a single unified entity?" Although economic and political boundaries may fall, social and cultural differences will remain. And companies marketing in Europe will face a daunting mass of local rules. Still, even if only partly successful, unification will make Europe a global force with which to reckon.[12]

In North America, the United States and Canada phased out trade barriers in 1989. In January 1994, the *North American Free Trade Agreement (NAFTA)* established a free trade zone among the United States, Mexico, and Canada. The agreement created a single market of 360 million people who produce and consume $6.7 trillion worth of goods and services. As it is implemented over a 15-year period, NAFTA will eliminate all trade barriers and investment restrictions among the three countries.

Thus far, the agreement has allowed trade between the countries to flourish. Each day the United States exchanges more than half a trillion dollars in goods and services with Canada, its largest trading partner. And in 1998, Mexico passed Japan to become America's second largest trading partner. Since the agreement was signed in 1993, merchandise trade between Mexico

■ Economic communities: The European Union represents one of the world's single largest markets. Its current 25 member countries contain more than 448 million consumers and account for 20 percent of the world's exports.

and the United States has more than tripled, now totaling $232 billion. Given the apparent success of NAFTA, talks are now under way to investigate establishing a Free Trade Area of the Americas (FTAA). This mammoth free trade zone would include 34 countries stretching from the Bering Strait to Cape Horn, with a population of 800 million, a combined gross domestic product of more than $13 trillion, and more than $3.4 trillion in annual world trade.[13]

Other free trade areas have formed in Latin America and South America. For example, MERCOSUR now links six members, including full members Argentina, Brazil, Paraguay, and Uruguay and associate members Bolivia and Chile. With a population of more than 200 million and a combined economy of more than $1 trillion a year, these countries make up the largest trading bloc after NAFTA and the European Union. There is talk of a free trade agreement between the EU and MERCOSUR, and MERCOSUR's member countries are considering adopting a common currency, the merco.[14]

Although the recent trend toward free trade zones has caused great excitement and new market opportunities, some see it as a mixed blessing. For example, in the United States, unions fear that NAFTA will lead to the further exodus of manufacturing jobs to Mexico, where wage rates are much lower. Environmentalists worry that companies that are unwilling to play by the strict rules of the U.S. Environmental Protection Agency will relocate in Mexico, where pollution regulation has been lax.[14]

Each nation has unique features that must be understood. A nation's readiness for different products and services and its attractiveness as a market to foreign firms depend on its economic, political-legal, and cultural environments.

Economic Environment

The international marketer must study each country's economy. Two economic factors reflect the country's attractiveness as a market: the country's industrial structure and its income distribution.

The country's *industrial structure* shapes its product and service needs, income levels, and employment levels. The four types of industrial structures are as follows:

- *Subsistence economies:* In a subsistence economy, the vast majority of people engage in simple agriculture. They consume most of their output and barter the rest for simple goods and services. They offer few market opportunities.

- *Raw material exporting economies:* These economies are rich in one or more natural resources but poor in other ways. Much of their revenue comes from exporting these resources. Examples are Chile (tin and copper), Zaire (copper, cobalt, and coffee), and Saudi Arabia (oil). These countries are good markets for large equipment, tools and supplies, and trucks. If there are many foreign residents and a wealthy upper class, they are also a market for luxury goods.

- *Industrializing economies:* In an industrializing economy, manufacturing accounts for 10 to 20 percent of the country's economy. Examples include Egypt, India, and Brazil. As manufacturing increases, the country needs more imports of raw textile materials, steel, and heavy machinery, and fewer imports of finished textiles, paper products, and automobiles. Industrialization typically creates a new rich class and a small but growing middle class, both demanding new types of imported goods.

- *Industrial economies:* Industrial economies are major exporters of manufactured goods, services, and investment funds. They trade goods among themselves and also export them to other types of economies for raw materials and semifinished goods. The varied manufacturing activities of these industrial nations and their large middle class make them rich markets for all sorts of goods.

The second economic factor is the country's *income distribution.* Countries with subsistence economies may consist mostly of households with very low family incomes. In contrast, industrialized nations may have low-, medium-, and high-income households. Still other countries may have households with only either very low or very high incomes. However, in many cases, poorer countries may have small but wealthy segments of upper-income consumers. Also, even in low-income and developing economies, people may find ways to buy products that are important to them:

> Philosophy professor Nina Gladziuk thinks carefully before shelling out her hard-earned zlotys for Poland's dazzling array of consumer goods. But spend she certainly does. Although she earns just $550 a month from two academic jobs, Gladziuk, 41, enjoys making purchases: Such purchases are changing her

■ Developing economies: In Central Europe, companies are catering to the new class of buyers with dreams of the good life and buying habits to match who are eager to snap up everything from western consumer goods to high fashions and the latest cell phones.

lifestyle after years of deprivation under communism. In the past year, she has furnished a new apartment in a popular neighborhood near Warsaw's Kabaty Forest, splurged on foreign-made beauty products, and spent a weekend in Paris before attending a seminar financed by her university. . . . Meet Central Europe's fast-rising consumer class. From white-collar workers like Gladziuk to factory workers in Budapest to hip young professionals in Prague, incomes are rising and confidence surging as a result of 4 years of economic growth. In the region's leading economies—the Czech Republic, Hungary, and Poland—the new class of buyers is growing not only in numbers but also in sophistication. Nearly one-third of all Czechs, Hungarians, and Poles—some 17 million people—are under 30 years old, with dreams of the good life and buying habits to match. And they've discovered the Internet. The online population in the region is growing by more than 25 percent each year, and online spending is growing at a much faster rate.[16]

Thus, international marketers face many challenges in understanding how the economic environment will affect decisions about which global markets to enter and how.

Political-Legal Environment

Nations differ greatly in their political-legal environments. At least four political-legal factors should be considered in deciding whether to do business in a given country: attitudes toward international buying, government bureaucracy, political stability, and monetary regulations.

In their *attitudes toward international buying,* some nations are quite receptive to foreign firms and others are quite hostile. For example, India has bothered foreign businesses with import quotas, currency restrictions, and limits on the percentage of the management team that can be nonnationals. As a result, many U.S. companies left India. In contrast, neighboring Asian countries such as Singapore, Thailand, Malaysia, and the Philippines court foreign investors and shower them with incentives and favorable operating conditions.

A second factor is *government bureaucracy*—the extent to which the host government runs an efficient system for helping foreign companies: efficient customs handling, good market information, and other factors that aid in doing business. Americans are often shocked by how quickly barriers to trade disappear in some countries if a suitable payment (bribe) is made to some official.

Political stability is another issue. Governments change hands, sometimes violently. Even without a change, a government may decide to respond to new popular feelings. The foreign company's property may be taken, its currency holdings may be blocked, or import quotas or new duties may be set. International marketers may find it profitable to do business in an unstable country, but the unstable situation will affect how they handle business and financial matters.

Finally, companies must also consider a country's *monetary regulations*. Sellers want to take their profits in a currency of value to them. Ideally, the buyer can pay in the seller's currency or in other world currencies. Short of this, sellers might accept a blocked currency—one whose removal from the country is restricted by the buyer's government—if they can buy other goods in that country that they need themselves or can sell elsewhere for a needed currency. Besides currency limits, a changing exchange rate also creates high risks for the seller.

Countertrade

International trade involving the direct or indirect exchange of goods for other goods instead of cash.

Most international trade involves cash transactions. Yet many nations have too little hard currency to pay for their purchases from other countries. They may want to pay with other items instead of cash, which has led to a growing practice called **countertrade**. Countertrade makes up an estimated 20 percent of all world trade.[17] It takes several forms: *Barter* involves the direct exchange of goods or services, as when Australian cattlemen swapped beef on the hoof for Indonesian goods including beer, palm oil, and cement. Another form is *compensation* (or *buyback*), whereby the seller sells a plant, equipment, or technology to another country and agrees to take payment in the resulting products. Thus, Goodyear provided China with materials and training for a printing plant in exchange for finished labels. Another form is *counterpurchase*, in which the seller receives full payment in cash but agrees to spend some of the money in the other country. For example, Pepsi sells its cola syrup to Russia for rubles and agrees to buy Russian-made Stolichnaya vodka for sale in the United States.

Countertrade deals can be very complex. For example, a few years back, DaimlerChrysler agreed to sell 30 trucks to Romania in exchange for 150 Romanian jeeps, which it then sold to Ecuador for bananas, which were in turn sold to a German supermarket chain for German currency. Through this roundabout process, DaimlerChrysler finally obtained payment in German money.[18]

Cultural Environment

Each country has its own folkways, norms, and taboos. When designing global marketing strategies, companies must understand how culture affects consumer reactions in each of its world markets. In turn, they must also understand how their strategies affect local cultures.

The Impact of Culture on Marketing Strategy

The seller must examine the ways consumers in different countries think about and use certain products before planning a marketing program. There are often surprises. For example, the average French man uses almost twice as many cosmetics and beauty aids as his wife. The Germans and the French eat more packaged, branded spaghetti than do Italians. Italian children like to eat chocolate bars between slices of bread as a snack. Women in Tanzania will not give their children eggs for fear of making them bald or impotent.

Companies that ignore such differences can make some very expensive and embarrassing mistakes. Here's an example:

> McDonald's and Coca-Cola managed to offend the entire Muslim world by putting the Saudi Arabian flag on their packaging. The flag's design includes a passage from the Koran (the sacred text of Islam), and Muslims feel very strongly that their Holy Writ should never be wadded up and tossed in the garbage. Nike faced a similar situation in Arab countries when Muslims objected to a stylized "Air" logo on its shoes, which resembled "Allah" in Arabic script. Nike apologized for the mistake and pulled the shoes from distribution.[19]

Business norms and behavior also vary from country to country. American business executives need to be briefed on these factors before conducting business in another country. Here are some examples of different global business behavior:[20]

- South Americans like to sit or stand very close to each other when they talk business—in fact, almost nose-to-nose. The American business executive tends to keep backing away as the South American moves closer. Both may end up being offended.

■ Fast and tough bargaining, which works well in other parts of the world, is often inappropriate in Japan and other Asian countries. Moreover, in face-to-face communications, Japanese business executives rarely say no. Thus, Americans tend to become impatient with having to spend time in polite conversation about the weather or other such topics before getting down to business. And they become frustrated when they don't know where they stand. However, when Americans come to the point quickly, Japanese business executives may find this behavior offensive.

■ When American executives exchange business cards, each usually gives the other's card a cursory glance and stuffs it in a pocket for later reference. In Japan, however, executives dutifully study each other's cards during a greeting, carefully noting company affiliation and rank. They show a business card the same respect they show a person. Also, they hand their card to the most important person first.

By the same token, companies that understand cultural nuances can use them to advantage when positioning products internationally. Consider the following example:

A television ad running these days in India shows a mother lapsing into a daydream: Her young daughter is in a beauty contest dressed as Snow White, dancing on a stage. Her flowing gown is an immaculate white. The garments of other contestants, who dance in the background, are a tad gray. Snow White, no surprise, wins the blue ribbon. The mother awakes to the laughter of her adoring family—and glances proudly at her Whirlpool White Magic washing machine. The TV spot is the product of 14 months of research by Whirlpool into the psyche of the Indian consumer. Among other things, [Whirlpool] learned that Indian homemakers prize hygiene and purity, which they associate with white. The trouble is, white garments often get discolored after frequent machine washing in local water. Besides appealing to this love of purity in its ads, Whirlpool custom-designed machines that are especially good with white fabrics. Whirlpool now is

■ Overlooking cultural differences can result in embarrassing mistakes. When Nike learned that this stylized "Air" logo resembled "Allah" in Arabic script, it apologized and pulled the shoes from the distribution.

■ Global cultural
environment: By
understanding nuances,
Whirlpool has become the
leading brand in India's fast-
growing market for automatic
washing machines. It
designed machines that keep
whites whiter.

the leading brand in India's fast-growing market for fully automatic washing machines.[21]

Thus, understanding cultural traditions, preferences, and behaviors can help companies not only to avoid embarrassing mistakes but also to take advantage of cross-cultural opportunities.

The Impact of Marketing Strategy on Cultures

Whereas marketers worry about the impact of culture on their global marketing strategies, others may worry about the impact of marketing strategies on global cultures. For example, some critics argue that "globalization" really means "Americanization."

> Down in the mall, between the fast-food joint and the bagel shop, a group of young people huddles in a flurry of baggy combat pants, skateboards, and slang. They size up a woman teetering past wearing DKNY, carrying *Time* magazine in one hand and a latte in the other. She brushes past a guy in a Yankees' baseball cap who is talking on his Motorola cell phone about the Martin Scorsese film he saw last night.
> It's a standard American scene—only this isn't America, it's Britain. U.S. culture is so pervasive, the scene could be played out in any one of dozens of cities. Budapest or Berlin, if not Bogota or Bordeaux. Even Manila or Moscow. As the unrivaled global superpower, America exports its culture on an unprecedented scale. . . . Sometimes, U.S. ideals get transmitted—such as individual rights, freedom of speech, and respect for women—and local cultures are enriched. At other times, materialism or worse becomes the message and local traditions get crushed.[22]

Critics worry that the more people around the world are exposed to American lifestyles in the food they eat, the stores they shop, and television shows and movies they watch, the more they will lose their individual cultural identities. They contend that exposure to American values and products erodes other cultures and westernizes the world (see Real Marketing 19.1).

Deciding Whether to Go International

Not all companies need to venture into international markets to survive. For example, most local businesses need to market well only in the local marketplace. Operating domestically is

Real Marketing 19.1

Globalization vs. Americanization: Does Globalization Wear Mickey Mouse Ears?

Many social critics argue that large American multinationals like McDonald's, Coca-Cola, Nike, Microsoft, Disney, and MTV aren't just "globalizing" their brands, they are "Americanizing" the world's cultures. "Today, globalization often wears Mickey Mouse ears, eats big Macs, drinks Coke or Pepsi, and does its computing on an IBM PC, using Windows [software]," says Thomas Friedman, in his book *The Lexus and the Olive Tree.*

The critics worry that, under such "McDomination," countries around the globe are losing their individual cultural identities. Teens in India watch MTV and ask their parents for more westernized clothes and other symbols of American pop culture and values. Grandmothers in small villas in northern Italy no longer spend each morning visiting local meat, bread, and produce markets to gather the ingredients for dinner. Instead, they now shop at Wal-Mart Supercenters. Women in Saudi Arabia see American films and question their societal roles. In China, most people never drank coffee before Starbucks entered the market. Now Chinese consumers rush to Starbucks stores "because it's a symbol of a new kind of lifestyle." Similarly, in China, where McDonald's operates 80 restaurants in Beijing alone, nearly half of all children identify the chain as a domestic brand.

An American reporter writing from Japan claimed:

[It will] only be a matter of time before an Asian family [will] take cash from their corner U.S. bank, "drive off to Wal-Mart and fill the trunk of their Ford with the likes of Fritos and Snickers," then stop at the American-owned movie theater to see the latest Disney film before returning home to check their U.S. mutual fund accounts on America Online (on their Dell computer with Microsoft software). Asians see this as no less than the U.S. "desire to bury Asian values," and they are not pleased.

Recently, such concerns have led to a backlash against American globalization. Well-known U.S. brands have become the targets of boycotts and protests in many international markets. As symbols of American capitalism, companies such as Coca-Cola, McDonald's, and KFC have been singled out by antiglobalization protesters in hot spots all around the world, especially when anti-American sentiment peaks. For example, resistance to U.S brands has grown in France recently, partly because Americanization is already so advanced, but also because of frustrations over the Iraq war. More broadly, France has repeatedly tried to mandate the use of the French language to check the advance of English. "But most of the time, the law is impossible to apply," notes a French professor, "because if you want to be understood around the world you have to speak English." And "you have to know English if you want to use the Internet," he adds.

Almost immediately after U.S. armed forces unleashed their attack on Afghanistan following the September 11, 2001, terrorist

■ Global marketing's impact on cultures: Concerns that "globalization" really means "Americanization" has sometimes led to a backlash against American globalization.

easier and safer. Managers don't need to learn another country's language and laws. They don't have to deal with unstable currencies, face political and legal uncertainties, or redesign their products to suit different customer expectations. However, companies that operate in global industries, where their strategic positions in specific markets are affected strongly by their overall global positions, must compete on a worldwide basis to succeed.

attacks, McDonald's and KFC stores in Pakistan, India, and elsewhere around the world came under attack. In Karachi, Pakistan, thousands of protesters, chanting "Death to America," mobbed the U.S. consulate. When police turned them back with barricades and tear gas, "they went for the next-best option: Colonel Sanders," said a reporter at the scene. "It didn't matter that the nearby KFC, one of 18 in Pakistan, was locally owned. The red, white, and blue KFC logo was justification enough." The protesters set fire to the store before police could turn them away.

Despite such images, defenders of globalization argue that concerns of "Americanization" are overblown. Most studies reveal that, although globalization may bridge cultural differences, it does not eliminate them. Instead, the cultural exchange goes both ways.

Hollywood dominates the global movie market—capturing 90 percent of audiences in some European markets. However, British TV is giving as much as it gets in serving up competition to U.S. shows, spawning such hits as "The Weakest Link," "Who Wants to Be a Millionaire," and "American Idol." And while West Indian sports fans are now watching more basketball than cricket, and some Chinese young people are daubing the names of NBA superstars on their jerseys, the increasing popularity of American soccer has deep international roots. Even American childhood has increasingly been shaped by Asian cultural imports. Most parents now know about the Power Rangers, Tamagotchi and Pokemon, Sega and Nintendo. For the moment, English remains cyberspace's dominant language, and having Web access often means that Third World youth have greater exposure to American popular culture. Yet these same technologies enable Balkan students studying in the United States to hear Webcast news and music from Serbia or Bosnia. Thanks to broadband communication, foreign media producers will distribute films and television programs directly to American consumers without having to pass by U.S. gatekeepers.

American companies have learned that to succeed abroad they must adapt to local cultural values and traditions rather than trying to force their own. McDonald's CEO Jack Greenberg notes that McDonald's is "a decentralized . . . network of locally owned stores that is very flexible and adapts very well to local conditions." This concept is echoed on the McDonald's Web site and throughout its corporate culture. The company encourages franchisees to introduce menu items that reflect local tastes, including the Maharaja Mac (made of mutton) in India, the Tatsuta Burger in Japan, the McPork Burger with Thai Basil in Thailand, and the McTempeh Burger (made from fermented soybeans) in Indonesia. In fact, McDonald's restaurants in Bombay and Delhi feature a menu that is more than 75 percent locally developed.

Similarly, Disneyland Paris flopped at first because it failed to take local cultural values and behaviors into account. According to Euro Disney Chief Executive Jay Rasulo, "When we first launched, there was the belief that it was enough to be Disney. Now we realize that our guests need to be welcomed on the basis of their own culture and travel habits." That realization has made Disneyland Paris the number one tourist attraction in Europe—even more popular than the Eiffel Tower. The park now attracts more the 13 million visitors each year. And Disney recently introduced The Walt Disney Studios Park, a movie-themed park to accompany the revitalized Paris attraction. The new park blends Disney entertainment and attractions with the history and culture of European film. A show celebrating the history of animation features Disney characters speaking six different languages. Rides are narrated by foreign-born stars, including Jeremy Irons, Isabella Rossellini, and Nastassja Kinski, speaking in their native tongues.

So, does globalization wear Mickey Mouse ears? American culture does seem to carry more weight these days than that of other countries—the United States is the world's largest exporter of culture. But globalization is a two-way street. As one expert concludes, "If globalization has Mickey Mouse ears, it is also wearing a French beret, [talking on a Nokia cell phone, driving a VW Beetle,] and listening to a Sony Walkman."

Sources: Quotes and other information from Thomas L. Friedman, *The Lexus and the Olive Tree: Understanding Globalization* (New York: Anchor Books, 2000); Karl Moore and Alan Rugman, "Does Globalization Wear Mickey Mouse Ears?" *Across the Board,* January–February 2003, pp. 11–12; Walter LaFeber, *Michael Jordan and the New Global Capitalism* (New York: W. W. Norton, 1999), p. 23; Moises Naim, "McAtlas Shrugged," *Foreign Policy,* May–June 2001, pp. 26–37; Suh-Kyung Yoon, "Look Who's Going Native," *Far Eastern Economic Review,* February 1, 2001, pp. 68–69; Elisabeth Rosenthal, "Buicks, Starbucks and Fried Chicken. Still China?" *New York Times,* February 25, 2002, p. A4; Brian O'Keefe, "Global Brands," *Fortune,* November 26, 2001, pp. 102–110; Susan Postlewaite, "U.S. Marketers Try to Head Off Boycotts," *Advertising Age,* March 31, 2003, pp. 3, 90; Henry Jenkins, "Culture Goes Global," *Technology Review,* July–August 2001, p. 89; Paulo Prada and Bruce Orwall, "A Certain 'Je Ne Sais Quoi' at Disney's New Park—Movie-Themed Site Near Paris Is Multilingual, Serves Wine and Better Sausage Variety," *Wall Street Journal,* March 12, 2002, p. B1; Mark Rice-Oxley, "In 2,000 Years, Will the World Remember Disney or Plato?" *Christian Science Monitor,* January 15, 2004, p. 16; and "Euro Disney S. C. A.," *Hoover's Online,* Hoover's Inc., Austin, Texas, 2004.

Any of several factors might draw a company into the international arena. Global competitors might attack the company's domestic market by offering better products or lower prices. The company might want to counterattack these competitors in their home markets to tie up their resources. Or the company's domestic market might be stagnant or shrinking, and foreign markets may present higher sales and profit opportunities. Or the company's customers might be expanding abroad and require international servicing.

Before going abroad, the company must weigh several risks and answer many questions about its ability to operate globally. Can the company learn to understand the preferences and buyer behavior of consumers in other countries? Can it offer competitively attractive products? Will it be able to adapt to other countries' business cultures and deal effectively with foreign nationals? Do the company's managers have the necessary international experience? Has management considered the impact of regulations and the political environments of other countries?

Because of the difficulties of entering international markets, most companies do not act until some situation or event thrusts them into the global arena. Someone—a domestic exporter, a foreign importer, a foreign government—may ask the company to sell abroad. Or the company may be saddled with overcapacity and need to find additional markets for its goods.

Deciding Which Markets to Enter

Before going abroad, the company should try to define its international *marketing objectives and policies*. It should decide what *volume* of foreign sales it wants. Most companies start small when they go abroad. Some plan to stay small, seeing international sales as a small part of their business. Other companies have bigger plans, seeing international business as equal to or even more important than their domestic business.

The company also needs to choose *how many* countries it wants to market in. Companies must be careful not to spread themselves too thin or to expand beyond their capabilities by operating in too many countries too soon. Next, the company needs to decide on the *types* of countries to enter. A country's attractiveness depends on the product, geographical factors, income and population, political climate, and other factors. The seller may prefer certain country groups or parts of the world. In recent years, many major new markets have emerged, offering both substantial opportunities and daunting challenges.

After listing possible international markets, the company must screen and rank each one. Consider the following example:

> Many mass marketers dream of selling to China's more than 1.3 billion people. For example, Colgate is waging a pitched battle in China, seeking control of the world's largest toothpaste market. Yet, this country of infrequent brushers offers great potential. Only 20 percent of China's rural dwellers brush daily, so Colgate and its competitors are aggressively pursuing promotional and educational programs, from massive ad campaigns to visits to local schools to sponsoring oral care research. Through such efforts in this $350 million market, Colgate has expanded its market share from 7 percent in 1995 to 35 percent today, despite competing with a state-owned brand managed by Unilever and Procter & Gamble's Crest. [23]

■ Colgate's decision to enter the huge Chinese market seems fairly straightforward. Using aggressive promotional and educational programs, Colgate has expanded its market share from 7 percent to 35 percent in less than a decade.

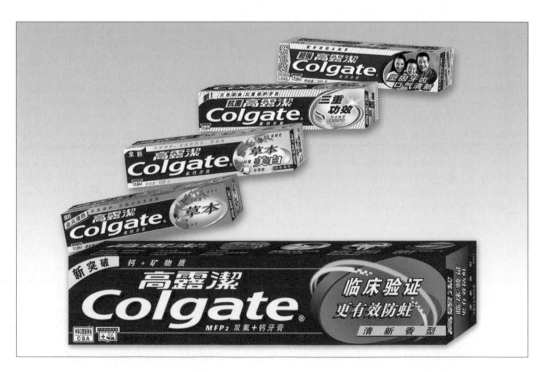

TABLE 19.1   **Indicators of Market Potential**

Demographic characteristics
Education
Population size and growth
Population age composition

Geographic characteristics
Climate
Country size
Population density—urban, rural
Transportation structure and market accessibility

Economic factors
GDP size and growth
Income distribution
Industrial infrastructure
Natural resources
Financial and human resources

Sociocultural factors
Consumer lifestyles, beliefs, and values
Business norms and approaches
Social norms
Languages

Political and legal factors
National priorities
Political stability
Government attitudes toward global trade
Government bureaucracy
Monetary and trade regulations

Colgate's decision to enter the Chinese market seems fairly simple and straightforward: China is a huge market without much established competition. Given the low rate of brushing, this already huge market can grow even larger. Yet we still can question whether market size *alone* is reason enough for selecting China. Colgate also must consider other factors: Will Colgate be able to overcome cultural barriers and convince Chinese consumers to brush their teeth regularly? Does China provide for the needed production and distribution technologies? Can Colgate continue to compete effectively with dozens of local competitors? Will the Chinese government remain stable and supportive? Colgate's current success in China suggests that it could answer yes to all of these questions. Still, the company's future in China is filled with uncertainties.

Possible global markets should be ranked on several factors, including market size, market growth, cost of doing business, competitive advantage, and risk level. The goal is to determine the potential of each market, using indicators such as those shown in Table 19.1. Then the marketer must decide which markets offer the greatest long-run return on investment.

Deciding How to Enter the Market

Once a company has decided to sell in a foreign country, it must determine the best mode of entry. Its choices are *exporting*, *joint venturing*, and *direct investment*. Figure 19.2 shows three market entry strategies, along with the options each one offers. As the figure shows, each succeeding strategy involves more commitment and risk, but also more control and potential profits.

Exporting

Exporting
Entering a foreign market by selling goods produced in the company's home country, often with little modification.

The simplest way to enter a foreign market is through **exporting**. The company may passively export its surpluses from time to time, or it may make an active commitment to expand exports to a particular market. In either case, the company produces all its goods in its home country. It may or may not modify them for the export market. Exporting involves the least change in the company's product lines, organization, investments, or mission.

Companies typically start with *indirect exporting*, working through independent international marketing intermediaries. Indirect exporting involves less investment because the firm does not require an overseas marketing organization or set of contacts. It also involves less risk. International marketing intermediaries bring know-how and services to the relationship, so the seller normally makes fewer mistakes.

Sellers may eventually move into *direct exporting*, whereby they handle their own exports. The investment and risk are somewhat greater in this strategy, but so is the potential return. A company can conduct direct exporting in several ways: It can set up a domestic export department that carries out export activities. It can set up an overseas sales branch that handles sales, distribution, and perhaps promotion. The sales branch gives the seller more presence and program control in the foreign market and often serves as a display center and

FIGURE 19.2
Market entry strategies

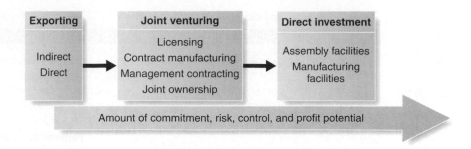

customer service center. The company can also send home-based salespeople abroad at certain times in order to find business. Finally, the company can do its exporting either through foreign-based distributors who buy and own the goods or through foreign-based agents who sell the goods on behalf of the company.

Joint Venturing

Joint venturing
Entering foreign markets by joining with foreign companies to produce or market a product or service.

A second method of entering a foreign market is **joint venturing**—joining with foreign companies to produce or market products or services. Joint venturing differs from exporting in that the company joins with a host country partner to sell or market abroad. It differs from direct investment in that an association is formed with someone in the foreign country. There are four types of joint ventures: licensing, contract manufacturing, management contracting, and joint ownership.[24]

Licensing

Licensing
A method of entering a foreign market in which the company enters into an agreement with a licensee in the foreign market, offering the right to use a manufacturing process, trademark, patent, trade secret, or other item of value for a fee or royalty.

Licensing is a simple way for a manufacturer to enter international marketing. The company enters into an agreement with a licensee in the foreign market. For a fee or royalty, the licensee buys the right to use the company's manufacturing process, trademark, patent, trade secret, or other item of value. The company thus gains entry into the market at little risk; the licensee gains production expertise or a well-known product or name without having to start from scratch.

Coca-Cola markets internationally by licensing bottlers around the world and supplying them with the syrup needed to produce the product. In Japan, Budweiser beer flows from Kirin breweries, Lady Borden ice cream is churned out at Meiji Milk Products dairies, and Marlboro cigarettes roll off production lines at Japan Tobacco, Inc. Online brokerage E*TRADE has set up E*TRADE-branded Web sites under licensing agreements in several countries. And Tokyo Disneyland is owned and operated by Oriental Land Company under license from the Walt Disney Company.[25]

Licensing has potential disadvantages, however. The firm has less control over the licensee than it would over its own production facilities. Furthermore, if the licensee is very successful, the firm has given up these profits, and if and when the contract ends, it may find it has created a competitor.

Contract Manufacturing

Contract manufacturing
A joint venture in which a company contracts with manufacturers in a foreign market to produce the product or provide its service.

Another option is **contract manufacturing**—the company contracts with manufacturers in the foreign market to produce its product or provide its service. Sears used this method in opening up department stores in Mexico and Spain, where it found qualified local manufacturers to produce many of the products it sells. The drawbacks of contract manufacturing are decreased control over the manufacturing process and loss of potential profits on manufacturing. The benefits are the chance to start faster, with less risk, and the later opportunity either to form a partnership with or to buy out the local manufacturer.

Management Contracting

Management contracting
A joint venture in which the domestic firm supplies the management know-how to a foreign company that supplies the capital; the domestic firm exports management services rather than products.

Under **management contracting**, the domestic firm supplies management know-how to a foreign company that supplies the capital. The domestic firm exports management services rather than products. Hilton uses this arrangement in managing hotels around the world.

Management contracting is a low-risk method of getting into a foreign market, and it yields income from the beginning. The arrangement is even more attractive if the contracting firm has an option to buy some share in the managed company later on. The arrangement is

■ Licensing: Tokyo Disneyland is owned and operated by the Oriental Land Co., Ltd. (a Japanese development company), under license from the Walt Disney company.

not sensible, however, if the company can put its scarce management talent to better uses or if it can make greater profits by undertaking the whole venture. Management contracting also prevents the company from setting up its own operations for a period of time.

Joint Ownership

Joint ownership

A joint venture in which a company joins investors in a foreign market to create a local business in which the company shares joint ownership and control.

Joint ownership ventures consist of one company joining forces with foreign investors to create a local business in which they share joint ownership and control. A company may buy an interest in a local firm, or the two parties may form a new business venture. Joint ownership may be needed for economic or political reasons. The firm may lack the financial, physical, or managerial resources to undertake the venture alone. Or a foreign government may require joint ownership as a condition for entry.

KFC entered Japan through a joint ownership venture with Japanese conglomerate Mitsubishi. KFC sought a good way to enter the large but difficult Japanese fast-food market. In turn, Mitsubishi, one of Japan's largest poultry producers, understood the Japanese culture and had money to invest. Together, they helped KFC succeed in the semiclosed Japanese market. Surprisingly, with Mitsubishi's guidance, KFC developed decidedly un-Japanese positioning for its Japanese restaurants:

> When KFC first entered Japan, the Japanese were uncomfortable with the idea of fast food and franchising. They saw fast food as artificial and unhealthy. To build trust, KFC Japan created ads depicting the most authentic version of Colonel Sanders's beginnings possible. The ads featured the quintessential southern mother and highlighted the KFC philosophy—the southern hospitality, old American tradition, and authentic home cooking. With "My Old Kentucky Home" by Stephen Foster playing in the background, the commercial showed Colonel Sanders's mother making and feeding her grandchildren KFC chicken made with 11 secret spices. It conjured up scenes of good home cookin' from the American South, positioning KFC as wholesome, aristocratic food. In the end, the Japanese people could not get enough of this special American chicken. The campaign was hugely successful, and in less than 8 years KFC expanded its presence from 400 locations to more than 1,000. Most Japanese now know "My Old Kentucky Home" by heart.[26]

Joint ownership has certain drawbacks. The partners may disagree over investment, marketing, or other policies. Whereas many U.S. firms like to reinvest earnings for growth, local firms often prefer to take out these earnings; and whereas U.S. firms emphasize the role of marketing, local investors may rely on selling.

■ Joint ownership: KFC entered Japan through a joint ownership venture with Japanese conglomerate Mitsubishi.

Direct Investment

Direct investment

Entering a foreign market by developing foreign-based assembly or manufacturing facilities.

The biggest involvement in a foreign market comes through **direct investment**—the development of foreign-based assembly or manufacturing facilities. If a company has gained experience in exporting and if the foreign market is large enough, foreign production facilities offer many advantages. The firm may have lower costs in the form of cheaper labor or raw materials, foreign government investment incentives, and freight savings. The firm may improve its image in the host country because it creates jobs. Generally, a firm develops a deeper relationship with government, customers, local suppliers, and distributors, allowing it to adapt its products to the local market better. Finally, the firm keeps full control over the investment and therefore can develop manufacturing and marketing policies that serve its long-term international objectives.

The main disadvantage of direct investment is that the firm faces many risks, such as restricted or devalued currencies, falling markets, or government changes. In some cases, a firm has no choice but to accept these risks if it wants to operate in the host country.

Deciding on the Global Marketing Program

Standardized marketing mix

An international marketing strategy for using basically the same product, advertising, distribution channels, and other elements of the marketing mix in all the company's international markets.

Adapted marketing mix

An international marketing strategy for adjusting the marketing mix elements to each international target market, bearing more costs but hoping for a larger market share and return.

Companies that operate in one or more foreign markets must decide how much, if at all, to adapt their marketing mixes to local conditions. At one extreme are global companies that use a **standardized marketing mix**, selling largely the same products and using the same marketing approaches worldwide. At the other extreme is an **adapted marketing mix**. In this case, the producer adjusts the marketing mix elements to each target market, bearing more costs but hoping for a larger market share and return.

The question of whether to adapt or standardize the marketing mix has been much debated in recent years. On the one hand, some global marketers believe that technology is making the world a smaller place, and that consumer needs around the world are becoming more similar. This paves the way for "global brands" and standardized global marketing. Global branding and standardization, in turn, result in greater brand power and reduced costs from economies of scale.

On the other hand, the marketing concept holds that marketing programs will be more effective if tailored to the unique needs of each targeted customer group. If this concept applies within a country, it should apply even more in international markets. Despite global convergence, consumers in different countries still have widely varied cultural backgrounds. They still differ significantly in their needs and wants, spending power, product preferences, and shopping patterns. Because these differences are hard to change, most marketers adapt their products, prices, channels, and promotions to fit consumer desires in each country.

However, global standardization is not an all-or-nothing proposition but rather a matter of degree. Most international marketers suggest that companies should "think globally but act locally"—that they should seek a balance between standardization and adaptation. These marketers advocate a "glocal" strategy in which the firm standardizes certain core marketing

■ Marketing mix adaptation: In India, McDonald's serves chicken, fish, and vegetable burgers, and the Maharaja Mac—two all mutton patties, special sauce, lettuce, cheese, pickles, onions, on a sesame-seed bun.

elements and localizes others. The corporate level gives global strategic direction; local units focus on the individual consumer differences across global markets. Simon Clift, head of marketing for global consumer goods giant Unilever, puts it this way: "We're trying to strike a balance between being mindlessly global and hopelessly local."[27]

L'Oreal, the highly successful international personal care products company, operates this way. It markets truly global brands but adapts them to meet the cultural nuances of each local market (see Real Marketing 19.2). Similarly, McDonald's uses the same basic operating formula in its restaurants around the world but adapts its menu to local tastes. It uses chili sauce instead of ketchup on its hamburgers in Mexico. In Korea, it sells roast pork on a bun with a garlicky soy sauce. In India, where cows are considered sacred, McDonald's serves chicken, fish, vegetable burgers, Pizza McPuffs, McAloo Tikki (a spiced-potato burger), and the Maharaja Mac—two all-mutton patties, special sauce, lettuce, cheese, pickles, onions on a sesame-seed bun.[28]

Product

Five strategies allow for adapting product and promotion to a global market (see Figure 19.3).[29] We first discuss the three product strategies and then turn to the two promotion strategies.

Straight product extension

Marketing a product in a foreign market without any change.

Straight product extension means marketing a product in a foreign market without any change. Top management tells its marketing people, "Take the product as is and find customers for it." The first step, however, should be to find out whether foreign consumers use that product and what form they prefer.

Straight extension has been successful in some cases and disastrous in others. Kellogg cereals, Gillette razors, Heineken beer, and Black & Decker tools are all sold successfully in about the same form around the world. But General Foods introduced its standard powdered Jell-O in the British market only to find that British consumers prefer a solid wafer or cake

FIGURE 19.3
Five international product and promotion strategies

	Product		
Promotion	Don't change product	Adapt product	Develop new product
Don't change promotion	1. Straight extension	3. Product adaptation	5. Product invention
Adapt promotion	2. Communication adaptation	4. Dual adaptation	

Real Marketing 19.2

L'Oréal: Adapting Global Brands to Local Cultures

How does a French company with a British CEO successfully market a Japanese version of an American lipstick in Russia? Ask L'Oréal, the hugely successful international personal care products company. Headquartered in France, L'Oréal sells more than $17 billion worth of cosmetics, hair-care products, fragrances, and perfumes each year in 150 countries across the globe, making it the world's biggest cosmetics company. That's 85 products sold every second, accounting for 13 percent of all cosmetics purchases made around the world.

L'Oréal's broad list of global brands includes, among others, Garnier, Maybelline, Redken, Lancome, Helena Rubinstein, Kiehl's, Biotherm, Softsheen-Carson, Vichy, and Ralph Lauren and Giorgio Armani Parfums. Impressively, L'Oréal has achieved 19 straight years of double-digit international profit growth. Last year, its sales jumped nearly 70 percent in China, 40 percent in Russia, and 30 percent in India.

What's the secret to L'Oréal's amazing international success? The company markets its brands globally by understanding how they appeal to cultural nuances in specific local markets. Says one observer, "L'Oréal is French only when it wants to be. The rest of the time, it's happy being African, Asian, or anything else that sells." The giant cosmetics retailer buys local brands, tweaks them, and exports them globally, presenting a different face to each consumer around the world.

For example, in 1996, the company bought the stodgy American makeup producer, Maybelline. To reinvigorate and globalize the brand, it moved the unit's headquarters from Tennessee to New York City and added "New York" to the label. The resulting urban, street-smart, Big Apple image played well with the mid-price positioning of the workaday makeup brand. The makeover earned Maybelline a 20 percent market share in its category in Western Europe. The young urban positioning also hit the mark in Asia. As one industry analyst recounts:

> It's a sunny afternoon outside Parkson's department store in Shanghai, and a marketing battle is raging for the attention of Chinese women. Tall, pouty models in beige skirts and sheer tops pass out flyers promoting Revlon's new spring colors. But their effort is drowned out by L'Oréal's eye-catching show for its Maybelline brand. To a pulsing rhythm, two gangly models in shimmering Lycra tops dance on a podium

■ What's the secret to L'oréal's amazing international success? The company markets its brands globally by understanding how they appeal to cultural nuances in specific local markets. It has become the Untied Nations of Beauty.

before a large backdrop depicting the New York City skyline. The music stops, and a makeup artist transforms a model's face while a Chinese saleswoman delivers the punch line. "This brand comes from America. It's very trendy," she

---

form. Likewise, Philips began to make a profit in Japan only after it reduced the size of its coffeemakers to fit into smaller Japanese kitchens and its shavers to fit smaller Japanese hands. Straight extension is tempting because it involves no additional product development costs, manufacturing changes, or new promotion. But it can be costly in the long run if products fail to satisfy foreign consumers.

Product adaptation

Adapting a product to meet local conditions or wants in foreign markets.

Product adaptation involves changing the product to meet local conditions or wants. For example, Procter & Gamble's Vidal Sassoon shampoos contain a single fragrance worldwide, but the amount of scent varies by country: more in Europe but less in Japan, where subtle scents are preferred. Gerber serves Japanese baby food fare that might turn the stomachs of many western consumers—local favorites include flounder and spinach stew, cod roe spaghetti, mugwort casserole, and sardines ground up in white radish sauce. And Finnish cell phone maker Nokia customized its 6100 series phone for every major market. Developers

shouts into her microphone. "If you want to be fashionable, just choose Maybelline." Few of the women in the crowd realize that the trendy "New York" Maybelline brand belongs to French cosmetics giant L'Oréal.

Although the Maybelline brand thrives on an infusion of American energy, L'Oréal does more than simply pitch a western ideal. Instead, it recognizes different cultural views of beauty throughout the world. In fact, the company often goes out of its way to challenge conventional preconceptions of beauty. For example, the cover of a recent annual report featured a Japanese model with red hair and purple lipstick. Ads for Garnier hair dye posted in Moscow picture bleach blonde African and Asian models.

L'Oreal's CEO, Lindsay Owens-Jones, insists that the secret to good brand management is hitting the right audience with the right product. "Each brand is positioned on a very precise segment," he says. For L'Oréal, that means finding local brands, sprucing them up, positioning them for a specific target market, and exporting them to new customers all over the globe. To support that effort, the company spends $4 billion annually to tailor global marketing messages to local cultures around the world.

Take, for example, L'Oréal's recent acquisition and merger of the Soft Sheen and Carson brands. Originally marketed only in the United States, the Soft Sheen-Carson brand now generates more than 30 percent of its revenues abroad. In South Africa, where the brand has a 41 percent market share, L'Oréal has worked locally to promote trial of its new products. In Senegal, the company's marketers are setting up training sessions for hairdressers.

Beyond tailored messages and promotions, L'Oréal's products themselves must suit local needs across the very diverse range of people, cultures, and climates. Toward that end, as a share of revenues, L'Oréal spends 50 percent more than the industry average on product research and development. It filed more than 490 patents last year alone. For example, research centers in Japan focus on the needs of Asian skin and hair types. The L'Oréal Institute for Ethnic Hair and Skin Research studies the needs of consumers of African descent. A climate-controlled wind tunnel in France provides insights into the impact of weather on cosmetics. R&D helps L'Oréal to formulate products for use in high-temperature, high-humidity environments like India. R&D also forms the basis for L'Oréal's fastest growing segment—so-called active cosmetics that

are biomedically engineered by the company's scientists and dermatologists.

A seemingly conflicting array of words could be used to describe L'Oréal's brands: scientific and spiritual, mass-market and word-of-mouth, French sophistication and New York street smarts, conformity and uniqueness, luxury and affordability. How can a company stake a claim to all ends of the spectrum on so many different dimensions? For L'Oréal, being different things to different people means "conveying the allure of different cultures through its many products," says an industry analyst. Notes another observer:

> In sharp contrast to other . . . western brands such as Coca-Cola and McDonalds, which offer only a single cultural icon, L'Oréal can entice Asian consumers, for example, with a taste of French *chic*, New York attitude, or Italian elegance. You are anxious to buy into a part of the American dream—then Maybelline New York is there for the taking. [Want] 'Le latin way of life'—then Giorgio Armani is there for the taking.

L'Oréal products are found in chic shops, beauty salons, pharmacies, department stores, and even grocery stores. The company goes where the customer is and delivers what that customer wants—Vichy Laboratories in pharmacies, Giorgio Armani in upscale shops, mid-priced Maybelline at Wal-Mart. When CEO Owens-Jones recently addressed a UNESCO conference, nobody batted an eyelid when he described L'Oréal as "the United Nations of Beauty."

Sources: Quotes and other information from Gail Edmondson, "The Beauty of Global Branding," *Business Week*, June 28, 1999, pp.70–75; Richard Tomlinson, "L'Oréal's Global Makeover," *Fortune*, Sept 30, 2002, p. 141; EuroFile Backgrounder: L'Oréal, Sept. 11, 2001, accessed online at www.hemscott.co.uk; "Top Global Brands," *Global Cosmetic Industry*, February 2003, pp. 28–34; "History: Making Sure the Hair Creams Taste OK," accessed online at www.iwon.com, July 2003; "Consumer Products Brief: L'Oreal," *Wall Street Journal*, February 23, 2004, p. 1; Vito J. Racanelli, "Touching Up," February 16, 2004, pp. 18–19; and information accessed at www.loreal.com, January 2005.

---

built in rudimentary voice recognition for Asia where keyboards are a problem and raised the ring volume so the phone could be heard on crowded Asian streets.

Product invention

Creating new products or services for foreign markets.

Product invention consists of creating something new for a specific country market. This strategy can take two forms. It might mean maintaining or reintroducing earlier product forms that happen to be well adapted to the needs of a given country. Volkswagen continued to produce and sell its old VW Beetle model in Mexico until just recently. Or a company might create a new product to meet a need in a given country. For example, Sony added the "U" model to its VAIO personal computer line to meet the unique needs of Japanese consumers, even though it wouldn't have much appeal in the United States and other world markets:

> The U may be the most "Japanese" product in the entire Sony VAIO line. The smallest laptop in the world, it is less than 7 inches wide, with a 6-inch diagonal screen,

it makes an ordinary laptop look sumo sized. Sony noticed that rush-hour trains to Tokyo were simply too crowded to allow many commuters to use their laptops. "The only people in Tokyo who have the luxury of a lap are the first people on the train," says Mark Hanson, a Sony vice president. The point of the U, he explains, gripping its base with two hands and resting his thumbs on the keyboard, "is to give users the experience of what I'd call a standing computer." How would that translate into the U.S. market? The cultural differences are daunting. Far more Americans touch-type than do Japanese (a few Japanese characters convey a lot), and touch typists are likely to resist typing with their thumbs. And few Americans face a Tokyo-type rush-hour commute.[30]

Promotion

Companies can either adopt the same promotion strategy they used in the home market or change it for each local market. Consider advertising messages. Some global companies use a standardized advertising theme around the world. Of course, even in highly standardized promotion campaigns, some small changes might be required to adjust for language and minor cultural differences. For example, Guy Laroche uses virtually the same ads for its Drakkar Noir fragrances in Europe as in Arab countries. However, it subtly tones down the Arab versions to meet cultural differences in attitudes toward sensuality.

Colors also are changed sometimes to avoid taboos in other countries. Purple is associated with death in most of Latin America, white is a mourning color in Japan, and green is associated with jungle sickness in Malaysia. Even names must be changed. In Sweden, Helene Curtis changed the name of its Every Night Shampoo to Every Day because Swedes usually wash their hair in the morning. And Kellogg had to rename Bran Buds cereal in Sweden, where the name roughly translates as "burned farmer." (See Real Marketing 19.3 for more on language blunders in international marketing.)

Communication adaptation
A global communication strategy of fully adapting advertising messages to local markets.

Other companies follow a strategy of **communication adaptation**, fully adapting their advertising messages to local markets. Kellogg ads in the United States promote the taste and nutrition of Kellogg's cereals versus competitors' brands. In France, where consumers drink little milk and eat little for breakfast, Kellogg's ads must convince consumers that cereals are a tasty and healthful breakfast. In India, where many consumers eat heavy, fried breakfasts, Kellogg's advertising convinces buyers to switch to a lighter, more nutritious breakfast diet.

Similarly, Coca-Cola sells its low-calorie beverage as Diet Coke in North America, the United Kingdom, and the Middle and Far East but as Light elsewhere. According to Diet Coke's global brand manager, in Spanish-speaking countries Coke Light ads "position the soft drink as

■ Some companies standardize their advertising around the world, adapting only to meet cultural differences. Guy Laroche uses similar ads in Europe (left) and Arab countries (right), but tones down the sensuality in the Arab version—the man is clothed and the woman barely touches him.

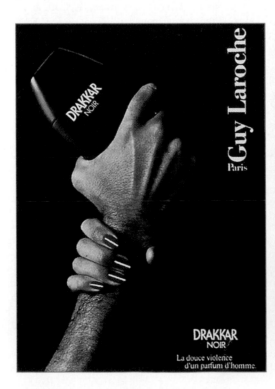

Real Marketing 19.3

Many global companies have had difficulty crossing the language barrier, with results ranging from mild embarrassment to outright failure. Seemingly innocuous brand names and advertising phrases can take on unintended or hidden meanings when translated into other languages. Careless translations can make a marketer look downright foolish to foreign consumers.

We've all run across examples when buying products from other countries. Here's one from a firm in Taiwan attempting to instruct children on how to install a ramp on a garage for toy cars: "Before you play with, fix waiting plate by yourself as per below diagram. But after you once fixed it, you can play with as is and no necessary to fix off again." Many U.S. firms are guilty of such atrocities when marketing abroad.

The classic language blunders involve standardized brand names that do not translate well. When Coca-Cola first marketed Coke in China in the 1920s, it developed a group of Chinese characters that, when pronounced, sounded like the product name. Unfortunately, the characters actually translated to mean "bite the wax tadpole." Now, the characters on Chinese Coke bottles translate as "happiness in the mouth."

Several U.S. carmakers have had similar problems when their brand names crashed into the language barrier. Chevy's Nova translated into Spanish as *no va*—"it doesn't go." GM changed the name to Caribe and sales increased. Buick scrambled to rename its new LaCrosse sedan the Allure in Canada after learning that the name comes too close to a Quebecois word for masturbation. And Rolls-Royce avoided the name Silver Mist in German markets, where *mist* means "manure." Sunbeam, however, entered the German market with its Mist Stick hair curling iron. As should have been expected, the Germans had little use for a "manure wand." A similar fate awaited Colgate when it introduced a toothpaste in France called Cue, the name of a notorious porno magazine.

One well-intentioned firm sold its shampoo in Brazil under the name Evitol. It soon realized it was claiming to sell a "dandruff contraceptive." An American company reportedly had trouble marketing Pet milk in French-speaking areas. It seems that the word *pet* in French means, among other things, "to break wind." Similarly, IKEA markets a children's workbench named FARTFULL (the word means "speedy" in Swedish). Hunt-Wesson introduced its Big John products in Quebec as Gros Jos before learning that it means "big breasts" in French. This gaffe had no apparent effect on sales.

Interbrand of London, the firm that created household names such as Prozac and Acura, recently developed a brand-name "hall of shame" list, which contained these and other foreign brand names you're never likely to see inside the local A&P: Krapp toilet paper (Denmark), Crapsy Fruit cereal (France), Happy End toilet paper (Germany), Mukk yogurt (Italy), Zit lemonade (Germany), Poo curry powder (Argentina), and Pschitt lemonade (France).

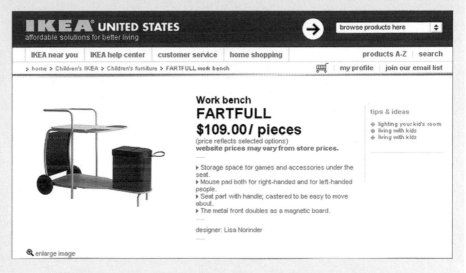

Global language barriers: Some standardized brand names do not translate well globally.

Travelers often encounter well-intentioned advice from service firms that takes on meanings very different from those intended. The menu in one Swiss restaurant proudly stated, "Our wines leave you nothing to hope for." Signs in a Japanese hotel pronounced, "You are invited to take advantage of the chambermaid." At a laundry in Rome, it was, "Ladies, leave your clothes here and spend the afternoon having a good time." The brochure at a Tokyo car rental offered this sage advice: "When passenger of foot heave in sight, tootle the horn. Trumpet him melodiously at first, but if he still obstacles your passage, tootle him with vigor."

Advertising themes often lose—or gain—something in the translation. The Coors beer slogan "get loose with Coors" in Spanish came out as "get the runs with Coors." Coca-Cola's "Coke adds life" theme in Japanese translated into "Coke brings your ancestors back from the dead." The milk industry learned too late that its American advertising question "Got Milk?" translated in Mexico as a more provocative "Are you lactating?" In Chinese, the KFC slogan "finger-lickin' good" came out as "eat your fingers off." And Frank Perdue's classic line, "It takes a tough man to make a tender chicken," took on added meaning in Spanish: "It takes an aroused man to make a chicken affectionate." Even when the language is the same, word usage may differ from country to country. Thus, the British ad line for Electrolux vacuum cleaners—"Nothing sucks like an Electrolux"—would capture few customers in the United States.

Sources: See David A. Ricks, "Perspectives: Translation Blunders in International Business," *Journal of Language for International Business,* 7:2, 1996, pp. 50–55; "But Will It Sell in Tulsa?" *Newsweek,* March 17, 1997, p. 8; Ken Friedenreich, "The Lingua Too Franca," *World Trade,* April 1998, p. 98; Sam Solley, "Developing a Name to Work Worldwide," *Marketing,* December 21, 2000, p. 27; Thomas T. Sermon, "Cutting Corners in Language Risky Business," *Marketing News,* April 23, 2001, p. 9; Lara L. Sowinski, "Ubersetzung, Traduzione, or Traduccion," *World Trade,* February 2002, pp. 48–49; Martin Croft, "Mind Your Language," *Marketing,* June 19, 2003, pp. 35–39; and Mark Lasswell, "Lost in Translation," *Business 2.0,* August 2004, pp. 68–70.

an object of desire, rather than as a way to feel good about yourself, as Diet Coke is positioned in the United States." This "desire positioning" plays off research showing that "Coca-Cola Light is seen in other parts of world as a vibrant brand that exudes a sexy confidence."[31]

Media also need to be adapted internationally because media availability varies from country to country. TV advertising time is very limited in Europe, for instance, ranging from 4 hours a day in France to none in Scandinavian countries. Advertisers must buy time months in advance, and they have little control over airtimes. Magazines also vary in effectiveness. For example, magazines are a major medium in Italy and a minor one in Austria. Newspapers are national in the United Kingdom but are only local in Spain.[32]

Price

Companies also face many problems in setting their international prices. For example, how might Black & Decker price its power tools globally? It could set a uniform price all around the world, but this amount would be too high a price in poor countries and not high enough in rich ones. It could charge what consumers in each country would bear, but this strategy ignores differences in the actual costs from country to country. Finally, the company could use a standard markup of its costs everywhere, but this approach might price Black & Decker out of the market in some countries where costs are high.

To deal with such issues, P&G adapts its pricing to local markets. For example, in Asia it has moved to a tiered pricing model.

> When P&G first entered Asia, it used the approach that had made it so successful in the United States. It developed better products and charged slightly higher prices than competitors. It also charged nearly as much for a box of Tide or bottle of Pantene in Asia as it did in North America. But such high prices limited P&G's appeal in Asian markets, where most consumers earn just a few dollars a day. Two-thirds of China's population earns less than $25 per month. So last year P&G adopted a tiered pricing strategy to help compete against cheaper local brands while also protecting the value of its global brands. It slashed Asian production costs, streamlined distribution channels, and reshaped its product line to create more affordable prices. For example, it introduced a 320-gram bag of Tide Clean White for 23 cents, compared with 33 cents for 350 grams of Tide Triple Action. Clean White doesn't offer such benefits as stain removal and fragrance, and it contains less advanced cleaning enzymes. But it costs less to make and outperforms every other brand at the lower price level. The results of P&G's new tiered pricing

■ International pricing: Twelve European Union countries have adopted the euro as a common currency, creating "pricing transparency" and forcing companies to harmonize their prices throughout Europe.

have been dramatic. Using the same approach for toothpaste, P&G now sells more Crest in China than in the United States.[33]

Regardless of how companies go about pricing their products, their foreign prices probably will be higher than their domestic prices for comparable products. A Gucci handbag may sell for $60 in Italy and $240 in the United States. Why? Gucci faces a *price escalation* problem. It must add the cost of transportation, tariffs, importer margin, wholesaler margin, and retailer margin to its factory price. Depending on these added costs, the product may have to sell for two to five times as much in another country to make the same profit. For example, a pair of Levi's jeans that sells for $30 in the United States typically fetches $63 in Tokyo and $88 in Paris. A computer that sells for $1,000 in New York may cost £1,000 in the United Kingdom. A Ford automobile priced at $20,000 in the United States might sell for more than $80,000 in South Korea.

Another problem involves setting a price for goods that a company ships to its foreign subsidiaries. If the company charges a foreign subsidiary too much, it may end up paying higher tariff duties even while paying lower income taxes in that country. If the company charges its subsidiary too little, it can be charged with *dumping*. Dumping occurs when a company either charges less than its costs or less than it charges in its home market. For example, the U.S. Southern Shrimp Alliance, which represents thousands of small shrimp operations in the southeast United States, recently complained that six countries (China, Thailand, Vietnam, Ecuador, and Brazil) have been dumping excess supplies of farmed shrimp on the U.S. market. The U.S. International Trade Commission agreed and has recommended that the Commerce Department impose duties on shrimp imports from the offending countries.[34] Various governments are always watching for dumping abuses, and they often force companies to set the price charged by other competitors for the same or similar products.

Recent economic and technological forces have had an impact on global pricing. For example, in the European Union, the transition to the euro is reducing the amount of price differentiation. As consumers recognize price differentiation by country, companies are being forced to harmonize prices throughout the countries that have adopted the single currency. Companies and marketers that offer the most unique or necessary products or services will be least affected by such "price transparency."

> For Marie-Claude Lang, a 72-year-old retired Belgian postal worker, the euro is the best thing since bottled water—or French country sausage. Always on the prowl for bargains, Ms. Lang is now stalking the wide aisles of an Auchan hypermarket in Roncq, France, a 15-minute drive from her Wervick home. . . . Ms. Lang has been coming to France every other week for years to stock up on bottled water, milk, and yogurt. But the launch of the euro . . . has opened her eyes to many more products that she now sees cost less across the border. Today she sees that "saucisse de campagne," is cheaper "by about five euro cents," a savings she didn't notice when she had to calculate the difference between Belgian and French francs. At Europe's borders, the euro is turning into the coupon clipper's delight. Sure, price-conscious Europeans have long crossed into foreign territory to find everything from cheaper television sets to bargain bottles of Coca-Cola. But the new transparency is making comparisons a whole lot easier.[35]

The Internet will also make global price differences more obvious. When firms sell their wares over the Internet, customers can to see how much products sell for in different countries. They might even be able to order a given product directly from the company location or dealer offering the lowest price. This will force companies toward more standardized international pricing.

Distribution Channels

Whole-channel view
Designing international channels that take into account all the necessary links in distributing the seller's products to final buyers, including the seller's headquarters organization, channels among nations, and channels within nations.

The international company must take a **whole-channel view** of the problem of distributing products to final consumers. Figure 19.4 shows the three major links between the seller and the final buyer. The first link, the *seller's headquarters organization*, supervises the channels and is part of the channel itself. The second link, *channels between nations*, moves the products to the borders of the foreign nations. The third link, *channels within nations*, moves the

FIGURE 19.4
Whole-channel concept for international marketing

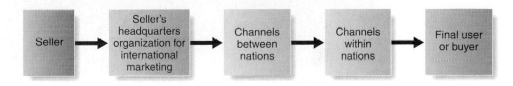

products from their foreign entry point to the final consumers. Some U.S. manufacturers may think their job is done once the product leaves their hands, but they would do well to pay more attention to its handling within foreign countries.

Channels of distribution within countries vary greatly from nation to nation. First, there are the large differences in the *numbers and types of intermediaries* serving each foreign market. For example, a U.S. company marketing in China must operate through a frustrating maze of state-controlled wholesalers and retailers. Chinese distributors often carry competitors' products and frequently refuse to share even basic sales and marketing information with their suppliers. Hustling for sales is an alien concept to Chinese distributors, who are used to selling all they can obtain. Working with or getting around this system sometimes requires much time and investment.

When Coke first entered China, for example, customers bicycled up to bottling plants to get their soft drinks. Many shopkeepers still don't have enough electricity to run soft drink coolers. Now, Coca-Cola has set up direct-distribution channels, investing heavily in refrigerators and trucks, and upgrading wiring so that more retailers can install coolers. The company has also built an army of more than 10,000 sales representatives that makes regular visits on resellers, often on foot or bicycle, to check on stocks and record sales. "Coke and its bottlers have been trying to map every supermarket, restaurant, barbershop, or market stall where a can of soda might be consumed," notes an industry observer. "Those data help Coke get closer to its customers, whether they are in large hypermarkets, Spartan noodle shops, or schools."[36]

Another difference lies in the *size and character of retail units* abroad. Whereas large-scale retail chains dominate the U.S. scene, much retailing in other countries is done by many small, independent retailers. In India, millions of retailers operate tiny shops or sell in open markets. Their markups are high, but the actual price is lowered through haggling. Supermarkets could offer lower prices, but supermarkets are difficult to build and open because of many economic and cultural barriers. Incomes are low, and people prefer to shop daily for small amounts rather than weekly for large amounts. They also lack storage and refrigeration to keep food for several days. Packaging is not well developed because it would add too much to the cost. These factors have kept large-scale retailing from spreading rapidly in developing countries.

Deciding on the Global Marketing Organization

Companies manage their international marketing activities in at least three different ways: Most companies first organize an export department, then create an international division, and finally become a global organization.

■ International distribution: Distribution channels vary greatly from nation to nation, as this picture from the streets of Beijing suggests.

A firm normally gets into international marketing by simply shipping out its goods. If its international sales expand, the company organizes an *export department* with a sales manager and a few assistants. As sales increase, the export department can expand to include various marketing services so that it can actively go after business. If the firm moves into joint ventures or direct investment, the export department will no longer be adequate.

Many companies get involved in several international markets and ventures. A company may export to one country, license to another, have a joint ownership venture in a third, and own a subsidiary in a fourth. Sooner or later it will create *international divisions* or subsidiaries to handle all its international activity.

International divisions are organized in a variety of ways. An international division's corporate staff consists of marketing, manufacturing, research, finance, planning, and personnel specialists. It plans for and provides services to various operating units, which can be organized in one of three ways. They can be *geographical organizations*, with country managers who are responsible for salespeople, sales branches, distributors, and licensees in their respective countries. Or the operating units can be *world product groups*, each responsible for worldwide sales of different product groups. Finally, operating units can be *international subsidiaries*, each responsible for its own sales and profits.

Many firms have passed beyond the international division stage and become truly *global organizations*. They stop thinking of themselves as national marketers who sell abroad and start thinking of themselves as global marketers. The top corporate management and staff plan worldwide manufacturing facilities, marketing policies, financial flows, and logistical systems. The global operating units report directly to the chief executive or executive committee of the organization, not to the head of an international division. Executives are trained in worldwide operations, not just domestic *or* international. The company recruits management from many countries, buys components and supplies where they cost the least, and invests where the expected returns are greatest.

Moving into the twenty-first century, major companies must become more global if they hope to compete. As foreign companies successfully invade their domestic markets, companies must move more aggressively into foreign markets. They will have to change from companies that treat their international operations as secondary, to companies that view the entire world as a single borderless market.

> Reviewing the Concepts <

In the past, U.S. companies paid little attention to international trade. If they could pick up some extra sales through exporting, that was fine. But the big market was at home, and it teemed with opportunities. Companies today can no longer afford to pay attention only to their domestic market, regardless of its size. Many industries are global industries, and firms that operate globally achieve lower costs and higher brand awareness. At the same time, *global marketing* is risky because of variable exchange rates, unstable governments, protectionist tariffs and trade barriers, and several other factors. Given the potential gains and risks of international marketing, companies need a systematic way to make their global marketing decisions.

1. Discuss how the international trade system, economic, political-legal, and cultural environments affect a company's international marketing decisions.

A company must understand the *global marketing environment*, especially the international trade system. It must assess each foreign market's *economic*, *political-legal*, and *cultural characteristics*. The company must then decide whether it wants to go abroad and consider the potential risks and benefits. It must decide on the volume of international sales it wants, how many countries it wants to market in, and which specific markets it wants to enter. This decision calls for weighing the probable rate of return on investment against the level of risk.

2. Describe three key approaches to entering international markets.

The company must decide how to enter each chosen market—whether through *exporting*, *joint venturing*, or *direct investment*. Many companies start as exporters, move to joint ventures, and finally make

a direct investment in foreign markets. In *exporting*, the company enters a foreign market by sending and selling products through international marketing intermediaries (indirect exporting) or the company's own department, branch, or sales representative or agents (direct exporting). When establishing a *joint venture*, a company enters foreign markets by joining with foreign companies to produce or market a product or service. In *licensing*, the company enters a foreign market by contracting with a licensee in the foreign market, offering the right to use a manufacturing process, trademark, patent, trade secret, or other item of value for a fee or royalty.

3. Explain how companies adapt their marketing mixes for international markets.

Companies must also decide how much their products, promotion, price, and channels should be adapted for each foreign market. At one extreme, global companies use a *standardized marketing mix* worldwide. Others use an *adapted marketing mix*, in which they adjust the marketing mix to each target market, bearing more costs but hoping for a larger market share and return.

4. Identify the three major forms of international marketing organization.

The company must develop an effective organization for international marketing. Most firms start with an *export department* and graduate to an *international division*. A few become *global organizations*, with worldwide marketing planned and managed by the top officers of the company. Global organizations view the entire world as a single, borderless market.

> Reviewing the Key Terms <

Adapted marketing mix 604
Communication adaptation 608
Contract manufacturing 602
Countertrade 595
Direct investment 604
Economic community 592

Embargo 590
Exchange controls 590
Exporting 601
Global firm 590
Joint ownership 603
Joint venturing 602

Licensing 602
Management contracting 602
Nontariff trade barriers 590
Product adaptation 606
Product invention 607
Quota 590

Standardized marketing mix 604
Straight product extension 605
Tariff 590
Whole-channel view 611

> Discussing the Concepts <

1. Explain how the addition of the World Trade Organization as a functioning body has changed the nature of international commerce.

2. The NAFTA and EU regional free trade agreements have benefited both North America's and Europe's trading partners. But not all affected groups support these trading pacts. What are some of the concerns raised by groups opposed to such regional trade arrangements? What is your position—are you for, against, or uncertain?

3. Discuss the advantages and disadvantages of direct investment in a foreign market. Name two foreign markets where a household appliance manufacturer would be interested in investing, and two foreign markets where it would have no interest in investing. Support your answers.

4. Assume your boss has asked you for your opinion on how your company should enter the Japanese, South Korean, and Vietnamese markets with a new line of women's athletic shoes. Would you recommend entering with a standardized marketing mix or an adapted marketing mix? Explain.

5. Figure 19.4 shows a "whole-channel view" of international distribution. Comment on why a company would or would not require the full range of international channel intermediaries discussed in the chapter?

6. The chapter discusses three forms of international marketing organizations. Identify the form for each of the companies listed below:

   ■ Bank of America
   ■ General Motors
   ■ Halliburton
   ■ Motorola
   ■ Raytheon
   ■ Starbucks
   ■ Time-Life
   ■ Weyerhaeuser

> Applying the Concepts <

1. The United States has a trade restriction on Cuba. Is this restriction a tariff, quota, or embargo? To what extent does this trade restriction allow U.S. businesses to export their products to Cuba?

2. Assess the joint-venture opportunities a software manufacturer would have available if it were looking to market to European Union countries?

3. Form a small group and suppose that you are members of BlockBuster's international division, headquartered in Dallas, TX. Chris Wyatt, president of the international division, wants your group to prepare a memo outlining the potential cultural, political, and economic issues facing the company if it expands directly into Lebanon? (Note: You already have a franchise dealer in Israel.)

> Focus on Technology <

Companies that conduct business internationally face many language skill requirements. Speaking the language of the host country is one requirement, but there are others. For example, how should the company go about converting its Web site and marketing literature? It's time to talk to Systran Language Translation Technologies or a similar language technology company. For a sample of what Systran does, visit www.systransoft.com/ and try the "free" translation tools on the homepage. Now visit http://french.about.com/library/bl-onlinetranslators.htm and read the article on machine translation. When you are finished with the demo and the article, respond to the following questions:

1. What are the advantages of language translation technologies like Systran's?

2. What problems might you encounter with such language translation technologies?

3. Given these advantages and problems, what can a company do to increase the chances of successfully translating its Web sites and marketing literature?

> Focus on Ethics <

Is it a gift or a bribe? U.S. businesses operating internationally often face this question. In addition to the Fair Practices Corruption Act (FPCA) of 1977 and the International Anti-Bribery and Fair Competition Act of 1998, there are a number of international laws designed to fight corruption and bribery in the global business community. In some cases, it's clear whether or not an exchange of money or goods is a gift or a bribe. In other cases, it's not at all clear. For example, consider American Rice case in which the defendants won a judgment based on the argument that the payments made to Haitian customs officials were within the FPCA guidelines because they were made to "assist in retaining or obtaining business." This judgment has since been reversed by the 5th Circuit Court of Appeals, and American Rice officials were scheduled for trial in Houston in late 2004. Visit www.sec.gov/litigation/complaints/comp17651.htm, read the original complaint filed by the SEC, and respond to the following questions.

1. What do you think about this case?

2. Do you feel that companies should be allowed to bribe officials to gain business if it is a common practice in the country or region?

3. What should be done to the companies and executives convicted of bribery? Fines? Jail?

Sources: See www.oecd.org/dataoecd/50/33/1827022.pdf.

Video Case

Nivea

In 1911, Nivea launched its first line of body care products, capitalizing on an innovation that created a new generation of skin crème. Today Nivea products are well known and widely used in more than 150 countries around the world. In each of those countries, the characteristic Nivea blue signifies a consistent promise—high quality, gentle body care products. Nivea's strong, consistent brand image is one of the company's most valuable assets.

Despite Nivea's worldwide presence, a quick survey reveals that, regardless of where they live, Nivea's customers believe that the company's products are locally manufactured and marketed. Why? Because Nivea carefully adjusts the marketing mix to cater to local cultures and preferences. This globally consistent but locally focused marketing cam-

paign has produced phenomenal results. To date, the company has sold more than 11 billion tins of the traditional Nivea Crème.

After viewing the video featuring Nivea, answer the following questions about the company and the global marketplace.

1. Does Nivea offer a standardized marketing mix or an adapted marketing mix?

2. Visit Nivea's Website, www.nivea.com, and tour the sites for several different countries. How does Nivea market its products differently in different countries? How does the company maintain the consistency of its brand?

Company Case

Wal-Mart Takes on the World

Wal-Mart is the largest retailer in the world. It has more than 4,900 stores, employs 1.5 million people, and has annual sales of $256 billion. The next largest global retailer, Carrefour (a French discount retailer), has sales of $79.7 billion, and Wal-Mart's nearest U.S. competitor in the general merchandise category, Target, has only $48.2 billion in sales. More than 60 percent of Wal-Mart's merchandise comes from China. If Wal-Mart were a country, it would be China's eighth largest trading partner, ahead of Russia and Great Britain.

While the bulk of Wal-Mart's sales come from the United States, its international division is growing rapidly and now accounts for more than 20 percent of sales. In order to appeal to consumers of differing levels of affluence and sophistication in various countries, one might expect that Wal-Mart would have to change its strategy. But that is not the case. The giant retailer's strategy is the same everywhere in the world—Everyday Low Prices (EDLP) and Everyday Low Costs (EDLC).

To achieve lower costs, Wal-Mart engages in its own version of global sourcing. At Wal-Mart, this isn't just a buying function. Instead, managers in the global sourcing unit focus on categories of goods or items where there is an opportunity to improve quality, lower price, or gain efficiencies. They first identify basic products that people use all over the world and then look for an opportunity to improve their supply. Then, they work with producers to

improve quality or lower price. Finally, the improved product is made available to all managers around the world. It's important that the managers make the purchase decisions based on their local expertise.

Fewer suppliers means less paperwork and fewer problems. It also engenders closer relationships between Wal-Mart and its suppliers. For suppliers, this relationship is especially important because they may need only to sell to Wal-Mart to gain access to the global marketplace. Selling to one customer means lower distribution, selling, and promotional expenses—just part of the EDLP and EDLC strategy.

WAL-MART'S INTERNATIONAL GROWTH

Wal-Mart operates in North and South America, Europe, and Asia and has used multiple entry strategies in various countries.

North and South America

Canada: Wal-Mart's first international venture was Canada—a market similar to the United States. Wal-Mart bought 122 Canadian Woolco stores, and by 2000 it had more than 200 Canadian stores.

Mexico: In Mexico, Wal-Mart used an acquisition strategy (buying Suburbia stores that sell clothing to young women, VIPS restaurants, Superama supermarkets, and 62 percent of Cifra, Mexico's largest retailer). It also established it's own Wal-Mart and Sam's Clubs. Mexico

(box continues)

has been a big success for Wal-Mart, largely because of Cifra's thorough understanding of the Mexican consumer. By 2004, Wal-Mart had nearly 1,000 outlets of some kind in Mexico and sales of more than $10.7 billion with a 4.5 percent net margin—better than the 3.5 percent overall Wal-Mart margin.

Puerto Rico: This is another big success for Wal-Mart. It established its own stores and bought the Supermercados Amigo—Puerto-Rico's second largest grocery retailer.

Brazil and Argentina: Wal-Mart entered these countries in the mid-1990s with disappointing results. The economic situation in both countries was miserable—inflation spiraling out of control, devaluation of currencies, and defaults on loans, plus a political maelstrom in which Argentina's presidency seemed to be a revolving door.

There were also competitive woes. Carrefour was well entrenched in both markets, having entered Brazil in 1975 and Argentina in 1982. Upon Wal-Mart's entry, Carrefour started a price war and located hypermarkets next to Wal-Mart stores. As a result, Carrefour is still the largest retailer in both countries. In retaliation, Wal-Mart opened smaller format stores called "Todo Dia," which sell mostly groceries and a little general merchandise. These smaller stores give Wal-Mart a presence in crowded Brazilian neighborhoods and enable it to sell to lower income consumers who buy daily.

In early 2004, Wal-Mart bolstered its market share from sixth to third by buying the 118-unit Bompreco supermarket chain. Increased market share will generate lower costs and lower prices and make Wal-Mart more competitive with Carrefour and with Companhania Brasiliera de Distribuicao (CBD), the largest grocery retailer in Brazil. Wal-Mart has 143 stores in these two countries, including 13 supercenters and 10 Sam's Clubs.

Europe

Germany: In 1998, Wal-Mart bought the 21-unit Wertkauf chain in Germany, and a year later it purchased the 74 unit Interspar hypermarkets. As the third largest retail market in the world (behind the United States and Japan), Germany initially looked very attractive. But from the start, it has been a nightmare. First, there were real estate issues: strict zoning laws, scarcity of land, and high real estate prices. Then there were well-entrenched unions, which were unlikely to allow their members to gather in the morning to respond to Wal-Mart's "Give me a W . . . Give me an A . . ." rallying cheer. In addition, competition in Germany was much greater—5 of the top world's top 25 global retailers are German, with two of them in the top 10. Finally, German consumers are among the most demanding in the world. They are extremely quality conscious and are less price conscious. On top of all that, Wal-Mart had purchased two chains with declining sales, poor locations, and dirty stores.

Wal-Mart executives admit in hindsight that they moved too fast in Germany and failed to take advantage of the managerial expertise in their acquisitions. Although Wal-Mart has not given up on Germany, it has had to close stores there because of poor performance.

United Kingdom: While Wal-Mart stuck out in Germany, it scored a homerun when it purchased the U.K's ASDA chain. These U.K. outlets are the biggest contributor to the profits of Wal-Mart's International Division. Why? ASDA had for years modeled itself on the Wal-Mart format—right down to the rah-rah philosophy and low prices. It was not a struggling chain; instead it is a top-notch retailer that "knows food retailing" and which shares that knowledge throughout Wal-Mart's other global operations. With Wal-Mart's backing, ASDA cut prices (undercutting rivals), added general merchandise, and took advantage of Wal-Mart's inventory prowess. ASDA has been so successful that its sales per square foot go as high as $2,000, four times higher than at Sam's Club. In Christmas 2003, nine of the ten top-selling Wal-Mart stores worldwide were in the U.K. This does not mean a lack of competition; two other U.K. retailers, Tesco and Sainsbury's, are also in the top 25 global retailers.

Asia

Hong Kong, Thailand and Indonesia: Wal-Mart's first stop in Southeast Asia was Hong Kong, where it entered a joint venture with Ek Chor Distribution System Co. Ltd. to establish Value Clubs. Because Ek Chor is actually owned by C. P. Pokphand of Bangkok, Wal-Mart was able to locate in Thailand and then Indonesia.

Peoples Republic of China: China is the largest market in the world, with more than 1.3 billion people and 170 cities with populations above 1 million. In 2000, Wal-Mart opened its first store there, and by April 2004, it had 35 stores with plans to open 7 more during the year. Its has 30 stores in shopping centers, three Sam's Clubs, and two community stores. Wal-Mart's eventual goal in China is 500 stores.

Given its size, China would appear to be the one other country in the world that could sustain a scale similar to that of the U.S. Wal-Mart operation, but it will take awhile to develop. Like Germany, there is a shortage of land and stores tend to be smaller. One of the first Wal-Mart's was in a subway station, located to cater to busy commuters.

But the biggest problem has been with the government. In an effort to limit competition, the government designated territories within which each retailer must locate, and Wal-Mart was confined mostly to southern China. By 2004, it had opened stores in 17 Chinese cities, but not in Shanghai, the fastest-growing, most western, highest income market in China. However, the government is starting to relax these restrictions, and growth in China should accelerate. To prepare for this growth, Wal-Mart China, Ltd. and CITIC Ltd. (China International Trust and Investment Company) founded the Wal-Mart South China Department Store Co., Ltd. in October 2003.

Carrefour is also in China and it has a number of advantages—more stores, all hypermarkets—and a greater presence in not only China, but also Korea. But Wal-Mart also has advantages. Its multiple formats offer greater expansion flexibility; it has a strong partner in CITIC; its stores are more exciting and entertaining; it has superior global sourcing; and it is more aggressive on price.

Japan: Wal-Mart entered Japan in 2002 by buying a stake in the Seiyu Ltd. chain, Japan's fifth largest supermarket chain. Although Seiyu had many stores (400) with good locations, the stores were shabby and the company had declining sales. Anxious not to repeat the German mistake in a land of demanding consumers, Wal-Mart is moving slowly to remodel Seiyu's stores. Unfortunately, this gives Japanese retailers such as Aeon time to get a jump on Wal-Mart.

There are many of the same problems in Japan as in China and Germany, such as pricey real estate and few locations. Until recently, laws restricted store size and opening hours in an effort to protect smaller Japanese retailers, who make up 58 percent of the Japanese retailing system. In addition, there are complicated and sometimes convoluted distribution systems in which retailers go through layers of middlemen with long-standing relationships instead of buying directly from suppliers. As a result, goods may pass through three or more hands before reaching a retailer.

And then there are the Japanese consumers, not only considered to be among the world's quirkiest but also among the most demanding. They want fresher foods, the most orderly and clean stores, short checkout lines, and an abundance of clerks. And they don't understand the EDLP strategy. Trained by Japanese retailers in the past to hunt through newspapers for discounts, consumers still expect discounts and they want to find these in newspaper ads, which have to be in color. Shoppers also don't understand jargon such as "rollback," so Wal-Mart has to translate terms that it considers standard in the rest of the world. Worse, Japanese consumers think very low prices indicate poor quality. Thus, a strategy of ever-lower prices could hurt sales.

In spite of Wal-Mart's elaborate planning, results in Japan have been disappointing. Seiyu has lost money and blames the sluggish economy and unusual weather—not to mention the competition.

WHAT'S NEXT?

The answer appears to be Russia. Although the Russia of the 1990s strongly resembled Argentina and Brazil with spiraling inflation, an economy in shambles, devaluation of the ruble, defaults on foreign debt, and an unstable political and governmental system, Vladimir Putin's government has brought stability to the Russian marketplace and economic growth of roughly 6 percent a year. Russia is a large market of 146 million consumers, many of whom are anxious to acquire western goods. The Russian grocery market is estimated at $89 billion and direct foreign investment in Russia is expected to be $8 billion in 2004 alone. Companies such as Italy's Enel SpA, Germany's Metro AG, and France's Auchan chain are already in Russia, along with the Swedish retailer IKEA.

Rumors have circulated since 2002 that Wal-Mart would enter the Russian market. One rumor involved an offer to purchase 75 percent of Promyshlenno-Finansovaya Kompaniya BIN, a 31-store chain. Another rumor hinted at an agreement with Metro AG in which Metro would use its Russian contacts to build 20 hypermarkets in Moscow costing $500 million, which Wal-Mart would then buy. In early 2004, "Russian sources" informed a London-based publication that Wal-Mart had a team researching the market that would shortly make a presentation to the Wal-Mart board on an entry strategy.

While there is nothing definite about Russia, we can be sure that Wal-Mart has plenty of moves up its sleeve for the global market in the future. Stay tuned!

Questions for Discussion

1. In what countries has Wal-Mart done well? Can you identify any common consumer, market, retailer traits, or entry strategies across these countries that might account for Wal-Mart's success?

2. In what countries has Wal-Mart done poorly? Can you identify any common consumer, market, retailer traits, or entry strategies across these countries that might account for Wal-Mart's lack of success?

3. In your opinion, will Wal-Mart be successful in Japan? Why or why not?

4. In your opinion, should Wal-Mart enter the Russian market? If so, how should it go about this?

5. Beyond Russia, What countries do you think Wal-Mart should consider entering? What factors are important in making this decision? Be prepared to defend the countries that you chose.

Sources: Laura Heller, "Latin Market Never Looked So Bueno," *DSN Retailing Today,* June 10, 2002, p. 125; Laura Heller, "Southern Hemisphere Woes Persist," *DSN Retailing Today,* June 10, 2002, p. 126; "Germany: Wal-Mart Closings," *The New York Times,* July 11, 2002, p. 1; Mike Troy, "Foothold in the Orient Keeps Growing," *DSN Retailing Today,* June 10, 2002, p. 121; Andrea Welsh and Ann Zimmerman, "Wal-Mart Snaps Up Brazilian Chain," *Wall Street Journal,* March 2, 2004, p. B3; "Wal-Mart to Take 34 Pct. Stake in Japan's Seiyu, *Jiji Press English News,* December 12, 2002, p. 1; Tony Lisanti, "Wal-Mart Has Edge in China Battle," *DSN Retailing Today,* October 28, 2002, p. 13; "Wal-Mart to Take on Russia with German Help," *Info-Product Research (Middle East),* November 2002, p. 1; and information accessed at www.walmartstores.com, December 2004.

> **After studying this chapter, you should be able to**

1. identify the major social criticisms of marketing
2. define *consumerism* and *environmentalism* and explain how they affect marketing strategies
3. describe the principles of socially responsible marketing
4. explain the role of ethics in marketing

CHAPTER

20

Marketing Ethics and Social Responsibility

Previewing the Concepts

In this final chapter, we'll focus on marketing as a social institution. First, we'll look at some common criticisms of marketing as it impacts individual consumers, other businesses, and society as a whole. Then, we'll examine consumerism, environmentalism, and other citizen and public actions to keep marketing in check. Finally, we'll see how companies themselves can benefit from proactively pursuing socially responsible and ethical practices. You'll see that social responsibility and ethical actions are more than just the right thing to do; they're also good for business.

Before moving on, let's visit the concept of social responsibility in business. Over the past several years, Nike has been a lightning rod for social responsibility criticisms. Critics have accused Nike of putting profits ahead of the interests of consumers and the broader public, both at home and abroad. You've probably read headlines alleging foreign "sweatshops" abuses and possible exploitation of inner-city consumers. Are these criticisms justified? Read on.

If you say "Nike" and "corporate social responsibility" in the same breath, most consumers will bring up the negatives. Many have read the headlines in recent years: "Nike Axes 'Sweatshop' after BBC Investigation," "Nike Accused of Exploiting Inner-City Youths with High-Priced Sneakers," or "Just Do It without Nike." However, while criticisms of Nike have grabbed the headlines, look a little deeper. You might be surprised to learn about all the socially responsible things that Nike does to make this world a better place.

Despite its success at selling shoes—or perhaps *because* of this success—Nike has been heavily criticized. As the headlines suggest, the company has been accused of everything from running sweatshops, using child labor, and exploiting low-income consumers to degrading the environment. The rights and wrongs concerning these issues are often hard to discern.

Consider the Nike "sweatshop" charges. Like many other companies these days, to be more cost and price competitive, Nike outsources production to contractors in low-wage countries, such as China, Vietnam, Thailand,

Indonesia, the Philippines, and Pakistan. The problem is that, through the eyes of affluent Westerners, workplace conditions in many third-world factories are truly appalling. These factories have long hours, unsafe working conditions, child labor, and substandard pay for people desperate to have any job at all.

As Nike has outsourced more manufacturing to foreign subcontractors, reports of such abusive conditions have surfaced. The issue became very public in 1996, when a *New York Times* editorial accused Nike of running sweatshops and using child labor. Other critics quickly joined in, painting a picture of a greedy Nike, reaping profits at the expense of low-paid foreign laborers, many of them children, who were forced to work in the dismal conditions in suppliers' factories.

Nike responded that, years earlier, it had created a Code of Conduct, which demanded more socially responsible labor practices by its contractors. What's more, according to Nike CEO Phil Knight, Nike was actually improving the working conditions in low-wage countries. "Nike has paid, on average, double the minimum wage as defined in countries where its products are produced under contract," he claimed. Besides, Nike argued, who are we to decide what rules are proper in other countries—to define who is a child, who has a right to work, and under what conditions? Some developing countries actually resent the paternalistic regulations of a multinational corporation.

Still, Nike took the charges seriously and accepted some of the criticisms as legitimate. It commissioned Andrew Young, a civil rights leader and former UN ambassador, to visit Nike factories abroad. Although Young suggested there was room for improvement, he found none of the alleged extreme examples of abuse. Despite Nike's responses, the criticisms of its foreign manufacturing practices continued.

Nike has also received criticism at home. For example, it has been accused of wrongly targeting its most expensive shoes to low-income families, making the shoes an expensive status symbol for poor urban street kids. Critics point to stories of youths gunned down in inner-city neighborhoods for a pair of $100 Nike sneakers. Nike isn't just selling utilitarian footwear, they claim. It's selling a hip athletic image created by a big-budget marketing campaign. The high price becomes the cost of membership in an artificial, "Just Do It" culture inhabited by the likes of Michael Jordan and LeBron James.

Although such criticisms have received most of the attention, a second look shows that Nike works hard at being a socially responsible global citizen. Click on the "Responsibility" tab at the company's Web site (www.nikebiz.com), and you'll learn that Nike pursues an active agenda of good works. "Our vision is to be an innovative and inspirational global citizen in a world where companies participate," says Nike. "As a company and as individuals, we ardently contribute to the communities where we live, work, and play throughout the world." Such words are cheap, but Nike backs this vision with actions.

Nike and the Nike Foundation contributed more than $30 million in cash and products last year to programs that encourage youth to participate in sports and that address challenges of globalization. The company's goal is to give 3 percent of annual pretax earnings to charities, nonprofit organizations, and community partners around the world. Here are just a few of the good things Nike is doing:

The NikeGO program works closely with Boys & Girls Clubs of America to combat obesity, diabetes, and eating disorders among American youth resulting from poor diet, inactivity, and lack of safe facilities. The program funds kid-designed programs that increase club member activity—programs that

get kids to "just Go!" The NikeGO Fund supports courts and facilities around the country. For example, it recently provided funds to refurbish every basketball court found in Portland's 10,000 acres of public parkland—new surfaces, rebuilt backboards, fresh nets, and all.

Nike's Jordan Fundamentals Grant Program awards grants to teachers or professionals who design innovative learning experiences for economically disadvantaged students in grades 6 to 12. Nike also supports Self Enhancement, Inc. (SEI), which works with schools and families to develop after-school programs in education, recreation, and the arts to help inner-city youth in Portland (Nike's home town) to realize their full potential.

Nike supports the Wings of America youth development program, which works with American Indian youth across the United States and Canada. The program uses running as a vehicle for leadership, self-esteem, wellness, and cultural pride among youths from 5 to 14 years of age.

Throughout the world, Nike works with governments, local communities, nongovernment organizations, and sports associations to actively promote kids' participation in sports through organized programs and better sports facilities. For example, Nike recently joined with its factory partners in China to donate a new, full-sized Nike Football Park located 15 minutes from Tiananmen Square. The facility is available to community soccer enthusiasts daily, free of charge. Nike also worked with the Shanghai Education Bureau to provide youth with safe places to play after school and on weekends.

Nike also donates money for education, community development, and small business loans in the countries in which it operates. For example, Nike set up the Nike Village in Thailand, which combines progressive manufacturing with community development. This program encourages Nike contractors to set up satellite production facilities in rural areas to halt the migration into overcrowded Bangkok. The Nike Village hosts a community center, micro-loan programs, ecology and health education, and a women's advocacy group that provides business education and empowerment training.

Regarding its manufacturing practices, Nike has pledged to "make responsible sourcing a business reality that enhances workers lives." For example, Nike's Code of Conduct is now available in 18 languages. It spells out Nike's position on child labor, forced labor, compensation, benefits, work hours, environment, safety, and health. Contractors must post the code where workers can read it and certify that they adhere to it. Today, Nike has 85 employees located in countries where Nike products are manufactured who visit suppliers' factories on a daily basis.

Nike is also committed to sustainable environmental practices. "Our [environmental] targets for products wearing the Nike name are simple and straightforward," claims Nike: "zero toxic substances, zero waste, and 100 percent recoverable product." For example, it has developed environmentally responsible products such as PVC-free footware and a line of 100 percent organic cotton apparel. Nike's Reuse-A-Shoe program collects old shoes of any brand—some 2 million pairs a year—then grinds them up and gives them new life as athletic surfaces or in other Nike products. Through its Air to Earth Program, Nike works with environmental organizations to educate students in grades 4 to 9 about conservation, reuse, and recycling.

Like most global companies, Nike isn't perfect when it comes to matters of social responsibility. But many marketing experts think that the company's corporate heart is now in the right place. "There's an argument to be made that [Nike's good deeds] do end up selling shoes," says one observer. But "what I've liked about Nike is that one of their maxims has always been 'Do the right thing.'"

"We made some mistakes," says CEO Knight. But the mistakes were not for a lack of trying to do what's right. Issues of social responsibility are seldom clear cut. Still, they are very, very important. In Knight's words:

> "As a citizen of the world, Nike must Do the Right Thing. I know what makes for good performance when I see it on the running track. I know it when I read quarterly results from the finance department. I have to admit, though, I'm not sure how we measure good performance in corporate responsibility. I'm not convinced anybody [knows how]. Why not? Because there are no standards, no agreed-on definitions. . . . Until [we have such standards], we have to figure it out for ourselves. [No matter what the standards, however,] the performance of Nike and every other global company in the 21st century will be measured as much by our impact on quality of life as it is by revenue growth and profit margins."[1]

Responsible marketers discover what consumers want and respond with marketing offers that create value for buyers in order to capture value in return. The *marketing concept* is a philosophy of customer value and mutual gain. Its practice leads the economy by an invisible hand to satisfy the many and changing needs of millions of consumers.

Not all marketers follow the marketing concept, however. In fact, some companies use questionable marketing practices, and some marketing actions that seem innocent in themselves strongly affect the larger society. Consider the sale of cigarettes. On the face of it, companies should be free to sell cigarettes and smokers should be free to buy them. But this private transaction involves larger questions of public policy. For example, the smokers are harming their health and may be shortening their own lives. Smoking places a financial burden on the smoker's family and on society at large. Other people around smokers may suffer discomfort and harm from secondhand smoke. Finally, marketing cigarettes to adults might also influence young people to begin smoking. Thus, the marketing of tobacco products has sparked substantial debate and negotiation in recent years.[2]

This chapter examines the social effects of private marketing practices. We examine several questions: What are the most frequent social criticisms of marketing? What steps have private citizens taken to curb marketing ills? What steps have legislators and government agencies taken to curb marketing ills? What steps have enlightened companies taken to carry out socially responsible and ethical marketing?

AQUÍ

Social Criticisms of Marketing

Marketing receives much criticism. Some of this criticism is justified; much is not. Social critics claim that certain marketing practices hurt individual consumers, society as a whole, and other business firms.

Marketing's Impact on Individual Consumers

Consumers have many concerns about how well the American marketing system serves their interests. Surveys usually show that consumers hold mixed or even slightly unfavorable attitudes toward marketing practices. Consumers, consumer advocates, government agencies, and other critics have accused marketing of harming consumers through high prices, deceptive practices, high-pressure selling, shoddy or unsafe products, planned obsolescence, and poor service to disadvantaged consumers.

High Prices

Many critics charge that the American marketing system causes prices to be higher than they would be under more "sensible" systems. They point to three factors—*high costs of distribution*, *high advertising and promotion costs*, and *excessive markups*.

HIGH COSTS OF DISTRIBUTION A long-standing charge is that greedy intermediaries mark up prices beyond the value of their services. Critics charge that there are too many intermediaries, that intermediaries are inefficient, or that they provide unnecessary or duplicate services. As a result, distribution costs too much, and consumers pay for these excessive costs in the form of higher prices.

How do resellers answer these charges? They argue that intermediaries do work that would otherwise have to be done by manufacturers or consumers. Markups reflect services that consumers themselves want—more convenience, larger stores and assortments, more service, longer store hours, return privileges, and others. In fact, they argue, retail competition is so intense that margins are actually quite low. For example, after taxes, supermarket chains are typically left with barely 1 percent profit on their sales. If some resellers try to charge too much relative to the value they add, other resellers will step in with lower prices. Low-price stores such as Wal-Mart, Best Buy, and other discounters pressure their competitors to operate efficiently and keep their prices down.

HIGH ADVERTISING AND PROMOTION COSTS Modern marketing is also accused of pushing up prices to finance heavy advertising and sales promotion. For example, a dozen tablets of a heavily promoted brand of pain reliever sell for the same price as 100 tablets of less promoted brands. Differentiated products—cosmetics, detergents, toiletries—include promotion and packaging costs that can amount to 40 percent or more of the manufacturer's price to the retailer. Critics charge that much of the packaging and promotion adds only psychological value to the product rather than functional value.

Marketers respond that advertising does add to product costs. But it also adds value by informing potential buyers of the availability and merits of a brand. Brand name products may cost more, but branding gives buyers assurances of consistent quality. Moreover, consumers can usually buy functional versions of products at lower prices. However, they *want* and are willing to pay more for products that also provide psychological benefits—that make them feel wealthy, attractive, or special. Also, heavy advertising and promotion may be necessary for a firm to match competitors' efforts—the business would lose "share of mind" if it did not match competitive spending. At the same time, companies are cost-conscious about promotion and try to spend their money wisely.

■ A heavily promoted brand of aspirin sells for much more than a virtually identical non-branded or store-branded product. Critics charge that promotion adds only psychological value to the product rather than functional value.

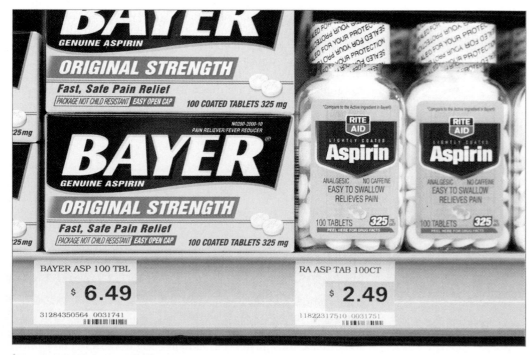

EXCESSIVE MARKUPS Critics also charge that some companies mark up goods excessively. They point to the drug industry, where a pill costing 5 cents to make may cost the consumer $2 to buy. They point to the pricing tactics of funeral homes that prey on the confused emotions of bereaved relatives and to the high charges for auto repair and other services.

Marketers respond that most businesses try to deal fairly with consumers because they want to build customer relationships and repeat business. Most consumer abuses are unintentional. When shady marketers do take advantage of consumers, they should be reported to Better Business Bureaus and to state and federal agencies. Marketers also respond that consumers often don't understand the reasons for high markups. For example, pharmaceutical markups must cover the costs of purchasing, promoting, and distributing existing medicines plus the high research and development costs of formulating and testing new medicines.

Deceptive Practices

Marketers are sometimes accused of deceptive practices that lead consumers to believe they will get more value than they actually do. Deceptive practices fall into three groups: pricing, promotion, and packaging. *Deceptive pricing* includes practices such as falsely advertising "factory" or "wholesale" prices or a large price reduction from a phony high retail list price. *Deceptive promotion* includes practices such as misrepresenting the product's features or performance or luring the customers to the store for a bargain that is out of stock. *Deceptive packaging* includes exaggerating package contents through subtle design, using misleading labeling, or describing size in misleading terms.

To be sure, questionable marketing practices do occur. For example, at one time or another, we've all gotten an envelope in the mail screaming something like "You have won $10,000,000!" Or a pop-up Web screen promises free goods or discounted prices. In recent years, sweepstakes companies have come under the gun for their deceptive communication practices. Sweepstakes promoter Publishers Clearing House recently paid heavily to settle claims that its high-pressure tactics had misled consumers into believing that they had won prizes when they hadn't. The Wisconsin Attorney General asserted that "there are older consumers who send [sweepstakes companies] checks and money orders on a weekly basis with a note that says they were very upset that the prize patrol did not come."[3]

Deceptive practices have led to legislation and other consumer protection actions. For example, in 1938 Congress reacted to such blatant deceptions as Fleischmann's Yeast's claim to straighten crooked teeth by enacting the Wheeler-Lea Act giving the Federal Trade Commission (FTC) power to regulate "unfair or deceptive acts or practices." The FTC has

■ Questionable marketing practices: Sweepstakes promoter Publishers Clearing House recently paid heavily to settle claims that its high-pressure tactics had misled consumers into believing that they had won prizes which they hadn't.

published several guidelines listing deceptive practices. Despite new regulations, some critics argue that deceptive claims are still the norm.

The toughest problem is defining what is "deceptive." For instance, an advertiser's claim that its powerful laundry detergent "makes your washing machine 10 feet tall," showing a surprised homemaker watching her appliance burst through her laundry room ceiling, isn't intended to be taken literally. Instead, the advertiser might claim, it is "puffery"— innocent exaggeration for effect. One noted marketing thinker, Theodore Levitt, once claimed that advertising puffery and alluring imagery are bound to occur—and that they may even be desirable: "There is hardly a company that would not go down in ruin if it refused to provide fluff, because nobody will buy pure functionality. . . . Worse, it denies . . . people's honest needs and values. Without distortion, embellishment, and elaboration, life would be drab, dull, anguished, and at its existential worst."[4]

However, others claim that puffery and alluring imagery can harm consumers in subtle ways, and that consumers must be protected through education:

The real danger to the public . . . comes not from outright lies—in most cases facts can ultimately be proven and mistakes corrected. But . . . advertising uses [the power of images and] emotional appeals to shift the viewer's focus away from facts. Viewers who do not take the trouble to distinguish between provable claims and pleasant but meaningless word play end up buying "the sizzle, not the steak" and often paying high. The best defense against misleading ads . . . is not tighter controls on [advertisers], but more education and more critical judgment among . . . consumers. Just as we train children to be wary of strangers offering candy, to count change at a store, and to kick the tires before buying a used car, we must make the effort to step back and judge the value of . . . advertisements, and then master the skills required to separate spin from substance.[5]

Marketers argue that most companies avoid deceptive practices because such practices harm their business in the long run. Profitable customer relationships are built upon a foundation of value and trust. If consumers do not get what they expect, they will switch to more reliable products. In addition, consumers usually protect themselves from deception. Most consumers recognize a marketer's selling intent and are careful when they buy, sometimes to the point of not believing completely true product claims.

High-Pressure Selling

Salespeople are sometimes accused of high-pressure selling that persuades people to buy goods they had no thought of buying. It is often said that insurance, real estate, and cars are *sold*, not *bought*. Salespeople are trained to deliver smooth, canned talks to entice purchase. They sell hard because sales contests promise big prizes to those who sell the most.

Marketers know that buyers often can be talked into buying unwanted or unneeded things. Laws require door-to-door and telephone salespeople to announce that they are selling a product. Buyers also have a "3-day cooling-off period" in which they can cancel a contract after rethinking it. In addition, consumers can complain to Better Business Bureaus or to state consumer protection agencies when they feel that undue selling pressure has been applied.

But in most cases, marketers have little to gain from high-pressure selling. Such tactics may work in one-time selling situations for short-term gain. However, most selling involves building long-term relationships with valued customers. High-pressure or deceptive selling can do serious damage to such relationships. For example, imagine a Procter & Gamble account manager trying to pressure a Wal-Mart buyer, or an IBM salesperson trying to browbeat a General Electric information technology manager. It simply wouldn't work.

Shoddy or Unsafe Products

Another criticism is that products lack the needed quality. One complaint is that many products are not made well and services not performed well. A second complaint is that many products deliver little benefit, or that they might even be harmful. For example, many critics have pointed out the dangers of today's fat-laden fast food. In fact, McDonald's recently faced a class-action lawsuit charging that its fare has contributed to a nationwide obesity epidemic:

[Three years ago,] the parody newspaper *The Onion* ran a joke article under the headline "Hershey's Ordered to Pay Obese Americans $135 Billion." The hypothesized class-action lawsuit said that Hershey "knowingly and willfully" marketed to

■ Responding to consumer concerns about today's fat-laden fast food, McDonald's cut the "super size" option from its menu and introduced healthier fare, such as its Go Active Happy Meal.

children "rich, fatty candy bars containing chocolate and other ingredients of negligible nutritional value," while "spiking" them with "peanuts, crisped rice, and caramel to increase consumer appeal." Some joke. Last summer New York City attorney Sam Hirsch filed a strikingly similar suit-against McDonald's—on behalf of a class of obese and overweight children. He alleged that the fast-food chain "negligently, recklessly, carelessly and/or intentionally" markets to children food products that are "high in fat, salt, sugar, and cholesterol" while failing to warn of those ingredients' links to "obesity, diabetes, coronary heart disease, high blood pressure, strokes, elevated cholesterol intake, related cancers," and other conditions. . . . Rates of overweight among small children—to whom junk-food companies aggressively market their products—have doubled since 1980; rates among adolescents have tripled.[6]

Industry defenders decried the suit as frivolous. It is ridiculous, they claimed, to blame the fast-food industry for consumers "own nutritional ignorance, lack of willpower, genetic predispositions, failure to exercise, or whatever else may play a role in [their] obesity." A federal judge agreed and dismissed the suit, explaining that "it is not the place of the law to protect them from their own excess." However, the fast-food industry is listening. For example, McDonald's, Kraft, and Frito-Lay are now working to reduce the amount of artery-clogging trans fats in their foods. McDonald's recently cut the "super size" option from its menu in an effort to trim the large serving sizes that may encourage overeating. And it introduced a Go Active Happy Meal, featuring a salad, bottled water, and a pedometer.[7]

A third complaint concerns product safety. Product safety has been a problem for several reasons, including company indifference, increased product complexity, and poor quality control. For years, Consumers Union—the nonprofit testing and information organization that publishes the *Consumer Reports* magazine and Web site—has reported various hazards in tested products: electrical dangers in appliances, carbon monoxide poisoning from room heaters, injury risks from lawn mowers, and faulty automobile design, among many others. The organization's testing and other activities have helped consumers make better buying decisions and encouraged businesses to eliminate product flaws (see Real Marketing 20.1).

However, most manufacturers *want* to produce quality goods. The way a company deals with product quality and safety problems can damage or help its reputation. Companies selling poor-quality or unsafe products risk damaging conflicts with consumer groups and regulators. Moreover, unsafe products can result in product liability suits and large awards for damages. The average compensatory jury award for product liability cases from 1993 through

Real Marketing 20.1

When Consumer Union Talks, Buyers Listen

For almost 70 years, Consumers Union (CU) has given buyers the lowdown on everything from SUVs and luggage to candy bars and lawn sprinklers. The nonprofit product-testing organization's mission is summed up by its motto: Test, Inform, Protect. CU's magazine, *Consumer Reports,* is one of the nation's most-read magazines. It reaches more than 4 million subscribers and—as dog-eared library copies will attest—has several times that many borrowers. CU's Web site (www.consumerreports.org) is the Web's largest paid-subscriber site with more than 1.6 million users and over 6.4 million subscribers to their newsletter.

One of world's the largest consumer organizations, Consumers Union is also one of the most influential. More recently, when it raved about Saucony's Jazz 3000 sneaker, sales doubled, leading to nationwide shortages.

Although some may view *Consumer Reports* as a deadly dull shopper's guide to major household appliances, Consumers Union does a lot more than rate cars and refrigerators. It has looked at almost anything consumable—from mutual funds, home mortgages, and public health policies to retirement communities and prostate surgery.

■ For almost 70 years, under its mission to "test, inform, protect," Consumers Union has given buyers the lowdown on everything from cars to candy bars.

Despite its serious mission, Consumers Union is rarely harsh or loud. Instead, it's usually understated, and it can even be funny. The very first issue in 1936 noted that Lifebuoy soap was itself so smelly that it simply overwhelmed your "B.O. with L.O." And what reader didn't delight to find in a 1990 survey of soaps that the most expensive bar, Eau de Gucci at 31 cents per hand washing, wound up dead last in a blind test.

To avoid even the appearance of bias, CU has a strict no-ads, no-freebies policy. It buys all of its product samples on the open market and anonymously. CU's steadfast editorial independence has made *Consumer Reports* the bible of con-

sumerism. "We're very single-minded about who we serve," says Rhoda Karpatkin, CU's recently retired president. "We serve the consumer."

A visit to CU's maze of labs confirms the thoroughness with which CU's testers carry out their mission. A chemist performs a cholesterol extraction test on a small white blob in a beaker: a ground-up piece of turkey enchilada, you are told. Elsewhere you find the remains of a piston-driven machine called "Fingers" that added 1 + 1 on pocket calculators hundreds of thousands of times or until the calculators failed, whichever came first. You watch suitcases bang into one another inside a huge contraption—affection-

2002 was $700,000, but individual or class action awards frequently run into the tens of millions of dollars.[8]

More fundamentally, consumers who are unhappy with a firm's products may avoid future purchases and talk other consumers into doing the same. Thus, quality missteps can have severe consequences. Today's marketers know that customer-driven quality results in customer value and satisfaction, which in turn creates profitable customer relationships.

Planned Obsolescence

Critics also have charged that some producers follow a program of planned obsolescence, causing their products to become obsolete before they actually should need replacement. For example, critics charge that some producers continually change consumer concepts of acceptable styles to encourage more and earlier buying. An obvious example is constantly changing clothing fashions.

ately dubbed the "Mechanical Gorilla"—that looks like an 8-foot-wide clothes dryer.

Down the hall in the appliance department, a pair of "food soilers" will soon load 20 dishwashers with identical sets of dirty dishes. A sample dinner plate is marked off with scientific precision into eight wedge-shaped sections, each with something different caked to it—dried spaghetti, spinach, chipped beef, or something else equally difficult to clean. Next door, self-cleaning ovens are being tested, their interiors coated with a crusty substance—called "Monster Mash" by staffers—that suggests month-old chili sauce. The recipe includes tapioca, cheese, lard, grape jelly, tomato sauce, and cherry pie filling—mixed well and baked one hour at 425 degrees. If an oven's self-cleaning cycle doesn't render the resulting residue into harmless-looking ash, 4 million readers will be so informed.

Some of the tests that CU runs are standard tests, but many are not. Several years ago, in a triumph of low-tech creativity, CU's engineers stretched paper towels across embroidery hoops, moistened the center of each with exactly 10 drops of water, and then poured lead shot into the middle. The winner held 7 pounds of shot; the loser, less than 1. Who could argue with that? There is an obvious logic to such tests, and the results are plainly quantifiable.

Beyond simply rating products, Consumers Union has long championed a broad range of consumer issues. In the 1930s, CU was one of the first organizations to urge a boycott of products imported from Nazi Germany, and it's been calling for nationalized health care since 1937. In the 1950s, it warned the nation that fallout from nuclear tests was contaminating milk supplies. In the 1960s and 1970s, it prodded automakers to install seat belts, then air bags.

More recently, when a Consumers Union study found that less than one-third of consumers trust Web commerce, it launched Consumer WebWatch (www.consumerwebwatch.org). The project's mission is to build online trust and provide consumer protection by investigating and improving the credibility of information published on the Web. The site gives ratings on everything from the disclosure of transaction fees to the publication of privacy policies and the labeling of pop-up ads.

To encourage consumers to voice their own complaints, Consumers Union launched a Take Action Center on its Web site.

The Center urges consumers to actively lobby companies and lawmakers on important issues. It even helps consumers craft letters to make their points better. Current Take Action campaigns include, among many others, Financial Privacy Now! (addressing identity theft issues); Escape Cell Hell! (promoting better cell phone service); and Healthy Kids, Healthy Schools (improving child access to health care and health insurance).

From the start, Consumers Union has generated controversy. The second issue of *Consumer Reports* dismissed the Good Housekeeping Seal of Approval as nothing more than a fraudulent ploy by publisher William Randolph Hearst to reward loyal advertisers. *Good Housekeeping* responded by accusing CU of prolonging the Depression. To the business community, *Consumer Reports* was at first viewed as a clear threat to the American way of doing business. During its early years, more than 60 advertising-dependent publications, including the *New York Times, Newsweek,* and the *New Yorker,* refused to accept CU's subscription ads. In 1939, in a move that would seem ludicrous today, Congress' new House UnAmerican Activities Committee (then known as the Dies Committee) branded CU a subversive organization.

However, the controversy has more often helped than hurt subscriptions. And through the years, only 15 makers of panned products have filed suit against CU challenging findings unfavorable to their products. To this day Consumers Union has never lost or settled a libel suit.

Sources: Portions adapted from Doug Stewart, "To Buy or Not to Buy, That Is the Question at *Consumer Reports,*" *Smithsonian,* September 1993, pp. 34–43. Other quotes and information from Robin Finn, "Still Top Dog, Consumers' Pitt Bull to Retire," *New York Times,* October 5, 2000, p. B2; Barbara Quint, "Consumers Union Launches Consumer WebWatch," *Information Today,* June 2002, p. 48; Jim Guest, "What's Bugging You?" *Consumer Reports: Publisher's Edition Including Supplemental Guides,* May 2003, p. 7; "Consumers Union of United States, Inc.," *Hoover's Company Capsules,* Austin, March 15, 2004; and Consumers Union Web sites at www.consumersunion.org, www.consumerreports.org, and www.consumerwebwatch.org, January 2005.

Other producers are accused of holding back attractive functional features, then introducing them later to make older models obsolete. Critics claim that this occurs in the consumer electronics and computer industries. For example, Intel and Microsoft have been accused in recent years of holding back their next-generation computer chips and software until demand is exhausted for the current generation. Still other producers are accused of using materials and components that will break, wear, rust, or rot sooner than they should. One writer put it this way: "The marvels of modern technology include the development of a soda can which, when discarded, will last forever—and a . . . car, which, when properly cared for, will rust out in two or three years."[9]

Marketers respond that consumers *like* style changes; they get tired of the old goods and want a new look in fashion or a new design in cars. No one has to buy the new look, and if too few people like it, it will simply fail. For most technical products, customers *want* the latest innovations, even if older models still work. Companies that withhold new features run the risk that competitors will introduce the new feature first and steal the market. For example, consider personal computers. Some consumers grumble that the consumer electronics industry's constant push to produce "faster, smaller, cheaper" models means that they must continually buy new machines just to keep up. Others, however, can hardly wait for the latest model to arrive.

> There was a time not so long ago when planned obsolescence was a troubling ghost in the machine. Four decades ago, consumer advocates described engineers at General Electric who intentionally shortened the life of lightbulbs and automotive engineers who proposed limiting the life spans of cars. That was then. In today's topsy-turvy world of personal computers, obsolescence is not only planned, it is extolled by marketers as a virtue. Moreover, there has been hardly a peep from consumers, who dutifully line up to buy each new generation of faster, more powerful machines, eager to embrace the promise of simpler, happier, and more productive lives. Today's computer chips are no longer designed to wear out; in fact, they will last for decades or longer. Even so, hapless consumers now rush back to the store ever more quickly, not to replace broken parts but to purchase new computers that will allow them to talk longer, see more vivid colors, or play cooler games.[10]

Thus, companies do not design their products to break down earlier, because they do not want to lose customers to other brands. Instead, they seek constant improvement to ensure that products will consistently meet or exceed customer expectations. Much of so-called planned obsolescence is the working of the competitive and technological forces in a free society—forces that lead to ever-improving goods and services.

Poor Service to Disadvantaged Consumers

Finally, the American marketing system has been accused of serving disadvantaged consumers poorly. For example, critics claim that the urban poor often have to shop in smaller stores that carry inferior goods and charge higher prices. A Consumers Union study compared the food-shopping habits of low-income consumers and the prices they pay relative to middle-income consumers in the same city. The study found that the poor do pay more for inferior goods. The results suggested that the presence of large national chain stores in low-income neighborhoods made a big difference in keeping prices down. However, the study also found evidence of "redlining," a type of economic discrimination in which major chain retailers avoid placing stores in disadvantaged neighborhoods.[11]

Similar redlining charges have been leveled at the insurance, consumer lending, and banking industries. Home and auto insurers have been accused of assigning higher premiums to people with poor credit ratings. The insurers claim that individuals with bad credit tend to make more insurance claims, and that this justifies charging them higher premiums. However, critics and consumer advocates have accused the insurers of a new form of redlining. Says one writer, "This is a new excuse for denying coverage to the poor, elderly, and minorities."[12]

Clearly, better marketing systems must be built to service disadvantaged consumers. Moreover, disadvantaged consumers clearly need consumer protection. The FTC has taken action against merchants who advertise false values, sell old merchandise as new, or charge too much for credit. The commission is also trying to make it harder for merchants to win court judgments against low-income people who were wheedled into buying something.

Marketing's Impact on Society as a Whole

The American marketing system has been accused of adding to several "evils" in American society at large. Advertising has been a special target—so much so that the American Association of Advertising Agencies launched a campaign to defend advertising against what it felt to be common but untrue criticisms.

False Wants and Too Much Materialism

Critics have charged that the marketing system urges too much interest in material possessions. People are judged by what they *own* rather than by who they *are*. This drive for wealth and possessions hit new highs in the 1980s and 1990s, when phrases such as "greed is good" and "shop till you drop" seemed to characterize the times.

In the new millennium, many social scientists have noted a reaction against the opulence and waste of the previous decades and a return to more basic values and social commitment. However, our infatuation with material things continues.

DESPITE WHAT SOME PEOPLE THINK, ADVERTISING CAN'T MAKE YOU BUY SOMETHING YOU DON'T NEED.

Some people would have you believe that you are putty in the hands of every advertiser in the country.

They think that when advertising is put under your nose, your mind turns to oatmeal.

It's mass hypnosis. Subliminal seduction. Brain washing. Mind control. It's advertising.

And you are a pushover for it.

It explains why your kitchen cupboard is full of food you never eat.

Why your garage is full of cars you never drive.

Why your house is full of books you don't read, TV's you don't watch, beds you don't use, and clothes you don't wear.

You don't have a choice. You are forced to buy.

That's why this message is a cleverly disguised advertisement to get you to buy land in the tropics.

Got you again, didn't we? Send in your money.

ADVERTISING
ANOTHER WORD FOR FREEDOM OF CHOICE.
American Association of Advertising Agencies

THIS AD IS FULL OF LIES.

LIE #1: ADVERTISING MAKES YOU BUY THINGS YOU DON'T WANT.
Advertising is often accused of inducing people to buy things against their will.

But when was the last time you returned home from the local shopping mall with a bag full of things you had absolutely no use for? The truth is, nothing short of a pointed gun can get *anybody* to spend money on something he or she doesn't want.

No matter how effective an ad is, you and millions of other American consumers make your own decisions. If you don't believe it, ask someone who knows firsthand about the limits of advertising. Like your local Edsel dealer.

LIE #2: ADVERTISING MAKES THINGS COST MORE. Since advertising costs money, it's natural to assume it costs *you* money. But the truth is that advertising often brings prices down.

Consider the electronic calculator, for example. In the late 1960s, advertising created a mass market for calculators. That meant more of them needed to be produced, which brought the price of producing each calculator down. Competition spurred by advertising brought the price down still further.

As a result, the same product that used to cost hundreds of dollars now costs as little as five dollars.

LIE #3: ADVERTISING HELPS BAD PRODUCTS SELL.
Some people worry that good advertising sometimes covers up for bad products.

But nothing can make you like a bad product. So, while advertising can help convince you to try something once, it can't make you buy it twice. If you don't like what you've bought, you won't buy it again. And if enough people feel the same way, the product dies on the shelf.

In other words, the only thing advertising can do for a bad product is help you find out it's a bad product. And you take it from there.

LIE #4: ADVERTISING IS A WASTE OF MONEY. Some people wonder why we don't just put all the money spent on advertising directly into our national economy.

The answer is, we already do.

Advertising helps products sell, which holds down prices, which helps sales even more. It creates jobs. It informs you about all the products available and helps you compare them. And it stimulates the competition that produces new and better products at reasonable prices.

If all that doesn't convince you that advertising is important to our economy, you might as well stop reading.

Because on top of everything else, advertising has paid for a large part of the magazine you're now holding.

And that's the truth.

ADVERTISING.
ANOTHER WORD FOR FREEDOM OF CHOICE.
American Association of Advertising Agencies

■ The American Marketing Association has run ads to counter common advertising criticisms.

It's hard to escape the notion that what Americans really value is stuff. Since 1987, we've had more shopping malls than high schools. We average 6 hours a week shopping and only 40 minutes playing with our children. Our rate of saving is 2 percent—only a quarter of what it was in the 1950s, when we earned less than half as much in real dollars. Nearly two-thirds of adults agree that wearing "only the best designer clothing" conveys status. Even more feel this way about owning expensive jewelry. Big homes are back in vogue, which means Americans have more space to fulfill their acquisitive fantasies, from master bathrooms doubling as spas and gyms to fully wired home entertainment centers. Some consumers will let nothing stand between them and their acquisitions. Last year, in a Florida Wal-Mart, post-Thanksgiving shoppers rushing to buy DVD players (on sale for $29) knocked down a woman, trampled her, and left her unconscious.[13]

The critics do not view this interest in material things as a natural state of mind but rather as a matter of false wants created by marketing. Businesses hire Madison Avenue (where the headquarters of many advertising agencies are located) to stimulate people's desires for goods, and Madison Avenue uses the mass media to create materialistic models of the good life. People work harder to earn the necessary money. Their purchases increase the output of American industry, and industry in turn uses Madison Avenue to stimulate more desire for the industrial output. Thus, marketing is seen as creating false wants that benefit industry more than they benefit consumers. Some critics even take their concerns to the streets.[14]

For the last 4 years Bill Talen, also known as Reverend Billy, has taken to the streets, exhorting people to resist temptation—the temptation to shop. With the zeal of a street-corner preacher and the schmaltz of a street-corner Santa, Reverend Billy will tell anyone willing to listen that people are walking willingly into the hellfires of consumption. He believes that shoppers have almost no resistance to the media

■ Materialism: With the zeal of a street-corner preacher and the schmaltz of a street-corner Santa, Reverend Billy—founder of the Church of Stop Shopping—will tell anyone who will listen that people are walking willingly into the hellfires of consumption.

messages that encourage them, around the clock, to want things and buy them. He sees a population lost in consumption, the meaning of individual existence vanished in a fog of wanting, buying and owning too many things. To further his message, Billy started the Church of Stop Shopping. As Reverend Billy, he wears a televangelist's pompadour and a priest's collar, and is often accompanied by his gospel choir when he strides into stores he considers objectionable or shows up at protests like the annual post-Thanksgiving Buy Nothing Day event on Fifth Avenue in Manhattan. When the choir, which is made up of volunteers, erupts in song, it is hard to ignore: "Stop shopping! Stop shopping! We will never shop again!"

These criticisms overstate the power of business to create needs, however. People have strong defenses against advertising and other marketing tools. Marketers are most effective when they appeal to existing wants rather than when they attempt to create new ones. Furthermore, people seek information when making important purchases and often do not rely on single sources. Even minor purchases that may be affected by advertising messages lead to repeat purchases only if the product performs as promised. Finally, the high failure rate of new products shows that companies are not able to control demand.

On a deeper level, our wants and values are influenced not only by marketers but also by family, peer groups, religion, ethnic background, and education. If Americans are highly materialistic, these values arose out of basic socialization processes that go much deeper than business and mass media could produce alone.

Too Few Social Goods

Business has been accused of overselling private goods at the expense of public goods. As private goods increase, they require more public services that are usually not forthcoming. For example, an increase in automobile ownership (private good) requires more highways, traffic control, parking spaces, and police services (public goods). The overselling of private goods results in "social costs." For cars, the social costs include traffic congestion, air pollution, gasoline shortages, and deaths and injuries from car accidents.

A way must be found to restore a balance between private and public goods. One option is to make producers bear the full social costs of their operations. The government could require automobile manufacturers to build cars with even more safety features, more efficient engines, and better pollution control systems. Automakers would then raise their prices to cover extra costs. If buyers found the price of some cars too high, however, the producers of these cars would disappear. Demand would then move to those producers that could support the sum of the private and social costs.

A second option is to make consumers pay the social costs. For example, many cities around the world are starting to charge "congestion tolls" in an effort to reduce traffic congestion. To unclog its streets, the city of London now levies a congestion charge of $8 per day per car to drive in an 8-square mile area downtown. The charge has not only reduced traffic congestion by 40 percent, it raises money to shore up London's public transportation system. Similarly, San Diego has turned some of its HOV (high-occupancy vehicle) lanes into HOT (high-occupancy toll) lanes for drivers carrying too few passengers. Regular drivers can use the HOV lanes, but they must pay toll ranging from $.50 off-peak to $4.00 during rush hour. If the costs of driving rise high enough, consumers will travel at nonpeak times or find alternative transportation modes.[15]

Cultural Pollution

Critics charge the marketing system with creating *cultural pollution*. Our senses are being constantly assaulted by advertising. Commercials interrupt serious programs; pages of ads obscure magazines; billboards mar beautiful scenery. These interruptions continually pollute people's minds with messages of materialism, sex, power, or status. Although most people do not find advertising overly annoying (some even think it is the best part of television programming), some critics call for sweeping changes.

Marketers answer the charges of "commercial noise" with these arguments: First, they hope that their ads reach primarily the target audience. But because of mass-communication channels, some ads are bound to reach people who have no interest in the product and are therefore bored or annoyed. People who buy magazines addressed to their interests—such as *Vogue* or *Fortune*—rarely complain about the ads because the magazines advertise products of interest. Second, ads make much of television and radio free to users and keep down the costs of magazines and newspapers. Many people think commercials are a small price to pay for these benefits. Finally, today's consumers have alternatives. For example, they can zip and zap TV commercials or avoid them altogether on many cable or satellite channels. Thus, to hold consumer attention, advertisers are making their ads more entertaining and informative.

Too Much Political Power

Another criticism is that business wields too much political power. "Oil," "tobacco," "auto," and "pharmaceuticals" senators support an industry's interests against the public interest. Advertisers are accused of holding too much power over the mass media, limiting media freedom to report independently and objectively. One critic has asked, "How can [most magazines] afford to tell the truth about the scandalously low nutritional value of most packaged foods ... when these magazines are being subsidized by such advertisers as General Foods, Kellogg's, Nabisco, and General Mills? . . . The answer is *they cannot and do not.*"[16]

American industries do promote and protect their own interests. They have a right to representation in Congress and the mass media, although their influence can become too great. Fortunately, many powerful business interests once thought to be untouchable have been tamed in the public interest. For example, Standard Oil was broken up in 1911, and the meatpacking

■ Balancing private and public goods: In response to lane-clogging traffic congestion like that above, London now levies a congestion charge. The charge has reduced congestion by 40 percent and raised money to shore up the city's public transportation system.

industry was disciplined in the early 1900s after exposures by Upton Sinclair. Ralph Nader caused legislation that forced the automobile industry to build safer cars, and the Surgeon General's Report resulted in cigarette companies putting health warnings on their packages.

More recently, giants such as AT&T, R.J. Reynolds, Intel, and Microsoft have felt the impact of regulators seeking to balance the interests of big business against those of the public. Moreover, because the media receive advertising revenues from many different advertisers, it is easier to resist the influence of one or a few of them. Too much business power tends to result in counterforces that check and offset these powerful interests.

Marketing's Impact on Other Businesses

Critics also charge that a company's marketing practices can harm other companies and reduce competition. Three problems are involved: acquisitions of competitors, marketing practices that create barriers to entry, and unfair competitive marketing practices.

Critics claim that firms are harmed and competition reduced when companies expand by acquiring competitors rather than by developing their own new products. The large number of acquisitions and rapid pace of industry consolidation over the past several decades have caused concern that vigorous young competitors will be absorbed and that competition will be reduced. In virtually every major industry—retailing, entertainment, financial services, utilities, transportation, automobiles, telecommunications, health care—the number of major competitors is shrinking.

Acquisition is a complex subject. Acquisitions can sometimes be good for society. The acquiring company may gain economies of scale that lead to lower costs and lower prices. A well-managed company may take over a poorly managed company and improve its efficiency. An industry that was not very competitive might become more competitive after the acquisition. But acquisitions can also be harmful and, therefore, are closely regulated by the government.

Critics have also charged that marketing practices bar new companies from entering an industry. Large marketing companies can use patents and heavy promotion spending, and can tie up suppliers or dealers to keep out or drive out competitors. Those concerned with antitrust regulation recognize that some barriers are the natural result of the economic advantages of doing business on a large scale. Other barriers could be challenged by existing and new laws. For example, some critics have proposed a progressive tax on advertising spending to reduce the role of selling costs as a major barrier to entry.

Finally, some firms have in fact used unfair competitive marketing practices with the intention of hurting or destroying other firms. They may set their prices below costs, threaten to cut off business with suppliers, or discourage the buying of a competitor's products. Various laws work to prevent such predatory competition. It is difficult, however, to prove that the intent or action was really predatory. In recent years, Wal-Mart, American Airlines, Intel, and Microsoft have all been accused of various predatory practices. Take Microsoft, for example:

> Competitors and regulators in both the U.S. and Europe have accused giant Microsoft of predatory "bundling" practices. That's the term used to describe Microsoft's practice of continually adding new features to Windows, the operating system installed on more than 90 percent of desktop computers. Because customers are essentially locked in to Windows, it's easy for the company to get them to use its other software—even if competitors make better products. That dampens competition, reduces choice, and could retard innovation. For example, in its zeal to become a leader not just in operating systems but on the Internet, Microsoft bundled its Internet Explorer browser into its Windows software. This move sparked an antitrust suit by the U.S. government, much to the delight of Microsoft's rivals. After all, Web-browsing innovator Netscape has seen its market share plummet as it tries to sell what Microsoft now gives away for free. In another action, the European Commission recently took dramatic steps to stop what it saw as predatory bundling by Microsoft. It ordered Microsoft to offer a version of Windows with its media-playing software stripped out. The Commission also fined Microsoft more than $600 million for using its "near monopoly" in the Windows operating system to squeeze out rivals in other types of software.[17]

Although competitors and the government charge that Microsoft's actions are predatory, the question is whether this is unfair competition or the healthy competition of a more efficient company against less efficient ones.

HASTA AQUÍ

Citizen and Public Actions to Regulate Marketing

Because some people view business as the cause of many economic and social ills, grassroots movements have arisen from time to time to keep business in line. The two major movements have been *consumerism* and *environmentalism*.

Consumerism

American business firms have been the target of organized consumer movements on three occasions. The first consumer movement took place in the early 1900s. It was fueled by rising prices, Upton Sinclair's writings on conditions in the meat industry, and scandals in the drug industry. The second consumer movement, in the mid-1930s, was sparked by an upturn in consumer prices during the Great Depression and another drug scandal.

The third movement began in the 1960s. Consumers had become better educated, products had become more complex and potentially hazardous, and people were unhappy with American institutions. Ralph Nader appeared on the scene to force many issues, and other well-known writers accused big business of wasteful and unethical practices. President John F. Kennedy declared that consumers had the right to safety and to be informed, to choose, and to be heard. Congress investigated certain industries and proposed consumer-protection legislation. Since then, many consumer groups have been organized and several consumer laws have been passed. The consumer movement has spread internationally and has become very strong in Europe.

Consumerism

An organized movement of citizens and government agencies to improve the rights and power of buyers in relation to sellers.

But what is the consumer movement? **Consumerism** is an organized movement of citizens and government agencies to improve the rights and power of buyers in relation to sellers. Traditional *sellers' rights* include:

- The right to introduce any product in any size and style, provided it is not hazardous to personal health or safety; or, if it is, to include proper warnings and controls.
- The right to charge any price for the product, provided no discrimination exists among similar kinds of buyers.
- The right to spend any amount to promote the product, provided it is not defined as unfair competition.
- The right to use any product message, provided it is not misleading or dishonest in content or execution.
- The right to use any buying incentive programs, provided they are not unfair or misleading.

Traditional *buyers' rights* include:

- The right not to buy a product that is offered for sale.
- The right to expect the product to be safe.
- The right to expect the product to perform as claimed.

Comparing these rights, many believe that the balance of power lies on the seller's side. True, the buyer can refuse to buy. But critics feel that the buyer has too little information, education, and protection to make wise decisions when facing sophisticated sellers. Consumer advocates call for the following additional consumer rights:

- The right to be well informed about important aspects of the product.
- The right to be protected against questionable products and marketing practices.
- The right to influence products and marketing practices in ways that will improve the "quality of life."

Each proposed right has led to more specific proposals by consumerists. The right to be informed includes the right to know the true interest on a loan (truth in lending), the true cost per unit of a brand (unit pricing), the ingredients in a product (ingredient labeling), the nutritional value of foods (nutritional labeling), product freshness (open dating), and the true benefits of a product (truth in advertising). Proposals related to consumer protection include strengthening consumer rights in cases of business fraud, requiring greater product safety, and giving more

Nutrition Information

Ingredients

■ Consumer desire for more information led to putting ingredients, nutrition, and dating information on product labels.

power to government agencies. Proposals relating to quality of life include controlling the ingredients that go into certain products and packaging, reducing the level of advertising "noise," and putting consumer representatives on company boards to protect consumer interests.

Consumers have not only the *right* but also the *responsibility* to protect themselves instead of leaving this function to someone else. Consumers who believe they got a bad deal have several remedies available, including contacting the company or the media; contacting federal, state, or local agencies; and going to small-claims courts.

Environmentalism

Whereas consumerists consider whether the marketing system is efficiently serving consumer wants, environmentalists are concerned with marketing's effects on the environment and with the costs of serving consumer needs and wants. **Environmentalism** is an organized movement of concerned citizens, businesses, and government agencies to protect and improve people's living environment.

Environmentalists are not against marketing and consumption; they simply want people and organizations to operate with more care for the environment. The marketing system's goal, they assert, should not be to maximize consumption, consumer choice, or consumer satisfaction, but rather to maximize life quality. And "life quality" means not only the quantity and quality of consumer goods and services, but also the quality of the environment. Environmentalists want environmental costs included in both producer and consumer decision making.

The first wave of modern environmentalism in the United States was driven by environmental groups and concerned consumers in the 1960s and 1970s. They were concerned with damage to the ecosystem caused by strip-mining, forest depletion, acid rain, loss of the atmosphere's ozone layer, toxic wastes, and litter. They also were concerned with the loss of recreational areas and with the increase in health problems caused by bad air, polluted water, and chemically treated food.

The second environmentalism wave was driven by government, which passed laws and regulations during the 1970s and 1980s governing industrial practices impacting the environment. This wave hit some industries hard. Steel companies and utilities had to invest billions of dollars in pollution control equipment and costlier fuels. The auto industry had to introduce expensive emission controls in cars. The packaging industry had to find ways to reduce litter. These industries and others have often resented and resisted environmental regulations, especially when they have been imposed too rapidly to allow companies to make proper adjustments. Many of these companies claim they have had to absorb large costs that have made them less competitive.

The first two environmentalism waves have now merged into a third and stronger wave in which companies are accepting responsibility for doing no harm to the environment. They are shifting from protest to prevention, and from regulation to responsibility. More and more companies are adopting policies of **environmental sustainability**—developing strategies that both sustain the environment *and* produce profits for the company (see Real Marketing 20.2). According to one strategist, "The challenge is to develop a *sustainable global economy:* an

Environmentalism
An organized movement of concerned citizens and government agencies to protect and improve people's living environment.

Environmental sustainability
A management approach that involves developing strategies that both sustain the environment and produce profits for the company.

Simply put, environmental sustainability is about generating profits while helping to save the planet. Sustainability is a crucial but difficult societal goal.

Today, almost every company is taking at least some measures to protect and preserve the environment. Sony has reduced the amount of heavy metals—such as lead, mercury, and cadmium—in its electronic products. Nike produces PVC-free shoes, recycles old sneakers, and educates young people about conservation, reuse, and recycling. P&G's Tide still gets clothes clean, but the back of the box also mentions that the soap is biodegradable, comes in recycled-content packaging, and is safe for septic systems. Wal-Mart has opened "eco-friendly" stores in which the air-conditioning systems use non-ozone-depleting refrigerant, rainwater is collected from parking lots and rooftops for landscaping, skylights supplement fluorescent lighting adjusted by photo sensors, and the electronic signs are solar powered.

Some companies, however, are going even further. They are making sustainability central to their core missions. Here are some examples:

DuPont: Known during much of the 20th century as America's worst polluter, DuPont is now transforming itself from a down-and-dirty oil-and-chemicals business into a twenty-first century, eco-friendly life sciences firm. How? For starters, DuPont is polluting less and reducing waste, emissions, and energy usage. But it's doing much more—it is recreating itself as a collection of businesses that can operate forever without depleting natural resources. To do that, DuPont is spinning off businesses such as its Conoco oil and gas unit. In turn, it's investing in new businesses such as Pioneer Hi-Bred International. Pioneer Hybrid's seeds "produce not only food for people and livestock," notes an analyst, "but renewable materials for commercial uses—turning corn into stretch T-shirts, for example." DuPont is also introducing a bevy of new environmentally responsible products, such as Tyvek, a housing-insulation wrap that saves far more energy than is required to produce it. Other products include Super Solids, a paint that can be applied to cars without discharging toxic solvents into the air; and Solae, a nutritional soy protein formulation that goes into more than 1,000 food products. Last year, the company generated 15 percent of its revenues from renewable resources. Its goal is to achieve 25 percent by 2010.

UPS: Every day, some 70,000 boxy brown UPS delivery trucks rumble to life across the nation. Each year they travel more than 1.3 billion miles, delivering 4.6 billion packages to almost 8 million customers. They also guzzle tens of millions of gallon of diesel fuel along the way, creating a significant environmental challenge. To meet this challenge, UPS is now turning its brown fleet "green," finding cleaner replacements for its old, smoke-belching diesels. UPS now operates some 1,800 alternative-fuel vehicles, 2,500 low-emissions vehicles, and a growing number of electric vehicles. In addition, it's working with DaimlerChrysler and the U.S. Environmental Protection Agency (EPA) to test fuel cells that run on hydrogen and other alternative fuels. UPS's goal is to reduce greenhouse gas emissions and air pollution, and to improve the renewability of the resources that it uses. As a side benefit, going green also reduces costs. For example, in addition to lowering emissions by 90 percent, hybrid electric vehicles can cut fuel costs by 50 percent. Such actions also reaffirm UPS's commitment to its consumers' well-being. UPS knows that every time one of its brown vehicles belches a malodorous cloud of black smoke, its brand is tarnished. The company's current ad campaign asks, "What can Brown do for you?" One of the answers, it seems: Brown can help you breathe a littler easier about the environment.

Dell: Like many companies, Dell understands that sustainability means more that just a clean factory. It also means proper handling its products at the ends of their useful lives. Electronics are a fast-growing portion of America's trash, with

$10 OFF when you recycle online! Recycle your old PC or other electronics using Dell Recycling online. Limited Time Offer ▸ **Offer Details**

Dell Recycling

FRIENDLY TO THE ENVIRONMENT.
FRIENDLY TO YOUR WALLET.

Commitment to Customers, Commitment to the Environment
As personal computers have become common in most homes, there is a growing concern about the environmental impact of old computers, computer parts and other electronic products. When you are ready to dispose of your old PC and computer-related devices, Dell is here to help.

Recycle	**Donate**
By choosing to recycle with Dell, you may receive a special offer towards your new computer or other new Dell Electronics & Accessories products. Plus, if you buy a new Dell desktop or notebook and select the free recycling option, we will recycle your old one at no cost to you, for a limited time.	Dell has partnered with the National Cristina Foundation (NCF) Cristina Foundation site ▦ (NCF) to help disabled and economically disadvantaged children and adults receive the gift of technology.

▸ Learn How to Get Free Dell Recycling

▸ How to Recycle with Dell

▸ Recycling FAQs

▸ Recycling Terms & Conditions

 Go Recycle

▸ Save on Electronics & Accessories!

▸ How to donate with NCF

▸ Donation FAQs

▸ NCF Policy for donations

 Go to Donate ▣

 Environmental News
Learn what Dell is doing to help the environment.
More Details

 Environmental Policies
Learn about computer equipment recycling practices.
More Details

Events Calendar
Find out about Dell's Recycling Programs
More Details

Large Business or Corporate Recycling
Click here if you are a business interested in recycling.
More Details

■ Environmental sustainability: Dell understands that sustainability means handling its products at the ends of their useful lives. Its Dell Recycling program helps customers to recycle or donate old computer equipment.

(box continues)

hundreds of millions of computers destined to become obsolete within just the next few years. These computers contain both toxic metals and useful, reusable materials, so Dell wants to keep them out of landfills. To accomplish this, the company set up Dell Recycling, an effort to reduce the environmental impact of old computers, monitors, keyboards, mice, and printers. Through this multi-pronged effort, Dell customers—big businesses and home buyers alike—can exchange, mail in, or drop off old computer equipment, or even have it picked up. Dell will accept any model of old computer, even competing brands. If the old machine is still useful, Dell will refurbish it and donate it to one of several charities. If the old machine is obsolete or broken beyond repair, Dell will recycle or safely dispose of component materials. To promote Dell Recycling, the company recently organized a 15-city recycling tour that collected almost 2 million pounds of old computer equipment from more than 7,500 consumers.

BP: BP sees the environmental sustainability challenge as an opportunity. "There are good commercial reasons to do right by the environment," says CEO John Browne. Under his leadership, BP has become active in public forums on global climate issues and has worked to reduce emissions in exploration and production. It has begun marketing cleaner fuels and invested significantly in exploring alternative energy sources, such as photovoltaic power and hydrogen. At the local level, BP opened "the world's most environmentally friendly service station" near London. The innovative station features an array of green initiatives that show BP's commitment to environmental responsibility. It runs entirely on renewable energy and generates up to half of its own power, using solar panels installed on the roofs and three wind turbines. More than 60 percent of the water needed for the restrooms

comes from rainwater collected on the shop roof, and water for hand washing is heated by solar panels. The site's vapor recovery systems collect and recycle even the fuel vapor released from customers' tanks as pump gas. BP has planted landscaping around the site with indigenous plant species. And, to promote biodiversity awareness, the company has undertaken several initiatives to attract local wildlife to the area, such as dragonflies and insect-feeding birds. The wildflower turf under the wind farm will even provide a habitat for bumble bees. "BP has a simply stated goal," says the company: "to do no damage to the environment."

Some companies have responded to consumer environmental concerns by doing only what is required to avert new regulations or to keep environmentalists quiet. Enlightened companies, however, are taking action not because someone is forcing them to, or to reap short-run profits, but because it is the right thing to do—for both the company and for the planet's environmental future.

Sources: Marc Gunther, "Tree Huggers, Soy Lovers, and Profits," *Fortune*, June 23, 2003 pp. 98–104; "DuPont Discusses Sustainability," *Electronic Materials Update*, April 2003, p. 1; "Social Commitment: Global Progress Report," accessed at www.dupont.com, June 2004; Charles Haddad, "Fedex and Brown Are Going Green," *Business Week,* August 11, 2003; "Sustainability Key to UPS's Environmental Initiatives," accessed online at http://pressroom.ups.com/, June 2004; "Recycling Programs at Dell," accessed at www.dell.com, December 2004; "BP Launches World's Greenest Service Station," BP press release, April 25, 2002, accessed at www.bp.com/centres/press/media_resources/press_release/index.asp; and "BP: Environment," accessed at www.bp.com/subsection.do?categoryId=41&contentId=2000030, December 2004.

economy that the planet is capable of supporting indefinitely. . . . [It's] an enormous challenge—and an enormous opportunity."[18]

Figure 20.1 shows a grid that companies can use to gauge their progress toward environmental sustainability. At the most basic level, a company can practice *pollution prevention*. This involves more than pollution control—cleaning up waste after it has been created. Pollution prevention means eliminating or minimizing waste before it is created. Companies emphasizing prevention have responded with "green marketing" programs—developing ecologically safer products, recyclable and biodegradable packaging, better pollution controls, and more energy-efficient operations. They are finding that they can be both green *and* competitive.

At the next level, companies can practice *product stewardship*—minimizing not just pollution from production but all environmental impacts throughout the full product life cycle. Many companies are adopting *design for environment (DFE)* practices, which involve thinking ahead to design products that are easier to recover, reuse, or recycle. DFE not only helps to sustain the environment, it can be highly profitable for the company. An example is Xerox Corporation's Equipment Remanufacture and Parts Reuse Program, which converts end-of-life office equipment into new products and parts:

> Xerox starts by including reuse considerations in its design process to maximize end-of-life potential of products and parts. Its machines contain fewer parts and are designed for easy disassembly. Parts are designed for durability over multiple product life cycles and are coded with disposition instructions. As a result, equipment returned to Xerox at end-of-life can be remanufactured reusing 70 to 90 percent by weight of old machine components, while still meeting performance standards for equipment made with all new parts. Xerox's remanufacture and reuse program creates benefits for both the environment and the company. It prevents more 150 mil-

	Internal	External
Tomorrow	**New environmental technology** Is the environmental performance of our products limited by our existing technology base? Is there potential to realize major improvements through new technology?	**Sustainability vision** Does our corporate vision direct us toward the solution of social and environmental problems? Does our vision guide the development of new technologies, markets, products, and processes?
Today	**Pollution prevention** Where are the most significant waste and emission streams from our current operations? Can we lower costs and risks by eliminating waste at the source or by using it as useful input?	**Product stewardship** What are the implications for product design and development if we assume responsibility for a product's entire life cycle? Can we add value or lower costs while simultaneously reducing the impact of our products?

FIGURE 20.1

The environmental sustainability grid

Source: Stuart L. Hart, "Beyond Greening: Strategies for a Sustainable World," Harvard Business Review, *January–February 1997, p. 74. Copyright © 1997 by the President and Fellows of Harvard College; all rights reserved. Reprinted by permission of* Harvard Business Review.

lions of pound of waste from entering landfills each year. And it reduces the amount of raw material and energy needed to produce new parts. Last year alone, energy savings from parts reuse totaled an estimated 400,000 megawatt hours—enough energy to light more than 320,000 U.S. homes for the year. Xerox estimates that its savings in raw materials, labor, and waste disposal in the first year of the program alone ranged between $300 million and $400 million. Today, 100 percent of Xerox equipment is designed with remanufacturing and reuse in mind.[19]

At the third level, companies look to the future and plan for *new environmental technologies*. Many organizations that have made good sustainability headway are still limited by existing technologies. To develop fully sustainable strategies, they will need to develop new technologies. Monsanto is doing this by shifting its agricultural technology base from bulk chemicals to biotechnology. By controlling plant growth and pest resistance through bioengineering, rather than through the use of pesticides or fertilizers, Monsanto hopes to fulfill its promise of environmentally sustainable agriculture. The Monsanto Pledge states the company's dedication to being capable stewards of the technologies it develops. The Pledge declares, "Monsanto is committed to providing high-quality products that benefit [both] our customers and the environment."[20]

Finally, companies can develop a *sustainability vision*, which serves as a guide to the future. It shows how the company's products and services, processes, and policies must evolve and what new technologies must be developed to get there. This vision of sustainability provides a framework for pollution control, product stewardship, and environmental technology.

Most companies today focus on the lower-left quadrant of the grid in Figure 20.1, investing most heavily in pollution prevention. Some forward-looking companies practice product stewardship and are developing new environmental technologies. Few companies have well-defined sustainability visions. Emphasizing only one or a few cells in the environmental sustainability grid in Figure 20.1 can be shortsighted. Investing only in the bottom half of the grid puts a company in a good position today but leaves it vulnerable in the future. In contrast, a heavy emphasis on the top half suggests that a company has good environmental vision but lacks the skills needed to implement it. Thus, companies should work at developing all four dimensions of environmental sustainability. Hewlett-Packard is doing just that:

Hewlett-Packard (H-P) has evolved through three distinct phases of environmental sustainability over the past two decades. In the 1980s, it focused mostly on pollution control and prevention, with an eye on reducing emissions from existing manufacturing processes. In the 1990s, the focus shifted to product steward-ship—on developing global processes for regulatory compliance, customer inquiry response systems, information management, public policy shaping, product take-back programs, green packaging, and integrating "design for environment" and life cycle analysis into product development. Today, sustainability is about developing technologies that actually contribute a positive impact to environmental challenges. Pollution prevention and product stewardship have become baseline market expectations. To be an environmental leader in the 21st century, H-P knows that it needs to integrate environmental sustainability into its fundamental vision and strategy. "At H-P," says the company, "we believe that environmentally sustainable development is not an option, it's an imperative."[21]

Environmentalism creates some special challenges for global marketers. As international trade barriers come down and global markets expand, environmental issues are having an ever-greater impact on international trade. Countries in North America, Western Europe, and other developed regions are developing strict environmental standards. In the United States, for example, more than two dozen major pieces of environmental legislation have been enacted since 1970, and recent events suggest that more regulation is on the way. A side accord to the North American Free Trade Agreement (NAFTA) set up a commission for resolving environmental matters. The European Union (EU) recently passed "end-of-life" regulations affecting automobiles and consumer electronics product. And the EU's Eco-Management and Audit Scheme provides guidelines for environmental self-regulation.[22]

However, environmental policies still vary widely from country to country. Countries such as Denmark, Germany, Japan, and the United States have fully developed environmental policies and high public expectations. But major countries such as China, India, Brazil, and Russia are in only the early stages of developing such policies. Moreover, environmental factors that motivate consumers in one country may have no impact on consumers in another. For example, PVC soft drink bottles cannot be used in Switzerland or Germany. However, they are preferred in France, which has an extensive recycling process for them. Thus, international companies have found it difficult to develop standard environmental practices that work around the world. Instead, they are creating general policies and then translating these policies into tailored programs that meet local regulations and expectations.

Public Actions to Regulate Marketing

Citizen concerns about marketing practices will usually lead to public attention and legislative proposals. New bills will be debated—many will be defeated, others will be modified, and a few will become workable laws.

Many of the laws that affect marketing are listed in Chapter 3. The task is to translate these laws into the language that marketing executives understand as they make decisions about competitive relations, products, price, promotion, and channels of distribution. Figure 20.2 illustrates the major legal issues facing marketing management.

Business Actions Toward Socially Responsible Marketing

At first, many companies opposed consumerism and environmentalism. They thought the criticisms were either unfair or unimportant. But by now, most companies have grown to accept the new consumer rights, at least in principle. They might oppose certain pieces of legislation as inappropriate ways to solve specific consumer problems, but they recognize the consumer's right to information and protection. Many of these companies have responded positively to consumerism and environmentalism as a way to create greater customer value and to strengthen customer relationships.

Enlightened marketing
A marketing philosophy holding that a company's marketing should support the best long-run performance of the marketing.

Enlightened Marketing

The philosophy of **enlightened marketing** holds that a company's marketing should support the best long-run performance of the marketing system. Enlightened marketing consists of five principles: *consumer-oriented marketing, innovative marketing, value marketing, sense-of-mission marketing,* and *societal marketing.*

FIGURE 20.2
Major marketing decision areas that may be called into question under the law

Selling decisions
Bribing?
Stealing trade secrets?
Disparaging customers?
Misrepresenting?
Disclosure of customer rights?
Unfair discrimination?

Product decisions
Product additions and deletions?
Patent protection?
Product quality and safety?
Product warranty?

Advertising decisions
False advertising?
Deceptive advertising?
Bait-and-switch advertising?
Promotional allowances and services?

Packaging decisions
Fair packaging and labeling?
Excessive cost?
Scarce resources?
Pollution?

Channel decisions
Exclusive dealing?
Exclusive territorial distributorships?
Tying agreements?
Dealer's rights?

Price decisions
Price-fixing?
Predatory pricing?
Price discrimination?
Minimum pricing?
Price increases?
Deceptive pricing?

Competitive relations decisions
Anticompetitive acquisition?
Barriers to entry?
Predatory competition?

Consumer-Oriented Marketing

Consumer-oriented marketing

The philosophy of enlightened marketing that holds that the company should view and organize its marketing activities from the consumer's point of view.

Consumer-oriented marketing means that the company should view and organize its marketing activities from the consumer's point of view. It should work hard to sense, serve, and satisfy the needs of a defined group of customers. Every good marketing company that we've discussed in this text has had this in common: an all-consuming passion for delivering superior value to carefully chosen customers. Only by seeing the world through its customers' eyes can the company build lasting and profitable customer relationships. By creating value *for* consumers, the company can capture value *from* consumers in return.

Innovative Marketing

Innovative marketing

A principle of enlightened marketing that requires that a company seek real product and marketing improvements.

The principle of **innovative marketing** requires that the company continuously seek real product and marketing improvements. The company that overlooks new and better ways to do things will eventually lose customers to another company that has found a better way. An excellent example of an innovative marketer is Samsung:

Less than a decade ago, Samsung was a copycat consumer electronics brand you bought off a shipping pallet at Costco if you couldn't afford a Sony. But today, the brand holds a high-end, cutting-edge aura. In 1996, Samsung Electronics made an inspired decision. It turned its back on cheap knock-offs and set out to overtake rival Sony. The company hired a crop of fresh, young designers, who unleashed a torrent of new products—not humdrum, me-too products, but innovative and stylish products, targeted to high-end users. Samsung called them "lifestyle works of art"—from brightly colored cell phones and elegantly thin DVD players to flat-panel TV monitors that hung on walls like paintings. Every new product had to pass the "Wow!" test: if it didn't get a "Wow!" reaction during market testing, it went straight back to the design studio.

Samsung supported the innovative new products with a $400 million marketing campaign, headed by ads proclaiming that Samsung is "DigitAll" and that "everyone's invited." Samsung also changed its distribution to match its new caché. It abandoned low-end distributors such as Wal-Mart and Kmart, instead building strong relationships with specialty retailers such as Best Buy and Circuit City. Samsung is now the world's fastest growing brand. It's No. 1 worldwide in ultra-thin computer and television screens, No. 2 in DVD players, and No. 3 in mobile phones. The Samsung brand is valued at an estimated $11 billion, almost tripled its value just 4 years ago.

■ Innovative marketing: In less than a decade, Samsung has given its brand a cutting-edge image by unleashing a torrent of new products—not humdrum, me-too products, but innovative and stylish products, targeted to high-end users.

Samsung's performance continues to astound brand watchers," says one analyst. The company has become a model for others that "want to shift from being a cheap supplier to a global brand." Says a Samsung designer, "We're not el cheapo anymore."[23]

Customer-Value Marketing

Customer-value marketing
A principle of enlightened marketing that holds that a company should put most of its resources into customer value-building marketing investments.

According to the principle of **customer-value marketing**, the company should put most of its resources into customer value-building marketing investments. Many things marketers do—one-shot sales promotions, minor packaging changes, direct response advertising—may raise sales in the short run but add less *value* than would actual improvements in the product's quality, features, or convenience. Enlightened marketing calls for building long-run consumer loyalty and relationships by continually improving the value consumers receive from the firm's marketing offer.

Sense-of-Mission Marketing

Sense-of-mission marketing
A principle of enlightened marketing that holds that a company should define its mission in broad social terms.

Sense-of-mission marketing means that the company should define its mission in broad *social* terms rather than narrow *product* terms. When a company defines a social mission, employees feel better about their work and have a clearer sense of direction. For example, defined in narrow product terms, the mission of Unilever's Ben & Jerry's unit might be "to sell ice cream and frozen yogurt." However, Ben & Jerry's states its mission more broadly as one of "linked prosperity," including product, economic, and social missions (see www.benjerrys.com/our_company/our_mission/). Reshaping the basic task of selling consumer products into the larger mission of serving the interests of consumers, employees, and others in the company's various "communities" gives Ben & Jerry's a vital sense of purpose. Like Ben & Jerry's, many companies today are undertaking socially responsible actions and building concern for their communities into their underlying cultures (see Real Marketing 20.3).

Chances are, when you hear the term *socially responsible business*, a handful of companies—and their founders—leap to mind, companies such as Ben & Jerry's Homemade (Ben Cohen, Jerry Greenfield) and The Body Shop International (Anita Roddick). Such social revolutionaries pioneered the concept of "values-led business" or "caring capitalism." Their mission: Use business to make the world a better place.

Ben Cohen and Jerry Greenfield founded Ben & Jerry's Homemade in 1978 as a company that cared deeply about its social and environmental responsibilities. It bought only hormone-free milk and cream and used only organic fruits and nuts to make its ice cream, which it sold in environmentally friendly containers. It went to great lengths to buy from minority and disadvantaged suppliers. From its early Rainforest Crunch to its more recent One Sweet Whirled flavors and awareness campaigns, Ben & Jerry's has championed a host of social and environmental causes over the years. From the start, Ben & Jerry's donated a whopping 7.5 percent of pre-tax profits to support projects that exhibited "creative problem solving and hopefulness . . . relating to children and families, disadvantaged groups, and the environment." By the mid-1990s, Ben & Jerry's had become the nation's number two superpremium ice cream brand.

Anita Roddick opened The Body Shop in 1976 with a similar mission: "to dedicate our business to the pursuit of social and environmental change." The company manufactured and retailed natural-ingredient-based cosmetics in simple and appealing recyclable packaging. All products were formulated without any animal testing, and supplies were often sourced from developing countries. Roddick became a vocal advocate for putting "passion before profits," and The Body Shop, which now operates over 1,900 stores in 50 countries, donates a percentage of profits each year to animal-rights groups, homeless shelters, Amnesty International, Save the Rain Forest, and other social causes.

Both companies set up shop in the late 1970s and grew fast and furiously through the 1980s and early 1990s. However, as competitors not shackled by their "principles before profits" missions invaded their markets, growth and profits flattened. In recent years, both Ben & Jerry's and The Body Shop have struggled. In 2000, after several years of less than stellar financial returns, Ben & Jerry's was acquired by giant food producer Unilever. And Anita Roddick eventually handed over The Body Shop's reins to a more business-savvy turnaround team, taking the role of consultant.

What happened to the founders' lofty ideals of caring capitalism? Looking back, both companies may have focused on social issues at the expense of sound business management. Neither Ben Cohen nor Anita Roddick really wanted to be businesspeople. In fact, according to one analyst, Cohen and Roddick "saw businesspeople as tools of the military-industrial complex and profits as a dirty word." Cohen once commented, "There came a time [when I had to admit] 'I'm a businessman.' And I had a hard time mouthing those words."

Likewise, Roddick admitted, "A lot of us would have slit our wrists if we ever thought we'd be part of corporate America or England. Big business was alien to me. . . . I was only ever interested in running a company that could break the rules of how business could be run. It wasn't about financial science or the science of retailing. It was about being a communications company."

HONEST TEA
Real Tea. Real Taste. Honest.

Real Tea.

We use only organic tea leaves. For generations, cultures around the world have enjoyed tea grown without chemical pesticides and fertilizers and we don't see any reason to include them in our recipes today.

Real Taste.

Our goal is to create a product in which the true taste of the leaves comes through. We don't pulverize, process or concentrate our tea leaves. Instead we brew the whole leaf in spring water in a way that Shen Nung would still recognize. We add just a touch of natural sweetener - enough to accentuate the tea's natural flavor, but not so much that the sweetener drowns out the tea taste.

Honest.

Tea is consumed by some of the world's wealthiest populations, yet it is produced by some of the poorest. We hope that by introducing new teas and exciting new tastes under the Honest Tea name, we can help to create greater economic opportunity in communities that are seeking to become more self-sufficient. We also try to present our teas in a culturally authentic context, using our labels to illustrate the tea's origin or story-a Crow Native American Chief, a Chinese rubbing from the Tang Dynasty, an oil painting from Guatemala or a hand-drawn sketch from Haarlem South Africa.

www.honesttea.com
800.865.4736

■ Societal marketing: Today's new activist entrepreneurs are not social activists with big hearts who hate capitalism, but well-trained business managers and company builders with a passion for a cause.

Having a "double bottom line" of values and profits is no easy proposition. In the words of one especially harsh critic, "Ben and Jerry wants to use ice cream to solve the world's problems. They call it running a values-led business; I call it a mess. Operating a business is tough enough. Once you add social goals to the demands of serving customers, making a profit, and returning value to shareholders, you tie yourself up in knots." For sure, it's often difficult to take good intentions to the bank.

The experiences of the 1980s and 1990s revolutionaries taught the socially responsible business movement some hard lessons. The result is a new generation of activist entrepreneurs—not social activists with big hearts who hate capitalism, but well-trained business managers and company builders with a passion for a cause. Here are some of the lessons, gleaned from an *Inc* magazine study of several new values-led businesses:

■ *What you sell is important:* The product or service, not just the mission, must be socially responsible. Hence, Honest Tea Inc. markets barely sweetened iced tea and totally biodegradable tea bags; WorldWise Inc. offers garden, home, and pet products made from recycled or organic materials; Sustainable Harvest Inc. sells organic, shade-grown coffee

(box continues)

Socially Responsible Marketing: Serving a Double Bottom Line of Values and Profits   *continued*

with a guaranteed base price for growers; CitySoft Inc. does Web development using urban workers; Wild Planet Toys Inc. creates nonsexist, nonviolent toys; and Village Real Estate Services revitalizes communities and neighborhoods.

■ *Be proud to be in business:* Unlike the old revolutionaries, the new young founders are businesspeople—and proud of it—and all appreciate solid business training. Honest Tea founder Seth Goldman won a business-plan competition as a student at the Yale School of Management and later started the company with one of his professors. Wild Planet CEO Daniel Grossman has an MBA from the Stanford Business School. Sustainable Harvest's David Griswold hires business school graduates because he believes that success "really depends on competing, using the rules of business. Good deeds alone don't work."

■ *Make a solid commitment to change:* Cohen and Greenfield stumbled into making ice cream to make ends meet; Roddick owned a small hotel in England before opening her first store. By contrast the new social entrepreneurs' companies are a natural outgrowth of their long-held values. For example, Wild Planet's Grossman served for 8 years in the U.S. Foreign Service. David Griswold co-founded and ran Aztec Harvest, a sales-and-marketing outfit for farmer-owned Mexican coffee cooperatives. And CitySoft CEO Nick Gleason was a community and labor organizer in Oakland, California, and ran his own urban-development consulting company, serving non-profits, foundations, school districts, and governments.

■ *Focus on two bottom lines:* Today's social entrepreneurs are just as dedicated to building a viable, profitable business as to shaping a mission. WorldWise's Lamstein comments, "You can't be successful if you can't do both." Lamstein's strategy for getting WorldWise up and running, built around the concept of environmentally responsible products, illustrates such double-bottom-line thinking. "Our whole concept was that our products had to work as well as or better than others, look as good or finer, cost the same or less, and be better for the environment," says Lamstein. Honest Tea's Goldman agrees: "A commitment to socially responsible business cannot be used

as an excuse to make poor business decisions. If we were to accept lower margins, then we'd be doing the . . . socially responsible business movement a disservice, because we wouldn't be as competitive or as attractive to investors."

■ *Forget the hype:* For these socially responsible companies, it's not about marketing and image. They go about doing their good deeds quietly. Village Real Estate Services concentrates primarily on marketing its services, not on publicizing the company's Village Fund, which funds the revitalization of urban neighborhoods. Honest Tea markets it's First Nation Tea in partnership with I'tchik Herb, a small woman-owned company on the Crow Reservation in Montana. I'tchik gets royalties from the sales of the tea, as does a Native American organization called Pretty Shield Foundation, which includes foster care among its activities. However, "when we first brought out our peppermint tea, our label didn't mention that we were sharing the revenues with the Crow Nation," says Goldman. "We didn't want people to think that was a gimmick."

It remains to be seen how these new socially responsible companies will fare down the road. Many are less than 5 years old and post sales from $2 million to $10 million. Ben & Jerry's, by contrast, has sales of some $150 million (down from more than $350 million at its peak), and cash registers in Body Shop stores rang up more than $600 in sales last year. Still, this much is clear: Social responsibility for the recent crop of company founders—at least at this early date—seems to be not about them nor even about their companies. It's about the mission.

Sources: Portions adapted from Thea Singer, "Can Business Still Save the World?" *Inc,* April 30, 2001, pp. 58-71. Other information from Harriot Marsh, "Has the Body Shop Lost Its Direction for Good?" *Marketing,* May 10, 2001, p. 19; "Anita Roddick," *Director,* June 2003, p. 60; Mike Hoffman, "Ben Cohen: Ben & Jerry's Homemade, Established in 1978," *Inc,* April 30, 2001, p. 68; "The Body Shop International PLC," *Hoover's Company Capsules,* Austin, March 15, 2004; and from the Ben & Jerry's and The Body Shop Web sites at www.benjerrys.com and www.bodyshop.com, July 2004.

Societal Marketing

Societal marketing

A principle of enlightened marketing that holds that a company should make good marketing decisions by considering consumers' wants, the company's requirements, consumers' long-run interests, and society's long run interests.

Following the principle of **societal marketing**, an enlightened company makes marketing decisions by considering consumers' wants and interests, the company's requirements, and society's long-run interests. The company is aware that neglecting consumer and societal long-run interests is a disservice to consumers and society. Alert companies view societal problems as opportunities.

A societally oriented marketer wants to design products that are not only pleasing but also beneficial. The difference is shown in Figure 20.3. Products can be classified according to their degree of immediate consumer satisfaction and long-run consumer benefit. **Deficient products**, such as bad-tasting and ineffective medicine, have neither immediate appeal nor long-run benefits. **Pleasing products** give high immediate satisfaction but may hurt consumers in the long run. Example include cigarettes and junk food. **Salutary products** have low appeal but may benefit consumers in the long run; for instance, seat belts and air bags. **Desirable products** give both high immediate satisfaction and high long-run benefits, such as a tasty *and* nutritious breakfast food.

Examples of desirable products abound. Philips Lightings Earth Light compact fluorescent lightbulb provides good lighting at the same time that it gives long life and energy sav-

FIGURE 20.3
Societal classification of products

	Immediate satisfaction	
	Low	High
Long-run consumer benefit — High	Salutary products	Desirable products
Long-run consumer benefit — Low	Deficient products	Pleasing products

Deficient products
Products that have neither immediate appeal nor long-run benefits.

Pleasing products
Products that give high immediate satisfaction but may hurt consumers in the long run.

Salutary products
Products that have low appeal but may benefit consumers in the long run.

Desirable products
Products that give both high immediate satisfaction and high long-run benefits.

ings. Toyota's gas-electric hybrid Prius gives both a quiet ride and fuel efficiency. Maytag's front-loading Neptune washer provides superior cleaning along with water savings and energy efficiency. And Herman Miller's office chairs are not only attractive and functional but also environmentally responsible:

Herman Miller, one of the world's largest office furniture makers, has received numerous awards for environmentally responsible products and business practices. More than a decade ago, the company formed a Design for the Environment team responsible for infusing the company's design process with its environmental values. The team carries out "cradle-to-cradle" life cycle analyses on the company's products, including everything from how much of a product can be made from recycled materials to how much of the product itself can be recycled at the end of its useful life. For example, the team redesigned the company's chairs for the lowest possible ecological impact and high recyclability. Herman Miller's Aeron chair is constructed of 66 percent recycled materials (from pop bottles and recycled aluminum) and is 90 percent recyclable. The frames need no paint or other finish. No ozone-depleting materials are used. Chairs are shipped partially assembled, thus reducing the packaging and energy needed to ship them. Finally, materials schematics are imbedded in the bottoms of chair seats to help recycle chairs at the ends of their lives. Herman Miller chairs are truly desirable products—they've won awards for design and function *and* for environmental responsibility. And it inspired future models of environmentally friendly chairs. Most recently, Herman Miller introduced the Mirra chair, which is made from 42 percent recycled materials and is 96 percent recyclable.[24]

Companies should try to turn all of their products into desirable products. The challenge posed by pleasing products is that they sell very well but may end up hurting the consumer.

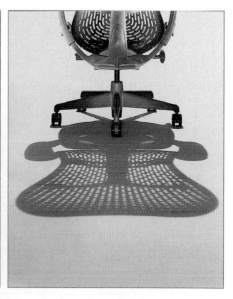

■ Herman Miller's Design for the Environment team is responsible for infusing the company's design process with its environmental values. For example, its Mirra chair is made from 42 percent recycled materials and is 96 percent recyclable.

The product opportunity, therefore, is to add long-run benefits without reducing the product's pleasing qualities. The challenge posed by salutary products is to add some pleasing qualities so that they will become more desirable in consumers' minds.

Marketing Ethics

Conscientious marketers face many moral dilemmas. The best thing to do is often unclear. Because not all managers have fine moral sensitivity, companies need to develop *corporate marketing ethics policies*—broad guidelines that everyone in the organization must follow. These policies should cover distributor relations, advertising standards, customer service, pricing, product development, and general ethical standards.

The finest guidelines cannot resolve all the difficult ethical situations the marketer faces. Table 20.1 lists some difficult ethical situations marketers could face during their careers. If marketers choose immediate sales-producing actions in all these cases, their marketing behavior might well be described as immoral or even amoral. If they refuse to go along with *any* of the actions, they might be ineffective as marketing managers and unhappy because of the constant moral tension. Managers need a set of principles that will help them figure out the moral importance of each situation and decide how far they can go in good conscience.

But *what* principle should guide companies and marketing managers on issues of ethics and social responsibility? One philosophy is that such issues are decided by the free market and legal system. Under this principle, companies and their managers are not responsible for making moral judgments. Companies can in good conscience do whatever the system allows.

A second philosophy puts responsibility not on the system but in the hands of individual companies and managers. This more enlightened philosophy suggests that a company should have a "social conscience." Companies and managers should apply high standards of ethics

TABLE 20.1   Some Morally Difficult Situations in Marketing

1. You work for a cigarette company. Public policy debates over the past few years now leave no doubt in your mind that cigarette smoking and cancer are closely linked. What would you do?
2. Your R&D department has changed one of your products slightly. It is not really "new and improved," but you know that putting this statement on the package and in advertising will increase sales. What would you do?
3. You have been asked to add a stripped-down model to your line that could be advertised to pull customers into the store. The product won't be very good, but salespeople will be able to switch buyers up to higher-priced units. You are asked to give the green light for the stripped-down version. What would you do?
4. You are thinking of hiring a product manager who has just left a competitor's company. She would be more than happy to tell you all the competitor's plans for the coming year. What would you do?
5. One of your top dealers in an important territory recently has had family troubles, and his sales have slipped. It looks like it will take him a while to straighten out his family trouble. Meanwhile you are losing many sales. Legally, you can terminate the dealer's franchise and replace him. What would you do?
6. You have a chance to win a big account that will mean a lot to you and your company. The purchasing agent hints that a "gift" would influence the decision. Your assistant recommends sending a fine color television set to the buyer's home. What would you do?
7. You have heard that a competitor has a new product feature that will make a big difference in sales. The competitor will demonstrate the feature in a private dealer meeting at the annual trade show. You can easily send a snooper to this meeting to learn about the new feature. What would you do?
8. You have to choose between three ad campaigns outlined by your agency. The first (a) is soft-sell, honest, straight-information campaign. The second (b) uses sex-loaded emotional appeals and exaggerates the product's benefits. The third (c) involves a noisy, somewhat irritating commercial that is sure to gain audience attention. Pretests show that the campaigns are effective in the following order: c, b, and a. What would you do?
9. You are interviewing a capable female applicant for a job as salesperson. She is better qualified than the men just interviewed. Nevertheless, you know that some of your important customers prefer dealing with men, and you will lose some sales if you hire her. What would you do?

and morality when making corporate decisions, regardless of "what the system allows." History provides an endless list of examples of company actions that were legal but highly irresponsible. Consider the following example:

> Prior to the Pure Food and Drug Act, the advertising for a diet pill promised that a person taking this pill could eat virtually anything at any time and still lose weight. Too good to be true? Actually the claim was quite true; the product lived up to its billing with frightening efficiency. It seems that the primary active ingredient in this "diet supplement" was tapeworm larvae. These larvae would develop in the intestinal tract and, of course, be well fed; the pill taker would in time, quite literally, starve to death.[25]

Each company and marketing manager must work out a philosophy of socially responsible and ethical behavior. Under the societal marketing concept, each manager must look beyond what is legal and allowed and develop standards based on personal integrity, corporate conscience, and long-run consumer welfare. A clear and responsible philosophy will help the company deal with knotty issues such as the one faced recently by 3M:

> In late 1997, a powerful new research technique for scanning blood kept turning up the same odd result: Tiny amounts of a chemical 3M had made for nearly 40 years were showing up in blood drawn from people living all across the country. If the results held up, it meant that virtually all Americans may be carrying some minuscule amount of the chemical, called perfluorooctane sulfonate (PFOS), in their systems. Even though they had yet to come up with definitive answers—and they insisted that there was no evidence of danger to humans—the company reached a drastic decision. In mid-2000, although under no mandate to act, 3M decided to phase out products containing PFOS and related chemicals, including its popular Scotchgard fabric protector. This was no easy decision. Since there was as yet no replacement chemical, it meant a potential loss of $500 million in annual sales. 3M's voluntary actions drew praise from regulators. "3M deserves great credit for identifying the problem and coming forward," says an Environmental Protection Agency administrator. "It took guts," comments another government scientist. "The fact is that most companies . . . go into anger, denial, and the rest of that stuff. [We're used to seeing] decades-long arguments about whether a chemical is really toxic." For 3M, however, it wasn't all that difficult a decision—it was simply the right thing to do.[26]

As with environmentalism, the issue of ethics provides special challenges for international marketers. Business standards and practices vary a great deal from one country to the next. For example, whereas bribes and kickbacks are illegal for U.S. firms, they are standard business practice in many South American countries. One recent study found that companies from some nations were much more likely to use bribes when seeking contracts in emerging-market nations. The most flagrant bribe-paying firms were from Russia and China, with Taiwan and South Korea close behind. Other countries where corruption is common include India, Pakistan, and Bangladesh. The least corrupt were companies from Australia, Sweden, Switzerland, Austria, and Canada.[27] The question arises as to whether a company must lower its ethical standards to compete effectively in countries with lower standards. In one study, two researchers posed this question to chief executives of large international companies and got a unanimous response: No.[28]

For the sake of all of the company's stakeholders—customers, suppliers, employees, shareholders, and the public—it is important to make a commitment to a common set of shared standards worldwide. For example, John Hancock Mutual Life Insurance Company operates successfully in Southeast Asia, an area that by western standards has widespread questionable business and government practices. Despite warnings from locals that Hancock would have to bend its rules to succeed, the company set out strict guidelines. "We told our people that we had the same ethical standards, same procedures, and same policies in these countries that we have in the United States, and we do," says Hancock Chairman Stephen Brown. "We just felt that things like payoffs were wrong—and if we had to do business that way, we'd rather not do business." Hancock employees feel good about the consistent levels of ethics. "There may be countries where you have to do that kind of thing," says Brown. "We haven't found that country yet, and if we do, we won't do business there."[29]

Many industrial and professional associations have suggested codes of ethics, and many companies are now adopting their own codes. For example, the American Marketing Association, an international association of marketing managers and scholars, developed the code of ethics shown in Table 20.2. Companies are also developing programs to teach

TABLE 20.2   American Marketing Association Code of Ethics

Ethical Norms and Values for Marketers

Preamble

The American Marketing Association commits itself to promoting the highest standard of professional ethical norms and values for its members. Norms are established standards of conduct that are expected and maintained by society and/or professional organizations. Values represent the collective conception of what people find desirable, important and morally proper. Values serve as the criteria for evaluating the actions of others. Marketing practitioners must recognize that they not only serve their enterprises but also act as stewards of society in creating, facilitating and executing the efficient and effective transactions that are part of the greater economy. In this role, marketers should embrace the highest ethical norms of practicing professionals and the ethical values implied by their responsibility toward stakeholders (e.g., customers, employees, investors, channel members, regulators and the host community).

General Norms

1. Marketers must do no harm. This means doing work for which they are appropriately trained or experienced so that they can actively add value to their organizations and customers. It also means adhering to all applicable laws and regulations and embodying high ethical standards in the choices they make.
2. Marketers must foster trust in the marketing system. This means that products are appropriate for their intended and promoted uses. It requires that marketing communications about goods and services are not intentionally deceptive or misleading. It suggests building relationships that provide for the equitable adjustment and/or redress of customer grievances. It implies striving for good faith and fair dealing so as to contribute toward the efficacy of the exchange process.

Marketers must embrace, communicate and practice the fundamental ethical values that will improve consumer confidence in the integrity of the marketing exchange system. These basic values are intentionally aspirational and include honesty, responsibility, fairness, respect, openness and citizenship.

Ethical Values

Honesty—to be truthful and forthright in our dealings with customers and stakeholders.
- We will tell the truth in all situations and at all times.
- We will offer products of value that do what we claim in our communications.
- We will stand behind our products if they fail to deliver their claimed benefits.
- We will honor our explicit and implicit commitments and promises.

Responsibility—to accept the consequences of our marketing decisions and strategies. We will make strenuous efforts to serve the needs of our customers.
- We will avoid using coercion with all stakeholders.
- We will acknowledge the social obligations to stakeholders that come with increased marketing and economic power.
- We will recognize our special commitments to economically vulnerable segments of the market such as children, the elderly and others who may be substantially disadvantaged.

Fairness—to try to balance justly the needs of the buyer with the interests of the seller.
- We will represent our products in a clear way in selling, advertising and other forms of communication; this includes the avoidance of false, misleading and deceptive promotion.
- We will reject manipulations and sales tactics that harm customer trust.
- We will not engage in price fixing, predatory pricing, price gouging or "bait-and-switch" tactics.
- We will not knowingly participate in material conflicts of interest.

Respect—to acknowledge the basic human dignity of all stakeholders.
- We will value individual differences even as we avoid stereotyping customers or depicting demographic groups (e.g., gender, race, sexual orientation) in a negative or dehumanizing way in our promotions.
- We will listen to the needs of our customers and make all reasonable efforts to monitor and improve their satisfaction on an ongoing basis.
- We will make a special effort to understand suppliers, intermediaries and distributors from other cultures.
- We will appropriately acknowledge the contributions of others, such as consultants, employees and coworkers, to our marketing endeavors.

Openness—to create transparency in our marketing operations.
- We will strive to communicate clearly with all our constituencies.
- We will accept constructive criticism from our customers and other stakeholders.
- We will explain significant product or service risks, component substitutions or other foreseeable eventualities that could affect customers or their perception of the purchase decision.
- We will fully disclose list prices and terms of financing as well as available price deals and adjustments.

Citizenship—to fulfill the economic, legal, philanthropic and societal responsibilities that serve stakeholders in a strategic manner.
- We will strive to protect the natural environment in the execution of marketing campaigns.
- We will give back to the community through volunteerism and charitable donations.
- We will work to contribute to the overall betterment of marketing and its reputation.
- We will encourage supply chain members to ensure that trade is fair for all participants, including producers in developing countries.

TABLE 20.2   Continued

Implementation

Finally, we recognize that every industry sector and marketing subdiscipline (e.g., marketing research, e-commerce, direct selling, direct marketing, advertising) has its own specific ethical issues that require policies and commentary. An array of such codes can be accessed through links on the AMA Web site. We encourage all such groups to develop and/or refine their industry and discipline-specific codes of ethics to supplement these general norms and values.

Source: Reprinted with permission of the American Marketing Association.

managers about important ethics issues and help them find the proper responses. They hold ethics workshops and seminars and set up ethics committees. Furthermore, most major U.S. companies have appointed high-level ethics officers to champion ethics issues and to help resolve ethics problems and concerns facing employees.

PricewaterhouseCoopers (PwC) is a good example. In 1996, PwC established an ethics office and comprehensive ethics program, headed by a high-level chief ethics officer. The ethics program begins with a code of conduct, called "The Way We Do Business." PwC employees learn about the code of conduct and about how to handle thorny ethics issues in a comprehensive ethics training program, called "Navigating the Grey." The program also includes an ethics help line and regular communications at all levels. "It is obviously not enough to distribute a document," says PwC's Global CEO, Samuel DiPiazza. "Ethics is in everything we say and do." The PwC training program has involved 40,000 employees. Thanks to the increased level of awareness, last year there was about a 50 percent increase in calls to the help line from people asking for guidance in working through difficult ethics dilemmas.[30]

■ Ethics programs: PricewaterhouseCoopers established a comprehensive ethics program, which begins with a code of conduct, called "The Way We Do Business," says PwC's CEO, "Ethics is in everything we say and do."

Still, written codes and ethics programs do not ensure ethical behavior. Ethics and social responsibility require a total corporate commitment. They must be a component of the overall corporate culture. According to PwC's DiPiazza, "I see ethics as a mission-critical issue . . . deeply imbedded in who we are and what we do. It's just as important as our product development cycle or our distribution system. . . . It's about creating a culture based on integrity and respect, not a culture based on dealing with the crisis of the day. . . . We ask ourselves every day, 'Are we doing the right things?'"[31]

> Reviewing the Concepts <

Well—here you are at the end of your introductory marketing travels! In this chapter, we've closed with many important concepts involving marketing's sweeping impact on individual consumers, other businesses, and society as a whole. You learned that responsible marketers discover what consumers want and respond with the right products, priced to give good value to buyers and profit to the producer. A marketing system should sense, serve, and satisfy consumer needs and improve the quality of consumers' lives. In working to meet consumer needs, marketers may take some actions that are not to everyone's liking or benefit. Marketing managers should be aware of the main *criticisms of marketing.*

1. Identify the major social criticisms of marketing.

Marketing's *impact on individual consumer welfare* has been criticized for its high prices, deceptive practices, high-pressure selling, shoddy or unsafe products, planned obsolescence, and poor service to disadvantaged consumers. Marketing's *impact on society* has been criticized for creating false wants and too much materialism, too few social goods, cultural pollution, and too much political power. Critics have also criticized marketing's *impact on other businesses* for harming competitors and reducing competition through acquisitions, practices that create barriers to entry, and unfair competitive marketing practices.

2. Define *consumerism* and *environmentalism* and explain how they affect marketing strategies.

Concerns about the marketing system have led to *citizen action movements. Consumerism* is an organized social movement intended to strengthen the rights and power of consumers relative to sellers. Alert marketers view it as an opportunity to serve consumers better by providing more consumer information, education, and protection. *Environmentalism* is an organized social movement seeking to minimize the harm done to the environment and quality of life by marketing practices. The first wave of modern environmentalism was driven by environmental groups and concerned consumers, whereas the second wave was driven by government, which passed laws and regulations governing industrial practices impacting the environment. Moving into

the twenty-first century, the first two environmentalism waves are merging into a third and stronger wave in which companies are accepting responsibility for doing no environmental harm. Companies now are adopting policies of *environmental sustainability*—developing strategies that both sustain the environment and produce profits for the company.

3. Describe the principles of socially responsible marketing.

Many companies originally opposed these social movements and laws, but most of them now recognize a need for positive consumer information, education, and protection. Some companies have followed a policy of *enlightened marketing,* which holds that a company's marketing should support the best long-run performance of the marketing system. Enlightened marketing consists of five principles: *consumer-oriented marketing, innovative marketing, customer-value marketing, sense-of-mission marketing,* and *societal marketing.*

4. Explain the role of ethics in marketing.

Increasingly, companies are responding to the need to provide company policies and guidelines to help their managers deal with questions of *marketing ethics.* Of course even the best guidelines cannot resolve all the difficult ethical decisions that individuals and firms must make. But there are some principles that marketers can choose among. One principle states that such issues should be decided by the free market and legal system. A second, and more enlightened principle, puts responsibility not in the system but in the hands of individual companies and managers. Each firm and marketing manager must work out a philosophy of socially responsible and ethical behavior. Under the societal marketing concept, managers must look beyond what is legal and allowable and develop standards based on personal integrity, corporate conscience, and long-term consumer welfare.

Because business standards and practices vary from country to country, the issue of ethics poses special challenges for international marketers. The growing consensus among today's marketers is that it is important to make a commitment to a common set of shared standards worldwide.

> Reviewing the Key Terms <

Consumerism 633
Consumer-oriented
   marketing 639
Customer-value marketing 640

Deficient products 643
Desirable products 643
Enlightened marketing 638
Environmental sustainability 634

Environmentalism 634
Innovative marketing 639
Pleasing products 643
Salutary products 643

Sense-of-mission marketing 640
Societal marketing 642

> Discussing the Concepts <

1. Review the claims made by consumers, consumer advocates, public policy makers, and others that marketers are harming consumers through planned obsolescence, shoddy or unsafe products, and poor service to disadvantaged consumers. Do you agree with these claims?

2. Review the responses offered by marketers to claims that high distribution costs, high advertising and promotional costs, and excessive markups lead to high prices harmful to consumers. Do you agree with the marketers' responses?

3. Review claims made by critics that marketing creates false wants and too much materialism, too few social goods, cultural pollution,

and too much political power. Do you agree or disagree with these claims?

4. Can an organization be focused on both consumerism and environmentalism at the same time? Explain.

5. Can a marketer have two sets of ethical values—a personal set and a business set? Explain.

6. Describe the two philosophies of ethics and social responsibility discussed in the chapter. Is one philosophy better than the other? Explain?

> Applying the Concepts <

1. Suppose you are a key person in the marketing department of your organization. You recently learned that your company is marketing an unsafe product, which has already resulted in a few consumer injuries. Publicly acknowledging the problem would damage your brand's image and would require an expensive product recall. However, you believe that you could quietly introduce an improved version of the product, avoiding both the recall and the harmful publicity. What would you do?

2. In a small group, search the Internet for companies that have included a discernable societal marketing goal in their mission/vision statements. Record and share these mission statements.

Rewrite the following Dell mission statement incorporating a more societal marketing focus.

> "Dell's mission is to be the world's most successful computer company, delivering the best customer experience in markets we serve."

3. Recent public concerns over children and the Internet resulted the Children's Online Privacy Protection Act (COPPA). Among other things, this act requires Web sites that are visited by children under the age of 13 to post a privacy policy detailing any personally identifiable information collected from those children. Do some research and answer the question: What consumer need is being met by COPPA?

> Focus on Technology <

Retail check-out scanners have been around for almost a generation. They save time for the consumer and are an integral part of the retailer's supply chain management system. But according to FTC reports, whether intentionally or unintentionally, 1 out of 30 scanner prices is wrong. Half of the incorrect prices are too high and the other half are too low.

1. How trusting are consumers of electronic scanning?

2. Do you believe some retailers intentionally mismark items? Why would they do this? Is it easy or difficult to prove that an item is intentionally mismarked?

3. Would Radio Frequency Identification (RFID) help to fix this problem? Why or why not?

Sources: See www.ftc.gov/reports/scanner2/scanner2.htm; and www.ftc.gov/reports/scanner1/scanners.htm.

> Focus on Ethics <

A *whistle-blower* is a person who reports illegal or unethical behavior to the public, to the government, or to those in positions of authority. If there ever was a whistle-blower poster-person, it's Sherron Watkins, of Houston, Texas. As you may recall, this ex-vice president of corporate development at Enron wrote a memo to Kenneth Lay, Enron's chairman and CEO, alerting him to the company's financial improprieties. Watkin's story is one of concern for a company she helped build and compassion for fellow employees. Visit www.time.com/time/personoftheyear/2002/poywatkins.html and read the Time Web site article selecting Watkins and two other whistle-blowers as "Time Magazine Person of the Year 2002." Then visit http://news.findlaw.com/hdocs/docs/enron/empltr2lay82001.pdf and read the now famous Watkins' memo. Respond to the following questions.

1. Did Sherron Watkins do the right thing in going to Kenneth Lay rather than to the media? Explain?

2. In the memo, is Watkins clear about Enron's alleged illegal financial dealings?

3. If you had been Kenneth Lay and had received Watkins' letter, what would you have done?

4. Do you think there is adequate protection for whistle-blowers?

Sources: See www.telltheboard.com/questions/definitions.html; and http://news.findlaw.com/hdocs/docs/enron/empltr2lay82001.pdf.

Video Case

NFL

When you think of the NFL, you probably think first of Monday night football and the Superbowl. Since 1920, the league has brought professional football to fans across the country and around the world. You may also know that the league provides more than just athletic entertainment for fans. The NFL also strives to have a positive impact on communities across America. So, in 1974, the league formed a partnership with the United Way. Today, that partnership had grown into a charitable enterprise that generates funds and services for more than 30 million people each year.

The benefit to the community and to the United Way is clear, but the NFL benefits from its charitable efforts as well. In addition to connecting more deeply with fans through community outreach and player volunteer efforts, the NFL sponsors a series of ad campaigns featuring the United Way that reminds fans that football players are regular people who want to do good in the communities where they work and live.

After viewing the video featuring the NFL, answer the following questions about marketing and social responsibility.

1. Why do you think the NFL partners with the United Way? How does the United Way benefit? How does the NFL benefit?

2. Make a list of criticisms about the NFL's marketing efforts. Does the NFL's partnership with the United Way lessen any of those concerns?

Company Case

Vitango: Fighting Malnutrition

Imagine teaching an elementary school class in which students are constantly inattentive and falling asleep—not because they are bored but because they are malnourished. In many countries, this is not an unusual problem. Two billion people around the globe suffer from anemia—an iron deficiency. Iron deficiency leads to reduced resistance to disease, lowers learning ability in children, and contributes to the death of one out of five pregnant mothers. Two hundred million children do not get enough Vitamin A. As a result 250,000 of them go blind each year and 2.2 million children under five die each year from diarrhea. Many malnourished children suffer from zinc deficiency, which leads to growth failure and infections. Close to 2 billion people do not get enough iodine, and iodine deficiency is the leading cause of preventable mental retardation in the world. If they only used the ordinary table salt found in homes and restaurants all across the United States, this wouldn't happen.

What can U.S. businesses do about this deplorable situation? Quite a bit. Companies such as Coca-Cola and Procter & Gamble have invested millions of dollars in research of micronutrients. They are learning how to fortify everyday food and beverages with additional minerals and vitamins to wipe out deficiencies and keep school children around the world alert and mentally prepared for school.

Fortified foods are common in the United States. Iodine has been added to ordinary table salt for decades; milk contains Vitamin D and calcium; and cornflakes list all the micronutrients found in them on the box. A quick check of your pantry reveals that many drinks and other foods have Vitamins and minerals added to them. Thus, adding micronutrients to foods is not new or unusual in this country.

What are new are the efforts of companies to identify specific deficiencies and to develop new technologies for adding micronutrients to foodstuffs in order to eliminate or reduce the deficiencies in specific countries. A good example is a Coca-Cola beverage product called Vitango in Botswana.

Coca-Cola spent years developing a powdered beverage that, when mixed with water, looks and tastes like a sweeter version of Hi-C. The beverage is fortified with 12 vitamins and with minerals that are chronically lacking in the diets of people in developing countries. Coke tested this product in Botswana in Project Mission. Every day for eight weeks, nurses visited schools where they mixed the beverage and passed out paper cups of the "new Hi-C." At the end of the test period, levels of iron and zinc in the children's blood levels had grown. Some parents noted that their children had become more attentive at school. After the Botswana tests, Coca-Cola also ran tests in Peru to determine how well the nutrients are absorbed into the bloodstream.

Coca-Cola, however, is not yet ready to launch Vitango. One issue is the powdered product form. Given the impurities of much water in Africa, Coca-Cola wants to package it in a ready-to-drink formula, not in the powdered version now available. That will require reformulation that could actually drive down the price.

P&G has also developed micronutrient-enriched drinks for distribution in developing countries. In the 1990s, P&G developed its own proprietary iron, Vitamin A, and iodine fortification technology, which it called GrowthPlus. GrowthPlus was the basic ingredient in a product called Nutridelight that P&G launched in the Philippines. Unfortunately it didn't sell well—primarily because it was priced at 50 percent above the market price of other powdered drinks.

More recently, P&G has launched another product, Nutristar, containing eight vitamins and five minerals in Venezuela. Sold at most food stores, it comes in flavors such as mango and passion fruit and promises to produce "taller, stronger, and smarter kids." To date, Nutristar is doing quite well. One reason is that it's available at McDonald's, where it is chosen by consumers with about half of all happy meals sold. P&G is also offering free samples in schools.

The major problem with both Coca-Cola's and P&G's nutritional products is price. These products were expensive to develop because of long lead times, the need to enlist the help of nutritional experts around the world, and the need to develop products that appeal to the local population's tastes. If offered at "reasonable" prices, they would be out of the reach of the world's desperately poor, the group that needs them most. Consider Coca-Cola's Vitango. The poor people in other countries are *not* eating at McDonald's. In countries such as Botswana, they are barely existing on cornmeal and rice. They simply cannot afford to buy fortified sweetened drinks or, for that matter, any sweetened drinks.

How can P&G and Coca-Cola market such products without pricing them too high for the intended market? Learning its lesson in the Philippines, P&G priced Nutristar about 25 percent higher than other powdered drinks and 30 percent below carbonated soft drinks. Even so, that's still too high for the poverty-stricken. Coca-Cola originally planned to sell Vitango for about 20 cents for an 8 ounce liquid serving but realizes that this price is too high. That's part of the reason continuing developmental work on the product.

One solution to the pricing problem is to work with governments, but many of them are too poor to be able to afford the products. Or they lack the resources to educate their people on the merits of fortified foods. Enter GAIN—the Global Alliance for Improved Nutrition—an international consortium set up by the Bill and Melissa Gates charitable foundation. GAIN offers companies assistance in lobbying for favorable tariffs and tax rates and for speedier regulatory review of new products in targeted countries. It also gives local governments money to increase the demand for fortified foods, including large-scale public relations campaigns or a government "seal of approval." This program is receiving $70 million over five years beginning in May 2002. Such actions should help Coca-Cola and P&G by educating target populations about the value of fortified foods and beverages so that they will buy such products.

Of course, Coca-Cola and P&G can work with governments on their own, but their actions may be distrusted. After all, these are "for profit" organizations whose motives may be suspect. GAIN has the advantage that it's a not-for-profit.

While GAIN seems like a wonderful resource for helping malnourished peoples, it does have its critics. They point out that selling or giving away fortified foods does not solve the underlying problem of poverty. Nor does it teach people good nutritional habits. Moreover, inn addition to their vitamins and minerals, many of the "fortified" foods also contain overly large amounts of fat, sugar, and salt. So, for example, whereas the foods might help reduce iron deficiency, they could also lead to obesity. Some observers claim that it would be better to teach people how to grow fruits and vegetables. The problem is that people will die from malnutrition before poverty is eliminated or trees bear fruit.

Other issues must also be addressed. A fortified beverage such as Vitango will help in dealing with malnutrition but can't eliminate it. People will still need to eat a variety of other foods, which makes education very important. Remember that these products contain no juice. They are intended as supplements, not as substitutes for a proper diet. Lack of understanding about how to use products has landed other companies, such as Nestle with its infant formula, in trouble when they were used inappropriately.

Given all these problems, why would Coca-Cola and P&G develop these products in the first place? One answer is future sales and profits. Products such as Nutristar and Vitango could create a basis from which to launch other Coca-Cola or P&G products, such as snack foods or juice drinks. As sales of carbonated beverages around the world have slowed, these fortified drinks pose a growth opportunity for the companies. Another answer is "goodwill," and not just goodwill for the companies involved. September 11, 2001 taught us in the United States that our country is the focus of both the world's envy and its hatred. Efforts to help share our wealth of technology and research in ways that improve the lot of other peoples may be a major deterrent to future attacks and the growth of terrorism. By helping other nations of the world, U.S. corporations can help create environments where freedom can flourish. One writer insists that when U.S. corporations help people as consumers to buy the goods and services that our companies sell, they also enhance our government's ability to sell our country.

Questions for Discussion

1. Which of the textbook's criticisms of marketing's impact on consumers, if any, are found in the cases of Vitango and Nutristar?

2. Which of the criticisms of marketing's impact on society are found in the Vitango and Nutristar case?

3. Could Vitango and Nutristar be considered enlightened marketing? Why or why not?

4. Are the development and marketing of such products as fortified foods and beverages ethical and socially responsible?

5. How should Coca-Cola proceed with the marketing of Vitango?

Sources: Jill Bruss, "Reaching the World," *Beverage Industry*, December 2001, p. 28+; Rance Crain, "U.S. Marketers Must Develop Products to Help Third World," *Advertising Age*, December 3, 2001, p. 20; Betsy McKay, "Drinks for Developing Countries," *Wall Street Journal*, November 27, 2001, p. B1, B6; Rachel Zimmerman, "Gates Fights Malnutrition with Cheese, Ketchup Incentives," *Wall Street Journal*, May 9, 2002, p. B1; George Carpenter, "P&G and Sustainable Development—Finding Opportunity in Responsibility," April 1, 2003, accessed at www.eu.pg.com/news/speeches/20030401insideoutcarpenter.html; and "GAIN to Help China Improve Soy Sauce," *SinoChina Daily Business News*, October 24, 2003, p. 1.

MARKETING PLAN

The Marketing Plan: An Introduction

As a marketer, you'll need a good marketing plan to provide direction and focus for your brand, product, or company. With a detailed plan, any business will be better prepared to launch a new product or build sales for existing products. Nonprofit organizations also use marketing plans to guide their fundraising and outreach efforts. Even government agencies put together marketing plans for initiatives such as building public awareness of proper nutrition and stimulating area tourism.

The Purpose and Content of a Marketing Plan

Unlike a business plan, which offers a broad overview of the entire organization's mission, objectives, strategy, and resource allocation, a marketing plan has a more limited scope. It serves to document how the organization's strategic objectives will be achieved through specific marketing strategies and tactics, with the customer as the starting point. It is also linked to the plans of other departments within the organization. Suppose a marketing plan calls for selling 200,000 units annually. The production department must gear up to make that many units, the finance department must have funding available to cover the expenses, the human resources department must be ready to hire and train staff, and so on. Without the appropriate level of organizational support and resources, no marketing plan can succeed.

Although the exact length and layout will vary from company to company, a marketing plan usually contains the sections described in Table X on page Y. Smaller businesses may create shorter or less formal marketing plans, whereas corporations frequently require highly structured marketing plans. To guide implementation effectively, every part of the plan must be described in considerable detail. Sometimes a company will post its marketing plan on an internal Web site, which allows managers and employees in different locations to consult specific sections and collaborate on additions or changes.

The Role of Research

Marketing plans are not created in a vacuum. To develop successful strategies and action programs, marketers need up-to-date information about the environment, the competition, and the market segments to be served. Often, analysis of internal data is the starting point for assessing the current marketing situation, supplemented by marketing intelligence and research investigating the overall market, the competition, key issues, and threats and opportunities issues. As the plan is put into effect, marketers use advertising and other forms of research to measure progress toward objectives and identify areas for improvement if results fall short of projections. Finally, marketers use marketing research to learn more about their customers' requirements, expectations, perceptions, and satisfaction levels. This deeper understanding provides a foundation for building competitive advantage through well-informed segmenting, targeting, and positioning decisions. Thus, the marketing plan should outline what marketing research will be conducted and how the findings will be applied.

The Role of Relationships

The marketing plan shows how the company will establish and maintain profitable customer relationships. In the process, however, it also shapes a number of internal and external relationships. First, it affects how marketing personnel work with each other and with other departments to deliver value and satisfy customers. Second, it affects how the company works with suppliers, distributors, and strategic alliance partners to achieve the objectives listed in the plan. Third, it influences the company's dealings with other stakeholders, including government regulators, the media, and the community at large. All of these relationships are important to the organization's success, so they should be considered when a marketing plan is being developed.

From Marketing Plan to Marketing Action

Companies generally create yearly marketing plans, although some plans cover a longer period. Marketers start planning well in advance of the implementation date to allow time for marketing research, thorough analysis, management review, and coordination between departments. Then, after each action program begins, marketers monitor ongoing results, compare them with projections, analyze any differences, and take corrective steps as needed. Some marketers design contingency plans, as in the sample plan below, for implementation if certain conditions emerge. Because of inevitable and sometimes unpredictable environmental changes, marketers must be ready to update and adapt marketing plans at any time.

For effective implementation and control, the marketing plan should define how progress toward objectives will be measured. Managers typically use budgets, schedules, and performance standards for monitoring and evaluating results. With budgets, they can compare planned expenditures with actual expenditures for a given week, month, or other period. Schedules allow management to see when tasks were supposed to be completed—and when they were actually completed. Performance standards track the outcomes of marketing programs to see whether the company is moving forward toward its objectives. Some examples of performance standards are: market share, sales volume, product profitability, and customer satisfaction.

Sample Marketing Plan for Sonic

This section takes you inside the sample marketing plan for Sonic, a hypothetical start-up company. The company's first product is the Sonic 1000, a multifunction personal digital assistant (PDA), also known as a handheld computer. Sonic will be competing with palmOne, Hewlett-Packard, and other well-established rivals in an increasingly crowded marketplace. The annotations explain more about what each section of the plan should contain—and why.

Executive Summary

This section summarizes the main goals, recommendations, and points as an overview for senior managers who must read and approve the marketing plan. Generally a table of contents follows this section, for management convenience.

Sonic is preparing to launch a new PDA product, the Sonic 1000, in a maturing market. Despite the dominance of PDA leader palmOne, we can compete because our offering combines exclusive features at a value-added price. We are targeting specific segments in the consumer and business markets, taking advantage of opportunities indicated by higher demand for easy-to-use, wireless-enabled PDAs with expanded communications functionality.

The primary marketing objectives of this plan are to achieve first-year U.S. market share of 3 percent and unit sales of 240,000. The primary financial objectives are to achieve first-year sales revenues of $60 million, keep first-year losses to less than $10 million, and break even early in the second year.

Current Marketing Situation

In this section, marketing managers discuss the overall market, identify the market segments they will target, and provide information about the company's current situation.

Sonic, founded 18 months ago by two entrepreneurs with experience in the PC market, is about to enter the PDA market dominated by palmOne. Now, however, overall PDA sales have slowed and profitability has suffered. The emergence of multifunction PDAs and advanced cell phones has increased competitive pressure. The estimated size of the market for multifunction PDAs and cell phones is $63.7 billion, with 50% growth expected within 4 years. To gain market share in this environment, Sonic must carefully target specific market segments.

Market Description

By describing the targeted segments in detail, marketers provide context for the marketing strategies and detailed action programs discussed later in the plan.

Sonic's market consists of consumers and business users who need to conveniently store, communicate, and exchange information on the go. Specific segments being targeted during the first year include professionals, students, corporations, entrepreneurs, and medical users. Table A1.1 shows how the Sonic 1000 addresses the needs of targeted consumer and business segments.

PDA purchasers can choose between models based on two different operating systems, one created by Palm and one created by Microsoft. Sonic licenses the market-dominant Palm system because thousands of software applications and hardware peripherals are compatible with this system. Product proliferation and increased competition have resulted in lower prices and lower profit margins. Lower prices are helping sales of PDAs in the lower end of the consumer market, but at the expense of gross margins. Customers with first-generation PDAs are reentering the market by buying newer, high-end multifunction units.

Exhibit 1 clarifies the benefits that product features will deliver to satisfy the needs of customers in each market segment.

Product Review

The product review should summarize the main features for all of the company's products. The information may be organized by product line, by type of customer, by market, or (as here) by order of product introduction.

Our first product, the Sonic PDA 1000, offers the following standard features:

- Voice recognition for hands free commands and communication
- Built-in cell phone functionality
- Wireless Web access and e-mail capabilities
- MP3 music downloading and player capabilities
- Full organization and communication functions, including calendar, address book, memo pad, Internet browser, e-mail program, and text and instant messaging programs

TABLE A1.1   Needs and Corresponding Features/Benefits of Sonic PDA

Targeted Segment	Customer Need	Corresponding Feature/Benefit
Professionals (consumer market)	• Stay in touch while on the go	• Wireless e-mail to conveniently send and receive messages from anywhere; cell phone capability for voice communication from anywhere
	• Record information while on the go	• Voice recognition for no-hands recording
Students (consumer market)	• Perform many functions without carrying multiple gadgets	• Compatible with numerous applications and peripherals for convenient, cost-effective functionality
	• Express style and individuality	• Case wardrobe of different colors and patterns allows users to make a fashion statement
Corporate users (business market)	• Input and access critical data on the go	• Compatible with widely available software
	• Use for proprietary tasks	• Customizable to fit diverse corporate tasks and networks
Entrepreneurs (business market)	• Organize and access contacts, schedule details	• No-hands, wireless access to calendar and address book to easily check appointments and connect with contacts
Medical users (business market)	• Update, access, and exchange medical records	• No-hands, wireless recording and exchange of information to reduce paperwork and increase productivity

- Connectors to accommodate all palmOne-compatible peripherals
- Ability to run any palmOne-compatible application
- Large color display
- Keyboard for input
- Cradle for synchronizing data with PC
- Interchangeable case wardrobe of different colors and patterns

First-year sales revenues are projected to be $60 million, based on sales of 240,000 Sonic 1000 units at a wholesale price of $250 each. During the second year, we plan to introduce the Sonic 2000 as a higher-end product with the following standard features:

- Global positioning system for identifying locations, obtaining directions
- Built-in digital camera
- Translation capabilities to send English text as Spanish text (other languages to be offered as add-on options)

Competitive Review

The purpose of a competitive review is to identify key competitors, describe their market positions, and briefly discuss their strategies.

Increased entry of established computer and cell phone companies has pressured industry participants to continually add features and cut prices. Competition from specialized devices for text and e-mail messaging, such as Blackberry devices, is also a factor. Key competitors include:

- **palmOne.** palmOne has had some financial struggles, in part because of the need to reduce prices for competitive reasons. Its acquisition of Handspring boosted its product

TABLE A1.2   Selected PDA Products and Pricing

Competitor	Model	Features	Price
palmOne	Tungsten C	PDA functions, wireless capabilities, color screen, tiny keyboard, wireless capabilities	$499
palmOne	M130	PDA functions, color screen, expandable functionality	$199
Handspring	Treo 270	PDA and cell phone functions, color screen, tiny keyboard, speakerphone capabilities; no expansion slot	$499
Samsung	i500	PDA functions, cell phone functions, MP3 player, color screen, video capabilities	$599
Garmin	iQue 3600	PDA functions, global positioning system technology, voice recorder, expansion slot, MP3 player	$589
Dell	Axim X5	PDA functions, color screen, e-mail capable, voice recorder, speaker, expandable	$199
Sony	Clie PEG-NX73V	PDA functions, digital camera, tiny keyboard, games, presentation software, MP3 player, voice recorder	$499

development strength and expanded its product mix. As the best-known maker of PDAs, palmOne has achieved good distribution in nearly every channel and is gaining distribution among U.S. cell phone service carriers. At present, palmOne products lack some the voice recognition software that is standard in the Sonic 1000.

- **Hewlett-Packard.** HP is targeting business markets with its iPAQ Pocket PC devices, many with wireless capabilities to accommodate corporate users. For extra security, one model allows access by fingerprint match as well as by password. HP enjoys excellent distribution, and its products are priced from below $300 to more than $600.

- **Garmin.** Garmin's iQue 3600 was the first PDA with built-in global position system (GPS) capability. Priced at $589, its mapping software and verbal commands eliminate the need for an automotive device. Garmin's PDA uses the Palm operating system and has other unique functions, such as a digital voice recorder for brief memos.

- **Dell.** Dell's basic PDA model is priced starting at $199. However, this product is larger than competing palmOne products, and it lacks wireless functionality as a standard feature. New, slimmer models are expected at regular intervals from this low-cost competitor, which markets directly to customers.

- **Samsung.** This is one of several manufacturers that has married cell phone capabilities with multifunction PDA features. Its i500 uses the Palm operating system, provides speedy e-mail and MP3 downloads, plays video clips and offers PDA functions such as address book, calendar, and speed dial.

Despite this strong competition, Sonic can carve out a definite image and gain recognition among the targeted segments. Our licensing arrangement with Cellport Systems allows us to provide the exclusive feature of voice recognition for hands-off operation, a critical point of differentiation for competitive advantage. Table A1.2 shows a selection of competitive PDA products and prices.

Distribution Review

In this section, marketers list the most important channels, provide an overview of each channel arrangement, and mention any new developments or trends.

Sonic-branded products will be distributed through a network of select store and non-store retailers in the top 50 U.S. markets. Among the most important channel partners being contacted are:

- **Office supply superstores.** Office Depot and Staples will both carry Sonic products in stores, in catalogs, and on Web sites.
- **Computer stores.** Gateway stores will carry Sonic products.
- **Electronic specialty stores.** Circuit City and Best Buy will carry Sonic PDAs.
- **Online retailers.** Amazon.com will carry Sonic PDAs and, for a promotional fee, will give Sonic prominent placement on its home page during the introduction.

Although distribution will initially be restricted to the United States, we plan to expand into Canada and beyond, according to demand. We will emphasize trade sales promotion in the first year.

Strengths, Weaknesses, Opportunities, and Threat Analysis

Sonic has several powerful strengths on which to build, but our major weakness is lack of brand awareness and image. The major opportunity is growing demand for multi-function PDAs that deliver communication-specific benefits. We also face the threat of ever-higher competition and downward pressure on pricing. Table A1.3 summarizes the main strengths, weaknesses, opportunities, and threats facing Sonic.

Strengths

> Strengths are internal capabilities that can help the company reach its objectives.

Sonic can build on three important strengths:

1. **Innovative product.** The Sonic 1000 includes a voice-recognition system that simplifies usage and allows hands-free operation. It also offers features such as built-in cell phone functionality, wireless communication, and MP3 capabilities.
2. **Compatibility.** Our PDA can work with the hundreds of Palm-compatible peripherals and applications currently available.
3. **Pricing.** Our product is priced lower than competing multifunction models—all of which lack voice recognition—which gives us an edge with price-conscious customers.

Weaknesses

> Weaknesses are internal elements that may interfere with the company's ability to achieve its objectives.

By waiting to enter the PDA market until the initial shakeout and consolidation of competitors has occurred, Sonic has learned from the successes and mistakes of others. Nonetheless, we have two main weaknesses:

TABLE A1.3
Sonic's Strengths, Weaknesses, Opportunities, and Threats

Strengths	Weaknesses
• Voice-recognition capabilities and multiple functions valued by customers • Value pricing • Compatibility with Palm add-ons	• Lack of brand awareness and image • Heavier than most competing models
Opportunities	**Threats**
• Increased demand for multiple communication methods • Availability of diverse add-ons cycle • Availability of applications for consumer and business use	• Increasing competition • Downward pricing pressure • Compressed product life

1. **Lack of brand awareness.** As a start-up, Sonic has not yet established a brand or image in the marketplace, whereas palmOne and other rivals have strong brand recognition. This is an area we will address with promotion.

2. **Heavier weight.** To accommodate the multifunction features, the Sonic 100 is slightly heavier than most competing models. To counteract this, we will emphasize our multifunction features and value-added pricing, two important competitive strengths.

Opportunities

Sonic can take advantage of three major market opportunities:

1. **Increasing demand for multiple communication methods.** The market for wireless Web-enabled PDAs with cell phone functionality is projected to grow faster than the market for nonwireless models. More prospects are seeing users with PDAs in work and educational settings, which is boosting primary demand. Also, customers who bought entry-level models are now trading up.

2. **Add-on peripherals.** More peripherals, such as digital cameras and global positioning systems are available for PDAs that use the Palm operating system. Consumers and business users who are interested in any of these peripherals will see the Sonic 1000 as a value-priced device able to be conveniently and quickly expanded for multiple functions.

3. **Diverse applications.** The wide range of Palm-compatible software applications available for home and business use allows the Sonic PDA to satisfy communication and information needs.

Threats

We face three main threats at the introduction of the Sonic 1000:

1. **Increased competition.** More companies are entering the U.S. PDA market with models that offer some but not all of the features and benefits provided by Sonic's PDA. Therefore, Sonic's marketing communications must stress our clear differentiation and value-added pricing.

2. **Downward pressure on pricing.** Increased competition and market-share strategies are pushing PDA prices down. Still, our objective of seeking a 10% profit on second-year sales of the original model is realistic, given the lower margins in the PDA market.

3. **Compressed product life cycle.** PDAs seem to be reaching the maturity stage of their life cycle more quickly than earlier technology products. We have contingency plans to keep sales growing by adding new features, targeting additional segments, and adjusting prices.

Objectives and Issues

We have set aggressive but achievable objectives for the first and second years of market entry.

First-year Objectives

During the Sonic 1000's initial year on the market, we are aiming for a 3 percent share of the U.S. PDA market through unit sales volume of 240,000.

Second-year Objectives

Our second-year objectives are to achieve a 6 percent share based on sales of two models and to achieve break-even early in this period.

Issues

One major issue is our ability to establish a well-regarded brand name linked to a meaningful positioning. We will have to invest heavily in marketing to create a memorable and

---

Opportunities are external elements that the company may be able to exploit to its advantage.

Threats are current or emerging external elements that may possibly challenge the company's performance.

The company's objectives should be defined in specific terms so management can measure progress and, if needed, take corrective action to stay on track. This section describes any major issues that might affect the company's marketing strategy and implementation.

distinctive brand image projecting innovation, quality, and value. We also must measure awareness and response so we can adjust our marketing efforts if necessary.

Marketing Strategy

Sonic's marketing strategy is based on a positioning of product differentiation. Our primary consumer target is middle- to upper-income professionals who need one portable device to coordinate their busy schedules and communicate with family and colleagues. Our secondary consumer target is high school, college, and graduate students who need a multifunction device. This segment can be described demographically by age (16–30) and education status.

Our primary business target is mid- to large-sized corporations that want to help their managers and employees stay in touch and input or access critical data on the go. This segment consists of companies with more than $25 million in annual sales and more than 100 employees. A secondary business target is entrepreneurs and small-business owners. We are also targeting medical users who want to reduce paperwork and update or access patients' medical records.

Each of the four marketing-mix strategies conveys Sonic's differentiation to the target market segments identified above.

Positioning

A positioning built on meaningful differences, supported by appropriate strategy and implementation, can help the company build competitive advantage.

Using product differentiation, we are positioning the Sonic PDA as the most versatile, convenient, value-added model for personal and professional use. The marketing strategy will focus on the voice-recognition system as the main feature differentiating the Sonic 1000.

Product Strategy

These sections summarize the broad logic that will guide decisions made about the marketing mix in the period covered by the plan.

The Sonic 1000, including all the features described in the earlier Product Review section, will be sold with a one-year warranty. We will introduce a more compact, powerful high-end model (the Sonic 2000) during the following year, with GPS functionality and other features. Building the Sonic brand is an integral part of our product strategy. The brand and logo (Sonic's distinctive yellow thunderbolt) will be displayed on the product and its packaging, and reinforced by its prominence in the introductory marketing campaign.

Pricing Strategy

The Sonic 1000 will be introduced at $250 wholesale/$350 estimated retail price per unit. We expect to lower the price of this first model when we expand the product line by launching the Sonic 2000, to be priced at $350 wholesale per unit. These prices reflect a strategy of (1) attracting desirable channel partners and (2) taking market share from palmOne.

Distribution Strategy

Our channel strategy is to use selective distribution to have Sonic PDAs sold through well-known stores and online retailers. During the first year, we will add channel partners until we have coverage in all major U.S. markets and the product is included in the major electronics catalogs and Web sites. We will also investigate distribution through cell-phone outlets maintained by major carriers such as Cingular Wireless. In support of our channel partners, Sonic will provide demonstration products, detailed specification handouts, and full-color photos and displays featuring the product. We will also arrange special trade terms for retailers that place volume orders.

Marketing Communications Strategy

By integrating all messages in all media, we will reinforce the brand name and the main points of product differentiation, especially our exclusive voice-recognition feature. Research about media consumption patterns will help our advertising agency choose appropriate media and timing to reach prospects before and during product introduction. Thereafter, advertising will appear on a pulsing basis to maintain brand awareness and communicate various differentiation messages. The agency will also coordinate public relations efforts to build the Sonic brand and support the differentiation message. To attract market attention and encourage purchasing, we will offer as a limited-time premium a leather carry-case. To attract, retain, and motivate channel partners for a push strategy, we will use trade sales promotions and personal selling to channel partners. Until the Sonic brand has been established, our communications will encourage purchases through channel partners rather than from our Web site.

Marketing Research

Using research, we are identifying the specific features and benefits that our target market segments value. Feedback from market tests, surveys, and focus groups will help us develop the Sonic 2000. We are also measuring and analyzing customers' attitudes toward competing brands and products. Brand awareness research will help us determine the effectiveness and efficiency of our messages and media. Finally, we will use customer satisfaction studies to gauge market reaction.

Management should explain in this section how marketing research will be used to support development, implementation, and evaluation of strategies and action programs.

Marketing Organization

Sonic's chief marketing officer, Jane Melody, holds overall responsibility for marketing strategy and direction. Figure A1.1 shows the structure of the eight-person marketing organization. Sonic has hired Worldwide Marketing to handle national sales campaigns, trade and consumer sales promotions, and public relations efforts.

The marketing department may be organized by function, as in this sample, by geography, by product, or by customer (or some combination).

Action Programs

The Sonic 1000 will be introduced in February. Following are summaries of the action programs we will use during the first six months of next year to achieve our stated objectives.

Action programs should be coordinated with the resources and activities of other departments, including production, finance, purchasing, etc.

January

We will initiate a $200,000 trade sales promotion campaign to educate dealers and generate excitement for the product launch in February. We will exhibit at the major consumer electronics trade shows and provide samples to selected product reviewers, opinion leaders, and celebrities as part of our public relations strategy. Our training staff

FIGURE A1.1
Sonic's marketing organization

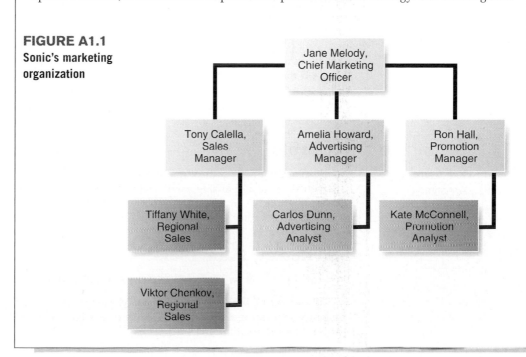

will work with sales personnel at major retail chains to explain the Sonic 1000's features, benefits, and competitive advantages.

February

We will start an integrated print/radio/Internet campaign targeting professionals and consumers. The campaign will show how quickly Sonic PDA users can accomplish tasks using voice recognition. This multimedia campaign will be supported by point-of-sale signage as well as online-only specials.

March

As the multimedia advertising campaign continues, we will add consumer sales promotion tactics such giving away leather carry-cases as a premium. We will also distribute new point-of-purchase displays to support our retailers.

April

We will hold a trade sales contest offering prizes for the salesperson and retail organization that sells the most Sonic PDAs during the 4-week period.

May

We plan to roll out a new national advertising campaign this month. The radio ads will feature celebrity voices using the voice-recognition system to operate their Sonic PDAs. The print ads will show these celebrities holding their Sonic PDAs.

June

Our radio campaign will add a new voice-over tag line promoting the Sonic 1000 as a graduation gift. We will also exhibit at the semiannual electronics trade show and provide channel partners with new competitive comparison handouts as a sales aid. In addition, we will tally and analyze the results of customer satisfaction surveys for use in future promotions and to provide feedback for product and marketing activities.

Budgets

> Budgets serve two main purposes: to project profitability and to help managers plan for expenditures, scheduling, and operations related to each action program.

Total first-year sales revenue for the Sonic 1000 is projected at $60 million, with an average wholesale price of $250 per unit and variable cost per unit of $150 for unit sales volume of 240,000. We anticipate a first-year loss of up to $10 million on the Sonic 1000 model. Break-even calculations indicate that the Sonic 1000 will become profitable after the sales volume exceeds 267,500, early in the product's second year. Our break-even analysis of Sonic's first PDA product assumes per-unit wholesale revenue of $250 per unit, variable cost of $150 per unit, and estimated first-year fixed costs of $26,750,000. Based on these assumptions, the break-even calculation is:

$$\frac{26,750,000}{\$250 - \$150} = 267,500 \text{ units}$$

Controls

> Controls help management measure results after the plan is implemented and identify any problems or performance variations that need corrective action.

We are planning tight control measures to closely monitor quality and customer service satisfaction. This will enable us to react very quickly in correcting any problems that may occur. Other early warning signals that will be monitored for signs of deviation from the plan include monthly sales (by segment and channel) and monthly expenses.

Marketing Plan Tools

Prentice Hall offers two valuable resources to assist you in developing a marketing plan:

■ *The Marketing Plan: A Handbook* by Marian Burk Wood explains the process of creating a marketing plan, complete with checklists, real-world examples, and a listing of marketing-related Web sites.

■ Marketing Plan Pro software is an award-winning package that includes sample marketing plans, step-by-step guides, help wizards, and customizable charts for documenting a marketing plan.

Sources: Background information and market data adapted from: Pui-Wing Tam, "Palm Unveils palmOne Name, after Breakup," Wall Street Journal, *August 18, 2003, p. B4; Elaine C.Y. Chen, "Lean, Mean Multimedia Machine,"* Laptop, *August 2003, p. 20; Michael V. Copeland, Om Malik, and Rafe Needleman, "The Next Big Thing,"* Business 2.0, *July 2003, pp. 62–69; Steve Hamm, "Tech Comes Out Swinging,"* Business Week, *June 23, 2003, pp. 62–66; "Dell Rides Wireless Wave,"* eWeek, *July 7, 2003,* http://www.eweek.com; *Stephen H. Wildstrom, "Wi-Fi Handhelds? Not for the Footloose,"* Business Week, *June 16, 2003, p. 24; Bob Brewin, "Palm to Buy Handspring to Bolster Hardware Unit,"* Computerworld, *June 9, 2003, p. 12; "PDAs with Phones,"* PC Magazine, *May 6, 2003, p. 108; "Handheld Market Declines in 2002,"* Health Management Technology, *March 2003, p. 6; Bob Brewin, "Palm Slashes Pricing to Match the Competition,"* Computerworld, *February 10, 2003, p. 36.*

Appendix 2

MEASURING AND FORECASTING DEMAND

When a company finds an attractive market, it must estimate that market's current size and future potential carefully. This appendix presents the principles and tools for measuring and forecasting market demand.

To develop effective targeting strategies, and to manage their marketing efforts effectively, companies must be good at both measuring *current* market demand and forecasting *future* demand. The company can lose a lot of profit by overestimating or underestimating the market. Overly optimistic estimates of current or future demand can result in costly overcapacity or excess inventories. Underestimating demand can mean missed sales and profit opportunities.

Measuring Current Market Demand

Marketers will want to estimate three different aspects of current market demand—*total market demand, area market demand,* and *actual sales and market shares.*

Estimating Total Market Demand

Total market demand

The volume of a product or service that would be bought by a defined customer group in a defined geographic area in a defined time period in a defined marketing environment under a defined level and mix of industry marketing effort.

The **total market demand** for a product or service is the total volume that would be bought by a defined consumer group in a defined geographic area in a defined time period in a defined marketing environment under a defined level and mix of industry marketing effort. Total market demand is not a fixed number but a function of the stated conditions. For example, next year's total market demand for ice cream in the United States will depend on how much the makers of Breyers, Häagen-Dazs, Ben & Jerry's, and other brands spend on marketing. It will also depend on many environmental factors, ranging from the level of consumer health concerns to the weather in key market areas. The demand for the premium ice cream brands will be affected by economic conditions.

Figure A2.1 shows the relationship between total market demand and various market conditions. The horizontal axis shows different possible levels of industry marketing expenditures in a given time period. The vertical axis shows the resulting demand level. The curve shows the estimated level of market demand at varying levels of industry marketing effort. Some minimum level of sales would take place without any marketing expenditures. Greater marketing expenditures would yield higher levels of demand, first at an increasing rate, and then at a decreasing rate. Marketing efforts above a certain level would not cause much more demand. This upper limit of market demand is called **market potential.** The industry market forecast shows the expected level of market demand corresponding to the planned level of industry marketing effort in the given environment.

Market potential

The upper limit of market demand.

Primary demand

The total demand for all brands of a given product or service.

Selective demand

The demand for given brand of a product or service.

Companies selling in mature markets often take **primary demand**—total demand for all brands of a given product or service—as given. They concentrate their marketing resources on building **selective demand**—demand for *their* brand of the product or service. For example, in the United States, where Coca-Cola faces a mature soft drink market, it directs most of its marketing energies toward building consumer preference for Coke, Diet Coke, Sprite, and its other brands. However, in countries such as China or Russia, which are characterized by huge but largely untapped market potential, Coca-Cola attempts to build the primary demand for soft drinks, as well as preference for its own brands.

FIGURE A2.1
Market demand

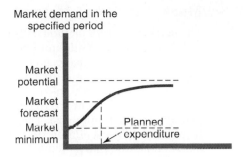

Market demand as a function of industry marketing expenditures

Companies have developed various practical methods for estimating total market demand. We will illustrate two here. Suppose Sony Music USA wants to estimate the total annual sales of recorded compact disks. A common way to estimate total market demand is as follows:

$$Q = n \times q \times p$$

where
Q = total market demand

n = number of buyers in the market

q = quantity purchased by an average buyer per year

p = price of an average unit

Thus, if there are 100 million buyers of compact disks each year, the average buyer buys 6 disks a year, and the average price is $14, then the total market demand for disks is $8.4 billion (= 100,000,000 × 6 × $14).

A variation of this approach is the *chain ratio method*. This method involves multiplying a base number by a chain of adjusting percentages. For example, suppose that Sony wants to estimate demand for its new line of premium digital cameras, which store a large number of high-quality digital images, which are later transferred to a personal computer to be resized, cropped, enhanced, grouped, and printed. Sony's new digital cameras are priced higher than previous digital models and ordinary film cameras. Thus, Sony first plans to target only serious amateur photographers who have home computers and enough money to afford the new cameras. Sony can make a U.S. demand estimate using a chain of calculations like the following:

Total number of U.S. households
× The percentage of U.S. households containing one or more serious amateur photographers
× The percentage of these households owning a personal computer
× The percentage of PC-owning households with enough discretionary income to buy Sony's new digital camera

This simple chain of calculations would provide only a rough estimate of potential demand. However, more detailed chains involving additional segments and other qualifying factors would yield more accurate and refined estimates.

Estimating Area Market Demand

Companies face the problem of selecting the best sales territories and allocating their marketing budget optimally among these territories. Therefore, they need to estimate the market potential of different cities, states, and countries. Two major methods are available: the *market buildup method*, which is used primarily by business goods firms, and the *market factor index method,* which is used primarily by consumer goods firms.

Market Buildup Method

Market buildup method

A forecasting method that identifies market factors that correlate with market potential and combines them into a weighted index.

The **market buildup method** calls for identifying all the potential buyers in each market and estimating their potential purchases. Suppose a manufacturer of mining instruments developed an instrument that can be used in the field to test the actual proportion of gold or silver in metal-bearing ores. By using it, miners would not waste their time digging deposits of ore containing too little gold or silver to be commercially profitable. The manufacturer wants to price the instrument at $10,000. It sees each mine as buying one or more instruments, depending on the mine's size. The company wants to determine the market potential for this instrument in each mining state. It would hire a salesperson to cover each state that has a market potential of over $300,000. The company wants to start by finding the market potential in Colorado.

To estimate the market potential in Colorado, the manufacturer can consult the North American Industrial Classification System (NAICS) developed by the U.S. Bureau of the Census. The NAICS is the government's coding system that classifies industries, for purposes of data collection and reporting, according to the processes they use to produce goods and services. Each major industrial group is assigned to a two-digit code—mining bears the code number 21. Within mining are further breakdowns (the gold-ore and silver-ore mining category has the code number 21222). Finally, gold and silver ores are subdivided into further NAICS groups, with six-digit code numbers (gold is 212221 and silver is 212222).

Next the manufacturer can turn to the U.S. Census of Mining to determine the number of gold- and silver-mining operations in each state, their locations within the state, and the number of employees, annual sales, and net worth. Suppose that in consulting the census for Colorado, the company finds the data located in columns 1 and 2 of Table A2.1. It can then prepare the market potential estimate shown. Column 1 classifies mines into three groups based on the number of employees. Column 2 shows the number of mines in each group. Column 3 shows the potential number of instruments that mines in each size class might buy. Column 4 shows the unit market potential (column 2 times column 3). Finally, column 5 shows the dollar market potential, given that each instrument sells for $1,000. In this example, Colorado has a market potential of $370,000. Therefore, the mining instrument manufacturer would hire one salesperson for Colorado. In the same way, companies in other industries can use the market buildup method to estimate market potential in specific market areas.

Market Factor Index Method

Consumer goods companies also have to estimate area market potentials. Consider the following example: A manufacturer of men's dress shirts wishes to evaluate its sales performance relative to market potential in several major market areas, starting with Indianapolis. It estimates total national potential for dress shirts at about $2 billion per year. The company's current nationwide sales are $140 million, about a 7 percent share of the total potential market. Its sales in the Indianapolis metropolitan area are $1,100,000. It wants to know

TABLE A2.1 Market Buildup Method Using NAICS: Instrument Potential in Colorado

NAICS	(1) Number of Employees	(2) Number of Mines	(3) Potential Number of Instruments per Size Class	(4) Unit Market Potential	(5) Dollar Market Potential (at $1,000 Each)
212221	Under 10	40	1	40	
(gold ore mining)	10 to 50	20	2	40	
	Over 50	10	3	30	
		70		110	$110,000
212222	Under 10	80	1	80	
(silver ore mining)	10 to 50	50	2	100	
	Over 50	20	4	80	
		150		260	$260,000
					$370,000

whether its share of the Indianapolis market is higher or lower than its national 7 percent market share. To find this out, the company first needs to calculate market potential in the Indianapolis area.

Market factor index method
A forecasting method that calls for identifying the potential buyers in each market and estimating their potential purchases.

A common method for calculating area market potential is the **market factor index method,** which identifies market factors that correlate with market potential and combines them into a weighted index. An excellent example of this method is called the *buying power index,* which is published each year by *Sales & Marketing Management* magazine in its *Survey of Buying Power.* This survey estimates the buying power, or "ability to buy," for each region, state, and metropolitan area of the nation. The buying power index is based on three factors: the area's share of the nation's *population, effective buying income,* and *retail sales.* The buying power index (BPI) for a specific area is given by

$$\text{BPI} = .2 \times \text{percentage of national population in the area}$$
$$+ .5 \times \text{the percentage of effective buying income in the area}$$
$$+ .3 \times \text{percentage of national retail sales in the area}$$

Using this index, the shirt manufacturer looks up the Indianapolis metropolitan area and finds that this market has .5596 percent of the nation's population, .5984 percent of the nation's effective buying income, and .6594 percent of the nation's retail sales. Thus, the buying power index for Indianapolis is:

$$\text{BPI} = (.2 \times .5596) + (.5 \times .5984) + (.3 \times .6594) = .6089$$

That is, Indianapolis should account for .6089 percent of the nation's total potential demand for dress shirts. Because the total national potential is $2 billion each year, total potential in Indianapolis equals $2 billion $\times$ .006089 = $12,178,000. Thus, the company's sales in Indianapolis of $1,100,000 amount to a $1,100,000 / $12,178,000 = 9.03 percent share of area market potential. Comparing this with its 7 percent national share, the company appears to be doing better in Indianapolis than in other parts of the country.

Many companies compute additional area demand measures. Marketers now can refine state-by-state and city-by-city measures down to census tracts or ZIP codes. Census tracts are small areas about the size of a neighborhood, and ZIP code areas (designated by the U.S. Post Office) are larger areas, often the size of small towns. Information on population size, family income, and other characteristics is available for each type of unit. Marketers can use this data to estimate demand in neighborhoods or other smaller geographic units within large cities.

Estimating Actual Sales and Market Shares

Besides estimating total and area demand, a company will want to know the actual industry sales in its market. Thus, it must identify its competitors and estimate their sales.

Industry's trade associations often collect and publish total industry sales, although not individual company sales. In this way, each company can evaluate its performance against the industry as a whole. Suppose the company's sales are increasing at a rate of 5 percent a year and industry sales are increasing at 10 percent. This company actually is losing its relative standing in the industry.

Another way to estimate sales is to buy reports from marketing research firms that audit total sales and brand sales. For example, Nielsen Media Research audits retail sales in various product categories in supermarkets and drugstores and sells this information to interested companies. A company can obtain data on total product category sales as well as brand sales. It can compare its performance with that of the total industry or any particular competitor to see whether it is gaining or losing in its relative standing.

Forecasting Future Demand

Forecasting
The art of estimating future demand by anticipating what buyers are likely to do under a given set of conditions.

Forecasting is the art of estimating future demand by anticipating what buyers are likely to do under a given set of future conditions. Very few products or services lend themselves to easy forecasting. Those that do generally involve a product with steady sales, or sales growth, in a stable competitive situation. But most markets do not have stable total and company demand, so good forecasting becomes a key factor in company success.

Companies commonly use a three-stage procedure to arrive at a sales forecast. First they make an *environmental forecast,* followed by an *industry forecast,* followed by a *company sales forecast.* The environmental forecast calls for projecting inflation, unemployment, interest rates, consumer spending and saving, business investment, government expenditures, net exports, and other environmental events important to the company. The result is a forecast of gross domestic product, which is used along with other indicators to forecast industry sales. Then the company prepares its sales forecast by assuming that it will win a certain share of industry sales.

Companies use several specific techniques to forecast their sales. Table A2.2 lists many of these techniques. All forecasts are built on one of three information bases: what people say, what people do, or what people have done. The first basis—*what people say*—involves surveying the opinions of buyers or those close to them, such as salespeople or outside experts. It includes three methods: surveys of buyer intentions, composites of sales force opinions, and expert opinion. Building a forecast on *what people do* involves putting the product into a test market to assess buyer response. The final basis—*what people have done*—involves analyzing records of past buying behavior or using time-series analysis or statistical demand analysis.

Survey of Buyers' Intentions

One way to forecast what buyers will do is to ask them directly. Surveys are especially valuable if the buyers have clearly formed intentions, will carry them out, and can describe them to interviewers. However, this is sometimes not the case, and marketers must be careful when using consumer survey data to make forecasts.

Several research organizations conduct periodic surveys of consumer buying intentions. These organizations ask questions such as the following:

Do you intend to buy an automobile within the next six months?										
0	.1	.2	.3	.4	.5	.6	.7	.8	.9	1.0
No chance		Slight chance		Fair chance		Good chance		Strong chance		For certain

This is called a *purchase probability scale.* In addition, the various surveys ask about the consumer's present and future personal finances, and his or her expectations about the economy. The various bits of information are combined into a *consumer sentiment measure* (Survey Research Center of the University of Michigan) or a *consumer confidence measure* (Sindlinger and Company). Consumer durable-goods companies subscribe to these indexes to help them anticipate major shifts in consumer buying intentions so that they can adjust their production and marketing plans accordingly. For *business buying,* various agencies carry out intention surveys about plant, equipment, and materials purchases.

Composite of Sales Force Opinions

When buyer interviewing is impractical, the company may base its sales forecasts on information provided by the sales force. The company typically asks its salespeople to estimate

TABLE A2.2   Common Sales Forecasting Techniques*

Based On	*Methods*
What people say	Surveys of buyers' intentions
	Composite sales force opinions
	Expert opinion
What people do	Test markets
What people have done	Past-sales analysis
	Leading indicators

*For more on measuring market demand, see Philip Kotler, *Marketing Management,* 11th ed. (Upper Saddle River, NJ: Prentice Hall, 2003), pp. 143–154; and Eric Almquist, Martin Kon, and Wolfgang Bock, "The Science of Demand," *Journal of Marketing Management,* March–April, 2004, pp. 20–26.

sales by product for their individual territories. It then adds up the individual estimates to arrive at an overall sales forecast.

Few companies use their sales force's estimates without some adjustments. Salespeople are biased observers. They may be naturally pessimistic or optimistic, or they may go to one extreme or another because of recent sales setbacks or successes. Furthermore, they are often unaware of larger economic developments, and they do not always know how their company's marketing plans will affect future sales in their territories. They may understate demand so that the company will set a low sales quota. They may not take the time to prepare careful estimates or may not consider it worthwhile.

Assuming these biases can be countered, a number of benefits can be gained by involving the sales force in forecasting. Salespeople may have better insights into developing trends than any other group. After participating in the forecasting process, the salespeople may have greater confidence in their quotas and more incentive to achieve them. Also, such "grassroots" forecasting provides estimates broken down by product, territory, customer, and salesperson.

Expert Opinion

Companies can also obtain forecasts by turning to experts. Experts include dealers, distributors, suppliers, marketing consultants, and trade associations. Thus, auto companies survey their dealers periodically for their forecasts of short-term demand. Dealer estimates, however, are subject to the same strengths and weaknesses as sales force estimates.

Many companies buy economic and industry forecasts from well-known firms. These forecasting specialists are in a better position than the company to prepare economic forecasts because they have more data available and more forecasting expertise.

Occasionally companies will invite a special group of experts to prepare a forecast. The experts may be asked to exchange views and come up with a group estimate (group discussion method). Or they may be asked to supply their estimates individually, with the company analyst combining them into a single estimate. Finally, they may supply individual estimates and assumptions that are reviewed by a company analyst, revised, and followed by further rounds of estimation (called the Delphi method).

Experts can provide good insights on which to base forecasts, but they can also be wrong. For example, in 1943, IBM chairman Thomas J. Watson predicted, "I think there's a world market for about five computers." A short time later, *Popular Mechanics* sagely observed that "Computers in the future may weigh no more than 1.5 tons." As recently as 1981, Bill Gates, a founder of Microsoft, proclaimed that "640K ought to be enough for anybody." In 1876, Western Union asserted, "This 'telephone' has too many shortcomings to be seriously considered as a means of communication. The device is inherently of no value to us." And in 1946, Daryl F. Zanuck, head of 20th Century Fox, made this pronouncement: "TV won't be able to hold on to any market it captures after the first six months. People will soon get tired of staring at a plywood box every night." Where possible, the company should back up experts' opinions with estimates obtained using other methods.

Test Marketing

Where buyers do not plan their purchases carefully or where experts are not available or reliable, the company may want to conduct a direct test market. A direct test market is especially useful in forecasting new-product sales or established-product sales in a new distribution channel or territory. Test marketing is discussed in Chapter 10.

Past-Sales Analysis

Sales forecasts can be developed on the basis of past sales. *Time-series analysis* consists of breaking down past time series into four components (trend, cyclo, seasonal, and erratic), and projecting these components into the future. *Exponential smoothing* consists of projecting the next period's sales by combining an average of past sales and the most recent sales, giving more weight to the latter. *Statistical demand analysis* consists of measuring the impact level of each of a set of causal factors (e.g., income, marketing expenditures, price) on the sales level. Finally, *econometric analysis* consists of building sets of equations that describe a system and proceeding to statistically fit the parameters.

Leading Indicators

Leading indicators
Time series that change in the same direction but in advance of company sales.

Many companies try to forecast their sales by finding one or more **leading indicators**—other time series that change in the same direction but in advance of company sales. For example, a plumbing supply company might find that its sales lag behind the housing starts index by about four months. The housing starts index would then be a useful leading indicator. The National Bureau of Economic Research has identified 12 of the best leading indicators, and their values are published monthly in the *Survey of Current Business* (see www.bea.doc.gov/bea/pubs.htm).

> Reviewing the Key Terms <

Forecasting A-15
Market buildup method A-14
Market factor index method A-15

Market potential A-12
Primary demand A-12

Selective demand A-12
Total market demand A-12

MARKETING MATH

One aspect of marketing not discussed within the text is marketing arithmetic. The calculation of sales, costs, and certain ratios is important for many marketing decisions. This appendix describes three major areas of marketing arithmetic: the *operating statement, analytic ratios,* and *markups and markdowns.*

Operating Statement

Balance sheet
A financial statement that shows assets, liabilities, and net worth of a company at a given time.

Operating statement (profit-and-loss statement, income statement)
A financial statement that shows company sales, cost of goods sold, and expenses during a given period of time.

The operating statement and the balance sheet are the two main financial statements used by companies. The **balance sheet** shows the assets, liabilities, and net worth of a company at a given time. The **operating statement** (also called **profit-and-loss statement** or **income statement**) is the more important of the two for marketing information. It shows company sales, cost of goods sold, and expenses during a specified time period. By comparing the operating statement from one time period to the next, the firm can spot favorable or unfavorable trends and take appropriate action.

Table A3.1 shows the 2004 operating statement for Dale Parsons Men's Wear, a specialty store in the Midwest. This statement is for a retailer; the operating statement for a manufacturer would be somewhat different. Specifically, the section on purchases within the "cost of goods sold" area would be replaced by "cost of goods manufactured."

The outline of the operating statement follows a logical series of steps to arrive at the firm's $25,000 net profit figure:

Net sales	$300,000
Cost of goods sold	−175,000
Gross margin	$125,000
Expenses	−100,000
Net profit	$ 25,000

Gross sales
The total amount that a company charges during a given period of time for merchandise.

The first part details the amount that Parsons received for the goods sold during the year. The sales figures consist of three items: *gross sales, returns and allowances,* and *net sales.* **Gross sales** is the total amount charged to customers during the year for merchandise purchased in Parsons's store. As expected, some customers returned merchandise because of damage or a change of mind. If the customer gets a full refund or full credit on another purchase, we call this a *return.* Or the customer may decide to keep the item if Parsons will reduce the price. This is called an *allowance.* By subtracting returns and allowances from gross sales, we arrive at net sales—what Parsons earned in revenue from a year of selling merchandise:

Gross sales	$325,000
Returns and allowances	−25,000
Net sales	$300,000

Cost of goods sold
The net cost to the company of goods sold.

The second major part of the operating statement calculates the amount of sales revenue Dale Parsons retains after paying the costs of the merchandise. We start with the inventory in the store at the beginning of the year. During the year, Parsons bought $165,000 worth of suits, slacks, shirts, ties, jeans, and other goods. Suppliers gave the store discounts totaling $15,000, so that net purchases were $150,000. Because the store is located away from regular shipping routes, Parsons had to pay an additional $10,000 to get the products delivered, giving the firm a net cost of $160,000. Adding the beginning inventory, the cost of goods available for sale amounted to $220,000. The $45,000 ending inventory of clothes in the store on December 31 is then subtracted to come up with the $175,000 **cost of goods sold.** Here again we have followed a logical series of steps to figure out the cost of goods sold:

TABLE A3.1   Operating Statement: Dale Parsons Men's Wear Year Ending December 31, 2004

Gross Sales			$325,000
Less: Sales returns and allowances			25,000
Net sales			$300,000
Cost of goods sold			
Beginning inventory, January 1, at cost		$ 60,000	
Gross purchases	$165,000		
Less: Purchase discounts	15,000		
Net Purchases	$150,000		
Plus: Freight-in	10,000		
Net cost of delivered purchases		$160,000	
Cost of goods available for sale		$220,000	
Less: Ending inventory, December 31, at cost		$ 45,000	
Cost of goods sold			$175,000
Gross margin			$125,000
Expenses			
Selling expenses			
Sales, salaries, and commissions	$ 40,000		
Advertising	5,000		
Delivery	5,000		
Total selling expenses		$ 50,000	
Administrative expenses			
Office salaries	$ 20,000		
Office supplies	5,000		
Miscellaneous (outside consultant)	5,000		
Total administrative expenses		$ 30,000	
General expenses			
Rent	$ 10,000		
Heat, light, telephone	5,000		
Miscellaneous (insurance, depreciation)	5,000		
Total general expenses		$ 20,000	
Total expenses			$100,000
Net profit			$ 25,000

Amount Parsons started with (beginning inventory)	$ 60,000
Net amount purchased	+150,000
Any added costs to obtain these purchases	+10,000
Total cost of goods Parsons had available for sale during year	$220,000
Amount Parsons had left over (ending inventory)	−45,000
Cost of goods actually sold	$175,000

Gross margin

The difference between net sales and cost of goods sold.

The difference between what Parsons paid for the merchandise ($175,000) and what he sold it for ($300,000) is called the **gross margin** ($125,000).

In order to show the profit Parsons "cleared" at the end of the year, we must subtract from the gross margin the *expenses* incurred while doing business. *Selling expenses* included two sales employees, local newspaper and radio advertising, and the cost of delivering merchandise to customers after alterations. Selling expenses totaled $50,000 for the year. *Administrative expenses* included the salary for an office manager, office supplies such as stationery and business cards, and miscellaneous expenses including an administrative audit conducted by an outside consultant. Administrative expenses totaled $30,000 in 2004. Finally, the general expenses of rent, utilities, insurance, and depreciation came to $20,000. Total expenses were therefore $100,000 for the year. By subtracting expenses ($100,000) from the gross margin ($125,000), we arrive at the net profit of $25,000 for Parsons during 2004.

Analytic Ratios

Operating ratios
Ratios of selected operating
statement items to net sales
that allow marketers to
compare the firm's
performance in one year
with that in previous years
(or with industry standards
and competitors in the
same year).

The operating statement provides the figures needed to compute some crucial ratios. Typically these ratios are called **operating ratios**—the ratio of selected operating statement items to net sales. They let marketers compare the firm's performance in one year to that in previous years (or with industry standards and competitors in the same year). The most commonly used operating ratios are the *gross margin percentage*, the *net profit percentage*, the *operating expense percentage*, and the *returns and allowances percentage*.

Ratio		Formula	Computation from Table A3.1
Gross margin percentage	$=$	$\dfrac{gross\ margin}{net\ sales}$	$=\dfrac{\$125{,}000}{\$300{,}000}=42\%$
Net profit percentage	$=$	$\dfrac{net\ profit}{net\ sales}$	$=\dfrac{\$\ 25{,}000}{\$300{,}000}=\ 8\%$
Operating expense percentage	$=$	$\dfrac{total\ expenses}{net\ sales}$	$=\dfrac{\$100{,}000}{\$300{,}000}=33\%$
Returns and allowances percentage	$=$	$\dfrac{returns\ and\ allowances}{net\ sales}$	$=\dfrac{\$\ 25{,}000}{\$300{,}000}=\ 8\%$

Another useful ratio is the *stockturn rate* (also called *inventory turnover rate*). The stockturn rate is the number of times an inventory turns over or is sold during a specified time period (often one year). It may be computed on a cost, selling price, or units basis. Thus the formula can be:

$$\text{Stockturn rate} = \frac{\text{cost of goods sold}}{\text{average inventory at cost}}$$

or

$$\text{Stockturn rate} = \frac{\text{selling price of goods sold}}{\text{average selling price of inventory}}$$

or

$$\text{Stockturn rate} = \frac{\text{sales in units}}{\text{average inventory in units}}$$

We will use the first formula to calculate the stockturn rate for Dale Parsons Men's Wear:

$$\frac{\$175{,}000}{(\$60{,}000 + \$45{,}000)/2} = \frac{\$175{,}000}{\$52{,}500} = 3.3$$

That is, Parsons's inventory turned over 3.3 times in 2004. Normally, the higher the stockturn rate, the higher the management efficiency and company profitability.

Return on investment (ROI) is frequently used to measure managerial effectiveness. It uses figures from the firm's operating statement and balance sheet. A commonly used formula for computing ROI is:

Return on investment (ROI)
A common measure of
managerial effectiveness—
the ratio of net profit to
investment.

$$\text{ROI} = \frac{\text{net profit}}{\text{sales}} \times \frac{\text{sales}}{\text{investment}}$$

You may have two questions about this formula: Why use a two-step process when ROI could be computed simply as net profit divided by investment? And what exactly is "investment"?

To answer these questions, let's look at how each component of the formula can affect the ROI. Suppose Dale Parsons Men's Wear has a total investment of $150,000. Then ROI can be computed as follows:

$$\text{ROI} = \frac{\$25{,}000(\text{net profit})}{\$300{,}000(\text{sales})} \times \frac{\$300{,}000(\text{sales})}{\$150{,}000(\text{investment})}$$

$$= 8.3\% \times 2 = 16.6\%$$

Now suppose that Parsons had worked to increase his share of market. He could have had the same ROI if his sales had doubled while dollar profit and investment stayed the same (accepting a lower profit ratio to get higher turnover and market share):

$$\text{ROI} = \frac{\$25,000(\text{net profit})}{\$600,000(\text{sales})} \times \frac{\$600,000(\text{sales})}{\$150,000(\text{investment})}$$

$$= 4.16\% \times 4 = 16.6\%$$

Parsons might have increased its ROI by increasing net profit through more cost cutting and more efficient marketing:

$$\text{ROI} = \frac{\$50,000(\text{net profit})}{\$300,000(\text{sales})} \times \frac{\$300,000(\text{sales})}{\$150,000(\text{investment})}$$

$$= 16.6\% \times 2 = 33.2\%$$

Another way to increase ROI is to find some way to get the same levels of sales and profits while decreasing investment (perhaps by cutting the size of Parsons's average inventory):

$$\text{ROI} = \frac{\$25,000(\text{net profit})}{\$300,000(\text{sales})} \times \frac{\$300,000(\text{sales})}{\$75,000(\text{investment})}$$

$$= 8.3\% \times 4 = 33.2\%$$

What is "investment" in the ROI formula? *Investment* is often defined as the total assets of the firm. But many analysts now use other measures of return to assess performance. These measures include *return on net assets (RONA), return on stockholders' equity (ROE),* or *return on assets managed (ROAM).* Because investment is measured at a point in time, we usually compute ROI as the average investment between two time periods (say, January 1 and December 31 of the same year). We can also compute ROI as an "internal rate of return" by using discounted cash flow analysis (see any finance textbook for more on this technique). The objective in using any of these measures is to determine how well the company has been using its resources. As inflation, competitive pressures, and cost of capital increase, such measures become increasingly important indicators of marketing and company performance.

Markups and Markdowns

Markup

The percentage of the cost or price of a product added to cost in order to arrive at a selling price.

Markdown

A percentage reduction from the original selling price.

Retailers and wholesalers must understand the concepts of **markups** and **markdowns.** They must make a profit to stay in business, and the markup percentage affects profits. Markups and markdowns are expressed as percentages.

There are two different ways to compute markups—on *cost* or on *selling price:*

$$\text{Markup percentage on cost} = \frac{\text{dollar markup}}{\text{cost}}$$

$$\text{Markup percentage on selling price} = \frac{\text{dollar markup}}{\text{selling price}}$$

Dale Parsons must decide which formula to use. If Parsons bought shirts for $15 and wanted to mark them up $10 to a price of $25, his markup percentage on cost would be $10/$15 = 67.7%. If Parsons based markup on selling price, the percentage would be $10/$25 = 40%. In figuring markup percentage, most retailers use the selling price rather than the cost.

Suppose Parsons knew his cost ($12) and desired markup on price (25%) for a man's tie, and wanted to compute the selling price. The formula is:

$$\text{Selling price} = \frac{\text{cost}}{1 - \text{markup}}$$

$$\text{Selling price} = \frac{\$12}{.75} = \$16$$

As a product moves through the channel of distribution, each channel member adds a markup before selling the product to the next member. This "markup chain" is shown for a suit purchased by a Parsons customer for $200:

		$ Amount	% of Selling Price
Manufacturer	Cost	$108	90%
	Markup	12	10
	Selling price	120	100
Wholeslaer	Cost	120	80
	Markup	30	20
	Selling price	150	100
Retailer	Cost	150	75
	Markup	50	25
	Selling price	200	100

The retailer whose markup is 25 percent does not necessarily enjoy more profit than a manufacturer whose markup is 10 percent. Profit also depends on how many items with that profit margin can be sold (stockturn rate) and on operating efficiency (expenses).

Sometimes a retailer wants to convert markups based on selling price to markups based on cost, and vice versa. The formulas are:

$$\text{Markup percentage on selling price} = \frac{\text{markup percentage on cost}}{100\% + \text{markup percentage on selling cost}}$$

$$\text{Markup percentage on cost} = \frac{\text{markup percentage on selling price}}{100\% - \text{markup percentage on selling price}}$$

Suppose Parsons found that his competitor was using a markup of 30 percent based on cost and wanted to know what this would be as a percentage of selling price. The calculation would be:

$$\frac{30\%}{100\% + 30\%} - \frac{30\%}{130\%} = 23\%$$

Because Parsons was using a 25 percent markup on the selling price for suits, he felt that his markup was suitable compared with that of the competitor.

Near the end of the summer Parsons still had an inventory of summer slacks in stock. Therefore, he decided to use a *markdown,* a reduction from the original selling price. Before the summer he had purchased 20 pairs at $10 each, and he had since sold 10 pairs at $20 each. He marked down the other pairs to $15 and sold 5 pairs. We compute his *markdown ratio* as follows:

$$\text{Markdown percentage} = \frac{\text{dollar markdown}}{\text{total net sales in dollars}}$$

The dollar markdown is $25 (5 pairs at $5 each) and total net sales are $275 (10 pairs at $20 + 5 pairs at $15). The ratio, then, is $25/$275 = 9%.

Larger retailers usually compute markdown ratios for each department rather than for individual items. The ratios provide a measure of relative marketing performance for each department and can be calculated and compared over time. Markdown ratios can also be used to compare the performance of different buyers and salespeople in a store's various departments.

> ## Reviewing the Key Terms <

Appendix 4

CAREERS IN MARKETING

Now that you have completed this course in marketing, you have a good idea of what the field entails. You may have decided you want to pursue a marketing career because it offers constant challenge, stimulating problems, the opportunity to work with people, and excellent advancement opportunities. But you still may not know which part of marketing best suits you—marketing is a very broad field offering a wide variety of career options. This appendix helps you discover what types of marketing jobs best match your special skills and interests, shows you how to conduct the kind of job search that will get you the position you want in the company of your choice, describes marketing career paths open to you, and suggests other information resources.

Marketing Careers Today

The field of marketing is booming in the twenty-first century, with nearly a third of all Americans now employed in marketing-related positions. Marketing salaries may vary by company, position, and region, and salary figures change constantly. In general, entry-level marketing salaries usually are only slightly below those for engineering and chemistry but equal or exceed starting salaries in economics, finance, accounting, general business, and the liberal arts. Moreover, if you succeed in an entry-level marketing position, it's likely that you will be promoted quickly to higher levels of responsibility and salary. In addition, because of the consumer and product knowledge you will gain in these jobs, marketing positions provide excellent training for the highest levels in an organization. A recent study by an executive recruiting firm found that more top executives come out of marketing than any other functional group.

Overall Marketing Facts and Trends

In conducting your job search, consider the following facts and trends that are changing the world of marketing.

Technology: Technology is changing the way marketers work. For example, price coding allows instantaneous retail inventorying. Software for marketing training, forecasting, and other functions is changing the ways we market. And the Internet is creating new jobs and new recruiting rules. Consider the explosive growth in new media marketing. Whereas advertising firms have traditionally recruited "generalists" in account management, "generalist" has now taken on a whole new meaning—advertising account executives must now have both broad and specialized knowledge.

Diversity: The number of women and minorities in marketing continues to rise. Traditionally, women were mainly in retailing. Now, women and minorities are rapidly moving into all industries. They also are rising rapidly into marketing management. For example, women now outnumber men by nearly two to one as advertising account executives. As marketing becomes more global, the need for diversity in marketing positions will continue to increase, opening new opportunities.

Global: Companies such as Coca-Cola, McDonald's, IBM, MTV, and Procter & Gamble have become multinational, with offices and manufacturing operations in hundreds of countries. Indeed, such companies often make more profit from sales outside the United States than from within. And it's not just the big companies that are involved in international marketing. Organizations of all sizes have moved into the global arena. Many new marketing opportunities and careers will be directly linked to the expanding global marketplace. The globalization of business also means that you will need more cultural, language, and people skills in the marketing world of the twenty-first century.

Nonprofit organizations: Increasingly, colleges, arts organizations, libraries, hospitals, and other nonprofit organizations are recognizing the need for effectively marketing their "products" and services to various publics. This awareness has led to new marketing positions—with these organizations hiring their own marketing directors and marketing vice presidents or using outside marketing specialists.

Looking for a Job in Today's Marketing World

To choose and find the right job, you will need to apply the marketing skills you've learned in this course, especially marketing analysis and planning. Follow these nine steps for marketing yourself: (1) Conduct a self-assessment and seek career counseling; (2) examine job descriptions; (3) develop job search objectives; (4) explore the job market and assess opportunities; (5) develop search strategies; (6) prepare a résumé; (7) write a cover letter and assemble supporting documents; (8) interview for jobs; and (9) follow up.

Conduct a Self-Assessment and Seek Career Counseling

If you're having difficulty deciding what kind of marketing position is the best fit for you, start out by doing some self-testing or get some career counseling. Self-assessments require that you honestly and thoroughly evaluate your interests, strengths, and weaknesses. What do you do well (your best and favorite skills) and not so well? What are your favorite interests? What are your career goals? What makes you stand out from other job seekers? The answers to such questions may suggest which marketing careers you should seek or avoid. For help in making an effective self-assessment, look at the following books in your local bookstore: Susan Johnston, *The Career Adventure: Your Guide to Personal Assessment, Career Exploration, and Decision Making* (Prentice Hall, 2001); Wilma R. Fellman, *Finding a Career That Works for You: A Step-by-Step Guide to Choosing a Career and Finding a Job* (Independent Publishers Group, 2000; and Richard Bolles, *What Color Is Your Parachute?* (Berkeley, CA: Ten Speed Press, 2005.).

For help in finding a career counselor to guide you in making a career assessment, Richard Bolles's, *What Color Is Your Parachute?* contains a useful state-by-state sampling. (Some counselors can help you in your actual job search, too.) You can also consult the career counseling, testing, and placement services at your college or university.

Career Counseling on the Internet

Today an increasing number of colleges, universities, and commercial career counselors offer career guidance on the Internet. In general, college and university sites are by far the best. But one useful commercial site you might look at is JobStar (www.jobstar.org/tools/career/index.cfm).

Examine Job Descriptions

After you have identified your skills, interests, and desires, you need to see which marketing positions are the best match for them. Two U.S. Labor Department publications in your local library, the *Occupation Outlook Handbook* and the *Dictionary of Occupational Titles,* describe the duties involved in various occupations, the specific training and education needed, the availability of jobs in each field, possibilities for advancement, and probable earnings.

Your initial career shopping list should be broad and flexible. Look for different ways to achieve your objectives. For example, if you want a career in marketing management, consider the public as well as the private sector, and regional as well as national firms. Be open initially to exploring many options, then focus on specific industries and jobs, listing your basic goals as a way to guide your choices. Your list might include "a job in a start-up company, near a big city, on the West Coast, doing new product planning, with a computer software firm."

Explore the Job Market and Assess Opportunities

At this stage, you need to look at the market and see what positions are actually available. You do not have to do this alone. Any of the following may assist you.

College Placement Centers

Your college placement center is an excellent place to start. Besides posting specific job openings, placement centers have the current edition of the *College Placement Annual,* which lists job openings in hundreds of companies seeking college graduates for entry-level positions, as well as openings for people with experience or advanced degrees. More and more, schools are also going on the Internet. For example, the Web site of the career center of Emory University in Atlanta, Georgia, has a list of career links (http://www.emory.edu/CAREER/Students/Links.htm).

In addition, find out everything you can about the companies that interest you by consulting business magazines, annual reports, business reference books, faculty, career counselors, and others. Try to analyze the industry's and the company's future growth and profit potential, advancement opportunities, salary levels, entry positions, travel time, and other factors of significance to you.

Job Fairs

College placement offices often work with corporate recruiters to organize on-campus job fairs. You might also use the Internet to check on upcoming career fairs in your region. For example, visit http://www.jobweb.com/employ/fairs/public_fairs.asp.

Networking and the Yellow Pages

Networking, or asking for job leads from friends, family, people in your community, and career centers, is one of the best ways to find a marketing job. An estimated 33 percent of jobs are found through networking. The idea is to spread your net wide, contacting anybody and everybody.

The phone book's yellow pages are another effective way to job search. Check out employers in your field of interest in whatever region you want to work, then call and ask if they are hiring for the position of your choice.

Summer Jobs and Internships

In some parts of the country one in seven students gets a job where he or she interned. On the Internet, many sites have separate internship areas. For examples, look at Wetfeet (www.wetfeet. internshipprograms.com), the Monster Board (www.monster.com), and Idealist (www.idealist. org). If you know a company for which you wish to work, go to that company's corporate Web site, enter the personnel area, and check for internships. If there are none listed, try e-mailing the personnel department, asking if internships are offered.

The Internet

A constantly increasing number of sites on the Internet deal with job hunting. You can also use the Internet to make contacts with people who can help you gain information on companies and research companies that interest you. The Riley Guide offers a great introduction to what jobs are available (www.rileyguide.com). Other helpful sites are Employment Opportunities for People with Disabilities (http://www.dol.gov/odep/joblinks/joblinks.htm) and HireDiversity (www.hirediversity.com/), which contains information on opportunities for African Americans, Hispanic Americans, Asian Americans, and Native Americans.

Most companies have their own Web sites upon which they post job listings. This may be helpful if you have a specific and fairly limited number of companies that you are keeping your eye on for job opportunities. But if this is not the case, remember that to find out what interesting marketing jobs the companies themselves are posting, you may have to visit hundreds of corporate sites.

Develop Search Strategies

Once you've decided which companies you are interested in, you need to contact them. One of the best ways is through on-campus interviews. But not every company you are interested in will visit your school. In such instances, you can write (this includes e-mail) or phone the company directly or ask marketing professors or school alumni for contacts.

Prepare Résumés

A résumé is a concise yet comprehensive written summary of your qualifications, including your academic, personal, and professional achievements, that showcases why you are the best candidate for the job. Many organizations use résumés to decide which candidates to interview.

In preparing your résumé, remember that all information on it must be accurate and complete. Résumés typically begin with the applicant's full name, telephone and fax numbers, and traditional mail and e-mail addresses. A simple and direct statement of career objectives generally appears next, followed by work history and academic data (including awards and internships), and then by personal activities and experiences applicable to the job sought. The résumé usually ends with a list of references the employer may contact. If your work or internship experience is limited, nonexistent, or irrelevant, then it is a good idea to emphasize your academic and nonacademic achievements, showing skills related to those required for excellent job performance.

There are three types of résumés. *Chronological* résumés, which emphasize career growth, are organized in reverse chronological order, starting with your most recent job. They focus on job titles within organizations, describing the responsibilities required for each job. *Functional* résumés focus less on job titles and work history and more on assets and achievements. This format works best if your job history is scanty or discontinuous. *Mixed,* or *combined,* résumés take from each of the other two formats. First, the skills used for a specific job are listed, then the job title is stated. This format works best for applicants whose past jobs are in other fields or seemingly unrelated to the position.

Your local bookstore or library has many books that can assist you in developing your résumé. Popular guides are Tom Jackson, with Ellen Jackson, *The New Perfect Résumé* (Garden City, NY: Anchor Press/Doubleday, revised, 1996); Yana Parker, *The Damn Good Résumé Guide* (Berkeley, CA: Ten Speed Press, 2002); and Arthur Rosenberg and David Hizer, *The Résumé Handbook* (Adams Media Corporation, 2003). Computer software programs such as *WinWay Résumé,* provides hundreds of sample résumés and ready-to-use phrases while guiding you through the résumé preparation process.

Online Résumés

Today more and more job seekers are posting their résumés on the Internet. Preparing an electronic résumé is somewhat different from preparing a traditional résumé. For example, you need to know the relevant rules about scanning (including that your computer will be unable to scan the attractive fonts you used in your original résumé) and keywords. Moreover, if you decide to post your résumé in a public area like a Web site, then for security purposes you might not want to include your street or business address or the names of previous employers or references. (This information can be mailed later to employers after you have been contacted by them.) JobStar (www.jobstar.org/tools/resume/index.cfm) might assist you in writing your online résumé. In addition, placement centers usually assist you in developing a résumé. (Placement centers can also help with your cover letter and provide job interview workshops.)

After you have written your résumé, you need to post it. The following sites may be good locations to start: Monster.com (www.monster.com) and Yahoo! hotjobs (www.hotjobs.yahoo.com).

Résumé Tips

- Communicate your worth to potential employers in a concrete manner, citing examples whenever possible.
- Be concise and direct.
- Use active verbs to show you are a doer.
- Do not skimp on quality or use gimmicks. Spare no expense in presenting a professional résumé.
- Have someone critique your work. A single typo can eliminate you from being considered.
- Customize your résumé for specific employers. Emphasize your strengths as they pertain to your targeted job.

- Keep your résumé compact, usually one page.
- Format the text to be attractive, professional, and readable. Avoid too much "design" or gimmicky flourishes.

Write Cover Letter and Assemble Supporting Documents

Cover Letter

You should include a cover letter informing the employer that a résumé is enclosed. But a cover letter does more than this. It also serves to summarize in one or two paragraphs the contents of the résumé and explains why you think you are the right person for the position. The goal is to persuade the employer to look at the more detailed résumé. A typical cover letter is organized as follows: (1) the name and position of the person you are contacting; (2) a statement identifying the position you are applying for, how you heard of the vacancy, and the reasons for your interest; (3) a summary of your qualifications for the job; (4) a description of what follow-ups you intend to make, such as phoning in two weeks to see if the résumé has been received; (5) an expression of gratitude for the opportunity of being a candidate for the job.

Letters of Recommendation and Other Supporting Documents

Letters of recommendation are written references by professors, former and current employers, and others that testify to your character, skills, and abilities. A good reference letter tells why you would be an excellent candidate for the position. In choosing someone to write a letter of recommendation, be confident that the person will give you a good reference. In addition, do not assume the person knows everything about you or the position you are seeking. Rather, provide the person with your résumé and other relevant data. As a courtesy, allow the reference writer at least a month to complete the letter and enclose a stamped, addressed envelope with your materials.

In the packet containing your résumé, cover letter, and letters of recommendation, you may also want to attach other relevant documents that support your candidacy, such as academic transcripts, graphics, portfolios, and samples of writing.

Interview for Jobs

As the old saying goes, "The résumé gets you the interview; the interview gets you the job." The job interview offers you an opportunity to gather more information about the organization, while at the same time allowing the organization to gather more information about you. You'll want to present your best self. The interview process consists of three parts: before the interview, the interview itself, and after the interview. If you successfully pass through these stages, you will be called back for the follow-up interview.

Before the Interview

In preparing for your interview, do the following:

1. Understand that interviewers have diverse styles, including the "chitchat," let's-get-to-know-each-other style; the interrogation style of question after question; and the tough-probing "why, why, why" style, among others. So be ready for anything.

2. With a friend, practice being interviewed and then ask for a critique. Or, videotape yourself in a practice interview so that you can critique your own performance. Your college placement service may also offer "mock" interviews to help you.

3. Prepare at least five good questions whose answers are not easily found in the company literature, such as "What is the future direction of the firm?" "How does the firm differentiate itself from competitors?" "Do you have a new-media division?"

4. Anticipate possible interview questions, such as "Why do you want to work for this company?" or "Why should we hire you?" Prepare solid answers before the interview. Have a clear idea of why you are interested in joining the company and the industry to which it belongs.

5. Avoid back-to-back interviews—they can be exhausting and it is unpredictable how long they will last.

6. Dress conservatively and professionally. Be neat and clean.

7. Arrive 10 minutes early to collect your thoughts and review the major points you intend to cover. Check your name on the interview schedule, noting the name of the interviewer and the room number. Be courteous and polite to office staff.

8. Approach the interview enthusiastically. Let your personality shine through.

During the Interview

During the interview, do the following:

1. Shake hands firmly in greeting the interviewer. Introduce yourself, using the same form of address the interviewer uses. Focus on creating a good initial impression.

2. Keep your poise. Relax, smile when appropriate, be upbeat throughout.

3. Maintain eye contact, good posture, and speak distinctly. Don't clasp your hands or fiddle with jewelry, hair, or clothing. Sit comfortably in your chair. Do not smoke, even if asked.

4. Carry extra copies of your résumé with you. Bring samples of your academic or professional work along.

5. Have your story down pat. Present your selling points. Answer questions directly. Avoid one-word or too-wordy answers.

6. Let the interviewer take the initiative but don't be passive. Find an opportunity to direct the conversation to things about yourself that you want the interviewer to hear.

7. To end on a high note, make your most important point or ask your most pertinent question during the last part of the interview.

8. Don't hesitate to "close." You might say, "I'm very interested in the position, and I have enjoyed this interview."

9. Obtain the interviewer's business card or address and phone number so that you can follow up later.

A tip for acing the interview: Before you open your mouth, find out *what it's like* to be a brand manager, sales representative, market researcher, advertising account executive, or other position for which you're interviewing.

After the Interview

After the interview, do the following:

1. After leaving the interview, record the key points that arose. Be sure to note who is to follow up and when a decision can be expected.

2. Analyze the interview objectively, including the questions asked, the answers to them, your overall interview presentation, and the interviewer's responses to specific points.

3. Immediately send a thank you letter, mentioning any additional items and your willingness to supply further information.

4. If you do not hear within the specified time, write or call the interviewer to determine your status.

Follow Up

If you are successful, you will be invited to visit the organization. The in-company interview will probably run from several hours to an entire day. The organization will examine your interest, maturity, enthusiasm, assertiveness, logic, and company and functional knowledge. You should ask questions about issues of importance to you. Find out about the working environment, job role, responsibilities, opportunity for advancement, current industrial issues, and the company's personality. The company wants to discover if you are the right person for the job, whereas you want to find out if it is the right job for you. The key is to determine if the right fit exists between you and the company.

Marketing Jobs

This section describes some of the key marketing positions.

Advertising

Advertising is one of today's hottest fields in marketing. In fact, *Money* magazine lists a position in advertising as among the 50 best jobs in America.

Job Descriptions

Key advertising positions include copywriter, art director, production manager, account executive, and media planner/buyer. *Copywriters* write advertising copy and help find the concepts behind the written words and visual images of advertisements. *Art directors,* the other part of the creative team, help translate the copywriters' ideas into dramatic visuals called "layouts." Agency artists develop print layouts, package designs, television layouts (called "storyboards"), corporate logotypes, trademarks, and symbols. *Production managers* are responsible for physically creating ads, in-house or by contracting through outside production houses. *Account development executives* research and understand clients' markets and customers and help develop marketing and advertising strategies to impact them. *Account executives* serve as liaisons between clients and agencies. They coordinate the planning, creation, production, and implementation of an advertising campaign for the account. *Media planners* determine the best mix of television, radio, newspaper, magazine, and other media for the advertising campaign.

Skills Needed, Career Paths, and Typical Salaries

Work in advertising requires strong people skills in order to interact closely with an often difficult and demanding client base. In addition, advertising attracts people with high skills in planning, problem solving, creativity, communication, initiative, leadership, and presentation. Advertising involves working under high levels of stress and pressure created by unrelenting deadlines. Advertisers frequently have to work long hours to meet deadlines for a presentation. But work achievements are very apparent, with the results of creative strategies observed by thousands or even millions of people.

Because they are so sought after, positions in advertising sometimes require an MBA. But there are many jobs open for business, graphics arts, and liberal arts undergraduates. Advertising positions often serve as gateways to higher-level management. Moreover, with large advertising agencies opening offices all over the world, there is the possibility of eventually working on global campaigns.

Starting advertising salaries are relatively low compared to some other marketing jobs because of strong competition for entry-level advertising jobs. You may even want to consider working for free to break in. Compensation will increase quickly as you move into account executive or other management positions. For more facts and figures, see the Web pages of *Advertising Age,* a key ad industry publication (www.adage.com, click on the Job Bank button), and the American Association of Advertising Agencies (www.aaaa.org).

Brand and Product Management

Brand and product managers plan, direct, and control business and marketing efforts for their products. They are involved with research and development, packaging, manufacturing, sales and distribution, advertising, promotion, market research, and business analysis and forecasting.

Job Descriptions

A company's brand management team consists of people in several positions. The *brand manager* guides the development of marketing strategies for a specific brand. The *assistant brand manager* is responsible for certain strategic components of the brand. The *product manager* oversees several brands within a product line or product group. The *product category manager* directs multiple product lines in the product category. The *market analyst* researches the market and provides important strategic information to the project managers. The *project director* is responsible for collecting market information on a marketing or product project. The *research director* oversees the planning, gathering, and analyzing of all organizational research.

Skills Needed, Career Paths, and Typical Salaries

Brand and product management requires high problem-solving, analytical, presentation, communication, and leadership skills, as well as the ability to work well in a team. Product management requires long hours and involves the high pressure of running large projects. In consumer goods companies, the newcomer—who usually needs an MBA—joins a brand team as an assistant and learns the ropes by doing numerical analyses and watching senior brand people. This person eventually heads the team and later moves on to manage a larger brand, then several brands. Many industrial goods companies also have product managers. Product management is one of the best training grounds for future corporate officers. Product management also offers good opportunities to move into international marketing. Product managers command relatively high salaries. Because this job category encourages or requires a master's degree, starting pay tends to be higher than in other marketing categories such as advertising or retailing.

Sales, Sales Management

Sales and sales management opportunities exist in a wide range of profit and nonprofit organizations and in product and service organizations, including financial, insurance, consulting, and government organizations.

Job Descriptions

Key jobs include consumer sales, industrial sales, national account manager, service support, sales trainers, sales management, and teleseller. *Consumer* sales involves selling consumer products and services through retailers. *Industrial sales* includes selling products and services to other businesses. *National account managers (NAM)* oversee a few very large accounts. *Service support* personnel support salespeople during and after the sale of a product. *Sales trainers* train new hires and provide refresher training for all sales personnel. *Sales management* includes a sequence of positions ranging from district manager to vice president of sales. The *teleseller* (not to be confused with the home consumer telemarketer) offers service and support to field salespeople.

Salespeople enjoy active professional lives, working outside the office and interacting with others. They manage their own time and activities. Competition for top jobs can be intense. Every sales job is different, but some positions involve extensive travel, long workdays, and working under pressure, which can negatively impact personal life. You can also expect to be transferred more than once between company headquarters and regional offices.

Skills Needed, Career Paths, and Typical Salaries

Selling is a people profession in which you will work with people every day, all day long. Besides people skills, sales professionals need sales and communication skills. Most sales positions also require high problem-solving, analytical, presentation, and leadership ability as well as creativity and initiative. Teamwork skills are increasingly important.

Career paths lead from salesperson to district, regional, and higher levels of sales management and, in many cases, to the top management of the firm. Today, most entry-level sales management positions require a college degree. Increasingly, people seeking selling jobs are acquiring sales experience in an internship capacity or from a part-time job before graduating. Although there is a high turnover rate (one in four people leave their jobs in a year), sales positions are great springboards to leadership positions, with more CEOs starting in sales than in any other entry-level position. Possibly this explains why competition for top sales jobs is intense.

Starting base salaries in sales may be moderate, but compensation is often supplemented by significant commission, bonus, or other incentive plans. In addition, many sales jobs include a company car or car allowance. Successful salespeople are among most companies' highest paid employees.

Other Marketing Jobs

Retailing

Retailing provides an early opportunity to assume marketing responsibilities. Key jobs include store manager, regional manager, buyer, department manager, and salesperson. *Store managers* direct the management and operation of an individual store. *Regional managers* manage groups of stores across several states and report performance to headquarters. *Buyers* select and buy the merchandise that the store carries. The *department manager* acts as store manager of a department, such as clothing, but on the department level. The *salesperson* sells merchandise to retail customers. Retailing can involve relocation, but generally there is little travel, unless you are a buyer. Retailing requires high people and sales skills because retailers are constantly in contact with customers. Enthusiasm, willingness, and communication skills are very helpful for retailers, too.

Retailers work long hours, but their daily activities are often more structured than some types of marketing positions. Starting salaries in retailing tend to be low, but pay increases as you move into management or some retailing specialty job.

Marketing Research

Marketing researchers interact with managers to define problems and identify the information needed to resolve them. They design research projects, prepare questionnaires and samples, analyze data, prepare reports, and present their findings and recommendations to management. They must understand statistics, consumer behavior, psychology, and sociology. A master's degree helps. Career opportunities exist with manufacturers, retailers, some wholesalers, trade and industry associations, marketing research firms, advertising agencies, and governmental and private nonprofit agencies.

New-Product Planning

People interested in new-product planning can find opportunities in many types of organizations. They usually need a good background in marketing, marketing research, and sales forecasting; they need organizational skills to motivate and coordinate others; and they may need a technical background. Usually, these people work first in other marketing positions before joining the new-product department.

Marketing Logistics (Physical Distribution)

Marketing logistics, or physical distribution, is a large and dynamic field, with many career opportunities. Major transportation carriers, manufacturers, wholesalers, and retailers all employ logistics specialists. Increasingly, marketing teams include logistics specialists, and marketing managers' career paths include marketing logistics assignments. Coursework in quantitative methods, finance, accounting, and marketing will provide you with the necessary skills for entering the field.

Public Relations

Most organizations have a public relations staff to anticipate problems with various publics, handle complaints, deal with media, and build the corporate image. People interested in public relations should be able to speak and write clearly and persuasively, and they should have a background in journalism, communications, or the liberal arts. The challenges in this job are highly varied and very people oriented.

Nonprofit Services

The key jobs in nonprofits include marketing director, director of development, event coordinator, publication specialist, and intern/volunteers. The *marketing director* is in charge of all marketing activities for the organization. The *director of development* organizes, manages, and directs the fund-raising campaigns that keep a nonprofit in existence. An *event coordinator* directs all aspects of fund-raising events, from initial planning through implementation. The *publication specialist* oversees publications designed to promote awareness of the organization. Although typically an unpaid position, the *intern/volunteer* performs various marketing functions, and this work can be an important step to gaining a full-time position. The nonprofit sector is typically not for someone who is money driven. Rather, most nonprofits look for people with a strong sense of community spirit and the desire to help others. So starting pay is usually lower than in other marketing fields. However, the bigger the nonprofit, the better your chance of rapidly increasing your income when moving into upper management.

Other Resources

Professional marketing associations and organizations are another source of information about careers. Marketers belong to many such societies. You may want to contact some of the following in your job search:

American Advertising Federation, 1101 Vermont Avenue, NW, Suite 500, Washington, DC 2005. (202) 898-0089 (www.aaf.org)

American Marketing Association, 250 South Wacker Drive, Suite 200, Chicago, IL 60606. (312) 648-0536 (www.marketingpower.com)

Council of Sales Promotion Agencies, 750 Summer Street, Stamford, CT 06901. (203) 325-3911

Market Research Association, 2189 Silas Deane Highway, Suite 5, Rocky Hill, CT 06067. (860) 257-4008 (www.mra-net.org)

National Council of Salesmen's Organization, 389 Fifth Avenue, Room 1010, New York, NY 10016. (718) 835-4591

National Management Association, 2210 Arbor Boulevard, Dayton, OH 45439. (513) 294-0421

National Retail Federation, 701 Pennsylvania Avenue NW, Suite 710, Washington, DC 20004. (202) 783-7971 (www.nrf.com)

Product Development and Management Association, 401 North Michigan Avenue, Chicago, IL 60611. (312) 527-6644 (www.pdma.org)

Public Relations Society of America, 33 Irving Place, Third Floor, New York, NY 10003. (212) 995-2230 (www.prsa.org)

Sales and Marketing Executives International, Statler Office Tower, Number 977, Cleveland, OH 44115. (216) 771-6650 (www.smei.org)

The Association of Women in Communications, 780 Ritchie Highway, Suite 28-S, Severna Park, MD 21146. (410) 544-7442

Women Executives in Public Relations, P.O. Box 609, Westport, CT 06881. (203) 226-4947 (www.wepr.org)

References

CHAPTER 1

1. Quotes and other information from Mark Woods, "Readers Try to Explain Why Racin' Rocks," *The Florida Times Union*, February 16, 2003, p. C1; Tina Grady, "NASCAR Fan Base More Than Just Blue Collar," *Aftermarket Business*, May 2002, p. 11; George Pyne, "In His Own Words: NASCAR Sharpens Winning Strategy," *Advertising Age*, October 28, 2002, p. S6; Peter Spiegel, "Heir Gordon," *Forbes*, December 14, 1998, pp. 42–46; Tony Kontzer, "Backseat Drivers—NASCAR Puts You in the Race," *InformationWeek*, March 25, 2002, p. 83; Matthew Futterman, "What Fuels NASCAR," *The Star-Ledger*, February 16, 2003, p. 1; Rich Thomaselli, "Sponsors Sweat New NASCAR Scoring System," *Advertising Age*, February 2, 2004, p. 4; Tom Lowry, "The Prince of NASCAR," *Business Week*, February 23, 2004, pp. 91–98; Thomas Heath and Greg Sandoval, "Baseball Adding Ads to On-Field Lineup," *Washington Post*, May 6, 2004, p. A01; and www.NASCAR.com, November 2004.

2. The American Marketing Association offers this definition: "Marketing is an organizational function and a set of processes for creating, communicating, and delivering value to customers and for managing customer relationships in ways that benefit the organization and its stakeholders." Accessed at www.marketingpower.com/live/mg-dictionary-view1862.php, July 2004. Also see Lisa M. Keefe, "Marketing Redefined," *Marketing News*, September 15, 2004, pp. 1, 16–18.

3. For an interesting discussion of creating customer value and extracting value in return, see Natalie Mizik and Robert Jacobson, "Trading Off Between Value Creation and Value Appropriation: The Financial Implications of Shifts in Strategic Emphasis," *Journal of Marketing*, January 2003, pp. 63–76.

4. Mark Ritson, "The Best Research Comes from Living the Life of Your Customer," *Marketing*, July 18, 2002, p. 16; June Lee Risser, "Customer Come First," *Marketing Management*, November–December 2003, pp. 22–26; Jack Neff, "Value Proposition Becomes a Priority," *Advertising Age*, February 23, 2004, p. 24; and Neff, "Q&A with Lafley: It's the Consumer, Stupid," *Advertising Age*, February 23, 2004, p. 20.

5. See Theodore Levitt's classic article, "Marketing Myopia," *Harvard Business Review*, July–August 1960, pp. 45–56. For more recent discussions, see James R. Stock, "Marketing Myopia Revisited: Lessons for Logistics," *International Journal of Physical Distribution & Logistics Management*, vol. 2, issue 1/2, 2002, pp. 12–21; and Yves Doz, Jose Santos, and Peter J. Williamson, "Marketing Myopia Re-Visited: Why Every Company Needs to Learn from the World," *Ivey Business Journal*, January–February 2004, p. 1.

6. Erika Rasmusson, "Marketing More than a Product," *Sales & Marketing Management*, February 2000, p. 99. Also see B. Joseph Pine II and James Gilmore, "Welcome to the Experience Economy," *Harvard Business Review*, July–August 1998, p. 99; Pat Esgate, "Pine and Gilmore Stage a Fourth ThinkAbout Experience," *Strategy & Leadership*, vol. 30, issue 3, 2002, pp. 47–48; Bernd Schmitt, *Customer Experience Management: A Revolutionary Approach to Connecting with Your Customers* (New York: John Wiley & Sons, 2003); and Lawrence A. Crosby and Sheree L. Johnson, "Manufacturing Experiences," *Marketing Management*, January–February 2004, pp. 12–14.

7. For more discussion on demand states, see Philip Kotler, *Marketing Management*, 11th ed. (Upper Saddle River, NJ: Prentice Hall, 2003), p. 6.

8. See James Bandler, "Kodak Advances in Marketing Share of Digital Cameras," *Wall Street Journal*, December 21, 2001, p. B2; Bandler, "Leading the News: Kodak Posts Disappointing Net, Plans New Layoffs," January 23, 2003, p. A3; and "Kodak Changes the Picture," *Global Agenda*, January 22, 2004, p. 1.

9. Kotler, *Marketing Management*, 11th ed., p. 19. Also see Kotler, *Marketing Insights from A to Z* (Hoboken, NJ: Wiley, 2003), pp. 32–34.

10. See Philip Kotler, *Kotler on Marketing* (New York: Free Press, 1999), pp. 20–24; Anthony W. Ulwick, "Turn Customer Input Into Innovation," *Harvard Business Review*, January 2002, pp. 91–97; and David Kirkpatrick, "Why 'Bottom Up' Is on Its Way Up," *Fortune*, January 26, 2004, p. 54.

11. See Jane E. Brody, "The Widening of America, or How Size 4 Became Size 0," *New York Times*, January 20, 2004, p. F.7; and Kenneth Hein, "Salad Days to Continue for Fast-Feeders," *Brandweek*, January 5, 2004, p. 12.

12. See Alex Taylor III, "Can J&J Keep the Magic Going?" *Fortune*, May 27, 2002. pp. 117–121; and www.jnj.com/our_company/our_credo/index.htm, November 2004.

13. See Neil A. Martin, "A New Ground War," *Barron's*, April 21, 2003, pp. 21–26; Kevin Kelleher, "Why FedEx Is Gaining Ground," *Business 2.0*, October 2003, p. 56; and "FedEx Corporation," Hoover's Company Capsules, accessed at http://proquest.umi.com, February 2004.

14. For more on customer satisfaction, see Regina Fazio Marcuna, "Mapping the World of Customer Satisfaction," *Harvard Business Review*, May–June 2000, p. 30; Marc R. Okrant, "How to Convert '3's and '4's into '5's," *Marketing News*, October 14, 2002, pp. 14, 17; and Frederick F Reichheld, "The One Number You Need," *Harvard Business Review*, December 2003, pp. 46–54.

15. Information about the Harley Owners Group accessed at www.hog.com, September 2004.

16. See Erika Rasmusson, "Wanted: Profitable Customers," *Sales & Marketing Management*, May 1999, pp. 28–34; Chris Serres, "Banks Get Customers' Numbers," *Raleigh*

News & Observer, March 19, 2002, pp. A1, A4; "Customer Profitability," *Chief Executive,* April 2003, pp. 1–4; and Larry Selden and Geoffrey Colvin, "How to Measure the Profitability of Your Customers," *Harvard Business Review,* June 2003, p. 74.

17. See Renee Houston Zemansky and Jeff Weiner, "Just Hang On to What You Got," *Selling Power,* March 2002, pp. 60–64; and Marc R. Okrant, "How to Convert '3's and '4's into '5's," *Marketing News,* October 14, 2002, pp. 14, 17.

18. Kotler, *Kotler on Marketing,* p. 20.

19. Adapted from Jennifer Gilbert, "Partners in Branding," *Sales & Marketing Management,* March 2004, p. 10.

20. Thor Valdmanis, "Alliances Gain Favor over Risky Mergers," *USA Today,* February 4, 1999, p. 3B. Also see Matthew Schifrin, "Partner or Perish," *Forbes,* May 21, 2001, pp. 26–28; and Kim T. Gordan, "Strong Partnerships Build Marketing Muscle," *CRN,* February 10, 2003, p. 14A.

21. See Frederick F Reichheld, "The One Number You Need," *Harvard Business Review,* December 2003, pp. 46–54; Thomas O. Jones and W. Earl Sasser Jr. "Why Satisfied Customers Defect," *Harvard Business Review,* November–December 1995, pp. 88–99; Fred Reichheld and Christine Detrick, "Loyalty: A Prescription for Cutting Costs," *Marketing Management,* September–October, 2003, pp. 24–25; Deborah L. Vence, "Keep 'em Coming Back for More," *Marketing News,* October 13, 2003, p. 19; and Jacquelyn S. Thomas, Robert C. Blattberg, and Edward J. Fox, "Recapturing Lost Customers," *Journal of Marketing Research,* February 2004, pp. 31–45.

22. Information from www.stew-leonards.com/html/about.cfm, November 2004.

23. See Mark McMaster, "A Lifetime of Sales," *Sales & Marketing Management,* September 2001, p. 55; Lauren Keller Johnson, "The Real Value of Customer Loyalty," *MIT Sloan Management Review,* Winter 2002, pp. 14–17; and Charlotte H. Mason, "Tuscan Lifestyles: Assessing Customer Lifetime Value," *Journal of Interactive Marketing,* Autumn 2003, pp. 54–60.

24. Erin Stout, "Keep Them Coming Back for More," *Sales and Marketing Management,* February 2002, pp. 51–52; and Fiona Haley, "Fast Talk," *Fast Company,* December 2003, p. 57.

25. See Roland T. Rust, Valerie A. Zeithaml, and Katherine A. Lemon, *Driving Customer Equity* (New York Free Press 2000); Rust, Lemon, and Zeithaml, "Where Should the Next Marketing Dollar Go?" *Marketing Management,* September–October 2001, pp. 24–28; Robert C. Blattberg, Gary Getz, Jacquelyn S. Thomas, *Customer Equity* (Boston, MA: Harvard Business School Press, 2001); John E. Hogan, Katherine N. Lemon, and Roland T. Rust, "Customer Equity Management: Charting New Directions for the Future of Marketing," *Journal of Service Research,* August 2002, pp. 4–12; and Rust, Lemon, and Zeithaml, "Return on Marketing: Using Customer Equity to Focus Marketing Strategy," *Journal of Marketing,* January 2004, pp. 109–127.

26. This example is adapted from Rust, Lemon, and Zeithaml, "Where Should the Next Marketing Dollar Go?" *Marketing Management,* p. 25. For deeper discussions of how to measure customer equity, see Blattberg, Getz, and Thomas, *Customer Equity*; Rust, Lemon, and Zeithaml, "Return on Marketing: Using Customer Equity to Focus Marketing Strategy," *Journal of Marketing,* pp. 109–127; and James D. Lenskold, "Customer-Centered Marketing ROI," *Marketing Management,* January/February 2004, pp. 26–32.

27. Ravi Dhar and Rashi Glazer, "Hedging Customers," *Harvard Business Review,* May 2003, pp. 86–92.

28. Werner Reinartz and V. Kumar, "The Mismanagement of Customer Loyalty," *Harvard Business Review,* July 2002, pp. 86–94. For more on customer equity management, see Blattberg, Getz, and Thomas, *Customer Equity,* chapters 3–6; Sunil Gupta and Donald R. Lehman, "Customers as Assets," *Journal of Interactive Marketing,* Winter 2003, pp. 9–24; Reinartz and Kumar, "The Impact of Customer Relationship Characteristics on Profitable Lifetime Duration," *Journal of Marketing,* January 2003, pp. 77–79; Bradley E. Hosmer, "Customer Equity: Building and Managing Relationships as Valuable Assets, *Consulting to Management,* June 2003, p. 59; Sunil Gupta, Donald R. Lehman, and Jennifer Ames Stuart, "Valuing Customers," *Journal of Marketing Research,* February 2004, pp. 7–18; and Gupta and Lehmann, *Managing Your Customers as Investments: The Strategic Value of Customer in the Long Run* (Philadelphia: Wharton School Publishing, 2005).

29. For another interesting discussion on managing the customer portfolio, see Michael D. Johnson and Fred Selnes, "Customer Portfolio Management: Toward a Dynamic Theory of Exchange Relationships." *Journal of Marketing,* April 2004, pp. 1–17.

30. "Internet Penetration Rate Slows," *Silicon Valley/San Jose Business Journal,* February 5, 2003, accessed at http://eastbay.bizjournals.com/sanjose; "Population Explosion!" *CyberAtlas,* March 14, 2003, accessed at www.cyberatlas.com; and information accessed online at www.internetworldstats.com, February 2004.

31. Robert D, Hof, "Survive and Prosper," *Business Week,* May 14, 2001, p. EB60; and Timothy Mullaney, "E-Biz Surprise," *Business Week,* May 12, 2003, pp. 60–68.

32. Steve Hamm, "E-Biz: Down but Hardly Out," *Business Week,* March 26, 2001, pp. 126–130; "B2B E-Commerce Headed for Trillions," March 6, 2002, accessed online at www.cyberatlas.internet.com; and Mullaney, "E-biz Surprise," pp. 60–68.

33. See Ben & Jerry's full mission statement online at www.benjerry.com.

34. Example adapted from Alison Stein Wellner, "Oh Come All Ye Faithful," *American Demographics,* June 2001, pp. 52–55. Other information is from www.marblechurch.org, May 2004.

35. For other examples, and for a good review of nonprofit marketing, see Philip Kotler and Alan R. Andreasen, *Strategic Marketing for Nonprofit Organizations,* 6th ed. (Upper Saddle River, NJ: Prentice Hall, 2003); Philip Kotler and Karen Fox, *Strategic Marketing for Educational Institutions* (Upper Saddle River, NJ: Prentice Hall, 1995); Norman Shawchuck, Philip Kotler, Bruce Wren, and Gustave Rath, *Marketing for Congregations: Choosing to Serve People More Effectively* (Nashville, TN: Abingdon Press, 1993); and Philip Kotler, John Bowen, and James Makens, *Marketing for Hospitality and Tourism,* 3d ed. (Upper Saddle River, NJ: Prentice Hall, 2003).

36. "100 Leading National Advertisers," *Advertising Age*, June 23, 2003, p. 2. For more on social marketing, see Philip Kotler, Ned Roberto, and Nancy R. Lee, *Social Marketing: Improving the Quality of Life*, 2nd ed. (Upper Saddle River, NJ: Prentice Hall, 2002).

CHAPTER 2

1. Marc Gunther, "Mouse Hunt," *Fortune*, January 12, 2004, p. 106; "Top 50 North American Amusement/Theme Parks," *Amusement Business*, December 22, 2004, p. 18; "The Walt Disney Company," *Hoover Company Profiles*, Austin, March 15, 2004, p. 11603; David J. Jefferson and Johnnie L. Roberts, "The Magic Is Gone," March 15, 2004, p. 52; and information accessed online at www.Disney.go.com/corporate, November 2004.

2. For a more detailed discussion of corporate- and business-level strategic planning as they apply to marketing, see Philip Kotler, *Marketing Management*, 11th ed. (Upper Saddle River, N.J.: Prentice Hall, 2003), Chapter 4.

3. See Forest David and Fred David, "It's Time to Redraft Your Mission Statement," *The Journal of Business Strategy*, January/February 2003, pp. 11–15; and "Crafting Mission Statements," *Association Management*, January 2004, p. 23.

4. The following discussion is based in part on information found at www.bcg.com/this_is_bcg/mission/growth_share_matrix.jsp, August 2004. For more on strategic planning, see Tom Devane, "Ten Cardinal Sins of Strategic Planning," *Executive Excellence*, October 2000, p. 15; Dave Lefkowith, "Effective Strategic Planning," *Management Quarterly*, Spring 2001, pp. 7–11; Dennis Rheault, "Freshening Up Strategic Planning: More than Fill-in-the-Blanks," *The Journal of Business Strategy*, Vol. 24, Iss. 6, 2004, pp. 33–37; and Anthony Lavia, "Strategic Planning in Times of Turmoil," *Business Communications Review*, March 2004, pp. 56–60.

5. H. Igor Ansoff, "Strategies for Diversification," *Harvard Business Review*, September–October 1957, pp. 113–124. Also see Philip Kotler, *Kotler on Marketing* (New York: Free Press, 1999), pp. 46–48; and Kevin Lane Keller, *Strategic Brand Management*, 2nd edition (Upper Saddle River, NJ: Prentice Hall, 2003) pp. 576–578.

6. Michael Krauss, "Starbucks Adds Value by Taking on Wireless," *Marketing News*, February 2003, p. 9; Brannon Boswell, "Say It with a Card," *Retail Traffic*, February 2004, pp. 10–11; and Jake Batsell, "Starbucks Steams Ahead with Aggressive Expansion Plans," *Knight Ridder Tribune Business News*, March 28, 2004, p. 1; and information. accessed online at www.starbucks.com, November 2004.

7. Dean Takahashi, "Hewlett-Packard Teams Up with Starbucks on Hybrid Music Store-Coffee Houses," *Knight-Ridder Tribune Business News*, March 16, 2004.

8. Nirmalya Kumar, "Kill a Brand, Keep a Customer," *Harvard Business Review*, December 2003, pp. 87–95.

9. Michael E. Porter, *Competitive Advantage: Creating and Sustaining Superior Performance* (New York: Free Press, 1985); and Michel E. Porter, "What Is Strategy?" *Harvard Business Review*, November–December 1996, pp. 61–78. Also see Kim B. Clark, et al, *Harvard Business School on Managing the Value Chain* (Boston: Harvard Business School Press, 2000); "Buyer Value and the Value Chain," *Business Owner*, September–October 2003, p. 1; and "The Value Chain," accessed at www.quickmba.com/strategy/value-chain/, July 2004.

10. Kotler, *Kotler on Marketing*, pp. 20–22. Also see Philip Kotler, *Marketing Insights from A to Z* (Hoboken, NJ: Wiley, 2003), pp. 102–107.

11. David Stires, "Fallen Arches," *Fortune*, April 29, 2002, pp. 74–76; Sherri Day, "After Years at the Top, McDonald's Strives To Regain Ground," *New York Times*, March 3, 2003, p. A1; and McDonald's Corporation Investor Fact Sheet January 2004, accessed at www.mcdonalds.com/corp/invest/pub/2004_fact_sheet.html.

12. Myron Magnet, "The New Golden Rule of Business," *Fortune*, February 21, 1994, pp. 60–63. For more on value network and supply chain management and strategic alliances, also see Philip Kotler, *Marketing Management*, 11th ed. (Upper Saddle River, NJ: Prentice Hall, 2003), pp. 70–71; and David A. Taylor, *Supply Chains: A Manager's Guide* (Boston: Addison-Wesley, 2004).

13. Accessed at Ad Age Dataplace, www.adage.com/dataplace, November 2004.

14. The four *Ps* classification was first suggested by E. Jerome McCarthy, *Basic Marketing: A Managerial Approach* (Homewood, IL: Irwin, 1960). For the 4Cs, other proposed classifications, and more discussion, see Robert Lauterborn, "New Marketing Litany: 4P's Passé; C-Words Take Over," *Advertising Age*, October 1, 1990, p. 26; Don E. Schultz, "Marketers: Bid Farewell to Strategy Based on Old 4Ps," *Marketing News*, February 12, 2001, p. 7, John Farrell, "Highlighting the 4Rs of Marketing," *Incentive*, April 2002, p. 101; and Elliott Ettenberg, "Goodbye 4Ps, Hello 4Rs," *Marketing Magazine*, April 14, 2003, p. 8.

15. Brian Dumaine, "Why Great Companies Last," *Business Week*, January 16, 1995, p. 129. See James C. Collins and Jerry I. Porras, *Built to Last: Successful Habits of Visionary Companies* (New York: HarperBusiness, 1995); Rob Goffee and Gareth Jones, *The Character of a Corporation: How Your Company's Culture Can Make or Break Your Business* (New York: HarperBusiness, 1998); Jeff Rosenthal and Mary Ann Masarech, "High-Performance Cultures: How Values Can Drive Vision," *Journal of Organizational Excellence*, Spring 2003, pp. 3–18; and Naomi Moneypenny, "Five Foundations for Developing a Corporate Culture," *The RMA Journal*, February 2004, p. 22.

16. For more on brand and product management, see Kevin Lane Keller, *Strategic Brand Management*, 2nd ed. (Upper Saddle River, N.J.: Prentice Hall, 2003).

17. See Roland T. Rust, Valerie A. Zeithaml, and Katherine N. Lemon, *Driving Customer Equity: How Lifetime Customer Value Is Reshaping Corporate Strategy* (New York: Free Press, 2000); Rust, Lemon, and Zeithaml, "Where Should the Next Marketing Dollar Go?" *Marketing Management*, September–October 2001, pp. 24–28; Sunil Gupta and Donald R. Lehman, "Customers as Assets," *Journal of Interactive Marketing*, Winter 2003, pp. 9–24; Michael D. Johnson and Fred Selnes, "Customer Portfolio Management: Toward a Dynamic Theory of Exchange Relationships," *Journal of Marketing*, April 2004, pp. 1–17; and Gupta and Lehmann, *Managing Your Customer as*

Investment: The Strategic Value of Customers in the Long Run (Philadelphia: Wharton School Publishing, 2005).

18. For details, see Kotler, *Marketing Management,* pp. 695–699. Also see Neil A. Morgan, Bruce H. Clark, and Rich Gooner, "Marketing Productivity, Marketing Audits, and Systems for Marketing Performance Assessment: Integrating Multiple Perspectives," *Journal of Marketing,* May 2002, pp. 363–375.

19. "Lenskold Group Announces 'Marketing ROI' Book Now Shipping," press release, July 25, 2003, accessed at www/lenskold.com/news/mroi_book.html; and Arundhati Parmar, "Barriers to Success," *Marketing News,* March 1, 2004, pp. 20–21. Also see Patrick Lapointe, "Marketing ROI: What's Next?" *B to B,* February 9, 2004, p. 11.

20. *Ibid.*; and Judann Pollack, "Marketers Slap Network TV in Survey on ROI," *Advertising Age,* October 13, 2003, p. 11.

21. Mark McMaster, "ROI: More Vital than Ever," *Sales & Marketing Management,* January 2002, pp. 51–52. Also see, Jim Lenskold, "CFOs Are from Mars, CMOs Are from Venus," accessed at www.marketingpower.com/live/content17702C5226.php, May 2004.

22. For a full discussion of this model and details on customer-centered measures of return on marketing, see Roland T. Rust, Katherine N. Lemon, and Valerie A. Zeithaml, "Return on Marketing: Using Customer Equity to Focus Marketing Strategy," *Journal of Marketing,* January 2004, pp. 109–127. Also see James D. Lenskold, "Customer-Centric Marketing ROI," *Marketing Management,* January–February 2004, pp. 26–32; and Sunil Gupta, Donald R. Lehmann, and Jennifer Ames Stuart, "Valuing Customers," *Journal of Marketing Research,* February 2004, pp. 7–18.

23. James D. Lenskold, "Marketing ROI: Playing to Win," *Marketing Management,* May–June 2002, pp. 30–36; Judann Pollack, "Marketers Slap Network TV in Survey on ROI," p. 1; Tim Donaldson, "Measure Returns with Process Integration," *Marketing News,* March 1, 2004, p. 23; and Michael D. Johnson and Fred Selnes, "Customer Portfolio Management: Toward a Dynamic Theory of Exchange Relationships." *Journal of Marketing,* April 2004, pp. 1–17.

CHAPTER 3

1. Sherri Day, "After Years at Top, McDonald's Strives To Regain Ground," *New York Times,* March 3, 2003, p. A.1; "McDonald's Real Life Choices Teaches Consumers How to Eat the McDonald's Food They Love and Stay on Track with Their Diets," McDonalds Press Release, January 6, 2004 accessed at www.McDonalds.com; Jonathan B. Cox, "From Burgers to Beans," *The News and Observer,* January 10, 2004, p. C1; Shirley Leung, "McDonald's Makeover," *Wall Street Journal,* January 28, 2004, p. B1; Steven Gray, "McDonald's Feels the Heat and Offers Some Healthier Fare," *Wall Street Journal,* April 16, 2004, p. A11; Sarah Hale Meiter, "McDonald's Bistro Gourmet Concept Spreads," *Chicago Tribune Online Edition,* May 12, 2004; David Stires, "McDonald's Keeps Right on Cookin'," *Fortune,* May 17, 2004, p. 174; "McDonald's Earnings Jump 56%," *Los Angeles Times,* April 28, 2004, p. C3; and Michael Arndt, "McDonald's: Fries with that Salad?" *Business Week,* July 5, 2004, pp. 82–84.

2. See Sarah Lorge, "The Coke Advantage," *Sales & Marketing Management,* December 1998, p. 17; "Coca-Cola Inks New Deal with Jack in the Box Chain," *Nation's Restaurant News,* January 13, 2003, p. 52; and Chad Terhune "Coke Wins a 10-Year Contract From Subway, Ousting PepsiCo," *Wall Street Journal,* November 28, 2003, p. B.3.

3. World POPClock, U.S. Census Bureau, accessed online at www.census.gov, November 2004. This Web site provides continuously updated projections of the U.S. and world populations.

4. Adapted from Frederik Balfour, "Educating the 'Little Emperors': There's a Big Market for Products that Help China's Coddled Kids Get Ahead," *Business Week,* November 10, 2003, p. 22. Also see Clay Chandler, "Little Emperors," *Fortune,* October 4, 2004, pp. 138–150.

5. Alison Stein Wellner, "The Next 25 Years," *American Demographics,* April 2003, pp. 23–27; and U.S. Census Bureau projections and POPClock Projection, U.S. Census Bureau, accessed at www.census.gov, May 2004.

6. Alison Stein Wellner, "The Wealth Effect," *American Demographics,* January 2003, p. 35; and Rebecca Gardyn, "Whitewashed," *American Demographics,* February 2003, pp. 13–15.

7. Diana McKeon Charkalis, "Boomers Remodel Empty Nests Their Way," *USA Today,* March 21, 2003, accessed online at www.usatoday.com; and "Baby Boomers," *Brand Strategy,* February 11, 2004, p. P.31.

8. See Michael Weiss, "Chasing Youth," American Demographics, October 2002, pp. 35–41; Joan Raymond, "The Joy of Empty Nesting," *American Demographics,* May 2000, pp. 49–54; David Rakoff, "The Be Generation," *Adweek,* March 5, 2001, pp. SR18–SR22; Gene Koretz, "Bless the Baby Boomers," *Business Week,* June 10, 2002, p. 30; Greg Schneider, "Rebels with Disposable Income: Aging Baby Boomers Line Up to Buy High-End Versions of Youthful Indulgences," *The Washington Post,* April 27, 2003, p. F01; and "Married Baby Boomers Heart of Cruise Market," March 31, 2004, accessed at www.hospitality.net.

9. "Mixed Success: One Who Targeted Gen X and Succeeded—Sort Of," *Journal of Financial Planning,* February 2004, p. 15.

10. See Jean Chatzky, "Gen Xers Aren't Slackers After All," *Time,* April 8, 2002, p. 87; Rebecca Ryan, "10 Questions with . . . Rebecca Ryan," *Journal of Financial Planning,* February 2004, pp. 12–17; "They're Not Aloof . . . Just Generation X," *CMA Management,* April 2004, p. 6; and "Overlooked and Under X-Plointed," *American Demographics,* May 2004, p. 48.

11. Example adapted from information found in Jura Koncius, "Chicago: In a Gritty Northside . . . ," *The Washington Post,* February 20, 2003, p. H1; "The Core CB2 Shopper," *The Washington Post,* February 20, 2003, p. H5. Also see Jo Napolitano, "Crate and Barrel Handles Its Offshoot with Care," *New York Times,* June 22, 2003, p. 3.4; and Tracy Turner, "Columbus, Ohio, to Get First Crate & Barrel Store," *Knight Ridder Tribune News,* March 19, 2004, p. 1.

12. See Ken Gronback, "Marketing to Generation Y," *DSN Retailing Today,* July 24, 2000, p. 14; and Joanna Krotz, "Tough Customers: How to reach Gen Y," accessed at www.bcentral.com, March 21, 2003.

13. Tobi Elkin, "Gen Y Quizzed about On-Demand," *Advertising Age,* February 14, 2003, p. 37. Also see Pamela Paul, "Getting Inside Gen Y," *American Demographics,* September 2001,

pp. 43–49; and Rebecca Gardyn, "Born to be Wired," *American Demographics*, April 2003, pp. 14–15; and "Teens Spent $175 Billion in 2003," press release, Teenage Research Unlimited, January 9, 2004, accessed at www.teenresearch.com.

14. Adapted from portions of Jean Halliday, "Automakers Mix It Up To Chase Young Buyers," *Automotive News*, April 26, 2004, p. 28B.

15. See J. Walker Smith and Ann Clurman, *Rocking the Ages* (New York: HarperBusiness, 1998); Mercedes M. Cardona, "Hilfiger's New Apparel Lines Getting Individual Efforts," *Advertising Age*, February 8, 1999, p. 24; and Alison Stein Wellner, "Generational Divide," *American Demographics*, October 2000, pp. 53–58.

16. Alison Stein Wellner, "The American Family in the 21st Century," *American Demographics*, August 2001, p. 20.

17. Information on household composition accessed online at www.census.gov/population/projections/nation/hh-fam, July 2004.

18. U.S. Census Bureau, "Women and Men in the United States," accessed online at www.census.gov/prod/2003pubs/p20-544.pdf, March 2003.

19. For these and other examples, see Kelly Shermach, "Niche Malls: Innovation for an Industry in Decline," *Marketing News*, February 26, 1996, p. 1; and Sue Shellenbarger, "'Child-Care Cams': Are They Good News for Working Parents?" *Wall Street Journal*, August 19, 1998, p. B1; and Michelle Conlin, "Mommy Is Really Home from Work," *Business Week*, November 25, 2002, pp. 101–104.

20. U.S. Census Bureau, "Geographical Mobility," March 2004, accessed online at www.census.gov/prod/2004pubs/p20-549.pdf.

21. See Alison Stein Wellner, "Size Doesn't Matter," *American Demographics*, May 2001, pp. 23–24; Roderick J. Harrison, "The New White Flight," *American Demographics*, June 2002, pp. 20–24; "About Metropolitan and Micropolitan Statistical Areas," U.S. Census Bureau, www.census.gov/population/www/estimates/aboutmetro.html, June 2004; and Redefining Where We Live: New Concepts and Definitions of Statistical Areas," *Industrial Relations*, January 2004, pp. 293–294.

22. See "FedEx Rebrands Kinko's," FedEx Press Release, April 27, 2004, accessed at http://fedex.com/us/about/news/update/officeprint.html; "Five Questions," *Sales & Marketing Management*," July 2004, p. 13; and information found at www.fedex.com/us/officeprint/main/?link=4, November 2004.

23. U.S. Census Bureau, "Women and Men in the United States," March 2003, p. 3, accessed at www.census.gov/prod/2003pubs/p20-544.pdf; and Peter Francese, "Top Trends for 2003," *American Demographics*, January 2003, pp. 48–51.

24. See Rebecca Piirto Heath, "The New Working Class," *American Demographics*, January 1998, pp. 51–55; *Digest of Education Statistics 1997*, National Center for Education Statistics, January 1998, at http://nces01.ed.gov/pubs/digest97; and U.S. Bureau of Labor Statistics, "Labor Force, Employment, and Earnings," p. 416, accessed at http://landview.census.gov/prod/2001pubs/statab/sec13.pdf, June 2004.

25. See "How to Succeed in Multicultural Marketing," special supplement to *American Demographics*, November 2003; Sabrina Jones, "Hispanics Surpass Blacks as Growth Market for Ads," *The Washington Post*, January 5, 2004, p. E.01; Brian Grow, "Hispanic Nation," *Business Week*, March 15, 2004, pp. 59–70; Deborah L. Vence, "You Talkin' to Me? Experts Offer Best Practices in Multicultural Marketing," *Marketing News*, March 1, 2004, pp. 1, 9; and U.S. Census Bureau reports accessed online at www.census.gov, November 2004.

26. Information accessed at www.rivendellmarketing.com/ngng/ngng_profiles_set.html, November 2004.

27. Ellen Florian, "Queer Eye Makes Over the Economy," *Fortune*, February 9, 2004, p. 38.

28. For these and other examples, see John Fetto, "In Broad Daylight," *American Demographics*, February 2001, pp. 16, 20; Sandra Yin, "Coming Out in Print," *American Demographics*, February 2003, pp. 18–21; Dianne Solis, "Mainstream Marketing Increasing in Gay Themes in Ads," *The Raleigh News and Observer*, August 8, 2003, pp. D1, D6; Todd Wasserman, "IBM Targets Gay Business Owners," *Adweek*, October 6, 2003, p. 8; and Jennifer Gilbert, "Small but Mighty," *Sales & Marketing Management*, January 2004, pp. 30–35.

29. Information accessed at Volkswagen's Web site (www.vw.com) and www.vsarts.org/programs/vw/, June 2004.

30. Alison Stein Wellner, "The Next 25 Years," *American Demographics*, April 2003, pp. 23–27.

31. See Alison Stein Wellner, "The Money in the Middle," *American Demographics*, April 2000, pp. 56–64; and Wellner, "The Wealth Effect," *American Demographics*, January 2003, p.35.

32. David Leonhardt, "Two-Tier Marketing," *Business Week*, March 17, 1997, pp. 82–90. Also see "MarketLooks: The U.S. Affluent Market," a research report by Packaged Facts, January 1, 2002; and Rebecca Gardyn, "Love Richly," *American Demographics*, April 2003, pp. 16–18.

33. For more discussion, see the "Environmentalism" section in Chapter 20. "Earth in the Balance," *American Demographics*, January 2001, p. 24; Subhabrata Bobby Banerjee, "Corporate Environmentalism: The Construct and Its Measurement," *Journal of Business Research*, March 2002, pp. 177–191; Marc Gunther, "Tree Huggers, Soy Lovers, and Profits," *Fortune*, June 23, 2003, pp. 98–104; Charles Haddad, "FedEx and Brown Are Going Green," *Business Week*, August 11, 2003; "Sustainability Key to UPS's Environmental Initiatives," accessed online at http://pressroom.ups.com/, June 2004; and information accessed at www.3m.com/about3m/sustainability/policies_ehs_tradition_3p.jhtml, November 2004.

34. See "Uncreased U.S. R&D Spending Expected in 2004," *JOM*, March 2004, p. 7.

35. A J Vogl, "Does It Pay to Be Good?" *Across the Board*, January/February 2003, pp. 16–23.

36. For more on online privacy, see William M. Savino, "Protecting Online Privacy," *Marketing Management*, September–October 2002, pp. 49–51; Deborah L. Vence, "Marketers Expect to See Federal Law on Online Privacy Soon," *Marketing News*, June 24, 2002, p. 4; Eric Goldman, "The

Internet Privacy Fallacy," *Computer and Internet Lawyer,* January 2003, p. 20; and "The Spies in Your Computer," *New York Times,* February 18, 2004, p. A18.

37. Information obtained from www.boxtops4education.com, July 2004.

38. See Kevin T. Higgins, "Marketing with a Conscience," *Marketing Management,* July–August 2002, pp. 12–15; Sonoo Singh, "Success Is All in a Good Cause," *Marketing Week,* April 10, 2003, pp. 28–19; Linda I. Nowak and T. K. Clarke, "Cause-Related Marketing: Keys to Successful Relationships with Corporate Sponsors," *Journal of Non-profit & Public Sector Marketing,* 2003, pp. 137–149; "Cause-Related Marketing Comes of Age in 2003," accessed online at www.porternovelli.com, April 2003; and Irwin S. Stoolmacher, "Cause-Related Marketing and Your Non-profit," *Board & Administrator; for Administrators Only,* February 2004, pp. 3–5.

39. For more on Yankelovich Monitor, see http://secure. yankelovich.com/solutions/monitor/monitor_new.asp.

40. Adapted from Becky Ebenkamp, "Fun/Duty Now, for the Future," *Brandweek,* January 5, 2004, p. 16.

41. Portions of this example are adapted from information in Eileen Daspin, "The End of Nesting," *Wall Street Journal,* May 16, 2003, p. W1. Also see "The Cocoon Cracks Open," *Brandweek,* April 28, 2003, pp. 32–36; and Dan Lippe, "Gimme Shelter," *Advertising Age,* special report, April 5, 2004, pp. S1–S8.

42. See Paula Szuchman, "Stars, Stripes . . . and Lines," *Wall Street Journal,* May 23, 2003, p. W1.

43. Steve Jarvis, "Red, White, and Blues," *Marketing News,* May 27, 2002, pp. 1, 9; Alison Stein Wellner, "The Perils of Patriotism," *American Demographics,* September 2002, pp. 49–51; and "Consumers Dislike Flag-Waving Promos," *Stores,* October 2003, p. 12.

44. See Debbie Howell, "Health Food, Like Bell Bottoms, Puts Mojo Back in Mass," *DSN Retailing Today,* April 16, 2001, pp. 21–22; Victoria Furness, "McDonald's Organic Bid to Lure Customers," *Marketing Week,* January 9, 2003, p. 5; Mark Machlis, "In a New Age Acting Naturally Can Build Traffic and Sales," *Nation's Restaurant News,* March 1, 2004, p. 28; and Christina Cheddar Berk, "Silk Soy Milk Looks to Strengthen Healthy Image with National Ads," *Wall Street Journal,* April 21, 2004, p. 1.

45. Quotes from Myra Stark, "Celestial Season," *Brandweek,* November 16, 1998, pp. 25–26; and Becky Ebankamp, "The Young and Righteous," *Brandweek,* April 5, 2004, p. 18.

46. See Philip Kotler, *Kotler on Marketing* (New York: Free Press, 1999), p. 3; and Kotler, *Marketing Insights from A to Z* (Hoboken, NJ: John Wiley & Sons, 2003), pp. 23–24.

47. Howard E. Butz Jr. and Leonard D. Goodstein, "Measuring Customer Value: Gaining the Strategic Advantage," *Organizational Dynamics,* Winter 1996, pp. 66–67.

CHAPTER 4

1. See "Coke 'Family' Sales Fly as New Coke Stumbles," *Advertising Age,* January 17, 1986, p. 1; Jack Honomichl, "Missing Ingredients in 'New' Coke's Research," *Advertising Age,* July 22, 1985, p. 1; Rick Wise, "Why Things Go Better with Coke," *The Journal of Business Strat-*

egy, January–February 1999, pp. 15–19; Catherine Fredman, "Smart People, Stupid Choices," *Chief Executive,* August/September 2002, pp. 64–68; "Top-10 U.S. Carbonated Soft Drink Companies and Brands for 2003," special issue, *Beverage Digest,* March 5, 2004, accessed at www.beverage-digest.com/pdf/top-10_2003.pdf; and "The Real Story of New Coke" accessed online at www2.coca-cola.com/heritage/cokelore_newcoke.html, January 2005.

2. See Christina Le Beau, "Mountains to Mine," *American Demographics,* August 2000, pp. 40–44; Diane Trommer, "Information Overload—Study Finds Intranet Users Overwhelmed with Data," *Electronic Buyers' News,* April 20, 1998, p. 98; Julie Schlosser, "Looking for Intelligence in Ice Cream," *Fortune,* March 17, 2003, pp. 114–120; Leslie Langnau, "Drowning in Data," *Material Handling Management,* December 2003, p. 22; and Rick Mullin, "Dealing with Information Overload," *Chemical and Engineering News,* March 22, 2004, p. 19.

3. Alice LaPlante, "Still Drowning!" *Computer World,* March 10, 1997, pp. 69–70; and Jennifer Jones, "Looking Inside," *InfoWorld,* January 7, 2002, pp. 22–26.

4. See Philip Kotler, *Marketing Insights from A to Z* (Hoboken, NJ: John Wiley & Sons, 2003), pp. 80–82.

5. See Geoffrey Brewer, "The Customer Stops Here," *Sales & Marketing Management,* March 1998, pp. 31–36; Andy Patrizio, "Home-Grown CRM," *Insurance & Technology,* February 2001, pp. 49–50; and "USAA," *Hoover's Company Capsules,* March 15, 2004, p. 40508.

6. Andy Serwer, "P&G's Covert Operation," *Fortune,* September 17, 2001, pp. 42–44.

7. Adapted from information in Ellen Neuborne, "Know Thy Enemy," *Sales & Marketing Management,* January 2003, pp. 29–33. Also see Gina Rollins, "Cast Deep to Sell," *Selling Power,* June 2003, pp. 26–28; and Deborah Lynne Wiley, "Super Searchers on Competitive Intelligence: The Online and Offline Secrets of Top CI Researchers," *Online,* May–June 2004, p. 62.

8. See James Curtis, "Behind Enemy Lines," *Marketing,* May 21, 2001, pp. 28–29; and Mei Fong, "The Enemy Within," *Far Eastern Economic Review,* April 22, 2004, p. 34–38.

9. For more on research firms that supply marketing information, see Jack Honomichl, "Honomichl 50," special section, *Marketing News,* June 15, 2004, pp. H1–H55.

10. Information from www.infores.com/public/global/content/consumernetwork/householdpanel.htm and http://secure. yankelovich.com/solutions/monitor/monitor_new.asp, July 2004.

11. Example adapted from Douglas McGray, "Babes in R&D Toyland," *Fast Company,* December 2002, p. 46.

12. Adapted from Linda Tischler, "Every Move You Make," *Fast Company,* April 2004, pp. 73–75.

13. Example adapted from Alison Stein Wellner, "The New Science of Focus Groups," *American Demographics,* March 2003, pp. 29–33.

14. This and other examples and quotes in this section, unless otherwise noted, are from "Market Trends: Online Research Growing," accessed at www.greenfieldcentral.com/research_solutions/rsrch_solns_main.htm, June 2003; Noah Shachtman, "Web Enhanced Market Research," *Advertising*

Age, June 18, 2001, p. T18; Thomas W. Miller, "Make the Call: Online Results Are a Mixed Bag," *Marketing News,* September 24, 2001, pp. 30–35; "Cybersurveys Come of Age," *Marketing Research,* Spring 2003, pp. 32–37; and Richard Lee, "Stamford, Conn.-Based Market Research Firm Able to Reach Millions," *Knight Ridder Tribune Business News,* May 6, 2004. p. 1. Also see Catherine Arnold, "Not Done Net," *Marketing News,* April 2004, p. 17.

15. For more on Internet privacy, see James R. Hagerty and Dennis K. Berman, "Caught in the Net: New Battleground Over Web Privacy," *Wall Street Journal,* August 27, 2004, p. A1; and "The Spies in Your Computer," *Wall Street Journal,* February 18, 2004, p. A18.

16. Adapted from examples in Gary H. Anthes, "Smile, You're on Candid Computer," *Computerworld,* December 3, 2001, p. 50; and Brandon Mercer, "Can Computers Read Your Mind?" *Techlive,* May 29, 2002, accessed at www.techtv.com/news/computing/story/0,24195,3386341,00.html.

17. For a good discussion, see Deborah L. Vence, "Better! Faster! Cheaper! Pick Any Three. That's Not a Joke," *Marketing News,* February 1, 2004, pp. 1, 31–32.

18. David Harding, David Chiefetz, Scott DeAngelo, and Elizabeth Ziegler, "CRM's Silver Lining," *Marketing Management,* March–April 2004, pp. 27–32.

19. See Marc L. Songini, "Fedex Expects CRM System to Deliver," *Computerworld,* November 6, 2000, p. 10. The Marks & Spencer example is adapted from "SAS Outfits Marks & Spencer with Customer Intelligence," accessed at www.sas.com/success/marksandspencer.html, June 2004.

20. Darrell K. Rigby, "Avoid the Four Perils of CRM," *Harvard Business Review,* February 2002, pp. 101–109; and Karl Flinders, "CRM Set for Spending Explosion," *VNUnet.com,* March 8, 2004.

21. Michael Krauss, "At Many Firms, Technology Obscures CRM," *Marketing News,* March 18, 2002, p. 5.

22. See Robert McLuhan, "How to Reap the Benefits of CRM," *Marketing,* May 24, 2001, p. 35; Sellar, "Dust Off That Data," p. 72; Stewart Deck, "Data Mining," *Computerworld,* March 29, 1999, p. 76; "Six Changes in CRM," *Selling Power,* source book, 2003, pp. 26–30; and Jason Compton, "CRM Gets Real," *Customer Relationship Management,* May 2004, pp. 11–12.

23. Ravi Kalakota and Marcia Robinson, *E-Business: Roadmap for Success* (Reading, MA: Addison-Wesley, 1999); "Maximizing Relationships," *Chain Store Age,* August 2001, pp. 21A–23A; and Pacific Research Consulting, "Seiyu Implementing Wal-Mart's Real-Time Sales/Inventory System," *Innovative New Packaging in Japan,* February 25, 2004, p. 1.

24. "Business Bulletin: Studying the Competition," *Wall Street Journal,* March 19, 1995, pp. A1, A5.

25. Alison Stein Wellner, "Research on a Shoestring," *American Demographics,* April 2001, pp. 38–39. Also see "Bissell, Inc.," *Hoover Company Profiles,* Austin, May 15, 2004, p. 47534.

26. For some good advice on conducting market research in a small business, see "Marketing Research . . . Basics 101," accessed at www.onlinewbc.gov/docs/market/mkt_res_basics.html, June 2004; and "Researching Your Market,"

U.S. Small Business Administration, accessed at www.sba.gov/library/pubs/mt-8.doc, June 2004.

27. Jack Honomichl, "Despite Acquisitions, Firms' Revenue Dips," *Marketing News,* August 13, 2003, pp. H3–H27; and the AC Nielsen International Research Web site, accessed at www.acnielsen.com/services/ir/, July 2004.

28. Phone, PC, and other country media stats are from www.nationmaster.com; December 2004.

29. Jain, *International Marketing Management,* 3d edition (Boston: PWS-Kent, 1990), p. 338. Also see Alvin C. Burns and Ronald F. Bush, *Marketing Research,* 3rd ed. (Upper Saddle River, NJ: Prentice Hall, 2000), pp. 317–318; and Debra L. Vence, "Leave It to the Experts," *Marketing News,* April 28, 2003, p. 37.

30. Steve Jarvis, "Status Quo = Progress," *Marketing News,* April 29, 2002, pp. 37–38; and Catherine Arnold, "Global Perspective," *Marketing News,* May 15, 2004, p. 43.

31. Adapted from Richard Behar, "Never Heard of Acxiom? Chances Are It's Heard of You," *Fortune,* February 23, 2004, pp. 140–148.

32. See "Too Much Information?" *Marketing Management,* January–February 2004, p. 4.

33. Margaret Webb Pressler, "Too Personal to Tell?" *The Washington Post,* April 18, 2004, p. F.05.

34. "ICC/ESOMAR International Code of Marketing and Social Research Practice," accessed at www.iccwbo.org/home/menu_advert_marketing.asp, June 2004.

35. Catherine Siskos, "In the Service of Guarding Secrets," *Kiplinger's Personal Finance,* February 2003, p. 26; John Schwartz, "Chief Privacy Officers Forge Evolving Corporate Roles," *New York Times,* February 12, 2001, p. C1; and Steve Ulfelder, "CPOs: Hot or Not?" *Computerworld,* March 15, 2004, p. 40.

36. Schwartz, "Chief Privacy Officers Forge Evolving Corporate Roles," p. C1.

37. Cynthia Crossen, "Studies Galore Support Products and Positions, But Are They Reliable?" *Wall Street Journal,* November 14, 1991, pp. A1, A9. Also see Allan J. Kimmel, "Deception in Marketing Research and Practice: An Introduction," *Psychology and Marketing,* July 2001, pp. 657–661.

38. Information accessed at www.casro.org/codeofstandards.cfm#intro, January 2004.

CHAPTER 5

1. Quotes and other information from Greg Schneider, "Rebels with Disposable Income; Aging Baby Boomers Line Up to Buy High-end Versions of Youthful Indulgences," *The Washington Post,* April 27, 2003, p. F1; Ian P. Murphy, "Aided by Research, Harley Goes Whole Hog," *Marketing News,* December 2, 1996, pp. 16, 17; Ted Bolton, "Tattooed Call Letters: The Ultimate Test of Brand Loyalty," accessed online at www.boltonresearch.com, April 2003; James D. Speros, "Why the Harley Brand's So Hot," *Advertising Age,* March 15, 2004, p. 26; Harley-Davidson Reports Record Fourth Quarter and 18th Consecutive Record Year," Harley-Davidson press release, January 21, 2004, accessed at www.Harley-Davidson.com; Jay Palmer, "Vroom at the Top," *Barron's,* March 29, 2004,

pp. 17–18; and the Harley-Davidson Web site at www. Harley-Davidson.com, January 2005.

2. World POPClock, U.S. Census Bureau, www.census.gov, December 2004. This Web site provides continuously updated projections of the U.S. and world populations.

3. Brad Weiners, "Getting Inside—Way Inside—Your Customer's Head," *Business 2.0*, April 2003, pp. 54–55.

4. Statistics from Eduardo Porter, "Buying Power of Hispanics Is Set to Soar," *Wall Street Journal*, April 18, 2003, p. B1; Allison Stein Wellner, "The Next 25 Years," *American Demographics,* April 2003, pp. 24–27; Brian Grow, "Hispanic Nation," *Business Week*, March 15, 2004, pp. 58–70; and "U.S. Interim Projections by Age, Sex, Race, and Hispanic Origin," March 18, 2004, accessed at www.census.gov/ipc/www/usinterimproj.

5. For these and other examples, see Catherine P. Taylor, "BarbieLatina Says 'Hola' to Net," *Advertising Age,* October 1, 2001, p. 54; Laurel Wentz, "Doors Opening Wide," *Advertising Age,* May 6, 2002, p. 24; Rebecca Garden and John Fetto, "Race, Ethnicity, and the Way We Shop," *American Demographics*, February, 2003, pp. 30–33; Grow, "Hispanic Nation," pp. 58–70; and Mercedes M. Cardona, "Home Chains Focus on Hispanic Market," *Advertising Age,* March 22, 2004, p. 6.

6. Calmetta Y. Coleman, "Attention Shoppers: Target Makes a Play for Minority Group Sears Has Cultivated," *Wall Street Journal*, April 12, 1999, p. A1; Robert Sharoff, "Diversity in the Mainstream," *Marketing News,* May 21, 2001, pp. 1, 131; Cecile B. Corral, "Sears Habla Espanol, ¿y Usted?" *Home Textiles Today,* February 3, 2003; and Miriam Jordan, "Hispanic Market Draws More Ad Spending," *Wall Street Journal*, April 21, 2004, p. B.3.

7. "The U.S. African American Market," Packaged Facts, January 2002; Garden and Fetto, "Race, Ethnicity, and the Way We Shop," p. 31; James Clingman, "Blackonomics; Turning Spending Power into $630B in Economic Power," *New York Beacon,* September 24, 2003, p. 8; Louise Witt, "Color Code Red," *American Demographics*, February 2004, pp. 23–25; and U.S. Census Bureau reports accessed online at www.census.gov, December 2004.

8. "Facts about Mahogany," accessed at http://pressroom. hallmark.com/mahogany_cards_facts.html, July 2004.

9. See Steve Jarvis, "Ethnic Sites Draw New Ad Wave," *Marketing News,* August 5, 2002; pp. 4, 6; information accessed at www.BlackPlanet.com, July 2004; and a list of most popular African American Web sites at www. freemaninstitute.com/AfAmSites.htm, December 2004.

10. Drawn from Garden and Fetto, "Race, Ethnicity, and the Way We Shop," p. 31; Wellner, "The Next 25 Years," p. 26; "How to Succeed in Multicultural Marketing," special supplement to *American Demographics,* November 2003; and U.S. Census Bureau reports accessed at www.census.gov, December 2004.

11. See Louise Lee, "Speaking the Customer's Language—Literally," *Business Week,* September 25, 2000, p. 178; Hassan Fattah, "Asia Rising," *American Demographics,* July–August 2002, pp. 38-43; and Robert Frank, "Affluence Rises for Asian Americans," *Wall Street Journal,* February 25, 2004, p. D8.

12. See Peter Francese, "Older and Wealthier," *American Demographics*, November 2002, pp. 40-41; Wellner, "The Next 25 Years," pp. 24–27; and information accessed at www.census.gov, April 2004.

13. See D. Allen Kerr, "Where There's Gray, There's Green," *Marketing News,* May 25, 1998, p. 2; "Fewer Seniors in the 1990s but Their Ranks Are Set to Explode," *Business Week,* May 28, 2001, p. 30; Laura Petrecca, "Savvy, Aging Boomers Buy into Pharma Mantra," *Advertising Age,* July 8, 2002, pp. S8–S9; Peter Francese, "Consumers Today," *American Demographics,* April 2003, pp. 28-29; and Robin Goldwyn Blumenthal, "Gray Is Good," *Barron's*, March 22, 2004, p. 37.

14. For more on social class, see Terrell G. Williams, "Social Class Influences on Purchase Evaluation Criteria," *Journal of Consumer Marketing,* vol. 19, iss. 2/3, 2002, pp. 248–276; Michael R. Solomon, *Consumer Behavior* 5th ed. (Upper Saddle River, NJ: Prentice Hall, 2002), chapter 13; and Leon G. Schiffman and Leslie L. Kanuk, *Consumer Behavior,* 8th ed. (Upper Saddle River, NJ: 2004), chapter 11.

15. See Edward Keller and Jonathan Berry, *The Influentials* (New York, NY: The Free Press, 2003); "The Chattering Class," *Fast Company*, January 2003, p. 48; and John Battelle, "The Net of Influence," *Business 2.0,* March 2004, p. 70.

16. Daniel Eisenberg and Laura Bradford, "It's an Ad, Ad, Ad, Ad World," *Time,* September 2, 2002, pp. 38–41.

17. Example adapted from Linda Tischler, "What's the Buzz?" *Fast Company*, May 2004, p. 76.

18. See Darla Dernovsek, "Marketing to Women," *Credit Union Magazine,* October 2000, pp. 90–96; Sharon Goldman Edry, "No Longer Just Fun and Games," *American Demographics,* May 2001, pp. 36–38; Hillary Chura, "Marketing Messages for Women Fall Short," *Advertising Age,* September 23, 2002, pp. 4, 14–15; and Jennifer Pendleton, "Ford at 100: Targeting the Female Market," *Advertising Age,* March 31, 2003, F38–F40.

19. Adapted from information in Bruce Upbin, "Merchant Princes," *Forbes,* January 20, 2003, pp. 52–56. Also see Fara Warner, "Yes, Women Spend (and Saw and Sand)," *New York Times*, February 29, 2004, p. 3.3.

20. Example drawn from Karl Greenberg, "The Kids Stay in the Future," *Brandweek,* March 31, 2003; and www.toyota. com/sienna, January 2005.

21. Tobi Elkin, "Sony Marketing Aims at Lifestyle Segments," *Advertising Age,* March 18, 2002, pp. 3, 72; and Kenneth Hein, "When Is Enough Enough?" *Brandweek,* December 2, 2002, pp. 26–28.

22. Quotes and examples from www.carhartt.com/rugged/ index.html, December 2004.

23. See Rebecca Piirto, "Measuring Minds in the 1990s," *American Demographics*, December 1990, pp. 35–39; and Rebecca Piirto, "VALS the Second Time," *American Demographics,* July 1991, p. 6. VALS information and examples accessed at www.sric-bi.com?VALS/types.shtml and www. sric-bi.com/VALS/projects.shtml, July 2004.

24. Accessed at www.forrester.com/Data/ConsumerTechno, July 2004.

25. Jennifer Aaker, "Dimensions of Measuring Brand Personality," *Journal of Marketing Research*, August 1997, pp. 347–356. Also see Aaker, "The Malleable Self: The Role of Self Expression in Persuasion," *Journal of Marketing Research*, May 1999, pp. 45–57; and Audrey Azoulay and Jean-Noel Kapferer, "Do Brand Personality Scales Really Measure Brand Personality?" *Journal of Brand Management*, November 2003, p. 143.

26. Charles Pappas, "Ad Nauseam," *Advertising Age*, July 10, 2000, pp. 16–18.

27. Bob Garfield, "'Subliminal' Seduction and Other Urban Myths," *Advertising Age*, September 18, 2000, pp. 4, 105. Also see "We Have Ways of Making You Think," *Marketing Week*, September 25, 2003, p. 14; and Si Cantwell, "Common Sense; Scrutiny Helps Catch Catchy Ads," *Wilmington Star-News*, April 1, 2004, p. 1B.

28. Kate Fitzgerald, "Milk Tailors Effort to Teens," *Advertising Age*, February 18, 2002, p. 16; Rebecca Flass, "'Got Milk?' Takes a Serious Look Inside the Body," *Adweek*, January 27, 2003, p. 5; Katie Koppenhoefer, "MilkPEP Ads Make Big Impact with Hispanics," press release, International Dairy Foods Association, March 3, 2003, accessed at www.idfa.org/news/gotmilk/2003/miklpepads.cfm; and information from www.whymilk.com, December 2004.

29. See Henry Assael, *Consumer Behavior and Marketing Action* (Boston: Kent Publishing, 1987), chapter 4. An earlier classification of three types of consumer buying behavior—routine response behavior, limited problem solving, and extensive problem solving—can be found in John A. Howard and Jagdish Sheth, *The Theory of Consumer Behavior* (New York: John Wiley, 1969), pp. 27–28. Also see John A. Howard, *Consumer Behavior in Marketing Strategy* (Upper Saddle River, NJ: Prentice Hall, 1989).

30. See Leon Festinger, *A Theory of Cognitive Dissonance* (Stanford, CA: Stanford University Press, 1957); Schiffman and Kanuk, *Consumer Behavior*, pp. 219–220; Jillian C. Sweeney, Douglas Hausknecht, and Geoffrey N. Soutar, "Cognitive Dissonance After Purchase: A Multidimensional Scale," *Psychology & Marketing*, May 2000, pp. 369–385; Patti Williams and Jennifer L. Aaker, "Can Mixed Emotions Peacefully Coexist?" March 2002, pp. 636–649; and Geoffrey Soutar and Jillian Sweeney, "Are There Cognitive Dissonance Segments?" *Australian Journal of Management*, December 2003, p. 227–263.

31. The following discussion draws from the work of Everett M. Rogers. See his *Diffusion of Innovations*, 5th ed. (New York: Free Press, 2003). Also see Peter J. Danaher, Bruce G. S. Hardie, and William P. Putsis, "Marketing-Mix Variables and the Diffusion of Successive Generations of a Technological Innovation," *Journal of Marketing Research*, November 2001, pp. 501–514; Eric Waarts, Yvonne M. van Everdingen, and Jos van Hillegersberg, "The Dynamics of Factors Affecting the Adoption of Innovations," *The Journal of Product Innovation Management*, November 2002, pp. 412–423; Jae H. Pae and Donald R. Lehmann, "Multigeneration Innovation Diffusion," *Academy of Marketing Science Journal*, Winter 2003, pp. 36–45; and Chuan-Fong Shih and Alladi Venkatesh, "Beyond Adoption: Development and Application of a Use-Diffusion Model," *Journal of Marketing*, January 2004, pp. 59–72.

CHAPTER 6

1. Quotes and other information from Dale Buss, "Up with Brown," *Brandweek*, Jan 27, 2003 p. 16; "Business as Usual for Ads on Sunday News Shows," *B to B*, April 14, 2003 p. 30; "UPS Service Helps Companies Go Global," *Transportation & Distribution*, May 2003 p. 19; "The New Mission of Synchronizing Global Supply Chains," *Inventory Management Report*, May 2003 p. 9; Robert McGarvey, "UPS Builds Millions in Sales," *Selling Power*, June 2004, pp. 56–61; and information gathered at www.UPS.com, December 2004.

2. See Kate Macarthur, "Teflon Togs Get $40 Million Ad Push," *Advertising Age*, April 8, 2002, p. 3; "Neat Pants for Sloppy People," *Consumer Reports: Publisher's Edition Including Supplemental Guides*, May 2003, p. 10; and "Sales Makes the Wearables World Go 'Round," *Wearables Business*, April 24, 2004, p. 22.

3. "How to Determine the Supplier Relationship Management Model," *Supplier Selection & Management Report*, July 2003, p. 4. Also see Steve Rogers, "Supply Management: Elements of Superior Design," *Supply Chain Management Review*, April 24, 2004, pp. 48–55; and Christopher Bouverie-Brine, "Business Relationship for Competitive Advantage," *Supply Management*, April 29, 2004, p. 35.

4. Patrick J. Robinson, Charles W. Faris, and Yoram Wind, *Industrial Buying Behavior and Creative Marketing* (Boston: Allyn & Bacon, 1967). Also see Erin Anderson, Weyien Chu, and Barton Weitz, "Industrial Purchasing: An Empirical Exploration of the Buyclass Framework," *Journal of Marketing*, July 1987, pp. 71–86; Michael D. Hutt and Thomas W. Speh, *Business Marketing Management*, 7th ed. (Upper Saddle River, NJ: Prentice Hall, 2001), pp. 56–66; and Junyean Moon and Surinder Tikoo, "Buying Decision Approaches of Organizational Buyers and Users," *Journal of Business Research*, April 2002, pp. 293–299.

5. See Philip Kotler, *Marketing Management*, 11th ed. (Upper Saddle River, NJ: Prentice Hall, 2003), pp. 219–220.

6. See Frederick E. Webster Jr. and Yoram Wind, *Organizational Buying Behavior* (Upper Saddle River, NJ: Prentice Hall, 1972), pp. 78–80. Also see James C. Anderson and James A. Narus, *Business Market Management: Understanding, Creating and Delivering Value* (Upper Saddle River NJ: Prentice Hall, 2004), chapter 3.

7. Frederick E. Webster, Jr., and Yoram Wind, *Organizational Buying Behavior*, pp. 33–37.

8. Robinson, Faris, and Wind, p. 14.

9. Unless otherwise noted, quotes and spending information in this section are from Michael A. Verespej, "E-Procurement Explosion," *Industry Week*, March 2002, pp. 24–28; "E-Procurement Still Less Popular than Paper Orders," *Supply Management*, March 13, 2003, p. 10; Jennifer Baljko, "Online Purchasing Activity on the Rise—But OEM Cost-Cutting Initiatives Are Limiting Process Changes," *EBN*, April 21, 2003, p. 6; and "Online Purchasing Still on the Rise," *Industrial Distribution*, December 2004, p. 24; and C. Subramaniam and M. Shaw, "The Effects of Process Characteristics on the Value of B2B E-Procurement," *Information Technology and Management*, January–April, 2004, p. 161.

10. Information obtained online at www.covisint.com/about/ and www.gxs.com/gxs/aboutus/, January 2005.

11. See Verespej, "E-Procurement Explosion," pp. 25-28; "E-Procurement: Certain Value in Changing Times," *Fortune,* April 30, 2001, pp. S2–S3; and Susan Avery, "Microsoft Moves Entire PC Buy Online, Saves 6%," *Purchasing,* January 16, 2003, pp. 14–18.

12. Paul E. Goulding, "Q&A: Making Uncle Sam Your Customer," *Financial Executive,* May–June 1998, pp. 55–57.

13. Kotler, p. 237.

14. See Ellen Messmer, "The Feds Get into Online Buying," *Network World,* March 5, 2001, p. 67; Patrick E. Clarke, "DLA Shifting from Managing Supplies to Managing Suppliers," May 30, 2002, accessed at www.dla.mil; and information accessed at http://progate.daps.dla.mil/home/ and www.gsa.gov/Portal/gsa/ep/contentView.do?contentId= 11887&contentType=GSA_OVERVIEW, January 2005.

CHAPTER 7

1. See Erin White and Sarah Ellison, "Unilever Ads Offer Tribute to Dirt," *Wall Street Journal,* June 2, 2003, p. B3; and information accessed at www.pg.com and www.tide.com, December 2004.

2. See "Home Depot Lite," *Chain Store Age,* January 2002, p. 39; Marianne Rohrlich, "Manhattanites Will Soon Find Depots Close to Home," *New York Times,* April 15, 2004, p. F10; Mike Troy, "Neighborhood Market Caps Year with Round of New Market Entries," *DSN Retailing Today,* January 27, 2003, pp. 3, 22; and Mel Duvall, "Wal-Mart Stores: the 'Neighborhood' Bully," *Baseline,* February 5, 2004, p. 34.

3. For these and other examples, see Patricia Sellers, "Gap's New Guy Upstairs," *Fortune,* April 24, 2003, pp. 110–116; Rob Turner, "Toothpaste for Women?" *Fortune,* March 3, 2003, p. 182; and information accessed at www.crest.com and www.rejuvenatingeffects.com, January 2005.

4. See information accessed at www.womenandco.com. July 2004; Bruce Upbin, "Merchant Princes," *Forbes,* January 20, 2003, pp. 52–56; and Debbie Howell, "Home Centers Focus on Females," *DSN Retailing Today,* May 3, 2004, p. 9.

5. Michelle Orecklin, "What Women Watch," *Time,* May 13, 2002, pp. 65–66; and information accessed online at www.iVillage.com and www.oxygen.com, December 2004.

6. Information accessed at www.neimanmarcus.com/store/ sitelets/incircle/index.jhtml, July, 2004.

7. Robert Berner, "Out-Discounting the Discounter," *Business Week,* May 10, 2004, pp. 78–79.

8. "Lifestyle Marketing," *Progressive Grocer,* August 1997, pp. 107–110; and Philip Kotler, *Marketing Management: Analysis, Planning, Implementation, and Control,* 11th ed. (Upper Saddle River, NJ: Prentice Hall, 2003), pp. 291–292.

9. See Jonathon Welsh, "Transport: The Summer of the Scooter: Boomers Get a New Retro Toy," *Wall Street Journal,* April 13, 2001, p. W1; Tammy Lieber, "Vroom, Vroom: Scooter Sales Motor after Slow Start," *Indianapolis Business Journal,* December 8, 2003, pp. 39–45; and Honda's Web site at www.powersports.honda.com/scooter, July 2004.

10. Information from www.kodak.com, January 2005.

11. See Jennifer Ordonez, "Fast-Food Lovers, Unite!" *Newsweek,* May 24, 2004, p. 56.

12. Kendra Parker, "How Do You Like Your Beef?" *American Demographics,* January 2000, pp. 35–37.

13. Based on an example from Christine Del Valle, "They Know Where You Live—and How You Buy," *Business Week,* February 7, 1994, p. 89; and PRIZM cluster information accessed at www.claritas.com, August 2004.

14. John Fetto, American Neighborhoods' First Page," *American Demographics,* July–August 2003, p. 34.

15. For more on geodemographic segmentation, see John MacManus, "Street Wiser," *American Demographics,* July–August 2003, p. 32–35. Information about the PRIZM segmentation system accessed at www.clusterbigip1.claritas. com/claritas/Default.jsp?main=3&submenu=seg&subcat= segprizm, August 2004.

16. Information from http://home.americanexpress.com/home/ mt_personal.shtml, August, 2004.

17. For more on segmenting business markets, see Turan Senguder, "An Evaluation of Consumer and Business Segmentation Approaches," *Journal of the Academy of Business,* March 2003, pp. 618–624; and James C. Anderson and James A. Narus, *Business Market Management,* 2nd ed. (Upper Saddle River, NJ: Prentice Hall, 2004), pp. 45–52.

18. See Arundhati Parmar, "Global Youth United," *Marketing News,* October 28, 2002, pp. 1, 49; the MTV Worldwide Web site, www.mtv.com/mtvinternational; "Teen Spirit," *Global Cosmetic Industry,* March 2004, p. 23; and "MTV: Music Television: The Facts," accessed online at www. viacom.com/prodbyunit1.tin?ixBusUnit=19, July 2004.

19. See Michael Porter, *Competitive Advantage* (New York: Free Press, 1985), pp. 4–8, 234–236. For more recent discussions, see Stanley Slater and Eric Olson, "A Fresh Look at Industry and Market Analysis," *Business Horizons,* January–February 2002, pp. 15–22; Kenneth Sawka and Bill Fiora, "The Four Analytical Techniques Every Analyst Must Know: 2. Porter's Five Forces Analysis," *Competitive Intelligence Magazine,* May–June 2003, p. 57; and Philip Kotler, *Marketing Management,* 11th ed. (Upper Saddle River, NJ: 2003), pp. 242–243.

20. Nina Munk, "Why Women Find Lauder Mesmerizing," *Fortune,* May 25, 1998, pp. 97–106; Christine Bittar, "New Faces, Same Name," *Brandweek,* March 11, 2002, pp. 28–34; Robin Givhan, "Estée Lauder, Sending a Message in a Bottle," *The Washington Post,* April 26, 2004, p. C.01; and information accessed at www.elcompanies.com, January 2005.

21. Peter Burrows, "How to Milk an Apple," *Business Week,* February, 3, 2003, p. 44; and Josh Quittner, "Steve Jobs," *Time,* April 26, 2004, p. 75.

22. See Gerry Khermouch, "Call it the Pepsi Blue Generation," *Business Week,* February 3, 2003, p. 96; Kathleen Sampey, "Sweet on Sierra Mist," *Adweek,* February 2, 2004, p. 20; and Nat Ives, "Mountain Dew Double-Dose for Times Square Passers-By," *New York Times,* April 8, 2004, p. C9.

23. Information accessed online at www.ostrichesonline.com, July 2004.

24. For a good discussion of mass customization and relationship building, see Don Peppers and Martha Rogers,

Managing Customers Relationships: A Strategic Framework (Hoboken, NJ: John Wiley & Sons, 2004), chapter 10.

25. See Faith Keenan, "A Mass Market of One," *Business Week,* December 2, 2002, pp. 68–72; and information accessed at http://shop.mms.com/customized/index.asp?UID=, August 2004.

26. Adapted from information found in Mark Tatge, "Red Bodies, Black Ink," *Forbes,* September 18, 2000. p 114; "Oshkosh Truck Corporation," *Hoover's Company Profiles,* Austin, May 15, 2004, p. 14345; and information accessed at www.oshkoshtruck.com, December 2004.

27. Sony A. Grier, "The Federal Trade Commission's Report on the Marketing of Violent Entertainment to Youths: Developing Policy-Tuned Research," *Journal of Public Policy and Marketing,* Spring 2001, pp. 123–132; Deborah L. Vence, "Marketing to Minors Still under Careful Watch," *Marketing News,* March 31, 2003, pp. 5–6; and Susan Linn, *Consuming Kids: The Hostile Takeover of Childhood* (New York: The New Press, 2004).

28. See Michelle Singletary, "Don't Get Baited by These Scams," *Washington Post,* February 5, 2004, p. 1; and information at the FBI's Internet Fraud Complaint Center Web site, www. ifccfbi.gov, July 2004.

29. Adapted from a positioning map prepared by students Brian May, Josh Payne, Meredith Schakel, and Bryana Sterns, University of North Carolina, April 2003. SUV sales data furnished by WardsAuto.com, June 2003. Price data from www.edmunds.com, June 2004.

30. See Kotler, *Kotler on Marketing,* pp. 59–63.

31. See Bobby J. Calder and Steven J. Reagan, "Brand Design," in Dawn Iacobucci, ed. *Kellogg on Marketing* (New York: John Wiley & Sons, 2001) p. 61. The Palm and Mountain Dew examples are from Alice M. Tybout and Brian Sternthal, "Brand Positioning," in Iacobucci, ed., *Kellogg on Marketing,* p. 54.

CHAPTER 8

1. Portions adapted from a case written by Peter Attwater, student at the University of North Carolina at Chapel Hill, April 2003. Other information and quotes from "It's Official: Krispy Kreme Coming to Clackamas," April 8, 2003, accessed online at www.katu.com; Sarah MacDonald, "It's a Drive-Thru or No Go," April 17, 2003, *Daily News Transcript,* accessed online at www.neponsetvalleydailynews.com; Andy Serwer, "The Hole Story," *Fortune,* July 7, 2003, pp. 62; Serwer, "A Hole in Krispy Kreme's Story," *Fortune,* June 14, 2004, p. 40; and information accessed online at www.krispykreme.com/presskit.pdf, January 2005.

2. Information accessed at www.wirednewyork.com/toys_rus. htm, December 2004.

3. For more on experience marketing, see B. Joseph Pine and James H. Gilmore, *The Experience Economy* (New York: Free Press, 1999); Stephen E. DeLong, "The Experience Economy," *Upside,* November 2001, p. 28; and "Brand Entertainment: Brands Play the World's Stage," *Brand Strategy,* August 2003, p. 20.

4. See Kate Fitzgerald, "Buick Rides the Tiger," *Advertising Age,* April 15, 2002, p. 41; "He Sold Fame; We Bought It,"

Los Angeles Times," May 20, 2003, p. B14; and "The Celebrity 100," *Forbes,* accessed at www.forbes.com, June 2004.

5. See Daniel Roth, "The Trophy Life," *Fortune,* April 19, 2004, p. 70; Trump, Donald. *Trump: The Art of the Comeback* (New York: Random House, 1997); Richard Linnett, "'Human Logo': Reconstructing the Trump Brand," *Advertising Age,* August 18, 2003, p. 1; Adam Lashinsky, "For Trump, Fame Is Easier than Fortune," *Fortune,* February 23, 2004, p. 38; and Daniel Roth, "The Trophy Life," *Fortune,* April 19, 2004, pp. 70–84.

6. Check out the tourism Web pages of these states at www.TravelTex.com, www.michigan.org, and www. iloveny.state.ny.us.

7. For more on marketing places, see Philip Kotler, Donald Haider, and Irving J. Rein, *Marketing Places: Attracting Investment, Industry, and Tourism to Cities, States, and Nations* (New York: Free Press, 2002). Examples information found at www.TravelTex.com, www.michigan.org, www.iloveny.state.ny.us, www.ireland.travel.ie, and www.ida.ie, December 2004.

8. Accessed online at www.social-marketing.org/aboutus. html, January 2005.

9. See Alan R. Andreasen, Rob Gould, and Karen Gutierrez, "Social Marketing Has a New Champion," *Marketing News,* February 7, 2000, p. 38. Also see Philip Kotler, Ned Roberto, and Nancy Lee, *Social Marketing: Improving the Quality of Life,* 2nd ed. (Thousand Oaks, CA: Sage Publications, 2002); and www.social-marketing.org, December 2004.

10. Quotes and definitions from Philip Kotler, *Kotler on Marketing* (New York: Free Press, 1999), p. 17; and www.asq. org, January 2005.

11. See Roland T. Rust, Anthony J. Zahorik, and Timothy L. Keiningham, "Return on Quality (ROQ): Making Service Quality Financially Accountable," *Journal of Marketing,* April 1995, pp. 58–70; Roland T. Rust, Christine Moorman, and Peter R. Dickson, "Getting Return on Quality: Revenue Expansion, Cost Reduction, or Both?" *Journal of Marketing,* October 2002, pp. 7–24; and Roland T. Rust, Katherine N. Lemon, and Valarie A. Zeithaml, "Return on Marketing: Using Customer Equity to Focus Marketing Strategy," *Journal of Marketing,* January 2004, p. 109.

12. Example adapted from Bruce Nussbaum, "The Power of Design," *Business Week,* May 17, 2004, pp. 86–94.

13. See Kate Fitzgerald, "Packaging Is the Capper," *Advertising Age,* May 5, 2003, p. 22.

14. Adapted from examples found in Julie Dunn, "Pouring Paint, Minus a Mess," *New York Times,* October 27, 2002, p. 3.2; "Look Ma, No Drip," *Business Week,* December 16, 2002, p. 74; Seth Godin, "In Praise of the Purple Cow," *Fast Company,* February 2003, pp. 74–85; Catherine Arnold, "Way Outside the Box," *Marketing News,* June 23, 2003, pp. 13, 15; and information accessed at www.dutchboy. com/twistandpour/index_store.asp, June 2004.

15. Robert M. McMath, "Chock Full of (Pea)nuts," *American Demographics,* April 1997, p. 60. For more on packaging, see Robert L. Underwood, "The Communicative Power of Product Packaging: Creating Brand Identity via Lived and Mediate Experience," *Journal of Marketing Theory and Practice,* Winter 2003, p. 62.

16. Bro Uttal, "Companies That Serve You Best," *Fortune*, December 7, 1987, p. 116; and American Customer Satisfaction Index ratings accessed at www.theacsi.org, December 2004.

17. Example adapted from Michelle Higgins, "Pop-Up Sales Clerks: Web Sites Try the Hard Sell," *Wall Street Journal*, April 15, 2004, p. D.1.

18. Information accessed online at www.marriott.com, December 2004.

19. Information about P&G's product lines accessed at www.pg.com/products/usa_product_facts.jhtml and www.crest.com, December 2004. For more on product line strategy, see Robert Bordley, "Determining the Appropriate Depth and Breadth of a Firm's Product Portfolio," *Journal of Marketing Research*, February 2003, pp. 39–53.

20. See "McAtlas Shrugged," *Foreign Policy*, May–June 2001, pp. 26–37; and Philip Kotler, *Marketing Management*, 11th ed. (Upper Saddle River, NJ: Prentice Hall, 2003), p. 423.

21. Douglas Holt, "What Becomes an Icon Most?" *Harvard Business Review*, March 2003, pp. 43–49.

22. David C. Bello and Morris. B. Holbrook, "Does an Absence of Brand Equity Generalize Across Product Classes?" *Journal of Business Research*, October 1995, p. 125; and Scott Davis, *Brand Asset Management: Driving Profitable Growth through Your Brands* (San Francisco: Jossey-Bass, 2000). Also see Kevin Lane Keller, *Building, Measuring, and Managing Brand Equity*, 2nd ed. (Upper Saddle River, NJ: Prentice Hall, 2003), chapter 2; and Kusum Ailawadi, Donald R. Lehman, and Scott A. Neslin, "Revenue Premium as an Outcome Measure of Brand Equity," *Journal of Marketing*, October 2003, pp. 1–17.

23. "The World's Most Valuable Brands," *Business Week*, August 2, 2004.

24. See Roland Rust, Katherine Lemon, and Valarie Zeithaml "Return on Marketing: Using Customer Equity to Focus Marketing Strategy," *Journal of Marketing*, January 2004, p. 109.

25. See Davis, *Brand Asset Management*; and Kotler, *Marketing Management*, pp. 419–420.

26. See Marc Gobe, *Emotional Branding* (New York: Allworth Press, 2001); and Jack Neff, "P&G Bets $100 Million on Crest Brand Plan," *Advertising Age*, March 22, 2004, pp. 5, 33.

27. Example adapted from Matthew Boyle, "Brand Killers," *Fortune*, August 11, 2003, pp. 89–100.

28. See "The Private Label Connection," *Beverage Industry*, February 2003, p. 48; and Shelley Branch, "Going Private (Label)," *Wall Street Journal*, June 12, 2003, p. B1. For more on private brands, see Tulin Erdem, Ying Zao, and Ana Valenzuela, "Performance of Store Brands: A Cross-Country Analysis of Consumer Store-Brand Preferences, Perceptions, and Risk," *Journal of Marketing Research*, February 2004, pp. 86–100; and Kusum Ailawadi and Bari Harlam, "An Empirical Analysis of Retail Margins: The Role of Store-Brand Share," *Journal of Marketing*, January 2004, pp. 147–165.

29. William Wilkie, "Marketing Research and Public Policy: The Case of Slotting Fees," *Journal of Public Policy and Marketing*, Fall 2002, pp. 275–289; Gene Epstein, "Envelope, Please," *Barron's*, November 4, 2002, p. 37; and Margaret Webb Pressler, "Shelf Game; When Stores Force Makers to Pay Them Fees, You Lose," *The Washington Post*, January 18, 2004, p. F.05.

30. Jay Sherman, "Nick Puts Muscle Behind everGirl," *TelevisionWeek*, January 5, 2004, p. 3

31. See Laura Petrecca, "'Corporate Brands' Put Licensing in the Spotlight," *Advertising Age*, June 14, 1999, p. 1; and Bob Vavra, "The Game of the Name," *Supermarket Business*, March 15, 2001, pp. 45–46.

32. Gabrielle Solomon, "Co-Branding Alliances: Arranged Marriages Made by Marketers," *Fortune*, October 12, 1998, p. 188; and "Martha Stewart, Kmart Continue Partnership," *Gourmet News*, June 2004, p. 14.

33. For more on the use of line and brand extensions and consumer attitudes toward them, see Vanitha Swaminathan, Richard J. Fox, and Srinivas K. Reddy, "The Impact of Brand Extension Introduction on Choice," *Journal of Marketing*, October 2001, pp. 1–15; Kalpesh Kaushik Desai and Kevin Lane Keller, "The Effect of Ingredient Branding Strategies on Host Brand Extendibility," *Journal of Marketing*, January 2002, pp. 73–93; Subramanian Balachander and Sanjoy Ghose, "Reciprocal Spillover Effects: A Strategic Benefit of Brand Extensions," *Journal of Marketing*, January 2003, pp. 4–13; and Eva Martinez and Leslie de Chernatony, "The Effect of Brand Extension Strategies Upon Brand Image," *The Journal of Consumer Marketing*, 2004, p. 39.

34. "Top 200 Megabrands," accessed at www.adage.com, June 2004.

35. See Kevin Lane Keller, "The Brand Report Card," *Harvard Business Review*, January 2000, pp. 147–157; Keller, *Strategic Brand Management*, pp. 766–767; and David A. Aaker, "Even Brands Need Spring Cleaning," *Brandweek*, March 8, 2004, pp. 36–40.

36. Steve Jarvis, "Refocus, Rebuild, Reeducate, Refine, Rebrand," *Marketing News*, March 26, 2001, pp. 1, 11; and "Top 10 Wireless Phone Brands," *Advertising Age*, June 24, 2002, p. S-18; and information accessed at www.myrateplan.com, June 2004.

37. See Ronald Henkoff, "Service Is Everybody's Business," *Fortune*, June 27, 1994, pp. 48–60; Valarie Zeithaml and Mary Jo Bitner, *Services Marketing*, 3d ed. (New York: McGraw-Hill, 2002), pp. 8–9; and Margaret Popper, "Services: Slowed but Still Strong," *Business Week*, December 12, 2002, accessed online at www.businessweek.com. For more on the importance of services to marketing and the economy, see Robert F. Lusch and Stephen L. Vargo, "Evolving to a New Dominant Logic for Marketing," *Journal of Marketing*, January 2004, p. 1.

38. Adapted from information in Leonard Berry and Neeli Bendapudi, "Clueing in Customers," *Harvard Business Review*, February 2003, pp. 100–106 and information accessed at www.mayoclinic.org, December 2004.

39. See James L. Heskett, W. Earl Sasser Jr., and Leonard A. Schlesinger, *The Service Profit Chain: How Leading Companies Link Profit and Growth to Loyalty, Satisfaction, and Value* (New York: Free Press, 1997); and Heskett, Sasser, and Schlesinger, *The Value Profit Chain: Treat Employees Like Customers and Customers Like Employees* (New York: Free Press, 2003).

40. Jeremy B. Dann, "How to Find a Hit as Big as Starbucks," *Business 2.0*, May 2004, pp. 66–68.

41. For discussions of service quality, see Valarie A. Zeithaml, A. Parasuraman, and Leonard L. Berry, *Delivering Quality Service: Balancing Customer Perceptions and Expectations* (New York: The Free Press, 1990); Zeithaml, Berry, and Parasuraman, "The Behavioral Consequences of Service Quality," *Journal of Marketing,* April 1996, pp. 31–46; Thomas J. Page Jr., "Difference Scores Versus Direct Effects in Service Quality Measurement," *Journal of Service Research,* February 2002, pp. 184–192; and Y H Hung, M L Huang, and K S Chen, "Service Quality Evaluation by Service Quality Performance Matrix," *Total Quality Management & Business Excellence,* January 2003, pp. 79–89.

42. See James L. Heskett, W. Earl Sasser Jr., and Christopher W. L. Hart, *Service Breakthroughs* (New York: Free Press, 1990).

43. See "Jury Awards in Product Liability Cases Increasing in Recent Years," *Chemical Market Reporter,* February 12, 2001, p. 5; and "Ford Motor Co.: Jury Orders Auto Maker to Pay $369 in Explorer Case," *Wall Street Journal,* June 4, 2004, p. 1.

44. See James A. Bruen, "Product Liability: The Role of the Product Steward," *Risk Management,* February 2002, p. 34.

45. See Philip Cateora, *International Marketing,* 8th ed. (Homewood, IL: Irwin, 1993), p. 270; David Fairlamb, "One Currency—But 15 Economies," *Business Week,* December 31, 2001, p. 59; and www.walkabouttravelgear.com, July 2004.

46. Information accessed online at www.deutsche-bank.com, July 2004.

47. Information accessed online at www.interpublic.com and www.mccann.com, December 2004.

48. See "Wal-Mart International Operations," accessed at www.walmartstores.com, July 2004; and "2004 Global Powers of Retailing," *Stores,* January 2004, accessed at www.stores.org.

CHAPTER 9

1. Portions adapted from Ian Wylie, "Calling for a Renewable Future," *Fast Company,* May 2003, pp. 4648. Also see Brad Smith, "Nokia: From Banks of Remote River Comes Innovation," *Wireless Week,* March 22, 2004, p. 26; and Andy Reinhardt, "Can Nokia Get the Wow Back?" *Business Week,* May 31, 2004, pp. 4850.

2. For these and other examples, see Simon Romero, "Once Proudly Carried, and Now Mere Carrion," *New York Times,* November 22, 2001, p. G5; Kelly Carroll, "Satellite Telephony: Not for the Consumer," *Telephony,"* March 4, 2002, p. 17; and Eric Almquist, Martin Kon, and Wolfgang Bock, "The Science of Demand," *Marketing Management,* March–April 2004, pp. 20–26.

3. See Bruce Tait, "The Failure of Marketing 'Science,'" *Brandweek,* April 8, 2002, pp. 20–22; Alison Stein Wellner, "The New Science of Focus Groups," *American Demographics,* March 2003, p. 30; Kevin J Clancy and Peter C Krieg, "Surviving Innovation," *Marketing Management,* March/April 2003, pp. 14–20; and "Market Research: So What's the Big Idea?" *Marketing Week,* March 11, 2004, p. 37.

4. Information and examples from Gary Slack, "Innovations and Idiocities," *Beverage World,* November 15, 1998, p. 122; Robert M. McMath and Thom Forbes, *What Were They Thinking? Money-Saving, Time-Saving, Face-Saving Marketing Lessons You Can Learn from Products That Flopped* (New York: Times Business, 1999), various pages; Melissa Master, "Spectacular Failures," *Across the Board,* March–April 2001, p. 24; and www.newproductworks.com/product_poll/hm_index.html, December 2004.

5. Gary Hamel, "Innovation's New Math," *Fortune,* July 9, 2001, pp. 130–131.

6. Paul Lukas, "Marketing: The Color of Money and Ketchup," *Fortune,* September 18, 2000, p. 38; Sonia Reyes, "Shopping List: Quick, Classic, and Cool for Kids," *Brandweek,* June 17, 2002, pp S52–S54; "Heinz EZ Squirt Shoots for the Stars with Its Latest Creation; Stellar Blue Has Landed on Store Shelves," Heinz press release, April 7, 2003, accessed at www.heinz.com/jsp/news_f.jsp; and information accessed at www.heinz.com/jsp/new_prod.jsp, July 2004.

7. Pam Weisz, "Avon's Skin-So-Soft Bugs Out," *Brandweek,* June 6, 1994, p. 4; and information accessed online at www.avon.com, January 2005.

8. Stefan Thomke and Eric von Hippel, "Customers as Innovators: A New Way to Create Value," *Harvard Business Review,* April 2002, pp. 74–81; and Faith Keenan, "A Mass Market of One," *Business Week,* December 2, 2002, pp. 68–72.

9. Robert Gray, "Not Invented Here," *Marketing,* May 6, 2004, pp. 34–37.

10. See Philip Kotler, *Kotler on Marketing* (New York, NY: The Free press, 1999), pp. 43–44. For more on developing new-product ideas, see Darrell Rigby and Chris Zook, "Open-Market Innovation," *Harvard Business Review,* October 2002, pp. 80–89; and Jacob Goldenberg, Roni Horowitz, Amnon Levav, and David Mazursky, "Finding Your Innovation Sweetspot," *Harvard Business Review,* March 2003, pp. 120–129.

11. See Katherine Mieszkowski, "Fill'er Up with Hydrogen," *Fast Company,* March 2003, p. 34; and "DaimlerChrysler Delivers the First Fuel Cell Cars to Customers in Berlin," June 18, 2004, accessed at www.daimlerchrysler.com.

12. Adrienne Ward Fawcett, "Oreo Cones Make Top Grade in Poll," *Advertising Age,* June 14, 1993, p. 30; Becky Ebenkamp, "The New Gold Standards," *Brandweek,* April 19, 1999, p. 34; Ebenkamp, "It's Like Cheers and Jeers, Only for Brands," *Brandweek,* March 19, 2001; and Ebenkamp, "The Focus Group Has Spoken," *Brandweek,* April 23, 2001, p. 24; and discussions with Mark Sneider, General Manager, AcuPOLL, October 2004.

13. "Hershey Research Sees Net Gain," *Marketing News,* November 25, 2002, p. 17.

14. Examples adapted from those found in Emily Nelson, "Focus Groupies: P&G Keeps Cincinnati Busy with All Its Studies—While Her Sons Test Old Spice; Linda Geil Gets Swabbed," *Wall Street Journal,* January 24, 2002, p. A1; Linda Grant, "Gillette Knows Shaving—and How to Turn Out Hot New Products," *Fortune,* October 14, 1996, pp. 207–210; and Carol Matlack, "The Vuitton Machine," *Business Week,* March 22, 2004, pp. 98–102.

15. Judann Pollack, "Baked Lays," *Advertising Age,* June 24, 1996, p. S2; Jack Neff and Suzanne Bidlake, "P&G, Unilever Aim to Take Consumers to the Cleaners," *Advertising Age,* February 12, 2001, pp. 1, 2; and Dean Takahashi, "Nokia's N-Gage Shakes Up the Gaming Market," *Electronic Business,* April 1, 2003, p. 28.

16. This and other examples can be found in Robert McMath, "To Test or Not to Test," *Advertising Age,* June 1998, p. 64; and Bret Thron, "Lessons Learned: Menu Miscues," *Nation's Restaurant News,* May 20, 2002, pp. 102–104. Also see Jerry W. Thomas, "Skipping Research a Major Error," *Marketing News,* March 4, 2002, p. 50.

17. Jack Neff, "Is Testing the Answer?" *Advertising Age,* July 9, 2001, p. 13; and Dale Buss, "P&G's Rise," *Potentials,* January 2003, pp. 26–30.

18. Information on BehaviorScan accessed at www.infores. com, December 2004.

19. Emily Nelson, "Colgate's Net Rose 10% in Period, New Products Helped Boost Sales," *Wall Street Journal,* February 2, 2001, p. B6; and "New Products Aid Colgate Net," *New York Times,* February 5, 2003, p. C.2.

20. For a good review of research on new-product development, see Rajesh Sethi, "New Product Quality and Product Development Teams," *Journal of Marketing,* April 2000, pp. 1–14; Shikhar Sarin and Vijay Mahajan, "The Effect of Reward Structures on the Performance of Cross-Functional Product Development Teams," *Journal of Marketing,* April 2001, pp. 35–54; Joseph M. Bonner, Robert W. Ruekert, and Orville C. Walker Jr, "Upper Management Control of New Product Development Projects and Project Performance," *Journal of Product Innovation Management*, May 2002, pp. 233–245; and Sandra Valle and Lucia Avella, "Cross-Functionality and Leadership of the New Product Development Teams," *European Journal of Innovation Management,* 2003, pp. 32–47. For an interesting view of an alternative new product development process, see Bruce Nussbaum, "The Power of Design," *Business Week,* May 17, 2004, pp. 86–94.

21. See Michael Arndt, "3M: A Lab for Growth," *Business Week,* January 21, 2002, pp. 50–51; Tim Studt, "3M—Where Innovation Rules," *R&D,* April 2003, pp. 20–24; Tim Stevens, "3M Reinvents Its Innovation Process," *Research Technology Management,* March/April 2004, p. 3; and "Innovation at 3M," accessed at www.3m.com/about3m/innovation/index.jhtml, December 2004.

22. Kevin Clancy and Peter Krieg, "Product Life Cycle: A Dangerous Idea," *Brandweek,* March 1, 2004, p. 26.

23. Laurie Freeman, "Study: Leading Brands Aren't Always Enduring," *Advertising Age,* February 28, 2000, p. 26.

24. This definition is based on one found in Bryan Lilly and Tammy R. Nelson, "Fads: Segmenting the Fad-Buyer Market," *Journal of Consumer Marketing,* vol. 20, no. 3, 2003, pp. 252–265.

25. See "Scooter Fad Fades, as Warehouses Fill and Profits Fall," *Wall Street Journal,* June 14, 2001, p. B4; Katya Kazakina, "Toy Story: Yo-Yos Make a Big Splash," *Wall Street Journal,* April 11, 2003, p. W-10; and Robert Johnson, "A Fad's Father Seeks a Sequel," *New York Times,* May 30, 2004, p. 3.2.

26. These and other uses found in "Always Another Uses: 2000 Uses List," http://fanclub.wd40.com/Members/FanSpeak/uses.cfm, July 2004.

27. Example adapted from Stephanie Thompson, "Sprucing Up Spam for New Generation," *Advertising Age,* October 28, 2002, p. 6. Additional information from "The Lighter Side of Spam," December 9, 2002, accessed at www.msn.com/id/2074884/; and information from www.spammobile.com, January 2005.

28. See Jack Neff, "Mr. Clean Gets $50 Million Push," *Advertising Age,* August 18, 2003, pp. 3, 32; and information accessed at www.homemadesimple.com/mrclean/, December 2004.

29. For a more comprehensive discussion of marketing strategies over the course of the product life cycle, see Philip Kotler, *Marketing Management*, 11th ed. (Upper Saddle River, NJ: Prentice Hall, 2003), chapter 10.

CHAPTER 10

1. Thomas T. Nagle and Reed K. Holden, *The Strategy and Tactics of Pricing,* 3d ed. (Upper Saddle River, NJ: Prentice Hall, 2002), p. 1.

2. Excerpts from "Business: It Was My Idea," *The Economist,* August 15, 1998, p. 54; Karl Taro Greenfeld, "Be Your Own Barcode," *Time,* July 10, 2000, pp. 96–97; Ben Rosier, "The Price Is Right," *Marketing,* February 22, 2001, p. 26; and www.priceline.com, July 2004. See also "Priceline.com's Online 'Reach' Up 810% vs. a Year Ago," June 7, 2002, accessed at www.priceline.com; Timothy J. Mullaney, "A Humbler, Happier Priceline," *Business Week,* August 11, 2003, p. 34; "Priceline, Incorporated," *Hoover's Company Profiles,* Austin, March 15, 2004; Brian Ek, "Priceline.com Launches New Airline Tickets Service with TV Ad Campaign Featuring William Shatner and Leonard Nimoy," January 16, 2004, accessed at www.priceline.com; and Christina Binkley, "The Making of a Star," *Wall Street Journal*, January 15, 2004, p. D.1.

3. Dean Foust, "Raising Prices Won't Fly," *Business Week,* June 3, 2002, p. 34; and Geoffery Colvin, "Pricing Power Ain't What It Used to Be," *Fortune,* September 15, 2003, p. 52.

4. Linda Tischler, "The Price is Right," *Fast Company,* November 2003, pp. 83–91.

5. Robert D. Hof, "Going, Going, Gone," *Business Week*, April 12, 1999, pp. 30–32. Also see Mui Kung, Kent B. Monroe, and Jennifer L. Cox, "Pricing on the Internet," *The Journal of Product and Brand Management,* 2002, pp. 274–287; Charles Fishman, "Which Price is Right?" *Fast Company,* March 2003, pp. 92–102; and Faith Keenan, "The Price is Really Right," *Business Week,* March 31, 2003, pp. 60–67.

6. "MusicRebellion: Dynamic Pricing for Music Starts with 10-Cent Tunes," *Wall Street Journal,* January 9, 2004; and "MusicRebellion, Inc." *Hoover's Company Capsules,* Austin, March 15, 2004, p. 132322.

7. For an excellent discussion of factors affecting pricing decisions, see Nagle and Holden, *The Strategy and Tactics of Pricing*, chapter 1.

8. See Robert Berner, "Why P&G's Smile Is So Bright," *Business Week,* August 12, 2002, pp. 58–60; Jack Neff, "Power Brushes a Hit at Every Level," *Advertising Age,* May 26, 2003, p. 10; and information accessed at www.spinbrush.com, December 2004.

9. Here accumulated production is drawn on a semilog scale so that equal distances represent the same percentage increase in output.

10. Joshua Rosenbaum, "Guitar Maker Looks for a New Key," *Wall Street Journal,* February 11, 1998, p. B1; "Gibson Guitar Corp.," *Hoover's Company Profiles,* Austin, March 15, 2004, p. 53672; and information accessed online at www.gibson.com, January 2005.

11. See Nagle and Holden, *The Strategy and Tactics of Pricing,* chapter 4.

12. Information and quotes accessed at www.greenmountain.com, October 2004.

13. The arithmetic of markups and margins is discussed in Appendix 2, "Marketing Math."

14. See "Hi-Lo versus EDLP: We Want Both!" *Retail World,* August 18, 2003, p. 30; and Laura Heller, "EDLP Has Only Scratched the Surface," *DSN Retailing Today,* January 26, 2004, pp. 35–36.

15. Erin Stout, "Keep Them Coming Back for More," *Sales & Marketing Management,* February 2002, pp. 51–52. Also see Alison Smith, "The Flip Side of Pricing," *Selling Power,* May 2003, pp. 29–30.

CHAPTER 11

1. Excerpts adapted from Ann Zimmerman and Amy Merrick, "Kmart Rivals Appear to Benefit from BlueLight," *Wall Street Journal,* September 7, 2001, p. B1; and Mark Danzig, "By Design: The BlueLight Brand Story," *Design Management Journal,* Winter 2002, pp. 26–32. Also see Amy Merrick, "Target Sues Kmart Claiming Ads Misstate Prices in Comparisons," *Wall Street Journal,* August 22, 2001, p. B8; Alice Z. Cuneo, "Ailing Kmart Surrenders in Price War," *Advertising Age,* January 21, 2002, pp. 1, 43, Constance L. Hays, "A New Start, a New Name. But Have Things Really Changed as Kmart Comes Out of Bankruptcy?" *New York Times,* May 7, 2003, p. C9; Tony Lisanti, "Kmart's Ten Deadly Sins," *DSN Retailing Today,* August 18, 2003, pp. 16–22; Sarah Karush, "Kmart's Finances Healthy; Shoppers Needed," *The Durham Herald-Sun,* May 6, 2004, p. C7; and Amy Merrick and Ann Zimmerman, "Can Sears and Kmart Take On a Goliath Named Wal-Mart?" *Wall Street Journal,* November 19, p. B1.

2. For comprehensive discussions of pricing strategies, see Thomas T. Nagle and Reed K. Holden, *The Strategy and Tactics of Pricing,* 3d ed. (Upper Saddle River, NJ: Prentice Hall, 2002); and Michael V. Marn, *The Price Advantage* (New York: John Wiley & Sons, 2004).

3. Philip Kotler, *Marketing Management,* 11th ed. (Upper Saddle River, N.J.: Prentice Hall, 2003), p. 474; Cliff Edwards, "HDTV: High-Anxiety Television," *Business Week,* June 10, 2002, pp. 142–146; Eric Taub, "HDTV's Acceptance Picks Up Pace as Prices Drop and Networks Sign On," *New York Times,* March 31, 2003, p. C1; and Stephen H. Wildstrom, "Buying the Right HDTV," *Business Week,* February 2, 2004, p. 22.

4. Seanna Browder, "Nintendo: At the Top of Its Game," *Business Week,* June 9, 1997, pp. 72–73; "Console Competition Lowers Opening Price Points," *DSN Retailing Today,* March 25, 2002, p. 18; and Ken Belson, "Sony Profits Climb 96% in Quarter," *New York Times,* January 30, 2003, p. W1.

5. Information accessed at www.hersheyscocoamulch.com/, January 2005.

6. Susan Krafft, "Love, Love Me Doo," *American Demographics,* June 1994, pp. 15–16; "That Zoo Doo that You Do So Well," accessed at www.csis.org/states/expzoodoo,html, March 2004; "Time Again for Zoo's Annual Spring Fecal Fest!" Woodland Park Zoo Press Release, February 27, 2004, accessed at www.zoo.org; and "Woodland Park Zoo Doo," accessed at http://zoo.org/zoo_info/special/zoodoo.htm#whatis, July 2004.

7. See Nagle and Holden, *The Strategy and Tactics of Pricing,* pp. 244–247; Stefan Stremersch and Gerard J. Tellis, "Strategic Bundling of Products and Prices: A New Synthesis for Marketing," *Journal of Marketing Research,* January 2002, pp. 55–72; and Chris Janiszewski and Marcus Cunha, Jr., "The Influence of Price Discount Framing on the Evaluation of a Product Bundle," *Journal of Marketing Research,* March 2004, pp. 534–546.

8. Example adapted from Charles Fishman, "Which Price Is Right?" *Fast Company,* March 2003, pp. 92–96. For more on yield management, see Susan Greco, "Are Your Prices Right?" *Inc.,* January 1997, pp. 88–89; Robert G. Cross, *Revenue Management: Hard-Core Tactics for Market Domination* (New York: Broadway Books, 1998); Anthony Ingold, Una McMahon-Beattie, and Ian Yeoman, *Yield Management* (New York, NY: Continuum Publishing, 2002); Edward Wong, "Airline Economics: Fasten Your Sear Belt," *New York Times,* December 9, 2003, p. G6; Sheryl E. Kimes and Jochen Wirtz, "Has Revenue Management become Acceptable?" *Journal of Service Management,* November 2003, p. 125; and Lynn DeLain and Edward O'Meara, "Building a Business Case for Revenue Management," *Journal of Revenue Management and Pricing Management,* January 2004, pp. 338–353.

9. Example adapted from Greco, "Are Your Prices Right?" *Inc.,* p. 88.

10. For more reading on reference prices and psychological pricing, see Eric Anderson and Duncan Simester, "Mind Your Pricing Cues," *Harvard Business Review,* September 2003, pp. 96–102; Keith S. Coulter, "Odd-Ending Price Underestimation: An Experimental Examination of Left-to-Right Processing Effects," *The Journal of Product and Brand Management,* Vol. 10, Iss. 4/5, 2001, pp. 276–393; Robert M. Schindler and Patrick N. Kirby, "Patterns of Right-Most Digits Used in Advertised Prices: Implications for Nine-Ending Effects," *Journal of Consumer Research,* September 1997, pp. 192–201; Tulin Erdem, Glenn Mayhew, and Baohong Sun, "Understanding Reference-Price Shoppers: A Within- and Across-Category Analysis," *Journal of Marketing Research,* November 2001, pp. 445–457; Michael A. Kamins, Xavier Dreze, and Valerie S. Folkes, "Effects of Seller-Supplied Prices on Buyers' Product Evaluations: Reference Prices in an Internet Auction Context," *Journal of Consumer Research,* March 2004, pp. 622–629; and Nagle and Holden, *The Strategy and Tactics of Pricing,* pp. 83–90.

11. Tim Ambler, "Kicking Price Promotion Habit Is Like Getting Off Heroin—Hard," *Marketing,* May 27, 1999, p. 24. Also see Robert Gray, "Driving Sales at Any Price?" *Marketing,* April 11, 2002, p. 24; and Lauren Kellere Johnson, "Dueling Pricing Strategies," *MIT Sloan Management Review,* Spring 2003, pp. 1011.

12. Adapted from Andrew Park and Peter Burrows, "Dell, the Conqueror," *Business Week,* September 24, 2001, pp. 92–102. See also Andy Serwer, "Dell Does Domination," *Fortune,*

January 21, 2002, pp. 70–75; Gary McWilliams, "Dell Computer's Kevin Rollins Becomes a Driving Force," *Wall Street Journal*, April 4, 2002, p. B6; and David Bank, "Leading the News: Hewlett Packard Earnings Get Lift from Weak Dollar," *Wall Street Journal*, February 20, 2004, p. A.3.

13. Philip R. Cateora, *International Marketing*, 7th ed. (Homewood, IL: Irwin, 1990), p. 540. Also see Barbara Stottinger, "Strategic Export Pricing: A Long and Winding Road," *Journal of International Marketing*, 2001, pp. 40–63; and Warren J. Keegan, *Global Marketing Management* (Upper Saddle River, NJ: Prentice Hall, 2002), chapter 12.

14. See John Greenwald, "Cereal Showdown," *Time*, April 29, 1996, p. 60; "Cereal Thriller," *The Economist*, June 15, 1996, p. 59; Terril Yue Jones, "Outside the Box," *Forbes*, June 14, 1999, pp. 52–53; "Kellogg Concedes Top Spot to General Mills," *New York Times*, February 22, 2001, p. C4; "Kellogg Company," *Hoover's Company Profiles*, March 15, 2004; and Stephanie Thompson, "Kellogg Bulls Its Way into Fruit Snacks," *Advertising Age*, February 9, 2004, p. 3.

15. Jack Neff, "Kimberly-Clark Looses 'Bounty Killer,'" *Advertising Age*, April 2, 2001, p. 34; and information accessed at www.scottbrand.com/products/towels, December 2004.

16. For discussions of these issues, see Dhruv Grewel and Larry D. Compeau, "Pricing and Public Policy: A Research Agenda and Overview of Special Issue," *Journal of Marketing and Public Policy*, Spring 1999, pp. 3–10; and Michael V. Marn, Eric V. Roegner, and Craig C. Zawada, *The Price Advantage* (Hoboken, NJ: John Wiley & Sons, 2004), appendix 2.

17. Ralph Blumenthal, "Ex-Executive of Christie's Tells of Collusion Scheme," *New York Times*, November 15, 2001, p. D1; Paul Hofheinz, "EU Accuses Auction Houses of Running Price-Fixing Cartel," *Wall Street Journal*, April 22, 2002, p. B6; and Brooks Barnes, "Sotheby's, Christie's to Settle Claims by Overseas Customers," *Wall Street Journal*, March 12, 2003, p. B.2.

18. Stephen Labaton, "The World Gets Tough on Fixing Prices," *New York Times*, June 3, 2001, p. 3.1; Scott Kilman, "Court Reinstates Suit Alleging Archer Rigged Sweetener Market," *Wall Street Journal*, June 19, 2002, p. D2; Jennifer Ordonez, "The Record Industry Owes You $20—For Music Buyers, a Deadline Is Approaching to File Claims in a Big CD Price-Fixing Case," *Wall Street Journal*, February 5, 2003, p. D1; "Vitamin Firms Are Guilty of Price Fixing," *Wall Street Journal*, June 16, 2003, p. B3; and DeBeers Is in Talks to Settle Price-Fixing Charge," *Wall Street Journal*, February 24, 2004, p. A.1.

19. "Predatory-pricing Law Passed by New York Governor," *National Petroleum News*, December 2003, p. 7.

20. Excerpts from Dan Carney, "Predatory Pricing: Cleared for Takeoff," *Business Week*, May 14, 2001, p. 50. Also see James Helgeson and Eric Gorger, "The Price Weapon: Developments in U.S. Predatory Pricing Law," *Journal of Business to Business Marketing*, 2003, pp. 3–22; "American Airlines Wins Appeal in Federal Lawsuit," *New York Times*, July 4, 2003, p. C.5.

21. See "Nike's Pricing Practices under investigation in Florida," *New York Times*, February 19, 2003, p. C4.

22. Grewel and Compeau, "Pricing and Public Policy: A Research Agenda and Overview of Special Issue," p. 8; and

Timothy Mullaney, "Overstock: The Price Isn't Always Right," *Business Week*, March 15, 2004, p. 11.

23. "FTC Guides Against Deceptive Pricing," accessed at www.ftc.gov/bcp/guides/decptprc.htm, January 2005.

CHAPTER 12

1. Quotes and other information from Donald V. Fites, "Make Your Dealers Your Partners," *Harvard Business Review*, March–April 1996, pp. 84–95; Sandra Ward, "The Cat Comes Back," *Barron's*, February 25, 2002, pp. 21–24; DeAnn Weimer, "A New Cat on the Hot Seat," *Business Week*, March 1998, pp. 56–62; *Hoover's Company Capsules*, March 15, 2004, p. 10304; Shirley A. Lazo, "The Cat's Meow," *Barron's*, June 14, 2004, p. 35; and information accessed at www.caterpillar.com, January 2005.

2. For definitions and a complete discussion of distribution channel topics, see Anne T. Coughlin, Erin Anderson, Louis W. Stern, and Adel El-Ansary, *Marketing Channels*, 6th ed. (Upper Saddle River, NJ: Prentice Hall, 2001), pp. 2–3.

3. Example adapted from "Sealing Their Fate: A Deal with Target Put Lid on Revival at Tupperware," *Wall Street Journal*, February 18, 2004, p. A.1.

4. Coughlin, Anderson, Stern, and El-Ansary, *Marketing Channels*, 6th ed., p. 160; Matthew Boyle, "Brand Killers," *Fortune*, August 11, 2003, pp. 89–100; and information accessed at www.giantfood.com and www.luxottica.com/english/profilo_aziendale/index_keyfacts.html, January 2005.

5. "Business Floating on Air," *The Economist*, May 19, 2001, pp. 56–57; Richard Heller, "Galician Beauty," *Forbes*, May 28, 2001, p. 98; Miguel Helft, "Fashion Fast Forward," *Business 2.0*, May 2002, p. 60; John Tagliabue, "A Rival to Gap That Operates Like Dell," *New York Times*, May 30, 2003, p. W-1; Susan Reda, "Retail's Great Race," *Stores*, March 2004, p. 36; and www.zara.com/v04/eng/home.php; December 2004.

6. See Ilan Alon, "The Use of Franchising by U.S.-Based Retailers," *Journal of Small Business Management*, April 2001, pp. 111–122; John Reynolds, "Economics 101: How Franchising Makes Music for the U.S. Economy," *Franchising World*, May 2004, pp. 37–40; and "Answers to the 21 Most Commonly Asked Questions About Franchising," accessed online at the International Franchise Association Web site: www.franchise.org, July 2004.

7. Amanda Miller, Peter Rose, and Machael Voeller, "General Mills, Inc.," Krause Fund Research, Fall 2002, accessed at www.biz.uiowa.edu/krause/General_Mills_F02.pdf; and information accessed at www.cerealpartners.co.uk/, January 2005.

8. See Subhash C. Jain, *International Marketing Management*, 3d ed. (Boston: PWS-Kent Publishing, 1990), pp. 489–491. Also see Warren J. Keegan, *Global Marketing Management* (Upper Saddle River, NJ: Prentice Hall, 2002), pp. 403–404.

9. See Aruna Chandra and John K. Ryans Jr, "Why India Now?" *Marketing Management*, March–April 2002, pp. 43–45; Dana James, "Dark Clouds Should Part for International Marketers," *Marketing news*, January 7, 2002, pp. 9, 13; Russell Flannery, "Red Tape," *Forbes*, March 3, 2003, pp. 97–100; and Russell Flannery, "China: The Slow Boat," *Forbes*, April 12, 2004, p. 76.

10. For more on channel relationships, see "Supply Chain Challenges," *Harvard Business Review,* July 2003, pp. 65–73; and James C. Anderson and James A. Narus, *Business Market Management,* 2nd ed. (Upper Saddle River, NJ: Prentice Hall, 2004), chapter 9.

11. Mitch Betts, "GE Appliance Park Still an IT Innovator," *Computerworld,* January 29, 2001, pp. 20–21; and "What Is GE CustomerNet?" accessed online at www.geappliances.com/buildwithge/index_cnet.htm, January 2005.

12. For a full discussion of laws affecting marketing channels, see Coughlin, Anderson, Stern, and El-Ansary, *Marketing Channels,* chapter 12.

13. Martin Piszczalksi, "Logistics: A Difference Between Winning and Losing," *Automotive Manufacturing & Production,* May 2001, pp. 16–18; and Andrew D. Beadle, "Logistics Costs, Quantified," *Journal of Commerce,* June 14, 2003, p. 1.

14. Shlomo Maital, "The Last Frontier of Cost Reduction," *Across the Board,* February 1994, pp. 51–52; and "Wal-Mart to Expand Supercenters to California," *Business Journal,* May 15, 2002, accessed online at http://sanjose.bizjournals.com; and information accessed online at www.walmart.com, December 2004.

15. Mike Troy, "Wal-Mart: Behind the Scenes Efficiency Keeps Growth Curve on Course," *DSN Retailing Today,* June 4, 2001, pp. 80, 91; Gail Braccidiferro, "One Town's Rejection Is Another's 'Let's Do Business,'" *New York Times,* June 15, 2003, p. 2; Christopher Dinsmore, "Wal-Mart to Add 1 Million Square Feet to Virginia Import Distribution Center," *Knight Ridder Tribune Business News,* May 29, 2004, p. 1; and "Wal-Mart Centers Benefit from Quick Start," accessed online at www.dtae.org/quickstart/News7/walmart.html, July 2004.

16. J. William Gurley, "Why Dell's War Isn't Dumb," *Fortune,* July 9, 2001, pp. 134–136; and Susan Kuckinskas, "Data-Based Dell," *Adweek Magazine's Technology Marketing,* September 2003, p. 20.

17. See "Business: The Best Thing Since the Bar-Code: The IT Revolution," *The Economist,* February 8, 2003, p. 57–58; Faith Keenan, "If Supermarket Shelves Could Talk," *Business Week,* March 31, 2003, pp. 66–67; Laurie Sullivan, "Reaching Down the Supply Chain," *InformationWeek,* March 22, 2004, p. 49; and information accessed online at www.autoidlabs.org, August 2004.

18. Judy Strauss and Raymond Frost, *E-Marketing,* 2nd ed. (Upper Saddle River, N.J.: Prentice Hall, 2001), p. 193; Jean Kinsey, "A Faster, Leaner Supply Chain: New Uses of Information Technology" *American Journal of Agricultural Economics,* November 15, 2000, pp. 1123+; and Carol Sliwa, "EDI: Alive and Well After All These Years," *Computerworld,* June 14, 2004, p. 1.

19. Tom Stein and Jeff Sweat, "Killer Supply Chains—Six Companies Are Using Supply Chains to Transform the Way They Do Business," *Information Week,* November 11, 1998, p. 36; Susan Reda, "Internet-EDI Initiatives Show Potential to Reinvent Supply Chain Management," *Stores,* January 1999, pp. 26–27; and Craig A. Hill and Gary D. Scudder, "The Use of Electronic Data Interchange for Supply Chain Coordination in the Food Industry," *Journal of Operations Management,* August 2002, pp. 375–387.

20. See William C. Copacino, "Supply Chain Software Still Has Much to Offer," *Logistics Management,* May 2003, p. 76; and Martin Grossman, "The Role of Trust and Collaboration in the Internet-Enabled Supply Chain," *Journal of American Academy of Business,* September 2004, p. 391.

21. Adapted from Dean Foust, "Big Brown's New Bag," *Business Week,* July 19, 2004, pp. 54–56. Also see Chuck Salter, "Surprise Package," *Fast Company,* February 2004, p. 62.

22. See "Add Value to Your Supply Chain—Hire a 3PL," *Materials Management and Distribution,* January–February 2004, p. A3.

23. Mike Verespej, "Logistics' New Look? Now It's Service," *Frontline Solutions,* June 2002, pp. 24–31.

CHAPTER 13

1. Quotes and other information from Bill Saporito, "Is Wal-Mart Unstoppable?" *Fortune,* May 6, 1991, pp. 50–59; Carol J. Loomis, "Sam Would Be Proud," *Fortune,* April 17, 2001, pp. 131–144; Cait Murphy, "Introduction: Wal-Mart Rules," *Fortune,* April 15, 2002, pp. 94–98; Jerry Useem, "One Nation Under Wal-Mart," *Fortune,* March 3, 2003, pp. 65–78; Steve Lohr, "Is Wal-Mart Good for America?" *New York Times,* December 7, 2003, p. 4.1; Bruce Upbin, "Wall-to-Wall Wal-Mart," *Forbes,* April 12, 2004, p. 76; and Sandra O'Loughlin and Barry Janoff, "Wal-Mart Keeps Smiling, and Rivals Are Not Happy," *Brandweek,* June 21, 2004, p. S62.

2. See Bob Tedeschi, "The History of Online Grocery Shopping: First as Web Farce, Now a Lucrative Field for Older Companies," *New York Times,* May 6, 2002, p. C7; Katy McLaughlin, "Back from the Dead: Buying Groceries Online," *Wall Street Journal,* February 25, 2003, p. D-1; and Sonia Reyes, "Online Grocers: Ready to Deliver?" *Brandweek,* May 3, 2004, p. 26.

3. See "2003 SOI Highlights," National Association of Convenience Stores, accessed online at www.cstorecentral.com; and "2004 NACS State of the Industry Reports Now Available, June 30, 2004, accessed at www.nacsonline.com/NACS/News/Press_Releases/2004/pr063004.htm.

4. Mike Duff, "Supercenters Take Lead in Food Retailing," *DSN Retailing Today,* May 6, 2002. pp. F8–F9; and Patricia Callahan and Ann Zimmerman, "Price War in Aisle 3—Wal-Mart Tops Grocery List with Supercenter Format," *Wall Street Journal,* May 27, 2003, p. B-1; and Mike Troy, "What Setback? Supercenters Proliferate," *DSN Retailing Today,* May 17, 2004, p. 1.

5. See Ray A. Smith, "Outlet Centers Go Upmarket with Amenities," *Wall Street Journal,* June 6, 2001, p. B12; Mervyn Rothstein, "At a Shoppers' Mecca, Now, Retail for Locals," *New York Times,* April 10, 2002, p. C6; and Sally Beatty, "Paying Less for Prada," *Wall Street Journal,* April 29, 2003, p. D.1.

6. Adapted from John Helyar, "The Only Company Wal-Mart Fears," *Fortune,* November 24, 2003, pp. 158–166. Also see Tiffany Meyers, "Marketers Learn Luxury Isn't Simply for the Very Wealthy," *Advertising Age,* September 13, 2004, pp. S2, S10.

7. See David Stires, "Fallen Arches," *Fortune,* April 29, 2002, pp. 74–76; Anne Field, "Your Ticket to a New Career,"

Business Week, May 12, 2003, pp. 100–101; information accessed online at www.subway.com, August 2004; and information accessed online at www.mcdonalds.com/corp.html, January 2005.

8. Portions adapted from Bridget Finn, "For Petco, Success Is a Bitch," *Business 2.0,* November 2003, p. 54; and Frank Green, "Petco Reports First-Quarter Earnings Rose 42 Percent, Boosts Outlook," *Knight Ridder Tribune Business News,* May 20, 2004, p. 1.

9. See Lorrie Grant, "Maytag Stores Let Shoppers Try Before They Buy," *USA Today,* June 7, 2004, p. 7B.

10. Myron Magnet, "Let's Go for Growth," *Fortune,* March 7, 1994, pp. 60–72. Also see Dierdre Donahue, "Bookstores: A Haven for the Intellect," *USA Today,* July 10, 1997, pp. D1, D2; and Christina Nifong, "Beyond Browsing," *Raleigh News & Observer*, May 25, 1999, p. E1.

11. "Mall of America Starts 10th Year Celebration," *Home Textiles Today,* June 24, 2002, p. 42; Kelly Barbieri, "Mall of America Debuts New Coaster in Camp Snoopy Area," *Amusement Business*, April 5, 2004, p. 8; and "The History of Mall of America," accessed online at www.mallofamerica.com, January 2005.

12. Andrea Bermudez, "Bijan Dresses the Wealthy for Success," *Apparel News.Net*, December 1–7, 2000, accessed online at www.apparelnews.net/Archieve/120100/News/newsfeat.htm; Mimi Avins, "FASHION; More is More; Over-the-Top Isn't High Enough for Bijan, Whose Boutique Embraces Excess," *The Los Angeles Times,* January 5, 2003, p. E.1; and information accessed at www.bijan.com/boutique, December 2004.

13. John Fetto, "Mall Rats," *American Demographics,* March 2002, p. 10; Robert Berner and Gerry Khermouch, "Retail Reckoning," *Business Week,* December 10, 2001, pp. 71–77; Brian Libby, "Shopping Around for Second Lives," *New York Times,* June 15, 2003, p. 32; and information accessed on the International Council of Shopping Centers website, www.icsc.org, December 2004.

14. Dean Starkman, "The Mall, Without the Haul—'Lifestyle Centers' Slip Quietly into Upscale Areas, Mixing Cachet and 'Curb Appeal,'" *Wall Street Journal,* July 25, 2001, p. B1; and "To Mall or Not to Mall?" *Buildings,* June 2004, p. 99.

15. See Amy Barrett, "A Retailing Pacesetter Pulls Up Lame," *Business Week*, July 12, 1993, pp. 122–123; and John Helyar, "The Only Company Wal-Mart Fears," *Fortune,* November 24, 2003, pp. 158–166.

16. See Malcolm P. McNair and Eleanor G. May, "The Next Revolution of the Retailing Wheel," *Harvard Business Review*, September–October 1978, pp. 81–91; Stephen Brown, "The Wheel of Retailing: Past and Future," *Journal of Retailing*, Summer 1990, pp. 143–147; Stephen Brown, "Variations on a Marketing Enigma: The Wheel of Retailing Theory," *Journal of Marketing Management*, 7, no. 2, 1991, pp. 131–155; Jennifer Negley, "Retrenching, Reinventing, and Remaining Relevant," *Discount Store News*, April 5, 1999, p. 11; and Don E. Schultz, "Another Turn of the Wheel," *Marketing Management,* March–April 2002, pp. 8–9.

17. Richard Karpinskr, "Web Delivers Big Results for Staples," *B to B*, November 11, 2002, p. 14; and Joseph Pereira, "Staples Posts Strong Earnings on High-Margin Internet Sales," *Wall Street Journal,* March 5, 2004, p. A13.

18. Excerpt adapted from Alice Z. Cuneo, "What's in Store?" *Advertising Age,* February 25, 2002, pp. 1, 30–31. Also see Robert Berner, "Dark Days in White Goods for Sears," *Business Week,* March 10, 2003, pp. 78–79.

19. See Jack Neff, "Wal-Mart Weans Suppliers," *Advertising Age,* December 1, 2003, pp. 1, 33; and "The Fortune 500," *Fortune,* April 5, 2004, p. F1.

20. Adapted from information found in Christina Rexrode, "Concept Store in Bloom," *The Herald-Sun,* June 6, 2004, pp. F1, F3; and "Food Lion Opens First Bloom Concept Store," press release, May 25, 2004, accessed at www.foodlion.com/news.asp?parm=323.

21. James Cox, "Red-Letter Day as East Meets West in the Aisles," *USA Today,* September 11, 1996, p. B1; and "Wal-Mart International Operations," July 2004, accessed online at www.walmartstores.com.

22. Carla Rapoport, "Retailers Go Global," *Fortune,* February 20, 1995, pp. 102–108; "Global Retailing in the Connected Economy," *Chain Store Age,* December 1999, pp. 69–82; Tim Craig, "Global Retailing's Defining Moments Are Getting Lost in the Mix," *Dsn Retailing Today,* April 21, 2003, p. 7; and "World's 100 Largest Retailers," accessed at www.chainstoreage.com, December 2004.

23. Adapted from Tim Craig, "Carrefour: At the Intersection of Global," *DSN Retailing Today,* September 18, 2000, p. 16. Additional information from Richard Tomlinson, "Who's Afraid of Wal-Mart?" *Fortune,* June 26, 2000, pp. 186–196; "Carrefour SA," *Euroweek,* April 25, 2003, p. 1; "Carrefour SA," *Wall Street Journal*, March 5, 2004, p. C.14; and www.carrefour.com, January 2005.

24. Nifong, "Beyond Browsing," p. E1. Also see Fred Brock, "Catering to the Elderly Can Pay Off," *New York Times,* February 2002, p. 3.11.

25. Kathleen Cholewka, "Standing Out Online: The Five Best E-Marketing Campaigns," *Sales & Marketing Management,* January 2001, pp. 51–58. Other information from www.playstation.com, July 2004.

26. "McKesson: Raising Expectations," *Modern Materials Handling,* February 2004, p. 53; and information from "About the Company" and "Supply Management Online," accessed online at www.mckesson.com, August 2004.

27. Facts accessed at www.supervalu.com, August 2004; and from "SuperValu Inc.," *Hoover's Company Capsules,* Austin, July 15, 2004, p. 11419.

CHAPTER 14

1. Extracts adapted from John Gaffney, "Most Innovative Campaign," *Business 2.0,* May 2002, pp. 98–99; and Warren Berger, "Dare Devils," *Business 2.0,* April 2004, pp. 111–116. Other quotes and information from Lisa Granatstein, "Crispin Porter + Bogusky," *Mediaweek,* June 23, 2003, p. SR6; Joan Voight, "Mini's Wild Ride" *Adweek,* June 2, 2003, p. 24; John T. Slania, "Mini Cooper's Big Ride," *Crain's Chicago Business*, April 21, 2003, p. 3; Monica Elliott, "High-Tech and High-Touch," *Industrial Engineer*, April 2003, pp. 28–32; "Mini Marketing Chief Proves Them Wrong," *Automotive News*, January 13, 2003, p. 8M; Alicia Griswold, "Off-Road Trip," *Adweek*, January 20, 2003, p. 26; Fara Warner, "What to Expect When Your

Expecting a Mini-Cooper," *The New York Times,* January 25, 2004, p. 3.7; and Joseph B. White, "Challenges Rise for BMW's Mini in U.S. Market," *Wall Street Journal,* March 24, 2004, p. 1.

2. The first four of these definitions are adapted from Peter D. Bennett, *Dictionary of Marketing Terms* (Chicago: American Marketing Association, 1995). Other definitions can be found at www.marketingpower.com/live/mg-dictionary.php?, August 2004.

3. Don E. Schultz, "New Media, Old Problem: Keep Marcom Integrated," *Marketing News,* March 29, 1999, p. 11. Also see Michael McLaren, "Key to Tech Marketing Is Integrated message," *B to B,* February 10, 2003, p. 16; and Claire Atkinson, "Integration Still a Pipe Dream for Many," *Advertising Age,* March 10, 2003, pp. 1, 47.

4. See, Chapters 3 and 4. Also see Don E. Schultz and Philip J. Kitchen, *Communication Globally: An Integrated Marketing Approach* (New York: McGraw Hill, 2000); and Don E. Schultz and Heidi Schultz, *IMC: The Next Generation* (New York: McGraw Hill, 2004).

5. For more on integrated marketing communications, see Don E. Schultz, Stanley I. Tannenbaum, and Robert F. Lauterborn, *Integrated Marketing Communications* (Chicago, IL: NTC, 1992); Don E. Schultz and Philip J. Kitchen, *Communication Globally: An Integrated Marketing Approach* (New York: McGraw Hill, 2000); Prasad A. Naik and Kalyan Raman, "Understanding the Impact of Synergy in Multimedia Communications," *Journal of Marketing Research,* November 2003, pp. 375–388; and Don E. Schultz and Heidi Schultz, *IMC: The Next Generation* (New York: McGraw Hill, 2004).

6. Carolyn Setlow, "Humorous, Feel-Good Advertising Hits Home with Consumers," *DSN Retailing Today,* April 22, 2002, p. 14.

7. Quotes and other information found in Hillary Chura, "A Creative Low Point," *Advertising Age,"* February 9, 2004, p. 49; and Stuart Elliott, "Can Beers Ads Extol Great Taste in Good Taste?" *New York Times,* April 2004, p. C2.

8. For these and other examples, see Pamela Paul, "Color by Numbers," *American Demographics,* February 2002, pp. 31–35; and Arundhati Parmar, "Marketers Ask: Hues on First?" *Marketing News,* February 15, 2004, pp. 8–10.

9. Adapted from Sandra Yin, "Degree of Challenge," *American Demographics,* May 2003, pp. 20–22. Also see Scott Donaton, "Marketing's New Fascination, Figuring Out Word of Mouth," *Advertising Age,* November 17, 2003, p. 18; and "Word of Mouth More Influential than Ads," *Campaign,* April 23, 2004, p. 5.

10. For more on advertising spending by company and industry, see the Advertising Age Data Center at www.adage.com.

11. For more on setting promotion budgets, see W. Ronald Lane, Karen Whitehill King, and J. Thomas Russell, *Kleppner's Advertising Procedure,* 16th ed. (Upper Saddle River, NJ: Prentice Hall, 2005), chapter 6.

12. "Super Bowl XXXVIII Drives CBS to Its Most Watched and Highest Rated Week in Adults," February 3, 2004, accessed online at www.viacom.com; Brian Steinberg, "Advertising: Newest TV Spinoffs: 'Situ-mercials,'" *Wall Street Journal,* March 2, 2004, p. B11, and "Friends' End Draws 51 Million Viewers," *CNN.com,* May 7, 2004.

13. Michele Marchetti, "What a Sales Call Costs," *Sales & Marketing Management,* September 2000, p. 80; and Harry J. Abramson, "Perfect Reasons to Stop Making Cold Calls in the Eyes of a Rep," *Agency Sales,* December 2003, p. 26.

14. Based on Matthew P. Gonring, "Putting Integrated Marketing Communications to Work Today," *Public Relations Quarterly,* Fall 1994, pp. 45–48. Also see Philip Kotler, *Marketing Management,* 11th ed. (Upper Saddle River, NJ: Prentice Hall, 2003), pp. 583–584.

15. Information accessed at www.tropicalforestfoundation.org/about.html and www.avoncompany.com/women/avoncrusade/, August 2004.

16. For more on the legal aspects of promotion, see Lane, King, and Russell, *Kleppner's Advertising Procedure,* chapter 25; and Douglas J. Dalrymple, William L. Cron, and Thomas E. DeCarlo, *Sales Management,* 8th ed. (New York: Wiley, 2004), chapter 10.

CHAPTER 15

1. Adapted from Warren Berger, "Dare-Devils," *Business 2.0,* April 2004, p. 110.

2. Information on U.S. and international advertising spending accessed at the Ad Age Dataplace, www.adage.com, August 2004; Mercedes M. Cardona, "Ad-Spending Soothsayers Optimistic on Year Ahead," *Advertising Age,* December 15, 2003, p. 8; and "100 Leading National Advertisers," *Advertising Age,* June 28, 2004, pp. 2–5.

3. For more on advertising budgets, see W. Ronald Lane, Karen Whitehill King, and J. Thomas Russell, *Kleppner's Advertising Procedure,* 16th ed. (Upper Saddle River, NJ: Prentice Hall, 2005), chapter 6.

4. Information from Gary Levin, "'Meddling' in Creative More Welcome," *Advertising Age,* April 9, 1990, pp. S4, S8; Sarah Theodore, "Absolut Secrets," *Beverage Industry,* July 2000, p. 50; Hillary Chura, "Absolut Vanilla Part of Plan to Boost Flat Market Share," *Advertising Age,* December 16, 2002, p. 8; "Absolut Vodka Turns 25 Tomorrow," press release, April 19, 2004, accessed at www.absolut.com; and the Q&A section at www.absolut.com, January 2005.

5. "500 Channels with Nothing On? Nah—No Channels at All," July 2, 2004, accessed at www.corante.com/importance/archives/004736.html; and information accessed online at www.magazine.org, December 2004.

6. Charles Pappas, "Ad Nauseam," *Advertising Age,* July 10, 2000, pp. 16–18; and Mark Ritson, "Marketers Need to Find a Way to Control the Contagion of Clutter," *Marketing,* March 6, 2003, p. 16.

7. Richard Linnett, "Super Bowl Busts Records, *Advertising Age,* January 12, 2004, p. 1; Stuart Elliott, "NBC's 'Friends' Finale is the Super Bowl of Sitcoms," *New York Times,* May 3, 2004, p. C.8; and Claire Atkinson, "'Idol' Tops TV Price Chart," *Advertising Age,* September 27, 2004, pp. 1, 77

8. Gary Ruskin, "A Death Spiral of Disrespect," *Advertising Age,* April 26, 2004, p. 18; and Andrew Green, "Clutter Crisis Countdown," *Advertising Age,* April 21, 2004, p. 22.

9. Wayne Friedman, "PVR Users Skip Most Ads: Study," *Advertising Age,* July 1, 2002, pp. 4, 46; and Ronald Grover, "Can Mad Ave Make Zap-proof Ads?" *Business Week,* February 2, 2004, pp. 36–37.

10. Edward A. Robinson, "Frogs, Bears, and Orgasms: Think Zany if You Want to Reach Today's Consumers," *Fortune,* June 9, 1997, pp. 153–156. Also see Tobi Elkin, "Courting Craftier Consumers," July 1, 2002, p. 28; and Devin Leonard, "Nightmare on Madison Avenue," *Fortune,* June 28, 2004, pp. 93–108.

11. Tobi Elkin, "Porsche, Acura Latest to Try Out TiVo Showcases," *Advertising Age,* February 24, 2003; Elkin, "Getting Viewers to Opt In, Not Tune Out," *Advertising Age,* November 4, 2002, p. 10; Jon Healey, "California; TiVo to Sell Statistics on Ads Skipped," *Los Angeles Times,* June 2, 2003, p. C2; and Joe Mandese, "Study Says DVRs, Ads Can Co-Exist," *TelevisionWeek,* June 7, 2004, p. 35.

12. "Media Multi-Taskers," *Journal of Marketing Management,* May–June 2004, p. 6.

13. *Newsweek* and *Business Week* cost and circulation data accessed online at http:/mediakit.businessweek.com and www.newsweekmediakit.com, January 2005.

14. See Marty Bernstein, "Why TV Commercials Are So Costly," *Automotive News,* May 10, 2004, p. 30H.

15. Information on advertising agencies from "World's Top 25 Ad Organizations," *Advertising Age,* April 19, 2004, p. S-2.

16. See George E. Belch and Michael A. Belch, *Advertising and Promotion* (New York: McGraw-Hill/Irwin, 2004), pp. 666–668.

17. *2002 Trade Promotion Spending & Merchandising Industry Study* (Wilton, CT: Cannondale Associates, 2002), p. 13; and *Trade Promotion Spending & Merchandising 2003 Industry Study* (Wilton, CT: Cannondale Associates, 2003), p. 7. Also see "Promotions and Incentives: Offers You Can't Refuse," *Marketing Week,* April 15, 2004, p. 31; and E. Craig Stacey, "Abandon TV at Your Own Risk," *Advertising Age,* June 7, 2004, p. 32.

18. Kenneth Hein, "Coke Puts New Twist on Plain Vanilla Sampler, Summer Tours," *Brandweek,* July 1, 2002, p. 35; and "Coca-Cola Unveils U.S. Launch Plans for its New Lower-Carb, Lower-Cal Cola, Coca-Cola C2," May 24, 2004, accessed at www.coca-cola.com.

19. Debra Aho Williamson, "P&G's Reformulated Pert Plus Builds Consumer Relationships," *Advertising Age,* June 28, 1999, p. 52; and Emily Rogers, "Eat Natural Raises Awareness with Sampling Drive," *Marketing,* May 12, 2004, p. 6.

20. See "Do Coupons Make Cents?" *Incentive,* May 2003, p. 19; Catherine Arnold, "No Coup Online," *Marketing News,* May 26, 2003, p. 3; and Natalie Schwartz, "Clipping Path," *Promo Magazine,* April 1, 2004.

21. See Lucia Moses, "Coupons Make Move Online," *Editor & Publisher,* February 24, 2003, p. 10; and information accessed at www.catalinamarketing.com/manufacturer_services/products.html, December 2004.

22. See Kate Bertrand, "Premiums Prime the Market," *Advertising Age's Business Marketing,* May 1998, p. S6; and Paul Nolan, "Promotions Come Alive with the Sound of Music," *Potentials,* April 1999, p. 10. For other examples, see Elinor Dumont, "Today's Version of the Toaster," *Bank Marketing,* September 2001, pp. 12–14; and Kenneth Hein, "Frito-Lay Supplies Pieces to the Star Wars Puzzle," *Brandweek,* March 25, 2002, p. 10.

23. See William F. Kendy, "The Great Giveaway," *Selling Power,* September 2002, pp. 98–105; and information found at the Promotional Products Association International Web site, www.ppai.org, December 2004.

24. See "Nearly Half a Million Attend Bauma Trade Show," *Pit & Quarry,* May 2004, p. 16; and information found at the consumer Electronics Association Web site, www.cesweb.org/press/default_flash.asp, December 2004.

25. Adapted from Scott Cutlip, Allen Center, and Glen Broom, *Effective Public Relations,* 8th ed. (Upper Saddle River, NJ: Prentice Hall, 2000), chapter 1. For additional definitions, see Fraser P. Seitel, *The Practice of Public Relations* (Upper Saddle River, NJ: Prentice Hall, 2004), chapter 1.

26. Diane Brady, "Wizard of Marketing," *Business Week,* July 24, 2000, pp. 84–87. Also see Dick Lynch, "The Magic of 'Harry Potter,'" *Advertising Age,* December 10, 2001, p. 26; Stephen Brown, "Marketing for Muggles: The Harry Potter Way to Higher Profits," *Business Horizons,* January–February 2002, pp. 6–14; and "Harry Potter and the Publishing Goldmine," www.Economist.com, June 23, 2003.

27. See Kathleen Sampey, "Crest Whitestrips to Get $90M Push," *Brandweek,* June 4, 2001, p. 27; Sampey, "Breaking the Rules of PR/Fashion Results in White-Hot Campaign," *PR News,* Feb. 25, 2002; Patricia Van Arnum, "Whitening Products Help to Drive Growth in Oral Care," *Chemical Market Reporter,* May 10, 2004, p. FR10; and Molly Prior, "Whiter, Cheaper, Faster Are the Latest Buzzwords in Oral Care," *Drug Store News,* July 19, 2004, pp. 23–24.

28. Al Ries and Laura Ries, "First Do Some Publicity," *Advertising Age,* February 8, 1999, p. 42. Also see Ries and Ries, *The Fall of Advertising and the Rise of PR* (New York: HarperBusiness, 2002). For points and counterpoints, see O. Burtch Drake, "'Fall' of Advertising? I Differ," *Advertising Age,* January 13, 2003, p. 23; Robert E. Brown, "Book Review: The Fall of Advertising & the Rise of PR," *Public Relations Review,* March 2003, pp. 91–93; and Mark Cheshire, "Roundtable Discussion—Making & Moving the Message," *The Daily Record,* January 30, 2004, p. 1.

29. Based on information from Kate Fitzgerald, "Marketing on the Move," *Advertising Age,* March 18, 2002, p. 59; Jeff St. John, "Microsoft Sends Mobile Marketing Van to Kennewick, Wash., Area," *Knight Ridder Tribune Business News,* April 28, 2004, p. 1; and "Microsoft Celebrates National Small Business Week with Technology and Service Offerings for Small Businesses," Microsoft press release, May 17, 2004.

30. See "Butterball Turkey Talk-Line Fact Sheet," accessed at www.butterball.com/en/files/PDF/Fact_Sheet_sheet.PDF, December 2004.

31. See Mark Gleason, "Edelman Sees Niche in Web Public Relations," *Advertising Age,* January 20, 1997, p. 30; Steve Jarvis, "How the Internet Is Changing Fundamentals of Publicity," *Marketing News,* July 17, 2000, p. 6; G. A. Markin, "Why Doesn't the Press Call?" *Public Relations Quarterly,* Spring 2002, pp. 9–10; and "Best Use of the Internet 2004," *PRweek,* March 8, 2004, p. S47.

CHAPTER 16

1. Quotes and other information from Jeff O'Heir, "Michael Krasny—IT Sales Innovator." *Computer Reseller News,* November 18, 2002; Ed Lawler, "Integrated Campaign Win-

ner: CDW Computer Centers," *B to B*, December 9, 2002 p. 20; "CDW Chooses Richardson to Strengthen Customer Focus," *Business Wire*, July 23, 2003, p. 5397; Mark Del Franco, Paul Miller, and Margery Weinstein, "Smooth Sailing in Choppy Waters," *Catalog Age*, March 2004, pp. 42–46; Scott Campbell, "CDW Snags Companywide Cisco Premier Status," *CRN*, April 12, 2004, p. 12; and www.cdw.com, July 2004.

2. Quote from Laurence Zuckerman, "Selling Airplanes with a Smile," *New York Times*, February 17, 2002, p. 3.2. Also see Bill Kelley, "How to Sell Airplanes, Boeing-Style," *Sales & Marketing Management*, December 9, 1985, pp. 32–34; J. Lynn Lunsford, "Boeing Beats Out Airbus to Sell Virgin Blue $3 Billion in Jets," *Wall Street Journal*, January 16, 2003, p. B6; and Joann Muller, "7 Digital 7," *Forbes*, June 21, 2004, p. 117.

3. Quotes and other information from Geoffrey Brewer, "Love the Ones You're With," *Sales & Marketing Management*, February 1997, pp. 38–45; and Erin Stout, "Blue Skies Ahead?" *Sales & Marketing Management*, March 2003, pp. 25–29.

4. "Selling Power 500," accessed at www.sellingpower.com/sp500/index.asp, August 2004.

5. For more on this and other methods for determining sales force size, see Mark W. Johnson and Greg W. Marshall, *Churchill/Ford/Walker's Sales Force Management* (New York: McGraw-Hall Irwin, 2003), pp. 142–147; and Douglas J. Dalrymple, William L. Cron, and Thomas E. DeCarlo, *Sales Management*, 8th ed. (New York: John Wiley & Sons, 2004), pp. 112–116.

6. Michele Marchetti, "What a Sales Call Costs," *Sales & Marketing Management*, September 2000, p. 80; and "How Many Personal Sales Calls Does It Take to Close a Sale?" accessed at www.cahnerscarr.com/5425d.htm, August 2004.

7. See Martin Everett, "Selling by Telephone," *Sales & Marketing Management*, December 1993, pp. 75–79. Also see Terry Arnold, "Telemarketing Strategy," *Target Marketing*, January 2002, pp. 47–48.

8. Adapted from Geoffrey Brewer, "Lou Gerstner Has His Hands Full," *Sales & Marketing Management*, May 8, 1998, pp. 36–41. Also see Michelle Cioci, "Marketing to Small Businesses," *Sales & Marketing Management*, December 2000, pp. 94–100.

9. See "A Phone Is Better than a Face," *Sales & Marketing Management*, October 1987, p. 29. Also see "Climax Portable Machine Tools Case Study," accessed online at www.selltis.com/case_climax.html, August 2004.

10. Karen J. Bannan, "Call Center's Role Evolves with CRM," *B to B*, May 5, 2003, p. 14. Also see Julia Chang, "Dialing for Dollars," *Sales & Marketing Management*, July 2003, p. 28.

11. William F. Kendy, "No More Lone Rangers," *Selling Power*, April 2004, pp. 70–74.

12. "Customer Business Development," accessed at www.pg.com/jobs/jobs_us/work_we_offer/advisor_overview.jhtml?sl=jobs_advisor_business_development, August 2004.

13. Quotes and other information in this section on super salespeople from Geoffrey Brewer, "Mind Reading: What Drives Top Salespeople to Greatness?" *Sales & Marketing Management*, May 1994, pp. 82–88; Andy Cohen, "The Traits of Great Sales Forces," *Sales & Marketing Management*, Octo-

ber 2000, pp. 67–72; Julia Chang, "Born to Sell?" *Sales & Marketing Management*, July 2003, pp. 34–38; and Henry Canaday, "Recruiting the Right Stuff," *Selling Power*, April 2004, pp. 94–96.

14. Robert Klein, "Nabisco Sales Soar after Sales Training," *Marketing News*, January 6, 1997, p. 23; and Geoffrey James, "The Return of Sales Training," *Selling Power*, May 2004, pp. 86–91.

15. Julia Chang, "No Instructor Required," *Sales & Marketing Management*, May 2003, p. 26.

16. See "SMM's Best of Sales and Marketing: Best Trained Sales Force—Cisco Systems," *Sales & Marketing Magazine*, September 2001, pp. 28–29; and "E-Learning: Field Training—How Cisco Spends Less Time in the Classroom and More Time with Customers," accessed at http://business.cisco.com/prod/tree.taf%3Fpublic_view=true&kbns=1&asset_id−86360.html, August 2003.

17. See Christen P. Heide, "All Levels of Sales Reps Post Impressive Earnings," press release, www.dartnell.com, May 5, 1997; *Dartnell's 30th Sales Force Compensation Survey*, Dartnell Corporation, August 1999; Christine Galea, "2003 Salary Survey," *Sales & Marketing Management*, May 2003, pp. 32–41; and Galea, "2004 Salary Survey," *Sales & Marketing Management*, May 2004, pp. 28–34.

18. See Gary H. Anthes, "Portal Powers GE sales," *Computerworld*, June 2, 2003, pp. 31–32. Also see Betsy Cummings, "Increasing Face Time," *Sales & Marketing Management*, January 2004, p. 12.

19. David Prater, "The Third Time's the Charm," *Sales & Marketing Management*, September 2000, pp. 101–104. For more on sales force automation (SFA), see Cheri Speier and Viswanath Venkatesh, "The Hidden Minefields in the Adoption of Sales Force Automation Technologies," *Journal of Marketing*, July 2002, pp. 98–111; Steve Levy, "A Call to Integrate CI, Customer Relationship Management, and Sales Force Automation," *Competitive Intelligence Magazine*, March–April 2003, pp. 36–39; and Betsy Cummings, "Tools of the Trade," *Sales & Marketing Management*, October 2003, pp. 46–51.

20. Melinda Ligos, "Point, Click, and Sell," *Sales & Marketing Management*, May 1999, pp. 51–56; Tim Wilson, "Salespeople Leverage the Net," *Internetweek*, June 4, 2001, pp. PG11, PG13; Amy J. Morgan and Scott A. Inks, "Technology and the Sales Force: Increasing Acceptance of Sales Force Automation," *Industrial Marketing Management*, July 2001, pp. 463–472; Eilene Zimmerman, "Casting the Net Wide," *Sales & Marketing Management*, April 2002, pp. 50–56; and Paul N. Romani, "The Internet and Personal Selling," *The American Salesman*, March 2003, pp. 3–10.

21. Christine Neuberger, "Incentives to Perform, *Selling Power Sourcebook*, 2002, pp. 12–16. Also see Heidi Waldrop-Bay, Catherine Carson, Barry LaBoy, and Mark Sullivan, "Sales Incentives 2004," *Potentials*, February 2004, pp. 8–12.

22. Quotes from Bob Donath, "Delivering Value Starts with Proper Prospecting," *Marketing News*, November 10, 1997, p. 5; and Bill Brooks, "Power-Packed Prospecting Pointers," *Agency Sales*, March 2004, p. 37.

23. Quotes from David Stamps, "Training for a New Sales Game," *Training*, July 1997, pp. 46–52; Erin Stout, "Throwing the Right Pitch," *Sales & Marketing Management*, April

2001, pp. 61–63; Andy Cohen, ""Customers Know Best," *Sales & Marketing Management,* January 2003, p. 10; and William F. Kendy, "How to Be a Good Listener," *Selling Power,* April 2004, pp. 41–44.

24. Adapted from Betsy Cummings, "On the Cutting Edge," *Sales & Marketing Management,* June 3, 2003, pp. 39–43.

25. Renee Houston Zemanski, "Well Connected," *Selling Power,* March 2003, pp. 32–34.

26. For these and other direct-marketing statistics in this section, see "Economic Impact: U.S. Direct Marketing Today," along with a wealth of other information, accessed at www.the-dma.org/research, August 2004.

27. Alicia Orr Suman, "Ideas You Can Take to the Bank! 10 Big Things All Direct Marketers Should Be Doing Now," *Target Marketing,* February 2003, pp. 31–33.

28. Dana Blakenhorn, "Marketers Hone Targeting," *Advertising Age,* June 18, 2001, p. T16; Thomas H. Davenport, "How Do They Know Their Customers So Well?" *MIT Sloan Management Review,* Winter 2001, pp. 63–73; and "The Customer Is Job 1 at Ford," accessed at www.sas.com/success/ford.html, August 2003.

29. For these and other examples, see Jonathan Berry, "A Potent New Tool for Selling: Database Marketing," *Business Week,* September 4, 1994, pp. 56–62; Weld F. Royal, "Do Databases Really Work?" *Sales & Marketing Management,* October 1995, pp. 66–74; Daniel Hill, "Love My Brand," *Brandweek,* January 19, 1998, pp. 26–29; "FedEx Taps into Data Warehousing," *Advertising Age's Business Marketing,* January 1999, p. 25; and Harriet Marsh, "Dig Deeper into the Database Goldmine," *Marketing,* January 11, 2001, pp. 29–30.

30. Gary Loveman, "Diamonds in the Data Mine," *Harvard Business Review,* May 2003, pp. 109–113; and Julie Schlosser, "Teacher's Bet," *Fortune,* March 8, 2004, pp. 158–163.

31. Statistics on direct media expenditures and sales throughout this section are from "Economic Impact: U.S. Direct Marketing Today," accessed at www.the-dma.org/research, August 2004.

32. Matthew L. Wald, "Third Area Code Is Added in the Land of the Toll-Free," *New York Times,* April 4, 1998, p. 10; and "AT&T Offers Toll-Free Number Availability Tool Online," *Direct Marketing,* May 2001, p. 24.

33. Excerpt from Dave Barry, "So What's Their Hang-up?" *Miami Herald,* October 5, 2003, accessed at www.miami.com/mld/miamiherald/living/columnists/dave_barry/6934584.htm?1c.

34. Facts about the catalog industry in this section are from "The DMA State of the Catalog Industry Report," accessed at www.the-dma.org, August 2004.

35. "Live from ACC: Catalog Sales Growth Outpaces Employment Growth," *Catalog Age,* June 2, 2003, accessed online at http://catalogagemag.com/ar/marketing_live_acc_catalog/; and "U.S. Catalog Sales to Top $175bn," *Precision Marketing,* May 14, 2004, p. 9.

36. "Catalog Study Now Available," *Business Forms, Labels, and Systems,* June 20, 2001, p. 24; Richard S. Hodgson, "It's Still the Catalog Age," *Catalog Age,* June 2001, p. 156; and Sherry Chiger, "It's Raining Catalogs," *Catalog Age,* June 2004, p. 12.

37. See "About Lillian Vernon," accessed at www.lillianvernon.com, August 2004; and "Lillian Vernon Corporation," *Hoover's Company Capsules,* Austin, March 15, 2004, p. 12111.

38. Ron Donoho, "One-Man Show," *Sales & Marketing Management,* June 2001, pp. 36–42; and information accessed at www.ronco.com, March 2004.

39. Nat Ives, "Infomercials Clean Up Their Pitch," *New York Times,* April 12, 2004, p. C1.

40. See Steve Sullivan, "Shopping Channels: Less Hard Sell," *Broadcasting & Cable,* November 27, 2000, pp. 86–90; Bob Tedeschi, "Television Shopping Channels May Become the Big Winners in the Competition for Online Sales," *New York Times,* April 16, 2001, p. C4; and "QVC, Inc.," *Hoover's Company Capsules,* March 14, 2004, p. 57399.

41. Larry Beck, "The Kiosk's Ship Has Come In," *DSN Retailing Today,* February 19, 2001, p. 14; Shayn Ferriolo, "The Key to Kiosks," *Catalog Age,* June 2003, pp. 103–108; and Charlotte Goddard, "Mobile Offers Kiosks a New Role," *Revolution,* January 2004, p. 21.

42. "Interactive: Ad Age Names Finalists," *Advertising Age,* February 27, 1995, pp. 12–14.

43. Yang, "No Web Site Is an Island," p. EB38; Matthew Haeberle, "REI Overhauls Its E-commerce," *Chain Store Age,* January 2003, p. 64; and Sarah McBride, "Virgin Group Plans New Venture to Enter Online Music Business," *Wall Street Journal,* March 8, 2004, p. B.4.

44. "Sweepstakes Groups Settles with States," *New York Times,* June 27, 2001, p. A14; and "PCH Reaches $34 Million Sweepstakes Settlement with 26 States," *Direct Marketing,* September 2001, p. 6.

45. Jennifer Lee, "Welcome to the Database Lounge," *New York Times,* March 21, 2002, p. G1.

46. Information on the DMA Privacy Promise obtained at www.the-dma.org/privacy/privacypromise.shtml, August 2004.

47. Debbie A. Connon, "The Ethics of Database Marketing," *Information Management Journal,* May–June 2002, pp. 42–44.

CHAPTER 17

1. Extracts adapted from Linda Tischler, "Bank of (Middle) America," *Fast Company,* March 2003, pp. 104–110. Quotes and other information from Michael Sisk, "WaMu Goes after the Middle Man," *USBanker,* November 2003, p. 60; Jacob Ward, "Should a Bank Be a Store?" *USBanker,* April 2004, pp. 36–40; "Washington Mutual, Inc." *Hoover's Company Capsules,* Austin, July 15, 2004, p. 15119; and "America's Most Admired Companies," *Fortune,* accessed at www.fortune.com/fortune/mostadmired/snapshot/2004/0,15020,117-1,00.html.

2. Beth Snyder Bulik, "Sony, Kodak Lead U.S. Battle for Share in Digital Cameras," *Advertising Age,* May 31, 2004, p. 12.

3. See Jonathan Gaw, "Britannica Gives In and Gets Online," LA Times, October 19, 2000, p. A1; Peter Jacso, "Britannica Concise Encyclopaedia," *Link-Up,* May–June 2002, pp. 16–17; Encyclopaedia Britannica Set Up Direct Unit," *Precision Marketing,* May 23, 2003, p. 1; and "Encyclopae-

dia Britannica, Inc.," *Hoover's Company Capsules,* Austin, July 15, 2004, p. 40871.

4. Jeffrey F. Rayport and Bernard J. Jaworski, *e-Commerce* (New York: McGraw-Hill, 2001), p. 53.

5. Smriti Jacob, "After 150 Years, Bausch & Lomb Keeps Focus on Eye-Care Industry," *Rochester Business Journal,* October 31, 2003, p. 1.

6. Andy Reinhardt, "Intel Is Taking No Prisoners," *Business Week,* July 12, 1999, p. 38; Brent Schlender, "Intel Unleashes Its Inner Attila," *Fortune,* October 15, 2001, pp. 169–184; and Edward F. Moltzen, "Intel, AMD Go At It Again," *CRN,* March 29, 2004, p. 80.

7. See Michael Porter, *Competitive Advantage: Creating and Sustaining Superior Performance* (New York: Free Press, 1998), chap. 6.

8. See Kotler, *Marketing Management,* pp. 4–5; Sam Hill and Glenn Rifkin, *Radical Marketing* (New York: HarperBusiness, 1999); Gerry Khermouch, "Keeping the Froth on Sam Adams," *Business Week,* September 1, 2003, p. 54; and information accessed at www.bostonbeer.com, December 2004.

9. Michael E. Porter, *Competitive Strategy: Techniques for Analyzing Industries and Competitors* (New York: Free Press, 1980), chap. 2; and Porter, "What Is Strategy?" *Harvard Business Review,* November–December 1996, pp. 61–78.

10. See Michael Treacy and Fred Wiersema, "Customer Intimacy and Other Value Disciplines," *Harvard Business Review,* January–February 1993, pp. 84–93; Michael Treacy and Mike Wiersema, *The Discipline of Market Leaders: Choose Your Customers, Narrow Your Focus, Dominate Your Market* (Perseus Press, 1997); Fred Wiersema, *Customer Intimacy: Pick Your Partners, Shape Your Culture, Win Together* (Knowledge Exchange, 1998); and Wiersema, *Double-Digit Growth: How Great Companies Achieve It—No Matter What* (Portfolio, 2003).

11. For more discussion on defense and attack strategies, see Philip Kotler, *Marketing Management,* 11th ed., pp. 254–272. Also see Eric K. Clemons and Jason A. Santamaria, "Maneuver Warfare: Can Modern Military Strategy Lead You to Victory?" *Harvard Business Review,* April 2002, pp. 57–65.

12. Adapted from an example found in George Stalk, Jr., and Rob Lachenaur, "Hardball: Five Killer Strategies for Trouncing the competition," *Harvard Business Review,* April 2004, pp. 62–71.

13. See Bulik, "Sony, Kodak Lead U.S. Battle for Share in Digital Cameras," p. 12; and Dean Foust, "Things Go Better with Juice," *Business Week,* May 17, 2004, pp. 81–82.

14. Jack Ewing, "The Beer Wars Come to a Head," *Business Week,* May 24, 2004, p. 68; and James B. Arndorfer, "Bud Declares Cease Fire in Beer Battles," *Advertising Age,* September 6, 2004, pp. 1, 23.

15. Jack Neff, "Unilever Cedes Laundry War," *Advertising Age,* May 27, 2002, pp. 1, 47; and "100 Leading National Advertisers," *Advertising Age,* June 29, 2004, p. 63.

16. "Logitech Aims at Convergence for New Growth," *Wall Street Journal,* June 16, 2004, p. 1.

17. Jim Kirk, "Company Finds Itself, Finds Success: Alberto-Culver Adopts Strategy of Knowing Its Strengths and Pro-

moting Small Brands, Rather Than Tackling Giants," *Chicago Tribune,* January 22, 1998, Business Section, p. 1; "Alberto-Culver Company, "Hoover's Company Profiles," July 15, 2004, p. 10048; and "Alberto Culver Posts Double-Digit Sales and Profit Increases for 2004 Third Quarter, " PRNewswire, July 22, 2004, accessed at www.alberto.com/investing.cfm.

CHAPTER 18

1. See Stewart Alsop, "I'm Betting on Amazon," *Fortune,* April 30, 2001, p. 48; Geoffrey Colvin, "Shaking Hands on the Web," *Fortune,* May 14, 2001, p. 54; "Firm May Prove to Be a Rare E-Commerce Site with Staying Power," *The Washington Post,* January 24, 2003; Jim Milliot, "Amazon.com Book Unit Sales Up 13%," *Publishers Weekly,* February 2, 2004, p. 7; David Stires, "Amazon's Secret," *Fortune,* April 19, 2004, p. 144; Susan Posnock, "Customer Satisfaction Up Online" *American Demographics,* April 2004, p. 16; and "Amazon.com, Inc." *Hoover's Company Records,* July 15, 2004, p. 51493.

2. See "U.S. Internet Population Continues to Grow," February 6, 2002, accessed at www.cyberatlas.com; "Population Explosion!" *CyberAtlas,* June 23, 2003, accessed at www.cyberatlas.com; and "Portrait of the Online Population," Jupiter Research, January 2004, accessed at www.jup.com.

3. Timothy J. Mullaney, "At Last, the Web Hits 100 MPH," *Business Week,* June 23, 2003, pp. 80–81; and "US Broadband Households by 2008," Jupiter Research, September 2003, accessed at www.jup.com.

4. Robyn Greenspan, "The Web as a Way of Life," accessed online at www.cyberatlas.internet.com, May 21, 2002; and "June 2003 Internet Usage Stats," accessed at www.cyberatlas.com, September, 2003.

5. Paola Hjelt, "Flying on the Web in a Turbulent Economy," *Business Week,* April 30, 2001, pp. 142–148; and Amy Spector, "Cheesecake Factory Staff, Execs Raise the Bar on Service Together," *Nation's Restaurant News,* May 24, 2004, p. 32.

6. Bob Parks, "Let's Remake a Dealership," *Business 2.0,* June 2004, pp. 65–67.

7. See Timothy Mullaney, "The E-Biz Surprise," *Business Week,* May 12, 2003, pp. 60–68; Patti Freeman Evans, "Market Forecast: Retail Spending Online," Jupiter Research, January 8, 2004, accessed at www.jup.com; and Carrie A, Johnson, "US eCommerce Overview: 2004 to 2010," August 2, 2004, accessed at www.forrester.com/Research/Document/Excerpt/0,7211,34576,00.html.

8. See Michael Totty, "E-Commerce (A Special Report): Selling Strategies—Demographics: The Masses Have Arrived— . . . And E-Commerce Will Never Be the Same," *Wall Street Journal,* January 27, 2003, p. R8; and Vipul Patel, "Portrait of the Online Population," Jupiter Research, March 18, 2004, accessed at www.jup.com.

9. Roger O. Crockett, "A Web That Looks Like the World," *Business Week,* March 22, 1999, p. EB46–EB47. Also see Robyn Greenspan, "Internet Not for Everyone," April 16, 2003, accessed at www.cyberatlas.com.

10. See Michael Pastore, "Internet Key to Communication Among Youth," January 25, 2002, accessed online at www.cyberatlas.internet.com; John Fetto, "Teen Chatter,"

American Demographics, April 2002, p. 14; and Pamela Paul, "Nouveau Niche," *American Demographics,* July–August, 2003, pp. 20–21.

11. See Joanne Cleaver, "Surfing for Seniors," *Marketing News,* July 19, 1999, pp. 1, 7; Sara Teasdale Montgomery, "Senior Surfers Grab Web Attention," *Advertising Age,* July 10, 2000, p. S4; Hassan Fattah, "Hollywood, the Internet, & Kids," *American Demographics*, May 2001, pp. 51–56; Robyn Greenspan, "Surfing with Seniors and Boomers," *CyberAtlas,* January 23, 2003, accessed at www.cyberatlas.com; and Vipul Patel, "Portrait of the Online Population," Jupiter Research, March 18, 2004, accessed at www.jup.com.

12. Information for this example accessed at http://quickenloans.quicken.com, August 2004.

13. See Steve Hamm, "E-Biz: Down but Hardly Out," *Business Week*, March 26, 2001, pp. 126–130; "B2B E-Commerce Headed for Trillions," March 6, 2002, accessed at www.cyberatlas.internet.com; and Timothy Mullaney, "The E-Biz Surprise," *Business Week*, May 12, 2003, pp. 60–68.

14. Darnell Little, "Let's Keep This Exchange to Ourselves," *Business Week,* December 4, 2000, p. 48. Also see Eric Young, "Web Marketplaces That Really Work," *Fortune/ CNET Tech Review,* Winter 2002, pp. 78–86.

15. Facts from eBay annual reports and other information accessed at www.ebay.com, September 2004; "EBay Realizes Success in Small-Biz Arena," *Marketing News,* May 1, 2004, p. 11; and Erick Schonfeld, "Corporate America's New Outlet Mall," *Business 2.0,* April 2004, pp. 43–45.

16. Adapted from Lev Grossman, "Meet Joe Blog," *Time,* June 21, 2004, p. 65.

17. Kris Oser, "Nike Assays Blog as Marketing Tool," *Advertising Age,* June 14, 2004, p. 26.

18. Michelle Slatalla, "Toll-Free Apology Soothes Savage Beast," *New York Times,* February 12, 2004, p. G4; and information from www.planetfeedback.com/consumer, August 2004.

19. Heather Green, "How to Reach John Q. Public," *Business Week*, March 26, 2001, pp. 132–134. Also see Ellen Florian, "Dot-Com Deathwatch: Dead and (Mostly) Gone," *Fortune,* December 24, 2001, pp. 46–47.

20. Bradley Johnson, "Out-of-Sight Spending Collides with Reality," *Advertising Age,* August 7, 2000, pp. S4–S8.

21. Gary Hamel, "Is This All You Can Build with the Net? Think Bigger," *Fortune*, April 30, 2001, pp. 134–138.

22. See Ann Weintraub, "For Online Pet Stores, It's Dog-Eat-Dog," *Business Week*, March 6, 2000, pp. 78–80; "Death of a Spokespup," *Adweek,* December 11, 2000, pp. 44–46; Jacques R. Chevron, "Name Least of Pet.com's Woes," *Advertising Age,* January 22, 2001, p. 24; Norm Alster, "Initial Offerings Take a Turn to the Traditional," *New York Times,* May 19, 2002, p. 3.4; "Marketing Hits and Misses," *Sales & Marketing Management,* August 2002, p. 16; and "Dot-com Craze Sparks IPO Flameouts," *Knight Ridder Tribune Business News,* November 2, 2003, p. 1.

23. Ranja Gulati and Jason Garino, "Get the Right Mix of Bricks and Clicks," *Harvard Business Review*, May–June 2000, pp. 107–108; "Office Depot, Inc.," *Hoover's Online,* Austin, July 15, 2004, p. 14308; and information accessed at www.officedepot.com, September 2004.

24. "E-Commerce Trudges through Current Slowdown," accessed at www.cyberatlas.internet.com, May 22, 2001. Also see Eyal Biyalogorsky and Prasad Naik, "Click and Mortar: The Effect of On-line Activities on Off-line Sales," *Marketing Letters,* February 2003, pp. 1–21.

25. Sharon Gaudin, "The Site of No Return," May 28, 2002, accessed at www.graphics-art.com/ Site%20of%20no%20return.htm.

26. Marty Bernstein, "Mitsubishi Super Bowl Ad Lures Viewer to Internet," *Automotive News,* March 29, 2004, p. 56B.

27. John Deighton, "The Future of Interactive Marketing," *Harvard Business Review,* November–December 1996, p. 154.

28. Don Peppers and Martha Rogers, "Opening the Door to Consumers," *Sales & Marketing Management*, October 1998, pp. 22–29; Mike Beirne, "Marketers of the Next Generation: Silvio Bonvini," *Brandweek*, November 8, 1999, p. 64; Bob Tedeschi, "Consumer Products Companies Use Web Sites to Strengthen Ties with Consumers," *New York Times,* August 25, 2003, p. C.6; and information from www.candystand.com, June 2004.

29. Jeffrey F. Rayport and Bernard J. Jaworski, *e-Commerce* (New York: McGraw-Hill, 2001), p. 116. Also see Goutam Chakraborty, "What Do Customers Consider Important in B2B Websites?" *Journal of Advertising,* March 2003, p. 50; and David Sparrow, "Get 'Em to Bite," *Catalog Age,* April 1, 2003, pp. 35–36.

30. Reid Goldsborough, "Creating Web Sites for Web Surfers," *Black Issues in Higher Education,* June 17, 2004, p. 120.

31. Lisa Bertagnoli, "Getting Satisfaction," *Marketing News,* May 7, 2001, p. 11.

32. Tobi Elkin, "Size Matters; So Does Price," *Advertising Age,* January 13, 2003, p. 46.

33. For these and other examples, see William M. Bulkeley, "E-Commerce (A Special Report): Cover Story—Pass It On: Advertisers Discover They Have a Friend in 'Viral' Marketing," *Wall Street Journal,* January 14, 2002, p. R6; and Pete Snyder, "Wanted: Standards for Viral Marketing," *Brandweek,* June 28, 2004, p. 21.

34. Eilene Zimmerman, "Catch the Bug," *Sales and Marketing Management,* February 2001, pp. 78–82. Also see Ellen Neuborne, "Viral Marketing Alert," *Business Week,* March 19, 2001, p. EB8.

35. *IAB Internet Advertising Revenue Report,* April 2004, p. 3; accessed at www.iab.net/resources/adrevenue/pdf/IAB_PwC_2003.pdf.

36. Tobi Elkin, "Net Advantages," *Advertising Age*, February 10, 2003, p. 29.

37. Adapted from information found in Stuart Elliott, "Seinfeld and Superman Join Forces Again in Spots for American Express, This Time on the Web," *New York Times,* March 30, 2004, p. C.5; and Michael Snider, "Internet: Watch Out for Adver-tainment," *McLean's,* May 17, 2004, p. 54.

38. Information from "iVillage Wins More Users than Rival," *New Media Age,* March 11, 2004, p. p.3; James Hibberd, "Web Spawns Reunion Show," *TelevisionWeek,* April 5, 2004, p. 3; the iVillage Top-Line Metrics section of www.ivillage.com, October 2004; and www.MyFamily.com, September 2004.

39. See Thane Peterson, "E-I-E-I-E-Farming," *Business Week*, May 1, 2000, p. 202; "Survival of the Fittest," *Agri Marketing*, March 2002, pp. 18–24; Bekah Reddick, "Ag Online Leads in the Polls," *Agri Marketing*, November/December 2003, p. 42; and www.agriculture.com, September 2004.

40. Rebecca Gardyn, "Target Practice," *American Demographics*, October 2002, pp. 18–20; "DoubleClick Marketing Spending Index," accessed online at www.DoubleClick.com, March 2003; and Juliana Deeks, "Online Advertising and E-mail Marketing through 2008," Jupiter Media, February 12, 2004, accessed at www.jup.com.

41. Heidi Anderson, "Nintendo Case Study: Rules Are Made to Be Broken," *E-Mail Marketing Case Studies*, March 6, 2003, accessed online at www.clickz.com.

42. Michael Porter, "Strategy and the Internet," *Harvard Business Review*, March 2001, pp. 614–678.

43. Timothy J. Mullancy, "Break Out the Black Ink," *Business Week*, May 13, 2002, pp. 74–76; and Timothy Mullaney, "The Web Is Finally Catching Profits," *Business Week*, February 17, 2003, p. 66.

44. See Peter Han and Angus Maclaurin, "Do Consumers Really Care About Online Privacy?" *Marketing Management*, January–February 2002, pp. 35–38; Eric Goldman, "The Internet Privacy Fallacy," *Computer and Internet Lawyer*, January 2003, p. 20; and Nancy Wong, "Getting Pragmatic about Privacy," *American Demographics*, June 2003, pp. 14–15.

45. See Jaikumar Vijayan, "First Online Data Privacy Law Looms in California," *Computerworld*, June 28, 2004, p. 12.

46. See Jennifer DiSabatino, "FTC OKs Self-Regulation to Protect Children's Privacy," *Computerworld*, February 12, 2001, p. 32; Laurie Flynn, "New Efforts Are Being Made to Keep Online Merchants from Collecting Personal Information from Children," *New York Times*, May 12, 2003, p. C4; and Ann Mack, "Marketers Challenged on Youth Safeguards," *Adweek*, June 14, 2004, p. 12.

47. Bob Tedeschi, "Everybody Talks about Online Privacy, but Few Do Anything about It," *New York Times*, June 3, 2002, p. C6; and Susan Johnson, "Reflecting a Global Reality," *Beyond Numbers*, April 2004, pp. 6–13.

48. Information on TRUSTe accessed at www.truste.com, September 2004.

49. See "Seventy Percent of US Consumers Worry About Online Privacy, But Few Take Protective Action, Reports Jupiter Media Metrix," Jupiter Media Metrix press release, June 3, 2002, accessed online at www.jup.com.

50. See Ira Sager, "The Underground Web," *Business Week*, September 2, 2002, pp. 67–74; "VeriSign Signs Pact with eBay to Fight Fraud on Auction Site," *Wall Street Journal*, May 8, 2002, p. A9; the Internet Fraud Complaint Center Annual Report, 2003, accessed online at www.ifccfbi.gov; and Katie Hafner, "With Internet Fraud Up Sharply, EBay Attracts Vigilantes," *New York Times*, March 20, 2004, p. A.1.

51. Facts from Mark Warschauer, "Demystifying the Digital Divide," *Scientific American*, August 2003, p. 42; quote from Richard J. Dalton Jr., "New York Libraries Try to Close Minorities' Digital Divide," *Knight Ridder Tribune Business News*, July 4, 2004, p. 1.

52. "114-Year-Old Bids over $3M for Items in eBay Auctions," *USA Today*, April 30, 1999, p. 10B.

CHAPTER 19

1. Hillary Chura and Richard Linnett, "Coca-Cola Readies Global Assault," *Advertising Age*, April 2, 2001, pp. 1, 34; Ken Hein, "Soft Drinks," *Mediaweek*, April 21, 2003, p. SR29; "Sprite Shows Off Hint of Mint Up North," *Packaging Digest*, May 2003, p. 4; The Advertising Age Global Advertising Report," *Advertising Age*, November 10, 2003, p. 3; Julie Creswell and Julie Schlosser, "Has Coke Lost Its Fizz?" *Fortune*, November 10, 2003, pp. 215–217; and "Our Company," accessed at www.coca-cola.com, January 2005.

2. George Melloan, "Feeling the Muscles of the Multinationals," *Wall Street Journal*, January 6, 2004, p. A19.

3. John Alden, "What in the World Drives UPS?" *International Business*, April 1998, pp. 6–7; Karen Pennar, "Two Steps Forward, One Step Back," *Business Week*, August 31, 1998, p. 116; Michelle Wirth Fellman, "A New World for Marketers," *Marketing News*, May 10, 1999, p. 13; Alan Greenspan, "International Trade: Globalization vs. Protectionism," *Vital Speeches of the Day*, April 15, 2001, pp. 386–388; and *International Trade Statistics 2002*, WTO, p. 1, accessed at www.wto.org/english/res_e/statis_e/its2002_e/its02_toc_e.htm, August 2004.

4. Gail Edmondson, "See the World, Erase Its Borders," *Business Week*, August 28, 2000, pp. 113–114.

5. Steve Hamm, "Borders Are So 20th Century," *Business Week*, September 22, 2003, pp. 68–73.

6. "The Unique Japanese," *Fortune*, November 24, 1986, p. 8; and James D. Southwick, "Addressing Market Access Barriers in Japan Through the WTO," *Law and Policy in International Business*, Spring 2000, pp. 923–976. For more on nontariff and other barriers, see Warren J. Keegan and Mark C. Green, *Principles of Global Marketing* (Upper Saddle River, NJ: Prentice Hall, 2000), chapter 8; and Simon P. Anderson and Nicholas Schmidt, "Nontariff Barriers and Trade Liberalization," *Economic Inquiry*, January 2003, pp. 80–98.

7. "What Is the WTO?" accessed at www.wto.org/english/thewto_e/whatis_e/whatis_e.htm, September 2004.

8. See Ping Deng, "Impact of GATT Uruguay Round on Various Industries," *American Business Review*, June 1998, pp. 22–29; Helene Cooper, "U.S. Seeks a New Rounds of WTO Talks," *Wall Street Journal*, July 18, 2001, p. A12; Michael Finger, Julio J. Nogues, "The Unbalanced Uruguay Outcome: The New Areas in Future WTO Negotiations," *The World Economy*, March 2002, pp. 321–340; and *WTO Annual Report 2003*, accessed at www.wto.org/english/res_e/booksp_e/anrep_e/anrep03_e.pdf, September 2004.

9. "Leaders: Deadlocked in Doha; World Trade," *The Economist*, March 29, 2003, p. 13; and Supachai Panitchpakdi, "Brave New World," *Wall Street Journal*, February 26, 2004, p. A.10.

10. Jeffrey Lewis, "The European Union," *AFP Exchange*, March/April 2003, pp. 46–50; Robert J. Samuelson, "The European Predicament," *The Washington Post*, February 4, 2004, p. A23; and "The European Union at a Glance," accessed online at http://europa.eu.int, December 2004.

11. "Finance and Economics: The Euro, Trade and Growth; Economic Focus," *The Economist*, July 12, 2003, p. 74; and "One Europe, United in Fiscal Misrule," *Global Agenda*, January 26, 2004, p. 1.

12. For more on the European Union, see "Around Europe in 40 Years," *The Economist,* May 31, 1997, p. S4; "European Union to Begin Expansion," *New York Times,* March 30, 1998, p. A5; Joan Warner, "Mix Us Culturally? It's Impossible," *Business Week,* April 27, 1998, p. 108; Paul J. Deveney, "World Watch," *Wall Street Journal,* May 20, 1999, p. A12; and Stephen J. Dannhauser, "Can Europe Become a Global Superpower? Europe Must Have Unification," *Vital Speeches of the Day,* April 1, 2003, pp. 382–385.

13. Fay Hansen, "World Trade Update," *Business Finance,* March 2002, pp. 9–11; Daniel T Griswold, "NAFTA at 10" *World Trade,* March 2003, p. 10; Kenneth G Weigel, "The FTAA," *World Trade,* July 2003, p. 44; Kelley Mullaney, "Importance of U.S.–Canada Trade Relationships Highlighted at Houston Partnership," January 14, 2004, accessed at www.partnershipforgrowth.org; and Michael O'Boyle, "Nafta's Birthday Party," *Business Mexico,* February 2004, pp. 28–34.

14. Bernard Malamud and Wayne A. Label, "The Merco: A Common Currency for Mercosur and Latin America," *American Business Review,* June 2002, pp. 132–139; Terry Wade, "Latin Trade Bloc Flexes Its Muscle—New Leaders in Argentina, Brazil Give Mercosur Clout; Another Challenge for U.S." *Wall Street Journal,* June 16, 2003, p. A.13; and K D Narendranate, "Preferential Mercosur Tariffs Likely by June," *The Economic Times,* February 28, 2004, accessed at http://economictimes.indiatimes.com.

15. See Geri Smith and Cristina Lindblad "Mexico: Was NAFTA Worth It?" *Business Week,* December 22, 2003, pp. 66–72.

16. See David Woodruff, "Ready to Shop until They Drop," *Business Week,* June 22, 1998, pp. 104–108; and James MacAonghus, "Online Impact of a Growing Europe," *New Media Age,* February 12, 2004, p. 15.

17. See Dan West, "Countertrade," *Business Credit,* April 2001, pp. 64–67; West, "Countertrade," *Business Credit,* April 2002, pp. 48–51; and Joao Pedro Taborda, "The Use of Countertrade and Offsets as a Tool for Strategic Advantage," *Competitive Intelligence Magazine,* May–June, 2003, p. 51.

18. For this and other examples, see Louis Kraar, "How to Sell to Cashless Buyers," *Fortune,* November 7, 1988, pp. 147–154; Nathaniel Gilbert, "The Case for Countertrade," *Across the Board,* May 1992, pp. 43–45; Darren McDermott and S. Karen Witcher, "Bartering Gains Currency," *Wall Street Journal,* April 6, 1998, p. A10; Anne Millen Porter, "Global Economic Meltdown Boosts Barter Business," *Purchasing,* February 11, 1999, pp. 21–25; S. Jayasankaran, "Fire-Fighting," *Far Eastern Economic Review,* May 31, 2001, p. 52; and Dalia Marin and Monika Schnitzer, "The Economic Institution of International Barter," *Economic Journal,* April 2002, pp. 293–316.

19. Rebecca Piirto Heath, "Think Globally," *Marketing Tools,* October 1996, pp. 49–54; and "The Power of Writing," *National Geographic,* August 1999, p. 128–129.

20. For other examples and discussion, see *Dun & Bradstreet's Guide to Doing Business Around the World* (Upper Saddle River, NJ: Prentice Hall, 2000); Betsy Cummings, "Selling Around the World," *Sales & Marketing Management,* May 2001, p. 70; James K. Sebenius, "The Hidden Challenge of Cross-Border Negotiations," *Harvard Business Review,* March 2002, pp. 76–85; Daniel Joseph, "Dangerous Assumptions," *Ceramic Industry,* January 2003, p. 120; and Ellen Neuborne, "Bridging the Culture Gap," *Sales & Marketing Management,* July 2003, p. 22.

21. Pete Engardio, Manjeet Kripalani, and Alysha Webb, "Smart Globalization," *Business Week,* August 27, 2001, pp. 132–136.

22. Adapted from Mark Rice-Oxley, "In 2,000 Years, Will the World Remember Disney or Plato?" *Christian Science Monitor,* January 15, 2004, p. 16.

23. See "Crest, Colgate Bare Teeth in Competition for China," *Advertising Age International,* November 1996, p. I3; and Jack Neff, "Submerged," *Advertising Age,* March 4, 2002, p. 14.

24. For a good discussion of joint venturing, see James Bamford, David Ernst, and David G. Fubini, "Launching a World-Class Joint Venture," *Harvard Business Review,* February 2004, pp. 91–100.

25. Robert Neff, "In Japan, They're Goofy about Disney," *Business Week,* March 12, 1990, p. 64; "In Brief: E*Trade Licensing Deal Gives It an Israeli Link," *American Banker,* May 11, 1998; John Engen, "Going Going Global," *USBanker,* February 2000, pp. 22S–25S; "Cowboys and Samuri: The Japanizing of Universal," *Wall Street Journal,* March 22, 2001, p. B1; Chester Dawson, "Will Tokyo Embrace Another Mouse?" *Business Week,* September 10, 2001; and Bruce Orwall, "Eisner Contends Disney Is Primed for Turnaround," *Wall Street Journal,* August 9, 2002, p. B1; and "Walt Disney Parks & Resorts," *Hoover's Company Capsules,* Austin, July 1, 2003, p. 104368.

26. See Cynthia Kemper, "KFC Tradition Sold Japan on Chicken," *Denver Post,* June 7, 1998, p. J4; and Milford Prewitt, "Chains Look for Links Overseas," *Nation's Restaurant News,* February 18, 2002, pp. 1,6.

27. For good discussions, see Laura Mazur, "Globalization Is Still Tethered to Local Variations," *Marketing,* January 22, 2004, p. 18; and Johny K. Johansson and Ilkka A. Ronkainen, "The Brand Challenge: Are Global Brands the Right Choice for Your Company?" *Marketing Management,* March/April 2004.

28. See "In India, Beef-Free Mickie D," *Business Week,* April 7, 1995, p. 52; Jeff Walters, "Have Brand Will Travel," *Brandweek,* October 6, 1997, pp. 22–26; David Barboza, "From Abroad, McDonald's Finds Value in Local Control," *New York Times,* February 12, 1999, p. 1; Suh-Kyung Yoon, "Look Who's Going Native," *Far Eastern Economic Review,* February 1, 2001, pp. 68–69; and Saritha Rai, "Tastes of India in U.S. Wrappers," *New York Times,* April 29, 2003 p. W1.

29. For more, see Warren J. Keegan, *Global Marketing Management,* 7th ed. (Upper Saddle River, NJ: Prentice Hall, 2002), pp. 346–351.

30. Adapted from Douglas McGray, "Translating Sony into English," *Fast Company,* January 2003, p. 38. Also see Jeffrey Selingo, "Newer, Smaller, Fasters, and Not in Stores Now," *New York Times,* May 8, 2003, p. G.5.

31. Kate MacArthur, "Coca-Cola Light Employs Local Edge," *Advertising Age,* August 21, 2000, pp. 18–19; and "Case

Studies: Coke Light Hottest Guy," *Advantage Marketing, msn India,* accessed at http://.advantage.msn.co.in, March 15, 2004.

32. See Alicia Clegg, "One Ad One World?" *Marketing Week,* June 20, 2002, pp. 51–52; and George E. Belch and Machael A. Belch, *Advertising and Promotion: An Integrated Marketing Communications Perspective,* 6th ed. (New York, NY: McGraw Hill, 2004), pp. 666–668.

33. Adapted from Normandy Madden and Jack Neff, "P&G Adapts Attitude toward Local Markets," *Advertising Age,* February 23, 2004, p. 28.

34. Michael Schroeder, "The Economy: Shrimp Imports to U.S. May Face Antidumping Levy," *Wall Street Journal,* February 18, 2004, p. A.2.

35. Sarah Ellison, "Revealing Price Discrepancies, the Euro Aids Bargain-Hunters," *Wall Street Journal,* January 30, 2002, p. A15.

36. See Patrick Powers, "Distribution in China: The End of the Beginning," *China Business Review,* July–August, 2001, pp. 8–12; Drake Weisert, "Coca-Cola in China: Quenching the Thirst of a Billion," *The China Business Review,* July–August 2001, pp. 52–55; and Gabriel Kahn, "Coke Works Harder at Being the Real Thing in Hinterland," *Wall Street Journal,* November 26, 2002, p. B1.

CHAPTER 20

1. Quotes and other information for this Nike story from Rebecca De Winter, "The Anti-Sweatshop Movement," *Ethics & International Affairs,* October 2001, pp. 99–117; Richard Locke, "The Promise and Perils of Globalization: The Case of Nike," in Thomas A. Kochan and Richard Schmalensee, *Management: Inventing and Delivering Its Future* (Boston: MIT Press, 2003); Ann M. Peterson, "Nike Boosts Indians' Health, Its Reputation," *Marketing News,* June 1, 2004, p. 10; and www.nikebiz.com, June 2004.

2. See Gordan Fairclough, "Study Slams Philip Morris Ads Telling Teens Not to Smoke—How a Market Researcher Who Dedicated Years to Cigarette Sales Came to Create Antismoking Ads,"*Wall Street Journal,* May 29, 2002, p. B1; Winnie Hu, "The Smoking Ban: Clean Air, Murky Economics," *The New York Times,* December 28, 2003, p. 1.1; and "Smoking Bans Have Their Place, but Outside Isn't One of Them," *The Washington Post,* February 5, 2004, p. T.04.

3. James Heckman, "Don't Shoot the Messenger: More and More Often, Marketing Is the Regulators' Target," *Marketing News,* May 24, 1999, pp. 1, 9; "Business Brief—Publishers Clearing House: Payment of $34 Million Set to Settle with 26 States," *Wall Street Journal,* June 27, 2001, p. B8; Helen Rothschild Ewald and Roberta Vann, "'You're a Guaranteed Winner': Composing 'You' in a Consumer Culture," *The Journal of Business Communication,* April 2003, pp. 98–128; and "Publishers Clearing House," *Hoover's Company Capsules,* March 15, 2004, accessed at http://proquest.umi.com.

4. Theodore Levitt, "The Morality(?) of Advertising," *Harvard Business Review,* July–August 1970, pp. 84–92. For counterpoints, see Heckman, "Don't Shoot the Messenger," pp. 1, 9.

5. Lane Jennings, "Hype, Spin, Puffery, and Lies: Should We Be Scared?" *The Futurist,* January–February 2004, p. 16.

6. Roger Parloff, "Is Fat the Next Tobacco?" *Fortune,* February 3, 2003, pp. 51–54; "'Big Food' Get the Obesity Message," *New York Times,* July 10, 2003, p. A22; and Carl Hulse, "Vote in House Offers Shield in Obesity Suits," *New York Times,* March 11, 2004, p. A1.

7. "McDonald's to Cut 'Super Size' Option," *Advertising Age,* March 8, 2004, p. 13; and Dave Carpenter, "Hold the Fries, Take a Walk," *The News & Observer,* April 16, 2004, p. D1.

8. Gary Bagin, "Products Liability Verdict—Study Releases," press release, Jury Verdict Research, January 15, 2004, accessed at www.juryverdictresearch.com.

9. Cliff Edwards, "Where Have All the Edsels Gone?" *Greensboro News Record,* May 24, 1999, p. B6. Also see Joel Dryfuss, "Planned Obsolescence Is Alive and Well," *Fortune,* February 15, 1999, p. 192; and Atsuo Utaka, "Planned Obsolescence and Marketing Strategy," *Managerial and Decision Economics,* December 2000, pp. 339–344.

10. Adapted from John Markoff, "Is Planned Obsolescence Obsolete?" *New York Times,* February 17, 2002, p. 4.6. Also see Kevin McKean, "Planned Obsolescence," *InfoWorld,* September 29, 2003, pp. 38–46.

11. See Judith Bell and Bonnie Maria Burlin, "In Urban Areas: Many More Still Pay More for Food," *Journal of Public Policy and Marketing,* Fall 1993, pp. 268–270; Kathryn Graddy and Diana C. Robertson, "Fairness of Pricing Decisions," *Business Ethics Quarterly,* April 1999, pp. 225–243; Gordon Matthews, "Does Everyone Have the Right to Credit?" *USBanker,* April 2001, pp. 44–48.

12. See Brian Grow and Pallavi Gogoi, "A New Way to Squeeze the Weak?" *Business Week,* January 28, 2002, p. 92; Mark A. Hofmann, "Redlining Becomes Less of an Issue for Agents, Brokers," *Business Insurance,* May 5, 2003, p. 14C; Todd Cooper, "Redlining Rears Its Ugly Head," *USBanker,* August 2003, p. 64; and Marc Lifsher, "Allstate Settles Over Use of Credit Scores," *Los Angeles Times,* March 2, 2004, p. C.1.

13. Information from John De Graaf, "The Overspent American/Luxury Fever," *The Amicus Journal,* Summer 1999, pp. 41–43; Tim Kasser, *The High Price of Materialism* (Cambridge, MA: MIT Press, 2003); Carolyn Setlow, "Profiting from America's New Materialism," *Discount Store News,* April 17, 2000, p. 16; and "Shop 'til They Drop?" *Christian Science Monitor,* December 1, 2003, p. 8. For interesting discussions on materialism and consumption, see Tim Kasser and Allen D. Kanner, *Psychology and Consumer Culture: The Struggle for a Good Life in a Materialistic World,"* (Washington, DC: American Psychological Association, 2003); Gregg Easterbrook, *The Progress Paradox* (New York: Random House, 2003); and J. Walker Smith, "More than Stuff," *Marketing Management,* March/April 2004, p. 56.

14. Adapted from Constance L. Hays, "Preaching to Save Shoppers from 'Evil' of Consumerism," *New York Times,* January 1, 2003, p. C1. Also see Penelope Green, "Consumer Beware," *New York Times,* November 23, 2003, p. 0.10; and www.revbilly.com.

15. See Lee Hultgreen and Kim Kawada, "San Diego's Interstate 15 High-Occupancy/Toll Lane Facility Using Value Pricing," *ITE Journal,* June 1999, pp. 22–27; Mark Rico Oxley,

"Britain Battles Clogged Streets," *The Christian Science Monitor,* February 18, 2003, p. 7; and Ben Walker, "Congestion Charge Is Cutting Jams, Say Chiefs," *Regeneration and Renewal,* June 13, 2003, p. 3.

16. From an advertisement for *Fact* magazine, which does not carry advertisements.

17. Adapted from information found in Steve Hamm, "Microsoft's Future," *Business Week*, January 19, 1998, pp. 58–68; Dan Carney and Mike France, "The Microsoft Case: Tying It All Together," *Business Week,* December 3, 2001, pp. 68–69; and Paul Meller and Matt Richtel, "Europeans Rule Against Microsoft; Appeal Is Promised," *New York Times,* March 25, 2004, p. C.1.

18. Stuart L. Hart, "Beyond Greening: Strategies for a Sustainable World," *Harvard Business Review,* January–February 1997, pp. 66–76. Also see Trevor Price and Doug Probert, "The Need for Environmentally-Sustainable Developments," *International Need for Environmentally-Sustainable Developments,* 2002, pp. 1–22; Subhabrata Bobby Banerjee, Easwar S. Iyer, and Rajiv K. Kashyap, "Corporate Environmentalism: Antecedents and Influence of Industry Type," *Harvard Business Review,* April 2003, pp. 106–122; Christopher Laszlo, *The Sustainable Company: How to Create Lasting Value through Social and Environmental Performance* (Washington, D.C.: Island Press, 2003); and Volkert Beekman, "Sustainable Development and Future Generations," *Journal of Agriculture and Environmental Ethics,* Vol. 17, Iss. 1, 2004, p. 3.

19. Information from "Xerox Equipment Remanufacture and Parts Reuse," accessed at www.xerox.com, August 2004.

20. Accessed at www.monsanto.com/monsanto/layout/our_pledge/default.asp, September 2004.

21. Adapted from Lynelle Preston, "Sustainability at Hewlett-Packard: From Theory to Practice," *California Management Review,* Spring 2001, pp. 26–36; and "Environmental Sustainability," accessed at www.hp.com/hpinfo/globalcitizenship/index.html, August 2004.

22. See "EMAS: What's New?" accessed at http://europa.eu.int/comm/environment/emas, August 2004; "NAFTA's Trade-Environment Regime and Its Commission for Environmental Cooperation: Contributions and Challenges Ten Years On," *The Canadian Journal of Regional Science,* Summer 2002, p. 207; "Bahadir Basdere and Guenther Seliger, "Disassembly Factories for Electrical and Electronics Products to Recover Resources in Product Materials Cycles," *Environmental Science and Technology,* December 1, 2003, p. 5354; and "Special Report: Free Trade on Trial—Ten Years of NAFTA," *The Economist,* January 3, 2004, p. 13.

23. Information and quotes from Andy Milligan, "Samsung Points the Way for Asian Firms in Global Brand Race," *Media,* August 8, 2003, p. 8; Katherine Chen, Michael Jakielski, Nadia Luhr, and Joseph Mayer-Salman, "DigitAll," student paper at the University of North Carolina at Chapel Hill, Spring 2003; Gerry Khermouch, "The Best Global Brands," *Business Week,* August 5, 2002, p. 92; John Larkin, "Samsung Tries to Snatch Sony's Crown," *Far Eastern Economic Review,* October 10, 2002, pp. 36–41; Leslie P. Norton, "Value Brand," *Barron's.* September 22, 2003, p. 19; and Samsung Electronics Co. Ltd., *Hoover's Company Capsules,* Austin, March 15, 2004; and www.samsung.com/DigitAll/BrandCampaign/index.htm, June 2004.

24. Jacquelyn A. Ottman, "Green Marketing: Wake Up to the Truth about Green Consuming," *In Business,* May–June 2002, p. 31; Marc Gunther, "Son of Aeron," *Fortune,* May 12, 2003, p. 134; and information accessed online at www.HermanMiller.com, June 2004.

25. Dan R. Dalton and Richard A. Cosier, "The Four Faces of Social Responsibility," *Business Horizons,* May–June 1982, pp. 19–27.

26. Joseph Webber, "3M's Big Cleanup," *Business Week,* June 5, 2000, pp. 96–98. Also see Kara Sissell, "3M Defends Timing of Scotchgard Phaseout," *Chemical Week,* April 11, 2001, p. 33; Peck Hwee Sim, "Ausimont Targets Former Scotchgard Markets," *Chemical Week,* August 7, 2002, p. 32; and Jennifer Lee, "E.P.A. Orders Companies to Examine Effect of Chemicals," *New York Times,* April 15, 2003, p. F2.

27. Barbara Crossette, "Russia and China Top Business Bribers," *New York Times,* May 17, 2002, p. A10; and Jakob Svensson, "Who Must Pay Bribes and How Much? Evidence from a Cross Section of Firms," *The Quarterly Journal of Economics,* February 2003, p. 207.

28. John F. Magee and P. Ranganath Nayak, "Leaders' Perspectives on Business Ethics," *Prizm,* Arthur D. Little, Inc., Cambridge, MA, first quarter, 1994, pp. 65–77. Also see Turgut Guvenli and Rajib Sanyal, "Ethical Concerns in International Business: Are Some Issues More Important than Others?" *Business and Society Review,* Summer 2002, pp. 195–206.

29. Ibid., pp. 71–72. Also see Thomas Donaldson, "Values in Tension: Ethics Away from Home," *Harvard Business Review,* September–October 1996, pp. 48–62; Patrick E. Murphy, "Character and Virtue Ethics in International Marketing: An Agenda for Managers, Researchers, and Educators," *Journal of Business Ethics,* January 1999, pp. 107–124; and Gopalkrishnan, "International Exchanges as the Basis for Conceptualizing Ethics in International Business," *Journal of Business Ethics,* February 2001, pp. 3–25.

30. See Samuel A. DiPiazza, "Ethics in Action," *Executive Excellence,* January 2002, pp. 15–16; Samuel A. DiPiazza, Jr., "It's All Down to Personal Values," accessed online at www.pwcglobal.com, August 2003; and "Code of Conduct: The Way We Do Business," accessed at www.pwcglobal.com/gx/eng/ins-sol/spec-int/ethics/index.html, June 2004.

31. DiPiazza, "Ethics in Action," p. 15.

Credits

CHAPTER 1 2 AP Wide World Photos. 7 © Earth Share. All rights reserved. 9 Porsche, Boxster and the Porsche Crest are registered trademarks and the distinctive shapes of PORSCHE automobiles are trade dress of Fr. Ing. h.c. F. Porsche AG. Used with permission of Porsche Cars North America, Inc. Copyrighted by Porsche Cars North America, Inc. 12 Courtesy of Johnson & Johnson. 14 Corbis Bettmann. © Alan Schein Photography/CORBIS. 20 Courtesy of Steve Niedorf, photographer; Harley Davidson and Carmichael Lynch. All rights reserved. 16 Courtesy of Southwest Airlines. 17 © 2004 Bank One Corporation. Reprinted with permission. All rights reserved. 20 Courtesy of Stew Leonard. 21 © General Motors Corp. Used with permission. GM Media Archives. 23 Courtesy of Workbookstock.com. 25 Coca-Cola, BMP, Fanta, NaturaAqua, Bitter Mar Rosso, and accompanying trade dress are trademarks of The Coca-Cola Company. Sprite Ice is a trademark of Coca-Cola Ltd. 26 Courtesy of Corbis/Bettmann. 27 Used with permission of Marble Collegiate Church and Follis Advertising. © John Follis. http://www.follisinc.com.

CHAPTER 2 35 Courtesy of Getty Images. 39 Used with permission of Girl Scouts of Northern California and Nevada and Amazon Advertising. 42 Courtesy of PhotoEdit. 45 Used with permission of Wal-Mart Stores, Inc. All rights reserved. 46 © Toyota Motor Sales U.S.A., Inc. All rights reserved. 48 Courtesy of Getty Images, Inc.—Liaison. 49 © Toyota Motor Sales U.S.A., Inc. All rights reserved; © General Motors Corp. Used with permission. GM Media Archives. 54 Courtesy of Jeff Zaruba, CORBIS. 56 © General Mills. All rights reserved.

CHAPTER 3 63 Courtesy of AP Wide World Photos. 67 Courtesy of Norm Betts. 68 Used with permission of Wal-Mart Stores, Inc. All rights reserved. 69 Courtesy of The Image Works. 71 Courtesy of Corbis/Bettmann. 73 © 2003 Avon Products, Inc. All rights reserved. mark™ is a registered trademark. 74 Courtesy of Rubin Postaer and Associates. 75 Courtesy of Picture Desk, Inc./Kobal Collection. 76 © 1995-2004 FedEx. All rights reserved. 78 Used with permission of Bank of America. 79 Used with permission of Volkswagen of America, Inc. All rights reserved. 82 Courtesy of Daimler Chrysler Corporation. 83 © Richard Schultz/Auto-ID Labs. Courtesy of Xplane (http://www.xplane.com) and the Auto-ID Center (http://www. autoidcenter.org). 85 Courtesy of Getty Images Inc.—Image Bank. 88 Used with permission of KitchenAid Home Appliances. Courtesy of Saatchi & Saatchi Worldwide. 90 Courtesy of Getty Images. 92 Courtesy of White Wave, Inc. Used with permission.

CHAPTER 4 99 Courtesy of Corbis/Bettmann. 101 Courtesy of Tom and Deann McCarthy, Corbis/Stock Market. 103 © 2002, USAA. All rights reserved. 104 Courtesy of Chris Volk Photography. 108 © The Dialog Corporation. Used with permission. 109 Courtesy of Fisher-Price Company. 111 Courtesy of David Sherman Photography. 114 © 2004 ActiveGroup. All rights reserved. 115 © 2004 Greenfield Online, Inc. All rights reserved. 118 Courtesy of Douglas A. Fidaleo. 119 SAS and all

other SAS Institute Inc. product or service names are registered trademarks or trademarks of SAS Institute Inc. in the USA and other countries. ® indicates USA registration. Other brand and product names are trademarks of their respective companies. Copyright © 2003. SAS Institute Inc. Cary, NC, USA. All rights reserved. 120 Courtesy of Richard B. Levine/Frances M. Roberts. 121 Courtesy of Getty Images. 123 © BISSELL Homecare, Inc. All rights reserved. 125 © 2004 ACNielsen. All rights reserved. 127 © 2003 by American Express Company. All rights reserved.

CHAPTER 5 135 Courtesy of AP/Wide World Photos. 139 Courtesy of PhotoEdit. 140 Courtesy of Charles Schwab & Company, Inc. All rights reserved. 143 Courtesy of BzzAgent; Getty Images, Inc.—Image Bank. 144 Copyright © 2004 by Lowe's®. 145 Courtesy of Carhartt Inc. 147 Courtesy of Pittsburgh Brewing Company. All rights reserved. 149 © 2004 Cable News Network. A Time Warner Company. All rights reserved. 150 Courtesy of Sergio Piumatti. 152 Courtesy of Richard B. Levine/ Frances M. Roberts. 153 Courtesy of the National Fluid Milk Processor Promotion Board. 156 © 2004 American Dairy Association® managed by Dairy Management, Inc.™ All rights reserved. The 3-A-Day™ of Dairy logo is a mark owned by Dairy Management, Inc.™ 158 Courtesy of Pearson Education/ PH College. 161 TM/®Snickers is a registered trademark of Mars, Incorporated and its affiliates. It is used with permission. Mars, Incorporated is not associated with the Prentice Hall Business Publishing.

CHAPTER 6 169 Copyright © 1994-2004 United Parcel Service of America, Inc. All rights reserved. Photo © STONE/ Phile Banko. 172 © Intel Corporation. All Rights Reserved. 173 Courtesy of Fujitsu. 175 © 2004 ChemStation International. All rights reserved. 177 Courtesy of Cardinal Health, Medical Products & Services. 178 © 1998 Volvo Trucks North America, Inc. © RIPSAW, Inc. 180 Courtesy of HSBC. 184 © 2004 Compuware Corporation. All Rights Reserved.

CHAPTER 7 193 Courtesy of Pearson Education/PH College. 197 © The Procter & Gamble Company. All rights reserved. Courtesy of Saatchi & Saatchi. 198 Used with permission of Leatherman Tool Group, Inc. All rights reserved. 199 © 2004 Neiman Marcus. All rights Reserved. 200 Courtesy of American Honda Motor Co. Inc. 201 Courtesy of the Pottery Barn. 203 Reprinted with permission of Callard & Bowser-Suchard, Inc. 204 Courtesy of Pepsi-cola North America. 205 Used with permission of Unilever. 206 © 2004 American Express Company. All Rights Reserved. Courtesy of Ogilvy & Mather. 208 Courtesy of Getty Images, Inc. 209 Courtesy of Anything Left Handed. All rights reserved. 211 Courtesy of Getty Images, Inc.; PhotoEdit; Sergio Piumatti. 212 Courtesy of PepsiCo, Inc. All rights reserved. 213 TM/®MM'S is a registered trademark of Mars, Incorporated and its affiliates. The MM'S® Milk Chocolate Candies and Peanut Chocolate Candies wrappers are trade dress of Mars, Incorporated and its affiliates. All are used with permission. Mars, Incorporated is not associated with the

Prentice Hall Business Publishing. 215 Used with permission of Nacara Cosmetiques. All rights reserved. Not for reproduction. 216 Used with permission of Olive Garden. 219 Courtesy of Getty Images. 220 Used with permission of Unilever. 222 Used with permission of General Mills, Inc. All rights reserved. HÄAGEN-DAZS is a registered trademark of General Mills, Inc. 223 Courtesy of Southwest Airlines.

CHAPTER 8 231 Courtesy of The Image Works. 233 Courtesy of Toys "R" Us, Inc. All rights reserved. 235 © 2004 Sony Electronics Incorporated. All rights reserved. 236 Courtesy of Pearson Education/PH College; PhotoEdit; Corbis Digital Stock. 237 © 2004 BASF Corporation. All rights reserved. 238 Courtesy of Corbis/Sygma. 240 Courtesy of the National Council for Crime Prevention. All rights reserved; Courtesy of the Ad Council of America; Courtesy of Keep America Beautiful, Inc. All rights reserved; Courtesy of United Negro College Fund. All rights reserved. 242 Courtesy of IDEO. 243 Courtesy of James Worrell Photography. 245 Used with permission of The Sherwin-Williams Co. 246 Courtesy of H.J. Heinz Company. 248 © 2004 Marriott International, Inc. All Rights Reserved. 249 Courtesy of Aaron Goodman. 251 Courtesy of Godiva Chocolatier Inc. All rights reserved. 252 Courtesy of Costco Wholesale. 254 Courtesy of Warner Brother Pictures, Inc./© 1966 Warner Brothers. 255 Courtesy of Morton International, Inc.: Morton Salt Division. 258 Courtesy of the United States Postal Service and Campbell-Ewald. Used with permission. 259 © 1998-2004 Mayo Foundation for Medical Education and Research. All rights reserved. 261 The Ritz-Carlton Hotel Company, LLC. All rights reserved. 263 © 2004 British Airways Plc. All rights reserved. 266 Courtesy of Munshi Ahmed Photography.

CHAPTER 9 273 © 2004 Nokia. All rights reserved. 275 New Products Showcase and Learning Center. 277 Copyright 1990-2004 Eureka! Institute. All rights reserved. 279 © 2004 Avon Products, Inc. All rights reserved. 281 DaimlerChrysler AG. 282 CLOROX® is a registered trademark of The Clorox Company. © 2003 The Clorox Company. Reprinted with permission. Photographer: Leigh Beisch. 284 Courtesy of Corbis/Sygma. 285 © 2004 Nokia. All rights reserved. 286 Courtesy of Getty Images, Inc.—Stone Allstock; © 2004 Information Resources, Inc. All Rights Reserved. 288 © 2004 Colgate-Palmolive Company. All rights reserved. 289 © 3M 1995-2004. All rights reserved. 291 The TABASCO® marks, bottles and label designs are registered trademarks and servicemarks exclusively of McIlhenny Company, Avery Island, LA 70513. www.TABASCO.com. 292 Getty Images/Time Life Pictures. 294 Courtesy of Volkswagen of America, Inc. 296 © 2004 WD-40 Company. All rights reserved. 297 SPAM and all SPAM derived terms are registered trademarks of Hormel foods, LCC and are used with permission from Hormel Foods. 298 Courtesy of Procter & Gamble Company. All rights reserved.

CHAPTER 10 305 Used with permission of priceline.com Inc. All rights reserved. 307 Courtesy of AP Wide World Photos. 308 © 2004 by Yahoo! Inc. YAHOO! And the YAHOO! Logo are trademarks of Yahoo! Inc. 310 Reprinted courtesy of Caterpillar Inc. 311 Porsche, Boxster and the Porsche Crest are registered trademarks and the distinctive shapes of PROSCHE automobiles are trade dress of Fr. Ing. H.C. F. Porsche AG. Used with permission of Porsche Cars North America, Inc. Copyrighted by Porsche Cars North America, Inc. 312 © 2004 Steinway & Sons. All rights reserved.

316 © 2004 Moen Incorporated. All rights reserved. 317 © 2004 Gibson Guitar Corp. All rights reserved. 319 © 2004 Green Mountain Energy Company. All rights reserved. 323 © 2004 Montblanc International GMBH. All rights reserved. 324 Reprinted courtesy of Caterpillar Inc.

CHAPTER 11 331 Courtesy of Big Kmart. 334 © 2004 Gramophone. All rights reserved. 336 © 2004 CityPass. All rights reserved. 338 Used with permission of Continental Airlines and MapQuest. All rights reserved; Used with permission of Continental airlines. 339 Courtesy of PhotoEdit. 340 Courtesy of Getty Images Inc.—Hulton Archive Photos. 342 Courtesy of Wide World Photos. 344 Courtesy of McDonald's. 346 Courtesy of Joy perfume. 348 © 2004 Kimberly-Clark. All rights reserved. 350 Courtesy of GlaxoSmithKline. 353 Courtesy of Photo Researchers, Inc.

CHAPTER 12 359 Reprinted courtesy of Caterpillar Inc. 361 © 2004 palmOne. All rights reserved. 362 © 1995-2004 FedEx. All rights reserved. 366 Courtesy of Churchill & Klehr Photography. 367 © 2004 Luxottica Group. All rights reserved. 369 Used with permission of Cereal Partners UK. 371 Courtesy of iTunes.com. 373 © 2004 Mary Kay Inc. All rights reserved. 374 © 2004 GEICO. All rights reserved. 375 © 2004 Rolls-Royce & Bentley Motor, Inc. All rights reserved. 376 Courtesy of Stock Boston. 378 © 2004 General Electric Company. All rights reserved. 380 Courtesy of Fine Image Photography. 382 Courtesy of Martyn Goddard. 383 © 2004 Roadway Express, Inc. All rights reserved. 385 © 2004 Oracle Corporation. All rights reserved. 386 Copyright © 1994-2004 United Parcel Service of America, Inc. All rights reserved. Photo © Michale Prince/CORBIS.

CHAPTER 13 395 Courtesy of Brian Coats Photography. 398 © 2004 Safeway. All rights reserved. 400 Courtesy of Baerbel Schmidt Photography. 402 © Geeks On Call America, Inc. All Rights Reserved. 404 Courtesy of Brad Hines Photography; Dwight Eschliman; 407 Courtesy of Getty Images, Inc.—Liaison. 408 Courtesy of Mall of America; CORBIS-NY. 410 Copyright 2004 Staples, Inc. All Rights Reserved; © 1996-2004 Travelocity.com LP. All rights reserved. 412 Courtesy of Wide World Photos. 414 Courtesy of W. W. Grainger, Inc. 419 Courtesy of McKesson, INC.

CHAPTER 14 425 © 2004 BMW of North America, LLC. All rights reserved. 428 © 2004 by Hearst Communications Inc. All rights reserved. 429 © DaimlerChrysler Corporation. All rights reserved. 433 © DaimlerChrysler Corporation. All rights reserved. 434 © Houghton Mifflin Company and Mullen. All rights reserved. 435 Used with permission of the Salvation Army. All rights reserved. Courtesy of Octaine Inc. 436 Courtesy of Volkswagen and Arnold Worldwide. Photography provided by permission of Bill Cash, Photographer. 438 Courtesy of Getty Images Inc.—Taxi. 440 Courtesy of Getty Images, Inc.—Agence France Presse; Getty Images, Inc.—Agence France Presse; Corbis/Bettmann. 442 Courtesy of PhotoEdit; Courtesy of Procter & Gamble Company. All rights reserved. 443 Courtesy of Masterfile Corporation. 445 Courtesy of Michael Newman. 447 © 2004 State Farm Insurance Companies. All rights reserved.

CHAPTER 15 453 © Copyright 2004 Virgin Atlantic Airways Ltd. All rights reserved. Courtesy of Crispin Porter + Bogusky. 457 © General Mills. All rights reserved. 458 Permission by V&S Vin & Sprit AB; ABSOLUT COUNTRY OF SWEDEN VODKA &

LOGO, ABSOLUT, ABSOLUT BOTTLE DESIGN AND ABSO-LUT CALLIGRAPHY ARE TRADEMARKS OWNED BY V&S VIN & SPRIT AB. 2004 V&S VIN & SPRIT AB. 459 Used with permission of TiVo Inc. TiVo and the TiVo Logo are registered trademarks of TiVo Inc. Home Media Option and TiVo Series2 are trademarks of TiVo Inc. All rights reserved. 460 Reprinted with permission of Callard & Bowser-Suchard, Inc. 462 Used with permission of Kraft Foods, Inc. All rights reserved. 465 Courtesy of PhotoEdit; Medialink WirePix Worlwide Photographic Solutions; Corbis/Bettmann; AP Wide World Photos. 467 © 2004 The Picture People Inc. All rights reserved. 469 Used with permission of Gillette. All rights reserved. 471 Used with permission of Lladro USA. 472 © 2004 Ferrero USA, Inc. All rights reserved. 474 Courtesy of CES International. 475 Used with permission of the Empire State Development. 477 Courtesy of John Storey Photography. 478 Courtesy of Microsoft.

CHAPTER 16 485 © 2004 CDW Corporation. All rights reserved. 488 Courtesy of Boeing Commercial Airplane Group. 490 Courtesy of Getty Images Inc.—Stone Allstock. 491 Courtesy of Corbis/Bettmann. 492 Courtesy of Corbis/Bettmann. 494 Courtesy of Ferorelli Enterprises, Inc. 495 Courtesy of AP/Wide World Photos. 499 Courtesy of Robin Nelson. 500 © 2004 Marriott International, Inc. All Rights Reserved. 502 Used with permission of Margi Systems. All rights reserved. 504 © Copyright 1999-2004 Boise Cascade Corporation. All Rights Reserved. 506 © 2001 Dell Inc. All rights reserved. 508 © 2001. Mars, Incorporated. Used with permission. 510 Used with permission of the Caroline Cookie Company. All rights reserved. 512 Courtesy of photographer: Amanda B. Kamen. 513 Courtesy of REI. 514 Courtesy of Ronco/Ron Popeil. 517 Courtesy of Getty Images. 518 Courtesy of the Direct Marketing Association.

CHAPTER 17 525 © 2004 Washington Mutual, Inc. All rights reserved. 528 © 2004 Encyclopedia Britannica, Inc. All rights reserved. 530 © 2004 Sub-Zero Freezer Company, Inc. All rights reserved. Courtesy of The Richards Group. 532 © 2004 Johnson & Johnson. All rights reserved. 535 © 2004 Hohner, Inc. All rights reserved. 536 © 2004 British Airways Plc. All rights reserved. 538 The Ritz-Carlton Hotel Company, LLC. All rights reserved. 540 Courtesy of Arm & Hammer. 543 © 2004 Logitech Inc. All rights reserved. 544 © 2004 Burt's Bees, Inc. All rights reserved.

CHAPTER 18 551 Courtesy of Amazon.com. 555 Copyright © 1999-2004 reflect.com LLC. 556 Courtesy of SuperStock, Inc. 557 © 2004 L.L. Bean, Inc. L.L. Bean® is a registered trademark of L.L. Bean, Inc. 558 Courtesy of PhotoEdit; PhotoEdit; SuperStock, Inc.; Superstock, Inc. 560 © 2000-2004 Quicken Loans Inc. All rights reserved. 561 © 2004 VertMarkets, Inc. All rights reserved. 562 Screenshot courtesy of Nike and Gawker Media. Published at http://www.gawker.com/artofspeed/. NIKE and the Swoosh Design logo are trademarks of Nike, Inc. and its affiliates. Used by permission. 563 © 1997-2004, Intelliseek, Inc. All rights reserved. 565 Courtesy of Getty Images, Inc.—Liaison. 567 © 2004 Office Depot, Inc. All rights reserved. 568 These materials have been reproduced with the permission of Ben & Jerry's Homemade Holdings Inc. Copyright © Ben & Jerry's Homemade Inc. All rights reserved. 570 Reprinted with permission of Callard & Bowser-Suchard, Inc. 573 © 2004 Google. All rights reserved. 575 Courtesy of iVillage. All rights reserved. 577 © 2004 Wherify Wireless, Inc. All rights reserved.

CHAPTER 19 587 Courtesy of Arthur Meyerson. 589 Courtesy of Network Aspen; Getty Images, Inc. Liaison; AP Wide World Photos. 591 Courtesy of Getty Images, Inc.—Agence France Presse. 592 Courtesy of the Audiovisual Library, European Commission. 594 Courtesy of Regina Maria Anzenberger. 596 Courtesy of Cary Sol Wolinsky/Trillium Studios. 597 Courtesy of Whirlpool of India, LTD. All rights reserved. 598 Courtesy of AP Wide World Photos. 600 © 2004 Colgate-Palmolive Company. All rights reserved. 603 Courtesy of Walt Disney Attractions Japan, Ltd. 604 Courtesy of Stock Boston. 605 Courtesy of Getty Images, Inc.—Agence France Presse. 606 Courtesy of L'Oréal. 608 Courtesy of L'Oréal. Photographer: Bernard Matussiere. All rights reserved. Used with permission. 609 © Inter IKEA Systems B.V. 1999-2004. All rights reserved. 610 Courtesy of Audiovisual Library of the European Commission. 612 Courtesy of AP Wide World Photos.

CHAPTER 20 619 © 2004 Nike, Inc. All rights reserved. 622 Courtesy of PhotoEdit. 623 Courtesy of AP Wide World Photos. 625 Courtesy AP Wide World Photos. 626 © 2004 by Consumers Union of U.S., Inc. Yonkers, NY 10703-1057, a non-profit organization. Reprinted with permission CONSUMER REPORTS® for educational purposes only. No commercial use or reproduction permitted. http://www.ConsumerReports.org. 629 Courtesy of the American Association of Advertising Agencies. 630 Courtesy of Rober Yager. 631 Courtesy of Wikipedia Foundation, Inc.; the Image Works. 634 © 2004 Campbell's Soup Company. All rights reserved. 635 © 2001 Dell Inc. All rights reserved. 640 © 2004 Samsung Electronics America, Inc. 641 Courtesy of Honest Tea. All rights reserved. 643 Courtesy of Herman Miller, Inc. 647 Reprinted with permission of PricewaterhouseCoopers LLP. © 2004 PWC. All rights reserved.

Glossary

Adapted marketing mix An international marketing strategy for adjusting the marketing mix elements to each international target market, bearing more costs but hoping for a larger market share and return.

Administered VMS A vertical marketing system that coordinates successive stages of production and distribution, not through common ownership or contractual ties, but through the size and power of one of the parties.

Adoption process The mental process through which an individual passes from first hearing about an innovation to final adoption.

Advertising Any paid form of nonpersonal presentation and promotion of ideas, goods, or services by an identified sponsor.

Advertising agency A marketing services firm that assists companies in planning, preparing, implementing, and evaluating all or portions of their advertising programs.

Advertising objective A specific communication task to be accomplished with a specific *target* audience during a specific period of time.

Advertising specialty Useful article imprinted with an advertiser's name, given as a gift to consumers.

Affordable method Setting the promotion budget at the level management thinks the company can afford.

Age and life-cycle segmentation Dividing a market into different age and life-cycle groups.

Agent A wholesaler who represents buyers or sellers on a relatively permanent basis, performs only a few functions, and does not take title to goods.

Allowance Promotional money paid by manufacturers to retailers in return for an agreement to feature the manufacturer's products in some way.

Alternative evaluation The stage of the buyer decision process in which the consumer uses information to evaluate alternative brands in the choice set.

Approach The step in the selling process in which the salesperson meets the customer for the first time.

Attitude A person's consistently favorable or unfavorable evaluations, feelings, and tendencies toward an object or idea.

B2B (business-to-business) e-commerce Using B2B trading networks, auction sites, spot exchanges, online product catalogs, barter sites, and other online resources to reach new customers, serve current customers more effectively, and obtain buying efficiencies and better prices.

B2C (business-to-consumer) e-commerce The online selling of goods and services to final consumers.

Baby boomers The 78 million people born during the baby boom following World War II and lasting until the early 1960s.

Basing-point pricing A geographical pricing strategy in which the seller designates some city as a basing point and charges all customers the freight cost from that city to the customer.

Behavioral segmentation Dividing a market into groups based on consumer knowledge, attitude, use, or response to a product.

Belief A descriptive thought that a person holds about something.

Benchmarking The process of comparing the company's products and processes to those of competitors or leading firms in other industries to find ways to improve quality and performance.

Benefit segmentation Dividing the market into groups according to the different benefits that consumers seek from the product.

Brand A name, term, sign, symbol, or design, or a combination of these intended to identify the goods or services of one seller or group of sellers and to differentiate them from those of competitors.

Brand equity The positive differential effect that knowing the brand name has on customer response to the product or service.

Brand extension Using a successful brand name to launch a new or modified product in a new category.

Break-even pricing (target profit pricing) Setting price to break even on the costs of making and marketing a product; or setting price to make a target profit.

Broker A wholesaler who does not take title to goods and whose function is to bring buyers and sellers together and assist in negotiation.

Business analysis A review of the sales, costs, and profit projections for a new product to find out whether these factors satisfy the company's objectives.

Business buyer behavior The buying behavior of the organizations that buy goods and services for use in the production of other products and services or for the purpose of reselling or renting them to others at a profit.

Business buying process The decision process by which business buyers determine which products and services their organizations need to purchase, and then find, evaluate, and choose among alternative suppliers and brands.

Business portfolio The collection of businesses and products that make up the company.

Buyer-readiness stages The stages consumers normally pass through on their way to purchase, including awareness, knowledge, liking, preference, conviction, and purchase.

Buyers The people who make an actual purchase.

Buying center All the individuals and units that participate in the business buying-decision process.

Buzz marketing Cultivating opinion leaders and getting them to spread information about a product or service to others in their communities.

By-product pricing Setting a price for by-products in order to make the main product's price more competitive.

C2B (consumer-to-business) e-commerce Online exchanges in which consumers search out sellers, learn about their offers, and initiate purchases, sometimes even driving transaction terms.

C2C (consumer-to-consumer) e-commerce Online exchanges of goods and information between final consumers.

Captive-product pricing Setting a price for products that must be used along with a main product, such as blades for a razor and film for a camera.

Cash refund offer (rebate) Offer to refund part of the purchase price of a product to consumers who send a "proof of purchase" to the manufacturer.

Catalog marketing Direct marketing through print, video, or electronic catalogs that are mailed to select customers, made available in stores, or presented online.

Category killer Giant specialty store that carries a very deep assortment of a particular line and is staffed by knowledgeable employees.

Causal research Marketing research to test hypotheses about cause-and-effect relationships.

Chain stores Two or more outlets that are owned and controlled in common, have central buying and merchandising, and sell similar lines of merchandise.

Channel conflict Disagreement among marketing channel members on goals and roles—who should do what and for what rewards.

Channel level A layer of intermediaries that performs some work in bringing the product and its ownership closer to the final buyer.

Click-and-mortar companies Traditional brick-and-mortar companies that have added e-marketing to their operations.

Click-only companies The so-called dot-coms, which operate only online without any brick-and-mortar market presence.

Closing The step in the selling process in which the salesperson asks the customer for an order.

Co-branding The practice of using the established brand names of two different companies on the same product.

Cognitive dissonance Buyer discomfort caused by postpurchase conflict.

Commercialization Introducing a new product into the market.

Communication adaptation A global communication strategy of fully adapting advertising messages to local markets.

Competition-based pricing Setting prices based on the prices that competitors charge for similar products.

Competitive advantage An advantage over competitors gained by offering consumers greater value, either through lower prices or by providing more benefits that justify higher prices.

Competitive marketing strategies Strategies that strongly position the company against competitors and that give the company the strongest possible strategic advantage.

Competitive-parity method Setting the promotion budget to match competitors' outlays.

Competitor analysis The process of identifying key competitors; assessing their objectives, strategies, strengths and weaknesses, and reaction patterns; and selecting which competitors to attack or avoid.

Competitor-centered company A company whose moves are mainly based on competitors' actions and reactions.

Complex buying behavior Consumer buying behavior in situations characterized by high consumer involvement in a purchase and significant perceived differences among brands.

Concentrated (niche) marketing A market-coverage strategy in which a firm goes after a large share of one or a few segments or niches.

Concept testing Testing new-product concepts with a group of target consumers to find out if the concepts have strong consumer appeal.

Consumer buyer behavior The buying behavior of final consumers-individuals and households who buy goods and services for personal consumption.

Consumer market All the individuals and households who buy or acquire goods and services for personal consumption.

Consumer-oriented marketing The philosophy of enlightened marketing that holds that the company should view and organize its marketing activities from the consumer's point of view.

Consumer product Product bought by final consumer for personal consumption.

Consumerism An organized movement of citizens and government agencies to improve the rights and power of buyers in relation to sellers.

Contests, sweepstakes, games Promotional events that give consumers the chance to win something-such as cash,

trips, or goods-by luck or through extra effort.

Contract manufacturing A joint venture in which a company contracts with manufacturers in a foreign market to produce the product or provide its service.

Contractual VMS A vertical marketing system in which independent firms at different levels of production and distribution join together through contracts to obtain more economies or sales impact than they could achieve alone.

Convenience product Consumer product that the customer usually buys frequently, immediately, and with a minimum of comparison and buying effort.

Convenience store A small store, located near a residential area, that is open long hours 7 days a week and carries a limited line of high-turnover convenience goods.

Conventional distribution channel A channel consisting of one or more independent producers, wholesalers, and retailers, each a separate business seeking to maximize its own profits even at the expense of profits for the system as a whole.

Corporate VMS A vertical marketing system that combines successive stages of production and distribution under single ownership-channel leadership is established through common ownership.

Corporate Web site A Web site designed to build customer goodwill and to supplement other sales channels, rather than to sell the company's products directly.

Cost-plus pricing Adding a standard markup to the cost of the product.

Countertrade International trade involving the direct or indirect exchange of goods for other goods instead of cash.

Coupon Certificate that gives buyers a saving when they purchase a specified product.

Cultural environment Institutions and other forces that affect society's basic values, perceptions, preferences, and behaviors.

Culture The set of basic values, perceptions, wants, and behaviors learned by a member of society from family and other important institutions.

Customer-centered company A company that focuses on customer developments in designing its marketing strategies and on delivering superior value to its target customers.

Customer database An organized collection of comprehensive data about individual customers or prospects, including geographic, demographic, psychographic, and behavioral data.

Customer equity The total combined customer lifetime values of all of the company's customers.

Customer lifetime value The value of the entire stream of purchases that the customer would make over a lifetime of patronage.

Customer perceived value The difference between total customer value and total customer cost.

Customer relationship management (CRM) The overall process of building and maintaining profitable customer relationships by delivering superior customer value and satisfaction.

Customer sales force structure A sales force organization under which salespeople specialize in selling only to certain customers or industries.

Customer satisfaction The extent to which a product's perceived performance matches a buyer's expectations.

Customer value analysis Analysis conducted to determine what benefits target customers value and how they rate the relative value of various competitors' offers.

Customer value marketing A principle of enlightened marketing that holds that a company should put most of its resources into customer value-building marketing investments.

Deciders People in the organization's buying center who have formal or informal power to select or approve the final suppliers.

Decline stage The product life-cycle stage in which a product's sales decline.

Deficient products Products that have neither immediate appeal nor long-run benefits.

Demand curve A curve that shows the number of units the market will buy in a given time period, at different prices that might be charged.

Demands Human wants that are backed by buying power.

Demarketing Marketing to reduce demand temporarily or permanently; the aim is not to destroy demand but only to reduce or shift it.

Demographic segmentation Dividing the market into groups based on demographic variables such as age, sex, family size, family life cycle, income, occupation, education, religion, race, and nationality.

Demography The study of human populations in terms of size, density, location, age, gender, race, occupation, and other statistics.

Department store A retail organization that carries a wide variety of product lines-typically clothing, home furnishings, and household goods; each line is operated as a separate department managed by specialist buyers or merchandisers.

Derived demand Business demand that ultimately comes from (derives from) the demand for consumer goods.

Descriptive research Marketing research to better describe marketing problems, situations, or markets, such as the market potential for a product or the demographics and attitudes of consumers.

Desirable products Products that give both high immediate satisfaction and high long-run benefits.

Differentiated (segmented) marketing A market-coverage strategy in which a firm decides to target several market segments and designs separate offers for each.

Direct investment Entering a foreign market by developing foreign-based assembly or manufacturing facilities.

Direct-mail marketing Sending an offer, announcement, reminder, or other item to a person at a particular address.

Direct marketing Direct communications with carefully targeted individual consumers—the use of telephone, mail, fax, e-mail, the Internet, and other tools to communicate directly with specific consumers.

Direct marketing channel A marketing channel that has no intermediary levels.

Direct-response television marketing Direct marketing via television, including *direct-response television advertising* or *infomercials* and *home shopping channels.*

Discount A straight reduction in price on purchases during a stated period of time.

Discount store A retail institution that sells standard merchandise at lower prices by accepting lower margins and selling at higher volume.

Disintermediation The displacement of traditional resellers from a marketing channel by radical new types of intermediaries.

Dissonance-reducing buying behavior Consumer buying behavior in situations characterized by high involvement but few perceived differences among brands.

Distribution center A large, highly automated warehouse designed to receive goods from various plants and suppliers, take orders, fill them efficiently, and deliver goods to customers as quickly as possible.

Diversification A strategy for company growth through starting up or acquiring businesses outside the company's current products and markets.

Downsizing Reducing the business portfolio by eliminating products or business units that are not profitable or that no longer fit the company's overall strategy.

Dynamic pricing Charging different prices depending on individual customers and situations.

E-business The use of electronic platforms-intranets, extranets, and the Internet-to conduct a company's business.

E-commerce Buying and selling processes supported by electronic means, primarily the Internet.

Economic community A group of nations organized to work toward common goals in the regulation of international trade.

Economic environment Factors that affect consumer buying power and spending patterns.

E-marketing The marketing side of e-commerce-company efforts to communicate about, promote, and sell products and services over the Internet.

Embargo A ban on the import of a certain product.

Engel's laws Differences noted over a century ago by Ernst Engel in how people shift their spending across food, housing, transportation, health care, and other goods and services categories as family income rises.

Enlightened marketing A marketing philosophy holding that a company's marketing should support the best long-run performance of the marketing.

Environmental sustainability A management approach that involves developing strategies that both sustain the environment and produce profits for the company.

Environmentalism An organized movement of concerned citizens and government agencies to protect and improve people's living environment.

Exchange The act of obtaining a desired object from someone by offering something in return.

Exchange controls Government limits on the amount of foreign exchange with other countries and on the exchange rate against other currencies.

Exclusive distribution Giving a limited number of dealers the exclusive right to distribute the company's products in their territories.

Experience curve (learning curve) The drop in the average per-unit production cost that comes with accumulated production experience.

Experimental research The gathering of primary data by selecting matched groups of subjects, giving them different treatments, controlling related factors, and checking for differences in group responses.

Exploratory research Marketing research to gather preliminary information that will help define problems and suggest hypotheses.

Exporting Entering a foreign market by selling goods produced in the company's home country, often with little modification.

Extranet A network that connects a company with its suppliers and distributors.

Factory outlet An off-price retailing operation that is owned and operated by a manufacturer and that normally carries the manufacturer's surplus, discontinued, or irregular goods.

Fad A temporary period of unusually high sales driven by consumer enthusiasm and immediate product or brand popularity.

Fashion A currently accepted or popular style in a given field.

Fixed costs Costs that do not vary with production or sales level.

FOB-origin pricing A geographical pricing strategy in which goods are placed free on board a carrier; the customer pays the freight from the factory to the destination.

Focus group interviewing Personal interviewing that involves inviting 6 to 10 people to gather for a few hours with a trained interviewer to talk about a product, service, or organization. The interviewer "focuses" the group discussion on important issues.

Follow-up The last step in the selling process in which the salesperson follows up after the sale to ensure customer satisfaction and repeat business.

Franchise A contractual association between a manufacturer, wholesaler, or service organization (a franchiser) and

independent businesspeople (franchisees) who buy the right to own and operate one or more units in the franchise system.

Franchise organization A contractual vertical marketing system in which a channel member, called a franchiser, links several stages in the production-distribution process.

Freight-absorption pricing A geographical pricing strategy in which the seller absorbs all or part of the freight charges in order to get the desired business.

Gatekeepers People in the organization's buying center who control the flow of information to others.

Gender segmentation Dividing a market into different groups based on gender.

General need description The stage in the business buying process in which the company describes the general characteristics and quantity of a needed item.

Generation X The 45 million people born between 1965 and 1976 in the "birth dearth" following the baby boom.

Generation Y The 72 million children of the baby boomers, born between 1977 and 1994.

Geographic segmentation Dividing a market into different geographical units such as nations, states, regions, counties, cities, or neighborhoods.

Global firm A firm that, by operating in more than one country, gains R&D, production, marketing, and financial advantages in its costs and reputation that are not available to purely domestic competitors.

Government market Governmental units-federal, state, and local-that purchase or rent goods and services for carrying out the main functions of government.

Group Two or more people who interact to accomplish individual or mutual goals.

Growth-share matrix A portfolio-planning method that evaluates a company's strategic business units in terms of their market growth rate and relative market share. SBUs are classified as stars, cash cows, question marks, or dogs.

Growth stage The product life-cycle stage in which a product's sales start climbing quickly.

Habitual buying behavior Consumer buying behavior in situations characterized by low consumer involvement and few significant perceived brand differences.

Handling objections The step in the selling process in which the salesperson seeks out, clarifies, and overcomes customer objections to buying.

Horizontal marketing system A channel arrangement in which two or more companies at one level join together to follow a new marketing opportunity.

Idea generation The systematic search for new-product ideas.

Idea screening Screening new-product ideas in order to spot good ideas and drop poor ones as soon as possible.

Income segmentation Dividing a market into different income groups.

Independent off-price retailer An off-price retailer that is either owned and run by an entrepreneur or is a division of a larger retail corporation.

Indirect marketing channel A channel containing one or more intermediary levels.

Individual marketing Tailoring products and marketing programs to the needs and preferences of individual customers-also labeled "markets-of-one marketing," "customized marketing," and "one-to-one marketing."

Industrial product Product bought by individuals and organizations for further processing or for use in conducting a business.

Influencers People in an organization's buying center who affect the buying decision; they often help define specifications and also provide information for evaluating alternatives.

Information search The stage of the buyer decision process in which the consumer is aroused to search for more information; the consumer may simply have heightened attention or may go into active information search.

Innovative marketing A principle of enlightened marketing that requires that a company seek real product and marketing improvements.

Inside sales force Inside salespeople who conduct business from their offices via telephone or visits from prospective buyers.

Institutional market Schools, hospitals, nursing homes, prisons, and other institutions that provide goods and services to people in their care.

Integrated direct marketing Direct-marketing campaigns that use multiple vehicles and multiple stages to improve response rates and profits.

Integrated logistics management The logistics concept that emphasizes teamwork, both inside the company and among all the marketing channel organizations, to maximize the performance of the entire distribution system.

Integrated marketing communications (IMC) The concept under which a company carefully integrates and coordinates its many communications channels to deliver a clear, consistent, and compelling message about the organization and its products.

Intensive distribution Stocking the product in as many outlets as possible.

Interactive marketing Marketing by a service firm that recognizes that perceived service quality depends heavily on the quality of buyer-seller interaction.

Intermarket segmentation Forming segments of consumers who have similar needs and buying behavior even though they are located in different countries.

Intermodal transportation Combining two or more modes of transportation.

Internal databases Electronic collections of information obtained from data sources within the company.

Internal marketing Marketing by a service firm to train and effectively motivate its customer-contact employees and all the supporting service people to work as a team to provide customer satisfaction.

Internet A vast public web of computer networks, which connects users of all types all around the world to each other and to an amazingly large information repository.

Intranet A network that connects people within a company to each other and to the company network.

Introduction stage The product lifecycle stage in which the new product is first distributed and made available for purchase.

Joint ownership A joint venture in which a company joins investors in a foreign market to create a local business in which the company shares joint ownership and control.

Joint venturing Entering foreign markets by joining with foreign companies to produce or market a product or service.

Learning Changes in an individual's behavior arising from experience.

Licensing A method of entering a foreign market in which the company enters into an agreement with a licensee in the foreign market, offering the right to use a manufacturing process, trademark, patent, trade secret, or other item of value for a fee or royalty.

Lifestyle A person's pattern of living as expressed in his or her activities, interests, and opinions.

Line extension Using a successful brand name to introduce additional items in a given product category under the same brand name, such as new flavors, forms, colors, added ingredients, or package sizes.

Local marketing Tailoring brands and promotions to the needs and wants of local customer groups-cities, neighborhoods, and even specific stores.

Macroenvironment The larger societal forces that affect the microenvironment-demographic, economic, natural, technological, political, and cultural forces.

Management contracting A joint venture in which the domestic firm supplies the management know-how to a foreign company that supplies the capital; the domestic firm exports management services rather than products.

Manufacturers' sales branches and offices Wholesaling by sellers or buyers themselves rather than through independent wholesalers.

Market The set of actual and potential buyers of a product or service.

Market-centered company A company that pays balanced attention to both customers and competitors in designing its marketing strategies.

Market challenger A runner-up firm that is fighting hard to increase its market share in an industry.

Market development A strategy for company growth by identifying and developing new market segments for current company products.

Market follower A runner-up firm that wants to hold its share in an industry without rocking the boat.

Market leader The firm in an industry with the largest market share.

Market nicher A firm that serves small segments that the other firms in an industry overlook or ignore.

Market penetration A strategy for company growth by increasing sales of current products to current market segments without changing the product.

Market-penetration pricing Setting a low price for a new product in order to attract a large number of buyers and a large market share.

Market positioning Arranging for a product to occupy a clear, distinctive, and desirable place relative to competing products in the minds of target consumers.

Market segment A group of consumers who respond in a similar way to a given set of marketing efforts.

Market segmentation Dividing a market into distinct groups of buyers who have distinct needs, characteristics, or behavior and who might require separate products or marketing mixes.

Market-skimming pricing Setting a high price for a new product to skim maximum revenues layer by layer from the segments willing to pay the high price; the company makes fewer but more profitable sales.

Marketing The process by which companies create value for customers and build strong customer relationships in order to capture value from customers in return

Marketing audit A comprehensive, systematic, independent, and periodic examination of a company's environment, objectives, strategies, and activities to determine problem areas and opportunities and to recommend a plan of action to improve the company's marketing performance.

Marketing channel (or distribution channel) A set of interdependent organizations involved in the process of making a product or service available for use or consumption by the consumer or business user.

Marketing communications mix (promotion mix) The specific mix of advertising, personal selling, sales promotion, and public relations a company uses.

Marketing concept The marketing management philosophy that holds that achieving organizational goals depends on knowing the needs and wants of target markets and delivering the desired satisfactions better than competitors do.

Marketing control The process of measuring and evaluating the results of marketing strategies and plans, and taking corrective action to ensure that objectives are achieved.

Marketing environment The actors and forces outside marketing that affect marketing management's ability to build and maintain successful relationships with target customers.

Marketing implementation The process that turns marketing strategies and plans into marketing actions in order to accomplish strategic marketing objectives.

Marketing information system (MIS) People, equipment, and procedures to gather, sort, analyze, evaluate, and distribute needed, timely, and accurate information to marketing decision makers.

Marketing intelligence The systematic collection and analysis of publicly available information about competitors and developments in the marketing environment.

Marketing intermediaries Firms that help the company to promote, sell, and distribute its goods to final buyers; they include resellers, physical distribution firms, marketing service agencies, and financial intermediaries.

Marketing logistics (physical distribution) The tasks involved in planning, implementing, and controlling the physical flow of materials, final goods, and related information from points of origin to points of consumption to meet customer requirements at a profit.

Marketing management The art and science of choosing target markets and building profitable relationships with them.

Marketing mix The set of controllable tactical marketing tools-product, price, place, and promotion-that the firm blends to produce the response it wants in the target market.

Marketing offer Some combination of products, services, information, or experiences offered to a market to satisfy a need or want.

Marketing research The systematic design, collection, analysis, and reporting of data relevant to a specific marketing situation facing an organization.

Marketing strategy The marketing logic by which the business unit hopes to achieve its marketing objectives.

Marketing strategy development Designing an initial marketing strategy for a new product based on the product concept.

Marketing Web site A Web site that engages consumers in interactions that will move them closer to a direct purchase or other marketing outcome.

Maturity stage The stage in the product life cycle in which sales growth slows or levels off.

Merchant wholesaler Independently owned business that takes title to the merchandise it handles.

Microenvironment The actors close to the company that affect its ability to serve its customers-the company, suppliers, marketing intermediaries, customer markets, competitors, and publics.

Micromarketing The practice of tailoring products and marketing programs to the needs and wants of specific individuals and local customer groups-includes *local marketing* and *individual marketing*.

Mission statement A statement of the organization's purpose-what it wants to accomplish in the larger environment.

Modified rebuy A business buying situation in which the buyer wants to modify product specifications, prices, terms, or suppliers.

Motive (drive) A need that is sufficiently pressing to direct the person to seek satisfaction of the need.

Multichannel distribution system (or hybrid marketing channel) A distribution system in which a single firm sets up two or more marketing channels to reach one or more customer segments.

Natural environment Natural resources that are needed as inputs by marketers or that are affected by marketing activities.

Need recognition The first stage of the buyer decision process, in which the consumer recognizes a problem or need.

Needs States of felt deprivation.

New product A good, service, or idea that is perceived by some potential customers as new.

New-product development The development of original products, product improvements, product modifications, and new brands through the firm's own R&D efforts.

New task A business buying situation in which the buyer purchases a product or service for the first time.

Nontariff trade barriers Nonmonetary barriers to foreign products, such as biases against a foreign company's bids, or product standards that go against a foreign company's product features.

Nonpersonal communication channels Media that carry messages without personal contact or feedback, including major media, atmospheres, and events.

Objective-and-task method Developing the promotion budget by (1) defining specific objectives; (2) determining the tasks that must be performed to achieve these

objectives; and (3) estimating the costs of performing these tasks. The sum of these costs is the proposed promotion budget.

Observational research The gathering of primary data by observing relevant people, actions, and situations.

Occasion segmentation Dividing the market into groups according to occasions when buyers get the idea to buy, actually make their purchase, or use the purchased item.

Off-price retailer Retailer that buys at less-than-regular wholesale prices and sells at less than retail. Examples are factory outlets, independents, and warehouse clubs.

Online advertising Advertising that appears while consumers are surfing the Web, including banner and ticker ads, interstitials, skyscrapers, and other forms.

Online databases Computerized collections of information available from online commercial sources or via the Internet.

Online (Internet) marketing research Collecting primary data through Internet surveys and online focus groups.

Open trading exchanges Huge e-marketspaces in which B2B buyers and sellers find each other online, share information, and complete transactions efficiently.

Opinion leader Person within a reference group who, because of special skills, knowledge, personality, or other characteristics, exerts influence on others.

Optional-product pricing The pricing of optional or accessory products along with a main product.

Order-routine specification The stage of the business buying process in which the buyer writes the final order with the chosen supplier(s), listing the technical specifications, quantity needed, expected time of delivery, return policies, and warranties.

Outside sales force (or *field sales force*) Outside salespeople who travel to call on customers.

Packaging The activities of designing and producing the container or wrapper for a product.

Partner relationship management Working closely with partners in other company departments and outside the company to jointly bring greater value to customers.

Patronage reward Cash or other award for the regular use of a certain company's products or services.

Percentage-of-sales method Setting the promotion budget at a certain percentage of current or forecasted sales or as a percentage of the unit sales price.

Perception The process by which people select, organize, and interpret information to form a meaningful picture of the world.

Performance review The stage of the business buying process in which the buyer assesses the performance of the supplier and decides to continue, modify, or drop the arrangement.

Personal communication channels Channels through which two or more people communicate directly with each other, including face to face, person to audience, over the telephone, or through the mail.

Personal selling Personal presentation by the firm's sales force for the purpose of making sales and building customer relationships.

Personality The unique psychological characteristics that lead to relatively consistent and lasting responses to one's own environment.

Pleasing products Products that give high immediate satisfaction but may hurt consumers in the long run.

Point-of-purchase (POP) promotion Display and demonstration that takes place at the point of purchase or sale.

Political environment Laws, government agencies, and pressure groups that influence and limit various organizations and individuals in a given society.

Portfolio analysis The process by which management evaluates the products and businesses making up the company.

Positioning statement A statement that summarizes company or brand positioning—it takes this form: To *(target segment and need)* our *(brand)* is *(concept)* that *(point-of-difference)*.

Postpurchase behavior The stage of the buyer decision process in which consumers take further action after purchase, based on their satisfaction or dissatisfaction.

Preapproach The step in the selling process in which the salesperson learns as much as possible about a prospective customer before making a sales call.

Premium Good offered either free or at low cost as an incentive to buy a product.

Presentation The step in the selling process in which the salesperson tells the "product story" to the buyer, highlighting customer benefits.

Price The amount of money charged for a product or service, or the sum of the values that consumers exchange for the benefits of having or using the product or service.

Price elasticity A measure of the sensitivity of demand to changes in price.

Price pack (cents-off deal) Reduced price that is marked by the producer directly on the label or package.

Primary data Information collected for the specific purpose at hand.

Private brand (or store brand) A brand created and owned by a reseller of a product or service.

Private trading exchanges B2B trading networks that link a particular seller with its own trading partners.

Problem recognition The first stage of the business buying process in which someone in the company recognizes a problem or need that can be met by acquiring a good or a service.

Product Anything that can be offered to a market for attention, acquisition, use, or consumption that might satisfy a want or need.

Product adaptation Adapting a product to meet local conditions or wants in foreign markets.

Product bundle pricing Combining several products and offering the bundle at a reduced price.

Product concept The idea that consumers will favor products that offer the most quality, performance, and features and that the organization should therefore devote its energy to making continuous product improvements.

Product development A strategy for company growth by offering modified or new products to current market segments.

Product invention Creating new products or services for foreign markets.

Product life cycle (PLC) The course of a product's sales and profits over its lifetime. It involves five distinct stages: product development, introduction, growth, maturity, and decline.

Product line A group of products that are closely related because they function in a similar manner, are sold to the same customer groups, are marketed through the same types of outlets, or fall within given price ranges.

Product line pricing Setting the price steps between various products in a product line based on cost differences between

the products, customer evaluations of different features, and competitors' prices.

Product/market expansion grid A portfolio-planning tool for identifying company growth opportunities through market penetration, market development, product development, or diversification.

Product mix (or product assortment) The set of all product lines and items that a particular seller offers for sale.

Product position The way the product is defined by consumers on important attributes—the place the product occupies in consumers' minds relative to competing products.

Product quality The ability of a product to perform its functions; it includes the product's overall durability, reliability, precision, ease of operation and repair, and other valued attributes.

Product sales force structure A sales force organization under which salespeople specialize in selling only a portion of the company's products or lines.

Product specification The stage of the business buying process in which the buying organization decides on and specifies the best technical product characteristics for a needed item.

Production concept The idea that consumers will favor products that are available and highly affordable.

Promotional pricing Temporarily pricing products below the list price, and sometimes even below cost, to increase short-run sales.

Proposal solicitation The stage of the business buying process in which the buyer invites qualified suppliers to submit proposals.

Prospecting The step in the selling process in which the salesperson identifies qualified potential customers.

Psychographic segmentation Dividing a market into different groups based on social class, lifestyle, or personality characteristics.

Psychological pricing A pricing approach that considers the psychology of prices and not simply the economics; the price is used to say something about the product.

Public Any group that has an actual or potential interest in or impact on an organization's ability to achieve its objectives.

Public relations Building good relations with the company's various publics by obtaining favorable publicity, building up a good "corporate image," and handling or heading off unfavorable rumors, stories, and events.

Pull strategy A promotion strategy that calls for spending a lot on advertising and consumer promotion to build up consumer demand. If the strategy is successful, consumers will ask their retailers for the product, the retailers will ask the wholesalers, and the wholesalers will ask the producers.

Purchase decision The buyer's decision about which brand to purchase.

Push strategy A promotion strategy that calls for using the sales force and trade promotion to push the product through channels. The producer promotes the product to wholesalers, the wholesalers promote to retailers, and the retailers promote to consumers.

Quota A limit on the amount of goods that an importing country will accept in certain product categories.

Reference prices Prices that buyers carry in their minds and refer to when they look at a given product.

Retailer A business whose sales come *primarily* from retailing.

Retailing All activities involved in selling goods or services directly to final consumers for their personal, nonbusiness use.

Return on marketing (or marketing ROI) The net return from a marketing investment divided by the costs of the marketing investment.

Sales force management The analysis, planning, implementation, and control of sales force activities. It includes setting and designing sales force strategy; and recruiting, selecting, training, supervising, compensating, and evaluating the firm's salespeople.

Sales promotion Short-term incentives to encourage the purchase or sale of a product or service.

Sales quota A standard that states the amount a salesperson should sell and how sales should be divided among the company's products.

Salesperson An individual acting for a company by performing one or more of the following activities: prospecting, communicating, servicing, and information gathering.

Salutary products Products that have low appeal but may benefit consumers in the long run.

Sample A segment of the population selected for marketing research to represent the population as a whole; a small amount of a product offered to customers for trial.

Secondary data Information that already exists somewhere, having been collected for another purpose.

Segmented pricing Selling a product or service at two or more prices, where the difference in prices is not based on differences in costs.

Selective distribution The use of more than one, but fewer than all, of the intermediaries who are willing to carry the company's products.

Selling concept The idea that consumers will not buy enough of the firm's products unless it undertakes a large-scale selling and promotion effort.

Selling process The steps that the salesperson follows when selling, which include prospecting and qualifying, preapproach, approach, presentation and demonstration, handling objections, closing, and follow-up.

Sense-of-mission marketing A principle of enlightened marketing that holds that a company should define its mission in broad social terms rather than narrow product terms.

Sequential product development A new-product development approach in which one company department works to complete its stage of the process before passing the new product along to the next department and stage.

Service Any activity or benefit that one party can offer to another that is essentially intangible and does not result in the ownership of anything.

Service inseparability A major characteristic of services—they are produced and consumed at the same time and cannot be separated from their providers.

Service intangibility A major characteristic of services—they cannot be seen, tasted, felt, heard, or smelled before they are bought.

Service perishability A major characteristic of services—they cannot be stored for later sale or use.

Service-profit chain The chain that links service firm profits with employee and customer satisfaction.

Service variability A major characteristic of services—their quality may vary greatly, depending on who provides them and when, where, and how.

Share of customer The portion of the customer's purchasing that a company gets in its product categories.

Shopping center A group of retail businesses planned, developed, owned, and managed as a unit.

Shopping product Consumer good that the customer, in the process of selection and purchase, characteristically compares on such bases as suitability, quality, price, and style.

Simultaneous (or team-based) product development An approach to developing new products in which various company departments work closely together, overlapping the steps in the product-development process to save time and increase effectiveness.

Single-source data systems Electronic monitoring systems that link consumers' exposure to television advertising and promotion (measured using television meters) with what they buy in stores (measured using store checkout scanners).

Social classes Relatively permanent and ordered divisions in a society whose members share similar values, interests, and behaviors.

Social marketing The design, implementation, and control of programs seeking to increase the acceptability of a social idea, cause, or practice among a target group.

Societal marketing concept A principle of enlightened marketing that holds that a company should make good marketing decisions by considering consumers' wants, the company's requirements, consumers' long-run interests, and society's long run interests.

Spam Unsolicited, unwanted commercial e-mail messages.

Specialty product Consumer product with unique characteristics or brand identification for which a significant group of buyers is willing to make a special purchase effort.

Specialty store A retail store that carries a narrow product line with a deep assortment within that line.

Standardized marketing mix An international marketing strategy for using basically the same product, advertising, distribution channels, and other elements of the marketing mix in all the company's international markets.

Straight product extension Marketing a product in a foreign market without any change.

Straight rebuy A business buying situation in which the buyer routinely reorders something without any modifications.

Strategic group A group of firms in an industry following the same or a similar strategy.

Strategic planning The process of developing and maintaining a strategic fit between the organization's goals and capabilities and its changing marketing opportunities. It involves defining a clear company mission, setting supporting objectives, designing a sound business portfolio, and coordinating functional strategies.

Style A basic and distinctive mode of expression.

Subculture A group of people with shared value systems based on common life experiences and situations.

Supermarket Large, low-cost, low-margin, high-volume, self-service store that carries a wide variety of food, laundry, and household products.

Superstore A store much larger than a regular supermarket that carries a large assortment of routinely purchased food products, nonfood items, and services.

Supplier development Systematic development of networks of supplier-partners to ensure an appropriate and dependable supply of products and materials that they will use in making their own products or resell to others.

Supplier search The stage of the business buying process in which the buyer tries to find the best vendors.

Supplier selection The stage of the business buying process in which the buyer reviews proposals and selects a supplier or suppliers.

Supply chain management Managing upstream and downstream value-added flows of materials, final goods, and related information among suppliers, the company, resellers, and final consumers.

Survey research The gathering of primary data by asking people questions about their knowledge, attitudes, preferences, and buying behavior.

Systems selling Buying a packaged solution to a problem from a single seller, thus avoiding all the separate decisions involved in a complex buying situation.

Target costing Pricing that starts with an ideal selling price, then targets costs that will ensure that the price is met.

Target market A set of buyers sharing common needs or characteristics that the company decides to serve.

Target marketing The process of evaluating each market segment's attractiveness and selecting one or more segments to enter.

Tariff A tax levied by a government against certain imported, designed to raise revenue or to protect domestic firms.

Team selling Using teams of people from sales, marketing, engineering, finance, technical support, and even upper management to service large, complex accounts.

Technological environment Forces that create new technologies, creating new product and market opportunities.

Telephone marketing Using the telephone to sell directly to customers.

Territorial sales force structure A sales force organization that assigns each salesperson to an exclusive geographic territory in which that salesperson sells the company's full line.

Test marketing The stage of new-product development in which the product and marketing program are tested in more realistic market settings.

Third-party logistics (3PL) provider An independent logistics provider that performs any or all of the functions required to get its client's product to market.

Total costs The sum of the fixed and variable costs for any given level of production.

Undifferentiated (mass) marketing A market-coverage strategy in which a firm decides to ignore market segment differences and go after the whole market with one offer.

Uniform-delivered pricing A geographical pricing strategy in which the company charges the same price plus freight to all customers, regardless of their location.

Unsought product Consumer product that the consumer either does not know about or knows about but does not normally think of buying.

Users Members of the buying organization who will actually use the purchased product or service.

Value analysis An approach to cost reduction in which components are studied carefully to determine if they can be redesigned, standardized, or made by less costly methods of production.

Value-based pricing Setting price based on buyers' perceptions of value rather than on the seller's cost.

Value chain The series of departments that carry out value-creating activities to design, produce, market, deliver, and support a firm's products.

Value-delivery network The network made up of the company, suppliers, distributors, and ultimately customers who "partner" with each other to improve the performance of the entire system.

Value pricing Offering just the right combination of quality and good service at a fair price.

Value proposition The full positioning of a brand-the full mix of benefits upon which it is positioned.

Variable costs Costs that vary directly with the level of production.

Variety-seeking buying behavior Consumer buying behavior in situations characterized by low consumer involvement but significant perceived brand differences.

Vertical marketing system (VMS) A distribution channel structure in which producers, wholesalers, and retailers act as a unified system. One channel member owns the others, has contracts with them, or has so much power that they all cooperate.

Viral marketing The Internet version of word-of-mouth marketing-e-mail messages or other marketing events that are so infectious that customers will want to pass them along to friends.

Wants The form human needs take as shaped by culture and individual personality.

Warehouse club An off-price retailer that sells a limited selection of brand name grocery items, appliances, clothing, and a hodgepodge of other goods at deep discounts to members who pay annual membership fees.

Web communities Web sites upon which members can congregate online and exchange views on issues of common interest.

Wheel-of-retailing concept A concept of retailing that states that new types of retailers usually begin as low-margin, low-price, low-status operations but later evolve into higher-priced, higher-service operations, eventually becoming like the conventional retailers they replaced.

Whole-channel view Designing international channels that take into account all the necessary links in distributing the seller's products to final buyers, including the seller's headquarters organiza-tion, channels among nations, and channels within nations.

Wholesaler A firm engaged *primarily* in wholesaling activity.

Wholesaling All activities involved in selling goods and services to those buying for resale or business use.

Word-of-mouth influence Personal communication about a product between tar-get buyers and neighbors, friends, family members, and associates.

Zone pricing A geographical pricing strategy in which the company sets up two or more zones. All customers within a zone pay the same total price; the more distant the zone, the higher the price.

Index

Subject

Name, Organization, Brand, Company